CIVIL PROCEDURE IN FRANCE

*Columbia University School of Law*
*Project on International Procedure*

HANS SMIT
Director and Editor

*Peter Herzog*

*with the collaboration of*

Martha Weser

# CIVIL PROCEDURE IN FRANCE

Springer-Science+Business Media, B.V.

1967

---

ISBN 978-94-017-5826-0 ISBN 978-94-017-6275-5 (eBook)
DOI 10.1007/978-94-017-6275-5

THE PREPARATION OF THIS BOOK WAS MADE POSSIBLE BY FUNDS GRANTED BY CARNEGIE CORPORATION OF NEW YORK
THE STATEMENTS MADE AND VIEWS EXPRESSED ARE SOLELY THE RESPONSIBILITY OF THE AUTHORS AND OF THE PROJECT ON INTERNATIONAL PROCEDURE OF THE SCHOOL OF LAW OF COLUMBIA UNIVERSITY

## ABOUT THE AUTHORS

**Peter E. Herzog,** B.A., Hobart College, 1952; LL.B., Syracuse University, 1955; Editor-in-Chief, Syracuse Law Review, 1954–1955; LL.M., Columbia University, 1956; Member, Bar of New York, since 1957; Deputy Assistant Attorney General, New York State Department of Law, 1956–57; Assistant Attorney General, New York State Department of Law, 1957–58; Legal Assistant, New York State Joint Legislative Committee on Metropolian Areas Studies, 1958–1960; Professor of Law, Syracuse University.

**Martha Weser,** *Docteur en Droit,* University of Paris, 1951; *Docteur en Droit International Privé,* University of Paris, 1952; Assistant Professor of Law, University of Brussels; Member, Belgian-Netherlands-Luxembourg Commission for the Study of the Unification of Laws; Member, Committee of Experts of the European Economic Community Charged With the Drafting of a Treaty on Bankruptcy; Collaborator, *Revue Critique de Droit International Privé*; Author, *Etude Critique du Traité Franco-Belge du 8 Juillet 1899* (Paris and Brussels, 1951).

# PREFACE

This book is the third in a series of books on foreign civil procedure published by the Project on International Procedure of the School of Law of Columbia University. Books on civil procedure in Sweden and Italy were published recently; a book on civil procedure in Japan is in preparation.

The Project's studies on foreign civil procedure have several objectives. First, they provide an opportunity to become familiar with the procedural systems of other countries; the differences between common law and foreign systems of procedure are pervasive and proper understanding of foreign substantive law cannot be achieved without knowledge of foreign procedure. Second, they are designed to permit critical evaluation of domestic procedure in the light of foreign procedural institutions. Third, they should promote better understanding and easier acceptance of procedure in international tribunals, which in large part, is patterned on foreign systems of procedure. And finally, they should facilitate comprehension and appreciation of the culture and customs of foreign countries in general.

The basic structure of the three books on civil procedure is the same. Each endeavors to discuss the problems encountered in litigating a civil controversy in the chronological order in which they are most likely to arise. By proceeding in this fashion, a coherent picture is presented, and, at the same time, abstract categorizations cutting across normal developments in a lawsuit which impede proper understanding of foreign rules in their functional context are avoided. Since civil procedure, as all law, is a product of historical developments and since it cannot be understood without reference to the political structure within which it is to operate, the first chapter is devoted to a discussion of the history of the foreign country, its political organization, and the history of its civil procedure. Also included in that chapter are a description and an evaluation of authoritative sources of civil procedure. By way of conclusion, each books describes the treatment extended to judgments rendered in foreign countries and domestic procedures of international cooperation in litigation. The practical importance of these subjects to foreign lawyers warrants their inclusion.

Each book is the product of co-operation between an American lawyer and a lawyer of the country whose procedure it describes. This form of collaboration was chosen to insure that the subject matter be presented in a form comprehensible to lawyers trained in the common law and that the content meet the standards of scholarship observed in the foreign country.

French civil procedure was selected for obvious reasons. Not only is it the system of procedure prevailing in one of the leading nations of the world, but it has also been an important part of France's cultural exports to many other countries of the world.

Dr. Weser and Professor Herzog commenced their work on the book in the fall of 1960. Because the preparation of this book required considerably more time than anticipated and Dr. Weser had to terminate her collaboration in the fall of 1962, it was impossible to adhere to the procedure followed in the preparation of the Project's other studies. Dr. Weser and Professor Herzog did collaborate on chapters 2, 4, 5, and 6, but Dr. Weser neither participated in the preparation of, nor is responsible for, any of the other chapters.

In 1962, Professor Herzog spent four months in France, working on the manuscript for this book. He acknowledges his particular gratitude for assistance willingly granted and information readily supplied to: the Honorable Judge Marc Ancel, *Conseiller* at the *Cour de Cassation*; Professor Henri Batiffol; the Honorable Judge Pierre Bellet, *Président de Chambre* at the *Cour d'Appel* in Paris; Professor René David; Me. René Després, *avoué* at the *Cour d'Appel* in Paris; Professor Christian Gavalda; Me. Fernand Jeantet, *avocat* at the *Cour d'Appel* in Paris; the Honorable Judge Louis Legorju, *Vice President, Tribunal de Grande Instance* in Paris; Me. J. Lot, chief clerk, *Cour d'Appel* in Paris; the Honorable Mr. Robert Onéto, *Substitut* of the *Procureur de la République* in Paris; Professor Roger Perrot; Me. Jean Ponelle, *avoué* at the *Tribunal de Grande Instance* in Paris; Me. Pradon, *avocat* at the *Conseil d'Etat* and *Cour de Cassation*; Professor Henri Solus; and Me. Juliette Veillier-Duray, *avocat* at the *Cour d'Appel* in Paris. Special thanks are also due to Mrs. G. S. Koopman of The Hague, The Netherlands, who is mainly responsible for the typing of the manuscript.

The manuscript for this book was completed in June, 1965. During its preparation, the French law of civil procedure was the subject of rather rapid changes. An effort has been made to take due account of these changes even when they affected chapters that had already been completed. After the manuscript had been completed, additional legislative changes occurred, including the promulgation of Décret No. 65–872 of October 13, 1965, and Décret No. 65–1006 of November 26, 1965. To the extent possible, these changes were taken into consideration in the correction of the printed proofs.

We are sincerely grateful to the Carnegie Corporation of New York which made the grant that permitted us to undertake the preparation of this book.

We also express our sincere gratitude to Andrew Cordier, Dean of the Columbia University School of International Affairs, who provided the funds that enabled us to publish this book in a form considerably more voluminous than anticipated, and to William C. Warren, Dean of the Columbia University School of Law, who was a moving force in the creation of the Project and through his benevolent supervision made light the burden of its administration.

The editor, finally, expresses his appreciation to Willis L. M. Reese, Charles Evans Hughes Professor of Law at Columbia University, for his kind and ready assistance.

HANS SMIT
*Professor of Law*
*Columbia University*

## SUMMARY OF CONTENTS

## DETAILED TABLE OF CONTENTS

## ABBREVIATIONS

Abbreviations conform substantially with *A Uniform System of Citations* (10th ed. 1958), copyright by the *Columbia, Harvard,* and *University of Pennsylvania Law Reviews* and the *Yale Law Journal.* However, in a number of instances, citation forms prescribed in this booklet have been altered in the interest of greater clarity or to conform more nearly to French practice. For an extensive list of French abbreviations, see also Szladits, *Guide to Foreign Legal Materials: French-German-Swiss* 113–116 (1959).

Because of their frequent recurrence, the following abbreviations are listed below:

1. *Books*

| | | |
|---|---|---|
| Batiffol | = | Henri Batiffol, Traité Elémentaire de Droit International Privé (3d ed. 1959) |
| Colin & Capitant | = | Cours Elémentaire de Droit Civil Français de Ambroise Colin et Henri Capitant, volumes 2 and 3 (10th ed., 1948–50); vol. 1 is entitled Traité de Droit Civil (rev. ed. by Julliot de la Morandière 1953) |
| Cornu & Foyer | = | Gérard Cornu et Jean Foyer, Procédure Civile (1958); *Mise à jour* (1960) |
| Cuche & Vincent | = | Paul Cuche et Jean Vincent, Précis de Procédure Civile et Commerciale (12th ed. 1960); *Mise à jour* (1961) |
| Garsonnet & Cézar-Bru | = | E. Garsonnet et Ch. Cézar-Bru, Traité Théorique et Pratique de Procédure Civile et Commerciale, in 10 volumes (3d ed. 1912–1938) |
| Julliot de la Morandière | = | Traité de Droit Civil de Ambroise Colin et Henri Capitant, completely revised by L. |

| | |
|---|---|
| | Julliot de la Morandière, volume 1 (1957), volume 2 (1959) |
| Morel | = René Morel, Traité Elémentaire de Procédure Civile (2d ed. 1949) |
| Solus & Perrot | = Henri Solus et Roger Perrot, Droit Judiciaire Privé, volume 1 (1961) |

2. *Periodicals and Reports*

| | |
|---|---|
| B.L.D. | = Bulletin Législatif Dalloz |
| Bull. Civ. | = Bulletin des arrêts de la Cour de Cassation = rendus en matière civile (Bulletin Civil) |
| Clunet | = Journal du Droit International |
| D. | = Recueil Dalloz (Dalloz Périodique) (until 1940). The figure immediately following the D. indicates the part. Thus, [1930] D. 2.200 means: Dalloz Périodique, for the year 1930, part 2, page 200 |
| D.H. | = Dalloz Hebdomadaire (until 1940) |
| D.A. (or D. Anal.) | = Dalloz Analytique (1941–1944) |
| D.Cr. (or D. Crit.) | = Dalloz Critique (1941–1944)<br>The individual parts for Dalloz Analytique and Dalloz Critique are abbreviated as follows: Chr. = Chronique, J. = Jurisprudence, L. = Législation |
| D.Chr. | = Recueil Dalloz, section Chronique (1945 – date) |
| D.J. | = Recueil Dalloz, section Jurisprudence (1945 – date) |
| D.L. | = Recueil Dalloz, section Législation (1945 – date) |
| D. Somm. | = Recueil Dalloz, section Sommaires (1945-date) |
| Gaz. Pal. | = Gazette du Palais |
| J.C.P. | = Jurisclasseur Périodique (La Semaine Juridique). The symbol No. in front of the item number has been omitted. Thus,[1960] J.C.P. 2.15552 means: Jurisclasseur Périodique, for the year 1960, part 2, item No. 15552. |
| J.O. | = Journal Officiel de la République Française |

| | |
|---|---|
| Rev. Cr. D.I.P. | = Revue critique de droit international privé |
| Rev. Trim. Dr. Civ. | = Revue trimestrielle de droit civil |
| S. | = Recueil Sirey. Depending upon the method of designation employed in the volume itself, the legislation part of this service is designated as S.L. Annot. (Sirey Lois Annotés) or as S. 5. (Sirey part 5). |

3. *Courts*

| | |
|---|---|
| Cass. Civ. | = Cour de Cassation, chambre civile |
| Cass. Com. | = Cour de Cassation, chambre civile, section commerciale |
| Cass. Crim. | = Cour de Cassation, chambre criminelle |
| Cass. Req. | = Cour de Cassation, chambre des requêtes |
| Cass. Soc. | = Cour de Cassation, chambre civile, section sociale |
| Cour | = Cour d'Appel |
| trib. | = tribunal civil (tribunal d'arrondissement) |
| trib. com. | = tribunal de commerce |
| trib. gde inst. | = tribunal de grande instance |
| trib. inst. | = tribunal d'instance |
| trib. paix | = tribunal de paix |

References to legislative materials are either in French or in English:

| | |
|---|---|
| Loi | = Law |
| Décret | = Decree |
| Décret-Loi | = Decree Law |
| Ordonnance | = Ordinance |

## CHAPTER 1

# INTRODUCTION

This chapter provides a background for the description of French civil procedure in subsequent chapters. It summarizes the political history of France (1.01–1.10), describes France's political organization (1.11–1.20), provides a summary history of French civil procedure (1.21–1.29), and describes the formal sources of French civil procedure (1.30–1.38).

## 1. THE POLITICAL HISTORY OF FRANCE

### 1.01. Early History

In the field of procedure, perhaps more than elsewhere, it is true that "the life of the law has not been logic, it has been experience." [1] Study of the history of France is therefore helpful in obtaining an understanding of present-day French Procedure.[2]

**a. The Gauls.** Archeological discoveries indicate that as early as the stone age a relatively highly developed culture must have existed in southwestern France. However, little is known about that region's early inhabitants.[3] Around 500 B.C., the Celts, a warlike people pro-

[1] HOLMES, THE COMMON LAW 1 (1881). On the different developments in England and in France, see 1 HOLDSWORTH, HISTORY OF ENGLISH LAW 304, 314–20 (7th ed. 1956); 2 HOLDSWORTH, HISTORY OF ENGLISH LAW 125 (3d ed. 1927); *cf.* 2 POLLOCK & MAITLAND, HISTORY OF ENGLISH LAW 674 (2d ed. 1899); SMITH, THE DEVELOPMENT OF EUROPEAN LAW XX (1928). On permanent and changeable elements in procedure generally, see CALAMANDREI, PROCEDURE AND DEMOCRACY (1956).

[2] The summary of French history presented here is based, in large measure, upon the following sources: BAINVILLE, HISTOIRE DE FRANCE (1924); COBBAN, HISTORY OF MODERN FRANCE (2 vols; 1961) (containing a fairly extensive bibliography); GUÉRARD, FRANCE, A SHORT HISTORY (1946); MAUROIS, HISTOIRE DE LA FRANCE (2 vols. 1954); ROMIER & ROWSE, A HISTORY OF FRANCE (1953); TIMBAL, HISTOIRE DES INSTITUTIONS ET DES FAITS SOCIAUX (1957). For larger works in French, see HANOTAUX, HISTOIRE DE LA NATION FRANÇAISE, DES ORIGINES PRÉHISTORIQUES JUSQU'À NOS JOURS (15 vols. 1929); LAVISSE, HISTOIRE DE FRANCE DEPUIS LES ORIGINES JUSQU'À LA RÉVOLUTION (9 vols. 1926); LAVISSE, HISTOIRE DE LA FRANCE CONTEMPORAINE (10 vols. 1922).

[3] Phoenician and Greek commercial settlements were early established along the southern coast of France, among them Marseilles (Marsilia 600 B.C.). However, the political influence of these towns never reached far inland.

bably coming from the Baltic region in northeastern Europe, conquered not only much of what is now French territory, but also England and Ireland. Those who settled in France came to be known as Gauls, the name given to them by the Romans.[4] The society of the Gauls was fairly primitive. Politically, they were organized into largely independent tribal units in which priests, called druids, appear to have held influential positions. The Gauls had no urban centers comparable to the cities of the Mediterranean peoples.

**b. The Roman conquest of Gaul.** The Romans, long interested in acquiring the portion of Gaul that bridged their Italian and Spanish possessions, conquered southern France in 121 B.C. and established that territory as the Roman province *Gallia Transalpina.*[5] Julius Caesar, who became governor of *Gallia Transalpina* in 59 B.C., encouraged by rivalries between the Gallic tribes, embarked upon a campaign to conquer all of Gaul. Despite the superior organization of the Roman army and the dissension among the Gauls, it took over seven years of arduous campaigning before the country was finally subdued.

During the first two centuries of Roman rule, introduction of varied elements of Mediterranean culture and technology brought relative prosperity to Gaul. However, in the third century A.D., unrest among the Germanic and other peoples of eastern and northern Europe as well as internal corruption and decay presaged the disintegration of the Roman Empire. The first barbarian invasions were repulsed, but insecurity mounted and commerce declined. Laying part of the foundation for the feudal system that was to come, small landowners put their persons and property under protection of more powerful lords.

**c. The Franks.** At the time of the collapse of the Western Roman Empire, in 476 A.D.,[6] Gaul was conquered by the Franks (from whom France received her name), a Germanic people governed by kings from the Merovingian family. In 496, hastening the process of assimilation

[4] Some information on the Gauls is provided in Julius Caesar's book on his conquest of Gaul, the COMMENTARII DE BELLO GALLICO, which became a popular text for the study of Latin.

[5] Translated literally, Gaul on the other side of the Alps; northern Italy was called *Gallia Cisalpina, i.e.*, Gaul on this (the Italian) side of the Alps.

[6] In the fifth century, the Roman Empire was divided into an Eastern and a Western half. The last Western Roman Emperor, Romulus Augustulus, was deposed by the Germanic leader Odoakar in 476. The Eastern Roman Empire continued until 1453, when Constantinople, its capital, was conquered by the Turks. Indeed, the great codification of Roman law under the Emperor Justinian, which became the basis for the revival of Roman law in the twelfth century, was prepared around 550 A.D., after the Western Empire had ceased to exist.

between conquered and conquerors, the King of the Franks, Clovis, accepted Christianity. He thereby gained the support of the Church, at that time about the only remaining organized force within the country.

The period following the death of King Clovis was one of internal strife and threats from abroad, the most serious of which came from the Arabs who had already conquered North Africa and Spain.[7] In 732, under the leadership of Charles Martell, mayor of the palace (chief officer of the king), the invading Arabs were turned back. In 758, with the approval of the Pope, Charles Martell's son and successor as mayor of the palace, Pipin (called the Short), made himself king, thereby placing formal authority where actual authority had existed for some time.

Charlemagne, son of Pipin, ruling from 771 to 814, consolidated the Frankish kingdom and extended its boundaries to include the territory of present-day France, Germany as far as the Elbe River, and substantial parts of Italy. In 800, Charlemagne was solemnly crowned Emperor of the Romans by the Pope. However, his rule did not abate the unsettled conditions that prevailed since the collapse of the Roman Empire. While Charlemagne's sons quarrelled about their inheritance rights, invasions by Norsemen and others continued to plague the population. By the Treaty of Verdun (843), Charlemagne's empire was divided among his sons into three parts: a western section, which became present-day France, an eastern section, which became Germany, and a narrow central section separating the two. The central section, called Lotharingia (Lorraine) after its first ruler, was to become a bone of contention between the two nations.

**d. The early Capetian kings.** Most of the Carolingian kings (descendants of Charlemagne) were weak rulers; during their reign, the local nobles, originally only officers of the crown, became virtually independent. In 987, Hugh Capet, a member of one of the more prominent noble families and supported by the powerful bishop of Rheims, was elected king; his election terminated the rule of the Carolingians.

Hugh Capet and his successors strengthened royal power. The Capetian kings abolished the elective system in force during the Carolingian period by making their sons co-rulers during their lifetime. They added territories to their own domain, which was strategically located in the

[7] According to a theory proposed by the Belgian historian Pirenne, the progress of the Arabs, more than the barbarian invasions, caused the downfall of Roman civilization. *Cf.* HEATON, ECONOMIC HISTORY OF EUROPE 75–79 (1948).

center of France around Paris, and asserted increasing authority over the feudal lords.

**e. The early Middle Ages.** The twelfth century marks the inception of a period of marked development and progress in the economic, political, and cultural life of France. Increasing commercial activity was attended by the growth of cities and trade centers. Paris University, founded around 1209, became an important center for theological studies. Construction of the Cathedral of Notre Dame commenced about the same time. A reform started at Cluny resulted in the correction of church abuses. The Crusades began, leading to the temporary conquest of the Holy Land and, of more enduring significance, commercial and intellectual contacts with the East.

Politically, this period saw a further consolidation of royal power. Louis VI (1108–1137) restored order in his own domain, thus laying the basis for further progress. The energetic Philippe Auguste (1180–1223) directed his efforts against the English and succeeded in adding to the royal domain Normandy, Poitou, and Maine.[8] The military expeditions of Louis VIII (1223–1226) won for the crown the Toulouse region of France. Under Louis IX (1226–1270), better known as Saint Louis, the king's reputation for justice, fairness, and holiness, rather than military might, served to augment royal authority and prestige. Under him, the famous *Parlement* of Paris was established as France's main court of law.[9] The methods of Philippe the Fair (1285–1314) were of a different character. Engaged in open conflict with both the church and the great nobles, he surrounded himself with persons learned in Roman law (the so-called *légistes*), who tried to show that the kings of France were entitled to all the prerogatives of emperors. In 1302, to obtain support against the church, Philippe convened the first Estates General (*Etats Généraux*) to which representatives of the nobility, the clergy, and the commoners (*bourgeoisie*) were summoned.[10]

[8] In the period preceding the reign of Philippe Auguste, the marriage of Eleanor of Aquitania, who held extensive possessions in western France, to the English King, Henry Plantagenet, had put almost the entire Atlantic seacoast under English control. Since the Norman invasion of England (1066), the King of England had also been Duke of Normandy.

[9] This was done by transferring the judical activities of his council to a separate body, which came to be called *Parlement*. See 1.23 *infra*. St. Louis also made the minting of coin a royal prerogative; earlier, the feudal nobles had minted their own coin. St. Louis did return some areas in western France to the English, but required that they recognize his overlordship over these territories (Treaty of Paris, 1259).

[10] Like the English parliament, the French Estates General were an outgrowth of the royal council (*curia regis*). Since they were usually subject to royal domination, they never attained the power of the English parliament.

**f. The Hundred Years' War.** Upon the death of Charles IV, son of Philippe the Fair, in 1328, the direct line of the Capetians came to an end. The accession to the throne of the Valois, a younger branch of the Capetian family, was contested by Edward III, King of England and grandson of Philippe the Fair. A bitter conflict between England and France, the Hundred Years' War ensued.

During the latter half of the fourteenth century and the beginning of the fifteenth century, military defeat at the hands of the better organized and equipped English troops, peasant revolts, and the alliance of the Dukes of Burgundy and the citizens of Paris with the English, appeared to seal the fate of France. In the Treaty of Troyes (1420), King Charles VI disinherited his own son and appointed Henry V, King of England, as Regent of France. France seemed destined to come completely under English domination. However, Charles VII, the son of Charles VI, refused to recognize the treaty of 1420; he continued the war, but with very little success until Joan of Arc appeared in 1429, liberated Orleans, and had the King crowned at Rheims. Despite Joan's subsequent capture and execution (1431), the French were to retain the upper hand. The Dukes of Burgundy broke their English alliance and aligned themselves with the Kings of France. In 1453, the war ended with an almost complete defeat for the English. They lost all of their French possessions with the exception of Calais.

The Hundred Years' War had disastrous effects in France. The French population declined sharply, commerce suffered, and production was impaired. Yet the war increased the feeling of national unity. It strengthened the power of the kings and weakened that of the feudal nobles who, in the emerging age of gunpowder, were no longer an effective fighting force.

## 1.02. Renaissance and Reformation

The period following the end of the Hundred Years' War was one of consolidation. Politically, the monarchy strengthened its power, largely through land annexations [11] and administrative reforms directed against the feudal lords. Officials and advisers were selected from the middle class, the feudal army was replaced by a standing army under direct royal control, and the powers of the remaining feudal lords to dispense justice were curtailed: Decisions of their courts were made subject to review by the royal tribunals. In addition, the kings began to legislate extensively for the whole kingdom, a prerogative rarely exer-

[11] Louis XI (1461–1483) acquired part of Burgundy and the province of Anjou.

cised during the Middle Ages. Of particular significance, through a royal ordinance of 1454, the various customs (*coutumes*) upon which the private law in the northern part of France was based were reduced to writing. [12] Economic expansion kept pace with political consolidation. Discoveries in the East and in America stimulated trade, while inventions such as the printing press resulted in the creation of new industries. The Renaissance with its new ideas in the arts, literature, and philosophy spread from Italy to France. In the legal field, interest in Roman law was revived and its study was organized on a more systematic, historical basis. [13]

During the first half of the sixteenth century, military expeditions in Italy brought the French into conflict with the Hapsburg Emperor of Germany, Charles V, who also controlled Austria, most of Burgundy, the Netherlands, Spain, and the Spanish possessions in Italy and the New World. The Hapsburg threat abated in 1556, when Charles V, wearied by the opposition he had encountered on all sides, abdicated and divided his realm between his two sons Ferdinand (who received the Austrian part) and Philippe (who received the Spanish part). Thereafter, the security of France was no longer endangered by the same power on her eastern and southern borders.

In the latter part of the sixteenth century, dissension created in France by the Reformation led to increasingly violent internal strife culminating in the massacre of thousands of protestants on the night of St. Bartholomew in 1572, and the assassination of King Henry III in 1589. Religious peace was restored by King Henry IV (Henry of Bourbon), a protestant who became a catholic in 1593 to overcome the opposition of the catholic party to his accession. In 1598, King Henry issued the Edict of Nantes which granted the protestants religious freedom and, as a safeguard for their rights, allowed them to occupy certain fortified cities.

### 1.03. The Rule of the Bourbons

**a. Henry IV.** Assisted by his protestant minister Sully, Henry IV endeavored to promote national prosperity through public work programs and other economic measures; his slogan was "a chicken in the pot for every French peasant on Sunday." Being of a practical bent, he formal-

[12] There are, however, earlier private collections of the *coutumes* of some areas.

[13] The best known representatives of the historical school are Cujas (1520–1590), whose main works appeared between 1554 and 1585, and Godefroy or Godofredus (1549–1622).

ized the system of selling judicial and other public offices – a system that had existed in France since the thirteenth century.

**b. Increasing absolutism: Louis XIII and Cardinal Richelieu.** Henry IV was assassinated in 1610, when his son, Louis XIII (1610–1643), was still a child. As Regent, Louis XIII's mother Marie de Medicis was unable to deal effectively with the insurgent nobles and the reins of government were soon taken up by Bishop (later Cardinal) Richelieu. On the domestic side, Richelieu continued the centralizing and absolutist tendencies of the French monarchs. He levied taxes without convening the Estates General, subdued opposition among the nobility, and, without attempting to curtail religious freedom, destroyed the political power of the French protestants by conquering La Rochelle, the last of the protestant fortifications established under the Edict of Nantes. By contrast, on the foreign scene, Richelieu allied himself with the protestant princes of Germany. Assisting them in their struggle against the Hapsburgs, whom he considered the most dangerous enemies of France, Richelieu ultimately brought France into the Thirty Years' War on the protestant side. Although the Treaty of Westphalia (1648), which terminated the war, was not concluded until after the death of Richelieu (1642), it represents the outstanding achievement of his foreign policy: France acquired a part of Alsatia, the Sundgau; the German princes became virtually independent of the Hapsburg Emperors; and France was made the guarantor of their independence. In short, the German Empire ceased to exist as a political force capable of jeopardizing the security of France.

**c. Absolute monarchy and its apex: Louis XIV**. Within a year of the death of Richelieu, Louis XIII died and the crown again devolved upon a child, Louis XIV. The regency conducted by his mother, Anne of Austria, resulted in a period of anarchy, known as *La Fronde*. Once again the nobility attempted to regain lost power, this time assisted by the members of the *parlements*.[14] By 1653, the rebellious nobles and judges were defeated. Thereafter, Cardinal Mazarin ruled France on the principles laid down by Richelieu.

In 1661, when Mazarin died, the personal rule of Louis XIV commenced. To eliminate the disorders of the *Fronde*, he sought to put a

[14] After the creation of the *Parlement* of Paris under Louis IX, other *parlements* were gradually established in some of the larger cities. Since the judges of the *parlements* had an hereditary title to their office, which they could sell, they were quite independent of the King and often opposed royal policy. See also 1.03.a, f *infra*.

permanent end to opposition from the nobility. He built and established his court at the palace of Versailles, attracted the great nobles there, and, while purporting to bestow favors upon them, deprived them of political power by entrusting the administration of governmental affairs to commoners, such as Colbert. [15] Afraid of the power of a prime minister, Louis XIV did not permit any of his advisers or officials to attain that position. Louis XIV's religious policy reflected his desire to secure absolute power in the hands of the monarch. Revoking the Edict of Nantes in 1684, he deprived the protestants of their religious freedom. [16] While supporting the Catholic Church in doctrinal matters, he engaged in a number of disputes with the Pope, insisting upon a large measure of control over the "Gallican" Church. [17] His foreign policy was one of expansion. Forays against Germany and Holland brought territorial acquisitions and political supremacy to France. However, during Louis' last years, France suffered a number of military reverses in the War of the Spanish succession (1701–1714) [18] and her economy was severely strained. The peace treaties (Paris and Utrecht, 1713, 1714) were inconclusive: Louis' grandson, Philippe, became King of Spain, but on the condition that France and Spain never be united. Louis XIV died soon after the war ended (1715). The people, wearied by his wars and autocratic regime, rejoiced at the news that he who had been called Louis the Great and the Sun-King (*Roi-Soleil*) was dead. [19]

**d. The regency of Philippe of Orléans.** A number of deaths in the royal family and the accession of Louis XIV's grandson to the Spanish throne left a five-year old child (Louis XV) as the only heir to the French crown. In his last will, Louis XIV appointed Philippe of Orléans as

[15] Colbert was Louis XIV's chief adviser on general administration, finance, commerce, and colonial and naval matters. His principal military adviser was Louvois, while his fortresses were designed by Vauban.

[16] He also intervened in the so-called Jansenist controversy and dissolved the abbey of Port-Royal, where the doctrine of Jansenism (so-called after its founder Jansenius who held views somewhat similar to those of Calvin) had its main support. One of the most famous Jansenists was Blaise Pascal, the writer, philosopher, and mathematician.

[17] The controversy with the Pope centered around the King's claim to the revenues of vacant bishoprics; Gallicanism (the doctrine of the independence of the French church from the Pope in temporal matters) found its chief expression in the "four articles" adopted by the general assembly of the French clergy in 1682. One of the main supporters of Gallicanism was Bossuet, the famous bishop of Meaux.

[18] Louis XIV was related to the Spanish Hapsburgs through marriage. The controversy arose when England, Austria, and Russia opposed his attempt to place his grandson, Philippe, on the vacant Spanish throne.

[19] The temper of the times was reflected in the sermon preached at Louis XIV's funeral. It began with the words: "God alone is great, my brethren."

Regent of France, but restricted his powers by directing that a regency council supervise his actions. Philippe persuaded the *Parlement* of Paris to invalidate the will and, in return, granted its judges the right to "remonstrate" – to oppose royal decrees.

**e. Louis XV.** The monarchy, weakened during Philippe's regency, suffered a further loss of prestige during the personal rule of Louis XV. The King's foreign policy was largely a failure. Although Lorraine (1766) and Corsica (1768) were acquired, giving France substantially her present frontiers, France lost Canada and her colonies in the Indies, as well as other overseas possessions. [20] At home, the war efforts caused a financial crisis. Exemptions enjoyed by the privileged classes – the clergy and the nobility – limited tax revenues. The *parlements* contended that new taxes, unless voted by the Estates General, required their approval. On the advice of his chancellor Meaupou, Louis XV finally abolished the *parlements* and replaced them by appellate courts without political powers.

**f. The prelude to the revolution: Louis XVI.** When Louis XVI acceded to the throne in 1774, it still seemed possible to solve existing problems: The young King had a genuine desire to do what was right. As the King's chief minister, the economist Turgot proposed a number of fiscal and economic reforms, which, however, encountered opposition from many quarters. The nobility, unwilling to give up any of its privileges, adopted an uncompromisingly hostile attitude toward the bourgeoisie. Further, the judges of the reinstated *parlements* – Louis XVI had been unable to refund to the judges the purchase price of their offices and had therefore abrogated the Meaupou reform – opposed reform vigorously. After only two years in office, Turgot was compelled to retire. Meanwhile, the War of Independence broke out in America; France assisted the American colonies, finally entering the war on the side of the United States. The Treaty of Paris (1783) brought victory to the two allies, but the financial cost of the war was crushing for France. Following a number of unsuccessful attempts to cope with the evergrowing deficit, it was suggested to the King that the urgently needed reforms could be effected only if the Estates General approved. The King accepted this advice, and on May 5, 1789, the Estates General convened for the first time since 1614.

[20] In the Wars of the Austrian Succession (1740–48) and the Seven Years War (1756–63), known in American history as King George's War and the French and Indian War.

### 1.04. Revolution and Empire (1789–1815)

**a. The constitutional monarchy.** When the Estates General – 300 deputies of the nobility, 300 of the clergy, and 600 of the third estate (*bourgeoisie*) – met on May 5, 1789, nobody advocated overthrowing the monarchy, at least not openly. Yet the convocation of the Estates General after such a long period of time was in itself an event of revolutionary significance. A dispute between the third estate and the King developed almost at once. The King thought that the voting should be by estates, so that the two privileged classes could outvote the third estate; the members of the third estate insisted on one vote for each delegate. When the King refused to accede to the wishes of the third estate, its members declared themselves the true representatives of the people. Taking the name *Assemblée Nationale* (National Assembly), they invited delegates of the nobility and the clergy who sympathized with their views to join them (June 17). A few days later, the King gave in and accepted this National Assembly (June 27).

The assembly began at once to enact a series of far-reaching reforms: During the famous night of August 4, 1789, all feudal rights and special privileges (including feudal rights to services, and rents) were abrogated; [21] on August 26, 1789, the Rights of Man were proclaimed. In addition, work was commenced upon a constitution. [22] As a means of solving the mounting financial crisis, a plan for the seizure and sale of church property was approved (November 2, 1789); as compensation, priests were to be paid a salary by the state, provided they obeyed a new law regulating the activities and organization of the Church. [23] The plan did not work well. Paper money (*assignats*) issued by the government, backed in theory by the value of the seized church property, depreciated rapidly. In the depressed market, church properties sold at inordinately low prices. Moreover, the measures were the beginning of an increasingly bitter religious conflict. The King ,who opposed legislation directed against the church, was forced by the populace to leave Versailles and return to Paris (October 5). [24]

[21] Some of these rights were subsequently restored to the landholders, the Assembly distinguishing between rights of contractual and servile origin. The final abolition of all dues owed the large noble landowners did not come until 1793.

[22] For this reason, the National Assembly became known as the Constituent Assembly.

[23] This legislation was called the "Civil Constitution of the Clergy." It gave the French government a very high degree of control over the Church and practically eliminated the influence of the Pope. It required all French priests to take an oath accepting the "Civil Constitution." A majority of the clergy refused to do so, and the legislation was eventually condemned by the Pope in its entirety.

[24] The "Civil Constitution of the Clergy" was one of the main bones of contention between the Assembly and the King, who was quite religious.

The following year, the Assembly continued its work of reform. The old courts, including the *parlements*, were abolished and a new court system created. [25] Freedom of trade was established and the ancient guilds, which had controlled most occupations in France, were abolished. On September 3, 1791, the Constitution was proclaimed. It provided for separation of executive and legislative power: Legislative power was vested in an assembly elected for two years by all citizens paying more than a certain sum in taxes; [26] executive power resided in the King who also had authority to suspend enactments of the Assembly for a period of four years. [27] The judiciary was originally envisioned as an appendage of the legislature rather than as an independent authority.

**b. The Legislative Assembly.** The Assembly elected under the constitution was increasingly dominated by its more radical elements. Alarmed at the turn of events in France, the European powers contemplated steps to halt the progress of radical ideas. Thereupon, the party then in control of the National Assembly (the *Girondins*) compelled the King to declare war upon Austria and Prussia (April 20, 1792). During the early part of the war, largely as a result of the effects of the revolution upon morale and discipline within the army, France suffered a series of reverses for which Louis XVI was held responsible. On August 20, 1792, a mob, intent on revenge, invaded the King's palace. The King fled to the National Assembly. It was the virtual end of the monarchy. [28]

**c. The Convention.** The new Assembly, elected shortly after the King's flight, soon came under the dominating influence of the radical *Jacobin* group. [29] The Assembly proclaimed France a republic (September 21, 1792) and adopted a new constitution (June 24, 1793) to become effective upon the restoration of normal circumstances; in fact, this constitution never came into effect. The internal and external situation of France deteriorated: Armed insurrection against the revo-

[25] See 1.24 *infra*. In its basic features the system established during the French Revolution is still in force today.

[26] Citizens having the right to vote were called "active" citizens; those without the franchise were called "passive" citizens.

[27] In addition, the King was authorized to appoint the various cabinet ministers, who were not directly responsible to the Assembly.

[28] The King had lost much of his power a year earlier, when he tried to flee from Paris to join royalist troops. However, he was recognized at Varennes and forced to return.

[29] The Jacobins received their name from the convent of the Jacobins (Dominicans) where they held their meetings.

lutionary government occurred in parts of western France, and the allied Austrian and Prussian armies penetrated into French territory. It became impractical for the National Assembly to try to govern the country; power was put in the hand of a small committee (*Comité du Salut Public*)[30] led by the *Jacobin*, Robespierre, an erstwhile *avocat*.

The committee took vigorous, indeed ruthless, steps to insure the victory of the revolutionary regime. During a period, appropriately called the Terror (1793–94), a large number of actual or supposed enemies of the regime, including the King (on January 21, 1793), were guillotined. Eventually, armed rebellion ceased. To oppose the highly trained professional armies of the allied powers, conscription was introduced. Vast mass armies were led into battle, the allied armies were repulsed, and French troops penetrated into Belgium (Battle of Fleurus, 1794). To check the mounting inflation, the committee promulgated a law establishing maximum prices. "Radical" legislation was also introduced in the field of private law. [31]

**d. The Directorate *(Directoire)*.** Ultimately, reaction to the terror methods took effect. Robespierre himself was executed and a new constitution was adopted vesting executive power in a Directorate (*Directoire*) of five members and legislative power in two assemblies, the Five Hundred and the Ancients. The right to vote was restricted to citizens with a certain minimum income.

The war with Austria continued, but French troops penetrated into Germany, and campaigns in Italy, led by General Napoleon Bonaparte, were highly successful. In 1797, Austria was compelled to abandon the war (Peace Treaty of Campo Formio). General Bonaparte, upon hearing that the French government was beset by difficulties, abandoned a campaign against the English in Egypt, [32] returned to France, and overthrew the *Directoire* government (1799).

[30] *Comité du Salut Public* is usually translated "Committee of Public Safety." Professor Guérin suggests as a more accurate translation: "Committee of Public Salvation."

[31] Notably in the field of family law (divorce, division of decedents' estates among all children).

[32] Napoleon's Egyptian campaign resulted in some important archeological discoveries, notably the famous Rosetta stone which made it possible to decipher the Egyptian hieroglyphics. Militarily, the campaign was less successful. Napoleon sought to hurt England's colonial interests, but the French Navy suffered a severe defeat at Abu Kir at the hands of the British fleet.

**e. The consulate.** The new constitution adopted after Napoleon's coup distributed legislative power among four bodies.[33] Executive power was nominally vested in three consuls. However, in fact, quasi-dictatorial power was exercised by Napoleon, who assumed the title of First Consul.

In both domestic and foreign matters, the new government was successful. Prosperity began to return to France. Relations with the Church were normalized by the Concordat of 1801,[34] and the members of the nobility who had left France during the revolution were invited to return. In rather rapid succession, a Civil Code (1804), a Code of Civil Procedure (1806),[35] a Commercial Code (1807), a Code of Criminal Procedure (1808), and a Penal Code (1810) were adopted. The Codes – particularly the Civil Code – represented a synthesis between pre-revolutionary French law and revolutionary principles. Napoleon also reorganized the administration, establishing the basic structure still existing in France. Peace on favorable terms was effected with Austria and England (1801).[36] On August 2, 1802, Napoleon was made consul for life.[37]

**f. The Empire.** In 1804, Napoleon Bonaparte was crowned Emperor. To add luster to his reign, he created a new nobility composed of persons who had served him well, most prominently, his military aides. Economic rehabilitation continued, and important military victories against Austria and Prussia were achieved. England posed the remaining threat. In 1805, the French navy was defeated at Trafalgar. A year later, from Berlin, Napoleon issued the continental blockade – a decree banning commerce between the nations of the continent and England. In 1812, because Russia was not observing the blockade, Napoleon declared war upon her. Troops from France as well as most other European nations (who had become Napoleon's unwilling allies) followed

[33] These were the Council of State (*Conseil d'Etat*), the Senate, the *Tribunat*, and the *Corps Législatif*. Of these, the Council of State still subsists as legal adviser to the government and as a kind of administrative tribunal. See 3.01 *infra*.

[34] By the *Concordat*, freedom of worship was once more granted to the Catholic Church. Bishops were to be nominated by Napoleon, but to receive their official investiture from the Pope. Parish priests were to be appointed by the bishops. Both bishops and priests were to swear loyalty to the government. Somewhat similar rules were adopted for the other religious bodies in France.

[35] See 1.24 *infra*.

[36] Austria's possessions in Italy were restriced to the area around Venice. French predominance over satellite republics (Holland, Switzerland, Northern Italy) was recognized (Treaty of Lunéville, February 1801).

[37] During this period, Napoleon effected the sale of the Louisiana Territory to the United States (April 30, 1803).

the Emperor into Russia. In the late fall of 1812, Moscow was conquered, but the great fire that broke out in that city and the onset of the Russian winter forced Napoleon to withdraw. Heavy losses at the hands of Russian forces attended the retreat. Soon Prussia and, after some hestitation, Austria joined the victorious Russians. Although Napoleon managed to raise and equip one more army, his forces were defeated at the battle of Leipzig (1813) by the combined armies of Russia, Prussia, and Austria. The following year, the allied powers penetrated into France and entered Paris. Napoleon abdicated and was taken to Elba.

### 1.05. The Restoration (1814–1830)

**a. Louis XVIII.** After the abdication of Napoleon, a brother of the executed King Louis XVI, assuming the name of Louis XVIII, took up the reins of government. He promulgated a reasonably liberal constitution (*Charte*) that vested executive power in the King and legislative power in a two-chamber parliament, a lower chamber elected by all persons satisfying a property requirement and an upper chamber (*chambre des pairs*) with a hereditary membership.

At the same time, a Congress met in Vienna to elaborate a peace treaty between France and the allied powers. Its labors were interrupted when Napoleon left the island of Elba and landed in France. The government of Louis XVIII collapsed very quickly, and Napoleon re-established the Empire. But war was renewed and Napoleon's army was decisively beaten at Waterloo, near Brussels (1815). Napoleon surrendered to the English and was taken to the island of St. Helena, in the South Atlantic, where he died a few years later (1821). The Second Empire had lasted only one hundred days.

After Napoleon's second downfall, Louis XVIII resumed his former position. France signed a peace treaty, in which she relinquished the conquests of the revolutionary and Napoleonic eras, but her pre-revolutionary boundaries remained substantially intact.

Louis XVIII, who had been a very conservative but basically moderate ruler, was succeeded by Charles X, who, supported by the ultra-royalist (*ultra*) party, sought a return to the days of absolute monarchy. When he attempted to enact legislation without observing the established constitutional procedures, a new revolution broke out, which accomplished its purpose in three days (*les trois glorieuses*): Charles X was forced to abdicate and a liberal government replaced the ultra-royalists (July 1830).

### 1.06. The Citizen-King: Louis Philippe (1830–1848)

The brief revolution of 1830 brought power to the well-to-do bourgeois, who sought to secure their position against extremists on both ends of the political spectrum. The crown was offered to Louis Philippe, of the house of Orléans, a younger branch of the Bourbon family with liberal tendencies. Under the new constitution, similar in most respects to the *Charte* of Louis XVIII, the franchise was broadened and membership in the upper house ceased to be hereditary.

Counseled by his prime minister, the historian Guizot, Louis-Philippe governed in a fashion designed to please his chief supporters, the members of the middle class. However, discontent arose in other quarters. The new class of wage-earners created by the beginnings of industralization agitated for abolition of property qualifications upon the right to vote. In addition, the memory of Napoleon was still an active influence. Twice, Louis Napoleon, a nephew of the Emperor, unsuccessfully attempted a Bonapartist coup. In February, 1848, armed clashes between demonstrators for an extension of the franchise and government troops broke out. France was in the midst of another revolution.

### 1.07. The Revolution of 1848 and the Reign of Napoleon III (1848–1871)

Louis Philippe did not want to use force to resist the revolutionaries; he abdicated and fled to England. An assembly met to elaborate a new constitution. This time the left had gained strength; for the first time in French politics, the socialists became influential. France was again proclaimed a republic, and universal suffrage was established. But after a few months, reaction set in in the provinces; the national workshops created for the unemployed in response to socialist demands were abolished, and bloody riots ensued.

In the meantime, the constitution had been drafted. It provided for a president with strong executive powers and a unicameral legislature. Although there were a number of candidates for the presidency, Louis Napoleon won by a wide margin. When the newly elected legislature, dominated by monarchists, voted to restrict the electoral franchise, Louis Napoleon utilized the resulting unrest and overthrew the assembly (December 2, 1851). Following this coup, Louis Napoleon was reelected president by an overwhelming majority. A new constitution was enacted granting him almost dictatorial powers. By a referendum conducted the following year, the title of Emperor was conferred upon him and he assumed the name of Napoleon III (December 2, 1852).

Domestic prosperity increased during Napoleon III's reign: Great factories were constructed, a network of railroads began to cover France, and extensive public works were undertaken. However, the foreign ventures of Napoleon III were unsuccessful. The Crimean War, in which France and England allied themselves against Russia, brought an inconclusive peace. Efforts to assist the cause of Italian unification fared somewhat better. As a reward for participating in the war to oust Austria from Italy, France obtained Nice and Savoy from the Kingdom of Piedmont. However, when an attempt was made to annex the Papal States to the new Kingdom of Italy, Napoleon and his Italian allies parted company. To remain on good terms with the catholic population in his own country, Napoleon put French troops at the disposal of the Pope. Napoleon III's third major foreign undertaking, the Mexican expedition, seemed even less required by the national interests of France than the Crimean and Italian campaigns. His plan to overthrow the Mexican Republic and to install the Archduke Maximilian, a brother of the Emperor Francis Joseph of Austria, as Emperor of Mexico miscarried, and Maximilian was shot by the Mexican leader, Juarez (1867).

Napoleon III's last war, that against Prussia-Germany (1870–1871), brought his downfall. When a relative of the King of Prussia became a candidate for the then vacant throne of Spain, France protested. The dispute seemed on its way to settlement when the Prussian chancellor, Bismarck, by publishing an inaccurate report of an interview between the French ambassador to Prussia and the King of Prussia, practically forced Napoleon to declare war upon Prussia. The French army was no match for the trained forces of Prussia, assisted by troops from most of the other German states. The bulk of the French army capitulated at Sedan (September 1870), and the Emperor was taken prisoner by the Prussians. [38] Soon thereafter, the republic was proclaimed in Paris.

However, the German armies continued to advance towards the interior of France and besieged Paris. After a winter of privation, the beleaguered inhabitants of Paris surrendered. The peace of Francfort, terminating the war (May 1871), deprived France of Alsace and Lorraine and imposed upon her a war indemnity of about five billion francs.

### 1.08. The Third Republic (1871–1940)

**a. The conservative Republic.** In february 1871, before the conclusion of the peace treaty with Germany, a general election was held. Con-

[38] Another French army under Marshal Bazaine was surrounded in the fortress Metz and had to capitulate there.

servative, monarchical elements obtained a majority. The new National Assembly ratified the Treaty of Francfort, but not without considerable opposition, particularly from its republican members. In Paris, where the population vividly recalled the hardships of the war, the conservative tendencies of the new government caused irritation. A revolt (the *Commune*) broke out; a number of buildings were destroyed, and hostages were shot by the insurrectionists. Finally, the government troops gained the upper hand and bloodily suppressed the revolution.

Because the rightist elements in control of the Assembly could not agree on a candidate, victory did not bring restoration of the monarchy. In 1875, a temporary solution was adopted. In a series of constitutional laws, a new governmental structure was outlined. [39] Provision was made for a bicameral legislature composed of a Senate with 75 permanent members and 225 members elected for nine year periods by an electoral college, a National Assembly elected by universal suffrage, and a president elected by both houses in joint session. Marshal MacMahon, who became the new president, was expected to resign when conditions made reintroduction of the monarchy feasible. The constitutional laws of 1875 were less provisional than anticipated: They remained the framework for the government of France until 1940.

The actual leader of the French government during the period following the Franco-Prussian war was Prime Minister Thiers, originally a monarchist, but later a moderate republican. Under his management, France recovered rather quickly from the effects of the war. The reparations exacted in the peace treaty were paid ahead of schedule; as a result, German troops evacuated the parts of France held as security for payment of the indemnity.

The 1876 lower house election brought victory to the republicans. In 1879, a republican majority was attained in the upper house as well. MacMahon, having failed to impose his will upon the Assembly, decided to resign. Later presidents of the Third Republic remained outside the political arena.

**b. The Republicans in control.** After the resignation of MacMahon, the power of the republicans was secure. Except for a dispute with the Church occasioned by legislation establishing free compulsory secular education (1881–82), and a series of scandals that gave rise to General Boulanger's abortive attempt to seize governmental power (1889), the

[39] The term "constitution" was avoided since permanence was not intended.

domestic scene was relatively calm until the turn of the century when sparks of dissension and political rivalries were ignited by the Dreyfus affair. Prominent writers, politicians, and intellectuals, convinced that Dreyfus was innocent, joined in a vigorous campaign to have the conviction for treason reversed. [40] Most (but not all) of Dreyfus' defenders were persons with leftist leanings. Reaction came from the right: The army, the monarchists, and many catholics viewed the pro-Dreyfus movement as an attack upon established authority. The hatred, anti-Semitism, and anti-clericalism engendered during the bitter controversy long survived the ultimate exoneration of Captain Dreyfus.

In the years following the war of 1870, France's relative weakness gave her scant opportunity for an active foreign policy in Europe. In 1894, to strengthen her external position, France concluded an alliance with Russia. Subsequently, disputes with England were settled, principally by delineation of the respective spheres of influence of the two nations in Africa; an alliance with that country was concluded in 1904 (the *Entente Cordiale*). As relationships with Germany deteriorated, these alliances became increasingly valuable to France.

**c. The First World War.** Following the assassination of the Austrian Archduke Francis Ferdinand by a Serbian nationalist on June 28, 1914, [41] and in fairly rapid succession, Austria declared war upon Serbia, Russia came to Serbia's aid, Germany entered the war on Austria's side, and France, pursuant to her alliance with Russia, was drawn into the conflict. At the outset of the war, German troops invaded neutral Belgium and advanced into northern France. England then entered the war on the side of France.

The principal thrust of the German attack was directed against the French. In September 1914, German troops reached the vicinity of Paris. They were brought to a halt near the river Marne by French forces under Marshal Joffre. [42] Both sides dug in; much of the remainder of the fight on the Western Front consisted of trench warfare in which both sides suffered severe losses, while neither succeeded in obtaining major territorial gains.

[40] The pro-Dreyfus writers included Emile Zola and Anatole France.

[41] Austria's demand that Serbia punish the murderer and that Austrian judges participate in the trial was rejected. The Austrian government apparently wanted to humiliate Serbia, hoping in this manner to discredit that country, which held a considerable attraction for the Slavic members of the Austro-Hungarian Monarchy.

[42] At the battle of the Marne, the French General Gallieni counterattacked with some reserves brought to the battlefield in Paris motor cabs. This was the first use of motor transport in modern warfare.

By 1917, war weariness among the French troops found open expression. Some mutinies occurred, but these were suppressed by Marshal Pétain, who had repulsed the German attack against Verdun the previous year. At about that time, the French cabinet was re-organized. Georges Clemenceau, who favored vigorous conduct of the war, became Prime Minister. Germany's last large-scale offensive in the West, attempted in the spring of 1918 when the allied blockade rendered her economic situation desperate, had initial success, but the allied forces, with a new unified high command under Marshal Foch, finally stopped further German advances. By July 1918, a large number of American troops under General Pershing had reinforced the allied armies, and a vigorous counteroffensive was begun. The exhausted German troops were unable to stop the allied advance. At the same time, the allied forces in the Balkans and the Middle East were successful. The German high command capitulated, and an armistice was concluded on November 11, 1918, at Compiègne.

In January, 1919, the victors met at Versailles to settle the peace. The French urged severe terms designed to immunize France against German attack, but the English and Americans favored a moderate approach. Compromise resulted. The treaty, signed on June 28, 1919 (five years to the day after the murder of Archduke Francis Ferdinand) returned Alsace-Lorraine to France. Germany also lost her colonies (as well as parts of Silesia and Pomerania, which were given to re-established Poland). In addition, she was to pay reparations, in an as yet undetermined amount. As security for Germany's performance, portions of the Rhineland were to be occupied by allied (mainly French) troops for varying lengths of time.

**d. The post-war period.** Large areas of northern and eastern France had been destroyed during the war, and casualties were extensive.[43] Nevertheless, recovery was fairly rapid. The government, under Poincaré, was able to avoid the catastrophic inflation that plagued Germany. With American assistance, the franc was stabilized at about one fifth its former value. Initially, France insisted upon strict enforcement of the Versailles treaty. In 1923, when Germany fell into arrears on reparation payments, French troops were dispatched to the industrial area of the Ruhr in northwestern Germany. The Germans answered with passive resistance. The reparations issue was settled in 1924 by the

[43] Total French casualties included about one and three quarter million military and civilian dead.

Dawes plan, providing for American loans enabling Germany to fulfill its obligations.[44] The following year, France evacuated the Ruhr region and, under the sponsorship of the French Foreign Minister Briand, who favored reconciliation with Germany, the Locarno agreements were concluded, leading to the acceptance of Germany into the League of Nations (1926).

**e. The great depression and its aftermath.** Economic crises became acute in the early 1930's. Politically, the left had the upper hand, but dissension among the leftist parties – communists, socialists, and radical socialists[45] – led to a series of shortlived, ineffectual governments. Eventually, the parties of the left began to compose their differences. In January 1936, the Popular Front – an association of radical-socialists, socialists, and communists – was created. Later that year, it won a resounding electoral success. A new government led by the socialist Léon Blum was formed. A forty-hour week, paid holidays, recognition of workers' delegates in the factories, the nationalizations of some defense industries, and a number of other reforms were the first order of business. However, the nation's economic situation did not improve, and Blum found it necessary to call a temporary halt to social reform. His decision aroused the ire of the communists, leading to the disintegration of the Popular Front and, in 1937, to Blum's resignation. After Blum's resignation, cabinets under the aegis of the radical-socialist party (Chautemps, Daladier) governed France. Their task at home was made easier by the eventual waning of the depression, but the worsening of the international situation provided them with another, more difficult problem.

**f. International relations before the outbreak of the Second World War.** Following the end of the First World War, to protect herself against a resurgence of German power, France entered into an alliance with many of the newly created (or enlarged) states of Eastern Europe (the little *entente*). After the Locarno treaty, a more conciliatory policy prevailed, evidenced by the Kellog-Briand Pact outlawing war. At the same time, the French General Staff, influenced by the memories of the

[44] The Dawes plan for German reparations was succeeded in 1930 by the Young plan, also of American origin. Eventually, the international financial crisis created by the great depression brought about the termination of reparation payments.

[45] The radical-socialist party is actually less radical than the socialist party and at times has been fairly conservative in economic matters. It is more a petty bourgeois than a workers' party.

First World War, in which tactical advantage was generally enjoyed by the defense, constructed the Maginot line from the Swiss to the Belgian border.

Hopes for improvement in international relations came to an end in 1933 when, upon Hitler's accession to power, Germany left the League of Nations as well as the disarmament conference. In 1935, contrary to the Versailles treaty, Hitler reintroduced compulsory military service, and the following year he reoccupied the Rhineland. France reacted by trying to strengthen her alliances and increase her military preparedness, but she could not keep pace with the rapidity of German rearmament.

In 1938, Germany occupied Austria, without noticeable opposition from the Western powers. A few months later, the French Premier Daladier and the English Prime Minister Chamberlain acceded to Hitler's demand for the Sudetenland, a portion of the territory of their ally, Czechoslovakia (Munich Pact, 1938). Disregarding assurances given in Munich, Hitler occupied the remainder of the Czech territory in March of 1939. Again, the Western powers failed to interfere, but the event convinced them that Hitler's expansionist drives had to be stopped. Strong guarantees were given to Poland. However, negotiations for a military alliance with the Soviet Union were abortive: In August 1939, the Soviet Union concluded a non-aggression pact with Germany. A few days after the pact was signed, Hitler invaded Poland. Faithful to their promise, France and England declared war upon Germany. The Second World War had begun.

### 1.09. The Second World War and Its Aftermath

**a. The Second World War.** In September, 1939, Hitler's armored divisions overran Poland in a few weeks. The Western powers provided no military assistance. During the whole fall and winter, French and English troops remained behind the Maginot line without displaying a substantial amount of activity. This was the period of the "phony war", the *drôle de guerre*. Presumably, the French General Staff wanted to induce Germany to engage in a war of attrition by frontal assaults on the Maginot line.

Germany took the initiative again in the spring of 1940. In April, Denmark and Norway were occupied. A month later, German troops invaded Holland, Belgium, and Luxemburg. French and English forces came to the assistance of the Belgians, but within a few days motorized German forces broke through the allied lines and, pushing westward until they reached the English Channel, put an end to the effort to save Belgium.

Soon thereafter, German troops entered Paris. Changes in the French government and high command could not arrest the catastrophe. On June 22, 1940, the aged Marshal Pétain, the hero of Verdun, who had become Prime Minister, concluded an armistice. Its terms were onerous: All of northern and central France, and the entire French Atlantic seacoast were to be occupied by Germany, and France was to bear all occupations costs. One dissenting voice was raised, however. On June 18, 1940, General De Gaulle, who had escaped to England, broadcast an appeal to the French people to continue the fight. He found few immediate adherents, but the circle of his followers was to grow steadily in the years that followed.

Soon after the armistice, what was left of the French National Assembly conferred quasi-absolute power on Marshal Pétain. Laval became Prime Minister. Domestic policy was right wing; pressure from Germany left little choice as to foreign policy. [46] However, in the field of private law and civil procedure, worthwhile projects were undertaken leading to enactments still in effect. [47]

In November 1942, when the Allies landed in French North Africa, Admiral Darlan, Pétain's commander-in-chief, aligned himself with the Allies. In reprisal for Darlan's part in facilitating the landing process, the Germans occupied all of France, including Vichy, the temporary seat of the government.

By the end of 1942, the Pétain government had lost substantially all its freedom of action. The Germans began to draft French workers for forced labor in Germany, a move which swelled the ranks and gave impetus to the activities of the anti-German underground. The increasing underground activities brought ever more violent reprisals from the Germans.

While the Vichy government became increasingly more powerless, another, which was eventually to replace it, came into being. In June 1940, General De Gaulle had organized his Free French movement in London. Subsequently, the movement was transformed into a quasi-governmental organization, the French National Committee. After the allied landing in North Africa, the Committee established headquarters in Algiers and took as its name the Committee of National Liberation.

[46] The confusion in Vichy as to whether to cooperate actively with Germany or to "wait and see" was compounded by the Mers-el-Kébir incident when the English navy sank a part of the French navy, apparently to avoid its falling into German hands.

[47] On these enactments, see 1.27 *infra*.

In June 1944, shortly before the Anglo-American forces landed in Normandy, the Committee of National Liberation declared itself the provisional government of the French Republic.

After the American forces had broken through the German lines in Normandy, the Germans evacuated most of France, taking Pétain and his cabinet with them. De Gaulle made Paris the seat of his provisional government soon after one of his Free French units entered the city. All laws promulgated by the Vichy government were declared void, unless ratified by the provisional government. [48] In the fields of private. law and civil procedure, however, the bulk of the Vichy legislation remained in effect.

De Gaulle's principal endeavor during the months following the liberation – to obtain recognition for France as an equal partner of the major allies (the United States, Great Britain, and Russia) – was successful. France became a permanent member of the Security Council of the newly created United Nations and, when Germany finally collapsed (May 8, 1945), France became one of the four occupying powers. [49]

**b. The Fourth Republic.** The first election after the war, in October 1945, was coupled with a referendum on the question whether the 1875 constitution should be retained. An overwhelming majority favored revision. However, De Gaulle and the newly elected legislature could not agree upon the structure of government to be outlined in the new fundamental law. The assembly, composed mainly of deputies of the left (socialists and communists) and the M.R.P. (a new middle of the road catholic party), wanted a powerful assembly. General De Gaulle, on the other hand, favored a strong executive. Eventually, the General resigned and retired from political life.

A proposed constitution submitted to the voters in May, 1946, was rejected. However, in a second referendum, held in October, 1946, a slightly modified version won approval. The new constitution embodied in substance practices developed under the constitutional laws of 1875. Legislative power resided in a National Assembly. A *Conseil de la République*, successor to the old Senate, had merely the right to suggest amendments. A president, largely a figurehead, was elected by joint vote of the two chambers. Executive power was entrusted to a cabinet responsible to the Assembly.

[48] The decrees and proclamations of the various organizations formed by General De Gaulle up to the time of his return to France are collected (with a note giving the constitutional laws of the Vichy regime) in 67–72 Clunet 166–196 (1940–1945).

[49] Paris also was the site of the conference leading to the signing of the peace treaties with Italy and Germany's allies in the Balkans.

From its inception, the Fourth Republic was faced with numerous problems. People who had collaborated with the Germans had to be punished, and the country had to be rebuilt. Special courts were set up for the trial of collaborators. In the immediate postwar period, Pierre Laval and a number of others were sentenced to death and executed. Marshal Pétain was imprisoned for life. In economic reconstruction, despite temporary setbacks caused by a number of strike waves, progress was rapid. In some industries, for example, the Renault automobile works, nationalized as punishment for the pro-German activities of the owners, pre-war production was surpassed. [50] A loan from the United States was negotiated to help finance the reconstruction program. In addition, a number of difficult foreign problems, such as the Saar question and the issue of German participation in the western defense effort were solved. France became an active force in the growing movement for European unity, participating in the European Coal and Steel Community, the European Common Market, and Euratom.

At the same time, the political situation of the country became unstable. The large communist party no longer participated in the government, and the number of parties at the center of the political spectrum had again increased. Middle of the road governments with a majority in the National Assembly could be formed only by reliance upon unwieldy coalitions of several parties.

The political climate did not promote formulation of the long-range policy needed to cope with the mounting demands of France's overseas possessions for independence. In Morocco and Tunis, which had always enjoyed semi-independence, the transition to complete sovereignty was fairly easy. But in Indochina a long, bloody war against communist-led guerrilla forces brought France only disappointments: In the Geneva agreements of 1954, France relinquished to the communists the northern half of Viet-Nam, the most important of the three Indochinese states, while the southern half of Viet-Nam and the two other states, Laos and Cambodia, gained shaky independence.

At about the same time, a guerrilla war against French rule began in French Algeria. The mounting crisis reached its peak in May 1958, when French inhabitants of Algeria, attempting to impose a "no compromise" policy upon the government, staged a revolt. The civil war in France that seemed almost inevitable, was averted when the

[50] Soon after the war, France also adopted a very complete system of compulsory health, old age, accident, and unemployment insurance.

middle of the road premier, Pfimlin, resigned and General De Gaulle returned to power (June, 1958).

### 1.10. The Fifth Republic: De Gaulle Again in Power

The new government set out immediately to revise the 1946 constitution. During the summer of 1958, a commission drafted a basic law expressing De Gaulle's idea of a strong executive power. Legislative power was still vested in a National Assembly and Senate, but henceforth legislation was to be necessary only in matters enumerated in the constitution, among them, taxation, the organization of government, and judicial independence. As to matters falling outside the enumeration, the executive was authorized to issue decrees with the force of law. During a six-month period following the adoption of the new constitution as well as during national emergencies, executive law-making power could be exercised without limitation.

The president, chief executive in both name and function, was to be chosen by a large electoral body composed of the members of the National Assembly, the mayors of all French municipalities, the city councils of the larger municipalities, and additional representatives of the biggest cities.

The constitution made no substantial changes in the French judicial system, but for the first time in French history it created a body with the power to declare laws unconstitutional. [51]

The constitution was submitted to the people in October, 1958; it received overwhelming approval. As anticipated, General De Gaulle was elected President. Moreover, a newly formed political party in sympathy with his views, the U.N.R., obtained the largest number of seats in the National Assembly. The Communist Party, which claimed the largest number of deputies during the Fourth Republic, lost seats, probably as a result of changes in the electoral system rather than a significant decrease in the number of communist voters.

In the period following the adoption of the new constitution, the machinery of the new governement was created and sweeping reforms were introduced in many areas, among them, judicial organization and civil and criminal procedure. [52] A number of African colonies achieved either complete independence, or at least a large measure of self-

[51] For a more detailed description of the French constitution of 1958, as well as of earlier developments, see ARON, FRANCE, THE NEW REPUBLIC (1959) and CHATELAIN, LA NOUVELLE CONSTITUTION ET LE RÉGIME POLITIQUE DE LA FRANCE (1959).

[52] See 1.29 *infra.*

government within the framework of the French Community (established by the 1958 constitution).

When the De Gaulle government began to negotiate with the Algerian Moslem independence movement (F.L.N.), the French settlers in Algeria, whose revolt had brought De Gaulle to power in 1958, felt cheated and began to oppose his regime. And when the French government concluded the Evian agreement with the F.L.N. which promised independence for Algeria (March 1962), the radical elements among the European settlers in Algeria organized an underground movement (O.A.S.) which tried to prevent Algerian independence by force. In spite of numerous terrorist attacks in Algeria and some in metropolitan France, including assassination attempts directed against De Gaulle, the O.A.S. was unable to bring a reversal of French policy, mainly because it found relatively few adherents in metropolitan France. Following a plebiscite, Algeria was declared independent (July 1962). A very large number of French Algerians, afraid of revenge by the Moslem population, left Algeria for France. Specially created military tribunals handed out some harsh sentences against a number of persons who had participated in O.A.S. inspired terrorist activities. [53]

Desirous of consolidating his position, De Gaulle now wanted to change the French constitution by providing for a direct popular election of the President. Since parliament objected, he proposed the submission of this issue to the voters in a referendum. Irked by this attempt to bypass them, the members of the National Assembly voted a motion of censure against the cabinet. [54] However, they were unable to prevent the referendum, which resulted in approval of the plan for direct election of the President. Shortly thereafter, new parliamentary elections were held, which gave the U.N.R. the largest number of seats and almost an absolute majority. Thus, De Gaulle's power seemed assured for some time to come.

[53] Some members of the O.A.S. were sentenced to death and executed. Of the top leaders, General Jouhaux was sentenced to death, but his sentence was later commuted to life imprisonment. General Salan was sentenced to life imprisonment. Georges Bidault, who had been one of the leaders of the anti-German underground during the second World War and frequently prime minister or foreign minister during the Fourth Republic, went abroad, but continued a violent campaign against General De Gaulle.

[54] The vote was formally directed against the cabinet of Georges Pompidou, the prime minister. In fact, it was a condemnation of De Gaulle's policies. Many politicans objected to De Gaulle's Algerian policy, his use of emergency powers to create and abolish special military tribunals to deal with subversive activities, his foreign policy, which in spite of a rapprochement with Germany became increasingly aloof, his anti-American and anti-British sentiments, and his often-stated dislike of politicians.

## 2. POLITICAL ORGANIZATION

### 1.11. Introduction

For close to a century, from the downfall of Napoleon III in 1870 to the accession of General de Gaulle to power in 1958, the *Parlement,* the legislative branch, occupied a position of dominating influence. Frequently, by compelling the resignation of the cabinet in power, it created protracted crises: Every new cabinet had to obtain the approval of a parliamentary majority, and the many parties, while willing to unite in bringing down the government, were often unable to agree on the formation of its successor. As a result, the preparation of long-range policy was often seriously impeded. [55]

The Constitution of October 1958 drastically reduced the powers of the French Parliament in favor of the executive. [56] However, the structure of the French Parliament has not changed significantly.

### 1.12. The French Parliament: The *Assemblée Nationale* and the *Sénat*

The Parliament is composed of a lower house, called *Assemblée Nationale,* and an upper house, called *Sénat.* [57] Members of the lower house are elected for five-year terms. [58] The members of the *Sénat* are elected by indirect vote for terms of nine years. The terms of senators are staggered: One third of the Senate's memberschip is re-elected every third year. [59] There are two regular sessions of Parliament each year, one lasting from October through December, and another one, beginning in April and lasting for not more than three months. [60]

[55] Because of the availability of many English source materials on France's political organization, the text has been kept brief. For more detailed discussions, see CHATELAIN, LA NOUVELLE CONSTITUTION ET LE RÉGIME POLITIQUE DE LA FRANCE (1959); DAVID & DE VRIES, THE FRENCH LEGAL SYSTEM 29–33 (1958); DUVERGER, THE FRENCH POLITICAL SYSTEM (1958).

[56] See CHATELAIN, *op. cit. supra* note 55, at 80–92.

[57] Constitution of 1958, art. 24. During the Fourth Republic the upper house was called *Conseil de la République,* but the 1958 Constitution readopted the name *Sénat,* which had been in use for the upper house under the Third Republic.

[58] Ordinance No. 58–1065 of Nov. 7, 1958, J.O. Nov. 9, 1958, p. 10128, [1958] D.L. 382, arts. 2, 3. The following deputies were elected to the National Assembly in 1962: 41 Communists, 5 left Socialists, 67 Socialists, 44 Radicals, 32 Independent Republicans, 38 MRP (catholic), 234 UNR (gaullist), 19 Independents. 1964 STATESMEN'S YEARBOOK 976.

[59] Constitution of 1958, art. 24; Ordinance No. 58–1097 of Nov. 15, 1958, J.O. Nov. 16, 1958, p. 10303 [1958] DL. 389, arts. 2–4. Article 1 of this Ordinance provides for 245 senators to represent France, and some additional senators to represent various overseas areas and French nationals living in foreign countries.

[60] Constitution of 1958, art. 28. The limitation on the length of the parliamentary sessions reduces the possibility of legislative interference in executive matters.

Since 1958, Parliament no longer elects the President. It may adopt only legislation concerning matters the constitution has specifically reserved for legislative regulation.[61]

Bills may be introduced or amended by the Prime Minister on behalf of the cabinet; [62] in practice, most bills are introduced by the cabinet.[63] Members of Parliament may also propose legislative measures, but may not submit bills or amendments which would reduce public revenues or increase the burden on the public treasury. [64] The cabinet has the power to cut off debate and eliminate unwelcome amendments by compelling an immediate vote on any bill debated on the floor. [65] In case of such a vote, amendments not approved by the cabinet are disreregarded. [66]

Both houses must ordinarily approve all legislation, [67] but only the Assembly can compel resignation of the cabinet by a vote of censure. [68]

The cabinet can put pressure on the Assembly by making the adoption of proposed legislation a question of confidence. If that is done, the proposed legislation is considered adopted, unless a motion of censure is made within fourty-eight hours by at least one tenth of the total membership of the Assembly and is adopted by a majority.

[61] Constitution of 1958, art. 34. The list of matters reserved for legislation includes the following: civil rights and civil liberties, compulsory military service, nationality, status of persons, succession, criminal law and criminal procedure, status of the judiciary, taxation, elections, and status of public and military officials. In the matters of national defense, local government, education, and the law of property and obligations, the establishment of basic principles, but not of detailed rules, are proper legislative concerns. Under the 1958 Constitution, Parliament retains the right to vote the budget; it must be approved in the manner provided for by an organic law. Constitution of 1958, art. 47.

[62] Constitution of 1958, arts. 39, 44.

[63] Bills introduced by the government receive priority on the calendars of the two chambers. Constitution of 1958, art. 48.

[64] Constitution of 1958, art. 40. This deprives members of Parliament of a means of embarrassing the government by submitting bills likely to be popular with the electorate, but which the government must oppose for fiscal reasons.

[65] Constitution of 1958, art. 44. The cabinet may also require submission of a bill to a special ad hoc committee for examination, instead of to one of the regular standing committees. Constitution of 1958, art. 43. This article was apparently designed to weaken the standing committees of the National Assembly who had formerly been quite powerful. See CHATELAIN, *op. cit. supra* note 55, at 103.

[66] Constitution of 1958, art. 44.

[67] If the National Assembly and Senate cannot agree on a bill, the cabinet may request submission of the bill to a conference committee of members of both houses. If this committee is unable to prepare an acceptable draft, or if the draft fails of passage, the government may submit the bill to the National Assembly, whose vote is final. Constitution of 1958, art. 45. "Organic" laws relating to the election of the President of the Republic, the appointment of public officials, the election of members of parliament, the organization of the Constitutional Council, and similar matters, must be submitted at least fifteen days before a final vote is taken; in case of deadlock between the National Assembly and the *Sénat*, the Assembly can override the *Sénat* only by a vote of a majority of all its members. See Constitution of 1958, art. 46.

[68] Constitution of 1958, art. 49.

A question of confidence may also be put to the Assembly by the cabinet on its general policy. A vote of censure leads to resignation of the cabinet. Even if no question of confidence has been raised, motions of censure may be made by one tenth of the membership of the Assembly, but members of the Assembly who have submitted a motion of censure that did not carry may not submit another motion during the same session. [69]

As a result of these restrictions, the power of Parliament to overthrow the cabinet, while still in existence, has lost most of its earlier significance. [70]

### 1.13. The Executive Branch

Until 1958, executive power rested mainly with the cabinet which was responsible to, ordinarily composed of members of, and, in a sense, merely the executive committee of, Parliament. The functions of the President of the Republic, elected in a joint session of both houses of Parliament, were mostly ceremonial in nature.

**a. The President and his cabinet.** Under the 1958 Constitution, the President is the effective head of the executive branch of government. In emergencies, he also possesses legislative powers. He appoints the Prime Minister, and, at the suggestion of the Prime Minister, the other ministers who make up the cabinet.[71] He presides over the meetings of the cabinet. [72] He promulgates the laws adopted by Parliament and signs the decrees adopted by the cabinet. Although he has no veto power, [73] he may dissolve the National Assembly. [74] He is the commander in chief of the armed forces. On the advice of the appropriate minister, he appoints the main civil and military offi-

[69] Constitution of 1958, art. 49.

[70] Before 1958, defeat of any government bill led to resignation of the cabinet.

[71] Constitution of 1958, art. 8. Under the Fourth Republic, the cabinet had to be formally approved by the National Assembly before it could begin to function. The new Constitution contains no such provision; the selection of the cabinet is the exclusive duty of the President and Prime Minister. The National Assembly retains a certain amount of indirect control over the cabinet, since it can compel the resignation of a new cabinet by disapproving the declaration of policy submitted to the National Assembly by the Prime Minister. The constitution does not make it entirely clear, however, whether a declaration of policy must be submitted to the National Assembly if a new cabinet is formed. *Cf.* CHATELAIN, *op. cit. supra* note 55, at 75–77

[72] Constitution of 1958, art. 18.

[73] However, he may return an approved bill to parliament within two weeks and request a new debate. Constitution of 1958, art. 10.

[74] Constitution of 1958, art. 12. The threat of dissolution by the President is an additional way of putting pressure on Parliament.

cials, including the members of the judiciary. [75] He negotiates treaties. [76] In times of crisis, he may assume dictatorial powers. [77]

The President of the Republic is elected for a term of seven years by universal suffrage. [78]

Governmental policy is determined by the President and the cabinet. [79] The cabinet consists of the ministers who head the various ministeries and of the Prime Minister, who directs and co-ordinates its work. [80] Until 1958, the Prime Minister was the chief governmental policy maker, but that function is now exercised in fact as well as in theory by the President. Whether the Prime Minister would remain in his present somewhat subordinate rôle if General De Gaulle were replaced by a less forceful figure is not clear.

**b. The ministries.** In contrast to pre-1958 practice, ministers may no longer be members of Parliament. Ministers usually, but not always, head governmental departments (*ministères*). [81]

Among the various ministries, including those of foreign affairs and health, the Ministry of the Interior occupies a central place in the governmental scheme. It is in charge of the entire French police system and deals with matters relating to internal security and public safety. In addition, the rather tight control to which the central government in France subjects local municipalities is exercised through the ministry of the Interior. The Minister of the Interior is also the head of the *préfets*, who act as the government's representatives in the various *départements*. [82] Another important ministry is the Ministry of Justice, which fulfills a prominent rôle in the legislative process and in the administration of justice.

Ultimate responsibility for all administrative matters rests with the ministries. There are no independent administrative agencies charged

[75] Constitution of 1958, arts. 13, 15.

[76] Constitution of 1958, art. 52.

[77] Constitution of 1958, art. 16.

[78] Constitution of 1958, art. 6, as amended by Law No. 62–1292 of Nov. 6, 1962, J.O. Nov. 7, 1962, p. 10762, [1962] D.L. 363. As originally enacted, the French constitution provided for the election of the President by an electoral college composed of various local officials.

[79] Constitution of 1958, arts. 9, 20.

[80] Constitution of 1958, art. 21.

[81] As of 1962, there were five Ministers of State (Overseas Areas; Administrative Reform; Cooperation; Science, Atom, and Space; Cultural Affairs) and fourteen regular ministries: Justice, Foreign Affairs, Interior, Armed Forces, Finance and Economy, Education, Public Works and Transport, Industry and Commerce, Agriculture, Labor, Health, Housing, Veterans, Post Office and Telecommunications. 1964 STATESMEN'S YEARBOOK 976.

[82] See, *e.g.*, WALINE, DROIT ADMINISTRATIF 297–98 (9th ed. 1963).

with the administration of public matters. In this context, it should be noted that the *Conseil d'Etat,* whose origin can be traced back to the royal council of pre-revolutionary France, is not an administrative body. Its main function is to furnish legal advice to the French government and to give its comments on proposed laws and *décrets*: While it is often discretionary with the government whether or not to consult the *Conseil d'Etat,* the cabinet must obtain, even though it needs not follow, the advice of the *Conseil d'Etat* before it adopts certain *décrets.* [83] A separate division of the *Conseil d'Etat,* called *section du contentieux,* acts as an administrative tribunal which reviews the legality of decisions of French administrative agencies. [84]

**c. The staffs of the ministries: the administration.** The ministries all have more or less the same organizational structure. [85] They are headed by a minister and consist of a central administration in Paris and field offices in various parts of the country.

The minister is the hierarchical superior of all employees in his ministry. He may issue directives to his subordinates, which may take the form of orders in individual cases or of circulars or rulings of general import. Circulars or rulings must be distinguished from *décrets* adopted by the cabinet as a whole and signed by the President of the French Republic: *Décrets* are quasi-legislative enactments binding the public in general; ministerial circulars or rulings are, at least in theory, binding only on public officials. [86]

The central administration of each ministry consists of several divisions (*directions* or *directions générales,* depending upon their importance), which are in turn divided into *sous-directions* and *bureaux.* [87] In addition, each minister has his own *cabinet,* composed of his personal confidential staff. [88]

The organization of the field services varies somewhat depending upon the nature of the activities concerned. Most ministries have a number of regional offices as well as offices in each of the 90 *départements.* [89]

[83] See, *e.g.*, WALINE, *op. cit. supra* 82, at 125; DAVID, LE DROIT FRANÇAIS 32, 33 (1960).

[84] On the *Conseil d'Etat,* see also 3.01 *infra.*

[85] The designation of *administration* is often given in France to the various governmental offices, agencies, and bureaus collectively. The term denotes the permanent elements of the executive branch which are not affected by political change, rather than the relatively few political appointees in the top positions.

[86] WALINE, *op. cit. supra* note 82, at 291.

[87] WALINE, *op. cit. supra* note 82, at 295–96.

[88] DAVID, *op. cit. supra* note 83, at 55.

[89] See DAVID, *op. cit. supra* note 83, at 29; WALINE, *op. cit. supra* note 82, at 296.

In fact, most of the work of the ministries is performed by permanent employees of the ministry with tenure who are called *fonctionnaires.* Only the members of the minister's *cabinet,* whose number is ordinarily quite small, leave office when he does. Most other positions are held by civil service employees whose appointment and promotion are based largely on educational qualifications, the passing of often difficult competitive examinations, and seniority. After the Second World War, the civil service system was subjected to a rather thorough reform and divided into a higher and lower level. Access to positions in the higher level is now available only to graduates of the National School of Administration. To be admitted to that school, one must either have a *licence en droit* or similar university degree, or four year's government service. Candidates for admission must also pass a competitive examination. They are paid while they are in training. Most persons who enter the civil service expect to make it a lifelong career. Even the top positions in the various ministries are held by civil service employees. [90] This explains why the numerous government crises under the Fourth Republic were not as harmful in their effects as might have been expected: Much of the work of the ministries continued to be carried on by civil servants and was little affected by changes in the cabinet. [91]

### 1.14. Local Government: The Centralized Structure of French Government

Much of early French history is taken up by the struggles of the monarchy against the powerful feudal lords, who in ruling the provinces enjoyed almost sovereign status. It is not astonishing that, once the monarchy had achieved control in all parts of the country, it was unwilling to part with power obtained with so much difficulty and permitted only a limited amount of local self-government. [92]

[90] For a more detailed description of the French civil service, see DAVID & DE VRIES, *op. cit. supra* note 55, at 38.

[91] The French bureaucracy has received varying evaluations. On the positive side, its members possess a long familiarity with the problems they deal with; they do not join a government office merely to obtain some expertness in the field and to exploit that expertness as soon as possible in some better paid private activity. The sense of belonging to a closely knit professional body fosters personal integrity. The same factors, however, may also produce a lack of initiative or imagination. Furthermore, it is often difficult for new ministers to put new programs into effect with collaborators appointed by their predecessors, who cannot be dismissed and who may not be in sympathy with the new minister's views. To the limited extent possible, ministers do, of course, favor persons of their own political persuasion when making promotions. *Cf.* 1 DAVID & DE VRIES, *op cit. supra* note 55, at 31.

[92] France's administrative system was never completely unified. Some of the provinces retained more privileges than others. Certain provinces, called *pays d'état,* had representative assemblies of the three estates; others did not and were under the absolute control of the royal *intendant.* See, *e.g.*, ESMEIN, COURS ELÉMENTAIRE D'HISTOIRE DU DROIT FRANÇAIS

The revolution abolished the old administrative subdivisions and replaced them with new ones with fairly artificial boundaries: (1) the *départements*, (2) the *districts* (later renamed *arrondissements*), and (3) the municipalities (*communes*), all to be governed by elected officials. Local self-government under the revolution did not work well. The new elective officials lacked experience and were unable to cope with the chaotic conditions which prevailed at the time.

The revolutionary system was profoundly revised by Napoleon. The division into *départements* and *arrondissements* was retained, but the *départements* were henceforth governed by a *préfet*, appointed by and responsible to the central government. Each *arrondissement* was put in charge of an appointive *sous-préfet* and the mayors of the various French municipalities were also made appointive. Thus, Napoleon created an almost military chain-of-command structure for the administration of France: The orders of the central government could be transmitted via the *préfets*, the *sous-préfets*, and the mayors to the inhabitants of the most remote villages in France.

After 1830, a measure of local autonomy was restored. Elective departmental councils (*conseils généraux*) and municipal councils were instituted in 1831; later, the powers of these councils were increased and eventually the mayors became elective officials. However, the *préfet* has always remained an appointed official. The financial crisis of the 1930's brought a return to more central control.

## 1.15. The *Départements*

France is subdivided into ninety *départements*. The population of the *départements* varies greatly. [93] Each *département* is a separate legal entity with limited powers of self government.

A *département* is administered by a *conseil général* (general council), elected by the voters of the *département*, and by a *préfet*, appointed by the central government. The *conseil général* votes the annual budget of, and the taxes levied by, the *département* and decides local matters. However, the scope of authority of the *conseil général* is limited, since many matters are handled by the central government. In fact, although some *départements* also operate bus lines or other facilities, their main

654-85 (13th ed. 1920). For a history of local government in France, see also WALINE, *op. cit. supra* note 82 at 307-310; VON MEHREN, THE CIVIL LAW SYSTEM 119-20 (1957) (citing numerous sources). The 1958 Constitution devotes only one article totalling less than eight lines in print to local government. Constitution of 1958, art. 72.

[93] See 1964 STATESMEN'S YEARBOOK 997-98 for statistics.

independent function seems to be the construction and maintenance of a network of departmental highways. [94]

The *préfet*, appointed by the central government, is the executive officer of the *département*. [95] At the same time, he is the delegate of the the central government in his *département*. [96] His main function as a delegate of the central government is the supervision and co-ordination of the field offices of the various ministries in his *département* and the maintenance of peace and order. He also has a certain amount of control over the decisions of the *conseil général* and of the municipal councils of his *département*, especially in budgetary matters, and may initiate proceedings to obtain the invalidation of decisions of the *conseil général* or of the municipal councils. His administrative control over the affairs of the *département* and the municipalities is usually called *tutelle administrative* (administrative guardianship). Unlike most other French public officials, the *préfet* does not have tenure, but may be dismissed at the almost complete discretion of the central government. [97]

**a. The Regions.** Although numerous fairly small *départements* do not always furnish an appropriate framework for governmental activities, until the very recent past, suggestions for the creation of larger units remained without much effect. However, in 1964, the French territory was divided into regions, each of which embraces several *départements*. The main purpose of the regions is to serve as units for purposes of regional planning and economic development; generally the administrative activities remain centered in the *départements*. Each region is headed by a regional *préfet* of the *département* whose seat serves as capital for the region. He must put the governmental policies of economic development and regional planning into effect, co-ordinate the activities of the *préfets*, economic agencies, and public authorities operating in his region and supervise the governmental agencies operating in

[94] WALINE, *op. cit. supra* note 82, at 372–73; VON MEHREN, *op. cit. supra* note 92, at 129–131.

[95] See WALINE, *op. cit. supra* note 82, at 376. VON MEHREN, *op. cit. supra* note 92, at 131.

[96] Constitution of 1958, art. 72; DÉCRET No. 64–250 of March 14, 1964, J.O. March 20, 1964, p. 2588, [1964] D.L. 121 (increasing powers of prefects.) Prefects exercise little control over local offices of government departments dealing with education, taxation, labor and judicial administration.

[97] WALINE, *op. cit. supra* note 82, at 363–65; VON MEHREN, *op. cit. supra* note 92, at 126–29. The *préfet* also represents the government in many court proceedings. Thus he must raise objections if one of the regular courts should render a decision interfering with the administrative authorities. See 3.03 *infra*; *cf.* generally DAVID & DE VRIES, THE FRENCH LEGAL SYSTEM 37 (1958).

more than one *département* in his region. He also prepares the regional portion of the national economic plan. He is assisted by a regional administrative conference consisting of the *préfets* of the region and various other administrative officials. [98]

## 1.16. The *Arrondissement* and the *Cantons*

Each of the 90 *départements* is subdivided into a number of *arrondissements*. At present, there are about 313 *arrondissements*. [99] The chief officer of the *arrondissement* is the *sous-préfet*. An elected *arrondissement* council was abolished by the Vichy regime and has not been re-instituted. In practice, the *arrondissement* does not play a very significant rôle. It has no legal personality, but is merely a subdivision of the *département*. The *sous-préfet* seems to be important mainly as a liaison between the *préfet* and the various mayors of the *départements*.[100]

*Arrondissements* are subdivided into *cantons*; there are about 3052 *cantons*. [101] The *cantons* have no separate administrative organs or self-governing powers. Until they were abolished by the reform of 1958, the *juge de paix* courts were organized on a *canton* basis. The *cantons* are still the constituencies for the election of councillors to the *conseils généraux*. [102]

## 1.17. The *Communes*

All local municipalities in France are legally called *communes*. With the exception of Paris, they have basically the same administrative organization. [103] *Communes* are governed by a council (*conseil municipal*) and an elected mayor (*maire*), who usually has some assistants (*adjoints*). The *conseil municipal* has at least nine members in *communes*

[98] DÉCRET No. 64–251 of March 14, 1964, J.O. March 20, 1964, p. 2589, [1964] D.L. 122. See also DÉCRET No. 64–252 of March 14, 1964, J.O. March 20, 1964, p. 2591, [1964] D. L.124 (Commissions for regional economic development).

[99] 1961 STATESMEN'S YEARBOOK 991.

[100] WALINE, *op. cit. supra* note 82, at 313–14.

[101] 1964 STATESMEN'S YEARBOOK 977. Usually, there are several *communes* in each canton but some large cities cover several cantons.

[102] WALINE, *op. cit. supra* note 82, at 370; DAVID & DE VRIES, *op. cit. supra* note 55, at 37.

[103] There are about 38,000 *communes* in France, most of them extremely small. In 1954, only 209 *communes* had a population of 20,000 or more, but 34.067 had a population of 1,500 or less, and 23,806 a population of 500 or less. In some *communes*, it is difficult to set up the nine-member municipal council because the number of eligible adult inhabitants is not much larger. By way of contrast, Paris has 2,850,189 inhabitants, Marseilles 661,492, Lyon 471,270, Toulouse 268,863, and Bordeaux 257,946. See 1961 STATESMEN'S YEARBOOK 991, 993. The large number of *communes* with a very small population and few resources has often been criticised but attempts at reform have not been successful. However, *communes* are authorized to provide joint services in some cases. *Cf.* WALINE, *op. cit. supra* note 82, at 315.

of 100 or less inhabitants and more in larger *communes*. Members of the *conseil municipal* are elected for six-year terms.

The *conseil municipal* is the main governing body of the *commune*. It votes the annual budget of the *commune* and, within rather rigid legislative limits, levies the municipal taxes. It also decides what municipal services the *commune* will provide. All *communes* are obliged by law to provide certain basic services, such as primary schools and registry offices for births, deaths, and marriages, but otherwise the public services provided vary greatly. The *conseil municipal* also creates all municipal offices, though it does not appoint the municipal employees. The *préfet* exercises a certain amount of control over the municipal budget and municipal elections. [104]

The mayor is elected by the municipal council from among its members for the same term as the council. [105] He must execute the decisions of the council, and he appoints and promotes the municipal employees within the framework of municipal offices created by the council. However, the mayor is not merely the executive officer of the municipal council. He, not the council, exercises the police power of the *commune*. Thus, it is the mayor (not the council) who adopts ordinances (*arrêtés*) for the maintenance of the health, safety, or morals of the *commune*. [106] In addition, the mayor is the delegate of the central government in his *commune* and responsible for the maintenance of peace and order. The *préfet* may suspend the mayor from office for one month. This suspension may be extended to three months by the Minister of the Interior. After notice and hearing, the mayor can be permanently dismissed by the cabinet. [107]

The municipal council also elects one or more *adjoints* (assistants to the mayor). Their exact number depends on the size of the council. The *adjoints* perform the duties delegated to them by the mayor. In larger *communes*, the mayor ordinarily delegates supervision over one particular city department to each *adjoint*. In rural areas, an *adjoint* may be in charge of a particular outlying area of a *commune*. [108]

Communes may engage in various types of cooperative undertakings. In addition, special districts (*districts*) may be created to study common

[104] The *préfet* may also annul a decision of the municipal council that is illegal. WALINE, *op. cit. supra* note 82, at 366; VON MEHREN, *op. cit. supra* note 92, at 131–34; 1 DAVID, LE DROIT FRANÇAIS 30 (1960).

[105] This means that the mayor ordinarily holds office for six years, but a mayor elected to fill a premature vacancy may hold office for a considerably shorter period.

[106] WALINE, *op. cit. supra* note 82, at 356, 643–44.

[107] WALINE, *op. cit. supra* note 82, at 353–54; VON MEHREN, *op. cit. supra* note 92, at 136.

[108] WALINE, *op. cit. supra* note 82, at 358–60; VON MEHREN, *op. cit. supra* note 92, at 135.

problems and provide certain services in lieu of the participating municipalities.

### 1.18. The Region of Paris

A special form of governmental organization has always been in effect for the Paris Metropolitan Area, which comprises more than ten percent of the French population. This organization was drastically revised in 1964. [109]

**a. The City of Paris.** The City of Paris, which is the capital of the Paris region, exercises the functions of a city as well as of a *département*. It has an elected municipal council (called *conseil de Paris*, rather than *conseil municipal*), which also acts as a departmental council (*conseil général*). The functions of mayor and the prefect are exercised by two officials appointed by the central government, the *préfet* of Paris and the Police Prefect (*préfet de Police*). The *préfet* deals mainly with matters of general administration, the Police Prefect with police matters and fire protection. Paris is divided into twenty *arrondissements* each with a mayor, who is in fact only a keeper of vital statistics records. [110]

**b. The *départements* of the region of Paris.** Generally speaking, the administrative structure of the various *départements* of the Paris region is the same as that of other *départements*, but there are some exceptions. Thus, the Police Prefect of Paris exercises some of his functions (including that of fire protection) not only in the city of Paris but also in the contiguous *départements* of the region. [111] The city of Paris and the *départements* of the Paris region may, by agreement, create joint agencies or institutions, which may include *départements* outside the region. The creation of such agencies and institutions may also be com-

[109] Until 1964, the city of Paris and the suburbs immediately surrounding it formed the *département* Seine. For most purposes, the *département* Seine performed the functions of a city administration in Paris. The *département* Seine was completely surrounded by the *département* Seine et Oise, which comprised the outer suburbs. See WALINE, *op. cit. supra* note 82, at 412. The reorganization of the Paris region was effectuated by Law No. 64-707 of July 10, 1964, J.O. July 12, 1964, p. 6204, [1964] D.L. 242. At the time this book was completed, court organization, based on the former administrative system, had not yet been changed; specifically, the *Tribunal de Grande Instance* in Paris is still called *Tribunal de Grande Instance de la Seine*. It may be noted that the total population of the Paris metropolitan region is over 6,500,000 inhabitants; the city of Paris alone has 2,790,000 inhabitants. 1965 STATESMEN'S YEARBOOK 679.

[110] Law No. 64-707, *supra* note 109, arts. 2–7, 10.

[111] Law No. 64-707, *supra* note 109, arts. 8, 10–11.

pelled by the central government. There is a complicated system for the equalization of tax revenues within the region of Paris. [112]

**c. The district of Paris.** The district of Paris was created in 1959 to study problems common to all or part of the Paris metropolitan area. It may assist localities and sometimes operate public services. It consists of the municipalities and *départements* of the Paris commuting area. A delegate general appointed by the central government is its chief executive officer. It also has a governing body composed in part of members appointed by the Prime Minister and Minister of the Interior and in part of members elected by the participating municipalities and *départements*. [113] The important *Régie Autonome des Transports Parisiens,* the public authority which operates the subway and bus lines throughout the Paris region, is, however, independent of the district.

### 1.19. *Sociétés Nationales* and *Etablissements Publics*

Even before the Second World War, the French government had nationalized certain private enterprises, such as the railroads; nationalization continued at an accelerated pace immediately after the war. Most of the nationalized enterprises, such as the railroads, the airline (Air France), and the Renault automobile works, although the government is the sole or major stockholder, are operated as regular corporations and are usually referred to as *sociétés nationales*. While they are under the ultimate control of the appropriate ministry, they have boards of directors and other corporate officers, are not subject to regular budget procedures, and sue and are sued in the ordinary courts. [114]

In addition to *sociétés nationales*, there are *établissements publics* which have legal personality and a certain amount of fiscal independence, but may be sued only in the administrative courts.

*Etablissements publics* may be created by the state, or by *départe-*

[112] Law No. 64–707, *supra* note 109, arts. 9, 33– 43.

[113] Ordinance No. 59–272 of Feb. 4, 1959, J.O. Feb. 11, 1959, p. 1858, [1959] D.L. 315 (creating district of Paris). The Ordinance has been implemented by a series of *décrets*. See WALINE, *op. cit. supra* note 82, at 412–13. The creation of the district of Paris, of the regions, and various related measures are all part of a planned administrative reform in France designed to facilitate regional planning and general administration on a level going beyond that of the *communes* and *départements*, considered to afford too narrow a base for such purposes in an age of ever increasing urbanization and faster communications. These measures have not always been welcomed by the *communes* and *départements* affected, who are sometimes hesitant to transfer some of their powers to larger administrative units.

[114] See De Vries & Hoeniger, *Post-Liberation Nationalizations in France*, 50 COLUM. L. REV. 629 (1950).

*ments* or *communes*, or by groups of *communes* acting in concert. Many of the older types of public services, such as universities and hospitals, are *établissements publics*. In addition, a few of the enterprises taken over by the government after the Second World War are operated as *établissements publics*; the most important of them is the national electrical utility, *Electricité de France*. At times, the distinction between *établissements publics* and *sociétés nationales* is nebulous. [115]

### 1.20. The Judicial Branch

In France, the judicial branch has traditionally been treated as less important than the executive and legislative branches. Indeed, to some extent, the judicial branch is considered merely as an appendage of the executive branch. The 1958 Constitution does not even speak of the judicial branch, but merely of judicial authority. [116] A more detailed description of French judicial organization is provided in chapter 3.

## 3. SUMMARY HISTORY OF FRENCH CIVIL PROCEDURE

### 1.21. The Origins of French Civil Procedure

French civil procedure finds its origins in Roman law, especially that of the later imperial period, in Germanic law, and in Canon law.

**a. Roman law procedure.** In classical Rome, civil proceedings were divided into two phases. [117] In the first phase (*in iure*), the parties presented their claims and defenses to a public official, called *praetor*, who had the right to grant various types of provisional relief (*interdicta*), but whose main function was to issue a *formula* setting forth the applicable law. The *formula* was a written instruction, not unlike a modern charge to a jury, to the trier of facts, the *iudex*. The *iudex* was a private individual selected with the consent of the parties from an

[115] WALINE, *op. cit. supra* note 82, at 380–90.

[116] Constitution of 1958, tit. VIII. Since a part of the legislative power has been given to the executive, the 1958 Constitution has not carried out the principle of the separation of powers consistently. Indeed, the 1958 Constitution does not speak of executive power or of an executive branch of government. Its title II is entitled "The President," without more, and its title III "The Government." Title III deals with the Prime Minister and the ministers.

[117] For a detailed description of Roman law procedure, see WENGER, INSTITUTES OF ROMAN LAW OF CIVIL PROCEDURE (1939). See also Wenger, *The Roman Law of Civil Procedure*, 5 TUL. L. REV. 353 (1931). For a criticism of some of Wenger's views, see DAWSON, A HISTORY OF LAY JUDGES 21–30 (1960). On Roman law procedure generally, see also BUCKLAND, A MANUAL OF ROMAN PRIVATE LAW 370-74 (1925); LEE, ELEMENTS OF ROMAN LAW (4th ed. 1956); RADIN, HANDBOOK OF ROMAN LAW (1927).

official list. In the second phase of the proceedings (*apud iudicem*), the *iudex* found the facts on the basis of the evidence presented by the parties and rendered a decision in accordance with the *formula*. [118] Although some extraordinary remedies were available against judgments rendered by corrupt judges, there was no appeal.

The classical Roman law procedure was not followed in the Roman provinces, where governors administered justice under their general administrative powers. In the later imperial period, the procedure used by these administrative officials was also introduced in Rome, at first only in extraordinary cases – hence, its name *extraordinaria cognitio* –, but later generally. Private individuals no longer functioned as fact finders. The use of writings increased: An action was initiated by a written pleading, called *libellus*. Courts were authorized to investigate facts on their own initiative, but lost the power to evaluate the evidence freely. Greater weight was given to documentary evidence than to other forms of proof. [119] Courts, like other public offices, were established on a hierarchical basis, and appeals could be taken to higher courts and, ultimately, to the emperor. Since the new procedure lent itself to dilatory tactics, parties often resorted to arbitration or submitted their disputes to their religious leaders for settlement.

**b. Germanic procedure.** The two main courts that administered civil justice in the Germanic tribes were the "hundred" court and the county court. The "hundred" court's territorial verge covered an area capable of supplying one hundred fighting men; the county court's competence embraced several "hundreds." These courts consisted usually of an assembly of all freeborn males of the "hundred" or county and dealt not only with legal disputes, but with all matters of interest to the community.

The plaintiff had to formulate his claim orally, using precisely prescribed, traditional language. Defenses were formulated in a similar manner. The judgment was rendered before, not after, the proof had been presented and, as a result, has sometimes been called a medial or intermediate judgment: It indicated what proof should be presented and what consequences would follow from a successful or unsuccessful

[118] As to the structure of the *formulae* for the various causes of action, see WENGER, *op. cit supra* note 117, at 140–58; RADIN, *op. cit. supra* note 117, at 46 (giving an English translation). A number of reconstructed Latin *formulae* are set forth in BUCKLAND, *op. cit. supra* note 117, at 419–20.

[119] See generally Ferguson, *A Day in Court in Justinian's Rome, Problems of Evidence, Proof and Justice in Roman Law*, 46 IOWA L. REV. 732 (1961).

proof presentation. Judicial combat between the parties or their champions, ordeals, or oaths constituted the means of proof. If oaths were used, the party who could muster more oath-helpers usually won.

In later times, since it became burdensome for all inhabitants of a district to attend court, the decision was often rendered by a small group of people called *scabini*, *rachimburgi*, or *Schoeffen*. Although lay men, they found the law, not the facts. Eventually, parties were permitted to be represented by forespeakers who possessed some legal learning. The parties could retract erroneous statements made by their forespeakers and thus avoid some of the formalism of the old procedure. [120]

**c. Canon law procedure.** On the advice of St. Paul[121], the early Christians brought their disputes before their priests and bishops, rather than before the secular courts of the Roman Empire. After the collapse of the Roman empire, the adjudicatory powers of these ecclesiastical officials expanded greatly and came to extend to all disputes involving ecclesiastics and all controversies relating to marriage, succession, and many matters involving sin, such as sex offenses. Eventually, an entire court system, based on the hierarchical structure of the church, came into being.

Procedure before the ecclesiastical courts was strongly influenced by the later Roman law procedure (*extraordinaria cognitio*). Unlike Germanic procedure, it was predominantely a written procedure. Actions were started by a written complaint (*libellus*). Later, both parties had to restate their factual allegations in detailed so-called positions which served to delineate the issues. Canon law used rational means of proof, such as documents and witnesses, not the ordeal or judicial combat. However, it also regulated in detail the weight to be given certain types of evidence. Thus, the testimony of two unimpeachable witnesses was conclusive on the judge, but the testimony of only one such witness made further evidence necessary. Evidence did not necessarily have to be submitted at one time.

While judgments in Roman law generally had to be for a sum of

[120] On court organization and procedure in the early period of Germanic law, see 1 BRUNNER, DEUTSCHE RECHTSGESCHICHTE 195–268 (3d ed. 1906) (best known, but somewhat antiquated, text). On the Frankish period, see 2 *Brunner, supra*, 435–698 (2d ed. 1928). See also ENGELMANN-MILLAR, A HISTORY OF CONTINENTAL CIVIL PROCEDURE (1927); SMITH, THE DEVELOPMENT OF EUROPEAN LAW 34–46 (1928). On court organization in the Frankish period, see DAWSON, *op. cit. supra* note 117, at 35–39; *cf.* 1 HOLDSWORTH, HISTORY OF ENGLISH LAW 3–17; 2 HOLDSWORTH, HISTORY OF ENGLISH LAW 102–18 (3d ed. 1927).

[121] I *Cor.* VI, 1–6.

money, Canon law developed a remedy of specific performance by threatening recalcitrant parties with ecclesiastical sanctions. Judgments of courts of first instance were appealable to tribunals ranking above them in the ecclesiastical hierarchy. The possibility ot several appeals and the written character of the procedure facilitated dilatory tactics. For this reason, an accelerated procedure was introduced in the Middle Ages. [122]

### 1.22. Medieval French Procedure

As a result of the Germanic invasions, the population of France at the beginning of the Middle Ages consisted of Germanic and Gallo-Roman elements. [123] Under the then prevailing system of personal law, the Germanic elements of the population were ruled by their customary law, while the Gallo-Roman elements were ruled by Roman law. After a fusion of the two ethnic groups had taken place, all inhabitants of northern France were governed by a customary law mainly of Germanic origin, while a modified Roman law predominated in southern France. Hence, northern France was called the country of customary law (*pays de droit coutumier*), while southern France was called the country of written (*i.e.*, Roman) law (*pays de droit écrit*). [124]

In the early Middle Ages, justice in France was administered mainly by the numerous feudal lords who had acquired the right to hold court during the period of the greatest weakness of the French monarchy. The King's judicial functions were generally restricted to his own private domain, where he rendered justice through his *prévots* (bailiffs) in less important cases and through his *baillis* or *sénéchaux* in cases of greater importance. Cases involving the great men of the Realm were brought before the King's council (*curia regis*). Later, a special section of the council, which always remained in Paris instead of following the King on his trips through the country, was created to handle its ju-

[122] See generally ENGELMANN-MILLAR, *op. cit. supra* note 120, at 453-503; SMITH, *op. cit. supra* note 120, at 193–95; Lobingier, LEX CHRISTIANA, *The Connecting Link between Ancient and Modern Law*, 20 GEO. L. J. 1 (1931). For the description of present-day procedure in an ecclesiastical tribunal, see *A Moot Ecclesiastical Trial - Smith v. Jones*, 5 CATHOLIC LAWYER 226 (1959).

[123] See 1.01. c *supra*.

[124] See, *e.g.*, TIMBAL, HISTOIRE DES INSTITUTIONS ET DES FAITS SOCIAUX 157–61 (1957); SMITH, *op. cit. supra* note 120, at 230. The boundary between the two areas was represented by a line running approximately from the Swiss border to the Loire valley. For a detailed discussion of French legal history, see GLASSON, HISTOIRE DES INSTITUTIONS ET DU DROIT DE LA FRANCE (1897).

dicial business. Eventually, it developped into a true court which became known as the *Parlement* of Paris. [125]

In the late Middle Ages, the increase of the King's power over the feudal lords limited the importance of the feudal courts. The more serious crimes were reserved for the royal courts. Also, the feudal courts ceased to be courts of last resort: Appeals became possible to the royal *baillis* and *sénéchaux*, and from there to the *Parlement* in Paris. When that court became overburdened with cases, additional *parlements* were created in some of the major French cities. At the same time, the judicial personnel became professionalized: The *baillis* and *sénéchaux* as well as the feudal lords who exercised judicial powers increasingly relied on deputies learned in the law who acted as judges in their stead. [126]

Originally, the procedure in the feudal courts was based largely on Germanic law. However, dissatisfaction with this procedure, especially its methods of prooftaking, led St. Louis, around 1260, to abolish judicial combat in the royal domain. Later, it also gradually disappeared in the rest of France. Canon law procedure, which had borrowed much from Roman law, began to supplant the Germanic procedure, first in the South, but later on, especially after adoption by the *Parlement* in Paris, in the North as well.

By the end of the Middle Ages, although there were local variations, civil procedure throughout France was fairly uniform. The parties were generally represented by professional counsel (*prolocutores*). Gradually, oral presentations were replaced by written pleadings, and written records were kept. As in the Roman-canonical system, documents became an important means of proof, though witnesses were considered superior (*témoins passent lettres*). Ordeal and judicial combat were no longer used. However, under the influence of the Germanic procedure, an interlocutory decision was rendered before proof could be taken: It defined the issues and determined the means of proof. Witnesses were examined neither by the parties nor by the court, but by a judge appointed for the purpose. He heard the witness, reduced the testimony to writing, and returned it to the court (*enquête*). Appeals to the royal courts, which became available at that time, were in reality retrials on

[125] ESMEIN, COURS ELÉMENTAIRE D'HISTOIRE DE DROIT FRANÇAIS 292–98 (13th ed. 1920) (feudal courts); *id.* at 394–409 (royal courts); *id.* at 409–26 (*parlement*). See also ROUSSELET, HISTOIRE DE LA MAGISTRATURE FRANÇAISE 4–14 (1957); *cf.* DAWSON, *op. cit. supra* note 117, at 39–43; SMITH, *op. cit. supra* note 120, at 239. Originally, the *parlement* was the section of the *curia regis* in which one speaks (*parle*), *i.e.*, argues, cases.

[126] ESMEIN, *op. cit. supra* note 125, at 434–41, 464–82; *cf.* 1 ROUSSELET, *op. cit. supra* note 125, at 45-50.

the merits. As a result, the appellate courts, such as the *Parlements*, required rather large judicial staffs. To compensate for the slowness in the handling of cases, special summary procedures were developed for cases involving minor matters, debts evidenced by writings under seal, and the like. [127]

The procedure of this period is described in an important treatise, the *Stylus Curiae Parlamenti* of Du Breuil, written around 1330.

### 1.23. Procedure in the 16th, 17th, and 18th Centuries

**a. The courts.** In the period from the end of the Middle Ages to the French Revolution, no drastic changes in French court organization were made. Although their importance declined, the feudal courts continued their existence, and so did the various royal courts. At the same time, the Kings attempted to restrict the powers of the ecclesiastical tribunals. As a result of the expansion of commerce, special courts composed of businessmen were created in commercial centers to handle litigation between merchants; these were called *tribunaux consulaires*. In port cities, admiralty courts (*amirautés*) dispensed justice in maritime matters. [128] The King, who was considered the supreme fountain of justice, exercised judicial functions in his council (*conseil privé* or *conseil des parties*). For example, an appeal could be taken from a decision of a *parlement* to the royal council on points of law. The procedure for such appeals was regulated by a 1738 ordinance, which is still, in part, the basis for the procedure before the present *Cour de Cassation*. The King could also draw unto himself any other litigation pending in a French court (*évocation*). However, an appeal to the King in his council was always considered an extraordinary remedy. [129]

Throughout this period, the *parlements* remained the most important courts in France. [130] Since they traced their origin to the old *curia regis*, they claimed not only judicial, but also legislative and administrative powers. In matters not governed by royal decree or customary law, they had the right to enact *arrêts de règlement*, rules of court concerning not only questions of procedure, but also matters of substantive law. More importantly, as a matter of tradition, royal ordinances did not become

[127] ENGELMANN–MILLAR, *op. cit. supra* note 120, at 651–93; 2 GARSONNET & CÉZAR-BRU at 15–16. For a discussion of the reasons which may have led to the adoption of the Roman-Canonical procedure instead of the jury system, see DAWSON, *op. cit. supra* note 117, at 43–53.

[128] For a listing of the various types of courts in existence in France at the time, see ESMEIN, *op. cit. supra* note 125 at 434–37; TIMBAL, *op. cit. supra* note 124, at 303, 304.

[129] ESMEIN, *op. cit. supra* note 125, at 531–35; TIMBAL, *op. cit. supra* note 124, at 237–39.

[130] They were mainly appellate courts, but appellate courts which retried the cases on the merits. They also had limited original competence.

effective until they had been registered by the local *parlement*. When the *parlements* disliked particular ordinances, they sometimes refused to register them and addressed remonstrances to the King, indicating the reasons for their objections. Although the King could overcome the resistance of the *parlements* by appearing personally in court, [131] he could not combat judicial opposition to his decrees by the removal of judges: The French King had, at an early date, begun to sell judicial offices and to give the holders a permanent, inheritable title. [132]

The resistance of the *parlements* to royal ordinances was one of the causes of the French Revolution. On the one hand, the *parlements* managed to stifle many reforms, which might have averted the Revolution; on the other hand, in their remonstrances, which were widely circulated in pamphlet form, they propagated many modern ideas. Among these were the idea that there were certain unalterable laws which the King could not modify, and the idea that new laws required the consent of the nation – that is, in the absence of an elected assembly, of the *parlements*. [133]

**b. Procedure.** Royal legislation, unimportant as a source of procedural law in the Middle Ages, gained significance in that regard in the 16th to the 18th centuries. Royal ordinances in the 16th century prescribed that courts throughout France had to use the French language (Ordinance of Villers-Cotterets, 1539), prohibited oral evidence of agreements involving more than 100 *livres* (Ordinance of

[131] On the rôle of the *parlements*, see ESMEIN, *op. cit. supra* note 125, at 582–607; TIMBAL, *op. cit. supra* note 124, at 206–08. For a detailed description of the history of the *parlements* and of their controversies with the French Kings, see DUFEY, HISTOIRE, ACTES ET REMONSTRANCES DES PARLEMENTS DE FRANCE (1826).

[132] Actually, it was not the title to the judicial office which was saleable and inheritable, but rather the right to present a qualified candidate to the King for appointment. As a result of the hereditary and saleable character of judicial offices, the judiciary became almost a traditional career in certain families. The system contributed to the expensive character of French justice before the Revolution: Since judges lived on the fees they received from the litigants, they naturally favored procedures which involved heavy costs, such as views of the premises in litigation. Furthermore, the Kings were often tempted to create many new judgeships to help their finances. On the other hand, the system made the judges largely independent of royal power. In the pre-revolutionary era, there were numerous judges famous for their learning. For an evaluation of the effect of the system of selling judicial offices, see 1 ROUSSELET, *op. cit. supra* note 125, at 113; *cf.* Bacon, *On A Ministry of Justice*, 22 VA. L. REV. 175 (1935).

[133] See, *e.g.*, 2 DUFEY, *op. cit. supra* note 131, at 244, 300; *cf.* 1 COBBAN, A HISTORY OF MODERN FRANCE 126–27 (1961). Many pamphlets published by the *parlements* in the 18th century with remonstrances are collected in a set, REMONSTRANCES DES PARLEMENTS, (Ranke Collection, Syracuse University). Towards the end of the reign of Louis XV, to end their interference in legislative matters, Chancellor Meaupou abolished the *parlements*. However, they were reinstituted soon afterwards by Louis XV's successor, Louis XVI.

Moulins, 1566), and enacted various other procedural rules (Ordinance of Orléans, 1560).[134]

Under the reign of Louis XIV, the *Ordonnance Civile* (also called *Code Louis*) of 1667 codified French civil procedure and made it uniform throughout France.[135]

The 1667 *Ordonnance* followed, in general, the procedures in use in the late Middle Ages. It prescribed written pleadings and regulated when specified defenses had to be raised. After the exchange of pleadings, a hearing was held before the court, during which counsel for the parties presented documentary evidence and tried, by oral argument, to persuade the court. If the court was not inclined to render a decision on the merits immediately, it could order an *appointement*, a proceeding consisting basically of an exchange of written memoranda on points of law. The restrictions on the use of oral evidence were continued. Public documents, unless attacked in a complex proceeding called *inscription de faux*, became almost conclusive. Non-documentary evidence could be used only pursuant to court order. Witnesses were heard by a commissioner, who reduced their testimony to writing (*enquête*). Experts also had to submit written reports (*expertise*). The final judgment was based on the oral arguments of the parties, the documentary evidence they had submitted, and the written reports of any *enquête*, *expertise*, or similar proof proceeding that had been conducted.

Time to appeal decisions was quite long (up to 10 years), and appeals, other than to the royal council, resulted in a readjudication on the merits. As a result, the procedure could become lengthy and expensive. However, summary proceedings could be used to adjudicate disputes as to small claims up to 400 *livres*.[136]

### 1.24. The Reforms of the Revolution and the Empire

**a. Court organization.** The defects in the system of judicial administration had been one of the chief grievances against the Monarchy. As a result, the new National Assembly turned its attention to court

[134] Engelmann-Millar, *op. cit. supra* note 120, at 708; 2 Garsonnet & Cézar-Bru at 17. On the ordinance of Moulins, which established a requirement of writing for contracts, see also Rabel, *The Statute of Frauds and Comparative Legal History*, 63 L.Q.R. 174 (1947); *cf.* 3 Schaeffner, Geschichte der Rechtsverfassung Frankreichs 482–84 (1850).

[135] The law was due to the efforts of Louis XIV's minister Colbert. It was drafted under the supervision of his uncle, the councillor of state Pussort, with the co-operation of Lamoignon, the presiding judge of the Paris *Parlement*. See, *e.g.*, 3 Schaeffner, *op. cit. supra* note 134, at 485. There are numerous commentaries on the 1667 law, including works by Bornier, Jousse, Pigeau, Rodier Serpillon. For a bibliography, see Cornu & Foyer 24.

[136] *E.g.*, Engelmann-Millar, *op. cit. supra* note 120, at 709–46; 2 Garsonnet & Cézar-Bru 18.

organization at an early date. During the famous night of August 4, 1789, feudal courts and the saleability of judicial offices were abolished along with all other feudal privileges. A Law of August 16–24, 1790, [137] abolished all courts, except the commercial courts, [138] and created a new judicial system. Minor matters were to be handled by justice of the peace (*juge de paix*) courts composed of a judge and two assessors. Ordinary non-commercial cases were to be handled by a district court of five judges. Appeals from one district court went to another district court. A *Tribunal de Cassation*, created a few weeks later, was to act as supreme court. Because of the revolutionary legislators' view that law making should be exclusively a function of the legislature, and because of their faith in the feasability of a legal system based entirely on statutes, the rôle of that court was narrowly circumscribed: It could reverse only in case of violation of a statutory provision and had to remand all cases reversed by it for a final decision on the merits. If the law were uncertain, an authentic interpretation was to be obtained from the National Assembly, which also had to be given periodic reports. [139]

The Law of August 16–21, 1790, also provided for an elected judiciary. To prevent the new judges from exercising a rôle similar to that of the members of the old *parlements*, they were forbidden from interfering with the legislative or executive branch of the government and from promulgating rules of court. As an additional check, they were ordered to write an opinion for every case decided by them.

During the radical phase of the Revolution, the so-called *Convention*, representation of parties by lawyers was abolished, and the number of courts was drastically reduced. Arbitration was considered the best means for settlement of disputes. [140] These radical notions did not per-

[137] The 1790 law is printed in CODE JUDICIAIRE 117 (Paris 1791). The speech of deputy Thouret, reprinted at 94–112 of this book, provides a good description of the objections raised against the old court system. Before adopting the 1790 legislation, the National Assembly first debated and voted on a number of basic issues, such as whether there should be a jury, whether there should be a jury in civil or only in criminal cases (it was decided to have a jury only in criminal cases), and whether the courts should ride circuit or be sedentary (it was decided that the courts should be sedentary). English influence on some of these questions is unmistakeable, but few Englisch institutions were actually adopted. The excesses of the *parlements* led to a deliberate avoidance of a powerful and creative judiciary. The preliminary questions and resolutions of the National Assembly are reprinted in CODE JUDICIAIRE, *supra*, at 112–17.

[138] Actually, the competence of the commercial courts, since they took over the functions of the abolished admiralty courts, was broadened.

[139] Law of 27 Nov.-1 Dec. 1790, reprinted in CODE JUDICIAIRE, *op. cit. supra* note 137, at 271. In the case of laws of the early revolutionary period, the first date given indicates the day of adoption by the National Assembly, the second date the day of royal assent.

[140] *E.g.*, MOREL at 90; 4 SCHAEFFNER, *op. cit. supra* note 134, at 193–94.

sist after Napoleon came to power. He re-established district courts (now consisting of three judges) in each *arrondissement* and called them *tribunaux civils* or *tribunaux d'arrondissement.* Appeals from one court of first instance to a neighbouring court of first instance were abolished Instead, a series of intermediate appellate courts, called *tribunaux d'appel* (later renamed *cours d'appel*), were created. The *Tribunal de Cassation* was renamed *Cour de Cassation,* a title more in accord with pre-revolutionary traditions. The judges were appointed for life, and law schools, abolished during the Revolution, were reorganized. Representation by professional lawyers was again required. [141]

**b. Procedure.** During the Revolution, no permanent changes were effected in civil procedure. Except during the radical *Convention* period, the 1667 Code remained in effect, though the parties were required to bring their disputes to the *juge de paix* for an attempt at settlement before they could start an action in the district courts, and a simplified procedure was created for the new *juge de paix* courts. [142]

Under Napoleon, the Civil Code of 1804 brought some changes in the field of civil procedure. It contained rules of procedure in divorce cases and a number of provisions concerning evidence. [143] At about the same time, a commission prepared a draft of a Code of Civil Procedure, which was adopted in 1806. [144] The new code continued the simplified procedure for justice of the peace (*juge de paix*) courts adopted during the revolution as well as the rule that all cases had to be submitted first to a *juge de paix* for an attempt at settlement. Otherwise, however, it followed the 1667 Code rather closely. As under that Code, the cornerstone of the proceeding was the *audience,* the hearing before the full court during which counsel for the parties submit documentary evi-

[141] See 4 SCHAEFFNER, *op. cit. supra* note 134, at 195; ENGELMANN-MILLAR, *op. cit. supra* note 120, at 751. Before the Revolution, the higher courts, especially the *parlements,* were referred to as *cours* and their judges as *conseillers* (councillors). In renaming the *tribunaux d'appel cours d'appel* and the *Tribunal de Cassation Cour de Cassation* and by granting the judges of these courts the title *conseillers,* Napoleon thus reestablished an old tradition.

[142] Law of 16–24 August 1790, *supra* note 137, tit. 10, art. 2 (settlement attempt before *juge de paix*); Law of 14–26 Oct. 1790, reprinted in CODE JUDICIAIRE, *op. cit. supra* note 137 (procedure before *juges de paix*).

[143] See CODE CIVIL arts. 234–266 (divorce, separation), 1341–1369 (various rules relating to evidence).

[144] The commission consisted, among others, of: Treilhard, a member of the *Conseil d'Etat*; Séguier, the presiding judge of the *Paris Cour d'Appel*; Berthereau, the presiding judge of the *Tribunal Civil* in Paris; and Pigeau who had practiced law in Paris before the Revolution. The procedural rules contained in the CODE CIVIL (as to divorce, separation, and certain evidentiary and other matters) as well as some special statutes remained in effect after the enactment of the 1806 Code. The 1806 Code has often been criticised for relying too much on the old 1667 legislation. See, *e.g.*, 2 GARSONNET & CÉZAR-BRU at 23.

dence and argue in favor of their clients. A special court order was required for the submission of non-documentary evidence. Such evidence was usually taken before a delegated judge, who submitted a report to the full court. After a new argument in an *audience,* the case was then decided on the merits. Final judgments could be executed anywhere in France without recourse to the *pareatis* procedure required for this purpose before the Revolution. Time to take an appeal to the *cours d'appel* was reduced to three months, but appeals to the intermediate appellate courts continued to be readjudications on the merits. As before the Revolution, defendants against whom default judgments had been entered could obtain a reopening of their case as a matter of right by the remedy of *opposition.*

The 1806 Code contained no rules for the procedure in the *Cour de Cassation,* which remained governed by the 1738 *Ordonnance* and the 1790 legislation setting up the *Tribunal de Cassation.* The *cours d'appel,* to which the *Cour de Cassation* had to remand in the event of reversal, remained free to disregard the decision rendered by the *Cour de Cassation.* However, if they disregarded that court's decision, the point in dispute was submitted to the legislature for an authentic interpretation of the law. A new appeal to the *Cour de Cassation* was not possible. [145]

## 1.25. Limited Reform in the 19th Century

Only limited changes were made in French civil procedure and court organization in the period between the fall of Napoleon and the beginning of the first World War. [146] Most significant was an expansion of the authority of the *Cour de Cassation.* A 1837 law permitted an appeal to the *Cour de Cassation* from the decision rendered on remand. Such an appeal was heard by the full court, rather than one of the panels who decided ordinary cases. In the event of a second reversal, the decision of the *Cour de Cassation* became binding on the court below. [147] Also significant were laws increasing the powers of the *juges de paix* and creating a system of legal aid (*assistance judiciaire*) providing not only for exemption from certain fees for poor people but also for the assignment of counsel, even in civil cases. Other laws dealt with various minor matters. [148] Finally, the reintroduction of divorce in

[145] For a general description of the procedure of the 1806 Code, see ENGELMANN-MILLAR, *op. cit. supra* note 120, at 756–79.

[146] Insofar as court organization is concerned, the 19th century has been called a century of stability. 1 SOLUS & PERROT at 50.

[147] Law of April 1, 1837, 1837 BULLETIN DES LOIS No. 6769, [1837] D. 3. 151.

[148] For a brief survey of the period, see 1 SOLUS & PERROT at 50; MOREL at 12.

1884 (divorce had been abolished in 1816) led to the passage of legislation regulating the procedure in divorce cases. [149]

A major study looking towards a revision of the Code of Civil Procedure was undertaken in the late 19th century, but no legislative action resulted. [150]

### 1.26. The Period between the Two World Wars

**a. Court organization.** Between the two World Wars, an enduring financial crisis produced various attempts to save money by reform of the judiciary. At one time, the number of courts of first instance (*tribunaux civils*) was drastically reduced. This measure encountered so much opposition that most abolished courts were re-established soon afterwards. However, the number of resident judges in many of the little occupied courts was reduced to one. To hear regular civil cases, courts with only one judge were to be completed by two other judges assigned on a temporary basis. [151]

On the other hand, the size of the *Cour de Cassation*, which handled an ever-growing number of cases, was increased. Until 1938, it had been sitting in three panels, one for the preliminary screening of civil cases (*chambre des requêtes*), one for civil matters (*chambre civile*), and one for criminal matters (*chambre criminelle*). In 1938, a fourth panel, called *chambre sociale*, was added to handle labor and related cases. [152]

**b. Procedure.** Through the treaty of Versailles, France regained Alsace-Lorraine, ceded to Germany in 1871. Though French substantive law was eventually introduced in that area, most of the German procedural legislation remained in effect. [153]

The French Code of Civil Procedure was repeatedly modified between the two wars. The rule requiring all actions to be brought at the domi-

[149] For a review of the history of divorce in France, see 1 COLIN & CAPITANT at 450–61.

[150] For a review of the proposals, see 2 GARSONNET & CÉZAR-BRU at 24; 1 SOLUS & PERROT at 65.

[151] See 1 SOLUS & PERROT at 530–35; MOREL at 96–7. The single resident judge could deal with all matters requiring only one judge – such as various types of interlocutory and exparte relief, certain rent control matters, and the like.

[152] Decree of June 17, 1938, J.O. June 30, 1938, [1938] D. 4. 321 (with report of Prime Minister explaining reasons for decree).

[153] The German ZIVILPROZESSORDNUNG, as modified by later French legislation, is in effect under the name of CODE DE PROCÉDURE LOCALE. Since it has occasionally served as a model for reform of French procedure and since some French institutions have, over the years, been introduced in Alsace-Lorraine, the gap between the two systems is narrowing. See 1 SOLUS & PERROT at 71.

cile of the defendant was liberalized in favor of plaintiffs; [154] arbitration clauses were declared legal in commercial matters; [155] a quick procedure for the recovery of small commercial debts was instituted; [156] and the *référé* procedure for the granting of provisional relief was made available in commercial cases. [157]

In addition to these piecemeal reforms, a major revision of the Code of Civil Procedure was undertaken in 1935. The new law provided that one of the judges of the *tribunal civil* was to be specially assigned to each new case to see to it that it was handled expeditiously. That judge, named *juge chargé de suivre la procédure* (judge charged with following the procedure), was also authorized to render certain interlocutory decisions. [158] In practice, this reform turned out to be rather ineffectual. The *juges chargés de suivre la procédure* did not play the active rôle that had been anticipated.

Although the 1935 reform also introduced the rule that violation of purely formal rules was not ground for reversal unless prejudice had been shown, the *Cour de Cassation* soon developed case law making violations of certain "essential" rules of form grounds for reversal even in the absence of any prejudice. [159]

Other changes made in 1935 were of minor importance. [160]

## 1.27. The Vichy Regime

The work of a commission created in 1934 to study the Code of Civil Procedure with a view to suggesting reforms was interrupted by the outbreak of the Second World War. However, the Vichy regime put into effect some of the recommendations of the commission. In 1942, the procedure for appeals to the *cours d'appel* was simplified. At the same time, the procedure for the interrogation of parties by written interrogatories (*interrogatoire sur faits et articles*) was abandoned in

[154] Law of Nov. 26, 1923, J.O. Nov. 27, 1923, p. 11066, [1923] BULLETIN DES LOIS 3477 (in tort actions, plaintiff may sue where tort was committed as well as at defendant's domicile); Law of July 13, 1930, J.O. July 18, 1930, [1931] D. 4. 1, arts. 2, 3 (actions against insurance companies may be brought at insured's domicile; in casualty insurance cases also where accident happened; in real property insurance cases also where property located).

[155] Law of December 31, 1925, J.O. Jan. 4, 1926, p. 199, [1926] S. 5.57–8 (with extensive discussion of legislative history).

[156] See 11.02.a *infra*.

[157] Law of March 11, 1924, J.O. March 20, 1924, p. 2682, [1924] D. 4. 142.

[158] CODE DE PROCÉDURE CIVILE arts. 80–82.

[159] For a detailed discussion, see 1 SOLUS & PERROT 372–86.

[160] Thus, the *instruction par écrit*, the equivalent of the *appointement* procedure of the 1667 Code, was abolished. The procedure had not been used in practice. Time to demand a reopening of a default through opposition was reduced. Changes effectuated in 1938 concerning execution against immovable property should also be mentioned. See 1 SOLUS & PERROT 66–7; MOREL 12.

favor of a procedure enabling the court to ask rather wide-ranging questions (*comparution personnelle*). Two years later, the powers of the *juge chargé de suivre la procédure* were increased, the *expertise* procedure was simplified and, for the first time, detailed rules were devised for certain *ex-parte* applications in non-litigious proceedings – such as applications in estate, guardianship, and related matters – as well as for litigated matters heard by the court in chambers (*chambre du conseil*). [161]

### 1.28. The Fourth Republic

The 1946 constitution guaranteed and created a special body, called *Conseil Supérieur de la Magistrature,* to safeguard judicial independence. [162] The Fourth Republic also added to the court system. Special courts to administer the laws newly enacted for the protection of farm tenants (*tribunaux paritaires de baux ruraux*) and other courts to administer the social security laws (*commissions de sécurité sociale*) were created. The unsettled conditions of the times and the prolific amount of legislation which needed authoritative interpretation caused an enormous backlog in the *Cour de Cassation.* To cope with it, the panel for the preliminary screening of cases (*chambre des requêtes*) was replaced by a panel hearing cases on the merits, one more panel was added, and the number of judges in the panels was increased. [163] Additional measures taken during the Fourth Republic included revision of legislation governing various law professionals and the extension of the law school curriculum from three to four years. [164]

In the procedural field, the Fourth Republic was less active. Notable are the abandonment of the compulsory pre-trial settlement attempt before the *juge de paix,* and the creation of a broadly available attachment procedure. In addition, the scope of the law providing a summary procedure for the recovery of small debts was expanded.

Soon after the liberation of France, a commission had been appointed to recommend reforms in the Code of Civil Procedure. Its recommendations were published in 1955, but were not enacted into law. [165]

[161] For a brief description, see MOREL 12; 1 SOLUS & PERROT 66–67. The Vichy régime had abolished the life tenure of French judges, but this legislation was declared invalid. See 1 SOLUS & PERROT 665.

[162] French Constitution of 1946, arts. 83–84.

[163] 1 SOLUS & PERROT 51, 665. As to the history of the *Cour de Cassation* during that period, see also 3.32 *infra.* As part of the reorganization of the *Cour de Cassation,* the procedure before that court was also revised.

[164] See 2.03 *infra.*

[165] 1 SOLUS & PERROT 66–67.

## 1.29. The Reforms of the De Gaulle Government

The new Constitution adopted after General De Gaulle returned to power reaffirmed the independence of the judiciary, but gave the President the power to appoint the members of the *Conseil Supérieur de la Magistrature.* [166] At the same time, the government was authorized to regulate a number of matters, including civil procedure, by *décret* (executive order). [167]

Acting under special powers granted by the 1958 Constitution, the government reorganized the French judicial system in 1958. A great many courts of first instance (*tribunaux civils*) were abolished. The remaining courts of first instance were located in larger cities with far more judicial business and renamed *tribunaux de grande instance.* The *juge de paix* courts were replaced by a smaller number of courts with limited adjudicatory powers called *tribunaux d'instance.* The judges of these courts were made members of the regular judicial hierarchy. An institute designed to train recent law graduates for a career in the judiciary was created, and more rapid promotions to higher courts were made possible. All these measures were designed to attract more qualified candidates to the judiciary. [168]

At the same time, steps were taken to speed up litigation. Thus, the availability of *opposition* as a means for the reopening of default judgments was curtailed, and the special procedure for the hearing of witnesses (*enquête*) was simplified. Various other procedural changes were made in subsequent years. However, the general revision of the French Code of Civil Procedure, promised again in 1958, has not yet been forthcoming. [169]

### 4. FORMAL SOURCES OF FRENCH CIVIL PROCEDURE

## 1.30. The Constitution and Legislation

In France, constitutional provisions have traditionally had little bearing on, [170] and legislation has been the primary source of, civil procedure. [171]

[166] French Constitution of 1958, arts. 64–65. It is interesting to note that article 64 provides that the President of the Republic is "the guarantor of the independence of the judiciary."

[167] French Constitution of 1958, arts. 34, 37.

[168] As to the 1958 reforms, see 3.11–3.15 *infra.*

[169] *Cf.* 1 SOLUS & PERROT 67–8. For further reforms, see 7.58–7.62 *infra.*

[170] See 1.20 *supra.* See also DAVID & DE VRIES, THE FRENCH LEGAL SYSTEM 60–63 (1958).

[171] In France, legislation is generally considered the main source of law. On the predominant role of statutory law in French legal theory, see DAVID & DE VRIES, *op. cit. supra* note 170, at 86.

Since French constitutional law created no serious obstacles to delegation of legislative powers, before adoption of the 1958 Constitution, numerous statutes empowered the executive branch – in practice, the cabinet – to amplify statutory rules by executive regulation. Many such regulations, traditionally referred to as *décrets*, were promulgated in the field of civil procedure. [172] Furthermore, some important measures in the field of court organization and civil procedure were enacted by *décrets-lois*. [173] These *décrets-lois* were promulgated by the executive pursuant to delegation of full legislative powers in times of political or economic crises and, unlike *décrets*, were not subject to attack in the courts.

The significance of *décrets* and *lois* was modified by the 1958 Constitution. It contains a rather narrow list of matters that may be regulated only by legislation enacted by Parliament. As a result, all subjects not included on the list may be regulated by *décrets* promulgated by the cabinet, [174] which now have the character of real legislation and may amend or abrogate prior law. Since the list of subjects reserved for legislation includes the status and tenure of the judiciary, but not civil procedure, the Code of Civil Procedure may now be revised by simple executive action. This has in fact been done in several instances. [175] In addition, the Constitution provides that, in case of certain emergencies, the executive branch of the government may assume complete legislative powers. [176] In such instances, even matters ordinarily subject only to legislative regulation, such as the status of the judiciary, may be dealt with by executive acts which are usually called *ordonnances*.

## 1.31. Treaties

Treaties are recognized as a source of law, though some treaties may require statutes to make them effective. [177] A number of countries

[172] 1 Colin & Capitant 131–35; in addition to formal decrees, which embody action of the executive branch of government as such, there are the less formal *arrêtés* of individual ministers.

[173] See note 172 *supra*.

[174] Constitution of 1958, arts. 34, 37. Laws relating to a limited number of matters mentioned in the Constitution (mainly government organization) require a somewhat more complex procedure for adoption than regular laws. They are called organic laws.

[175] Cuche & Vincent 10–11. For criticism of this procedure, see 1 Solus & Perrot 67–68, who consider the executive power to modify civil procedure a threat to civil liberties.

[176] Constitution of 1958, art. 16. In 1961, the De Gaulle government used the powers conferred by article 16, *i.a.*, to modify the laws governing the appointment and promotion of judges serving in Algeria. 1 Solus & Perrot 1000–01. Solus criticises these measures as grave attacks upon the independence of the judiciary.

[177] See 1 David, Le Droit Français 1, 143 (1960).

have concluded treaties with France covering some phases of civil procedure, especially competence of courts and the enforcement of foreign judgments. The United States is not a party to any of these treaties.[178] However, the Convention of Establishment concluded with France in 1959 grants nationals of both contracting countries free access to the courts and also deals with the enforcement of arbitration awards.[179]

## 1.32. Judicial Decisions (*Jurisprudence*)

In French legal theory, in the absence of a formal principle of *stare decisis*, judicial decisions (*jurisprudence*) are not, strictly speaking, a source of law.[180] Nevertheless, court decisions are by no means unimportant and are constantly studied and cited by French lawyers.

While the *Cour de Cassation* never cites a judicial decision, it always follows decisions rendered by *toutes chambres réunies* – that is, in a solemn session of all its divisions; ordinarily, unless it has become convinced that the decision has outlived its usefulness, it also follows a decision rendered by an individual division. Decisions of lower courts, however, seem to carry little weight with the *Cour de Cassation*, unless there is a whole line of consistent cases (*jurisprudence constante*). The lower courts, on the other hand, ordinarily follow decisions of the *Cour de Cassation*, unless they believe that the *Cour de Cassation* itself may be ready to reconsider its former holdings.[181]

The importance of court decisions has perhaps been greater in civil procedure than in other areas of French law. Some procedural rules, such as the requirement that all actions must involve an actual controversy ripe for judicial decision, are almost entirely based on court

[178] See 4.07 and 15.01 *infra*.

[179] As to the Convention of Establishment of 1959, see 6.03.b and 14.07 *infra*.

[180] On the broad French techniques of statutory interpretation which make it possible to base the decision of cases on legislative enactments, even though such enactments may not have covered the situation explicitly, see DAVID & DE VRIES, *op. cit. supra* note 171. A decision need not be justified by reference to statutory rules. Occasionally, the courts rely on one of the traditional rules which have never been codified, such as *fraus omnia corrumpit* (fraud vitiates everything).

[181] For a discussion of the rôle of case law (*jurisprudence*) in French law, see 1 COLIN & CAPITANT 104–07; DAVID, *op. cit. supra* note 177, at 160–68; DAVID & DE VRIES, *op. cit. supra* note 170, at 113–21. French opinions are ordinarily very brief and couched in the form of a syllogism, in which a short statement of the facts is the minor premise and the statement of the applicable law the major premise, the decision being the conclusion following from the two premises. The brevity of French opinions makes it difficult to distinguish cases on their facts.

decisions. In other instances, decisions of the *Cour de Cassation* have limited the scope of new legislation. [182]

## 1.33. Textbooks, Treatises, and Articles (*Doctrine*)

In France, the writings of learned experts, whether in the form of multi-volume treatises, one volume texts, short monographs, or articles [183] in legal periodicals are collectively referred to as *la doctrine.* [184] Legal writers exercise considerable influence on the development of the law. They not only collect and systematize existing materials, but also attempt to provide solutions for new legal problems. Their opinions carry a great deal of weight and, indeed, the predominating rôle of legal writers is often considered one of the distinctive features of civil law systems.

In recent years, however, legal literature may not have played as significant a rôle in the development of civil procedure as in other areas of the law. All of the large multi-volume treatises on French civil procedure are of advanced age and fail to deal with recent statutory changes and other developments. Several excellent short texts and numerous articles do not quite make up for this deficiency.

## 1.34. Customs

Procedure, perhaps more than other branches of the law, is influenced by the customs of judges and attorneys. These customs are often local in scope, reflecting problems prevailing at a particular court. [185] Thus, although commercial courts are authorized to appoint referees (*arbitres-rapporteurs*) to examine complex accounts, the commercial court for the Seine department (Paris), which must handle a large number of

[182] 1 Solus & Perrot 71–72. See also 6.02 (requirement of an actual controversy), 6.02.c (requirement of timeliness), 7.09.c (only rules which are not "substantial" may be disregarded if their violation has caused no prejudice), 6.04.d (*nul ne plaide par procureur*, *i.e.*, every action must be brought by the real party in interest) *infra.*

[183] Articles in French legal periodicals are of two types: They are either fairly long discussions of a particular topic or a shorter comment on a particular case, the latter generally appended to the report of the case in one of the unofficial reports, such as Dalloz, Sirey, or J.C.P. These comments on recent decisions are prepared by some of the leading French scholars. In view of the short, and sometimes almost cryptic, nature of French opinions, these critical evaluations by experts are most valuable.

[184] For more extensive citiations of authorities on the rôle of *la doctrine* and for a more detailed treatment of the topic, see David & de Vries, *op. cit. supra* note 170, at 122–26; 1 David, *op. cit. supra* note 177, at 169–73; 1 Colin & Capitant 109–11.

[185] On the rôle of custom in French law generally, see David & de Vries, *op. cit. supra* note 170, at 106; David, *op. cit. supra* note 177, at 152–59; 1 Colin & Capitant at 104–05. French authors do not always use the word custom in the same sense. Ordinarily, it is used in the sense in which it has been used in the text to denote a traditional way of handling certain matters, which is not based on any formal authority. Occasionally, however, custom is considered almost a synonym for case law.

cases with an inadequate staff, uses *arbitres-rapporteurs* in a manner going far beyond the statutory scheme: Its *arbitres-rapporteurs* hear all phases of commercial cases, including oral argument; the full court limits its activity to approval of the referee's report. [186] A somewhat similar practice exists in the labor court (*conseil de prud'hommes*) in Paris.

In other instances, customs are national or almost national in scope. Thus, the procedure known as *instruction par écrit*, which was the equivalent of the *appointement* of pre-revolutionary French law, remained practically unused, and the relevant sections of the *Code de Procédure Civile* were abrogated in 1935, long after they had been made inoperative by custom. [187]

Customs are not always of ancient vintage. The institution of the *juge chargé de suivre la procédure* in 1935 remained a dead letter in most parts of France, because the judiciary and the legal practitioners ignored this reform. [188]

While customs are, to some extent, considered as a source of law, not all customs are necessarily valid. Thus, the court at Toulouse developed the practice of referring certain cases to an *avocat* to hear the evidence and report. Although this device was somewhat similar to the use made of *arbitres-rapporteurs* by the commercial court in Paris, the *Cour de Cassation* eventually declared this practice illegal. [189] Whether and to what extent rules of law can be modified by custom is therefore not clear.

### 1.35. Absence of Court Rules

French courts may make rules concerning their internal administration – such as rules regulating the rotation of judges among the various divisions –, but, although the limits to their powers are not always observed very closely in borderline cases, [190] they may not transgress this limited authority. The reasons for their limited powers in this regard are historical. The rule-making power possessed, but not always prudently used, by the pre-revolutionary *parlements* was withdrawn during the Revolution. [191] Though merely statutory, the rule that the courts have no power to issue regulations of a nature binding

[186] See 7.17 *infra*.
[187] See note 160 *supra*.
[188] See 1.26.b *supra*.
[189] See Dame Veuve Barthe v. Barreau, Cass. Civ., April 8, 1935, [1935] D. 1. 94 and note.
[190] Thus, there are fairly detailed regulations governing the conduct of experts in Paris. See 7.54 *infra*.
[191] See 1.24.a supra; *cf.* DAVID & DE VRIES, *op. cit. supra* note 170, at 113.

on the public at large is viewed in France as a corollary of the separation of powers doctrine and an almost constitutional principle. It has been honored since the days of the Revolution. [192] When, in 1958, the presiding judges of the *cours d'appel* received very limited power to deal by rules with some problems arising from the transition to the new court system created in December 1958, even the grant of that limited and temporary power was criticised, because it was not in accord with French legal tradition. [193]

The absence of judicial rule-making power has not stood in the way of desirable reform. The close ties between the *Ministère de la Justice* (Ministry of Justice) and the courts have permitted the Ministry of Justice to propose the reforms that were deemed desirable by the judiciary. The broad legislative powers of the executive branch have further facilitated efficient procedural reforms. [194]

## 5. SELECTED BIBLIOGRAPHY

### 1.36. Works on Civil Procedure Proper

General works in this category usually include discussions of court organization, the status of the judiciary, and law professionals.

#### a. Works of historical interest.

Du Breuil, Stylus Curiae Parlamenti is the most important work for the medieval period.

The following are a number of commentaries on the *Ordonnance* of 1667:

Jousse, Nouveau commentaire sur l'Ordonnance Civile (2 volumes 1767);

Pigeau, La Procédure civile du Châtelet de Paris et de toutes les juridictions ordinaires du royaume (1787);

Pothier, Traité de procédure civile (1778).

Pigeau, who became one of the main draftsmen of the Code of 1806, also published commentaries on that code: Pigeau, La procédure civile des tribunaux de France (2 volumes); Pigeau, Commentaire sur le code de procédure civile (2 volumes).

Other 19th century works:

[192] See, *e.g.*, 1 David, *op. cit. supra* note 177, at 21, 161.
[193] See Cuche & Vincent 83–84.
[194] See 1.30 *supra*; 3.05 *infra*.

BERRIAT SAINT PRIX, COURS DE PROCÉDURE CIVILE (1811);

RODIÈRE, TRAITÉ DE COMPÉTENCE ET DE PROCÉDURE EN MATIÈRE CIVILE (2 volumes)

CARRÉ ET CHAUVEAU, LOIS DE PROCÉDURE CIVILE ET COMMERCIALE (13 volumes). This is the most important work on civil procedure for the second half of the 19th century. It went through numerous editions.

**b. Multi-volume treatises.** There is no large multi-volume treatise on French civil procedure that is completely up-to-date. The following two works, however, contain a wealth of information and are still very important:

GARSONNET & CÉZAR-BRU, TRAITÉ THÉORIQUE ET PRATIQUE DE PROCÉDURE CIVILE ET COMMERCIALE (3d ed. 9 volumes); a tenth volume brings the third edition, publication of which was started in 1912, up to date as far as 1938.

GLASSON, TISSIER & MOREL, TRAITÉ THÉORIQUE ET PRATIQUE D'ORGANISATION JUDICIAIRE, DE COMPÉTENCE, ET DE PROCÉDURE CIVILE (3d. ed. 5 volumes). Publication of the third edition was started in 1925 and terminated in 1936. The fifth volume of the work brings the earlier volumes up to date as far as 1936.

All the authors of the two works mentioned above are noted scholars in the field of procedure. Garsonnet and Glasson were deans at the faculty of law of the University of Paris; Glasson is also the author of a work on the history of French civil procedure. Cézar-Bru was dean of the faculty of Law of the University of Toulouse. Morel, professor of civil procedure at the University of Paris, is chiefly famous for his one volume text on civil procedure.

**c. *Répertoires* (Encyclopedias).**

As a successor to earlier encyclopedias, the best-known French law publisher, Dalloz, publishes an ENCYCLOPÉDIE DALLOZ, destined to cover all of French law. The ENCYCLOPÉDIE DALLOZ consists of separate sets (called *répertoires*) for the various fields of law. The set dealing with civil procedure is the RÉPERTOIRE DE PROCÉDURE CIVILE ET COMMERCIALE (2 volumes, 1956, and annual supplements). Within the *Répertoire*, individual topics are arranged alphabetically. The articles evidence considerable scholarship, are signed, and contain useful bibliographies.

The JURISCLASSEURS publishing firm publishes a set of loose-leaf treatises on various fields of law including JURISCLASSEUR DE PRO-

CÉDURE CIVILE (8 volumes). Arrangement of the individual topics follows the scheme of the code of civil procedure. The set is kept up to date by a somewhat complicated system of supplementary sheets.

**d. Shorter texts.** A number of shorter one or two volume texts have been published mainly for use by students. However, they usually have eminent scholars as authors and are also used by members of the legal profession.

The most extensive of these is SOLUS & PERROT, DROIT JUDICIAIRE PRIVÉ (v. 1. 1961, v. 2 in course of publication). The work is quite detailed; one of its remarkeable features is the amount of comparative law material, including material on Anglo-American law, it contains. Both authors are members of the law faculty of the University of Paris.

The best known and most comprehensive of the one volume works, though out of date in some aspects, is: MOREL, TRAITÉ ÉLÉMENTAIRE DE PROCÉDURE CIVILE (2d ed. 1949).

More sketchy, but valuable as a brief survey of the field is: CUCHE & VINCENT, PROCÉDURE CIVILE ET COMMERCIALE (12th ed. 1960). Cuche was dean of the faculty of law at Grenoble; Vincent is professor at Lyon.

CORNU & FOYER, PROCÉDURE CIVILE ET COMMERCIALE (1958; a supplement published in 1960 deals with the 1958 reforms) contains much interesting statistical and sociological information. It is at times sketchy in its treatment of details of procedure. Cornu is professor in Poitiers; Foyer, formerly a professor in Lille, is now Minister of Justice.

Two works were especially written for students in the abbreviated two-year program leading to the *capacité* degree. They are less detailed than the works mentioned above:

CRÉMIEU, TRAITÉ ÉLÉMENTAIRE DE PROCÉDURE CIVILE ET DES VOIES D'EXÉCUTION (1956);

PARISOT & JAUFFRET, MANUEL DE PROCÉDURE CIVILE ET DES VOIES D'EXÉCUTION (1958).

**e. Monographs and works dealing with specific topics.**

(1) *On the reforms of 1958:*

GIVERDON & LARGUIER, PROCÉDURE CIVILE, DROIT PÉNAL, PROCÉDURE PÉNALE (1959) (containing a collection of pertinent *ordonnances et décrets*);

BLANC, LA NOUVELLE PROCÉDURE CIVILE (1959).

(2) *On judicial organization:*

COSTA, LES INSTITUTIONS JUDICIAIRES (1959). Costa is a member of the *Cour de Cassation.*

ROUSSELET, HISTOIRE DE LA MAGISTRATURE (2 volumes 1957);

FAYE, LA COUR DE CASSATION (1903).

(3) *On the legal professions:*

APPLETON, TRAITÉ DE LA PROFESSION D'AVOCAT (2d ed. 1929);

CRÉMIEU, TRAITÉ DE LA PROFESSION D'AVOCAT (2d ed. 1954).

(4) *On proof and evidence:*

Questions of proof and evidence, especially questions relating to burden of proof and the admissibility of evidence, are usually treated in works on civil or commercial law. Texts and treatises on civil procedure usually deal only with the mechanics of the introduction of proof. There is only one recent work dealing comprehensively with questions of proof:

SICARD, LA PREUVE EN JUSTICE APRÈS LA RÉFORME JUDICIAIRE (1960).

It is indicative of the attitude of French scholars towards problems of proof that this work was written by a judge of the *tribunal de grande instance* in Rennes rather than by a professor.

LEGEAIS, LES RÈGLES DE PREUVE EN DROIT CIVIL. "PERMANENCES ET TRANSFORMATIONS" (1955) (monograph making some suggestions for changes in the law of proof).

(5) *On interlocutory relief and ex-parte remedies:*

CÉZAR-BRU, HÉBRAUD & SEIGNOLLE, TRAITÉ DES RÉFÉRÉS ET DES ORDONNANCES SUR REQUÊTE (3 volumes 1954).

(6) *On execution of judgments and provisional remedies tending to insure execution:*

French books on civil procedure (with the exception of the multivolume treatises) do not usually cover either provisional remedies tending to insure execution, such as *saisie conservatoire,* or the various proceedings for the execution of judgments. These matters are dealt with in separate works:

CUCHE & VINCENT, VOIES D'EXÉCUTION ET PROCÉDURES DE DISTRIBUTION (8th ed. 1961);

LABORDE-LACOSTE, EXPOSÉ MÉTHODIQUE DES VOIES D'EXÉCUTION (2d ed. 1952).

(7) *On arbitration:*

ROBERT, ARBITRAGE CIVIL ET COMMERCIAL (3d ed. v. 1. 1961; v. 2 to be published).

**f. Formbooks.**

Books with less exhaustive treatment of theoretical legal problems, but with numerous practical suggestions and forms, have been written for the use of practitioners. They are usually called *formulaires* (formbooks), or *traité formulaire* (treatise with forms). The forms given are not very detailed and leave much to the draftmanship of the user. Thus, the forms for pleadings (*conclusions*) give the formal parts of pleadings, but usually do not contain separate forms for pleadings in specified actions. The best known formbooks are:

RAVIART, TRAITÉ FORMULAIRE DE PROCÉDURE GÉNÉRALE (2 volumes, 8th ed. 1956);

JURISCLASSEUR FORMULAIRE DE PROCÉDURE (loose-leaf).

**1.37. Works that Deal Primarily with Subjects other than Procedure**

French treatises in the field of civil procedure usually do not deal at length with questions of evidence or problems with international aspects, such as the competence of French courts in suits with international contacts, enforcement of foreign judgments, and similar problems. Problems of that nature are usually discussed more fully in works on general civil law (*droit civil*), commercial law (*droit commercial*), or conflict of laws (*droit international privé*).

**a. Works on general civil law.**

All the general treatises on civil law devote considerable space to the law of evidence, mainly for the reason that it is covered in the Civil Code. They also contain good introductory discussions on the history of French law in general, its sources, and court organization. The best known are:

COLIN & CAPITANT, TRAITÉ DE DROIT CIVIL (10th ed. 3 volumes), Publication of a completely revised edition to be in four volumes has been started by Julliot de la Morandière under the title TRAITÉ DE DROIT CIVIL FRANÇAIS v. 1, 1957 (supp. 1960); v. 2, 1959 (supp. 1961); volume 1 of this edition deals fairly extensively with some aspects of procedure and evidence.

PLANIOL & RIPERT, TRAITÉ ÉLÉMENTAIRE DE DROIT CIVIL (3 volumes; 4th ed. 1951). An earlier edition of this work has been translated by the Louisiana State Law Institute into English (6 volumes 1959).

Both of the above works are destined mainly for students, but are also much consulted by practitioners and scholars.

There also are longer works, such as:

PLANIOL & RIPERT, TRAITÉ PRATIQUE DE DROIT CIVIL FRANÇAIS (14 volumes, 2d ed. 1952). Questions of evidence are discussed in volume 7.

AUBRY & RAU, DROIT CIVIL FRANÇAIS (12 volumes; 6th ed. by Esmein 1958). Questions of evidence are discussed in volume 12.

**b. Commercial law.**

Procedure before the commercial courts, especially the competence of commercial courts and the special rules of evidence in commercial cases, are usually treated in works on commercial law. Some of the better-known ones are:

RIPERT, TRAITÉ DE DROIT COMMERCIAL (3d ed. 1954);

ESCARRA, COURS DE DROIT COMMERCIAL (2d ed. 1952);

HAMEL & LAGARDE, TRAITÉ DE DROIT COMMERCIAL (vol. 1, 1954; a second volume to be published).

**c. Conflict of laws.**

Treatises on conflict of laws deal with questions of competence in international cases, proof of foreign law, capacity of aliens to sue and be sued, international co-operation in litigation, proof of facts with a foreign situs, enforcement of foreign judgments and similar problems. The most authoritative one-volume treatise is:

BATIFFOL, TRAITÉ ÉLÉMENTAIRE DE DROIT INTERNATIONAL PRIVÉ (3d ed. 1959).

Two of the larger and somewhat older multi-volume works are also important:

NIBOYET, TRAITÉ DE DROIT INTERNATIONAL PRIVÉ FRANÇAIS (7 volumes 1951);

ARMINJON, PRÉCIS DE DROIT INTERNATIONAL PRIVÉ (3 volumes 1958).

One work of a rather theoretical nature has had a great influence on the formulation of French concepts of jurisdiction:

BARTIN, PRINCIPES DE DROIT INTERNATIONAL PRIVÉ (3 volumes 1935).

## 1.38. General Materials

### a. Codes, laws, and *décrets*.

The most convenient edition of the CODE DE PROCÉDURE CIVILE is the edition in the PETIT CODES DALLOZ series. The CODE DE PROCÉDURE CIVILE, as most other codes in that series, is published annually in paperbound form. The CODE DE PROCÉDURE CIVILE volume includes the text of the Code and of supplementary legislation relating to civil procedure, court organization, the judiciary, and the legal professions. Each yearly edition contains the current text, as well as older (abrogated) provisions, and references to articles in periodicals and case annotations. The usefulness of this otherwise extremely practical book is somewhat impaired by extremely small print.

A larger annotated edition of the CODE DE PROCÉDURE CIVILE, quite out of date, is:

TISSIER, DARRAS & LOUICHE-DESFONTAINES, CODE DE PROCÉDURE CIVILE ANNOTÉ (2 volumes and supplement, 1911).

Current French laws and *décrets* are published in the official *Journal Officiel de la République Française*, which publishes parliamentary debates, reports, and other legislative material as well as new laws, *décrets*, and other executive acts. However, laws and *décrets* are published in a separate part.

Most laws and *décrets* are also published in the unofficial biweekly BULLETIN LÉGISLATIF DALLOZ, which has a much handier format. The more important legislative and quasi-legislative materials are also available in the various services mentioned in the following section.

**b. Reports, services, and periodicals.**

**(1) Reports:**

At present, only the decisions of the *Cour de Cassation* are officially reported. There are two series: The BULLETIN DES ARRÊTS DE LA COUR DE CASSATION RENDUS EN MATIÈRE CIVILE (generally referred to as BULLETIN CIVIL) reports the decisions of the court in civil cases, including decisions relating to civil procedure; decisions in criminal cases are reported in the BULLETIN DES ARRÊTS DE LA COUR DE CASSATION RENDUS EN MATIÈRE CRIMINELLE.

**(2) *Recueils* (Services):**

The most important legal periodicals for the French practitioner are the *recueils*. They serve for the publication of cases, new laws, and *décrets*, and articles. The best-known is the:

RECUEIL DALLOZ. It consists of weekly pamphlets with three sections, *chronique* (articles), *jurisprudence* (cases), and *législation* (laws and decrees). The reports of cases are often accompanied by notes by legal scholars explaining their significance. New laws and *décrets* may be accompanied by scholarly comment on their significance, or by legislative reports. The three sections of the weekly RECUEIL DALLOZ are separately paginated, on a volume basis. At the end of the year, a general index is provided. The subscriber can then separate the monthly pamphlets into their three constituent parts and have them bound with the index so as to have a volume with three sections, each continuously paginated.

Though their frequency of publication varies from that of DALLOZ, the other *recueils* follow substantially the same scheme. They include the following:

RECUEIL SIREY (merged with Dalloz on Jan. 1, 1965);

GAZETTE DU PALAIS (also publisher of a legal newspaper appearing several times a week);

JURISCLASSEUR PÉRIODIQUE (also called SEMAINE JURIDIQUE). In this set, both the individual items as well as the pages are numbered. Citation is usually to the item, rather than to page number.

Access to these four publications is facilitated by cumulative indexes covering five or ten years of publication.

**(3) Periodicals:**

French legal periodicals tend to specialize. The most important periodical for the study of French civil procedure is the REVUE TRIMESTRIELLE DE DROIT CIVIL. It contains a special section devoted to new developments in the field of civil procedure, edited by professors Raynaud and Hébraud.

For persons interested in litigation with international aspects the REVUE CRITIQUE DE DROIT INTERNATIONAL PRIVÉ and the JOURNAL DU DROIT INTERNATIONAL, popularly known as CLUNET, are important. In addition to articles, they also contain full reprints or digests of cases and legislation affecting private international law, sometimes with English translations or summaries.

Commercial procedure is often discussed in the REVUE TRIMESTRIELLE DE DROIT COMMERCIAL.

Various professional organizations also publish periodicals (such as LE BARREAU DE FRANCE) dealing with questions of procedure and court organization.

CHAPTER 2

# PROFESSIONAL LEGAL ASSISTANCE

This chapter surveys the various types of professional legal assistance available. After a brief introduction (1.01–1.02), it discusses *avocats* (2.03), *officiers ministériels* (2.04), *avocats* before the *Cour de Cassation* (2.05), *avoués* (2.06), *agréés* (2.07), *huissiers* (2.08), *greffiers* (2.09), *notaires* (2.10), and special professionals involved in the administration or sale of property (2.11). The chapter concludes with a prognosis of future developments (2.12).

## 2.01. Introduction

In France, any person, whether or not legally trained, may give legal advice. [1] As a consequence, many persons, although not members of one of the legal professions and sometimes without possessing any legal education, practice law in France under such names as *conseil juridique* or *agent d'affaires*. In addition, French business organizations frequently have persons on their legal staffs, who, although legally trained, are not members of any of the professions. The freedom to practice law is subject to only two limitations: First, no one, not meeting the prescribed requirements, may engage in activities explicitly reserved by law to the legal professions – such as the legally required representation by a member of a legal profession in most litigated and certain non-litigated matters; second, it is unlawful falsely to hold oneself out as belonging to a legal profession. [2] Notwithstanding this large degree of freedom, the assistance of a member of one of the recognized legal professions is ordinarily invoked in every case involving a substantial client or problem.

Formerly, non-professionals were permitted to represent parties in litigation before the *juge de paix* who was competent in certain minor

[1] David, Le Droit Français 59 (1960).

[2] *Id.* See, *e.g.*, Code Pénal art. 259 (forbidding illegal use of the title *avocat*); X., Trib. correctionnel Seine, March 8, 1950, [1950] D.J. 375 (only *avocat* may use title *avocat international*); Radulesco, Trib. correctionnel Seine, June 24, 1948, [1948] D.J. 454 (unlicensed legal adviser may not use title *avocat-conseil*).

civil and criminal cases, and in litigation before the commercial courts. At present, parties may act as their own attorneys, or be represented by a member of their family or one of their employees, before the *tribunaux d'instance*, which replaced the *juges de paix* in 1959. However, if they desire other assistance, they must ordinarily procure the services of an *avocat* or *avoué*.

The use of unofficial legal advisers before the labor and social security courts is also restricted: Although parties may act as their own attorneys, they may be represented only by one of their employees or fellow workers, by officials of trade organizations or labor unions, or by an *avocat* or *avoué*. [3] Other unofficial legal advisers may now appear in a representative capacity only before the commercial courts, before which any layman may still represent litigants. However, even before the commercial courts a body of specialized counsellors, called *agréés*, has come into existence.

## 2.02. The Various Legal Professions

Professional legal assistance in France is provided by the members of various legal professions. [4] Oral argument before the courts (with the exception of the two highest French courts, the *Cour de Cassation* and the *Conseil d'Etat*), lies within the exclusive province of the *avocat*. [5] His position is somewhat analogous to that of an English barrister. Before the ordinary civil courts of general competence, the *tribunaux de grande instance*, as well as before the intermediate courts of appeal, the *cours d'appel*, the *avoués* have a monopoly for the representation of the parties in procedural matters and the preparation of the various written papers. Their function resembles that of an English solicitor. [6] They may not present oral argument, since that activity is reserved to the *avocats*. Before the *Cour de Cassation* and the *Conseil d'Etat*, the combined

[3] DÉCRET No. 58–1291 of December 22, 1958, J.O. Dec. 23, 1958, p. 11613, [1959] B.L.D. 77, art. 69. Before the rural lease courts, parties may either act as their own attorneys, or use the services of an *avocat* or *avoué*; they may also be represented by a member of their household, or a *huissier*, or a member of an argricultural organization. DÉCRET No. 58–1293 of Dec. 22, 1958, J.O. Dec. 23, 1958, p. 11627, [1959] B.L.D. 87, art. 12.

[4] For a description in English of the various persons who give professional legal assistance in France, see AMOS & WALTON, INTRODUCTION TO FRENCH LAW 22–23 (2d ed. 1963); DAVID & DE VRIES, THE FRENCH LEGAL SYSTEM 21–28 (1958); BURDICK, THE BENCH AND BAR OF OTHER LANDS 258–79 (1939); Lepaulle, *Law Practice in France*, 50 COLUM. L. REV. 945–58 (1950); Conard, *Forming a Subsidiary in the European Common Market*, 59 MICH. L. REV. 26–31 (1960).

[5] See 2.03 *infra*. The *avocats* may not practice before some of the specialized courts, such as the prize courts.

[6] See 2.06 *infra*.

functions of *avocat* and *avoué* are exercised by a small group of men called *avocats au Conseil d'Etat et à la Cour de cassation.* [7]

The preparation of certain legal documents is the responsibility of the *notaire.* In addition, the *notaire,* who is legally trained, is usually consulted in cases involving decedents' estates and marital property and in matters of property law. His functions are vastly more important than those of an American notary public. [8] Among the persons rendering professional legal assistance in France, French authors usually also include the *greffiers* and the *huissiers.* The *greffiers* are the clerks of the courts. Like the *notaires* and *avoués,* they derive their compensation mainly from fees collected from the parties and only in small part from a salary. [9] The same is true of the *huissiers* who act as process servers and levy execution. [10]

## 2.03. The *Avocats*

**a. Educational requirements.** To become a French *avocat,* one must have the degree of *licencié en droit* from the law faculty of one of the French universities. [11] Admission to a university requires the completion of five years of primary education [12] and seven years of secondary education. Secondary education is given in a *lycée* or *collège.* There are several types of these institutions, some emphasizing the classics, others the sciences. Though students may choose the type of institution they attend, they have generally no choice in the selection of individual courses. In French high schools, considerable emphasis is put on linguistic skills, logic, and memory. Many children seek gainful employment when they are fourteen or fifteen years old and obtain no secondary education or do not complete it. Until recently, French high school graduates tended to be of middle class origin, but this situation is changing. The number of high school graduates of lower class origin

[7] See 2.05 *infra.*
[8] See 2.10 *infra.*
[9] See 2.09 *infra.*
[10] See 2.08 *infra.*
[11] See notes 17–22 *infra.* The regular French universities are all state institutions. The University of Paris, founded in 1200, is the oldest French institution of higher learning. There are 16 other French universities. There are also some municipal and some Catholic institutions at which law is taught, but diplomas issued by these institutions have no official value. The present official title of the faculties in France is: "*Faculté de Droit et des Sciences Economiques.*"
[12] Primary education has been free and compulsory in France since the Laws of June 16, 1881, [1882] D. 4.26 and March 28, 1882, [1882] D. 4.64. See also 1.08.b *supra.* Attendance at a secondary school is not required in France, but students not attending secondary institutions must go to primary school for eight years.

has increased rapidly in recent years. [13] Graduation from high school requires the passing of a final examination (uniform throughout France), called *baccalauréat.* [14] A French high school graduate has roughly the equivalent of the general education in the arts and sciences of an American college student after his sophomore year. All students who have successfully passed the *baccalauréat* may register at the law faculties; the type of high school attended is not material. Recently, a so-called equivalency examination was instituted to permit persons who did not complete their high school education to obtain the right to register at a university by passing that examination. [15] Tuition at French universities is extremely low, especially by American standards. [16]

To obtain the degree of *licencié en droit,* the completion of a four-year course is required.

French law faculties, known in French as *facultés de droit et des sciences économiques* (faculties of law and economic sciences), teach many courses in the social sciences in addition to those of a more strictly legal nature. They award two basic degrees both of which require four years of study: [17] The *licence en sciences économiques* is

[13] According to recent statistics, about 12% of all university students are children of small tradesmen or little shop owners, 3% sons of workers, 17% sons of salaried employees. About 13% are children of professional men, 6% children of business executives. About one third of the students in law and in the sciences are women.

[14] The *lycée* is a state-owned institution; other schools, whether private, religious, or municipal, are called *collèges*. Students begin attendance at these schools at the age of 11 or 12. Those completing only three years receive a diploma called B.E.C.P. (*brevet d'études du premier cycle*). About 200,000 students take the *baccalauréat* examination each year, about 60% of whom pass. About 85% of those who pass subsequently obtain some form of higher education. *Cf.* generally GUIDE NÉRET DES CARRIÈRES: LE BACC ET LES DÉBOUCHÉS DES ÉTUDES SECONDAIRES 8 (1961). The *baccalauréat* examination points out the general characteristics of French secondary education. In 1962, the examination in French, identical for all students, consisted of a long essay in which the students could either comment on the works of La Fontaine or on a poem by Verlaine or on a passage by St. Exupéry on human responsibility. The philosophy examination varied according to the type of school attended. The students of high schools emphasizing the classics could choose among the following essay topics: What is the difference between a technical and a magical process; does the will need the help of habit; does the feeling of guilt have a moral value? A sample question for students of technical and commercial high schools: Is efficiency a sufficient norm for human action? For students of science high schools: Is there room for the concept of finality in scientific explanation? France Soir, June 26, 1962, p. 7F. The *baccalauréat* has recently been subjected to some revisions. See DÉCRETS No. 62–1172 and No. 62–1173 of Sept. 29, 1962, J.O. Oct. 11, 1962, p. 9943–44.

[15] DÉCRET No. 56–1201 of Nov. 27, 1956, J.O. Nov. 29, 1956, p. 11433, [1956] B.L.D. 999; DÉCRET No. 61–440 of May 5, 1961, J.O. May 6, 1961 p. 4193, [1961] B.L.D. 323.

[16] Annual charges were only about 40 F. (about $10.—) in 1959. 1 DAVID, LE DROIT FRANÇAIS 187 (1960). This may be one reason for the large number of French law students.

[17] The four-year *licence* curriculum was instituted by the DÉCRET of March 27, 1954, J.O. March 28, 1954, p. 2966, [1954] D.L. 141. The official memorandum preceding the DÉCRET contains a good summary of the new program and a criticism of the former 3-year curriculum. The 1954 DÉCRET has now been superseded by DÉCRET No. 62–768 of July 10, 1962, J.O.

destined for students specializing in economics and related fields; the *licence en droit* (roughly corresponding to an American LL.B. degree) is destined for students seeking to enter one of the legal professions, but is also valued as preparation for a wide variety of careers in government or business. [18]

The course of studies for the *licence en droit* is established by government decree and is substantially uniform throughtout France. The program for the first two years is prescribed. It includes elementary courses in basic subjects, such as private law (*droit civil*) which includes the law of persons, of property and of obligations, a few courses in the public law field, such as constitutional law, and a number of introductory courses in political science and legal history. The political science courses are designed to give the French law student, who begins his studies when he is about eighteen years of age and who has not attended a college (in the American sense of the term), a basic knowledge of the social sciences. Examinations are held at the end of each academic year.

The student who successfully completes the first two years of law study is granted a certificate of *études juridiques générales* (general legal studies) which gives access to some civil service positions. [19] During the third year of his studies, the candidate for the *licence en droit* must take

July 11, 1962, p. 6780, [1962] D.L. 224. However, the length of the program has not been changed. For a description of the 1954 program, see also Piret, *La réforme des études de droit en France*, 69 JOURNAL DES TRIBUNAUX 257 (1954); L'INDICATEUR DE L'ÉTUDIANT EN DROIT 108–14 (1958); Tunc, *New Developments in Legal Education in France*, 4 AM. J. COMP. L. 419-25 (1955). The 1962 changes are described in Trotabas, *Le nouveau régime de la licence en droit*, [1962] D. CHR. 203.

[18] Because some knowledge of legal matters is viewed as helpful in a large number of careers, the number of law students in France, especially at the University of Paris, is extremely large but the number of students who finish their studies and obtain the *licencié en droit* degree is very much smaller. During the academic year 1953–54, 19.509 students were registered at the Faculty of Legal and Political Sciences (now Faculty of Law and Economic Sciences) of the University of Paris, of whom 1.507 were women, but during the same year only 1.309 *licencié* degrees and about 600 other degrees (*doctorat* and *capacité*) were conferred. Subsequently, the number of students decreased. In 1958–59, there were 14.165 students, of whom 3.665 were women, 1368 foreign students, and 785 students from the French overseas territories. Of these students 6.915 were registered in the *licencié* program, 2.954 were doctoral candidates, and the rest candidates for various other degrees. During the same year, 792 *licencié* degrees were conferred and 167 doctoral degrees. While the changeover from a three to a four-year curriculum, which occurred during that period, makes it difficult to draw any definite conclusions, these figures would tend to show that perhaps only 50% of the students beginning legal studies in France actually complete them. In future years, the number of students obtaining the *licencié en droit* degree will undoubtedly be smaller, since students concentrating in economics no longer obtain the *licencié en droit* degree, as they did until recently. See notes 19–21 *infra*.

In the universities outside Paris the number of students is considerably smaller; the number of *licencié* degrees conferred by the provincial universities varied in 1959 from 102 (Rennes) to 29 (Poitiers). For more complete statistics see 1 DAVID, LE DROIT FRANÇAIS 192–93 (1960).

[19] DÉCRET No. 62–768, *supra* note 17, arts. 3–6.

a number of additional compulsory courses, including courses in commercial law, labor law, and civil liberties. For the balance of his course work, he may either choose a group of courses falling within the private law area – including courses on civil procedure and such advanced *droit civil* subjects as suretyship, real property, and the like –, or a group of courses falling within the public law-political science area – including courses on public international law and the methodolgy of the social sciences. The third year also terminates with an examination.

For his fourth year, the student must elect between two major fields of concentration: private law (broadly defined) or political science. Students selecting private law must take courses in conflict of laws, business taxation, advanced *droit civil*, history of private law, and similar advanced private law courses. Students selecting political science must take courses on European organizations, the history of political ideas, and similar subjects. In addition to the required number of courses in his area of concentration, each student must take five additional one-semester courses. As to the latter, he has a very wide choice: He may select additional courses either within or without his field of concentration; even courses taken in institutes not belonging to a law faculty or courses taken abroad may be counted towards fulfillment of this requirement.

The examination at the end of the fourth year covers both the area of concentration and the elective courses. [20] All students completing the *licence en droit* program have the same rights of access to the various legal professions, whether their field of concentration is private law or political science. Although French universities do have political science institutes, they do not have political science faculties. As a result, a student who wishes to specialize in political science at a university must qualify either for the *licence en sciences économiques* or for the *licence en droit.* [21]

Instruction at French law schools is largely in the form of lectures, which the students frequently do not attend, preferring to study from

[20] For the rules governing the third and fourth year of the curriculum, see DÉCRET No. 62–768, *supra* note 17 arts. 6, 7, 15–18.

[21] Originally, the DÉCRET of March 27, 1954, *supra* note 17, provided, in addition, for an economic section with a heavy concentration of courses in the field of economics and business administration and a very limited number of law courses. The successful completion of the program of the economic section also gave the student the right to the *licencié en droit* degree with all its advantages. This system was criticized because of the limited legal education obtained by the graduates of the economic section. See Piret, *supra* note 17. Since 1960, graduates of the economic section no longer receive the title of *licencié en droit* with all its privileges, but the title *licencié en sciences économiques*, which does not give access to the legal professions. See 1 DAVID, LE DROIT FRANÇAIS 194 (1960).

mimeographed or printed transcripts of the professor's lectures, which are widely available. However, since 1954, students must attend one three-hour course of *exercices pratiques* in civil law. The *exercices pratiques* may involve the preparation of a written comment on court decisions, the drafting of written pleadings (*conclusions*), or similar practical work. Only students who have done satisfactory work in the *exercices pratiques* may take the final year-end examinations.

Except for the *exercices pratiques*, instruction is fairly theoretical. While there are variations of emphasis, the lectures tend to deal more with general principles than with their practical application. Thus, in a course on civil procedure a great deal of time will be spent on attempts to define the nature of the judicial function or the concept of cause of action and comparatively little time on a discussion of the various procedural steps which must be taken in a concrete case. As a result, many graduates of French law schools tend to retain a fondness for broad general concepts throughout their careers. [22]

The theoretical approach of French legal education is also apparent from the scope of the four yearly examinations. They are partly oral and partly written, and always require the preparation of a written essay on some point of legal theory as well as the solution of more practical problems. [23] Contacts between students and faculty tend to be infrequent; this is in part due to the emphasis on formal lectures, which give the students no opportunity for class discussion. However,students are free to come to their professors' offices if they have problems, and faculty members ordinarily try to render assistance.

While the degree of *licencié* is sufficient as preparation for *avocats* and judges, some students continue their studies in order to obtain the degree of *docteur en droit*, which requires additional course work and the preparation of a written thesis. This degree is sought after particularly by students who contemplate university teaching or research as a career.

To be distinguished from the regular *docteur en droit* degree, sometimes called *doctorat d'état*, is the *doctorat d'université*, which the Uni-

[22] See DAVID, LE DROIT FRANÇAIS 44–47 (1960); DAVID & DE VRIES, THE FRENCH LEGAL SYSTEM, *supra* note 4, at 27, 28. As a corollary, French legal discussion ordinarily centers around rights, rather than around remedies; indeed, no precise translation for the English term remedy exists in French. The *exercices pratiques*, introduced by the 1954 DÉCRET, are now prescribed by arts. 8 and 9 of the DÉCRET No. 62–768, *supra* note 17. A certain amount of lecturing seems to go on even in the *exercices pratiques*.

[23] See DÉCRET No. 62–768, *supra* note 17 arts. 14–18. French legal education is not of quite as theoretical a nature as German or Italian legal education, however, and tends to put more emphasis on the cases. See DAVID, *op. cit. supra* note 21, at 65.

versity of Paris confers upon foreign graduate students who have completed a special program. [24]

**b. Professional examination.** To supplement the somewhat theoretical legal education leading to the degree of *licencié*, special compulsory one year programs for future *avocats* have been established at the French universities. They may be attended either during the last (fourth) year of studies for the *licencié en droit* degree, or after that degree has been obtained. [25] The program consists of courses, special lectures, and *exercices pratiques*; the courses are given by law teachers, *avocats*, *avoués*, and judges and deal with the rôle of the *avocat* in society, his professional obligations, and the practical aspects of his work, such as litigation. [26] At the completion of the course, the students must pass an oral and written examination designed to test their general education, as well as their knowledge of the law and of the duties of the *avocat*. Students having passed this examination receive the *certificat d'aptitude à la profession d'avocat* (certificate of fitness for the profession of avocat). In case of failure, the examination may be repeated, but not more than three times. [27] Since this examination is given before the candidate has had any experience with actual practice of law, it bears some resemblance to the bar examinations of many American states rather than to the examinations given prospective lawyers in Germany or Austria after the completion of an extended clerkship period. Some French authors have suggested the adoption of a system somewhat similar to the German and Austrian systems. [28]

**c. Clerkship *(Stage)*.** To become a full-fledged *avocat*, the holder of a *certificate d'aptitude pour la profession d'avocat* must complete a *stage* (trial period) of three to five years, designed to give him additional

[24] See L'INDICATEUR DE L'ÉTUDIANT EN DROIT 66 (1958). The University of Paris seems to be the only European university which has a special doctoral program for foreign students who want to obtain advanced training in a specialized field, such as international law. It is attended by students from all over the world.

[25] DÉCRET of October 13, 1954, J.O. Oct. 14, 1954, p. 9618, [1954] D.L. 417. The *certificat d'aptitude* had orginally been instituted by the Vichy régime in 1941, but the applicable law was declared invalid by Law No. 54–390 of April 8, 1954, J.O. April 9, 1954, p. 3420, [1954] D.L. 158.

[26] DÉCRET of Oct. 13, 1954, *supra* note 25, art. 5.

[27] The board of examiners consists of two law professors, two *avocats*, one *magistrat* (judge or prosecutor), and one *avoué*. DÉCRET of October 13,1954, *supra* note 25, art. 7. The examination seems to be fairly strict. In 1959-60, over 500 students attended the program, but only 131 obtained the certificate. 1 DAVID, LE DROIT FRANÇAIS (1960).

[28] Joly, *Réflexions sur le certificat d'aptitude à la profession d'avocat*, [1956] D. CHR. 33; Solus, *Autres réflexions sur le certificat d'aptitude à la profession d'avocat*, [1956] D. CHR. 63.

skills in his chosen profession and to test his character and integrity. The *stage* is largely under the control of the local professional organizations of the *avocats* (*ordres*). To be admitted to the *stage*, the candidate must submit proof to the executive council (*conseil de l'ordre*) of the organization at his residence that he has been a French national for at least five years, [29] holds a *licencié en droit* degree from a French university and the *certificat d'aptitude*, and is of good moral character. [30] Candidates admitted to the *stage* take an oath of office before the *cour d'appel*; they promise never to say anything contrary to law or morals, and to respect the courts and public authorities.[31] Henceforth, they may take the title of *avocat stagiaire*.

The professional organization must conduct courses dealing with professional ethics, the duties of the *avocat*, and similar topics for the benefit of the *avocats stagiaires*. In practice, the bar organizations do not always organize these courses very effectively.

The *avocat stagiaire* must work for at least one year as a clerk in the office of an *avocat, avoué*, or *agréé*, or with the *ministère public*. He must also handle all the legal aid (*assistance judiciaire*) cases that are assigned to him. [32] These cases are quite numerous, since in France indigent parties have a right to assigned counsel in civil as well as in criminal cases. As a clerk in the office of an *avocat*, the *avocat stagiaire* performs legal research for his employer, argues in less important cases, and prepares drafts of legal instruments. *Avocats stagiaires* may not appear in court or give legal advice while they are clerks of an *avoué, notaire* or *agréé*. However, *avocats stagiaires* who have completed the one-year clerkship period have the same rights as a full-fledged *avocat* except that they may not vote in the elections for officers of their professional organizations [33] and must always use the title of *avocat stagiaire* rather than that of *avocat*.

[29] ORDONNANCE of October 19, 1945 (Code of French Nationality), J.O. Oct. 20, 1945, p. 6700, [1946] D.L. 10, art. 81. In the case of naturalized French citizens, the *conseil de l'ordre* also examines their knowledge of the French language and their adaptation to French society; decisions of the *conseil* in that respect are subject to review by the courts. X., Cass. Req., June 2, 1937, [1937] D.H. 345.

[30] DÉCRET No. 54–406 of April 10, 1954, J.O. April 11, 1954, p. 3494, [1954] B.L.D. 165, as modified by DÉCRET No. 56–1232 of Nov. 30, 1956, J.O. Dec. 5, 1956, p. 11616, [1956] B.L.D. 1050, art. 22 and DÉCRET No. 60–126 of Feb. 12, 1960, J.O. Feb. 16, 1960, p. 1487, [1960] D.L. 92.

[31] DÉCRET No. 54–406, *supra* note 30, art. 23. The application for admission to the *stage* must be made at the actual, not a fictitious, domicile. X., Cass. Req., Nov. 9, 1925, [1926] D. 1.41.

[32] DÉCRET No. 54–406, *supra* note 30 art. 26.

[33] CUCHE & VINCENT 168 n.l. Thus, *avocats stagiaires* who have completed the one-year clerkship period are theoretically free to handle the most complicated cases. In practice, they limit their activities to fairly simple ones.

At the end of the three-year *stage* period, the president of the local organization of *avocats* may issue the *avocat stagiaire* a certificate attesting to the completion of the *stage* and conferring the right to practice as an *avocat*. If the performance of the *avocat stagiaire* has not been satisfactory, he may be required to continue his *stage* for an additional one or two-year period. At the end of the fifth year of the *stage*, a certificate must be issued to the *avocat stagiaire*, unless the executive council of the bar organization (*conseil de l'ordre*) decides not to issue the certificate. Such a decision, which means in effect that the candidate cannot become an *avocat*, is reviewable by the *cour d'appel*. [34]

Since the *avocat stagiaire* receives only a very small salary while he is employed as a clerk, and since thereafter the bulk of his own cases consists either of legal aid matters for which he ordinarily receives no pay at all or of cases of small importance, the requirement of the *stage*, coming after a period of four years' study at the university, causes financial problems. As a result, *avocats* tend to come from a middle-class background; children of less wealthy families attracted by a legal career are more likely to become *avoués* or *notaires* who do not require such a long course of studies. [35] As a further consequence, the number of *avocats stagiaires* and therefore also of *avocats* has been diminishing. [36] On the other hand, the proportion of women among the *avocats stagiaires* has increased.

**d. Functions, rights, and obligations of the *avocat*.** After having received the certificate attesting to the completion of the *stage*, the newly formed *avocat* will ordinarily open his own office. While an *avocat* may and does give legal advice in other than litigated matters, his work in this area is usually not very significant. His main activity consists in the presentation of oral argument in court. Since a French civil suit often involves several interlocutory decisions, there may be several oral arguments in one suit. Before the regular courts of first instance, the *tribunaux de grande instance*, and before the intermediate courts of ap-

[34] DÉCRET No. 54–406, *supra* note 30, art. 27. *Avoués* holding the *licencié en droit* degree who wish to become *avocats* must go through a *stage*, but its length may be reduced. They must resign as *avoués* before entering the *stage*. DÉCRET No. 54–406, *supra* note 30, art. 28. Members of the *Conseil d'Etat*, judges, and other *magistrats* with more than three years' experience and some other persons with legal experience are excepted from the *stage*. DÉCRET No. 54–406, *supra* note 30, art. 29.

[35] DAVID, *op. cit. supra* note 22, at 56. In addition, *avoués* and *notaires* are more certain to obtain at least a minimum income, since the number of *avoués* and *notaires* is limited. However, the office of an *avoué* or *notaire* must be purchased; thus, some initial capital is required to enter these professions.

[36] In 1937, there were 7.321 *avocats* in France, and 2,464 *avocats stagiaires*; in 1960, there were 6565 *avocats*, and only 923 *stagiaires*, of whom one-third were women.

peal, the *cours d'appel*, only *avocats*, or the parties themselves, may present oral argument.[37] Since parties rarely argue on their own behalf, the *avocats* have a practical monopoly before these courts. There is no such monopoly before most of the other courts, such as the *tribunaux d'instance*, commercial courts, and the labor courts.

Since the *avocat* does not question witnesses, which is ordinarily done by the judge, the art of examination and cross-examination is foreign to him. It is rather the function of the *avocat* to make the court view the facts and the law in a light favorable to his client. As a result, the *avocats* are mainly experts on substantive law and skilled orators, who rely to a considerable extent on oral arguments. The speeches of *avocats* in court are sometimes quite long and not always confined to matters that are strictly relevant. Judges rarely interrupt the argument of *avocats* to ask questions.[38]

Since the *avocat* is considered an adviser, not an agent, the parties are not bound by statements of their *avocats*.[39] However, before courts in which the assistance of an *avoué* is not required, *avocats* sometimes act as *avocats* and de facto *avoués*. Since *avocats* are not considered as agents of their clients, they have not, until recently, been allowed to accept funds on their clients' behalf. This prohibition has now been abandoned in cases in which the *avocat* also acts as *avoué*.[40] The *avocat* enjoys immunity from suits based on statements made during argument, as long as these statements are relevant to the case.[41]

The *avocat* is free to accept or refuse employment, except if a case is assigned to him.[42] He enjoys a great deal of latitude in the manner of

[37] CUCHE & VINCENT 171; *cf.* Ordre des Avocats à la Cour de Paris v. Epoux Pergent et autres, Cass. Civ., Jan. 19, 1942, [1942] D. CR. 61. Article 85 of the *Code de Procédure Civile* permits the parties, including corporations, who may use one of their officers, to argue for themselves, but provides that the court may deprive them of that right when they act improperly.

[38] DAVID & DE VRIES, *op. cit. supra* note 4, at 21-23.

[39] CUCHE & VINCENT 171 n. 2. In this respect, an *avocat* resembles the forespeaker of the Germanic procedure.

[40] The local *ordres* of *avocats* may authorize their members to handle their clients' funds in cases in which the client has no *avoué*; this authorization may be granted only if the *ordre* has contracted for indemnity insurance to protect clients. DÉCRET No. 56–1232, *supra* note 30 art. 48.

[41] Law of July 29, 1881, [1881] D. 4.65, as amended by ORDONNANCE of Nov. 17, 1958, J.O. Nov. 1958, [1958] D.L. art. 41; CRÉMIEU, TRAITÉ DE LA PROFESSION D'AVOCAT 240 (2d ed. 1954); *cf.* Muret v. Mignard, Cass. Req. May 2, 1893, [1893] D.I. 288. Third parties may always sue *avocats* on account of a statement not relevant to the action; the parties themselves may sue only if authorized by the court. Law of July 29, 1881, art. 41 (last sentence). The immunity covers statements made before all courts, but not during an *expertise* ordered by the court. 1 DALLOZ, RÉPERTOIRE DE PROCÉDURE CIVILE ET COMMERCIALE, *Avocat*, No. 186 (1955).

[42] CUCHE & VINCENT 173; DÉCRET No. 54–406, *supra* note 30, art. 44.

presenting his client's case. He may terminate his employment at will, at least if he obtains another *avocat* to replace him, and he should terminate his employment if his client asks him to violate the rules of professional ethics. [43] The *avocat* has the right to wear a gown, and must wear it when appearing in court. [44]

The *avocat* owes complete loyalty to his client and may not accept employment in a matter in which he has been employed by the other side. [45] It is generally assumed that an *avocat* may become liable to his client for failure to exercise the care of a prudent *avocat*, but there is some authority to the effect that, since he is not the client's agent, an *avocat* is not liable as long as he acts in good faith. [46]

An *avocat* may not reveal confidential communications made to him by his client. [47] As a corollary, he cannot be compelled to testify concerning such communications when called as a witness, [48] and searches in his office by the police are subject to severe restrictions. [49]

The *avocat* must treat his opponent and his colleagues fairly; in argument he may not use documents, unless he has first sent them to his opponent's *avocat* for inspection. [50] The *avocat* must not make offending remarks concerning the courts or individuals judges. [51] However, the *avocats* consider themselves in no way as subordinates of the judiciary; due to mutual respect, incidents between judges and *avocats* are quite rare. [52] If a court lacks a quorum, an *avocat* may be called upon to act as a temporary judge. [53]

[43] Cuche & Vincent 174; *cf.* Les Barreaux dans le Monde 230 (1959); Dalloz, *op. cit. supra* note 41, at No. 206.

[44] *Cf.* X. v. Proc. Gén. Cour de Paris, Cass. Civ., July 1, 1958, [1958] D.J. 526 (duty to wear gown when appearing in disciplinary proceeding)

[45] Crémieu, *op. cit. supra* note 41, at 267, 270.

[46] Décret No. 54–406, *supra* note 30, art. 43 (responsibility for violations constituting crimes); 1 Mazeaud & Tunc, Traité Théorique et Pratique de la Responsabilité Civile No. 515 (4th ed. 1947); Cuche & Vincent 171. Liability insurance for attorneys is available in France, Crémieu, Traité de la profession d'avocat 297 (1st ed. 1939).

[47] Décret No. 54–406, *supra* note 30, art. 41; Code Pénal art. 378.

[48] The client cannot waive the privilege. Crémieu, *op. cit. supra* note 41, at 288.

[49] A search may be made only to discover some specified object, such as a forged document, but not circumstantial evidence of a crime generally; in addition, it is a traditional rule that the *bâtonnier* (president of the local bar association) must accompany the police. The permission of the *procureur général* is required. 1 Dalloz, *op. cit. supra* note 41, at No. 192.

[50] See 7.34 *infra*.

[51] The oath of office of the *avocat* includes this undertaking. See text accompanying note 31 *supra*. An *avocat* may not publish a newspaper article in which he states that he despises the judiciary in general or one court in particular. Min. Public. v. Me. X., Cour Montpellier, Dec. 4, 1912, [1913] D. 2.269. The relations between members of the bench and bar are much more formal in France than in the United States.

[52] Les Barreaux dans le Monde, *op. cit. supra* note 43, at 236–38. The *bâtonnier* (president of the local bar organization) ordinarily acts as mediator in case a dispute does arise.

[53] Cuche & Vincent 173. Ordinarily, the *avocat* with the greatest amount of seniority must act as a temporary judge.

Advertising and the solicitation of business are forbidden. To prevent possible conflicts of interest, the *avocat* may hold practically no other position. Thus, he may not act as a business executive or real estate agent. Law teaching and the holding of elective political office represent almost the only exceptions to this rule. [54] In fact, a large number of French politicians have come from the ranks of *avocats*. *Avocats* holding political office may not ordinarily handle suits against the French republic or other public bodies. [55]

**e. Fees.** Traditionally, the French *avocat* has been viewed as a defender of the rights of the oppressed, who exercises his profession more to render a public service than to obtain private gain. French *avocats* are extremely proud of this tradition. [56] Originally, the fee paid by the client was supposed to be an expression of spontaneous gratitude. As a result, the right of the *avocat* to sue his client for his fee was doubted, and some *barreaux* subjected members who sued their clients to disciplinary proceedings. This created no serious hardship at a time when many *avocats* had independent means, but was inappropriate in modern conditions. [57] Since 1957, the French *avocats* have a clear legal right to sue for unpaid fees; however, every such action must be preceded by an attempt at conciliation made by the *bâtonnier* (president of the local bar organization). [58]

There is no official fee schedule for French *avocats*; they may freely contract with their clients in that respect, but the fee must be reasonable in view of the importance and difficulty of the case, the time spent, and other similar factors. [59] Contingent fee contracts and fee-splitting are illegal. [60] However, since 1958, counsel assigned to an indigent

[54] DÉCRET No. 54–406, *supra* note 30, art. 45. It is one consequence of this rule that French *avocats*, or even *avocats stagiaires*, cannot be employed by American law firms in France without losing their status as *avocats*.

[55] DÉCRET No. 54–406, *supra* note 30, art. 46.

[56] LES BARREAUX DANS LE MONDE, *op. cit. supra* note 43, at 266; DAVID, *op. cit. supra* note 21, at 55, 56. Art. 16 of DÉCRET No. 54–406, *supra* note 30, states that the profession of the *avocats* rests on principles of honesty, disinterested service, moderation, and brotherliness.

[57] CRÉMIEU, *op. cit. supra* note 41, 238–246; Chapelet, *Commentaire, Loi du 21 décembre 1957*, [1958] B.L.D. (Comm.) 15.

[58] Law No. 57–420 of Dec. 31, 1957, J.O. Jan. 5, 1958. p. 194, [1958] B.L.D. 35.

[59] DALLOZ, *op. cit. supra* note 41, at No. 208–09; LES BARREAUX DANS LE MONDE, *op. cit. supra* note 43, at 256; X. v. Grima & Escoffier, Trib. Marseille, Feb. 22, 1955, [1955] J.C.P. II. 8738, [1956] D. SOMM. 93 (*avocat* may sue for fee, but fee must be reasonable); X. v. Courtinade, Trib. Paix Toulouse, July 5, 1955, [1955] J.C.P. II. 8927 (facts to be considered in fixing fee include experience of *avocat*, difficulty of case, and result achieved).

[60] CRÉMIEU, *op. cit. supra* note 41, at 243 (fee splitting forbidden); X., Cour Orléans, June 25, 1946, [1946] D.J. 364 (contingent fee contract void as against public policy). Indigent parties may obtain the services of assigned counsel, even in civil cases; this eliminates one reason for contingent fee contracts.

party under the French system of legal aid (*assistance judiciaire*) may make a charge if he has obtained a sufficient recovery. [61] *Avocats* may agree to provide legal advice for a fixed annual retainer; they may not bind themselves in advance to handle all the litigation of a party for a fixed annual fee, since such an arrangement would interfere with their right to refuse their co-operation in cases they consider unjustified. [62] The fees charged by French *avocats* for comparable work vary widely.

The government collects comparatively small fees from all parties making use of the services of an *avocat* for purposes of litigation. These fees, payable when the *enrégistrement* tax on the judgment is collected, are paid into a special fund called *Caisse nationale des barreaux français*. From that fund, an old age pension is paid to retired *avocats*. [63] It might be added that a French *avocat* who is retiring may not sell the goodwill of his office. [64]

**f. Professional organization.** French *avocats* enjoy a high degree of self-government. There is a separate organization of *avocats*, called *ordre*, at the seat of each intermediate court of appeal (*cour d'appel*) and at the seat of each court of first instance (*tribunal de grande instance*). [65] Each *avocat* must be enrolled in the *ordre* for the area in which he resides. [66] Collectively, the *avocats* enrolled in one *ordre* are often referred to as a *barreau*. [67] The affairs of each *ordre* are administered by an executive

[61] A charge may be made if the recovery is so large that the benefit of legal aid (*assistance judiciaire*) would not have been granted had the party owned the equivalent of the recovery at the beginning of the suit. DÉCRET No. 58–1289 of Dec. 22, 1958, J.O. Dec. 23, 1958, p. 11608, [1959] B.L.D. 58, art. 12.

[62] CRÉMIEU, *op. cit. supra* note 41, at 243, 256.

[63] The fee is ordinarily 15 francs (about $3,—) for each suit; another fee becomes payable on appeal. Law of Jan. 12, 1948, J.O. Jan. 13, 1948, p. 373, [1948] D.L. 49 (setting up fund); DÉCRET No. 65–379 of May 19, 1965, reprinted in CODE DE PROCÉDURE CIVILE 671 (62d ed. Dalloz 1966). *Avocats* become entitled to a pension if they are 65 years old and have practiced for at least 30 years. The pensions paid under this program are fairly small. CRÉMIEU, *op. cit. supra* note 41 at 351. Recently, the *Caisse nationale des barreaux* has also been authorized to operate a life insurance and disability fund based on members' contributions. Law No. 61–1384 of Dec. 19, 1961, J.O. Dec. 20 1961, p. 11660, [1962] D.L. 11 and DÉCRET No. 62–702 of June 27, 1962, J.O. June 29, 1962, p. 6283, [1962] D.L. 206. See also Law No. 62–905 of Aug. 3, 1962, J.O. Aug. 7, 1962, p. 7816, [1962] D.L. 267.

[64] LES BARREAUX DANS LE MONDE, *op. cit. supra* note 43, at 244.

[65] DÉCRET No. 54–406, *supra* note 30, art. 1. However, in cities in which there is a *tribunal de grande instance* and a *cour d'appel* there is only one *ordre*.

[66] DÉCRET No. 54–406, *supra* note 30, art. 1. *Avocats* must ordinarily reside in the *arrondissement* in which the court is located to which their *ordre* is attached, even if that court is competent in a much larger area.

[67] Each *ordre* prepares an annual roll of its members, by seniority. DÉCRET No. 54–406, *supra* note 30, art. 2. An *avocat* may not be a member of two *ordres* at the same time; if he changes his residence, he must seek admission to the *barreau* of his new residence. In such a case, the procedure for the admission of *avocats* is generally applicable but no *stage* is required of an *avocat* with ten ore more years practice. DÉCRET No. 54–406, *supra* note 30, art. 29.

council called *conseil de l'ordre,* and a president called *bâtonnier.* [68] The members of the *conseil* and the *bâtonnier* are elected by all enrolled members, except the *avocats stagiaires.* [69] Each *ordre* has legal personality; it may own property and often operates funds for the relief of widows or orphans of *avocats.* [70]

The numerous *ordres* in France are independent of each other. While there is a national association of French *avocats,* it has no supervisory rights over the individual *ordres.* [71] Nevertheless, a French *avocat* may argue anywhere in France, except before the *Conseil d'Etat, Cour de Cassation, Tribunal des Conflits, Cour des Comptes,* and *Conseil des Prises.* [72] By special permission, counsel admitted in a foreign country may argue in a French court, provided he is assisted by a French *avocat.* [73]

**g. Discipline.** One of the most important functions of each *ordre,* in addition to the organization of the *stage,* is the maintenance of high professional standards and of professional discipline. The executive committee (*conseil*) of each *ordre* may – and does – issue regulations governing the conduct of all member *avocats.* [74] Sitting as a disciplinary council, it has the power to impose disciplinary sanctions against *avocats* guilty of unprofessional conduct. The penalties which may be imposed include warnings, reprimands, temporary suspension, and permanent disbarment. [75] Official disciplinary action is ordinarily preceded

[68] The size of the *conseil* (executive committee) varies from three members for *ordres* of six members or less to twenty-six members for the *ordre* in Paris which has over 2000 members. DÉCRET No. 54–406, *supra* note 30, arts. 8, 10 and DÉCRET No. 60–126 of February 12, 1960, J.O. February 16, 1960, p. 1487, [1960] D.L. 92.

[69] DÉCRET No. 54–406, *supra* note 30, arts. 9, 11, 14. In addition to the elections, the general membership of each *ordre* is supposed to meet twice a year to discuss matters of common interest. Resolutions passed at these meetings have no binding force. DÉCRET No. 54–406, *supra* note 30, art. 21.

[70] In all legal transactions, the *bâtonnier* acts as representative of the *ordre.* DÉCRET No. 54–406, *supra* note 30, art. 18.

[71] DAVID, *op. cit. supra* note 21, at 57; *cf.* MOREL No. 185.

[72] DÉCRET No. 54–406 *supra* note 30, art. 6. An *avocat* arguing in a court outside the area of his own *ordre* must introduce himself to the presiding judge of the court, the member of the *ministère public* in attendance, the opposing *avocat* and the president of the local *ordre.* Ordinarily, *avocats* may not argue before the *Cour de Cassation, Conseil d'Etat, Tribunal des Conflits, Cour des Comptes* and *Conseil des Prises* because the right to argue before these agencies is reserved to others. As to the persons entitled to argue before the *Conseil d'Etat* and *Cour de Cassation,* see 2.05 *infra.* The *Tribunal des Conflits* decides disputes between the regular and administrative courts. See 3.03 *infra.* The *Cour des Comptes* has funtions somewhat analogous to those of the U.S. Comptroller General; the *Cour des Prises* is a prize court.

[73] CRÉMIEU, *op. cit. supra* note 41, at 19; DALLOZ, *op. cit. supra* note 41, at No. 303.

[74] DÉCRET 54–406, *supra* note 30, art. 16. Concerning the functions of the *ordre* in connection with the regulation of the *stage* and the admission of *avocats,* see 2.03.f *infra.*

[75] DÉCRET No. 54–406, *supra* note 30, arts. 31, 32. Eight day's notice must be given of a diciplinary proceeding to the *avocat* in question, who has a right to be heard. DÉCRET No.

by an attempt on the part of the *bâtonnier* to settle the matter. [76] In many cases, the moral authority of the *bâtonnier* is sufficient to produce the desired result. Official disciplinary proceedings are therefore fairly rare. Decisions of the *ordres* in disciplinary matters may be reviewed by the intermediate courts of appeals (*cours d'appel*). [77] Further review by the *Cour de Cassation* is possible but seldom elicited.

Quite apart from disciplinary sanctions, an *avocat* may be removed from the roll of attorneys if he has accepted a position incompatible with that of *avocat*, if he has moved to a place outside the district of the *ordre* to which he belongs, or if he has in fact ceased to exercise his profession. [78]

**h. Associations of *avocats*.** Afraid of losing their prized independence by any form of association, French *avocats* have traditionally practiced only as single practitioners. Recently, however, the argument has been advanced that partnerships of several *avocats* increase efficiency by permitting a division of labor and a lowering of general overhead, to the advantage of the *avocats* concerned, as well as of their clients. [79] Since 1954, the individual *ordres* of *avocats* may authorize their members to form partnerships. [80] Partnerships, which are limited to not more than five members, have not become very prevalent. In Paris, where there are well over two thousand *avocats*, there are about thirty partnerships with a total of about seventy members. About twenty more law firms exist in the provinces. [81] Undoubtedly, the number of law firms will increase in the future.

**i. The social and economic position of the *avocat*.** The young French *avocat* usually strikes out on his own after he has completed the *stage*. Especially in Paris, he often finds it difficult to find office space at

54–406, *supra* note 30, art. 33. Details of procedure in disciplinary cases are regulated by rules promulgated by each *ordre*.

[76] LES BARREAUX DANS LE MONDE, *op. cit. supra* note 43, at 260.

[77] DÉCRET No. 54–406, *supra* note 30, arts. 38, 39. The *avocat* in question as well as the *procureur général* (public prosecutor at the seat of the *cour d'appel*) have the right to appeal.

[78] DÉCRET No. 54–406, *supra* note 30, art. 4.

[79] CRÉMIEU, *op. cit. supra* note 41, at 111; LES BARREAUX DANS LE MONDE, *supra* note 43, at 244.

[80] DÉCRET No. 54–406, *supra* note 30, at 49.

[81] Choffel, *Les Avocats sont condamnés à s'associer*, LA VIE ECONOMIQUE, May 5, 1961, p. 24. According to Choffel, partnerships, when they exist, are of one of three types: in some cases, an older *avocat* close to retirement age becomes associated with a younger member of the profession, turning some of his duties over to him; sometimes, *avocats* unite merely to share an office and reduce overhead; in some instances, French law firms are associations of specialists in several fields.

reasonable rates. Unless he has a numerous circle of acquaintances, the number of his clients will initially be quite small. The net income of a young *avocat* is therefore usually quite modest. However, after a few years most able *avocats* are reasonably successful financially. A few famous *avocats* have even become fairly wealthy.

In addition, the *avocats* occupy a rather favorable social position. They are the most prominent of the various legal professions. This may be due in part to the longer academic preparation which the *avocats* receive and also to the circumstance that in the past *avocats* have traditionally come from higher-class families. [82] It is interesting to note that women are much attracted by the profession of *avocat*. More than one quarter of the Paris bar consists of women. [83]

**j. The changing *rôle* of the *avocat*.** Traditionally, the main activity of the French *avocat* was the presentation of oral argument in court. He had rather little to do with clients not already engaged in litigation. [84] However, the rôle of the *avocat* is slowly changing. Increasingly, the *avocat* is becoming the legal adviser of business firms, attempts to negotiate settlements before litigation is actually started, and engages in other similar activities. The permission to handle clients' funds recently granted to *avocats* recognizes this tendency. The regulations of some *ordres* have likewise been amended recently to facilitate the *avocat*'s rôle as a counselor. [85] However, the French *avocat* still does not seem to take a rôle in the purely business aspects of negotiations, nor does he deal with real property transfers, a matter traditionally handled by the *notaire*.

While these changes are considered as quite progressive by many of the older members of the bar, many younger members do not think they have gone far enough. They feel that the increasing complexity of the

[82] DAVID, *op. cit. supra* note 21, at 56. In evaluating the social position of the French *avocat*, differences in the social structure between France and the United States should be kept in mind; in France, a learned profession requiring extended academic preparation confers a certain prestige, even if the financial rewards realized are meager; a business, even if more lucrative, will not confer a similar prestige.

[83] There are about 2501 *avocats* in Paris and the former Seine *département*; 654 of these are women. The percentage of women is likely to increase in the future, since there are 104 woman among the 311 *avocats stagiaires* in the Seine *département*. These figures were taken from the lists of *avocats* and *avocats stagiaires* contained in ANNUAIRE OFFICIEL DU TRIBUNAL DE GRANDE INSTANCE DU DÉPARTEMENT DE LA SEINE (1961).

[84] LES BARREAUX DANS LE MONDE, *op. cit. supra* note 43, at 226.

[85] Choffel, *Les avocats veulent s'adapter à la vie des affaires*, LA VIE FRANÇAISE, May 24, 1957, p. 1. Mr. Choffel is one of the main protagonists of change in the traditional French conception of the role of the *avocat*. See also BARRAINE, PROCÉDURE CIVILE 96 (1959).

law makes it desirable that the *avocat* should become an effective legal counselor specializing in some particular field.

## 2.04. *Officiers Ministériels* in General

*Avoués, notaires, huissiers, greffiers,* and some other occupations are often given a common designation in France, that of *officiers publics et ministériels* or simply *officiers ministériels*. While these persons engage in widely different activities, certain common rules apply to all.

All *officiers ministériels*, whether they are officers of the courts (such as the *greffiers*, who are the court clerks) or the agents of private parties (such as the *avoués*), are appointed by the Minister of Justice. Candidates for appointment must fulfill educational requirements, which vary with each class of *officiers ministériels*. The number of *officiers ministériels* in each category is limited. Even qualified candidates are not appointed as *officiers ministériels* unless they have been "presented" to the Minister of Justice by another *officier ministériel* whose office (including its good will) they have purchased.[87] If an *officier ministériel* dies before having sold his office, his heirs can sell it and "present" the purchaser. However, the Ministry of Justice must be informed about the sale price, and controls its reasonableness. Ordinarily, the Ministry of Justice will not approve a sale unless the sale price is about 4–5.5 times the average annual income of the office sold. However, in the case of *greffiers* (court clerks) the price may be as high as eight times the average annual income.[88] Secret agreements to pay a higher price than that made public are void and subject the parties to penalties.[89] The rule that persons who want to become *officiers ministériels* must purchase the right to exercise their occupation goes back to pre-revolutionary France, when most public offices were subject to purchase and sale.

Even those *officiers ministériels* who exercise a profession, such as the *avoués* or *notaires*, are to some extent considered quasi-public officers. As a result, they may not refuse their services to a client unless they have a valid excuse,[90] and documents prepared in due form by *officiers*

[86] See Choffel, *supra* note 85.

[87] Law of April 28, 1816, 13 BULLETIN ANNOTÉ DES LOIS 482 (1837), art. 91; DÉCRET No. 53–1342 of Dec. 30, 1953, J.O. Jan. 5, 1954, p. 260, [1954] D.L. 62.

[88] GOYET, LE MINISTÈRE PUBLIC 72 (3d ed. 1953). Profit and loss statements covering the operations of the office during the last few years must be included in each application to the Ministry of Justice.

[89] CODE GÉNÉRAL DES IMPÔTS art. 1793. The penalties include loss of the right to practice and a fine equal to one-half the sum involved.

[90] DAVID & DE VRIES, *op. cit. supra* note 24, at 24; CUCHE & VINCENT 179.

*ministériels* ordinarily have a higher probative value than ordinary writings. [91] Each *officier ministériel* may act only within a specified territory. [92]

All *officiers ministériels* must be members of their respective professional organizations. These organizations have important duties in connection with the admission of new *officiers ministériels* and professional discipline. The local professional organizations of the *officiers ministériels* are not autonomous, such as the *ordres* of the *avocats*, but under the control of regional and national bodies. [93] In addition, the *ministère public* also supervises the *officiers ministériels.*

All *officiers ministériels* must have been French citizens for at least five years at the time of their appointment. [94] Women as well as men may be *officiers ministériels.* [95] Partnerships between *officiers ministériels* are not authorized. [96]

## 2.05. Representation of Parties Before the Highest French Courts: The *Avocat au Conseil d'Etat et à la Cour de Cassation*

Before the highest of the regular French courts, the *Cour de Cassation,* and before the highest of the administrative courts, the *Conseil d'Etat,* parties must be represented by a special group of lawyers called *avocats au Conseil d'Etat et à la Cour de Cassation,* sometimes abbreviated *avocats aux Conseils.* These lawyers attend not only to all procedural details and prepare all writtings, but also present oral argument.

There are only sixty *avocats aux Conseils* in France, [97] who are organized in an *ordre* of their own. To become an *avocat aux Conseils,* one must practice as a regular *avocat* for three years, pass an examination given by the *ordre* of the *avocats aux Conseils,* and receive the approval of the

[91] See 7.25 and 7.43 *infra.*

[92] Cuche & Vincent 179.

[93] Cuche & Vincent 180–82.

[94] Code of French Nationality, Law of Oct. 19, 1945, *supra* note 29, art. 81.

[95] Law of March 20, 1948, J.O. March 21, 1948, p. 2827, [1948] D.L. 129.

[96] Cuche & Vincent 178. There is an exception (unimportant for the purposes of this study) in the case of *agents de change* (brokers).

[97] This number was established by the Ordonnance of September 10, 1817, 14 Bulletin Annoté des Lois 254 (1837), art. 1, and has not varied since. The few *avocats aux Conseils* are apparently able to handle the very large amount of business before the *Conseil d'Etat* and the *Cour de Cassation,* because each one employs a number of assistants, usually young scholars preparing themselves for a career as law teachers, to help in the preparation of cases. In addition, the *avocats aux Conseils* usually have great experience in handling cases before the *Cour de Cassation* and *Conseil d'Etat* and thus can work rather fast. Besides, the *avocat* who has handled the case before the lower court always transmits his files to the *avocat aux Conseils,* which facilitates preparation of the case. In cases pending before the *Cour de cassation, mémoires ampliatifs* are prepared, which are very similar to an American brief in structure, but are very concise and rarely exceed 15 pages in length.

*Cour de Cassation*. If these requirements have been met, the *avocat* may be appointed an *avocat aux Conseils* by the French government. [98] Since the *avocats aux Conseils* are considered as *officiers ministériels*, the government appoints only persons who have purchased the office from a retiring *avocat aux Conseils*. [99] Thus, the number of *avocats aux Conseils* remains stationary, while there are no legal limitations upon the number of persons who may be admitted as ordinary *avocats*.

The traditions and rules of conduct of the *avocats aux Conseils* are quite similar to those of the regular *avocats*.[100] The *avocats aux Conseils* occupy a very prominent social position.

## 2.06. The *Avoués*

**a. Educational requirements.** To become an *avoué*, one must have at least the so-called *capacité* degree in law from a French university. The *baccalauréat* is not a prerequisite to registration for the *capacité* degree; the completion of three years of high school is sufficient. [101] The program leading to the *capacité* degree requires course work for two years, and the passing of two examinations, each covering work of one year. The candidate for the *capacité* takes courses in private law, civil procedure, public law, criminal law and procedure, administrative law, political economy, and some other subjects. The practical aspects of the law seem to be emphasized somewhat more than in the *licencié* program. [102] Of course, persons holding the degree of *licencié* or *docteur* in law are also qualified to become *avoués*. [103] While many women are *avocats*, there seem to be practically no women *avoués*.

**b. Other requirements.** To become an *avoué*, a person holding the *capacité* degree must work for at least five years as a clerk in the office of an *avoué*. For persons holding the *licencié* degree a clerkship of only three years is required. [104] In addition, all prospective *avoués* must pass

[98] Cuche & Vincent 190; Dalloz, *op. cit. supra* note 41, at No. 67.

[99] 2 Dalloz, Répertoire de Procédure Civile et Commerciale, *Office Public ou Ministériel* No. 29 (1956).

[100] 1 Dalloz, Répertoire de Procédure Civile et Commerciale, *Cassation* No. 66 (1955). The fees of the *avocats aux Conseils*, just as the fees of ordinary *avocats*, depend on the agreement between them and their clients; on the other hand, the *avoués* are governed by an official fee schedule.

[101] The so-called B.E.C.P. certificate is sufficient. See note 14 *infra*. Since French students begin high school at age 11 or 12, the B.E.C.P. can be obtained at about the age of 14 or 15.

[102] The curriculum leading to the *capacité* degree is described in Crémieu, Procédure Civile 303–06 (1956).

[103] Ordonnance of November 2, 1945, J.O. Nov. 3, 1945, p. 7367, [1945] D.L. 310, art. 2(5). In fact, most *avoués* seem to have the *licence*, and some even a doctoral, degree.

[104] Ordonnance of Nov. 2, 1945, *supra* note 103, art. 2(6). The law requires only a two-year clerkship for holders of the *docteur en droit* degree.

a qualifying examination given by a commission composed of four *avoués* and a judge, and receive the approval of the *tribunal de grande instance* or *cour d'appel* of the place where they want to practice. The examination involves the preparation of written pleadings (*conclusions*) and other legal documents and oral questions designed to test the candidates general legal knowledge. The *avoué* must also obtain a certificate of good conduct from the local organization of *avoués*. [105] Since *avoués* are *officiers ministériels*, candidates must purchase an existing office and be "presented" to the Minister of Justice by their predecessor in office. If they fulfill all these requirements, they receive their official nomination and may begin to practice.

c. **Functions, rights, and obligations.** The *avoué* is basically a specialist in civil procedure. He prepares the papers and takes all other steps that are required to set the French court machinery into motion and to bring the various phases of a French civil suit to a conclusion. He prepares the original process which is served on the other side to begin the suit and the various *conclusions* (pleadings) which contain the allegations and prayers for relief of the parties. [106] The *avoué* also sees to it that the case is placed on the calendar and takes necessary steps if the plaintiff must enforce his judgment by execution. In actual practice, however, it often happens that the *avocat* prepares draft *conclusions* which the *avoué* puts in final form and files. In such cases, the *avoué* concerns himself more with the procedural clauses of the document and the *avocat* with its substantive aspects. However the relationship between *avocat* and *avoué* is not subject to very definite rules. Sometimes, the *avoué* will do substantially all the drafting involved in the preparation of *conclusions*, and the *avocat* very little; sometimes, the opposite will be true. Local traditions, the respective familiarity of *avocat* and *avoué* with the points of law involved, and their work habits seem to be some of the determining factors. The *avoué* may engage in negotiations on behalf of his client, and perform related services, but in fact his main activity relates to litigation.

The parties must use an *avoué* when they are involved in litigation before a *tribunal de grande instance* or a *cour d'appel*. [107] Before the

[105] ORDONNANCE of Nov. 2, 1945, *supra* note 103, arts. 2(7), 2(8) 3; DÉCRET of Dec. 19, 1945, J.O. Dec. 22, 1945, p. 8482, [1946] D.L. 64, as modified by DÉCRET of Feb. 5, 1947, J.O. Feb. 8, 1947, p. 12015, [1947] D.L. 80, art. 5.

[106] The French state that the function of the *avoué* consists of *postuler* and *conclure*. *Postuler* means the taking of procedural steps; *conclure*, informing the court about the contentions of the parties. MOREL 163.

[107] Law of 27 ventôse year VIII, reprinted in CODE DE PROCÉDURE CIVILE 523 (58th ed. Dalloz 1962); 1 DALLOZ, RÉPERTOIRE DE PROCÉDURE CIVILE ET COMMERCIALE, *Avoués* No. 57 (1955).

other courts of first instance (*tribunaux d'instance*, commercial courts, labor courts), the parties may use the services of an *avoué* but are not obliged to do so. [108]

The *avoué* is considered the agent of his client and binds his client by his statements. [109] The *avoué* can impliedly ratify statements made by the *avocat*, if he is present in court during the *avocat*'s argument and remains silent. [110] A party wishing to contest the authority of his *avoué* must initiate a special proceeding called *action en désaveu.*

*Avoués* have no right to engage in oral argument, since oral argument is the prerogative of the *avocats*. By way of exception to this rule, *avoués* may present oral argument in connection with purely procedural matters not concerning the merits of the case. [111] In certain localities, where the number of *avocats* is insufficient, *avoués* have the right to argue and are then called *avoués plaidants*. [112] In 1958, many courts sitting in small towns with few *avocats* were abolished; this will eventually reduce the number of *avoués* with the right to engage in oral argument. [113]

Each *avoué* is attached to a particular *tribunal de grande instance* or *cour d'appel*. He must reside in the city in which that court is sitting. While *avocats* may argue before courts anywhere in France, an *avoué* may practice only before the *tribunal de grande instance* or *cour d'appel* to which he is attached and before inferior courts in his area. The division of labor between *avocats* and *avoués* creates a certain amount of latent friction between the two professions. *Avoués*, like all other *officiers ministériels*, may not form partnerships. However, they are usually assisted by clerks (*clercs*). These clerks are ordinarily law graduates who may eventually become *avoués*.

**d. Fees.** *Avoués* are compensated according to an official fee schedule. At present, an *avoué* practicing before a court of first instance is ordinarily entitled to a flat fee of F. 25.– (about $5) for each suit handled

108 Before these courts, the parties often use *avocats* to represent them and take necessary procedural steps. See notes 3 and 4 *supra*.

109 CUCHE & VINCENT 189. However, the binding effect of offers, settlements, and admissions may be contested in a special proceeding called the *action en désaveu*. CODE DE PROCÉDURE CIVILE arts. 352–362.

110 A party is not otherwise bound by statements made by his *avocat*. See 2.03.d *supra*.

111 *E.g.*, Proc. Gén. de la Martinique v. André et autres, Cass. Civ., Dec. 30, 1878, [1881] D.I. 57; CRÉMIEU, *op. cit. supra* note 41, at 204.

112 See Choffel, *supra* note 85, at 18. The list of courts where the *avoués* may argue is established each year by the *cours d'appel*.

113 For transitory provisions allowing present *avoués plaidants* to continue their activities, see DÉCRET No. 58–1281 of Dec. 22, 1958, J.O. Dec. 23, 1958, p. 11574, [1959] B.L.D. 44, art. 16.

by him [114] and to a proportional fee based on the amount in controversy. The proportional fee is 3% for amounts below F. 7,000; the percentage decreases as the amount in controversy increases. [115] Additional amounts (usually one-half flat fees) become payable, if the suit involves procedures leading to interlocutory orders or judgments, or certain other complications. [116] These may increase the total fees of the *avoué* considerably. The *avoué* is also entitled to receive reimbursement for his expenses and to an additional allowance designed to compensate him for the cost of paper and other similar outlays. [117] The fees of *avoués* practicing before the *cours d'appel* are about one-third higher than the fees of *avoués* before the courts of first instance.[118] If *avoués* perform services which are not listed in the official schedule, they may freely determine what charges they will make. [119] In the case of a dispute between the *avoué* and his client concerning fees or disbursements, they must be taxed by the president judge of the court in which the *avoué* has been acting and an *avoué* may sue his client only for fees or disbursements so taxed. However, the *avoué* has a kind of retaining lien on his clients' papers until he is paid. [120]

Although the fees of *avoués* seem small, it must be remembered that the *avoué* deals only with the procedural aspects of litigation and that the problems of substantive law are handled by the *avocat,* who must also be paid by his client. Since the number of *avoués* in any one area is limited (in Paris, for instance, with its enormous amount of litigation, there are about 150 *avoués* who practice before the *tribunal de grande instance,* and 51 who practice before the *cour d'appel*), an *avoué* can ordinarily be certain of a reasonable income, which often exceeds that of a young or little known *avocat.* But since his work is limited to procedural matters, he has little chance of increasing his income and prestige beyond a certain point. On the other hand, French *avocats* sometimes achieve considerable fame and a correspondingly large income.

[114] DÉCRET No. 60–323 of April 2, 1960, J.O. April 7, 1960, p. 3194, [1960] D.L. 133, art. 2.

[115] DÉCRET of April 2, 1960, *supra* note 114, art. 4. The fee is 3% of all amounts between F. 1 and F. 7.000 (20 cts.–$1400); 2% of amounts between F. 7001 and F. 14.000 ($1400–$2400); 1% of amounts between F. 14.001 and F. 26.000 ($2400–$5200); 0.5% of all amounts between F. 26.001 and F. 60.000 ($5200–$12000); 0.25% of all amounts above F. 60.000 ($12.000).

[116] DÉCRET of April 2, 1960, *supra* note 114, art. 20.

[117] DÉCRET of April 2, 1960, *supra* note 114, arts. 67–68, as amended by DÉCRET No. 63–959 of Sept. 17, 1963, J.O. Sept. 21, 1963, p. 8520, [1963] D.L. 294 and ARRÊTÉ of July 10, 1963, J.O. July 24, 1963, p. 6853, [1963] D.L. 235.

[118] DÉCRET of April 2, 1960, *supra* note 114, arts. 69–71.

[119] DÉCRET of April 2, 1960, *supra* note 114, art 82(d).

[120] DÉCRET of April 2, 1960, *supra* note 114, art. 84.

**e. Professional organizations.** All *avoués* of a *département* who practice before the *tribunaux de grande instance* of that area (usually there is one such court per *département*; there are more in some large *départements*) must belong to a professional organization called *chambre départementale des avoués.* [121] The *chambre départementale* represents the interests of the *avoués* of the *département*; it issues regulations concerning the conduct of *avoués*, hears grievances against them, decides disputes between *avoués* of the same *département*, and imposes disciplinary sanctions upon its members. The chamber also deals with the working conditions and the professional education of the clerks and employees of the *avoués.* [122] When acting upon matters concerning clerks or employees of *avoués*, delegates of the clerks and employees join the *chambre.* [123] Each year, an executive committee is elected by the whole membership of the organization. The committee which is also called *chambre* selects a president and the other officers. [124]

There is also a regional *chambre* of *avoués* at the seat of each *cour d'appel.* It represents the interests of *avoués* on a regional level and settles disputes between *avoués* from different *départements.* At the seat of each *cour d'appel*, there is also a *chambre* for the *avoués* practicing before that court. As to these *avoués*, it has the same functions as the *chambres départmentales* for the *avoués* practicing before the *tribunaux de grande instance.* A national *chambre* represents the interests of the *avoués* attached to the *tribunaux de grande instance* on a national level, manages their welfare funds, and performs similar functions. The *avoués* practicing before the *cour d'appel* also have a national organization. [125]

When dealing with disciplinary matters, the *chambres départmentales* are called *chambres de discipline.* [126] The penalties they can impose include a warning, simple censure, censure before the full *chambre*, and an injunction not to relapse. If the *chambre* finds more severe penalties to be appropriate, it requests the *procureur de la République* (public prosecutor) to cite the *avoué* before the *tribunal de grande instance*, which may suspend or disbar him. [127] *Avoués* failing to exercise due care

[121] ORDONNANCE of Nov. 2, 1945, *supra* note 105, art. 4.

[122] ORDONNANCE of Nov. 2, 1945, *supra* note 105, art. 6.

[123] ORDONNANCE of Nov. 2, 1945, *supra* note 105, art. 6; DÉCRET of Dec. 19, 1945, *supra* note 105, art. 21.

[124] The size of the committee (*chambre*) varies from four (for *départements* with twenty *avoués* or less) to eleven (for the Seine *département*). DÉCRET of Dec. 19, 1945, *supra* note 105, arts. 13, 14.

[125] ORDONNANCE of Nov. 2, 1945, *supra* note 105, arts. 4, 11.

[126] DÉCRET of Dec. 19, 1945, *supra* note 105, art. 13.

[127] ORDONNANCE of June 28, 1945, J.O. June 29, 1945, p. 3926, [1945] D.L. 134, arts. 3, 9–15. Thus, the *avoués* enjoy less self-government than the *avocats.*

are liable to their clients in damages, in addition to being subject to disciplinary penalties. [128]

**f. The relationship between *avocats* and *avoués*.** The required division of labor between two different types of legal counsel in French litigation has been criticized. [129] However, a speedy change in that situation seems unlikely. The division of labor between *avocats* and *avoués* enables the *avocat* to concern himself mainly with general principles of substantive law, which are his chosen field, without worrying about procedural details [130] on which the *avoué* is an expert. Since each *avoué* always practices before the same court, he is well informed about the special procedures and traditions of the court in which he practices and knows the judges and his fellow *avoués* well. [131] This helps to speed up litigation. The *avocats*, who may practice their profession throughout France and usually know more substantive law than the *avoués*, are not so well informed about local practices. Thus, it is not astonishing that the judges are among the most strenuous defenders of the *avoués*. [132] Some protagonists of a fusion between the professions of *avocats* and *avoués* have favored the creation of law firms, in which one or more members would be specialists in procedure. [133] However, since the *avoués* have been independent of the *avocats* for centuries, a change in their status is unlikely to occur soon. [134]

## 2.07. The *Agréés*

Before the commercial courts, the parties may be represented by any person they choose. [135] A number of persons have made it their occupation to represent clients before these courts. Some of these organized

[128] See DALLOZ, *op. cit. supra* note 107, at No. 142–194. However, the *avoué* is responsible only for acts falling within his official duties; he is not responsible for incorrect documents falling within the official duties of the *huissier*, even if they have actually been prepared by him. Consorts de Scoraille v. Lalisse, Cour Riom, July 21, 1910, [1911] D.II. 51.

[129] Choffel, *supra* note 85; L'AVOUÉ DANS LE MONDE MODERNE 28–29 (1957).

[130] DAVID, *op. cit. supra* note 21, art. 57. Professor David states that the institution of the *avocat* enables a French court to keep the lawsuit in the realm of principles, independently of procedural contingencies. The statement illustrates the French tendency to consider legal rights in the abstract without regard to the procedural means by which they may be enforced.

[131] L'AVOUÉ DANS LE MONDE MODERNE, *op. cit. supra* note 129, at 23–24.

[132] See the introduction of M. Rousselet, *Premier Président* (Presiding Judge) of the *Cour d'Appel* in Paris, to L'AVOUÉ DANS LA VIE MODERNE, *op. cit. supra* note 129.

[133] Choffel, *supra* note 81, art. 24.

[134] *Les Avoués à travers l'histoire nationale*, in L'AVOUÉ DANS LA VIE MODERNE, *op. cit. supra* note 129, at 10–14. It should be noted that the distinction between *avocats* and *avoués* does not exist in the *départements* Haut-Rhin, Bas-Rhin, and Moselle (Alsace-Lorraine) which have a procedure based largely on the German ZIVILPROZESSORDNUNG.

[135] Except *huissiers*. CODE DU COMMERCE art. 627.

groups sought to improve professional standards and to have their members placed on a list of persons approved (*agréés*) by the commercial court as representatives of parties. They were therefore called *agréés*. Originally, this arrangement was entirely voluntary in nature. Since 1941, the *agréés* have been subject to official regulation. [136]

**a. Qualifications.** Strictly speaking, the *agréés* are not *officiers ministériels*. They are not appointed by the Minister of Justice, but by the commercial court before which they intend to practice. [137] While the number of *agréés* before each court is not limited by law, only a person who has purchased the office of a deceased or retiring *agréé* will be appointed. The position of *agréés* and of *officiers ministériels* is thus fairly analogous. [138]

To become an *agréé* one must have at least a *capacité* degree of a French university. In a few places, the professional organizations of *agréés* require their members to be *licenciés en droit*. [139] The future *agréé* must work for at least five years in the office of an *agréé* and pass a qualifying examination. The examination involves the preparation of various written documents which may be used in actions or bankruptcy proceedings before the commercial courts and a series of oral questions relating mainly to civil and commercial law. He must also obtain a certificate of good conduct from the professional organization of *agréés* and the approval of the *procureur de la République*. [140] Having met these conditions and purchased the office of his predecessor, the candidate can request the commercial court to accept him officially as *agréé*.

**b. Functions, rights, and obligations.** The *agréé* represents his clients before the commercial court which has appointed him. He may perform the functions of an *avocat* as well as those of an *avoué*, but may not represent parties before any other court. [141] The *agréé* has no monopoly.

[136] RIPERT, DROIT COMMERCIAL 55–56 (3rd ed. 1954). The status of the *agréés* is regulated by an ORDONNANCE of November 2, 1945, J.O. Nov. 8, 1945, p. 7367, [1945] D.L. 312. Supplementary provisions are found in a DÉCRET of Dec. 19, 1945, J.O. Dec. 22, 1945, p. 8492, [1946] D.L. 75.

[137] ORDONNANCE of Nov. 2, 1945, *supra* note 136, art. 4.

[138] RIPERT, *op. cit. supra* note 136.

[139] ORDONNANCE of Nov. 2, 1945, *supra* note 136, art. 2; CUCHE & VINCENT 194, n. 2.

[140] *Ibid.*; DÉCRET of Dec. 19, 1945, *supra* note 136, art. 3.

[141] ORDONNANCE of Nov. 2, 1945, *supra* note 136, art. 1. The territorial limitation imposed upon their activity is a further point of analogy between the *agréés* and the regular *officiers ministériels*.

Parties involved in litigation before the commercial courts may use the services of *avocats, avoués,* or of any other person.

Legally, the *agréé* may freely contract with his client concerning his fees. However, many commercial courts have established semi-official fee schedules. [142] Practicing *agréés* may not engage in any other occupation. [143] They wear a traditional professional costume when arguing in court, but may not use the gown of the *avocats.* [144] Like the *avocats* and the *officiers ministériels,* they may not reveal confidential communications of their clients. [145]

**c. Professional organizations.** As in the case of the *avocats* and of all *officiers ministériels,* membership in their professional organization is compulsory for the *agréés.* Since the number of commercial courts is smaller than that of the regular courts of first instance and since only a few *agréés* practice before some commercial courts, the *agréés* have been organized on a regional, rather than on a local or *département,* basis: There is an organization of *agréés* at the seat of each *cour d'appel,* unless fewer than five *agréé*s practice in that region. Collectively, the *agréés* of one region are referred to as a *compagnie.* [146] The members of each *compagnie* elect a *chambre.* The duties and functions of the *chambre* are substantially the same as those of the *chambres* of the *avoués.* [147] *Agréés* are subject to the same disciplinary penalties as *avoués.* Temporary suspension and permanent disbarment may be imposed only by the commercial court. [148] There is also a national *chambre* of *agréés* which represents the interests of the *agréés* on a national level. [149]

## 2.08. *Huissiers*

**a. Qualifications for appointment.** The French term *huissier* has no precise common law equivalent. Although the *huissier* performs functions that are performed in the United States by process servers and

[142] 1 DALLOZ, RÉPERTOIRE DE PROCÉDURE CIVILE ET COMMERCIALE, *Agréé,* Nos. 25–28 (1955).

[143] ORDONNANCE of Nov. 2, 1945, *supra* note 136, art. 1.

[144] Ordre des avocats de Lille v. Agréés de Roubaix et de Tourcoing, Cass. Civ., July 29, 1936, [1936] D.I. 86; Barreau de Lille v. Cie des agréés de Roubaix-Tourcoing, Cour Amiens, Feb. 16, 1938, [1938] D.H. 168; 1 DALLOZ, *op. cit. supra* note 141, No. 21.

[145] CODE PÉNAL art. 378.

[146] ORDONNANCE of Nov. 2, 1945, *supra* note 136, art. 7. However, there is a special organization for the *agréés* practicing before the commercial court in Paris. In regions with fewer than five *agréés,* they join the organization of a neighboring region.

[147] ORDONNANCE of Nov. 2, 1945, *supra* note 136, art. 11.

[148] ORDONNANCE of Nov. 2, 1945, *supra* note 136, arts. 5, 6; *cf.* X., Conseil d'Etat, May 31, 1925, [1925] D.III. 80.

[149] ORDONNANCE of Nov. 2, 1945, *supra* note 136, art. 8.

marshals, these terms are not adequate translations of the French word *huissier*. [150] *Huissiers* may serve as official court attendants, serve legal papers, levy execution, and perform various other related functions. In matters of relatively minor importance, *huissiers* frequently also serve as collection agents.

Considered an *officier ministériel*, an *huissier* must purchase his office from another *huissier* before he qualifies for official appointment by the Minister of Justice. [151] Other legal prerequisites for appointment are: French nationality, good character, a three years' clerkship in a *huissier*'s office, the passing of an examination, and approval of the court in the district in which he resides. The period of clerkship is reduced for holders of law degrees. [152]

**b. Functions and duties.** The main function of the *huissier* is the service of legal papers. Except when the law expressly provides for service by mail, [153] only *huissiers* may make service; service by others is void. The *huissiers* are also exclusively authorized to levy attachments and executions [154] and may draw the legal documents necessary for their activities. However, since *avocats* and *avoués* usually prefer to draft *ajournements* (summonses) and similar papers themselves, *huissiers* merely serve these documents if the parties are represented by *avocats* and *avoués*. When they levy execution on the basis of certain notarial contracts in the nature of cognovit notes, *huissiers* ordinarily draw their own papers.

*Huissiers* are also used for the service of formal notifications, such as

[150] Although since 1955 their full legal title has been *huissiers de justice*, they are generally called *huissiers*. The basic law governing the *huissiers* is the ORDONNANCE of Nov. 2, 1945, J.O. Nov. 3, 1945, p. 7163, [1945] D.L. 311, amended by a DÉCRET (actually DÉCRET-LOI) of May 20, 1955, J.O. May 22, 1955, p. 5136, [1955] D.L. 260 and a Law of Feb. 11, 1958, J.O. Feb. 12, 1958, p. 1571, [1958] D.L. 99. The ORDONNANCE of 1945 was implemented by a regulation enacted by DÉCRET of Feb. 29, 1956, J.O. March 3, 1956, p. 2214, [1956] D.L. 110, amended by DÉCRET of Nov. 9, 1956, J.O. Nov. 14, 1956, p. 10880, [1956] D.L. 476, DÉCRET No. 58–1282 of Dec. 22, 1958, J.O. Dec. 23, 1958, p. 11574, [1959] D.L. 37, by DÉCRET No. 59–1217 of Oct. 23, 1959, J. O. Oct. 28, 1959, p. 10266, [1959] D.L. 629, and by DÉCRET No. 64–640 of June 29, 1964, J.O. July 1, 1964, p. 5715, [1964] D.L. 219.

[151] See generally ARGENSON & CHODKIEWIEZ, GUIDE DES HUISSIERS 1 (1954); 2 DALLOZ, RÉPERTOIRE DE PROCÉDURE CIVILE, *Huissier de Justice* (1956). The government may increase the number of *huissiers* in a particular area; the newly appointed *huissiers* must then pay an indemnity to their established colleagues.

[152] DÉCRET of Feb. 29, 1956, *supra* note 150, arts. 30–30K. Women, as well as men, may become *huissiers*.

[153] The trend of modern legislation is to increase the situations in which service by mail is allowed, but attempts to replace service by *huissier* generally by service by mail have never been successful. French authors feel that service by a responsible, closely regulated, professional, such as the *huissier*, affords guarantees not available in the case of service by mail. See 1 SOLUS & PERROT 321–25.

[154] ORDONNANCE of November 2, 1945, as amended, *supra* note 150, art. 1.

notices of protest of negotiable instruments and notices to vacate leased premises. [155]

In places in which there are no official *commissaires priseurs*, auction sales of personal property may be conducted by *huissiers*. They may also be appointed to make certain factual inverstigations for the parties or for the court. [156]

An *huissier* may act validly only within the district of the *tribunal d'instance* in which he resides. Usually, a number of *huissiers* practice within a particular district, and the parties may use the services of any one of these. [157] However, in some instances in which receipt of actual notice is particularly important, papers may be served only by an *huissier* specially designated for that purpose by the court, who is then called *huissier commis*. His services must be used to serve default judgments [158] and summonses in proceedings in which the time to appear is particularly short. [159]

In addition to serving as agents of private parties, some *huissiers* act as official court attendants. The *huissiers* acting in that capacity are called *huissiers audienciers*. Their main duty is to preserve order in the court and to call the calendar. They are selected each year by the court from among all the *huissiers* practicing in the area. [160] The *huissiers audienciers* receive no salary from the government, [161] but they are entitled to a fee payable by the parties. They also have a monopoly for the service of papers in situations in which service may be made upon an *avoué* in the court house. [162] In addition, the judges usually select a

[155] 1 SOLUS & PERROT 891.

[156] ORDONNANCE of Nov. 2, 1945, as amended, *supra* note 150, art. 1. On the rôle of *huissiers* in making investigations and preparing reports, see 5.02 *infra*. On the rôle of the official *commissaires prisures*, see 2.11.a *infra*; *cf.* ARGENSON & CHODKIEWIEZ, *op. cit. supra* note 151, at 13.

[157] DÉCRET of Feb. 29, 1956, as amended, *supra* note 150, art. 5. Under some special circumstances, the Minister of Justice may expand the areas in which *huissiers* may act. DÉCRET of February 29, 1956, as amended, *supra* note 150, art. 6; *cf.* also arts. 7–8. An act performed by an *huissier* outside the district (usually the *arrondissement*) in which he may perform his functions is void. 1 SOLUS & PERROT 895.

[158] CODE DE PROCÉDURE CIVILE arts. 20, 150, 156, 435.

[159] CODE DE PROCÉDURE CIVILE art. 808; Veuve Vellé v. Versé, Cour Grenoble, May 10, 1905, [1905] D. II. 180 (When the use of a *huissier* specially designated by the court is required, service by any other *huissier* is void). For another situation in which notice by a specially designated *huissier* is required, see CODE DE PROCÉDURE CIVILE art. 832 (certain proceedings to remove mortgages and other liens from real property); *cf.* also CODE CIVIL arts. 2183, 2185.

[160] DÉCRET of Feb. 29, 1956, as amended, *supra* note 150, arts. 11–14.

[161] ORDONNANCE of Nov. 2, 1945, as amended, *supra* note 150, art. 10.

[162] DÉCRET of Feb. 29, 1956, as amended, *supra* note 150, art. 11. The fees payable in these two cases are not paid to individual *huissiers*, but are pooled and eventually distributed in equal shares to all the *huissiers audienciers* of the court.

*huissier audiencier* when they must designate an *huissier* (*huissier commis*) for the service of documents. [163]

Although he receives no salary from the government, the *huissier*, like the other *officiers ministériels*, has rights and obligations as a public officer. The *huissier* may wear an official badge. [164] An attack upon his person or an interference with his official functions is a crime more serious than an assault upon a private individual. [165] Like the official assertions of other public officers, statements made by a *huissier* in a document prepared by him are deemed true unless attacked by the complicated proceeding known as *inscription de faux*. [166]

Unless prohibited by law from acting, [167] the *huissier*, as a quasi-public officer, must lend his services to any person who requests them .[168] He must keep duplicate originals of all papers served by him and prepare appropriate indexes. [169] There are only a limited number of outside activities in which *huissiers* may engage, and the approval of the Ministry of Justice is needed even for these. [170] Each *huissier* may have one or more clerks (*clercs assermentés*). They may perform most of the functions of regular *huissiers*, but their employers remain responsible for the faithful performance of their duties. [171] *Huissiers* may participate in an office sharing arrangement or combine in a regular partnership. [172]

[163] However, there is no legal requirement that this be done.

[164] DÉCRET of Feb. 29, 1956, as amended, *supra* note 150, art. 17.

[165] 1 SOLUS & PERROT 898; CODE PÉNAL arts. 209, 224, 258, 259.

[166] *Cf.* CODE CIVIL arts. 1317, 1319. Statements made by the *huissier* are conclusive only to the extent they relate to actions by the *huissier* himself and not insofar as they relate to conclusions drawn by the *huissier* from the facts. Thus, a statement in a return that the *huissier* has served the summons (*ajournement*) personally on a particular date is conclusive, absent *inscription de faux*. But an added statement that the defendant seemed to the *huissier* to be mentally competent is not conclusive. Reports made by *huissiers* when they act as a kind of special investigator are merely evidence of the facts reported. ORDONNANCE of Nov. 2,1945, as amended, *supra* note 150, art. 1. See also note 220 *infra*.

[167] An *huissier* may not act on behalf of his relatives in direct line, nor for his brothers, sisters, in-laws, and some others. CODE DE PROCÉDURE CIVILE arts. 4, 66; 1 SOLUS & PERROT 904–05.

[168] DÉCRET of Feb. 29, 1956, as amended, *supra* note 150, art. 15.

[169] ORDONNANCE of Nov. 2, 1945, as amended, *supra* note 150, art. 2; DÉCRET of February 29, 1956, as amended, *supra* note 150, arts. 24-29.

[170] ORDONNANCE of Nov. 2, 1945, as amended, *supra* note 150, art. 1; DÉCRET of Feb. 29, 1956, as amended, *supra* note 150, arts. 18–21. Art. 20 of the DÉCRET authorizes an *huissier* to act as an insurance agent, secretary of an agricultural cooperative, manager of buildings, and in a few other similar capacities.

[171] Law of Dec. 27, 1923, J.O. Dec. 29, 1923, p. 12132, [1924] D.IV. 207, arts. 6–11. Returns of service and other papers are always signed by the *huissier*, not by his clerk.

[172] DÉCRET of Feb. 29, 1956, as amended, *supra* note 150, arts. 31–39. A peculiar form of cooperation between *huissiers* is the "common bureau" they have in some large cities such as Paris or Lyon. Papers to be served are forwarded daily from the offices of the *huissiers* to the "common bureau" which sorts them geographically; the clerks of the *huissiers* then go to

**c. Professional organization and discipline.** All *huissiers* must be members of their official professional organization. Its structure is similar to that of the organization of the *avoués.* [173] There is a basic association, *Chambre départementale,* in each *département.* Regional associations, *Chambres régionales,* composed of the departmental organizations located within the region, exist at the seat of each *cour d'appel.* The national organization, *Chambre nationale,* encompasses all departmental and regional groups in France.

These organizations represent the interests of the *huissiers* in all matters of professional interest; they administer a loan fund and see to it that proper standards of professional conduct are observed. [174] The *Chambre départmentale* may inspect the books of all member *huissiers,* [175] and the disciplinary committee, *Chambre de discipline,* of the departmental organization may impose the lighter disciplinary penalties such as censure. Penalties for more serious violations of professional ethics are imposed by the *tribunal de grande instance* at the request of the *Chambre de discipline.* [176] The treasury of the departmental organization serves as an indemnity fund for clients who have suffered damages as a result of the misconduct of an *huissier.* [177] In addition, *huissiers* are personally liable for misconduct, such as negligence in the observance of the numerous formal rules governing the service of legal papers.

The supervision exercised by the professional organizations of the *huissiers* seems to be quite effective. There are very few complaints about the manner in which *huissiers* perform their duties. The official organizations of the *huissiers* are not the only organizations of which

the bureau and each one picks up the papers to be served in one particular area, whether they orginated in the office of his employer or not. This procedure seems of somewhat doubtful legality. 1 SOLUS & PERROT 327.

[173] See 2.06.e *supra.*

[174] ORDONNANCE of Nov. 2, 1945, as amended, *supra* note 150, arts. 4–9; DÉCRET of Feb. 29, 1956, as amended, *supra* note 150, arts. 41–54; *cf.* DALLOZ, *op. cit. supra* note 150, at No. 145.

[175] ORDONNANCE of Nov. 2, 1945, as amended, *supra* note 150, arts. 6(5); DÉCRET of Feb. 29, 1956, as amended, *supra* note 150, art. 56.

[176] Disciplinary proceedings concerning *officiers ministériels* in general, including *huissiers,* are governed by an ORDONNANCE of June 28, 1945, J.O. June 29, 1945, p. 3926, [1945] D.L. 134. This ORDONNANCE is discussed in more detail in connection with *avoués.* See 2.06.e *supra. Huissiers* may be disciplined not only for misconduct directly relating to their official functions, but for any kind of conduct that shows a lack of honesty or probity. Disciplinary penalties may include revocation of their right to practice. X., Cour Colmar, June 12, 1951, GAZ. PAL. 2.55; S. v. Proc. Gén. Colmar, Cass. Civ. March 10, 1954, [1954] D. J. 348 (*huissier* may be disbarred for conduct preceding his appointment if it resulted in criminal conviction after his appointment).

[177] DÉCRET of Feb. 29, 1956, as amended, *supra* note 150, art. 55.

*huissiers* are members. They may form unofficial associations for any purpose not conflicting with that of the official organizations. [178]

**d. Fees.** The fees of the *huissiers* are specified in an official and quite complex fee schedule established by *décret.* [179] Since the fees specified in the schedule are considered full compensation for the performance of the various functions listed, [180] an *huissier* may charge neither more nor less. [181] The charging of smaller fees is considered unfair competition and may be ground for disciplinary proceedings and even an action for damages by his professional brethren. [182]

For services not specified in the official schedule, the *huissier* may receive compensation in any amount agreed upon by him and his client. If they cannot agree, the fee is taxed by the court. [183] A *huissier* performing services unconnected with litigation, for instance in attempting to collect debts, is usually paid a percentage of the sum to be collected. [184] The *huissiers audienciers* (*huissiers* acting as court attendants) are also paid on a fee basis. [185] Although the income of a *huissier* depends on the amount of litigation going on in the area in which he works, most *huissiers* make a fairly comfortable living. [186]

[178] ORDONNANCE of Nov. 2, 1945, as amended, *supra* note 150, art. 10.

[179] The latest fee schedule is contained in a DÉCRET of Oct. 30, 1958, J.O. Nov. 5, 1958, p. 10020, [1958] D.L. 374, since amended in minor respects. The total fee of an *huissier* is usually composed of the fee proper, an additional fee as compensation for the cost of paper and supplies, and mileage. However, the mileage fee is always the same and is paid into a central pool that reimburses the *huissiers* on the basis of actual mileage travelled. The purpose of this system is to reduce the cost of litigation in the rural areas, where parties might be living at a greater distance from the residence of the *huissier*. The fee payable to a *huissier* for the preparation and service of a summons (*ajournement*) is about F. 16.80 or about $3.40. When a stamp tax and an *enregistrement* tax are payable, the total cost of a summons is about twice the amount mentioned. See 1 SOLUS & PERROT 320 n. 1.

[180] DÉCRET of Oct. 30, 1958, *supra* note 179, art. 13.

[181] DÉCRET of Oct. 30, 1958, *supra* note 179, art. 23.

[182] 2 DALLOZ, *op. cit. supra* note 151, at No. 124; X. v. Z., Cour Toulouse, June 22, 1911, [1913] D. 2. 186.

[183] DÉCRET of October 30, 1958, *supra* note 179, art. 14.

[184] See 2 DALLOZ, RÉPERTOIRE DE PROCÉDURE CIVILE ET COMMERCIALE, *Frais et Dépens* No. 70 (1956).

[185] See notes 160–163 *supra*. The fees payable to the *huissiers audienciers* are regulated in art. 7 of the DÉCRET of Oct. 30, 1958, *supra* note 179. They receive F. 1.85 (about $0.35) for each new case called before the *tribunal de grande instance*, F. 2.65 for each case before the *cour d'appel* and F. 3.60 for each case before the *Cour de Cassation* and F. 0.95 – F. 1.85 for each paper served in the courthouse. In actual practice, the service of papers in the courthouse can be handled very expeditiously, because the number of *avoués* attached to any one court is limited and they all have mail boxes at the courthouse.

[186] It should be remembered that while the fees payable to *huissiers* are not large, the number of *huissiers* in any one area is limited and cannot increase.

## 2.09. The *Greffiers*

**a. Prerequisites to appointment.** The *greffiers* are the clerks of the courts. The chief clerks of the courts, called officially *greffiers titulaires de charge* and frequently simply *greffiers*, are *officiers ministériels*. Although they are appointed by the Minister of Justice and receive a small salary, they derive their main income from fees payable by litigants and may sell their office. [187]

To qualify for official appointment to the office he has purchased, the candidate *greffier* must be a French national, [188] over 25 years old, of good moral character, and have the approval of the court in which he is to act. Candidates for appointment as head clerk of a *cour d'appel* or the *Cour de Cassation* must also possess the *licencié* degree in law. Although clerks to all other courts need not possess a law degree, all candidates for appointment must have three years of practical experience as clerks in a court clerk's office, or in the office of a notary, an *avoué*, or a person similarly situated, and pass an examination. [189]

**b. Functions.** The duties of the *greffier* are fairly similar to those of his American counterpart. [190] He must be present at all court sessions: [191] A court sitting without its *greffier* cannot act legally. [192] In

[187] On *officiers ministériels* in general, see 2.04 *supra*. Law No. 65–1002 of Nov. 30, 1965, J.O. Dec. 2, 1965, p. 10660, [1965] B.L.D. 671, enacted after the manuscript of this book had been completed, substantially modifies the position of the *greffiers* in the *Cour de Cassation, cours d'appel, tribunaux de grande instance, tribunaux d'instance* and the State Security Court. The new law will go into effect on a date to be fixed by decree, but no later than January 1, 1967. After its effective date, the work of the *greffiers* is to be transferred to salaried government employees, though *greffiers* now in office may retain their position for up to ten more years. However, they no longer have the right to "present" their successor, in other words to sell their office. They are to be indemnified by the government for this loss. If they fulfill the necessary requirements, they will be able to receive positions as *magistrats* or employees of the Ministry of Justice. The *greffiers* of the *Cour de Cassation* and State Security Court have no ten-year grace period, however.

[188] ORDONNANCE of October 19, 1945, J.O. Oct. 20, 1945,p. 6700, art. 81 (code of French nationality). Women may now become *greffiers*. Law of March 20, 1948, J.O. March 21, 1948, p. 2827, [1948] D.L. 129.

[189] Previous legal experience or education may justify reduction of the three year clerkship period. See generally DÉCRET No. 57–43 of Jan. 14, 1957, J.O. Jan. 16, 1957, p. 740, modified by DÉCRET No. 58–534 of June 14, 1958, J.O. June 19, 1958, p. 5711, [1958] D.L. 224, and DÉCRET of July 18, 1959, J.O. July 24, 1959, p. 7349, [1959] D.L. 545.

[190] On the functions of the *greffiers* generally, see 2 DALLOZ, RÉPERTOIRE DE PROCÉDURE CIVILE ET COMMERCIALE, *Greffiers* (1956) and, on the changes introduced by the 1958 reforms, the 1963 supplement.

[191] In the language of the 1808 DÉCRET which provided for the internal organization of the French courts, "The *greffier* shall hold the pen at the hearings from the beginning until they are terminated." DÉCRET of March 30, 1808, art. 91, reprinted in CODE DE PROCÉDURE CIVILE 541 (58th ed. Dalloz 1962). The minutes are signed by the presiding judge and the *greffier*.

[192] CODE DE PROCÉDURE CIVILE art. 1040. The *greffier* must also be present when the court transacts business outside the courthouse, *e.g.*, when viewing the premises in litigation or hearing a witness too ill to be heard in court. Since the *greffier* must always be present when the court is in session, he is in a sense a member of the court.

addition, he keeps the official copies (*minutes*) of the judgments which he must countersign and file [193] and prepares summaries of the court's proceedings. An official stenographic transcript of the proceedings is never made, though occasionally some *avocats* use the services of a private stenographer to obtain the verbatim text of their own or their opponent's argument.

The *greffier*, who must keep his office open for eight hours on week-days, [194] preserves the records of the court [195] and prepares and issues certified copies upon proper request. [196] On the first certified copy of every judgment the *greffier* apposits the so-called *formule exécutoire* (executory formula). The *formule exécutoire* is a direction to any *huissier* shown the judgment to levy execution according to its tenor. [197] The *greffier* must also prepare the various required reports and statistics concerning the work of the court and transmit them to the appropriate authorities. [198] In some special proceedings, especially those relating to decedent's estates, certain declarations concerning the parties' intentions, such as whether they accept or reject an inheritance, must be made to the *greffier*. [199] The *greffier* also keeps duplicate copies of all vital statistics records. [200]

The *greffiers* of the commercial courts have, in addition, the duty to keep the *régistre du commerce* (commercial register) in which all business firms of the area are listed, to file copies of the articles of incorporation of all new companies created within their district, and to file certain instruments establishing security interests in the property of business enterprises. They also perform important functions in bankruptcy proceedings. [201]

[193] The judgment must also be signed by the presiding judge. CODE DE PROCÉDURE CIVILE art. 138.

[194] DÉCRET of March 30, 1808, *supra* note 191, art. 90.

[195] DÉCRET of March 30, 1808, *supra* note 191, art. 93.

[196] Certified copies must be delivered to all persons requesting them and willing to pay the fee. CODE DE PROCÉDURE CIVILE art. 853.

[197] The text of the *formule exécutoire* has been prescribed by DÉCRET of June 12, 1947, J.O. June 13, 1947, p. 5487, [1947] D.L. 225, as modified by DÉCRET No. 58–1289, J.O. Dec. 23, 1958, p. 11608, [1959] D.L. 95.

[198] As to these reports, see 3.20 *infra*; *cf.* the Circular of the Ministry of Justice of Oct. 12, 1950; GOYET, LE MINISTÈRE PUBLIC 69 (1953).

[199] *Ibid.*; *cf.*, *e.g.*, CODE CIVIL arts. 784, 793.

[200] CODE CIVIL art. 43. The *greffiers* of the *tribunaux d'instance* also keep certain public records regarding security interests in crops. *Cf.* 1 SOLUS & PERROT 911.

[201] Only firms and individuals who are *commerçants* are subject to bankruptcy proceedings in France. As to who is a *commerçant* (businessman) in French law, see 4.39.b *infra*. Concerning the filing of instruments creating liens, see mainly Law of March 17, 1909, J.O. March 19, 1909, [1909] D.4. 41, art. 1.

**c. Assistants and office organization.** Since in most courts, especially those having many divisions, the head *greffier* cannot be present at all court sessions and perform all clerical duties of his office, he usually has a number of assistants. Some of these assistants are state employees appointed by the Minister of Justice whose status is somewhat different from that of regular civil servants. Their main function is to participate in court proceedings and to keep the minutes.[202] In addition, the *greffier* usually hires a number of assistants at his own expense. They perform mostly clerical work, such as the filing of papers and the preparation of certified copies of judgments, for which the *greffier* collects a fee from the parties. The employees of the *greffier* are governed by the laws regulating private employment relationships in France.[203] The *greffier* is responsible for all actions of his own employees on a *respondeat superior* basis. Whether he is also responsible for the negligence or other misfeasance of the government employees working in his office is disputed.[204]

Some of the larger courts have a very substantial clerical staff. Thus, the head *greffier* of the *tribunal de grande instance* of the Seine *département* has 131 government employees as assistants, in addition to those he hires himself; the *greffier* of the *Cour d'appel* in Paris has about 53 assistants paid by the government and 30 office employees paid by himself. At the *Cour de Cassation*, in addition to a head *greffier* for the entire court, there are eight so-called *greffiers de chambre* and numerous *greffiers*.[205]

The head *greffiers* also own the office equipment used in their offices. As a result, there are variations in the efficiency with which the various *greffes* operate. The office machines and filing equipment of the *greffe* of the *Cour d'appel* in Paris would be the envy of any court clerk in the United States and papers are processed with extraordinary speed. In some courts in France, on the other hand, it is still usual to prepare copies of judgments in longhand.

[202] 1 Solus & Perrot 919-24. The status, conditions of appointment, and promotion of these assistants to the *greffier* are governed by a Décret of Nov. 26, 1962, J.O. Dec. 1, 1962, p. 11708, [1962] D.L. 395.

[203] 1 Solus & Perrot 924.

[204] 1 Solus & Perrot 916, 917.

[205] The *greffiers de chambre* are government employees, not *officiers ministériels*; they are appointed by the Minister of Justice. Law of Sept. 26, 1952, J.O. Sept. 30, 1952, p. 9391, [1952] D.L. 349. The number of the *greffiers de chambre*, whose titles imply that they are the head clerks for the five divisions – *chambres* – of the court, has, somewhat illogically, been raised to eight in 1956. Law of Aug. 4, 1956, J.O. Aug. 14, 1956, p. 7791, [1956] D.L. 289, art. 51. The *greffiers de chambre* who are not head clerks for the five divisions of the court perform supervisory functions in the civil, criminal, and "social" branch of the clerk's office.

**d. Supervision and discipline.** The *greffiers* have no self-policing organization, such as the *huissiers* or *avoués*. [206] The presiding judges of each court and the *procureurs de la République* supervise the *greffiers*, [207] and the presiding judges of the *cours d'appel* also exercise a certain amount of control over the *greffiers* in their region.

In the case of misconduct of a *greffier*, the presiding judge of his court may give him a warning. In more serious cases, the *greffier* may be censured by the presiding judge of the appropriate *cour d'appel*. The Minister of Justice, acting on the advice of a special disciplinary council, may remove *greffiers* from office. [208] The professional obligations of the *greffier* include the duty to reside in the city in which the court he serves is located. [209] A *greffier* may engage only in a very limited number of outside occupations. [210]

**e. Salary and fees.** The head *greffier* of each court receives a comparatively small salary from the government. In addition, he collects fees from the parties for the various activities he performs in the course of a lawsuit, such as putting the case on the calendar, preparing and filing the judgment, and delivering certified copies of the judgment. The fees payable to the *greffiers* are specified in an official fee schedule. [211] These fees are comparatively modest, but can amount to a considerable total in a busy court. [212] As a result, the income of *greffiers* varies greatly.

In addition to their regular fees, *greffiers* are entitled to mileage fees whenever they accompany judges on a view of the premises. [213] The

[206] However, there are some unofficial associations of *greffiers* in the nature of clubs.

[207] ORDONNANCE of Nov. 5, 1823, 16 BULLETIN ANNOTÉ DES LOIS 143 (1837), art. 2. A power of supervision is also vested in the *procureur général* of each *cour d'appel*. Law of April 20, 1810, 12 BULLETIN ANNOTÉ DES LOIS 3, 19, art. 45 (1836).

[208] DÉCRET of April 26, 1954, J.O. April 27, 1954, p. 4034, [1954] D.L. 181, arts. 1–22; 1 SOLUS & PERROT 918–19. As part of the penalty of removal from office, the *greffier* may be deprived of his right to sell his office. This amounts in effect to a confiscation of the sum he has invested in his office.

[209] DÉCRET of March 30, 1808, *supra* note 191, art. 100.

[210] *Cf.* 1 SOLUS & PERROT 915–16.

[211] DÉCRET of May 3, 1958, J.O. May 6, 1958, p. 4431, [1958] D.L. 205, amended by DÉCRET No. 59–1959 of May 5, 1959, J.O. May 6, 1959, p. 4825, [1959] B.L.D. 876.

[212] The *greffier* of the *tribunal de grande instance* is entitled to a fee of F. 7.20 (about $1.80) for putting a case on the calendar and to a fee of F. 2 (about $0.50) for each typewritten page of the orginal copy of the judgment. The *tribunal de grande instance* for the Seine *département* (Paris) decided 25.837 cases during the 1958–1959 judicial year. 1 SOLUS & PERROT 541 n.l. Thus, the fees payable to the head *greffier* must have supplied him with a comfortable income, even though he had to pay the salaries of a considerable number of assistants. *Greffiers* in rural areas are obviously less well off.

[213] DÉCRET of May 3, 1958, as amended, *supra* note 211, art. 24. It will be recalled that a *greffier* must always accompany the court.

*greffiers* may not charge fees in excess of those listed in the official schedule. [214]

## 2.10. *Notaires*

**a. Qualifications.** The duties of a *notaire* are far more extensive than those of an American notary, who generally does no more than take acknowledgements. [215] The main function of the *notaire* is the drawing of legal instruments, especially in the field of property, family, and corporate law. In many cases, transactions, in order to be valid, must be incorporated in notarial deeds. The *notaire* is the principal legal adviser of French families, especially in rural areas. As an *officier ministériel,* he must buy another *notaire*'s office before he qualifies for official appointment. However, the government, under complex rules, may increase the number of *notaires* in a district. [216]

To qualify for appointment, a person who aspires to be a *notaire* must pass a professional examination that is reputed to be quite difficult. It involves the preparation of at least two notarial acts and an oral examination concerning fields of law in which the *notaires* are mainly active. In practice, although a law degree is not required, most notaries have a law degree which facilitates their passing the professional examination. The aspiring *notaire* must also meet the qualifications generally required for the appointment of *officiers ministériels* (French nationality, good character, fulfillment of military service

[214] DÉCRET of May 3, 1958, as amended, *supra* note 211, art. 23. It should be added that by DÉCRET No. 58–1282 of December 22, 1958, J.O. Dec. 23, 1958, p. 11574, [1959] B.L.D. 44, arts. 1–12, a number of measures were taken to assist *greffiers* whose courts were abolished; otherwise they would have lost not only their livelihood, but also the capital invested in their offices.

[215] On the differences between an American notary public and a French *notaire,* see SCHLESINGER, COMPARATIVE LAW 11–13 (2d ed. 1959); Schlesinger, *The Notary and the Formal Contract in Civil Law,* [1942] REP. N.Y.L. REV. COM. 403; Brown, *The Office of the Notary in France,* 2 INT'L & COMP. L. Q. 60–71 (1953).

[216] On *officier ministériels* in general, see 2.04 *supra.* Many of the rules governing the *notaires* go back to the time of the revolution. The principal statutes are a Law of the 25 *ventôse,* Year XI (1803), reprinted in CODE CIVIL 497 (61st ed. Dalloz 1962), amended by a Law of Aug. 12, 1902, J.O Aug. 14, 1902, [1902] D. 4.73; a Law of August 21, 1936, J.O. Aug. 23, 1936, p. 9090, [1936] B.L.D. 619; an ORDONNANCE of Nov. 2, 1945, J.O. Nov. 3, 1945, p. 7160, [1945] D.L. 309; a DÉCRET No. 58–1282 of December 22, 1958, J.O. Dec. 23, 1958 p. 11574, [1959] D.L. 37. The ORDONNANCE of Nov. 2, 1945, has been implemented in several particulars by DÉCRET of Dec. 19, 1945, J.O. Dec. 22, 1945, p. 8478, [1946] D.L. 60, since amended repeatedly. DÉCRETS of Feb. 5, 1947, J.O. Feb. 8, 1947 p. 1301, [1947] D.L. 85; July 19, 1948, J.O. July 21, 1948, p. 7125, [1948] D.L. 258; March 29, 1949, J.O. March 30, 1949, p. 3299, [1949] D.L. 213; Nov. 29, 1951, J.O. Dec. 2, 1951, p. 11892, [1951] D.L. 405; April 2, 1955, J.O. April 9, 1955, [1955] D.L. 152; DÉCRET No. 59–50 of Jan. 3, 1959, J.O. Jan. 7, 1959, p. 380, [1959] D.L. 209; DÉCRET No. 64–742 of July 20, 1964, J.O. July 24, 1964, p. 6572, [1964] D.L. 262. On the creation of new notarial offices, see DÉCRETS Nos. 64–26 and 64–27 of Jan. 9, 1964, J.O. Jan. 15, 1964, p. 524, [1964] D.L. 73.

obligation). Candidates must ordinarily have worked as clerks in a notary's office for six years before they receive an official appointment. The period of clerkship is only four years for candidates who have a degree of *docteur* or *licencié* in law, or who have attended one of the accredited training institutes for *notaires*. [217]

**b. Functions.** French law gives no profession a monopoly for the drawing of ordinary contracts. For the preparation of contracts, French businessmen invoke professional legal assistance far less frequently than their United States counterparts. [218] However, in order to protect the parties and the public in general, French law requires that certain documents be prepared by a *notaire* in the special form prescribed for notarial documents. The law thus insures that documents that are important or the subject of complex legal rules governing their form and substance are drawn by a competent person. In addition, the use of the notary prevents fraud and, perhaps even more importantly, claims of fraud: Before preparing any instrument, the notary is under a strict obligation to ascertain the correct identity of the parties and to make sure that they have legal capacity to act. Furthermore, the notary does not give the original instrument prepared by him (*minute*) to the parties; it is kept permanently in his office and thus protected against alterations. Certified copies (*expéditions*) of notarial documents may be issued to interested parties. [219] Since the *notaire* is a quasi-public officer, a notarial document offers the additional advantage of having "authentic" force: Subject to the possibility of attacking the accuracy of

[217] Law of 25 *ventôse*, Year XI, as amended, *supra* note 216, arts. 35-43.

[218] This may be due to the less casuistic character of French law, which does not put quite as high a premium on draftsmanship as American law. *Cf.* Van Hecke, *A Civilian Looks at the Common Law Laywer*, in INTERNATIONAL CONTRACTS: CHOICE OF LAW AND LANGUAGE 5–13 (Reese ed. 1962).

[219] The basic rules of form concerning notarial documents are contained in articles 8 through 30 of the Law of 25 *ventôse*, Year XI, as amended, *supra* note 216. See especially art. 8 (*notaire* may not act in matters in which close relatives are involved); art. 11 (*notaire* must ascertain name, residence, and capacity of person appearing before him); art. 13 (writing materials, such as ink and typewriter ribbon, used by a *notaire*, must be of type approved by Minister of Justice; no abbreviations, interlineations or blanks are allowed; violations subject *notaire* to fine); art. 15 (documents not written by hand in their entirety must be initialled at the bottom of each page by the parties, the *notaire*, and any witnesses); art. 20 (*notaires* must ordinarily keep originals of all documents prepared by them); art. 22 (*notaires* may not give up original (*minute*), except pursuant to court order); art. 23 (in the absence of a court order copies may be issued only to parties, their heirs, and assignees). Ordinarily, witnesses are not required for notarial acts, but article 9 of the Law requires two ordinary persons or one (additional) notary as witnesses for acts establishing gifts *inter vivos*, acceptances of gifts, revocations of wills and gifts, and recognition of natural children. Notarial documents are kept in the notary's office for 125 years; thereafter, they may be transferred to public archives. Law of March 14, 1928, J.O. March 15, 1928, [1928] D.4. 307.

the document in a special proceeding (*inscription de faux*), any statement made in the notarial document by the notary as to matters he has performed or seen performed and as to the date on which the document was executed has conclusive force. [220] In an appropriate case, the *notaire* may, by putting the "executory formula" on the first copy (*grosse*) of the notarial document, convert it into a title for execution, on the basis of which execution may be levied without court proceedings. [221]

Instruments that *must* be prepared by a notary include *contrats de mariage*, [222] deeds of gifts, [223] mortgages, [224] and all instruments concerning the transfer of real property that must be recorded. [225] Notaries may also draw all other instruments unless exclusive power to do so has been granted to another public officer or *officier ministériel*. [226]

In some instances, the power of *notaires* to perform certain functions is not exclusive, but concurrent with that of other *officiers ministériels*. Thus, they share the power to protest negotiable instruments with the *huissiers*, and the power to conduct public sales of movable property with both the *commissaires priseurs* and the *huissiers*. [227] In view of the virtually conclusive probative force of notarial documents, the aid of a *notaire* in the preparation of important legal instruments is frequently invoked even if the instrument may be prepared by any lay person. Thus, partnership contracts or articles of incorporation are often drawn as notarial acts, [228] and a special notarial testament (*testament par acte public*) [229] is often preferred over the simple holographic will. A

[220] CODE CIVIL arts. 1317, 1319, 1328. The authentic character of notarial documents extends only to matters within the sphere of competence of the notary. Thus, a statement in a notarial will that it has been made by such and such a person on such and such a date has binding probative force, but a statement that the testator seemed to the notary to beof sound mind does not. See also AMOS & WALTON, *op. cit. supra* note 4, at 24–25.

[221] Law of 25 *ventôse*, Year XI, as amended, *supra* note 216 arts. 19, 25.

[222] CODE CIVIL art. 1394.

[223] CODE CIVIL art. 931. A deed of gift must also be accepted by notarial act. CODE CIVIL art. 932.

[224] CODE CIVIL art. 2127.

[225] DÉCRET No. 55–22 of January 4, 1955, J.O. Jan. 7, 1955, p. 346, [1955] D.L. 44, art. 4; *cf.* 1 COLIN & CAPITANT 11 (Suppl. 1955).

[226] As to instruments that may not be prepared by notaries, see, *e.g.*, CODE CIVIL arts. 55-78 (birth and death certificates); CODE CIVIL art. 477 (declaration of emancipation of minor which must be made before judge of *tribunal d'instance* and *greffier*); CODE CIVIL art. 784 (renunciation of inheritance must be made before *greffier*).

[227] Sometimes, judges have a concurrent power to prepare "authentic" acts. See, *e.g.*, CODE CIVIL art. 392 (designation of assistant (*conseil*) to surviving mother acting as guardian may be made by will or notarial act or declaration before judge).

[228] *Cf.* MOREAU, FRENCH CORPORATIONS 6 (1951); Conard, *Forming a Subsidiary in the European Common Market*, 59 MICH. L. REV. 1 (1960); Becker, The *Société Anonyme and the Société à Responsabilité Limitée in France*, 38 N.Y.U.L. REV. 835 (1963).

[229] CODE CIVIL art. 971. It is to be noted that in this case two notaries or a notary and two witnesses are required.

*notaire* may also act as a depository of documents not drawn by him. In that case, however, he may not prepare copies. [230]

Generally, parties to a contract use only one *notaire* selected by common accord. The use of independent legal advisers, in addition to the *notaire* preparing the document, is common only when a contract has some bearing on actual or threatened litigation, such as property settlements in connection with matrimonial difficulties. The rôle of independent adviser may be played by a party's *avocat*; it may also be played by another *notaire*. However, the rôle of *avocats* in the preparation of contracts and other documents has been increasing. Often, *notaires*, especially *notaires* having a long-continuing relationship with a client, also act as general advisers and representatives, and take care of purchases and sales (especially of real property), and also of loans, investments, and similar transactions. *Avocats* do not play an important rôle in that field. [231]

In addition to his work on behalf of private clients, the *notaire* may be delegated by the court to perform certain quasi-judicial functions, especially in partition proceedings or in connection with the division of community property after a divorce. [232]

**c. Duties.** The duties of the *notaire* are prescribed in considerable detail by law. A *notaire* must make his services available to any person requesting them for a lawful purpose; he may not refuse to act in a matter in which he is competent. [233] On the other hand, no *notaire* may perform any of his functions outside the district for which he has been appointed. [234] A *notaire* must reside in the municipality in which he has his office. [235]

The *notaire* is under a strict duty to observe all formal requirements for the preparation of notarial acts. He must ascertain the identity of the parties as well as their capacity to act and is personally responsible

[230] DALLOZ, PETIT DICTIONNAIRE DE DROIT, *Notaire*, No. 9 (1951).

[231] See 2.03 *supra*. A *notaire* has an obligation to protect the interests of both parties to a contract prepared by him. X. v. Digonnet, Cass. Civ., Dec. 6, 1949, [1950] D.L. 141 (notary selected by debtor bound to inform creditor that mortgage likely to be insufficient security).

[232] CODE DE PROCÉDURE CIVILE art. 969.

[233] Law of 25 *ventôse*, Year XI as amended, *supra* note 216, art. 3. However, the *notaire* may not act on behalf of close relatives. See note 219 *supra*.

[234] Law of 25 *ventôse*, Year XI, as amended, *supra* note 216, art. 6. *Notaires* having their office in a city in which a *cour d'appel* has its seat may exercise their profession within the district for which the *cour d'appel* is competent; *notaires* having their office in a city in which a *tribunal de grande instance* has its seat may exercise their profession in the whole area, usually a *département*, in which the *tribunal de grande instance* is territorially competent; all other *notaires* must ordinarily exercise their profession within the *arrondissement* in which they have their office. Law of 25 *ventôse*, Year XI, as amended, *supra* note 216, art. 5.

[235] Law of 25 *ventôse*, Year XI, as amended, *supra* note 216, art. 4.

for the validity of the instruments he prepares. [236] A *notaire* may handle funds belonging to his clients, but is subject to very detailed regulations as to the books he must keep. [237] In no event may a *notaire* keep funds of a client for more than three months. Funds not withdrawn by clients within three months must be deposited with a special government agency. [238]

No *notaire* may engage in speculative transactions of any sort, whether involving shares of stock, other intangibles, or real property. He may have no personal interest in any transaction in which he participates, nor may he become a surety for a loan negotiated by him. [239] Each *notaire* must carry liability insurance as protection for his clients. [240]

**d. Professional organization and discipline.** The structure of the professional organization of the French *notaires* is substantially similar to that of the *avoués* and that of the *huissiers*. Membership in the organization is compulsory. There is a local organization of *notaires* in each *département*, called *Chambre des Notaires*. The local organizations within the district of a *cour d'appel* form a regional council (*Conseil Régional*). An all-encompassing central body, the National Council of Notaries (*Conseil Supérieur du Notariat*), is established in Paris. The officers of these organizations are elected by their members.

These associations represent the interests of the *notaires* before the public authorities, such as the Ministry of Justice. [241] In addition, they administer welfare institutions for *notaires* and an indemnity fund

[236] Law of 25 *ventôse*, Year XI, as amended, *supra* note 212, art. 12; *cf.* art. 18 (each notary to keep list of incompetents in his district) X. v. Digonnet, *supra* note 231.

[237] The legal rules governing the books to be kept by *notaires* go into minute detail. The *notaire* must keep indexes of all documents in his office. He is required to use special numbered receipt forms, which are obtainable only from the local *chambre* of *notaires*, for all funds received by him. In addition, all books kept by notaries must conform to models approved by the Minister of Justice. DÉCRET of Dec. 19, 1945, as amended, *supra* note 216, arts. 16–20C.

[238] These funds must be deposited in the *Caisse des Dépôts et Consignations*, a government agency which also serves as a custodian for all funds paid into court. DÉCRET of Dec. 19, 1945, *supra* note 216, art. 15.

[239] DÉCRET of Dec. 19, 1945, *supra* note 216, art. 13.

[240] DÉCRET of May 20, 1955, J.O. May 22, 1955, p. 5136, [1955] D.L. 260, art. 13.

[241] The present structure of the professional organization of the French *notaires* is based on arts. 2–6 of the ORDONNANCE of Nov. 2, 1945, *supra* note 216, which replaced an earlier law of the Vichy government on the subject. In addition to the organizations mentioned in the text, there are so-called joint committees of *notaires* and their clercs, which consist of the governing bodies of the various organizations of *notaires* supplemented by an equal number of delegates of clerks. The *conseil régional* at the *cour d'appel* in Paris has authority only over the *chambres des notaires* outside the Seine *département* (Paris). The *chambre départementale* for the Seine *département* performs the functions of a regional council for its members. ORDONNANCE of Nov. 2, 1945, *supra* note 216, art. 8.

which protects clients who suffer losses due to the misconduct of a *notaire* and are unable to collect the full amount of the loss from the *notaire* or his insurer. [242] The professional organizations of *notaires* also exercise general supervision over their members and may enact rules supplementing statutory provisions that govern the *notaires*. Periodically, these organizations also audit the books of all *notaires* to make sure that no unauthorized use is made of clients' funds and that the complex rules governing their books are observed. [243]

The local organizations of *notaires* also exercise a disciplinary power. Sitting as disciplinary councils (*chambres de discipline*) they may either issue a warning, or a simple censure, or a censure before the full *chambre*. If the *chambre* finds that a more stringent penalty is appropriate, it forwards the charges to the *procureur de la République*, who summons the wayward *notaire* before the *tribunal de grande instance*. That court may put the *notaire* on probation or suspend him either temporarily or permanently. A *notaire* permanently suspended from office suffers a loss of his political rights, including the right to vote. [244] It should be added that the need for disciplinary proceedings arises rarely and that French *notaires* usually fulfill their professional obligations conscientiously.

**e. Fees.** The fees of the *notaires*, like those of the other *officiers ministériels*, are specified in an official fee schedule. [245] Charges in excess of those specified in the official schedule are illegal. The fees are sometimes flat fees for the performance of a particular act and sometimes percentage fees that depend on the amount involved. Thus, a father

[242] At the seat of each *cour d'appel* there is a regional indemnity fund which is primarily liable. Claims for which the resources of a regional fund are insufficient are paid out of a central fund in Paris. In practice, recourse to these funds is rare. Reserves of the central fund that are not needed currently may be used to make loans to candidate *notaires* who wish to purchase an office. DÉCRET of May 20, 1955, *supra* note 216.

[243] ORDONNANCE of Nov. 2, 1945, *supra* note 216, art. 4. The books of each office must be audited at least once every four years. The inspection is made by two *notaires* from a city other than that of the *notaire* inspected. The inspecting *notaires* are entitled to examine all books, registers, and records kept in the office and to ask for the assistance of an accountant. DÉCRET of Dec. 19, 1945, *supra* note 216, arts. 21–22. The manner in which the organizations of *notaires* must audit the books of their members is prescribed in detail in arts. 5–18 of a DÉCRET of March 16, 1931, J.O. March 18, 1931, [1931] D. 4.57, since amended in minor details.

[244] ORDONNANCE of June 28, 1945, J.O. June 29, 1945, p. 3926, *Rectificatif* (correction of error), J.O. July 4, 1945, p. 4061, [1945] D.L. 134 arts. 1–17.

[245] DÉCRET of Sept. 29, 1953, J.O. Sept. 30, 1953, p. 8559, [1953] D.L. 367 amended by DÉCRETS of Aug. 14, 1954, J.O. Aug. 18, 1954, p. 7955, [1954] D.L. 355; July 29, 1955, J.O. August 4, 1955, p. 7787, [1955] D.L. 4370; May 7, 1956, J.O. May 12, 1956, p. 4432, [1956] D.L. 180; Nov. 21, 1956, J.O. Nov. 23, 1956, p. 11.200, [1956] D.L. 487; May 3, 1958, J.O. May 6, 1958, p. 4431, [1958] D.L. 205 and June 18, 1958, J.O. June 20, 1958, p. 5742, [1958] D.L. 225.

establishing a dowry for his daughter must pay a fee of 3% for amounts up to F. 6000 (about $1500), 2% for amounts up to F. 20.000 (about $5000), 1% for amounts up to F. 60.000, and 1/2% for amounts in excess of that sum. [246] Other proportionate fees are at about the same level. A *notaire* representing clients in business dealings or other matters not described in the schedule may charge a fee to be agreed upon between him and his client. In case the parties fail to come to an agreement, the fee may be determined by the court. Although the total fees collected in any given year depend upon the amount of business handled, [247] the average *notaire* appears to earn a quite comfortable income.

**f. Social position.** The *notaire* plays a rôle of considerable importance in day-to-day life in France. [248] He is the only one of the law professionals whose main work is not connected with litigation. The very nature of the instruments for which his assistance is required, such as ante-nuptial agreements, gifts, authentic testaments, and real estate transactions, brings him in close contact with family problems. As a result, there is often a close relationship between a *notaire* and his client. Many a French family has a family *notaire*, who is a trusted adviser.

Nevertheless, some of the younger *notaires* are not satisfied with the present situation and long for more freedom of action. A number of reforms have been suggested, but they have all failed of adoption because of the resistance of the French Parliament. Some changes, however, are probably inevitable. Perhaps, it will eventually be necessary to autorize partnerships between *notaires*, or at least office sharing

[246] See table annexed to DÉCRET of Sept. 29, 1953, *supra* note 245, item 76B.

[247] It might be added that in some matters concerning paupers *notaires* may not charge fees. DÉCRET of Sept. 29, 1953, *supra* note 245, arts. 21, 22. In matters involving impecunious persons, some fees are deliberately set at a fairly low rate; by way of compensation fees for some business transactions are higher. Since a new *notaire* may ordinarily be admitted only if he purchases the office of a retiring *notaire*, *notaires* are necessarily somewhat protected from competition. There is about one *notaire* per 6,000 inhabitants in the larger cities, and usually one *notaire* per canton in rural areas. Brown, *supra* note 215 at 62. The total number of *notaires* in the city of Paris is only about 122. By *décret*, the government may increase, and under some circumstances decrease, the number of *notaires* in any one area, if the amount of business makes this desirable. If the number of *notaires* is increased, the newly established *notaires* must pay a certain sum to those already there; if the number of *notaires* is reduced, the remaining *notaires* must pay a sum to those whose offices have been abolished. The same rule prevails as to the other *officiers ministériels*. Law of 25 *ventôse*, Year XI, as amended, *supra* note 216, arts. 31–32. Special measures were taken in connection with the court reorganization of December 1958.

[248] There are at present about 6,300 *notaires* in France, who have a total of about 26,000 clerks. LE MONDE, Dec. 12, 1961. Even the chief clerks of *notaires* (*premiers clercs*) enjoy a certain amount of social status and seem to be in fair demand as legal advisers for business firms. *Cf.* Brown, *supra* note 215.

arrangements to facilitate the use of modern office machinery. The same reasons may require modification of the strict rules governing account books of *notaires* which were devised in the days of handwritten entries in heavy ledgers. Finally, the ever growing complexity of legal relations and special expertise possessed by a *notaire* may well result in his playing a growing rôle as adviser to business firms as well as to individuals. [249]

## 2.11. Persons Involved in Legal Proceedings in Connection with the Administration or Sale of Property

Ordinarily, only professionals are judicially charged with the sale of property on execution and with the temporary operation or liquidation of a business ordered by the courts. Some of these professionals are *officiers ministériels*; others, though not properly *officiers ministériels*, function in a similar manner. The duties of most of these professionals are more administrative than legal.

**a. *Commissaires-priseurs.*** The *commissaires-priseurs* have a virtual monopoly in the judicially ordered appraisal, and sale on auction, of tangible personal property. [250] *Commissaires-priseurs*, who are *officiers ministériels*, are lacking only in some of the smaller communities in France, [251] in which the *huissiers* or *notaires* may fulfill their functions. [252] The qualifications required for admission as *commissaire-priseur* are quite similar to the requirements for admission as *huissier*. [253] Like the other *officiers ministériels*, the *commissaires-priseurs* are organized in a professional organization, membership in which

[249] In the business field, *notaires* are quite active in matters involving the sale of business enterprises and the creation of partnerships, corporations, and other business organizations. *Cf.* Le Monde, Dec. 12, 1961.

[250] Ordonnance of Nov. 2, 1945, J.O. Nov. 3, 1945, p. 7164, [1945] D.L. 312, art. 1. This *ordonnance* was implemented by a Décret of Dec. 19, 1945, J.O. Dec. 22, 1945, p. 8459, [1946] D.L. 72, amended by a series of further Décrets of Feb. 5, 1947, J.O. Feb. 8, 1947, p. 1297, [1947] D.L. 81; Nov. 29, 1951, J.O. Dec. 2, 1951, p. 11898, [1951] D.L. 410; Nov. 9, 1956, J.O. Nov. 14, 1956 p. 10880, [1956] D.L. 476; Jan. 3, 1959, J.O. Jan. 7, 1959, p. 380, [1959] D.L. 209. The activity of the *commissaires-priseurs* is not limited to auction sales of property seized on execution. They conduct all kinds of auction sales.

[251] Originally, *commissaires-priseurs* were instituted only in Paris, Law of 27 *ventôse*, Year XI (1801); they were established in other places in France by art. 89 of a Law of April 28, 1816, implemented by an Ordonnance of June 26, 1816. Parts of these enactments are still in force.

[252] See 2.06, 2.08 *supra.*

[253] The requirements are: French nationality, good character, successful passing of an examination in which the *commissaire-priseurs'* ability to appraise property is tested, three years' clerkship in the office of a *commissaire-priseur* or *notaire*, at least one of which must have been in the office of a *commissaire-priseur*. The local organization of *commissaires-priseurs* may, in addition, require a law degree. The clerkship period is two years for holders of the degree *licencié* or *docteur en droit*. Ordonnance of Nov. 2, 1945, *supra* note 250 arts. 2–3.

is compulsory and which exercises supervision and may impose disciplinary penalties. The *commissaires-priseurs,* because of their comparatively small number, are organized on a regional, rather than on a departmental, basis. [254]

**b. *Syndics administrateurs judiciaires* and *liquidateurs judiciaires.*** Occasionally, for instance in case of a suit between the members of a partnership or in case of bankruptcy, a business may have to be taken over by an agent of the court for the purpose of temporary control during litigation or for liquidation. For a long time, the French courts were not restricted by law in the choice of persons who could be appointed to such a position. Often, *avoués* were appointed, but in the larger cities these functions were eventually taken over by a body of specialists. They organized professional associations somewhat similar to those of the *avoués* or *notaires,* but without official standing. [255]

A Decree-Law of May 20, 1955, [256] has formalized this situation at least insofar as commercial matters are concerned. It provides that only persons mentioned on a special list prepared by the regional *cour d'appel* may be appointed by the commercial courts. [257] The list has a separate section for each commercial court, or civil court acting in lieu of a commercial court, within the region of the *cour d'appel* and includes the professional *syndics administrateurs judiciaires* and *liquidateurs judiciaires* approved by the court. If warranted by the amount of available business, the list may also include *avoués, huissiers, commissaires-priseurs,* and *greffiers* of the *tribunaux d'instance,* but not *greffiers* of the higher courts.

Professional trustees or *syndics administrateurs judiciaires* and receivers or *liquidateurs judiciaires* may be admitted to practice if they fulfill qualifications that are fairly similar to those required of *huissiers*

[254] In addition to the regional organizations, there is also a national organization. ORDONNANCE of Nov. 2, 1945, *supra* note 250, arts. 4–9. The regional organizations usually comprise the areas of several *cours d'appel.* DÉCRET of Dec. 19, 1945, as amended *supra* note 250, art. 7.

[255] CUCHE & VINCENT 197; 1 SOLUS & PERROT 940, 941.

[256] J.O. May 21, 1955, p. 5086, [1955] D.L. 237. It was amended by ORDONNANCE No. 58–1037 of Oct. 29, 1958, p. 9982, [1958] D.L. 373, a DÉCRET of Dec. 19, 1958, J.O. Dec. 20, 1958, p. 11460, [1959] D.L. 18, and a DÉCRET No. 59–670 of May 19, 1959, J.O. May 29, 1959, p. 5442, [1959] D.L. 503. It has been implemented by two DÉCRETS, one of June 18, 1956, J.O. June 21, 1956, p. 5686, [1956] D.L. 210 amended by DÉCRET of Nov. 9, 1956, J.O. Nov. 14, 1956, p. 10880, [1956] D.L. 476 and another of May 29, 1959, No. 59–708, J.O. June 12, 1959 p. 5828, [1959] D.L. 513.

[257] Actually, the law is applicable to all commercial cases, those handled by the regular commercial courts and those handled by regular civil courts sitting in lieu of a commercial court. It is not applicable to ordinary civil cases, in which anyone may be appointed as a receiver. The need for the appointment of a trustee in bankruptcy cannot arise in a civil court, since only business firms can be declared bankrupt. *Cf.* 1 SOLUS & PERROT 942.

In addition, they must be proposed to the *cour d'appel* by the commercial court in the district of which they wish to practice. They must become members of their professional association, which is organized on a regional and national level. Because some regional organizations have a fairly small membership, the power to discipline members has been conferred on the national association.

*Avoués*, *huissiers*, and other qualified persons who wish to be inscribed on the list of authorized receivers and trustees must meet the minimum requirements prescribed for the *syndics administrateurs judiciaires* and *liquidateurs judiciaires*. In addition, they must have the consent of their own professional organization. [258]

All persons acting as receivers or trustees in bankruptcy are paid on the basis of an official fee schedule. They are subject to rather close supervision, especially insofar as their books of accounts are concerned. [259]

c. ***Arbitres-rapporteurs.*** In commercial cases, the courts are authorized to appoint so-called *arbitres-rapporteurs* to examine accounts, attempt to conciliate the parties, and report to the court. [260] Commercial courts with crowded calendars use *arbitres-rapporteurs* quite extensively even in cases not involving an examination of accounts. It is uncertain to what extent courts may delegate their functions to *arbitres-rapporteurs*. [261]

*Arbitres-rapporteurs* are neither judges nor *avocats*, and no law prescribes their professional qualifications. However, their position has developed along the same lines as that of the *syndics*. In the larger cities, a limited number of persons began to specialize as *arbitres-rapporteurs* and to organize unofficial professional organizations requiring certain minimum qualifications for admission to membership, which in Paris include possession of a law degree. By appointing only members of these organizations, the commercial courts have co-operated in the development of a professional class of *arbitres-rapporteurs*. It may be expected that this scheme will eventually be embodied in legislation. [262]

[258] *Avoués* and *huissiers* who act as receivers and trustees do not become members of the professional organizations of the *syndics*.

[259] See generally CUCHE & VINCENT 197–98; 1 SOLUS & PERROT 940–54.

[260] CODE DE PROCÉDURE CIVILE art. 429. The name of the *arbitres-rapporteurs* emphasizes their dual function; *Arbitre* means arbitrator or rather conciliator, and *rapporteur* means reporter.

[261] For further discussion, see 7.17 *infra*, dealing with proceedings before the commercial courts.

[262] See CUCHE & VINCENT 196–97; 1 SOLUS & PERROT 955–59.

## 2.12. Conclusion

During the formative era of French law, the period of the Revolution and the Consulate, the opinion was widespread that substantive law, once properly codified, would not be too difficult of ascertainment. This may explain why the giving of legal advice as such was not regulated: Lay people were considered quite competent to understand the meaning of a code. [263] Professional assistance was made mandatory only in specific areas with inherent complexities, such as the procedure before the higher courts and the preparation of certain documents. In such areas, specialists such as the *avoués* and *notaires*, were given exclusive competence. Even the *avocat*, whose assistance is not required, has traditionally performed a fairly narrow, specialized, function. On the other hand the French legislator has shown considerable concern for the potential misconduct of members of the legal professions. To a large extent, the emphasis has been on the prevention of unprofessional conduct rather than on its punishment after the event by disciplinary proceedings. Detailed fee schedules regulate the remuneration of all law professionals except the *avocats*. Strict rules limiting outside activities prevent conflicts of interests and remove the temptation to neglect professional duties in favor of possibly more lucrative business. Professional organizations with far-reaching self-governing and disciplinary powers are a strong factor tending to ensure maintenance of professional standards. By subjecting those professionals who may handle their clients' funds to strict rules concerning bookkeeping procedures, misuse of such funds is made less likely. That the law professionals ordinarily exercise their profession [264] as solo practitioners may also have contributed to the development of a strong sense of individual responsibility. [265]

However, the situation in France is far from static. Its legal system, which has become vastly more complex since the enactment of the original codes, will require increased co-operation between the law professionals, and lead to greater emphasis on their counselling functions. This may result in breaking down some of the present divisions. A fusion between *avocats* and *avoués* may eventually come about, and more and larger law firms may emerge.

[263] Tradition and history, in addition to the factors mentioned in this section, undoubtedly were largely responsible for the development of the legal professions in France in their present form. The separate professions have roots considerably antedating the French Revoluiton, and the idea of strict professional self-regulation goes back to the Middle Ages. But it is significant that the Revolution, which produced such important permanent changes in the administrative and judicial system of France, did not lead to a more profound reorganization of the legal professions.

[264] Although *avocats* may form partnerships with a limited number of members, few actually do. See 2.03.h *supra*. Other professionals must generally practice as individuals.

CHAPTER 3

# JUDICIAL ORGANIZATION

This chapter discusses administrative courts (3.01–3.04), the rôle of the Ministry of Justice in judicial organization and administration (3.05–3.10), the schooling, appointment, promotion, remuneration, and discipline of *magistrats* (3.11–3.21), and the regular courts (3.22–3.32) – particularly, the *tribunaux de grande instance* (3.24), the *tribunaux d'instance* (3.25), the *tribunaux de commerce* (3.26), the *conseils de prud'hommes* (3.27), the *tribunaux paritaires de baux ruraux* (3.28), the social security courts (3.29), the *cours d'appel* (3.30), the *Commission Nationale Technique* (3.31), and the *Cour de Cassation* (3.32).

## 1. ADMINISTRATIVE COURTS

### 3.01. The Development of Administrative Courts

When, during the course of the French Revolution, the framers of the new institutions created a new judicial system for France, they were well aware of the rôle which the *parlements*, the ancient appellate courts in the various provinces, had played in opposing the reforming and centralizing influence of the monarchy. [1] To prevent the recurrence of such events, a law was enacted forbidding judges from interfering in any manner with administrative officials. [2] This law, which is still in effect, precluded relief to individuals injured by administrative action. Only appeal within the executive branch of the government – which does not seem to have been effective [3] – was available.

This situation was changed when Napoleon, as First Consul, created the *Conseil d'Etat*. This body of experts was to act as legal adviser to the government and took a leading part in the preparation of the French codes. At the same time, Napoleon developed the practice of referring

[1] SCHWARTZ, FRENCH ADMINISTRATIVE LAW AND THE COMMON-LAW WORLD 6 (1954) [hereinafter cited as SCHWARTZ]; WALINE, DROIT ADMINISTRATIF 24 (29th ed. Paris 1963) [hereinafter cited as WALINE].

[2] Law of 16th and 24th of August 1789, 1 BULLETIN ANNOTÉ DES LOIS 221 (1834), translated in SCHWARTZ, *op. cit. supra* note 1; *cf.* WALINE, *op. cit. supra* note 1, at 25. At the same time, the courts were forbidden from enacting general rules. This provision is presently contained in CODE CIVIL art. 5.

[3] WALINE, *op. cit. supra* note 1, at 21–33.

petitions for relief against administrative action which had been addressed to him to the *Conseil d'Etat.* A special division (*section du contentieux*) was created within the *Conseil d'Etat* to handle these grievances. In the course of time, this section became, in fact, a court charged with the duty of reviewing administrative acts. [4] Due to a lack of legislative rules in the field of French administrative law, the *Conseil d'Etat* created a substantial body of case law.

For a long time, the *Conseil d'Etat* was substantially the only agency with general power to review administrative action. It became swamped with a flood of cases when the extension of administrative activities in recent years led to a corresponding increase in the number of cases brought before it. [5] To alleviate this situation, in 1953, competence to review most types of administrative action was conferred on a number of administrative courts throughout France. Their decisions can be appealed to the *Conseil d'Etat,* which has become a court of last resort in most administrative matters. [6]

The *Conseil d'Etat* and the administrative tribunals are not part of the regular court system. Neither the constitutional provisions concerning the independence of judges, [7] nor the legislation concerning the status and duties of the judiciary and the organization of the courts, are applicable to these agencies. Nevertheless, the *Conseil d'Etat* and the administrative tribunals exercise part of the judicial, rather than merely administrative, power of the state. As a result, in France judicial power is divided between two court systems (*ordres*). [8] This division goes so far that, as a rule, the regular courts may not deal with administrative matters that are raised incidentally in the course of a proceeding concerned with questions within their subject matter competence. In such cases, the regular courts must obtain a decision from the proper administrative tribunal and stay their own proceedings in the meantime. [9]

[4] *Ibid.*

[5] SCHWARTZ 45-50; WALINE 143,

[6] DÉCRET No. 53–934 of September 30, 1953, J.O. Sept. 30, 1953, p. 8593, [1953] D.L. 376.

[7] Constitution of 1958, arts. 64–65. For history and prior law, see also CHATELAIN, LA NOUVELLE CONSTITUTION ET LE RÉGIME POLITIQUE DE LA FRANCE 135–40 (1959).

[8] MOREL 83; CORNU & FOYER 84.

[9] Thus, the regular courts may not hold an administrative act invalid, nor may they ordinarily interpret an individual administrative decision if its meaning is doubtful. They may, however, interpret administrative regulations of a general nature. MOREL 235; CUCHE & VINCENT 268.

### 3.02. The Competence of the Administrative Courts

**a. Review of administrative acts.** In most instances, the administrative tribunals and the *Conseil d'Etat* [11] may review the propriety of administrative acts in proceedings generally referred to as *recours pour excès de pouvoir*. The power to review administrative acts is exercised in four situations: (1) if the administrative agency fails to observe procedural rules, [12] (2) if there is an error of law, [13] (3) if the administrative agency uses its power for an improper purpose (*détournement de pouvoir*), [14] and (4) if no proper basis for the administrative decision is given (*défaut de motif légal*). [15]

**b. Actions for money damages against public agencies.** The *Conseil d'Etat* and the administrative tribunals are also competent to determine governmental liability, whether based on contract or on tort. [16] The rules applied by the administrative courts, both in contract [17] and in tort [18] cases, are different from the rules applicable in ordinary civil suits.

**c. Cases in which administrative matters are brought before the regular civil courts.** In a number of instances, special statutes have conferred competence on the regular civil courts in matters that would otherwise have been regarded as administrative. Examples are actions for damages caused by vehicles owned by governmental bodies, [19] actions for damages due to injuries suffered by students in public schools, [20] and proceedings to establish the nationality of a party. [21]

[10] In some cases, administrative action is not subject to review. The number of cases is limited, involving chiefly matters with international implications. WALINE 216–25. At times, the scope of review may also be broader than indicated here.

[11] For a list of all administrative courts in France, see Kock, *The Machinery of Law Administration in France*, 108 U. PA. L. REV. 366, 377–81 (1960).

[12] WALINE 458–62.

[13] WALINE 462–73. As Waline points out, this rule is fairly broad. There is violation of law by an administrative agency not only when it violates or wrongly interprets a statute, but also when an administrative regulation, or even one of the fundamental principles of law (such as the principle against retro-active decisions), is violated.

[14] WALINE 480–88, citing numerous examples.

[15] For example, if no or insufficient facts to support the decision are stated. WALINE 472–79.

[16] SCHWARTZ 250. These proceedings are referred to as *recours de pleine juridiction*.

[17] See WALINE 11–15.

[18] See WALINE 835–40.

[19] Law No. 57–1424 of December 31, 1957, J.O. Jan. 5, 1958, p. 190, [1958] D.L. 30.

[20] Law of April 5, 1937, J.O. April 6, 1937, p. 3923, [1937] B.L.D. 337; *cf.* Hamson, *Tribunal des Conflits in France, Affaire Gavillet*, 67 L. Q. REV. 44 (1951). See also note Debré appended to Lhomme, Cons. d'Etat, June 4, 1937, [1937] D. 3.48.

[21] Code of French nationality, October 19, 1945, J.O. Oct. 20, 1945, p. 6700, art. 124. However, when the validity of a specific administrative act, such as a decree of the government

Special statutes have also conferred competence upon the regular courts to deal with certain matters pertaining to elections and taxation. [22] Sometimes, case law, rather than a specific statutory grant, enables the regular courts to deal with cases in the administrative area, such as those in which the administration has acted without color of right (*voies de fait*). [23] Examples of such cases include the arrest of a person without a warrant, seizure of private property without regular proceedings, the arbitrary tearing down of a building, and the requisitioning of an apartment for persons in need without statutory authority. [24]

Difficult problems arise in connection with public enterprises engaged in commercial activities. Whether the regular or the administrative courts are competent in disputes involving such enterprises depends on the nature of the enterprise [25] and on the type of contract involved. [26] Actions to hold an individual public officer liable for his wrongs must be brought before the ordinary courts. However, instances in which an action can be brought against an individual public officer are rather limited: Ordinarily, the governmental unit involved is the proper defendant. [27]

A special solution has been found for disputes involving the various social security agencies. Their decisions can be reviewed by special commissions, but appeals from these commissions go ordinarily to the regular intermediate courts of appeal (*cours d'appel*) and to the highest of the regular French courts, the *Cour de Cassation*, and not to the *Conseil d'Etat*.

## 3.03. The *Tribunal des Conflits*

In 1872, to solve conflicts of competence between the regular and administrative courts, a special court, called *Tribunal des Conflits*, was

conferring French nationality on a person, is in question, the power of review belongs to the administrative tribunals, not to the regular courts. BATIFFOL 173.

[22] Decree No. 58–1284 of December 22, 1958, J.O. Dec. 23, 1958, p. 11579, [1959] B.L.D. 52, arts. 6(10), 9–12.

[23] VIZIOZ, ETUDES DE PROCÉDURE 329–30 (1956).

[24] *Id.* at 331–35; WALINE 90–93. Cases involving non-authorized seizure of apartments (for bombed-out persons and other war victims) were very frequent in the immediate postwar era.

[25] Thus, many of the enterprises nationalized after World War II are considered as private enterprises as far as the competence of the regular courts is concerned. See 1 COLIN & CAPITANT 801–02; SCHLESINGER, COMPARATIVE LAW 246–48 (2d. ed. 1959); de Vries & Hoeniger, *Post Liberation Nationalizations in France*, 50 COLUM. L. REV. 629, 647 (1950).

[26] WALINE 565–47

[27] Thus, the statutes mentioned *supra* notes 19 and 20 specify that the action must be brought against the governmental body concerned, not against the individual teacher or

created.[28] The basic statute under which it operates has recently been revised to expedite the solution of conflicts between the civil and administrative courts.[29]

The *Tribunal des Conflits* consists of three judges of the highest regular court, the *Cour de Cassation,* and of three judges of the highest administrative court, the *Conseil d'Etat.* If there is an even division of votes among the members of the court, the Minister of Justice joins the court and casts the deciding vote. This happens very rarely.[30]

The adjudicatory power of the court can be invoked in a number of situations. If both the administrative and the regular courts have decided that they are not competent and the plaintiff is thus left without remedy (a so-called negative conflict), the court may invalidate either the decision of the regular courts or that of the administrative courts and thus compel the court whose decision has been invalidated to take the case. When a case is filed in a regular court, which, in the opinion of the executive branch, belongs before the administrative courts, but the parties involved have made no objections, the *préfet,* as representative of the executive branch, may request the court to dismiss the case. If the case is not dismissed by the court, the proceedings must be stayed and the question of competence must be submitted to the *Tribunal des Conflits.* The *Cour de Cassation,* the *Conseil d'Etat,* or any other court whose decisions are non-reviewable, may transfer a case pending before it to the *Tribunal des Conflits* if the case involves the question of whether it belongs before the regular or the administrative courts.

As a rule, the *Tribunal des Conflits* does not decide cases on the merits, but merely determines which court system must handle the case.[31] However, in certain situations involving inconsistent decisions of the administrative and of the regular courts, the court may render a decision on the merits.[32] The statute empowering it to do so was enacted mainly to provide relief to persons injured as a result of a

driver. As a general rule, there is no personal liability on the part of a public officer as long as he stays within the scope of his employment. SCHWARTZ 255–66.

[28] Law of May 24, 1872, [1872] BULL. DES LOIS No. 1160, [1872] D. 4.88. The law also definitely established the *Conseil d'Etat* as an agency independent of the executive.

[29] DÉCRET No. 60–728 of July 25, 1960, J.O. July 28, 1960, p. 6960, [1960] S.l. 246.

[30] Only five or six times between 1872 and 1950. Hamson, *supra* note 20.

[31] DÉCRET No. 60–728, *supra* note 29; Kock, *supra* note 11, at 381–84; WALINE 42–44. Until 1960, cases involving "negative" conflicts had to be appealed to the *Conseil d'Etat* and to the *Cour de Cassation* before they could be brought before the *Tribunal des Conflits.* Now two inconsistent decisions, even if rendered by lower courts, constitute sufficient ground for recourse to the *Tribunal des Conflits,* provided either the decision of the regular or of the administrative court has become non-reviewable.

[32] Law of April 20, 1932, J.O. April 22, 1932, [1932] D. 4. 273.

collision between a private and a government vehicle, who were denied relief when the civil courts held that the governmental vehicle had caused the accident and the administrative courts held that it was the private vehicle. [33] Since all vehicular tort cases must now be brought in the civil courts, the statute has lost much of its significance. [34]

### 3.04. The *Conseil Constitutionnel*

Neither the *Conseil d'Etat*, nor the *Tribunal des Conflits*, nor the regular courts (including the *Cour de Cassation*), have the power to review the constitutionality of French legislation. A constitutional committee set up under the French constitution of 1946 to supervise the constitutionality of legislation had no real powers and was quite ineffective. [35] The French Constitution of 1958 established for the first time machinery for some control over the constitutionality of legislative acts. Its seventh title [36] establishes a *Conseil Constitutionnel,* composed of nine members, of whom three are appointed by the President of the Republic, and three each by the presiding officers of the two houses of the legislature.

All newly enacted "organic" laws – laws which deal with the organization of the government and require a qualified majority [37] – and all rules adopted by either house of the legislature must be submitted to this body before they are promulgated or put into operation. International agreements and regular statutes may be submitted to the Council by the President of the Republic, by the Prime Minister, or by the presiding officer of either house of the legislature before promulgation or ratification. [38] A treaty that has been declared unconstitutional may not be ratified; if declared unconstitutional, a statute may not be promulgated and a rule of either house of the French legislature

[33] This was the famous Rosay affair; the various cases involved are summarized by WALINE 56.

[34] See note 19 *supra.*

[35] CHATELAIN, *op. cit. supra* note 7 at 176, 177; *Cf.* Letourneur and Drago, *The Rule of Law as Understood in France,* 7 AM. J. COMP. L. 147 (1958).

[36] Constitution of 1958, arts. 56–63. The provisions of these articles concerning the Constitutional Council are amplified by Organic Law No. 58–1067 of November 7, 1958, J.O. Nov. 9, 1958 p. 10129, [1958] D.L. 383, modified by ORDINANCE No. 59–223 of February 4, 1959, J.O. Feb. 7, 1959, p. 1683, [1959] B.L.D. 521. See generally Engel, *Judicial Review and Political Preview of Legislation in Post-War France,* 6 INTER-AM. L. REV. 53 (1964).

[37] Constitution of 1958, art. 46; Sirat, *La Loi Organique de La Constitution de 1958,* [1960] D. CHR. 153.

[38] Constitution of 1958, art. 61.

may not be applied.[39] The *Conseil Constitutionnel* may not deal with statutes once they have been promulgated.

## 2. THE MINISTRY OF JUSTICE

### 3.05. The Functions of the Ministry of Justice

The provision in the French constitution which guarantees the independance of the judiciary[40] does not assure the French judiciary of control over matters of judicial administration. Rather, the Ministry of Justice, headed by the Minister of Justice,[41] exercizes a considerable measure of control over such matters. In addition, it plays an important rôle in the administration of criminal justice, is the main source of proposals for law reform, and prepares the budget for the courts and related agencies.[42]

In the field of civil litigation, the Ministry of Justice (1) participates in some civil suits through its agents, the members of the *ministère public*, (2) plays an important rôle in the appointment, promotion, and discipline of judicial officers, and (3) supervises the courts.

[39] Constitution of 1958, art. 62. The Constitutional Council also performs functions in the field of elections (arts. 58–60) and in the case of certain disputes between the executive branch and the legislative branch (art. 41). It must decide whether the President of the Republic is incapable of performing his duties (art. 7) and whether an emergency situation exists, enabling the President to use his special powers (art. 16).

[40] Article 65 of the Constitution of 1958 provides that the "President of the Republic is the guarantor of judicial independence" and that the judges shall be *inamovible, i.e.*, may not be dismissed by the executive without cause.

[41] The Minister of Justice (*Ministre de la Justice*) is frequently referred to as the Keeper of the Seals (*Garde des Sceaux*).

[42] The Ministry of Justice has recently been reorganized by DÉCRET No. 64–754 of July 25, 1964, J.O. July 28, 1964, p. 6708, [1964] D.L. 265 (report of Prime Minister explaining reasons for change). The Ministry now consists of the cabinet of the Minister, which forms his small personal staff and the following divisions: Judicial Services (matters relating to the administration of justice, appointment and promotion of judges, and, in cooperation with the civil division, preparation of legislation relating to civil procedure); Civil Affairs (preparation of legislation in private law matters, advising other government departments in private law matters, supervision of the *ministère public* in private law matters and questions of nationality); Criminal Affairs (preparation of legislation in the criminal field, supervision over the *ministère public* in the criminal field; investigation of applications for executive clemency); Penitentiary Administration (administration of penal institutions; administration of probation and parole); Supervised Education (administration of institutions for delinquent minors, juvenile delinquency and protection of youth matters in general); General Administration and Equipment (centralized accounting, purchasing and maintenance services). There is also an inspector general for the judicial services who supervises the periodic inspection of the courts and *ministère public*. For general, somewhat dated, discussions of the functions of the Ministry of Justice in France, see Edwards, *The Ministry of Justice in France*, 8 N.C.L. REV. 328 (1930). See also Perraud, *The Organization of the Courts and the Judicial Bench in France*, 11 J. COMP. LEGIS. (3rd ser.) 1 (1929); Garner, *The French Judiciary*, 26 YALE L. J. 349 (1916); Bacon, *On a Ministry of Justice*, 22 VA. L. REV. 175 (1935) Bacon, *The Subjection of Judges to the Executive*, 25 VA. L. REV. 745 (1937) (both articles by Bacon are highly critical of the French system).

### 3.06. The *Ministère Public*

The Ministry of Justice supervises and directs a body of public officers, collectively called the *ministère public*, who are attached to nearly all the regular courts in France. In the more serious criminal cases, these officials act as prosecutors. [43] They also perform important functions in civil cases. The *ministère public* can be traced historically to a group of attorneys acting as counsel for the King of France. [44]

The hierarchical head of the *ministère public* is the Minister of Justice. [45] Under him is a *Procureur Général*, who heads the *ministère public* attached to the highest of the regular French courts, the *Cour de Cassation*. The *Procureur Général* for the *Cour de Cassation* has a rather large staff. There is also a *procureur général* for each of the 27 *cours d'appel* (intermediate appeal courts). Since, in practice, the *Procureur Général* for the *Cour de Cassation* does not exercise the supervisory rights over the *procureur généraux* at the 27 *cours d'appel*, the Minister of Justice is their direct superior. [46]

The *procureurs généraux* for the *cours d'appel* each have a staff for the work before their own courts. [47] In addition, they are the hierarchical superiors of the members of the *ministère public* attached to the courts of first instance. The head of the *ministère public* before the court of first instance (*tribunal de grande instance*) is called *procureur de la République*. Together with their assistants (called *substituts*), the *procureurs de la République* act as public prosecutors in most criminal cases. [48] They also have administrative functions, including the supervision over certain public officers, [49] and participate in many civil cases. The numerous duties of the members of the *ministère public*

[43] Code de Procédure Pénale art. 111.

[44] 1 Colin & Capitant 182.

[45] See Ordinance No. 58–1270 of Dec. 22, 1958, J.O. Dec. 23, 1958, p. 11551, [1959] B.L.D. 15, art. 5.

[46] See Cuche & Vincent 152–53.

[47] The senior assistants of the *Procureur Général* at the seat of each *cour d'appel* are called *avocats généraux*.

[48] They handle all the cases before the tribunal de grande instance, called tribunal correctionnel in criminal cases. See Code de Procédure Pénale art. 111. They may also handle minor cases in which the *tribunal d'instance*, called *tribunal de police* in criminal cases, is competent, but police commissioners or mayors ordinarily act as prosecutors in these cases. Code de Procédure Pénale art. 45. See also Cornu & foyer 328; Kock, *Criminal Proceedings in France*, 9 Am. J. Comp. L. 253 (1960). Before the *cour d'assises*, which handles the most serious crimes, the *procureur général* of the regional *cour d'appel*, or one of his assistants, acts as prosecutor.

[49] These functions include supervision over the clerks of the courts (*greffiers*), the registrars of vital statistics, supervision over the administration of legal aid, and supervision over all *officiers ministériels*. See Morel 149; Goyet, Le Ministère Public (3d ed. Rousselet & Patin 1953).

can perhaps be summarized in the words of a statute enacted in the early days of the French Revolution: They are the representatives of the executive branch before the courts. [50]

### 3.07. The Status of the *Ministère Public*

Since the work of the members of the *ministère public* is so closely connected with that of the courts, they and the judges are often given a common designation, that of *magistrats*. Many (but not all) rules concerning appointment, promotion, discipline, and professional responsibility are the same for all *magistrats*. Both groups of public servants are considered equal, so that the judges have no power to discipline or control the members of the *ministère public*. [51] Members of the *ministère public* and judges in corresponding positions are in the same salary grade. The equality between the judges and the members of the *ministère public* is also apparent from the similarity of their professional costumes and the fact that both sit on a dais, while the benches for the parties' counsel stand on the courtroom floor. [52]

If a member of the *ministère public* refuses to obey the orders of his superiors, disciplinary sanctions may be imposed upon him. [53] However there are some limitations upon this rule. Traditionally, the obligation of the members of the *ministère public* to follow the orders of their superiors has related only to the preparation and filing of written papers; on oral argument, they have been considered free to take any position they choose. [54] This rule has received statutory sanction by the reform legislation of December 1958. [55] In actual practice, interference of the Minister of Justice in the work of the members of the *ministère public* is quite unusual, especially in civil matters.

### 3.08. The *Rôle* of the *Ministère Public* in Civil Actions

French scholars usually distinguish participation in civil actions by the *ministère public* as a joined party (*partie jointe*) from its participation as a main party (*partie principale*).

As *partie jointe*, the *ministère public* acts in litigation between other parties – not so much as representative of the executive, but as repre-

[50] Law of 16–24 Aug. 1790, 1 BULLETIN ANNOTÉ DES LOIS 221 (1834), tit. 8, art. 1.

[51] *E.g.*, CUCHE & VINCENT 153.

[52] *Cf.* Bacon, *supra* note 42, at 179.

[53] Ordinance No. 58–1270 of December 22, 1958, J.O. Dec. 23, 1958, p. 11551, [1959] B.L.D. 15, art. 43.

[54] This has been expressed by the saying: "*La plume est serve, mais la parole est libre*" (The pen is slave, but the word is free). See, *e.g.*, MOREL 148.

[55] ORDONNANCE No. 58–1270, *supra* note 53, art. 5.

sentative of the public interest. [56] As *partie principale,* it acts as, or on behalf of, a litigant – in the latter case, for a governmental agency.

### 3.09. The *Ministère Public* as *Partie Jointe*

If the *ministère public* chooses to participate in a civil proceeding as *partie jointe,* its representative addresses the court at the hearing (*audience*), during which the *avocats* of the parties present oral argument. However, the *ministère public* does not participate in proceedings devoted only to the production of proof. [57] The representative of the *ministère public* speaks last, after the argument by counsel for the parties. [58] He may also file written papers (*conclusions*) in which he suggests a decision to the court.

Generally, it is discretionary with the *ministère public* whether to intervene in a proceeding. However, it has an obligation to do so whenever the court request its participation, [59] or, in certain cases, when a statute specifically so provides. The latter cases include all actions concerning personal status (divorce, guardianship matters, and related cases), proceedings to obtain a declaration of presumed death, matters involving infants or incompetents, matters concerning charitable bequests, matters concerning the state or other public bodies, actions involving the personal liability of judges, cases involving attacks upon the competence of courts, and all cases in the highest French court, the *Cour de Cassation.* [60]

In most of the less important cases (including practically all divorce and separation cases), the representatives of the *ministère public* usually limit their participation to the statement that they rely on the wisdom of the court. [61]

The *ministère public* has no right of appeal when it acts as a *partie jointe.* [62]

[56] CODE DE PROCÉDURE CIVILE art. 83(8).

[57] GOYET, *op. cit. supra* note 49, at 24.

[58] CUCHE & VINCENT 156. While the representative of the *ministère public* may not raise issues not raised by the parties, he may make his own independent arguments concerning the issues that have been properly raised.

[59] CODE DE PROCÉDURE CIVILE art. 83(8).

[60] CODE DE PROCÉDURE CIVILE art. 83. CUCHE & VINCENT 156–58. In these cases, the parties must transmit (*communiquer*) their files to the *ministère public* three days before the hearing (a rule frequently not observed). Hence, these cases are usually called cases that are *communicables.*

[61] CORNU & FOYER 336.

[62] CUCHE & VINCENT 155. However, in certain cases, the *ministère public* may lodge a *pourvoi* in the *Cour de Cassation,* although it is not a party. See 9.11, 9.15 *infra.*

### 3.10. The *Ministère Public* as *Partie Principale*

Although some French governmental agencies are represented in court by the *ministère public,* [63] the rôle of the *ministère public* in this area is limited. French governmental agencies are often represented in court by regular *avoués* and by other public officials, especially by an officer of the French Treasury called *agent judiciaire du trésor.* [64]

In a number of instances, the *ministère public* may bring civil actions in its own name, rather than as counsel for a governmental agency. [65] These actions include: (1) actions for the annulment of a void marriage; [66] (2) adoption proceedings; (3) proceedings concerning the custody of infants; [67] (4) actions to deprive a parent of his parental authority; [68] (5) actions to correct official birth, death, and marriage records;[69] (6) in the absense of close relatives, proceedings to have an insane person adjudicated an incompetent; [70] (7) actions in certain cases involving testamentary dispositions in the nature of future interests; [71] and (8) all actions for a declaratory judgment that a party is, or is not, a French national. [72]

A statute enacted in 1810 provides that the *ministère public* shall "...watch over the execution of laws and judgments; in matters which concern the public interest (*ordre public*) it shall take steps to ensure their proper execution." [73] Since the same statute also provides that the *ministère public* must act *ex officio* in the cases provided by statute, a controversy has arisen whether the *ministère public* may bring civil suits only in the cases mentioned in the preceding paragraph, or whether

[63] MOREL 152.

[64] See generally ROSSIGNOL, LA REPRÉSENTATION DE L'ÉTAT DEVANT LES TRIBUNAUX JUDICIAIRES (1952).

[65] The *ministère public* does so infrequently. CORNU & FOYER 338. However, the *ministère public* will act if necessary to defend the rights of persons who cannot adequately represent themselves and also in cases involving strong public policy.

[66] CODE CIVIL arts. 184, 191. Since the main purpose of the action brought by the *ministère public* is to terminate a relationship which created a public scandal, its right to sue terminates with the death of one of the spouses, even though the death of a spouse does not ordinarily terminate the right to demand an annulment. CODE CIVIL art. 109; 1 COLIN & CAPITANT 224.

[67] CODE CIVIL 353 (adoption; here the *ministère public* acts at the request of the adopting parents and in essence, to save counsel fees); CODE CIVIL art. 302 (custody in divorce cases).

[68] Law of July 24, 1889, J.O. July 25, 1889, [1889] D. 4.15, as modified by Law of November 15, 1921, J.O. Nov. 15, 1921, [1921] B.L.D. 624, art. 3.

[69] CODE CIVIL art. 99. In addition, the *ministère public* supervises the public officials who keep birth, death, and marriage records.

[70] CODE CIVIL art. 491. In the case of dangerous lunatics, the *ministère public* may even act when there are relatives capable of bringing the proceedings.

[71] CODE CIVIL art. 1057.

[72] ORDONNANCE of October 19, 1945 (Code of French Nationality) J.O. Oct. 20, 1945, p. 6700, arts. 129, 130.

[73] Law of April 20, 1810, 12 BULLETIN ANNOTÉ DES LOIS 3 (1836).

it may sue whenever in its judgment the public interest requires such action. [74] The case law has gone through various phases. The more recent cases authorize the *ministère public* to bring a civil action in its own name, even in the absence of direct statutory authority, if the public interest is *directly* involved. [75]

The members of the *ministère public* may act in courts which have no *ministère public*, such as the commercial courts. [76] In cases in which the *ministère public* acts as a party or as counsel for a party, it is not bound by the restrictions imposed upon it when it acts as *partie jointe*. [77] Specifically, it may appeal an adverse decision. [78] However, it may never be ordered to pay costs.[79]

## 3. THE *MAGISTRATS*

### 3.11. Introductory Remarks

In France, the career of a *magistrat*, a denomination commonly given to both members of the judiciary and members of the *ministère public*, is begun at a comparatively young age and usually offers a rather unattractive position in the beginning. Selection and promotion under such a system create serious problems.

In the past, it had been argued that the French system of judicial selection and promotion put too much emphasis on examinations that tested the candidates' power to reason logically rather than on their judgment and experience and failed to avoid political influence. [80] In December 1958, pursuant to powers granted earlier that year, [81] the French government decreed a sweeping reform in the method of judicial selection.

[74] See, *e.g.*, MOREL 153–54.

[75] The cases are reviewed in CORNU & FOYER 337–39. See also Ministère public c. Soc. d'armement maritime et de transports, Cour Paris, March 5, 1956, [1956] D.J. 632 (*ministère public* may sue to compel reconversion of office building into apartment building; due to war-caused damages, housing matters are affected with public interest); Procureur général près la cour de Douai c. Epoux Cheval-Tomaxzyk, Cass. Civ., March 29, 1955, [1955] D.J. 429 (*ministère public* may not bring filiation proceeding when parties do not want to do so).

[76] CUCHE & VINCENT 161.

[77] CODE DE PROCÉDURE CIVILE art. 381.

[78] *E.g.*, CUCHE & VINCENT 155–56.

[7] *Id.* at 156. Ordinarily, the losing party is responsible for costs, CODE DE PROCÉDURE CIVILE art. 130.

[80] See the two articles by Bacon, *supra* note 42.

[81] Constitution of 1958, art. 92 (authorizing the government for limited period of time to enact laws having the force of statutes by action of the Council of Ministers, taken with the advice of the *Conseil d'Etat*).

### 3.12. Prerequisites for Appointment

The 1958 legislation followed earlier models by providing substantially similar methods of selection for all *magistrats,* whether judges or members of the *ministère public,* but it brought innovation by creating a special institute, the *Centre National d'Etudes Judiciaires* (National Center of Judicial Studies) for the training of future *magistrats.* [82] Subject to a few exceptions, all persons wishing to obtain a position as *magistrat* must now pass through the *Centre.*

To be admitted to the *Centre,* one must have the degree of *licencié* in law from a French university. Thus, candidates for positions in the judiciary and in the *ministère public* have the same educational background as *avocats.* During their last two years at the university, law students who contemplate a judicial career can obtain special scholarships. Candidates for admission to the *Centre* must be French nationals and in good health. [83] They must also pass a competitive examination [84] held annually. [85] This examination is reputed to be quite difficult. About 60 candidates are admitted to the *Centre* each year out of a total of three to four times that many applicants.

Persons holding the degree of doctor of laws who have been assistants at the faculty of law of a university for two years, or *avocats, avoués,*

[82] Ordinance No. 58–1270, *supra* note 53, art. 14. Concerning the organization of the Institute, which is under the control of the Minister of Justice, see Ordinance No. 59–77 of Jan. 7, 1959, J.O. Jan. 8, 1959, p. 563, [1959] B.L.D. 378 and Decree No. 59–83 of January 7, 1959, J.O. Jan. 8, 1959, p. 567, [1959] B.L.D. 380. Before the 1958 reforms the original appointment to a position as *magistrat* was dependent upon the passing of a competitive examination.

[83] Ordinance No. 58–1270, *supra* note 53, art. 16. Candidates must have been French nationals for at least five years. Under certain circumstances foreign nationals may be admitted as students, but they can never receive an appointment in the French judicial system. Women can be candidates for admission to the Center for Judicial Studies as well as for judicial positions generally.

[84] Ordinance No. 58–1270, *supra* note 53, arts. 15, 22. The text of the ordinance relating to the examination was implemented by a number of regulations, reprinted in a brochure, CENTRE NATIONAL D'ETUDES JUDICIAIRES, L'ACCÈS À LA MAGISTRATURE 75–100 (1962). To help students prepare for the examination, special *Instituts d'Etudes Judiciaires* have been created at the French law faculties; however, attendance at these institutes is not compulsory for students who wish to take the entrance examination for the *Centre National d'Etudes Judiciaires.*

[85] The examination consists of a written and an oral part; the written part involves a long essay on a topic of general cultural interest (sample question; "The individual and the state at the beginning of the 19th century and to-day"); an essay on a topic involving private law (sample question: "Legal transactions of insane persons"); an essay on a criminal or public law topic (sample question: "The criminal responsibility of corporations"); and a translation from a foreign language. The oral examination consists of an interrogation of the candidate by the examiners in which his general legal knowledge is tested; in addition, the candidate receives a short excerpt from some author dealing with a topic of general cultural interest on which he must present a 10 minute speech after a brief preparation and then discuss his text with the examiners (sample authors used: Raymond Aron, Blaise Pascal, Simone Weil). See CENTRE NATIONAL D'ETUDES JUDICIAIRES, *op. cit. supra* note 84, at 58–64.

notaries or *greffiers* (court clerks) for three years, may be admitted to the institute without competitive examination. The same is true of civil servants with the degree of *licencié en droit* who have unusual experience in the legal or economic field. The number of candidates admitted to the institute without competitive examination ordinarily may not exceed one-sixth of the number admitted after examination. [86] Candidates admitted to the Institute are called *auditeurs de justice* (auditors of justice) and must take an oath of office. [87] While they are in training, they receive a salary. [88] They must promise to remain in public service for at least ten years if they receive an appointment at the end of their training period. [89]

The training period of the auditors is divided into three parts of one year each. During the first year the auditors are in turn legal assistants for regular judges, the *ministère public*, children's court judges, and *juges d'instruction* (investigating magistrates) in various places outside Paris, but always away from their home town. [90]

During the second year, in Bordeaux, the auditors attend a program of courses, seminars, and special lectures designed to broaden their general cultural horizon, to increase their legal knowledge, and to provide information about non-legal matters, such as legal medicine and accounting, with which they may have to deal during their career. For their third year of studies, the auditors move to Paris and are assigned duties at the courts mainly to familiarize themselves with the special problems existing in large metropolitan centers. [91]

At the end of their training period, the auditors are graded according to their achievements. They can then choose positions among the openings for *magistrats* of the lowest rank, but the choice must be made by them in the order of their class standing. Thus, the best students can choose the more desirable positions. The formal appointment is made by the President of the Republic, on the proposal of the Minister of

[86] Ordinance No. 58–1270, *supra* note 53, arts. 15, 22. The study period of persons admitted without examination because of their prior experience is shortened by one third (art. 24).

[87] Ordinance No. 58–1270, *supra* note 53, art. 20.

[88] At present (1962), the salary is 662 F. (about $132,40) per month during the first two years, and about 740 F. ($148) during the last year. During the first and third year, they may receive an additional allowance as compensation for the fact that they must live away from home.

[89] Ordinance No. 58–1270, *supra* note 53, art. 18; Decree No. 59–83, *supra* note 82, art. 32.

[90] Ordinance No. 58–1270, *supra* note 53, art. 20.

[91] Ordinance No. 58–1270, *supra* note 53, art. 21. For a more detailed description of the studies of the *auditeurs*, see CENTRE NATIONAL D'ETUDES JUDICIAIRES, *op. cit. supra* note 84, at 65–70 (listing all the courses and special lectures); Loignon & Valon, *Le Centre National d'Etudes Judiciaires*, LE POUVOIR JUDICIAIRE 6 (Febr. 1962).

Justice. [92] The newly appointed *magistrats,* whether judges or members of the *ministère public,* must take an oath of office before being solemnly installed in their new positions. [93]

Auditors who do not qualify for an appointment as a *magistrat* may be given positions as *attachés de justice* (legal assistants). [94]

At present, the *Centre National d'Etudes Judiciaires* graduates about 60 students per year. This is almost, but not quite, equal to the number of openings created each year by retirement, death, and similar circumstances. [95]

Persons having received an appointment as *magistrats* may not hold other public offices. They need special permission to exercize any private professional or salaried occupation, but may engage in scholarly, literary, or artistic activities. [96] There are even restrictions on the activities of the spouses of *magistrats.* [97] The *magistrats* are usually required to live in the city in which the court to which they are attached sits.

### 3.13. Classification

For purposes of promotion, all positions open to *magistrats* in France have been grouped in 5 classes in the following somewhat illogical manner (listing the classes from the lowest to the highest): first group of the second degree; second group of the second degree; first group of the first degree; second group of the first degree; unclassified service. [98]

[92] Ordinance No. 58–1270, *supra* note 53, art. 26.

[93] Ordinance No. 58–1270, *supra* note 53, art. 6.

[94] These legal assistants (*attachés de justice*) may be assigned to a court to perform administrative functions or to do legal research. See Decree No. 59–84 of January 7, 1959, J.O. Jan. 8, 1959, p. 569, [1959] B.L.D. 385.

[95] The remaining positions are apparently filled with *magistrats* returning from the former colonies and appointments of outsiders. Until 1958, there was a serious personnel crisis, because far too few young persons wanted a career as *magistrat,* but this situation has been largely remedied since the 1958 reforms. The responsible French officials seem quite pleased with the quality of the students at the *Centre National d'Etudes Judiciaires.*

[96] Ordinance No. 58–1270, *supra* note 53, arts. 8–9.

[97] Ordinance No. 58–1270, *supra* note 53, art. 9 (wife of a magistrat may not be a member of the French legislature).

[98] Ordinance No. 58–1270, *supra* note 53, as amended by Organic Law No. 63–805 of Aug. 6, 1963, J.O. Aug. 8, 1963, p. 7347, [1963] D.L. 265, arts. 2–3; DÉCRET No. 58–1277 of December 22, 1958, J.O. Dec. 23, 1958, p. 11560, [1959] B.L.D. 29, arts. 1–3. The DÉCRET has received numerous, though minor, modifications. For a list of amendments see DALLOZ, RÉPERTOIRE DE PROCÉDURE CIVILE ET COMMERCIALE, *Juge,* at No. 2 (Supp. 1964).

Classification of the various positions in the French judiciary and in the *ministère public* (within each group the positions are listed in an arbitrary fashion):

Second Degree

First Group

Judge of the *tribunal d'instance*

Judge of the *tribunal de grande instance* (outside Paris)

Most of the rules regarding the promotion of *magistrats* are inapplicable to positions in the unclassified service. Positions with higher courts are in a higher category than positions in lower courts, and the presiding judge of a court is usually ranked one category higher than the associate judges. Positions with courts in Paris are graded higher than corresponding positions elsewhere. Judicial positions are classified together with positions in the *ministère public*, so that a person holding a judicial position may obtain promotion to a position in the *ministère public* and vice versa. [99]

### 3.14. Promotion

To reduce political influence in the promotion of all *magistrats*, a *Commission d'Avancement* (promotion commission) has been established. It consists of the *Premier Président* of the *Cour de Cassation*, who is the chairman of the commission, three *magistrats*, appointed by the Minister of Justice from a list of at least six *magistrats* (half of whom must be judges) submitted to him by the *Cour de Cassation*, and of high officials in the Ministry of Justice. [100] The commission compiles annual

Children's judge (*juge des enfants*)
*Substitut* of the *procureur de la République* (outside Paris)
Second Group
Judge of the *tribunal de grande instance* (Paris)
Children's Court judge in Paris
*Substitut* of the *procureur de la République* in Paris
President of a *tribunal de grande instance* (outside Paris)
*Procureur de la République* (outside Paris)

First Degree

First Group
Judge of a *cour d'appel*
*Substitut général* at a *cour d'appel*
Second Group
Judge at the *cour d'appel* in Paris
*Substitut général* at the *cour d'appel* in Paris
President of a *chambre* (panel) of a *cour d'appel*
*Avocat général* at a *cour d'appel*
*Vice président* of the *tribunal de grande instance* of the Seine (Paris)

Unclassified Service

All the *magistrats* of the *Cour de Cassation*
The Presidents and *procureurs généraux* of all the *cours d'appel*
The presidents of the *chambres* (panels) and *avocats généraux* of the *Cour d'Appel* of Paris
The President of the *Tribunal de grande instance* in Paris and its senior vice-presidents
The *Procureur de la République* of the *tribunal de grande instance* in Paris and his senior assistants

(This table has been adapted from Decree No. 58–1277 of Dec. 22, 1958, J.O. Dec. 23, 1958, p. 11560, [1959] B.D.L. 29, arts. 1–3, since amended in minor details. Some of the less important positions have been omitted).

[99] Generally, there seem to be somewhat more promotions from positions in the *ministère public* to judicial positions (35 versus 47 in 1961) than vice versa. Pinelli, *Une année de mouvements judiciaires*, POUVOIR JUDICIAIRE 8 (Feb. 1962).

[100] Ordinance No. 58–1270, *supra* note 53, arts. 34–35.

lists of *magistrats* qualified to be promoted from a position in the first group of the second degree to the second group of the second degree, and from the second degree to the first degree. [101] Promotion requires a certain amount of seniority in each category, usually two years. In its work, the promotion commission is guided mainly by annual reports prepared by the *premiers présidents* and by the *procureurs généraux* of the *cours d'appel* concerning the work of the judges and members of the *ministère public* in their respective areas. [102]

There are no promotion lists for appointments in the unclassified service; the government may choose its appointees from among *magistrats*, officials of the Ministry of Justice, law teachers, certain attorneys, and others.

Appointments to the *Cour de Cassation* may be given only to persons who have, at some time, held the office of first president or president of a division, or *procureur* or *avocat général* of a *cour d'appel*, or *président* or senior vice-president or *procureur de la République* or senior assistant *procureur de la République* of the *Tribunal de Grande Instance* [103] of Paris.

Even in the four lower categories, one appointment in ten may be made outside the regular hierarchy of *magistrats*. These appointments may be given to members of the legal professions, public officials, or law teachers with a certain number of years' experience. [104] In actual practice, appointments of outsiders are not very frequent, and those that are made are regarded with a somewhat jaundiced eye by many career *magistrats*.

### 3.15. Special Rules for the Promotion of Judges

While the rules governing the promotion of members of the *ministère public* and of judges are substantially the same, there are some differences. A *magistrat* eligible for a position in the *ministère public* is appointed to that position by the President of the Republic acting on the suggestion of the Minister of Justice. [105] Except as to positions in the unclassified service, promotion may, of course, be given only to persons on the promotion lists.

A similar procedure is followed for most judicial appointments. How-

[101] Ordinance No. 58–1270, *supra* note 53, art. 36.

[102] Decree No. 58–1277, *supra* note 98, art. 4.

[103] Ordinance No. 58–1270, *supra* note 53, art. 40.

[104] Ordinance No. 58–1270, *supra* note 53, arts. 37–39; Decree No. 61–1093 of Sept. 29, 1961, J.O. Oct. 4, 1961, p. 9059, [1961] D.L. 315.

[105] Ordinance No. 58–1270, *supra* note 53, arts. 28, 38.

ever, suggestions for judicial appointments must be submitted to a special body, called *Conseil Supérieur de la Magistrature* (High Council on the Judiciary), created to preserve the independence of the judiciary.

The *Conseil Supérieur de la Magistrature* consists of eleven members. The President of the French Republic is its *ex officio* president, and the Minister of Justice its vice-president. In addition, it consists of two judges and an *avocat général* of the *Cour de Cassation,* three judges from other courts, a member of the *Conseil d'Etat,* and two members of the general public. [106] The members of the *Conseil Supérieur de la Magistrature* are appointed by the President of the French Republic. He must select the five judges and the *avocat général* from a list of twelve persons submitted to him by the *Cour de Cassation.* The members of the *Conseil d'Etat* must be chosen from a list of three submitted by the *Conseil d'Etat.*

Concerning most judicial appointments, the *Conseil Supérieur de la Magistrature* has merely the right to give advice. [107] However, for positions on the *Cour de Cassation* and for positions as *premier président* (presiding judge) of a *cour d'appel,* the *Conseil,* not the Minister of Justice, proposes the names of the appointees to the French President, and thus effectively controls the appointment. [108] For positions on the *Cour de Cassation,* the requirements as to prior experience must be observed.

### 3.16. Discipline

**a. Disciplinary proceedings against judges.** In the field of professional discipline, the differences between the judges and the members of the *ministère public* are more marked than elsewhere. To ensure judicial independence, the French Constitution has traditionally granted judges freedom from arbitrary dismissal. [109] Without his consent, a judge may not even be transferred to a similar or higher position than the one he is holding. [110] In cases of urgent need, judges may temporarily be

[106] Constitution of 1958, art. 65; Ordinance No. 58–1271 of December 22, 1958, J.O. Dec. 23, 1958, p. 11556, [1959] B.L.D. 23, arts. 1–4.

[107] Ordinance No. 58–1271, *supra* note 106, art. 12. The Council is entitled to make comments concerning the promotion lists; in advance of any Council meeting dealing with promotions, the Minister of Justice must submit the personal files of the candidates to the Council. The Council also has functions concerning petitions for executive clemency. See Decree No. 59–305 of February 19, 1959, J.O. Feb. 20, 1959, p. 2147, [1959] B.L.D. 595.

[108] Ordinance No. 58–1271, *supra* note 106, art. 12.

[109] Constitution of 1958, art. 64; CHATELAIN, LA NOUVELLE CONSTITUTION ET LE RÉGIME POLITIQUE DE LA FRANCE 137–41 (1959). The powers of the executive branch have been increased by the 1958 Constitution.

[110] Ordinance No. 58–1270, *supra* note 53, art. 4.

assigned to a different court, but such assigments are permissible only for brief periods of time.[111]

Disciplinary sanctions against judges may be decreed only by the *Conseil Supérieur de la Magistrature.* In disciplinary proceedings the Minister of Justice must act as the complaining party.

When the Council sits in a disciplinary matter, neither the French President nor the Minister of Justice may be present; the presiding judge of the *Cour de Cassation* acts as presiding officer. The accused judge and his counsel are entitled to examine the complete file of the case, and the judge is entitled to be heard.[112] If the judge is found guilty, a number of sanctions are available, including censure, transfer, downgrading, retirement, and dismissal with or without forfeiture of pension rights.[113] The decision of the Council can apparently not be reviewed by the *Conseil d'Etat.*[114]

Sanctions may be imposed not only for professional misconduct as such, or conduct unbecoming a judge, but also for concerted activity which may interfere with the administration of justice (strikes) and certain political activities, including "manifestations of hostility towards the ... form of government of the Republic."[115] Disciplinary proceedings against judges are very rare.

**b. Disciplinary proceedings against members of the *ministère public.*** Originally, the members of the *ministère public* could be removed from their positions at the will of the Minister of Justice. Some restraints on the Minister's freedom developed eventually.[116] Under the 1958 reform legislation, the Minister of Justice retains his diciplinary powers. However, he must submit complaints against members of the *ministère public* to a board composed of the *Procureur Général* at the *Cour de Cassation* and other high-ranking officials of the *ministère public.* This

[111] Decree No. 58–1281 of December 22, 1958, J.O. Dec. 23, 1958, p. 11572, [1959] B.L.D. 40, art. 15. The temporary transfer may not exceed two months, except that it may be extended to four months with the consent of the Minister of Justice. The transfer is to be made by the presiding judge of the *cour d'appel.*

[112] Ordinance No. 58–1271, *supra* note 106, arts. 13–14; Ordinance No. 58–1270, *supra* note 53, arts. 49–58; Decree No. 59–305, *supra* note 107, arts .9–13.

[113] Ordinance No. 58–1270, *supra* note 53, arts. 45–46.

[114] Before the 1958 reforms, it was doubtful whether the *Conseil d'Etat* could review decisions by the *Conseil Supérieur de la Magistrature.* CORNU & FOYER 249. The 1958 reform legislation seems to exclude such review. See Ordinance No. 58–1270, *supra* note 53, art. 57, providing that the decisions of the *Conseil Supérieur de la Magistrature* shall not be subject to any review. *Cf.* GIVERDON ET LARGUIER, PROCÉDURE CIVILE, DROIT PÉNAL, PROCÉDURE PÉNALE 41 n. l. (1959).

[115] Ordinance No. 58–1270, *supra* note 53, arts. 10, 43.

[116] CORNU & FOYER 243–245.

board, after having investigated the matter and having given the accused an opportunity to be heard, suggests a penalty to the Minister of Justice.[117] The penalties that can be imposed are similar to those that may be imposed upon judges. If the Minister of Justice wishes to impose a more severe penalty than that suggested by the board, he must inform the board of his decision and request its renewed opinion on the matter.[118] The decision of the Minister is apparently reviewable by the *Conseil d'Etat*. The safeguards with which the disciplinary power of the Minister over the members of the *ministère public* is now surrounded suggest that the French government has become increasingly aware of the quasi-judicial nature of many of their functions. Two recent French authors have stated that the Ministry of Justice may be somewhat the Trojan horse of the executive branch in the judiciary.[119] This may not be as dangerous as it seems, since the main agents of the Ministry of Justice, the members of the *ministère public*, have achieved a fairly independent position.

### 3.17. Damage Suits against *Magistrats (Prise à Partie)*

Disciplinary sanctions are not the only means to enforce the professional obligations of *magistrats*. Serious violations of professional duties are criminal offenses.[120] Furthermore, judges as well as entire courts may be sued for damages on account of their official actions. To avoid burdening judges with numerous suits by disgruntled parties, the procedure for bringing suits of this nature, called *prise à partie*, has intentionally been made cumbersome.

A person desiring to sue a judge must first obtain leave from the *premier président* of the proper *cour d'appel*. The presiding judge must hear a representative of the *ministère public* before making a decision. Although denial of permission may be appealed to the *Cour de Cassation*, an unsuccessful appellant may be subjected to a fine.[121] Suit can be brought only in a limited number of cases, including fraud, intentional wrongful conduct or gross professional negligence on the part

[117] Ordinance No. 58–1270, *supra* note 53, arts. 59–65.

[118] Ordinance No. 58–1270, *supra* note 53, art. 66.

[119] CORNU & FOYER, MISE À JOUR 1960, at 3.

[120] Included are bribery, rendering a decision out of favor or hatred, denial of justice (*i.e.*, refusal to decide a case ripe for decision). CODE PÉNAL arts. 183, 185. Judges involved in criminal proceedings as defendants enjoy certain privileges as to the court before which they may be tried, CODE DE PROCÉDURE PÉNALE arts. 679–87.

[121] CODE DE PROCÉDURE CIVILE art. 510. The plaintiff must avoid all discourteous remarks against the defendant (art. 512).

of the judge or court, [122] and unreasonable delay in rendering a decision. [123] The proceedings must ordinarily be brought before a *cour d'appel*; but if a judge of a *cour d'appel* or a whole division (*chambre*) of such a court is the defendant, the proceeding must be brought before the *Cour de Cassation.* [124] No actions seem possible against the *Cour de Cassation* or one of its divisions. [125] The French state is liable for judgments rendered against judges, but retains a right of recovery over against them. [126] The *prise à partie* procedure is also available against members of the *ministère public* and certain officers involved in criminal investigations. [127]

### 3.18. Salaries

The salaries of judges and of members of the *ministère public* are based on a system inaugurated in 1946 for all public employees. Under this system, positions are assigned index numbers, the lowest paying position receiving the number 100. The index number indicates the salary for the position as a percentage of the lowest salary. Thus, a person holding a position rated 300 receives three times the minimum salary. [128] Some top positions are not included in this scheme (*positions hors échelle*).

An *auditeur de justice*, who has just been appointed judge or *substitut* in a *tribunal de grande instance*, receives a salary corresponding to the index 480, or F. 12.120 (about $2424) per annum, the number 100 corresponding in 1962 to a salary of F. 2.525 per annum. As long as he holds a position within the second degree, his salary is automatically raised from time to time, generally by 75 index points, which correspond at present to F. 1893 (about $379). Automatic raises ordinarily take place every four years as long as the *magistrat* occupies a position within the second degree; once he is promoted to a position in the higher (second) group, the automatic raises come every third year. [129]

[122] CODE DE PROCÉDURE CIVILE art. 505. Even a serious legal error is not necessarily gross negligence. *Cf.* VIZIOZ, ETUDES DE PROCÉDURE 301–05 (1956).

[123] CODE DE PROCÉDURE CIVILE arts. 506–08.

[124] CODE DE PROCÉDURE CIVILE art. 509.

[125] MOREL 145.

[126] CODE DE PROCÉDURE CIVILE art. 505.

[127] MOREL 145.

[128] WALINE, DROIT ADMINISTRATIF 775 (7th ed. 1957).

[129] See DÉCRET No. 58–1278 of Dec. 22, 1958, J.O. Dec. 23, 1958, p. 11570, and the accompanying ARRÊTÉ of the Minister of Justice in CENTRE NATIONAL D'ETUDES JUDICIAIRES, *op. cit. supra* note 84, at 39–42 (with detailed tables). The first increase comes 18 months after nomination; the second, two years and six months thereafter. Thus, a young *magistrat* who has served four years will receive an annual salary of (excluding fringe benefits) about F. 15.150 ($3.030); at that time, he is probably about 30–32 years old.

If a *magistrat* is promoted from the second grade to the first grade, he receives a salary indexed 750, or F. 18.937 (about $3787) with the same periodic increases thereafter, which, however, come more rapidly: every three years as long as he is in the lower group, and every two years if he is in the higher group.

Salaries, including those for positions *hors échelle*, do not go beyond about $12.000 per annum.

In practice, the financial position of the French *magistrat* is improved by a number of fringe benefits. Thus, he receives a family allowance, which includes a modest flat sum (F. 80 to F. 160 ($16 – $32)) per child per annum, and a salary increment of 3 to 5 per cent of the base salary for each child beyond the first one. [130] There are additional allowances (*indemnité de fonctions* and *indemnité de résidence*), which depend on the position held and the place where the *magistrat* lives and may increase the base salary by another 10 to 25 percent. Certain high judges also receive a representation allowance: The presiding judge of the *tribunal de grande instance* in Paris and the presiding judges of the *cours d'appel* in the provinces receive about F. 1.200 ($240). [131]

A small deduction (6% plus a flat F. 17.50) is made from all judicial salaries for retirement and social security purposes.

Retired judges receive pension benefits, which amount to about 50–60% of their last salary before retirement, the exact percentage depending on the length of service. Retirement may be demanded by a *magistrat* after he has reached the age of sixty. Retirement is mandatory at the age of sixty-eight for all *magistrats* in the second group, and at the age of seventy for all others. Special provisions for the granting of premature retirement benefits were made for judges whose position was abolished by the reform of 1958. [132] Provisions for sick leave with pay are liberal. [133]

### 3.19. Social Position of Judges

The judiciary in France holds a respected position. Accusations of partiality or political motivation are most rare.

On the other hand, it is quite difficult for a French judge to attain

[130] WALINE *op. cit. supra* note 128, at 776; CENTRE NATIONAL D'ETUDES JUDICIAIRES, *op. cit. supra* note 84, at 42.

[131] DÉCRET No. 58–1280 of Dec. 22, 1958, J.O. Dec. 23, 1958, p. 11571; DÉCRET No. 58–1279 of Dec. 22, 1958, J.O. Dec. 23, 1958, p. 11571 (*indemnité de fonction*). The purpose of these benefits is apparently to adjust salaries to variations of the cost of living in France and to compensate for not otherwise reimbursable expenses occasioned by official duties.

[132] WALINE, *op. cit. supra* note 128, at 789–90.

[133] *Id.* at 775.

personal fame. The principle that cases are decided by a panel without dissenting opinions and the tradition of making opinions brief and casting them in a standard style make it virtually impossible for an individual judge to put his personal stamp on his decisions. [134]

### 3.20. Supervision by the Ministry of Justice

The Ministry of Justice supervises the functioning of the French court system quite closely, and collects pertinent data and reports. Thus, the clerks of the courts must file various periodic and detailed reports concerning the status of the court calendar, types of litigation handled, and similar matters. [135] Copies of the orders of the presiding judges regulating the internal administration of the courts must also be filed. There is even a requirement that the minutes of the first court session after the end of the vacation period (July 15 – September 15) be transmitted to the Ministry of Justice. These minutes list the names of the judges who are present and of those who are absent, [136] so that the Ministry knows what judges have not returned from their vacations on time. In addition, the presiding judges of the twenty-seven *cours d'appel* in France must annually inspect the courts within their district and report their findings to the Minister of Justice. A similar inspection and report must be made by the *procureur général* at the seat of each *cour d'appel* concerning the work of his subordinates. The Minister of Justice may also appoint a special commission consisting of one or more *magistrats* or of high officials of the Ministry of Justice to inspect the courts generally or to investigate specific matters. [137] The reports filed with the Ministry of Justice are quite important in connection with its functions concerning the appointment and promotion of judges. They

[134] Some French courts, especially those in Paris, have a very large staff. In 1962, the *Cour d'Appel* in Paris has 165 judges; the *Tribunal de Grande Instance* in Paris about 250 judges. The total number of all French *magistrats*, including the *ministère public*, was 3737 in 1955, of which 212 were women. POUVOIR JUDICIAIRE, June 1955.

[135] DÉCRET of November 28, 1900, J.O. Nov. 30, 1900, [1900] D. 4, 79, as modified by the DÉCRETS of May 13, 1948, J.O. June 3, 1948, p. 5321, [1948] D.L. 213; September 23, 1949, J.O. Sept. 24, 1948, p. 9522, [1949] D.L. 407; and June 28, 1952, J.O. June 29, 1952, p. 6492, [1952] D.L. 221. Actually, these reports must be sent to the *procureur général* of the appropriate *cour d'appel*, who sends all the reports collected by him, together with his comments, to the Ministry of Justice.

[136] DÉCRET of July 4, 1885, J.O. July 5, 1885, [1886] D. 4. 7.

[137] DÉCRET No. 58–1281 of December 22, 1958, J.O. Dec. 23, 1958, p. 11572, [1959] B.L.D. 40, as amended by DÉCRET No. 63–582 of Aug. 13, 1963, J.O. Aug. 22, 1963, p. 7738, [1963] D.L. 279, arts. 17–18. See also DÉCRET No. 58–1290 of December 22, 1958, J.O. Dec. 23, 1958, p. 11613, [1959] B.L.D. 66. (Minister of Justice must appoint two *magistrats* of the *Cour de Cassation* each year to inspect courts). The inspection functions of the Ministry of Justice are under the control of an inspector general of the judicial services. DÉCRET No. 64–754, *supra* note 42, art. 8.

may also induce the Ministry to begin disciplinary proceedings or, in appropriate cases, to give warnings to judges.[138]

### 3.21. The *Conseil de l'Organisation Judiciaire*

Since the Ministry of Justice supervises the French court system closely and collects numerous data as to its operation, it is in a position to suggest remedial action if this seems appropriate. New legislation concerning the courts is traditionally proposed to the French parliament by the Ministry of Justice. In addition, the 1958 Constitution has authorized the cabinet to issue *décrets* (decrees) in the field of civil procedure and to some extent also in the field of court organization.[139] So that the views of all persons affected by reform projects may be heard, the 1958 legislation has provided for the creation of a *Conseil de l'Organisation Judiciaire* (Council on Judicial Organization). The Council is presided by the Minister of Justice; in addition, it consists of the *Premier Président* (presiding judge) of the *Cour de Cassation,* the *Procureur Général* at that court, and other representatives of the judiciary and the *ministère public.* It also includes a representative of the *Conseil d'Etat* and of the *Cour des Comptes* as well as high officials in the Ministry of Justice.[140] The Council may be consulted on all questions concerning judicial organization; it must be consulted concerning all reform projects involving the establishment of a new *cour d'appel* or a new *tribunal de grande instance,* or the discontinuation of such a court. It must also be consulted, if the creation of new (specialized) courts will affect the subject matter competence of the *cours d'appels, tribunaux de grande instance,* and *tribunaux d'instance.* The Council may request professional organizations and other interested parties to state their opinion on any reform project which it has under discussion.[141] It remains to be seen whether the creation of the Council will prevent the introduction of new reforms in the abrupt manner in which the 1958 legislation was enacted.

[138] Ordinance No. 58–1270, *supra* note 53, art. 44.

[139] By virtue of articles 34 and 37 of the 1958 Constitution, legislation is necessary to create new court systems or to modify the status of the *magistrats.* However, other matters, such as civil procedure and the geographical distribution of the courts can be regulated by *décret* (administrative regulation). *Cf.* Ordinance No. 58–1273 of December 22, 1958, J.O. Dec. 23, 1958, p. 11557, [1959] B.L.D. 25, art. 2. The geographical distribution of courts of first instance, the number of panels they are to have, and the size of their staff are to be determined by *décret.*

[140] DÉCRET No. 58–1281, supra note 137, art. 9. The *Cour des Comptes* deals with matters of public finance. See Kock, *The Machinery of Law Administration in France,* 108 U. PA. L. REV. 366, 378 (1960).

[141] DÉCRET No. 58–1281, *supra* note 137, art. 10. According to art. 12 of the DÉCRET, the Council must hold at least one meeting a year; it meets at the Ministry of Justice.

## 4. THE REGULAR COURTS

### 3.22. The Principle of the Unity of Criminal and Civil Courts

Ordinarily, civil and criminal cases are handled by the same courts. French authors describe this phenomenon as the "principle of the unity of criminal and civil courts." [142] It should be noted, however, that French courts usually have a large number of judges who sit in separate *chambres* (divisions), each of which handles special types of cases and that criminal cases are brought before the criminal divisions. The regular court of first instance, the *tribunal de grande instance,* is usually referred to as *tribunal correctionnel* when it sits as a criminal court, whether or not it has a separate division for criminal cases. The *tribunal d'instance* is ordinarily composed of only one judge, who handles both civil and criminal cases. When it sits as a criminal court, the *tribunal d'instance* is called *tribunal de police.* [143]

There is some rotation among the judges of the various divisions of a court; thus, the judges of the criminal division are not all specialists in criminal law.

One court in the regular French court system, the *Cour d'Assises,* has exclusively criminal competence. It handles the most serious crimes after they have been referred to it by a division of the *cour d'appel,* called *chambre d'accusations,* which has functions somewhat analogous to those of a grand jury. The *Cour d'Assises* is composed of three professional judges and nine lay jurors. The presiding judge must be a judge of a *cour d'appel.* [144] All questions of law and fact are decided jointly by the lay and the professional judges.

A court with competence predominantly, but not exclusively, in the criminal field is the children's court. Children's courts have been established at the seat of certain *tribunaux de grande instance.* [145] The presiding judge of the children's court is a judge of the *tribunal de*

[142] MOREL 83–84; CORNU & FOYER 85; *cf.* Garner, *The French Judiciary,* 26 YALE L. J. 349, 350 (1917).

[143] Before the 1958 reforms, the *tribunal de police* was called *tribunal de simple police.* In a few cities, there is a *tribunal de police* separate from the *tribunal d'instance.* See generally Kock, *Criminal Proceedings in France,* 9 AM. J. COMP. L. 262 (1960).

[144] CODE DE PROCÉDURE PÉNALE arts. 191–230; 231–54. Among the other criminal courts which might be mentioned, is the *Haute Cour de Justice,* which must deal with crimes committed by the President of France or members of the cabinet in the course of their official functions (Constitution of 1958, arts. 67–68), the courts martial (see COSTA, LES INSTITUTIONS JUDICIAIRES 230–32 (1959)), and the special court created in 1963 to deal with crimes against national security (see Law No. 63–22 of Jan. 15, 1963, J.O. Jan. 16, 1963, p. 507, [1963] D.L. 48).

[145] ORDONNANCE No. 58–1274 of Dec. 22, 1958, J.O. Dec. 23, 1958, p. 11559, [1959] B.L.D. 26.

*grande instance,* called *juge des enfants* (children's judge). In addition, the court is composed of two lay assessors appointed by the Minister of Justice. [146] As assessors, the Minister must select persons who have shown an outstanding interest in the welfare of children. [147] The children's judge may hear simpler cases sitting alone; more serious matters must be brought before the children's court as a whole. [148]

### 3.23. Civil Cases in Criminal Courts

In cases in which a crime also constitutes a civil wrong, such as cases involving criminal negligence or assault, the person wronged may become a party to the criminal proceedings brought by the public prosecutor. [149] The court, simultaneously with passing sentence on the defendant, may also award damages to the injured party. [150] Even if the victim prefers to bring his action in the civil court, the criminal proceedings will have some influence on the civil case. If a crime also amounts to a civil wrong, the much shorter period applicable to criminal prosecutions, rather than the thirty year statute of limitations generally applicable to torts in France, [151] applies in the civil case. [152] If criminal proceedings are started after the civil action has been begun, the civil action must be stayed until a decision has been rendered in the criminal case. [153] Finally, the decision in the criminal case is *res judicata* in the civil action. [154]

[146] ORDONNANCE No. 58–1274, *supra* note 145, art. 5.

[147] ORDONNANCE No. 58–1274, *supra* note 145, art. 5.

[148] See COSTA, LES INSTITUTIONS JUDICIAIRES 229–30 (1959).

[149] CODE DE PROCÉDURE PÉNALE art. 3.

[150] 1 DALLOZ, RÉPERTOIRE PRATIQUE, *Action Civile* (1910). As a rule, the plaintiff may not pursue his remedy both in the civil and in the criminal courts. CODE DE PROCÉDURE PÉNALE art. 5.

[151] CODE CIVIL art. 2262.

[152] CODE DE PROCÉDURE PÉNALE art. 10. The application of this principle may cause difficulties when it is not certain whether the defendant's actions amount to a crime. See, *e.g.*, Lecasse v. Pentaux, Jan. 22, 1935, Cass. Civ., [1935] D. 1. 41; Putinier v. Donabedian, July 23, 1934, *ibid.* (thirty year, not shorter, limitation applicable to damage action in criminal prosecution for traffic infraction). The cases show the courts' hostility to the rule. The following limitation periods are applicable in the case of torts based on crimes: 10 years when the crime is a felony (CODE DE PROCÉDURE PÉNALE art. 7); 3 years when the crime is a misdemeanor (CODE DE PROCÉDURE PÉNALE art. 8); 1 year when there is a mere infraction (CODE DE PROCÉDURE PÉNALE art. 9); three months for damages caused by various offenses committed by the public press, including criminal libel, and assorted violations of fish and game laws. See the statutes cited in 2 COLIN & CAPITANT 415.

[153] CODE DE PROCÉDURE PÉNALE art. 4.

[154] CORNU & FOYER 86. A criminal conviction is conclusive proof that the defendant committed the act involved. An acquittal is conclusive evidence that the defendant did not commit the act he was accused of. However, in a civil case he may still be held liable on some other basis. 1 JULLIOT DE LA MORANDIÈRE 333–36; Epoux Bessières v. Cie des voitures l'Abeille, July 29, 1924, Cass. Civ., [1925] D.I. 5 (automobilist acquitted on criminal negligence charge can be held liable in tort action on basis of rule providing for liability without fault).

### 3.24. The *Tribunal de Grande Instance*

The most important courts in France are the ordinary courts of first instance, which, since the 1958 reforms, are called *tribunaux de grande instance*. They replaced the old *tribunaux civils*, of which there were 353, one in each *arrondissement*. [155]

At present, there is a *tribunal de grande instance* in each of the 90 *départements* in France (including Corsica). Additional courts have been provided where the volume of litigation or transportation difficulties make this desirable. A heavier concentration of courts exists particularly in the highly industrialized and densely populated areas of northern France. [156] Although the department Seine, which comprised most of the Paris metropolitan area, was abolished, its *tribunal de grande instance*, which has 27 separate panels (*chambres*), [157] has thus far been retained. The total number of all *tribunaux de grande instance* is 172. [158] They handle a very large number of cases each year, and the intake of new cases exceeds the number of cases decided. In spite of the resulting backlog, the waiting period for an *audience* (hearing) usually does not exceed a few months, even in large metropolitan centers. [159]

**a. The staff.** The *tribunal de grande instance*, in accordance with French tradition, is a collegiate court; three judges must hear and de-

[155] Cornu & Foyer, Mise à jour 1960, 32; Ordinance No. 58–1273 of December 22, 1958, J.O. Dec. 23, 1958, p. 11557, [1959] B.L.D. 25, art. 2.

[156] There are 31 *départements* with 1 court, 41 with 2, 16 with 3, one with 4 (Pas de Calais), and one with 7 (Nord). For a complete list of all the courts in France, see Blanc, La Nouvelle Procédure Civile 181–233 (1959), reprinting the official tables from Decree No. 58–1286 of December 22, 1958, J.O. 23, 1958, p. 11582.

[157] Cornu & Foyer, Mise à jour 1960, 33.

[158] *Ibid.*

[159] Case load of the *tribunaux civils* (predecessors of the *tribunaux de grande instance*)* (in thousands):

| Year | New Cases | Pending cases | Decided |
|---|---|---|---|
| 1946 | 189.4 | 313.2 | 182.5 |
| 1947 | 162.4 | 292.6 | 171.0 |
| 1948 | 147.3 | 269.3 | 155.6 |
| 1949 | 137.7 | 251.7 | 148.8 |
| 1950 | 135.4 | 249.2 | 141.7 |
| 1951 | 131.2 | 239.3 | 138.8 |
| 1952 | 131.0 | 231.8 | 132.2 |
| 1953 | 130.8 | 230.3 | 128.7 |
| 1954 | 153.7 | 255.1 | 138.8 |
| 1955 | 144.5 | 261.9 | 146.8 |
| 1956 | 139.7 | 254.6 | 141.1 |
| 1957 | 141.0 | 255.4 | 137.9 |
| 1958 | 145.8 | 263.5 | 143.3 |

* Source: Annuaire statistique de la France Rétrospectif 80 (1961).

cide a case.[160] As a result, each *tribunal de grande instance* has at least three judges, one of whom is the presiding judge. The associate judges of the *tribunal de grande instance* belong to the lowest category of the judicial hierarchy, the first group of the second degree. The presiding judge (*président*) is one class above them.[161] Courts with a heavy case load may have additional personnel and are usually divided into panels (*chambres*), each of which deals with a specified class of cases.[162] If a panel has a heavy workload, the president of the court may assign some of its cases to a different panel.[163] Ordinarily, matters concerning the internal administration of each court are determined in a meeting of all the judges of the court.[164] However, the presiding judge decides annually how the various judges are to be allocated among the panels of the court.[165] A judge may sit in more than one panel.[166] The presiding judges of the panels are called *vice-présidents* of the court. At least one judge who previously sat in a particular panel must be returned to that panel when the annual reallocation of judges takes place.[167] A copy of the order by which the president of each court allocates the judges among the various panels must be transmitted to the Ministry of Justice.[168] The *procureur de la République* as representative of the *ministère public* is entitled to be heard concerning the allocation of judges.[169] Close relatives may not be members of the same court, although dispensation from this rule may be granted by government

[160] CUCHE & VINCENT 88, 94.

[161] Decree No. 58–1277 of December 22, 1958, J.O. Dec. 23, 1958, p. 11560, [1959] B.L.D. 29, art. 2.

[162] A court may be divided into several panels if it has five judges or more. CUCHE & VINCENT 95. Generally speaking, the most important and delicate cases are assigned to the first panel (*chambre*); ordinarily the most brilliant judges, who have the greatest chances for promotion, are assigned to the first, or other low-numbered panels. The chances for promotion of the judges assigned to the other panels are generally less good. This is also true of the *cours d'appel*. In Paris, the division of labor among the first five panels of the *tribunal de grande instance* is about as follows: 1st *chambre:* all suits involving judges, *avocats* as parties; filiation cases, others that are quite important on account of subject matter or parties involved; 2nd: succession cases; 3d: intellectual property (copyright, *etc.*); 4th: accidents; 5th: enforcement of judgments, including foreign judgments. This specialization helps the various panels achieve a considerable expertise.

[163] Law of August 18, 1810, art. 35, 12 BULLETIN ANNOTÉ DES LOIS 77 (1836).

[164] Half the judges of the court constitute a quorum. Law of April 11, 1838, art. 11, [1838] D. 3. 87.

[165] Law of August 14, 1943, J.O. Sept. 26, 1943, p. 2530, [1943] D. ANAL. L. 132, as modified by Law of March 15, 1955, J.O. March 16, 1955, p. 2680, [1955] D.L. 119.

[166] Law of August 14, 1943, *supra* note 165, art. 10.

[167] Law of August 14, 1943, *supra* note 165, art. 9. The rule presumably has as its purpos the avoidance of overspecialization in the judiciary, without sacrificing continuity of experience.

[168] Law of August 14, 1943, *supra* note 165, art. 11.

[169] Law of August 14, 1943, *supra* note 165, art. 5.

decree if the court is large enough so that the relatives can sit in different panels. [170]

Floorplan of *Tribunal de Grande Instance* courtroom

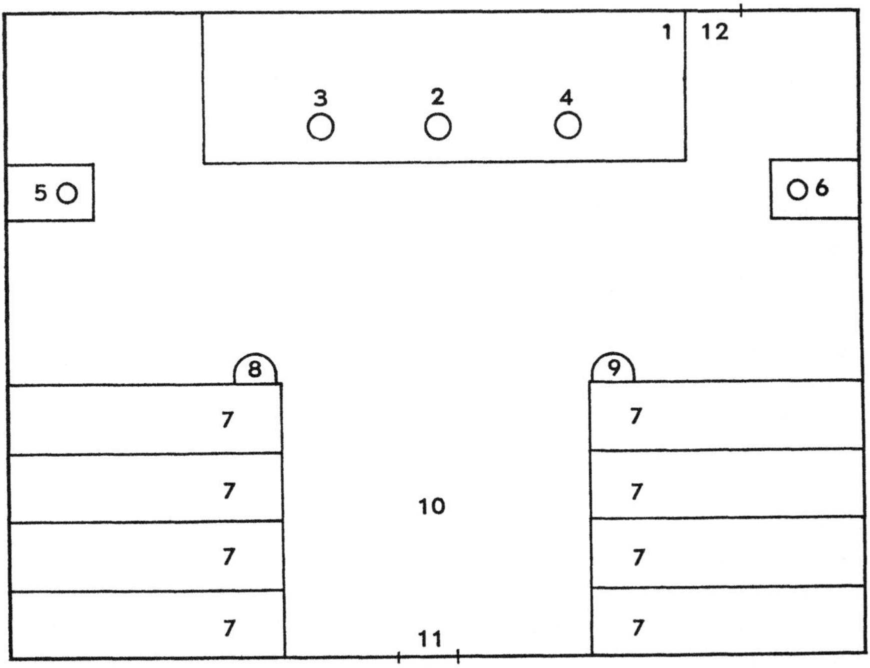


1. Elevated platform on which judges sit.
2. Chair for presiding judge (vice-president or president).
3–4. Chairs for associate judges.
5. Elevated platform on which chair for *greffier* (clerk) stands.
6. Elevated platform on which chair for *procureur de la République* or his *substitut* stands.
7. Benches on courtroom floor for counsel, parties, and spectators.
8–9. Seats and pulpits for the *avocats* arguing case (on courtroom floor).
10. Aisle.
11–12. Doors.

Details of floorplans vary somewhat depending on the space available and the age of the building. Sometimes, the platform of the judges is curved rather than straight; sometimes, there are no special places for the *avocats* arguing, who simply place themselves in the first row of the benches (7).

**b. The *ministère public*.** A representative of the *ministère public* is attached to each *tribunal de grande instance*. He has the title of *pro-*

[170] Ordinance No. 58–1281 of December 22, 1958, J.O. Dec. 23, 1958, p. 11572, [1959] B.L.D. 40, art. 13.

*cureur de la République* and may have a number of assistants, designated as *substituts*. The *procureur de la République* is equal in grade to the presiding judge of the court, and his assistants are equal in grade to the judges. [171]

**c. The clerk and court attendants.** The clerical work of the *tribunal de grande instance* is handled by an official, called *greffier* (clerk), and by his assistants. [172] The main income of the *greffier* is derived from the fees he collects from the public for the filing and certification of papers. [173]

Court attendants (*huissiers audienciers*) are selected annually by the court from among the *huissiers* practicing in the district. They call the calendar and maintain order in court. [174] In addition, uniformed guards and ushers police the court house, supply information to the public, and perform related functions.

## 3.25. The *Tribunaux d'Instance*

Next in importance to the *tribunal de grande instance* is the *tribunal d'instance*. In 1958, it became the successor of the abolished *juge de paix* (justice of the peace), [175] who handled – usually quite expeditiously – cases involving small claims. While there were over two thousand justice of the peace courts – usually one in each *canton* –, there are presently only 455 *tribunaux d'instance*, generally one per *arrondissement*, which may comprise ten or more *cantons*. [176]

The abolition of the old justice of the peace courts did not involve the abolition of their clerk's offices (*greffes*). They remain in existence

[171] See 3.07 *supra*.
[172] See 2.09.b *supra*.
[173] See 2.09.e *supra*.
[174] See 2.08.b *supra*.
[175] Ordinance No. 58–1273 of Dec. 22, 1958, J.O. Dec. 23, 1958, p. 11557, [1959] B.L.D. 25, arts. 1–2.
[176] Decree No. 58–1286, *supra* note 156.
Cases handled by the *juge de paix* courts (predecessors of the *tribunaux d'instance*) *
(in thousands):

| Year | Cases | Year | Cases |
|---|---|---|---|
| 1946 | 138.1. | 1953 | 146.2 |
| 1947 | 132.8 | 1954 | 147.8 |
| 1948 | 128.9 | 1955 | 154.0 |
| 1949 | 129.3 | 1956 | 157.5 |
| 1950 | 125.8 | 1957 | 157.5 |
| 1951 | 127.4 | 1958 | 159.3 |
| 1952 | 138.4 | | |

* Source: ANNUAIRE STATISTIQUE DE FRANCE RÉTROSPECTIF 80 (1961).

(at least temporarily) and function as additional clerk's offices for the new *tribunaux d'instance.* [177] Thus, it is possible to transact much of the clerical business of the new courts in all the places in which justice of the peace courts used to be located. In addition, clerk's offices may be created where geographical, economic, or social conditions make this desirable. [178]

The *tribunal d'instance* may also be authorized by the *premier président* (presiding judge) of the *cour d'appel* in the district of which it is located to hold court in places other than the municipality in which it has its seat. [179]

**a. The staff.** Cases brought before the *tribunal d'instance* are heard by one judge, not by a panel of judges, [180] and many *tribunaux d'instance,* especially in rural areas, are composed of only one judge. However, certain *tribunaux d'instance* in urban areas have two or more (up to a maximum of nine) judges.

If the court comprises more than two judges, one of them is appointed *directeur* of the court and has charge of its administrative affairs. If there are two judges, these duties are performed by the senior judge. [181] The old justices of the peace, while law trained, were not a part of the regular judicial hierarchy, and could not gain promotion to other courts. The judges of the *tribunal d'instance* are part of the ordinary hierarchy of *magistrats* and belong to the same category as the judges of the *tribunal de grande instance.* [182] However, presumably because the judges of the *tribunal d'instance* cannot benefit from the experience of colleagues sitting with them, a *magistrat* must have been a judge in a *tribunal de grande instance* for at least two years before he can be appointed to a *tribunal d'instance.* [183]

The clerical officials and attendants of the *tribunal d'instance* (*greffiers* and *huissiers*) occupy a position substantially similar to that of their counterparts before the *tribunal de grande instance.* While no

[177] Decree No. 58–1281 of December 22, 1958, J.O. Dec. 23, 1958, p. 11572, [1959] B.L.D. 40, art. 4; Decree No. 58–1282 of December 22, 1958, J.O. Dec. 23, 1958, p. 11574, [1949] B.L.D. 44, art. 3. The reason for these measures was only in part the convenience of the persons having business with the court; the government was also influenced by the fact that the *greffiers* had paid for their offices and was therefore unwilling to abolish these offices too abruptly. Unneeded *greffes* are to be abolished within ten years. Decree No. 58–1282, art. 5.

[178] Decree No. 58–1281, *supra* note 177, art. 4.

[179] Decree No. 58–1281, *supra* note 177, art. 5.

[180] Decree No. 58–1281, *supra* note 177, arts. 1, 3.

[181] Decree No. 58–1281, *supra* note 177, art. 3.

[182] *I.e.,* to the first group of the second degree, the lowest of the five categories. Decree No. 58–1277 of December 2, 1948, J.O. Dec. 28, 1958, p. 11560, [1959] B.L.D. 29, art. 2.

[183] Decree No. 58–1277, *supra* note 182, art. 5.

member of the *ministère public* is permanently attached to the *tribunal de grande instance*, the *procureur de la République* attached to the *tribunal de grande instance* in the area, or one of his assistants (*substituts*), may appear before it in any matter. [184]

### 3.26. The *Tribunaux de Commerce*

In the middle ages, non-maritime commerce was largely concencentrated at certain fairs. In France, those of the Champagne were particularly famous. Since these fairs lasted only for short periods of time, disputes between merchants attending the fairs had to be settled quickly. Because recourse to the ordinary courts with their slow procedures was impractical, courts, which were staffed by merchants and administered justice on the basis of the customs of the merchants, sprang up at the fairs. The customs of the merchants were quite similar throughout Europe, and there emerged a fairly uniform commercial law distinct from the ordinary civil law of the European countries.

In France, the commercial courts came to be called *tribunaux consulaires*, a name which is still used occasionally. Commercial law was largely codified in France by an *Ordonnance* of 1673. When the French court system was reorganized during the French revolution, the special courts for commercial matters were combined with the admiralty courts (*amirautés*) and renamed *tribunaux de commerce*. French commercial law was codified in the *Code de Commerce* of 1807. That code borrowed much from prior law, especially from the *Ordonnance* of 1673. A large amount of subsequent legislation in the commercial field remains outside the Commercial Code. The 1958 reform laws affected the commercial courts only slightly. [185]

There are about 230 commercial courts in France. [186] They are not set up according to a uniform scheme of territorial distribution, but are created by government decree in the cities where they are needed.[187]

[184] Ordinance No. 58–1273 of December 22, 1958, J.O. Dec. 28, 1958, p. 11557, [1959[ B.L.D. 25, art. 4.

[185] Concerning the history of the French commercial courts, see 1 LYON-CAEN & RENAULT, TRAITÉ DE DROIT COMMERCIAL 15–44 (5th ed. 1921); RIPERT, TRAITÉ ÉLÉMENTAIRE DE DROIT COMMERCIAL 9–19 (3d ed. 1954); *cf.* Fuller, *French Courts of Commerce*, 12 COLUM. L. REV. 145 (1912); Thayer, *Comparative Law and the Law Merchant*, 6 BROOKLYN L. REV. 139 (1936). In the *Départements* of Alsace-Lorraine, there are no commercial courts, only commercial panels of the regular civil courts, in which a professional judge sits with two lay assessors. RIPERT, *supra*, at 53.

[186] 1 ESCARRA, MANUEL DE DROIT COMMERCIAL 9–19, 52–55 (1947).

[187] CORNU & FOYER 218; Decree No. 59–348 of Feb. 27, 1959, J.O. March 1, 1959, p. 2534, [1959] B.L.D. 740, art. 2.

Their competence extends usually through one *arrondissement.* [188] Where there is no commercial court, commercial matters are brought before the *tribunal de grande instance.* [189]

**a. The judges and the staff.** The judges of the commercial courts are not law trained, but are businessmen elected – indirectly – by their peers. Each commercial court consists of one *président* (presiding judge), two or more associate judges, and a number of alternates. [190] Nobody can be elected associate judge unless he has first been an alternate, and nobody can be elected *président* of the court unless he has been an associate judge. [191] The *président* is elected for a term of three years, the judges for terms of two years, but the terms are staggered so that elections take place annually. There are some restrictions on the number of successive terms to which the members of the commercial courts can be elected. [192] The judges of the commercial courts do not receive pay, but election to the court is considered a considerable honor. [193]

The *président* and the judges of the commercial courts are elected by a small group of delegates, called *délégués consulaires.* [194] These in turn are elected annually by: (1) all businessmen or branch establishments registered in the commercial register of the appropriate commercial court, provided they fulfill certain conditions as to nationality and previous good conduct; they have one vote each, regardless of the size of their business; (2) all *sociétés commerciales,* including public corporations administered as commercial ventures rather than as governmental services and branch establishments; these may cast three votes each in the place where they are registered in the com-

[188] Unless there is more than one commercial court in the *arrondissement.* CORNU & FOYER 218.

[189] Decree No. 58–1283 of December 22, 1958, J.O. Dec. 23, 1958, p. 11578, [1959] B.L.D. 51, art. 1.

[190] See Decree No. 59–348, *supra* note 187, art. 2.

[191] The method of electing judges for the commercial courts was considerably revised in 1961 by Decree No. 61–923 of August 3, 1961, J.O. August 18, 1961, p. 7750, [1961] D.L. 277. This Decree abandoned the method of direct election of the judges of the commercial courts by the businessmen of the area. See 1 SOLUS & PERROT 565–66, 992. To be eligible as president, a judge must have been in office for three years, and an alternate must likewise have been in office for three years to be eligible as judge. Decree No. 61–923, art. 39.

[192] The president and the judges may be elected for three terms in a row; after that, they must wait for at least one year before becoming candidates again. Decree No. 61–923, *supra* note 191, art. 40.

[193] MOREL 107.

[194] Actually, the judges of the commercial courts are elected by the *délégués consulaires* to which are added the present and former judges of the commercial courts and the delegates of the chambers of commerce and industry. Decree No. 61–923, *supra* note 191, art. 29.

mercial register; (3) all harbour and river pilots as well as captains in the merchant marine and commercial aircraft pilots, who are actually in command of a ship or plane; they may cast one vote each; and (4) all present and former members of the commercial courts and delegates to the chambers of commerce who do not have voting rights on some other basis. [195] Candidates for judgeships must belong to one of the four classes just mentioned. They must be at least thirty years of age and have exercised their occupation for five years. Persons who have lost their right to vote due to retirement from business but are not actively exercizing any other occupation are still eligible as judges. [196] There are detailed regulations concerning the commission which must establish the voting lists and the conduct of the elections. At least three judges must sit in every commercial case. [197]

The clerical work of the commercial court is handled by a *greffier* and his assistants, whose functions are similar to those of the *greffier* of the *tribunal de grande instance*; in addition, he keeps the commercial register. [198] No representative of the *ministère public* is attached to the commercial courts, perhaps because justice is supposed to be rendered there not only for, but also by, businessmen.

Some French scholars have advocated abolition of the commercial courts, or at least the inclusion of one professional judge among the members of each tribunal, in order to give commercial litigants a greater guarantee that the decisions reached by the court will be in accordance with the rules of law. However, these suggestions have not made much headway, and businessmen generally seem to be quite satisfied with the manner in which the commercial courts in France handle their very considerable caseload. They apparently fear that the somewhat informal atmosphere of the commercial courts, which is conducive to the settlement of cases, may be lost by "professionalization" of these tribunals. [199]

[195] Decree No. 61–923, *supra* note 191, arts. 1, 4. The number of votes available to branch establishments depends on the number of their employees.

[196] Decree No. 61–923, *supra* note 191, art. 14.

[197] Decree No. 61–923, *supra* note 191, art. 41. The newly elected judges are presented to the *cour d'appel* or *tribunal de grande instance* of the area, and then officially installed in their offices each October 15th. Decree No. 61–923, *supra* note 191, art. 37.

[198] See 2.09 *supra*.

[199] Besides, many of the businessmen who sit as judges in the commercial courts are law trained. The commercial courts handled about 268.000 cases throughout France in 1945. This was about 100.000 more than the number of cases handled by the *tribunaux civils*. The commercial court in Paris alone handles about 24.000 cases annually. Concerning these statistics and the reform projects relating to the commercial courts, see 1 Solus & Perrot 557–61.

### 3.27. The *Conseils de Prud'Hommes*

Even in pre-revolutionary days, [200] there existed specialized courts that dealt with disputes between employers and employees. At present, labor courts (*conseils de prud'hommes*) can be created by government decree in every place where this seems desirable. A labor court must be created, if its creation is requested by the municipal council of the city where it is to be established and the municipal councils of the other communities within the proposed area of its competence concur in this request. Before a labor court is created, public notice of its proposed creation must be given, and all interested parties must be invited to make their views known to the Ministry of Labor. [201] Labor courts may have special sections for various trades or occupations. At present, a labor court may consist of one or more of the following sections: industrial occupations section, commercial occupations section, agricultural occupations section, miscellaneous occupations section. The area for which a labor court is to be competent must be specified in the decree creating it. That decree must also list the sections of which the court is to be composed. [202]

Each labor court – or each section, if a court has more than one section – has a conciliation office consisting of one employer judge and one employee judge. [203] The conciliation offices seem to succeed in settling about one third of the cases brought before them. [204]

**a. The judges and the staff.** Each labor court is composed of at least twelve judges, more if there are several sections. Half the judges are elected by employers; the other half is elected by employees. The judges' term of office is six years, half the membership of each court being elected every three years. [205] Outgoing judges may be re-elected.

[200] The labor courts (*conseils de prud'hommes*) are said to have been derived from a court operating in Lyon in pre-revolutionary days, re-established in the Napoleonic era. See CORNU & FOYER 179.

[201] Decree No. 58–1292 of December 22, 1958, J.O. Dec. 23, 1958, p. 11621, [1959] B.L.D. 77, as amended by Decree No. 63–992 of Oct. 2, 1963, J.O. Oct. 3, 1963, p. 8867, [1963] D.L. 308, arts. 1, 2.

[202] Decree No. 58–1292, *supra* note 201, arts. 3, 4.

[203] Decree No. 58–1292, *supra* note 201, arts. 54–6; Ordinance No. 58–1276 of December 22, 1958, J.O. Dec. 23, 1958, p. 11560, [1959] B.L.D. 28, art. 1.

[204] CORNU & FOYER 180. The statistics there cited show the following figures for 1954: cases brought before the conciliation offices of the Labor Courts, 54,043; cases settled by the conciliation offices, 16,912; cases brought before the litigation offices, 29,865; cases actually decided, 21,128. The figures for other years are comparable. Apparently, a considerable number of cases that have withstood the efforts at settlement of the conciliation offices are discontinued or settled in some other manner before final judgment.

[205] Decree No. 58–1292, *supra* note 201, arts. 3, 6–7.

If the court is divided into sections, the elections take place for each section as a separate unit. All persons who may vote in the political elections and have exercised a trade or occupation mentioned in the decree instituting the court for a period of at least three years may vote vote in the elections for judges of the labor court. [206] Each labor court has a president and vice-president; if the court is composed of several sections, there is a president and vice-president for each section, as well as a general president responsible for administrative affairs. [207] The members of the court are unpaid. In contrast to general French practice, the expenses of the labor courts are not paid from funds of the French Government, but from funds of the municipalities in which they function. [208] An even number of judges sits in each case. If a suit before the labor court results in a deadlock between the employer and employee judges, a judge of the *tribunal d'instance* must join the court and cast the tie-breaking vote. [209] Regulations for the internal administration of each labour court are enacted in a meeting of all the judges of the court. The clerical work of the labor courts is not performed by a *greffier*, but by a clerk who is an official of the *département* in which the court is situated. [210] No member of the *ministère public* is attached to the court.

### 3.28. The *Tribunaux Paritaires de Baux Ruraux*

Special courts to deal with litigation involving farm tenancies were originally instituted during the Vichy régime, [211] and have been continued by the Fourth as well as the Fifth Republic. However, these courts are far less independent of the regular judiciary than the other specialized courts. Rural lease courts exist at the seat of the various *tribunaux d'instance*. [212] A judge of the *tribunal d'instance* acts as presiding judge of the court, and the *greffier* of the *tribunal d'instance*

[206] Decree No. 58–1292, *supra* note 201, art. 21. The actual voting process is quite complex, being designed not only to give even representation to employers and employees, but also make sure that all voters are qualified in terms of length of exercise of their occupation and of residence. See arts. 22–35.

[207] These offices are rotated among employer and employee members in such a manner that the president is an employer and the vice president an employee, or vice versa. See Decree No. 58–1292, *supra* note 201, arts. 8–15.

[208] Decree No. 58–1292, *supra* note 201, arts. 98–99. However, certain travel expenses are borne by the French Republic.

[209] Decree No. 58–1292, *supra* note 201, arts. 57–60.

[210] Decree No. 58–1292, *supra* note 201, arts. 16–18. The secretary of the court is not an *officier ministériel*, but a government employee, who cannot sell his office nor generally keep the fees collected by him.

[211] CORNU & FOYER 183.

[212] Decree No. 58–1293 of December 22, 1958, J.O. Dec. 23, 1958, p. 11627, [1959] B.L.D. 87, art. 1.

acts as its clerk. [213] When presiding over a rural lease court, the judge of the *tribunal d'instance* sits with at least four lay *assesseurs*. If there are regular farm tenants in an area as well as share croppers, the Minister of Justice may establish two sections within each rural lease court: one for regular farm tenants, the other for share croppers. In that case, each section is composed of four assessors and of the judge of the *tribunal d'instance.* [214]

**a. The *assesseurs*.** Assessors are elected for five year terms by the tenant farmers and by the landlords in the *arrondissement* in which the rural lease court is competent. [215] An equal number of assessors elected by tenants and by landlords must sit in every case. [216] When there are separate sections, the assessors of the two sections are elected separately by regular landlords and tenants and sharecropper landlords and tenants. [217] In the past, absenteeism of the elected judges seems to have been a serious problem. [218] Two measures are now possible to meet this problem. If, due to the absence of assessors, the court is incomplete, the judge of the *tribunal d'instance* who presides may decide the case alone, after having asked the assessors who are present for their advice. [219] If a rural lease court is consistently hampered in its operation by absenteeism, the government may abolish it and transfer its functions to the appropriate *tribunal d'instance.* [220]

### 3.29. The Social Security Courts

Special courts to deal with social security legislation owe their existence to the creation, in 1945, of a comprehensive system of social insurance. [221] Earlier laws in the field were administered by a variety

[213] Decree No. 58–1293, *supra* note 212, arts. 2, 21.

[214] Decree No. 58–1293, *supra* note 212, art. 2.

[215] Voters must be tenants or landlords, who have been French nationals for at least five years, are over 21 years of age, and are domiciled or have their residence in the district. Candidates for the office of assessor must be qualified voters of at least 26 years, who have been landlords or tenants for at least five years. For the rules governing the elections, see Decree No. 58–1293, *supra* note 212, arts. 3–6.

[216] Decree No. 58–1293, *supra* note 212, art. 2.

[217] See note 215 *supra.*

[218] See CORNU & FOYER, MISE À JOUR 1960, at 22.

[219] Decree No. 58–1293, *supra* note 212, art. 18. This may discourage absenteeism, because there is no requirement that an equal number of landlord and tenant assessors must be present to give that advice.

[220] Decree No. 58–1293, *supra* note 212, arts. 7, 22.

[221] The basis for the comprehensive scheme of social insurance in France was laid by an Ordinance of Oct. 19, 1945, J.O. Oct. 20, 1945, p. 6721, [1945] D.L. 294, since repeatedly amended. For a general survey of social insurance in France, see Rodgers, *Social Security in France*, 31 PUBLIC ADMINISTRATION 377 (1953).

of courts and commissions.[222] The actions of the social security courts are reviewable in the last resort by the *Cour de Cassation* and judges of the regular courts usually serve on them; they are thus part of the regular, and not of the administrative, court system.[223]

Social insurance in France, as in many other European countries, is administered not by the government directly, but by autonomous regional bodies supervised by the government. These bodies (*caisses de sécurité sociale*) collect contributions from employers and employees and pay out benefits. The social security courts have been created mainly to decide disputes between these bodies and employers and employees concerning the payment of contributions and the award of benefits.

There are two main types of social security courts: (1) first instance commissions for general litigation in social security matters, and (2) regional commissions for so-called technical litigation.

**a. The *Commissions de première instance*.** The first instance commissions consist of the president of the *tribunal de grande instance* (or a judge of that court designated by the president) and two *assesseurs*, one of whom represents employers and the other employees. The assessors for each case are taken from a list of employer and employee representatives established by the president of the *tribunal de grande instance*. In establishing the list, the president is limited to names supplied him by various employer and employee organizations. The assessors serve for terms of five years, but may be reappointed.[224] The assessors are not entitled to a salary, but may receive expenses and some compensation for lost wages or profits.[225] An assessor who, although duly summoned, is absent without excuse, may forfeit his office.[226] The clerical work of the first instance commissions is handled by an employee of a regional social security office rather than by the

[222] Prior to the creation of an unified system of social insurance, employers were liable for all accidents arising out of the employment, without regard to fault, but the amounts recoverable by injured employees were limited to fixed sums. 2 COLIN & CAPITANT 279. The basis for the present system of social security courts, which deal with industrial accidents as well as all other matters covered by social insurance, is the Law of October 24, 1946, J.O. Oct. 25, 1946, p. 9038, [1946] D.L. 417.

[223] Decree No. 58–1291 of December 22, 1958, J.O. Dec. 23, 1958, p. 11613, [1959] B.L.D. 66, art. 7.

[224] Decree No. 58–1291, *supra* note 223, art. 8. Article 9 of the same decree provides that persons may not be appointed assessors unless they meet specified requirements as to nationality, absence of criminal convictions, and similar qualifications.

[225] Decree No. 58–1291, *supra* note 223, art. 8.

[226] Decree No. 58–1291, *supra* note 223, art. 11. An assessor must be summoned to sit on a case at least fifteen days in advance; if he is excusedly absent, a person from a special list of alternates must sit.

*greffier* of the *tribunal de grande instance.* [227] There is a complex system for the allocation of the costs arising from the operation of the first instance commissions among the various interested parties.

**b. The *Commissions régionales techniques.*** The regional technical commissions, which handle mostly cases involving medical problems, consist of an official of the governmental office supervising the administration of the social security laws by the autonomous *caisses,* acting as chairman, one other governmental representative appointed by him, a physician appointed by him, a physician appointed by the plaintiff, and one appointed by the social security body (*caisse*) whose decision is the subject of the litigation. In some cases, the commission may have additional members. [228] The clerical work of the commissions is performed by an official of a social security office. [229]

### 3.30. The *Cours d'Appel*

**a. Historical introduction.** During the French Revolution, there were no special intermediate appellate courts. An appeal from one district court was heard in another district court. This system of so-called circular appeals was abolished under Napoleon, who created separate appellate courts, called *tribunaux,* and later *cours d'appel.* However, appeals from the justice of the peace courts went to the regular courts of first instance, renamed *tribunaux civils.* Eventually, additional, sometimes short-lived, appellate courts were created to deal with appeals in certain special cases.

The reform legislation of 1958 brought drastic changes. With the exception of certain social security matters, practically all appeals, from whatever court, now go to a *cour d'appel.* The power of the *tribunaux de grande instance* to hear appeals from inferior courts has been abolished. However, the executive branch of the government has retained the right to restore the limited appellate powers of the *tribunaux de grande instance* by decree. [230] Some favor the exercise of that right to reduce congestion in the *cours d'appel* and to give litigants involved in small cases an appellate tribunal closer to their home.

[227] Decree No. 58–1291, *supra* note 223, art. 14. The official involved is not an official of one of the autonomous bodies administering the social security laws (*caisses de sécurité sociale*) but of the government agency supervising the working of the social security system.

[228] Decree No. 58–1291, *supra* note 223, art. 31; Ordinance No. 58–1275 of December 22, 1958, J.O. Dec. 23, 1958, p. 11559, [1959] B.L.D. 27.

[229] Decree No. 58–1291, *supra* note 223.

[230] Decree No. 58–1284 of December 22, 1958, J.O. Dec. 23, 1958, p. 11579, [1959] D.L. 41, art. 35.

The articles of the *Code de Procédure Civile* relating to the procedure before the *cours d'appel* were amended several times [231] and subjected to a general revision in 1942. [232] The reform legislation of 1958 affected primarily the organization of the *cours d'appel.* [233]

**b. Number and organization.** There are twenty-seven *cours d'appel* in Metropolitan France, a number which has remained unchanged since 1927. [234] Of the several *cours d'appel* in the French overseas territories, only those in Réunion and Martinique are still in existence. The size of the area for which the various *cours d'appel* are competent varies. Thus, the *Cour d'Appel* in Bastia hears appeals from only one *département,* Corsica. Most others cover two to four *départements.* The *Cour d'Appel* in Paris, the largest of all, hears cases which originate in an area with a total population approximating nine million inhabitants. [235] *Cours d'appel* are frequently, but not always, located in large cities: There is a *Cour d'Appel* in Aix, but none in nearby Marseille, which is much larger.

The *cours d'appel* do not usually sit *en banc,* but in panels, called *chambres.* Like the panels of the *tribunaux de grande instance,* [236] they are composed of three judges. The number of *chambres* of each court depends on the amount of litigation handled. Thus, the *Cour d'Appel* in Paris has 25 *chambres* In addition, most of its *chambres* are divided into two *sections,* which are, in fact, independent, so that there are

[231] Especially the Law of April 11, 1938 and the Decree-Law of October 30, 1935, J.O. Oct. 31, 1935, [1935] D. 4. 421. See also 1 DALLOZ, RÉPERTOIRE DE PROCÉDURE CIVILE ET COMMERCIALE, *Appel,* Nos. 5–8 (1955).

[232] Law of May 23, 1942, J.O. June 11, 1942, p. 2035, [1942] D. ANAL. L. 120. See also Hébraud, *Commentaire, Loi du 23 mai 1942,* [1943] D. ANAL. L. 1.

[233] See Decree No. 58–1289 of December 22, 1958, J.O. Dec. 23, 1958, p. 11608, [1959] D.L. 45.

[234] The number of *cours d'appel,* their location, and the number of their panels and judges is determined by executive regulation (*décret*). See Ordinance No. 58–1273 of Dec. 23, 1958, J.O. Dec. 23, 1958, p. 11557, [1959] D.L. 26, art. 8. The number and composition of the *cours d'appel* is now governed by Decree No. 58–1286 of December 22, 1958, J.O. Dec. 23, 1958, p. 11582, [1959] D.L. 44, since amended several times as regards the number of judges, but not as to the location of the courts. See Decree No. 61–259 of March 23, 1961, J.O. March 25, 1961, p. 2997. *Cours d'appel* are located in Agen, Aix, Amiens, Angers, Bastia, Besançon, Bordeaux, Bourges, Caen, Chambéry, Colmar, Dijon, Douai, Grenoble, Limoges, Lyon, Montepellier, Nancy, Nîmes, Orléans, Paris, Pau, Poitiers, Rennes, Riom, Rouen, and Toulouse. In addition, two *chambres* formally belonging to the Colmar *Cour d'Appel* sit permanently in Metz.

[235] SOLUS & PERROT 547–48; Decree No. 58–1286, *supra* note 234. The area in which a *cour d'appel* is territorially competent is usually called its *ressort.*

[236] See 3.24 *supra.* Originally, seven judges had to sit on every panel; this number was later reduced to five, and eventually to three. This development has been criticized on the ground that cases on appeal should be handled by a larger number of judges than cases in first instance. See 1 SOLUS & PERROT 550.

forty-nine separate panels. [237] Most other courts are far smaller, having two to six *chambres*, while the courts at Bastia and Chambéry have only one panel each. [238]

In courts having several *chambres*, there is a good deal of specialization. *Chambres criminelles* deal with appeals in criminal cases. Another panel deals with juvenile delinquents and related problems, [239] while a panel, called *chambre d'accusation*, performs functions somewhat similar to those of a grand jury, screening indictments involving the more serious felonies and remanding the criminals to the *Cour d'Assises* for trial. [240] Since 1958, the courts have a special panel, called *chambre sociale*, for appeals involving employment contracts and social security and related matters. [241] Even among the *chambres* having no distinctive name, there is a certain division of labor. [242] The various *chambres* are numbered consecutively; traditionally, the most important cases, including cases in which judges or members of the legal professions are involved personally, are handled by the first *chambre*.[243] The presiding judge of the court, or some official designated by him, such as the chief clerk of the court, assigns the new cases to the various panels. [244]

Each *cour d'appel* supplies the presiding judges for the various *cours d'assises* in its district and may supply the associate judges. [245] In addition, the clerk of the *cour d'appel* acts as clerk of the *cour d'assises* sitting in the same *département*, which, from an administrative point of view, is practically an appendage of the *cour d'appel*. [246]

[237] Decree No. 58–1286, *supra* note 234. See also the official directory of the court, COUR D'APPEL DE PARIS, ANNÉE JUDICIAIRE 1961–1962.

[238] Decree No. 58–1286, *supra* note 234. The second largest *cour d'appel* in France following Paris sits in Aix en Provence and has 12 *chambres*.

[239] CODE DE PROCÉDURE PÉNALE art. 510 (criminal panels); Ordinance No. 58–1274 of Dec. 22, 1958, J.O. Dec. 23, 1958, p. 11559, [1959] D.L. 27 (special panels dealing with infants).

[240] CODE DE PROCÉDURE PÉNALE art. 191.

[241] Decree No. 58–1281 of Dec. 22, 1958, J.O. Dec. 23, 1958, p. 11572, [1959] D.L. 35, art. 8.

[242] For example, one panel will specialize in landlord and tenant matters, and another in copyright cases. There is also a *chambre* dealing with condemnation cases, the composition of which is governed by somewhat special rules.

[243] There is a general assumption that the *chambres* with the lowest numbers deal with the cases raising the most difficult legal problems, but that assumption is not altogether true.

[244] 1 SOLUS & PERROT 541–49. The number of cases in the Paris *Cour d'Appel* is so large that the chief clerk must subdelegate part of his duties in that respect to several of his assistants. In the case of panels whose duties are not prescribed by law, the assignment is a matter of court custom.

[245] CODE DE PROCÉDURE PÉNALE arts. 244–53.

[246] CODE DE PROCÉDURE PÉNALE art. 380. An additional tribunal, called *cour régionale des pensions*, which deals with cases involving veterans' pensions, is also an appendage of the *cour d'appel*. See COUR D'APPEL DE PARIS, *op. cit. supra* note 237, at 27.

Cases remanded from the *Cour de Cassation* and *prise à partie* proceedings to impose damages upon judges must be heard by a panel of five judges sitting in a solemn session, an *audience solennelle,* at which the judges wear red robes. The presiding judge of the court always presides at an *audience solennelle*; the judges of the first *chambre* together with as many judges trom another *chambre* as are needed to bring their number up to five act as judges. A regular panel would commit reversible error if it heard a case reserved for an *audience solennelle.* [247]

From time to time, all panels of a *cour d'appel* meet together in general assembly in order to deal with matters of internal court administration. [248] A special general assembly, composed only of the first two *chambres* – the first three in Paris – hears appeals from decisions of the disciplinary councils of the *avocats* [249] and various other matters.

c. **The judges.** At the head of each *cour d'appel* is a presiding judge called *premier président.* [250] Each *chambre* is presided over by a *président*; if a *chambre* is divided into sections, the head of each section bears that title. The judges of the *cours d'appel* are called *conseillers.* Many *cours d'appel* have extremely large judicial staffs. During the 1961–62 judicial year, the *Cour d'Appel* in Paris consisted of the *Premier Président,* 49 *présidents,* and 115 judges. [251] While the other courts are much smaller, their staffs are still sizeable. [252] In spite of this, there are complaints about delay and calendar congestion in some of the *cours d'appel,* indicating that the number of judges is still inadequate. The reasons for this condition are varied. The possibility to obtain an adjudication de novo seems to encourage appeals. [253] Each appeal,

[247] 1 SOLUS & PERROT 551; CUCHE & VINCENT 99–100; *cf.* Decree of July 6, 1810, art. 7.As to the *prise à partie,* see 3.17 *supra.*

[248] In addition, questions of general interest to the courts (*e.g.*, proposed new procedural legislation) may be discussed by the *assemblée générale.* 1 DALLOZ, RÉPERTOIRE DE PROCÉDURE CIVILE ET COMMERCIALE, *Cour d'Appel,* No. 90 (1956); Decree of July 6, 1810, arts. 61–69; CUCHE & VINCENT 100.

[249] Decree No. 54–406 of April 10, 1954, J.O. April 11, 1954, p. 3994, [1954] B.L.D. 165 art. 40. As to disciplinary measures against *avocats* generally, see 2.03.g *supra.*

[250] Literally, first president. The *premier président* may preside sessions of any panel of his court.

[251] See COUR D'APPEL DE PARIS, *op. cit. supra* note 237, at 5–11.

[252] Ordinarily, a *président* and two *conseillers* for each *chambre,* in addition to the *premier président.* As to the number of *chambres* of the various courts, see 3.30.b *supra.*

[253] During 1961, 13.200 new civil and 8.900 new criminal cases were put on the calendar of the Paris *Cour d'Appel* alone. In addition, the *chambre d'accusation* had to deal with 2.400 cases, and the *Cour d'Assises* in Paris, staffed in part by judges from the *Cour d'Appel,*

since it involves relitigation of both facts and law, [254] makes great demands on judicial time. The obligation to write an opinion in every case imposes an additional burden. Furthermore, the judges have little or no research assistance, and a number of judges are occasionally doing non-appellate work, especially as members of a *cour d'assises.* [255]

The judges of the *cours d'appel,* and even more so the *présidents* of the various panels and the *premiers présidents* of the courts, rank rather high in the French judicial hierarchy. The members of the Paris *Cour d'Appel,* like other Paris judges, rank one or more grades higher than their brethren holding corresponding positions elsewhere. [256]

There is a certain amount of annual rotation among the various panels of each *cour d'appel* to prevent overspecialization. The rules governing rotation are similar to those applied in the case of the *tribunaux de grande instance.* [257] However, the members of the *chambre sociale* are not affected by this rotation, since they are selected on the basis of their interest and learning in social and labor legislation and are intended to develop a special expertise in this area. [258] In spite of

handled 160 more cases. As the following table shows, the statistics for France as a whole are also extremely high.

Business handled by all *Cours d'Appel* in France (in thousands):

| Year | New Cases | Backlog | Decided Cases |
|---|---|---|---|
| 1950 | 26.1 | 60.6 | 27.0 |
| 1951 | 27.3 | 61.0 | 27.5 |
| 1952 | 28.8 | 62.3 | 28.4 |
| 1953 | 27.1 | 61.2 | 26.5 |
| 1954 | 28.4 | 63.2 | 26.9 |
| 1955 | 31.2 | 67.8 | 29.5 |
| 1956 | 31.8 | 70.3 | 29.7 |
| 1957 | 31.5 | 72.3 | 30.2 |
| 1958 | 29.3 | 71.6 | 31.1 |

[Source: ANNUAIRE STATISTIQUE DE LA FRANCE RÉTROSPECTIF 80 (1961)].

However, delays, even in Paris, where the situation is worst, do not exceed 1½ years.

[254] The abolition of the appellate powers of the *tribunaux de grande instance* has apparently contributed to the backlog of cases, in spite of an increase in judicial manpower. See 1 SOLUS & PERROT 494–97.

[255] French judges, in spite of their large numbers, are generally quite busy. Thus, the various panels of the Paris *Cour d'Appel* sit three times a week for a whole morning or afternoon – some regularly on Saturdays –, except during the two-months summer recess. There is no alternation between terms during which the court hears cases and periods during which no cases are heard.

[256] See 3.13 *supra.*

[257] See 3.24.a *supra.*

[258] See Decree No. 58–1281, *supra* note 241, art. 8. The compartments between the various panels are not airtight, however: Panels having a lighter case load may, to some extent, be assigned cases belonging to other panels. If necessary, judges of one panel may temporarily sit on other panels. *But see,* as to the *chambre d'accusation,* CODE DE PROCÉDURE PÉNALE art. 191.

the annual rotation of judges, the members of the first *chambre* and of the other *chambres* with low numbers have more prestige then their brethren from the other panels of the same court and apparently also a greater chance for promotion. A specially important rôle is played by the *premier président* of each *cour d'appel*. He is responsible for the internal administration of the court. In addition, he is, in a sense, the hierarchical superior of all judges in his district. He may give them an admonition if necessary. He must make an annual inspection of all the courts under his supervision and make reports to the Ministry of Justice. He may authorize the *tribunaux d'instance* in his district to hold court in places other than their regular seat. He also has the power to assign judges from the *tribunaux d'instance* and *grande instance* to other courts for periods not to exceed two months. [259]

**d. The *ministère public*.** The head of the *ministère public* attached to each *cour d'appel* is called *procureur général*. Under him are a number of *avocats généraux* and *substituts généraux*. The *procureur général* is equal in rank to the *premier président*. There is a similar correspondence between the positions of the *avocats généraux* and the *présidents* of the *chambres*, and between those of the *substituts généraux* and of the judges. [260] However, the number of judges is ordinarily considerably larger than that of the members of the *ministère public*. [261] The duties of the *ministère public* before the *cours d'appel* are substantially similar to its duties before the courts of first instance. The *procureur général* has general supervisory and disciplinary powers not only over the members of his own staff, but also over all the *procureurs de la République* and their assistants in his district. [262]

**e. Other staff.** The clerk's office is headed by a *greffier*, who, being an *officier ministériel*, must purchase the right to his office from his predecessor. He ordinarily has quite a large staff. Those members of his staff who act as clerks for the various panels of the court and attend the hearings are usually government employees. The office personnel is paid by the *greffier* out of the fees he collects from litigants. [263]

[259] 1 Solus & Perrot 555; Cornu & Foyer, Mise à Jour 1960, at 28–29.

[260] See 3.07 *supra*. The correct title of the *substituts généraux* is *substituts du procureur général*; the expression *substituts généraux* is used by way of abbreviation.

[261] Thus, the *Cour d'Appel* in Paris has 1 *procureur général*, 22 *avocats généraux*, and 32 *substituts généraux*, and 1 *premier président*, 49 *présidents*, and 115 judges.

[262] See 3.06 *supra*.

[263] See 2.09 *supra*.

*Huissiers audienciers* act as court attendants, though part of the burden of maintaining order in the courthouse ordinarily falls on uniformed guards. [264] There are also a number of other employees, such as librarians and messengers, who belong to the regular civil service. Only the presiding judge, who has heavy administrative duties, seems to have special secretarial assistance.

### 3.31. The *Commission Nationale Technique*

The only appellate tribunal of any significance in the hierarchy of the regular courts [265] other than the *cours d'appel* is the *Commission Nationale Technique* (National Technical Commission). It hears appeals from all regional technical social security commissions. [266]

Like the *cours d'appel*, the *Commission Nationale Technique* is divided into panels. The panels have a somewhat heterogeneous composition. There are two judges on every panel, but they may be selected either from the regular or from the administrative courts; the third permanent member is a high official either of the Ministry of Labor or of the Ministry of Agriculture, depending on whether the particular panel deals mainly with cases of industrial or agricultural employment. These three members are selected by joint action of the Minister of Justice and of the Minister of Labor or the Minister of Agriculture, as the case may be. Each panel is completed by one employer and one employee representative, who are selected from lists furnished by representative employer and employee organizations. The employer and employee representatives are not appointed on a permanent basis, but are selected for each particular case on the basis of their special competence.

Three members of a panel constitute a quorum. [267] One of the members of each panel acts as its president. There is also a president and a vice president for the entire *Commission*; both are selected from among the panel presidents. The president assigns the cases to the

[264] See 2.08.b *supra*.

[265] The main reason for classifying the National Technical Commission with the regular rather than the administrative courts is the fact that a *pourvoi* from its decisions must be taken to the *Cour de Cassation*, not to the *Conseil d'Etat*. See Decree No. 58–1291 of Dec. 22, 1958, J.O. Dec. 23, 1958, p. 11613, [1959] D.L. 49, art. 53. In certain other respects (written procedure, absence of *ministère public*), the National Technical Commission resembles the administrative courts more than the regular courts.

[266] See Decree No. 58–1291, *supra* note 265, art. 37. The employer and employee representatives are on call for terms of 5 years. Art. 49.

[267] Decree No. 58–1291, *supra* note 265, art. 48.

various panels. He may preside any panel he wants and combine two or more panels for the hearing of cases if he deems it desirable. [268]

No representative of the *ministère public* is attached to the National Technical Commission; however, officials of the Ministries of Labor and Agriculture perform somewhat analogous functions under the title of *commissaires du gouvernement.* [269] The clerk's office is staffed not by a *greffier,* who has purchased his appointment, but by active or retired employees of the Ministries of Labor or Agriculture. [270]

Since the cases before the National Technical Commission usually involve medical evidence, there is also a provision for the establishment of a list of physicians by the Ministries of Labor and Agriculture. Although these physicians are not members of the *Commission,* the files of all cases must be submitted to one of the doctors on that list for his comments. [271]

### 3.32. The *Cour de Cassation*

**a. Introduction.** At the apex of the judicial pyramid stands the *Cour de Cassation,* sometimes called *Cour Suprême.* Its main function is to review decisions of the *cours d'appel* and certain other decisions that are not subject to any further *appel.*

Review by the *Cour de Cassation* is restricted to questions of law. In case of reversal, the court must remand the case for further proceedings. To distinguish recourse to the *Cour de Cassation* from the much broader *appel* to a *cour d'appel,* the former is called a *pourvoi.* [272]

The *Cour de Cassation* was created in 1790 as part of the reorganization of the French judicial system initiated during the early days of the Revolution. [273] Originally, it was conceived of merely as an appendage of the French legislature. The courts to which cases were remanded were not bound to follow its view of the law. However, a Law of April 1, 1837, [274] strengthened the position of the *Cour de Cas-*

[268] Decree No. 58–1291, *supra* note 265, arts. 38, 46.

[269] Decree No. 58–1291, *supra* note 265, art. 40.

[270] Decree No. 58–1291, *supra* note 265, art. 41.

[271] Decree No. 58–1291, *supra* note 265, art. 46.

[272] See 6 GARSONNET & CÉZAR-BRU 604–10. While *appel* is usually called an ordinary method of review (*voie de recours ordinaire*), *pourvoi* is considered as one of the extra-ordinary methods of review (*voies de recours extraordinaires*), to be used only sparingly.

[273] Law of November 27, 1790, reprinted in DALLOZ, CODE DE PROCÉDURE CIVILE 436 (58th ed. 1960), and in CODE JUDICIAIRE 271 (1791). Concerning the history of the *Cour de Cassation,* see also 1 DALLOZ, RÉPERTOIRE DE PROCÉDURE CIVILE ET COMMERCIALE, *Cassation,* at Nos. 2–21 (1955) (the author of the article on *Cassation* is the *Procureur-Général,* Mr. Besson); *cf.* 6 GARSONNET & CÉZAR-BRU 591–603. For books on the *Cour de Cassation,* see CRÉPON, LA COUR DE CASSATION (1892); FAYE, LA COUR DE CASSATION (1903).

[274] Law of April 1, 1837, (1837) BULLETIN DES LOIS No. 6769, [1837] D. 3. 151 (with report of Minister giving reasons for new legislation).

*sation* by compelling courts to which a case was remanded to follow the decision by the *Cour de Cassation*, but only if, after an earlier refusal by the lower court to do so, the case had been remanded for a second time. It is mainly as a result of that law that the *Cour de Cassation* is able to fulfill the function of ensuring a reasonable degree of consistency among the court decisions in France and of preventing a recurrence of the regional differences in law which prevailed before the Revolution. [275]

The *Code de Procédure Civile* deals only marginally with the procedure before the *Cour de Cassation*. Until 1947, that procedure was largely governed by a pre-revolutionary *ordonnance* [276] dealing with the procedure before the royal council (*Conseil des parties*). Though now largely superseded by a 1947 statute, a few provisions of the *ordonnance* are still important. The 1958 reforms had only a very limited impact on the *Cour de Cassation*.

**b. The various panels.** Like most other French courts, the *Cour de Cassation* does not usually sit *en banc*, but in panels called *chambres*. Originally, there were only three such panels, the *chambre civile*, the *chambre criminelle*, and the *chambre des requêtes*. The *chambre criminelle* dealt with all criminal cases. Civil cases were submitted to the *chambre des requêtes* for initial *ex parte* scrutiny. If that body decided that there was some substance to the contentions of the party asking for a review, the case was referred to the *chambre civile* for a full adversary hearing; otherwise, it was dismissed. [277] In 1938, to cope with the increasing amount of litigation, an additional panel called *chambre sociale*, dealing mainly with cases arising under labor and related legislation, was added. [278]

After the end of the Second World War, the *Cour de Cassation* became swamped with a veritable flood of litigation and fell far behind in its work. In 1947, to cope with this situation, the *chambre des requêtes*

[275] For this reason the *Cour de Cassation* is sometimes called the *cour régulatrice*, the court that regulates the case law. On the rôle of the *Cour de Cassation* in the development of French law, see 1 SOLUS & PERROT at 600–02, 617–19. For a brief description of the *Cour de Cassation*, see also Kock, *The Machinery of Law Administration in France*, 108 U. PA. L. REV. 366, 375 (1960); Pugh, *Administration of Criminal Justice in France*, 23 LA. L. REV. 1, 7 (1962).

[276] This was the Royal Ordinance of June 28, 1738. See 1.23.a *supra*.

[277] In fact, the *chambre des requêtes* which was intended only as a preliminary screening device eventually gave rather detailed consideration to the cases before it so that it delayed, rather then expedited, the work of the court. This was one of the reasons for its abolition. See 1 SOLUS & PERROT 606; Hébraud, *La Loi du 23 Juillet 1947 Sur La Cour de Cassation*, [1947] D. CHR. 125.

[278] Decree of June 17, 1938, J.O. June 30, 1938, [1938] D. 4. 321 (with report of Prime Minister explaining reasons for enactment).

was abolished and transformed into an additional civil panel hearing cases on the merits. [279] Since the caseload of the *Cour de Cassation* still kept increasing, an additional civil panel was added in 1952, [280] and in 1956 the membership of the various panels was expanded. [281]

As a result of these measures, the *Cour de Cassation* now consists of five panels – a criminal panel (*chambre criminelle*) and four civil panels. Often, the four civil panels, though independent of each other, are called collectively *chambre civile*. The individual civil panels are ordinarily designated as *chambre civile, 1. section civile* (civil panel, first civil section), *chambre civile, 2. section civile* (civil panel, second civil section), *chambre civile, section commerciale et financière* (civil panel, commercial and financial section), and *chambre civile, section sociale* (civil panel, social section). [282] Each panel consists of 15 judges, with the exception of the criminal panel which has 17 judges. [283] Seven judges constitute a quorum. [284] To be able to hear more cases, the criminal panel frequently sits in two sub-panels, a procedure made possible by the low quorum requirement. [285] The division of labor among the four civil panels of the court is based on a rule promulgated by the so-called *bureau* of the *Cour de Cassation*, a board consisting of several high-ranking members of that court. [286]

At present, the first civil panel (*chambre civile, 1. section civile*) deals

[279] Law No. 47–1366 of July 23, 1947, J.O. July 24, 1947, p. 7142, [1947] D.L. 275 (with circular of Minister of Justice at [1947] D.L. 278 explaining new law). This law was amended by Law No. 52–853 of July 21, 1952, J.O. July 22, 1952, p. 7356, [1952] D.L. 269; Law No. 56–734 of July 27, 1956, J.O. July 28, 1956, p. 7023, [1956] D.L. 266; Law No. 56–780 of August 4, 1956, J.O. August 7, 1956, p. 7439, [1956] D.L. 289; Ordinance No. 58–889 of Sept. 24, 1958, J.O. Sept. 27, 1958, p. 8883, [1958] D.L. 320; and Ordinance No. 58–1281 of December 22, 1958, J.O. Dec. 23, 1958, p. 11572, [1959] D.L. 35. Unless otherwise noted, a reference to an article of the 1947 law will always refer to the text as amended by the subsequent legislation. Concerning the 1947 law, see Hébraud, *supra* note 277; Perrin, *Commentaire*, [1948] S. 5. 1137 (tracing historical development and analyzing new law).

[280] Law No. 52–853, *supra* note 279. On this law, see Ropers, *La Loi du 21 Juillet créant une Nouvelle Chambre Civile à la Cour de Cassation*, [1952] J.C.P. 1. 1054. In 1952, to lower the costs caused by the creation of an additional panel, the number of judges per panel had been slightly reduced.

[281] Law No. 56–780, *supra* note 279, art. 51. For a comment concerning the 1956 legislation, see Huguet, *Chronique Législative*, [1957] D. CHR. 29, 36. The 1956 law again increased the number of judges per panel.

[282] See, *e.g.*, 1 SOLUS & PERROT 608. *But cf.* CUCHE & VINCENT 121, who speak of 4 *chambres civiles* (civil panels). The law of 1947 speaks only in terms of a criminal panel, whose competence is governed by a specific legislative enactment (CODE DE PROCÉDURE PÉNALE art. 567) and four civil panels, without giving them any particular name. The names used in the text are apparently derived from the ARRÊTÉ of the Ministry of Justice concerning the official reports (*bulletins*) of the court. See ARRÊTÉ of August 8, 1950, J.O. August 11, 1950, p. 8408, [1950] D.L. 178. Quite often, the term *chambre sociale* is used to designate the social panel, and the term *chambre commerciale* to designate the commercial panel.

[283] Law No. 47–1366, *supra* note 279, art. 1.

[284] Law No. 47–1366, *supra* note 279, art. 7.

[285] In important cases, however, the entire criminal panel will sit.

with cases involving questions of nationality, personal status, property, non-commercial contracts, liens and mortgages, successions, gifts, copyright, separation of powers problems, war damage claims, and disciplinary proceedings against *avocats* and *officiers ministériels*; it also acts as a *chambre d'accusation* in criminal prosecutions against *magistrats* who commit crimes in their official capacity.

The second civil panel (*chambre civile, 2. section civile*) deals with cases involving torts, divorce and separation, civil procedure, elections, and social security.

The social panel (*chambre civile, section sociale*) and the commercial and financial panel (*chambre civile, section commerciale et financière*) deal with the subject matters indicated by their respective names. [287]

An additional temporary panel, called *chambre de la Communauté* (panel for the French Community), was created in 1959 to hear *pourvois* in cases pending in the former French colonies which had just been granted their independence, but had not yet completed the establishment of their own judicial system. Subsequently, most of the newly independent African states established their own judicial system or agreed that cases arising in their territory be heard by one of the regular panels of the *Cour de Cassation*. [288] Consequently, a recent *décret* authorizes the presiding judge of the *Cour de Cassation* to assign the additional judges appointed for the *chambre de la Communauté* to any panel on which their services may be needed. [289] The judges of the *Cour de Cassation* are not rotated among the various panels of the court, but if a panel does not have its quorum of seven members, judges from another panel are called in. [290]

**c. The *assemblée plénière civile*.** Since the reforms of 1947–1956, the *Cour de Cassation* consists of so many separate panels dealing with

[286] Law No. 47–1366, *supra* note 279, art. 3.

[287] This allocation of functions is based on a decision of the *bureau* of the *Cour de Cassation* of July 30, 1952. The second civil panel also has certain functions in connection with the prosecution of *magistrats* for crimes not committed within the scope of their official duties. See 1 DALLOZ, *op. cit. supra* note 273, at Nos. 127–31; 1 SOLUS & PERROT 608.

[288] See 1 SOLUS & PERROT 611, 998.

[289] Decree No. 61–117 of February 3, 1961, J.O. February 4, 1961, p. 1331, [1961] D.L. 83, modified by Decree No. 62–1199 of October 12, 1962, J.O. October 17, 1962, p. 10116, [1962] D.L. 334. A DÉCRET No. 64–837 of August 6, 1964. [1964] D.L. 279, amended by DÉCRET No. 65–635 of July 28, 1965, [1965] D.L. 264 has created a temporary additional panel for eminent domain cases. It consists of the presiding judge originally appointed for the *chambre de la Communauté* and of four judges, one from each of the four civil panels, who are designated by the *bureau* of the court. This new panel is to function until abolished by decree.

[290] As each panel now has 15 members and the quorum is only 7, this is at present an unlikely occurrence. The rule mentioned is based on the Ordinance of January 15, 1826, art. 4, reprinted in DALLOZ, CODE DE PROCÉDURE CIVILE 440 (58th ed. 1962).

often closely related matters that there is a serious danger of inconsistent decisions. To avoid this danger and to enable the court to fulfill what is one of its prime functions, the development of a reasonably homogeneous case law, the *assemblée plénière civile* was instituted in 1947. The *assemblée plénière civile* consists ordinarily of the members of all the civil panels, though its quorum is rather low: Only 15 of the 45 judges of the civil panels need be present. However, the presence of the *premier président* of the *Cour de Cassation,* of the *présidents* of the civil panels, and of the *doyens* (senior associate judges) of these panels is required. [291]

A case is referred to the *assemblée plénière civile* by the *premier président* of the *Cour de Cassation,* if it involves either a question of principle or if there is danger of inconsistent decisions. In ordering the transfer of a case from an individual panel to the *assemblée plénière civile,* the *premier président* acts on the suggestion of the presiding judge of the panel to which the case was originally assigned. In two cases, the *premier président* must, rather than may, transfer a case to the *assemblée plénière civile*: (1) if the *procureur général* at the *Cour de Cassation* requests it in writing, and (2) if the judges of the panel to which the case has been assigned are evenly divided. [292]

The *assemblée plénière civile* seems to have been helpful in avoiding inconsistent decisions by the *Cour de Cassation,* but even greater coordination between the various panels of the court would be necessary to make it fully effective in that respect. [293]

It should be added that in cases in which there is a possible inconsistency of decisions between the civil panels and the criminal panels – this occurs especially in tort cases – the judges of the criminal panel are also a part of the *assemblée plénière civile.* [294] Decisions of the *as-*

[291] Law No. 47–1366, *supra* note 279, arts. 6–7. Since the quorum for the *assemblée plénière* is so small, judges with special experience in the particular question under discussion usually predominate. 1 DALLOZ, *op. cit. supra* note 273, at No. 97.

[292] Law No. 47–1633, *supra* note 279, art. 41. The parties have no right to either request or oppose the transfer of a case to the *assemblée plénière.* MOREL 520. The panel president acts on the advice of the reporting judge to whom the case was originally assigned and who remains the reporting judge for the *assemblée plénière civile,* unless he is replaced by another judge by order of the presiding judge. For an example of the use of the *assemblée plénière civile* to reconcile conflicting views of several panels, see Lovera v. Rinaldi, Cass. Ass. Plén., June 22, 1949, [1949] S. 1. 161 (note Niboyet) (effect of war on treaties).

[293] This co-ordination is, to some extent, provided by the research and documentation unit of the court, but could probably be improved. See 3.32.i *infra.*

[294] In cases in which the criminal panel participates in the *assemblée plénière civile,* at least four members of the criminal panel must sit as judges. Law No. 47–1633, *supra* note 279, arts. 5–7.

*semblée plénière civile* are considered as more authoritative than decisions of the individual panels of the court. [295]

**d. The *chambres réunies*.** A second, somewhat indirect, method for avoiding or overcoming inconsistent decisions is the use of the *chambres réunies* (court sitting *en banc*). The *chambres réunies* consist of all the panels of the court. The quorum is only thirty-five, although most members of the court are likely to be present. The *premier président* of the *Cour de Cassation* acts as presiding officer. [296] When the *chambres réunies* meet, the court is said to sit in solemn session (*audience solennelle*). A meeting of the *chambres réunies* is indeed a rather imposing spectacle; the seventy-odd judges in their colorful red gowns almost fill the huge courtroom in which the first civil panel ordinarily sits, leaving little room for counsel and spectators.

The *chambres réunies* meet on certain solemn occasions – for instance, for the first session of court following the summer vacation, the installation of new members of the court, eulogies for deceased judges, and similar events. [297] More importantly, the *chambres réunies* must hear cases coming to the *Cour de Cassation* on a second *pourvoi*. As mentioned, a court to which a case is remanded by the *Cour de Cassation* after a reversal is not bound to follow the decision of the *Cour de Cassation*. If a new *pourvoi* is taken, based on the same grounds as the original *pourvoi*, the second *pourvoi* must be referred to the *chambres réunies* by the panel which would normally be competent. [298] If, on this second *pourvoi*, the *chambres réunies* adhere to the position taken by the individual panel of the court on the first *pourvoi*, the decision becomes binding upon the court to which the case is thereafter remanded. [299]

As decisions of individual panels are followed in the large majority of cases, the *chambres réunies* do not meet too often, ordinarily not more than twice a year, shortly before the beginning of the court's

[295] In the former German Supreme Court (*Reichsgericht*) there seems to have been a tendency to avoid the use of the full bench if at all possible, commentators speaking of a *horror pleni* (fear of the full bench). See, *e.g.*, SCHLESINGER, COMPARATIVE LAW 233 (2d ed. 1959). As far as can be ascertained, there is no equivalent reluctance in France to resort to the *assemblée plénière civile*. Nevertheless, the number of cases decided each year by that body seems rather small. None is mentioned for the 1961–62 term in the (selective) Dalloz reports.

[296] Law No. 47–1633, *supra* note 279, art. 7.

[297] The *chambres réunies* also meet when a decision of the *ordre* of the *avocats* at the *Cour de Cassation* in a disciplinary matter must be approved. 1 DALLOZ, *op. cit. supra* note 273, at No. 98.

[298] Law No. 47–1633, *supra* note 279, arts. 58–59.

[299] Law No. 47–1633, *supra* note 279, art. 60. See also 9.26 *infra*.

summer vacation, and shortly after the end of the vacation period. Each session lasts one or two weeks. Decisions of the *chambres réunies* have a special authority, and are hardly ever departed from. [300]

The use of the *chambres réunies* has been criticized by some authors because it is slow and tedious. [301] It is unlikely, however, that the *chambres réunies* will be abolished. In the early days of the *Cour de Cassation*, there was a considerable amount of experimentation to arrive at a method which would achieve a uniform interpretation of the law without abandoning the notion that no court is legally bound to follow any views other than its own. Resort to the *chambres réunies* on a second *pourvoi* in the same case appeared as a reasonable way to harmonize these two conflicting principles. [302] It is unlikely that any more acceptable compromise can be found. Additionally, this procedure makes it possible for the whole *Cour de Cassation* to review a decision of one of its panels if the decision is controversial enough to be disregarded by the lower court on the first remand, and thus to prevent possibly ill-considered rulings. It is also helpful in resolving conflicts among the panels.

**e. The judges.** The *Cour de Cassation* has an extremely large judicial staff. It consists of a presiding judge for the whole court, called *premier président*; a presiding judge, called *président*, for each of the five panels of the court; and sixty-seven associate judges (*conseillers*), 17 for the criminal panel, and fifteen for each of the four civil panels. [303] Besides, there are the three additional judges originally intended for the *chambre de la Communauté*.

The *premier président* acts as presiding officer for the *chambres réunies*, the *assemblée plénière civile*, and the so-called *bureau* of the court and its general assembly, two bodies which deal with problems of internal court administration. Traditionally, the *premier président* also acts as presiding officer of the first civil panel. He may preside any other panel he choses. [304] The *premier président* also presides the *Conseil*

[300] See 1 Solus & Perrot 617–18; 1 Collin & Capitant 104–09 (good discussion of importance of cases in French law); David & de Vries, The French Legal System 113–21 (1958). It might be noted that, although these cases are usually important and thus more likely to be published, the (selective) Dalloz reports published only 2 cases from the *chambres réunies* for the 1961–1962 term.

[301] *E.g.*, Morel 106; 1 Solus & Perrot 616–17.

[302] See 1.24.b and 1.25 *supra*.

[303] Law No. 47–1366, *supra* note 279, art. 1; Law No. 56–780, *supra* note 280, art. 51.

[304] Law No. 47–1366, *supra* note 279, arts. 1–2, 6; Ordinance of January 15, 1826, *supra* note 290, art. 28.

*Supérieur de la Magistrature* when that body exercises its disciplinary functions. [305] In addition, the *premier président* is the chief administrative officer of his court. To help him in his administrative duties, the *premier président* has a clerical staff under the direction of an official called *secrétaire général*, [306] who is a kind of administrative assistant.

The *présidents* act as presiding officers for the various panels, unless the *premier président* choses to preside. In the absence of the *premier président* and of the panel *président*, a panel must be presided by its senior associate judge, called *doyen*. [307]

The *premier président* of the *Cour de Cassation* is, of course, the highest ranking judicial officer in France. The panel presidents and judges of the *Cour de Cassation* (*conseillers*) also occupy a very high and respected position among French public servants. They wear distinctive red gowns.

Judges of the *Cour de Cassation* may be delegated by the Minister of Justice to inspect courts throughout France. [308] In addition, judges of the *Cour de Cassation* have often been members of special courts created on a temporary emergency basis, such as the *Haute Cour Militaire* which dealt with a number of prosecutions resulting from the Algerian conflict. [309]

**f. The *ministère public*.** The *ministère public* attached to the *Cour de Cassation* consists of a *procureur général*, who acts as its chief officer; a *premier avocat général*, who is his principal deputy; and seventeen *avocats généraux*. [310] The *ministère public* performs an important rôle even in civil cases, since it must be heard in every case before that court. [311] The written arguments of the *ministère public* in such cases are often quite lengthy and detailed.

The *procureur général* personally presents oral argument before the *chambres réunies* and the *assemblée plénière civile*. He may also argue

[305] See 3.16 *supra*; Ordinance No. 58–1270 of December 22, 1958, J.O. Dec. 23, 1958, p. 11551, [1959] D.L. 21, art. 51; French Constitution of Oct. 4, 1958, tit. VIII. art. 65.

[306] For a more detailed description, see 1 DALLOZ, *op. cit. supra* note 273, at No. 26.

[307] Ordinance of January 15, 1826, *supra* note 290, art. 28.

[308] On the appointment, promotion, and salaries of judges and the use of judges of the *Cour de Cassation* for the inspection of courts, see 3.11–3.20 *supra*.

[309] For a brief description of the various special tribunals created during the period of the Algerian troubles, and immediately thereafter, see SPECIAL COURTS IN FRANCE, BULLETIN OF THE INTERNATIONAL COMMISSION OF JURISTS No. 15, p. 16 (April 1963).

[310] Law No. 47–1633, *supra* note 279, art. 1. The figure given in the text includes the additional *avocat général* provided for the *chambre de la Communauté*.

[311] Ordinance of January 15, 1826, *supra* note 290, art. 44.

before any of the panels. [312] He is the administrative head of the *ministère public* attached to the *Cour de Cassation* and assigns his *avocats généraux* to the various panels of the court as the need may arise. [313] A *secrétaire général* acts as his chief assistant for administrative matters. [314] Although the *procureur général* has a power of supervision over all the members of the *ministère public* in France, he does not seem to exercise it. Since 1958, he is the presiding officer of the disciplinary commission for the *ministère public*. [315]

**g. The *bureau* and the *assemblée générale*.** The *bureau* of the *Cour de Cassation* is a kind of executive committee with important duties in the field of court administration. It consists of the *premier président*, the *président* and *doyen* of each panel, the *procureur général*, and the senior *avocat général*; the chief clerk of the court (*greffier en chef*) acts as its secretary.[316] The *bureau* adopts the rules which determine the competence of the various civil panels; it also determines the times and dates when court is to be open. It may assign the judges to the various panels and establishes the time limit within which the reporting judge and the *ministère public* must be ready to present their report or recommendations. [317] It also performs some related functions. [318]

Other questions of internal court administration are decided by the *assemblée générale*, which also designates the members of the *Cour de Cassation* who are to be part of the *Tribunal des Conflits*. Like the *chambres réunies*, the *assemblée générale* consists of a joint session of all the panels. While meetings of the *chambres réunies* are open to the public, it is excluded from meetings of the *assemblée générale*. [319]

[312] Ordinance of January 15, 1826, *supra* note 290, art. 45; Law No. 47–1366, *supra* note 279, art. 6.

[313] Ordinance of January 15, 1826, *supra* note 290, arts. 43, 46, and 47. The *avocats généraux* at the *Cour de Cassation* are in a sense considered as always representing the *procureur général*.

[314] See 1 DALLOZ, *op. cit. supra* note 273, at No. 56.

[315] Ordinance No. 58–1270, *supra* note 305, art. 60.

[316] Law No. 47–1366, *supra* note 279, art. 2.

[317] Law No. 47–1633, *supra* note 279, arts. 3–4, 23, 26, 41.

[318] For example, it prepares the list of nine members of the *Cour de Cassation* and nine lower court judges out of which the French President must select six appointees for the *Conseil Supérieur de la Magistrature*. Ordinance No. 58–1271 of December 22, 1958, J.O. Dec. 23, 1958, p. 11556, [1959] D.L. 25, art. 1.

[319] Law No. 47–1633, *supra* note 279, art. 5. The general assembly includes the members of the *ministère public*. It is also the body to which proposed legislation is submitted if the government wishes to obtain the opinion of the *Cour de Cassation*. 1 DALLOZ, *op. cit. supra* note 273, No. 99. On the *Tribunal des Conflits*, see 3.03 *supra*.

**h. The *greffier*.** The chief clerk of the court, called *greffier en chef*, is an *officier ministériel*, like the head clerks of the other courts. [320] He must be "presented" to the Minister of Justice by his predecessor before he can be appointed. In practice, this means that he purchases his office. Unlike the *greffiers* of the other courts, however, the chief clerk of the *Cour de Cassation* does not derive his main income from fees collected from litigants, which he must turn over to the government, but from his salary. [321] The main assistants of the chief clerk are eight so-called *greffiers de chambre*, only five of whom act as clerks for the panels of the court; the other three have supervisory functions in the three divisions (civil, criminal, and social) of the clerk's office. [322] In addition, there is a fair-sized clerical staff. The court uses eight *huissiers* selected by it from among the huissiers for the Seine *département* as court attendants. They have the sole right to serve certain documents used before the *Cour de Cassation*. [323]

**i. The *service de documentation et d'études* and the *bulletin*.** One of the measures taken during the 1947 reorganization of the *Cour de Cassation* to speed up the work of the court, to ensure greater consistency in the decisions of the various panels of the court, and to make its decisions more accessible, was the creation of a *service de documentation et d'études*. At present, it consists of a professional staff of about twenty *magistrats* in the lower echelons of the hierarchy and of a small clerical staff. It is under the direct supervision of the *premier président*. [324] The research and documentation unit has established a central card file of summaries of all *Cour de Cassation* decisions grouped by subject matter. [325] This facilitates case law research, difficult because of the absence of a true digest system, and makes it less likely that one panel will overlook a decision in point rendered by another

[320] On *officiers ministériels* in general and court clerks in particular, see 2.04, 2.09 *supra*. The chief clerk of the *Cour de Cassation* must always be the holder of a *licence* degree in law. Ordinance of January 15, 1826, *supra* note 290, art. 73.

[321] 1 Dalloz, *op. cit. supra* note 273, No. 60.

[322] Concerning the number of the *greffiers de chambre*, see Law No. 47–1366, *supra* note 279, art. 1. The *greffiers de chambre* are appointed to their post by the Minister of Justice on the suggestion of the *bureau* of the *Cour de Cassation*, which must evaluate the merits of each candidate who is proposed to it by the chief clerk.

[323] The eight court attendants (*huissiers audienciers*) have the sole right (1) to serve all papers which are served by one *avocat* at the *Cour de Cassation* on one of his colleagues and (2) to serve other papers concerning *Cour de Cassation* proceedings, provided they can be served within the city limits of Paris. 1 Dalloz, *op. cit. supra* note 273, No. 89.

[324] Law No. 47–1633, *supra* note 279, arts. 11–13; 1 Dalloz, *op. cit. supra* note 273, No. 57 (Supp. 1963).

[325] This is required by Law No. 47–1633, *supra* note 279, art. 10. In 1952, the file consisted already of well over 20,000 cards. Ropers, *supra* note 280.

panel. If the second panel does not wish to follow the decisions of the first panel, the case may be referred to the *assemblée plénière civile* to resolve the conflict. The *service de documentation et d'études* also renders research assistance to the members of the *Cour de Cassation.*

As part of the 1947 reorganization of the *Cour de Cassation*, its official reports (*Bulletin des arrêts de la Cour de Cassation*) were also improved. Until that time, they had contained only reversals and no affirmances. Since 1947, all civil cases decided by the *Cour de Cassation* are reported. [326]

**j. Sessions.** The *Cour de Cassation* has its official seat in Paris. It has never held court elsewhere, except during periods of emergencies. [327] Its official quarters are located in the huge and ancient *Palais de Justice*, where most of the other Paris courts also hold their sessions. However, most of the rooms used by the *Cour de Cassation* are in a nineteenth century addition to the building that is lavish but not as impressive as its older parts. The civil panels of the court do not meet during the official vacation period from August 1 to October 1. The criminal panel meets throughout the year. Judges from the civil panels periodically relieve the members of the criminal panel to enable the latter to get a vacation. During the vacation period, urgent civil cases are handled by the criminal panel. [328] The period during which the court is in session (October 1 to July 31) is usually referred to as its judicial year (*année judiciaire*).

**k. Calendar congestion.** Originally, the *Cour de Cassation* carried only a very small caseload. There were about 520 cases in 1840 and 700 around 1900. This load began to increase in the twentieth century, in part, perhaps, because the *Cour de Cassation* sometimes took a rather broad view as to what were matters of law subject to its review, and thus encouraged the filing of *pourvois*. [329] The unsettled social con-

[326] Publication of all civil cases is required by Law No. 47–1633, *supra* note 279, art. 62. Criminal cases are still published on a selective basis. The reports of the *Cour de Cassation* are published in two separate series, one for the criminal cases, called *bulletin criminel* and abbreviated *bull. crim.*, and one for the civil cases, usually called *bulletin civil*, abbreviated *bull. civ.* In the *bulletin civil*, there are separate parts for each of the four civil panels. The *bulletin* appears monthly, in pamphlet form, but continuously paginated per year, so that binding is easy.

[327] 1 DALLOZ, *op. cit. supra* note 273, Nos. 27–28 (giving detailed history of the peregrinations of the *Cour de Cassation* during various emergencies).

[328] Decree No. 53–586 of June 25, 1953, J.O. June 27, 1953, p. 5707, [1953] D.L. 228 (vacation of the *Cour de Cassation*); Ordinance of January 15, 1826, *supra* note 290, art. 64 (criminal panel not to have vacations; judges to be relieved by judges from other panels).

[329] *Cf.* Ropers, *supra* note 280.

ditions of the Second World War and its aftermath and the large volume of often poorly drafted legislation enacted at the time brought a veritable explosion of cases. [330] Slightly over 5000 civil and about the same number of criminal *pourvois* were filed in 1951. Both civil and criminal *pourvois* increased to well over 7,000 in 1956 and then declined again to about 5300 in 1961, the civil *pourvois* decreasing more steadily than the criminal *pourvois*. In 1947, the backlog of cases was about 5000; the number rose to 15,000 in 1952, and reached a maximum of over 23,000 in 1956. Then the effect of the various reforms – mainly expansion of the court – began to make itself felt, and the *Cour de Cassation* was able to decide substantially more cases than were added to its calendar (about 1200 more civil cases in 1961). At present, the calendar of criminal cases is up to date, and in the civil field, where congestion had been worst (four to five years delay), the court is close to up to date. [331]

The structure of the regular court system in France

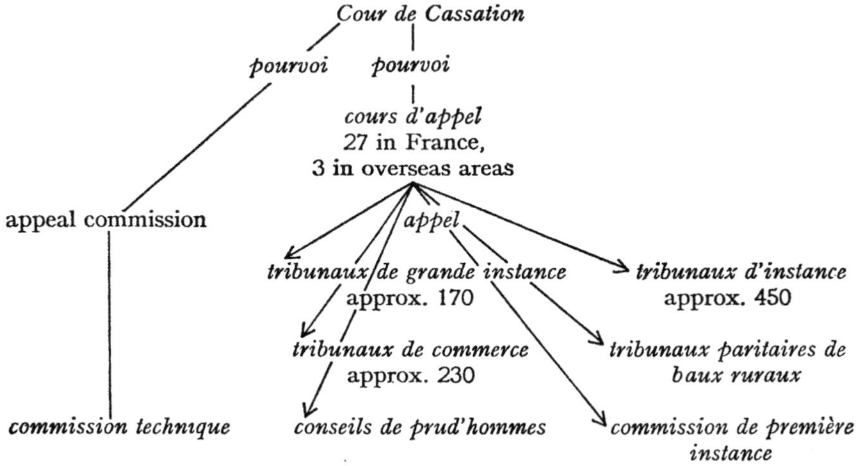


[330] Housing shortage and resulting rent control measures produced especially heavy litigation; between 1951 and 1958 an average of about 1200 rent control cases yearly came to the *Cour de Cassation*. In addition, in many matters involving social legislation the requirement that an *avocat aux conseils* be used was abolished. This increased *pourvois* by making them less costly, and added to the burden of the court, as some of the work was in fact shifted from counsel to the judges. Also, the decline in the value of the French currency made the fine payable by an unsuccessful appellant less of a deterrent. As part of the general program to reduce delay in the *Cour de Cassation*, the fine was increased, and the number of instances in which the assistance of an *avocat aux conseils* is not required was reduced. See 1 SOLUS & PERROT 607.

[331] Figures taken from ANNUAIRE STATISTIQUE DE LA FRANCE RÉTROSPECTIF 75 (1961) and from 1 DALLOZ, *op. cit. supra* note 273, at No. 105. Some were supplied by M. Marc Ancel, *Conseiller* at the *Cour de Cassation*. Figures that are considerably smaller, both concerning the number of *pourvois* filed and the total backlog, are given in 1 SOLUS & PERROT 608–09. These apparently exclude criminal cases.

## CHAPTER 4

# ADJUDICATORY AUTHORITY

This chapter surveys French rules regulating the exercise of adjudicatory power in civil cases. It provides definitions of terms used (4.01–4.02), discusses extraordinary (4.03–4.10) as well as ordinary rules of general competence (4.11–4.36), describes rules regulating the subject matter competence of the various tribunals that may hear civil cases (4.37–4.44), and concludes with a reference to the discussion of rules of territorial competence in earlier parts (4.44).

## 1. INTRODUCTION

### 4.01. Jurisdictional Concepts In General

A discussion in English of jurisdictional problems involving French law must cope with semantic difficulties. First, the terms *juridiction* and jurisdiction sound alike, but have different meanings: The French word *juridiction*, although often mistranslated as jurisdiction, [1] ordinarily means tribunal. [2] Second, in each language jurisdictional terms are often used in an imprecise manner. Discussion of the various meanings of the term jurisdiction and definition of the terms that will be used in this chapter should, therefore, precede elaboration on specific French rules.

In the United States, the term jurisdiction usually refers to the power of a political body, such as a state, or an organ of a political body, such as a court. However, it may also designate the territory within which the power may be exercised. [3] The term jurisdiction is further used to denote the manner of the exercise of a power rather than

[1] Thus, art. III of the recent Convention of Establishment with France of November 25, 1959, [1960] 2 U.S.T. & O.I.A. 2398, TIAS No. 4625, states that nationals of the contracting parties shall have access to courts in all degrees of jurisdiction. This is a literal translation of the French *tribunaux à tous degrès de juridiction*, meaning courts of all instances.

[2] Sometimes the term *juridiction* is also used to denote the judicial function or a group of courts. See, *e.g.*, MOREL 77. The French word *juridiction* and the English word jurisdiction are both derived from the Latin term *jurisdictio*. As to its meaning, see *Gai Institutiones* I 6; *Codex Justiniani* III, 13; and *Digesta* IIX, 1. On the terms jurisdiction and competence generally, see Smit, *The Terms Jurisdiction and Competence in Comparative Law*, in 10 AM. J COMP. L. 64 (1961).

[3] See, *e.g.*, 28 U.S.C. § 1783(a)(2) (1958).

its existence. Thus, it has been stated that in a criminal case the federal courts do not have jurisdiction if the defendant is deprived of his right to counsel. [4] Failure to give notice of the proceedings and to afford an opportunity to be heard has likewise been viewed as affecting jurisdiction. [5] Even the failure to state a cause of action has been alleged to deprive the court of jurisdiction. [6] In this study, the term jurisdiction is used only in its primary sense of denoting power.

**a. The meanings of the term jurisdiction.** In the United States, the term jurisdiction may describe legislative, executive, or judicial power.[7] However, since in this study problems of legislative and executive jurisdiction do not loom large, the term jurisdiction, when used, will refer to judicial jurisdiction.

Judicial jurisdiction has been defined as the power of a political body to subject a given person or thing to its judicial processes. [8] However, some further particularization seems desirable. In describing a power, the framework within which the power may be exercised must be defined. The term jurisdiction is often used to designate the power of a state to subject a given person or thing to its judicial processes under a higher body of law, such as the United States Constitution. However, in many cases, the scope of the jurisdictional power of a political body is determined under the law of some other, but not higher, body. When recognition is sought in the United States of a French judgment, American courts apply their own jurisdictional concepts to determine whether France had the power to render the judgment. [9] Nussbaum, following the example of Bartin, has proposed that jurisdiction in this latter sense be called indirect. [10] The term international jurisdiction is also used to indicate this form of judicial power, [11] but will be avoided here because it may lead to confusion with the term international competence, which is discussed below.

[4] Johnson v. Zerbst, 304 U.S. 458 (1938).

[5] See, *e.g.*, RESTATEMENT (SECOND), CONFLICT OF LAWS, *Introductory Note* c.4. (Tent. Draft No. 3, 1956). See also EHRENZWEIG, CONFLICT OF LAWS, 77–79 (1962).

[6] See Montana-Dakota Util. Co. v. Northwestern Public Service Co., 341 U.S. 246, 249 (1950).

[7] See RESTATEMENT (SECOND), CONFLICT OF LAWS, *Introductory Note* § 42, § 43c, § 43e (Tentative Draft No. 3, 1956).

[8] See RESTATEMENT (SECOND), CONFLICT OF LAWS § 74 (Tentative Draft No. 3, 1956).

[9] See, *e.g.*, Reese, *The Status in This Country of Judgments Rendered Abroad*, 50 COLUM. L. REV. 783, 789–90 (1950).

[10] Nussbaum, *Jurisdiction and Foreign Judgments*, 41 COLUM. L. REV. 221 (1941). The equivalent French term is *compétence indirecte*.

[11] Nussbaum, *supra* note 10, at 225.

**b. Jurisdiction and competence distinguished.** The situation in which the power of a state is defined under some higher or different law must be distinguished from the situation in which the power of a court is defined under the internal law of the governmental unit in which the court is sitting. The power of a court to act in a specific situation by virtue of the law of the state in which it is sitting will be described by use of the term competence.[12] However, when the question arises whether a state has the power to subject certain persons or things to its judicial processes as that power is defined by some higher law or by the law of a different state, then, and only then, will the term jurisdiction be used.[13] When necessary in discussing the enforcement of foreign judgments, the term jurisdiction will be used to indicate that the reference is to the judicial jurisdiction of one state as defined by the law of another.

The power of the French state to submit persons or things to its judicial processes is not limited by a higher body of law. As a result, problems as to French judicial jurisdiction arise only in connection with the enforcement of French judgments abroad. French law does provide, however, whether and which French courts have the power to deal with certain controversies. From those provisions, French courts have derived rules determining whether a foreign court has judicial jurisdiction under French law. Consequently, rules of competence of the French courts are of vital importance. If the six-nation European Common Market becomes an independent political force with the power to restrict the powers of the constituent nations, French judicial jurisdiction may become a more important topic.[14]

[12] The term competence or competency in the sense here used is known to, but not particularly popular with, American courts and commentators. For proper use of the term competence, see, *e.g.*, Strank v. Mercy Hospital, 376 Pa. 305, 309, 102 A. 2d 172 (1954); 2 BEALE, CONFLICT OF LAWS 1377 (1935); Nussbaum, *supra* note 10.

Both the Restatement of Judgments and the proposed revision of the Restatement of Conflict of Laws use the term competency. RESTATEMENT, JUDGMENTS § 7 (1942); RESTATEMENT (SECOND), CONFLICT OF LAWS § 47, *Comment* g (Tent. Draft No. 4, (1957). However,Ehrenzweig disapproves of the term. EHRENZWEIG, CONFLICT OF LAWS 73 (1962). Goodrich, CONFLICT OF LAWS (4th ed. Scoles 1964) uses the term only in passing, while STUMBERG, CONFLICT OF LAWS (3d ed. 1963), does not seem to use it at all. A court of competent jurisdiction is a term frequently encountered. And a competent court is often described as one having "lawful jurisdiction." See, *e.g.*, People *ex rel.* Fisher v. Morhous, 183 MISC. 51, 58, 49 N.Y.S. 2d 110, 116 (1944). These examples illustrate the desirability of more discriminate use of the terms competence and jurisdiction. See further Nussbaum, *supra* note 10.

[13] *Accord*, RESTATEMENT (SECOND), CONFLICT OF LAWS, *Introductory Note* c.4 (Tent. Draft No. 3, 1956); Nussbaum, *supra* note 10, at 221.

[14] Some steps in that direction have been taken. See 3.24 *infra*.

**c. General competence and specific competence distinguished.** In discussing the competence of the French courts, two distinct problems must be dealt with. The first, from a logical point of view, is the problem of whether, under French law, an action may be brought in France before any French court. This problem is resolved by application of what French scholars and this study call rules of *compétence générale* or sometimes *compétence internationale.* [15] Once it has been determined that the French courts are generally competent, the second problem that arises is before what specific court in France the action must be brought. The rules governing the answer to that problem are called rules of specific competence.

The logical distinction between the two kinds of competence, general and specific, seems clear. Nevertheless, that distinction was not, orginally, well understood in France. It is the merit of Bartin, the leading French scholar in the field, to have demonstrated its significance. [16] The confusion in this area is perhaps due to the fact that, notwithstanding the distinction between rules of general and of specific competence, they are interrelated in French law.

The only explicit statutory rules as to the general competence of the French courts are found in articles 14 and 15 of the French Civil Code. These articles provide generally that every action involving either a plaintiff or a defendant who is a French national may be brought in France. [17]

Rules as to the specific competence of French courts are found in a large number of disparate statutory provisions. [18] These rules are also of significance in determining the general competence of the French courts. It has been held that, even when articles 14 or 15 of the French Civil Code are not applicable, an action may nevertheless be brought in France if rules of specific competence point to a particular French court. [19] For example, one of the statutory provisions governing the specific competence of the French courts, article 59 of the Code of Civil Procedure, provides that the court specifically competent in an ordinary civil case is, subject to some exceptions, the court sitting at the defendant's domicile. This article has been interpreted to permit the

[15] The terms *compétence générale* and *compétence internationale* are used interchangeably by French authors.

[16] 1 BARTIN, PRINCIPES DE DROIT INTERNATIONAL PRIVÉ 303 *et seq.* (1930).

[17] See 4.04 *infra.*

[18] See 4.11–4.36 *infra.*

[19] See 4.11 *infra.*

bringing of an action in France whenever the defendant is a French domiciliary, even though Articles 14 and 15 may be inapplicable.

**d. Specific competence with respect to the subject matter or *compétence d'attribution*.** The determination of what French court is specifically competent to hear a given controversy requires the answer to two questions: First, before what kind of court must the case be brought; [20] and second, in what part of France must the proceedings be initiated. [21] The rules providing the answer to the first of these problems are called in France rules of *compétence d'attribution*, *compétence ratione materiae*, or *compétence absolue*. [22] In this study, the term competence with respect to subject matter or the French term *compétence d'attribution* will be used.

**e. Territorial competence.** In France, rules determining where in France an action must be brought are called rules of *compétence territoriale* or sometimes rules of *compétence relative* or *compétence ratione personae*. [23] This latter term is used because the place where the action must be brought depends frequently on the domicile of the parties to the suit. However, these rules have nothing in common with the American concept of jurisdiction over the person. Since they determine where in France a particular action must be brought, they are rather analogous to Anglo-American rules of venue. [24] This study will use the term territorial competence.

## 4.02. Some Basic Differences in Jurisdictional Concepts

Differences in approach to legal problems, even more than difficulties of language and terminology, may impede understanding of French

[20] On the rules determining the answer to this question, see 4.37–4.43 *infra*.

[21] On the rules providing the answer to this question, see 4.11–4.36, 4.44 *infra*.

[22] CUCHE & VINCENT 199–200; *Morel* 177–78.

[23] *Ibid*.

[24] One distinction between venue and territorial competence, as that term is understood in France, should be pointed out. Traditionally, the common law term venue does not refer to the court in which a certain action must be brought, but only to the place where the trial, which is only one phase of the action, must be had. Nussbaum, *supra* note 14, at 222. Thus, it is usually possible to take procedural steps not amounting to a trial in various places. See, *e.g.*, N.Y.C.P.L.R. § 2212 (motions may be made in any county within judicial district in which action is pending and in adjoining counties). There is no such option in France. All procedural steps must be taken before the court which is territorially competent. The only exception relates to provisional remedies and execution of judgments. See 4.26 *infra*. Nor was it possible, until recently, simply to transfer a case that had been brought before a court lacking territorial competence. The case had to be dismissed. Now a transfer is possible. See 7.09.b *infra*.

concepts of jurisdiction and competence. A few basic differences between French and common-law thinking are here indicated.

**a. Service of process does not affect the competence of French courts.** It is a traditional common-law notion that, except in actions *in rem* or *quasi in rem*, the court must obtain jurisdiction over the person of the defendant, frequently by service of process on the defendant within the state. [25]

Although this view has been attacked as an outgrowth of "outmoded power ideas," [26] personal service within the State is still a significant means for obtaining jurisdiction over the person in the United States. The same is not true in France. Service of process never confers competence on a French court. Accordingly, improper service, though it has certain procedural consequences, does not affect the competence of the court. [27]

**b. No collateral attack on judgments of incompetent French courts.** Under American law, lack of jurisdiction or competence usually renders a judgment void even in the state in which it was rendered. As a consequence, it is usually possible to attack such a judgment collaterally even in the state of rendition. [28]

French courts examine the existence of jurisdiction of the foreign state, or, as the French courts and commentators call it, the *compétence indirecte*, when they are asked to recognize a judgment rendered abroad. In doing this, they apply French concepts of jurisdiction and usually refuse to enforce the foreign judgment if the action was one that could have been brought in France under the sweeping provisions of articles 14 and 15 of Civil Code. [29]

A different rule prevails as to domestic French judgments. The general rule is that no collateral attack is allowed against a French judgment that has become final. [30] Therefore, it is impossible to attack a French judgment in France, even if it has been rendered by an incompetent court, once all means for direct attack have been exhausted.

[25] See Pennoyer v. Neff, 95 U.S. 714 (1878).

[26] EHRENZWEIG, *op. cit. supra* note 12, at 77–79.

[27] See 7.09.c *infra*.

[28] RESTATEMENT, JUDGMENTS § 11 (1942).

[29] See 14.04.a *infra*.

[30] The usual expression of this rule is: *Voies de nullité n'ont lieu contre jugements*. CUCHE & VINCENT 62–63. For a recent case, see Bouchet v. Lamberty, Cass. Civ., Febr. 25, 1964, [1964] D.J. 312.

**c. Easy waiver of jurisdictional objections.** As a general rule, in the United States, lack of competence over the subject matter is never waived, and the defendant may raise that issue at any stage of the proceedings. [31] In France, however, since the 1958 reforms, the defendant must raise objections to the competence of the court very early in the proceedings, and he is precluded from doing so once he raises an issue on the merits. It is quite immaterial in this connection whether the objection goes to the general competence or to the subject-matter or territorial competence of the court. Only in cases in which public policy is particularly involved, may the court dismiss an action on its own motion. In such a case, it may do so even if the defendant is precluded from raising the issue. [32]

## 2. RULES OF GENERAL COMPETENCE

### 4.03. Introduction

Only two statutory provisions, articles 14 and 15 of the French Civil Code, deal specifically with the general competence of the French courts. According to these articles, any action to which a French national is a party may be brought in France. As a result of the meagerness of these statutory provisions, much of the law concerning the general competence of the French courts is case law.

French rules of general competence are derived from two sources. They are contained not only in articles 14 and 15 of the French Civil Code, but have also been construed by the French courts to be embodied in the rules governing territorial competence. [33] The latter rules are often called in France ordinary rules of general competence, or *règles de compétence de droit commun*, or *règles de compétence ordinaires*. On the other hand, the rules derived from articles 14 and 15 of the Civil Code, which have no counterpart in internal French law, are frequently referred to as extraordinary or exceptional rules, as *règles exorbitantes* or *règles exceptionnelles*. [34] Although the extraordinary rules based on articles 14 and 15 of the Civil Code have often been attacked by French and foreign authors, they have been retained in the 1955 draft for a

[31] See, *e.g.*, FED. R. CIV. P. 12(b).

[32] CUCHE & VINCENT 280–82; CODE DE PROCÉDURE CIVILE arts. 168, 171, as amended by DÉCRET No. 58–1289 of Dec. 22, 1958, J.O. Dec. 23, 1958, p. 11608, [1959] D.L. 45.

[33] 6 NIBOYET No. 1804; BATIFFOL No. 683.

[34] Franceskakis, *Compétence étrangère et jugement étranger*, 42 REV. CRIT. DR. INT. PRIVÉ 17 (1853); 1 DALLOZ, RÉPERTOIRE DE PROCÉDURE CIVILE ET COMMERCIALE, *Compétence Internationale* No. 53 (1955).

revised Civil Code prepared by the Commission on the Revision of the Civil Code. [35]

## 4.04. The Nationality of the Parties as a Basis of General Competence

Articles 14 and 15 of the French Civil Code are found in the chapter dealing with the rights of aliens. They read in translation: [36]

> Art. 14: An alien, even if he does not reside in France, may be summoned before the French courts on account of the execution of obligations he has contracted in France with a Frenchman; he may be brought before the French courts on account of obligations he has contracted in a foreign country with a Frenchman.
>
> Art. 15. A Frenchman may be brought before a French court for all obligations contracted in a foreign country even with an alien.

Articles 14 and 15, although ordinarily discussed by French courts and writers as if they were one, deal with different situations. Article 14 permits a French plaintiff to sue an alien in France on all obligations contracted by the alien, wherever incurred. According to article 15, a French defendant may be sued in France irrespective of the nationality of the plaintiff. [37]

The critical factor determining the applicability of articles 14 and 15 is nationality. Whether any party is domiciled in France is immaterial.[38] According to article 14, a French national domiciled in New York may sue a citizen and resident of New York in France on a contract made in New York. Conversely, under article 15, an American citizen domiciled in New York may bring an action in France against a French national domiciled in New York on a contract made in New York. Articles 14 and 15 enable French nationals, whether as plaintiffs or defendants, to litigate with aliens in French courts [39] and thus create privileges attaching to French nationality. [40]

[35] Nadelmann, *Jurisdictionally Improper Fora*, in 20TH CENTURY COMPARATIVE AND CONFLICTS LAW, LEGAL ESSAYS IN HONOR OF HESSEL E. YNTEMA, 321, 322 (1961), BATIFFOL No. 684.

[36] The translation is substantially similar to that given in Lowenfeld and De Vries, *Jurisdiction in Personal Actions, A Comparison of Civil Law Views*, 44 IOWA L. REV. 306, 317 (1958). On the history of the rules, see also 3 ARMINJON, PRÉCIS DE DROIT INTERNATIONAL PRIVÉ 180–88 (2d ed. 1952).

[37] BATIFFOL No. 683; 6 NIBOYET Nos. 1733, 1754.

[38] Rougeron v. Veuve Rougeron, Cass. Civ., May 5, 1959, 48 REV. CRIT. DR. INT. PRIVÉ 501 (1959); 86 CLUNET 1158 (1959); Epoux Morris, Cass. Req., April 29, 1931, 59 CLUNET 98 (1932).

[39] BATIFFOL No. 684.

[40] 6 NIBOYET No. 1733.

## 4.05. Persons to Whom Articles 14 and 15 of the Civil Code Apply

In determining whether articles 14 and 15 apply, the French courts have given the requirement of French nationality a rather liberal interpretation.

**a. Natural persons.** Every natural person who is a national of France is covered by articles 14 and 15. [41] A person having more than one nationality, one of which is French, is considered French. [42]

The burden of proof is on the party who raises an issue involving nationality. Accordingly, a plaintiff relying on article 14 must show that he is a French national. [43] Refugees domiciled in France, although not French nationals, may also rely on articles 14 and 15. This judicial conclusion has been based on the Geneva convention on refugees which gives such refugees a de facto position quite similar to that of French nationals. [44]

Whether a person is a French national must be determined as of the time the suit is begun; nationality at the time the cause of action accrued or the judgment is rendered is immaterial. [45]

[41] BATIFFOL No. 685.

[42] BATIFFOL No. 78.

[43] Code of French Nationality, ORDONNANCE of Oct. 19, 1945; J.O. Oct. 20, 1945, p. 6700, [1946] D.L. 17, art. 138; Comité de défense des porteurs d'obligations de la Soc. de gaz de Bucarest v. Soc. du gaz de Bucarest, Trib. Seine, April 20, 1932, 60 CLUNET 70 (1933). *But see* Jahr v. Verdier, Trib. Gde. Inst. Seine, March 1, 1960, 88 CLUNET 448 (1961) (defendant contesting applicability of article 15 has burden of proving he is not a French National); *cf.* Plaisant, *French Law of Nationality*, 35 CORN. L.R. 373 (1948). Any person wanting documentary proof of his French nationality may ask the *tribunal d'instance* to issue him a certificate of French nationality. Code of French Nationality arts. 149–51. Since the issuance of such a certificate is considered an administrative matter, an appeal from a decision of the court refusing a certificate lies to the Ministry of Justice. In the case of a naturalized French citizen, the certificate of naturalization fulfills the same role. *Id.* art. 138; *cf.* BATIFFOL Nos. 151–54; 6 NIBOYET 1733. When lack of French nationality was still sufficient to defeat competence, a defendant relying on alienage had to show that he was not a French national. Papazoglu v. Cassatelli, Cass. Req., April 12, 1918, 15 REV. CRIT. DR. INT. PRIVÉ 86 (1919).

[44] Ermolieff v. Sa femme, Cour Paris, June 27, 1957, 47 REV. CRIT. DR. INT. PRIVÉ 1944 (1958) (note Francescakis). *But see* Sarraute & Tager, Le nouveau statut des réfugiés (Convention de Genève du 28 juillet 1951), 42 REV. CRIT. DR. INT. PRIVÉ 245, 269 (1953). Until abrogated by article 13 of the Law of August 10, 1927, J.O. Aug. 14, 1927, p. 8697, [1927] B.L.D. 400, article 13 of the Civil Code provided that the government could issue a decree authorizing an alien to obtain an official domicile in France and that such an alien enjoyed full civil rights. As long as the old article 13 was in force, for the purpose of determining judicial competence, aliens having such an officially authorized domicile in France were treated as French nationals. BATIFFOL No. 658; For a New York case discussing former article 13, see Dupuy v. Wurtz, 53 N.Y. 556 (1873).

[45] Comte de Bari v. Comte de Caserte, Cass. Req. Jan 9, 1906, [1906] S.I. 262; De Kosserki v. Colmar, Cour Paris, June 7, 1928, [1928] D.H. 453, [1928] GAZ. PAL. 613, 56 CLUNET 353 (1929); Dame Vidal v. Marshall, Trib. Gde Inst. Seine, January 16, 1959, 87 CLUNET 114 1960).

**b. The effect of assignment on the competence of the French courts.** Problems arise when the person bringing suit is not the one in whose favor the cause of action accrued. In such a case, the nationality of the person bringing the suit, not that of the original holder of the cause of action, ordinarily governs. This rule is applicable to holders of negotiable instruments and also to persons suing on a cause of action that has descended by death. [46] It is not entirely clear to what extent the rule is applicable to a mere assignee of a contract right. [47]

If a contract originally made by persons who are not French nationals, which contains an arbitration clause or a clause specifying that actions on the contract must be brought before a specified foreign court, is subsequently assigned to a French national, the French national is bound by the provisions of the contract and cannot rely on articles 14 or 15. [48] This result is in accord with the usual French rule that the competence of courts may be modified by agreement of the parties. [49]

**c. Suits between French nationals.** Some early decisions held that article 14, by its own terms, applied exclusively when only one party was a French national. [50] On that reasoning, they dismissed suits between French nationals when the nationality of the plaintiff was the only possible basis for the competence of the French courts. [51] However, the more numerous and recent decisions hold that, since actions involving a French national and an alien may be brought in France even when both parties are non-domiciliaries, it follows *a fortiori* that two French nationals may sue each other before French courts though neither of them is domiciled in France. [52] This solution receives additional support from article 15 of the Civil Code. This article, which

[46] BATIFFOL No. 685.

[47] BATIFFOL No. 685; the problem is discussed extensively in 6 NIBOYET No. 1734. See also the cases cited in DALLOZ, RÉPERTOIRE DE PROCÉDURE CIVILE ET COMMERCIALE, *Compétence Internationale* No. 39.

[48] Montane v. Cie des chemins de fer portugais, Cass. Civ. July 12, 1950, 41 REV. CRIT. DR. INT. PRIVÉ 514 (1952) (note Francescakis) (arbitration clause); *cf.* Loustalet v. Balbis, Cass. Civ. April 9, 1935, 21 REV. CRIT. DR. INT. PRIVÉ 168 (1936) (election of domicile clause); BATIFFOL No. 686.

[49] See 4.28 *infra*.

[50] For the translation of article 14, see 4.04 *supra*.

[51] *E.g.*, Saad et Trad v. Emile et Jaques Tabet, Trib. Seine, July 2, 1930, 59 CLUNET 967 (1932).

[52] Dame Boulaud v. Boulaud, Cour Lyon, February 27, 1929, 58 CLUNET 1023 (1931); P.L.W. v. Dame P.L.W., Trib. civ. Seine, Nov. 30, 1956, [1957] D. SOMM. 8, [1957] J.P.C. 2 9806; X v. Dame X., Cour Paris, April 29, 1958, [1958] D.SOMM. 127, [1958] GAZ. PAL. 1.227. The cases on both sides of the question are collected in Perroud, *La compétence des tribunaux français pour les procès entre Français*, 59 CLUNET 867 (1932). See also DALLOZ, RÉPERTOIRE DE PROCÉDURE CIVILE ET COMMERCIALE, *Compétence Internationale* No. 37 and MISE À JOUR 1964.

must be read together with article 14, applies to defendants who are French nationals without specifying that the plaintiff may not be a French national.

**d. *Sociétés* (companies).** The rules of articles 14 and 15 are not restricted to natural persons. Any French *société* may also sue or be sued in France.[53] Though implying an organization with a separate legal personality, the French concept of *société* is broader than the American concept of corporation. The two French forms of business organization with limited liability that correspond most closely to American corporations, the *société anonyme* and the *société à responsabilité limitée*, are undoubtedly *sociétés*. But partnerships (*sociétés en nom collectif*) and partnerships with limited liability (*sociétés en commandite*) also answer that description. Although there is no limited liability for the active partners in the last two types of organizations, they are considered legal entities separate and distinct from the persons of the partners.[54] To avoid confusion, the term company will be used as a translation of *société*.

In determining the nationality of companies, French courts do not necessarily consider a company a national of the state in which it is incorporated.[55] The traditional rule is that a company has the nationality of the state in which its seat or *siège social* is located[56] and that the *siège social* is located where the management of the company's business is centered.[57] In determining the latter question, the courts now seem to use a sort of grouping of contacts approach, which permits them to disregard the more or less fictional offices some companies maintain.[58]

[53] BATIFFOL No. 685.

[54] RIPERT, TRAITÉ ELÉMENTAIRE DE DROIT COMMERCIAL 118–19, 252–53 (3d ed. 1954). There is no limited liability for the active partners in French partnerships. *Cf.* article 14 of the Convention of Establishment, *supra* note 1 (defining *société*). The French draftsman of the treaty seems to have believed that American partnerships have independent legal personality.

[55] BATIFFOL Nos. 193, 194; *cf.* Conard, *Forming a Subsidiary in the European Common Market*, 59 MICH. L. REV. 1, 21 (1960).

[56] Banque franco-serbe v. Danske Landmandsbank Cour Paris, May 21, 1957; 85 CLUNET 130 (1958), 47 REV. CRIT. DR. INT. PRIVÉ 128 (1958). Société Italo-Française v. Attenborough, Trib. com. Seine, June 7, 1938, 66 CLUNET 628 (1939) (seat of corporation in French colony).

[57] Banque Franco-Serbe v. Danske Landmandsbank, *supra* note 56.

[58] Magnard et autres v. Garnier, Cour Paris, Oct. 31, 1957, 47 REV. CRIT. DR. INT. PRIVÉ 345 (1958). Occasionally, French courts have determined the nationality of corporations on the basis of the nationality of the stockholders, but this approach has generally been limited to cases involving the seizure of alien property. BATIFFOL Nos. 196–98, 658 n. 9b. According to Delaume, its extension into the area of competence of courts is a distinct possibility. DELAUME, AMERICAN-FRENCH PRIVATE INTERNATIONAL LAW 145 (2d ed. 1961). Niboyet argues that the nationality of the stockholders ought to determine the nationality of corporations for all purposes. 6 NIBOYET No. 1736.

In the case of associations, the nationality of its members is probably controlling. [59]

## 4.06. Actions to Which Articles 14 and 15 Apply

Although articles 14 and 15 refer to *obligations* involving French nationals, and, in French law, the term *obligation* includes principally contracts and torts, articles 14 and 15 have received a liberal interpretation. They have been interpreted to apply not only to contract or tort actions, [60] but to constitute rules of general competence [61] applicable in many cases that are not based on any *obligation*, such as actions for divorce [62] or for annulment of a marriage, [63] filiation proceedings,[64] and the like. It has been said that articles 14 and 15 grant a personal privilege to French nationals and are therefore, *a fortiori*, applicable in actions involving personal status. [65] Some French courts have held the rule, embodied in the Civil Code, that proceedings involving decedents' estates must be brought at the last domicile of the decedent, [66] applicable even when the decedent had died outside of France and have refused to entertain suits in such cases. [67] Others, however, have permitted suits in France on the basis of articles 14 and 15 if either the plaintiff or defendant was a French national. [68] Recent cases in the *Cour de Cassation* approve of the latter solution. [69]

[59] See Comité de défense des porteurs d'obligations de la Société du gaz de Bucarest v. Société du gaz de Bucarest, *supra* note 43 (bondholders' protective committee cannot sue foreign corporation in France under the provision of article 14 unless there is proof that all its members are French nationals); *cf.* NIBOYET No. 1736, who approves of the decision, but is of the view that there should be no requirement that *all* members of the association be French nationals.

[60] See 2 COLIN & CAPITANT 7.

[61] BATIFFOL No. 687; DE LAPRADELLE & NIBOYET, RÉPERTOIRE DE DROIT INTERNATIONAL, *Compétence en matiere civile et commerciale*, No. 83 (1934) and authorities cited; 6 NIBOYET No. 1741; Consorts Bonnet v. Souris, Cass Civ., February 1, 1955, 44 REV. CRIT. DR. INT. PRIVÉ 327 (1955), [1955] J.C.P. II 8657, 83 CLUNET 684 (1956). For a very rare case giving a restrictive interpretation, see Dame Dougour v. son mari, Cour Aix, April 18, 1955, 83 CLUNET 682 (1956).

[62] *E.g.*, Epoux Morris, *supra* note 38; Ermolieff v. sa femme, *supra* note 44; 3 ARMINJON, *op. cit. supra* note 36, at 227.

[63] Weiler v. Dame Aliki Diplarakos et autre, Cour Paris, December 15, 1948, [1949] S. II 69 (note Delaume); 40 REV. CRIT. DR. INT. PRIVÉ 113 (1940) (note Francescakis).

[64] 6 NIBOYET No. 1742; BATIFFOL No. 687.

[65] BATIFFOL No. 687.

[66] Arts. 110, 822. For a more detailed discussion, see 4.17 *infra*.

[67] *E.g.*, Beer v. Beer-Webster, Cour Aix, January 5, 1953, [1953] J.C.P. 2. 7665; 80 CLUNET 372 (1953).

[68] Woltner v. Cons. Ziegler, Trib. Seine, January 29, 1948, 73–76 CLUNET 43 (1946–1949). Other cases are contained in a note appended to the report of Beer v. Beer-Webster, *supra* note 67, in CLUNET.

[69] Cons. Bonnet v. Souris, *supra* note 61; Rougeron v. Veuve Rougeron, *supra* note 38.

## 4.07. Exceptions to the Applicability of Articles 14 and 15

Two judicially made exceptions limit the tendency of the French courts to broaden the scope of articles 14 and 15. First, French courts will not entertain suits concerning immovables located outside of France even if one or both of the parties are French nationals. [70] This rule is applicable to all actions involving title to immovables, including actions for partition. [71] However, if the action is a so-called mixed action, one based on a personal obligation though involving real estate, the general rule remains applicable. Thus, an action for the rescission of a contract involving foreign real estate may be brought in France if the plaintiff is a French national, since that action is not concerned exclusively with property interests in realty. [72]

The second exception to the general rule is that orders relating to execution issued by foreign courts cannot be attacked in France, either directly or by means of an action for abuse of process based on the execution. [73] It is to be noted that, in the French view, execution refers not only to the execution of final judgments, but also to provisional remedies such as attachment. Indeed, the leading French case concerned an attachment of the account of a French national with the Irving Trust Co. by another French national. The *Cour de Cassation* held that a French court was not competent to annul the attachment which had been ordered by the United States District Court for the Southern District of New York. [74]

## 4.08. Territorial Competence in Actions Brought Under Articles 14 and 15

Articles 14 and 15, which are rules of general competence, determine merely whether an action may be brought in France. The specific French court in which the action must be brought is determined by applying rules of territorial competence. It usually depends on the defendant's domicile, although sometimes other contacts, such as the place of tort or the place of making of the contract, may also determine where the action may be brought.

[70] BATIFFOL No. 688; 6 NIBOYET No. 1744.

[71] Nagalingampoullé v. Saminadapoullé et autres, Cass. Civ., July 5, 1933, 61 CLUNET 892 (1934). The principle has recently been reaffirmed by the *Cour de Cassation* in Rougeron v. Veuve Rougeron, *supra* note 38.

[72] Villerelle v. Vinot, Cour Paris ,June 7, 1928, 56 CLUNET 351 (1929). For a definition of so-called mixed actions see MOREL, TRAITÉ ÉLÉMENTAIRE DE PROCÉDURE CIVILE 60–62 (2d ed. 1949).

[73] Société Cyprien Fabre v. Banque privée, Cas. Civ., May 12, 1931, 59 CLUNET 387 (1932), [1931] D.H. 60.

[74] Société Cyprien Fabre v. Banque privée, *supra* note 73.

Since nationality of the parties alone is sufficient to give the French courts competence, an action may be brought in France, although none of the usual rules of territorial competence point to a particular court in which the action may be brought. In such cases, the rules of territorial competence are modified. [75] For example, a defendant who has his residence but not his domicile in France may be sued at his residence in France. [76] A company having its *siège social* outside of France, but a branch office in France, may be sued where its branch office is located.[77] Actions concerning decedents' estates are generally brought at the decedent's domicile. [78] When articles 14 and 15 apply, suits concerning the real property of the decedent may be brought at the location of the property in France, regardless of the decedent's last domicile. [79]

If the action is based on a contract between a Frenchman and a foreigner that has been concluded in the foreign country and is to be performed there, it may be brought at the plaintiff's domicile in France. [80] If even that choice is unavailable because the plaintiff is also domiciled outside France, the plaintiff may choose the place in France where he will sue, provided his choice be reasonable. [81]

### 4.09. Waiver of Reliance on Articles 14 and 15

In spite of the nationalistic character of articles 14 and 15, their impact is often not as pervasive as that of American jurisdictional rules. It is doubtful whether American rules can be modified by agreement of the parties. [82] However, since no strong public policy (*ordre public*)

[75] See generally BATIFFOL No. 690; 6 NIBOYET at Nos. 1746–57.

[76] But this is true only when articles 14 and 15 of the Civil Code are applicable. See 4.13 *infra*.

[77] 1 DALLOZ, RÉPERTOIRE DE PROCÉDURE CIVILE ET COMMERCIALE, *Compétence Internationale* No. 51 (1956).

[78] CODE CIVIL arts. 110, 822. See 4.17 *infra*.

[79] See cases cited *supra* note 69.

[80] Epoux Testasecca, Cass. Req., August 1, 1930, [1930] D.H. 521, [1931] S. I. 43, 58 CLUNET 385 (1931).

[81] This means that the action should be brought in a court close to the frontier of the country where defendant lives, if he lives in a country bordering on France, or in some other place that has a reasonable connection with the parties. Dame Boulaud v. Boulaud, *supra* note 52; Weiller, Cass. Civ. April 23, 1959, 48 REV. CRIT. DR. INT. PRIVÉ 549. (1959); BATIFFOL No. 766. The rule stated in the text was applied most recently in Dal Fiume v. dame Dal Fiume, Cass. Civ., Feb. 14, 1962, 52 REV. CRIT. DR. INT. PRIVÉ 87 (1963) (note Lagarde). The court stated that the place chosen by the plaintiff for bringing the action – the last common residence of the parties in France – was appropriate from the point of view of proper administration of justice. The author of the extensive note interprets this as a possible limitation on the plaintiff's freedom in selecting a court.

[82] *Compare* Meachem v. Jamestown, Franklin and Clearfield R.R., 211 N.Y. 346, 105 N.E.

demands their application, [83] French law freely permits agreements in derogation of the rules enunciated in articles 14 and 15. [84] In this respect, French case law has followed rules governing territorial competence, which may be waived or modified by the parties. [85] Waiver may be made in two ways: either by agreement of the parties or by bringing suit outside France.

**a. Waiver by agreement of the parties.** Whether there is waiver by agreement of the parties is a question of fact that is not reviewable by the *Cour de Cassation.* [86] However, a few rules can nevertheless be marked out.

Reliance on article 14, which enables a French national to sue any foreigner in France, can be waived by the French national, while reliance on article 15, which may benefit either party, can be waived by either party.[87]

Waiver does not have to be explicit. A clause in a contract providing that all suits on the contract must be brought in a foreign court deprives the French courts of competence, even if the parties do not state expressly that they waive reliance on articles 14 and 15. [88] However, French courts tend to decide factual issues concerning the existence of waiver in favor of French nationals who desire to invoke

653 (1914) and Carbon Black Export Co. v. The S.S. Monrosa, 254 F.2d 297 (5th Cir. 1958), *petition for cert. dismissed,* 359 U.S. 180 (1959) *with* Wm. H. Muller & Co. v. Swedish American Line Ltd., 224 F.2d 806 (2d Cir. 1955), *cert. denied,* 350 U.S. 903 (1955). For a comparative discussion, see Lenhoff, *The Parties' Choice of a Forum: "Prorogation Agreements."* 15 RUTGERS L. REV. 414 (1961).

[83] See Comp. Luxembourgeoise d'assurance Le Foyer v. Dulac, Cass. Civ., Nov. 13, 1957, 86 CLUNET 828 (1959); 47 REV. CRIT. DR. INT. PRIVÉ 735 (1958), [1959] D.J. 595; NIBOYET No. 1745; BATIFFOL No. 684.

[84] BATIFFOL No. 692; *cf.* Delaume, *Jurisdiction of Courts and International Loans,* 6 AM. J. COMP. L. 189 (1957); Reboul v. Société Tekkah, Cass. Civ., Jan. 19, 1931, [1931] D.H. 145, 58 CLUNET 1039 (1931).

[85] In this respect, French cases have followed the law governing rules of territorial competence, which are likewise subject to waiver or modification by the parties. See 4.27–4.30 *infra.*

[86] Millet v. Dame Siosterzoneck, Cass. Req., May 4, 1935, [1936] S.I. 781, 63 CLUNET 634 (1936); Dollfus v. National Provincial Bank, Ltd., Cass. Civ., Feb. 13, 1950, 77 CLUNET 200 (1950); Consorts Bonnet v. Souris, *supra* note 61.

[87] BATIFFOL No. 768.

[88] Oualid & Cie v. Deutsche Orient Linie, Cass. Req., June 19, 1928, 56 CLUNET 336 (1929); Nègre v. Capitaine du San Giusto et Cie. Française de Marine, Cass. Req., November 30, 1927, 57 CLUNET 362 (1930); Reboul v. Société Tekkah, *supra* note 84; Cie d'assurance La Confiance v. Soc. Smit et Cie Internationale Sleepdienst, Cour Paris, Oct. 19, 1959, 49 REV. CRIT. DR. INT. PRIVÉ 208, 57, (1960); BATIFFOL No. 684.

If the parties merely waive reliance on articles 14 and 15, the possibility that the suit can still be brought in France is not excluded, since a waiver of articles 14 and 15 does not exclude application of other rules.

articles 14 and 15. Therefore, as a practical matter, it is desirable to be as specific as possible in drawing a waiver clause. [89]

Parties to French contracts often insert clauses to the effect that they elect a domicile in a particular place. In a purely internal French situation, such a clause makes it possible to bring suit where domicile has been elected as well as where the defendant has his real domicile. [90] When such a clause is inserted in an international contract, it may deprive the French courts of their competence under articles 14 and 15, [91] but only if it is clear that that is the purpose of the clause. [92] The use of an arbitration clause, in cases in which its validity is recognized by French law, also avoids application of articles 14 and 15. [93]

Whether a clause dealing with competence is valid depends on the law governing the contract, [94] but under French internal law such a clause need not be in writing. It may be implied from a course of dealings between the parties, [95] as long as it is clear that both parties have freely given their assent. A party having no actual knowledge of a waiver clause is not ordinarily bound by it. [96] The assignee of a contract [97] or bill of lading [98] is usually bound by a clause agreed to by the original parties which waives reliance on articles 14 and 15.

**b. Waiver by bringing suit abroad.** Frequently, French courts state that participation in a suit abroad amounts to waiver. [99] This is par-

[89] The best way to make sure that no suit can be brought in France is to provide by contract that reliance on articles 14 and 15 is waived and that all suits concerning the contract must be brought in a specified foreign court. See 4.36 *infra*.

[90] CODE CIVIL art. 111; CODE DE PROCÉDURE CIVILE art. 59. See also 4.29 *infra*.

[91] DE LAPRADELLE & NIBOYET No. 378; 1 DALLOZ, RÉPERTOIRE DE PROCÉDURE CIVILE ET COMMERCIALE, *Compétence Internationale*, No. 45.

[92] Comp. Le Foyer v. Dulac, *supra* note 83.

[93] BATIFFOL No. 694. Under French internal law, arbitration clauses are ordinarily valid only in commercial matters, but a different rule applies in contracts with international contacts. See 11.07.b *infra*; DALLOZ, *op. cit. supra* note 91, at No. 46. An arbitration clause subject to the condition that the parties must agree on the arbitrator does not result in waiver of reliance on article 14, since the clause is not unconditional. Sté Caribian v. Sté Wildenstein, New York, Cour Paris, Jan. 22, 1957, 46 REV. CRIT. DR. INT. PRIVÉ 486 (1957); [1957] GAZ. PAL. 1 249.

[94] BATIFFOL No. 769.

[95] *E.g.*, Grutter v. Syndic. Laury, Cour Colmar, April 8, 1933, 61 CLUNET 888 (1934).

[96] See Crédit foncier et agricole de l'Etat de Minas Geraes v. Marquet et autres, Cass. Req., June 20, 1932, 60 CLUNET 344 (1933) (French bondholder of Brazilian corporation not bound by provision in by-laws providing for exclusive adjudicatory power of Brazilian courts in all suits against corporation, when no mention of clause on bonds); Schuman et Cie v. Banque nationale du Méxique, Cour Paris, June 8, 1949, 77 CLUNET 206 (1949) (similar facts). However, a stockholder may be bound by such a clause in the by-laws.

[97] Montané v. Cie des Chemins de fer portugais, Cass. Civ., July 12, 1950, 77 CLUNET 1206 (1950), 41 REV. CRIT. DR. INT. PRIVÉ 514 (1952).

[98] Oualid et Cie v. Deutsche Orient Linie, *supra* note 88.

[99] Millet v. Dame Siosterzoneck, *supra* note 86; Tanneries lyonnaises v. Shirazi and sons et

ticularly true as to the party who acts as a plaintiff in the suit outside France. [100] At times, it is also true of the defendant, especially when he files a counter-claim. [101] Here again, whether articles 14 and 15 have been waived is basically a question of fact. Since the French courts seem to put some, although not conclusive, emphasis on whether the defendant in the foreign suit objected to the proceedings in the foreign court, [102] it may be advantageous to a French party who is sued abroad to make at least token objections to the competence of the foreign court. If objection is made, the French courts are likely to hold that the defendant has participated in the foreign suit unwillingly, [103] will refuse to enforce the foreign judgment in France, and will allow a second suit in France by the defendant in the foreign action. [104]

### 4.10. Treaties Limiting the Applicability of Articles 14 and 15

Many treaties modify the effect of articles 14 and 15. They are discussed in some detail below.

### 4.11. General Competence Based on Rules of Territorial Competence – Introduction

Articles 14 and 15 govern the general competence of the French courts only when at least one of the parties is a French national. Soon after the enactment of the French Civil Code the question arose whether, since no specific statutory provision authorized them to act in such cases, French courts were competent if all parties were aliens. Early decisions held that they were not.

This rule was unfair to the numerous foreigners living in France who had no ready access to other courts and was gradually modified. It was soon decided that French courts would hear suits concerning an interest in French land. [105] Reasons of commercial convenience caused

Mannet, Cour Lyon, July 24, 1929, 57 Clunet 116 (1950); Dame Cruheras Teran v. Sieur Cruheras Teran, Cour Paris, June 6, 1958, 86 Clunet 830 (1959); Quindandon v. Dame Delageneste, Trib. Gde Inst. Seine, June 10, 1959, 87 Clunet 160 (1960).

[100] Batiffol No. 771.

[101] *E.g.*, Tanneries lyonnaises v. Shirazi and sons et Mannet, *supra* note 99; Dollfus v. National Provincial Bank, Ltd. *supra* note 86 (counterclaim, waiver). *But see* Consorts Bonnet v. Souris, *supra* note 61. In determining whether the bringing of suit outside France amounts to a waiver, the courts seem to take into consideration where the parties' assets are, whether there has been a need to bring the action or defend it to protect local interests, and similar circumstances.

[102] *Cf.* Banque d'Italie v. Ferrand, Cass Civ., May 2, 1928, [1928] S. I. 781, 56 Clunet 76 (1929). Dumont et Cie. v. Verdoja, Cour Paris, April 3, 1930, 59 Clunet 636 (1932).

[103] Batiffol No. 694.

[104] See 4.36 *infra*.

[105] Batiffol Nos. 697, 698.

French courts to hold that they were competent in matters involving commercial contracts, [106] if the defendant's domicile was in France, or the contract was made and to be performed there, or payment was to be made there. [107] Practical necessity also compelled the courts to deal with cases, such as custody proceedings, in which delay would be harmful. [108] In subsequent cases, the French courts either acted if the defendant was a French domiciliary, or noted that suit before a foreign court would have been practically impossible, [109] or stressed some additional factor militating in favor of French competence. [110]

After the Second World War, the *Cour de Cassation*, in the famous *Patino* cases, abandoned the last vestiges of the rule that French courts lack competence in suits in which only aliens are involved. [111] In these cases, in which articles 14 and 15 could not be applied, the court used rules of territorial competence to determine general competence and held that, when rules of territorial competence, applied to a case with international ramifications, point to a French court, that court is generally as well territorially competent. Rules of territorial competence must therefore be discussed in conjunction with rules of general competence, even though logically the question of general competence precedes that of territorial competence.

When the French courts are generally competent both under articles 14 and 15 and under rules of territorial competence interpreted as embodying rules of general competence, the plaintiff may rely on either set of rules. For example, an American citizen suing a Frenchman domiciled in Paris may invoke either article 15 of the Civil Code or article 59 of the Code of Civil Procedure as a basis for the French court's

[106] BATIFFOL No. 698. Banque de commerce de Sibérie v. Slenoff, Cass. Req., July 29, 1929, 57 CLUNET 643 (1930).

[107] *Cf.* CODE DE PROCÉDURE CIVILE art. 420; BATIFFOL No. 698.

[108] BATIFFOL No. 698.

[109] *E.g.*, Sciaky v. Dame Sciaky, Cass. Req., July 5, 1926, 54 CLUNET 392 (1926); Epoux Grosberg, Cour Paris, October 24, 1929, 58 CLUNET 1025 (1931); Epoux Zilberberg, Cour Paris, December 31, 1931, 59 CLUNET 641 (1932).

[110] Herskowitz v. Herskowitz et Brandes, Trib. Strasbourg, Oct. 24, 1930, 59 CLUNET 1009 (1932) (goods involved in suit France); Prince de Colloredo-Mansfeld v. sa femme, Trib. Seine, December 1, 1932, 60 CLUNET 82 (1933) (validity of marriage celebrated in France). *But see* Preussische Staatsbank v. B., Cour Paris, December 11, 1930, 60 CLUNET 82 (1933) (no competence, since foreign court more convenient for witnesses); La Velle-Blackburn v. Wilbur, Trib. Seine, April 3, 1930, 58 CLUNET 1028 (1931) (no competence in case involving validity of marriage celebrated between American nationals in United States).

[111] Dame Patino, née Bourbon v. son mari, Cass. Civ., June 21, 1948, 73–76 CLUNET 20 (1946–1949), [1948] J.C.P. 2, 4422, [1949] S. 1, 121; Patino v. Dame Patino, Cour Paris, July 7, 1954, 82 CLUNET 636 (1955) (note); *cf.* 2 DALLOZ, RÉPERTOIRE DE DROIT CIVIL, *Etranger*, Nos. 329–37 (1952).

competence. Since nationality is a less elusive concept than domicile, reliance on article 15 may be convenient from a practical point of view. Nevertheless, it may often be more advantageous to rely on rules of territorial competence, since many foreign courts are reluctant to enforce French judgments based on articles 14 or 15. [112]

### 4.12. Competence Based on the Domicile of the Defendant

According to article 59 of the Code of Civil Procedure, most actions in France must be brought at the defendant's domicile. [113] That rule is often expressed by the Latin phrase *actor sequitur forum rei*. It is, therefore, generally possible to sue a defendant in France if he is domiciled there, regardless of the nationality of the parties.

In determining where the defendant is domiciled, French law uses criteria that are fairly similar to those prevailing in the United States. Every person usually has one domicile and one domicile only, [114] and that domicile is at the place of his principal establishment. [115] A change of domicile requires both an intent to change it and an actual physical change. [116] A minor is domiciled with his parents; a wife with her husband. [117] However, when a married woman operates a business within the meaning of French commercial law, she may have an independent domicile for the purpose of that business. [118] If the defendant's actions have misled the plaintiff as to his true domicile, the defendant may not complain if he is sued at his apparent domicile. [119]

[112] Nadelmann, *supra* note 35, at 327.

[113] As to the *tribunal de grande instance*, see CODE DE PROCÉDURE CIVILE art. 59. This article states somewhat cryptically that an action must be brought at defendant's domicile if a "personal" action or one concerning movables is involved, but has been interpreted broadly to cover all cases for which nothing else is specifically provided. A recent decree concerning the *tribunal d'instance* affirms this interpretation. DÉCRET No. 58–1284 of December 22, 1958, J.O. Dec. 23, 1958, p. 11579, [1959] B.L.D. 52 art. 20; *cf.* MOREL 218; CORNU & FOYER 224; CODE DE COMMERCE art. 420.

[114] 1 COLIN & CAPITANT 293.

[115] CODE CIVIL art. 102. The *Cour de Cassation* usually refuses to interfere with findings of the lower courts relating to domicile on the ground that they involve questions of fact only. 1 COLIN & CAPITANT 292.

[116] CODE CIVIL art. 103. Proof of intent is simplified because a person intending to change his domicile may record an official declaration to that effect at the clerks' offices of the municipalities he leaves and moves to. CODE CIVIL art. 104. Otherwise intent must be determined on the basis of all the facts. CODE CIVIL art. 105.

[117] CODE CIVIL art. 108. As to the application of the rule in divorce and separation cases, see 11.04.b *infra*.

[118] This is one of the rare instances in which a person can have a double domicile under French law. See 1 COLIN & CAPITANT 292–93, 298.

[119] 1 COLIN & CAPITANT 298; Sélim Seymour v. Epoux Catalano, Cour Paris, Oct. 14, 1958, [1959] D. SOMM. 12.

### 4.13. Competence Based on the Residence of the Defendant

Article 59 (1) of the Code of Civil Procedure provides that, when the defendant has no domicile, the action may be brought at his residence. This rule, when used as a rule of general competence, is given a rather literal interpretation: It applies only to a person having a residence in France who has no domicile either in or outside France. [120] Of course, this rule does not prevent a French national from suing a foreigner in France who has a residence there, but a domicile in some other country. The action must then be brought on the basis of article 14 of the Civil Code at the place in France where the defendant has his residence. [121]

### 4.14. Competence Based on the Domicile of Companies

The rule that civil actions must ordinarily be brought at the defendant's domicile also applies to *societés*. [122] A French company has its domicile where its *siège social* is located. [123] Since this rule would create hardship for plaintiffs, especially in the case of large companies with far-flung activities, the courts also entertain actions against companies in the place in which the defendant company maintains a branch establishment in charge of an agent with power to bind the company. However, the cause of action must arise out of the activities of the branch office or have some connection with it. [124] Because the rule was orginally developed in connection with actions against railroad companies whose principal stations were considered branch establishments, it was called the principal stations rule. It also applies to non-business companies, such as religious associations. [125]

Since rules of territorial competence may be relied on as embodying rules of general competence, article 59 of the Code of Civil Procedure makes it possible to sue a company in France which has its domicile there. As a corporation having its domicile in France is considered a French national, it may also be sued in France on the basis of article 15 of the Civil Code.

**a. Competence based on a branch in France of a company having its seat abroad.** Under French law, the seat or *siége social* of a company

[120] 1 DALLOZ, RÉPERTOIRE DE PROCÉDURE CIVILE, *Compétence Internationale*, No. 60 (1956); NIBOYET No. 1810.

[121] See 4.08 *supra*; Capitaine Peterson v. Lapeer -Estrade, Cour Rouen, Nov. 20, 1930, 58 CLUNET 1033 (1931).

[122] 6 NIBOYET No. 1812.

[123] See 4.05.d *supra*; CODE DE PROCÉDURE CIVILE art. 59(6).

[124] CUCHE & VINCENT 244-45.

[125] CORNU & FOYER 232; MOREL 221.

determines its nationality and a company having its seat outside France is not considered a French national, even if it has a branch office in that country, [126] and may, therefore, not be sued in France on the basis of article 15 of the Civil Code. However, since the principal stations rule may be used as a rule of general competence, a foreign company with a branch office in France may be sued there if the suit has some connection with the operation of the branch office. [127] Of course, a French citizen may sue a foreign company in France on any cause of action by relying on article 14 of the Civil Code.

### 4.15. Cases in Which Competence Does Not Depend on the Defendant's Domicile

In a number of cases, the defendant's domicile does not necessarily determine the place of suit. Exceptions to the rule *actor sequitur forum rei* have increased steadily. In some instances, they provide merely an alternative rule, allowing suit at the defendant's domicile as well as elsewhere. In others, they make the domicile of the defendant immaterial for purposes of territorial competence. Exceptions to the domicile rule usually attempt either to facilitate the administration of justice by allowing suit in a place convenient for the determination of factual issues or to assist the plaintiff.

### 4.16. Competence in Actions Concerning Real Property

All actions involving title to immovables (*actions réélles immobilières*) must be brought at the situs of the land, [128] where factual issues involving the property can be determined most easily.

Actions concerning leases, rights to possession of property, and boundary markers, among others, must also be brought where the land is located. [129] The same is true of actions involving the application of special laws for the protection of tenants [130] and of actions involving insurance of real property. [131] However, actions of a contractual nature,

[126] See 4.05.d *supra.*

[127] The Commercial Company of Salonica v. Misrachi, Cass. Civ., May 12, 1959, 49 Rev. cr. dr. int. privé 714 (1959) (note Loussouarn); Batiffol No. 699 and authorities cited.

[128] Code de Procédure Civile art. 59(4); Batiffol No. 688. However, no action concerning title to foreign land can be brought in France even if articles 14 and 15 of the Civil Code are applicable. See 4.07 *supra.*

[129] Décret No. 58–1284, *supra* note 113, art. 23.

[130] Décret No. 58–1293 of December 22, 1958, J.O. Dec. 23, 1958, p. 11627, [1959] B.L.D. 87, art. 8 (farm tenancies); Décret No. 53–960 of Sept. 30, 1953, J.O. Oct. 1, 1953, [1953] D.L. 393, arts. 30, 32–33 (commercial or business property); Law No. 48–1360 of September 1, 1948, J.O. Sept. 1948, [1948] D.L. 300, art. 48 (residential property).

[131] Law of July 13, 1930, J.O. July 18, 1930, [1931] D. 4.1, art. 3.

which also involve title to land, the so-called *actions mixtes*, may be brought at the situs of the property or at defendant's domicile. [132] The typical example of a mixed action is an action to have a contract for the sale of land declared void.

Irrespective of the nationality of the parties, actions involving immovable property located in France may be brought in France. The principle that the rules determining territorial competence also imply rules of general competence is fully applicable in these cases.

### 4.17. Competence in Actions Concerning Decedents' Estates

All suits concerning decedents' estates [133] must be brought in the court of the place in which the "succession has been opened" – that is, at the last domicile of the decedent. [134] Insofar as purely internal rules of territorial competence are involved, both the location in France and the character of the decedent's property are immaterial. However, this general rule is subject to an exception. If a person dies a domiciliary of France, the French courts that are competent to deal with his estate [135] do not exercise adjudicatory power in regard to immovable property located outside France. [136] Furthermore, this exception prevails even if a French national is a party to the action. [137] Conversely, if a person dies domiciled outside France leaving no immovable property in France, the French courts will ordinarily refuse to assume adjudicatory power with respect to his estate unless articles 14 and 15 of the Civil Code are

[132] CODE DE PROCÉDURE CIVILE art. 59(5); CUCHE & VINCENT 248; BATIFFOL No. 588; NIBOYET No. 1814; Villerelle v. Vinot, *supra* note 72. French courts tend to restrict the option granted by this article. An action for a judgment declaring that defendant is bound by a valid contract for the purchase of land and seeking recovery of the purchase price has been held to be an action for a sum of money only – not one involving title to property – that should be brought at defendant's domicile. Soc. Franck-Arthur et Weisweiler v. Soc. générale d'éditions et de publications, Cour Amiens, Jan. 7, 1948, [1948] D.J. 121. Actions to have contracts for the purchase of land declared void are considered "mixed" actions (*i.e.*, actions incidentally involving title), because under French law the mere signing of a purchase contract transfers title as between the parties. CODE CIVIL art. 1138; 1 COLIN & CAPITANT 1087–88.

[133] The term estate does not describe accurately the property left by a French decedent; in most cases, there is (at least in theory) no estate with separate legal personality, since all assets and liabilities of the decedent are transferred to his heirs at the moment of his death. A will contest or other litigation is therefore likely to take the form of an ordinary suit between the heirs and others. *Cf.* Rheinstein, *European Methods for Liquidation of the Debts of Deceased Persons*, 20 IOWA L. REV. 431–75 (1935).

[134] CODE CIVIL arts. 110, 822; CODE DE PROCÉDURE CIVILE art. 59 (8); *cf.* de Loriol v. Vve de Bioncourt, Cour Paris, July 10, 1956, 35 REV. CRIT. DR. INT. PRIVÉ 142 (1947). As to the exact scope of the rules, see CUCHE & VINCENT 243; MOREL 263.

[135] 1 DALLOZ, RÉPERTOIRE DE PROCÉDURE CIVILE ET COMMERCIALE, *Compétence Internationale*, No. 79 (1955).

[136] 1 DALLOZ, *op. cit. supra* note 135, No. 78; BATIFFOL No. 700; Succession Vve Bonnefoy, Trib. civ. Seine, Jan. 1, 1950, 39 REV. CRIT. DR. INT. PRIVÉ 79 (1950).

[137] See 4.07 *supra*.

applicable.[138] But the French courts will always entertain an action involving a decedent's immovable property located in France, regardless of the decedent's last domicile.[139]

### 4.18. Competence in Bankruptcy Proceedings

Suits arising from the bankruptcy of French business organizations must be brought at the domicile of the owner of the firm, or, in the case of a *societé*, at the place in which its seat is located.[140] Foreign bankruptcy does not affect assets in France, but French courts are empowered to declare bankrupt a foreigner domiciled outside of France or a company having its seat outside of France, as long as there are assets, or there is a branch office or agency, in France. Judicial action in France results in an independent state of bankruptcy as to the French assets of a foreign business organization.[141]

### 4.19. Actions by *Officiers Ministériels*

Actions for expenses advanced by *officiers ministériels* on behalf of their clients, such as sums expended during litigation by *avoués* for clerk's fees and stamp taxes, must be brought before the court that handled the litigation giving rise to the expense.[142]

### 4.20. Tort actions

In 1923,[143] legislation was enacted permitting suits involving a *délit* or *quasi-délit* to be brought in the court of the place in which the tort was committed[144] as well as in that of the place in which the

[138] Batiffol Nos. 690, 700; Niboyet No. 1838. French courts do hear suits involving the estates of persons who have died domiciled outside France – except suits concerning immovables outside France – as long as one of the parties to the suit is a French national and articles 14 and 15 are applicable. Such actions must ordinarily be brought at the domicile of defendant if that is in France. Consorts Bonnet v. Souris, *supra* note 61.

[139] See 4.16 *supra*.

[140] Code de Commerce art. 437; Code de Procédure Civile art. 59(8). A recent case indicates that article 15 of the Civil Code authorizes a foreign corporation to elicit in France a declaration in bankruptcy of a French "merchant" whose principal business establishment is located outside France. Chavanne v. Société Panafric, Cass. Civ., June 7, 1962, 90 Clunet 106 (1963) (note Ponsard); *cf.* Batiffol No. 774. A foreign trustee may sue in France without obtaining an ancillary appointment, but only in connection with his foreign functions. In France, persons other than businessmen or firms (*commerçants*) cannot be declared bankrupt.

[141] Batiffol No. 774; 6 Niboyet No. 1637.

[142] Code de Procédure Civile art. 60.

[143] Law of November 26, 1923, J.O. Nov. 27, 1923; [1923] Bulletin des Lois 3477, adding a subsection to articles 2 and 59 of the Code de Procédure Civile. This law is now codified in Code de Procédure Civile art. 59(11) (*tribunal de grande instance*) and Décret No. 58–1284, *supra* note 113, art. 21 (*tribunal d'instance*). See also 6 Niboyet No. 1829.

[144] The French definition of tort (*délit*) does not necessarily correspond to the American definition. An action by the owner of a semi-trailer against the owner of the tractor which was pulling the trailer and caused it to turn over has been considered a contract action which

defendant has his domicile. This legislation was enacted mainly to permit French courts to decide cases relating to automobile accidents at the place where the accident occurred. For example, an American tourist travelling in France and injured there by a German motorist domiciled in Bonn may sue the German motorist in France. [145]

### 4.21. Competence in a Case with Multiple Defendants

When the joinder of several co-defendants in one action is proper, the plaintiff may sue all co-defendants in the court of the place of the domicile of any defendant. [146] However, joinder of several defendants is allowed only if the causes of action against them are identical or closely related. [147] Furthermore, joinder is not permitted if the defendants must be sued before different types of courts: A person who may be sued only before a regular civil court may not be made a co-defendant in an action pending before a commercial court. [148]

The action may be brought only in the court of the actual domicile of one of the defendants, not before a court competent to proceed against one of the defendants for some other reason, such as an election of domicile. [149]

If, for the protection of the defendant, a clause has been inserted in a contract specifying that *all* actions must be brought at a particular place, suit must ordinarily be brought in that place, even though potential co-defendants are sued at some other place. [150] However, if the co-defendants are bound by an "indivisible" obligation, even a co-defendant who has protected himself by a clause specifying that he may be sued only at a particular place cannot object if he is sued jointly

could not be brought at the place of accident. Calopin et Cie d'assurances La Providence v. Soc. des transports Rozanne, Trib. Saverne, July 24, 1957, [1958] D.J. 343. That seduction may be a wrongful act furnishes no basis for bringing a filiation proceeding at the place where the mother has been seduced. Consorts I.v. Epoux C., Cass. Civ., October 29, 1935, [1935] D.H. 554.

145 *Cf.* BATIFFOL No. 700. French law authorizes a direct action against the insurer in automobile accident cases. However, this authorization has no influence on the place where the action may be brought. DELAUME, AMERICAN-FRENCH PRIVATE INTERNATIONAL LAW 152 (2d ed. 1961).

146 CODE DE PROCÉDURE CIVILE art. 59(3); DÉCRET No. 58–1284, *supra* note 113, art. 20 (*tribunal d'instance*); *cf.* Andreotti v. Caisse nationale des retraites, Cass. Civ., Jan. 8, 1947, [1947] D.J. 164.

147 1 DALLOZ, RÉPERTOIRE DE PROCÉDURE CIVILE ET COMMERCIALE, *Compétence civile des tribunaux de première instance*, No. 67 (1955). Under French terminology, *connexité* is said to exist between closely related causes of action.

148 1 DALLOZ, *op. cit. supra* note 147 at No. 74; Cie d'assurances v. Manutention marocaine et Cie. des Chargeurs réunis, Cass. Civ., May 12, 1958, [1958] D.J. 712 (note Ponchon).

149 1 DALLOZ, *op. cit. supra* note 147, at 75.

150 Soc. immob. Lacretelle-Vaugelas et Soc. immob. du Boulevard Devoust v. C., Cour Paris, Feb. 16, 1958, [1958] D.J. 215.

with the other co-defendants at the domicile of one of them. What amounts to an "indivisible" obligation is a matter of some dispute.[151]

The rule that several co-defendants may be sued at the domicile of one of them is also a rule of general competence. When one of several co-defendants is domiciled in France, all co-defendants may be sued there, regardless of their nationality.[152] The question has arisen whether several co-defendants may be sued together in France if only one is a French national and subject to article 15 of the Civil Code and neither he nor any of his co-defendants is domiciled in France. The courts seem to allow a joinder in these cases.[153] As a result, it seems that an American citizen domiciled in New York who has a joint cause of action against two persons also domiciled in New York, one of whom is a French national and the other an American citizen, may sue the French national in France under article 15 of the French Civil Code and join the American citizen as a co-defendant. Finally, by virtue of articles 14 and 15, a French plaintiff may always sue foreign nationals in France, regardless of their domicile[154] or number.

## 4.22. Competence in Cases of Impleader

When French law allows impleader, the party impleaded must be brought before the court in which the original action is pending.[155] This rule also applies in actions having international implications.[156] The *Cour de Cassation* recently approved impleader of a third-party defendant, who was a national and domiciliary of Italy, even though the pendency of the action in France constituted the only basis for assert-

[151] *Compare* Soc. Legay v. Capitaine du S.S. "W. H. Carruth" Cass. Civ., May 3, 1957, [1958] D.J. 167, 46 Rev. crit. dr. int. privé 495 (1957) (note Mezger), *with* Soc. des éleveurs du Bourbonnais v. Cie des Chemins de fer britanniques et Soc. de navigation A.L.A., Cass. Civ., Dec. 23, 1957, [1958] D.J. 294, 47 Rev. crit. dr. int. privé 385 (1958) (note Mezger), *and* Eleveurs du Bourbonnais, Villefranche d'Allier v. Soc. Torby Meat Products Ltd., Cass. Civ., May 3, 1957, [1958] D.J. 167; Dalloz, *op. cit. supra* note 149, at No. 76.

[152] Herskowitz v. Herskowitz et Brandes, *supra* note 110; Wilson v. Sté Allied Artists and United Artists Co., Metro-Goldwyn-Mayer et Sté nouvelle des Etablissements Gaumont, Trib. Gde. Inst. Seine, May 5, 1959, [1959] D.J. 235, 87 Clunet 166 (1960), *aff'd sub. nom.* Allied Artists Pictures Co. v. Soc. Metro-Goldwyn-Mayer et Wilson, Cour Paris, May 5, 1960, 49 Rev. crit. dr. int. privé 603 (1960); 1 Dalloz, Répertoire de Procédure Civile et Commerciale, *Compétence Internationale,* No. 95 (1956).

[153] Duhamel v. Delcourt et autres, Trib. civ. Lille, Nov. 9, 1955, 43 Rev. crit. dr. int. privé 832 (and cases cited in the note by Weser); 6 Niboyet No. 1842.

[154] *But see* Montané v. Cie des chemins de fer portugais et autres, July 12, 1950, Cass. Civ., 41 Rev. crit. dr. int. privé 509 (1950) (note Francescakis). There is language in this case to the effect that, even if article 14 is applicable, several co-defendants may be joined only if one of them is domiciled where the action is brought. The case can be explained on other grounds and the language of the court has been severely criticized in the note.

[155] Code de Procédure Civile arts. 59(10) and 181; Décret No. 58-1284, *supra* note 113, art. 28.

[156] 1 Dalloz, *op. cit. supra* note 152, at No 98; 6 Niboyet No. 1845.

ing competence over him. [157] The case is significant because it definitely established the principle that, apart from the operation of articles 14 and 15 of the Civil Code, an action may be entertained in France if a rule of territorial competence gives competence to a specific French court.

### 4.23. Competence in Contract Cases

French law distinguishes between two types of contracts: (1)commercial and (2) non-commercial or civil contracts. These two types are subject to different rules of substantive law; in addition, actions on commercial contracts must ordinarily be brought in the commercial courts.

**a. Competence in commercial contract cases.** In actions on commercial contracts, under article 420 of the Code of Civil Procedure, the plaintiff may sue the defendant at any of three places: (1) at defendant's domicile, (2) where the contract was made and the goods delivered, [158] or (3) where payment is to take place. [159] These rules of territorial competence are also interpreted as embodying rules of general competence. For example, an action on a contract made in France for the delivery of goods may be brought in France if the goods are to be delivered there.

Difficulties have been encountered in determining, for the purpose of applying article 420, the place of making of the contract, the place of delivery, and the place of payment. If a contract is not made *inter praesentes*, the place from where the acceptance was mailed is usually considered the place where the contract was made. [160] Unless the con-

[157] Pelassa v. Charrière et Dame Barral, Cass. Civ., Oct. 19, 1959, 87 CLUNET 846 (1960), 49 REV. CRIT. DR. INT. PRIVÉ 215 (note Loussouarn). Even a clause in a contract giving exclusive competence to the courts of some foreign country may not protect a third-party defendant against impleader in France. Maurel v. Desmouraux, Cass. Req., July 4, 1889, [1890] D. 1.376.

[158] 1 DALLOZ, RÉPERTOIRE DE PROCÉDURE CIVILE ET COMMERCIALE, *Compétence Commerciale*, No. 159 (1955) and cases cited; PARISOT & JAUFFRET, MANUEL DE PROCÉDURE CIVILE 90 (3d ed. 1947).

[159] Fernand Granier et Cie v. Lauro, Cass. Civ., July 11, 1923, [1923] D.I. 127; DALLOZ, RÉPERTOIRE DE PROCÉDURE CIVILE ET COMMERCIALE, *Compétence Commerciale*, No. 177 (Supp. 1963). If the contract does not specify the place of payment, the domicile of the obligee usually controls. CODE CIVIL art. 1247; 1 DALLOZ, *op. cit. supra* note 152, at No. 171. Sometimes a battle of the forms arises concerning the place of payment. See Fabrique de Biscuits Poults v. Soc. Béricol, Cour Toulouse, April 23, 1956, [1956] D.J. 511. In case of payment by check, the place of payment is not the place where the check has been issued but where it is payable. Vve Fournier v. Hermet, Cass. Civ., July 9, 1895, [1896] D. 1. 349.

[160] *E.g.*, Vins de Banyuls naturels v. Grenouillet, Cass. Civ., April 22, 1955, [1955] D. SOMM. 62; Le Lloyd de France v. Faucheux, Cass. Req., March 21, 1932, [1932] D.H. 217 (extensive note by Salle de la Marnière).

tract provides otherwise, the place of delivery is ordinarily the place from which the goods were sent.[161]

Although article 420 speaks only of contracts for the sale of goods, it has been applied to all other kinds of commercial contracts.[162] When the contract is not for the sale of goods, the place of performance is considered the place of delivery.[163] If there is a *bona fide* controversy concerning the existence of the contract, competence cannot be based on article 420 of the Code of Civil Procedure, and the action must be brought at the defendant's domicile.[164]

**b. Competence in non-commercial contract cases.** As a general rule, actions on non-commercial contracts must be brought at the domicile of the defendant, but actions concerning the sale of goods at retail, contracts for repairs or services, and related matters may be brought not only at the domicile of the defendant, but – if one of the parties has his domicile there – also at the place at the place where the contract was made or executed.[165] This makes it possible for a small shopkeeper to sue his customers, who may be tourists from a distant city, at the shopkeeper's domicile. The same rule applies to certain actions involving purchases of farmers' supplies, such as seed and fertilizer, and to litigation involving farm animals.[166]

**c. Competence in transportation contract cases.** Actions against common carriers for damage to property entrusted to them may, at the plaintiff's option, be brought at the domicile of either the consignor or the consignee.[167] Unless a treaty provides otherwise, this is also a rule of international competence. The Warsaw Convention on air transportation[168] is of particular interest to American litigants in this connection, since both the United States and France are parties. In

[161] 1 DALLOZ, *op. cit. supra* note 159, at No. 165–168.

[162] Le Lloyd de France v. Faucheux, *supra* note 160 and cases cited.

[163] MOREL No. 266.

[164] See, *e.g.*, Guille v. Soc. Louis Riguet et Fils, Cour Rouen, June 12, 1958, [1958] D.J. 666; MOREL 228; DALLOZ, *op. cit. supra* note 159, at Nos. 144, 156.

[165] CODE DE PROCÉDURE CIVILE art. 59(2); DÉCRET No. 58–1284, *supra* note 113, art. 22 (*tribunal d'instance*); 6 NIBOYET 1823. However, the rule is interpreted strictly. It has been held inapplicable to a physician suing for his fee. Dr. Maurice Parin v. Barrès, Cass. Civ., July 13, 1937, [1937] D.H. 571.

[166] DÉCRET No. 58– 1284, *supra* note 113, art. 22.

[167] DÉCRET No. 58–1294, *supra* note 113, art. 25; 1 DALLOZ, RÉPERTOIRE DE PROCÉDURE CIVILE ET COMMERCIALE, *Compétence civile des tribunaux d'instance*, No. 203 (Supp. 1963).

[168] T.S. 876, 49 STAT. 3000 (1934). Article 28 of the convention, which deals with jurisdiction, excludes reliance on articles 14 and 15 of the Civil Code. 6 NIBOYET No. 1907.

intra-European transactions, the Berne Convention on Rail Transport is significant.[169]

**d. Competence in employment contract cases.** Actions between employers and employees falling within the competence of the labor courts must be brought before the court at the place of employment. When an employee, such as an outside salesman or a person doing piecework at home, does not work in his employer's establishment, suit must be brought in the court of the place where the employment contract was made.[170] Some litigation involving employment contracts may be brought before the *tribunal d'instance*[171] at the domicile of the defendant or, if it is also the domicile of one of the parties,[172] at the place where the employment contract was made.

**e. Competence in insurance contract cases.** In insurance actions, for the protection of the insured, the rule that all suits must be brought at the defendant's domicile is further modified. Most actions involving insurance companies are brought at the domicile of the insured. In casualty insurance cases, the action may also be brought where the accident happened. In real property insurance cases, suit must be brought at the site of the property.[173]

These rules express a strong public policy. Consequently, territorial competence and general competence derived from rules of territorial competence in insurance matters cannot be modified by agreement of the parties.[174]

[169] See 6 NIBOYET No. 1905. Concerning treaties affecting sea transportation to which France is a party, see 2 RIPERT, DROIT MARITIME No. 1419 (2d ed. 1958). In actions based on ocean bills of lading, the general rules of competence are applicable; however, if the port of destination is in France, the consignor, the consignee, and their assigns may sue the carrier before the court of that port. Law of April 2, 1936 on maritime bills of lading, J.O. April 11, 1936, [1937] D. 4. 1. art. 10. In cases of maritime collisions, articles 14 and 15 of the Civil Code apply. In addition, the plaintiff may sue the defendant at his domicile or at the court of the place where one of the ships first sought refuge. If the collision occurred in French waters, the action may also be brought in the court within whose territorial competence the event took place. 1 DALLOZ, RÉPERTOIRE DE PROCÉDURE CIVILE ET COMMERCIALE, *Compétence Internationale*, No. 76 (1956 and Supp. 1963); CODE DE COMMERCE art. 407.

[170] DÉCRET No. 58–1292 of Dec. 22, 1958, J.O. Dec. 23, 1958, p. 11621, [1959] B.L.D. 77, art. 80.

[171] DÉCRET No. 58–1284 *supra* note 113, art. 4. See 4.38.b *infra*.

[172] DÉCRET No. 58–1284, *supra* note 113, art. 22; DALLOZ, *op. cit. supra* note 167, at No. 203.

[173] Law of July 13, 1930, *supra* note 131, art. 3.

[174] Law of July 13, 1930, *supra* note 131, art. 2; 1 DALLOZ, RÉPERTOIRE DE PROCÉDURE CIVILE ET COMMERCIALE, *Compétence civile des tribunaux de première instance*, No. 86 (1956); The Ocean Accident [*sic*] v. Vve Dewinter, Cour Douai, July 4, 1934, 63 Clunet 142 (1936); DALLOZ, RÉPERTOIRE DE PROCÉDURE CIVILE ET COMMERCIALE, *Compétence Internationale*, No. 74 (1956);

## 4.24 Competence in Support Actions

French law imposes an obligation upon children and other descendants to support their parents. These support actions may be brought at the domicile of either the plaintiff [175] or the defendant. [176] Thus, regardless of their nationality, parents domiciled in France may sue their children for support in France, no matter where the children are domiciled. [177]

## 4.25. Competence in Proceedings Involving Provisional Relief

In cases in which speed is essential, the presidents of several courts are authorized to grant provisional relief after a summary hearing. [178] The rules of competence applicable to these *référé* proceedings are usually the same as in ordinary actions. [179] In some cases, however, the *référé* proceedings must be commenced where the remedy sought is to be put into effect. Thus, a debtor using the *référé* procedure to cancel an attachment granted *ex parte* must usually pursue his remedy before the president of the court who authorized the attachment. [180] When disputes arise concerning the execution of judgments, a *référé* proceeding may be brought at the place where the *huissier* attempted to levy execution. [181]

## 4.26. Competence in Cases of Attachment and Garnishment

French law authorizes creditors to attach property of their debtors when speed is important and payment of the debt is endangered. [182] This attachment, called *saisie conservatoire,* became available only recently [183] and may also be used to create a lien against real property. [184] A somewhat different form of attachment, called *saisie-arrêt,*

6 Niboyet No. 1824. *But see* Fraenkel et Cie., Trib. Seine, May 5, 1949, [1949] Gaz. Pal. II 28; *cf.* Weser, Traité Franco-Belge du 8 Juillet 1899, at No. 123 (1951).

[175] Code de Procédure Civile art. 59(1) (*tribunal de grande instance*); Décret No. 58–1284, *supra* note 113, art. 24 (*tribunal d'instance*).

[176] 1 Dalloz, Répertoire de Procédure Civile et Commerciale, *Compétence civile des tribunaux de première instance,* No. 85 (1955).

[177] 6 Niboyet No. 1831b.

[178] See 4.43 and 5.07 *infra.*

[179] Cuche & Vincent 249–50; Morel No. 260; *cf.* Ermolieff v. sa femme, née Popoff, Cass. Civ., June 16, 1958, 47 Rev. crit. dr. int. privé 751.

[180] Décret No. 58–1284, *supra* note 113, art. 26.

[181] Code de Procédure Civile art. 554. By analogy the rule has been extended to other cases in which speed is essential; in such cases, a *référé* proceeding to obtain provisional relief exists. Morel 223.

[182] Code de Procédure Civile art. 48. See 5.05 *infra.*

[183] Law No. 55–1475 of Nov. 12, 1955, J.O. Nov. 15, 1955, [1955] D.L. 499.

[184] Code de Procédure Civile art. 54.

must be used to garnish claims due debtors by a third party. [185] In addition, a simplified form of attachment, called *saisie foraine*, is available when a debtor has neither domicile nor residence in the municipality in which the creditor resides. In the case of *saisie foraine*, the nationality of the debtor or creditor is immaterial. [187]

Permission to effectuate a *saisie conservatoire* must be granted by the president of the *tribunal de grande instance* or the judge of the *tribunal d'instance* of the district in which the debtor resides or the goods to be attached are located. [188] Permission for a *saisie-arrêt* must be granted by the president of the *tribunal de grande instance* or judge of the *tribunal d'instance* competent in the district in which the debtor or the garnishee is domiciled. [189] A *saisie foraine* may be granted only as to property located in the municipality in which the creditor lives. The competent judge is the president of the *tribunal de grande instance* or judge of the *tribunal d'instance* of the place in which the creditor resides. [190]

It is disputed whether it is possible to create competence by attaching property or garnishing a debt in a case in which the French courts are not otherwise competent. [191] Once property has been attached, the attaching creditor may generally sue on his underlying cause of action by relying on usual rules of competence. [192] However, when property has been attached or a third party garnished, the creditor may usually also realize on the attached property by bringing an action

[185] CODE DE PROCÉDURE CIVILE arts. 557–82. See 5.06.c *infra*.

[186] CODE DE PROCÉDURE CIVILE arts. 822–25. See 5.06.c *infra*.

[187] 2 DALLOZ, RÉPERTOIRE DE PROCÉDURE CIVILE, *Saisie Foraine*, No. 786 (1956); 4 GLASSON, MOREL & TISSIER, TRAITÉ DE PROCÉDURE CIVILE 459 (3d ed. 1932). Thus, *saisie foraine* may not be used against an alien who, while traveling extensively, has maintained an apartment in Paris for years. Chalon v. Rubens, Trib. Seine, Feb. 27, 1907, 4 REV. CRIT. DR. INT. PRIVÉ 959 (1908). However, it was allowed against a non-commissioned officer of the United States Army in France, who had lived for one year in an apartment in the city where the *saisie* was to take place; the court felt that as a member of the armed forces he could be transferred at any moment and thus had no stable domicile, especially since court-martial proceedings were pending against him. Hallberg v. Hiles, Trib. Orléans, Jan. 14, 1955, [1955] J.C.P. II. 8648, 46 REV. CRIT. DR. INT. PRIVÉ 94 (1957) (note Simon-Depitre). *Saise foraine* was likewise held available against a foreigner who had lived in France for years, but had fled the country at the time the *saisie* proceedings were brought against him in order to avoid a criminal prosecution. Wilson v. Pingué, August 7, 1877, Cass. Civ., [1878] D.I. 150, 4 CLUNET 379 (1878).

[188] CODE DE PROCÉDURE CIVILE art. 48.

[189] CODE DE PROCÉDURE CIVILE art. 558; DÉCRET No. 58–1284, *supra* note 113, arts. 3, 26.

[190] CODE DE PROCÉDURE CIVILE art. 822; DÉCRET No. 58–1284 of Dec. 22, 1958, J.O. Dec. 23, 1958, p. 11575, [1959] D.L. 41, arts. 3, 26. However, it probably suffices if the creditor has a branch establishment where the property to be attached is located. Gomez v. Herpich, Trib. Seine, March 1, 1913, 40 CLUNET 1270 (1913).

[191] Nadelmann, *Jurisdictionally Improper Fora*, in TWENTIETH CENTURY COMPARATIVE AND CONFLICTS LAW, LEGAL ESSAYS IN HONOR OF HESSEL E. YNTEMA, 321, 326 (1961).

[192] See 2 DALLOZ, RÉPERTOIRE DE PROCEDURE CIVILE ET COMMERCIALE, *Saisie et Mesures Conservatoires*, No. 832 (1956).

called *en validité de saisie.* [193] While the creditor must show that his basic claim is well founded and that the *saisie* is proper when he brings an action *en validité de saisie,* the rules regarding the competence of courts are somewhat different. Decree No. 58–1284 of December 22, 1958, [194] which governs the competence of the *tribunal d'instance,* provides that actions *en validité de saisie* must be brought before the court of the place in which the attachment took place; in the case of *saisie arrêt,* the court of the debtor's or the garnishee's domicile is competent. [195] Since rules of territorial competence may also embody rules of general competence, it may be possible to create competence by attaching property or garnishing a third party in France if the claim is small enough to fall within the subject matter competence of the *tribunal d'instance.* [196]

More doubt exists in regard to claims that must be brought before the *tribunal de grande instance.* In the case of *saisie-arrêt,* the Code of Civil Procedure provides that the action *en validité de saisie* must be brought at the debtor's domicile. [197] If the debtor does not have a domicile in France, the action *en validité de saisie* is sometimes entertained at the place of the *saisie.* If the *saisie* is based on an instrument entitling its holder to immediate execution, such as a judgment or notarial document, [198] final judgment will be rendered. If the plaintiff cannot base his claim on such an instrument, the proceedings in the action *en validité* will be stayed to enable the plaintiff to obtain a judgment in a competent foreign court. [199] Once judgment has been rendered, the action *en validité* is continued, and the third party is ordered to turn the assets in its possession over to the plaintiff. No stay of the action *en validité* is necessary if general competence can be based

[193] Actually, it is sometimes necessary to combine an action *en validité de saisie* and an action on the underlying cause of action, and this is frequently done as a matter of practice even when not necessary. Giverdon, *Commentaire, Loi du 12 Novembre 1955,* [1956] D.L. 499.

[194] See note 113 *supra.*

[195] DÉCRET No. 58–1284, *supra* note 113, art. 26.

[196] The *tribunal d'instance* is usually competent if the claim involves 300 Francs or less, though in some cases the limit is 1000 Francs. DÉCRET No. 58–1284, *supra* note 113, arts. 1, 2.

[197] CODE DE PROCÉDURE CIVILE art. 567. If articles 14 and 15 of the Civil Code are applicable because either plaintiff or defendant is a French national, the action *en validité de saisie* may be brought in France. De Sonnaz v. Pizzart, May 16, 1869, Cour Chambéry, [1874] D. 5. 441.

[198] A notary may add the *clause exécutoire* to documents prepared by him, thus rendering them enforceable as judgments. See 2.10.b *supra.*

[199] The stay is usually granted for a six months period. Potocki v. Tanieowski, Cass. Civ., March 23, 1868, [1868] D. 1. 369; Sandoz v. Pioda, Cass. Req. Dec. 30, 1929, 58 CLUNET 94 (1931); Chrysostomos v. Wiener Bank, Cour Paris, December 13, 1933, 61 CLUNET 1208 (1934). French courts are not competent to entertain *actions en validité* if the underlying attachment or garnishment did not take place in France. See 4.07 *supra.*

on articles 14 or 15 of the Civil Code or on any other rule of competence.[200]

The Code of Civil Procedure provides that actions *en validité* of a *saisie conservatoire* must be brought before a "competent" court.[201] In domestic cases, this is apparently the court at the debtor's domicile.[202] In international cases, the same rules as those relating to *saisie-arrêt* seem to govern.[203] Thus, once the amount in the litigation exceeds the subject matter competence of the *tribunal d'instance*, competence can be based on *saisie conservatoire* or *saisie-arrêt* only to a limited extent.[204] While the matter is not free from doubt, there is some authority for the view that in case of *saisie foraine* the action *en validité* may be brought before the court that authorized the *saisie*.[205] Thus, *saisie foraine* may possibly create competence in actions that fall within the subject matter competence of the *tribunal de grande instance*.

As a practical matter, the various forms of *saisie* are rather unimportant as bases of general competence. Articles 14 and 15 and the numerous other bases of competence usually make it unnecessary to resort to *saisie* in order to create a basis for suit in France.[206] This is particularly true in the case of *saisie foraine* which is mainly designed to enable local merchants, repairmen, and the like, to collect money owed by tourists or travelling salesmen.[207] In these cases, since 1932, local merchants may sue at the court of their domicile.[208] Nevertheless, *saisie* may have some importance in actions involving American citi-

[200] Banque Franco-Serbe v. Danske Landsmandsbank, Cour Paris, May 21, 1957, 47 REV. CRIT. DR. INT. PRIVÉ 128 (1958) (note Francescakis).

[201] CODE DE PROCÉDURE CIVILE art. 48.

[202] 2 DALLOZ, RÉPERTOIRE DE PROCÉDURE CIVIL ET COMMERCIALE, *Saisie et Mesures Conservatoires* No. 832 (1956); Giverdon, *supra* note 193, at 506.

[203] *Cf.* BATIFFOL No. 700.

[204] It may be that even the *tribunaux d'instance* would stay their proceedings in an *action en validité* if a real controversy on the merits arose. See also Samuel et Cie. v. Comp. des Chemins de fer de Madrid à Saragosse et à Alicante, Cour Paris, Dec. 14, 1907, [1908] GAZ. PAL. 1. 367 (French courts competent to apply French statute concerning replacement of lost bearer bonds if bonds negotiated at Paris exchange, even though all parties, including issuer of bonds, are foreign nationals; case explained on ground that applicable statute amounts to a police measure).

[205] 4 GLASSON, MOREL & TISSIER, *op. cit. supra* note 187, at 459; LABORDE-LACOSTE, VOIES D'EXÉCUTION 130 (2d ed. 1939); Cavanagh v. Aninat, Cour Paris, Feb. 22, 1909, 5 REV. CRIT. DR. INT. PRIVÉ 607 (1909); *cf.* Morris v. Rizarelli, Trib. Seine, April 27 and May 31, 1878, 4 CLUNET 379 (1878).

[206] In fact, since plaintiffs are unlikely to rely on articles 14 and 15 unless the defendant has assets in France, there is a certain functional equivalence between articles 14 and 15 of the Civil Code, Anglo-American rules of quasi-in-rem jurisdiction, and German *forum arresti* rules. See note by Francescakis to Banque Franco-Serbe v. Danske Landsmandsbank, *supra* note 200.

[207] 4 GLASSON, MOREL & TISSIER, *op. cit. supra* note 187, at 456.

[208] Now CODE DE PROCÉDURE CIVILE art. 59(3). See also 4.23.b *supra*.

zens, as American courts may be more inclined to recognize a judgment if it is based on a familiar jurisdictional ground, such as attachment, than when it is based on articles 14 or 15 of the Civil Code. Thus, even if reliance on articles 14 or 15 is necessary, it may be advantageous for a plaintiff suing in France to begin the action with a form of *saisie*.

### 4.27 Modification of the Usual Rules by Action of the Parties

Failure to object to the competence of the court during the initial phase of the litigation precludes the defendant from doing so later and renders an initially incompetent court competent. This rule obtains irrespective of whether the French court is generally or territorially incompetent. [209]

Since rules of territorial competence do not express a strong public policy, they may also be modified by agreement. [210] Such an agreement may give a French court competence which it does not otherwise have or waive competence it does have. However, when a clause modifying usual rules has been inserted in an invoice, a bill of lading, or a printed form, it must be specifically accepted by the other party. [211] International competence may be waived irrespective of whether it is based on articles 14 and 15 or on rules of territorial competence. [212]

### 4.28. The Election of Domicile Clause

A clause providing that domicile is "elected" at a particular place is particularly popular with French draftsmen. According to the provisions of the Civil Code and Code of Civil Procedure, a person who has elected a domicile in a particular place may be sued both at that place and at his true domicile. [213] An election of domicile clause in a contract thus amounts to a consent to suit in the place where domicile has been

[209] Salendre v. Turrettini, Cour Lyon, March 14, 1909, [1914] S. 2. 225; Duhamel v. Delcourt, Trib. Lille, Nov. 9, 1953, 43 REV. CR. DR. INT. PRIVÉ 832 (1954) (note Weser); BATIFFOL No. 699. CODE DE PROCÉDURE CIVILE art. 171 provides that a court may dismiss a case for lack of territorial competence on its own motion only if the case may not be settled by the parties. This rule applies mainly to divorce cases. Dame Massimo v. son mari, Trib. Gde. Inst. Seine, Sept. 28, 1959, 48 REV. CRIT. DR. INT. PRIVÉ 504 (1959) (note Francescakis); Dawn Adams, épouse Massimo v. Massimo, Cour Paris, Nov. 10, 1959, 49 REV. CR. DR. INT. PRIVÉ 218 (1960).

[210] See 4.09 *supra*; *cf.* MOREL No. 269.

[211] Such an acceptance should ordinarily be express, but may also be implied. 1 DALLOZ, RÉPERTOIRE DE PROCÉDURE CIVILE ET COMMERCIALE, *Compétence Civile*, No. 59 (1956).

[212] 6 NIBOYET No. 1825; BATIFFOL No. 699.

[213] CODE CIVIL art. 111; CODE DE PROCÉDURE CIVILE art. 59(11); DÉCRET No. 58-1284, *supra* note 113, art. 29 (*tribunal d'instance*). An election of domicile need not necessarily be express if the intent of the parties is clear. CORNU & FOYER 232.

elected.[214] However, when an election of domicile clause has been inserted in a contract exclusively at the instance of the defendant, it may be construed as the substantial equivalent of a clause specifying that all suits concerning the contract *must* be brought in the particular place where domicile has been elected and preventing the defendant from being sued at his actual domicile.[215] If the elected domicile is outside France, French courts will usually refuse to hear the case, no matter where the actual domicile is.[216]

### 4.29. Arbitration Clauses

In France, arbitration clauses are valid only in commercial contracts and a few other cases.[217] However, an arbitration clause that is valid under the law governing the contract[218] is recognized even if it is invalid under French internal law.[219]

### 4.30. Cases in Which Competence Cannot be Modified by Agreement

Competence cannot be modified by parties in violation of strong public policy (*ordre public*).[220] For example, competence based on the special rules prevailing in insurance cases may not be modified by

[214] Sometimes a person specifies not merely that he elects domicile in a particular city, but that he elects domicile at the office of a particular *notaire* or *avoué* in the city. This amounts to a consent to suit in the city and in addition to an appointment of the particular *notaire* or *avoué* to accept service of legal papers on behalf of the party. By serving process on defendant, the plaintiff elects domicile in the office of his *avoué* enabling the defendant to serve legal papers upon him there. CODE DE PROCÉDURE CIVILE art. 61.

[215] CUCHE & VINCENT 248.

[216] 6 NIBOYET No. 1825; BATIFFOL No. 699.

[217] Mainly commercial contracts and agreements between members of a business firm. CODE DE COMMERCE art. 631.

[218] Montané v. Cie des Chemins de fer portugais et autres, *supra* note 154; Cies d'assurances v. Manutention marocaine et Cie des chargeurs réunies, *supra* note 148.

[219] 6 NIBOYET No. 1826; 1 DALLOZ, RÉPERTOIRE DE PROCÉDURE CIVILE ET COMMERCIALE, *Compétence Internationale*, Nos. 20–21 (1956).

[220] DALLOZ, *op. cit. supra* note 219, at No. 26, 89; BATIFFOL No. 700. The French concept of *ordre public* is fairly similar to, but not identical with, the common law concept of public policy. See DELAUME, AMERICAN–FRENCH PRIVATE INTERNATIONAL LAW 83 (2d ed. 1961).

The application of this rule in cases of divorce is somewhat doubtful. Before 1958, it was apparently possible for spouses to agree to have their divorce action heard before a specified, but otherwise incompetent, court in France. Ines Bueno v. Arao Bueno, Cour Paris, March 15, 1956, 45 REV. CRIT. DR. INT. PRIVÉ 504 (1956) (competence of French courts based on failure to raise timely objection). However, present article 171 of the CODE DE PROCÉDURE CIVILE provides that the court may raise the issue of competence on its own motion in cases the parties may not settle. Consequently, French courts tend to raise issues of international (general) competence on their own motion in divorce cases. De Brandenbourgh v. dame de Brandenbourgh, Cour Paris, Dec. 23, 1960, 51 REV. CRIT. DR. INT. PRIVÉ 339 (1962) (note Bellet); *cf.* note by Francescakis to Dame Massimo v. son mari, *supra* note 209. *Ordre public* (public policy) is also said to be involved in patent matters, and agreements concerning the competence of courts in such matters are invalid. BATIFFOL No. 700.

contract. [221] The same is true of competence based on the special rules prevailing in actions concerning decedents' estates, [222] bankruptcy, [223] and the expenses of notaries and *avoués*. [224]

### 4.31. Effect of Pendency of Another Action

In two situations, rules of territorial competence do not affect international competence.

First, if two actions are brought in France involving the same parties and the same subject matter – a situation usually described by the term *litispendence* –, the second action is ordinarily consolidated with the first [225] by following a procedure called *règlement de juges*. [226] However, French courts will not dismiss an action instituted in France on the ground that an earlier action involving the same parties and the same subject matter was brought in a foreign country. [227] Various ingenious reasons have been given for the rule. [228] The desire of French courts to expand the area of their competence, exemplified by the broad interpretation given articles 14 and 15, may be the most plausible explanation. The general rule here stated is subject to exceptions. Treaties may provide that the pendency of another action abroad is a good defense. [229] There are also dicta in a few opinions that the defendant

[221] See, *e.g.*, note 174 *supra*.

[222] This is specifically provided by article 822 of the *Code Civil* as to actions for the partition of decedents' estates, but is presumably applicable also in other matters relating to estates. MOREL 253; DALLOZ, *op. cit. supra* note 211, at No. 55; *Contra*, 2 GLASSON, MOREL & TISSIER, TRAITÉ THÉORIQUE ET PRATIQUE D'ORGANISATION JUDICAIRE No. 380 (1925–1936).

[223] As to bankruptcy there is less certainty. MOREL 833; CUCHE & VINCENT 264; DALLOZ, *op. cit. supra* note 211, at No. 55.

[224] CODE DE PROCÉDURE CIVILE art. 60; CUCHE & VINCENT 265. Contractual modifications of rules of territorial competence are also forbidden in some cases of lesser importance, such as those involving disputes arising from sale of fertilizer. *Cf.* DÉCRET No. 58–1294, *supra* note 113, arts. 5(4) and 22

[225] 1 DALLOZ, RÉPERTOIRE DE PROCÉDURE CIVILE ET COMMERCIALE, *Litispendence* No. 3 (1955). See cases cited in note by Weser to Forest v. Punski, Cour Amiens, Feb. 18, 1959, 48 REV. CRIT. DR. INT. PRIVÉ (1959).

[226] CODE DE PROCÉDURE CIVILE art. 172. See 7.09.b *infra*.

[227] Dame Lasserre v. Lasserre, Cass. Civ., March 21, 1950, 40 REV. CR. DR. INT. PRIVÉ 666 (1951); Allied Artists Pictures Co. v. Soc. Metro-Goldwyn-Mayer et Wilson, Cour Paris, May 5, 1960, 49 REV. CRIT. DR. INT. PRIVÉ 603 (1960) (action pending in U.S. no defense); BATIFFOL No. 701; NIBOYET No. 1844.

[228] For example, (1) the *règlement de juges* procedure is applicable only if both actions are pending in France, or (2) the foreign decision will not affect the French decision in any event since a foreign decision is not entitled to automatic recognition in France. 1 DALLOZ, *op. cit. supra* note 219, at No. 18; BATIFFOL No. 701. See also note by Metzger to Allied Artists Pictures Co. v. Soc. Metro-Goldwyn-Mayer et Wilson, *supra* note 227.

[229] Treaty between France and Belgium of July 8, 1899, published by DÉCRET of July 30, 1900, J.O. Aug. 1, 1900, art. 4; Treaty between France and Italy of June 3, 1930, published by DÉCRET of November 22, 1933, J.O. Nov. 26, 1933, 26 REV. CRIT. DR. INT. PRIVÉ 193 (1931), art. 19.

may obtain dismissal of the second action when the plaintiff has first instituted suit abroad. [230]

Second, if an action is pending in France and another action is brought elsewhere in France involving the same parties and a related subject matter – a situation generally described by use of the term *connexité* –, the second action is consolidated with the first by following a procedure indentical to that used in a case of *litispendence.* [231] However, French courts refuse to consider the pendency of an action abroad a good defense if it involves a related cause of action. [232] This follows *a fortiori* from their refusal to recognize *litispendence* as a defense if a foreign action is involved. It should be noted that, in the converse situation, when an action in France is followed by an action involving the same parties and a related cause of action in another country, French courts assert their right to deal with both the first and the second cause of action. [233]

### 4.32. Competence Independent of Rules of Territorial Competence

**a. Competence in proceedings to enforce foreign judgments.** French courts are always competent to entertain an action to enforce a foreign judgment. [234] The place where such a proceeding must be maintained is usually the judgment debtor's domicile or residence. If the judgment debtor has no domicile or residence in France, the action may be brought where property can be levied upon, where the plaintiff has his domicile, or at some other place having a reasonable contact with the case. [235]

**b. Competence based on denial of justice.** Denial of justice may form a basis of competence even if no existing rule of general competence warrants the assumption of adjudicatory power. However, the case

[230] Dame Lasserre v. Lasserre, *supra* note 227; Wilson v. Sté Allied Artists Co., *supra* note 227. In neither of these cases was the defense of another action pending (*litispendence*) allowed. In a recent case, the *Cour de Cassation* reaffirmed the rule that an action pending in France. will not be dismissed on account of another action pending in a foreign country (*litispendence*). It emphasized, however, that the French action had been started before the foreign action. Professor Batiffol believes this foreshadows a limitation of the rules to instances in which the French action was brought before the foreign action. Dame Zins v. Verdier, Cass. Civ., May 5, 1962, 52 REV. CRIT. DR. INT. PRIVÉ 99 (1963) (note Batiffol).

[231] CODE DE PROCÉDURE CIVILE arts. 168, 172. See 7.09.b *infra.*

[232] Allied Artists Pictures Co. v. Soc. Metro-Goldwyn-Mayer et Wilson, *supra* note 227; BATIFFOL No. 701; 1 DALLOZ, *op. cit. supra* note 219, at No. 99.

[233] BATIFFOL No. 701; 1 DALLOZ, *op. cit. supra* note 219, at 99.

[234] Forest v. Punski, *supra* note 225, and cases cited in note Holleaux; 1 DALLOZ, *op. cit. supra* note 219, at No. 88.

[235] Forest v. Punski, *supra* note 225.

must have some contact with France, and resort to foreign courts must be either practically or legally impossible. [236]

### 4.33. Competence in Miscellaneous Proceedings Relating to Personal Status

It has been asserted that, since under French conflict of laws rules questions of personal status are governed by the law of one's nationality, [237] French courts should not deal with cases involving the personal status of aliens in France. [238] However, the need to protect persons living in France has often led to different results [239] and to the development of special rules of competence.

**a. Protection of infants and incompetents.** French rules concerning the protection of minors and incompetents are quite complex. They require the appointment of a *tuteur* [240] (guardian) who is supervised by a "family council" of close relatives presided over by a judge of the local *tribunal d'instance.* [241] The family council meets at, and is subject to the control of, the *tribunal de grande instance* of the domicile of the minor or incompetent. [242] Guardians for minors must be appointed

[236] 1 Dalloz, *op. cit. supra* note 219, at No. 92; 6 Niboyet No. 1818.
Denial of justice in this sence is present when the plaintiff has access to no other court. See note Francescakis to Dame Massimo v. son mari, *supra* note 209.

[237] Code Civil art. 3; Batiffol No. 393; Epoux Ahmed ben Hassem v. Epoux Silva, Cass. Civ., June 23, 1957, 46 Rev. crit. dr. int. privé 680 (1957).

[238] See note to Im Thurm v. sa femme, Cour Nîmes Feb. 28, 1881, [1882] D. 2. 106. The rule is presumably based at least in part on the now discarded idea that French courts are incompetent in suits involving only aliens.

[239] Proceedings in which there is no defendant (involving the so-called *juridiction gracieuse* or *volontaire*) and a number of proceedings involving domestic relations do not take place in open court, but in the room used for the deliberations of the judges called *chambre du conseil.* The procedure in the *chambre du conseil* is simpler than the regular procedure, but the statute governing it (Law of July 15, 1944, J.O. July 27, 1944, p. 1902, [1944] D. Anal. 82) contains no rules of territorial competence. It is generally assumed that in adversary proceedings in the *chambre du conseil* the domicile of the defendent determines the territorial competence and that the domicile of the party affected is determinative in non-adversary proceedings. Hébraud, *Commentaire, Loi du* 15 *Juillet* 1944, [1946] D.L. 333, 1 Dalloz, Répertoire de Procédure Civile, *Chambre du Conseil,* Nos. 28–29 (1955); 8.03 *infra.* These general rules are inapplicable, if specific rules exist. *Cf.* Epoux Paats v. De Rothchild, May 21, 1940, [1940] J.C.P. 2. 1527 (French courts competent to determine validity of marriage of foreigners always domiciled and married in France).

[240] See 1 Planiol & Ripert, Traité pratique de droit civil français 486 (2d ed. 1952) (giving a description of the system). In addition to the *tuteur* and the family council there is also a *subrogé tuteur* who acts as an associate guardian in some cases and as a supervisor of the guardian in others. *Cf.* Le droit international privé de la famille en France et en Allemagne 409 (1954). Legislation concerning *tuteurs* was recently amended by Law No. 64–1230 of Dec. 14, 1964, J.O. Dec. 15, 1964, p. 11140, [1965] D.L. 4. This amendment came too late for detailed discussion here.

[241] Code Civil art. 306.

[242] 1 Planiol & Ripert 582.

immediately after the death of either parent. [243] A guardian for an insane adult may be appointed only after the adult has been judicially declared an incompetent. Incompetency and guardianship proceedings must be brought at the domicile of the incompetent. [244]

If protective measures can be taken by the authorities of the country concerned, [245] French courts may refuse to appoint *tuteurs* for infants or incompetents who are not French nationals. For example, France has treaties with a number of countries allowing their consuls to appoint guardians. [246] If recourse to the national authorities is not possible French courts will entertain guardianship and incompetency proceedings and apply the national law of the person concerned. [247] French courts are always competent to take steps under French law for the temporary protection of infants or incompetents in France if the national authorities have not acted and if speed is essential. [248]

Proceedings to deprive an unworthy father of his parental powers,

[243] See CODE CIVIL art. 390. If only one of the parents has died, the other becomes *tuteur* by operation of law. The surviving spouse can provide by will who is to be *tuteur* after his or her death. In the absence of such a designation, the *tuteur* is appointed by the family council. CODE CIVIL arts. 397, 405. The husband must be the *tuteur* of his incompetent wife; otherwise, the rules relating to *tuteurs* of minors apply to incompetents. CODE CIVIL arts. 505, 506. Because of their complex nature, the rules relating to guardians are often disregarded in actual practice. See 1 PLANIOL & RIPERT 490. Emancipated minors are assisted by a *curateur* rather than by a *tuteur*; for persons who are not completely incompetent, but are spendthrifts or subject to other mental infirmities, a *conseil judiciaire* rather than a *tuteur* is appointed. CODE CIVIL arts. 499, 513. A *curateur* or *conseil judiciaire* has fewer powers than a *tuteur*. The same rules of competence seem applicable in their case.

[244] 1 PLANIOL & RIPERT 722.

[245] Antoniotti v. Antoniotti, Nov. 19, 1923, Cass. Civ., 51 CLUNET 164 (1924).

[246] *E.g.*, Greece. See Comp. des Chemins de fer de l'Est. v. Godefroy ès. noms, Cass. Civ., Nov. 10, 1896, [1897] D. 342; *cf.* the Treaty with Switzerland of June 15, 1869, mentioned in Im Thurm v. sa femme, *supra* note 238. Article 6 of the Treaty of July 8, 1899, between France and Belgium, *supra* note 229, provides that all suits concerning guardians or committees of incompetents must be brought where the guardian or committee has been appointed. The article seems to relate only to suits arising after the appointment of a guardian or committee, not to the appointment itself. NIBOYET No. 1624; 10 DE LAPRADELLE & NIBOYET, RÉPERTOIRE DE DROIT INTERNATIONAL, *Tutelle* No. 62 (1931).

[247] Antoniotti v. Barbier, May 7, 1928, Cass. Civ., [1928] S. 238, 56 CLUNET 431 (1929) (minor); Epoux Granger v. dame de Santa-Cruz, March 23, 1899, Cour Paris, [1900] D. 2. 21 (incompetent). In one case, the international competence of the French courts to appoint a *conseil judiciare* was based on article 14 of the Civil Code; however, the incompetent was domiciled in France. C. v. dame C., Aug. 1, 1894, Cour Paris, 21 CLUNET 997 (1894); *cf.* Zamitt v. Ricardeau, Dec. 22, 1874, Cass. Req., [1875] S. 423. The indiscriminate use of article 14 in cases of guardianship does not seem advisable. French courts will not act in the case of alien infants or incompetents if the foreign law applicable under the nationality principle requires the French courts to perform functions too much out of line with their duties as prescribed by French legislation relating to guardianship or committees. BATIFFOL No. 424; *cf.* Vlatkovic, Trib. Chalons sur Marne (*référé*), Dec. 20, 1948, [1949] GAZ. PAL. 1. 102 (appointment of *subrogé tuteur* to represent foreign minor in French estate proceeding).

[248] BATIFFOL No. 425; Comp. des Chemins de fer de l'Est v. Godefroy ès noms, *supra* note 246 (parents of Greek child killed in railroad accident; Greek consul refused to appoint guardian, but guardian had to be appointed quickly to prosecute wrongful death action against railroad).

which are also entertained in regard to aliens living in France,[249] must be brought at the father's domicile.[250] Domicile also determines the court before which declarations for the emancipation of minors must be made.[251]

**b. Adoption.** There are two forms of adoption in France: (1) *adoption*, which does not usually destroy the bonds between the adopted child and his natural parents; and (2) *légitimation adoptive* – a somewhat inappropriate name, since it has nothing to do with legitimation –, which does destroy these bonds.[252] Proceedings to obtain court approval for *adoption* must be brought at the domicile of the adopting parents; if their domicile is abroad, the proceedings may be brought at the child's domicile.[253] The same seems to be true for *légitimation adoptive*.[254] French courts may entertain adoption proceedings even if the parties are not French. Foreign law is then applied.[255] Actions for the revocation of an adoption must be brought at the domicile of the defendants.[256]

**c. Proceedings for the modification of registers of vital statistics and for declarations of death and absence.** In France, the only admissible evidence to prove birth, death, or marriage is ordinarily an excerpt from the register of vital statistics. Entries in such registers may be modified only by court order. Proceedings to obtain such orders must usually be brought where the registers are located. In the case of registers kept by French diplomatic officers, the action must be brought before the *tribunal de grande instance* in Paris.[257] Regardless of the

[249] See Assistance publique v. ministère public, March 28, 1935, Cour Colmar, 63 CLUNET 642 (1936). The law seems to be considered as a quasi-criminal enactment applicable to all persons on French territory. French courts are also competent to take steps for the protection of the physical and moral welfare of minors actually residing in France, even if not domiciled there, as long as no change in status (such as guardianship) is involved. BATIFFOL No. 493; NIBOYET No. 1622 bis; *cf.* Netherlands v. Sweden, Int. Court of Justice, Oct. 28, 1958, [1958] I.C.J. 55, 74 JOURNAL DES TRIBUNAUX 149 (1959) (note Weser); McChesney, *Judical Decisions*, 53 AM. J. INT'L L. 436 (1959). French administrative law must be applied whenever French public welfare agencies take custody of foreign minors. BATIFFOL No. 493.

[251] Barat v. Beth, March 13, 1888, Cour Pau, [1888] D. 2. 183. After the death of his parents, a minor may be emancipated by his family council. CODE CIVIL art. 378.

[252] 2 PLANIOL & RIPERT 859–64.

[253] CODE CIVIL art. 353. If no other court is available, adoption proceedings may be brought in the *tribunal de grande instance* in Paris.

[254] CODE CIVIL art. 369 (making CODE CIVIL art. 353 applicable in adoption proceedings)

[255] Unless foreign law violates French public policy. BATIFFOL No. 484.

[256] CODE CIVIL art. 367 provides that the regular rules of competence are applicable.

[257] CODE CIVIL art. 99. On birth, death, and marriage records generally, see 7.35 *infra*.

nationality of the parties, [258] French courts are always competent to entertain proceedings for the correction of French registers. Declaratory judgment actions concerning matters of personal status must be brought at the domicile of the interested party, unless the purpose of the action is to obtain merely completion of the official registers of vital statistics. In that case, the action must be brought at the place of the register. [259]

If a person has disappeared from his ordinary residence and his body has not been found, a regular death certificate may not be issued. If the person who has disappeared has not been involved in some catastrophe, a *déclaration d'absence* leading to the appointment of an administrator for his property may be obtained. After thirty years, the property is distributed to the heirs. [260] There are no other effects upon the status of the absent person. A *déclaration d'absence* must be obtained at the last domicile of the person who has disappeared. [261] When French courts were thought to be incompetent in suits involving only aliens, especially in matters of personal status, it was argued that they could not issue declarations of absence for foreign nationals. However, even then the *Cour de Cassation* took the position that, because the protection of property was the main purpose of the *déclaration d'absence*, French courts were competent if the absent person had his last domicile and property in France. [262] *A fortiori*, this rule is applicable now. In addition, a French court at the situs may take temporary measures for the protection of the French property of aliens who have disappeared even if they are not French domiciliaries. [263]

If a person has disappeared under circumstances that make his death likely – for instance, in an airplane or maritime disaster, or as a result of war or of racial extermination –, a declaration of death may be issued,

[258] See Dame Ostano Emilia, Cour Alger, Nov. 17, 1926, [1927] GAZ. PAL. I. 331. French courts are ordinarily incompetent to order the correction of foreign registers; if foreign registers concern French nationals, they must be recopied in the registers of the appropriate French consulate. French courts may then order the modification of the consular register. INSTRUCTION DU GARDE DES SCEAUX, MINISTRE DE LA JUSTICE, RELATIVE À L'ÉTAT CIVIL of Sept. 21, 1955, art. 439, J.O. Sept. 22, 1955, p. 9322, 44 REV. CR. DR. INT. PRIVÉ 574 (1955).

[259] 1 PLANIOL & RIPERT 307; *cf*. Cesaruk-Mamas, Oct. 26, 1955, Cour Montpellier, [1955] GAZ. PAL. 423 (French courts competent to issue declaratory judgments re birth of child born to displaced persons in Germany, as parents and child now live in France).

[260] CODE CIVIL arts. 120–34.

[261] 1 PLANIOL & RIPERT 66; Hébraud, *supra* note 239.

[262] Ramond v. Delplancq, Dec. 27, 1897, Cass. Civ., [1901] D.I. 140, 25 CLUNET 334 (1898). The court also relied on article 14 of the Civil Code, as the person who had disappeared was a Belgian national and the proceedings were initiated by a French national. Due to the Treaty between France and Belgium of July 8, 1899, *supra* note 229, article 14 of the French Civil Code is no longer applicable in suits between French and Belgian nationals. See 4.34 *infra*.

[263] BATIFFOL No. 406.

which is transcribed in the registers of vital statistics and has all the effects of a regular death certificate. [264] A declaration of death may be obtained for French nationals, for persons with a domicile or habitual residence in France, and for other aliens who have disappeared in France, regardless of the place of their death. [265] The proceedings may include an administrative investigation. [266] Proceedings to obtain a declaration of death must be initiated in the *tribunal de grande instance* of the place of death or disappearance, if that is in France; otherwise, at the last domicile or residence of the presumed decedent or at the home port of the ship or plane on which he disappeared. If several persons have disappeared together, a collective petition may be presented to the court at the place of disappearance or, in the case of an air or sea disaster, at the home port of the ship or plane. If no other French court is available, the petition may be submitted to the *tribunal de grande instance* in Paris. [267]

**d. Nationality.** An action for a judgment declaring that a person is, or is not, a French national must be brought at the domicile of the person whose nationality is in question. If the person has no domicile in France, the action may be brought at his residence. In the absence of a residence in France, the action must be brought before the *tribunal de grande instance* in Paris. [268] General competence presents no problem in these cases, since French courts are always competent to determine whether a person is a French national.

### 4.34. International Agreements Affecting the Competence of the French Courts

At present, France is a signatory to only two treaties dealing with general competence. The older of the two, the treaty of June 15, 1869,

[264] CODE CIVIL arts. 88–92.

[265] CODE CIVIL art. 88. A French court may be competent if the last news about an alien came from France, though his death probably occurred at some unknown place outside France. Nussbaum, Trib. Seine, April 25, 1947, [1947] J.C.P. II. 3665; INSTRUCTION DU GARDE DES SCEAUX, *supra* note 258. In a case antedating the effective date of present articles 88–92, it was held that a French child could obtain a declaratory judgment that her father, an Italian national, had died in Spain. The court based its decision on article 14 of the Civil Code and on the impossibility of obtaining relief in Spain. Dame Usala, Oct. 26, 1943, Cour Nancy, [1946] S. 2.1. The note by Niboyet approves the decision on the ground that due to the war no relief could be obtained elsewhere, but criticizes the reliance on article 14, since the only defendant in the proceeding was the *ministère public*.

[266] CODE CIVIL art. 90. The court may order such an investigation on its own motion if the facts do not seem sufficiently clear.

[267] CODE CIVIL art. 89.

[268] Code of French Nationality, *supra* note 43, art. 127.

between France and Switzerland, avoids the impact of articles 14 and 15 of the French Civil Code. [269] Because of its defective draftsmanship, [270] it has raised problems of interpretation. On the other hand, the treaty of July 8, 1899, between France and Belgium has proved to be quite helpful. [271]

The treaty with Belgium provides that French nationals in Belgium are to be treated as Belgian nationals, and vice versa: Articles 14 and 15 of the Civil Code are therefore inapplicable. [272] In addition, the treaty contains a number of detailed rules of competence, allocating cases either to Belgian or to French courts. [273] For example, a party electing a domicile in one of the two countries must be sued at the elected domicile. The treaty governs not only suits involving French and Belgian nationals, but most suits involving Belgian nationals pending in France, irrespective of the nationality of the other parties. The same rule applies, *mutatis mutandis*, to suits pending in Belgium. [274]

An action pending in one of the two countries is a good defense in another action between the same parties covering the same or a related subject. [275] The treaty gives a judgment rendered in one of the contracting states formal *res judicata* effect in the other state. [276]

Since the treaty is not limited to nationals of France and Belgium, it is of some importance to American citizens. An American firm sued in Belgium cannot be subjected to a subsequent suit in France covering the same subject matter; an action involving a contract between a French national, an American national, and a Belgian national, which provides for an elected domicile in France, must be brought at the elected domicile because the treaty so provides. It may not be brought at any other place, including the actual domicile of the defendant in France and Belgium. [277]

France has also concluded a treaty with Italy which concerns the

[269] 6 NIBOYET No. 1849.

[270] 6 NIBOYET No. 1848; SIEGRIST, DE LA DÉVOLUTION SUCCESSORALE EN APPLICATION DE LA CONVENTION FRANCO-SUISSE DU 15 JUIN 1869 (1953).

[271] WESER, TRAITÉ FRANCO-BELGE DU 8 JUILLET 1899, No. 301 (1951); Weser, *Convention Franco-Belge du 8 Juillet 1899 sur la compétence et l'exécution des jugements*, JURISCLASSEUR DE DROIT INTERNATIONAL fasc. 591, at No. 1 (1960).

[272] Treaty between France and Belgium of July 8, 1899, J.O. Aug. 1, 1900, art. 1; 6 NIBOYET Nos. 1877–79.

[273] Treaty between France and Belgium of July 8, 1899, *supra* note 272, arts. 2–9; WESER, *op. cit. supra* note 271, at Nos. 60–230; BATIFFOL No. 715.

[274] Treaty between France and Belgium of July 8, 1899, *supra* note 272, art. 3.

[275] Treaty between France and Belgium of July 8, 1899, *supra* note 272, art. 4; BATIFFOL No. 716; 6 NIBOYET No. 1888.

[276] Treaty between France and Belgium of July 8, 1899, *supra* note 272. Concerning the French concept of res judicata, see 13.02 *infra*.

[277] *Cf.* 6 NIBOYET No.1884; Weser, *supra* note 271, at No. 49.

execution of judgments. [278] It avoids the impact of article 14 of the French Civil Code, but leaves article 15 unaffected. [279]

At present, France is negotiating a multilateral treaty with the six countries of the European Common Market regarding the execution of judgments. [280] This treaty may avoid the impact of articles 14 and 15 of the Civil Code in regard to the Common Market countries and thus satisfy the guiding principles of the European Common Market. [281]

No treaty concerning competence exists between the United States and France. The Convention of Establishment of November 25, 1959,[282] grants nationals, including companies of the two countries, national treatment for access to courts and administrative agencies. [283] Since treaties of friendship having most favored nation or similar clauses do not affect competence, [284] the Convention of Establishment does not improve the status of American nationals. [285] Two treaties dealing mainly with other topics have some effect on the competence of French courts. The status of forces agreement occasionally causes the dismissal of tort actions brought against a United States national, [286] and the Warsaw Convention on International Air Transportation regulates the competence of French courts [287] in aircraft accident cases.

[278] Treaty between France and Italy of June 3, 1930, *supra* note 229. Since the treaty deals almost exclusively with the execution of judgments, it is discussed in greater detail below. See 14.07.a *infra*. For an unusual case in which the treaty rules were applied directly to determine the competence of the French courts, see Soc. Ludiprim di Costanzo v. Cooperative ortofrutti coltori Ravennati, Cour Paris, Feb. 4, 1964, [1964] D.J. 497.

[279] Treaty between France and Italy, *supra* note 229, art. 30; Weser, *Faut-il reviser la Convention franco-italienne du 3 juin 1930 sur l'exécution des jugements*, 43 REV. CRIT. DR. INT. PRIVÉ 451, 693 (1954), 44 REV. CRIT. DR. INT. PRIVÉ 63 (1955).

[280] See Weser, *Conflits de juridictions dans le cadre du Marché commun: Difficultés et remèdes*, 48 REV. CRIT. DR. INT. PRIVÉ 613 (1959), 49 REV. CRIT. DR. INT. PRIVÉ 21, 151 (1960).

[281] Convention establishing the European Economic Community, March 25, 1957, J.O. Febr. 2, 1958, p. 1188, 29 U.N.T.S. 11, art. 7. The character of the European common market prohibits discrimination based on nationality. See Van Hecke, *La notion de discrimination*, in LES ASPECTS JURIDIQUES DU MARCHÉ COMMUN 149 (1958); Nadelmann, *Jurisdictionally Improper Fora*, in TWENTIETH CENTURY COMPARATIVE AND CONFLICTS LAW, LEGAL ESSAYS IN HONOR OF HESSEL E. YNTEMA 321, 333 (1961). On the most recent draft, see Bellet, 92 CLUNET 833 (1965).

[282] See note 1 *supra*.

[283] Art. III(1).

[284] Banque France-Serbe v. Danske Landmansbank, *supra* note 200.

[285] However, the Convention affects the recognition of arbitration awards. Convention of Establishment, *supra* note 1, art. III.

[286] North Atlantic Treaty, Status of Forces, June 19, 1951, T.I.A.S. No. 2846, [1953] 2 U.S.T. & O.I.A. 1792. Under article 7 of the treaty, French criminal courts may have to surrender, in favor of American military authorities, their right to deal with an American serviceman who has committed a crime. In that case, a private party injured by the crime loses the possibility to obtain compensation for the wrong by becoming a civil party in a French criminal suit. Gadois, Cour Paris, Dec. 14, 1953, 81 CLUNET 736 (1954).

[287] 4.23.b *supra*.

## 4.35. Diplomatic and Sovereign Immunity

Sovereign immunity of the French state has largely disappeared from French law. [288] However, ordinarily, foreign countries and foreign diplomats may not be sued in France.

**a. Immunity of foreign countries.** Only countries sovereign under international law and not member states of a federal union are immune from suit. [289] If they perform a governmental function, [290] agencies of a sovereign government that may be sued separately are entitled to sovereign immunity. The growing tendency of states to engage in commercial activities has created troublesome problems. A number of decisions [291] have held that the commercial representation of the Soviet Union in France acted as a private import-export firm and was therefore not entitled to sovereign immunity; the Spanish Commercial Agency, which engaged only in trade promotion, [292] and the financial agency of Yugoslavia, [293] which limited its activities to the servicing of government loans, were held to enjoy sovereign immunity.

**b. Immunity of diplomatic agents.** In France, immunity from suit extends to all persons with diplomatic status, including those accredited by international organizations [294] established pursuant to a treaty to which France is a party. [295]

It is immaterial whether or not persons claiming immunity are sued

[288] See SCHWARTZ, FRENCH ADMINISTRATIVE LAW AND THE COMMON-LAW WORLD 270 (1954).

[289] Etat de Cerea v. Dorr, Cass. Civ., Oct. 24, 1932, [1932] D.I. 196, 60 CLUNET 644 (1933) (Brazilian state).

[290] *E.g.*, Lahalle et Levard v. The Battle Monuments Commission, Cour Paris, February 28, 1936, 63 CLUNET 924 (1936) (agency of U.S. government); Epoux Martin v. Banque d'Espagne, Cass. Civ., Nov. 3, 1952, 42 REV. CRIT. DR. INT. PRIVÉ 425 (1953) (note Freyria). Sometimes, French courts seem to import French notions of "administrative contracts" into sovereign immunity questions. In *Etats Unis d'Amérique, Directeur du Foreign Service of the United States of America à Paris* v. *Pérignon*, Cour Paris, Feb. 7, 1962, 89 CLUNET 1016 (1962), a French contractor had agreed to build apartment houses for non-diplomatic American personnel in Paris. The contract provided that all disputes between the United States and the contractor were to be determined by the Director of the U.S. Foreign Service in Paris or the Secretary of State. The court held that the United States enjoyed sovereign immunity in connection with any action on the contract. The annotation indicates that, in the absence of the "settlement of disputes" clause mentioned, the result may well have been otherwise.

[291] They are collected (with a note by Mr. Tager) in 58 CLUNET 410–19 (1931).

[292] La Forest v. Office commercial de l'ambassade d'Espagne, Cour Paris, June 5, 1959, 87 CLUNET 482 (1960).

[293] Banque Ottomane et Société Financière d'Orient v. Philippe, Trib. Seine, December 30, 1930, 58 CLUNET 1040 (1931).

[294] BATIFFOL No. 703.

[295] 1 DALLOZ, RÉPERTOIRE DE PROCÉDURE CIVILE ET COMMERCIALE, *Compétence Internationale*, No. 119 (1955) and cases cited.

in connection with their official function.[296] As to causes of action arising after their marriage, immunity extends to the wives of diplomats.[297] Consuls, who are not members of the diplomatic corps, are not entitled to immunity,[298] but French courts do not entertain suits that interfere with their official functions.[299]

**c. Waiver of sovereign immunity.** Sovereign immunity is usually asserted by the country or diplomat concerned and sometimes by the French government through the *ministère public.*[300] Sovereign immunity may be waived by the country concerned; in the case of diplomatic immunity, the country as well as the diplomat involved may waive.[301] Sovereign immunity may be waived by contract, but French courts interpret contracts alleged to contain a waiver rather strictly.[302] Participation in an action without timely objection amounts to waiver,[303] but a default does not. In default cases, the French government occasionally raises the issue of sovereign immunity itself.[304] Even if foreign countries or diplomats are not entitled to immunity, French courts are reluctant to permit the execution of judgments that interfere with the foreign country's or diplomat's public functions.[305]

## 4.36. Sumary: When an American National May Sue or Be Sued in France

French rules of international competence fall into two broad groups: (1) those derived from articles 14 and 15 of the Civil Code, and (2) those derived from rules of territorial competence. It may be helpful to

[296] 1 DALLOZ, *op. cit. supra* note 295, at No. 111 (citing also a few cases *contra*). Immunity lasts only as long as the diplomatic status of the defendant. It is not clear whether a diplomat may be sued on account of a cause of action which arose before he acquired his diplomatic status. See note to Sté Centrale de Construction à Paris v. Dame de Guiroye, épouse de Ayala, Cour Paris, January 11, 1955, 82 CLUNET 390 (1955).

[297] Sté Centrale de Construction à Paris v. Dame de Guiroye, épouse de Ayala, *supra* note 296.

[298] BATIFFOL No. 702; 1 DALLOZ, *op. cit. supra* note 295, at No. 121.

[299] Kroehly v. Gouvernement de sa Majesté Britannique, Cour Colmar, May 7, 1958, 86 CLUNET 828 (1959) (British consul cannot be evicted from his apartment in which he performs his official functions).

[300] Hanukiew v. Etat Afghan, Cass. Req., Jan. 23, 1933, [1933] S. 1. 249, 61 CLUNET 96 (1934); Procureur Général v. Franco-Franco, Cass. Civ., Feb. 5, 1954, 81 CLUNET 782 (1954).

[301] BATIFFOL No. 706.

[302] Hanukiew v. Etat Afghan, *supra* note 300 (standard election of domicile clause not an effective waiver of sovereign immunity); Kroehly v. Gouvernement de sa Majesté Britannique, *supra* note 299.

[303] *E.g.*, Grey v. Grey, Cour Paris, April 16, 1953, 80 CLUNET 886 (1953).

[304] See cases cited *supra* note 300.

[305] See Officina del Aceite v. Domeneck, Cour Aix, December 9, 1938, 66 CLUNET 596 (1939); Kroehly v. Gouvernement de sa Majesté Britannique *supra* note 299.

summarize these rules by discussing very briefly under what circumstances an American national may either sue or be sued in France.

Even if he has never been there and the suit has no contact with France, an American defendant may always, by virtue of article 14 of the Civil Code, be sued there by a French national. [306] This rule has only three exceptions: A French national may not sue an American national in France (1) if the suit concerns immovables located outside France, (2) if the suit concerns orders relating to execution or attachment issued by foreign courts, [307] or (3) if the French plaintiff has waived his right to rely on article 14. [308] When article 14 of the Civil Code is inapplicable, an American national may be sued in France if the rules of territorial competence indicate some place in France where the action may be brought. [309] For this reason, an American national having contractual relations with a French national is not necessarily protected against suit in France if the French national merely waives reliance on article 14 of the Civil Code, since this will not destroy other bases of competence. It is preferable to state specifically that the parties waive the right to rely on article 14 and 15 and that any action concerning the contract must be brought before a specified foreign court. An American national may be sued in France by another American national or by a national of a third country if he has his domicile in France, [310] but not if he has merely a residence there and is domiciled in the United States. [311] An American company may be sued in France at the site of its French branch. [312] It may also be declared bankrupt at that place.[313]

In the case of a commercial contract, an American national may be sued in France at the place of contracting if it is also the place of delivery, or at the place of payment. [314] In the case of a non-commercial

[306] See 4.03–4.10 *supra*. As a practical matter, a suit against an American national who is not present in France will rarely be undertaken there unless he has assets in France. Thus, article 14 is to some extent a substitute for common law rules of *quasi-in rem* jurisdiction. However, a judgement against a defendant is not limited to his property in France. *Cf.* Nadelmann, *supra* note 281, at 327. Nadelmann suggests that article 14 may become unnecessary in the event the competence of the French courts based on the attachment of property within France, now doubtful, becomes well-established. See also 4.26 *supra*.

[307] See 4.07 *supra*.

[308] See 4.09 *supra*.

[309] See 4.11 *supra*. For a recent case applying this principle, see Ranft v. Soc. Piereisnard et Fils, Cass. Civ., Oct. 19, 1959, 49 REV. CRIT. DR. INT. PRIVÉ 216 (1960).

[310] See 4.12 *supra*.

[311] See 4.13 *supra*.

[312] See 4.14 *supra*. If the plaintiff is not a French national who is able to invoke article 14 of the Civil Code, the suit must have some connection with the operation of the branch office.

[313] But only as to assets located in France. See 4.18 *supra*.

[314] See, *e.g.*, Ranft v. Soc. Piereisnard et Fils, *supra* note 309 (place of payment of contract at Bordeaux; French courts competent to hear case). See also 4.23.a *supra*.

contract, an American national may be sued at the place where he made the purchase. [315] An American national may be made a co-defendant in an action pending in France; he may be impleaded there if a party to an action pending in France has a right of indemnity against him. [316] An American national who has committed a tort in France may be sued there. [317] In none of these cases, service of process within France is required.

By virtue of article 15 of the Civil Code, an American plaintiff may always sue a French national in France, unless the suit concerns foreign immovables or execution of orders of foreign courts or unless reliance on article 15 has been waived. [318] In addition, an American national may sue any person in France if the rules of territorial competence point to a French court. Since French courts refuse to enforce foreign judgments rendered against French nationals who may be sued in France under article 15, [319] it is often desirable for an American national having contractual dealings with a French national to obtain a waiver of reliance on articles 14 and 15 by both parties to the contract. Since a waiver of reliance on article 15 does not deprive French courts of the general competence derived from rules of territorial competence, it will not unduly limit the plaintiff. The refusal of many countries to recognize French judgments rendered on the basis of article 15 [320] provides an additional incentive for waiving application of that article.

### 3. RULES OF SUBJECT MATTER COMPETENCE

#### 4.37. The Subject Matter Competence *(Compétence d'attribution)* of the *Tribunal de Grande Instance*

Since it possesses the "fullness of judicial power" or *plénitude de juridiction,* the *tribunal de grande instance* is often called the *tribunal de droit commun,* the regular or ordinary court. [321] The significance of this phrase is limited, since the *tribunal de grande instance* may not hear cases specifically assigned to other courts. However, the law confers

[315] See 4.23.b *supra.*
[316] See 4.21–4.22 *supra.*
[317] See 4.20 *supra.*
[318] See 4.03–4.10 *supra.*
[319] See 14.04.a *infra.*
[320] Nadelmann, *supra* note 281, citing Schisby v. Westenholz, L.R. 6 Q.B. 155 (1870); BATIFFOL No. 754; 6 NIBOYET No. 1748, RÉPERTOIRE PRATIQUE DE DROIT BELGE, *Compétence en Matière Civile et Commerciale* No. 1777; NUSSBAUM, DEUTSCHES INTERNATIONALES PRIVATRECHT 432 (1932); Perassi, *La cittadinanza dell' attore come criterio di competenza giurisdizionale nelle relazioni italo-francesi,* 1954 RIVISTA DI DIRITTO INTERNAZIONALE 239.
[321] CUCHE & VINCENT 203; CORNU & FOYER 12–13; *cf.* MOREL 181–86.

upon it a general residual competence: It hears all cases not specifically assigned to other courts.[322] In addition, the *tribunal de grande instance* hears cases important because of their subject matter or the amount in controversy. Thus, most civil cases – excluding commercial, labor, or rural lease cases – in which the amount of controversy exceeds 3,000 Francs must be brought before it.[323] Many actions involving strong public policy (*ordre public*) must be brought before the *tribunal de grande instance,* regardless of the amount in controversy. Included in this category are matters of nationality,[324] cases of personal status – such as, for instance, divorce or filiation actions –,[325] matters involving property rights in land,[326] special proceedings for contesting the genuineness of written documents,[327] actions involving the professional liability of an *officier ministériel,* and others.[328] Actions involving vehicular torts may be brought in the *tribunal d'instance* if they involve less than 3,000 francs, but must be brought in the *tribunal de grande instance* if they involve a larger amount. They may not be brought in administrative or commercial courts.[329] In addition, the *tribunal de grande instance* decides most disputes relating to execution of judgments, even of judgments rendered by other courts.

**a. Subject matter competence in matters raised incidentally or by way of defence.** The *tribunal de grande instance* may decide matters raised incidentally even if it is not allowed to hear such matters when they are the basis of the plaintiff's cause of action.[330] The rule stated is sometimes expressed by the maxim *le juge de l'action est le juge de l'ex-*

[322] DÉCRET No. 58–1284 of Dec. 22, 1958, J.O. Dec. 23, 1958, p. 11579, [1959] B.L.D. 52, [1959] D.L. 41, art. 31.

[323] In most cases, this is the limit of the competence of the *tribunal d'instance.* DÉCRET No. 58–1284, *supra* note 322, art. 1.

[324] Code of French Nationality, ORDONNANCE of October 19, 1945, *supra* note 43, art. 124.

[325] See, *e.g.*, CODE CIVIL arts. 234–53 (divorce); art. 307 (separation); art. 326 (*réclamation d'état, i.e.*, proof of legitimate filiation).

[326] CUCHE & VINCENT 203; *cf.* MOREL 182. But the competence of the *tribunal de grande instance* is not exclusive in other cases involving land, such as actions concerning merely possession rather than title or actions dealing with contracts concerning realty or with leases.

[327] See 7.44–7.45 *infra.*

[328] These include: matters relating to patents and trade marks and certain tax matters. CUCHE & VINCENT 206.

[329] Law No. 57–1424 of December 31, 1957, J.O. Jan. 5, 1958, p. 190, [1958] D.L. 30 (no competence in administrative courts); DÉCRET No. 58–1285 of Dec. 22, 1958, J.O. Dec. 23, 1958, p. 11582, [1959] B.L.D. 57 (no competence in commercial courts); the plaintiff's right to recover damages by becoming a private party in a criminal prosecution under article 3 of the Code of Criminal Procedure remains unaffected if the tortfeasor is prosecuted for a violation of law. See 3.23 *supra*; *cf.* the commentary of Prof. Auby on the Law of Dec. 31, 1957, at [1958] D.L. 299.

[330] CUCHE & VINCENT 268. This rule furnishes the main basis for the expression that the *tribunal de grande instance* possesses the fulness of judicial power or *plénitude de juridiction.*

*ception*. Thus, controversies concerning the legal existence of a corporation must usually be brought before the commercial court, but a defendant sued by a corporation before the *tribunal de grande instance* on account of a debt may raise the question of the plaintiff corporation's legal existence by the way of defense. [331] The same rule applies if other commercial matters are raised. [332]

In limited areas, the rule is not applicable. Ordinary civil courts may not deal with the validity of an administrative order. [333] French courts also refuse to interpret a treaty when this may interfere with the conduct of French foreign relations. [334] If the defendant is the object of a criminal prosecution, the civil courts may not determine questions of tort liability for the same wrong until the criminal case has been concluded. [335] In addition, the *tribunal de grande instance* is also precluded from dealing with matters of bankruptcy [336] and perhaps rural leases.[337] If an issue of this nature is raised, the suit must be stayed until a determination of the issue by a competent authority has been obtained. Such issues are therefore called *questions préjudicielles* or questions requiring a preliminary decision.

**b. Subject matter competence in case of joinder of causes of action.** The rule that the *tribunal de grande instance* has the fullness of judicial power is also of importance in connection with joinder of causes of action. A claim that falls within the subject matter competence of the

[331] Schmitz et Lumière ès qualités v. Rougier, Cass. Req., April 26, 1880, [1880] D.I. 425.
[332] *E.g.*, Morel 235.
[333] See 3.01 *supra*.
[334] The distinguishing line between treaties which may be interpreted by the courts and treaties which may be interpreted only by the executive branch of the government is hazy. Batiffol No. 38. The courts have interpreted a boundary treaty when this was necessary for the determination of private property rights. Rawane Boyé v. Chem. de fer de Dakar à Saint Louis, Cass. Civ., March 7, 1910, [1911] D. I. 233. They have also interpreted the treaty establishing the protectorate over Morocco to determine whether Morocco was entitled to sovereign immunity in the French courts. Gouvernement Impérial du Maroc, Maspero, et Soc. Marseilleise de crédit v. Laurans, Cour Aix, Dec. 30, 1929, [1932] S.I. 103. But they have refused to interpret a treaty defining consular powers and consider themselves bound by an official interpretation of a treaty, even if they are willing to interpret it in the absence of an official interpretation. Bigelow v. Dame Zizainoff, Cass. Crim., Dec. 15, 1928, [1932] D.I. 113. The most recent decision of the *Cour de Cassation* suggests a possible extension of the scope of judicial interpretation. Moss v. Procureur Général près la Cour d'Appel de Paris, Cass. Civ., March 22, 1960, 88 Clunet 150 (1961) (courts may interpret treaty provision relating to boundary when necessary to establish nationality). *But cf.* Union régionale algérienne de la C.F.T.C., Cons. d'Etat, Oct. 16, 1962, 90 Clunet 402 (1963) (protocol of August 22, 1962, with Algeria defining competence of French courts as to litigation pending at time of Algeria's attainment of independence must be interpreted by Ministry of Foreign Affairs).
[335] See 3.23 *supra*.
[336] Cuche & Vincent 269; *cf.* Code de Commerce art. 635.
[337] The point is not certain. Cuche & Vincent 269; see note 408 *infra*.

specialized courts may be joined with a claim before the *tribunal de grande instance* if there is *connexité*. This situation exists when there are common questions that make it desirable to adjudicate all claims in one action. [338] Since other French courts do not enjoy a similarly wide power to deal with matters not within their competence, they are said not to possess the fullness of judicial power.

### 4.38. The Subject Matter Competence *(Compétence d'Attribution)* of the *Tribunal d'Instance*

**a. Subject matter competence based on the amount in controversy.** The *tribunal d'instance* may not hear cases that are within the exclusive competence of the *tribunal de grande instance* – such as matters relating to personal status, nationality, or title to land –, [339] nor cases reserved to the specialized courts – such as commercial, labor, or rural lease matters. In most other instances, it is competent if the amount in controversy does not exceed 3,000 francs. [340] In cases involving suits for rent due, for damages for wrongful eviction, for repairs to leased property, and other matters involving the landlord-tenant relationship, the *tribunal d'instance* is competent if the rent is a maximum of 1500 francs *per annum* or, in the case of furnished apartments, 300 francs per month. [341] If the rent exceeds these amounts, the case must ordinarily be brought before the president of the *tribunal de grande instance.* [342]

When competence depends on the amount in controversy, the last *conclusions* (pleadings) of the parties, rather than the amount claimed at the beginning of the action, [343] control. The amount in controversy includes the principal and interest demanded, but not costs or interest accruing after commencement of the action. [344] If several claims based on the same or related transactions between one plaintiff and one defendant are consolidated, the *tribunal d'instance* may lose competence since the sums demanded in the various causes of action must be added. If the various claims are unrelated, the amount in controversy must be determined for each one separately. [345] If there are several plaintiffs or

[338] MOREL 241–43. The discretionary power of the lower courts to decide whether several matters may be tried together because of their close relationship (*connexité*) is not subject to review by the *Cour de Cassation.*

[339] *Cf.* ORDONNANCE No. 58–1273 of Dec. 22, 1958, J.O. Dec. 23, [1958] D.L. 25, arts. 1–2; MOREL 191–94.

[340] DÉCRET No. 58–1284, *supra* note 322, art. 1.

[341] DÉCRET No. 58–1284, *supra* note 322, art. 2.

[342] See 4.42 *infra.*

[343] CUCHE & VINCENT 233.

[344] *Ibid.*

[345] DÉCRET No. 58–1284, *supra* note 322, art. 14.

defendants, the total amount sued for must be divided by the number of defendants or plaintiffs in order to determine whether the *tribunal d'instance* is competent. [346] Counterclaims do not affect the competence of the *tribunal d'instance* over the original claim: The court may either dismiss a counterclaim for a sum in excess of its competence and determine the original claim or transfer the whole matter to the *tribunal de grande instance.* Irrespective of the amount demanded, the *tribunal d'instance* may always hear counterclaims based on allegations that the suit before it amounts to malicious prosecution or abuse of process. [347]

**b. Subject matter competence in other cases.** In some cases, the *tribunal d'instance* is competent without regard to the amount in controversy. These include cases involving bailments to a common carrier and some other bailments, and cases involving assault, battery, and defamation if the press is not involved. [348] Convenience of the parties, who may want to bring their case before a nearby court, is the reason why the *tribunal d'instance* is competent in support cases [349] and in many cases involving farming – such as actions for damage to growing crops, actions concerning the sale of domestic animals, seed, or fertilizer, actions on notes secured by liens on farm products, and the like. [350] The *tribunal d'instance* also has competence over certain actions involving land – such as actions to determine the right to possession of, but not title to, immovables; [351] actions to have markers put up on a boundary line; actions concerning certain rights in the nature of easements; actions to obtain compensation for rights of way taken by eminent domain on behalf of electric or gas companies; and similar actions. [352] The proximity of the court permits it to view the premises

[346] The statute itself is silent on the point. *But see* CORNU & FOYER, *Mise à jour 1960*, at 18 n. 3.

[347] DÉCRET No. 58–1284, *supra* note 322, art. 17. Counterclaims based on the fact that plaintiff's suit has been brought without good cause are allowed more readily under French law than under the common law. *Cf.* VIZIOZ 181–82. The rule mentioned in the text is necessary to deprive defendants of an easy means to obtain removal from the *tribunal d'instance* to the *tribunal de grande instance.*

[348] DÉCRET No. 58–1284, *supra* note 322, art. 63(3).

[349] DÉCRET No. 58–1284, *supra* note 322, art. 7(1). This includes: (1) support due parents by their children (CODE CIVIL art. 205) or by their son or daughter-in-law (CODE CIVIL art. 206); (2) support due to children (CODE CIVIL art. 207); and (3) support actions between spouses (CODE CIVIL art. 214).

[350] DÉCRET No. 58–1284, *supra* note 322, art. 5.

[351] DÉCRET No. 58–1284, *supra* note 322, art. 7(2). Under French law, a person dispossessed of real property, within one year of eviction, may bring a so-called possessory action to regain possession. In that action, title is not an issue. CODE DE PROCÉDURE CIVILE arts. 23–27; CODE CIVIL arts. 2228, 2236, 2243.

[352] DÉCRET No. 58–1284, *supra* note 322, arts. 7(3)-7(9); *cf.* arts. 7(14) and 7(15).

during these proceedings [353] without causing undue expense. When there is no *conseil de prud'hommes* (labor court) in the district, the *tribunal d'instance* hears cases involving individual employment contracts. [354] Finally, the *tribunal d'instance* has limited competence in the administrative area: It hears cases concerning customs duties, [355] certain fees payable to municipalities, [356] and some elections. [357] It also performs the purely administrative functions of the old *juge de paix* (justice of the peace). [358] As a general rule, controversies involving the execution of judgments, even those rendered by other courts, must be heard by the *tribunal de grande instance,* [359] but the *tribunal d'instance* may determine such controversies if it is competent to hear the underlying dispute. [360]

**c. Subject matter competence in regard to matters raised incidentally or by way of defense.** Generally, the *tribunal d'instance* may not decide matters that are within the exclusive competence of another court. [361] It must, for example, stay its proceedings until a determination of the *tribunal de grande instance* has been obtained [362] whenever an issue of personal status is raised. However, it may deal with questions relating to title to land raised incidentally even though the *tribunal civil,* the predecessor of the *tribunal de grande instance,* had exclusive competence over such questions.

### 4.39. The Subject Matter Competence of the *Tribunaux de Commerce*

Determination of the competence of the commercial courts requires preliminary discussion of the French concept of commercial law. Protagonists of the so-called subjective view consider commercial law as the special law of a class of people called "businessmen" or "merchants" (*commerçants*), which is applicable to all their transactions. According to others, adherents of the so-called objective view, commercial law is

[353] See Code de Procédure Civile arts. 295–301; *cf.* 7.55.b *infra.*

[354] Décret No. 58–1284, *supra* note 322, art. 4. This article also provides that the *tribunal d'instance* is competent in cases involving wet nurses, tuition of educational institutions, fees of institutions or persons providing board for children, and related matters.

[355] Décret No. 58–1284, *supra* note 322, art. 7(10).

[356] Décret No. 58–1284, *supra* note 322, art. 7(11).

[357] Décret No. 58–1284, *supra* note 322, arts. 9–12.

[358] See Ordonnance No. 58–1273, *supra* note 339, art. 3.

[359] See 4.37 *supra.*

[360] Décret No. 58–1284, *supra* note 322, art. 3.

[361] See 4.37.a *supra.*

[362] Cuche & Vincent 269–71.

[363] Décret No. 58–1284, *supra* note 322, art. 16.

the law applicable to all commercial transactions, irrespective of the persons who are parties thereto. [364] French law blends these views.

**a. Subject matter competence based on the nature of the transaction.** French commercial courts are competent in all cases involving "commercial acts" (*actes de commerce*), whether or not the parties before the court are technically merchants or businessmen. [365] The basic commercial acts are specifically listed in the *Code de Commerce.* [366] A person signing a draft always performs a commercial act, but signing other negotiable instruments, such as promissory notes or checks, does not have the same effect. [367] Another typical commercial act is the purchase for resale of goods, excluding real estate but including intangibles, unless it is merely an incident of non-commercial activity [368] – such as the occasional purchase of drugs by a doctor who later administers them to his patients. Purchases by farmers, unless they represent a distinct commercial sideline, are specifically excluded. [369] Certain activities are commercial only if they constitute a course of conduct rather than mere isolated acts. These include: (1) mining; [370] (2) manufacturing; (3) transportation by land, air, and inland waterways; [371] (4) supplying of gas, water, and the like; (5) the operation of public spectacles of all sorts; (6) the conduct of various types of agencies, such as travel agencies, public relations agencies, and real estate agencies; [372] and (7) operations relating to exchange of foreign currency, the transfer of capital from one place to another, and banking. [373] Operations on the stock exchange, even by a private speculator, also qualify as commercial acts if there is a sufficiently persistent course of conduct. [374]

[364] See Von Mehren, The Civil Law System 49–55 (1957) and materials cited. The denominator for all "commercial acts" has variously been said to be their speculative character, the circulation of goods, or the existence of an enterprise. 1 Hamel & Lagarde, Traité de Droit Commercial 172 (1954).

[365] Code de Commerce art. 631(3).

[366] Code de Commerce art. 632. For the definition of drafts, prommissory notes, and checks, see Code de Commerce art. 110; 2 Escarra, Manuel de Droit Commercial 681–742 (1948).

[367] Code de Commerce art. 632(1); 1 Hamel & Lagarde, *op. cit. supra* note 364, at 178. The purchase of goods to be leased to patrons also comes under this article.

[368] 1 Escarra, Manuel de Droit Commercial 64–65 (1947).

[369] Code de Commerce art. 638(1).

[370] Code Minier, Décret of Aug. 16, 1956, J.O. Aug. 21, 1956, p. 8004 [1956], B.L.D. 624, art. 23.

[371] Code de Commerce art. 632(2); *cf.* Décret No. 55–1590 of Nov. 30, 1955, J.O. Dec. 6, 1955, p. 11815, [1955] B.L.D. 1, art. 114 (air transport).

[372] Code de Commerce art. 632(3); 1 Hamel & Lagarde, *op. cit. supra* note 364, at 197.

[373] Code de Commerce arts. 632(4), 632(5); 1 Hamel & Lagarde, *op. cit. supra* note 364.

[374] 1 Escarra, *op. cit. supra* note 368, at 74.

In addition, the commercial courts are competent in admiralty matters, such as those relating to the purchase, sale, and construction of seagoing ships, marine insurance, the hiring of crews, and other matters relating to marine transportation. [375]

**b. Subject matter competence based on the character of the parties.** The French commercial courts also possess "subjective" subject matter competence: They decide all cases involving business transactions in which *both* parties are *commerçants*, irrespective of whether "commercial acts" listed in the *Code de Commerce* are involved. Merchant, the usual translation for *commerçant*, is perhaps too narrow a term, since a *commerçant* need not be a dealer in goods. [376]

The Commercial Code provides that all obligations involving *commerçants* and bankers are commercial in nature. [377] What constitutes a business transaction is thus usually not in doubt. The Commercial Code classifies as *commerçant* everybody who engages in the acts of commerce specifically enumerated. [378] Not only individual proprietors but also the active partners in a partnership are *commerçants*. Various types of *sociétés*, including partnerships, though they do not necessarily enjoy limited liability, [379] have legal personality under French law. Whether a company is a *commerçant* depends upon the nature of its activities. If it engages in commercial activities, such as the purchase of goods for resale, it is a *commerçant*. If it engages in non-commercial activities, such as the operation of an agricultural enterprise, it is not. [380] The two forms of business organizations most closely resembling an American corporation, the *société anonyme* and the *société à responsabilité limitée*, are *commerçants*, regardless of the activities in which they engage. [381]

Persons and firms who are *commerçants* are subject to the compe-

[375] CODE DE COMMERCE art. 633.

[376] CODE DE COMMERCE art. 631(1).

[377] CODE DE COMMERCE art. 632(6).

[378] CODE DE COMMERCE art. 1; 1 ESCARRA, *op. cit. supra* note 368, at 1.

[379] See 4.05.d *supra*.

[380] 1 ESCARRA, *op. cit. supra* note 168, at 117; RIPERT, TRAITÉ ELÉMENTAIRE DE DROIT COMMERCIAL 63 (3d ed. 1959).

[381] Law of July 24, 1867, [1867] D. 4.98, art. 68 (*société anonyme*); Law of March 7, 1925, [1925] D. 2.169, art. 3 (*société à responsabilité limitée*); CHURCH, BUSINESS ASSOCIATIONS UNDER FRENCH LAW 29–33, 531–32 (1960). The *société anonyme* resembles the publicly held American corporation, while the *société à responsabilité limitée* resembles the small privately held corporation. On the various forms of French business organizations, see also Conard, *Forming a Subsidiary in the European Common Market*, 59 MICH. L. REV. 1 (1960). The limited partnership on shares (*société en commandite par actions*) is also always "commercial." Public (government-owned) corporations may be *commerçants* if they are operated as commercial enterprises rather than govermental services. 1 ESCARRA, *op. cit. supra* note 368, at 274.

tence of the commercial courts, may vote in the elections for judges of the courts, must obey the rules relating to registration in commercial registries kept at the seat of each commercial court, must keep certain books of account, and must maintain a bank account. [382] Since only *commerçants* can go through bankruptcy, the commercial courts are competent in all bankruptcy matters. [383] The commercial courts are also competent in suits between members of a firm involving the firm, or between the firm and its members. [384]

The Commercial Code provides that all notes signed by *commerçants* are presumed to be commercial acts. [385] This principle has been extended to include all other acts of *commerçants* that form part of the conduct of their business. [386] Consequently, in addition to the specifically enumerated commercial acts, which are commercial no matter by whom they are effectuated, other acts are commercial if they are accomplished by a person who is a *commerçant*. [387] Since the commercial courts possess subject matter competence whenever commercial acts are involved, [388] *commerçants* may be sued in the commercial courts for all acts performed in the conduct of their business, even if the plaintiff is not a *commerçant* and the act is not one of those specifically listed. [389] Thus, a retail merchant who is a *commerçant*, since he engages in one of the listed commercial activities, may be sued by a retail customer in the commercial court. However, in this area the competence of the commercial courts is only permissive, and the customer may bring his action in the regular courts. And if the dealer wishes to sue the customer, he must sue him in the regular courts. [390]

[382] Failure to register does not deprive a businessman of his status as a *commerçant* or affect the competence of the commercial court (1 ESCARRA, *op. cit. supra* note 368, at 117), but registration creates a rebuttable presumption that the registrant is a *commerçant*. DÉCRET No. 58–1355 of Dec. 27, 1958, J.O. Dec. 29, 1958, p. 11971, [1959] B.L.D. 225, art. 15.

[383] CODE DE COMMERCE art. 635. The commercial courts are competent in suits directly related to bankrupcty, but not in other actions not within their ordinary "commercial" competence brought by the trustee in lieu of the bankrupt and without direct relation to the bankruptcy. MOREL 187.

[384] CODE DE COMMERCE art. 631(2).

[385] CODE DE COMMERCE art. 638.

[386] 1 HAMEL & LAGARDE, *op. cit. supra* note 364, at 205–06.

[387] In contradistinction to the enumerated "commercial acts," which are sometimes called "commercial acts by nature" (*par nature*), the acts which are deemed "commercial" because transacted by a businessman as part of his business are sometimes called "accessorily commercial" (*actes de commerces par accessoire*). They include all sorts of contracts, even the purchase of a going business, but apparently not the purchase of real estate. 1 ESCARRA, *op. cit. supra* note 368, at 79–81.

[388] See 4.39.a *supra*.

[389] 1 ESCARRA, *op. cit. supra* note 368, at 229.

[390] MOREL 187–88; CORNU & FOYER 164. A transaction, "commercial" from the point of view of one of the parties and "non-commercial" from the point of view of the other party, is called a "mixed" transaction.

Because the courts considered the operation of vehicles as part of regular business activity, it was possible to sue *commerçants* in the commercial courts for personal injuries caused by their cars or trucks. However, since the 1958 reforms, the regular courts have been exclusively competent in vehicular tort cases.[391] Actions between employers and employees are not ordinarily within the competence of the commercial courts, but must be brought before the labor courts.[392] Employees at the executive level, the so-called *cadres*, however, may sue their employers before the commercial courts.[393] The Code of Commerce also states that the commercial courts are competent in certain cases involving custodians of public funds and clerks or agents of businessmen;[394] this competence seems to be of little practical importance today. The amount in litigation has no bearing on the competence of the commercial courts, though it may affect the right of appeal.

**c. Subject matter competence in regard to matters raised incidentally or by way of defense.** Since the commercial courts possess very specialized powers, they have only a limited right to deal with matters not within their regular competence that are raised incidentally. In particular, they may not deal with matters of personal status or questions involving title to land.[395] If such issues, called *questions préjudicielles*, are raised, the action must be stayed until a decision of the *tribunal de grande instance* has been obtained. In suits involving promissory notes, the commercial courts are competent as soon as the note bears the signature of a *commerçant*; but they are not competent if the note bears only the signature of non-*commerçants*.[396] Counterclaims in regard to which the commercial courts have no competence must ordinarily be dismissed.[397]

[391] DÉCRET No. 58–1285, *supra* note 329.

[392] See 4.40 *infra*.

[393] CODE DE COMMERCE art. 634; DÉCRET No. 58–1292 of Dec. 22, 1958, J.O. Dec. 23, 1958, p. 11621, [1959] B.L.D. 77, art. 81.

[394] CODE DE COMMERCE art. 634.

[395] CUCHE & VINCENT 270–71. Disputes over patents, even if they arise incidentally, are also included among the matters over which the commercial courts do not have adjudicatory power; furthermore, the commercial courts may not deal with matters that are reserved for the administrative courts or the executive and are beyond the competence of even the civil courts.

[396] CODE DE COMMERCE art. 637.

[397] There may be an exeption if the original claim and the counterclaim are "indivisible.' MOREL 244.

## 4.40. The Subject Matter Competence of the *Conseils de Prud'hommes*

The *conseils de prud'hommes* or labor courts generally hear suits between employers and employees arising out of employment or apprenticeship contracts. Employees of executive rank, *cadres*, may sue their employers in the commercial courts. [398] Clauses in employment contracts aimed at depriving the labor courts of their competence are void. [399] The labor courts may hear disputes involving public employees only if they are employed by a public agency operated in the form of a business enterprise rather than in the form of a public service. [400] Each individual labor court and each section of each court may hear only disputes arising in the occupations for which it has received competence by the decree creating it. [401] This decree must also specify the area in which the court has competence. [402] Labor courts may not deal with collective labor disputes. [403]

If a dispute between an employer and an employee arises in a district in which there is no competent labor court, the dispute must be brought before the *tribunal d'instance.* [404]

Labor courts, like the commercial courts, have only limited power to deal with issues not within their basic competence that are raised incidentally. They may not decide questions of nationality, personal

[398] See note 393 *supra.*

[399] ORDONNANCE No. 58–1276 of Dec. 22, 1958, J.O. Dec. 23, 1958, p. 11560, [1959] B.L.D. 28, art. 1; DÉCRET No. 58–1292, *supra* note 393, art. 81. The courts are competent in disputes *between* workers (but not salaried employees) arising out of the employment contract. CODE DU TRAVAIL, Book I, art. 17.

[400] CUCHE & VINCENT 226.

[401] See 3.27 *supra.* The occupations are generally classified by trade, not by industry. DÉCRET No. 58–1292, *supra* note 393, art. 80. Until 1957, the labor courts were not competent in disputes between domestic servants and their employees. *Cf.* MOREL 188. As a consequence, they were never mentioned in the decrees creating individual labor courts. In 1957, labor court competence was extended to all disputes between employers and employees; in order to make amendments including domestic service in the numerous decrees creating the individual labor courts unnecessary, it has been provided that the individual labor courts are competent in this area even if domestic service is not listed in the instituting decree. *Cf.* Law No. 57–31 of Jan. 10, 1957, J.O. Jan. 11, 1957, p. 582, [1957] D.L. 36.

[402] DÉCRET No. 58–1284, *supra* note 322, art. 3.

[403] CUCHE & VINCENT 227. Compulsory arbitration of labor disputes existed immediately before the second World War. *Cf.* Heneman, *The French Superior Court of Arbitration,*9 BROOKLYN L. REV. 33–50 (1939). For a brief summary of present French procedure for the mediation, conciliation, and voluntary arbitration of collective labor disputes, see 2 COLIN & CAPITANT (*Mise à Jour* 1957) 2–3; Colton, *The Rejection of Compulsory Arbitration in France, The New Law on the Settlement of Labor Disputes,* 6 ARB. J. (N.S.) 42 (1951); *cf.* 11.05 *infra.* The labor courts have certain administrative functions, serving as repositories for regional collective agreements and plant rules, and they may be consulted in connection with labor problems. CUCHE & VINCENT 224.

[404] See 4.38.b *supra.*

status, or title to land. [405] They may hear only counterclaims involving matters within their competence. [406] The amount claimed by the plaintiff does not affect the competence of the labor courts, [407] though it may affect the right of appeal.

### 4.41. The Subject Matter Competence of the *Tribunaux Paritaires de Baux Ruraux*

The rural lease courts (*tribunaux paritaires de baux ruraux*) are competent in cases between farm tenants and landlords concerning the application of laws relating to farm leases, [408] including litigation relating to the termination of leases, the tenant's right of preemption, and landlord's liens. [409] When a rural lease court has two sections, one for sharecroppers and one for regular tenants, each section may, if the other section is not functioning, hear cases falling within the competence of the other section. [410] The restrictions on the power of the other specialized courts to deal with matters that are raised incidentally during a suit, but are not within their basic competence, also apply to the rural lease courts. [411]

### 4.42. The Subject Matter Competence of the Social Security Courts

**a. The subject matter competence of the *commissions de première instance.*** The first instance commissions deal with litigation arising out of the application of social security laws except for matters specifically assigned to other tribunals, especially the regional technical commissions. [412] The first instance commissions handle disputes concerning liability for contributions, benefits, and the like between the autono-

[405] *Cf.* 4.39.c *supra.*
[406] DÉCRET No. 58–1292, *supra* note 393, art. 82.
[407] DÉCRET No. 58–1292, *supra* note 393, art. 81.
[408] DÉCRET No. 58–1293 of Dec. 22, 1958, J.O. Dec. 23, 1958, p. 11627, [1959] B.L.D. 87, art. 1. Before the 1959 reform legislation, the applicable statute provided that the rural lease courts were to have exclusive competence in rural lease matters. The word exclusive has not been continued in the 1958 draft of the statute. Presumably, this means that the regular courts may now deal with rural lease matters at least when these are raised incidentally in the course of another proceeding. *Compare* CORNU & FOYER 183–185 *with* CORNU & FOYER (MISE À JOUR 1960) 22. The 1958 legislation seems also to have restricted the competence of the rural lease courts in other respects.
[409] The legislation administered by the rural lease courts is contained in CODE RURAL bk. 6, tit. 1–5. *Cf.* CUCHE & VINCENT 231. For a summary of that legislation, see 2 COLIN & CAPITANT 699–714 and MISE À JOUR 1957, at 8.
[410] DÉCRET No. 58–1293, *supra* note 408, art. 13.
[411] They may not deal with questions of personal status, nationality, or title to real property. *Cf.* 4.39.c *supra.*
[412] ORDONNANCE No. 58–1275 of Dec. 22, 1958, J.O. Dec. 23, 1958, p. 11550, [1959] B.L.D. 27, art. 1 (amending CODE DE LA SÉCURITE SOCIALE arts. 190–91).

mous bodies administering, and liable for payment under, the social security laws, the so-called *caisses de sécurité sociale,* [413] and the insured employees and their employers.

**b. The subject matter competence of the *commissions régionales techniques.*** The regional technical commissions hear cases involving mainly medical questions, in which the presence of physicians among the members of the court may present an advantage. They decide disputes between claimants and social security organizations relating to the existence or the degree of disability caused by industrial accidents, occupational disease, or illness. [414]

### 4.43. The Powers of the Presidents of the Various Courts

Ordinarily, all French courts, with the exception of the *tribunal d' instance,* hear and decide cases by panels of three or more judges. However, the presidents of most French courts may decide certain controversies acting alone. Usually, this power, often and especially in large cities delegated by the presidents, is limited to situations involving provisional relief. In some instances, decisions on the merits may also be rendered.

**a. The powers of the president of the *tribunal de grande instance* to decide cases on the merits.** The most extensive powers have been given to the president of the *tribunal de grande instance.* He, not the full court, decides controversies concerning apartments rented for residential or professional use arising between landlords and tenants under French rent control legislation [415] if the rent is more then 1,500 Francs annually or, in the case of furnished apartments, more than 300 Francs monthly. [416] The *tribunal d'instance* is competent if the rent is lower. When there is a dispute over the tenant's statutory right to obtain a renewal of his lease in suits involving the rent control laws applicable to

[413] *Cf.* CUCHE & VINCENT 229.

[414] There are separate regional commissions to deal with permanent disability in non-agricultural occupations, with temporary disability in non-agricultural occupations, and with temporary or permanent disability in agricultural occupations. ORDONNANCE No. 59–1275, *supra* note 412, amending CODE DE LA SÉCURITE SOCIALE arts. 193–96; DÉCRET No. 58–1291 of Dec. 22, 1958, J.O. Dec. 23, 1958, p. 11613, [1959] B.L.D. 66, arts. 29–30.

[415] Various rent control laws relating to space used for residential and professional purposes were codified by Law No. 48–1360 of Sept. 1, 1948, J.O. Sept. 2, 1948, p. 8659, [1948] D.L. 300, since amended in details. The law provides for the establishment of fair rents and the right of the tenant to remain in possession after the expiration of the lease unless the landlord needs the premises for himself. Operating costs, such as utilities, water, and sewer charges, may ordinarily be added to the rent. *Cf.* 2 COLIN & CAPITANT 714 and MISE À JOUR 1957, at 8.

[416] DÉCRET No. 58–1284, *supra* note 322, art. 38.

premises used for commercial purposes, [417] the *tribunal de grande instance* as such is competent. Other questions involving premises used for commercial purposes must ordinarily be brought before the president of the *tribunal de grande instance.* The amount of the rent is immaterial. [418]

**b. The power of the president of the *tribunal de grande instance* to grant *ex parte* provisional relief.** The president of the *tribunal de grande instance* may grant provisional relief upon *ex parte* application in many cases, including cases involving *saisie conservatoire, saisie foraine,* and other forms of attachment, [419] and divorce and estate matters. [420] *Ex parte* relief may be granted only if speed is important and if notice to the other side will defeat the purpose of the remedy. [421]

**c. The power of the president of the *tribunal de grande instance* to grant provisional relief in *référé* proceedings.** The president of the *tribunal de grande instance* may grant additional forms of provisional relief after notice to adverse parties and a summary hearing. In some cases – including disputes concerning the execution of judgments, [422] certain disputes concerning the *compulsoire* procedure by which the production of notarial documents may be compelled, [423] and several other instances –, [424] use of this *référé* procedure is specifically prescribed by law. In addition, the *référé* procedure may be used in urgent cases. The determination of what is an urgent matter lies within the discretion of the lower courts and is not reviewable by the *Cour de Cassation.* [425] The *référé* procedure is often used in divorce cases to obtain

[417] Rental of commercial premises is regulated by DÉCRET No. 53–960 of Sept. 30, 1953, J.O. Oct. 1, 1953, p. 8618, [1953] D.L. 393, since amended in details. As opposed to tenants of residential space, tenants of commercial space have no absolute right to hold over after the expiration of their lease, but may become entitled to an indemnity if the landlord refuses to renew the lease.

[418] DÉCRET of Sept. 30, 1953, *supra* note 417, arts. 30–33.

[419] See 4.25–4.26 *supra.*

[420] See, *e.g.*, CODE CIVIL art. 236 (divorce); CODE CIVIL art. 1008 (estate matters). See also 11.03 *infra.*

[421] CUCHE & VINCENT 208–09.

[422] CODE DE PROCÉDURE CIVIL art. 806 ( this article includes not only judgments, but also notarial documents which may be the basis of execution). See 2.10.a *supra.*

[423] CODE DE PROCÉDURE CIVILE art. 845. If a demand for a document is made while a suit is in progress, the matter must be brought before the court. CODE DE PROCÉDURE CIVILE arts. 846–52.

[424] *E.g.*, CODE CIVIL art. 1244 (stay of proceedings against debtor). For other examples, see 2 DALLOZ, RÉPERTOIRE DE PROCÉDURE CIVILE ET COMMERCIALE, *Référé Civil,* Nos. 53–62 (1956).

[425] 2 DALLOZ, *op. cit. supra* note 424, at No. 21.

alimony *pendente lite.* [426] It may also be used by the father to obtain the return of a child who has been removed from the parental household. [427] Before commencing litigation on the merits, victims of automobile accidents frequently ask the president of the *tribunal de grande instance,* sitting *en référé,* to appoint an expert to investigate the circumstances of the accident. [428] This is one of the limited means of discovery available under French law. The *référé* procedure is used in so many situations and its scope is so constantly expanded by French practitioners that no complete list can be given. The decision of the president of the *tribunal de grande instance,* acting *en référé,* may not and does not prejudge the merits. [429]

**d. The powers of the president of the *tribunal de commerce.*** The president of the commercial court decides controversies on the merits when the summary procedure to recover small commercial debts is used. [430] In addition, he is authorized to grant *ex parte* provisional relief, though his power in that respect is more restricted than that of the president of the *tribunal de grande instance.* [431] Since 1942, the president of a commercial court has also been authorized to grant provisional relief in urgent matters under the *référé* procedure. However, he may hear neither disputes concerning the execution of judgments – even of the commercial courts – nor disputes concerning the validity of attachment, [432] since litigation involving these matters must generally be initiated before the *tribunal de grande instance.* The president of a commercial court may grant provisional relief only if the underlying cause of action is within the competence of the commercial courts. [434]

[426] 2 Garsonnet, Tissier & Morel 16.

[427] See the cases cited in 2 Dalloz, *op. cit. supra* note 424, at No. 27.

[428] *E.g.,* Coppe et Comp. La Concorde v. Moskoleff, Oct. 23, 1955, Cour Paris, [1953] D.J. 686; the case cited in 2 Dalloz, *op. cit. supra* note 424, at No. 27.

[429] Code de Procédure Civile art. 809; 2 Dalloz, *op. cit. supra* note 424, at Nos. 75–86.

[430] Law No. 57–756 of July 4, 1957, J.O. July 7, 1957, p. 6690, [1957] D.L. 210, arts. 1–10. See also the commentary on that law by Deleau-Deshayes at [1957] D.L. 315 (contract obligations under 2500 Francs or any suit on an accepted draft or promissory note). The procedure is discussed below. See 11.02.a *infra.* The presidents of the commercial courts also have some administrative functions concerning the registers of commerce and related matters.

[431] Code de Procédure Civile art. 417. The president of the commercial court may not authorize the creation of a provisional lien on real property; such a lien may be authorized only by the president of the *tribunal de grande instance.* See Code de Procédure Civile art. 54.

[432] Law of March 11, 1924, J.O. March 20, 1924, [1924] D. 4. 142, [1924] B.L.D. 158, amending art. 417 of the Code de Procédure Civile. *Cf.* especially as to prior law, Morel 204–06.

[433] See 4.37 *supra.*

[434] *Cf.* Loisel, femme Comard, Cour Rouen, July 15, 1948, [1948] D.J. 23; Cornu & Foyer 165.

**e. The powers of the president of the *tribunal paritaire de baux ruraux*.** Perhaps because he is a professional judge and a member of the *tribunal d'instance*, the president of a rural leases court has been given fairly wide powers to grant provisional relief under the *référé* procedure. In derogation of the rule that only the *tribunal de grande instance* or its president may deal with questions relating to the execution of judgments, the president of a rural lease court, acting *en référé*, may also hear disputes concerning the execution of judgments of the rural lease court. [435] In addition, he may authorize certain types of *ex parte* provisional remedies. [436]

**f. The powers of the presidents of other courts.** The presiding judges of the remaining courts do not seem to have any special powers.

### 4. RULES OF TERRITORIAL COMPETENCE

#### 4.44. Rules of Territorial Competence – Crossreference

French rules of territorial competence, which have been interpreted to embody rules of general competence, have been discussed above. [437] They need no further elaboration here.

[435] DÉCRET No. 58–1293, *supra* note 408, art. 20.
[436] CUCHE & VINCENT at 232.
[437] See 4.11–4.33 *supra*.

CHAPTER 5

# PRE-COMMENCEMENT ACTIVITIES

This chapter describes the rôle of the legal practitioners in gathering factual information preparatory to the commencement of an action (5.01–5.02) and pre-commencement conciliation procedures (5.03). The second part deals with provisional remedies and other pre-commencement relief (5.04–5.07).

## 1. PREPARATION FOR LITIGATION

### 5.01. Introductory Remarks

As a general rule, French practitioners display only limited activity in gathering factual information preparatory to and during litigation in the civil courts. [1] This is due in part to the rule which makes any conversation between an attorney and prospective witnesses – whether his own or those of his adversary – a breach of professional ethics. [2] A further factor limiting the rôle of the French lawyer in fact gathering is the preference of French attorneys and courts for documentary evidence. [3] There are no rules as to whether the *avocat* or the *avoué* bears the burden of case preparation. In practice, the burden may be assumed by either or both, depending on the case, the lawyers involved, and similar circumstances. [4]

[1] On the respective rôles of the *avocat* and *avoué*, see 2.06.f *supra*.

[2] See, *e.g.*, LES BARREAUX DANS LE MONDE 254 (1959). To some extent, this rule is fortified by a criminal sanction. CODE PÉNAL art. 365 provides that a person using any kind of pressure, offer of gifts, artifice, and similar device, in order to induce another person to make a false statement or deposition or to give a false written certificate relating to any legal action, may be punished by imprisonment of one to three years in jail, and a fine of F. 1500 (about $300) to F. 15000 (about $3000), whether or not a false statement was actually obtained.

[3] For a more detailed discussion, see 7.22, 7.33 *infra*.

[4] Case preparation that involves routine work, such as obtaining files from the police or prosecutor's office, is more likely to be done by the *avoué* than by the *avocat*. Some *avoués* seem to think that the factual preparation of the case is properly their function and that it has been taken over to some extent by the *avocats* only because some *avoués* have not been active enough in the area.

## 5.02. The Gathering of Factual Information

To obtain factual information, the *avocat* or *avoué* will examine his client's file and tell his client what further factual investigations he should make in the light of the applicable law. The client may also be asked to obtain statements from witnesses or experts. In accident cases and other instances in which there has been a police investigation, the *avocat* or *avoué* will endeavor to obtain the file of the police or prosecutor. [5] If the case involves a highly technical matter, the *avocat* or *avoué* may discuss it with an expert to obtain the necessary background information. Discovery of papers and tangible evidence in the hands of an adverse party is possible only in very limited cases. [6] However, attorneys may ask an *huissier* to go to a specified place, to inspect the locality, and to make a report, which is called a *constat*. When it is to be feared that the *huissier* may not be admitted to the premises in question, *avoués* try to obtain an *ex parte* court order authorizing the *huissier* to enter the premises. [7] The procedure is popular especially in divorce cases as a means of obtaining proof of adultery; the *huissier*'s report in such a case is called a *constat d'adultère*. [8]

Courts may also appoint impartial experts to investigate and report,

[5] These may be obtained only with the consent of the appropriate *procureur de la République or procureur général*. CODE DE PROCÉDURE PÉNALE arts. R. 155, R. 156. The police investigation in an accident case is ordinarily more detailed than in the United States. If a criminal action is actually brought against a person responsible for an accident or other tort, the victim may be awarded damages in the criminal action if he joins it as a civil party. See 3.23 *supra*. This means that, in practice, the major job of preparation is shifted to the public prosecutor. In accident cases, CODE CIVIL art. 1384 (see 7.30.b *infra*) often creates a presumption of negligence, which materially reduces the need for factual investigations.

[6] A party wishing to use a document must make it available to the other side. CODE DE PROCÉDURE CIVILE art. 188–99; 7.34 *infra*. This rule is of no help to a party who needs a document his opponent does not want to use. In non-commercial cases, unless there is a special relationship such as co-ownership between the parties, there is usually no duty to make available documents or other tangible evidence one does not wish to use. This rule is expressed by the Latin saying *nemo tenetur edere contra seipsum* (nobody is bound to produce documents against himself). A few courts have occasionally permitted discovery beyond this by a so-called *actio ad exhibendum*, however. See 9 BEUDANT, COURS DE DROIT CIVIL FRANÇAIS 246, 247 (2d ed. 1953); 2 DALLOZ, RÉPERTOIRE DE PROCÉDURE CIVILE ET COMMERCIALE, *Preuve*, at Nos. 169–75 (1956). In bankruptcy and a few other cases, production of commercial books of account may be obtained, and in all other commercial cases such books must at least be submitted to the court so that the judge may copy the relevant entries. CODE DE COMMERCE arts. 14–16. See also 7.34 *infra*.

[7] When acting under court order, the *huissier* must be admitted.

[8] Because it would involve an unnecessary interference with privacy, this discovery device may not be available in litigation merely to modify an existing alimony decree. Perry v. Orban, Trib. Clermont-Ferrand, Jan. 23, 1954, [1954] D. SOMM. 39. Occasionally, French practitioners use a somewhat roundabout way to obtain evidence of adultery. They have their client file with the police a complaint charging adultery. Since adultery is a crime in France, the police makes an investigation. As soon as the investigation is made, the complaint is withdrawn, which stops further prosecution. However, the police file is then used in the divorce action.

even before a law suit has been started, if there is danger that evidence may be lost unless immediate action be taken (*expertise*). The appointment of an expert must be demanded in the *référé* procedure.

Experts have very far reaching powers of investigation. They may examine relevant places or equipment, and even hear witnesses, though not under oath. As a result, the appointment of an impartial expert before the beginning of the action is a rather effective discovery device, which enjoys increasing popularity. [9] However, except for an informal examination of witnesses, which is sometimes conducted by an expert, there is no way by which the testimony of witnesses, let alone that of an adverse party, may be obtained before the hearing. [10]

As a rule, the view that rhetorical skill at the time of the hearing before the court (*audience*) is more important than a thorough factual preparation is still quite prevalent in France. However, as the increasing use of the *constat* and the *expertise* indicate, this view may be changing.

### 5.03. Conciliation and Settlement

Before 1949, an action before the *tribunal civil* (now *tribunal de grande instance*) could ordinarily be brought only if the parties had first appeared before a *juge de paix* to attempt a settlement. However, the courts had the power to dispense with this requirement, and they were so liberal in granting dispensations that in 1949 the requirement was abandoned as ineffectual. [11] At present, a compulsory conciliation attempt must precede the commencement of an action only in certain matters, notably divorce and separation [12] and some other proceedings. [13]

Of course, the court before which an action is pending retains the right to attempt a settlement on a voluntary basis. Before the beginning of the formal hearing (*audience*), the reporting judge (*juge chargé*

[9] On reports of experts (the so-called *expertise*), see 7.54 *infra*. On the *référé* procedure, see 5.07 *infra*.

[10] See generally 1 SOLUS & PERROT 213–16. However, a recent statute authorizes courts to order parties and tax officials to produce tax documents relevant to a suit. Law No. 62-896 of Aug. 4, 1962, J.O. Aug. 5, 1962, p. 7778, [1962] D.L. 261.

[11] In 1948, about 147,000 new cases were brought before the *tribunaux civils* in France; of these, only about 30,000 seem to have been submitted to a *juge de paix* for an attempt at settlement. In about 9,700 cases a settlement could be reached. See the figures given in ANNUAIRE STATISTIQUE DE LA FRANCE RÉTROSPECTIF at 80–81 (1961) and CORNU & FOYER 174. Dispensation could be given whenever speed was essential.

[12] As to the settlement attempt in divorce cases, which must take place before a judge of the *tribunal de grande instance*, see 11.04.d *infra*.

[13] A settlement must be attempted in all cases before the *tribunal d'instance* (former *juge de paix*) and before the *conseil de prud'hommes*. As to settlement attempts by the court in cases involving the collection of small commercial debts, see 11.02.a *infra*.

*de suivre la procédure*) may always attempt to bring the parties to an agreement; after the beginning of the hearing, the full court may meet with the parties *in camera* for this purpose. If the case is settled, an official settlement agreement is prepared which has the effects of a judgment. [14]

## 2. PROVISIONAL REMEDIES AND OTHER PRE-COMMENCEMENT RELIEF

### 5.04. Introductory Remarks

In some instances, relief of a provisional nature, which does not prejudge the merits, may be obtained even before an action has been started. Included in such relief are provisional remedies granted *ex parte* as well as the many types of relief which may be granted after a hearing by a judge sitting *en référé.*

### 5.05. Attachment *(Saisie Conservatoire)* and Other Provisional Remedies Granted *Ex Parte*

Until 1955, provisional remedies were available rather broadly only in commercial cases. Since 1955, attachment (*saisie conservatoire*) has been available in *all* cases involving money obligations. [15]

A petition (*requête*) requesting authority to attach the debtor's property is presented *ex parte* to the presiding judge (or the judge acting as his delegate) of the *tribunal de grande instance*, or, in appropriate cases, of the *tribunal d'instance*, at the domicile of the defendant or at the place where the property is located. [16]

The petition indicates briefly why the attachment is requested and what property is to be attached. At the bottom of the petition, the *avoué* customarily puts a draft order (*ordonnance*) authorizing the attachment.

[14] Code de Procédure Civile art. 80. The agreement (*procès-verbal de conciliation*), like a judgment, may be a basis for execution. On the power of the *juge des mises en état* under the new amendments, see 7.58, 7.62 *infra*; Code de Procédure Civile arts. 81-83 (as amended).

[15] *Saisie conservatoire* is available only in actions on claims for a sum of money. See, *e.g.*, Prévost v. Bottos, Cour Paris, May 5, 1959, [1959] D.J. 304. *Saisie conservatoire* is available against a motorist responsible for an accident who has not complied with the French compulsory insurance legislation. Law No. 58–208 of Feb. 27, 1958, J.O. Feb. 28, 1958, p. 2148, [1958] D.L. 123, art. 8. Otherwise, *saisie* does not seem available in tort cases. However, the claim on which the attachment is based need not necessarily be liquidated. On *saisie* generally, see Giverdon, *Saisies et mesures conservatoires au terme de deux années d'application*, [1957] D. Chr. 209, and Giverdon, *Commentaire*, [1956] D.L. 499.

[16] Code de Procédure Civile art. 48. In commercial matters, the application must be presented to the president of the commercial court. Code de Procédure Civile art. 417. See also 4.43.d *supra.*

Attachment may be granted only if the plaintiff's claim seems well-founded and if speedy action is essential to ensure the eventual payment of the judgment. [17] Whether these conditions are fulfilled is a factual question. [18]

To grant the petition, the judge simply completes the skeleton order at the bottom. He may, but need not, order the plaintiff to post security for the payment of possible damages for wrongful attachment. The order granting the attachment must always indicate within what time the plaintiff must commence his action against the defendant. [19]

The order is delivered to an *huissier*, who may seize the designated property, whether it is in the hands of the debtor or of a third party.

After seizure, the property is delivered to a custodian, who must keep it until further order of the court. [20]

If the court refuses to grant the attachment, the plaintiff may appeal. The defendant may obtain cancellation of the attachment by contesting its validity in a *référé* proceeding before the judge who granted it or by giving security for the payment of any judgment which may be recovered against him. [21]

In cases in which an attachment may be granted, the court may authorize the plaintiff to register a temporary lien (*nantissement*) against his debtor's business if the debtor is a merchant registered in the Commercial Register. The lien must be recorded in the Commercial

[17] CODE DE PROCÉDURE CIVILE art. 48. For a form of a petition and order, see 1 RAVIART, TRAITÉ FORMULAIRE DE PROCÉDURE CIVILE 5 (Supp. 1956). Decisions by a single judge granting provisional relief are called *ordonnances* (orders), as opposed to decisions by a regular three man panel of the *tribunal de grande instance*, which are called *jugements* (judgments) even if only an interlocutory decision has been rendered.

[18] 2 DALLOZ, RÉPERTOIRE DE PROCÉDURE CIVILE ET COMMERCIALE, *Saisie et mesures conservatoires*, No. 5 (1956). A holder of a bill of exchange or promissory note protested for non-payment may request permission to attach the property of drawers, acceptors, and endorsers. CODE DE COMMERCE art. 158 (bill of exchange); art. 185 (promissory note).

[19] CODE DE PROCÉDURE CIVILE art. 48. This article also provides that the order must be executed even if it is attacked by way of *oppossition* or appeal. Whenever property has been attached, the plaintiff must sue his debtor within the time specified in the court order. He has two actions available to him: (1) the regular action, which would lie in the absence of attachment and which must be brought in the court competent to hear it, and (2), in most cases, an action called *en validité de saisie* (to validate a seizure), which is brought in the court having ordered the *saisie*, but which, in fact, has the same effect as the regular action. See 4.26 *supra*, especially at notes 191–205.

[20] If all parties agree, the debtor may be the custodian. The *huissier* must prepare a detailed report (*procès-verbal*) of his actions. CODE DE PROCÉDURE CIVILE arts. 51–52, 557–85, 587–93, 596–602. Any gratuitous transfer by the debtor made after the attachment is void. CODE DE PROCÉDURE CIVILE art. 56.

[21] A petition for cancellation of an attachment must be addressed to a judge sitting *en référé*. CODE DE PROCÉDURE CIVILE art. 50. In fact, the order granting the attachment must always include a clause that, in case of difficulties, the parties must have recourse to the judge sitting *en référé*.

Register in which the merchant is listed. If a judgment is later obtained against the debtor, the lien becomes permanent; otherwise, it is cancelled. [22]

Attachment is not available against a debtor's real property. However, in circumstances in which attachment is proper, the court may authorize the recording of a temporary lien against such property. The lien is effective for not more than three years. [23]

### 5.06. Other Forms of *Ex Parte* Relief

As a result of the fairly broad availability of *saisie conservatoire,* other forms of *ex parte* relief have lost some of their former importance. They are mentioned here only briefly.

**a. *Saisie-arrêt.*** A creditor who whishes to garnish claims belonging to his debtor may use a procedure known as *saisie-arrêt.* [24]

**b. *Saisie-gagerie.*** This is the proper procedure to make effective the lien of a lessor of a farm on property of his tenant. It does not require a court order. [25]

**c. *Saisie foraine.*** A creditor may attach property of a debtor who has neither a domicile nor a residence at the place at which the creditor lives, provided the property to be attached is located there. [26]

**d. *Saisie-revendication.*** The Code also permits the seizure of a chattel in the hands of a third party if the plaintiff either alleges that he owns the chattel or claims a lien. [27] Its importance is limited as a

[22] Code de Procédure Civile art. 53. Ordinarily, the term *nantissement* refers to a pledge (Code Civil art. 2071), but here and in a few other cases it is used to designate a lien created without change of possession.

[23] Code de Procédure Civile art. 54.

[24] On *saisie-arrêt,* see Code de Procédure Civile arts. 557–82 and 4.26 *supra. Saisie-arrêt* may be used only by a creditor having some written evidence of indebtedness. It may be used to garnish or attach any kind of property in the hands of a third party. When *saisie-conservatoire* became available, French authors assumed that it could not be used to garnish debts and that *saisie-arrêt* was the proper remedy for that purpose. However, some recent cases indicate that *saisie-conservatoire* may also be used to garnish debts. This seems to leave rather little scope for *saisie-arrêt* considered as a provisional remedy (*saisie-arrêt* may also be used after judgment). *Compare* 2 Dalloz, *op. cit. supra* note 92, at No. 11 (1956), *with Id.,* Supplement 1963.

[25] Code de Procédure Civile arts. 819–21.

[26] Code de Procédure Civile arts. 822–25; *cf.* 4.26 *supra. Saisie foraine,* a very expeditious procedure, was primarily intended to protect merchants who give credit to travelling salesmen and other persons spending very little time in one place.

[27] Code de Procédure Civile arts. 826–31.

result of the far-reaching protection given to third parties who acquire personal property.[28]

e. ***Saisie-contrefaçon.*** More importantly, machinery, equipment, books, works of art, products of manufacture, and similar articles, which violate an existing patent or copyright or a right existing under the laws for the protection of designs and similar laws may be seized by so-called *saisie-contrefaçon*. The seizure is designed at least in part to prevent the disappearance of evidence. In the case of patents, designs, trademarks, and models, actual seizure may therefore be replaced by the taking of photographs or the preparation of drawings, descriptions, or models.[29]

### 5.07. *Référé*

In case of difficulties concerning the execution of a judgment, and, much more importantly in this context, in all *urgent* matters, parties may make an application for provisional relief to a single[30] judge sitting *en référé*. The application may be made independently of any pending action, and the relief granted does not prejudge the merits.[31] Whether the matter is urgent is determined by the exercise of judicial discretion.[32]

The power to grant relief *en référé* resides in the presiding judge of the *tribunal de grande instance*, or, in commercial cases, of the commercial court. In case of necessity, the power may be delegated to another judge.[33]

Special sessions for the hearing of *référé* applications are usually held once a week in each court, more often in the larger cities.

A party making an application must summon his opponent to the hearing by a regular *ajournement* (summons), indicating the date when

[28] This protection extends even to third parties who acquire personal property without parting with value. CODE CIVIL art. 2279.

[29] Law of July 5, 1844, [1845] JOURNAL DU PALAIS 2. 29 arts. 47–48 (patents); Law No. 57–298 of March 11, 1957, J.O. March 11, 1957, p. 2723, [1957] D.L. 102 arts. 66–69 (literary property, copyright); Law of July 14, 1909, J.O. July 1, 1909, [1909] D. 4. 81, art. 12 (designs, models); Law No. 64–1360 of Dec. 31, 1964, J.O. Jan. 1, 1965, [1965] D.L. 59, art. 25 (trademarks). The expression *saisie-contrefaçon* means, literally, attachment of an imitation.

[30] The *tribunal de grande instance*, when it decides cases on the merits, sits in panels of three judges, see 3.24 *supra*.

[31] CODE DE PROCÉDURE CIVILE art. 806; *cf.* Maurin v. Epoux Gallard, Cass. Civ., Oct. 22, 1923, [1926] D. 1. 30.

[32] *E.g.*, Sutter v. Dame Sutter, Cass. Civ., May 11, 1953, [1953] D.J. 477. *But see* Soc. Vinification beaujolaise v. Soc. Et. Fruhinholz, Cour Lyon, March 19, 1956, [1956] D. SOMM. 172.

[33] CODE DE PROCÉDURE CIVILE art. 807 and art. 417 (commercial cases).

the hearing is to be had, and, in summary fashion, the grounds on which the application is based. There is no fixed rule as to how many days' notice must be given. The time must simply be reasonable. [34] In cases of extreme urgency, a *référé* application may be heard by the judge outside the regular session – by special permission, even in the judge's home. [35]

The matter is put on the calendar by filing with the clerk of the court a paper called *placet*, which is in essence a copy of the *ajournement*. The arguments are quite brief and are usually conducted by the parties' *avoués*, not by their *avocats*. The court may ask the parties to bring in additional documents or to provide other means of proof if that is required for a decision of the application, but seems to do so only infrequently.

The *référé* procedure is used in a great many different instances, and French practitioners constantly apply it to new situations. It may be used to obtain the appointment of an expert for discovery purposes. [36] In succession cases and other situations in which property is left without proper management as a result of death or absense, a judge sitting *en référé* may appoint a temporary administrator. [37] In some instances, the *référé* procedure may even be used to obtain the removal of a person occupying real property without right. [38] In divorce and separation cases, the *référé* procedure is frequently used to determine alimony and the custody of children *pendente lite*. [39] It is also frequently used to obtain preliminary injunctions.

The decision of the judge in a *référé* case is called *ordonnance* (order). Its execution is not stayed by an appeal. In case of default, a *référé* decision may not be reopened by way of *opposition*. However, *référé* decisions are subject to appeal. Time to appeal is only two weeks. [40]

[34] On the procedural details to be observed in *référé* matters and for forms, see 1 RAVIART, *op. cit. supra* note 17, at 654–73; CODE DE PROCÉDURE CIVILE art. 807 (2).

[35] CODE DE PROCÉDURE CIVILE art. 808.

[36] *E.g.*, Bouix v. Soc. Péreire, Cass. Req., June 9, 1931, [1931] D.H. 396; Guérard v. Dame veuve Robin, Cass. Req., Feb. 27, 1935, [1935] D.H. 194; *cf.* 5.02 *supra*.

[37] *E.g.*, Dame Lefebvre v. Badin, Cass. Req., June 1, 1934, [1934] D.H. 379; Berthet v. Latour, Cass. Req., April 15, 1924, [1924] D.I. 169.

[38] That is especially true if there is no real controversy on the merits. *E.g.*, Carlo v. Gilli, Cass. Civ., March 5, 1930, [1930] D.H. 250; Epoux Faurez v. Thomassin, Cass. Req., July 15, 1930, [1930] D.H. 476

[39] 2 DALLOZ, RÉPERTOIRE DE PROCÉDURE CIVILE ET COMMERCIALE, *Référé civil*, No. 27 (1956). A judge sitting *en référé* may apparently not make an order concerning the temporary custody of children if there is a serious controversy as to custody. Dame Hurot v. Legros, Cour Paris, Feb. 7, 1924, [1924] GAZ. PAL. 1. 151. On the use of the *référé* procedure to confer custody on a public welfare organization, see Demousseaux, Cour Paris, Oct. 4, 1941, [1941] S. 2. 47, 49 REV. TRIM. DR. CIV. 1226 (1942).

[40] CODE DE PROCÉDURE CIVILE art. 809.

CHAPTER 6

# PARTIES AND CLASSIFICATIONS OF ACTIONS

This chapter discusses the rules regulating who may function as parties in civil litigation (6.01–6.04), including rules relating to the requirement of an *intérêt* (6.02), rules concerning capacity to sue or to be sued (6.03), and rules determining who are proper parties (6.04). The second part of this chapter deals with classifications of actions (6.05–6.08).

## 1. PARTIES

### 6.01. Introduction

A person may bring a civil action only if he has a right (*droit*), an interest (*intérêt*), capacity (*capacité*), and is a proper party – that is, has what the French call *qualité*. [1]

### 6.02. The Requirement of *Intérêt*

A person may not bring a civil action unless he has a present, actual, personal, and lawful interest in its outcome. [2] Under this rule (to give some often-cited examples), a distributee who has been disinherited by by both an earlier and a later will cannot sue to have the second will annulled: Since the earlier will prevents his receiving a portion of the inheritance in any event, he has no real *intérêt*; [3] an unsecured creditor cannot object to proceedings for the distribution of a debtor's estate if the debtor's assets are insufficient to make a distribution to unsecured creditors; and a partner cannot bring a proceeding to have a partnership agreement declared void if the firm is already in liquidation and the liquidation procedure will produce the same results. [4]

[1] See Cuche & Vincent 18 (with some citations to authors who do not entirely agree with this analysis).

[2] *E.g.*, Cuche & Vincent 19; Cornu & Foyer 290–92; 1 Solus & Perrot 198–200. The rule has no general statutory basis; it is largely judge-made. Morel 31.

[3] See the cases cited in 1 Dalloz, Répertoire de Procédure Civile et Commerciale, *Action*, No. 19 (1955).

[4] Examples cited in Morel 31; *cf.* Solus & Perrot 198–99.

**a. The interest must be lawful.** Only parties with a lawful interest may bring a civil action. This rule is in essence a restatement in different form of the principle that every civil action must be based on a substantive right. [5] It is invoked mainly when the courts wish to reject a claim which is not supported by existing law. Thus, a concubine, although she was dependent upon her paramour for support and consequently had an interest, since her interest was not lawful, has been held not entitled to recovery under a wrongful death action for the death of her paramour. [6]

**b. The interest may be "moral" (non-pecuniary).** The rule that only parties having an interest may bring a civil action does not exclude litigation relating to non-pecuniary matters. Suits involving family names, titles of nobility, and other matters relating more to prestige than financial interest have often been allowed on the ground that the plaintiff had a moral interest in their outcome. [7]

**c. The interest must be present and actual.** Only persons with a "present" and "actual" interest may bring an action. This means in substance that claims may not be brought prematurely. [8] Beyond this, the rule has been used as the basis for restricting declaratory judgment actions and actions concerning potential or threatened harm. [9]

In a few instances, however, special statutory provisions permit relief in a case of merely potential harm or authorize declaratory judgments. A landowner, whose rights may be jeopardized by proposed

[5] This traditional rule (see 1 Dalloz, *op. cit. supra* note 3, at Nos. 26–27) has been attacked as irrational. 1 Solus & Perrot 203. Of course, an action may be brought only if there is some legal basis for it. It does not seem helpful to rephrase this by saying there must be a lawful interest. The controversy in this respect may be due to historical reasons. France has abandoned the Roman law classification of the law on the basis of actions in favor of a classification based on substantive rights. However, this process has not been carried as far as in some other European countries. Hence, the relationship between actions and rights is not too well defined. There is a voluminous theoretical literature on this subject. 1 Solus & Perrot 104–09 (citing many authorities).

[6] Méténier v. Epoux Luce, Cass. Civ., July 27, 1937, [1938] D. 1. 5 (note Savatier), [1938] S. 1. 321 (note Marty); *cf.* Mazeaud, *La lésion d'un "intérêt légitime juridiquement protégé", condition de la responsabilité civile,* [1954] D. Chr. 39. In the case cited the court also pointed out that concubinage creates no rights.

[7] *E.g.*, 1 Solus & Perrot 201. Examples are cited at 1 Dalloz, *op. cit. supra* note 3, at Nos. 30, 33–37.

[8] Thus, a party may not sue to obtain an interpretation of a contract as long as no dispute concerning the contract has arisen. On the other hand, if there is litigation concerning a contract, the plaintiff may bring up questions concerning installments which are not yet due. 1 Dalloz, *op. cit. supra* note 3, at Nos. 41–42.

[9] In the absence of specific statutory authorization, the courts tend to disallow actions to prevent mere threatened or future harm. They are more liberal as to declaratory judgment actions. 1 Solus & Perrot 207–09; Cuche & Vincent 29.

construction on an adjacent lot may bring an action to prevent such construction. [10] A party to a contract the authenticity of which may be subject to some doubt does not have to wait until the validity of the contract is contested: He may bring an action to have the contract declared valid. [11] The statutes regulating the acquisition of French citizenship provide that a person in doubt about his French nationality may petition the court for a declaration as to his nationality. [12]

Even in the absence of a specific statutory authorization, relief has sometimes been afforded in cases of merely threatened or potential harm on the ground that mere doubt as to the existence of a legal relationship gives a person an interest to litigate the matter. This has been particularly true in situations involving personal status. Thus, legatees have been permitted to obtain a judicial declaration concerning the validity of clauses in wills restricting their choice of future spouses.[13] On the other hand, declaratory judgments have not been allowed with any consistency in situations involving disputed clauses in commercial contracts. As stated by one French court: "The judiciary has not been instituted to give legal consultations." [14]

**d. The requirement that the interest be personal.** Often, organizations and associations bring actions to vindicate a right of their members. Thus, regional winegrowers' associations may sue to prevent growers in other areas from misrepresenting the origin of their product. Sportsmen's associations frequently bring actions to protect the rights of hunters. It has long been debated whether such actions, since they do not seek to protect the rights of the association as such and therefore do not seek to promote a "personal" interest, are permissible. [15]

The question has been solved in part by a 1920 statute [16] allowing

[10] This is the action known as *dénonciation de nouvel oeuvre* (complaint about new works). See 6.08 *infra.*

[11] CODE CIVIL arts. 1323–24 (*vérification d'écritures* procedure).

[12] ORDONNANCE No. 45-2441 of October 19, 1945 (Code of French nationality), J.O. Oct. 20, 1945, p. 6700, [1946] D.L. 10, art. 129.

[13] See, *e.g.*, the examples given by 1 SOLUS & PERROT 211–12; *cf.* Weiller v. Dame Diplarkos, Cour Paris, Dec. 15, 1948, [1949] D.J. 461 (note Savatier), *aff'd sub nom.* Epoux Russel v. Weiller, Cass. Civ., Jan. 22, 1951, 40 REV. CR. D.I.P. 167 (1951) (spouse against whom an ex parte divorce has been obtained in the United States may bring a declaratory judgment action in France to have the divorce declared void, even though the spouse who had obtained the divorce had taken no steps to have it recognized in France).

[14] See the cases cited in 1 DALLOZ, *op. cit. supra* note 3, at No. 15.

[15] Ordinarily, a party has a personal interest only if his own rights are directly affected. *E.g.*, MOREL 33–34.

[16] Law of March 12, 1920, J.O. March 14, 1920, [1922] S. 5.462, authorizing certain organizations (*syndicats*) to bring actions relating to matters causing a direct or indirect prejudice to the group they represent.

designated professional organizations, such as labor unions, to bring actions in defense of their members' rights, at least if the controversy is not lacking in actuality. Authority to bring actions for the protection of the collective interest of their members has also been granted to certain associations working in the public welfare area. It has, however, been denied to most other associations, although recently the courts have tended to become more liberal. [17]

## 6.03. Capacity to Sue or Be Sued *(Capacité d'Ester en Justice)*

French authors generally distinguish between capacity to bring an action as an abstract right, called *capacité de jouissance du droit d'ester en justice,* and the concrete procedural rules designating the persons authorized to bring or defend actions on behalf of minors, incompetents, and similar persons (*capacité d'exercice du droit d'ester en justice*).

**a. *Capacité de jouissance.*** Since the abolition of civil death as a penalty, all persons have the abstract capacity to sue or be sued. [18] It makes no difference whether they are physical persons or corporations or associations, provided they have legal personality. [19] Foreigners as well as French nationals enjoy this right. American citizens are doubly protected in this respect, since their right to sue in France is also guaranteed by the Convention of Establishment of November 25, 1959. [20]

**b. Security for costs.** Foreigners who want to initiate litigation as plaintiffs must, however, give security for any costs and damages which may be caused by the lawsuit (*cautio judicatum solvi*). [21] The *cautio judicatum solvi* need not be furnished if the plaintiff owns real property in France of a value sufficient to ensure payment of any

[17] See generally MOREL 35–37; CORNU & FOYER 299–300. For a more detailed discussion, see 1 SOLUS & PERROT 220–43.

[18] CUCHE & VINCENT 313. There is at least one exeption to the rule that all persons have (abstract) capacity to sue or to be sued. Under certain circumstances, a person having committed a felony (*crime*) who is a fugitive from justice can be declared to be *en contumace.* He is then considered a rebel against the law and loses his right to sue. CODE DE PROCÉDURE PÉNALE art. 627.

[19] To some extent, even associations without legal personality have been allowed to sue. In addition, in order to prevent a miscarriage of justice, associations lacking legal personality may sometimes be sued even if they are unable to bring an action themselves. CUCHE & VINCENT 314. On the legal personality of various types of associations in France, see also AMOS & WALTON, INTRODUCTION TO FRENCH LAW 52–54 (2d ed. 1963).

[20] [1960] 2 U.S.T. & O.I.A. 2398, T.I.A.S. No. 4625, art. III.

[21] Literally, security for the payment of the judgment (against the plaintiff).

judgment for costs and damages against him. [22] Unfortunately, the Convention of Establishment does not modify the rules concerning *cautio judicatum solvi*, which must therefore be furnished by American citizens suing in France. [23] As a result, article III of the treaty, which provides that American citizens in France must be allowed to sue *in forma pauperis* under the same conditions as French nationals is of little practical advantage when an American plaintiff is unable to post security. [24]

c. ***Capacité d'exercice du droit d'ester en justice.*** While all persons have the abstract right to sue and be sued, certain individuals, such as infants or incompetents, must exercise that right through or with the assistance of a person designated by law. The rules governing the capacity of infants and incompetents generally also govern their capacity to sue. [25] Some persons can sue only through a representative who acts in their behalf. Thus, an action on behalf of a non-emancipated minor must ordinarily [26] be brought by his father or other person acting as *tuteur* or *administrateur* (guardian). [27] Incompetents (*interdits*) must be represented by their *tuteur*.[28] Bankrupts (*faillis*) are represented in court by the trustee in bankruptcy. [29] Some other persons may bring an action in their own name, but only if they are "assisted" by a third person, which means in practice that they must have the approval

[22] Code Civil art. 16; Code de Procédure Civile arts. 166–67; *cf.* Batiffol Nos. 733–37; Soc. Krebs et Cie. v. Glenn, Cour Paris, Nov. 28, 1961, 51 Rev. cr. D.I.P. 58 (1962) (note Simon-Depitre) (purpose of *cautio judicatum solvi* is to ensure that the defendant can recover his costs if he wins as well as a possible judgment on a counterclaim for abuse of process; the appended note states that the *cautio judicatum solvi* has outlived its usefulness).

[23] Paragraph 3 of the protocol annexed to the Convention of Establishment, *supra* note 20, states specifically that the convention does not abrogate any legal requirements in that respect.

[24] See generally Lepaulle, *Réflexions sur la Convention d'établissement franco-américaine du novembre 25, 1959*, 50 Rev. cr. D.I.P. 291, 297 (1961); *cf.* Smit and Miller, International Co-Operation in Civil Litigation, A Report on Practices and Procedures Prevailing in the United States 81 (1961). For a recent French case indicating that American plaintiffs must post security in France in spite of the Convention, see Barker Bros. Co. v. Bussoz, Trib. Gde. Inst. Seine, Apr. 18, 1961, [1961] D.J. 499.

[25] On general capacity of infants and incompetents, see also 4.33 *supra*.

[26] The rule is not applicable in certain paternity actions. 1 Solus & Perrot 272.

[27] See Code Civil art. 389 (father ordinarily *administrateur* of his child while both parents alive); Code Civil art. 390 (after death of one spouse, surviving spouse represents minor under title of *tuteur*); Code Civil arts. 402, 405 (*tuteur* of infant without any parent). In actions involving the minor's real property and in partition actions, the *tuteur* needs the consent of a "family council." Code Civil arts. 464–65.

[28] The rules governing minors are also applicable to judicially declared incompetents. Code Civil art. 509.

[29] At least as to actions being part of the estate administered by the *syndic* (trustee). Code de Commerce art. 473. For a brief description of the two forms of bankruptcy in France, *faillite* and *règlement judiciaire*, see Amos & Walton, *op. cit. supra* note 19, at 370–78.

of that person for the various procedural steps to be taken. Thus, an emancipated minor needs the consent of his *curateur*, though not in all cases, and a spendthrift that of his *conseil judiciaire.* [30]

For persons committed to a mental institution without a judicial declaration of incompetency a special *mandataire ad litem* must be appointed by the court. [31]

Since the Law of February 28, 1938, married woman in France may sue and be sued without permission of their husbands. [32]

If the rules relating to the capacity of parties are violated, the proceedings may be declared void at the request of the person lacking capacity or his legal representative. Since the purpose of the rules is the protection of the incompetent party, the proceedings may not be declared void at the request of his adversary, but the adversary of an incompetent party may refuse to plead until the incompetent party is properly represented in court. [33]

**d. Capacity to sue under conflict of laws.** The *Cour de Cassation* has held that the capacity of a married woman to sue in France depends on her nationality. If she may sue without the authorization of her husband under her national law, she may also do so in France; if she needs the authorization of her husband, that authorization is also required for a suit in France. [34] The same principle seems to be applicable to other individuals and even to corporations or associations. If they have capacity to sue according to their national law, they may sue in France. [35]

[30] Code Civil art. 482 (emancipated minor may not be plaintiff or defendant in action involving his real property without the approval of his *curateur*); Code Civil art. 513 (court may prohibit spendthrift from suing without approval of a *conseil judiciaire* appointed by the court). One distinction between a *curateur* or *conseil judiciaire* and a *tuteur* should be noted: the *tuteur* is formally a party to the action, though only in a representative capacity; the *curateur* or *conseil judiciaire* is not a formal party, he merely "assists" the party, though this must be noted in the various procedural documents. See generally 1 Solus & Perrot 272–80.

Law No. 65–1230 of Dec. 14, 1964, J.O. Dec. 15, 1964, p. 11140, [1965] D.L. 4, which came too late for inclusion in the text, has to some extent modified the rules just given. A minor is now represented by a parent acting in the capacity of *administrateur.* If only one parent survives, the *administrateur* usually needs approval for his actions by a newley created guardianship judge (*juge des tutelles*). Infants without parents continue to be represented by a *tuteur* who needs the approval of the "family council" for partition, but not for other actions. The *tuteur* is under the control of the guardianship judge. An emancipated minor now has practically unlimited capacity in most cases (for all *actes de la vie civile*). See the amended articles in Code Civil arts. 389–481.

[31] Law of June 30, 1838, [1838] Bull. des Lois No. 7443, [1838] D. 3. 162, art. 33.

[32] Law of Feb. 18, 1938, J.O. Febr. 19, 1938, [1939] D. 4. 1, amending Code Civil art. 215. See also Code Civil art. 1428 (as amended in 1965) (each spouse administers own *propres*).

[33] *E.g.*, Schulz-Rolland v. Dame Pompejus, Cass. Civ., Oct. 31, 1934, [1935] S. 1. 6.

[34] Gesling v. Viditz, Cass. Civ., July 29, 1901, [1903] S. 1. 73, 28 Clunet 971 (1901) (English wife sued without consent of her Austrian husband; held, court below should have checked whether she could sue under her national law and her matrimonial régime).

[35] Batiffol No. 724A.

## 6.04. Proper Parties *(Qualité)*

In addition to legal capacity, a party beginning a lawsuit in France must also be a proper party, or, in French terminology, have *qualité*. A person – whether a private individual or an organization enjoying corporate personality – whose rights have been violated always has *qualité* to bring an action to defend these rights.[36] The question of *qualité* becomes troublesome only when a claim is asserted by someone who is not its true owner. As a general rule, three groups of persons whose rights are not directly affected nevertheless have *qualité*: (1) the *héritiers* (heirs) of a decedent; (2) the creditors of a person, who may sue under the circumstances mentioned in article 1166 of the Civil Code to enforce rights of their debtor; and (3) certain legal representatives and agents.

**a. The *qualité* of heirs.** Under French law, the assets of a decedent do not pass to his executor or administrator. At least in the case of intestacy, the decedent's assets and liabilities pass directly to his distributees (*héritiers*). For this reason, the distributees (*héritiers*) have *qualité* to bring or defend an action involving the decedent. If there are several *héritiers*, they act as joint plaintiffs or defendants.[37]

The rule that the *héritiers* may act in lieu of the decedent is not applicable to strictly personal actions, such as actions for divorce or separation. These abate with the death of the party directly concerned.[38] A few actions abate if they have not been initiated at the time of the death of the plaintiff, but they may be continued by the *héritiers* of the plaintiff, if the *ajournement* (summons) had been served at the time of his death. These actions include the action which a donor can institute in France to revoke a gift on account of the donee's ingratitude[39] and the action by a child for a declaration that he is the legitimate child of

[36] *Cf., e.g.*, 1 DALLOZ, *op. cit. supra* note 3, at No. 67. The rules determining whether an organization or association has a sufficient interest to sue also determine whether it has *qualité*. See 6.02.d *supra*; *cf.* Confédération nationale des Combattants volontaires de la Résistance v. Association pour défendre la mémoire du Maréchal Pétain, Trib. Seine, June 19, 1957, [1958] D.J. 67 (note Raynaud) (association of Resistance fighters may not sue to obtain dissolution of association created to uphold memory of Marshall Pétain; appended note discusses at length problem of *qualité* of associations).

[37] For a discussion of French methods of settling decedents' estates, see Rheinstein, *European Methods for the Liquidation of the Debts of Deceased Persons*, 20 IOWA L. REV. 181 (1935); Brown, *French Practice of Administration of Estates*, 3 INT'L & COMP. L.Q. 624 (1951). In at least four fifths of all cases, the property of a decedent passes to his *héritiers*, because no will is made. If a valid will is made, the *successeurs universels*, whose position is somewhat similar to that of American residuary legatees, exercise most of the rights of *héritiers*.

[38] See CODE CIVIL arts. 244, 307; 1 DALLOZ, *op. cit. supra* note 3, at No. 241.

[39] CODE CIVIL art. 957.

a designated couple. [40] The same solution seems applicable to actions for damages for pain and suffering caused by tortious conduct.

**b. The *qualité* of creditors.** Under article 1166 of the *Code Civil,* creditors may prosecute all actions belonging to their debtor which the latter refuses or neglects to prosecute. An action brought by creditors in the name of the debtor is called an *action oblique.* [41] The *action oblique* is not permissible in matters involving personal status, such as divorce actions, actions to disown a child, and actions to annul a marriage. [42] In actions with international elements, the law governing the action between the original parties determines whether an *action oblique* can be brought. The competence of the French courts must also be determined with reference to the original parties to the obligation, not with reference to the creditor who brings the *action oblique.* Thus, an American creditor of a French businessman may invoke article 14 of the Civil Code as the basis for an *action oblique* against a German national owing money to the French firm. [43]

**c. The *qualité* of legal representatives.** Law suits involving the rights of persons who have no capacity to sue or be sued must be brought or defended by representatives designated by law, such as fathers, guardians, and similar persons. These persons are called *représentants légaux. Représentants légaux* sue on behalf of the person lacking capacity, but bring the action – at least formally – in their own name; in other words, they are the parties who sue or are sued. [44]

[40] CODE CIVIL art. 330. For other examples, see Lemarchand v. Lemarchand, Cass. Civ., May 18, 1897, [1897] S. 1. 433 (note Lyon-Caen) (action to disown child may continue after death of child); 1 DALLOZ, *op. cit. supra* note 3, at No. 240.

[41] On the *action oblique* in general, see AMOS & WALTON, *op. cit. supra* note 19, at 241–43; Enregistrement v. Hérit. d'Herman, Cass. Civ., Jan. 23, 1848, [1849] D. 1. 42 (creditors may bring action to recover excess taxes paid by their debtor); Epoux Bascon v. Bonychon, Cass. Civ., April 14, 1886, [1886] D. 1. 220. However, creditors cannot make themselves parties to an existing action, Bignon v. Dreux, Cass. Civ., July 13, 1915, [1921] D. 1. 29. Unless an attachment is desired, the debtor need not be summoned. Borgne v. Soc. H. et P. Chasles, Cass. Civ., Sept. 25, 1940, [1943] D. Cr. J. 133 (note Carbonnier). It is generally assumed that creditors may sue in lieu of their debtors only if the debt is due, but there is some authority contra. 2 COLIN & CAPITANT 318–19.

[42] *E.g.*, Soc. "Réalisation d'Etudes" v. Dame Elissabide, Cass. Req., May, 26, 1941, [1942] D. Cr. J. 133 (creditors of husband may not bring action to have alimony reduced).

[43] BATIFFOL Nos. 543, 686.

[44] As to these various representatives, see 6.03.c *supra*. In the title of a French action as given in the standard French reports, the name of the infant or incompetent in whose behalf an action is brought is not even given, only the name of the *tuteur* who is the formal party; however, the words *ès qualités* (in the capacity of) are added to the name of the *tuteur* or similar representative to indicate that he is acting in a representative capacity. In the actual papers submitted to the court, it must, of course be made clear on whose behalf the action is brought. It will also be noted that husbands had standing to bring certain actions for their

**d. The *qualité* of agents or attorneys in fact: the rule *nul ne plaide par procureur*.** Whether or not the services of an *avoué* are required, a party may appoint any person who has legal capacity as its agent or attorney in fact to conduct litigation in its behalf. [45] The agent will then select an *avoué* or an *avocat* and do everything else required in connection with the litigation. However, a private individual may act as agent (attorney in fact) for purposes of litigation only if he has a special written power of attorney designating the lawsuit to which it relates. A power of attorney appointing someone to conduct all present and future litigation is invalid. [46]

The usefulness of attorneys in fact for the conduct of litigation is somewhat limited by the traditional French rule *nul ne plaide par procureur*, which, translated literally, means that no one sues by attorney. In the old French law, this was, in fact, its true meaning: All litigants had to appear in court personally; only the King had the privilege of appearing by attorney. [47] In modern French law, the rule means something different: The true owner of a claim may not hide his identity by having an agent assert it.

The present effect of the rule is essentially that even parties represented by an attorney in fact must be named in all papers relating to the litigation and must be served with copies of all papers. This is a source of additional expense and delay, if multiple parties are involved, especially since stamp taxes must ordinarily be paid for each copy served. [48]

The rule *nul ne plaide par procureur* has been somewhat restricted by the courts in order to limit its inconveniences. Thus, one agent may at times represent parties who form an association. Only the name of the association need then be mentioned in the various legal papers. [49]

wives under the French community property system. CODE CIVIL art. 1428; 1 SOLUS & PERROT 250. On present law, see note 32 *supra*.

[45] Other law professionals may also perform such functions in some instances. On the various persons who may represent litigants in lieu of an *avoué* in certain instances, see 2.01 *supra*. On the functions of the *avoué*, see 2.06 *supra*.

[46] *E.g.*, Proc. Gén. près la Cour de Cassation, intérêt de la loi, aff. Lampe v. Tiberghem frères, Cass. Civ., July 15, 1924, [1924] D. 1. 201 (note Appleton). *Avocats* and *avoués* do not need written powers of attorney.

[47] For a more detailed historical explanation of the rule, see MOREL 271–72.

[48] *Id.* at 272–73. For example, the rule has been applied in a case in which an attorney in fact sued to recover on a claim belonging to several co-heirs. It was held that all the co-heirs had to be parties to the action. Villarejo v. Davinroy, Cour Paris, Oct. 15, 1962, [1963] D. SOMM. 24. It is obvious that the cost of service of legal papers is substantially increased if there are many co-heirs. Joint ownership of a claim by several heirs is a frequent occurrence in France where estates are often held jointly rather than liquidated.

[49] There is no problem if an organization enjoying legal personality, such as a *société*, brings an action. It may, of course, sue in its own name; the members of the organization need not

The rule *nul ne plaide par procureur* does not seem to reflect a very strong public policy [50] (*ordre public*). For this reason, it may not be invoked by the court on its own motion [51] and may also be avoided by contract. [52] Furthermore, since the reform of 1958, a defense based on violation of the rule *nul ne plaide par procureur* is apparently waived unless asserted at the beginning of the law suit. [53]

Since the rule *nul ne plaide par procureur* is considered procedural for purposes of conflict of laws, it is applicable to all actions brought before French courts. [54] As a result, it may be necessary for an American trustee suing in France to indicate the persons for whose real benefit the suit is brought. [55] However, a lawfully appointed executor or trustee is not seriously hampered by the fact that the precise institution of executor, administrator, or trustee is unknown in France. Such a person, if lawfully appointed in the United States, may sue in France.[56] The lawfulness of the appointment is determined by the French courts in accordance with French conflict of law rules. Thus, the appointment of a guardian or committee depends on the nationality of the person involved, and the appointment of an executor or administrator will be

be made parties. The organization acts in court through its duly appointed officers. See 1 SOLUS & PERROT 255. In the case of unincorporated associations, the courts have occasionally permitted suit by an agent in fact if the unincorporated association could be analogized to an organization possessing corporate personality. *Cf.* Chollet v. Société vosgienne d'encouragement pour l'amélioration de la race chevaline, Cass. Civ., May 25 1887, [1888] S. 1. 161. *But see* Vizioz, *Chronique*, 44 REV. TRIM. DR. CIV. 246 (1946). The rule *nul ne plaide par procureur* is, obviously, not applicable to actions brought by persons who lack capacity. There are also limited exeptions in maritime law and in actions by stockholders. MOREL 274. On stockholders' actions see also 1 SOLUS & PERROT 257; CHURCH, BUSINESS ASSOCIATIONS UNDER FRENCH LAW § 417 (1960).

[51] Likewise, a defense based on this rule may not be raised for the first time before the *Cour de Cassation*. Casta Lumio v. Cie des messagéries maritimes, Cass. Civ. Febr. 9, 1921, [1924] D. 1. 110.

[52] French apartment houses are now frequently owned jointly by the occupants of the various apartments and administered by a *syndic* appointed by them. The agreement between the co-owners generally provides that the *syndic* may sue any of the co-owners in the name of all the owners. In such a case, the defendant has no right to demand that each of the other co-owners be named individually as plaintiff. See, *e.g.*, Griffaton v. Vve Fournol, *supra* note 50; Law of June 28, 1938, J.O. June 30, 1938, [1939] D. 4. 73, art. 7 (standing of *syndic*).

[53] Under the case law before the 1958 reform, a defense based on the rule *nul ne plaide par procureur* could be raised at any time before the courts of first instance and the *cours d'appel*, although some authors were of the view that this issue had to be raised at the beginning of the suit. MOREL 275; 1 DALLOZ, *op. cit. supra* note 3, at No. 154. However, in 1958, CODE DE PROCÉDURE CIVILE art. 192 was amended to require the raising of practically all defenses at the outset of the suit.

[54] BATIFFOL No. 724.

[55] *Cf.* Dame Zand v. Marmonnier, Cour Paris, Feb. 22, 1957, 84 CLUNET 722 (1957) (Austrian mother bringing support action on behalf of her illegitimate daughter must comply with rule *nul ne plaide par procureur*, but court will ignore her failure to entitle action properly where body of complaint left no doubt as to the true party in interest).

[56] As to actions by a trustee in France, see, *e.g.*, Gesling c. Viditz, *supra* note 34. See also 14.04.a and 14.04.b *infra*.

considered lawful if made according to the rules prevailing at the last domicile of the decedent. [57]

## 2. CLASSIFICATIONS OF ACTIONS

### 6.05. Introduction

Although it has been said that in France actions are merely reflections of underlying rights, [58] it is desirable for various procedural purposes, especially to determine questions of competence, to classify actions. [59] French authors usually divide actions either – according to the underlying right they are intended to protect – into real (*in rem*), personal, and mixed actions, or – according to the subject matter of the litigation – into actions concerning movables and actions concerning immovables. Actions may be classified in both groups mentioned: There may be actions concerning immovables which are personal, or real, or mixed; likewise, there may be actions concerning movables that have any of these characteristics. [60]

### 6.06. Personal, Real, and Mixed Actions

Real actions (*actions réelles*) are brought to protect a right *in rem* – for instance, a right of ownership (whether of a chattel or of land) or an easement. The best known of the real actions is the *revendication*, by which the owner of property seeks its restitution. Personal actions are brought to vindicate an *in personam* right, such as the payment of damages or the delivery of an item of property pursuant to a contractual stipulation. While real actions are limited in number and have been given specific names, personal actions largely lack specific designation. [61]

[57] Likewise, the law governing succession matters determines who has *qualité* to bring an action for the damages of a decedent. See generally BATIFFOL No. 724.

[58] 1 SOLUS & PERROT 117, 122.

[59] On competence, see ch. 4 *supra*.

[60] For domestic French purposes it is usually unnecessary to determine whether actions involving personal status are personal or real. For conflict of laws purposes, they are analogized to personal actions concerning movables, but the matter is not entirely free from doubt. See, *e.g.*, 1 SOLUS & PERROT 118; *cf.* Gonzalve de Cordone v. de Belissen, Cour Toulouse, June 4. 1879, [1880] D. 2. 113 (action for declaration of nullity of mariage is personal as far as CODE DE PROCÉDURE CIVILE art. 59 (place where action to be brought) is concerned); Dubroe v. Guérin, Trib. Bordeaux, Oct. 28, 1947, [1948] GAZ. PAL. 1. 74 (action for annulment of recognition of natural child considered personal). It has also been held that the jurisdictional provisions of the treaty between France and Switzerland of June 15, 1869, which mention only personal actions, apply to actions involving personal status as well. Dame Michoud v. Michoud, Cour Paris, Oct. 20, 1951, [1952] J.C.P. 2.6813 (note Delaume and Flattet.) French law knows a great many different actions relating to personal status. As to divorce and separation, see 11.04 *infra*. As to questions of competence in proceedings involving personal status, see 4.33 *supra*.

[61] 1 SOLUS & PERROT 123–25; MOREL 58–60.

Mixed actions involve both a personal right and a right *in rem*. Actions for the rescission of a contract of sale are considered mixed actions: The action for rescission of the contract is an *in personam* action, but, since in French law the mere conclusion of a contract of sale (ordinarily) also passes title, rescission also affects title to the property and therefore has an *in rem* effect. For somewhat similar reasons, actions for the delivery of property purchased under a contract may also be mixed actions. If the purchaser under a contract of sale sues the vendor to obtain possession of the house, the action is personal to the extent that the purchaser seeks to obtain the fulfillment of the vendor's obligation to deliver possession. But to the extent that the action involves the effectiveness of the contract – which, if valid, passes title –, it is real. [62]

## 6.07. Actions Concerning Movables and Actions Concerning Immovables

As indicated, another distinction made is that between actions concerning movables (*actions mobilières*) and actions concerning immovables (*actions immobilières*). Actions concerning movables may, in turn, be real, personal, or mixed, and so may actions concerning immovables. However, because of the limited protection given the ownership of movables under French law, real actions concerning movables are comparatively rare. Such actions are much more likely to concern immovables. [63]

## 6.08. *Actions Pétitoires* and *Actions Possessoires*

French authors subdivide real actions concerning immovables into two distinct types: *actions pétitoires* and *actions possessoires*. *Actions pétitoires* are used to adjudicate title, either to the immovable itself or to a lesser right concerning the immovable, such as an easement. [64]

Possessory actions are summary remedies for the protection of possession regardless of title. Although present statutes mention only possessory actions in general, three possessory actions have traditionally been discussed: [65] (1) the *réintegrande*, by which a person who has been

[62] 1 Solus & Perrot 125–32; Morel 60–62.

[63] 1 Solus & Perrot 132–37; Morel 62–64. On the distinction between movables and immovables, see also Code Civil art. 516 (all property either movable or immovable); 1 Colin & Capitant 821–48.

[64] 1 Solus & Perrot 139; Cornu & Foyer 35; Morel 65. The possessory actions have two purposes: (1) to prevent resort to self-help – and thus a possible breach of the peace; and (2) to afford a speedy remedy, not requiring proof of title.

[65] See Code de Procédure Civile arts. 23–27. The three actions mentioned in the text have traditionally been considered as part of French law. They were mentioned in the statutes dealing with the procedure before the *juge de paix* in effect from 1838 until 1958; they have

forcefully evicted from his land obtain its return; (2) the *complainte*, by which a person whose possession has been disturbed by acts not amounting to an eviction may obtain relief; and (3) the *dénonciation de nouvel oeuvre* (denunciation of new works), by which a person who feels himself threatened by construction on adjacent land may obtain a court order halting the construction. [66]

Possessory actions are always brought before the *tribunal d'instance*.[67] Title is not in issue, [68] and litigation concerning title may not be joined with a possessory action. [69] The defendant in a possessory action must wait until it is terminated before he may bring an *action pétitoire* to establish his title; [70] the plaintiff in a petitory action loses the right to bring a possessory action. [71] A person bringing a possessory action must ordinarily have been in possession for, and his right to relief must have accrued within, one year. [72]

not been mentioned expressly in the 1958 reform legislation, but this does not seem to have changed existing law. See generally 1 SOLUS & PERROT 143–44.

[66] 1 SOLUS & PERROT 140; MOREL 64–72. The *complainte* might be used if a neighbor, asserting an easement, passes over the plaintiff's land; the *dénonciation de nouvel oeuvre* if new construction may interfere with an easement of light and air.

[67] See 4.38.b, at n. 351 *supra*.

[68] CODE DE PROCÉDURE CIVILE art. 24.

[69] CODE DE PROCÉDURE CIVILE art. 25.

[70] CODE DE PROCÉDURE CIVILE art. 27. In addition, the defendant must comply with the judgment in the possessory action before he may try title. Cf. Alexandre Janot v. Lacheray, Trib. Inst. Reims, Feb. 3, 1960, [1960] D.J. 253 (traditional rule not changed by 1958 reforms).

[71] CODE DE PROCÉDURE CIVILE art. 26; *cf.* Chevallier v. Etienne, Cass. Req., June 22, 1897, [1897] D. 1. 560.

[72] CODE DE PROCÉDURE CIVILE art. 23. The possession must comply with the requirements of CODE CIVIL art. 2229 – *i.e.*, it must be peaceful, public, uninterrupted, and by a person considering himself as owner. However, in the case of the *réintégrande*, these requirements need not all be fulfilled, nor is possession for one year required. 1 SOLUS & PERROT 182–83.

CHAPTER 7

# PROCEEDINGS BEFORE COURTS OF FIRST INSTANCE

This chapter describes ordinary proceedings before the courts of first instance. A discussion of proceedings before the *tribunal de grande instance* (7.01–7.15) is followed by brief descriptions of proceedings before the *tribunal d'instance* (7.16) and before various specialized courts (7.17–7.21). The chapter concludes with a detailed treatment of proof proceedings and rules of evidence (7.22–7.58) and a summary of the 1965 reforms (7.59–7.62).

## 1. PROCEEDINGS BEFORE THE *TRIBUNAL DE GRANDE INSTANCE*

### 7.01. Introductory Remarks

The procedure before the *tribunal de grande instance* is generally considered as the ordinary type of procedure (*procédure de droit commun*). Procedures before other courts, such as the *tribunal d'instance* and the commercial court, are ordinarily described in terms of their differences from the procedure before the *tribunal de grande instance*.

Basic characteristics of procedure before the *tribunal de grande instance* are the following: First, the procedure is *contradictoire* – that is, the court must decide a case on the basis of materials submitted by the parties and not on the basis of factual materials it has gathered itself, and it must give each side a chance to be heard on all issues. Secondly, the court does not usually take the initiative. Litigation progresses from one step to the next only on the basis of papers, known collectively as *actes de procédures*, and oral arguments, presented by the parties. Although recent legislation has authorized the courts to play a more active rôle, they have been reluctant to avail themselves of their new powers. Thirdly, the procedure has both oral and written elements.

### 7.02. Original Process *(Ajournement* or *Assignation)*

A civil action before the *tribunal de grande instance* is initiated by a document called *ajournement* or *assignation*.[1] It is served on the defen-

[1] In divorce, separation, and some other cases, service of the *ajournement* must be preceded

dant by an *huissier de justice*, more commonly known simply as an *huissier*. [2] In essence, an *ajournement* is a combined summons, complaint, and return of service. These elements are ordinarily combined into one extremely long – and confusing – sentence.[3]

**a. Contents.** An *ajournement* must: (1) state the name, occupation, and domicile of the plaintiff and the name of the *avoué* who represents him; (2) contain a consent to the service of papers on the plaintiff at the *avoué*'s office; [4] (3) state the name and address of the *huissier* serving it; (4) indicate the court in which the action is pending and the number of days the defendant has to appear, and (5) state the defendant's name and domicile. It must be signed by an *huissier*. [5] The courts are inclined to insist on strict compliance with these rules, especially when their non-observance is likely to mislead the defendant. [6]

An *ajournement* must contain a summary statement of the grounds (*moyens*) for the action and state the relief requested. [7] While the relief requested must be indicated with sufficient preciseness, [8] with very few narrow exceptions, [9] there are no rules as to how the grounds (*moyens*) must be alleged. Specifically, no requirement exists that plaintiff state facts sufficient to constitute a cause of action. It is usually a question of fact for the trial court whether the grounds (*moyens*) for the action have been set out in adequate detail. [10] In practice, a brief conclusory statement of the facts and of the applicable law is

by an attempt at conciliation. See, *e.g.*, 11.04.d *infra*. MOREL 355. Persons wishing to sue the French Republic or its territorial subdivisions (*départements*) must ordinarily first address a memorandum (*mémoire*) to the appropriate public body. See CODE DU DOMAINE DE L'ETAT art. R. 161 (actions concerning public domain); Law of Aug. 10, 1871, [1871] D. 4. 128, art. 55 (*départements*).

The *ajournement* or *assignation* is one of the several papers (*exploits*) served by the *huissiers*.

[2] As to the functions of the *huissiers* and additional details concerning the service of papers by them, see 2.08 *supra*.

[3] For the form of an *ajournement*, see Appendix Form No. 1. The Ministry of Justice has requested *huissiers* to use simple language in preparing *ajournements*, and to make their meaning clearer by the use of appropriate headings and paragraphs, but these admonitions seem to have had little impact. See 1 SOLUS & PERROT 311–12.

[4] This is done in the form of a clause stating that the plaintiff "elects a domicile" at his *avoué's* office. *Cf.* MOREL 357.

[5] As to the contents of the *ajournement*, see CODE DE PROCÉDURE CIVILE art. 61.

[6] For a detailed discussion of the extent to which strict compliance with these rules is required, see 1 SOLUS & PERROT 314.

[7] CODE DE PROCÉDURE CIVILE art. 61.

[8] *Cf.* MOREL 357.

[9] In actions concerning land, the parcel in litigation must be described in some detail. CODE DE PROCÉDURE CIVILE art. 64. In personal injury cases, the plaintiff must indicate his social security status. CORNU & FOYER 525.

[10] 1 DALLOZ, RÉPERTOIRE DE PROCÉDURE CIVILE ET COMMERCIALE, *Ajournement*, No. 7 (1955).

given, which is expanded in later pleadings (called *conclusions*) which are freely permissible. A reference to the code article or other legal basis of the claim is often included, but is not necessary.

Since the rôle of pleadings (*conclusions*) is limited, the development of more precise rules of pleading has not generated much interest. The pleadings limit the relief that may be awarded: A court may not grant relief different from that demanded in the pleadings. The pleadings must also give adequate notice of the transaction upon which the action or defense is based. However, they are not designed to create issues of fact in the common law sense. Evidence is not limited to facts mentioned in the pleadings, particularly not to facts mentioned in the original pleadings of the parties. The delineation of the precise factual issuses is rather the function of oral argument presented during an *audience*. In a case involving a complex factual situation, the facts are likely to be developed in the course of several of these hearings. [11] The sufficiency of the pleadings cannot be tested by motions.

An *ajournement* is always prepared by an *huissier*, who usually follows a draft given him by his client's *avocat* or *avoué*. The *huissier* must obey strict rules concerning the form of the instrument. [12] Two duplicate originals of an *ajournement*, and as many copies as there are defendants to be served, are required. Ordinarily, a stamp tax of 2.50 francs ($ 0.50) is payable for each page of the original and of all copies. All stamps are affixed to one of the originals. In addition, an *enregistrement* tax of 5 francs (about $ 1) must be paid. [13]

**b. Manner of service.** Natural persons may be served either personally or at their home (*domicile*). [14] Personal service, formerly little used, has become more important as a result of the 1958 reforms: Since 1958, by making service personally, the plaintiff can prevent reopening of a

[11] A special court order is required if non-documentary evidence is to be submitted. This order defines the precise issue on which proof is to be taken. *Cf.* CLARK, CODE PLEADING 9 (2d ed. 1947); Millar, *Some Comparative Aspects of Civil Pleading under Anglo-American and Continental Systems*, 12 A.B.A.J. 401 (1926). Standard French form books generally give forms for the formal part of an *ajournement*, but not for the statement of the claim.

[12] *E.g.*, 1 SOLUS & PERROT 310–13 (standard size paper to be used; instrument must be in French; no blank spaces or erasures are permitted).

[13] No tax is payable if the amount in controversy is below F. 1500 (about $ 300), nor for certain special proceedings. See Law No. 63–254 of March 15, 1963, J.O. March 17, 1963, p. 2579, [1963] D.L. 97, arts. 3–4, 6–7, 39, 56. CODE DE PROCÉDURE CIVILE art. 65 requires that copies of all documents intended to be used later on be attached to the *ajournement*. This rule is often ignored. MOREL 357. Of course, the defendant retains the right to see all documents to be used against him before they are actually used. See 7.34 *infra*.

[14] CODE DE PROCÉDURE CIVILE art. 68.

default judgment. [15] To make personal service, the *huissier*, or one of his sworn clerks, must deliver a copy of the *ajournement* to the addressee personally. The *huissier* may make service anywhere within the district for which he is competent. [16] Service may not be made after 9 p.m., nor before 6 a.m. Except with court permission, it is also prohibited on Sundays and legal holidays. [17] At the time of service, recitals of the details of service are inserted in the appropriate places of the *ajournement.* [18] The original is filed by the *huissier* in his office, while the duplicate original is given to his client. [19]

A natural person may also be served at his home (*à domicile*). The ordinary rules of the Civil Code on domicile determine the place of the addressee's home. [20] A person who has elected domicile in a particular place may be served at that place. [21] A person who has no domicile, but a residence, in France may be served at his residence.

In case of service at the domicile, the *huissier* (or clerk) making service may leave the document to be served with a relative or a servant. The courts are quite liberal in interpreting these terms. If no relative or servant can be found, the *huissier* may leave the paper with a neighbor willing to deliver it to the addressee. [22] In large cities, *huissiers* frequently leave the *ajournement* with the janitor of the apartment house in which the addressee lives. This practice seems to be legal only if there has first been an unsuccessful attempt to serve a servant or relative. [23]

If neither a servant or relative nor a neighbor willing to transmit the document can be found, the *huissier* may take the instrument to the local mayor's office and deliver it to the mayor or one of his assistants. He must then inform the defendant by registered mail that an *ajournement* is waiting for him at the mayor's office. [24]

[15] Cuche & Vincent 332. See 7.04.a *infra.*

[16] *E.g.*, 1 Solus & Perrot 332–36.

[17] Code de Procédure Civile art. 1037.

[18] This is known as the *parlant à* because the *huissier* indicates the person with whom he has left the *ajournement* by stating that he was speaking to (*parlant à*) that person.

[19] Law No. 58–127 of Feb. 11, 1958, J.O. Feb. 12, 1958, p. 1571, [1958] D.L. 99; 1 Solus & Perrot 312.

[20] Code Civil arts. 102–11.

[21] Code Civil art. 111. Code de Procédure Civile art. 59(11). On election of domicil, see 4.28 *supra.* Under Code Civil art. 108, a married woman's domicile is that of her husband, but a husband may not serve his wife at his own domicile in a matrimonial action if there has been a *de facto* separation. 1 Solus & Perrot 337.

[22] Code de Procédure Civile art. 68. If the document is not given to the defendant personally, the *huissier* must put it in a sealed envelope before leaving it with a relative, servant, or neighbor.

[23] 1 Solus & Perrot 341. On service at the domicile generally, see *id.* 337–40.

[24] Code de Procédure Civile art. 68. If a copy of the instrument is left with a neighbor

If, because the defendant has no known domicile or residence, even this method of service is impractical, service may be made by delivering a copy to the *procureur de la République* and by posting a copy on the court house bulletin board. [25] This method of service may be used only after the *huissier* has attempted with "diligence and good faith" to locate the defendant. [26]

The law specifies in some detail on whom service must be made if an action is brought against the French Republic or one of its territorial subdivisions or agencies. [27] *Sociétés* (commercial companies) are served by leaving a copy of the *ajournement* at their seat (*siège social*). Service upon partnerships having no seat may be made at the domicile of one of the partners, but service on a general manager or similar employee is also valid. [28] In case of actions arising out of operations of the branch office of a large company, service may be made on the company at the branch establishment. [29]

The *Code de Procédure Civile* also provides how service is to be effected on individuals or companies with a known address outside France. [30]

Service in compliance with the applicable rules is valid, even if the addressee has not received actual notice. However, if the *huissier* attempts to serve an individual personally outside his home, service is valid only if the proper addressee has been served. [31]

or in the mayor's office, the orginal must be signed by the person on whom the copy has been served; when the defendant has been served in person, or when one of his servants or relatives has been served, this is unnecessary. However, *huissiers* frequently ask the person served to sign to obtain additional proof of service.

[25] CODE DE PROCÉDURE CIVILE art. 69(8).

[26] This method of service is not available if the defendant has a known address outside France. *Cf.* 1 SOLUS & PERROT 343–44, 356–58.

[27] CODE DE PROCÉDURE CIVILE art. 69; CODE DU DOMAINE DE L'ETAT art. R 158.

[28] CODE DE PROCÉDURE CIVILE art. 69(6); 1 DALLOZ, RÉPERTOIRE DE PROCÉDURE CIVILE ET COMMERCIALE, *Exploit*, at Nos. 228–30 (1955).

[29] *Id.* at Nos. 233–36. This is the so-called principal stations rule also applicable to questions of competence. See 4.14.a *supra*. French law contains no rules as to the person on whom an *ajournement* destined for a *société* must be served. While it seems preferable to serve the person who has the power to bring actions in the name of the *société*, service on any other employee found at its seat is apparently valid. However, service on the person having power to bring actions in the name of the *société* (*i.e.*, the president of a *société anonyme* or the *gérant* of a *société à responsabilité limitée*) has the same effect as personal service on an individual, while service on any other employee has only the effect of service at the domicile. The matter is not free from doubt. 1 SOLUS & PERROT 361–62.

[30] See 15.02 *infra*.

[31] This explains why, traditionally, so little effort has been made to serve a defendant personally; service at his home (*domicile*) was not only easier, but also less risky. *Cf.* MOREL 319.

**c. Effects of service on substantive rights.** Service of an *ajournement* interrupts the running of the statute of limitations. [32] In addition, service of an *ajournement* prevents the abatement of most personal actions including those, such as actions for damages for pain and suffering, that ordinarily abate on the death of the plaintiff. Only divorce and separation actions abate as a result of the death of either party even after service has been effectuated. [33] In some cases, service of an *ajournement* may cause interest (*intérêts moratoires*) to run against the defendant, may put the risk of loss on him, or may make him liable for the fruits of property he holds. [34]

### 7.03. Appearance and Time to Appear

Before the *tribunal de grande instance*, the defendant appears by appointing an *avoué* to represent him. The *avoué* serves a notice of appearance on his colleague who represents the plaintiff. Service of this notice is effected rather informally by *acte d'avoué à avoué*. [35] The notice of appearance states that a named *avoué* will represent the defendant. If the defendant is domiciled in the *département* in which the action is brought or in a neighboring *département*, the notice of appearance must be served within eight days; if he is domiciled in any other part of continental France, service must be effectuated within fifteen days. [36] Persons with a domicile elsewhere in Europe or in one of the countries on the North Shore of the Mediterranean (including Morocco), are granted one month to appear; domiciliaries of North America, the Near East, and most parts of Africa, two months; domiciliaries of Central and South America, three months; and domiciliaries of all other parts of the world, five months. [37] These time periods are so-called *franc* (free) time periods: In determining whether an appearance

[32] Code Civil art. 2244; Morel 46. If the service of the *ajournement* is later declared void for violation of a rule relating to one of the formalities of service, service is considered as having never occurred. Code Civil art. 2247.

[33] In addition, filiation actions always abate on the death of the child. Whether so-called separation of property actions abate after the service of the *ajournement* is debated. Morel 47.

[34] See generally Cornu & Foyer 454; Morel 47. On *intérêts moratoires*, see also Code Civil art. 1153. A simple demand has the same effect on *intérêts moratoires* as service of an *ajournement*.

[35] Code de Procédure Civile art. 75; Cuche & Vincent 339. The French Republic and its agencies need not appear by *avoué*, though they sometimes do so. *Cf.* 3.10 *supra*. For a form of notice of appearance, see Appendix, Form No. 2.

[36] Code de Procédure Civile art. 72.

[37] Code de Procédure Civile art. 73. This article also provides that the time limitations are doubled in the case of a war at sea, but special statutes are usually enacted in the case of war to protect the rights of absent litigants. As of right, a person domiciled outside France, but personally served in France, is entitled only to the regular time periods. However, the court may extend his time to appear. Code de Procédure Civile art. 74.

is timely, both the days on which the *ajournement* is served on the defendant and the day on which the notice of appearance is served on plaintiff's *avoué* must be disregarded; accordingly, if a defendant has been served on the first of the month and has eight days to appear, his notice of appearance may be served until the tenth of the month. [38] Once the defendant has appeared, neither side may dismiss his *avoué* without immediately replacing him. [39]

In cases in which speed is essential, the plaintiff's *avoué* may address an *ex parte* petition (*requête*) to the presiding judge of the court asking him to shorten the time period (*assignation à bref délai*) or to order the defendant to appear on a day certain (*à jour fixe*).[40] The order must be served together with the *ajournement*. If an *ajournement* is for a day certain, the first hearing takes place on that date and the defendant may appear by having an *avoué* present at the hearing. However, the *avoué* must later serve a formal notice of appearance. When the defendant is summoned *à jour fixe*, later procedures are also expedited and the case may come up for a hearing (*audience*) without waiting for its turn on the calendar. [41]

## 7.04. Default and Remedies for Default

If the defendant fails to appear within the time specified by law, the plaintiff may request a default judgment. [42] In such a case, French authors speak of a *défaut faute de comparaître* (default for lack of appearance), as opposed to a *défaut faute de conclure* (default for lack of pleading), which occurs when the defendant appears, but either side fails to submit its pleading (*conclusions*) to the court. [43]

The plaintiff may request a default judgment as soon as the defendant's time to appear has run out, but the defendant may appear until the hearing on the default judgment is terminated. Generally

[38] In computing time periods prescribed in procedural laws, the day on which the event occurs which sets the time period running is never counted. However, if the time period is considered *franc* (as, *e.g.*, the time to appear), the last day to perform the act is not the day on which the time period runs out, but the day thereafter. CODE DE PROCÉDURE CIVILE art. 1033; MOREL 334–35; 1 SOLUS & PERROT 396–401. If the last day available to appear (or perform any other procedural act) is a Saturday, Sunday, or legal holiday, the time period is extended to the next working day. CODE DE PROCÉDURE CIVILE art. 1033; 1 SOLUS & PERROT 401–02.

[39] CODE DE PROCÉDURE CIVILE art. 75.

[40] CODE DE PROCÉDURE CIVILE art. 72.

[41] CODE DE PROCÉDURE CIVILE art. 75; CUCHE & VINCENT 339. For a discussion of the practical aspects of this procedure, known as *assignation à jour fixe*, see Madray, *L'assignation à jour fixe à compter du 2 mars 1959*, [1959] J.C.P. 1. 1480.

[42] CODE DE PROCÉDURE CIVILE art. 149.

[43] On *défaut faute de conclure*, see 7.06 *infra*. On the distinction between *défaut faute de conclure* and *défaut faute de comparaître*, see also CUCHE & VINCENT 411–12.

speaking, French practitioners are inclined to wait some time beyond the time specified by law before asking for a default judgment and thus afford their opponents ample opportunity to make an appearance. [44]

The procedure for obtaining a default judgment is generally the same as that for obtaining a judgment in a contested case, except that the case does not have to await its turn on the calendar. The plaintiff does not obtain a default judgment automatically; the court must examine in summary fashion whether plaintiff's claim is well founded. Documentary evidence is often presented, though proof measures, such as the examination of witnesses (*enquête*), are rarely ordered in matters in which public policy is not strongly involved. The court may not grant relief more extensive than that asked for in the original *ajournement*. [45]

The judgment in a default case must generally be served on the defendant by an *huissier* specially appointed for this purpose by the presiding judge of the court. [46]

**a. Remedies against default: *opposition* and appeal.** Formerly, every defendant against whom a default judgment had been entered could obtain reopening of his case by *opposition*. In recent years, to avoid dilatory tactics, the remedy of *opposition* has been drastically curtailed. [47] In cases involving only one defendant, reopening may no longer be obtained if the judgment is subject to appeal to an intermediate appellate court (*cour d'appel*) or if the *ajournement* was served on the defendant personally. [48] If the defendant was not personally served and failed to appear within the time specified by law, the plaintiff may serve him a second time, or the *juge chargé de suivre la procédure* may, but need not, order the plaintiff to attempt a second service. [49]

[44] *Id.* 339; MOREL 338, 361; 2 DALLOZ, RÉPERTOIRE DE PROCÉDURE CIVILE ET COMMERCIALE, *Procédure Civile*, at No. 15 (1956).

[45] CUCHE & VINCENT 414–17.

[46] CODE DE PROCÉDURE CIVILE art. 156; *cf.* CODE DE PROCÉDURE CIVILE art. 158. The judgment must indicate the time available to defendant to demand a reopening (*opposition*) or to make an appeal. In case of personal service of the judgment, the *huissier* making service must orally remind the defendant of these time limitations. The judgment must be served within six months, or it becomes void. The requirement for service by an *huissier* specially appointed by the presiding judge of the court does not apply if there are several defendants who have no right to *opposition*. See text at note 50 *infra*.

[47] See generally Giverdon, *La réforme de la procédure par défaut*, [1959] D. CHR. 201. The most drastic restrictions on *opposition* were enacted as part of the 1958 reform legislation.

[48] CODE DE PROCÉDURE CIVILE art. 149. Default judgments not subject to reopening (*opposition*) are called *jugements réputés contradictoires*, *i.e.*, judgments that are considered contested.

[49] CODE DE PROCÉDURE CIVILE art. 150.

Personal service upon either first or second attempt cuts off the right to reopening.

In the case of several defendants, there may likewise be no reopening (*opposition*) if the judgment is subject to appeal or if all defaulting defendants were served personally. If no appeal is possible and if there was no personal service, the plaintiff must again serve all the defaulting defendants either personally or at their homes (*domiciles*). This second service is essential for the validity of the subsequent default judgment. A default judgment may be requested only after time to appear for the defendant having the longest time period available to him has expired. A default judgment is not subject to reopening by any of the defendants if at least one of them was personally served or appeared; otherwise, reopening may be obtained. [50]

A defendant may make *opposition* against a default judgment by appointing an *avoué* to represent him and by having the *avoué* serve a notice on the plaintiff's *avoué* indicating that a reopening is demanded. At least in summary fashion, the notice must give defendant's reasons for his attack on the default judgment. [51] The *opposition* is recorded in a special register in the court clerk's office. [52]

Ordinarily, the defendant has one month to demand a reopening. If the default judgment was served upon him personally, this time period begins to run upon service of the judgment. An *huissier* making personal service of a default judgment must remind the defendant of this time period and must ask him to sign the return of service. [53] If there is no personal service of the judgment, but the judgment is executed in the presence of the defendant and with his knowledge, he must make *oppo-*

[50] CODE DE PROCÉDURE CIVILE arts. 151–52. In older French terminology, this was called *défaut profit-joint*. The second *ajournement* must indicate that no reopening may be possible if a default judgment is entered. CODE DE PROCÉDURE CIVILE art. 153; *cf.* CUCHE & VINCENT 419–22.

[51] CODE DE PROCÉDURE CIVILE art. 162. Some facts showing that defendant has a good defense must be stated. *E.g.*, Abouhamad v. Dame Abouhamad, Cass. Req., Jan. 30, 1939, [1939] D. I. 45; Vitus v. Auran, Cour Aix, July 5, 1938, [1938] D.H. 523. The notice is served on the plaintiff's *avoué* in the form of an *acte d'avoué à avoué*, but other forms of notice may also be sufficient. In determining whether a person is entitled to demand a reopening, the general rules as to capacity and standing apply. CUCHE & VINCENT 433. In determining whether a judgment is a default judgment, the true facts govern; the qualification given the judgment by the court that rendered it is not necessarily conclusive. Schwab v. Etabl. Grauss et Cie., Cass. Comm., June 4, 1951, [1951] D.J. 526.

[52] CODE DE PROCÉDURE CIVILE art. 163. After a default judgment, acts of execution affecting a third party are permissible only if the court clerk certifies that no reopening has been demanded. CODE DE PROCÉDURE CIVILE art. 164. The register mentioned in the text enables the clerk to determine whether reopening has been demanded.

[53] CODE DE PROCÉDURE CIVILE art. 158. In proceedings to deprive parents of parental powers, time for *opposition* is only 8 days if the judgment was personally served. Law of July 24, 1889, J.O. July 25, 1889, [1890] D. 4. 15, art. 6.

*sition* immediately. [54] This may be done by an oral statement to the *huissier*, which must later be reiterated in writing. [55] If the defendant receives notice of the default judgment against him in any manner other than by personal service of the judgment or execution, he has one month from the day on which he received notice to demand a reopening In cases in which it is impossible to give the defendant any other notice, the presiding judge of the court which rendered the judgment may authorize its publication in a newspaper at the last domicile of the defendant. Time to demand an *opposition* begins to run upon publication. For defendants who are not domiciliaries of France, time to demand a reopening is extended by the time periods available for appearance to non-domiciliaries. [56]

*Opposition* automatically stays all execution not specifically permitted in spite of it. [57] It brings the whole case before the court anew. In no event may the plaintiff be awarded a greater recovery than on the first judgment. If the defendant wins, the plaintiff must return everything he has collected on execution of the default judgment. The plaintiff may even be liable for damages for wrongful execution. [58] However, certain costs are always payable by a defaulting defendant.[59]

A defaulting defendant may not obtain reopening through *opposition* if the judgment is subject to appeal to an intermediate appellate court. An appeal to an intermediate appellate court involves reconsideration of the merits, which enables the defendant to assert whatever defenses he

[54] Code de Procédure Civile art. 158 *bis*. Code de Procédure Civile art. 159 defines what constitutes execution. Generally, any act of execution which necessarily brings the fact of execution to the knowledge of the defendant is sufficient. *E.g.*, Laboual v. Consorts Chagneaud, Cass. Civ., July 6, 1937, [1937] D.H. 487 (making defendant temporary custodian of attached chattels). In all events, the defendant has one month from the service of the judgment for *opposition*, even if execution is levied sooner. Cuche & Vincent 435.

[55] Code de Procédure Civile art. 162. The written declaration must be made no later than eight days after the oral statement.

[56] Code de Procédure Civile art. 158 *bis*. Publication of a default judgment in France is not proper if the defendant has a known address outside France. An attempt must then be made to give him actual notice of the judgment. See 15.02.c *infra*. Actual notice of a default judgment always starts the time for *opposition* running, even if there is a formal defect causing the service of the judgment to be void. Cappelo v. Denonque, Cass. Civ., Nov. 22, 1956, [1957] D. Somm. 104.

[57] Cuche & Vincent 439. No default judgment may be executed for eight days after its service on the defendant, unless *exécution provisoire* (provisional execution) has been granted as part of the judgment. On *exécution provisoire*, see 8.15 *supra*.

[58] Cuche & Vincent 440–41. Since *opposition* leads to readjudication of the entire case, it is sometimes called *une voie de rétractation*, a means of retraction.

[59] Code de Procédure Civile art. 162 *bis* (even if successful on *opposition*, defendant must pay cost for the copy of the judgment, its service on him, its execution, and its publication, unless the court, taking into account the special circumstances of the case, decides otherwise).

may have. [60] As a rule, time to appeal, like time to demand a reopening, is one month. [61] Generally, in cases in which an appeal is a substitute for *opposition*, the rules determining when time to make *opposition* begins to run determine when time to appeal commences. [62] In an appropriate case, the decision rendered after *opposition* may be attacked by appeal. [63] In no event, however, is it possible to ask for a new *opposition* against a judgment rendered on reopening. [64]

## 7.05. Calendar Practice

After the defendant has appeared or defaulted, plaintiff must put his case on the calendar [65] by filing a *placet* in the court clerk's office. It is in essence the *ajournement* recopied on a special form having a number of blanks for the use of the clerk. If the plaintiff fails to file the *placet* within two weeks after defendant's appearance or after defendant's time to appear has run out, defendant may file it. [66]

After the court clerk has received the *placet* and the appropriate filing fee, he puts the case on the general calendar. [67] If the court has several panels (*chambres*), the clerk transmits the *placet* to the office of the presiding judge, who assigns the case to one of the panels (*cham-*

[60] Since the 1958 reforms, the possibility of appeal precludes *opposition*. *Cf.* Giverdon, *supra* note 47. On appeal generally, see ch. 8 *infra*. The new rule has met with criticism. It greatly reduces the scope of *opposition* before the *tribunal de grande instance*, since most decisions of that court are subject to appeal.

[61] See 8.06 *infra*.

[62] The defendant has one month from the time the judgment is executed in his presence to file an appeal; an immediate appeal is not necessary. CODE DE PROCÉDURE CIVILE art. 445. See also 8.07 *infra*.

[63] If on a reopening the court holds for the plaintiff, the original judgment is considered as becoming fully effective. The original decision and the decision on reopening are therefore considered as indivisible and the appeal must be taken against both decisions. Duc de Duras-Chastellux v. Dr. Heller, Cour Paris, June 30, 1958, [1958] D.J. 765; Niqueux v. Saiter, Trib. Pont-l'Evêque, Nov. 13, 1956, [1957] D. SOMM. 76.

[64] CODE DE PROCÉDURE CIVILE art. 165. At present, since *opposition* is impossible if both sides have appeared, the significance of the rule is quite limited.

[65] Until the case is put on the calendar, the court has no information concerning its pendency.

[66] CODE DE PROCÉDURE CIVILE art. 76. The word *placet* is a latin translation of the first words sometimes put on the document, *viz., plaise au tribunal* (may it please the court). If the plaintiff has been authorized to summon the defendant to appear on a day certain, the *placet* must be filed before that day. On the various topics discussed in this section, see also the DÉCRET of March 30, 1808, arts. 55–63, reprinted in DALLOZ, CODE DE PROCÉDURE CIVILE 65 (58th ed. 1962). For a *placet*, see Appendix, Form No. 3.

[67] CUCHE & VINCENT 340–41; MOREL 362. For the practical aspects of these procedures, see also 1 RAVIART, TRAITÉ FORMULAIRE DE PROCÉDURE CIVILE 182, 187 (8th ed. 1956). The filing fee for the *placet* is now F. 7.20 (about $ 1.50). DÉCRET of May 3, 1958, concerning the fees of *greffiers*, J.O. May 6, 1958, p. 4431, [1958] D.L. 205, art. 6; DÉCRET No. 59–1959 of May 5, 1959, J.O. May 6, 1959, p. 4825, [1959] B.L.D. 876. See Appendix, Form No. 4.

*bres*).[68] One of the judges of the panel is assigned to the case as *juge chargé de suivre la procédure.*[69] The case is then put on the separate calendar of the particular panel. The plaintiff's *avoué* is sent a notice informing him of the position of the case on the panel's calendar.[70]

When the clerk puts the case on the calendar, he starts a file for the case, in which are deposited copies of all pleadings (*conclusions*) exchanged by the parties, interlocutory judgments, and all other procedural documents prepared in the course of the litigation. The file enables the court or the *juge chargé de suivre la procédure* to obtain quick information about the status of any pending litigation.[71] In cases requiring transmittal of the file to the *ministère public*, the transmittal takes place when the above-mentioned formalities have been accomplished.[72]

### 7.06. Preliminary Hearing

After the case has been assigned to one of the panels, the first hearing takes place. The practice in conducting this hearing varies. In some places, it is conducted before a full three-judge panel; in Paris, it is conducted before the *juge chargé de suivre la procédure.* The clerk of the court sends plaintiff's *avoué* a notice indicating when the hearing is to take place. At least fifteen days before the hearing date, plaintiff's *avoué* serves a notice called *avenir* on defendant's *avoué* requesting him to serve his defensive pleading and to be present in court on a specified date.

While practice as to the preliminary hearing is subject to some regional variations, the hearing is generally a mere formality. Plaintiff's *avoué* puts a copy of his pleading (*conclusions*) on the court's desk. De-

[68] Traditionally, the more important cases are assigned to the lower-numbered, the less important cases to the higher numbered, panels. See DÉCRET of March 30, 1808, *supra* note 66, art. 60; *Cf.* 1 RAVIART, *op. cit. supra* note 67, at 187–88.

[69] In courts having only one panel, the *juge chargé de suivre la procédure* is designated by the presiding judge of the court. The name of the *juge chargé de suivre la procédure* must be indicated on the court calendar. CODE DE PROCÉDURE CIVILE art. 77. The presiding judge of the court or panel may replace the *juge chargé de suivre la procédure* during the course of a lawsuit. See 2 DALLOZ, RÉPERTOIRE DE PROCÉDURE CIVILE ET COMMERCIALE, *Procédure Civile*, at No. 74 (1956); MOREL 366. In very busy courts, the assignment of cases to the various panels is often made in the name of the presiding judge by the chief clerk or another court officer.

[70] 1 RAVIART, *op. cit. supra* note 67, at 188. Occasionally, however, the parties' *avoués* seek to obtain an interview with the presiding judge of the court to induce him to assign the case to a particular panel. 2 DALLOZ, *op. cit. supra* note 69, at No. 23; *cf.* Appendix, Form No. 5.

[71] CODE DE PROCÉDURE CIVILE art. 79. The file must be kept by the court for ten years. In the case of an appeal to a *cour d'appel* or a *pourvoi* to the *Cour de Cassation*, the file must be sent to the appropriate court by the clerk.

[72] 1 RAVIART, *op. cit. supra* note 67, at 189. On matters requiring transmittal of the file to the *ministère public*, see 3.09 *supra*.

fendant's *avoué* does likewise with a copy of his *conclusions*. The judge initials these pleadings and the *avoués* subsequently hand them to the clerk of the court for inclusion in the case file. [73] The hearing is said to result in the *mise en état initiale,* the preliminary putting of the case at issue, as distinguished from the final *mise en état,* which occurs at the beginning of the later hearing (*audience*) before the full court. [74] Once the *mise en état initiale* has taken place, the plaintiff may no longer abandon the case (*se désister*) without the consent of the defendant. [75] Many defenses must be raised in *conclusions* served before the *mise en état initiale*; [76] requests for disqualification of a judge or transfer of the action to an other court for reasons of prejudice must also be made before that time. [77]

If either the plaintiff or the defendant fails to submit his *conclusions* at the time of the original hearing, *défaut faute de conclure* (default for failure to submit *conclusions*) occurs. [78] Formerly, such a default was followed by a true default judgment which could be reopened by *opposition.* At present, if the defendant fails to submit his *conclusions,* a new *avenir* must be served on his *avoué.* If defendant still fails to serve his *conclusions* and to submit them to the court, plaintiff may obtain a judgment in his favor. That judgment is not subject to reopening. [79] An analogous procedure is available if the plaintiff has failed to submit his *conclusions.* [80]

## 7.07. Proceedings before the *Juge Chargé de Suivre la Procédure*

From the time of the preliminary hearing until the case is reached for the *audience* before the full court or panel, the case is under the

[73] Code de Procédure Civile art. 78. The *conclusions* must be filed in the court clerk's office within eight days of the hearing. The notice which the plaintiff's *avoué* sends the defendant's *avoué* is called an *avenir* because it invites the defendant to come (*à venir*) before the court. See generally Cornu & Foyer 527; Cuche & Vincent 342; 1 Raviart, *op. cit. supra* note 67, at 197. On defendant's *conclusions,* see 7.08–7.09 *infra.* On the way the hearing is conducted in Paris, see Cornu & Foyer 536. For an *avenir,* see Appendix, Form No. 6.

[74] Code de Procédure Civile art. 78; Cuche & Vincent 343.

[75] 2 Dalloz, *op. cit. supra* note 69, at No. 35; Morel 364.

[76] See 7.08–7.09 *infra.*

[77] Morel 364. It is sometimes said that the *lien d'instance* is created by the first hearing; for this reason, the first hearing is sometimes called *audience de liaison d'instance.* The concept of *lien d'instance* (literally bond of the suit) is quite vague; it seems to emphasize that from the time of the first hearing, the parties owe each other a modicum of good faith. The duty to submit for inspection all papers used in court to the other side is said to be a consequence of the *lien d'instance.*

[78] See 7.04.a *supra.*

[79] Code de Procédure Civile art. 154 *bis.* The second *avenir* must contain a statement indicating that it is served pursuant to article 154 *bis.* See Appendix, Form No. 7.

[80] Code de Procédure Civile art. 154; *cf.* Cuche & Vincent 423. The procedure for obtaining a judgment in case of a *défaut faute de conclure* is the same as in the case of a *défaut faute de comparaître.*

control of the *juge chargé de suivre la procédure*. This office was created in 1935 in the hope that it would contribute to faster disposition of the cases and less calendar congestion: It was expected that the *juge chargé de suivre la procédure* would be able to induce settlements, clarify issues, and accelerate the work of the *avoués*. On several occasions since that time, the powers of the *juge chargé de suivre la procédure* were increased. [81] At present, the *juge chargé de suivre la procédure*: (1) must ensure that the various time limitations relating to the preliminary hearing are observed; (2) may call in the parties and their counsel at any time and attempt a conciliation; [82] (3) has the power to decide certain issues which formerly had to be brought before the full three-judge court, such as requests for provisional counsel fees in matrimonial actions and requests for security for costs; (4) more importantly, may authorize all proof proceedings, such as *enquêtes* (examination of witnesses) and *expertises* (experts' reports); and (5) may order a party to submit to the opponent for examination the documents it plans to use in court. [83]

The court is not bound by any order made by the *juge chargé de suivre la procédure* in matters of proof. It may order a proof proceeding denied by the *juge chargé de suivre la procédure* and has full freedom in valuating any evidence secured through a proof proceeding authorized by that judge. [84]

In most parts of France, especially in the large cities, the institution of the *juge chargé de suivre la procédure* did not lead to the expected results. French *avoués* resented this attempt to oversee their activities. In addition, most *juges chargés de suivre la procédure* in large cities have so many cases under their supervision (sometimes several hundred) that it is practically impossible for them to play a very active rôle in attempting to conciliate the parties, clarify the issues, and encourage prompt action on the part of the *avoués*. Furthermore, French judges frequently have only their conference room (*chambre du conseil*) as

[81] *E.g.*, Cornu & Foyer 528-29; 1 Solus & Perrot 14. On a somewhat analogous institution in Germany which seems to have served as a model for the *juge chargé de suivre la procédure*, see Kaplan, von Mehren & Schaefer, *Phases of German Civil Procedure I*, 71 Harv. L. Rev. 1193, 1206 (1958).

[82] Code de Procédure Civile art. 80. On settlement and conciliation, see also 5.03 *supra*.

[83] Code de Procédure Civile art. 81. However, the *juge chargé de suivre la procédure* has no power to decide other matters of a non-final character, such as questions of competence or temporary alimony. Morel 366.

[84] Code de Procédure Civile art. 81 provides specifically that orders of the *juge chargé de suivre la procédure* shall not prejudge the merits. Orders authorizing certain proof proceedings may also be obtained by addressing a petition to a judge sitting *en référé*. See 5.07 *supra*. That procedure is even faster than the one before the *juge chargé de suivre la procédure*. See 2 Dalloz, *op. cit. supra* note 69, at Nos. 82–88.

chambers. This lack of private chambers makes conferences with the parties and their counsel, envisioned by the French legislator, difficult. Finally, French law professionals are so used to allowing the case to come to a hearing (*audience*) before the full court and to then obtaining a proof proceeding followed by another hearing that they often ignore the possibility of saving one *audience* before the full court by requesting the *juge chargé de suivre la procédure* to order a proof measure. [85]

If an application for a proof proceeding or other relief is made, the *juge chargé de suivre la procédure* must be asked to designate a day on which he will hear it. [86] The party's *avoué* then sends his opponent a notice (*avenir*) inviting him to the hearing. Ordinarily, the hearing takes place in the judges' conference room. Argument is rather brief. The decision of the *juge chargé de suivre la procédure* is called *ordonnance.* [87]

The *juge chargé de suivre la procédure* has some additional duties relating to calendar practice. After the exchange of the *conclusions*, he must transmit to the presiding judge the files of all default cases, all cases involving only limited issues (for instance, cases in which the defendant, at the outset, has raised merely a procedural defense), and cases requiring great speed, so that they may be heard at once. Such cases come to an *audience* before the full court (panel) without having to wait for their turn on the calendar. In other cases, the *juge chargé de suivre la procédure* must call in the parties' *avocats* and ask whether they wish to waive argument before the full court. If both sides agree, the *avocats* may argue before, and submit their papers and memoranda to, the *juge chargé de suivre la procedure.* The full court then decides the case on the basis of the documents and memoranda submitted and the report of the *juge chargé de suivre la procédure.* [88] If argument before the full court is waived, the case may be decided at once, without awaiting its turn on the calendar. [89]

[85] See Cornu & Foyer 536–37 (describing variations in practice in various parts of France); 2 Dalloz, *op. cit. supra* note 69, at No. 76. For a description of the duties of the *juge chargé de suivre la procédure* in one court where he plays a very active rôle, see Schewin, *L'expérience du juge chargé de suivre la procédure au tribunal de grande instance de Pontoise* (*S. et O.*), [1964] D. Chr. 185.

[86] This can be done orally at the preliminary hearing before the *juge chargé de suivre la procédure* or by a written *ex parte* petition. In the latter case, the judge notes the time he will hear the parties at the foot of the petition. 1 Raviart, *op. cit. supra* note 67, at 198–200.

[87] Code de Procédure Civile art. 81; Cuche & Vincent 355–56; 2 Dalloz, *op. cit. supra* note 69, at No. 89. No demand for a reopening (*opposition*) can be lodged against a decision of the *juge chargé de suivre la procédure,* which is appealable on the same terms on which other interlocutory decisions may be appealed. See 8.05.b *infra.*

[88] Code de Procédure Civile art. 80.

[89] Code de Procédure Civile art. 81. This interview with parties' counsel must take place after the parties have exchanged the documents on which they rely.

This procedure, instituted in 1958, seems to be practically unused. French *avocats* seem unwilling to forego their chance of coming into direct contact with the court.

### 7.08. Defenses in General

Like the plaintiff, the defendant, in formulating his pleadings, [90] is not bound by strict pleading rules. French authors distinguish between three types of defenses: (1) defenses going to the merits; (2) *exceptions*; and (3) *fins de non-recevoir*.

Defenses going to the merits (*défenses au fonds*) include what, by common law standards, would be considered denials and affirmative defenses. Thus, in case of a contract calling for payment of a sum of money, absence of a meeting of the minds or payment are defenses on the merits. [91] Defenses on the merits may be raised at any time before the case is ready for judgment, and defendant may amend his *conclusions* at a later date to include such defenses. [92] As a consequence, *avoués* wanting to raise only issues going to the merits, but no *exceptions* or *fins de non-recevoir*, frequently limit their original pleading to the statement that plaintiff's action must be dismissed because it is *irrecevable et mal fondée*, thus indicating that defendant's action is (procedurally) defective and ill-founded on the merits. This kind of pleading is possible since failure specifically to deny a factual allegation made by plaintiff is not considered an admission. This uninformative type of pleading is used especially in larger cities where calendar congestion leads to a long waiting period before the *audience*, so that there is ample opportunity for amendment. [93]

Rules are less liberal as to *exceptions* and *fins de non-recevoir*. These defenses are waived unless they are raised at the beginning of the suit (*in limine litis*), [94] before a preliminary hearing at which *conclusions*

[90] The terms pleadings and *conclusions* have been used interchangeably. However, French *conclusions* do not correspond strictly to common law pleadings. They are not intended to define the precise factual issues at the outset of the litigation. Rather, they serve to inform the court and adverse parties of the general character of the matters that will be raised at the next hearing. Many *conclusions* may be submitted at the various stages of the litigation. Pleadings more closely resembling common law pleadings, the so-called *conclusions grossoyés* which were used in earlier times, fell into disuse and were abolished in 1935. See generally Millar, *supra* note 11.

[91] 1 DALLOZ, RÉPERTOIRE DE PROCÉDURE CIVILE ET COMMERCIALE, *Exceptions et Fins de Non-Recevoir*, at No. 8 (1955); 1 SOLUS & PERROT 281–82.

[92] CODE DE PROCÉDURE CIVILE art. 78 (defendant's *conclusions* may be amplified or modified at a later date), art. 464 (new facts may be raised on appeal, if they amount to defense on merits). *Cf.* also 1 SOLUS & PERROT 283.

[93] 1 RAVIART, *op. cit. supra* note 67, at 211. For sample *conclusions*, see Appendix, Forms Nos. 8, 11, and 14.

[94] CODE DE PROCÉDURE CIVILE art. 192.

going to the merits are submitted. Unfortunately, it is not always easy to distinguish between *exceptions*, *fins de non-recevoir*, and defenses on the merits. Writers on substantive law often use the term *exception* to designate any defense. In a procedural context, however, the term *exception* designates a defense relating to the manner in which the action has been brought, such as lack of competence. In addition, the word *exception* designates some defenses which lead merely to a temporary stay of the action and not to dismissal. [95] Examples of some of the more important *exceptions* are given below. [96]

While there is a reasonably well-defined catalogue of *exceptions*, it is quite difficult to determine the nature of *fins de non-recevoir*. The original *Code de Procédure Civile* contained no reference to *fins de non-recevoir*. The concept seems to have been developed by the courts and authors in order to avoid the rule that all *exceptions* are waived unless they are raised at the beginning of the suit. [97] *Fins de non-recevoir* are said to fall between true *exceptions* and defenses on the merits because they deal neither with procedural defenses in a narrow sense nor with the merits, but with issues that prevent the court from reaching the merits, such as lack of plaintiff's standing to sue. [98] However, current terminology is quite imprecise, and at least some defenses on the merits, which if proven must lead to a judgment for defendant, are called *fins de non-recevoir*. [99]

This terminological confusion has been compounded by the recent rule requiring all *fins de non-recevoir* to be raised at the outset of the suit. [100] To avoid this rule, the courts, by a process which is in fact the converse of that responsible for the creation of the *fins de non-recevoir*, increasingly refer to *fins de non-recevoir* as defenses on the merits. Sometimes they also speak of a separate class of *fins de non-recevoir* called *fins de non-recevoir liés au fond*, which are subject to the

[95] See generally 1 DALLOZ, *op. cit. supra* note 91, at Nos. 1, 6; CUCHE & VINCENT 524; 1 SOLUS & PERROT 284. On the historical reasons for the confused terminology, see *id.* at 286. *Exceptions* by which defendant merely seeks a stay are sometimes called *exceptions dilatoires* (dilatory exceptions).

[96] See 7.09 *infra.*

[97] *E.g.*, 1 DALLOZ, *op. cit. supra* note 91, at Nos. 5, 58. There was some precedent in pre-revolutionary legal terminology for the concept of *fin de non-recevoir*.

[98] *E.g.*, 1 DALLOZ, *op. cit. supra* note 91, at No. 59; 1 SOLUS & PERROT 290.

[99] Thus, in a paternity proceeding, the defendant automatically wins if he can show that the mother was of notoriously bad conduct or had intercourse with another man at the time of conception, or that defendant cannot be the father because of non-access or accidental injuries, or that a blood grouping test excludes him as father. CODE CIVIL art. 340. In these cases, French authors frequently speak of *fins de non-recevoir*, though, obviously, no procedural issues are involved.

[100] CODE DE PROCÉDURE CIVILE art. 192, as amended by DÉCRET No. 58-1289 of Dec. 22, 1958, J.O. Dec. 23, 1958, p. 11608, [1959] D.L. 49.

rules on defenses on the merits. As a consequence, many defenses that, at one time or another, were considered as *fins de non-recevoir* may be raised at any time, and no special reference to them is required in defendant's original *conclusions*. Although court decisions are not unanimous, these defenses include *res judicata* and statute of limitations. [101] With greater justification, the defenses against paternity actions listed in the Civil Code, such as notorious misconduct on the part of the mother, are now considered as going to the merits and may be raised at any time. [102]

*Exceptions* and *fins de non-recevoir* must be interposed in a prescribed order: First, a demand for security for costs must be made; then the defenses of lack of competence and of the pendency of another or related action (*litispendence* and *connexité*) must be interposed; finally, all other *exceptions* and *fins de non-recevoir* must be advanced. [103] There will be a separate hearing, usually obtainable quickly, on each of these defenses. [104] After they have been decided, the defendant submits his *conclusions* on the merits, and the case then has to await its turn on the calendar for an *audience* on the merits. [105]

### 7.09. Specific *Exceptions*

Some of the more important *exceptions* are listed below in the order in which they must be raised. In the absence of an indication to the contrary, the regular procedure applies: *Exceptions* must be raised in *conclusions*, and they are the subject of later argument at a hearing (*audience*).

**a. *Cautio judicatum solvi* (security to be posted by foreign plaintiffs).** Foreign plaintiffs and intervenors must post security for costs and any possible judgment on a counterclaim for abusive procedure. [106] The defendant waives his right to security unless he demands it before

[101] 1 SOLUS & PERROT 293–96; 1 DALLOZ, *op. cit. supra* note 91, at Nos. 62–68 (and Supp. 1964).

[102] 1 DALLOZ, *op. cit. supra* note 91, at No. 66; *cf.* note 101 *supra.*

[103] CODE DE PROCÉDURE CIVILE art. 192 (generally), art. 166 (security for costs), art. 168 (incompetence), art. 173 (formal defects in *ajournement* and other papers).

[104] These defenses will ordinarily fall into the class of cases involving only limited issues, which are not required to await their turn on the calendar. The demand for security for costs may be brought before the *juge chargé de suivre la procédure.* See 7.09.a *infra.*

[105] The hearing on the merits may not be the last hearing the case receives. If proof-taking is requested at that hearing, proof will be taken, and a new hearing will follow.

[106] On the rules concerning security for costs, see 6.03.b *supra.* The demand for security is considered as an *exception,* and thus a kind of a defense, because plaintiff's action must be stayed until security has been posted. See CUCHE & VINCENT 522.

raising any other issue. [107] The demand for security may be addressed to the *juge chargé de suivre la procédure*; a hearing before the full panel is not required. [108]

**b. Incompetence; pendency of other action *(litispendence)* and of a related action *(connexité).*** The defenses of lack of competence – whether international competence, competence *ratione materiae,* or competence *ratione personae* – and of the pendency of an other action (*litispendence*) or a related action (*connexité*) must be raised simultaneously immediately after security for costs has been demanded. [109]

Even in cases strongly affected by public policy (*ordre public*), the right to raise these defenses is waived unless it is exercised at the outset of the suit. However, incompetence *ratione materiae* may be raised by the court on its own motion if the case should have been handled by an administrative or criminal tribunal or by a *tribunal d'instance* acting in last resort, or if it involves divorce, separation, other matters of personal status, or public policy (*ordre public*). Incompetence *ratione personae* may be raised on the court's own motion in cases in which the parties may not make settlements as to their rights, such as divorce or separation actions and other matters involving public policy. [110] Parties may also suggest to the court informally during argument that it should declare itself incompetent on its own motion. [111] A court wishing to

[107] CODE DE PROCÉDURE CIVILE art. 166.

[108] CODE DE PROCÉDURE CIVILE art 81.

[109] CODE DE PROCÉDURE CIVILE art. 168 (as amended in 1958). The defenses of *incompétence, litispendence,* and *connexité* are sometimes referred to as *déclinatoires.* If no security for costs is demanded, the issue of *incompétence* is the first one that must be raised. However, if defendant needs access to documents in plaintiff's possession in order to determine whether the case has been brought before a competent court, he may initiate proceedings (*communication des pièces*) to obtain these documents without waiving his right to raise an issue as to the competence of the court.

[110] CODE DE PROCÉDURE CIVILE art. 171. See generally Le Gall, *Requiem pour un ordre public,* [1963] D. CHR. 165.

[111] See Pochon, *Le nouveau régime des exceptions d'incompétence,* [1959] D. CHR. 233. According to the prevailing view, it is discretionary with a court whether to declare itself incompetent on its own motion, but there are some decisions indicating that a court failing to declare itself incompetent in an appropriate case may commit reversible error. Courts have a fair amount of freedom in deciding what cases are affected by public policy (*ordre public*). If a case belonging before the *tribunal de grande instance* is brought before one of the specialized tribunals, such as the commercial court, the latter may declare itself incompetent on its own motion. Soc. d'assurances "Les travailleurs français" v. Soc. de construction de chaudronnerie et tuyauterie, Cour Paris, May 18, 1961, [1962] D.J. 78; *cf.* Dlle Arduini v. Soc.Marseillaise de crédit, Cour Paris, Feb. 5, 1962, [1962] D. SOMM. 116. On the other hand, the rules of international competence embodied in CODE CIVIL arts. 14 and 15 do not involve *ordre public* and may not be raised by the court on its own motion. Cie marocaine des boissons v. Société vinicole du Languedoc, Cass. Civ., May 21, 1963, [1963] GAZ. PAL. 2. 235, 91 CLUNET 113 (1964). For a review of the cases, see DALLOZ, RÉPERTOIRE DE PROCÉDURE CIVILE ET COMMERCIALE, *Incompétence,* at Nos. 32–47 (Supp. 1964).

declare itself incompetent on its own motion must give the parties a chance to be heard on that issue. [112]

Before 1958, lack of competence was raised in *conclusions* and at a hearing. If the court declared itself incompetent, the case was dismissed and plaintiff had to start a new action in the proper court. That procedure has now been modified. [113] At present, the defendant must indicate in his *conclusions* what court would be competent. When the court holds its hearing on the issue of competence, it must announce the day on which it will render its decision. If factual issues arise, the court may order a proof proceeding. [114] If the court declares itself competent, the defendant may acquiesce and litigate on the merits. If the court declares itself incompetent, the plaintiff may acquiesce and institute another action in a competent court. [115]

A decision on the issue of competence may be appealed in all cases. If an appeal is taken, the court must stay its proceedings. An appeal is taken in a rather unusual manner: Within ten days of the judgment, the losing party must record a so-called *contredit,* a kind of notice of objections, in a register at the court clerk's office. The *contredit* must indicate briefly the reasons on which it is based. The clerk of the court sends the entire case file to the clerk of the competent *cour d'appel.* A date for the hearing is set by the appellate court, and the parties are notified of the hearing date by mail. The matter does not have to await its turn on the calendar. A decision must be rendered within one month and is mailed to the parties by the clerk. A *pourvoi* to the *Cour de Cassation* lies from the *cour d'appel* decision. [116]

In its decision, the *cour d'appel* indicates which court is competent. After the file is transmitted to that court, either party may continue the proceedings before that court by serving a notice on all other parties. No new contest on the issue of competence is possible. As a check on

[112] CODE DE PROCÉDURE CIVILE art. 171. The *contredit* procedure mentioned in the next paragraph of the text must be used by a party seeking review of the court's determination.

[113] On the changes made in 1958 and further modifications in procedure effectuated in 1960, see Giverdon, *Commentaire* (*Décret No. 60–802*), [1961] D.L. 113; Lindon, *La Récente Réforme en matière de conflits d'attribution,* [1960] J.C.P. 1. 1544 CUCHE & VINCENT 272–96 and Supp. 1960, at 5–19; CORNU & FOYER 62–66 (Supp. 1960). The new procedure was intended to discourage dilatory tactics. It has been criticized because it gives the courts more initiative than is traditional.

[114] CODE DE PROCÉDURE CIVILE art. 169.

[115] Giverdon, *supra* note 113, at 114–15.

[116] CODE DE PROCÉDURE CIVILE art. 169. The register mentioned in the text is the one also serving to record *oppositions.* CODE DE PROCÉDURE CIVILE art. 163. Use of a *contredit* (instead of a regular notice of appeal) within 10 days is an essential formality. Soc. Nationale des Chemins de fer Français v. Soc. coopérative des cheminots de Lens, Cour Douai, March 11, 1961, [1961] D.J. 395.

dilatory tactics, if it loses, the party having raised the issue of incompetence is ordinarily liable for a fine from 100 francs to 10,000 francs. In addition, on remand, the court of first instance may hold it liable for damages for abusive procedure. [117]

This special procedure is inapplicable in *référé* matters, in divorce and separation cases, and in cases which are alleged to belong before an administrative tribunal. [118] Its applicability in cases in which the incompetence of the court is due to an arbitration agreement is doubtful. [119] If a foreign court is alleged to be competent, the procedure is applicable, although the *cour d'appel* has, of course, no power to transfer the case to the foreign court. [120] The special procedure may not be used when no true case of incompetence, but rather a defense on the merits, is presented. [121]

With minor variations, the procedure for dealing with questions of competence is also applicable if the defenses of *litispendence* or *connexité* are raised: The decision of the *cour d'appel* then leads to joinder of both actions before the proper court (*règlement de juges*). [122]

**c. Violation of rules relating to formalities *(nullités)*.** A defense based on a defective *ajournement* is raised by claiming that the *ajournement* is suffering from nullity (*nullité*). [123] This terminology is misleading: A claim that the *ajournement* is void is waived unless it is advanced immediately after the defenses of incompetence, *litispendence*, and *connexité*. [124] A defaulting defendant may raise a defect in the *a-*

[117] CODE DE PROCÉDURE CIVILE art. 169. If several courts are competent, the *cour d'appel* must allow plaintiff to choose among them. *Cf.* Duflot v. Soc. "Sols et fondations," Cour Douai, June 29, 1962, [1962] D.J. 560.

[118] CODE DE PROCÉDURE CIVILE art. 170. On divorce and separation actions, see 11.04 *supra*. On administrative courts, see 3.01–3.03 *supra*.

[119] Chevallier v. Société civile immobilière M.A.B., Cour Paris, June 12, 1962, [1963] D.J. 24 (holding special procedure to be inapplicable) (some cases contra are cited in the appended note by Giverdon).

[120] Compagnie El Al v. Maydek, Cour Paris, March 27, 1962, 90 CLUNET 142 (1963); Koeberl v. Cie La Paix, Cour Paris, Feb. 14, 1961, 88 CLUNET 1080 (1961); Mourgnot v. Civoro, Trib. Gde Inst. Seine, Jan. 31, 1961, 88 CLUNET 1084 (1961) (with note Sialelli arguing that special procedure should not be applicable).

[121] Sovereign immunity is not a defense going to the competence of the court but rather one going to the merits, so that the special procedure cannot be used. Gouvernement des Etats Unis v. Raynal, Cour Nancy, May 18, 1961, [1961] J.C.P. 12421. The distinction creates difficulties if competence and merits depend on the same issue, *e.g.*, whether a party is a merchant (*commerçant*). See U.R.S.S.A.F. de Maine-et-Loire v. Guerault, Cour Agen. Dec. 13, 1960, [1961] D.J. 135. *Cf.* Giverdon, *Pour qui sonne le glas de la procédure du contredit*, [1964] D. CHR. 73; Cons. Terrail v. "La Vie au grand air pour l'enfance," Cass. Soc., March 12, 1964, [1964] D.J. 445 (note Giverdon).

[122] CODE DE PROCÉDURE CIVILE art. 172. On *litispendance* and *connexité*, see 4.31 *supra*.

[123] A defense based on a procedural defect is therefore called *exception de nullité*.

[124] CODE DE PROCÉDURE CIVILE arts. 173, 192. There is an inconsistency between the two

*journement* only through one of the regular means of review (*opposition* or *appel*). Once a judgment is no longer subject to one of the means of review, it is unimpeachable no matter how defective the *ajournement* may have been and even if defendant received no notice of the action against him. Unless the judgment is not merely void but non-existent, collateral attack against a judgment is not possible. [125]

The rules relating to *ajournements* generally also apply to other documents (*actes de procédure*) prepared in the course of litigation. [126] In case of a procedural infirmity, they may be declared void by the court. While, in the absence of motion practice, this cannot be done in the early stages of the litigation, a party seeking to have one of the subsequent papers declared void must submit *conclusions* to that effect before submitting *conclusions* going to the merits. [127]

If an *ajournement* is declared void, it loses its effect of tolling the statute of limitations, [128] and the entire case must be started again by service of a new *ajournement*. [129] If another procedural document is declared void, it likewise becomes ineffective as do all other documents based on it. [130] The *avoué, huissier*, or clerk responsible for a defective document may become liable for damages and various penalties. [131]

Unfortunately, it is not always easy to determine when a procedural defect renders an *ajournement* or other document void. The *Code de Procédure Civile* expressly deprives the courts of discretionary powers to disregard defects. [132] It also provides that a procedural irregularity

articles. While both require that a defect in the *ajournement* be raised at the outset of the litigation, article 173 seems to contemplate a separate defense, while article 192 requires that all *exceptions* and *fins de non-recevoir*, except security for costs and incompetence, be raised at the same time. *Cf.* MOREL 330.

[125] By virtue of the rule *voies de nullité n'ont lieu contre jugements en France*. See, *e.g.*, CORNU & FOYER 442–44; *cf.* 4.02.b *supra*. A judgment may be non-existent and therefore subject to collateral attack if rendered by a person who has no judicial powers or if entirely unrecorded. *Id.* 447. Cases holding a judgment to be non-existent are rare.

[126] This includes *conclusions* and other papers served in the course of litigation, testimony obtained during an *enquête*, experts' reports, and the like. For the purposes of this subsection, it is immaterial whether the document itself or the manner of its service is defective. The rules stated are not necessarily applicable to judgments. For additional rules concerning defects in *enquêtes*, see 7.51.g *infra*.

[127] CODE DE PROCÉDURE CIVILE arts. 173, 192. Thus, a party wishing to have an *enquête* declared void must file *conclusions* seeking a declaration to that effect before raising any issue as to the substance of the testimony.

[128] As far as the statute of limitations is concerned, the *ajournement* is considered as never having been served. CODE CIVIL art. 2247.

[129] CUCHE & VINCENT 534; CORNU & FOYER 430; 1 SOLUS & PERROT 390.

[130] *E.g.*, CUCHE & VINCENT 534; 1 SOLUS & PERROT 390. The act declared void may be repeated, unless a time limitation has run. If a notice of appeal is declared void, since the thirty-day appeal period has usually run by that time, the right to appeal is ordinarily lost.

[131] CODE DE PROCÉDURE CIVILE art. 1031 (disciplinary penalties, damages for malpractice, and no reimbursement for expenses relating to void document).

[132] CODE DE PROCÉDURE CIVILE art. 1029 provides that the rules relating to procedural

leads to nullity of a document only if the Code so prescribes. In other situations, procedural irregularities are sanctioned merely by a fine against the offending *avoué*. [133] However, under present case law, if the rule violated is "substantial," its violation may void the offending document, even though the Code does not specifically so provide. [134]

Amendments to the *Code de Procédure Civile* enacted in 1933 and 1935 provide that no defective *ajournement*, notice of appeal, or other procedural act may be declared void unless the defect causes prejudice to the other side. [135] Giving the reform a restrictive interpretation, the *Cour de Cassation* has held that a defective document may be declared void even in the absence of prejudice if there has been a failure to observe a "substantial" rule. There is no satisfactory definition of the term "substantial." [136] An *ajournement* suffers from a "substantial" defect if it does not have a date, or lacks the designation of its addressee, or fails to indicate defendant's time to appear, and so does any paper that is not signed. [137] On the other hand, failure to insert the number of the panel before which the action is pending is not violation of a "substantial" rule if the name of the court is given, and neither is the failure to insert a party's first name if there can be no doubt as to its identity, nor the failure of the *huissier* serving a document to indicate his address in its body, especially if he serves the document in an envelope bearing his complete name and address. [138]

defects shall not be *comminatoires*. The term *comminatoire* implies that the court has discretionary power to disregard procedural defects. This was the rule before the French revolution. 1 SOLUS & PERROT 364.

[133] CODE DE PROCÉDURE CIVILE art. 1031 (fine from F. 50 (about $ 12.50) to F. 200 (about $ 40)).

[134] In many cases, the CODE DE PROCÉDURE CIVILE states expressly that violation of specified rules makes the defective document void. On the *ajournement*, see, *e.g.*, CODE DE PROCÉDURE CIVILE art. 70 (violation of the rules contained in articles 61 (contents of *ajournement*), 64 (statements required if action concerns land), 68 and 69 (manner of service) void the *ajournement*). For a listing of some of the formalities considered so substantial by the courts that their violation leads to nullity, see text at notes 137–38 *infra*. See generally CUCHE & VINCENT 531–32; MOREL 327; 1 SOLUS & PERROT 368–70.

[135] CODE DE PROCÉDURE CIVILE art. 173. On the 1933 and 1935 amendments, see, *e.g.*, CUCHE & VINCENT 531.

[136] According to one definition, a formality is substantial if it relates to the essence of a procedural act and is necessary for the act to accomplish its purpose. See, *e.g.*, Durrmeyer v. Vacher de Lapouge, Cour Paris, March 13, 1958, [1958] D.J. 489. The cases seem based in part on pragmatic considerations.

[137] *E.g.*, Dillet v. Lebrun, Cass. Com., Nov. 18, 1947, [1948] D.J. 177; Dlle Merle v. Montal, Cass. Soc., June 27, 1951, [1952] D. SOMM. 50; Dame Collin v. Le Bellec, Cass. Civ., May 9, 1950, [1950] D.J. 429 (failure to mail defendant required letter when *ajournement* destined for him was left at mayor's office); Durrmeyer v. Vacher de Lapouge, *supra* note 136 (failure to specify judgment in notice of appeal); 1 SOLUS & PERROT 378.

[138] For detailed lists of matters which have been held to be substantial or non-substantial, see CORNU & FOYER 432; 1 SOLUS & PERROT 378–81.

The rule that an irregularity may be disregarded if no prejudice has been caused is also inapplicable if a non-waivable time limitation is involved. In such a case, late action is ineffective, whether or not there has been prejudice. [139] The same applies if one of the rules of court organization is violated – for example, if a document is served by an *huissier* acting outside the district for which he is competent. [140]

French authors frequently criticize the courts for disregarding legislative attempts to liberalize rules dealing with procedural defects. [141]

Procedural defects may be raised only by the party aggrieved, but, when public policy (*ordre public*) is involved, the court may apparently raise them on its own motion or they may be raised by the *ministère public*. Even in cases involving public policy, the party responsible for a defect may never rely on it to attack the validity of any procedural act. [142]

**d. Other *exceptions*.** In some cases, a defendant may raise *exceptions* which lead merely to a temporary stay of proceedings. In an action against the heir of a person recently deceased or against a recently divorced, separated, or widowed wife based on liabilities of the estate or on community property liabilities, the defendant may ask for a stay of three months and forty days from the time of death or termination of the marriage to enable him to make an inventory and to deliberate whether to accept the inheritance or the benefits of community property. [143] Thus, the defendant is able to avoid the personal liability which French law imposes upon heirs accepting an inheritance without reservation. [144]

Since the defendant can obtain a stay until the third-party has been brought into the action, impleader constitutes an additional *excep-*

[139] *E.g.*, Mattei v. Préfet de la Corse, Cour Bastia, June 12, 1950, [1950] D.J. 622 (time for *opposition*); Durand v. Percepteur du 9e arr. de Paris, Cour Paris, Feb. 20, 1941, [1941] D. ANAL. J. 216 (time to register appeal in clerk's office). Binding time limitations are sometimes referred to as *déchéances*. Not all time limitations are subject to these strict rules. A defendant may appear even after his time to appear has run out if no default judgment has been obtained. See 7.03–7.04 *supra*.

[140] Veuve Fougeroux v. Cattanéo, Cass. Soc., Dec. 1, 1951, [1952] D.J. 71.

[141] *E.g.*, MOREL 327; 1 SOLUS & PERROT 384. However, Solus and Perrot are of the view that there must be strict compliance with formalities going to the merits. See *id.* 375–76. French *avoués* frequently do not take advantage even of "substantial" irregularities if no harm has been caused to their client. MOREL 362. Nevertheless, the number of cases involving procedural defects is quite large. Undoubtedly, the number of formalities required by the Code could be greatly reduced without encouraging fraud or oppression.

[142] MOREL 330; 1 SOLUS & PERROT 386; *cf.* Dame Collin v. Le Bellec, *supra* note 137.

[143] CODE DE PROCÉDURE CIVILE art. 174.

[144] On the personal liability of French heirs and means of avoiding it, see AMOS & WALTON, INTRODUCTION TO FRENCH LAW 305–08 (2d ed. 1963). On the analogous right of a wife to "renounce" the community, see *id.* 268.

*tion.* [145] The same is usually true of lack of capacity on the part of plaintiff, because the action must be stayed until proper steps have been taken by the plaintiff's guardian or committee. [146] Other *exceptions* are of minor importance. [147]

## 7.10. Counterclaims

The *Code de Procédure Civile* contains only a few incidental references to counterclaims. The rules relating to counterclaims are mainly judge-made. [148]

A counterclaim may be interposed if the defendant wishes to use an unliquidated debt owed him by plaintiff as a set-off against the – not necessarily related – claim of plaintiff. This is known as *compensation judiciaire.* No counterclaim is required if the defendant wants to set off a liquidated debt against the plaintiff's claim. Such a set-off, called *compensation légale,* is considered a defense on the merits. [149]

Counterclaims are also possible when the defendant, though seeking an affirmative judgment on his counterclaim, is interested mainly in blocking plaintiff's action. This occurs most frequently when the defendant sued for non-performance of a contract interposes a counterclaim for rescission. [150]

More importantly, a counterclaim may be interposed whenever there is *connexité* between the main action and the counterclaim. Such a relation exists when the main action and the counterclaim are based on the same underlying transaction - for instance, when they arise from the same automobile accident. The courts have a rather wide discretion in determining when the main action and the counterclaim are sufficiently related. [151] Counterclaims are not permissible if the relationship between the two actions is too tenuous. [152]

[145] CODE DE PROCÉDURE CIVILE art. 175. See also 7.14 *infra* (third-party practice).

[146] This is disputed. 1 DALLOZ, *op. cit. supra* note 91, at No. 21. On capacity, see 6.03 *supra.*

[147] *E.g.*, CODE CIVIL art. 1225 (right of heir sued for liabilities of decedent to demand stay to bring co-heirs into action); CODE CIVIL art. 2170 (on foreclosure, stay available to owner of mortgaged premises who is not personally liable for the debt to enable him to start proceedings against the party personally liable).

[148] For one of the few statutory references, see CODE DE PROCÉDURE CIVILE art. 464 (permissibility of certain counterclaims on appeal). See generally MOREL 294; 1 SOLUS & PERROT 301 (with historical discussion).

[149] 1 DALLOZ, RÉPERTOIRE DE PROCÉDURE CIVILE ET COMMERCIALE, *Demande Reconventionelle,* at No. 14 (1955); MOREL 294.

[150] 1 DALLOZ, *op. cit. supra* note 149, at Nos. 11–13; 1 SOLUS & PERROT 303.

[151] *E.g.*, Allagnat v. Paufique, Cass. Civ., March 12, 1953, [1953] D.J. 322 (some of the participants in a brawl between five men sued the other participants who interposed counterclaims). The most frequent instance of a counterclaim based on *connexité* occurs in automobile collision cases. See generally 1 SOLUS & PERROT 303.

[152] Thus, an insurance agent sued by his company for the return of certain equipment

Counterclaims for divorce or separation are freely permitted in divorce or separation actions.[153] Furthermore, a defendant may counterclaim against plaintiff on the ground that plaintiff's very action against him amounts to an abuse of procedure.[154] However, counterclaims are not lawful in cases other than those here indicated.

Counterclaims are interposed by means of regular *conclusions*.[155] Defendant need not use his first *conclusions* for this purpose, but may interpose his counterclaim at any time before the end of the case. However, the courts retain the power to reject a counterclaim interposed merely for dilatory purposes. In addition, the court may always order severance if the counterclaim is likely to delay the main action.[156]

A plaintiff served with a counterclaim usually submits *conclusions* in which he asks for its dismissal.[157] Generally, however, a counterclaim against a counterclaim is not permissible.[158] If the main action is dismissed for a reason unrelated to the merits, the counterclaim must ordinarily also be dismissed.[159]

### 7.11. Exchange of Final *Conclusions*

**a. Time when final *conclusions* must be exchanged.** While the case is awaiting its turn on the calendar, the parties may exchange additional *conclusions*. However, court permission must be obtained for the service of *conclusions* within the last ten days preceding the hearing (*audience*). *Conclusions* in reply to *conclusions* filed within the last fifteen days before the *audience* may be served within five days of the *audience*. The court may not take into consideration *conclusions* that

loaned to him was not permitted to interpose a counterclaim for commissions due, nor could a counterclaim asking that certain business deals be declared invalid be interposed in an action concerning entirely unrelated contracts. See cases cited in 1 DALLOZ, *op. cit. supra* note 149, at No. 19.

[153] See 11.04.c *infra*.

[154] MOREL 296; 1 DALLOZ, *op. cit. supra* note 149, at No. 14. On when the institution of an action may amount to tortious abuse of procedure, see CUCHE & VINCENT 17.

[155] On problems of competence arising in connection with counterclaims, see 4.37–4.39 *supra*.

[156] 1 DALLOZ, *op. cit. supra* note 149, at Nos. 34–38; 1 SOLUS & PERROT 300. Facts brought out in connection with the counterclaim may be considered by the court on the main claim, and vice versa. Allagnat v. Paufique, *supra* note 151.

[157] Quite often, these are as brief as defendant's *conclusions* on the merits and state merely that the counterclaim is defective and must also be dismissed on the merits.

[158] 1 DALLOZ, *op. cit. supra* note 149, at 22. *But see* Dame Thévenon-Danière v. Thévenon-Danière, Trib. Belley, Dec. 10, 1952, [1953] D. SOMM. 34 (counterclaims possible against counterclaim if both have same basis).

[159] 1 DALLOZ, *op. cit. supra* note 149, at No. 42. *But see* Epoux Salomon v. Chambon, Cass. Com., Nov. 27, 1951, [1952] D.J. 71 (counterclaim may be entertained even if main action dismissed, especially if the parties consent by litigating the merits of the counterclaim).

have been submitted in violation of this rule, [160] but the point is waived absent objections by the adverse party. If no objections are made, *conclusions* may be submitted until the case is closed at the end of the *avocats'* argument. [161]

The court may grant a party an extension of time, but it must then give the adverse party five days to file reply *conclusions*. If necessary, the hearing must be adjourned. [162]

**b. Permissible changes in original *conclusions*.** Since the original pleadings of the parties on the merits are often quite brief, submission of new pleadings before the final hearing is the rule. In the absence of detailed statutory regulation, the rules concerning the permissibility of changes in the original pleadings are largely judge-made.

Unless they are related (*connexes*) to the original claim, new claims (*demandes*) may not be introduced by way of amended *conclusions*. However, new *moyens*, the facts and legal arguments on which the claim is predicated, may be so introduced. This distinction has created difficulties. [163]

Apparently, new evidentiary facts may always be alleged in amended pleadings. These are considered *moyens*.[164] But if the relief demanded or the ultimate fact upon which the action is based is different, there may be a new claim. A mere change in legal theory of the action seems permissible. Thus, in a personal injury action, one may rely on the liability for fault rule of article 1382 of the *Code Civil* in the original *conclusions* and on the absolute liability rule of article 1384 in amended *conclusions*. [165]

Amended pleadings may allege a new claim that is based on the same ultimate facts as the original claim: Such claims are considered *con-*

[160] CODE DE PROCÉDURE CIVILE art. 82; *cf.* Soc. des Etablissements Maire v. Maurice Conrad, Cour Paris, March 15, 1958, [1958] D. SOMM. 151.

[161] *E.g.*, Société Payet et Pluchet v. Chanteloube, Cass. Req., Feb. 25, 1941, [1941] D. ANAL. J. 151; Lavandier v. Leroy, Cass. Civ., Nov. 27, 1940, [1941] D. ANAL. J. 19.

[162] CODE DE PROCÉDURE CIVILE art. 82. A decision denying an extension of time may be appealed, but only together with the judgment on the merits.

[163] CODE DE PROCÉDURE CIVILE art. 337 contains practice provisions as to additional claims, but does not indicate when they are permissible. Analogous problems arise on appeal, since new claims are not permissible on appeal. CODE DE PROCÉDURE CIVILE art. 464. Indeed, most of the cases involving the permissibility of new claims are cases involving appeals. For additional materials, see 8.17 *infra.*

[164] *Cf.*, *e.g.*, Dame Lenoury v. Lenoury, Cass. Civ., Jan. 24, 1957, [1957] D. SOMM. 52.

[165] MOREL 290. Since 1935, CODE DE PROCÉDURE CIVILE art. 464 has allowed new claims on appeal involving the same relief (*objet*) as the claim in first instance, even if the claim is based on a different ultimate fact (*cause*). It is assumed that, *a fortiori*, the same rule must be applied to new claims presented before a court of first instance. See also 1 RAVIART, *op. cit. supra* note 67, at 367.

*nexes*. Thus, a creditor may sue the debtor for the principal amount of a debt and later demand interest accrued since the beginning of the action, [166] or sue a jointly and severally liable debtor for his pro-rata share of the debt and later amend his pleadings to demand the entire debt. [167] However, denial of costs discourages late interposition of claims that could have been submitted earlier. [168]

New claims that bear little relation to the old claim may not be advanced in amended *conclusions*. Thus, a person suing to enforce a right of way may not allege later that he is the owner of the property. [169] In practice, the courts, in determining whether amended *conclusions* are permissible, seem to emphasize the element of unfair surprise. The courts tend to approve them if the same defenses will be good against both the original and the new claim.

**c. Format of final *conclusions*.** The final *conclusions* exchanged by the parties are usually similar to those submitted at the outset of the litigation. Ordinarily, they consist of one very long sentence made up of individual clauses beginning with the word *attendu* (whereas). Except for the last which contains the prayer for relief, each clause contains an allegation of one of the facts or legal arguments (*moyens*) advanced. Since they contain references to subsequent developments – for instance, to a proof proceeding ordered by the *juge chargé de suivre la procédure* or to documents submitted –, amended *conclusions* are ordinarily more extensive than the original *conclusions*. However, no absolute rules exist. Counsel enjoy great freedom in formulating their *conclusions*, and *conclusions* sometimes show more resemblance with a memorandum of law or very long affidavit than with a common law pleading.

## 7.12. Hearing *(Audience)*

**a. Obtaining a hearing date (calendar practice).** After the preliminary hearing, the case must await its turn on the calendar for the hearing before the full panel of three judges, one of whom is the *juge chargé de suivre la procédure*. The length of this waiting period varies greatly throughout France, and even for different panels of the same court.

[166] MOREL 292. Similarly, a landlord suing a tenant for rent instalments past due could amend his pleadings and demand rent since the institution of the action. In both cases, the original and amended *conclusions* were considered as based on the same ultimate fact (*cause*).

[167] Caisse régionale d'Alger v. Valette, Trib. Orléansville, March 22, 1938, [1938] D.H. 414.

[168] CODE DE PROCÉDURE CIVILE art. 338.

[169] MOREL 290; *cf.* Philippe d'Ornano, Cour Paris, Dec. 5, 1962, [1963] D.J. 168 (claims for provisional relief, such as alimony *pendente lite*, may always be modified).

While in some more rural areas a hearing may be obtained very quickly, in Paris the waiting period is likely to be in excess of one year. Default cases, cases involving only limited argument, and urgent cases in which the summons is returnable on a day certain do not have to await their turn on the calendar. [170]

When a case is reached on the calendar, the clerk of the court sends a notice to the *avoués* informing them when it will be called. Cases that will be called during the next week are also posted in the courthouse. [171] In some of the more rural areas of France where cases move quickly and only a few *avoués* practice before each court, it is customary for the presiding judge of the court to meet periodically with all *avoués* to determine which cases should be heard soon and which ones should be kept waiting on the calendar. Even in Paris, it is possible to request the presiding judge to expedite or to delay the hearing. [172]

The call of the calendar takes place at the beginning of a hearing (*audience*). The *huissier audiencier* assigned to the court room calls the cases one by one and the *avoués* for both sides answer and indicate when they wish the case to be heard. [173] For this purpose, each *avoué* must first have determined when the *avocat* who will argue his case will be available. [174] Ordinarily, the presiding judge tries to accommodate the parties as to the date of the hearing. If neither side answers, the case may be struck from the calendar. This is not done very often, and it is easy to get the case back on the calendar. If only one side answers the calender call, its *avoué* may request the court to render judgment in its favor. [175]

On the day fixed for the hearing, there is a separate call of the calendar for all cases set down for that day. The parties' *avoués* or their *avocats* either answer that they are ready and indicate how much time they will need or ask for an adjournment. The court tries to cooperate if an adjournment is requested. [176] In places with crowded calendars, such as Paris, because all earlier dates have already been reserved, a request for an adjournment usually means a delay of several months.

[170] CODE DE PROCÉDURE CIVILE art. 80. The cases are referred to the full court for an immediate hearing by the *juge chargé de suivre la procédure*. See note 7.06 *supra*.

[171] There is a separate poster for each *chambre* (panel) of the court. See DÉCRET of March 30, 1808, *supra* note 66, art. 67. See also Appendix, Form No. 16.

[172] 2 DALLOZ, *op. cit. supra* note 69, at No. 41.

[173] DÉCRET of March 30, 1808, *supra* note 66, art. 62.

[174] Sometimes the calendar call will be answered by the parties' *avocats*; occasionally, both *avocats* and *avoués* are present.

[175] DÉCRET of March 30, 1808, *supra* note 66, art. 69; 2 DALLOZ, *op. cit. supra* note 69, at No. 42.

[176] *E.g.*, CORNU & FOYER 529.

Adjournment causes inconvenience to counsel who must be present at the beginning of the session: They cannot be sure when their case will be reached and may have to wait for a few hours. [177] A number of steps to discourage adjournments have been tried in the course of time, but they have not been too effective. [178]

**b. Argument.** After the call of the calendar, the reading of judgments of cases heard during previous hearings [179] precedes the hearing of new cases. During the hearing of new cases, the *conclusions* of the parties are first read by their *avoués*. Then the *juge chargé de suivre la procédure* reads his report, which is intended to summarize the contentions of the parties and the proceedings to date, but does not disclose the opinion of the *juge chargé de suivre la procédure* about the merits of the case. [180] Although, ordinarily, the report is brief and is handled in a routine fashion, [181] its preparation is considered as a substantial formality and its absence will make the judgment void. Since 1958, the filing of a written report by the judge is no longer required; an oral statement at the hearing suffices. [182]

The report has some procedural consequences. It is said to result in the definitive *mise en état* (putting at issue) of the case. Thereafter, various events that ordinarily lead to suspension of the proceedings, such as the death of a party or a change of status, remain without effect. [183] After the *juge chargé de suivre la procédure* has read his report, the composition of the court must remain the same. Thus, if the argument of counsel is so long that there must be an adjournment to another day, the court on the adjourned date must be composed of the

[177] Sessions of the court begin either in the morning or in the afternoon. They should last a minimum of four hours and thirty minutes. In Paris, the courts usually schedule more cases than can be heard, because they expect some adjournments. See generally 1 Raviart, *op. cit. supra* note 67, at 215.

[178] At present, the clerk of the court must send a letter specifying the hearing date to the parties. Code de Procédure Civile art. 81. It was hoped that parties aware of the hearing date would object if their *avocats* requested an adjournment. In practice, this measure has had little effect.

[179] This order is sometimes inverted. 1 Raviart, *op. cit. supra* note 67, at 215–18.

[180] Code de Procédure Civile art. 82.

[181] This is due to the preponderant rôle played by the subsequent oral argument. *Cf.* 2 Dalloz, *op. cit. supra* note 69, at No. 60.

[182] Consorts Marduel v. Bonjean, Cass. Civ., Oct. 24, 1962, [1963] D.J. 98 (oral report suffices, but if written report is prepared, it must be filed). Before the requirement of a written report was eliminated by the 1958 amendment to Code de Procédure Civile art. 82, the *Cour de Cassation*, contrary to its usual practice, did not hold itself bound by a recital in the judgment that the report had been given, but checked the case file to determine if a report was in existence. In the absence of a report, the judgment was reversed. Bensoussan v. Pocquet, Cass. Ass. Plén., Feb. 15, 1950, [1950] D.J. 298.

[183] On the events which may lead to a suspension of proceedings, see 7.15 *infra*.

same three judges as on the day of the original hearing. Even on the date the judgment of the court is read, the same judges must be present. [184]

After the report of the *juge chargé de suivre la procédure* has been given, the *avocats* [185] for both sides present their argument (*plaidoirie*). Plaintiff's *avocat* begins; he is followed by defendant's *avocat*. Plaintiff's *avocat* may then rebut. Sometimes defendant's *avocat* will in turn present argument to rebut plaintiff's rebuttal. However, the court has a discretionary power to limit argument. [186] The length of the argument varies greatly depending on the difficulty of the case; it may take only a few minutes or several hours. Generally, argument is much longer in rural areas where the courts are not so busy. Counsel for both sides usually begin their argument by stating the facts of the case. When they come to a point than can be proven by documentary evidence, they mention the document, show it to the court, and frequently quote from it. It is customary for French *avocats* to read their argument verbatim from notes put on folders (called *cotes*) which contain the pertinent documents. After the facts are presented, the law is discussed; during argument on the law, applicable code and statutory provisions are always cited. However, in courts of first instance, not many cases or other authorities, such as leading texts (*doctrine*), are cited. The few cases used are generally treated more as examples than as true precedents. The prayer for relief contained in the *conclusions* is always repeated as part of the argument. [187]

Ordinarily, the main emphasis during argument is on the facts, not on the law. Because they want to avoid the delay and expense of a proof proceeding, such as an *enquête* or *expertise*, counsel often attempt to induce the court to find the facts in their favor merely on the basis of the documentary evidence submitted. Considerable rhetorical skill is

[184] MOREL 369; CUCHE & VINCENT 349; 2 DALLOZ, *op. cit. supra* note 69, at No. 65. The rule requiring the same judges to be present may be avoided if the *avoués* of the parties reread their *conclusions* at the beginning of the adjourned hearing, and the *juge chargé de suivre la procédure* repeats his report. This amounts to a new *mise en état*. The argument need not be repeated. Poggio v. Faucou, Cass. Civ., May 18, 1953, [1953] D.J. 477; Epoux Charretier v. Trésor Public, Cass. Civ., June 11, 1953, [1953] D.J. 630. If, following the hearing, a proof measure is ordered which is followed by another hearing, the judges at that hearing do not have to be the same ones as at the original hearing.

[185] The parties may argue themselves. In a few instances, persons other than *avocats* or the parties may present argument. See 2.01–2.02 *supra*.

[186] *Cf.* Alaphilippe, Cour Toulouse, Jan. 17, 1951, [1951] D.J. 146 (criminal cases); CUCHE & VINCENT 350; MOREL 369.

[187] The prayer for relief in the *conclusions* and in the argument is sometimes phrased in the alternative. The court is asked to give judgment outright, but to order a proof measure should the court find that it does not possess sufficient evidence to warrant an immediate decision.

frequently displayed to show that the facts are established directly by the documents submitted or can be derived from them by a process of logical deduction. In a recent case brought to recover damages for the death of a secretary killed while riding in a car driven by her employer, the defendant contended that no personal injury action was permissible because the secretary was covered by the French equivalent of workmen's compensation. Plaintiff used only documentary evidence to counter this defense: (1) a police report showing that the young woman had her arm around her employer's back when extricated from the car; (2) a photograph of her taken while visiting a nightclub with her employer; and (3) a letter from her to a friend indicating that her feelings for her employer were unusually warm. On this basis and without any resort to testimonial evidence, plaintiff's *avocat* argued successfully that she had been outside the scope of her employment at the time of the accident.

Since this type of proceeding makes it difficult effectively to rebut factual arguments, counsel sometimes register their disapproval quite graphically when their opponent states facts with which they disagree: Violent head-shaking or lifting of the arms towards the ceiling is not considered unprofessional conduct. Questioning of counsel by the court is infrequent. If it occurs, it is usually innocuous.

After the parties have presented argument, the *ministère public* may do so, but exercises that right only in special cases.[188] No rebuttal against argument presented by the *ministère public* is possible. However, the parties may submit memoranda (*notes*) dealing with arguments presented by the *ministère public*. In an appropriate case, additional argument may be ordered.[189]

At the close of the argument, both parties submit to the court the files wich contain their argument in written form as well as all other documents on which they rely. All documents, including memoranda submitted in reply to the arguments of the *ministère public*, must be made available to the other side.[190]

**c. Public character of hearing; maintenance of order in court.** Ordinarily, the hearing (*audience*) must be conducted in court open to the public and the press.[191] However, proceedings at which no argument is

[188] On situations in which the *ministère public* acts in a civil case, see 3.08–3.10 *supra*.
[189] CORNU & FOYER 530; CUCHE & VINCENT 351; MOREL 370. This rule applies when the *ministère public* acts as *partie jointe*, not when it acts as a regular party (*partie principale*).
[190] On the duty to make documents available, see 7.34 *infra*.
[191] CODE DE PROCÉDURE CIVILE art. 87.

presented, such as examinations of witnesses (*enquête*) or of parties, do not have to be conducted in public. [192] Divorce and separation actions and a few other proceedings are not conducted in open court, but in the judges' conference room (*chambre du conseil*) from which the public is excluded. [193] Even in cases that must normally be conducted in open court, the public may be excluded if the court finds that "scandal or grave inconvenience" may otherwise result. The courts seem to have a rather wide discretionary power in deciding when this consequence is likely to ensue, but must report each instance of exclusion to the competent *procureur général*. [194]

While the press may freely report events occurring in open court, neither broadcasting, nor telecasting, nor photographing, is permissible in a court room. [195]

Persons present in court must conduct themselves with due decorum. [196] If a disturbance arises, the *huissier audiencier* on duty tells the disorderly person to be quiet and may order him to leave. In case of refusal, the presiding judge may summarily commit the recalcitrant person to jail for twenty-four hours. [197] Persons insulting an officer of justice may be arrested then and there and may be fined and sentenced to a prison term. These penalties must be imposed within twenty-four hours. [198] If misconduct in the court room amounts to a crime, the guilty party must be proceeded against before a criminal court. [199] Law professionals who misbehave in the court room may be summarily suspended. [200]

A clerk (*greffier*) must always be present during the hearing. He makes summary notes indicating, among other things, the time court opened, what judges were present, and what cases have been heard. However, he does not take down the argument of counsel. For that reason, *avocats* sometimes bring their own stenographers in order to

[192] On *enquêtes*, see 7.51 *infra*. On examination of parties, see 7.53 *infra*.

[193] On proceedings conducted in the conference room (*chambre de conseil*), see 11.03 *infra*. On divorce and separation, see 11.04 *infra*.

[194] CODE DE PROCÉDURE CIVILE art. 87; 2 DALLOZ, *op. cit. supra* note 69, at No. 47.

[195] Law No. 54–1218 of Dec. 6, 1954, J.O. Dec. 8, 1954, p. 11445, [1954] D.L. 480. The courts may prohibit the reporting of events occurring in the courtroom in all civil cases. Reporting is always prohibited in certain defamation and in paternity, divorce, and separation actions.

[196] The law provides that all persons present in the court room must have their heads bared, be silent and respectful, and obey the orders of the presiding judge. CODE DE PROCÉDURE CIVILE art. 88.

[197] CODE DE PROCÉDURE CIVILE art. 89.

[198] CODE DE PROCÉDURE CIVILE art. 91.

[199] CODE DE PROCÉDURE CIVILE art. 92.

[200] CODE DE PROCÉDURE CIVILE art. 90.

obtain a complete transcript of the proceedings. This is done especially if argument is likely to be continued over more than one day. The transcript prepared by such a stenographer has no official character.

## 7.13. Judgment

**a. Conference preceding judgment.** Although the court sometimes renders its judgment immediately after the argument following a brief conference in the court room or in the conference room, [201] this is unusual. Ordinarily, the court merely announces when it will render its judgment – usually, one to four weeks from the date of the argument. [202] Within that period, the judges confer. The conference is chaired by the presiding judge of the panel. The judges speak and vote in inverse order of seniority. [203] They may not consider material not regularly produced; it would, for instance, be improper for them informally to view the premises in litigation. [204]

The case is decided by a simple majority of the judges. If a majority cannot be found, two additional judges must be called in, and the case must be re-argued. [205] The judgment, which includes the opinion, will usually be drafted by the *juge chargé de suivre la procédure* or sometimes by the presiding judge. There are no dissenting opinions, and the votes of individual judges may not be revealed. [206]

**b. Rendition of judgment.** The judgment is rendered by being read at a public hearing (*audience*). Until its reading, the judgment is not final and may be changed [207] by the court. The same judges who heard the case must be present when the judgment is read. [208] After the

[201] CODE DE PROCÉDURE CIVILE art. 116

[202] The *greffier* prepares a *plumitif*, a summary statement in addition to the official registers and statistics. See 2 DALLOZ, RÉPERTOIRE DE PROCÉDURE CIVILE ET COMMERCIALE, *Jugement*, at Nos. 146–50 (1956).

[203] However, the juge *chargé de suivre la procédure* gives his opinion first. DÉCRET of March 30, 1808, *supra* note 66, art. 35.

[204] *E.g.*, 2 DALLOZ, *op. cit. supra* note 202, at Nos. 24–28.

[205] CODE DE PROCÉDURE CIVILE arts. 117–18. For additional rules concerning voting, see DÉCRET of March 30, 1808, *supra* note 66, art. 35, and Law of August 30, 1883, J.O. Aug. 31, 1883, [1883] D. 4. 58. See also CUCHE & VINCENT 386; 2 DALLOZ, *op. cit. supra* note 202, at Nos. 72–74. The clerk and members of the *ministère public* may not be present during the conference.

[206] See 3.19 *supra*.

[207] CODE DE PROCÉDURE CIVILE art. 116; CUCHE & VINCENT 387; MOREL 439. Ordinarily, judgments must be read at a public hearing even if the argument took place in the conference room (*chambre de conseil*).

[208] See note 184 *supra*. If there has been a change in the court's composition, as in the case of an adjourned hearing, the *avoués* repeat their *conclusions* and the *juge chargé de suivre la procédure* repeats his report before the judgment is read. Percepteur de Juvisy-sur-Orge

judgment has been read, the clerk of the court must write it on a paper called *feuille d'audience*. It is then signed by the presiding judge and the clerk. Minor changes in style or grammar but not changes of substance may be made at that time. The judgment as written on the *feuille d' audience* is ordinarily referred to as *minute* and kept in the court clerk's office. [209] Informal copies are sent to the *avoués* of the parties. Official copies certified by the clerk may be obtained by all interested persons upon payment of the proper fee. If the prevailing party wishes to levy execution, it must obtain a copy called *grosse* upon which the clerk puts the executory formula, a command to all *huissiers* and public authorities to execute the judgment. [210]

The prevailing party must serve a copy of the judgment on the opponent and on the opponent's *avoué* before execution may be levied. If the judgment does not terminate the litigation, however, service on the *avoué* suffices unless the judgment orders the party to do something in person – for instance, to appear for an examination (*comparution personnelle*). [211]

**c. Contents of judgment.** The most important part of the judgment (*jugement*) is the *dispositif*, the decretal paragraph in which the court awards relief or otherwise disposes of the case. In addition, each judgment, with unimportant exceptions, must also contain *motifs* – that is, an opinion indicating the court's reasoning. [212] Traditionally, the opinion is couched in the form of one, very long, sentence. Each statement of fact or law constitutes a separate subordinate clause introduced

v. Andrivon, Cass. Comm., June 5, 1950, [1950] D.J. 498; Dame Veyre v. Veyre, Cass. Comm., Dec. 19, 1950, [1951] D. Somm. 30.

[209] Code de Procédure Civile art. 138. For additional rules on the formalities to be observed in the preparation of the *minute*, see Code de Procédure Civile arts. 139–140, and Décret of March 30, 1808, *supra* note 66, arts. 36–38, 73–74. The sheets on which the *minutes* are written must be bound into annual volumes. In practice, some courts simply file them by date to facilitate their photo-reproduction. On permissible differences between the *minute* and the text of the judgement read at the hearing, see 2 Dalloz, *op. cit. supra* note 202, at No. 157.

[210] All *grosses* begin with the words "French Republic-In the Name of the French People," which are followed by the opinion and at the end, the "executory formula." Ordinarily, though unlimited numbers of regular copies may be obtained, a party may obtain only one *grosse*. Code de Procédure Civile art. 146; Décret No. 47–1047 of June 12, 1947, J.O. June 13, 1947, p. 5487, [1947] D.L. 225; *cf.* Cuche & Vincent 388. See Appendix, Form No. 22.

[211] Code de Procédure Civile art. 147; *cf.* Code de Procédure Civile art. 148 (no service on *avoué* necessary if he is deceased or retired). See also Morel 447. For service of the judgment on a party, the rules governing service of an *ajournement* are generally applicable.

[212] This requirement goes back to a law adopted in 1790. See 1.24 *supra*. An opinion is not required in adoption cases ( Code Civil art. 355), nor for *jugements préparatoires* or judgments involving a purely discretionary act, such as the granting of an adjournment. Cuche & Vincent 392; Morel 438.

by the word *attendu* (whereas). The decretal paragraph forms the main clause. The length of opinions varies, though they are usually brief. The opinion must be sufficiently explicit. Cases are cited infrequently. An opinion consisting only of a reference to another decided case is considered no opinion at all. The opinion must deal with each claim made by the parties in their *conclusions*, but need not refer to all arguments advanced. [213]

The law requires that each judgment contain: (1) the names of the judges who rendered it; (2) the name of the clerk; (3) the name of the member of the *ministère public* who argued (if one did); (4) the names, occupations, and addresses of the parties; (5) the names of their *avoués*; (6) the date of the decision; (7) a recital to the effect that the *juge chargé de suivre la procédure* read his report; and (8) a summary of the parties' contentions. [214] This information is usually given in a brief paragraph preceding the *motifs*, but the inclusion of these data in the *motifs* is also permissible.

Failure to observe a prescribed formality may make a judgment void if the omitted formality is a substantial one or if a statute expressly states that the omission makes the judgment void. [215] However, the defect must be raised by one of the regular methods of review, such as appeal or *opposition*. Collateral attack is not allowed even against a void judgment. [216] Until 1958, the recitals in a judgment were conclusive as to the formalities observed. If the judgment failed to recite that the *juge chargé de suivre la procédure* had rendered his report, the fact that he had nevertheless done so was immaterial and the judgment was void. Since 1958, failure of recital in the judgment is no longer fatal, if compliance with the formality can be shown by documentary evidence. [217]

[213] 2 DALLOZ, *op. cit. supra* note 202, at Nos. 249–77, 330; MOREL 439; *cf.* Soc. Fourmar v. Etat Espagnol, Cass. Comm., July 4, 1951, [1951] D.J. 656 (opinion may not contain ambiguous or imprecise statements, such as "... certain facts lead one to think that the plaintiff had doubts as to his claim ..."). Complete absence of an opinion (*défaut de motifs*) and lack of sufficient specificity (*manque de base légale*, literally, lack of a legal basis) are grounds for reversal by the *Cour de Cassation*.

[214] CODE DE PROCÉDURE CIVILE art. 141 (as amended in 1958). Before 1958, the prevailing party's *avoué* had to draft a detailed statement reciting all the contentions of the parties and the proceedings, which became part of the judgment and was called *qualités*. This requirement was abolished because it led to delay and controversy.

[215] The rule is the same as that governing in the case of *ajournements* and other procedural documents. A judgment is void if it lacks the names of the judges, or of the parties, or the summary recital of the parties' contentions, or has no decretal paragraph, or is not signed by the presiding judge, or fails to mention that the *juge chargé de suivre la procédure* gave his report. CUCHE & VINCENT 394; 2 DALLOZ, *op. cit. supra* note 202, at No. 359.

[216] MOREL 447; 2 DALLOZ, *op. cit. supra* note 202, at Nos. 370, 377; *cf.* 1.07.c *supra*.

[217] CODE DE PROCÉDURE CIVILE art. 142 (as amended in 1958); *cf.* Marquiset v. Schlinger, Cass. Civ., July 7, 1961, [1961] D.J. 721.

**d. Types of judgments.** The word *jugement* (judgment) has a broad meaning. Sometimes, any decision of any court is designated as a *jugement*. More frequently, this designation is reserved for decisions of the *tribunaux de grande instance* and of the commercial courts. Decisions of the *tribunaux d'instance* and of the *conseils de prud'hommes* (labor courts) are referred to as *sentences*, while decisions of the *cours d'appel* and of the *Cour de Cassation* are known as *arrêts*. Decisions of a single judge of a multi-judge court, such as decisions of the *juge chargé de suivre la procédure*, are referred to as *ordonnances*. [218]

Although decisions rendered by a full panel of the *tribunal de grande instance*, whether final or not, are always referred to as *jugements*, some distinctions are drawn. Judgments that decide the merits of a case are known as *jugements définitifs*. The same name is given to judgments that, although not terminating the case, finally determine an issue – for instance, judgments on the issue of the court's competence. Other judgments are known as *jugements avant dire droit*. If they relate to provisional relief, such as alimony *pendente lite*, they are also known as *jugements provisoires*. Such judgments have no *res judicata* effect and are subject to modification by the court. Judgments relating to the conduct of the suit, such as judgments ordering an examination of witnesses, are either *interlocutoires* or *préparatoires*. A judgment is *interlocutoire* when it gives some indication of the court's disposition towards the merits of the case, and *préparatoire* when it does not. Formerly, since *jugements interlocutoires* were immediately appealable, while *jugements préparatoires* were appealable only together with judgments on the merits, this distinction, though extremely hazy, was very important At present, both types of judgments are immediately appealable. However, the distinction remains important when review of a judgment by the *Cour de Cassation* is sought. Furthermore, *jugements préparatoires* lack *res judicata* effect. [219]

**e. Effect of judgment; the rule against modification of judgments.** A judgment: (1) declares the rights of the parties or creates new rights;

[218] Morel 431; 2 Dalloz, *op. cit. supra* note 191, at Nos. 1–2.

[219] Cuche & Vincent 382–84; Morel 432–35; 2 Dalloz, *op. cit. supra* note 202, at No. 15. On the immediate appealability of *jugements interlocutoires* and *préparatoires*, see Code de Procédure Civile art. 451 and 8.05.b *infra*. On *pourvois* to the *Cour de Cassation*, see 9.05 *infra*. Since 1958, all judgments dealing with *enquêtes*, formerly considered as *interlocutoires*, are appealable only together with the judgment on the merits. Code de Procédure Civile art. 258. See 5.51.a *infra*. In addition to the types of judgments mentioned in the text, French authors sometimes refer to *jugements d'expédient*, which merely incorporate an agreement of the parties.

(2) has *res judicata* effect; (3) may provide the basis for execution; and (4) terminates the court's power over the case. The first three of these consequences are discussed elsewhere. [220] The fourth is dealt with here.

Unless the case is formally re-opened by *opposition*, the court may not modify a judgment once it has been rendered. [221] However, courts may correct minor errors or interpret the decretal paragraphs of their judgments if they are so ambiguous that they cannot be executed. [222] In addition, courts sometimes render judgments that finally determine a case, but leave some issues for later decision. Thus, a court may decide a personal injury action for plaintiff on the issue of liability, but defer the issue of damages until after a medical *expertise* has been conducted or until the injuries are capable of more precise ascertainment. [223] In such a case, temporary damages are sometimes awarded to the plaintiff on an installment basis until final judgment is rendered.

### 7.14. Multiple Parties

Various procedures enable a third party to participate in a pending action or make it possible for a party to bring in others. The Code of Civil Procedure regulates the pertinent procedures in some detail, but the substantive rules determining when a party may intervene or be brought into an action are largely products of case law. [224]

**a. Intervention *(intervention volontaire)*.** French law distinguishes between two types of intervention, aggressive or principal intervention (*intervention agressive ou principale*) and conservatory or accessory intervention (*intervention conservatoire ou accessoire*). In a case of principal intervention, the intervenor seeks independent relief in his favor; in a case of conservatory intervention, the intervenor merely supports the position of one of the parties. [225] Often, since *amici curiae* are unknown to French law, conservatory intervention is used as a substitute for participation as *amicus curiae*. [226]

[220] See ch. 13 *infra*.

[221] MOREL 447–48; 2 DALLOZ, *op. cit. supra* note 202, at No. 377.

[222] *E.g.*, MOREL 448; 2 DALLOZ, *op. cit. supra* note 202, at Nos. 392–97, 441–26. Permissible changes include the correction of spelling mistakes, the correction of names of parties if there is no doubt as to their identity, or the correction of erroneous mathematical computations.

[223] MOREL 449.

[224] See MOREL 299; 2 DALLOZ, RÉPERTOIRE DE PROCÉDURE CIVILE ET COMMERCIALE, *Intervention*, No. 1 (1956). Occasionally, the CODE CIVIL contains some rules as to intervention. See *e.g.*, CODE CIVIL art. 882 ( creditors may intervene in partition action); CODE CIVIL art. 1447 (creditors of husband may intervene in separation of property action).

[225] *E.g.*, CORNU & FOYER 400; MOREL 300–01.

[226] See 3.09 *supra*.

Only true third parties may intervene. [227] They must enjoy procedural capacity and their claim must be related (*connexe*) to the main claim. Since a person acting as a principal intervenor is treated as a plaintiff, he must fulfill the ordinary requirements for parties; specifically, he must have a present, personal, and lawful interest in his claim. In addition, a principal intervenor who is not a French national must post security for costs. [228]

In case of conservatory intervention, the intervenor need not seek enforcement of a personal claim. However, he must have an interest, whether economic or "moral," in the outcome of the litigation. The problem of what constitutes a sufficient interest is most acute in the case of associations who frequently attempt to intervene in litigation affecting the rights of their members. [229] Intervening associations may defend the interests of their members if these are directly involved in the suit, but, as a rule, may not act merely to obtain a favorable judicial precedent. [230] Conservatory intervention is not permissible in proceedings relating to personal status, such as divorce or separation.[231]

A party intervenes by addressing a petition (*requête*) to the presiding judge of the court in which the action is pending. [232] Copies must be served on the parties. If the right to intervene is contested, the court must decide the issue at once. Intervention is possible at any time, provided decision of the main action is not delayed. If necessary to avoid delay, the two proceedings may be severed. [233]

A principal intervenor always submits his own *conclusions*, presents his own argument, and may demand proof measures. Since it merely supports the position taken by one of the original parties to the suit, a

[227] A person who is represented by a party to the action may not intervene. 2 DALLOZ, *op. cit. supra* note 224, at No. 15. As to representation, see 6.04.c *supra*.

[228] *E.g.*, MOREL 301–03. The interest need not necessarily be economic. Grandparents may intervene in a divorce action and demand that the custody of the children be awarded to them; similarly, a person mentioned as co-respondent in a divorce action may intervene to clear his name. 2 DALLOZ, *op. cit. supra* note 224, at No. 19.

[229] *Id.* at Nos. 17–18, 24–29; MOREL 301. In the case of intervening associations, the *amicus curiae* function of "conservatory" intervention is most pronounced.

[230] *Compare* Dlle Abragam v. Dame Janine Solane, Cour Paris, Jan. 6, 1953, [1953] D.J. 198 (note Lalou) (writers' association allowed to intervene in action by dancer against reviewer since action could have substantial impact on rights of reviewers) *with* Dutourt v. Royer de la Bastie, Cour Paris, July 10, 1957, [1957] D.J. 622 (author's association may not intervene in action against author of book who allegedly had used name very similar to that of plaintiff for character in book; mere interest in establishing case law favorable to authors is not sufficient to permit intervention). See also Laborie v. Henriquez de Zubereia, Cour Aix June 9, 1959, [1960] D.J. 376.

[231] MOREL 301; 2 DALLOZ, *op. cit. supra* note 224, at No. 7.

[232] CODE DE PROCÉDURE CIVILE art. 339.

[233] CODE DE PROCÉDURE CIVILE art. 340; MOREL 303. On the possibility of intervention by serving *conclusions* on adverse parties, see 2 DALLOZ, *op. cit. supra* note 224, at No. 47.

party acting only in a conservatory capacity may not submit independent *conclusions.* [234] If the main action is dismissed for a procedural reason, such as lack of competence, the intervenor's action fails; [235] the same is true, but only in the case of conservatory intervention, if the suit is abandoned. [236]

**b. Impleader and other methods of adding parties *(appel en garantie* and *intervention forcée).*** Impleader (*appel en garantie*) is possible when a defendant has a claim over against a third party. The name of this institution (literally, vouching in on warranty) suggests that it is available only to assert claims against warrantors. However, its availability is not so narrowly limited. If a third person claims ownership, the purchaser of movable or immovable property may implead his immediate vendor. A debtor sued for the entire amount of a joint and several obligation may implead his co-debtors. Each party to a partition action may implead the others if he is threatened in the ownership of the share allotted to him on partition. A surety may implead his principal, and a person liable for damage inflicted by another may implead the person whose fault caused the harm. [237] Some relationship (*connexité*) between the principal claim and the claim against the third-party defendant is required. Ordinarily, the same underlying facts must form the basis for both actions. [238]

French authors distinguish between *garantie formelle* and *garantie simple. Garantie formelle* exists only in the case of real actions involving land: If the plaintiff claims ownership of, or another real right in, land, the defendant may assert that his vendor owes him *garantie formelle.* All other situations involve only *garantie simple.* [239]

In case of *garantie formelle,* the vendor is not only obliged to pay damages to the defendant who is evicted from his land, but must also defend the action in the defendant's place. Once he has impleaded the vendor, the defendant may demand to be left out of the action and is not liable for costs should the plaintiff win. However, a judgment of

[234] *Id.* at No. 59.

[235] *E.g.,* Dupré v. Gasson, Trib. Mantes-Gassicourt, April 12, 1951, [1951] D.J. 466.

[236] See Trésorier-payeur général de la Gironde v. Echapasse, Cass. Com., July 15, 1952, [1952] D.J. 704.

[237] MOREL 308; 2 DALLOZ, *op. cit. supra* note 224, at No. 67; Soc. Guérineau v. Schmitter, Cour Nancy, April 25, 1951, [1951] D.J. 516 (landlord sued for injuries to child who fell from window while guest in tenant's apartment may implead tenant); *cf.* Lingelser v. Soc. Mallèvre, Cour Paris, Dec. 18, 1954, [1957] D.J. 40 (extensive note by Crémieu) (insured may implead his insurer).

[238] 2 DALLOZ, RÉPERTOIRE DE PROCÉDURE CIVILE ET COMMERCIALE, *Garantie,* No. 51 (1956).

[239] CUCHE & VINCENT 526–27; MOREL 309.

eviction is also binding on the defendant.[240] By invoking this procedure, the defendant does not abandon his claim against the vendor (third-party defendant). In cases involving only *garantie simple,* the defendant must remain a party to the principal action.

Impleader is effectuated by serving an *ajournement* and a copy of the original *ajournement* received by the defendant upon the third-party defendant. Service must ordinarily take place within eight days from the day defendant was served with the original *ajournement.*[241] If service on the third-party defendant is timely, the principal action may be stayed until the third-party defendant has effectively been brought into the action.[242] It is generally possible to bring the third-party defendant before the court in which the main action is pending even if that court would not otherwise be competent. However, if the original claim was brought for the purpose of compelling the third-party defendant to litigate before a court not located at his domicile, the proceedings against him may be remanded to the appropriate court at his domicile.[243]

There are two additional situations in which a person, originally not a party to the action, may be made a party: *mise en cause* and *assignation en déclaration de jugement commun.* Ordinarily, in case of *mise en cause,* a person who could have been made a party at the outset of the case is added subsequently. The existence of the remedy seems to be due in part to the absence of rules concerning necessary parties. Thus, a creditor may first sue one of a number of jointly and severally liable debtors, and then, through *mise en cause,* bring in the other debtors; a mortgage creditor bringing a (foreclosure) action against the present owner of the mortgaged land may later bring in the original mortgagor; and a person claiming to be owner of a parcel of land may sue the record title holder and later bring the holder of an easement into the action.[244]

[240] Code de Procédure Civile arts. 182, 185. Code de Procédure Civile art. 182 allows a defendant who has left the action to participate in a limited way. In such a case, he is not liable for costs, but is entitled to receive copies of all documents. In practice, this procedure is rarely used. 2 Dalloz, *op. cit. supra* note 238, at Nos. 104–07; Cuche & Vincent 528.

[241] Impleader must occur within the time limits set for an appearance. Code de Procédure Civile art. 175 (eight days for defendants in the same or neighboring *département;* fifteen days for defendants elsewhere in France). The time limitation is intended merely as protection for the principal plaintiff. Admin. des P.T.T. v. Bassino, Cour Nîmes, Dec. 21, 1953, [1954] D. Somm. 72. See also Appendix, Forms Nos. 9, 10, and 13.

[242] To obtain a stay, the defendant must give the plaintiff notice of the impleader. In practice, since the third party can usually be brought into the action before the first hearing takes place, a stay is requested rarely. 2 Dalloz, *op. cit. supra* note 238, at No. 76.

[243] Code de Procédure Civile art. 181. See also 4.22 *supra.* The court may, in its discretion, render one judgment in the main action and the impleader, or two separate judgments. Decaux ès qual. v. de Lagrange-Chancel, Cass. Comm., May 14, 1952, [1953] D.J. 625.

[244] 2 Dalloz, *op. cit. supra* note 238, at Nos. 64–65.

Through *assignation en déclaration de jugement commun* (literally, summons for a declaration that the judgment be considered joint), the plaintiff brings a third party into the litigation so that the judgment may be binding upon him. This is useful in a case in which a creditor brings an action belonging to his debtor. By *assignation en déclaration de jugement commun,* the creditor can ensure that the debtor will be bound by the judgment. [245]

To be brought into an action for purposes of *mise en cause* or *assignation en déclaration de jugement commun,* a party must be served with a regular *ajournement*; notice of such service must be given to all adverse parties. [246]

### 7.15. Interruption or Termination by Means other than Final Judgment.

Certain events interrupt the course of a French lawsuit or bring it to an end although no final judgment has been rendered. They are discussed briefly below.

**a. Interruption by death of party or *avoué* or by termination of *avoué*'s functions.** If a party dies before the final *mise en état* – that is, before the *juge chargé de suivre la procédure* has read his report –, all further proceedings are temporarily suspended, provided the other side has been given notice of the death. The same is true if the *avoué* of one of the parties dies or ceases to exercise his profession. In that event, the giving of notice is not required. [247]

The heirs of a deceased party may continue the action voluntarily by a notice served on all adverse parties, as may a party who has lost his *avoué,* if he has obtained a replacement. [248] If the action is not continued voluntarily, the other side may serve a regular *ajournement* on the heirs of the deceased or on the party having lost his *avoué,* requesting that

[245] *Id.* at No. 66. The procedure is intended primarily to avoid the rule (CODE CIVIL art. 1351) that a judgment has res judicata effect only between the parties to the action. For an extended discussion of the distinction between *mise en cause* and *assignation en déclaration de jugement commun,* see note Crémieu appended to Lingelser v. Soc. Mallèvre, *supra* note 237. While in *mise en cause* damages are frequently sought against the party brought into the action, this is not the case in an *assignation en déclaration de jugement commun.*

[246] *E.g.,* MOREL 307.

[247] CODE DE PROCÉDURE CIVILE arts. 342–44. It was apparently assumed that death, retirement, or suspension of an *avoué* would immediately be known by his colleagues practicing before the same court, so that notification would not be necessary. In case of death of a party notice is essential; adverse parties may validly continue the proceedings in the absence of such a notice. Caisse régionale assurances vieillesse de Limoges v. Bedin, Cass. Civ., Feb. 13, 1957, [1957] D. SOMM. 124. Death after the reading of the report of the *juge chargé de suivre la procédure* has no effect.

[248] MOREL 421; CORNU & FOYER 462.

the action be continued. [249] If there is no response to this *ajournement* within the ordinary time period for an appearance, the court may order the action continued. [250] This decision is treated as a default judgment and must be served by an *huissier* specially designated by the court.

Change of status of the parties, such as marriage, divorce, or declaration of incompetency, does not interrupt the proceedings. However, if the plaintiff dies before the defendant has appeared, his heirs must serve a new *ajournement* on the defendant. Service of a new *ajournement* is also required if the defendant changes his status before he has appeared. [251]

**b. Voluntary discontinuance *(désistement).*** The plaintiff may voluntarily discontinue the action (*désistement d'action*).[252] If he does so, all proceedings up to the time of discontinuance are considered as never having taken place and the statute of limitations as never having been tolled. However, the underlying cause of action is not affected; plaintiff may sue again unless the statute of limitations has run in the meantime. [253]

Discontinuance of the action is possible in all actions except when prohibited by public policy. In a divorce action, it is permissible only if it leads to continuation of the marriage. [254] Notice of discontinuance must be given to the defendant, but no particular form is required. [255] However, once the initial *mise en état* of the case has taken place, discontinuance is effective only if the defendant gives his consent. The courts have sometimes stated that consent may not be withheld

[249] CODE DE PROCÉDURE CIVILE art. 346.

[250] CODE DE PROCÉDURE CIVILE arts. 349–50. If the opponent appears and contests his duty to continue the action, the issue should be decided summarily. CODE DE PROCÉDURE CIVILE art. 348. When the interruption of the action is due to the death of a party, the heirs are likely to demand the three months and forty days stay provided for by CODE DE PROCÉDURE CIVILE art. 174. *Cf.* 6.04.a *supra*. If there is no appearance, the right to demand a stay is waived. CODE DE PROCÉDURE CIVILE art. 349.

[251] CODE DE PROCÉDURE CIVILE art. 345. Apparently, it was thought that under those circumstances the defendant might assume that the action would not be continued unless service was repeated. *Cf.* MOREL 422.

[252] In addition, a party may abandon any proceeding that is part of the action, such as a proof proceeding. No consent is required. See, *e.g.*, CUCHE & VINCENT 590–93.

[253] CODE DE PROCÉDURE CIVILE art. 403; CORNU & FOYER 464; MOREL 423. For example, a plaintiff may wish to discontinue the action if he notices that he does not have sufficient evidence but expects to obtain more evidence subsequently, or if he has brought the action before an incompetent court and wishes to begin a new suit before a competent court.

[254] CUCHE & VINCENT 591; Haentzler v. Dame Haentzler, Cour Paris, Nov. 19, 1952, [1953] D. SOMM. 5.

[255] CODE DE PROCÉDURE CIVILE art. 402; MOREL 424; CORNU & FOYER 465. It is usual to ask the court for a decision taking official notice of the discontinuance.

unreasonably.[256] The party discontinuing the action is liable for costs.[257]

If the plaintiff abandons his cause of action (*désistement d'action*), he may not bring another action. For that reason, acceptance of the abandonment by the defendant is generally not required. Causes of action relating to personal status may not be abandoned.[258]

**c. Termination of suit through inactivity over a period of time *(péremption* and *prescription).*** If for a period of three years neither side takes any action in the course of a law suit, so-called *péremption* occurs. Either side may thereafter request the court to declare the action abandoned.[259] Any procedural activity before this request has been made revives the action and avoids *péremption* even after a lapse of more than three years.[260] The courts view *péremption* as resting on an implied intention to discontinue the action. Therefore, they refuse to declare the action discontinued, if the facts clearly negate such an intention.[261] *Péremption* does not destroy the plaintiff's underlying right. He may begin a new action if the statute of limitation has not barred his claim. However, he becomes liable for costs incurred up to the time of the decision declaring the action abandoned.[262]

256 If defendant merely interposes a defense going to the competence of the court or the validity of the summons (*ajournement*), his consent is not required. It becomes necessary only after he has submitted his first *conclusions* going to the merits. MOREL 424; Haentzler v. Dame Haentzler, *supra* note 254. On the right of the court to override defendant's refusal to accept the discontinuance, see Société d'armement Belship v. Etat Français (Impex), Cour Paris, Dec. 6, 1950, [1951] D.J. 98 (defendant must consent to discontinuance of French action that had been brought only as a precautionary measure should the American court, before which the same action had been brought, declare itself incompetent).

257 CODE DE PROCÉDURE CIVILE art. 403.

258 *E.g.*, CUCHE & VINCENT 593; Fédération nationale de films v. Soc. le Capitole, Cour Lyon, Jan. 7, 1957, [1957] D. SOMM. 120.

259 CODE DE PROCÉDURE CIVILE art. 397, 399. Six additional months must be added in the event of the intervening death of a party, or the death of his *avoué*, or the termination of his functions. The three-year period runs against all persons, including the French Republic, its subdivisions, and minors. CODE DE PROCÉDURE CIVILE art. 398. *Péremption* is usually claimed by the defendant.

260 MOREL 426. For a discussion of various acts which would revive the action, see the note by Lobin appended to Labyorie v. Henriquez de Zuberia, *supra* note 230.

261 Thus, the period does not run against a party who cannot conduct the litigation. See Veuve de Colstonn v. Soc. Broko, Trib. Seine, Nov. 29, 1948, [1949] D.J. 190. It also does not run against a party actively litigating another action against the same defendant involving the same subject matter. Mezin v. Dlle Mezin, Cour Grenoble, Dec. 5, 1957, [1958] D. SOMM. 124; *cf.* Dame Mur v. Lamarche, Trib. Com. Toulouse, Nov. 26, 1930, [1932] D. 2. 49 (with very extensive note by Holleaux on the history and development of *péremption*). For a historical explanation, see also CORNU & FOYER 466–67.

262 CODE DE PROCÉDURE CIVILE art. 401.

If neither side displays any procedural activity for a period of thirty years, the action is automatically extinguished. [263]

**d. Acquiescence by defendant.** A suit also terminates upon defendant's acquiescence in plaintiff's claim. Such acquiescence may be either express or tacit and always affects the merits. Acquiscence is not possible if it would lead to divorce by agreement or to other results contrary to public policy. [264] An *avoué* may not abandon an action on behalf of his client unless he has a special power of attorney to do so. [265] Somewhat analogous to acquiescence in a claim is the acquiescence in a judgment. It amounts in substance to a waiver of the right to appeal or to resort to other methods of review. [266]

## 2. PROCEEDINGS BEFORE THE *TRIBUNAL D'INSTANCE*

### 7.16. General Characteristics

The procedure in use before the *tribunal d'instance* is designed for a single-judge court [267] in which representation by professional counsel is not required. [268] It is simple and expeditious.

Before an action may be started, unless the defendant lives too far away or the matter is urgent, an attempt at settlement must be made by the judge. A letter from the clerk of the court summons the defendant to appear for a settlement attempt. [269] A fair number of cases are terminated by settlement. [270]

If no settlement can be obtained, the plaintiff must summon the defendant to a hearing before the judge of the *tribunal d'instance* by means of a citation. [271] It is substantially similar to the *ajournement* used be-

[263] This rule is an application of the general thirty year limitation of CODE CIVIL art. 2262. Its applicability to actions has been contested. CORNU & FOYER 465–67; MOREL 430.

[264] *E.g.*, CUCHE & VINCENT 596–97.

[265] *Cf.* Soc. "Les véhicules automobiles d'occasion" v. Lesould, Cass. Soc., Jan. 13, 1960, [1960] D.J. 190.

[266] On acquiescence, see also 8.02, 9.06 *infra*.

[267] On the organization of the *tribunal d'instance*, see 3.25 *supra*.

[268] Parties may act as their own counsel in the *tribunal d'instance*. They may also use certain other persons as representatives. See 2.01–2.02 *supra*.

[269] Law of May 25, 1838, as amended by Law of May 2, 1855, cited in DALLOZ, CODE DE PROCÉDURE CIVILE art. 17 (61st ed. 1964). No attempt at settlement is required unless the defendant lives in the canton or city in which the court is located. If the case is urgent, the judge may give permission to summon defendant without a preliminary settlement attempt. This permission must be noted on the summons.

[270] For statistics, see CORNU & FOYER 174. They indicate that a settlement results in about one fifth of all cases.

[271] CODE DE PROCÉDURE CIVILE art. 1. The citation must be served by an *huissier*.

fore the *tribunal de grande instance*. At least three days must elapse between the date of service and the date of the hearing if the defendant lives in the *canton* in which the court is located or in a neighboring *canton*; at least five days when he lives in another *canton* in the same or a neighboring *département*; and at least fifteen days if he lives elsewhere in France. [272] In case of urgency, the judge may reduce these time periods. [273] Parties may also appear before, and submit their dispute to, a judge of a *tribunal d'instance* voluntarily. [274]

On the day of the hearing, the parties must appear before the judge either in person or through a person authorized to act for them. No written pleadings (*conclusions*) are to be exchanged. The law contemplates that the case will be decided on the basis of oral statements made by the parties in court. [275] The use of documentary evidence, of course, is permissible. If the defendant contends that the court is incompetent, the special procedure created for that purpose in 1958 must be followed .[276] Some difficulties arise because this procedure contemplates a separate judgment on the issue of incompetence, while an old, but unrepealed, statute authorizes the *tribunal d'instance* to render one judgment on both the issue of incompetence and the merits. [277]

If the defendant does not appear at the hearing to which he has been summoned, the judge may render a default judgment against him, which is subject to reopening by *opposition* only if it is not appealable and the defendant was not served personally or if it was impossible for him to appear. [278]

For proof measures, a special court decision is generally necessary, but the procedure is simplified. [279] No formal service of interlocutory

[272] Code de Procédure Civile art. 5. If the defendant lives outside France, the limitations of Code de Procédure Civile art. 73 are applicable. See 7.03 *supra*.

[273] Code de Procédure Civile art. 6.

[274] Code de Procédure Civile art. 7. This avoids the need for a citation.

[275] Code de Procédure Civile arts. 9, 12–13. Although this provision absolutely prohibits use of written *conclusions*, they are used occasionally. See Cuche & Vincent 367. If the parties misbehave during their appearance in court, the judge may fine them from 5 francs ($1) to 20 francs ($4) and commit them to jail for a maximum of three days. Code de Procédure Civile arts. 10–11.

[276] Décret No. 58–1289, of Dec. 22, 1958, J.O. Dec. 23, 1958, p. 11608, [1959] D.L. 45. Article 7 provides that the special procedure is applicable to all courts whose judgments are ultimately subject to review by the *Cour de Cassation*. On the special procedure, see 7.09.b *supra*.

[277] Law of May 25, 1838, *supra* note 269, art. 14. Presumably, that article must be considered as repealed by implication. See Dalloz, Répertoire de Procédure Civile et Commerciale, *Incompétence*, at No. 72 (Supp. 1964); Giverdon, *supra* note 113.

[278] Code de Procédure Civile arts. 19–22.

[279] Thus, witnesses who appear voluntarily may be heard without further procedure.Code de Procédure Civile art. 36. See 7.51 *infra*. The procedure for other proof is also simplified Code de Procédure Civile arts. 29–30. However, before the *tribunal d'instance*, appeal-

judgments rendered in the presence of both parties is necessary, [280] but service of the final judgment is required. The opinion and decretal paragraph are preceded by a short summary (*qualités*) of the proceedings prepared by the clerk of the court. [281]

### 3. PROCEEDINGS BEFORE THE *TRIBUNAL DE COMMERCE*

### 7.17. General Characteristics

Before the *tribunal de commerce* (commercial court), the assistance of professional counsel is not required. In most cases, however, parties are represented by *agréés*. [282]

Actions before the *tribunal de commerce* are initiated by a regular *ajournement*, which must be served on the defendant by an *huissier*. [283] There must be at least three days between the date of service of the *ajournement* and the hearing if the defendant lives in the district for which the commercial court is competent; eight days if he lives in the same *département* or in a neighboring *département*; and fifteen days if he lives elsewhere in France. [284] If speed is required, these time limitations may be shortened by order of the presiding judge of the court. This is especially true in maritime cases. [285]

At the hearing, the parties must be present in person or by a representative. [286] Otherwise, they are in default. The ordinary rules on defaults apply. [287] If the defendant denies that the court is competent, he must use the special procedure created for this purpose. [288] However,

ability of non-final judgments still depends upon the distinction between *jugements préparatoires* and *jugements interlocutoires*. See 8.05.b *infra*; CODE DE PROCÉDURE CIVILE arts 30–31.

[280] CODE DE PROCÉDURE CIVILE art. 28. If an interlocutory judgment has been rendered, the case must be finally decided within four months.

[281] *Cf.* CODE DE PROCÉDURE CIVILE art. 18; CUCHE & VINCENT 407. On the *qualités*, see also note 214 *supra*. On the procedure before the *tribunal d'instance* (formerly the *juge de paix*), see also CORNU & FOYER 560–63; MOREL 417–18. On the several special procedures in use before the *tribunal d'instance*, see 6.08 *supra* and 11.02.b *infra*.

[282] CODE DE PROCÉDURE CIVILE art. 414; CODE DE COMMERCE art. 627 (*avoués* not to be used before commercial courts). On persons who may act as representatives before commercial courts, see 2.01–2.02 *supra*. On *agréés*, see 2.07 *supra*.

[283] CODE DE PROCÉDURE CIVILE art. 415.

[284] CODE DE PROCÉDURE CIVILE art. 416. If the defendant lives outside of continental France, the one to five months time periods of CODE DE PROCÉDURE CIVILE art. 73 apply. See 7.03 *supra*.

[285] CODE DE PROCÉDURE CIVILE arts. 417–18. In maritime cases, the presiding judge may authorize service of a summons for a hearing on the same day.

[286] CODE DE PROCÉDURE CIVILE art. 421. See also note 281 *supra*.

[287] CODE DE PROCÉDURE CIVILE arts. 434–39. See 7.04 *supra*.

[288] The same is true if the defenses of *litispendance* or *connexité* are raised. CODE DE PROCÉDURE CIVILE art. 424.

the commercial court may decide the merits and the issue of competence in one judgment. A regular appeal rather than a *contredit* must then be used to obtain review by the *cour d'appel.* [289]

While no written *conclusions* need be submitted, in fact they are often used. [290] Oral statements suffice, however. If the case cannot be decided immediately at the end of the first hearing, the defendant must consent to service of papers on him at some place in the city in which the commercial court is located. [291] When proof measures are to be used, a special judgment is ordinarily required. [292] If accounts or complex documents are to be examined, the court may order their submission to one or three referees (*arbitres-rapporteurs*) who must examine the documents and report to the court. [293] In order to expedite proceedings, courts frequently submit cases to referees even when this is not specifically authorized by the Code of Civil Procedure. [294]

The commercial court in Paris, which has an extremely crowded calendar, uses an additional extra-legal procedure, known as the *délibéré* procedure, to increase the number of cases it can decide. Only *conclusions* are submitted at the first hearing. The case is then put on the calendar for another hearing. However, if the parties agree, the case is assigned to one of the judges of the court. In that case, the parties send their files to that judge and later argue briefly before him. The judge then prepares a draft judgment which he submits to the full court. Approval of the draft judgment by the court is practically automatic. Detailed argument before a full bench is extremely rare. [295]

Judgments of commercial courts are governed by rules substantially

[289] But a regular appeal may be taken only if the judgment on the merits is appealable; if it is not, the issue of competence must be reviewed through the *contredit* procedure. CODE DE PROCÉDURE CIVILE art. 425; *cf.* DALLOZ, *op. cit. supra* note 277, at No. 71; Giverdon, *supra* note 113.

[290] *E.g.*, CUCHE & VINCENT 372; CORNU & FOYER 555.

[291] If such consent is not given, service of papers on the clerk of the court constitutes sufficient service on the defendant. CODE DE PROCÉDURE CIVILE art. 422. Decision of the case at the first hearing is rare. At least one more hearing is usually required. See CORNU & FOYER 555.

[292] See CODE DE PROCÉDURE CIVILE art. 432 (ordinary rules applicable if witnesses to be heard by *enquête*). To some extent rules of evidence are more liberal in commercial cases. See 7.38 (requirement of writing) and 7.49 (commercial books of account) *infra.*

[293] CODE DE PROCÉDURE CIVILE art. 429. The procedure is somewhat like an *expertise.* See 7.54 *infra.* The referee is analogized to a judge; within three days of his nomination, unless both parties agreed to his appointment, his disqualification may be demanded. CODE DE PROCÉDURE CIVILE art. 430.

[294] This procedure has been approved by the courts. See, *e.g.*, MOREL 415.

[295] On the *délibéré* procedure, which conserves judicial manpower, as one judge does the work of an entire panel consisting of at least three judges, see, *e.g.*, CORNU & FOYER 559; MOREL 416. On calendar practice before the commercial court, see 2 RAVIART, *op. cit. supra* note 67, at 500.

similar to those applicable to judgments of the *tribunaux de grande instance*. However, for each judgment the clerk of the court must prepare a summary of the proceedings (*qualités*) which must accompany the judgment proper. [296]

French commercial courts also act as courts of bankruptcy and courts of admiralty. [297] Since there exists a statutory prohibition against judicial rule-making, [298] it is interesting to note that the somewhat sketchy provisions of the Code of Civil Procedure are sometimes amplified by rules promulgated by various commercial courts.

In areas in which no commercial court exists, commercial matters are handled by the competent *tribunal de grande instance*. In such cases, [299] the *tribunal de grande instance* must follow the procedure prescribed for commercial courts. [300]

## 4. PROCEDURE BEFORE *CONSEILS DE PRUD'HOMMES*

### 7.18. General Characteristics

The procedure before the *conseils de prud'hommes* (labor courts) is extremely simple. The parties, who do not need professional counsel, have a rather wide choice of persons authorized to represent them. [301] An action before a labor court [302] must be preceded by a settlement attempt before its conciliation *bureau*. Unless both parties voluntarily appear before the conciliation *bureau*, the defendant is summoned by letter of the clerk of the court. The summons to the defendant must include all claims arising out of the same employment contract. [303]

[296] See, *e.g.*, CUCHE & VINCENT 408.

[297] For a brief discussion of the two French forms of bankruptcy, *faillite*, which leads to a distribution of the bankrupt's assets but not to his discharge, and *règlement judiciaire*, which involves a discharge, see AMOS & WALTON, INTRODUCTION TO FRENCH LAW 370–78 (2d ed. 1963); CODE DE COMMERCE arts. 437–626. Both proceedings are limited to merchants. On maritime matters, see CODE DE COMMERCE arts. 190–436. On the procedure for the recovery of small commercial debts, see 11.02.a *infra*.

[298] CODE CIVIL art. 5.

[299] CODE DE COMMERCE art. 640.

[300] CODE DE COMMERCE art. 641.

[301] Fellow workers and employees may act as representatives. See 2.01 *supra*.

[302] On the organization of the labor courts, see 3.27 *supra*. On the types of cases they may hear, see 4.40 *supra*.

[303] DÉCRET No. 58–1292 of Dec. 22, 1958, J.O. Dec. 23, 1958, p. 11621, [1959] B.L.D. 77, art. 68. The amount in controversy may be increased before the conciliation bureau. Either party may be put under oath before it. Failure to summon the defendant before the conciliation bureau renders the proceedings void. CORNU & FOYER 563; CUCHE & VINCENT 375. If the plaintiff does not appear at the settlement hearing, the case must be struck from the calendar and may be put back only once.

If some, but not all, points can be settled by the conciliation *bureau*, the action may deal only with the remaining issues. [304]

The action is started either by a *citation* served by an *huissier* or by registered letter, return receipt requested, addressed to the defendant. [305] The defendant must appear in court on the hearing date indicated in the summons. Time to appear is extremely short, ordinarily only one "free" day. [306] The court may order an *enquête* which is conducted before the court itself. [307] In most other respects, the procedure before the *tribunal d'instance* is followed. [308] Since the labor courts are composed of equal numbers of employer and employee representatives, a deadlock may occur. In that case, the judge of the local *tribunal d' instance* must be called in and the proceeding must be repeated before the court now augmented by that magistrate. [309] In districts in which no labor court exists, the *tribunal d'instance* handles the cases for which the labor courts are competent. It follows the procedure prescribed for these courts. [310]

### 5. PROCEDURE BEFORE SOCIAL SECURITY COURTS

### 7.19. General Characteristics

Two specialized courts deal with disputes between the various agencies (*caisses*) dispensing social security benefits and the persons liable for contributions or entitled to benefits: The first instance commissions (*commissions de première instance*) handle most general litigation, while the regional technical commissions (*commissions régionales techniques*) deal with disability evaluation and related predominantly medical matters.

In case [311] of a dispute with a *caisse*, an attempt at settlement must

[304] DÉCRET No. 58–1292, *supra* note 303, art. 68; CORNU & FOYER 563.

[305] DÉCRET No. 58–1292, *supra* note 303, art. 65. Either procedure is authorized by the DÉCRET, but the individual courts have rules prescribing which procedure must be used. If the defendant is summoned by registered letter and no return receipt is received, a *citation* must be served by *huissier*.

[306] In other words, if the defendant receives the letter or citation on January 2, he may be asked to appear at a hearing scheduled for January 4. The time limits are extended if the defendant does not live in the municipality where the court is located; the defendant has three days if he lives in the same canton or in a neighboring canton, five days if he lives elsewhere in the same or a neighboring *département*, and fifteen days if he lives in another part of continental France.

[307] DÉCRET No. 58–1292, *supra* note 303, art. 67.

[308] DÉCRET No. 58–1292, *supra* note 303, art. 74. However, written *conclusions* are expressly authorized before the labor court. DÉCRET No. 58–1292, *supra* note 303, art. 69.

[309] DÉCRET No. 58–1292, *supra* note 303, art. 60.

[310] DÉCRET No. 58–1292, *supra* note 303, art. 74.

[311] On the organization of the social security commissions, see 3.29 *supra*. On the types of cases they hear, see 4.42 *supra*.

first be made by recourse to a conciliation board forming part of the *caisse* itself. [312]

Parties have two months from the date of an unfavorable decision [313] to bring the matter before the first instance commission by a petition filed in its clerk's office or mailed to the commission by registered mail. [314] Parties are called to a hearing by letter sent by the clerk. They must get at least fifteen days' notice and do not need the assistance of professional counsel. [315] Both parties may submit written memoranda. Such memoranda may also be submitted by various officials supervising the operation of the social security agencies. [316] The commission may request all parties to submit documents or other information. The rules concerning the contents of the judgment are rather similar to those applicable to the *tribunal d'instance*. The judgment is sent to the interested parties by the clerk of the commission. [317]

In cases falling within the competence of a regional technical commission, the parties have one month from the date they received notice of the decision of a *caisse* to request review. The request is made by registered letter, return receipt requested. The procedure is almost entirely written. The decision is based on the records and memoranda submitted by the parties. However, a medical examination of the person entitled to benefits may be ordered. [318]

## 6. PROCEDURE BEFORE *TRIBUNAUX PARITAIRES DE BAUX RURAUX*

### 7.20. General Characteristics

The procedure before the *tribunaux paritaires de baux ruraux* follows generally that before the *tribunaux d'instance*. [319] Before any action is brought, an attempt at settlement must be made before the court. A

[312] DÉCRET No. 58–1291 of Dec. 22, 1958, J.O. Dec. 23, 1958, p. 11613, [1959] D.L. 49, arts. 1–6.

[313] DÉCRET No. 58–1291, *supra* note 312, art. 15. The two months period runs from the final decision of the conciliation board. If the board fails to render a decision, recourse to the first instance commission must be taken within one month from the time the matter was submitted.

[314] DÉCRET No. 58–1291, *supra* note 312, art. 15.

[315] On the persons authorized to represent parties before the social security commissions, see 2.01 *supra*.

[316] DÉCRET No. 58–1291, *supra* note 312, art. 17.

[317] DÉCRET No. 58–1291, *supra* note 312, art. 23. Article 18 permits the presiding judge of the commission to decide a case if its regular membership is not present. The commission should try to settle the case if at all possible.

[318] DÉCRET No. 58–1291, *supra* note 312, arts. 33–37.

[319] DÉCRET No. 58–1293 of Dec. 22, 1958, J.O. Dec. 23, 1958, p. 11627, [1959] B.L.D. 87, art. 10.

party failing to appear for the settlement attempt may be fined up to 20 francs (about $ 4.—).[320] If the settlement attempt fails, the proceeding is initiated by registered letter addressed to the clerk of the court. The presiding judge of the court, who is the judge of the local *tribunal d'instance*, sets a date for the hearing. The assessors are summoned to the hearing by the clerk.[321]

Unless they have a legitimate excuse, parties must be personally present at the hearing. They may be assisted by a member of their family, an *avocat*, *avoué*, or *huissier*, or by a member of an agricultural organization.[322] Either party may demand the disqualification of an assessor related to the other side.[323] The issue of disqualification must be decided by the presiding judge alone.[324] Hearings before a *tribunal paritaire* are ordinarily public, but the court may exclude spectators. The judgment must always be rendered at a public hearing. Judgments are mailed to the parties by registered mail and may be used as a basis for execution without further formality.[325] The presiding judge of the court may render provisional relief under the *référé* procedure.[326] If a *tribunal paritaire* is abolished, its functions are taken over by the local *tribunal d'instance* which follows its own procedure.[327]

## 7. PROCEDURE BEFORE THE PRESIDING JUDGE OF THE *TRIBUNAL DE GRANDE INSTANCE* ACTING AS A SINGLE JUDGE IN RENT CONTROL CASES

### 7.21. General Characteristics

Disputes between landlords and tenants involving apartments subject to rent control are brought before the presiding judge of the *tribunal de grande instance* of the locality in which the demised premises are located if the annual rental exceeds 1500 francs (about $ 300), or – in

[320] DÉCRET No. 58–1293, *supra* note 319, art. 14.

[321] DÉCRET No. 58–1293, *supra* note 319, art. 11. The court consists of the judge of the local *tribunal d'instance* and of an equal number of lessor and tenant representatives acting as assessors. See 3.28 *supra*. On the types of cases which may be heard by the *tribunal d'instance*, see 4.41 *supra*.

[322] DÉCRET No. 58–1293, *supra* note 319, art. 12. If the parties have a valid excuse, the persons authorized to assist them may appear in their behalf.

[323] Disqualification of an assessor may be demanded if he is related to a party, or was involved in a law suit with a party within the last five years, or has given a written consultation on the case, or is an employee, employer, tenant or lessor of one of the parties. DÉCRET No. 58–1923, *supra* note 319, art. 16.

[324] DÉCRET No. 58–1293, *supra* note 319, art. 17.

[325] DÉCRET No. 58–1293, *supra* note 319, art. 19. Decisions are rendered by a simple majority. They must be accompanied by an opinion.

[326] DÉCRET No. 58–1293, *supra* note 319, art. 20.

[327] DÉCRET No. 58–1293, *supra* note 319, art. 22.

the case of furnished apartments – if the monthly rental exceeds 300 francs (about $ 60). [328] When hearing such cases, the presiding judge sits alone. Either an *avocat* or an *avoué* may fulfil the regular functions of both *avocat* and *avoué*. An *ajournement* is used; time to appear is the same as that before the *tribunaux de grande instance*. At any stage of the proceedings the judge may attempt a settlement. In all other respects, the *référé* procedure must be followed. [329]

## 8. PROOF PROCEEDINGS

### 7.22. Introduction

The drafters of the rules of evidence embodied in the French codes notably the *Code Civil* and the *Code de Procédure Civile* – were subject to divergent influences. On the one hand, the medieval tradition of mechanical rules of proof, which left the judges no leeway in the evaluation of evidence, continued to exercise its influence. On the other hand, the notion that the judges should decide controversies on the basis of their *conviction intime* (inner conviction) and should be free to take into account any evidence they considered proper was in steady ascendance. The draftsmen's efforts to blend these disparate trends into a harmonious scheme did not lead to success. [330]

Furthermore, the chief familiarity of the draftsmen was with litigation in contract, property, and decedent estate matters, in which litigation may be reduced by careful preparation of documentary evidence. Accordingly, they concentrated their efforts on detailed regulation of such evidence, which was called *preuve préconstituée* (proof prepared in advance). At present, however, accident and divorce cases, in which the preparation of documentary evidence contemporaneously with the event is difficult, constitute the bulk of litigation. In these cases, resort must ordinarily be taken to other types of evidence which have not received as detailed and careful consideration from the legislators. [331]

[328] Law No. 48–1360, of Sept. 1, 1948, J.O. Sept. 2, 1948, p. 8659, [1948] D.L. 300, as amended, art. 48. If the rental is less than that indicated in the text, the case is brought before the *tribunal d'instance*, which follows its ordinary procedure. Law No. 48–1360, *supra*, art. 47.

[329] Law No. 48–1360, *supra* note 328, art. 48.

[330] *Cf.* MOREL 378; CUCHE & VINCENT 540. For discussions of French law of evidence, see Giverdon, *The Problem of Proof in French Civil Law*, 31 TUL. L. REV. 28 (1956); Hamson, *Civil Procedure in France and England*, 10 CAMB. L. J. 411 (1950); Millar, *The Mechanism of Fact Discovery*, 32 ILL. L. REV. 261 (1937); Tyndale, *Outline of French Procedure with respect to the Production of Evidence*, 13 CAN. B. REV. 655 (1935); BODINGHAM, OUTLINE OF THE FRENCH LAW OF EVIDENCE (1904).

[331] See LEGEAIS, LES RÈGLES DE PREUVE EN DROIT CIVIL "PERMANENCES ET TRANSFOR-

Additional factors responsible for present-day deficiencies in French rules of evidence include (1) the traditional attenuated interest of French scholars in the subject, [332] (2) the absence of an integrated treatment of the subject in the standard commentaries due to the distribution of pertinent statutory provisions between the *Code Civil* and the *Code de Procédure Civile,* and (3) the very limited rôle played by the *Cour de Cassation* in reviewing and bringing uniformity to lower court decisions involving applications of rules of evidence. [333]

### 7.23. The Rôle of the Court in Ascertaining Facts

French civil courts determine both the law and the facts: There is no distribution of adjudicatory functions between the judges and a jury. Although the French procedural system has been described as inquisitorial, the basic principle in civil matters is that of neutrality of the judge. [334] As a general rule, the court, in finding facts, may take and consider only evidence suggested and submitted by the parties; indeed, it is even questionable whether French courts may judicially notice "notorious" facts. [335] To describe the French procedural system, although the introduction of other than documentary or tangible proof ordinarily requires an affirmative decision by the court, [336] the term inquisitorial therefore seems inapposite.

### 7.24. Waiver of Rules of Evidence

As a general rule, application of rules of evidence may be waived, [337] either explicitly by contract [338] or implicitly by conduct. [339] Rules of

MATIONS" 4–14 (1955); SICARD, LA PREUVE EN JUSTICE APRÈS LA RÉFORME JUDICIAIRE 19–20, 66 (1960). The general rules concerning the admissibility and effect of evidence were put in the CODE CIVIL section on obligations, CODE CIVIL arts. 1315–69.

[332] This may be due to a predilection of French scholars for topics of a more abstract nature. *Cf.* 1 DAVID, LE DROIT FRANÇAIS 130–31 (1960).

[333] SICARD, *op. cit. supra* note 331, at 3; DAVID & DE VRIES, THE FRENCH LEGAL SYSTEM 77 (1958). French courts must write an opinion in every case. If the decision of the court indicates that one of the rules of proof has been violated, the *Cour de Cassation* reverses. Dlle Gramont v. Dlle Manabé, Cass. Civ., Dec. 15, 1930, [1932] D. 1. 144.

[334] See, *e.g.*, 1 JULLIOT DE LA MORANDIÈRE 268.

[335] 12 AUBRY & RAU, DROIT CIVIL FRANÇAIS 58 (6th ed. Esmein 1958) (citing numerous cases); MOREL 378. Of course, the courts take judicial notice of French law. The problem of judicial notice is frequently ignored because the *Cour de Cassation,* when reviewing a judgment, rarely goes beyond recitals in the opinion. As a result, facts judges learned unofficially may not be clearly identified as such. See Chevallier, *Remarques sur l'utilisation par le juge de ses informations personnelles,* 61 REV. TRIM. DR. CIV. 5 (1962).

[336] See 7.01 *supra.*

[337] LEGEAIS, *op. cit. supra* note 331, at 134. Legeais favors strict application of the rules of evidence.

[338] *E.g.*, Laroche v. Mesnard, Cass. Req., March 20, 1876, [1877] S. 1. 338 (agreement between parties that they would rely on the account books given effect, though account books of non-merchants are not ordinarily evidence).

[339] *E.g.*, Le Corbusier v. Cie La Nation, Cass. Civ., July 11, 1947, [1949] GAZ. PAL. 2. 318

evidence of which application is waived may neither be applied by the lower courts on their own motion nor be invoked for the first time before the *Cour de Cassation.* [340]

By way of exception, application of some rules of evidence cannot be waived. Among these rules are those relating to proof in actions involving personal status, rules relating to the probative effect of notarial and other official documents, [341] and rules guarding against disclosure of confidential communications. [342]

### 7.25. The Probative Effect of the Various Means of Proof

The probative weight of some types of evidence is prescribed by law. [343] Thus, a decisory oath (*serment décisoire*) is absolutely conclusive; [344] notarial and other authentic documents are conclusive unless impeached in a special proceeding (*inscription de faux*); [345] and a private writing, acknowledged to have been signed, constitutes conclusive proof against the signatory in the absence of countervailing proof. [346]

The weight of other types of proof may be freely determined by the court. For example, the testimony of witnesses, extra-judicial admissions, and reports of experts are subject to free judicial evaluation. [347]

Finally, certain types of evidence are not independently sufficient. Included in these is the testimony of criminals, who may not be sworn. [348]

Because of the limited scope of review by the *Cour de Cassation* and the great freedom of lower courts to rely on *présomptions de fait* (infer-

(person who collected rent in building estopped from questioning date of lease, though ordinarily documents not subjected to *enregistrement* have no evidentiary value as far as their date is concerned); Etourneau v. consorts Hélie, Cass. Req., Aug. 1, 1906, [1909] D. 1. 398; *cf.* Halbritter v. Wieser, Cass. Civ., July 7, 1949, [1949] BULL. CIV. III. 806 (by calling a witness himself, defendant waived the right to object to oral testimony that would otherwise have been inadmissible).

340 This is in accord with the general rule concerning questions involving public policy (*ordre public*). 1 JULLIOT DE LA MORANDIÈRE 267.

341 *Ibid.* On notarial instruments, see 7.43 *infra.*

342 Waiver of evidentiary rules is discussed in greater detail below. See, *e.g.*, 7.38.d *infra.*

343 *Cf.* LEGEAIS, *op. cit. supra* note 331, at 91.

344 See 7.56.a *infra.*

345 Such documents must be impeached by *inscription de faux.* See 7.43–7.44 *infra.*

346 See 7.45 *infra.*

347 Thus, even uncontradicted testimony may be disbelieved. See 7.51.f *infra.*

348 In this case, the French speak of evidence that has the value of *simples renseignements* (simple information). In addition to the unsworn testimony of criminals, this class includes inferences.

ences of fact), the differences between these categories is not always of great practical significance.

### 7.26. Rules Regulating the Admissibility of Evidence in Proof Proceedings

A court may authorize the taking of evidence in a proof proceeding only if the facts to be shown by that evidence are *admissibles, pertinents*, and *concluants*. [349]

**a. The requirement that the facts to be shown be *admissible*.** The requirement of admissibility has a dual aspect: First, no evidence may be admitted to establish facts the proof of which is prohibited; [350] second, when the law requires a particular method of proof, such as documentary evidence, other proof may not be used.

**b. The requirement that the evidence be *pertinent et concluant*.** According to a recent French author, the requirement that only facts that are *pertinents* and *concluants* may be shown is the equivalent of the common law rule requiring evidence to be relevant and material. [351]The requirement has three distinct meanings. First, facts to be shown must be legally relevant. [352] Second, proof offered by a party must have a

[349] These requirements are mentioned in the CODE DE PROCÉDURE CIVILE only in connection with the *enquête*, but it is generally assumed that they are applicable in all cases. 2 DALLOZ, RÉPERTOIRE DE PROCÉDURE CIVILE, *Preuve*, No. 26 (1956); Chevallier, *Le contrôle de la Cour de Cassation sur la pertinence de l'offre de preuve*, [1956] D. CHR. 37, 39.

[350] Thus, in order to avoid public scandal, proof tending to show that a child is the issue of an adulterous or incestuous relationship is prohibited. CODE CIVIL art. 342; *cf.* also CODE CIVIL art. 340 (facts excluding paternity suits).

A person accused of defamation may show the truth of his statements, unless they concern merely the private life of the plaintiff or involve facts more than 10 years old or certain criminal convictions. ORDONNANCE of May 6, 1944, J.O. Sept. 12, 1944, p. 87, [1944] D. ANAL. LEG. 99; *cf.* Alric, Cass. Crim., March 3, 1949, [1949] D.J. 205 (denouncing persons to *gendarmes* not matter of private life). See generally 1 MAZEAUD & TUNC, TRAITÉ THÉORIQUE ET PRATIQUE DE LA RESPONSABILITÉ CIVILE 896 (5th ed. 1957). The opposition of French legislation against the disclosure of scandalous matters in law suits seems to be waning.

[351] Chevallier, *supra* note 349. It is perhaps a reflection on the relatively undeveloped condition of the French law of evidence that Chevallier uses several (untranslated) English terms. One of the leading older French texts suggests that *pertinent* refers to facts that will convince the court that plaintiff has established his claim, while *concluant* refers to facts showing that defendant has established his defense. 2 GARSONNET & CÉZAR-BRU 375. This seems wrong. Though the meanings of *pertinent* and of *concluant* tend to coalesce and both terms are nearly always used together, *pertinent* implies the requirement of relevance and *concluant* the requirement of probative value. *Cf.* DALLOZ, *op. cit. supra* note 349, at 32–35; 7 PLANIOL & RIPERT, TRAITÉ PRATIQUE DE DROIT CIVIL 837–39; 12 AUBRY & RAU 68.

[352] In an action against a principal, evidence concerning the negligence of an agent will, therefore, have to be rejected whenever the rule of *respondeat superior* is not applicable. *Cf.* La Courade et Mouillefarine v. Soc. d'assurances mutelles Seine et Seine et Oise, Cass. Civ., Nov. 27, 1929, [1930] S. 1. 247; Chevallier, *supra* note 349.

reasonable degree of probative value. While there is no hearsay rule, [353] testimony may properly be rejected if the witness has only very remote knowledge of the facts. [354] Third, a proof offer must be rejected if it is useless, either because the court has already made up its mind [355] or because the court believes that it cannot possibly be successful. [356]

**c. Review of rulings on admissibility by the *Cour de Cassation.*** Rulings on whether the evidence proffered is admissible are always subject to review by the *Cour de Cassation.* [357] However, rulings on whether the evidence is reasonably probative involve the exercise of the lower court's discretion in evaluating the proposed evidence and, as a consequence, are ordinarily not subject to *Cour de Cassation* review. [358] Although the *Cour de Cassation,* in some recent cases, has departed from the principle of non-reviewability of rulings on the probative effect of proposed evidence, [359] the facts of these cases were exceptional and do not warrant the conclusion that the principle has been relinquished. [360]

### 7.27. The Standard of Proof in Civil Cases

**a. General observations.** No legislative provision of general import defines the standard of proof to be met in civil cases. The problem of

[353] See 7.51.d *infra.*

[354] *Cf.* Dame Guemassia v. Guaemassia, Cass. Civ., Dec. 17, 1954, [1955] D.J. 255 (court properly rejected request by wife to hear friend testify to fact that friend had been instructed by wife to tell wife's mother that defendant was engaging in unnatural practices).

[355] Couture v. Dlle Escure, Cass. Civ., June 17, 1953, [1953] D.J. 611, [1953] J.C.P. 2. 7822 (putative father in paternity proceeding not granted blood grouping test when letters by him submitted to the court showed that he considered the child as his); Sté La Manufacture Weill v. Dame Dutestre, Cass. Civ., July 20, 1955, [1955] Bull. Civ. 508.

[356] A proof proceeding is considered useless if, under all the facts, a party is unlikely to prove the facts it wants to establish. Thus, in a filiation case a request for a blood grouping test may be rejected if the mother and the presumed father of the child are close relatives. Likewise, a request to authorize the examination of a dead body by an expert may be rejected if death has occurred so long ago that the examination is unlikely to discover anything useful. *Cf.* Comp. d'assurances "La Prévoyance" v. S.A.R.L. Malta Steamship, Cass. Com., March 15, 1955, [1955] Bull. Civ. 3. 101.

[357] La Courade et Mouillefarine v. Soc. d'assurances mutuelles Seine et Seine et Oise, *supra* note 352 (since relevance of evidence depends on application of *respondeat superior* doctrine, exclusion of evidence may be reviewed by *Cour de Cassation*); Teulade v. Vve Bonnefoy, Cass. Civ., July 20, 1925, [1926] S. 1. 221 (since relevance of evidence depending on rules governing co-ownership, question reviewable by *Cour de Cassation*).

[358] Thus, the *Cour de Cassation* did not interfere with the decision of a lower court rejecting a blood grouping test on the ground that other evidence firmly established the paternity of the defendant. Couture v. Dlle Escure, *supra* note 355.

[359] Bezombes v. Dlle Teyssie, Cass. Civ., July 25, 1949, [1949] D.J. 585 (note by Carbonnier) (rejection of blood grouping test held reversible error).

[360] *Cf.* Sicard, La Preuve en Justice après la réforme judiciaire 29 (1960), to the effect that the courts have tried to be realistic rather than to create an intellectually satisfying system.

defining that standard arises in all cases in which the probative effect to be attached to the particular evidence introduced is not defined by a mechanical rule. Because of the large degree of freedom in evaluating evidence enjoyed by the courts,[361] the problem is of little practical interest. French authors usually state that the conclusions reached need not be absolutely true, but that it is sufficient if they are probable. [362]

### 7.28. Rules Allocating the Burden of Proof *(Charge de la Preuve)*

Of greater practical importance are the rules determining the allocation of the burdens of proof. French law and doctrine make no sharp distinction between the burden of going forward – that is, the burden of producing sufficient evidence to permit the court to find in favor of the proponent of the evidence – and the burden of persuasion [363] that is, the burden of actually persuading the court to find in favor of the proponent of the evidence. Since the court must determine both the law and the facts and no procedural motion is available to test whether sufficient evidence has been introduced to permit the court to find a certain way before the court decides which way it will actually find, the distinction between the two burdens is of no practical significance. Some French cases and authors state that the party having the burden of proof must lose if the evidence for both sides is evenly balanced [364] and that the party having the burden of proof must also go forward with the evidence, but a clear distinction is not usually made. [365]

There are no general statutory rules allocating burdens of proof. Article 1315 of the *Code Civil* provides that he who demands the fulfillment of an obligation must prove its existence and that, conversely, he who asserts that an obligation has been extinguished must so prove. These rules, embodied in the Civil Code chapter on contracts, have been extended by way of expansive interpretation to all other situations

[361] *Compare* Dame Moulinier v. Moulinier, Cass. Civ., July 30, 1951, [1951] J.C.P. 2. 6526, *with* Rousseau v. Rousseau, Cass. Civ., July 4, 1912, [1913] S. 1. 390. Both cases involved practically identical fact situations, but the lower courts came to opposite conclusions. Both were affirmed by the *Cour de Cassation* on the ground that the lower courts have a large degree of discretion in the evaluation of evidence.

[362] *E.g.*, 7 PLANIOL & RIPERT, TRAITÉ PRATIQUE DE DROIT CIVIL FRANÇAIS Nos. 98–101 (1952).

[363] For common law definitions of these terms, see 9 WIGMORE, EVIDENCE 2485–89 (3d ed. 1940); 2 CONRAD, MODERN TRIAL EVIDENCE §§ 931–32 (1956).

[364] LEGEAIS, LES RÈGLES DE PREUVE EN DROIT CIVIL, "PERMANENCES ET TRANSFORMATIONS" 177 (1955); *cf.* Consorts Bonnard v. Consorts Bowers, Cour Paris, Jan. 19, 1953, [1953] J.C.P. 2. 7427.

[365] *E.g.*, ben Mohamed v. Tannucci, Cass. Com., June 12, 1950, [1950] D.J. 615; *cf.* Dewavrin v. Pion, Cass. Civ., April 5, 1927, [1927] S. 1. 222; Guillemette v. Tondut, Cass. Civ., March 3, 1926, [1926] S. 1. 167.

not covered by a specific statutory provision:[366] The plaintiff must prove all elements of his claim for relief, and the defendant must prove all affirmative defenses. Since it requires determination of what is an element of plaintiff's cause of action and what is an affirmative defense, this more general rule merely shifts the problem.

At one time, the now abandoned view was espoused that, since *negativa non sunt probanda*, the burden of proof rests on the party who asserts the affirmative of a proposition.[367] In more recent times, the realization has gained ground that no satisfactory rule of general application can be formulated.[368] On the whole, the courts have been influenced by considerations of policy and fairness and have frequently imposed the burden of proof on the party most likely to be in possession of pertinent evidence.[369] Some more specific examples may illustrate.

**a. Burden of proof in contract cases.** In an action on a contract, plaintiff has the burden of proving the existence of the contract and its breach.[370] However, lack of capacity to contract and fraud are affirmative defenses which must be proven by the defendant.[371] In actions on promissory notes and other so-called unilateral obligations, in which no *cause*[372] appears on the face of the instrument, the defendant has the burden of proving absence of *cause*.[373]

These general rules have been modified by statute in actions on contracts of insurance. In an action on a life insurance policy,[374] the insurance company has the burden of proving suicide, but in the case of an accident policy the beneficiary must show the insured died as a

[366] SICARD, *op. cit. supra* note 331, at 39; 2 GARSONNET & CÉZAR-BRU 376.

[367] *E.g.*, Casamajou-Puyou-Coos v. Larrieu-Baluhet, Cass. Req., July 26, 1934, [1935] S. 1. 5.

[368] See the discussion in 12 AUBRY & RAU, DROIT CIVIL FRANÇAIS 76 (6th ed. Esmein 1958), concerning attempts made in earlier editions of the work, especially the fifth edition edited by Bartin, to provide a classification of various situations.

[369] SICARD, *op. cit. supra* note 331, at 42. As an example, Sicard cites the rule that, while the burden of proof on causation is ordinarily on the plaintiff, the railroad must prove that an injury ostensibly sustained during a railroad accident was not caused by it.

[370] *E.g.*, Casamajou v. Larrieu-Balubet, *supra* note 367; Humeau v. Consorts Galory, Cass. Civ., Dec. 19, 1944, [1945] GAZ. PAL. 73 (plaintiff showed he had given money to defendant, but did not show what transaction was involved; defendant asserted he had received the money for investment purposes; held, plaintiff had the burden of showing what transaction was involved and must lose since he failed to do so).

[371] *E.g.*, 12 AUBRY & RAU 76.

[372] On *cause*, as an element of the French law of contracts, see VON MEHREN, THE CIVIL LAW SYSTEM 515 (1957).

[373] This is the rule established by case law. Many legal writers have a contrary opinion. See SICARD, *op. cit. supra* note 331, at 45; 2 GARSONNET & CÉZAR-BRU 378.

[374] Law of July 13, 1930, J.O. July 18, 1930, [1931] D. 4. 1, art. 62. Under this article, the insurer need not pay the policy amount in case of voluntary suicide; if the insurer has shown suicide, the beneficiary has the burden of showing the suicide was not voluntary.

result of an accident and not by suicide. [375] In actions on public liability policies, the insurer has the burden of proof of facts that would exclude his liability. [376] On the other hand, in the case of actions on casualty policies excluding coverage for war risks, the insured must prove the loss not to have been due to an act of war. [377]

**b. Burden of proof in property matters.** Although in property matters the burden of proof is usually on the party not in possession, [378] there are some exceptions. A person relying on adverse possession against the holder of the title of record must show when his adverse possession began. [379] If the existence of an easement is in question, the owner of the dominant estate must show that his easement has not been extinguished by non-user. [380]

**c. Burden of proof in tort cases.** In tort cases, the plaintiff ordinarily has the burden of proving fault, causation, and harm. However, in automobile cases and in other accidents caused by equipment for which defendant is responsible, article 1384 of the *Code Civil* creates a presumption of liability by imposing on the defendant the burden of showing that the accident was not caused by the automobile or other equipment. [381]

In building accident cases, the burden is on the defendant to show the damage was not due to faulty construction or maintenance. [382]

A defendant relying on rules protecting persons carrying passengers gratuitously must show that in fact no compensation was received. [383]

[375] Vve Blardone v. Cie d'assurances L'Abeille, Cass. Civ., Oct. 29, 1940, [1940] D.H. 196.

[376] For example, if an automobile policy excludes liability for accidents caused by unlicensed drivers, the insurer must show the driver was unlicensed. Cie d'assurances La Mutuelle Richelieu v. Epoux Carpentier, Cass. Civ., Jan. 7, 1936, [1936] D. 1. 84. If a policy excludes damage done by intoxicated drivers, the insurer must show intoxication. Vve Menessier v. Comp. d'assurances La Zurich, Cour Lyon, Dec. 15, 1952, [1953] S. 2. 112.

[377] Law of July 13, 1930, *supra* note 374, art. 34.

[378] SICARD, *op. cit. supra* note 331, at 41, 43 (1961).

[379] Maury v. Giron, Cass. Civ., Jan. 9, 1893, [1894] D. 1. 339 (defendant who relies on adverse possession must show when it started). However, in case of the special summary proceeding for the recovery of possession of land (*complainte*), which must be brought within one year from ouster, the plaintiff must show that the ouster occurred within a year. Vve Prouteau v. Vve Gaulthier, Cass. Civ., Oct. 28, 1891, [1892] S. 1. 183.

[380] Duvivier v. Poulet et consorts, Cass. Req., Feb. 15, 1842, [1842] S. 1. 344.

[381] SICARD, *op. cit. supra* note 331, at 43. *But see* 2 COLIN & CAPITANT 225 (plaintiff does not have to show excessive speed caused accident, but defendant must show his excessive speed did not cause accident). On the presumption of fault of article 1384, see also 7.30.b *infra*.

[382] CODE CIVIL art. 1386 provides that the owner of a building is liable for damages caused by its ruin, if due to defective construction or maintenance. See also 2 COLIN & CAPITANT 262–64.

[383] SICARD, *op. cit. supra* note 331, at 43. The presumption of fault of article 1384 is inapplicable to gratuitous passengers. 2 COLIN & CAPITANT 231. Contracts exempting from

A plaintiff suing a physician on account of an unauthorized operation has the burden of proving that he was not sufficiently informed of the nature and seriousness of the treatment. [384]

A person seeking reformation of a contract on account of fraud or duress is under a duty to show the existence of these facts. [385]

In tort cases, the statute of limitations is considered an affirmative defense to be proved by the defendant. [386]

## 7.29. *Présomptions* (Presumptions and Inferences)

*Présomptions* are one of the important means of legal proof provided for by the Civil Code. Article 1349 of the Civil Code defines *présomptions* as conclusions about unknown facts that the law or the court draws from known facts. When the conclusion to be drawn is prescribed by law, it is called a *présomption légale* (presumption); when it is merely an inference that may be drawn by the court, it is called a *présomption simple* or *présomption de fait.* [387] The distinction between presumptions and inferences is not always clearly discerned.[388] Furthermore, the statutory provisions frequently do not indicate with clarity whether *présomptions* are rebuttable or irrebuttable. [389] Consequently, the rules in this field have largely been developed by *doctrine* and the courts.

Some general rules concerning *présomptions* are contained in a special section of the *Code Civil.* In addition, specific provisions for *présomptions* are found in a large number of sundry statutory provisions. [390]

liability for fault are illegal, but the parties may modify the rules as to burden of proof. *Id.* at 228–30.

[384] Cons. Y. v. B., Cass. Civ., May 29, 1951, [1952] D.J. 53 (note by Savatier) (it was assumed that the patient had voluntarily consented to some sort of treatment).

[385] Comp. d'assurances la Paternelle v. Breuil, Cass. Civ., Feb. 5, 1894, [1894] D. 1. 134, [1894] S. 1. 277.

[386] SICARD, *op. cit. supra* note 331, at 44. The rule is applicable not only to the general thirty-year limitation of CODE CIVIL art. 2262, but also to the special ten-year limitation concerning the liability of builders and architects of article 2270.

[387] The French term *présomption* (*présomption simple, présomption de fait*) is sometimes translated as circumstantial evidence. *Cf.* 7.31 *infra.*

[388] See, *e.g.*, RIPERT, TRAITE ELÉMENTAIRE DE DROIT COMMERCIAL 143 (3d ed. 1954), as translated in VON MEHREN, THE CIVIL LAW SYSTEM 628 (1957) (proof by simple presumptions). The CODE CIVIL section on presumptions (articles 1349–52) have been called "the worst" of the Code. Mimin, *Les Présomptions Quasi-Légales*, [1946] J.C.P. 1. 58.

[389] See 7.30 *infra.* Additionally, rules of substantive law are sometimes phrased in terms of presumptions. The principle of res judicata is called a presumption. CODE CIVIL art. 1350; *cf.* also CODE CIVIL art. 1759 (tenant overstaying lease is presumed to be governed by lease usual in community).

[390] A list enumerating a large number of French presumptions is contained in 2 DALLOZ, RÉPERTOIRE DE PROCÉDURE CIVILE ET COMMERCIALE, *Preuve*, No. 104 (1956). Article 1350 of the CODE CIVIL, which, like all other articles dealing with evidence in general, is found in the Code chapter on contracts, contains a classification scheme for presumptions. According to it, presumptions involve either (1) rules that declare an act void because presumed in fraud of the law, or (2) rules that establish ownership or payment on the basis of certain facts, or (3) the rule

Although it is often stated that only *présomptions* prescribed by statute may be recognized, [391] the courts, by giving pertinent statutory texts an embracive interpretation, have in fact created *présomptions* not envisioned by the legislator. [392]

## 7.30. Effects of *Présomptions Légales*

*Présomptions légales* (presumptions) may be rebuttable or irrebuttable. Since, as a rule, the pertinent statutory provisions are silent, the courts have been saddled with the task of determining whether a presumption is rebuttable or irrebuttable. In carrying out this task, the courts have made further distinctions between (1) presumptions that may be rebutted without any special limitation, (2) presumptions that may be rebutted only by specified persons or by proof of specified facts, and (3) presumptions that may be rebutted only by specified means of proof. [393]

**a. Presumptions that may be rebutted freely.** Some *présomptions* may be rebutted freely, without limitations of any kind. These include the presumption that a person registered as a *commerçant* in the commercial register is actually a *commerçant*, [394] the presumption of payment implied from surrender of the original copy (*grosse*) of a notarial document embodying recognition of the debt, [395] and the presumptions relating to simultaneous deaths. [396]

of res judicata, or (4) rules governing the effect of admissions and of the party-oath. There are many presumptions that cannot be classified under any of these headings (*e.g.*, the simultaneous death presumptions of articles 720–22). Besides, the rules governing the effect of admissions and of the party-oath are really rules of evidence, not presumptions, and the rule of res judicata is essentially a rule of substantive law. *Cf.* 1 JULLIOT DE LA MORANDIÈRE 308. It seems to make no difference in which subdivision a particular presumption belongs.

[391] 2 DALLOZ, *op. cit. supra* note 349, at Nos. 108–10.

[392] Mimin, *supra* note 388. Mimin lists among others: the presumption that a pregnancy lasts between 180 and 300 days, prescribed by CODE CIVIL art. 312, which creates a presumption of legitimacy of children born during marriage, has been extended to cases involving illegitimate children (*e.g.*, Lhuillier v. Langrognet, Cass. Civ., July 11, 1923, [1924] S. 1. 113); the presumption of joint (*solidaire*) liability of co-debtors in commercial law, created by analogy to the rules governing the liability of partners; and also the presumption of fault of article 1384 of the CODE CIVIL which was discovered by the courts only with the advent of automobiles.

[393] CODE CIVIL art. 1352 (second sentence) provides that, unless counterproof is specifically allowed, a presumption is irrebuttable if on the basis of the presumption certain acts are annulled or an action at law denied. For criticism of this provision, see 2 DALLOZ, *op. cit. supra* note 349, at Nos. 120–21. The presumptions listed below are merely examples of presumptions falling into each of the classes listed in the text. No effort has been made to include all presumptions.

[394] DÉCRET No. 58–1355 of Dec. 27, 1958, J.O. Dec. 29, 1958, p. 11971, [1959] B.L.D. 225, art. 15; *cf.* Jouffret, *La réforme du régistre du commerce*, [1953] D. CHR. 145, 147.

[395] CODE CIVIL art. 1283.

[396] CODE CIVIL arts. 720–22. These articles provide that if two persons under fifteen die

**b. Presumptions rebuttable only by specified persons or by proof of specified facts.** Presumptions that may be rebutted only by specified persons include the presumption of legitimacy, which may be rebutted only by the husband and, in exceptional circumstances, by his heirs. [397]

Presumptions that may be rebutted only by proof of specified facts include the presumption of legitimacy of a child conceived during marriage, which may be rebutted only by proof that absence or accidental injury prevented the husband from having intercourse with his wife between the three hundredth and one hundred and eightieth day before the child's birth. [398] Another example of a presumption so limited is that prescribed by article 1384 of the *Code Civil* which permits rebuttal of the presumption of fault in the case of an accident involving an automobile or other equipment under the control of the defendant only by proof that the accident was due to *force majeure* or to the act of a third party. [399]

**c. Presumptions that may be rebutted only by specified means of proof.** Certain presumptions can be rebutted only by specified means of proof. Thus for example, the presumption that the interest has been

under circumstances making it impossible to determine who died first, the older person is presumed to have survived; if the persons are all over sixty, the younger is presumed to have survived; if some are under fifteen and others over sixty, those under fifteen are presumed to have survived; if they are between fifteen and sixty, men are presumed to have survived women; if the age difference between them is less than one year, but if they are all of the same sex, the younger are presumed to have survived the older. The courts have disregarded these presumptions on slight proof as to the actual sequence of deaths. Bèsse v. Carrat, Cour Rouen, Feb. 8, 1949, [1950] J.C.P. 5269; *cf.* Vve Netter et Dame Mosbacher v. Emile Weil, Trib. Strasbourg, June 20, 1948, [1948] GAZ. PAL. 2. 217.

[397] CODE CIVIL art. 312 (presumption of legitimacy of child conceived during marriage). The husband's heirs may attack the legitimacy of the child only if the very short period for contesting legitimacy by the husband has not run at the time of his death and the child either acquires possession of the inheritance or threatens the heirs' possession of the inheritance. CODE CIVIL art. 317; Robert v. Fontaine, Cass. Req., Feb. 1, 1876, [1876] D. 1. 323; Ahmed ben Said v. Dame Russak, Cass. Civ., Oct. 10, 1955, [1956] D.J. 3. For another example, see CODE CIVIL arts. 1499, 1500–04.

[398] CODE CIVIL arts. 312–13. In case of spouses who have obtained a decree of divorce or judicial separation or who are suing each other for such relief, the presumption of legitimacy does not apply to children born more than three hundred days after an interlocutory order authorizing them to maintain separate residences.

[399] 12 AUBRY & RAU, *op. cit. supra* note 335, at 88; 2 COLIN & CAPITANT 264–78. Article 1384 has become one of the basic elements of present-day French tort law. See VON MEHREN, THE CIVIL LAW SYSTEM 382–413 (1957); LAWSON, NEGLIGENCE IN THE CIVIL LAW (1950); AMOS & WALTON, INTRODUCTION TO FRENCH LAW 203–06 (2d ed. 1963). The presumption of fault of article 1384 does not apply in favor of gratuitous passengers. Soc. Monnot et Cie v. Veuve Dusson, Cass. Civ., Feb. 19, 1945, [1945] D.J. 181; Huguonnet v. Guignard, Cass. Civ., Jan. 9, 1957, [1957] D.J. 196. *But see* Calais-Aulpis, *La chambre civile a-t-elle créé une présomption de faute à la charge du transporteur bénévole?*, [1963] D. CHR. 21. The courts must make a finding of special negligence if article 1384 is inapplicable; a general finding that the defendant must have been negligent in some manner is not sufficient.

paid when a receipt without reservation is given for the repayment of capital can be rebutted only by a party oath or an admission in court.[400] Similarly, the presumption that a wall, fence, or other structure located on a boundary is a party structure can be rebutted only by a title of record or specified marks on the property. [401]

**d. Irrebuttable presumptions.** Presumptions that are irrebuttable are actually rules of substantive law, disguised in the form of presumptions. For example, the French rule of *res judicata* is cast in the form of an irrebuttable presumption. [402] Similarly, the rule of *respondeat superior* [403] is often stated as an irrebuttable presumption of fault on the part of the principal. [404] Even the thirty-year statute of limitations is sometimes treated as an irrebuttable presumption of payment.

### 7.31. *Présomptions de Fait* (Inferences): Escape from Formal Rules of Evidence

The *Code Civil* provides that *présomptions de fait, présomptions simples,* or *présomptions de l'homme* (inferences) may be used as means of proof only in cases in which oral evidence is admissible. [405] This provision has received an extremely liberal interpretation. As construed by the courts, it authorizes not only the drawing of inferences from facts proven by legal means of proof, but also the drawing of inferences from any factual information submitted to the court, irrespective of whether such information was furnished by legal means of proof. [406] The consequences of this liberal construction have been pervasive and, as a practical matter, have deprived of any significant effect the rule that facts may be proven only by legal means of evidence: If the proof furnished is not in the appropriate form and therefore not a legal means of proof,

[400] Baudet v. Administration des Domaines, Cass. Civ., Jan. 13, 1875, [1875] S. 1. 244 (admission); *cf.* CODE CIVIL arts. 911 and 1100 (presumptions as to illegal gifts.)

[401] CODE CIVIL art. 666.

[402] CODE CIVIL art. 1350.

[403] CODE CIVIL art. 1384 (3).

[404] COLIN & CAPITANT 255–59.

[405] CODE CIVIL art. 1353. 12 AUBRY & RAU 306; 2 DALLOZ, *op. cit. supra* note 349, at 971–74. This excludes the use of inferences in many actions relating to personal status, since official birth, death, or marriage records are frequently the only admissible proof. See 7.35 *infra*. Inferences are also excluded in all the situations in which written evidence of contracts or of payment is required. See CODE CIVIL art. 1341; 7.36–7.43 *infra*.

[406] 12 AUBRY & RAU 308; SICARD, *op. cit. supra* note 331, at 296; 2 DALLOZ, *op. cit. supra* note 349, at No. 949; Epoux Barrau et Glaudis v. Brassier, Cass. Soc., Nov. 12, 1952, [1952] BULL. CIV. 3. 603.

the court may nevertheless rely on the deficient proof as the premise for a permissible inference. [407]

The rule permitting reliance on *présomptions de fait* thus has brought great flexibility to the law of evidence. In its practical application, it has been subject to only one important restriction: All documentary materials provided to the court as a basis for judicial inference must be submitted to all adverse parties to permit their comments and the introduction of counter proof. [408]

## 7.32. The Probative Weight of Inferences

According to article 1353 of the *Code Civil*, the drawing of inferences is left to the prudence of the court, which is cautioned to draw only inferences that are weighty, precise, and consistent. The requirement of consistency may be interpreted to prohibit reliance on a single unsupported inference. This interpretation finds support in the argument that otherwise almost all incentives to submit evidence by legal means of proof would be eliminated. [409] However, most French authors reject this limiting interpretation. [410]

The position of the *Cour de Cassation* has remained unclear. Although it has repeatedly declared that the admissibility and weight of inferential evidence are to be decided by the lower courts in the exercise of their discretion, [411] the *Cour de Cassation* did reverse a lower court

[407] Thus, parties sometimes avoid the *expertise* procedure by submitting written certificates of doctors or their experts, which the court may use as a basis for inferences; while the expert used on a regular *expertise* is always an impartial court appointee, certificates submitted by the parties are often partisan and in direct contradiction to each other. Generally speaking, courts put more faith in the report of an impartial expert secured through an *expertise* than in informal certificates. *Cf.* SICARD, *op. cit. supra* note 331, at 302–03. The *enquête* procedure may be avoided by the use of written statements secured from witnesses. Police files can likewise be used in civil actions and in fact often are. Sometimes, courts even prefer statements of witnesses contained in police reports over their oral testimony on the ground that the original statement may be less distorted by lapses of memory or collusion. See generally Deschamps v. Delprat, Cass. Req., Jan. 2, 1940, [1940] D.H. 89; Dame Costaceque v. Costaceque, Cass. Civ., March 29, 1949, [1949] D.J. 290.

[408] Additionally, as noted earlier, inferences are excluded in a considerable number of cases in which documentary evidence is required. See note 405 *supra*.

[409] A court may decide a case on the basis of the testimony of one single witness submitted during a formal *enquête*, or on the basis of the report of one single expert submitted during a regular *expertise*. See 7.51.f and 7.54.h *infra*.

[410] 12 AUBRY & RAU 308; 1 JULLIOT DE LA MORANDIÈRE 307; 2 DALLOZ, *op. cit. supra* note 349, at 979. They treat the Code requirement that inferences be consistent as directory only.

[411] See also Dame Tonnelier v. Tonnelier, Cass. Civ., Dec. 21, 1954, [1955] D.J. 271 (lower court refusal to make finding of adultery on basis of police report affirmed); Hargumdeguy v. Doulon Frères, Cass. Com., May 15, 1956, [1956] BULL. CIV. 3. 126 (lower court refusal to look at books not kept in accordance with legal rules affirmed); Dame Pitiot v. Pitiot, Cass. Civ., Dec. 12, 1949, [1950] GAZ. PAL. 1. 135 (rejection in divorce case of written statement of witness affirmed).

decision that rejected unsworn written statements of witnesses as lacking all probative value. [412] In any event, the exercise of judicial discretion in using inferential proof is not completely withdrawn from *Cour de Cassation* review, and, upon occasion, the court has reversed lower court decisions based on only one inference drawn from an otherwise inadmissible item of proof. [413]

### 7.33. Documentary Evidence

The framers of the codes expected documentary evidence to be the most important means of proof and carefully regulated the various means of documentary proof. In this way, they hoped to encourage the preparation of contemporaneously constituted written proof (*preuve préconstitué*) of as many transactions as possible. [414] Since at present a great deal of civil litigation relates to matters, such as divorce and tort cases, in which written proof of the kind envisaged by the legislators is ordinarily not available, their expectations have not been met. However, the liberal interpretation given to the rule permitting inferential proof has greatly stimulated reliance on documentary materials other than those specifically designated in the Code as legal means of proof: Documentary evidence is freely introduced to provide the premises on which the court can build inferences. [415]

### 7.34. Introduction of Documentary Evidence

A further factor favoring reliance on documentary evidence is the ease of its introduction. No court order permitting the introduction of the evidence, required in regard to all other means of proof, is necessary: Documentary evidence of all kinds [416] may simply be submitted at one of the hearings (*audiences*).

[412] Demoiselles Gayon v. Badet et autres, Cass. Civ., June 1, 1954, [1954] D.J. 589. The case can perhaps be explained on the ground that the court below seemed to create a kind of hearsay rule, which is no part of French law.

[413] Cazin v. Messain, Cass. Com., May 9, 1951, [1951] D.J. 472 (lower court decision based solely on entry in "irregular" books reversed). Campion v. Fauvel, Cass. Civ., June 26, 1889, [1890] D. 1. 135, and appended note; Dame Tritsch v. son mari, Trib. Seine, Feb. 16, 1957, [1957] G.P. 1. 309 (tape recording); *cf.* Consorts Gaumer v. Tissier, Cass. Civ., Nov. 29, 1932, [1933] S. 1. 70 (irregular expertise may be used, but court must specifiy what other, regular, evidence it has used to support its decision). *But see* Ihasusta v. Bianchi, Cass. Civ., March 17, 1938, [1938] D. 1. 115 (note by Mimin).

[414] Legeais, *op. cit. supra* note 331, at 112 (1955); Levy, *The Evolution of Written Proof*, 13 Am. U. L. Rev. 133 (1964); 7.22 *supra*.

[415] See Legeais, *op. cit. supra* note 331, at 133.

[416] Code Civil art. 1333 analogizes so called *tailles* to written evidence. *Tailles* are marks made in sticks of wood as evidence of the sale of bread or other household items. With the disappearance of illiteracy, *tailles* have practically disappeared. Sicard, *op. cit. supra* note

The lack of a special procedure for the introduction of documentary evidence prevents preliminary consideration of its admissibility or probative force. However, before being introduced in the proceedings, all documents must be submitted in advance for examination to adverse parties. [417] Usually, an *avoué* who wishes to introduce documentary evidence transmits it to the *avoué* of his client's opponent who returns it after a few days. In the rare case in which this procedure, called *communication des pièces,* is not followed, examination of any document may be requested by an *exception de communication des pièces* within three days after an adverse party has relied on the document or has served a copy thereof on the party requesting the examination. Production is requested by a simple notice (*acte d'avoué à avoué*). The time for examination is fixed by order of the *juge chargé de suivre la procédure* or court order or agreement between the *avoués*. The *avoué* who fails to return the document after examination is subject to penalties. [418]

In regard to books of account, in order to prevent disclosure of business secrets, the right to production is limited. Usually, the court orders the books to be turned over to the court itself or to an impartial court appointed expert who makes a report of this examination. Under this so-called *représentation* procedure, since the expert reports only on matters relating to the controversy, disclosure is limited to matters relating directly to the controversy. [419]

Full production of books of accounts can be obtained only in exceptional cases, including controversies concerning the estate or community property of a deceased *commerçant*, liquidation of a *société*, and bankruptcy. Even in those cases, however, the books are usually deposited with the court rather than temporarily surrendered to adverse parties. [420]

331, at 181. Boundary markers, license plates, and other items of quasi-documentary evidence are used as a basis for inferences. *Id.* at 181–82.

[417] CUCHE & VINCENT 537. If an *avoué* distrusts his opponent, he may deposit the documents at the court clerk's office to be inspected there, but this is done rarely. The requirement that all documents used in court must be made available to adverse parties is not satisfied by the production of copies, but copies are usually made available in addition.

[418] CODE DE PROCÉDURE CIVILE arts. 81, 189–91 .There is a special summary procedure to compel restitution of documents detained by an *avoué*. CODE DE PROCÉDURE CIVILE art. 191. See Appendix, Form No. 15.

[419] CODE DE COMMERCE arts. 15–17; 1 HAMEL & LAGARDE, TRAITÉ DE DROIT COMMERCIAL 305 (1954).

[420] CODE DE COMMERCE art. 14; 1 HAMEL & LAGARDE, *op. cit. supra* note 419, at 302–04. However, a businessman may obligate himself by contract to produce his books in case of litigation.

## 7.35. The Requirement of Documentary Proof of Personal Status

As a general rule, birth, marriage, and death may be proved only by authenticated copies of entries in official registers. [421] Registers of birth, marriage, and death are kept in each *commune* by the mayor or his delegate, who, when functioning in this capacity, is referred to as *officier de l'état civil.* [422] Entries in these registers are, and have the probative force of, official documents. They constitute conclusive proof of all facts recorded as having been witnessed by the public official, and their probative effect may be attacked only in a special proceeding called *inscription de faux.* In regard to matters recorded as having been reported to the public official – such as the birth of a child –, these records constitute complete proof, but their probative effect may be rebutted by any kind of counterproof. [423]

The rule that birth, marriage, or death must be proven by an authenticated copy of the official record is inapplicable if an official record of the event to be proved was never prepared or if it has since been destroyed. [424] This provision has been given a liberal interpretation: It may be invoked whenever the record, although perhaps in existence, is unavailable. [425] In all cases to which the exception applies, proof may be provided in the form of entries in personal papers and by all other kinds of evidence. [426]

In some cases, special rules apply. The death of a person who has disappeared in a disaster or war may be proven by a judicial declaration

[421] On proof of marriage, see CODE CIVIL art. 194. This rule has been generalized. *Cf.* 1 COLIN & CAPITANT 214.

[422] The rules for the keeping of the official birth, death, and marriage records are now contained in DÉCRET No. 62–921 of August 3, 1962, J.O. Aug. 9, 1962, p. 7918, [1962] D.L. 272. They are quite elaborate in order to avoid alteration or fraud. A system of cross-references between marriage, birth, and death records makes it easy to determine whether any person whose place of birth is known is alive, and whether he is single, married or divorced. *Cf.* AMOS & WALTON, *op. cit. supra* note 399, at 37–38.

[423] In France, marriages must be celebrated by an *officier de l'état civil*; entries concerning marriages are thus always made on the basis of his own knowledge. Entries concerning births and deaths are based on reports made to an *officier de l'état civil* by others, such as relatives or a physician. They are conclusive only as to the fact that the report was made on the date indicated in the register. See Consorts Dufour, Cass. Civ., Dec. 9, 1924, [1925] D.H. 46 (when bodies of husband and wife were found in house destroyed by bomb, death record calling wife widow of husband was not conclusive on issue whether husband predeceased wife). Similarly, a birth certificate is not conclusive on the issue of legitimacy, but counterproof is restricted by the presumption of legitimacy. See 7.30.b *supra*; *cf.* 1 COLIN & CAPITANT 239–41.

[424] CODE CIVIL art. 46.

[425] 1 JULLIOT DE LA MORANDIÈRE 456; Achard v. Dame Achard, Cass. Req., Nov. 14, 1922, [1924] D. 1. 79 (in view of difficulties of communication, proof of marriage celebrated in Russia before revolution by other means allowed).

[426] CODE CIVIL art. 46. The person failing to produce the official records must show two things: their unavailability and the facts in question. 1 JULLIOT DE LA MORANDIÈRE 458.

of his death. In cases to determine inheritance rights, the death of persons long deceased may be shown by any evidence. [427]

### 7.36. The Requirement of a Writing for Legal Transactions

The requirement that a contract or other legal act be in writing may be either of an evidentiary or of a substantive nature. If it is an evidentiary requirement only, its disregard does not render the act void, but merely difficult or even impossible to prove. If the requirement is of a substantive nature, the act cannot validly exist without being in writing. [428] The most embracive requirement of a writing in French law, that embodied in article 1341 of the *Code Civil*, is of an evidentiary character. Requirements of a writing of a substantive nature are of rather infrequent occurrence.

### 7.37. Article 1341 of the *Code Civil*

Article 1341 of the *Code Civil* provides:

> "A notarial instrument or an instrument under private signature must be prepared for all matters exceeding 50 francs in amount or value, even in the case of voluntary bailments, and no proof by witnesses may be received against or beyond the contents of instruments, or as to what was said before, or at the time of, or after, an instrument was prepared, even in the case of an amount or value of less than 50 francs. All of this is without prejudice to what has been prescribed in the laws relating to commerce."

Its provisions are of comprehensive scope. It requires a writing for all acts – not only contracts, but also such unilateral acts as payments – exceeding the value of fifty francs. Furthermore, it forbids, irrespective of the value of the act, oral evidence against or beyond the writing or of what was said before, during, or after preparation of the writing. [430]

Any form of writing, whether handwritten, typed, or printed, that is signed, is within the compass of article 1341. The value of the act is determined as of the time of its occurrence, not as of the time of commencement of the litigation. [431] If capital and interest are demanded in one action, they must be added to determine the value of the trans-

[427] 1 JULLIOT DE LA MORANDIÈRE 566. On judicial declarations of death, see CODE CIVIL arts. 88–92.

[428] See 7 PLANIOL & RIPERT, TRAITÉ PRATIQUE DE DROIT CIVIL FRANÇAIS 830 (1954).

[429] *Cf.* SCHLESINGER, COMPARATIVE LAW 221 (1959); VON MEHREN, THE CIVIL LAW SYSTEM 93–96, 618–28, 869 (1957). On historical relationships between the English statute of frauds and the ORDONNANCE OF MOULINS, the predecessor of article 1341, see Rabel, THE STATUTE OF FRAUDS AND COMPARATIVE LEGAL HISTORY, 63 L. Q. REV. 174 (1947). See also the note by Mimin appended to Debiesse v. Bonnière, Cass. Civ., July 10, 1945, [1946] D.J. 181.

[430] 2 GARSONNET & CÉZAR-BRU 512; 2 COLIN & CAPITANT 515.

action. [432] The impact of article 1341 cannot be avoided by iimiting the claim to an amount below fifty francs [433] nor by splitting the claim. Claims arising from the same transaction and joined in one action must be added to determine the pertinent value. [434]

While oral evidence may not be used to show facts at variance with the writing, it may be adduced to clarify obscure terms [435] or to prove facts, such as novation or cancellation, that occurred after the legal act and modified its effect. [436]

### 7.38. Cases in which the Requirement of a Writing Embodied in Article 1341 Need not be Met

The requirement of a writing need not be met in a number of cases otherwise within the ambit of article 1341. Since the requirement of a writing is directed primarily against oral testimony, an act of a value exceeding fifty francs may be established by a party oath or an admission in court. [437] The requirement of a writing is also dispensed with in "commercial" cases. However, a limited number of commercial contracts require a written form by virtue of other statutory provisions. [438]

**a. Beginning of written proof.** Oral evidence to prove an act within the ambit of article 1341 may be used, by way of exception, if there is a *commencement de preuve par écrit* (beginning of written proof). The *Code Civil* defines beginning of written proof as "every written act coming from the person against whom the action is brought ... and making

[431] Thus, in a case involving the purchase of a lottery ticket, article 1341 was held inapplicable, since the price of the ticket did not exceed the monetary limitation of article 1341, even though the ticket had won a prize in the meantime. 2 GARSONNET & CÉZAR-BRU 527.

[432] CODE CIVIL art. 1342.

[433] CODE CIVIL art. 1343. Nor is oral evidence admissible to substantiate a claim for less than 50 francs if it involves a balance on a transaction involving more than 50 francs. CODE CIVIL art. 1344.

[434] CODE CIVIL art. 1346.

[435] Giovanetti v. Gregory, Cass. Civ., May 31, 1948, [1948] D. SOMM. 25; Hecker v. Harant, Cass. Civ., Nov. 22, 1954, [1955] D. SOMM. 27; *cf.* De Biesse v. Bonnière, *supra* note 429.

[436] 2 COLIN & CAPITANT 516; Epoux Urbain v. Raychler, Cass. Civ., May 14, 1946, [1946] D.J. 374 (abandonment of contract).

[437] On the party-oath, see 7.56 *infra*. On admissions, see 7.52 *infra*. An oral admission made out of court is not admissible in cases governed by article 1341. A written admission may be a beginning of written proof.

[438] CODE CIVIL art. 1341 excepts from its coverage the "laws relating to commerce." CODE DE COMMERCE art. 109 permits parole proof of purchases and sales if the court finds that this form of proof should be admitted. By judicial interpretation, this rule has been extended to all other commercial cases except those for which the CODE DE COMMERCE specifically requires a writing. SICARD, LA PREUVE EN JUSTICE APRÈS LA RÉFORME JUDICIAIRE 373 (1960); 2 ESCARRA, MANUEL DE DROIT COMMERCIAL 582 (1949).

the alleged facts probable." [439] This definition has received a liberal interpretation.

A contract, invalid for failure to meet formal requirements, and letters emanating from the party to be charged, even if unsigned, have been held to constitute beginning of written proof. [440] Furthermore, the requirement that the beginning of written proof come from the adverse party has been construed liberally: A post card written by a wife who was acting on behalf of her husband has been held to come from the latter, [441] and a letter written by an association of water users to the water company has similarly been held to have issued from a member of the association. [442]

Even writings prepared after commencement of litigation, such as written minutes of statements made by a party during a *comparution personelle* (interrogation of a party), may form beginning of written proof. [443]

Whether a writing satisfies the statutory requirement of making the facts probable is a question of fact the *Cour de Cassation* leaves for resolution by the lower courts.

**b. Production of written proof is impossible.** Production of written proof is not required when it is impossible. Events enumerated in the *Code Civil* of which written proof is not required include torts, acts giving rise to quasi-contractual obligations, [444] bailments in case of fire, revolt, or other emergencies, bailments by guests in inns, obligations contracted in emergencies generally, and transactions of which written proof has been lost as a result of *force majeure*. [445] The courts have gone

[439] CODE CIVIL art. 1347. A beginning of written proof has also been defined as incomplete written proof. LEGEAIS, *op. cit. supra* note 331, at 118.

[440] Marchand v. Merle, Cass. Civ., Oct. 27, 1903, [1903] D. 1. 574. Bastenti v. Gambini, Cass. Req., Dec. 6, 1933, [1934] D.H. 20 (letter dictated by party charged, but not signed).

[441] Epoux Sylvestre v. Le Fresne, Cass. Civ., July 7, 1955, [1955] D.J. 737.

[442] Demoiselle Pradel v. Cie. générale des eaux, Cass. Req., June 13, 1936, [1936] D.H. 393.

[443] Of course, if the admission is complete, the claim of the opponent has been established, and there is no need to treat the admission as a beginning of written proof authorizing oral testimony. Failure to appear for a *comparution personnelle* ordered by the court may be considered beginning of written proof. CODE DE PROCÉDURE CIVILE art. 336. This provision is not mandatory.

[444] CODE CIVIL art. 1348(1). That the drafters of the CODE CIVIL considered it necessary to state specifically that the requirement of written evidence is inapplicable to tort cases shows how far reaching they intended article 1341 to be. Article 1341 is argued to be applicable only in the case of *actes juridiques* (legal acts), *i.e.*, acts designed to have legal consequences, but not in the case of *faits juridiques*, such as accidents, not designed to have such consequences. LEGEAIS, *op. cit. supra* note 331, at 113; 2 COLIN & CAPITANT 513–14. Even in tort actions or actions on quasi-contracts, written proof may be necessary to show the existence of a contract having an incidental significance in the case. 2 COLIN & CAPITANT 519.

[445] CODE CIVIL art. 1348(2) and (4).

beyond the statutory enumeration and have allowed oral evidence in cases not statutorily prescribed in which production of written evidence was actually or practicably impossible. [446]

**c. Cases of fraud.** Parol evidence is also permitted when there is a claim of fraud. The rule providing for this exception has been given liberal application. [447]

**d. Waiver.** Article 1341 is applied only when its provisions are invoked: The court may not apply it on its own motion. [448] Furthermore, a party may waive application of article 1341. Waiver may be evidenced by submission of oral evidence by the party who may rely on article 1341 or by failure to raise a timely objection to an *enquête* requested by the opponent. [449]

### 7.39. Other Formalities that May Be Required

If a contract creates obligations that must be satisfied simultaneously by all parties, a separate original must be prepared for each party having a distinct interest. This requirement is of an evidentiary nature, so that its disregard does not vitiate the contract. The rule is inapplicable to contracts embodied in a notarial instrument. [450]

An instrument not in notarial form containing a unilateral promise to pay money or deliver goods must either be entirely handwritten or at least contain the words *bon pour* (good for) or *approuvé* and state the

[446] 2 COLIN & CAPITANT 520; 2 GARSONNET & CÉZAR-BRU 521. Compliance with article 1341 is not required if it would be "morally impossible" to insist on a writing – for instance, in the case of a fee paid to a doctor or wages paid to a servant. Ihasusta v. Bianchi, Cass. Civ. March 17, 1938, [1938] D. 1. 15 (with note by Mimin, giving as additional examples contracts between a farmer and farm laborer, a small retail merchant and his client, a parent and his child, a husband and his wife). Epoux Munudtey v. Veuve St. Jean, Cass. Civ., March 17, 1958, [1958] D. SOMM. 78 (brother and sister); Cons. Conchs v. Dlle Bertheaume, Cass. Civ., May 20, 1957, [1957] D. SOMM. 101; Dlle Chatelet v. Epoux Le Groux, Cour Paris, April 9, 1957, [1957] D.J. 455 (concubines).

[447] COLIN & CAPITANT 549.

[448] 2 COLIN & CAPITANT 516. Since it does not involve *ordre public* (public policy), reliance may not be placed on article 1341 for the first time before the *Cour de Cassation.*

[449] Hauer v. Etablissements Jules Erny, Cass. Civ., Jan. 6, 1936, [1936] D.H. 115; Le Guen v. Cossaert, Cass. Req., March 24, 1942, [1942] D. CR. J. 64.

[450] CODE CIVIL art. 1325. Each copy must state how many separate originals have been prepared. Failure to state the number of originals cannot be invoked by a party which has executed its obligation. The requirement of multiple originals is apparently intended to enable each party to a transaction to prove it if necessary. See VON MEHREN, THE CIVIL LAW SYSTEM 623 (1957). See also 2 GARSONNET & CÉZAR-BRU 410. The rule is inapplicable to agreements completely executed as to one party or to obligations arising in succession. 2 COLIN & CAPITANT 494; VON MEHREN, *supra* 624. In commercial cases, an instrument not complying with the rule stated may be considered as the basis for an inference. 2 ESCARRA, *op. cit. supra* note 438, at 583.

amount of money or quantity of goods in letters, not figures, in the handwriting of the person to be charged. This rule is inapplicable to merchants, to farm and day laborers, house servants, and persons similarly situated. [451]

## 7.40. Stamp Taxes and Registration

Many instruments of legal significance are subject to two kinds of taxes. Ordinarily, a tax stamp must be affixed to each sheet of paper,[452] and a registration tax must be paid upon compulsory registration with the office of the *enregistrement.* [453]

Failure to affix the tax stamp or to pay the registration tax may lead to punishment, but does not affect the validity of the instrument. Although an instrument to which the tax stamps are not affixed or which has not been registered may not be used in court, any party may remove this impediment by affixing the stamps or by registering the document. [454]

## 7.41. Transactions not Covered by Article 1341 that Require a Writing

Although the *Code Civil* provides that a lease may be either oral or in writing, [455] neither parol evidence nor beginning of written proof may be used to prove a lease that is wholly executory. [456] Disputes as to the amount of rent due under an oral lease that is no longer wholly executory must ordinarily be settled by rent receipts or, unless the tenant demands that the rental value be determined by an expert, by

[451] CODE CIVIL art. 1326. On the reasons for its enactment, see VON MEHREN, *op. cit. supra* note 450, at 624. If there is a difference between the sum or amount mentioned in the body of the instrument and the sum or amount mentioned in the *bon pour* clause, the smaller of the two controls. CODE CIVIL art. 1327.

[452] Ordinarily, this tax depends on the number of sheets and the size of the paper. It increases with the length of the instrument. *Cf.* 1 JULLIOT DE LA MORANDIÈRE 277.

[453] The instruments subject to this form of taxation are listed in CODE GÉNÉRAL DES IMPÔTS art. 646–II and Law No. 63–254 of March 15, 1963, J.O. March 17, 1963, p. 2843, [1963] D.L. 98. A copy of the instrument may be kept at the *enregistrement* office, which may deliver duplicates. CODE GÉNÉRAL DES IMPÔTS art. 815. Though the *enregistrement* office has some aspects of a public records office, *enregistrement* is basically a tax measure.

[454] Ordinarily, instruments must be subjected to *enregistrement* within a period of one month after execution. CODE GÉNÉRAL DES IMPÔTS art. 646–II. Parties waiting until later are subject to additional duties, often amounting to twice the original sum. Nevertheless, *enregistrement* is often neglected in order to save taxes, the parties hoping that no litigation will result. *Enregistrement* duties are ordinarily based on the value of the transaction.

[455] CODE CIVIL art. 1714.

[456] CODE CIVIL art. 1715. This provision allows a party-oath by the person denying existence of the lease. See also 2 COLIN & CAPITANT 669–70. Article 1715 contains a proviso excepting from its operation leases of farm land, which are governed by special legislation of fairly recent origin.

the landlord's statement under oath. [457] Parol evidence as to other conditions of executed oral leases is not admissible. [458]

A writing is also required for all agreements of compromise, settling disputes either before or after the initiation of litigation. [459] This requirement of a writing, like that concerning contracts of marine insurance, is of an evidentiary nature. [460]

## 7.42. Transactions Requiring a Writing for their Substantive Validity

In a number of cases, a writing, often in notarial form, is required for the substantive validity of a transaction. A notarial instrument is required to create a valid mortgage, [461] to transfer interests in land, [462] for *contrats de marriage* (ante-nuptial agreements), [463] and for promises of gifts. [464]

A writing is required for the formation of a *société* (company), [465] for the transfer of a *fonds de commerce* (business enterprise), [466] to make a negotiable instrument, for charter parties, and for bills of lading. [467]

Disregard of any of these requirements results in the substantive invalidity of the legal act. Powers of attorney must be cast in the same form required for the transaction authorized. [468]

## 7.43. Probative Effect of Notarial and other Authentic Instruments

Instruments prepared by *officiers ministériels* – including notaries [469] and other public officials – who act within the scope of their authority,

[457] CODE CIVIL art. 1716. The lessee must bear the cost of the expertise if the expert determines that the rental value is in excess of the amount indicated by the lessee.

[458] 2 COLIN & CAPITANT 671.

[459] CODE CIVIL art. 2044.

[460] SICARD, *op. cit. supra* note 331, at 374.

[461] CODE CIVIL arts. 2127–28. The rule applies only to mortgages of French land.

[462] DÉCRET No. 55–22 of January 4, 1955, J.O. Jan. 7, 1955, p. 346, [1955] D.L. 44, art. 4 (requiring instruments to be recorded to be in notarial form); *cf.* 1 COLIN & CAPITANT 1. (Supp. 1955).

[463] CODE CIVIL art. 1394.

[464] CODE CIVIL art. 931. Even acceptances of gifts must be in authentic (notarial) form. CODE CIVIL art. 932.

[465] CODE DE COMMERCE art. 41. The term *société* includes all business associations, including general and limited partnerships and the various forms of companies. This rule is applicable only to companies that are commercial in character. See 4.05.d, 4.39.b *supra*. No special formal requirements exist for civil (non-commercial) companies, but a writing is required by virtue of CODE CIVIL art. 1341, if a sum over 50 francs is involved.

[466] Law of March 17, 1909, J.O. March 19, 1909, [1909] D. 4. 41.

[467] SICARD, *op. cit. supra* note 331, at 374–75. This list is not intended to be exhaustive.

[468] SCHLESINGER, COMPARATIVE LAW 404 (2d ed. 1959). In addition, article 1341 is applicable. See CODE CIVIL art. 1985.

[469] For a partial list of transactions for which a notarial instrument is required, see 2.10.b and 7.42 *supra*. There are strict formal rules concerning the manner in which authentic documents must be prepared. Even the writing materials used for their preparation are subject to regulation by the Ministry of Justice.

are called *actes authentiques* and form conclusive proof of – that is, must be accepted by the court as establishing – the facts recorded as having been witnessed by the *officiers ministériels*. Although the *Code Civil* provides only that they are conclusive (*font foi*) between the parties to the transaction recorded, [470] the courts have extended this conclusive effect to third persons. [471] The conclusive effect of authentic instruments can be attacked only in a special proceeding, called *inscription de faux*.

The conclusive probative effect of authentic instruments is limited to acts the notary has performed or observed himself. [472] It attaches to so-called dispositive clauses – that is, clauses intended to have legal effect – and clauses related thereto, not to recitals of unrelated matters. [473] Furthermore, fraud, duress, or mistake may be shown even in attack upon an authentic instrument. [474]

### 7.44. *Inscription de Faux*

The conclusive probative effect of authentic instruments can be attacked in only two ways: First, a criminal complaint alleging forgery may be filed with the proper authorities; [475] a finding of forgery, as distinguished from an acquittal, in a criminal action is conclusive in a subsequent civil proceeding. [476] Second, a special proceeding, called *inscription de faux* or *faux incident civil*, may be instituted.

An *inscription de faux* may be instituted either to establish that the instrument has been altered after its execution (*faux matériel*) or to

[470] Code Civil art. 1319.

[471] 2 Garsonnet & Cézar-Bru 400; *cf.* 2 Colin & Capitant 498.

[472] Thus, a recital in a notarial bill of sale of real property that it was executed on a certain date and that the purchase price was paid in cash in the view of the notary would be binding, since the recital concerns matters within the personal knowledge of the notary; a recital to the effect that the property was of a certain acreage would not be conclusive since the notary could not have determined that matter for himself. 2 Colin & Capitant 498. See also Levesque v. Loubinoux, Cour Paris, July 2, 1956, [1956] D. Somm. 159. Likewise, a recital in a notarial will that it was dictated to the notary on a certain date would be conclusive as to the fact of dictation and the date; a further recital that the testator was, in the notary's opinion, of sound mind, would not be conclusive as to the sanity of the testator, since a determination of sanity is not within the competence of a notary. See Epoux Rougerie v. Vve Dubois, Cour Bordeaux, July 12, 1951, [1951] D.J. 630; Vve Duquenne v. Consorts Duquenne, Cass. Req., May 4, 1943, [1943] D. Anal. J. 66.

[473] Code Civil art. 1320; Sicard, *op. cit. supra* note 331, at 83.

[474] Renouard v. Boittin, Cour Agen, Dec. 7, 1951, [1952] D.J. 275 (mistake of parties in listing lot numbers in sale of property); Moulin v. Consorts Guichard, Cass. Req., Dec. 8, 1937, [1938] D.H. 114 (use of dummy party); Dame Hallé v. Maillard, Cass. Civ., Jan. 7, 1935, [1935] D. H. 131 (same). The formalities surrounding the execution of a notarial instrument make claims of fraud or duress quite rare.

[475] In that case, the civil action in which the incriminated document is to be used is stayed until termination of the criminal proceeding. Code de Procédure Civile art. 250.

[476] Morel 391.

prove that the draftsman made a false statement (*faux intellectuel*).[477] The initiation of an *inscription de faux* leads to a stay of the principal action.

To discourage its use, the *inscription de faux* proceeding has deliberately been made cumbersome. Before initiation of the proceeding, the party who wishes to attack an authentic instrument must notify his opponent that, unless his opponent will forego reliance on the instrument, he will commence an *inscription de faux*. If the opponent answers that he does not wish to forego reliance, the proceeding is commenced by a declaration (*inscription*) at the clerk's office, which is followed by a hearing (*audience*). After the hearing, the court must decide (1) either that the proceeding has been commenced frivolously and terminate it, (2) or that the proceeding should continue, (3) or that the instrument is so obviously false that no further proceedings are necessary. If the court decides that the proceeding should continue, a second hearing is held at which the means of proof to be used must be identified. The court then renders a second decision specifying what evidence may be introduced and appointing a commissioner before whom the evidence must be adduced. Alternatively, in a proper case, it may declare the document not false, impose a fine on the attacking party, and terminate the proceeding. If proof is permitted, the court renders a third decision after the proof has been taken before the commissioner. If the instrument is found not false, a fine may be imposed on the party who attacked it; if the instrument is found false, the court may order either that it be destroyed or that it be corrected.[478]

The cumbersomeness of this proceeding combined with the high degree of integrity of *officiers ministériels* and the safeguards surrounding the custody of authentic instruments make the *inscription de faux* of rare occurrence.

## 7.45. Probative Effect of Signed Instruments *(Actes Sous Seign Privé)*

An instrument drawn privately to record a legal transaction or act, such as a contract or a payment, constitutes conclusive proof (*fait foi*) – that is, must be accepted by the court as establishing the facts it relates – against the person who signed it. However, any form of counterproof may overcome this effect.

A person against whom a signed instrument is introduced as evidence

[477] MOREL 387; 2 GARSONNET & CÉZAR-BRU 397.

[478] CODE DE PROCÉDURE CIVILE arts. 214–51; 2 GARSONNET & CÉZAR-BRU 436; MOREL 387. The *ministère public* must always intervene in a *faux incident* civil.

may be required formally to deny or acknowledge his signature. If the instrument is introduced against general successors in interest, such as heirs, of the person who signed it, they may, in a proper case, assert lack of knowledge of the genuineness of the signature. [479]

a. ***Vérification d'écritures.*** If the signature is not acknowledged, the party who wishes to rely on the instrument must institute a special proceeding, called *vérification d'écritures*, to obtain a judicial declaration affirming the genuineness of the signature. The *vérification d'écritures* proceeds much in the same way as an *inscription de faux*. The principal difference is that in a *vérification d'écritures* proceeding the burden of proving the instrument genuine rests on the party who seeks to rely on it, while in the *inscription de faux* the burden of proving falsity rests on the party attacking the document. [480]

A *vérification d'écritures* proceeding may also be commenced independently of a pending action by anyone who wishes to obtain a judicial declaration of genuineness of an instrument. [481] Whether an instrument judicially affirmed to be genuine may be attacked by an *inscription de faux* is disputed. [482]

### 7.46. Probative Effect of the Date of a Signed Instrument

The conclusive probative effect of signed instruments is subject to one exception. Article 1328 of the *Code Civil* provides that, insofar as third persons are concerned, these instruments " have no date" unless (1) the instrument has been registered (*enregistré*), in which case the date of registration stamped on by the tax officials controls, or (2) it is embodied in a notarial instrument, in which case the date of the deed governs, or (3) the signer of the instrument has died, in which case the date of his death is decisive. Third persons within the meaning of Article 1328 are all persons other than the persons who signed the instrument and their general successors in interest, such as heirs.

Article 1328 is designed to prevent fraudulent ante-dating of legal instruments. It is inapplicable to commercial instruments. [483]

[479] CODE CIVIL art. 1323.
[480] 2 COLIN & CAPITANT 498.
[481] CODE DE PROCÉDURE CIVILE arts. 193–213; 2 GARSONNET & CÉZAR-BRU 406–20. If the signature is later judicially declared genuine, the person who has denied it may be fined.
[482] See CODE DE PROCÉDURE CIVILE art. 214.
[483] SICARD, *op. cit. supra* note 331, at 3.

### 7.47. Probative Effect of Copies

As a general rule, copies of legal instruments do not have the probative effect of originals. [484] Birth, death, and marriage records form an exception: Properly authenticated copies of such records have the same probative weight as the originals. [485]

In case of notarial instruments, production of the original is excused if the instrument has been destroyed and the first copy, the so-called *grosse*, is produced; other copies may substitute for a missing original only if they are more than thirty years old. [486]

The rules limiting the probative effect of copies have been criticized as old-fashioned when applied to photocopies. [487] Notaries have for some time been authorized to issue photocopies of authentic instruments, [488] but this reform has not modified the probative effect of such copies. Of late, the courts seem to be taking a friendlier attitude towards photocopies. [489]

### 7.48. Admissibility and Probative Effect of Letters

Reliance on letters as evidence is limited by a strong policy favoring confidential communications: As a general rule, courts may not rely on confidential letters as evidence. Whether letters are confidential cannot be determined by reference to a general formula; much depends on the facts of the individual case. [490] To be confidential, a letter need not

[484] SICARD, *op. cit. supra* note 331, at 128. CODE CIVIL art. 1334 provides that, when an original exists, its production may always be demanded.

[485] See 7.35 *supra*. Original birth, death, and marriage records always stay in the office where they are kept.

[486] CODE CIVIL art. 1335. Copies of copies may form the basis for inferences, however, and copies prepared by the notary but without court order and without the consent of the parties may be a beginning of written proof. The record of an instrument in the public (land) records can serve only as beginning of written proof, and even that only if the original has been destroyed. CODE CIVIL art. 1336.

[487] Carel, *Les Modes de preuve au XXe siècle*, [1957] GAZ. PAL. DOCTR. 32.

[488] DÉCRET of Dec. 2, 1952, J.O. Dec. 5, 1952, [1952] GAZ. PAL. 2. 695; ARRÊTÉ of the Minister of Justice of May 22, 1954, J.O. June 2, 1954, [1954] GAZ. PAL. 1. 711. When some birth, death, and marriage records in Paris were beginning to wear out from use, they were reproduced by photographic methods, but it was felt necessary to have the *procureur de la République* obtain a court decision certifying the accuracy of the copies. Trib. Seine, Oct. 31, 1952, [1953] J.C.P. 2. 7367.

[489] L. v. Dlle S., Cass. Civ., July 20, 1953, [1953] J.C.P. 2. 7813 (photostatic copies of letters father had written to mother, but which she had returned to him before the beginning of suit were held admissible in filiation case to show that the father had admitted his paternity in writing, the *Cour de Cassation* stating that they are truthful images of the original, but also relying on the absence of a timely objection to their use); *cf.* Camus v. Geoffroy, Cour Bourges, May 12, 1942, [1942] D. ANAL. J. 132, [1942] S. 2. 27.

[490] 2 DALLOZ, RÉPERTOIRE DE PROCÉDURE CIVILE, *Preuve*, Nos. 751–53 (1956). Often, cases with similar facts situations reach opposite results: Dlle Nicon v. De Chabre, Cour Rennes, Feb. 24, 1894, [1894] D. 2. 295 (offer of settlement from *avocat* to *avoué* not confidential);

necessarily be addressed to a lawyer, physician, or clergyman. Even commercial correspondence can be confidential, [491] although letters reflecting a contract are not. [492]

In actions between the sender and the receiver of a letter, even confidential letters may be relied on if they contain threats, attempts at extortion, libellous statements, or in general anything evidencing or creating an obligation. [493]

In actions between the receiver and a third person, the receiver generally needs the consent of the sender before a confidential letter may be relied on by the court. [494]

If someone who is neither the sender nor the receiver wants to use a letter, he must show that he has obtained it lawfully, and neither by trespass nor by abuse of trust nor by accident. [495] If the letter is confidential, there must, in addition, be consent on the part of the sender and of the receiver. However, consent has sometimes been implied from the mere fact of possession. [496] Consent is also unnecessary if the letter has been written in the interest of the third person, [497] or if the third person and the recipient have a common interest. Partial publication of a letter may waive the right to protect its confidential character. [498]

Recently, the rules prohibiting reliance on confidential letters have been relaxed. [499] If an attempt is made to use a confidential letter in the course of litigation, the writer or recipient, if not a party, may intervene and object to its being used. The opponent, even if neither writer nor recipient, may also object. [500]

The probative force of letters depends on their content. If the letter was not written by a party to the litigation, it may form only the basis for such inferences as the court may see fit to draw. If the letter ema-

X... v. Procureur général Tunis, Cass. Civ., June 14, 1957, [1957] D.J. 556, [1958] J.C.P. 2.10372 (*avocat* censured for revealing letter concerning settlement sent him by other *avocat*).

491 *E.g.*, Girardey v. Vermot, Cour Besançon, March 27, 1889, [1890] D. 2. 176 (letter by businessman to travelling salesman).

492 2 Dalloz, *op. cit. supra* note 349, at 654.

493 2 Dalloz, *op. cit. supra* note 349, at 755; Blanchonnet v. Théry, Cass. Civ., Dec. 31, 1913, [1917] D. 1. 143 (fraud).

494 3 Encyclopédie Dalloz, *Lettre Missive* 77 (1954).

495 Proc. gén. de Rennes v. De Chabre, Cass. Req., May 11, 1887, [1887] D. 1. 332 (letter removed from estate of decedent by person making inventory); Nguyen Van Hut v. Ministère public, Cass. Crim., Jan. 17, 1935, [1935] D.H. 132 (accidental misdelivery).

496 2 Dalloz, *op. cit. supra* note 349, at No. 759.

497 L. v. G., Cass. Civ., July 26, 1864, [1864] D. 1. 347 (letter by father of illegitimate child to midwife); 2 Dalloz, *op. cit. supra* note 349, at No. 760.

498 Syndicat des marchands de vins v. Lafosse, Cour Nancy, April 19, 1902, [1903] D. 2. 29; *cf.* note by Savatier appended to R. v. Dames C.B., Cour Poitiers, Dec. 31, 1918, [1920] D. 2. 62.

499 Poignard v. Epoux Jauvier, Cass. Civ., Feb. 17, 1955, [1955] D.J. 360.

500 2 Dalloz, *op. cit. supra* note 349, at No. 779.

nates from a party to the litigation, it may either contain extra-judicial admissions of facts which may be freely evaluated by the court [501] or, if it was drawn to record a legal transaction, have the conclusive probative effect attached to all signed instruments of that nature.

Since letters are written instruments, article 1341 of the *Code Civil* prevents recourse to oral testimony to contradict or modify agreements they embody. If the letter is not handwritten, compliance with the formality of the *bon pour* may be required. [502] The date of a letter has probative value against third persons only in the circumstances specified in article 1328 of the *Code Civil.* [503]

The requirement of double originals for contracts creating mutual unexecuted obligations does not seem applicable to agreements embodied in letters. [504] If a letter does not contain sufficient information to amount to a contract, it may still form the basis for inferences or amount to a beginning of written proof.

Copies of letters are treated as copies of other writings; ordinarily they do not have the probative effect of originals, but may form the basis for inferences. Although telegrams are considered copies, they have occasionally been treated in the same manner as letters. [505]

### 7.49. Admissibility and Probative Effect of Commercial Books of Account

Since 1953, the *Code du Commerce* prescribes that all *commerçants* must keep two kinds of books of account: a journal book and an inventory book. The journal book must contain entries for all transactions, but if original records are kept, periodic summaries are sufficient. The inventory book contains the annual inventories. To avoid subsequent alterations, these books must be firmly bound before use and their pages must be numbered and initialled by the presiding judge of the commercial court or one of a number of other public officers. [506] Before 1953, more complicated rules, which made it impossible to use

[501] *Id.* at 768; SICARD, *op. cit. supra* note 331, at 176.

[502] 2 DALLOZ, *op. cit. supra* note 349, at 770–76; Pirard v. Casson, Cass. Req., Feb. 6, 1928, [1928] D. 1. 148 ( in case of agreement embodied in letters, no oral testimony as to additional conditions admissible).

[503] Le Joncour v. Soc. des chantiers navals de la côte de Nacre, Cour Caen, March 4, 1949, [1949] S. 2. 197.

[504] 2 DALLOZ, *op. cit. supra* note 349, at No. 779.

[505] Clément v. Guarinos, Cour Alger, April 7, 1884, [1886] D. 2. 92 (telegram treated as original letter when no real dispute as to genuineness).

[506] CODE DU COMMERCE arts. 8–11 as amended by DÉCRET No. 53–875 of Sept. 22, 1953, J.O. Sept. 23, 1953, p. 8374, [1953] D.L. 353.

typewriters, let alone modern accounting machines, were honored in the breach rather than in the observance. [507]

Properly kept books of account are admissible evidence in suits between *commerçants* in commercial matters. [508] Even books not properly kept may be used, though only as a basis for inferences rather than as evidence. [509]

In actions between businessmen and non-businessmen, commercial books of account are always admissible as evidence against the businessman. However, the non-business party who relies on commercial books of account must take them as they are. If he submits such books, the court may consider all information they contain, whether favorable or unfavorable to the non-businessman. [510] Commercial books seem to be admissible against businessmen even in cases in which documentary evidence is required by article 1341 of the *Code Civil.*

The *Code Civil* provides that commercial books are not proof of deliveries made against non-businessmen. [511] The view has been propounded that this rule is not limited to deliveries of goods. [512]

Whatever its scope, the rule applies only in cases in which written evidence is required by article 1341 of the *Code Civil.* If this article is inapplicable, oral evidence is admissible, [513] and commercial books, whether or not they have been kept properly, may therefore be used by a businessman against a non-businessman as a basis for inferences. [514] In cases involving the delivery of goods to non-businessmen, commercial books may be used as a foundation for a supplementary oath. [515] Invoices may be used as evidence only if they have been accepted. [516]

Books of some businessmen, such as brokers, if and to the extent that they contain confidential information, may not be used. [517] Courts are never bound by information contained in commercial books. It may be evaluated freely.

[507] 1 Hamel & Lagarde, *op. cit. supra* 419, at 295–96 (1954). See also the official report preceding Décret No. 53–875, supra note 506.

[508] Code de Commerce art. 12; 1 Hamel & Lagarde, *op. cit. supra* note 419, at 300.

[509] See 7.31 *supra.*

[510] Code Civil art. 1330; 1 Hamel & Lagarde, *op. cit. supra* note 419, at 301.

[511] Code Civil art. 1329.

[512] 2 Colin & Capitant 510; Sicard, *op. cit. supra* note 331, at 171.

[513] See 7.37–7.38 *supra.*

[514] *E.g.*, Ihasusta v. Bianchi, Cass. Civ., March 17, 1938, [1938] D. 1. 115. *But see* Cazin v. Messain, Cass. Com., May 9, 1951, [1951] D.J. 472 (entry in butcher's book not sufficient proof of delivery of meat).

[515] This is true even if article 1341 remains applicable. 2 Colin & Capitant 510. On the supplementary oath (party-oath), see 7.56.c *infra.*

[516] 2 Escarra, Manuel de Droit Commercial 584 (1949).

[517] *Id.* at 583–84.

### 7.50. Admissibility and Probative Effect of Household Records, Family Account Books, and other Unsigned Statements

Household account books and household records have limited probative effect. If no official birth, death, or marriage record exists, birth, death, and marriage may be shown by family records of deceased fathers or mothers. [518] In some cases, family records may form a beginning of written proof and thus authorize recourse to oral evidence in an action to determine the parentage of a child. [519]

In actions involving legal transactions, household account books and family records have no probative value (*ne font pas foi*) in favor of the party who has prepared them. [520] They may be admitted to complete or explain other proof, but by themselves they are insufficient. They are sufficient proof of a transaction if used *against* the person who has prepared them, but only in two cases: (1) if they show receipt of a payment, and (2) if there is an entry stating expressly that it was made in *lieu* of a promissory note or other instrument establishing a claim against the person making the entry. [521] Since it is usually difficult to obtain documents from one's opponent, these rules are of limited practical importance.

In some cases, unsigned and undated statements put on legal instruments have probative value. Thus, a statement relating to partial payment made in the handwriting of the creditor on the *original* of an instrument is proof of such payment, but only if the instrument has always remained in the creditor's possession. Such a statement put on a *copy* in the debtor's possession is also proof of partial payment. [522]

All of these rules are subject to the exception that the documents discussed may always form the basis for inferences if the action is one in which oral evidence may be used. Furthermore, evidence to contradict family records, household account books, or unsigned statements on legal instruments is always admissible. [523]

### 7.51. Testimony

Fear of perjury led the drafters of the *Code de Procédure Civile* to look with disfavor upon testimony – another means of legal evidence recognized by the *Code Civil* – and to provide a rather cumbersome procedure,

[518] Code Civil art. 46.
[519] Code Civil art. 324.
[520] Code Civil art. 1331.
[521] Code Civil art. 1332; 2 Garsonnet & Cézar-Bru 406–08; 2 Colin & Capitant 510.
[522] Code Civil art. 1332; 2 Garsonnet & Cézar-Bru 409; 2 Colin & Capitant 511.
[523] 2 Colin & Capitant 509.

the *enquête*, for hearing witnesses. However, in 1958, the *enquête* procedure was considerably simplified, and courts were given greater powers to seek out facts and test the credibility of witnesses. Although this reform indicated a change of attitude in regard to testimony, the principle that witnesses may be heard in an *enquête* only pursuant to special court order was not modified. [524]

**a. Manner of requesting an *enquête*.** Authorization to conduct an *enquête* may be sought either from the court hearing the case, or, if the suit is pending before the *tribunal de grande instance*, from the *juge chargé de suivre la procédure*. The request for an *enquête* is contained in a pleading (*conclusions*) often in the form of an alternative prayer for relief. Although the court may order an *enquête* on its own motion, it does so rarely. An *enquête* may be requested at any stage of the proceedings. [525]

The party requesting an *enquête* must state in detail and item by item (*articuler*) the facts it seeks to prove. [526] French courts have required fairly strict compliance with this rule on the ground that it is designed to promote proper preparation by, and to prevent surprise of, adverse parties. [527] This requirement, which serves a useful purpose in a system that has few discovery devices and no motions addressed to the pleadings, [528] has lost some of its importance as a result of the 1958 reforms which eliminated the rule that the court, in interrogating the witness, may not go beyond the facts articulated.

Any adverse party may argue in his *conclusions* that an *enquête* should not be held. A denial of the facts articulated automatically authorizes introduction of testimony in support of the denial if an *enquête* is granted (*contre-enquête*). [529] However, if a party wishes to introduce proof of facts not articulated by his opponent, it must request an *enquête* of its own, which is called an *enquête respective*. [530]

[524] For an explanation of the 1958 reform, see the report of the Minister of Justice concerning DÉCRET No. 58–1289 of Dec. 22, 1958, J.O. Dec. 23, 1958, p. 11608, [1959] D.L. 45, at [1959] D.L. 335. Additional modifications, affecting chiefly the procedure before the *tribunal d'instance*, were enacted in 1960. DÉCRET No. 60–802 of Aug. 2, 1960, J.O. Aug. 5, 1960, p. 7250, [1960] D.L. 287 (with Minister's report).

[525] CODE DE PROCÉDURE CIVILE arts. 252–253. See Appendix, Form No. 12.

[526] MOREL 393; CORNU & FOYER 539.

[527] *E.g.*, Dlle Hermsdorff v. Jollivet, Cour Paris, Feb. 3, 1959, [1959] D. SOMM. 45; Legrand v. Dame Legrand, Cour Paris, March 3, 1959, [1959] D. SOMM. 64.

[528] SCHLESINGER, COMPARATIVE LAW 222 (2d ed. 1959); *cf.* Millar, *The Mechanism of Fact Discovery, A Study of Comparative Civil Procedure*, 32 ILL. L. REV. 261 (1937).

[529] CODE DE PROCÉDURE CIVILE art. 252.

[530] If an *enquête respective* is granted, the opponent is, of course, permitted to call witnesses to counter the proof adduced in the *enquête respective*. See MOREL 394; 2 GARSONNET & CÉZAR-BRU 554–55.

The court may authorize an *enquête* only as to facts which are relevant, material, and admissible (*pertinents, concluants, et admissibles*).[531]

If the court finds that an *enquête* would be appropriate, it or the *juge chargé de suivre la procédure,* as the case may be, renders a decision authorizing it, which lists the facts about which testimony is to be given. The *greffier* (clerk) must give a copy of the decision to the parties or their *avoués,* or send a copy by registered mail to every party who is in default or has no *avoué.*[532] An appeal from a decision granting or denying an *enquête* is possible only simultaneously with an appeal from a final judgment on the merits.[533]

If the decision authorizing the *enquête* is rendered by the court, it designates a day on which the witnesses will be heard. The decision may provide for hearing the witnesses in open court or in the judges' conference room (*chambre de conseil*). It may also provide for the appointment of a delegated judge (*juge commissaire*) to hear the witnesses, who may be the *juge chargé de suivre la procédure* or some other member of the court. In the latter event, the decision need indicate only a terminal date for completion of the *enquête.*[534]

Until 1958, the civil court of general competence, the *tribunal civil* (now *tribunal de grande instance*), heard witnesses only through a delegated judge. In practice, the *tribunal de grande instance* still follows this practice.

If the request for an *enquête* has been authorized by the *juge chargé de suivre la procédure,* he appoints himself to hear the witnesses.[535] In cases pending before the *tribunal d'instance,* the witnesses are heard by the judge who hears the whole case. The *enquête* may take place in open court or in the judge's office.[536]

If all witnesses live away from the place in which the court is sitting, the decision ordering the *enquête* may provide that it be held before a judge to be appointed by the presiding judge of another *tribunal de grande instance,* or before a judge of a *tribunal d'instance*: A court near the witnesses' residence is then selected to conduct the *enquête.* If only some of the witnesses reside at a distance from the court in which the case is pending, a similar arrangement may be used.[537]

[531] See 7.26 *supra.*
[532] Code de Procédure Civile art. 257.
[533] Code de Procédure Civile art. 258.
[534] Code de Procédure Civile arts. 254–55.
[535] Code de Procédure Civile art. 81.
[536] Code de Procédure Civile art. 34.
[537] Code de Procédure Civile art. 256.

**b. Witnesses: competence and privilege.** Each party must serve on the other and on the clerk of the court a list of the witnesses to be heard. The decision ordering the *enquête* must specify when these formalities have to be met. Five days before the date of the *enquête*, the clerk of the court must summon the witnesses whose names appear on the list. [538]

Neither parties nor experts may be heard as witnesses in an *enquête*. The commission of certain crimes automatically disqualifies the perpetrators to be heard as sworn witnesses; [539] in other cases, disqualification may be imposed as additional punishment. [540] Persons so disqualified may still be heard, but, since they are not sworn, their statements do not constitute testimony, but may form the basis for inferences. [541] Ascendants, descendants, and spouses of parties, including divorced spouses, are also disqualified from testifying. Relatives of parties, with the exception of descendants, may testify in actions relating to personal status, such as divorce of filiation proceedings, [542] but this exception has received a fairly strict interpretation. [543] Minors under fifteen years of age may be heard as witnesses, but are not sworn. [544]

Formerly, the *Code de Procédure Civile* listed additional persons whose past activities or ties with the parties cast suspicion upon their credibility and whose testimony could be excluded by resort to the *reproche* (reproach) procedure. [545] These provisions were eliminated by the 1958 reforms.

Article 378 of the Penal Code (*Code Pénal*) prohibits the disclosure of confidential information acquired by physicians, surgeons, pharmacists, midwives, and other persons in the course of their professional duties. This article has been interpreted as conferring upon these persons the privilege of refusing to disclose confidential information when called upon to testify in court. The privilege is not restricted to speci-

[538] CODE DE PROCÉDURE CIVILE arts. 254, 259. Since 1960, the list of witnesses must be served even upon a party in default. CODE DE PROCÉDURE CIVILE art. 259, as amended by DÉCRET No. 60–802, *supra* note 524, art. 10.

[539] CODE PÉNAL art. 34 (all persons under *dégradation civique*).

[540] CODE PÉNAL art. 54.

[541] CODE DE PROCÉDURE CIVILE art. 262. The Code uses the term *simples renseignements* rather than *présomptions de fait*, but in legal effect these two terms seem to be identical.

[542] CODE DE PROCÉDURE CIVILE art. 262.

[543] Consorts Paparic v. Faure, Cass. Civ., Nov. 20. 1950, [1951] D.J. 57; Jacquet v. Demoiselle Monnerat, Cour Paris, Feb. 19, 1959, [1959] D.J. 250; Paré v. Dame Paré, Cass. Civ., Dec. 12, 1958, [1959] D.J. 52; Raynaud, *Chronique*, 58 REV. TRIM. DR. CIV. 360 (1960).

[544] CODE DE PROCÉDURE CIVILE art. 262.

[545] CODE DE PROCÉDURE CIVILE arts. 282–84 (old). The articles relating to *reproche* were eliminated by DÉCRET No. 58–1289, *supra* note 524.

fied occupations, but may be invoked by any person who has acquired confidential information in a professional capacity. [546]

Article 378 has not received a uniform interpretation. In some cases, waiver of the privilege has not been allowed, [547] while in others the courts have been more lenient and have allowed waiver, at least if the information to be elicited from the doctor was unlikely to contain anything derogatory about the patient. [548]

**c. Conduct of the *enquête*.** The hearing of the witnesses takes place in the presence of the court or judge and of the parties and their counsel who wish to be present. [549] In Paris, as a rule, only the *avoués*, not the *avocats*, attend. If the examination is conducted by a single judge, it is usually held in the judge's office, and the public is excluded. If the *enquête* is conducted by the full court, it is held in open court or in the judges' conference room (*chambre de conseil*), depending on the directions in the judgment ordering the *enquête*.

In proceedings before the *tribunal d'instance*, witnesses need not be formally summoned, nor need lists of witnesses be exchanged. The court may hear any witness a party brings to the hearing. [550]

If a witness fails to appear at the appointed time, he may be subjected to a fine ranging from 100 to 500 francs (about $ 20–100). He may also be cited by an *huissier*, in which case he becomes liable for the latter's fees. If the witness is still recalcitrant, he may be subjected to a fine of up to 5000 francs (about $ 1000) or ordered brought to court by the police. The same penalties may be imposed if the witness refuses to be sworn or to answer. [551]

If a witness shows a valid excuse, he may not be fined and may be heard at an adjourned date. [552] In practice, French judges avoid harsh

[546] 10 Dalloz, Répertoire Pratique, *Secret Professionel*, Nos. 675–76 (1924); Hammelmann, *Professional Privilege*, 28 Can. B. Rev. 750, 756–57 (1950).

[547] Dr. Degraene, Cass. Crim., May 8, 1947, [1948] D.J. 109 (combined civil and criminal action against man having criminally assaulted child; refusal to testify by doctor who treated child upheld, though father of child called doctor as witness); Dame D. v. D., Cour Grenoble, May 29, 1952, [1952] D.J. 729 (in suit in which wife wanted to show that her husband knew of her pre-marital pregnancy before their marriage, statement by doctor, introduced by wife, that he examined wife before marriage and told her and her future husband that she was pregnant, not admissible); *cf.* R. v. Dames D.C.B. et L., Cour Poitiers, December 31, 1918, [1920] D. 2. 62 (note by Savatier).

[548] Dr. Delavierre v. Bouché, Cass. Civ., July 13, 1936, [1936] D.H. 588 (industrial accident); Consorts Danigo v. Le Gulludec, Cass. Civ., March 29, 1927, [1928] S.I. 5 (in will contest, medical certificates to effect testator was sane admissible, but others to effect he was insane inadmissible) (leading, but criticized, case).

[549] Code de Procédure Civile art. 263.

[550] Décret No. 60–802 of August 2, 1960, *supra* note 524.

[551] Code de Procédure Civile art. 269.

[552] Code de Procédure Civile art. 270.

measures against witnesses. There is no privilege against self-incrimination in civil actions. [553]

At present, witnesses for both sides are heard in one proceeding. [554] Before being sworn, each witness states his name, age, address, and occupation, and whether he is a servant or relative of a party. [555] If the answers disclose that the witness belongs to one of the classes of persons prohibited from testifying, he may not be heard. If it is doubtful whether the witness belongs to one of the classes who may not testify and the case is heard by a single judge rather than the full court, the witness is sworn and allowed to testify, and the full court subsequently rules on the admissibility of the testimony. [556]

After being sworn, the witness tells in narrative form what he knows about the facts to be proved. He may not read from a prepared statement. The judge dictates the substance of the testimony to the clerk for inclusion in the minutes. A verbatim transcript is not prepared. The text dictated by the judge is often considerably more literate than the testimony of the witness, though it may contain quotations of key words. After the witness has finished his statement, the clerk reads the minutes to him, and the witness may make any changes he sees fit.[557] Thereafter, the court or judge conducting the *enquête* may ask any questions which seem pertinent, whether or not relating to facts which have been articulated, provided only that oral evidence as to these facts is admissible. The court or judge may even call witnesses not summoned by the parties, if he feels that their presence may be helpful, [558] but this is done rarely. Neither the parties nor their counsel may question the witnesses directly, though they may suggest questions to the judge. [559] The answers given by the witnesses to these additional questions are also recorded in the minutes. The minutes must mention

[553] Pieck, *Witness Privilege against Self-Incrimination in the Civil Law*, 5 VILLANOVA L. REV. 375, 377, 386 (1960).

[554] Until 1958, the *enquête* and the *contre-enquête* were two entirely different proceedings.

[555] CODE DE PROCÉDURE CIVILE art. 238.

[556] CUCHE & VINCENT 556. But *quaere* whether that rule has not been changed by the 1958 reform. CODE DE PROCÉDURE art. 276 now provides that, subject to review by the full court, the delegated judge or *juge chargé de suivre la procédure* may decide all issues raised before him. Perjury may subject a witness to imprisonment from two to five years, and from five to ten years if he has accepted a bribe; in addition, a fine is imposed and the witness' „civil rights" may be revoked for a number of years. CODE PÉNAL arts. 362–64.

[557] CODE DE PROCÉDURE CIVILE art. 263. No minutes are prepared if the *enquête* is conducted by the full court rather than a delegated judge, and no appeal is possible. However, the *enquête* must be mentioned in the judgment. CODE DE PROCÉDURE CIVILE art. 271.

[558] CODE DE PROCÉDURE CIVILE art. 264.

[559] CODE DE PROCÉDURE CIVILE art. 265. Violation of the rule may be punished by a fine up to F. 100.

the accomplishment of the various formalities required by law. They are signed by the witness, the judge, and the clerk. [560]

Upon conclusion of his testimony, each witness must remain available to the court. He may be recalled and be asked additional questions, which may have suggested themselves to the judge in the light of subsequent testimony. The witness may also be confronted with other witnesses and with the parties. [561] Before being finally dismissed, witnesses may request the legal witness fee. [562] If all witnesses cannot be heard on the appointed day, the *enquête* may be continued with court permission to an adjourned date. This may also be done at the request of a party so that additional witnesses not named in the original list may be heard. The judge or court conducting the *enquête* has a discretionary power to grant or reject such a request. [563]

**d. Hearsay testimony.** In interrogating a witness, the judge is not limited to matters the witness has observed personally. The *Cour de Cassation* has held repeatedly that lack of personal knowledge on the part of the witness is no reason for exclusion of his testimony. [564] However, the court does seem to have a discretionary power to exclude hearsay evidence that it deems unreliable. [565]

Although, as a rule, hearsay evidence is admissible, the general rule – not followed consistently [566] – is that a witness may not testify as to a statement made to him by a person who is disqualified from testifying. [567]

Hearsay evidence – that is, testimony as to information obtained from others – is distinguished from proof by common repute (*commune*

[560] Code de Procédure Civile art. 273.

[561] Code de Procédure Civile arts. 263, 266. The court may hear the witnesses in whatever order it chooses.

[562] Code de Procédure Civile art. 279. Witnesses receive a fee similar to that payable in criminal cases (Code de Procédure Criminelle art. R 129) and travel expenses. See 12.05.b *infra*.

[563] Code de Procédure Civile arts. 267–268.

[564] Veuve Serre v. Julien, Cass. Civ., March 12, 1929, [1929] Gaz. Pal. 479; Zaoui v. Dlle Pat, Cass. Civ., October 23, 1950, [1950] Gaz. Pal. 2. 424; Demoiselles Gayon v. Badet, Cass. Civ., June 1, 1954, [1954] D.J. 589. At one time, the point was controversial. See note by Labbé appended to Preterre v. Preterre, Cass. Civ., Jan. 3, 1893, [1893] S. 1. 337, citing authorities on both sides of the question.

[565] Dame Guénassia v. Guénassia, Cass. Civ., Dec. 17, 1954, [1955] D.J. 255.

[566] De Lagoy v. Le Mée de La Salle, Cass. Req., June 6, 1899, [1900] S. 1. 39 (witness in divorce case may testify as to what children told him to show father instigated misbehavior of children).

[567] Dame Guénassia v. Guénassia, supra note 565 (words of plaintiff may not be repeated); Dame Therreau v. Therreau, Trib. Laval, Oct. 16, 1951, [1951] D.J. 781 (information gathered from children inadmissible in divorce case); L. v. L., Cour Poitiers, May 8, 1890, [1891] D. 5. 180 (same).

*renommée*), which is popular belief of the existence of facts that is not derived from a particular source of information. [568] Proof by common repute is admissible only in certain matrimonial property cases, when the husband has neglected to prepare an inventory, to prove contributions by the wife to the common household. [569]

**e. Proceedings subsequent to the *enquête*.** Within two weeks after conclusion of the *enquête*, the clerk (*greffier*) of the court must transmit certified copies of the minutes to the parties. [570] A party in default must be re-summoned at this stage of the proceedings. Either side may have the case put back on the calendar for a hearing (*audience*). [571]

At the hearing, unless the *enquête* has been conducted by the court, the minutes of the *enquête* are read and counsel for both sides present argument concerning the testimony, its credibility, and its legal effect.

**f. Probative effect of testimony.** In evaluating testimony, the court is not bound by mechanical rules. The credibility of evidence may be evaluated freely, and factors, such as whether the witness related facts from direct observation or from hearsay, may be given appropriate weight. [572] The court may believe one witness, rather than many, or none at all. However, in proceedings before the regular courts of first instance, the *tribunaux de grande instance*, in which witnesses are usually heard by a single judge delegated by the full court, the court, since it must rely merely on the minutes of the *enquête*, will ordinarily not rely on the demeanor of the witness to determine credibility. [573]

**g. Invalidity of the *enquête*.** At the hearing, if one of the formal rules has not been observed, either party may demand that the *enquête*, or at least its vulnerable part, be declared void. [574] In 1935, a law was enacted providing in general terms that no procedural step should be considered void because of the violation of a rule of form, unless the

[568] Preterre v. Preterre, *supra* note 564; 12 AUBRY & RAU 237.

[569] CODE CIVIL arts. 1413, 1442, 1499, 1504. Proof *par commune renommée* is thus mainly a means to sanction the absence of an inventory. 12 AUBRY & RAU 238; SICARD, LA PREUVE EN JUSTICE APRÈS LA RÉFORME JUDICIAIRE 290–93 (1960). On hearsay generally, see Hammelmann, *Hearsay Evidence, A Comparison*, 67 L. Q. REV. 67 (1951); Morgan, *Hearsay Dangers and the Application of the Hearsay Concept*, 62 HARV. L. REV. 177 (1935).

[570] CODE DE PROCÉDURE CIVILE art. 274. The original of the *minutes* goes into the file of the case in the court clerk's office.

[571] CODE DE PROCÉDURE CIVILE art. 275.

[572] 2 GARSONNET & CÉZAR-BRU 543–45.

[573] This may be one of the reasons why written evidence is often preferred.

[574] CORNU & FOYER 541–42; 2 GARSONNET & CÉZAR-BRU 580–85.

violation was prejudicial.[575] The courts have restricted the effect of this provision by holding it applicable only to formalities that are not of a substantial nature.[576] The law was re-affirmed in 1958.[577] It remains to be seen whether this re-affirmation will reduce the number of *enquêtes* declared void.

Since the 1958 reforms, the court, in determining whether a formality has been complied with, may rely on the minutes as well as on any other documentary evidence that may be available.[578] Before the 1958 reforms, the minutes were conclusive.[579]

An *enquête* or any part that has been declared void may be repeated with the court's permission. The person through whose fault an *enquête* has been declared void must bear the cost of the second proceeding.[580] In addition, the minutes of an *enquête* that has been declared void may be used as a basis for inferences. This may be of particular utility if the witness has become unavailable at the time of the second *enquête*. However, a court relying on the minutes of a void *enquête* as a basis for inferences must make this clear in its decision.[581]

The *enquête* procedure, as revised in 1958, has generally met with approval.[582] However, there has been some objection to the increased power given to the judges.[583] Even the *reproche* procedure, the object of general criticism before 1958, has found a defender, who argues that, though means for testing their credibility may be at hand, witnesses whose credibility is not above reproach should not be heard at all.[584]

### 7.52. Admissions

Although parties cannot be witnesses, they may be heard in a *comparution personnelle*. A *comparution personnelle*, although not limited to that purpose, is usually considered mainly a means of extracting admissions. It need not be used if a party voluntarily makes a statement at an appropriate point during his *avocat*'s argument, in which case no court order is necessary and the statement is not made under oath.

[575] CODE DE PROCÉDURE CIVILE art. 173.

[576] CORNU & FOYER 429, 431–32 (citing many cases); 1 SOLUS & PERROT 378–86.

[577] CODE DE PROCÉDURE CIVILE art. 278, as enacted in 1958 by DÉCRET No. 58-1289, *supra* note 524, expressly states that an *enquête* may be declared void only if article 173 requiring a showing of prejudice is applicable.

[578] CODE DE PROCÉDURE CIVILE arts. 142, 278.

[579] CUCHE & VINCENT 394

[580] CODE DE PROCÉDURE CIVILE art. 278.

[581] See 7.31 *supra*.

[582] CUCHE & VINCENT 551–52; CORNU & FOYER, SUPP. 1960, at 79.

[583] *E.g.*, CORNU & FOYER, SUPP. 1960, at 75.

[584] Raynaud, *Chronique*, 59 REV. TRIM. DR. CIV. 536 (1960).

Such a statement, if not amounting to an admission, may be at most a basis for inferences. Voluntary statements by parties are rare.

**a. Extra-judicial admissions.** French law distinguishes between admissions made in court and admissions made out of court. [585] As a general rule, oral admissions made out of court are admissible only in actions in which oral evidence may be produced; [586] even then, they may not be used if the actions involve personal status or other inalienable rights. [587]

When extra-judicial oral admissions are admissible, the courts may give them whatever weight seems appropriate.

Extra-judicial written admissions are treated as other writings. [588]

**b. Admissions made in court.** A formal admission in court may be made in writing in the *conclusions* (pleadings) or orally. An oral admission is usually made at a *comparution personnelle.*

As a rule, admissions made in court are effective in all types of actions, even in actions in which article 1341 of the *Code Civil* requires written evidence. However, admissions have no effect in actions involving personal status, such as divorce or separation actions. [589] Only a person having legal capacity to dispose of the right in litigation can make an admission. An admission by a guardian is effective only if the right involved in the litigation is one over which the guardian has a right of disposition. [590] Agents, including *avocats*, but excluding *avoués*, [591] can make effective admissions only if they have a power of attorney specifically authorizing them to do so. [592] A party is bound by an admission by its *avoué* unless it uses a special procedure called *désaveu* to disavow it. [593] If the *avoué* is in court when his *avocat* makes an admission, he must object promptly; otherwise, he will be considered to have ratified the admission. [594]

The *Code Civil* provides that an admission made in court is binding

[585] CODE CIVIL art. 1354.

[586] CODE CIVIL art. 1355.

[587] 2 COLIN & CAPITANT 537. The rule is not applied too strictly when there is no danger of collusion. *E.g.*, Drichemont v. Dame Schmitt, Cass. Civ., July 29, 1929, [1930] S. 1. 20.

[588] 2 COLIN & CAPITANT 537.

[589] 1 JULLIOT DE LA MORANDIÈRE 427.

[590] 2 COLIN & CAPITANT 536.

[591] Nor to *huissiers*. A party is not bound by statements made during argument by his *avocat*, though he is bound by statements made by his *avoué*. 2 COLIN & CAPITANT 536–37.

[592] CODE CIVIL art. 1356.

[593] However, no *désaveu* is possible if the *avoué* has been specifically authorized to make the admission. CODE DE PROCÉDURE CIVILE arts. 352–62.

[594] 2 COLIN & CAPITANT 537.

on the party who makes it and conclusively establishes the facts to which it relates. No counterproof of any kind can overcome this conclusive effect. However, a party may withdraw an admission made in court by showing that it was due to an error of fact, as distinguished from an error of law. [595]

An admission which contains qualifications or additional facts weakening its effect may not be "divided" against the party who has made it. [596] Thus, the court may not believe only those portions of the admission that favor the opponent and disbelieve the portions that favor the party who made the admission. The rule does not prevent proof by regular evidence that the part of the declaration that does not favor the party who made the admission is contrary to the facts. [597]

The rule that an admission is indivisible has some limitations. It applies only to facts that are so closely related to the admission that they could not exist without it. [598] The rule of indivisibility of admissions is also inapplicable if the actual admission and the additional statement contradict each other or if the second statement is so unlikely as to be almost impossible. [599]

### 7.53. Examination of Parties *(Comparution Personnelle)*

Until 1942, two procedures were available for the interrogation of parties: the *interrogatoire sur faits et articles* and the *comparution personnelle.* The *interrogatoire sur faits et articles* was an examination of a party by a delegated judge on the basis of written interrogatories settled in advance. Although the *Code de Procédure Civile* regulated it in detail, it was used rarely.

The *comparution personnelle* was developed mainly by the practitioners; the Code mentioned it only briefly. It was an examination of parties somewhat analogous to the examination of witnesses, but by the full court. It was used frequently.

In 1942, the *interrogatoire sur faits et articles* was abolished and the *comparution personnelle* received its present detailed regulation. [600]

595 CODE CIVIL art. 1356.

596 CODE CIVIL art. 1356; 2 COLIN & CAPITANT 538.

597 2 COLIN & CAPITANT 539.

598 If a party admits that he has received a loan, but states at the same time that he has repaid it, the court may not disregard the statement that the loan has been repaid since the statement that there has been a repayment makes no sense without the statement that there has been a loan. However, an admission that one of several instalments due has been paid only in part, coupled with the declaration that the next instalment has been paid in full, may be divided, since the two statements are independent.

599 2 COLIN & CAPITANT 538–39.

600 Law of May, 23, 1942, J.O. June 11, 1942, p. 2043, [1942] D. ANAL. L. 120.

Any person who is a party may be heard in a *comparution personnelle.* Corporations and associations with standing to sue are heard by an officer. [601] Unless the court directs the appearance of a specified officer, public bodies are heard by an agent designated by the public body. [602] Even incompetents and others under legal disability may be examined, either personally or by their guardian or other legal representative. [603] Since only parties may be heard in the *comparution personnelle,* a person interested in the outcome of a case, though not a party, may be examined only after he has been made a party. However, in actions involving community property, a wife may be examined, though only her husband is a formal party. [604]

The request for a *comparution personnelle* may be made either to the full court or to the *juge chargé de suivre la procédure.* It is made in the form of *conclusions.* [605]

If the request for a *comparution personnelle* is made to the full court, argument on it is heard in the judge's conference room (*chambre de conseil*), not in open court. [606] A *comparution personnelle* may also be ordered on the court's own motion. It may be ordered at any stage of the proceedings, and in any matter, even in cases, such as divorce actions, in which admissions are not effective. [607] The decision ordering a *comparution personnelle* is appealable immediately. [608]

The *comparution personnelle* takes place on the date specified in the decision ordering it. It is always conducted by the full court, never by a delegated judge or the *juge chargé de suivre la procédure.* [609] The party to be examined is summoned to appear by an *acte d'avoué à avoué.* If he fails to appear, he may be re-summoned by an *huissier.* [610] The examination is conducted in open court or in the judges' conference room (*chambre de conseil*), to which the public has no access. The court will choose the method that, under the circumstances seems more con-

[601] Code de Procédure Civile art. 334.

[602] Code de Procédure Civile art. 335.

[603] Code de Procédure Civile art. 334. An admission made by a person lacking legal capacity is not effective. See 7.52.b *supra.*

[604] Morel 408.

[605] Code de Procédure Civile arts. 324, 326.

[606] Code de Procédure Civile art. 327. This rule is waived if no timely objection is made to argument in open court. Esparbie v. Boutie, Cour Toulouse, Feb. 28, 1944, [1944] D. Cr. J. 101.

[607] Code de Procédure Civile art. 324.

[608] Code de Procédure Civile art. 327. This article provides that the decision is appealable in the same manner as *référé* decisions.

[609] Code de Procédure Civile art. 325.

[610] Code de Procédure Civile art. 328.

ducive to elucidation of the truth. [611] The party interrogated is not put under oath.

The interrogation is conducted by the judge. Counsel for both sides may be present. The court may conduct the interrogation in the presence of both parties, or it may confront the parties after the interrogation is over.

The party interrogated is first asked to make a narrative statement about the facts in question and may then be asked additional questions. Although counsel may not ask questions themselves, they may suggest questions to the court. [612]

The minutes of the interrogation are prepared in the same manner as in an *enquête*. Upon conclusion of the interrogation, the minutes are read to the party, and the court asks the party whether it has told the truth and whether it wishes to make any changes. Changes may be made at that time. The minutes are then signed by the presiding judge, the clerk, and the parties. The parties may obtain a copy of these minutes. [613]

A party who refuses to appear or to answer is not subject to a criminal penalty; however, his refusal may be considered a beginning of written proof under article 1347 of the *Code Civil* and thus relieve his opponent from the burden of producing documentary evidence. [614]

If illness or disability prevents a party from appearing in court, a judge may be delegated to conduct the examination in the party's home. [615] If a party lives at a distance from the place of examination, the examination may be conducted by another court selected for that purpose by letters rogatory. [616]

**a. Effects and purposes of the *comparution personnelle*.** The provisions of the *Code de Procédure Civile* concerning the *comparution personnelle* and the rules of the *Code Civil* concerning evidence are not in complete harmony. [617] The *Code Civil* considers parties only as sources of admissions, not as witnesses. The *comparution personnelle* procedure should therefore have been allowed only in cases in which admissions are valid evidence. However, the *Code de Procédure Civile*

[611] Code de Procédure Civile art. 325.
[612] Code de Procédure Civile arts. 329–30; Morel 409.
[613] Code de Procédure Civile art. 331.
[614] Code de Procédure Civile art. 336.
[615] Code de Procédure Civile art. 332.
[616] Code de Procédure Civile art. 333.
[617] *Cf.* Hébraud, *Commentaire, Loi du 23 mai 1942*, [1943] D. Cr. L. 10.

permits it to be used in all cases. [618] As a result, in divorce or separation actions and other actions in which admissions are not valid evidence, parties may be heard in a *comparution personnelle* to clarify other evidence in the case, to permit the court to form an opinion of the parties, [619] and in an effort to promote a settlement, [620] but not to elicit admissions.

To some extent, a *comparution personnelle* may also be used as a discovery device: Information gathered in a *comparution personnelle* may be used to obtain leads concerning additional witnesses or documents. [621]

The *comparution personnelle* further provides a means for evading article 1341 and various other rules requiring documentary evidence. Since the *comparution personnelle* may be used in every case, nothing prevents its use in actions in which written evidence is needed. If the person under examination appears and admits the existence of an agreement or other fact, his admission is full proof against him, even though no written document has been produced. [622] If he fails to appear or to answer, his failure constitutes beginning of written proof, which enables his opponent to prove the agreement by oral evidence. This is true whether evidence is required by article 1341 of the *Code Civil* or some other provision of law. [623]

## 7.54. Expert's Report *(Expertise)*

**a. When an *expertise* may be ordered.** An *expertise*, a special proceeding to obtain an expert's report, usually goes beyond eliciting expert testimony in response to hypothetical questions. [624] When only an expert opinion on established facts is required, counsel, rather than

[618] The *comparution* is possible in various actions (such as divorce) in which admissions are not allowed, as well as to hear persons, such as incompetents, whose admissions are not effective.

[619] MOREL 408.

[620] Hébraud, *supra* note 617, at 11.

[621] However, the *comparution personnelle*, for a variety of reasons, is not a very effective device in that respect. See SCHLESINGER, COMPARATIVE LAW 219 n. 19 (2d ed. 1959).

[622] *E.g.*, B. v. Dlle. Hunault, Cass. Civ., Nov. 5, 1957, [1958] D.J. 149 (admission in filiation case equivalent to signed admission of paternity, *minutes* of *comparution personnelle* being signed by party).

[623] CODE DE PROCÉDURE CIVILE art. 336 provides only that failure to appear and answer is a beginning of written proof under article 1347 of the Code Civil. Failure to appear or answer has also been considered as a beginning of written proof in other cases. *E.g.*, T. v. Dlle W., Cour Paris, Feb. 22, 1952, [1952] D.J. 401; Lévêque v. Dlle Péchinot, Cass. Civ., Feb. 7, 1950, [1950] S. 1. 189 (filiation cases).

[624] For a general discussion, see Hammelmann, *Expert Evidence*, 10 MODERN L. REV. 32 (1947). The *expertise* procedure was revised and simplified in 1944 by Law of July 15, 1944, J.O. July 27, 1944, p. 1903, [1944] D. ANAL. L. 82. For a commentary, see Hébraud, *Commentaire, Loi du 15 juillet 1944*, [1945] D.L. 49.

initiate an *expertise*, frequently submit written certificates containing the experts' opinions, which are admissible as inferences (*présomptions de fait*). [625]

Usually, in an *expertise*, the expert, in addition to forming his expert opinion, gathers facts on which to base it. Thus, he may perform an autopsy before reporting on the cause of death or he may examine an automobile involved in an accident before reporting on whether a defect in the manfacture caused the accident.

An *expertise* must be authorized by court order. [626] Ordinarily, the court may determine in its discretion whether to allow an *expertise*. In making its decision, it will be guided by the general rules governing the admissibility of evidence: The *expertise* may be ordered only as to facts which are *pertinents*, *concluants*, and *admissibles*. [627] Furthermore, in the case of the *expertise*, an additional requirement must be met. The *Code de Procédure Civile* provides that an expertise may be ordered only as to purely technical questions. [628] The term technical includes all matters requiring special knowledge not ordinarily possessed by a judge. [629] French judges have a tendency to disregard this requirement and to appoint experts to determine issues of fact, even if no questions requiring specialized knowledge are involved. [630]

In a few actions, an *expertise* is mandatory rather than optional. These include: (1) an action for the rescission of a sale of immovables on account of *lésion* (sale price amounting to less than 7/12th of the value of the property), (2) an action for the rescission of the sale of animals on account of certain defects (*vices rédhibitoires*), [631] (3) a partition action involving real property, [632] (4) an action involving the rental value of property, if there is no documentary evidence and the

[625] See 7.31 *supra*. Of course, judges are inclined to put more faith in the report of an expert than in a mere certificate submitted by a party. For restrictions on such certificates by official experts, see note 650 *infra*.

[626] Code de Procédure Civile art. 302.

[627] See 7.26 *supra*.

[628] Code de Procédure Civile art. 302.

[629] Bouton v. Vve Mion, Cour Paris, Oct. 24, 1957, [1958] D. Som. 56, Gaz. Pal. 12–15 Feb., 1958 (as to pure question of fact *expertise* not allowed); Lemaire v. Berthon, Cour Paris, July 2, 1943, [1944] D. Anal. J. 7 (as to accident case involving violation of right-of-way rules *expertise* not allowed); Coppe v. Moskaleff, Cour Paris, Oct. 23 1953, [1953] D.J. 686 (*expertise* allowed for purpose of preparing survey of accident site and examining various engineering questions bearing on accident).

[630] *E.g.*, Taki Meziane v. Hattab bey Akli, Cass. Soc., May 13, 1954, [1954] D.J. 591 (court appointed expert to find out whether tenant used apartment in "abusive" manner); Epoux Darnis v. Consorts Espeillac, Cass. Civ., [1954] D.J. 184 (expert appointed to find out extent of user of easement).

[631] Morel 403; Code Civil art. 1678 (*lésion*).

[632] Code Civil art. 824.

tenant refuses to be bound by the oath of the landlord, [633] and (5) filiation proceedings. [634]

**b. Who may order an *expertise*.** An *expertise* may be ordered in a pending case either by the court or by the *juge chargé de suivre la procédure*. [635] As a rule, the presiding judge of the *tribunal de grande instance* or his delegate sitting *en référé* may not order an *expertise* in a pending action, [636] except in cases of extreme urgency, when the delays of the regular procedure threaten to make an *expertise* impossible. [637] However, as long as some allegation of urgency is made, the courts have been fairly lenient in allowing a judge sitting *en référé* to order an *expertise* outside of any pending action.

**c. *Expertise* as a discovery device.** French practitioners have transformed the *expertise* ordered by the *référé* judge into a discovery device. In the case of automobile accidents, it is common practice to ask the *référé* judge, even before suit is brought, to appoint an expert with very broad powers to investigate all the circumstances of the accident, survey the scene, talk to all persons who may know anything about the event, and prepare a report. [638]

**d. Procedure for obtaining an *expertise*.** An *expertise* is ordinarily requested by means of *conclusions*. Service of the request on adverse parties is essential: An *expertise* ordered *ex parte* is void even if the opponent has participated in the activities of the expert. [639] After service of the *conclusions*, both sides present argument as to whether and on what issues an *expertise* should be ordered. If the court orders an

[633] CODE CIVIL art. 1716.

[634] CODE CIVIL art. 340, as amended in 1955, seems to make a blood grouping test mandatory in filiation cases upon request by the putative father. Such a blood grouping test is conducted in the form of an *expertise*.

[635] CODE DE PROCÉDURE CIVILE art. 81 (*juge chargé de suivre la procédure* may order any proof proceeding); CODE DE PROCÉDURE CIVILE art. 302.

[636] *E.g.*, Plesner v. Trost, Trib. Valence, April 23, 1956, [1956] J.C.P. 2. 9506 (note G.M.).

[637] Dothan v. Lamasson, Trib. Bayeux, Feb. 15, 1958, [1958] D. SOMM. 116 (witness necessary for *expertise* dying); Martineaux v. Epoux Boulingaud, Cass. Civ., March 16, 1960 [1960] D.J. 558 (building falling into disrepair).

[638] See, *e.g.*, Coppe v. Moskaleff, supra note 629; Raynaud, *Chronique*, 51 REV. TRIM. DR. CIV. 159 (1954). In the Coppe case, an expert was appointed to visit the scene of the accident, hear all persons knowing anything about the accident, obtain statements from the parties, prepare a survey of the accident scene, establish the paths of the vehicles up to the point of impact, and generally to reconstruct the accident.

[639] Soc. française des transports Gondrand v. Pech, Cass. Civ., Oct. 29, 1959, [1960] D. SOMM. 20. Even an *expertise* ordered *ex parte* and therefore void may apparently be used as the basis of an inference, at least if the opponent has received a copy. Soc. Friedenstadt et comp. v. Jeanclerc et comp., Cass. Req., Aug. 6, 1906, [1906] D. 1. 384.

*expertise*, its decision must state the names of the persons who are to act as experts and set forth in considerable detail the facts to be investigated.[640] Although the decision also includes a stock phrase to the effect that the expert is to conciliate the parties, if possible, few cases are settled through the good offices of experts. Within five days after the decision ordering the *expertise*, the *greffier* (clerk) of the court sends the expert a letter informing him of his appointment.[641] Also included in this letter is a form containing an oath of office, which the expert must sign and return within five days; otherwise, he is considered to have declined his appointment. The parties may, and frequently do, waive application of the rule that the expert must take an oath.

**e. Who may be appointed as an expert.** An expert is an officer of the court and must be impartial. In selecting an expert, the court is, therefore, not bound by the wishes of the parties.[642] Only French nationals may be experts, unless a treaty provides otherwise.[643] The parties may demand *récusation* (*disqualification*) of an expert if there are legitimate grounds for doubting his impartiality.[644] Demands for disqualification of an expert are very rare, perhaps because they are discouraged by the *Code de Procédure Civile*: The *avoué* making the demand must have a special power of attorney from his client;[645] if it is rejected, the expert as well as adverse parties may demand damages.[646] The demand is made to the court which has appointed the expert.[647]

As a rule, the court is quite free in the choice of the expert. However, an *avocat* may not be used as expert.[648] At one time, lists of sworn

[640] CODE DE PROCÉDURE CIVILE art. 302. The experts must limit their report to the matters listed in the decision unless the parties waive reliance on this rule. CODE DE PROCÉDURE CIVILE art. 304.

[641] CODE DE PROCÉDURE CIVILE art. 307. No *grosse* of the decision ordering the *expertise* has to be procured or served.

[642] MOREL 404.

[643] CODE DE PROCÉDURE CIVILE art. 306. The rule is apparently based on the idea that an expert is a quasi-public officer.

[644] The disqualification of an expert may be demanded if there are legitimate reasons to doubt his impartiality. Whether such reasons exist is apparently left to the discretion of the courts. DALLOZ, RÉPERTOIRE DE PROCÉDURE CIVILE ET COMMERCIALE, *Expertise*, at No. 114 (Supp. 1964); Le Roy, *Expertise*, in 3 JURISCLASSEUR FORMULAIRE ANALYTIQUE DE PROCÉDURE (Supp. 1962).

[645] CODE DE PROCÉDURE CIVILE art. 309.

[646] CODE DE PROCÉDURE CIVILE art. 314. But if the expert has obtained damages, he may not remain as expert.

[647] CODE DE PROCÉDURE CIVILE art. 308. The demand must be made within twenty days after the appointment of the expert.

[648] Raynaud, *Chronique*, 52 REV. TRIM. DR. CIV. 158 (1955); *cf.* Epoux Darnis v. Cons. Espeillac, Cass. Civ., Jan. 5, 1954, [1954] D.J. 184.

experts were used, from which the court had to make its choice. Such official lists no longer exist. However, there are lists of a semi-official character, from which the judges customarily select the experts they appoint. [649] These lists are prepared by the presiding judge of the court or by a judge delegated by him. The list is ordinarily prepared in co-operation with professional organizations of the various trades and professions. It may be very extensive; in Paris, it is over forty pages long and contains numerous specialties, from agriculture, accounting, and chemistry to medicine, physics, surveying, and wine growing. Larger courts may have a special office, called *service du contrôle des experts*, which keeps these lists up-to-date. This office is headed by one of the judges of the court, who is assisted by a staff. The office exercises some disciplinary power over experts: It receives complaints against experts based on demands for excessive fees or other improper conduct, and, in an appropriate case, removes an expert from the list. The *service du contrôle des experts* in Paris enforces rigorous standards of professional conduct. [650] Since the list of experts itself is not binding, removal of an expert from the list does not legally prevent his appointment, but in practice an appointment will not ordinarily be given to a person who has been struck from the list.

Ordinarily, the court may appoint either one or three experts. [651] To save expenses, usually only one expert is appointed. However, in *inscription de faux* [652] and *vérification d'écritures* [653] proceedings, the appointment of three experts is mandatory. An expert need not accept his appointment. If he declines the appointment, or fails to return the signed form containing the oath within five days, another expert must be appointed by the *juge chargé de suivre la procédure*. [654]

[649] MOREL 403.

[650] CODE CIVIL art. 5 deprives the courts of any rule-making power, but the *service du contrôle des experts* in Paris has established a number of rules for the conduct of experts. Some of these are mere paraphrases of statutory regulations, but others go further. Thus, no medical expert may become an expert for an insurance company; experts may never demand fees directly from parties, only through the *avoué*; they may demand payments on account before completion of their work, but only with court approval. They must file annual statistics of their work. The parties may use certificates given by listed experts only if they are unsigned and contain no indication that the person who has given the certificate is on the official list. TRIBUNAL DE GRANDE INSTANCE DE LA SEINE, LISTE DES SPÉCIALISTES ET TECHNICIENS LE PLUS SOUVENT DÉSIGNÉS COMME EXPERTS EN MATIÈRE CIVILE PAR LA COUR D'APPEL DE PARIS ET LE TRIBUNAL DE GRANDE INSTANCE DE LA SEINE (1961).

[651] CODE DE PROCÉDURE CIVILE art. 196. Three experts are more likely to be appointed before a *cour d'appel*.

[652] See CODE DE PROCÉDURE CIVILE arts. 236, 196.

[653] CODE DE PROCÉDURE CIVILE art. 196. Three experts must also be used in cases involving rescission of a contract on account of *lésion* (gross insufficiency of price). CODE CIVIL art. 1678.

[654] CODE DE PROCÉDURE CIVILE art. 316.

**f. Conduct of the *expertise*.** Parties must attend the conduct of an *expertise*, except when purely technical operations are being performed. They are notified of the opening of an *expertise* by an *acte d'avoué à avoué*, usually by the *avoué* of the party who requested the *expertise*. [655] At the opening of the *expertise*, the parties meet with and present memoranda, containing their contentions, called *dires* (sayings), to the expert. [656] The actual conduct of the *expertise* depends on the facts to be investigated. The expert may conduct scientific experiments, blood grouping tests, compare samples of handwritings, examine art objects, and engage in similar activities and may also examine witnesses. Witnesses questioned by experts are not put under oath. Their statements, when embodied in the expert's report, may be considered by the court, but only as the basis for an inference, not as testimony. [657]

A somewhat simplified procedure exists for conducting a formal *enquête* of witnesses whose testimony appears useful to the expert. Upon application, the *juge chargé de suivre la procédure* may order witnesses to be heard in an *enquête*. [658] The experts may either be present at, or consult the minutes of, the *enquête*. [659] These minutes qualify as testimony.

Ordinarily, an expert must perform his duties in person and may not delegate them to others. [660] However, the courts do not seem to object if experts rely on the assistance of outsiders in minor matters. [661] If there are three experts, all three should be present at all investigations, but that rule is not enforced strictly. [662] The *juge chargé de suivre la procédure* must be kept informed about the progress of the *expertise* and may be present when it is conducted. [663]

Unless the expert requests an extension of time from the *juge chargé de suivre la procédure*, the *expertise* must be terminated on the day

[655] CODE DE PROCEDURE CIVILE art. 315; de la Marnierre v. Poitou, Cass. Civ., April 23, 1964, [1964] D.J. 601 (*expertise* concerning damage done by game void as parties not present when expert inspected premises).

[656] CODE DE PROCÉDURE CIVILE art. 317. This article also provides that the expert must be given a copy of the judgment ordering the *expertise* and of all pertinent papers.

[657] CUCHE & VINCENT 572; Bordier v. Cons. Eon-Voisin, Cass. Civ., June 28, 1954, [1954] D.J. 612.

[658] CODE DE PROCÉDURE CIVILE art. 303.

[659] Janvier v. Creste, Cour Anger, Feb. 12, 1960, [1960] D.J. 252; Raynaud, *Chronique* 59 REV. TRIM. DR. CIV. 359.

[660] *E.g.*, Soc. des transports urbains et ruraux v. LaLanne, Cour Pau, Sept. 27, 1960, [1960] D. SOMM. 119.

[661] Dr. Secret v. Briquet, Cass. Civ., May 29, 1937, [1937] D.H. 393.

[662] Commune de Bône v. Jumel de Noiaterre, Cass. Civ., June 5, 1894, [1894] D. 1. 123 (although of the three experts appointed to determine extent of damage caused by fire one only prepared a survey, decision based on opinion of experts affirmed).

[663] CODE DE PROCÉDURE CIVILE art. 315.

mentioned in the decision. If that is not done and if the *expertise* is not terminated in time, the *juge chargé de suivre la procédure* must request an explanation from the expert. An expert who does not offer a satisfactory explanation for his tardiness may be summoned to appear before the full court, which may replace him. In that case, the expert must bear the costs of the *expertise* and may even have to pay damages to the parties. [664] As a practical matter, these provisions are not always effective in expediting *expertises*. Since the parties must ordinarily be present when the *expertise* is conducted, some delay is encountered in finding days that are convenient for all persons concerned. In addition, the experts themselves are likely to be busy practitioners in their own specialty. Delays are especially long when an *expertise* is conducted by three experts. Its completion may take up to one year, or even longer.

At the conclusion of the *expertise*, the expert prepares his report. First the *dires* (statements) submitted by the parties are listed, then the expert describes the factual investigations made, and finally, he expresses his opinion. The parties must be present while the expert prepares that part of the report that deals with factual investigations, but not while the expert prepares the portion of the report that contains his opinion. The report is signed by the expert; if there are three experts and one dissents, the dissent is noted in the report, but the name of the dissenting expert is not given. [665]

At the bottom of the report, the expert lists his fee and his expenses If there is a dispute between the expert and the parties, the expert's fee may be taxed by the court. The courts keep fees to reasonable amounts. While complaints about excessive fees of experts are sometimes heard, the fees of experts are ordinarily reasonable; even a fairly prominent medical man is likely to charge only 500 francs (about $ 100) for an *expertise*. The highest fees, higher than those of physicians, are charged by accountants.

**g. Proceedings subsequent to the *expertise*.** When the *expertise* is completed, the original of the report prepared by the expert is filed in the office of the *greffier* (clerk) [666] and copies are transmitted to the parties. [667] Subsequently, there is another *audience* before the full

[664] Code de Procédure Civile art. 320; Morel 406.
[665] Morel 406; Code de Procédure Civile art. 318.
[666] Code de Procédure Civile art. 319.
[667] This is not automatic. One of the *avoués* must get copies at the clerk's office and serve one on all adverse parties. Code de Procédure Civile art. 321.

court, [668] at which the *avocats* of the parties may make all appropriate arguments regarding the *expertise*.

They may argue that the *expertise* should be declared void because one of the rules regulating the conduct of *expertises* has not been observed. In theory, an *expertise* declared void may not be used by the court as a basis for its decision. However, even *expertises* declared void are sometimes used as the basis for inferences. [669] A decision declaring the *expertise* void cannot be requested once argument on the merits of the experts' report has been presented. [670]

The *avocats* of the parties may also present argument addressed to the substance of the report. In making such argument, counsel may rely on inconsistencies, or conflicts with recognized authorities, such as textbooks, and on other similar forms of attack. The court may, but rarely does, request the expert to attend the *audience* to explain his report. [671]

**h. Probative effect of *expertise*.** French judges are free to give whatever weight they consider proper to the report of the expert. [672] Only in paternity proceedings, a blood grouping test showing that the defendant cannot be the father of the child is conclusive. [673] The results of an *expertise* are also conclusive if the parties have stipulated in advance of the *expertise* that they will accept them. [674]

The court may order a new *expertise* on its own motion to obtain additional information. The original experts must give the experts appointed by the court to perform this additional *expertise* all data requested. [675]

As a practical matter, French courts generally accept reports of

[668] The party having obtained and served a copy of the report summons adverse parties to a new *audience* by *acte d'avoué à avoué*. CODE DE PROCÉDURE CIVILE art. 321. For sample *conclusions*, see Appendix, Form No. 12.

[669] See 7.31 *supra*.

[670] See 7.09 *supra*; *cf.* CODE DE PROCÉDURE CIVILE art. 192; CUCHE & VINCENT 533. The rules governing requests to have an *expertise* declared void are the same as those applicable in the case of *enquêtes*. See 7.51.g *supra*.

[671] MOREL 407.

[672] CODE DE PROCÉDURE CIVILE art. 323 provides expressly that judges need not follow the opinion of experts against their conviction. However, the rule of free evaluation of the report seems to be applicable only to the opinions and conclusions of the experts. As far as the report relates things the experts have done, it is generally treated as an authentic act which can be impeached only by an *inscription de faux*. See also 9.07 n. 52 *infra*.

[673] Such a test is listed among the defenses (*fins de non-recevoir*) leading to summary dismissal of paternity proceedings. CODE CIVIL art. 340.

[674] See Caillon v. Bardel, Cass. Civ., April 19, 1944, [1945] D.J. 56.

[675] CODE DE PROCÉDURE CIVILE art. 322.

experts.[676] The judicial tendency to accept the results of an *expertise* without question has often been criticized and makes an *expertise* somewhat of a risk.[677]

**i. *Enquête sociale.*** A special kind of *expertise* is in use in divorce and separation proceedings in order to determine the custody of children.[678] In these cases, the court appoints a social worker to investigate the circumstances of the parties, talk to all persons who may know anything about the case, and then make suggestions to the court. As in the case of a regular *expertise,* the court is not bound by the suggestions of the social worker.[679]

### 7.55. Direct Proof

**a. Demonstrative evidence.** Movable objects or pictures may be presented to the court by the *avocat* during his argument at the *audience* (hearing). Although the production of such demonstrative evidence is not regulated by any statute, this procedure is in current use and its legality is not doubtful.[680] However, reliance on this type of evidence is limited: The absence of general discovery procedures ordinarily restricts each party to the production of objects which are in its own possession.

**b. Viewing the premises: *descente sur les lieux.*** To permit the court to inspect real property or personal property which is too large to be brought into the courtroom, recourse must be taken to the *descente sur les lieux* (literally, descent upon the premises). The drafters of the *Code de Procédure Civile* designed this procedure mainly for use in actions involving land, but it is now used in many other situations in which judicial inspection of an object may be of value. Thus, courts

[676] MOREL 402; Hébraud, *supra* note 617. This tendency persists in spite of a number of decisions of the *Cour de Cassation,* in accord with CODE DE PROCÉDURE CIVILE art. 323, that judges are not bound to follow the opinion of the experts. *E.g.,* Chossegros v. Chossegros, Cass. Req., Oct. 28, 1935, [1936] D.H. 34; Vve David Chassagnole v. Terne et Durand-Ruel, Cass. Req., Dec. 23, 1892, [1892] D. 1. 409 (court need not follow opinion of experts and may base its decision on inferences, as long as the parties have an opportunity to discuss the materials submitted as a basis for inferences).

[677] *Cf.* SCHLESINGER, COMPARATIVE LAW 227 (2d ed. 1959).

[678] CODE CIVIL art. 238.

[679] In spite of its name, the *enquête sociale* is an *expertise* rather than an *enquête*: The court is more interested in the opinion of the social worker than in the unsworn statements of the persons to whom she has talked. For commentaries on the *enquête sociale*, see Raynaud, *Chronique*, 57 REV. TRIM. DR. CIV. 372; Carbonnier, *Commentaire*, [1945] D.L. 145, 149.

[680] See SICARD, LA PREUVE EN JUSTICE APRÈS LA RÉFORME JUDICIAIRE 310, 324 (1960); MOREL 382.

frequently view the site, and may even proceed to a fairly elaborate reconstruction, of an accident. [681]

A *descente sur les lieux* may take place only pursuant to an interlocutory court decision. [682] However, the parties waive the right to argue that a *descente sur les lieux* conducted by the court without a formal interlocutory decision is void by accompanying the court on its inspection. [683]

A *descente sur les lieux* is requested by the parties by *conclusions*. The *tribunal d'instance* may order a *descente sur les lieux* on its own motion; [684] the *tribunal de grande instance* may do so on its own motion only in those cases in which an *expertise* is not specifically authorized by law. [685]

In passing upon a request for a *descente sur les lieux*, the court is guided by the usual principles determining the admissibility of evidence. If the court authorizes a *descente sur les lieux*, it must also designate one of the judges who have heard the case to execute the *descente*. [686] At the request of the *avoué* for either party, the designated judge issues an order fixing the day on which he will view the premises. This order must be served on the other side by the *avoué* who has obtained it and constitutes an invitation to be present at the *descente*. [687] Although the *Code de Procédure Civile* provides specifically that a *descente sur les lieux* must be executed by one judge, inspection by all three judges sitting in the case does not invalidate the *descente*. [688] However,

[681] MOREL 382. On its use in accident cases, see Le Roy, *La reconstitution sur place des accidents de la circulation par les juridictions de jugement*, [1956] D. CHR. 157. The *descente sur les lieux* is also used in suits concerning alleged plagiarism; in such cases, the court frequently decides to view the performances involved. SICARD, *op. cit. supra* note 680, at 324.

[682] CODE DE PROCÉDURE CIVILE art. 41 (*tribunal d'instance*); CODE DE PROCÉDURE CIVILE art. 295; *cf.* Chabaud v. Charmasson, Cass. Civ., Oct. 21, 1907, [1908] D. 1. 64 ( reversing judgment based on inspection by one of court's judges of place where alleged illegal cutting of timber had taken place, performed without an official decision authorizing it and in the absence of the parties).

[683] Breton v. Descamp, Cour Anger, Feb. 8, 1897, [1899] D. 2. 20 (when all three members of court viewed premises without prior interlocutory decision and without preparing formal report, parties waived right to object by participating in proceedings); Soc. Lilloise v. Duhot, Cass. Req., June 27, 1915, [1916] D. 2. 262.

[684] CODE DE PROCÉDURE CIVILE art. 41.

[685] CODE DE PROCÉDURE CIVILE art. 295; *cf.* CODE CIVIL art. 1678 prescribing *expertise* in actions involving the rescission of a contract for the sale of land on account of *lésion*, *i.e.*, gross insufficiency of the purchase price. The rule has historical reasons: Before the ORDONNANCE of 1667, the courts, because of the large fees they collected, ordered this procedure too freely. CUCHE & VINCENT 566.

[686] CODE DE PROCÉDURE CIVILE art. 296. If the case is pending before the *tribunal d'instance*, the judge who hears the case executes the *descente sur les lieux* with his clerk. CODE DE PROCÉDURE CIVILE art. 41.

[687] CODE DE PROCÉDURE CIVILE art. 297.

[688] Breton v. Descamps, *supra* note 683.

only the expenses and mileage of one judge may be taxed as costs. [689]

On the appointed day, the judge and his clerk (*greffier*) proceed to the premises. [690] If specialized knowledge is required for appreciation of the facts, the judge of the *tribunal d'instance* may request experts to accompany him. [691] Although no specific statutory authority for following this procedure exists, the *tribunal de grande instance* may also combine an *expertise* with a view of the premises. [692] If the parties are present at the premises, they may make comments for the benefit of the judge. To gather additional information, the judge may also talk to other persons who may be present. After having viewed the premises, the judge dictates to the clerk a report (*procès-verbal*), which also mentions the comments made by the parties. Either party may obtain copies of the report at the clerks' office. The party who has first obtained copies must serve one on adverse parties.

After the *descente*, the case is re-instated on the calendar for another *audience* (hearing). [693] The parties proceed as in the case of other *audiences* following proof proceedings.

The judge and the clerk who view premises are entitled to mileage fees and travel expenses. A schedule of the fees payable in this case was established by a decree of 1920. In practice, this schedule is not used, as the devaluation of the French franc has rendered it completely unrealistic. The courts now use the much more recent schedule of travel expenses contained in the *Code de Procédure Pénale*. [694] The expected travel expenses must be deposited in the court clerk's office by the party who has requested the *descente sur les lieux*. [695]

[689] CUCHE & VINCENT 567. If the premises to be viewed are too far away from the place where the court sits, the court may designate another *tribunal de grande instance* or one of its judges, or even a judge of a *tribunal d'instance*, to view the premises. CODE DE PROCÉDURE CIVILE art. 1035.

[690] CORNU & FOYER 542; CODE DE PROCÉDURE CIVILE art. 30 (*tribunal d'instance*).

[691] CODE DE PROCÉDURE CIVILE art. 42.

[692] For examples see Le Roy, *supra* note 681.

[693] CODE DE PROCÉDURE CIVILE arts. 298–99. Since the judge viewing the premises must also decide the case, no report (*procès-verbal*) need be prepared in case of a *descente sur les lieux* undertaken by a *tribunal d'instance* unless an appeal is possible. In fact, the judge of the *tribunal d'instance* is authorized to render his decision while still on the premises and without a new *audience*. CODE DE PROCÉDURE CIVILE arts. 42–43.

[694] See the note in DALLOZ, CODE DE PROCÉDURE CIVILE 591 (61st ed. 1964).

[695] If means of mass transportation are available, judge and clerk are entitled to the price of a first-class ticket if they must go to a place further than four kilometers (about 2.5 miles) from the municipality in which they live; otherwise, they receive a mileage fee. An additional flat fee of F. 7 (about $ 1.40) is payable if a trip of more than 10 kilometers (about 6 miles) is involved. It is doubled if the trip is longer than 50 kilometers (about 31 miles). CODE DE PROCÉDURE PÉNALE arts. R 203, R 204.

### 7.56. Party-Oath *(Serment)*

The party-oath (*serment*) is a remnant of the formalistic medieval procedure.[696] In present times, it is used very infrequently. A party swearing a party-oath does not testify as to the facts in litigation and is not subject to cross-examination; he merely swears under oath as to the existence of the fact or facts specified in the court decision authorizing the oath.

Party-oaths are usually divided into three categories: (1) the *serment décisoire* (decisory oath), (2) the *serment supplétoire* (supplemental oath), and (3) the *serment in litem* or *serment in plaids* (oath relating to damages).

**a. *Serment décisoire* (decisory oath).** The *serment décisoire* (decisory oath) is a means for settling a factual issue conclusively and without further proof. A decisory oath sworn on an issue decides it absolutely; no counterproof can overcome the oath.[697] Nor is this result changed if the party who swore the oath is subsequently convicted of perjury.[698]

A party may swear a party-oath only if it is tendered by his opponent and the court authorizes it. A party-oath has been compared to a settlement or compromise, since it amounts in substance to an agreement to lose the case if the other side is willing to take the oath.[699] The party to whom the oath has been tendered may tender it back and will lose if the party who originally tendered the oath swears to the negative of the proposition sought to be established by his opponent. The oath may not be tendered a third time.[700]

Although the *Code Civil* provides that the decisory oath may be tendered in any action,[701] it may not be taken in cases strongly affected with public policy, such as actions involving personal status, including divorce.[702] However, since the party-oath may be tendered

[696] See generally Silving, *The Oath*, 68 YALE L. J. 1329, 1528–29 (1959).

[697] CODE CIVIL art. 1361. Conversely, a party who has been tendered the oath and who refuses to take it must lose the case unless the oath can be tendered back.

[698] This follows from CODE CIVIL art. 1363, which provides that an opponent may never prove the falsity of the party oath. The party who has lost its case because of perjury may join in the criminal perjury proceeding as a "civil party" to demand damages. See 2 COLIN & CAPITANT 543; 2 GARSONNET & CÉZAR-BRU 490.

[699] 2 COLIN & CAPITANT 542; 2 GARSONNET & CÉZAR-BRU 490.

[700] See CODE CIVIL art. 1361; 2 COLIN & CAPITANT 541.

[701] CODE CIVIL art. 1358.

[702] 2 COLIN & CAPITANT 542. Ordinarily, either party may tender the decisory oath to the other. However, in cases involving unexecuted oral leases, the decisory oath may be tendered only to the party who denies existence of the lease. CODE CIVIL art. 1715.

in a case in which article 1341 of the *Code Civil* or a similar rule requires documentary evidence, [703] it is a possible means for avoiding these rules.

The decisory oath may be tendered only upon a factual issue that is within the direct personal experience of the party to whom the oath has been tendered. [704] Thus, the plaintiff may tender an oath to the defendant on whether he has received money from the plaintiff, but not on whether somebody else (for whom defendant may be a surety) has received money.

The rule stated is subject to one exception. A number of comparatively short [705] statutes of limitation, which are really presumptions of payment, apply to claims arising from negotiable instruments, [706] to claims of innkeepers, laborers, teachers, [707] doctors, and *avoués*, [708] and to a few similar claims. Persons relying on these presumptions of payment may be asked to state under oath whether they have actually made payment. An oath to that effect may be tendered not only to the debtor himself, but also to his widow or universal successors, and to the guardian of a minor, [709] and even to a corporation, which may swear it through one of its officers. [710]

Since the decisory oath is considered as a kind of compromise, it may be tendered only by a party having legal capacity to conclude a compromise. The same capacity is required of the party to whom the oath is tendered. [711]

[703] No beginning of written proof is necessary. CODE CIVIL art. 1360. While a party may try to avoid the effect of article 1341 by tendering an oath, the party-oath is no substitute for a writing if a writing is required as a condition for the existence of the contract itself.

[704] CODE CIVIL art. 1359. A party to whom the oath has been tendered may tender it back only if the fact is within the personal experience of both sides. CODE CIVIL art. 1369.

[705] The ordinary French statute of limitations in contract and tort cases is 30 years. CODE CIVIL art. 2262.

[706] Limitation period: three years against the acceptor and one year against the endorsers in the case of bills of exchange (CODE DE COMMERCE art. 179) and promissory notes (CODE DE COMMERCE art. 185); three years against the drawee, and six months against the drawer and the endorsers, in the case of checks. DÉCRET-LOI of Oct. 30, 1935, J.O. Oct. 31, 1935, [1935] D. 4. 467, art. 52.

[707] Limitation period: six months. CODE CIVIL art. 2271.

[708] Limitation period: two years. CODE CIVIL art. 2272 (doctors, dentists, and midwives); CODE CIVIL art. 2273 (*avoués*).

[709] CODE CIVIL art. 2275 (claims of teachers, laborers, doctors, and *avoués*); CODE DE COMMERCE arts. 179, 185 (bills of exchange, and promissory notes); DÉCRET-LOI of Oct. 30, 935, *supra* note 706, art. 53.

[710] In case of a corporation, the oath is necessarily taken by a corporate officer rather than by the corporation itself, but does not concern the officer personally, as is ordinarily required in the case of the party-oath. For this reason, older cases did not permit the tendering of an oath to a corporation, but a recent *Cour de Cassation* case has held to the contrary. Mohamed ben Abdallah v. Soc. des Travaux souterrains, Cass. Soc., June 28, 1957, [1957] D.J. 711 (with note discussing the problem).

[711] 2 COLIN & CAPITANT 542.

If one of several joint creditors tenders an oath to the debtor on the issue of whether he owes the debt and the debtor takes the oath, only the pro-rata claim of the joint creditor who has tendered the oath is barred; the claims of the other creditors are not affected. However, the converse is not true: If either the principal or his surety asserts in a decisory oath that no debt is due, both principal and surety are freed from any obligation; a denial under oath by one of several joint debtors that the debt exists will likewise exonerate all the joint debtors. [712]

**b. Procedure followed in swearing a decisory oath.** A party wishing to tender a decisory oath must request court permission, by way of *conclusions*. [713] A judge sitting *en référé* is apparently not authorized to allow the tendering of a decisory oath. [714] If permission to tender the decisory oath is not sought by the party personally, but by its *avoué* or other representative, the representative must receive a special power of attorney from his client. [715] Permission to tender a decisory oath may be requested at any stage of the proceedings, even in cases in which article 1341 of the *Code Civil* is applicable; no beginning of written proof is necessary. [716]

Though the *Code Civil* seems to contemplate that permission for a decisory oath will be granted automatically in every case in which such an oath is tendered, [717] permission will not be granted if the court has already made up its mind about the facts to be sworn to. [718] Further, a decisory oath may not be imposed upon a party by the court acting on its own motion.

If the court authorizes the taking of the decisory oath, its decision must state the date on which the oath must be taken and the fact or facts which are to be sworn to. [719] The decision must be served upon the *avoué* of the party which is to take the oath, as well as on the party itself. [720]

[712] Code Civil art. 1365.

[713] CUCHE & VINCENT 565.

[714] Veuve Simonetti v. Gunzberg, Trib. Toulouse, June 28, 1950, [1950] GAZ. PAL. 2. 184; Kettar Mohand v. Chelouah Ahmed, Cour Lyon, Nov. 8, 1954, [1955] J.C.P. 8636.

[715] 2 COLIN & CAPITANT 542. Ordinarily, an *avoué* needs no written power of attorney.

[716] CODE CIVIL art. 1360.

[717] CODE CIVIL art. 1358 provides that the decisory oath may be tendered in any case.

[718] Nor will the oath be authorized in divorce cases. See 2 GARSONNET & CÉZAR-BRU 498 2 COLIN & CAPITANT 544.

[719] CODE DE PROCÉDURE CIVILE art. 120. If both parties are present at the *audience* at which the oath is requested and make no objections, the court may decide that the oath be taken at once. CUCHE & VINCENT 565.

[720] CODE DE PROCÉDURE CIVILE art. 121 seems to require only service upon the *avoué*, if

The oath is taken in open court during an *audience*; both sides should be present. [721] Although judicial practice has developed certain ceremonies, no specific formula beyond the words *je le jure* (I swear) is required. [722] Since the oath conclusively settles the issue on which it is taken, it is ordinarily not followed by another *audience*.

**c. *Serment supplétoire* (supplemental oath).** Under certain circumstances, the court may, on its own motion, request a party to take an oath as to one of the facts in issue. Since it is used to supplement existing proof, this oath is called *serment supplétoire* (supplemental oath).

A court may request a party to take a supplemental oath when there is some evidence in the case, but it is not sufficient to permit the court to render a proper decision. [723] In cases in which documentary evidence is required by article 1341 of the Code Civil or a similar provision, unless there is a beginning of written proof, [724] a supplemental oath may not be used. Nor, apparently, may a supplemental oath be used in matters involving strong public policy, such as divorce cases.

The court will ordinarily ask the party it considers more worthy of belief to take the supplemental oath. The supplemental oath is not necessarily restricted to matters within the direct personal knowledge of the party taking it. The court is not bound to decide in favor of the party which has taken the supplemental oath, but may evaluate the proof freely. [725] A party which has been asked by the court to take the supplemental oath may not tender it to the other side. [726]

A variant of the supplemental oath is the oath which may be imposed under article 17 of the *Code de Commerce*: If a party in commercial litigation states that it agrees to be bound by the entries in his opponent's books of account, the opponent must bring them into court for inspection. If he fails to do so, the party which has agreed to be bound

there is one, but, since the oath is an act which must be performed by the party directly, rather than by its *avoué*, the courts also require service upon the party. CUCHE & VINCENT 566.

[721] If the party is unable to come to court on account of illness or otherwise, the court may delegate one of its judges to go to the party's home with a clerk (*greffier*) and take the oath there. If a party lives at a distance from the court, the oath may be taken before the court where the party resides. The other side must always be notified of the time and place of the oath-taking by an *acte d'avoué à avoué*, and must have a chance to be present. CODE DE PROCÉDURE CIVILE arts. 121, 1035.

[722] MOREL 410.

[723] CODE CIVIL arts. 1366–1367.

[724] 2 GARSONNET & CÉZAR-BRU 505; 2 COLIN & CAPITANT 544.

[725] *Ibid.*

[726] CODE CIVIL art. 1368.

by the books may be authorized by the court to take a supplemental oath as to the facts in issue.

The procedural aspects of the supplemental and of the decisory oath are similar.

**d. *Serment in litem* or *serment in plaids*.** The *serment in plaids*, also called *serment in litem*, oath during the suit, has many aspects of the supplemental oath. [727] It may be used if the basic factual issues are no longer in doubt, but it is impossible to determine by other means the value of an object for the loss of or injury to which damages are demanded. In such a case, the court may ask the plaintiff – never the defendant – to state the value of the object under oath. [728] In its decision ordering a *serment in litem*, the court must specify a maximum value. This does not mean that the court must believe the plaintiff's statement if it is below that figure: The court may grant damages that are lower than those asserted by the plaintiff, but it may not go above the maximum it has set. [729] The oath *in litem* is used more than other forms of party-oath.

### 7.57. Proof in Actions with Foreign Elements

**a. Substance and procedure in the law of evidence.** The general rule is that matters of procedure are governed by the law of the forum. [730] However, only parts of the law of evidence are considered procedural. Whenever an evidentiary question is closely related to the substantive rights of parties, the courts treat it as substantive for conflict of laws purposes. For this reason, questions relating to presumptions and burden of proof are resolved in accordance with the law determining the parties' substantive rights. [731] Similarly, the law of the nationality, which usually governs in matters of personal status, [732] determines

[727] The French Civil Code considers it merely as a variant of the supplemental oath. See CODE CIVIL arts. 1357, 1366.

[728] CODE CIVIL art. 1369. For example, since nobody except the plaintiff himself will ordinarily have any knowledge of its contents, the *serment in plaids* may be used in a case in which damages for the loss of a suit-case are demanded from a common carrier. *Cf.* 2 COLIN & CAPITANT 545.

[729] CODE CIVIL art. 1369; 2 COLIN & CAPITANT 545; 2 GARSONNET & CÉZAR-BRU 509–10.

[730] *E.g.*, BATIFFOL 803.

[731] *Id.* 809. *But see* Garinau v. Pierre, Cass. Civ., Jan. 10, 1951, 78 CLUNET 882 (1951) (in will contest, question of due execution governed by French law of place of making of will, not by Egyptian law which governs succession).

[732] CODE CIVIL art. 3; BATIFFOL 434–43. In divorce cases, however, French courts apply the law of the domicile rather than that of the nationality if the spouses are of different nationality. *Id.* 441, 514.

questions relating to the use of admissions in divorce proceedings [733] and to the effect of a birth certificate as evidence of the recognition of a natural child or as evidence of filiation. [734]

**b. Evidentiary matters that are considered procedural.** The manner in which proof is presented, since it is considered procedural, is governed by French law. Accordingly, expert evidence must be introduced in the form of an *expertise*, and a witness must be heard in an *enquête*.

French law also determines the capacity of witnesses and the scope of privileged communications: Matters falling within the orbit of article 378 of the *Code Pénal* prohibiting the disclosure of professional secrets may not be introduced as evidence in a suit pending in France. [735]

The very liberal French rules as to *présomptions de fait* (inferences) are likewise considered procedural [736] and permit reliance on hearsay or opinion evidence outlawed by the law of the place determining the substantive rights of the parties.

**c. Impact of the rule *locus regit actum*.** As a general rule, the law of the forum governs the admissibility of proof. However, in the case of documentary evidence, this rule is tempered by the maxim *locus regit actum*. The maxim implies (1) that written evidence of a transaction or an event is required only if it is required at the place at which the event or transaction took place and (2) that the form of writing that is required is governed by the same law. In some cases, however, the courts have applied an alternative reference rule: French law, rather than the law of the place of the transaction, has been used when the French proof rules were less restrictive. [737]

[733] This is considered as substantive since permitting the use of admissions amounts to permitting divorce by consent. See BATIFFOL 810; *cf.* Figue v. Dedykère, Cass. Civ., June 17, 1958, [1958] J.C.P. 2. 10761 (Guatemalan divorce not given effect since based entirely on admission and thus amounting to divorce by consent).

[734] See De Torres v. Méchain, Cour Paris, Aug. 2, 1876, [1879] S. 2. 250 (birth certificate issued in Philippines mentioning father does not amount to recognition of child by father; when father is a French national recognition of child may take place only according to rules provided by French law); *cf.* Lathoud v. consorts Col, Cass. Civ., June 26, 1889, [1891] D. 1. 129 (birth certificate as evidence of filiation). In the French view, illegitimate filiation creates a status having some of the characteristics of legitimate filiation, but paternity proceedings may be brought only under certain conditions. See CODE CIVIL arts. 334–42. For this reason, in this area evidentiary rules are considered as substantive.

[735] BATIFFOL 813; *cf.* Dame Ancel v. Ancel, Cass. Req., Nov. 22, 1916, [1918] S. 1. 121 (evidence procured in Italy through letters rogatory not usable in French suit since it contained "professional secrets" privileged under CODE PÉNAL art. 378).

[736] BATIFFOL 814.

[737] *Id.* 811. The rule *locus regit actum* deals only with formal requirements, not with

These liberal conflict of laws rules make the requirements of French internal law concerning documentary evidence less burdensome in international litigation. [738] Thus, a marriage may be proved by cohabitation and reputation if the parties have always lived in an American state in which such proof is admissible. [739] Similarly, a certificate of baptism or a medical certificate may be used to show the date of birth if there are no official birth records at the place of birth.[740]

The rule *locus regit actum* is also applicable to contracts and other legal transactions: Thus, the date of a contract made abroad does not have to be corroborated by the formalities mentioned in article 1328 of the *Code Civil*. [741] French law does not seem to be concerned with

substance. It governs the question whether a marriage certificate issued by a public officer must be used as proof of marriage. See note 739 *infra*. The substantive validity of the marriage, being a question of status, depends ordinarily on the nationality of the parties. See note 732 *supra*. Capacity to contract is likewise governed by the nationality of the parties; the substantive validity of a contract in other respects depends on the intent of the parties or is determined by a grouping of contacts theory. BATIFFOL 618–27. Only the question whether a contract must necessarily be shown by a writing, and if so, by what type of a writing, is governed by the law of the place where the contract has been made.

[738] On the situations in which documentary evidence is required by French internal law, see 7.35–7.42 *supra*.

[739] Bousquet v. Dasque, Cass. Req., Dec. 20, 1841, [1842] S. 1. 322 (principle of common law marriage in Pennsylvania recognized, but evidence of cohabitation and reputation considered insufficient); De Valmy v. Ridgway, Cass. Req., Jan. 13, 1857, [1857] S. 1. 82 (marriage of parties in Pennsylvania shown by cohabitation and reputation); *cf.* Cherskowski-Leitner v. Hirsch Leitner, Trib. Seine, March 15, 1883, [1883] GAZ. PAL. 1. 51 (marriage certificate not required to prove marriage concluded in Poland, since Polish law quite liberal in allowing proof of marriage by witnesses).

[740] Consorts Justamond v. Epoux Delbreil, Cour Bordeaux, Dec. 21, 1886, [1887] D. 2. 163 (baptismal certificate may be used as proof of birth having occurred in Louisiana since such certificates are admissible there); Dussance v. Dussance, Cour Paris, Jan. 20, 1873, [1873] D. 59 (birth certificate issued by doctor in New York admissible as proof of birth there). In cases in which births, deaths, or marriages in other countries have to be proved, French courts, when permitting introduction of proof other than official birth, death, or marriage records, do not always rely on the rule *locus regit actum*. Sometimes, they base their decisions on CODE CIVIL art. 46, which allows such evidence whenever official certificates are not in existence. See Achard v. Dame Chaput, Cass. Req., Nov. 14, 1922, 50 CLUNET 304 (1923) (marriage concluded in Russia may be shown by means other than official certificate, since no official marriage registers available) (note criticizes case on ground that decision should have been based on rule *locus regit actum*); Rosa Anton v. Bartolo, Cass. Req., Dec. 24, 1889, [1890] D. 1. 171 (marriage in Malta need not be proved by official certificates as none in existence). In the case of events taking place in countries that have no official birth, death, or marriage registers, the result will be the same whether the rule *locus regit actum* or CODE CIVIL art. 46 is used. However, if a birth or death takes place in a country that has official registers but does not require official certificates for evidentiary purposes, a court relying on the rule *locus regit actum* will not require an official certificate, but a court relying on article 46 will. *Cf.* the case mentioned in 1 DALLOZ, RÉPERTOIRE DE PROCÉDURE CIVILE, *Actes de l'Etat Civil*, at No. 87 (1956), in which the court required an official death certificate as proof of a death occurring in New York, absent proof that there were no official registers of deaths in New York.

[741] Princesse Roukia v. Kraner, Cass. Civ., May 23, 1892, [1892] D. 1. 173 (in case of contract made in Turkey, formalities required by CODE CIVIL art. 1328 for proof of date of contract affecting third parties not applicable); Soc. Técalémite v. Comp. française pour l' exploitation des procédés Thomson-Houston, Cass. Civ., Feb. 1, 1944, [1944] S. 1. 108 (re-

whether the law prevailing at the place of the transaction considers its own formal requirements as substantive or procedural.

**d. Probative effect of written documents.** The rule *locus regit actum* also governs the probative value of foreign documents. If the law prevailing at the place of issuance of written documents permits rebuttal of the facts recorded by ordinary evidence, evidence to contradict them will also be admissible in France. If the contents of foreign written documents may not be proved false by ordinary evidence, French courts usually analogize them to French authentic instruments and require an *inscription de faux* procedure to contradict them. [742] However, the courts occasionally refuse to give credence to documentary evidence coming from abroad, although admissible under the law of the place of origin, if its value is seriously impeached by outside circumstances. [743]

## 9. THE REFORMS ADOPTED IN 1965

### 7.58. Introduction.

After this book had gone to press, two important *Décrets* were promulgated: *Décret* No. 65–872 of October 13, 1965, which makes substantial innovations in the procedure before the *tribunal de grande instance* and the *cour d'appel*, [744] and *Décret* No. 65–1006 of November 26, 1965, which simplifies procedural time limitations, improves the procedure for service of the *ajournement* and all other documents that must be served in a formal manner, and modifies rules concerning default judgments. [745] *Décret* No. 65–1006 is to become effective on July 1, 1966. [746] *Décret* No. 65–872 has been in effect since January 1, 1966,

quirements of CODE CIVIL art. 1328 not applicable in case of patent assignment made in New York).

[742] BATIFFOL 461 (birth, death, and marriage certificates), 812 (other documentary evidence); INSTRUCTION GÉNÉRALE DU GARDE DES SCEAUX, MINISTRE DE LA JUSTICE RELATIVE À L'ÉTAT CIVIL du 21 Sept. 1955, J.O. Sept. 22, 1955, p. 9322, at No. 424 (restates rules as to birth, death, and marriage certificates); *cf.* CODE CIVIL art. 47 (foreign birth, death, and marriage records, whether relating to French nationals or foreigners, are proof of the facts therein contained if made in accordance with the law of the place where issued).

[743] BATIFFOL 462–63 (citing a case refusing to give credence to a birth certificate delivered in Argentina where the original birth records had been prepared over a year after the event). See also 15.05 *infra*.

[744] J.O. Oct. 14, 1965, p. 9076, as corrected by J.O. Oct. 19, 1965, p. 9235, [1965] B.L.D. 600 (with report of Minister of Justice).

[745] J.O. December 2, 1965, p. 10664, [1965] B.L.D. 678.

[746] DÉCRET No. 65–1006, *supra* note 745, art. 25.

but, for the time being, is applicable only to a small number of *cours d'appel* and *tribunaux de grande instance.* It is to be put into effect in other courts only after adequate office space, secretarial assistance, and similar facilities have been provided. [747]

### 7.59. Changes in Time Limitations

*Décret* No. 65–1006 simplifies the rules as to time limitations. Henceforth, all procedural time limitations are to be *franc* – in other words, neither the day of the event that starts the running of the time period nor the day on which the procedural act is accomplished is counted to determine whether the act is timely. [748] Furthermore, no additional time periods are available to parties residing in France on account of their distance from the court. To avoid resulting hardship, time periods of less than one week have generally been extended to eight days. [749] Some other time periods have also been extended, often to fifteen days. [750] The schedule of additional time periods available to parties outside France has been simplified. For such parties, time for appearance, appeal, or *opposition* (reopening of a judgment) is increased by one month if they reside elsewhere in Europe, and by two months if they reside in any other part of the world. [751] The court retains the power to shorten the time to appear if the matter is urgent, or to order an appearance on a day certain. [752] As a practical result, the former greatly

[747] DÉCRET No. 65–872, *supra* note 744, arts. 20–21. By ARRÊTÉ of the Minister of Justice, the DÉCRET has been put into effect before the *cours d'appel* in Aix, Caen, Lyon, Montpellier, and Poitiers and about 29 *tribunaux de grande instance*, including those in Lyon, Marseilles, and Poitiers. The DÉCRET is not now in effect in Paris. ARRETÉ of October 13, 1965, J.O. Oct. 14, 1965, p. 9076, [1965] B.L.D. 606. A gradual extension of the applicability of the DÉCRET is contemplated. See report of the Minister of Justice, *supra* note 744.

[748] DÉCRET No. 65–1006, *supra* note 745, art. 28, modifying CODE DE PROCÉDURE CIVILE art. 1033. The new rule removes the uncertainties as to which time limitations are *franc*. For a more detailed discussion, see 7.03 and authorities cited in notes 37 and 38 *supra*.

[749] Time to appear is now uniformly eight days, regardless of the court involved and regardless of the place of the residence of the parties in France: DÉCRET No. 65–1006, *supra* note 745, art. 3 (*tribunal d'instance*); art. 8 (*tribunal de grande instance*); art. 15 (commercial court); arts. 36–37 (labor courts and various labor matters before *tribunal d'instance*); art. 38 (social security court); art. 40 (*tribunal paritaire de baux ruraux*); *cf.* art. 14 (time to demand admission of genuineness of document and time for summoning witnesses eight days).

[750] *E.g.*, DÉCRET No. 65–1006, *supra* note 745, art. 5 (*opposition* against judgments of *tribunal d'instance* within fifteen days); art. 19 (change of status extends time to appeal to fifteen days); art. 31 (*opposition* against decisions in bankruptcy matters must be brought within fifteen days); arts. 36–38 (time for *opposition* and appeal in labor and social security matters fifteen days); art. 14 (time for *contredit* against decision on competence fifteen days).

[751] DÉCRET No. 65–1006, *supra* note 745, arts. 29, 43 (replacing old article 73 of the CODE DE PROCÉDURE CIVILE, which provided for a variety of time periods ranging from one to five months (and twice that time in case of war at sea), by a new article 1033–1).

[752] The application must be made to the presiding judge of the court. DÉCRET No. 65–1006, *supra* note 745, art. 29.

varying time periods in the case of suits with domestic parties have been reduced to three: eight days, fifteen days, and one month. [753] Suits before the *Cour de Cassation* are not affected by these changes.

### 7.60. Service of Process

*Décret* No. 65–1006 contains new rules for service of *ajournements*, judgments, and notices of appeal. The new decree makes more explicit what has always been the law, namely that substantially identical rules govern service of these three documents. [754] The rules concerning the contents of these documents have not been changed to any very great extent, though they must now indicate not only the date of their preparation, and the name, domicile, and occupation of the party on whose behalf service is made, but also his nationality and place of birth, in addition to data as to the identity of the *huissier* effecting service. [755]

The new rules are designed to create greater certainty that the paper served will actually reach the addressee. A physical person present in France must now be served personally. Service upon another person found at the defendant's home (*signification à domicile*) is permissible only if personal service cannot be made. [756] This spells the end of the practice of *huissiers* in larger cities who frequently leave documents to be served with the janitor (*concierge*) of the house in which the addressee lives. When personal service is possible, any other type of service is apparently ineffective, [757] but the new rules indicate neither the nature nor the extent of the efforts the *huissier* must make to reach the defendant in person. Corporations of all kinds must also be served personally. In their case, personal service consists of service upon a person who legally represents the corporation, or upon his agent, or any other person having authority to accept service of process. [758]

[753] To achieve this end, in addition to the changes noted, some thirty day periods have been increased to one month. *E.g.*, DÉCRET No. 65–1006, *supra* note 745, art. 5 (time to appeal for *tribunal d'instance*). There is one exception to this new uniformity: time for *requête civile* remains at two months, plus the one or two months periods for parties residing abroad. DÉCRET No. 65–1006, *supra* note 745, art. 20.

[754] DÉCRET No. 65–1006, *supra* note 745, art. 7, modifies the heading of title II of book 2 of the CODE DE PROCÉDURE CIVILE and inserts three new articles explicitly applicable to service of all formal documents. The rules concerning informal service (*signification d'avoué à avoué*) have not been changed. See generally 7.02 *supra*.

[755] CODE DE PROCÉDURE CIVILE art. 58, as added by DÉCRET No. 65–1006, *supra* note 745, art. 7. Article 1 of the same DÉCRET contains some additional changes affecting the citation by which an action before the *tribunal d'instance* is started.

[756] CODE DE PROCÉDURE CIVILE art. 58–1, as amended by DÉCRET No. 65–1006, *supra* note 745, art. 7.

[757] CODE DE PROCÉDURE CIVILE art. 70, as amended by DÉCRET No. 65–1006, *supra* note 745, art. 3, provides, *i.a.*, that art. 58–1, which requires personal service, must be obeyed on pain of nullity.' On the meaning of this phrase, see 7.09.c. *supra*.

[758] See note 756 *supra*.

If personal service is not possible, the paper to be served may be left with any person at the home (domicile or residence) of the party to be served, but the person accepting the paper must indicate his identity. If no such person can be found, the paper may be left with a neighbor willing to identify himself and to transmit it. In that case, the *huissier* must leave a note at the home of the party to be served indicating what he has done with the instrument. If no person willing to accept the instrument can be found, it may be left in the local mayor's office.In every case in which no personal service has been made, the *huissier* must send a registered letter, return receipt requested, to the party to be served in which he must indicate with whom he has left the document he was to serve. That letter must be sent the day of formal service or the following day. [759]

If a person to be served has no known domicile, residence, or place of work, service may, as in the past, be effectuated by serving the *procureur de la République*. However, the *procureur* is now required to investigate the whereabouts of the party to be served and to transmit the document to him if he is successful in finding him. [760]

If possible, persons residing abroad must be served personally in France. Otherwise, formal service must be made by serving the *procureur de la République,* who, as before, transmits the documents through official channels. On the day of service on the *procureur,* the *huissier* must send a certified copy of the instrument to the party to be served by registered letter, return receipt requested. Time to appear begins to run at the time of service on the *procureur,* but only if it is shown by the return receipt that the defendant actually received the instrument. [761]

The remaining rules as to the manner of service remain unchanged.

## 7.61. Default Judgments and Remedies against Default

The rules relating to default judgments before the *tribunal de grande instance* and to the reopening of defaults (*opposition*) have been made more flexible. They give defendants who are ignorant of an action or

[759] CODE DE PROCÉDURE CIVILE arts. 58–2, 58–3 as added by DÉCRET No. 65–1006, *supra* note 745, art. 7.

[760] CODE DE PROCÉDURE CIVILE art. 69(8), as amended by DÉCRET No. 65–1006, *supra* note 745, art. 8 (*ajournement*); art. 158–2, added by DÉCRET No. 15–1006, *supra* note 745, art. 12 (judgments).

[761] The rule applies to persons residing in foreign countries and French overseas possessions. CODE DE PROCÉDURE CIVILE arts. 69(9) and 69(10), as amended by DÉCRET No. 65–1006, *supra* note 745, art. 8; art. 1033–3, as added by DÉCRET No. 65–1006, *supra* note 745, art. 29. When the *procureur* receives a receipt from the person abroad he must transmit it to the *huissier* who gave him the document to be served.

judgment against them greater protection, but reduce the time period for attacking default judgments in other cases.

Upon the defendant's failure to appear in due time, entry of a default judgment is no longer automatic if the service was made by serving the *procureur de la République*, either because he had no known domicile, residence, or place of employment at all or because he had to be served abroad. If service on the defendant had to be effectuated by serving the *procureur* because he had no known domicile, residence, or place of work, the *procureur* must inform the court in writing of his efforts to locate the defendant and their results. A copy of the notice is sent to the plaintiff's *avoué* by the clerk of the court. If the *procureur* was able to locate the defendant, the court may grant a postponement to enable the defendant properly to prepare his defense. However, if the defendant cannot be located, a default judgment may be entered. [762]

In case of service on persons residing abroad or in French overseas territories, a default judgment may be entered only if it appears from the return receipt that the copy of the *ajournement* mailed to the defendant has actually reached him. If the return receipt is not shown to the court, time to appear begins to run against the defendant only upon his receipt of actual notice of the action. Even if no return receipt is available, a default judgment may be entered after three months, provided the court notes in its decision that all necessary steps were taken to inform the defendant of the action. The court may order additional measures calculated to bring the action to the defendant's attention and to preserve the rights of the parties. [763]

Additional protection is also granted defendants by a new rule prohibiting the execution of default judgments until the time to demand a reopening or to appeal has expired, unless provisional execution is available by law or pursuant to court order. [794]

As a counterpart of this increased protection granted to defendants, time to demand a reopening of a default judgment by *opposition* has been reduced from one month to fifteen days. As noted, a judgment should be served on the defendant personally, but time to demand *opposition* now begins to run with the service of the judgment, even if it was

[762] Code de Procédure Civile art. 74–1, added by Décret No. 65–1006, *supra* note 745, art. 9. Article 16 makes the rules stated in this section applicable to the commercial courts.

[763] Code de Procédure Civile art. 1033–3, added by Décret No. 65–1006 *supra* note 745, art. 29.

[764] Code de Procédure Civile art. 155, as amended by Décret No. 65–1006, *supra* note 745, art. 10. Formerly, execution could be levied eight days after the service of the judgment unless a reopening had been demanded within that time.

left at the defendant's domicile or at his residence. [765] The legislator apparently assumed that the new rules on service ensure that the defendant will become aware of the judgment even in the last two circumstances.

A novel procedure has been created for situations in which it may be doubtful whether the defendant received notice of the judgment entered against him. If the default judgment was served upon the defendant by leaving it at the mayor's office, but it was not picked up by the defendant, the plaintiff must petition the presiding judge of the court for permission to levy execution. If the judge is convinced that the defendant received actual notice of the judgment against him (through the letter mailed to him by the *huissier*), [766] he must make an order stating in substance that time to demand a reopening began to run on the day the judgment was left in the mayor's office. In case of doubt, or if the judge is certain that the defendant did not receive the judgment, he must request the *procureur de la République* to investigate the whereabouts of the defendant through the police and to give him a copy of the judgment if he is found. If this happens, time to demand a reopening runs from the day defendant received the copy of the judgment. The presiding judge must note that day in his order.

If the defendant cannot be served by the police, but the *procureur's* investigation shows that the domicile, residence, or place of work indicated by the plaintiff is the correct one, the judge must make an order stating that time for *opposition* begins to run on the day of the order. Execution is possible as soon as the time for opposition has run. If the address turns out to be incorrect, the service is void. [767] If service of the judgment must be made on the *procureur* in the first place because the defendant has no known domicile, residence, or place of work anywhere, the *procureur* must again investigate his whereabouts and attempt to deliver the judgment to him through a police officer. If the defendant is found, time for *opposition* runs from the date he received a copy of the judgment. If he is not found, the judge makes an order noting this. Time for *opposition* runs from the date of the order. [768]

[765] CODE DE PROCÉDURE CIVILE arts. 156, 158, as amended by DÉCRET No. 65–1006, *supra* note 745, art. 11. See also note 756 *supra*. The rule that a default judgment must be served by an *huissier* specially appointed for the purpose has been continued. Formerly, time for *opposition* did not begin to run upon service of the judgment if it was not served personally. See 7.04.a *supra*.

[766] *Cf.* text at note 759 *supra*.

[767] CODE DE PROCÉDURE CIVILE art. 158–1, as added by DÉCRET No. 65–1006, *supra* note 745, art. 12.

[768] CODE DE PROCÉDURE CIVILE art. 158–2, added by DÉCRET No. 65–1006, *supra* note 745, art. 12.

In the case of defendants living abroad, time for *opposition*, increased by the one and two-months periods mentioned above, [769] begins to run on the day the judgment was served on the *procureur*, but only if it can be shown by return receipt that the defendant received the copy sent to him by mail. If the return receipt is not received within three months, the plaintiff may ask the presiding judge for permission to levy execution.

It should be granted, if the judge believes that everything possible has been done to inform the defendant of the judgment. The judge must note in his order that time for *opposition* has run. In an appropriate case the judge may order further steps to inform the defendant of the judgment. [770]

In cases in which immediate execution of a default judgment through "provisional execution" is available, time for *opposition* begins to run with the first act of execution. [771]

As has been noted, reopening of a default judgment is not possible if the judgment can be appealed to an intermediate appellate court (*cour d'appel*). [772] In such a case, the rules determining when time to appeal begins to run are the same as those determining the beginning of the time period for *opposition*. [773]

## 7.62. Changes in the Procedure before the *Tribunal de Grande Instance*

**a. Introductory remarks.** *Décret No.* 65–872 [774] attempts to speed up proceedings before the *tribunal de grande instance* after the case has been put on the calendar, [775] It does so mainly by giving the judges greater powers of supervision over the progress of pending cases. For the time being, this *Décret* affects only a limited number of courts. The old procedure continues in effect in all others. [776]

[769] See text at note 751 *supra*.

[770] Code de Procédure Civile art. 158–3, added by Décret No. 65–1006 *supra* note 745, art. 12.

[771] Code de Procédure Civile art. 158–4, added by Décret No. 65–1006 *supra* note 745, art. 12.

[772] See 7.04.a *supra*.

[773] Code de Procédure Civile art. 445–1, added by Décret No. 65–1006 *supra* note 745, art. 18. The rule noted in the text applies to true default judgments – that is, when the defendant fails to appear. If there is an appearance but a party subsequently fails to proceed (*défaut faute de conclure*), time to appeal starts to run from the day of service of the judgment on the party, except if the party resides abroad, in which case time to appeal begins to run on the day the judgment is served on his *avoué*.

[774] See note 744 *supra*.

[775] As to this, see 7.05 *supra*.

[776] See note 747 *supra*.

**b. The *juge des mises en état*.** The keystone of the reform is the creation of the *juge des mises en état*. The *juge des mises en état* performs all the functions of the *juge chargé de suivre la procédure* from the time the case has been put on the calendar by the *placet* until the formal hearing (*audience*), but his powers are, in some respects, substantially greater. [777] At the hearing, the powers once granted the *juge chargé de suivre la procédure* are exercised by a reporting judge (*juge rapporteur*) who is granted increased powers. [778] One or more *juges des mises en état*, who also exercise general supervision over the clerk's office and experts appearing before the court, must be appointed each year by the presiding judge of each *tribunal de grande instance*. A judge who has acted as *juge des mises en état* in a case may act as reporting judge, but the presiding judge may appoint another judge for this purpose. [779] The assumption is that in smaller courts both functions will be performed by the same judge. In the larger courts, the *juges des mises en état* will presumably be too occupied to perform any other function, and reporting judges will be designated among all the members of the court in turn. [780]

The reform does away with the original (informal) hearing destined solely for the exchange of *conclusions* (pleadings) by the parties. This will undoubtedly reduce confusion as to when the *mises en état*, the putting of the case at issue, occurs. [781] Under the new rules, once the case has been put on the calendar, the *juge des mises en état* must set a time limit for the filing of defendant's pleading (*conclusions*) and then a further time limit for the plaintiff's reply. On his own motion or that of a party, he may either permit or require additional pleadings. Every pleading must be served on the *avoué* of the opposing party, and a copy must be given to the *juge des mises en états* who initials it and then sees to its being included in the file of the case in the clerk's office. There are no particular rules the *juge des mises en état* must observe in fixing time limits for the submission of pleadings, except that he should see to it that default cases, cases involving only limited issues, and urgent matters are handled with dispatch. The judge may extend the time

[777] See the report of the Minister of Justice, *supra* note 744. A number of articles of the DÉCRET No. 65–872, *supra* note 744, amend various articles of the CODE DE PROCÉDURE CIVILE by substituting the expression "*juge des mises en état*" for "*juge chargé de suivre la procédure*." Some of the additional functions of the *juge des mises en état* are noted below.

[778] See text at notes 787–790 *infra*.

[779] CODE DE PROCÉDURE CIVILE art. 77, as amended by DÉCRET No. 65–872, *supra* note 744, art. 3.

[780] See Report of the Minister of Justice, *supra* note 744.

[781] Furthermore, as noted, the practice as to the hearing for the exchange of pleadings differed widely. See 7.06 *supra* and the Report of the Minister of Justice, *supra* note 744.

limits he has set. [782] If either side fails to submit *conclusions* within the time limited by him, the judge may issue an order stating that the case is at issue. If both sides fail to submit pleadings, he may strike the case from the calendar. [783]

The *juge des mises en état* has some additional powers. He may call in the parties and attempt a settlement; the same power is also granted to the reporting judge and the full court. [784] He may call in the parties' *avoués* for a conference, request information, or order the production of documents. He retains the *juge chargé de suivre la procedure*'s power to order proof measures, such as an *enquête* (hearing of witnesses), *expertise*, or a view of the premises. If he orders an *enquête*, he may delegate another judge to hear the witnesses if he is unable to do so. [785] If one of the parties demands security for costs or the production of documents used by the other side, he may grant appropriate relief. He must also rule on any defense based on the invalidity of the original *ajournement* or any other procedural document used before the case is at issue (*en état*). Furthermore, he may grant various types of provisional relief in matrimonial actions. In all the situations mentioned in this paragraph, the judge decides the matter by an order (*ordonnance*) rendered at a hearing. Ordinarily, the only remedy against such orders is an appeal taken at the time of an appeal of the decision on the merits. However, if the order of the *juge des mises en état* terminates the case, the matter may be brought before the full *tribunal de grande instance* within fifteen days. [786]

**c. Submission of documents.** It has been the customary practice of French *avocats* to submit the documents used at a formal hearing (*audience*) only after its completion. [787] To enable the court, and especially the reporting judge, to be better informed and thus to direct

[782] CODE DE PROCÉDURE CIVILE arts. 78–80, as amended by DÉCRET No. 65–872, *supra* note 744, art. 3.

[783] On the order stating that the case is at issue, see text at notes 787–88 *infra*. Following the order, the court may proceed with the case even in the absence of one of the parties. The resulting decision is not subject to reopening. CODE DE PROCÉDURE CIVILE art. 154, as amended by DÉCRET No. 65-872, *supra* note 744, art. 5; CODE DE PROCÉDURE CIVILE arts. 154–1 and 154–2, as added by DÉCRET No. 65–872, *supra* note 744, art. 6.

[784] CODE DE PROCÉDURE CIVILE art. 81–3, as added by DÉCRET No. 65–872, *supra* note 744, art. 4.

[785] The decree states that the *juge des mises en état* has the power to issue orders (*injonctions*); however, the only penalty for a failure to produce documents is apparently the drawing of unfavorable inferences as to their contents. CODE DE PROCÉDURE CIVILE arts. 80, 81, as amended by DÉCRET No. 65–872, *supra* note 744, art. 3.

[786] CODE DE PROCÉDURE CIVILE arts. 81–1, 81–2, as added by DÉCRET No. 65–872, *supra* note 744, art. 4.

[787] See 7.12.b *supra*, especially text at note 190.

argument at the hearing to the crucial issues, the new *Décret* provides that the *juge des mises en état* must order both sides to submit their files of documents to the court by a certain date. After the expiration of that date, the *juge des mises en état* makes an order stating that the case is at issue (*en état*). The entire file is then sent to the presiding judge of the court so that he may establish a date for the formal hearing. After issuance of the order putting the case at issue, the parties may not submit new pleadings or additional documents, except, at the request of the court, memoranda on points of law or statements as to facts. However, the *juge des mises en état*, the reporting judge, and, after the beginning of the formal hearing, the court may reopen the order putting the case at issue and permit the submission of new documents or pleadings if there are good grounds for doing so. [788]

**d. Report by reporting judge.** Until the new reforms, the report of the reporting judge or *juge chargé de suivre la procédure* read at the beginning of the formal hearing (*audience*) was usually a routine affair not shedding much light on the case. Furthermore, few questions were traditionally asked of counsel during their argument. [789] But since under the reforms the reporting judge has all the documents used by the parties at his disposal before the hearing date, he should submit a more detailed report based on those documents and on his own research, in which he summarizes the points of fact and law involved in the case. He may not indicate how the case should be decided. [790] If the study of the file suggests questions to the reporting judge he wishes to ask the parties, he may do so orally or in writing. Answers to these questions must apparently be given in writing. After the beginning of the hearing oral or written questions may also be asked by the court. The questions asked may not change the *objet* and the *cause* of the suit. In spite of the

[788] CODE DE PROCÉDURE CIVILE art. 81–4, as added by DÉCRET No. 65–872, *supra* note 744, art. 4. The order putting the case at issue is called *ordonnance de clôture* because it closes the preliminary phase of the case and prevents the submission of further pleadings or documents. It may be made only after the *juge des mises en état* has established that each side has seen the documents the other side wishes to use. In connection with this and the following three paragraphs, the overriding importance of documentary evidence in French law suits should be kept in mind. See 7.33–7.34 *supra*.

[789] See 7.12 *supra*, especially text at notes 180–182.

[790] CODE DE PROCÉDURE CIVILE art. 81–6, as added by DÉCRET No. 65–872, *supra* note 744, art. 4. The report of the reporting judge must be in writing. The parties may waive argument before the full court and argue before the reporting judge instead. In such a case, the report is given to the full court after the argument. It seems unlikely that many parties will be inclined to waive argument before the full court, however.

rule that the court can always raise issues affected by a strong public policy on its own motion, the court may not do so unless it has given the parties an opportunity to be heard on the issues it wishes to raise.[791]

**e. Proof measures.** If the court decides after the hearing to order a proof measure instead of deciding the case on the merits, the proof measure is carried out under the supervision of the *juge des mises en état*. After its completion, he must make a new order putting the case at issue again for a further formal hearing (*audience*). Presumably, however, the changes made in the procedure will render it less likely than before that proof measures will be necessary after the formal *audience*.[792]

**f. Procedure before *cours d'appel*.** The procedure before the *cours d'appel* as affected by the *Décret* conforms in substance to the new procedure before the *tribunaux de grande instance*.[793]

**g. Conclusion.** *Décret* No. 65–872, which has also made a number of changes of minor importance not accorded textual treatment here,[794] is designed principally to speed up litigation. It continues the tradition that was begun with the creation in 1935 of the office of *juge chargé de suivre la procédure*. At the time, the hopes were great that this institution would lead to a speed-up of litigation. The fact is, however, that in most parts of France it never achieved this result. It remains to be seen what the practical impact of the changes effected by *Décret* No. 65–872 will be.[795]

[791] CODE DE PROCÉDURE CIVILE art. 82, as amended by DÉCRET No. 65–872 *supra* note 744, art. 5. While the court could always ask questions, there was formerly no way of getting written answers to questions as to fact or law before the hearing; furthermore, more meaningful questions and questions more likely to narrow the issues may now be asked, since the court already has a substantial amount of information about the case when the questions are put. On the meaning of the terms *objet* and *cause*, see notes 165–66 *supra*.

[792] CODE DE PROCÉDURE CIVILE art. 81–7, as added by DÉCRET No. 65–872, *supra* note 744, art. 4.

[793] DÉCRET No. 65–872, *supra* note 744, arts. 13–17. See also c. 8 *infra*.

[794] See, *e.g.*, DÉCRET No. 65–872, *supra* note 744, art. 1, amending CODE DE PROCÉDURE CIVILE art. 64 (in actions involving land, the *ajournement* must describe property in the same manner that is required for recording purposes): art. 2, adding CODE DE PROCÉDURE CIVILE art. 75–1 (procedure when time to appear shortened or defendant summoned for a day certain conformed to new procedural rules); art. 3, amending CODE DE PROCÉDURE CIVILE art. 79 (more complete file to be kept at clerk's office); art. 19 (*juge des mises en état* may, on his own motion, call meeting of court's legal aid bureau).

[795] *Cf.* 7.07 *supra*. One recent change made by DÉCRET No. 65–464 of June 10, 1965, art. 1 (reprinted in CODE DE PROCÉDURE CIVILE at 131 (62 ed. Dalloz 1966)) should be mentioned. While the choice of experts is usually within the discretion of the court (see 7.54.e *supra*), in civil actions relating to patents the court must consult on the choice of an expert one of the organizations designated by joint decision of the interested ministers.

CHAPTER 8

# PROCEEDINGS ON APPEAL

After defining the term appeal (8.01), this chapter discusses what decisions are appealable (8.02), courts from which an appeal may be taken (8.03), appealability of final (8.04) and non-final (8.05) decisions, time limits within which an appeal must be taken (8.06–8.08), who may appeal (8.09–8.10), appeals in actions with multiple parties (8.11), intervention on appeal (8.12), the manner of taking an appeal (8.13), the effect of appeal on execution (8.14–8.15), the scope of the powers of the *cours d'appel* (8.16–8.18), the scope of appeal (8.19), procedure on appeal (8.20), appeals from decisions of specialized tribunals (8.21) and the impact of the 1965 reforms (8.22).

## 8.01. Introduction

In common law terminology, the term appeal is used to denote review by an intermediate appellate tribunal as well as review by a court of last resort. [1] The term *appel* has a narrower meaning. It covers only appeal from a decision by a court of first instance to an intermediate appellate tribunal. The means by which review is sought in the French Supreme Court, the *Cour de Cassation*, is called *pourvoi*. The distinction is one of substance, not merely of terminology. Ordinarily, an *appel* from a court of first instance to an intermediate appellate tribunal results in examination *de novo* of the whole case. [2] A *pourvoi* to the *Cour de Cassation* on the other hand leads merely to re-examination of questions of law. [3] It is usually restricted to review of the opinion below in order to ascertain whether it is based on correct rules of law; only rarely does a *pourvoi* involve examination of the whole record. [4] In order to avoid confusion, the word appeal will here be used to refer

[1] For a general comparative and historical discussion, see 5 POUND, JURISPRUDENCE 606 (1959).

[2] See, *e.g.*, Du Vivier, *The Appellate Courts and Appellate Procedure in France*, 6 AM. LAW SCHOOL REV. 1 (1926); Lepaulle, *Comparative Civil Procedure*, 12 CORNELL L. Q. 24, 36 (1927) (both discussions somewhat dated). The rule stated in the text is a manifestation of the principle of *double degré de juridiction*, according to which a party is ordinarily entitled to complete consideration of the issues – both factual and legal – in two instances. Review by the *Cour de Cassation* is not considered a *degré de juridiction*, because it is restricted to examination of questions of law. See generally 1 SOLUS & PERROT 492–94.

[3] See 9.07 *infra*.

[4] For further detail, see 9.07 and 9.09 *infra*.

exclusively to an appeal from a court of first instance to an intermediate appellate tribunal, never to describe a *pourvoi* to the *Cour de Cassation.*

## 8.02. Appealable Decisions

The right to appeal is broadly available: Ordinarily, a judicial decision is non-appealable only if a specific statutory rule expressly so provides. However, there can never be two successive appeals of any one decision. [5]

To some extent, the rules regulating the right to appeal are subject to modification by the parties. As to matters falling within the competence of the *tribunal d'instance,* [6] the commercial court [7] and the labor court, [8] as well as in cases of arbitration, [9] there is express authorization for contractual waiver of the right to appeal. [10] In addition, acquiescence in a decision or failure to appeal within the time provided by law constitutes, for all practical purposes, waiver of the right to appeal. On the other hand, the consent of the parties cannot make a decision appealable which, by law, is non-appealable. [11] Likewise, the parties may not bring a dispute before an appellate court initially, bypassing the courts of first instance. [12]

## 8.03. Courts from which an Appeal May Be Taken

Appeals may be taken from decisions by all courts of first instance. Even decisions of arbitrators can be appealed unless the right to appeal has been waived. An appeal is also possible from decisions of the *ordres* of *avocats* in diciplinary matters. [13] However, no appeal can be taken from decisions of a *cour d'appel,* even in those instances, such as *prise à partie,* in which a *cour d'appel* decides a case in first instance. [14]

[5] Since interlocutory decisions are ordinarily immediately appealable, there may be several appeals in one case. See generally MOREL 480; 6 GARSONNET & CÉZAR-BRU 12; 1 DALLOZ, RÉPERTOIRE DE PROCÉDURE CIVILE, *Appel,* Nos. 2–9 (1955).

[6] CODE DE PROCÉDURE CIVILE art. 7.

[7] CODE DE COMMERCE art. 639.

[8] CODE DU TRAVAIL liv. IV, art. 74.

[9] CODE DE PROCÉDURE CIVILE art. 1010. See also 11.11.b *supra.*

[10] However, waiver of the right to appeal before the beginning of an action is possible only if the parties have legal capacity and the matter is one in which a settlement is not unlawful. 1 DALLOZ, *op. cit. supra* note 5, at 28–29. Accordingly, the right to appeal may not be waived in divorce actions. See 11.04.f *supra.*

[11] 6 GARSONNET & CÉZAR-BRU 22; 1 SOLUS & PERROT 505.

[12] X..., Cass. Civ., Dec. 27, 1960, [1961] D.J. 469; 1 SOLUS & PERROT 505. For some older cases to the contrary, see 1 DALLOZ, *op. cit. supra* note 5, at Nos. 33–34. For a recent case to a contrary effect, see Soc. René Philippe v. Dame Léon, Trib. Seine, May 2, 1953, [1953] D.J. 380.

[13] See 2.03.g *supra.*

[14] 1 DALLOZ, *op. cit. supra* note 5, No. 4. Non-availability of an appeal does not preclude *pourvoi* to the *Cour de Cassation.*

## 8.04. Appealability of Final Decisions

Appeal is the proper method of review for substantially all final decisions, whether the appeal is based on questions of fact, on questions of substantive law, or on alleged procedural mistakes of the court below. [15] However, the decision appealed from must be a true judicial decision, not one that has an administrative character. [16] An appeal is likewise precluded in case of a decision that gives merely official sanction to an agreement entered into by the parties or that is based on a statement a party may not withdraw. [17]

Although ordinarily the nature of the right to relief has no influence on appealability, appeal is excluded in a few matters in which speed is essential, including litigation involving stamp and indirect taxes, [18] and certain bankruptcy proceedings. [19] Decisions in cases involving disputes relating to elections brought before the *tribunal d'instance* are also non-appealable. [20]

**a. Influence of the amount in controversy on appealability.** Appeal is not available if the amount in controversy is very small. However, a decision that is not appealable may still be reviewed on a point of law by *pourvoi* to the *Cour de Cassation.* [21] The minimum amount required to make a case appealable has been increased several times to keep pace with the decline in value of the franc. It varies depending on the nature of the claim and the court. [22]

Actions involving movables that are brought in the *tribunal de grande*

[15] 1 DALLOZ, *op. cit. supra* note 5, at 10. Indeed, when appeal is available, other methods of review, such as *opposition*, are generally not available.

[16] A decision by a judge or court is administrative if, in a broad sense, it relates to internal court administration. A ruling that, in the interest of effective administration of justice, a party may not act as his own *avocat* is considered administrative; the same is true of a decision adjourning a case to permit the introduction of further evidence. 1 DALLOZ, *op. cit. supra* note 5, at No. 23. Decisions of the *ordres*, the professional organizations of the *avocats*, rendered in disciplinary matters have specifically been made appealable by DÉCRET No. 54–406, 2.03.g, at n. 77 *supra*. In a recent case, an *ordre* admitted a lady applicant, but inserted a proviso in the document of admission that she was never to move her office to the building in which her husband, who was an *avoué*, had his office. It was held that this proviso was more than a mere administrative act and hence appealable. Mme X., Cour Amiens, April 21, 1959, [1959] D.J. 445.

[17] 6 GARSONNET & CÉZAR-BRU 74–75. This means, for example, that a party cannot appeal from a decision certifying that it has refused to take a decisory oath. The question whether the oath has been properly tendered is, of course, appealable.

[18] CODE GÉNÉRAL DES IMPÔTS art. 1919.

[19] CODE DE COMMERCE art. 457.

[20] DÉCRET No. 58–1284 of Dec. 22, 1958, J.O. December 23, 1958, p. 11579, [1959] D.L. 41, arts. 9–11.

[21] See 9.04 *infra*.

[22] For tables indicating the changes since 1810 and for present figures for the various courts, see 1 SOLUS & PERROT 498–99.

*instance* [23] are appealable if the amount in controversy exceeds 1500 francs (approximately $ 300). Since *in personam* actions must ordinarily be heard by the *tribunal d'instance* if the amount in controversy is less than 3000 francs (about $ 600), this means that substantially all *in personam* actions that may be brought before the *tribunal de grande instance* are appealable. The 1500 francs limit is of significance only in those instances in which the *tribunal de grande instance* must hear the case even if the claim is less than 3000 francs. [24] In actions involving property interests in land, appealability depends on the rental value of the property in litigation. An appeal lies if the rental value exceeds 300 francs (about $ 60) annually. [25]

Decisions of the *tribunal d'instance* on *in personam* claims are appealable if the amount in controversy exceeds 1500 francs (about $ 300). [26] However, disputes between landlords and tenants for which the *tribunal d'instance* is competent are appealable if the amount in controversy exceeds 1000 francs (about $ 200). [27] Decisions involving possessory actions, actions to fix boundary lines, certain other actions involving land, and support actions are always appealable. [28]

In the commercial courts, the monetary limit for appeals is 1500 francs, [29] and the same is true of the labor courts. [30] In the rural lease courts, however, the monetary limit for appeals (1000 francs) is the

[23] DÉCRET No. 58–1284, *supra* note 20, art. 32.

[24] 1 SOLUS & PERROT 497; CUCHE & VINCENT 204. For example, the 1500 francs limit may be of importance to determine the appealability of a decision granting the wife counsel fees in a divorce action. Divorce actions must always be brought in the *tribunal de grande instance*, so that the decision concerning counsel fees will be appealable if the amount demanded is over 1500 francs.

[25] DÉCRET No. 58–1284, *supra* note 20, art. 32. To determine rental value, even an expired lease, if not too remote in time, may be used. No deduction is made for property taxes; if these are paid by the tenant, they must be added to the rent. If property rights are involved for which no rent is payable, the claim is considered as indeterminate and always appealable. Problems arise when an action involves property rights in land as well as rights in personam, as occurs in mortgage foreclosures and actions to rescind land contracts. The majority opinion seems to be that the nature of the main issue controls. See 1 DALLOZ, *op. cit. supra* note 5, at Nos. 156–63, 6 GARSONNET & CÉZAR-BRU 160–66.

[26] DÉCRET No. 58–1284, *supra* note 20, art. 1 (in personam actions involving movables and all matters not covered specifically by the DÉCRET), art. 4 (actions involving employment contracts and related matters as well as actions involving tuition), art. 5 (actions involving damages to fields and certain other matters relating to agriculture), art. 6 (actions involving bailments and certain tort actions).

[27] DÉCRET No. 58–1284, *supra* note 20, art. 2.

[28] DÉCRET No. 58–1284, *supra* note 20, art. 7. Also included in this category are various unrelated proceedings concerning customs duties, certain easements, disputes concerning funerals, and the like.

[29] CODE DE COMMERCE art. 639.

[30] DÉCRET No. 58–1292 of Dec. 22, 1958, J.O. December 23, 1958, p. 11621, [1959] B.L.D. 77, art. 81.

same as that in actions between landlords and tenants pending before the *tribunal d'instance.* [31]

Matters brought before a single judge of a *tribunal de grande instance* in rent control cases are always appealable. If such matters are brought before a judge of a *tribunal d'instance,* they are appealable if the claim involves more than 1000 francs. [32]

Decisions by the regular first instance social security commissions are appealable if the amount in controversy exceeds 1500 francs. Decisions of the technical commissions are always appealable. [33]

The amount that determines whether a case is appealable is thus quite low. [34] A number of rules reduce even further its effectiveness as a restraint upon appeals.

An appeal is always open if the amount in controversy is undetermined. [35] Thus, divorce and separation actions, declaratory actions to determine a person's nationality, and all other actions not involving property interests are always appealable. The same is true of actions concerning property, such as partition actions, or actions for the return of a specified chattel if the plaintiff puts no value on the property. However, an exception is made if its value can be determined by recourse to official stock exchange quotations or to other official market reports. The value of a claim is also undetermined if its amount depends on future circumstances. An example of such a claim is one for an amount *per diem* until the happening of a certain event.

Furthermore, the so-called principal amount controls. This means that interest or rent accruing up to the date of suit is included in determining the amount in controversy. [36] The amount of the judgment

[31] DÉCRET No. 58–1293 of Dec. 22, 1958, J.O. Dec. 23, 1958, p. 11627, [1959] B.L.D. 87 art. 9.

[32] DÉCRET No. 58–1284, *supra* note 20, art. 38. Under this article, disputes involving rent control laws applicable to apartments used for residential or professional purposes are brought before the *tribunal d'instance* if the rent is less than 1500 francs per annum (less than 300 francs per month in the case of furnished apartments), before a judge of the *tribunal de grande instance* (not the full court) if the rent is above these amounts. See 4.43.a *supra.*

[33] DÉCRET No. 58–1291, of Dec. 22, 1958, J.O. Dec. 23, 1958, p. 11613, [1959] B.L.D. 66, art. 21.

[34] However, since it is rather inexpensive, there is a fair amount of litigation involving quite small claims.

[35] CUCHE & VINCENT 234; 6 GARSONNET & CÉZAR-BRU 170–77; 1 Dalloz, *op. cit. supra* note 5, at Nos. 128–45. The rule that indeterminate claims are always appealable affords an easy means for making almost every action appealable. A legislative attempt to curb the practice of making claims indeterminate in value proved ineffectual, largely because the law (now LOI No. 51–686 of May 24, 1951, J.O. June 2, 1951, p. 5819, [1951] D.L. 260) is extremely vague. See 1 SOLUS & PERROT 502–04; Lesire, *La demande de condamnation aux droit fiscaux perçus à l'occasion de l'instance,* [1952] D. CHR. 61.

[36] However, claims maturing during suit and cost are not included. 6 GARSONNET & CÉZAR-BRU 145; 1 DALLOZ, *op. cit. supra* note 5, at Nos. 194–209.

actually awarded is quite immaterial, as is a recital in the judgment that it is non-appealable: [37] The amount demanded in plaintiff's final *conclusions*, even if obviously inflated, determines appealability. [38]

Ordinarily, defenses asserted by the defendant do not influence appealability, but if a question of personal status is injected into an otherwise non-appealable matter, the case becomes subject to appeal. The same rule applies to defenses involving title to land. [39]

Counterclaims which, viewed as independent claims, are appealable, render the whole case subject to appeal. However, a counterclaim based on the ground that the principal action amounts to abuse of process does not make the main action appealable, no matter what sum has been demanded. [40] If the plaintiff joins several claims, the appealability of each one is determined separately if they are unrelated; if they are related, all claims must be added together to determine whether the decision is appealable. [41] An action involving several plaintiffs or several defendants which concerns a joint claim is appealable if the amount in controversy exceeds 5000 francs (about $ 1000); [42] in case of separate claims, the appealability of each individual claim depends on its amount.

## 8.05. Appealability of Non-Final Decisions

The appealability of non-final decisions has been a source of controversy. [43] Even after some recent legislative changes, the law is not altogether clear. For purposes of appeal, non-final decisions fall into two classes: (1) decisions granting or denying provisional relief, and (2)

[37] Code de Procédure Civile art. 454; 6 Garsonnet & Cézar-Bru 16, 92.

[38] Code de Procédure Civile art. 454; 1 Dalloz, *op. cit. supra* note 5, at Nos. 61–62. As a result, except when he is suing on a promissory note or other instrument for the payment of a specific sum of money, the plaintiff will always be able to make his action appealable.

[39] 1 Dalloz, *op. cit. supra* note 5, at No. 68; 6 Garsonnet & Cézar-Bru 118–19.

[40] Law of April 11, 1838, art. 2 (*tribunal de grande instance*); Décret No. 58–1284, *supra* note 20, art. 17 (*tribunal d'instance*); Code de Commerce art. 639 (commercial courts). The rule is designed to prevent the assertion of counterclaims based on the ground that the principal action amounts to be an abuse of justice merely in order to make a non-appealable matter appealable. Since counterclaims are often brought to make a non-appealable matter appealable, the courts have a tendency to hold that a counterclaim is based on the main action rather on an independent wrong. See Raynaud, *Chronique*, 42 Rev. trim. dr. civ. 132, 139 (1943) (the main action may be abusive if it is brought maliciously and in bad faith, or merely for the purpose of injuring the defendant's credit, or if the pleadings contain defamatory statements, or, if in a situation in which several courts are competent, the plaintiff brings his action in the court most inconvenient to defendant). 6 Garsonnet & Cézar-Bru 130–32).

[41] Décret No. 58–1284, *supra* note 20, art. 14.

[42] Décret No. 58–1284, *supra* note 20, art. 15.

[43] Interlocutory appeals often create considerable delay. However, they may also save time by avoiding unnecessary or improper proceedings subsequent to the interlocutory judgment.

decisions affecting the conduct of the main action, such as decisions concerning proof offers.

**a. Appealability of decisions concerning provisional relief.** Decisions granting or denying provisional relief are appealable, just as final decisions on the merits. It makes no difference whether the decision has been rendered by a judge sitting *en référé*, [44] a *juge chargé de suivre la procédure*, or the full court. [45] However, no appeal is possible from decisions granted *ex parte*, [46] and the time to appeal may be less than in the case of final judgments. [47]

The rules that make appealability depend on the amount in controversy create some uncertainty, for it is not clear whether the right to appeal depends on the amount mentioned in the petition for provisional relief or on the appealability of the main action. Most authors espouse the view that petitions for provisional relief, such as provisions for counsel fees in divorce actions, should be evaluated independently, [48] but the cases are split. [49]

**b. Appealability of decisions affecting the main action.** Prior to 1942, non-final decisions affecting the main action, such as decisions ordering an *enquête* or *expertise*, were divided into two classes: (1) *jugements préparatoires*, which could be appealed only together with the final judgment, and (2) *jugements interlocutoires*, which could be appealed immediately. A decision was *préparatoire* if it had merely a procedural character and did not prejudge the merits; a decision prejudging the merits was *interlocutoire*. [50]

The distinction was difficult to apply in practice, and the 1942 law

[44] See CODE DE PROCÉDURE CIVILE art. 809.

[45] 1 DALLOZ, *op. cit. supra* note 5, at 23.

[46] A person prejudiced by an *ex parte* decision ordinarily attempts to obtain an order from a judge sitting *en référé* annulling it. *Opposition* may also be available. See CUCHE & VINCENT 78–79.

[47] See 8.06 *infra*.

[48] *E.g.*, 6 GARSONNET & CÉZAR-BRU 126; Raynaud, *Chronique*, 42 REV. TRIM. DR. CIV. 132, 139 (1943). These writers argue that, even though a divorce action is always appealable, a request for counsel fees *pendente lite* which involves less than 1500 francs should not be appealable.

[49] For two cases from the same court reaching opposite results, see Dame Morel v. Morel Cour Paris, Jan. 2, 1942, and Blot v. Blot, Cour Paris, Jan. 6, 1944, both reported in [1945] D.J. 36.

[50] See CODE DE PROCÉDURE CIVILE arts. 451–52, abrogated in 1942; 6 GARSONNET & CÉZAR-BRU 258–61. A judgment is final if it definitely disposes of an issue, even though other issues remain. A decision on the issue of liability in a negligence case is therefore considered final, though the court must still rule on the extent of damages. Blanc et Cie d'assurances maritimes v. Paulet, Cour Aix, June 7, 1943, [1944] D. CRIT. J. 75.

concerning appeal procedure rendered it largely obsolete by making all non-final decisions, whether *interlocutoires* or *préparatoires*, immediately appealable.[51] Special measures were taken to avoid excessive delay caused by interlocutory appeals,[52] but these did not prove satisfactory.

Since 1958, a decision ordering or denying an *enquête* – formerly cited as the most notable example of a *jugement interlocutoire* subject to immediate appeal – is appealable only together with the final judgment.[53] However, the rules concerning other interlocutory judgments remain unchanged.

Although the 1942 legislation which abolished the distinction between *jugements préparatoires* and *jugements interlocutoires* dealt specifically only with appeals from the *tribunaux civils* (now *tribunaux de grande instance*) and the commercial courts, it was generally assumed that the distinction between *jugements préparatoires* and *jugements interlocutoires* had been abrogated by implication in proceedings before the *juges de paix* (now *tribunaux d'instance*) and labor courts. Some recent cases indicate, however, that this assumption may be unfounded.[54]

Even a non-final decision subject to immediate appeal may be appealed only if the amount in controversy in the main action warrants an appeal. If that amount is insufficient, no appeal is possible in any event.[55] Special rules govern appeals from decisions relating to the competence of courts.[56]

## 8.06. Time Limits Within Which an Appeal Must Be Taken

At one time, the losing party had thirty years to appeal.[57] Under the *Code de Procédure Civile* as originally enacted, time to appeal was three months. This period was gradually reduced as methods of com-

[51] Law of May 23, 1942, J.O. June 11, 1942, p. 2035, [1942] D. ANAL. L. 120, substituting new CODE DE PROCÉDURE CIVILE art. 451 for old articles 451 and 452. See also MOREL 482–83.

[52] Time to appeal was reduced to 15 days and the case had to be put on the calendar within one month. See 8.06 and 8.20.b *infra*.

[53] CODE DE PROCÉDURE CIVILE art. 258, as enacted by DÉCRET No. 58–1289 of Dec. 22, 1958, J.O. Dec. 23, 1958, p. 11608, [1959] D.L. 45. Since immediate appeals are possible from decisions ordering other proof measures, some French practitioners consider the prohibition against immediate appeals from decisions ordering or denying *enquêtes* as illogical.

[54] Raynaud, *Chronique*, 59 REV. TRIM. DR. CIV. 541 (1960) (surveying some recent cases); S.A.R.L. Raph v. Marchand, Cour Paris, June 25, 1959; Sté Anonyme Xavier Lambert v. Denys, Jan. 21, 1960, both in [1960] J.C.P. 2. 11657 (note Bizière).

[55] *E.g.*, CUCHE & VINCENT 448.

[56] See 7.09.b *supra*.

[57] *Cf.* MOREL 482.

munication improved. [58] The rules as to time to appeal have been changed recently. [59]

Time to appeal is one month for most decisions of the *tribunaux de grande instance,* [60] commercial courts, [61] *tribunaux d'instance* (with some exceptions), [63] rural lease courts, [64] and social security commissions. [65] In some cases, time to appeal is only fifteen days. These include appeals from the labor courts, [66] bankruptcy matters, [67] rent control cases, [68] and some matters relating to the execution of judgments. [69] Very occasionally, time to appeal is even shorter.[70] The time for appealing is always *franc*: neither the day on which the judgment is served in order to start the running of the appeal period nor the day on which the notice of appeal is served are counted in determining the timeliness of the appeal. [71]

To prevent delaying tactics, appeals from interlocutory decisions must usually be filed within fifteen days. [72] This is presently the proper period even before the labor courts. [73] The fifteen-day period also applies to *référé* decisions [74] and decisions of the *juge chargé de suivre la procédure.* [75]

As long as it is in metropolitan France, the domicile of the parties has no bearing on the appeal period. If the parties are domiciled or residing outside of metropolitan France, time to appeal is increased by one month for residents of Europe and by two months for inhabitants of all other parts of the world. [76]

[58] For a historical survey, see 6 GARSONNET & CÉZAR-BRU 266; *cf.* 1.22–1.23 *supra.*

[59] DÉCRET No. 65–1006 of Nov. 26, 1965, J.O. Dec. 2, 1965, p. 10664, [1965] B.L.D. 678. For a more detailed discussion of the changes made by this *Décret*, see 7.58, 7.59 *supra.* CODE DE PROCÉDURE CIVILE and other statutory references in subsequent footnotes are to the Code or statute as amended by this DÉCRET.

[60] CODE DE PROCÉDURE CIVILE art. 444.

[61] CODE DE COMMERCE art. 645 (by reference to CODE DE PROCÉDURE CIVILE).

[62] CODE DE PROCÉDURE CIVILE art. 16 (formerly 30 days).

[63] CODE DU TRAVAIL, bk. I, art. 68 (certain labor matters); DÉCRET No. 65–1006, *supra* note 59, art. 33 (actions for damage done by game).

[64] DÉCRET No. 58–1293 of Dec. 22, 1958, J.O. Dec. 23, 1958, p. 11627, [1959] B.L.D. 87, art. 23.

[65] DÉCRET No. 58–1291, *supra* note 33, arts. 24, 43.

[66] DÉCRET No. 58–1292, *supra* note 30, art. 89.

[67] CODE DE COMMERCE, art. 456.

[68] DÉCRET No. 58–1294, *supra* note 20, art. 38. *But see* CUCHE & VINCENT 481–482.

[69] See CODE DE PROCÉDURE CIVILE arts. 651, 696, 762.

[70] *E.g.*, under the quasi-penal action to deprive fathers of their parental rights. Law of July 24, 1889, [1890] D.4.15, art. 7.

[71] CODE DE PROCÉDURE CIVILE art. 1033.

[72] CODE DE PROCÉDURE CIVILE art. 452. The reference is to the interlocutory decisions mentioned 8.05.b *supra.*

[73] *Cf.* note 66 *supra.* Formerly, the time period was ten days.

[74] CODE DE PROCÉDURE CIVILE art. 809.

[75] CODE DE PROCÉDURE CIVILE art. 81. But see 8.22 *infra.*

[76] CODE DE PROCÉDURE CIVILE arts. 444, 1033–2.

Time limitations for appeals must be strictly observed; the courts have no powers of extension. An appeal filed too late is invalid; the defect is not cured by failure on the part of the respondent to make a timely objection. The appeal may be dismissed on the court's own motion, and its untimeliness is ground for reversal by the *Cour de Cassation.* [77]

At one time, appeals were prohibited during an eight-day period immediately following the rendition of most judgments. This truce period was designed to discourage rash appeals. [78] At present, it survives only in the case of decisions of the *tribunaux d'instance* [79] and of the labor courts, [80] which cannot be appealed during the first three days following their rendition. Appeals from decisions of all other courts may be filed immediately after they have been rendered. The formal service of a copy of the decision need not be awaited.

## 8.07. Commencement of Appeal Period

When there has been no default, the appeal period starts to run the day after the judgment of the lower court was served on the appellant, rather than on the day the judgment was rendered. [81] If no judgment is served, time to appeal runs only if execution is levied. In that case, an appeal may be taken within thirty years from the day of execution. [82]

Service of the judgment must be by an *huissier*, who must observe the same formalities that must be met in case of service of an *ajournement*. Usually, the prevailing party serves a copy of the judgment on the losing side, but there is no rule prohibiting the inverse procedure.

Ordinarily, it is not sufficient to serve a copy of the judgment on the party's *avoué* or at the party's elected domicile; service must be made on the party in person or, if this is impossible, at his residence. Actual notice of a judgment not properly served is irrelevant. [83]

[77] CODE DE PROCÉDURE CIVILE art. 445; MOREL 484; 1 SOLUS & PERROT 420.

[78] See 1 DALLOZ, *op. cit. supra* note 5, at 485; 6 GARSONNET & CÉZAR-BRU 261–66.

[79] Law of May 25, 1838, *supra* note 69, art. 13. An immediate appeal is possible if the decision is subject to provisional execution.

[80] In which the rules applicable to the *tribunaux d'instance* apply. 1 DALLOZ, *op. cit. supra* note 5, at No. 487; CUCHE & VINCENT 478.

[81] By virtue of CODE DE PROCÉDURE CIVILE art. 1033, the day of service is not counted in computing a time limitation. See 1 SOLUS & PERROT 397.

[82] Apparently on the theory that execution without service of judgment is illegal, thirty years being the time available to obtain annulment of an illegal execution. 6 GARSONNET & CÉZAR-BRU 273.

[83] CODE DE PROCÉDURE CIVILE art. 445–2 now states that time to appeal against a judgement which is not a true default judgment begins to run when the judgment has been served as provided by arts. 58–1 and 58–2, *i.e.*, on the party in person, or on someone at his residence,

If the respondent is a minor under guardianship, the judgment must be served on the *tuteur* as well as on the *subrogé tuteur*. [84] In the case of parties residing outside France, the judgment must be served on the *ministère public* which transmits it through diplomatic channels in the same manner as an *ajournement*. A copy of the judgment must be forwarded to the respondent by registered mail, return receipt requested. [85] However, if there has been no default, time to appeal runs against nonresidents of France as soon as a copy of the judgment has been served on their French *avoué*. [86] In a few cases, the clerk of the court mails a copy of the judgment to the parties. This starts the running of the appeal period. [87]

In the case of default judgments due to a lack of appearance (*défaut faute de conclure*), the same principles as in the case of *opposition* determine when time to appeal begins to run: If the judgment was delivered to the mayor's office but not claimed by the defendant, the president of the court may make an order determining that time to appeal started to run upon delivery of the judgment to the mayor's office, provided the judge believes the defendant received actual notice of the judgment; otherwise, he should instruct the *procureur de la République* to attempt service through the police. If this is also unsuccessful, the judge may, by order, establish when the time to appeal begins to run. If the judgment was served initially on the *procureur de la République*, he should attempt to locate the defendant through the police. If the defendant cannot be located, plaintiff may secure a judicial order determining when the time to appeal begins to run.

or on a neighbor. See 7.59 *supra*. However, article 445–2 provides that in commercial cases, in order to set the appeal period running, the judgment may be served at the elected domicile, or, if none has been elected, on the clerk of the commercial court. See CODE DE PROCÉDURE CIVILE art. 422.

[84] CODE DE PROCÉDURE CIVILE art. 446. On the functions of these persons, see 4.33.a *supra*. The rules apply to incompetents. MOREL 482; CUCHE & VINCENT 452.

[85] CODE DE PROCÉDURE CIVILE art. 147 requires service of the judgment upon party as well as *avoué*. In the case of a party residing outside France, this must evidently be done in the manner provided for *ajournements*. See 7.59 *supra*. *Quaere* whether this result is changed by new article 445–2 under which, in the case of parties residing outside France, service upon the *avoué* starts the running of the appeal period.

[86] CODE DE PROCÉDURE CIVILE art. 445–2. Article 9 requires all non-resident parties to actions in the *tribunaux d'instance* to "elect a domicile" in France. In such a case, service of the judgment at the elected domicile, or, in case of failure to elect a domicile, service upon the clerk of the court starts the running of the appeal period against appearing non-residents.

[87] *E.g.*, in social security matters (DÉCRET No. 58–1291, *supra* note 33, art. 24) or in rural lease matters (DÉCRET No. 58–1293, *supra* note 64, art. 19); *cf.* CODE CIVIL art. 380 (proceedings concerning minors whose health, education or morals are in danger).

If the defendant resides abroad, the default judgment must be served on the *procureur de la République* and a copy sent to the defendant by mail, return receipt requested. The time to appeal begins to run as the time to appear in the case of an *assignation* served abroad.[88] If the defendant appeared initially but defaulted at a later stage of the proceedings in first instance (*défaut faute de conclure*), valid service of the judgment starts the running of the appeal period.[89]

In a few cases, including proceedings to obtain disqualification of a judge, [90] adoptions, [91] and proceedings to deprive a father of his parental powers, [92] the time to appeal starts to run as soon as the judgment is rendered.

Service of a copy of the judgment makes the appeal period run against the party who has served it as well as against the party on whom it has been served. [93] Other parties are not affected by such service, however, except in the case of indivisible obligations. [94] If there are several prospective respondents, it is sufficient if the notice of appeal is timely as to one. If the appellant reports the appeal to the office of the clerk of the court as required by law, he may appeal against any other parties within one month thereafter. [95]

## 8.08. Events Extending the Time to Appeal

The death of a party after service of a copy of the judgment tolls the running of the appeal period. To start it running again, a copy of the judgment must be served on the heirs of the decedent at the decedent's last residence. The heirs need not be identified by name. The time to appeal commences to run again fifteen days after such service or three months and forty days from the date of death, whichever is

[88] Code de Procédure Civile art. 445–1.

[89] Code de Procédure Civile art. 445–2.

[90] Code de Procédure Civile art. 392.

[91] Code Civil art. 356.

[92] Law of July 24, 1889, *supra* note 70, art. 7.

[93] Code de Procédure Civile art. 445. On cross-appeals, see 8.13.b *infra*. Until fairly recently, service of a copy of the judgment made the appeal period run only against the person on whom service had been made, but not against the party who had served it. This was based on the ancient French principle *nul ne se forclôt soi-même*.

[94] 6 Garsonnet & Cézar-Bru 242–52, 282; *cf*. Soc. Andréas Alibrantis v. Crédit Lyonnais, Cass. Civ., May 23, 1957, [1957] D.J. 465.

[95] Code de Procédure Civile art. 457 provides that every appeal must be reported to the clerk's office of the *cour d'appel* within one month.

later. [96] The statutory three months and forty days period is available to the heirs to make an inventory of the decedent's property and deliberate as to whether they want to accept the inheritance, including its liabilities.

The ordinary rules apply if a party dies before the judgment has been served.

The appeal period is also tolled if there is a change of capacity of one of the parties – for instance, if a party is adjudicated incompetent. In such an event, the judgment must be served again, and the appeal begins to run anew fifteen days thereafter. [97]

If a judgment is based on a forged document, time to appeal does not begin to run until the party guilty of the forgery has admitted it or the forgery has been established by a judicial decision, such as a criminal conviction. An analogous rule applies if a party has lost a case because a document has been concealed by his opponent. In such an event, time to appeal does not start to run again until the document has been recovered, but there must be written proof of the date of recovery. [98]

A complete interruption of communication services, whether caused by a strike of post office and telegraph employees, or by war, or some other cause, may also toll the appeal period. However, the courts seem to be rather strict in evaluating whether it is really impossible to file a timely appeal. During the last two wars, this matter was to some extent regulated by special statutes. [99]

## 8.09. Who May Appeal

Except for the cases in which a new party may intervene, [100] an appeal may be taken only by and against parties who were parties to, or represented in, the action in first instance. The French idea of representation is quite similar to the common law concept of privity. Thus, heirs may appeal in an action to which their decedent was a party, and,

[96] CODE DE PROCÉDURE CIVILE art. 447. As a rule, the decedent's heirs, *i.e.*, in case of intestacy his statutory distributees, succeed to all his assets and liabilitites upon his death. However, they may delay acceptance of the estate and elect to be afforded three months from the date of death to make an inventory and forty days thereafter to deliberate if they want to accept the inheritance, including liabilities. See CODE CIVIL art. 795; CODE DE PROCÉDURE CIVILE art. 174. The three months and forty day period is not applicable in case of express acceptance of the inheritance. See Dame Veuve Vergauwe v. Dame Nicaise, Trib. Gde Inst. Seine, April 28, 1959, [1959] J.C.P. 2. 11264 (when death occurred on October 31, 1957, and service of judgment was renewed on December 16, appeal on Jan. 25, 1958, timely). See generally 6 GARSONNET & CÉZAR-BRU 292.

[97] CODE DE PROCÉDURE CIVILE art. 450. The *exploit* by which the judgment is served must make express reference to this article.

[98] CODE DE PROCÉDURE CIVILE art. 449; CUCHE & VINCENT 452; 1 DALLOZ, *op. cit. supra* note 5, at Nos. 544–46.

[99] 6 GARSONNET & CÉZAR-BRU 292; 1 DALLOZ, *op. cit. supra* note 5, at Nos. 577–81.

[100] On intervention, see 8.12 *infra*.

to the extent that creditors stand in the shoes of their debtor, they may appeal in his stead. [101]

In actions in which the *ministère public* has been *partie principale,* it may, of course, appeal, but it may not do so in actions in which it has been *partie jointe.* However, in actions involving public policy (*ordre public*) the *ministère public* may always appeal. An appeal on behalf of the *ministère public* may be taken either by the *procureur de la République,* who handled the case in the first instance, or by the *procureur général* attached to the *cour d'appel* to which the appeal is to be taken. [102] Ordinarily, it is not possible to appeal against a person who has been on the same side as the appellant in the court below. [103]

### 8.10. Extent to Which an Appellant Must Be Aggrieved

In accordance with the general rule, a party may appeal only if it has an interest [104] in the appeal, which means, in substance, that it must be aggrieved by the judgment below. To be aggrieved, a party need not necessarily have lost below as long as it has not been awarded everything demanded in the pleadings. Thus, a denial of costs is sufficient basis for an appeal.

Mere displeasure with the opinion, as opposed to the decretal portion of the judgment, does not render a party aggrieved. [105] The courts are sometimes fairly liberal in determining who may appeal. Thus, it has been held that a defendant in a divorce action who had filed a counterclaim for divorce and won, but changed her mind afterwards, should be allowed to appeal so that she could formally abandon the divorce proceedings. [106]

### 8.11. Appeals in Actions with Multiple Parties

In actions with multiple parties, an appeal is usually effective only between the party who has taken the appeal and the party against whom the appeal has been taken. The rights of other parties are not

[101] CUCHE & VINCENT 448. Privity also exists between purchaser and seller of a litigious object and in some other cases. See 6 GARSONNET & CÉZAR-BRU 27; 1 DALLOZ, *op. cit. supra* note 5, at Nos. 259–62. The rules as to the required capacity to be a party on appeal are the same as those applicable in first instance. 6 GARSONNET & CÉZAR-BRU 361.

[102] 6 GARSONNET & CÉZAR-BRU 27; 1 DALLOZ, *op. cit. supra* note 5, at Nos. 263–66. On the rôle of the *ministère public* in civil actions, see 3.08–3.10 *supra.* In social security matters certain social security officials, in addition to the parties, have a right to appeal. Their rôle is analogous to that of the *ministère public.* See DÉCRET No. 58–1291, *supra* note 33, art. 23.

[103] 6 GARSONNET & CÉZAR-BRU 331; CUCHE & VINCENT 449.

[104] On the requirement of interest, see 6.02 *supra*

[105] 6 GARSONNET & CÉZAR-BRU 272, 273.

[106] Dame Grandury v. Grandury, Cour Amiens, Nov. 25, 1953, [1953] J.C.P. 2. 7887 (note Granier). *But see* Dame Nicolle v. Nicolle, Cour Rouen, Feb. 11, 1959, [1959] D.J. 254 (since she won below, wife who successfully counterclaimed for divorce may not appeal to abandon action on ground *avoué* filed counterclaim against her will).

affected, except when an indivisible obligation is involved. An appeal by or against one of several parties to an indivisible obligation affects all parties. A similar result obtains in the case of a joint obligation. If one of the parties bound by a joint obligation takes a timely appeal, his co-debtors may intervene on appeal or file an appeal even after expiration of the time to appeal. However, they do not profit from the timely appeal if they fail to take any action. If several joint debtors are defendants, the plaintiff must take a separate, timely, appeal against each. [107]

### 8.12. Intervention on Appeal

In spite of the rule that only parties to the action in the court ot first instance may appeal, the law presently [108] allows an intervention on appeal by any person who has an interest in the proceeding, even if he has not been a party before the lower court. [109] This very liberal rule is due to the concept of an appeal's involving complete readjudication rather than correction of specific errors.

The rules determining who has standing to appeal also determine who has an interest sufficient to allow intervention on appeal: The intervening party must in some manner be aggrieved by the decision below. [110] The courts have sometimes compensated for the absence of a concept of a private *amicus curiae* by granting professional organizations the right to intervene on appeal in cases affecting the rights or duties of their members. [111] To some extent, parties who may intervene may also be impleaded on appeal. The procedure in the case of intervention on appeal is analogous to the procedure applicable to intervention in the courts of first instance. [112]

[107] CUCHE & VINCENT 460–61; 6 GARSONNET & CÉZAR-BRU 309–31. The distinction between joint obligation (*solidarité*) and indivisible obligation (*indivisibilité*) is not always easy to make. An example of an indivisible obligation is an obligation imposed on several people to deliver an item of property which cannot be divided, such as an automobile. See CODE CIVIL arts. 1217–19; 2 COLIN & CAPITANT 458. On joint obligations, see *id.* at 466–80.

[108] Since the 1942 amendments to the CODE DE PROCÉDURE CIVILE articles relating to appeal. On prior law, see 6 GARSONNET & CÉZAR-BRU 361–61.

[109] CODE DE PROCÉDURE CIVILE art. 466. A person who has been a party to the proceedings in the court below must appeal and may not intervene on appeal. 6 GARSONNET & CÉZAR-BRU 358.

[110] *Cf.* 1 DALLOZ, *op. cit. supra* note 5, at Nos. 270, 684. There is sometimes a duplication of remedies since persons aggrieved by a judgment in an action to which they were not parties may also obtain a reopening by means of *tierce opposition*.

[111] Thus, the national organization of French notaries, the *Conseil Superieur du Notariat*, was allowed to intervene on appeal in an action involving the validity of a contract clause used by French notaries in certain types of agreements as a matter of standard practice. May v. consorts Mary, Cour Rennes, April 28, 1959, [1959] J.C.P. 2. 11227; *cf.* the note Crémieux appended to Mme. X, *supra* note 16.

[112] On appeal, *mise en cause*, but not impleader in the American sense (*appel en garantie*), is possible. Garantie mutuelle des fonctionnaires v. Goujon, Cass. Civ., April 10, 1964, [1965]

## 8.13. Manner of Taking an Appeal

**a. Notice of appeal.** To stop the running of the appeal period and to initiate the appeal, the appellant must ordinarily serve on the respondent a document called *acte d'appel.* [113] In essence a summons requesting the respondent to appear in the appellate proceedings, the *acte d'appel* is governed by substantially the same rules as an *ajournement.* [114] Differences are that the *acte d'appel* must indicate the judgment appealed from [115] and that no ground for the appeal need be indicated. [116]

The *acte d'appel* must be served by an *huissier* who must deliver it to the respondent in person or, if this is impossible, at his residence. Service on the respondent's [117] *avoué* or at a domicile elected merely for purposes of suit is not sufficient. However, service is validly made at a domicile elected in a contract concluded before the beginning of the action. In the case of minors or incompetents, service must usually be made on their guardian or committee. [118] If the opponent has died after service of the judgment, the *acte d'appel* must be served on all the opponent's heirs collectively at the decedent's last residence. Their individual

D.J. 1 (note Lobin); *cf.* Raynaud *Chronique*, 59 REV. TRIM DR. CIV. 541 (1960). See also 7.14 *supra.*

[113] For a form, see Appendix, Form No. 17.

[114] CODE DE PROCÉDURE CIVILE art. 457; *cf.* 6 GARSONNET & CÉZAR-BRU 308. Since an appeal is considered as a new action before a higher court, it is logical to give the notice of appeal the form of a summons citing the respondent to appear before the appellate court. However, the courts seem to be more lenient in cases of defective notices of appeal than in cases of defective *ajournements.* See, *e.g.*, 1 DALLOZ, *op. cit. supra* note 5, at 373. As before the courts of first instance, the original appearance of respondent before the *cour d'appel* is merely symbolic and consists only in the appointment of an *avoué* to represent him. See 8.20.b *infra.*

[115] The judgment appealed from must be indicated with definiteness. An appeal from a final judgment does not automatically include an appeal from an as yet unappealed interlocutory judgment. The interlocutory judgment must be specifically mentioned. 6 GARSONNET & CÉZAR-BRU 181.

[116] Haurillon v. Soc. Pierre et Roumazeilles, Cour Toulouse, Jan. 16, 1956, [1956] D.J. 187; MOREL 483; 1 DALLOZ, *op. cit. supra* note 5, at No. 373. Statements of the ground for appeal may be exchanged later. As a practical matter, *actes d'appel* usually contain some indication of the grounds for appeal, but only in a very general manner. One form is often used, no matter what the case is about. See Appendix, Form No. 17 *infra.* However, in case of appeals from decisions concerning requests for the disqualification of a judge, or for a change of venue because a party is related to one of the judges of the court, the *acte d'appel* itself must specify the reasons for the appeal. CODE DE PROCÉDURE CIVILE arts. 392, 377. In case of disputes relating to priorities among judgments (the so-called *ordre*), the *acte d'appel* must indicate with precision the portions of the judgment that aggrieve the appellant. CODE DE PROCÉDURE CIVILE art. 762.

[117] CODE DE PROCÉDURE CIVILE art. 457. The rule is the same as that governing an *ajournement* initiating an action in the first instance.

[118] 1 DALLOZ, *op. cit. supra* note 5, at Nos. 432–39. On election of domicile, see 4.28 and 7.02 *supra.* An election made in first instance is not effective on appeal, since an appeal is considered a new proceeding.

names need not be specified in the *acte d'appel*. Such service is sufficient to stop the running of the appeal period. However, no further proceedings concerning the appeal may be taken by the appellant until he has delivered additional copies of the *acte d'appel* to each heir individually. [119]

In some instances, an *acte d'appel* is not necessary for taking an appeal. In case of requests for the disqualification of a judge, a declaration at the court clerk's office is sufficient. [120] The same is true in case of petitions for change of venue because of a relationship between one of the parties and a judge of the court. [121] In *ex parte* matters handled by the *chambre du conseil*, the appeal is taken by filing a petition with the presiding judge of the *cour d'appel*. [122] In social security matters, the appeal is taken either by addressing a registered letter to the clerk of the *cour d'appel* or by a declaration made to the clerk of the first instance commission. [123] Some recent cases hold that appeals from labor courts must be taken in the regular manner, through an *acte d' appel* served by an *huissier*, but there is authority that a declaration at the clerk's office is sufficient. [124]

Within one month from the date of the appeal, the *avoué* of the appellant must file a statement in the clerk's office of the *cour d'appel* indicating the names and addresses of the parties and the judgment appealed from. [125] This statement seems to have mainly statistical purposes and is not sufficient to get the case on the calendar.

**b. Cross-appeal.** Generally speaking, the judgment appealed from may be modified only in favor of the appellant. [126] This rule is subject to only a few exceptions. In a limited number of instances, new claims may be formulated on appeal by the respondent. Respondents may also

[119] Code de Procédure Civile art. 448.

[120] Code de Procédure Civile art. 392.

[121] Code de Procédure Civile art. 377 (making article 392 applicable). This provision refers to a relationship between one of the members of the court who is not sitting and a party. A judge sitting in a case may not be a relative of a party.

[122] *Cf.* 1 Dalloz, *op. cit. supra* note 5, at No. 365. This is generally the method by which *ex parte* proceedings of the *chambre du conseil* are appealed.

[123] Décret No. 58-1291, *supra* note 33, art. 24.

[124] They are reviewed in Raynaud, *Chronique*, 59 Rev. trim. dr. civ. 542 (1960).

[125] Code de Procédure Civile art. 457. The *avoué* failing to file such a statement is subject to a fine, but failure to file does not affect the validity of the proceedings. If there are several respondents, it is sufficient if the notice of appeal is timely as to one of them; the others may be served within one month from the date the appeal has been reported to the clerk's office. See text at note 97 *supra*. However, this report must subsequently be amended to show that additional parties have been served. See Appendix, Form No. 18.

[126] See, *e.g.*, 1 Dalloz, Répertoire de Procédure Civile et Commerciale, *Appel Incident*, at No. 25 (1956).

raise affirmative defenses on appeal. [127] In both instances, modification of the judgment in respondent's favor may result. Ordinarily, however, the respondent must formulate a cross-appeal if he wishes to obtain modification of the judgment below.

A cross-appeal may be taken by means of a regular *acte d'appel* served within the period specified by law, but this is not necessary. A cross-appeal may also be taken by *appel incident*. An *appel incident* may ordinarily be taken by the respondent at any time during the proceedings on the main appeal by serving *conclusions* stating his objections to the judgment below on the opponent's *avoué*. [128] An *appel incident* is possible only against an appellant or a party united in interest with him, however. [129] As far as capacity and standing to appeal are concerned, the rules governing appeals and cross-appeals are the same. [130]

Sometimes, a respondent is well advised to take a formal appeal within the time provided by law instead of relying on the possibility of lodging an *appel incident* later on. If the main appeal is dismissed – for instance, because it is not timely or the appellant has no standing to appeal –, the *appel incident* falls too. [131] A regular appeal taken by the respondent by serving a timely *acte d'appel* is not affected by such a dismissal. A voluntary discontinuance of his appeal by the appellant after the respondent has taken an *appel incident* seems to leave the *appel incident* unimpaired. [132]

[127] Code de Procédure Civile art. 464. For a more extensive discussion, see 8.17 *infra*.

[128] Code de Procédure Civile art. 445–3. The rule of Code de Procédure Civile art. 82 prohibiting the filing of new *conclusions* within the last ten days before the hearing of the case does not seem applicable; however, the question whether the taking of an *appel incident* is possible by a simple oral statement to that effect at the hearing is controverted. See 1 Dalloz, *op. cit. supra* note 126, at Nos. 5, 91; 6 Garsonnet & Cézar-Bru 47; Cuche & Vincent 457. The *appel incident* has two advantages over a formal appeal: (1) it need not be taken within the regular appeal period, and (2) since no formal service on the party but only service on an *avoué* is required, *huissier*'s fees are considerably less.

[129] 6 Garsonnet & Cézar-Bru 57. This is in line with the general rules applicable to appeals in cases with multiple parties. See 8.11 *supra*.

[130] Thus, acquiescence in the lower court decision or formal waiver may deprive respondent of his right to take an *appel incident* (see, *e.g.*, Consorts Garnier v. Consorts Lansalot, *infra* note 132), but failure to formulate an *appel incident* in his original *conclusions* on appeal does not deprive respondent of the right to do so later on. Lebas v. Dame Veuve Puginet Boshard, Cass. Civ., Oct. 11, 1957, [1957] D.J. 686.

[131] *E.g.*, Dame Nicolle v. Nicolle, Cour Rouen, Feb. 11, 1959, [1959] D.J. 254 (when the appellant in the main appeal no standing to appeal because he is not aggrieved, *appel incident* must fall too); 6 Garsonnet & Cézar-Bru 55.

[132] The point is controverted. *Compare* Calmel v. Dame Lecante, Cass. Civ., March 30, 1925, [1926] S. 1. 69, and Consorts Garnier v. Consorts Lansalot, Cass. Civ., April 1, 1925, [1926] S. 1. 229 (abandonment of main appeal by appellant does not affect *appel incident* unless accepted by respondent), *with* Jouanneau v. Soc. Anon. Foncière des Champs Elysées, Cour Paris, April 30, 1958, [1958] D.J. 364 (when respondent accepted lower court judgment

**c. Cross-appeal by others than the respondent.** Originally, an *appel incident* could be taken only by the respondent in the main appeal. Other parties had to appeal by a timely *acte d'appel.* [133] Thus, a third-party defendant liable over to a principal defendant against whom an appeal had been taken was unable to protect his interests if he did not learn about the appeal in time to serve a formal *acte d'appel.* [134] At present, however, all parties whose interests are affected by an appeal may file a kind of cross-appeal by simple *conclusions* served on the other parties, even after expiration of the time ordinarily available for an appeal. [135] Such a cross-appeal, which is merely a variant of the *appel incident,* is referred to in the Code of Civil Procedure as an appeal provoked by the main appeal, an *appel provoqué par l'appel principal.* [136] It is governed by the same rules as the *appel incident.* However, it may not delay decision of the main appeal. [137]

## 8.14. Effect of Appeal on Execution

Formerly, a judgment could be executed as soon as it had been served, even though the time to appeal had not yet expired. [138] There were only a few cases, such as divorce and incompetency proceedings [139] and *inscription de faux* cases in which the destruction or alteration of a document had been ordered, [140] in which this rule did not find application.

At present, however, unless "provisional execution" is available, execution of a judgment is not possible as long as the time to appeal has not yet expired. [141] Third parties never need execute a judgment unless they receive certificates from the *avoué* of the prevailing party and the clerk of the court showing that time to appeal has expired and that no appeal has been taken. [142]

by making voluntary payment under it and his opponent appealed, but withdrew before respondent had filed an appearance in the appeal, *appel incident* held not possible).

[133] For a discussion of this rule, see 6 GARSONNET & CÉZAR-BRU 53.

[134] Assuming, of course, that the third party defendant was not served with a notice of appeal.

[135] This was first authorized in 1935. The present rule goes back to the 1942 reform of appeal procedure. See Hébraud, *Commentaire,* [1943] D. CR. L. 1, at 3.

[136] CODE DE PROCÉDURE CIVILE art. 445–3. For an example, see Veau v. Tafforin et autres, Feb. 19, 1958, [1958] D.J. 447 (tort action involving impleaded parties).

[137] CODE DE PROCÉDURE CIVILE art. 445–3.

[138] *E.g.,* MOREL 486.

[139] See 11.04.f *supra*; CODE CIVIL art. 505; CODE DE PROCÉDURE CIVILE art. 895.

[140] CODE DE PROCÉDURE CIVILE art. 241.

[141] CODE DE PROCÉDURE CIVILE art. 445. Execution is possible whenever provisional execution has been granted by the court or is available as a matter of law, as in the cases mentioned in notes 145–48 *infra.*

[142] CODE DE PROCÉDURE CIVILE art. 548. The term execution is used here, as in French law

In addition, the appeal itself has a stay effect.[143] Any procedural step taken in violation of this rule is void, unless "provisional execution" has been granted. It is immaterial whether a final or interlocutory judgment is involved. A court may therefore not rely on an *expertise* conducted pursuant to a judgment that has been appealed.[144] In some cases in which speed is important, neither appeal period nor appeal stay execution. Decisions by a judge sitting *en référé*,[145] decisions granting petitions for the disqualification of a judge,[146] decisions in proceedings to obtain documents in the custody of public officials,[147] and a few others[148] are subject to execution though an appeal may have been taken. If a decision of a court of first instance recites that it is non-appealable but the losing party believes that this recital is erroneous and takes an appeal, there is likewise no automatic stay. However, it is possible to obtain an immediate decision from the *cour d'appel* as to whether the appeal is proper and stays execution.[149]

## 8.15. Avoiding Stay of Execution by Provisional Execution

The stay of execution during the appeal period or occasioned by an appeal may be avoided by obtaining court authorization for provisional execution.[150] Provisional execution may be granted by the court of first instance if delay in executing the judgment is likely to be dangerous or if the matter is otherwise

generally, in a broad sense. It refers to all types of acts giving effect to a judgment. Thus, persons holding funds belonging to one of the parties need not pay these out by virtue of a judgment until time to appeal has run out; even the official keeping the public land records (*conservateur des hypothèques*) does not have to make any entries in his records – *e.g.*, cancel a mortgage judicially declared invalid – until that time. An analogous rule applies to officials keeping birth, death, and marriage records. *Cf.* MOREL 486.

[143] CODE DE PROCÉDURE CIVILE art. 458. This is called the suspensive effect of an appeal. The appellant need not give any security to obtain this benefit.

[144] 6 GARSONNET & CÉZAR-BRU 205–07. It is quite immaterial whether or not the judgment appealed from is ultimately reversed. 1 DALLOZ, *op. cit. supra* note 5, at No. 592.

[145] CODE DE PROCÉDURE CIVILE art. 809. The reason seems to be that, at least in theory, *référé* decisions always involve urgent matters.

[146] CODE DE PROCÉDURE CIVILE art. 312. If certain procedural steps are not taken, an analogous rule is applied to decisions denying petitions for the disqualification of a judge. CODE DE PROCÉDURE CIVILE art. 396.

[147] CODE DE PROCÉDURE CIVILE art. 848.

[148] These include decisions punishing a party who disturbs court proceedings (CODE DE PROCÉDURE CIVILE arts. 89–90) and certain proceedings relating to sureties (CODE DE PROCÉDURE CIVILE art. 521); *cf.* CODE GÉNÉRAL DES IMPÔTS art. 1915 (recovery of indirect taxes not withstanding review of administrative decision by court).

[149] If the respondent has appeared, the appellant serves *conclusions* on his *avoué*, which may be submitted to the court immediately. If the respondent has not appeared, he must be summoned by *huissier* to appear at the hearing. A judge of the court on *ex parte* application determines how many days notice of the hearing must be given. CODE DE PROCÉDURE CIVILE art. 458.

[150] CODE DE PROCÉDURE CIVILE art. 458.

urgent.[151] Whether these conditions are present is essentially a question of fact within the discretion of the court authorizing the provisional execution. However, in its decision, the court must indicate the factual bases for its holding.[152] It may, in its discretion, authorize provisional execution of only part of the judgment.[153] Provisional execution may never be granted for the part of the judgment dealing with costs,[154] nor may it be authorized if execution of the judgment pending appeal may cause irreparable harm.[155]

The court may award provisional execution only if one of the parties has requested it before judgment has been rendered.[156] As a result, requests for provisional execution have become a standard element of the prayer for relief in the pleadings.[157] In accordance with the rule that a final judgment terminates the court's power to deal with the matter in litigation,[158] the parties may not request amendment of a decision that has not granted provisional execution. However, authorization for provisional execution may be requested for the first time from the *cour d'appel*.[159] A party levying provisional execution does so at his peril: In case of reversal on appeal, it must return everything collected on execution and becomes liable for all damages occasioned by the execution.[160]

To ensure payment of damages and the return of all sums collected, the court may condition the levying of provisional execution on the posting of security. Security may be provided either by a deposit of cash or securities or by a surety. Whether security must be posted is ordinarily discretionary with the court. However, the court may not require

[151] CODE DE PROCÉDURE CIVILE art. 135a; MOREL 487. The rules concerning provisional execution (*exécution provisoire*) were simplified and unified by the 1942 reforms. *Cf.* CUCHE & VINCENT 400.

[152] Burg v. Soc. Limoges-spectacles, Cass. Soc., April 27 ,1944, [1944] D. ANAL. J. 77; (*cour d'appel* authorized to prohibit levying of provisional execution if lower court decision contains no findings of fact showing urgency); Soc. C.O.M.A.V.A. v. Soc. du garage Magdebourg, Cour Paris, July 2, 1956, [1956] D. SOMM. 146; CUCHE & VINCENT 402.

[153] CODE DE PROCÉDURE CIVILE art. 135b. This rule emphasizes the discretionary character of provisional execution.

[154] CODE DE PROCÉDURE CIVILE art. 137.

[155] This seems to be the meaning of CODE DE PROCÉDURE CIVILE art. 135a, which states that provisional execution is not available if the nature of the action excludes it. The rule applies mainly in cases affecting personal status. See CUCHE & VINCENT 401.

[156] CODE DE PROCÉDURE CIVILE art. 135a.

[157] See, *e.g.*, 1 RAVIART, TRAITÉ FORMULAIRE DE PROCÉDURE CIVILE 179 (8th ed. 1956).

[158] On this rule, see 7.13 *supra*.

[159] CODE DE PROCÉDURE CIVILE art. 136. Whether *exécution provisoire* can be requested from an appellate court if the court of first instance has denied it, is controverted. *Cf.* CUCHE & VINCENT 462. Under article 136, *exécution provisoire* may also be requested during the *opposition* procedure.

[160] *E.g.*, MOREL 489.

security in actions based on written instruments if there is no contest as to the validity of the instrument, nor in actions based on earlier judgments that have become non-appealable. The same rule applies to judgments ordering proof measures, such as *expertises*. A party can ordinarily avoid the posting of security by agreeing, pending the outcome of the appeal, to pay into court all sums collected on execution.[161]

Except in personal injury and support actions, a party whose opponent has been authorized to levy provisional execution may pay into court the amount of the judgment against him. If this has been done, execution may not be levied. The funds paid into court remain there until the appeal has been decided.[162] A party against whom provisional execution has been awarded may request the *cour d'appel* before which the appeal is pending to rule on its lawfulness. The issue is heard and decided very rapidly. In determining the matter, the *cour d'appel* examines if the action is one in which provisional execution may be granted;[163] it also checks whether the lower court has listed sufficient facts to support the finding of urgency.[164] If the *cour d'appel* finds that the grant of provisional execution has been improper, it issues an order prohibiting the levying of execution. Except for this instance, an appellate court may not interfere with the execution of judgments rendered by lower courts.[165]

## 8.16. Scope of the Powers of the *Cours d'Appel*

As noted, an appeal ordinarily leads to complete readjudication of the case rather than to review of specifically assigned errors of law.[166] A *cour d'appel* may not restrict its review to questions of law and remand for a new adjudication of factual issues: It must itself decide the entire case on the merits.[167] Since an appeal brings the whole case be-

[161] CODE DE PROCÉDURE CIVILE arts. 135b–135c. Provisional execution of a proof judgment, such as one ordering an *expertise*, is unlikely to cause the other side much harm since reversal of the proof order will automatically lead to exclusion of the report of the proof proceedings.

[162] CODE DE PROCÉDURE CIVILE art. 135. The sums paid into court, whether to avoid provisional execution or the need to post security, are not paid to the clerk of the court but either to a person appointed by the court or – which is the usual rule – to a government agency created to hold sums paid into court and certain other funds, the *Caisse des Dépôts et Consignations*. CODE DE PROCÉDURE CIVILE art. 135e.

[163] CODE DE PROCÉDURE CIVILE art. 459. The procedure is similar to that used to determine whether the appeal stays execution. See note 149 *supra*.

[164] See cases cited note 152 *supra*.

[165] CODE DE PROCÉDURE CIVILE art. 461. Of course, reversal of a decision on appeal makes it illegal to execute the reversed decision, but an appellate court may not interfere directly with execution of a lower court decision.

[166] See 8.01 *supra*.

[167] See, *e.g.*, MOREL 489–90; CUCHE & VINCENT 463–64; 6 GARSONNET & CÉZAR-BRU 185. Stern et Soc. Sogetec v. Levy Lecornue, Cass. Soc., June 4, 1957, [1957] D.J. 579.

fore the *cour d'appel* for a new and independent determination, it is said to have an *effet dévolutif*. In its practical application, the principle of complete readjudication creates at least three interrelated problems.

First, if an appeal were viewed as an entirely new action, the parties would not be limited by the pleadings below, but could interpose new claims or defenses. This result would conflict with the principle of the *double degré de juridiction*, according to which the parties are ordinarily entitled to have each issue determined twice, once in the court of first instance and once on appeal. Further, this view would encourage dilatory tactics. It is clear that some restrictions on new matters that may be raised on appeal is necessary. [168]

Second, the appellant may ordinarily restrict his appeal to designated issues; this is expressed by the latin phrase *tantum devolutum quantum appellatum* (as much is brought up on appeal as has been appealed from). [169] However, if an appeal were viewed as always leading to re-examination of the whole case, any appeal would enable the *cour d' appel* to review all issues.

Third, the principle that the *cour d'appel* must re-examine the entire case is fully applicable only to appeals from final decisions. On appeals from interlocutory decisions, such as proof orders, the *cour d'appel* is ordinarily empowered to deal only with the decision appealed from; after the appeal from the interlocutory judgment has been decided, the case must be remanded so that it may continue its way through the lower court. [170] However, on certain interlocutory appeals, the *cour d' appel* may draw the entire case onto itself and decide it on the merits, though no final judgment has yet been rendered by the court below. This procedure, known as *évocation*, is evidently in conflict with the French rule of the *double degré de juridiction*. [171] Unfortunately, its precise scope is not well defined. [172] As a result, it is often difficult to determine whether the *cour d'appel* must decide the entire case on appeal or whether it must remand. [173]

These problems have been quite troublesome. A narrow view of the

[168] On the extent to which new matters may be brought up on appeal, see 8.17–8.18 *infra*.

[169] Of course, the respondent may broaden the scope of the appeal by formulating an *appel incident*. See 8.13.b *supra*. The difficult problem is the extent to which the respondent, or the court on its own motion, may broaden the scope of the appeal in the absence of an *appel incident*. See 8.19 *infra*.

[170] See 8.20.g *infra*.

[171] See 8.01 *supra*.

[172] This is particularly true as to decisions dealing with standing to sue, validity of the service of summons, or other issues not directly involving the merits.

[173] See 8.19.b *infra*.

powers of the *cours d'appel* may expedite appeals by reducing the number of issues. Yet, a greater willingness of appellate courts to determine all phases of a controversy may in the end speed up litigation by eliminating the need for readjudications or separate actions.[174]

## 8.17. The Rule Restricting New Claims on Appeal

The *Code de Procédure Civile* provides that, subject to some exceptions, new claims may not be presented on appeal.[175] However, the Code gives no definition of the term new claim. Because the courts have often been actuated by pragmatic rather than purely logical considerations, general formulas attempting a definition have not been successful.[176]

A few things are nevertheless certain. A claim is not new if it has been raised before the court of first instance and has not been formally withdrawn. It matters little whether the alleged new claim has been mentioned in the *ajournement* by which the action was initiated or in one of the *conclusions* exchanged during its course. The failure of the court of first instance to deal with a matter properly raised does not deprive it of its status of an old matter, which may be brought up again on appeal.[177]

Even a matter not raised before the lower court does not necessarily amount to a new claim. It has been stated that a new claim requires (1) new parties or parties acting in a different capacity, or (2) a new purpose.[178]

[174] One French authority has spoken of labyrinthine problems. See Motulski, *Nouvelles Réflexions sur l'Effet Dévolutif de l'Appel et l'Evocation*, [1958] J.C.P. 1. 1423. The matter is made even more complicated by the rather complex rules governing execution of judgments of the *cours d'appel*, see 8.20.g *infra*, and by the broad interpretation given the term execution. For a good discussion of the conflicting concepts bearing on appeals, see the note by Perrot appended to Bénit et Thonnerieux v. Labouré, Trib. Meaux, April 2, 1952, [1952] D.J. 564.

[175] CODE DE PROCÉDURE CIVILE art. 464. The Code speaks of new *demandes*. The English expression claim has been used because it probably comes closest to *demande*, a term the contours of which are rather imprecise. According to the standard definition given by textwriters, the *demande* is the procedural act by which the allegations of a party are brought before the court, in other words the *ajournement* by which an action is initiated or any other writing which may serve the same purpose. 1 SOLUS & PERROT 109, 192; CUCHE & VINCENT 17. However, article 464 rather seems to refer to the second meaning of *demande*, *viz.*, what the plaintiff claims in these documents. *Cf.* 1 SOLUS & PERROT 193. French authors distinguish the *demande* from the *moyens*, the factual allegations and legal arguments, which are used to support it. The prohibition against new *demandes* is not directed against reliance on new *moyens*.

[176] Some authors have suggested that a claim that would be barred by res judicata if brought in an independent action is not new, while a claim that would not be so barred is. See 1 DALLOZ, RÉPERTOIRE DE PROCÉDURE CIVILE ET COMMERCIALE, *Demande Nouvelle*, at No. 19 (1955).

[177] 1 DALLOZ, *op. cit. supra* note 176, at 63–70.

[178] On the often hazy distinction between prohibited new claims (*demandes*) and permissible new allegations supporting the claim (*moyens*), see note 175 *supra*. Originally, the dis-

The rule as to new parties is fairly easy to apply. Except to the extent intervention is allowed, [179] a person who is not a party to the proceedings in first instance may not participate in the appeal. On appeal, even persons who have been parties below may not ordinarily formulate claims against other parties with whom they had no direct contest in the first instance. The plaintiff may not demand direct judgment against an impleaded third-party defendant on appeal if he has not done so before the court of first instance and if the third-party defendant has raised no issue as to the validity of the plaintiff's claim against the main defendant. A new party may participate in appellate proceedings if it represents a person who was a party before the court of first instance. Thus, if an accident victim dies after the court of first instance has pronounced judgment in his personal injury action, his widow may take an appeal as her husband's representative. However, on appeal she may not file a claim for the damages suffered by her personally as a result of the wrongful death of her husband. [180]

The rule that a point raised on appeal is to be considered a new claim if it involves a new purpose has created more difficulties. [181] It is well established that a party may bring up new facts on appeal if they do not change the nature of the action. According to the predominant view, facts that have occurred after the decision of the court below may be alleged on appeal, since the *cour d'appel* must decide on the basis of the factual situation as it exists when it deals with the case. Thus, the plaintiff in a divorce action based on adultery may show an act of adultery committed after the decision of the lower court was rendered.[182] Except in cases of waiver, it is also possible to use new evidence to support existing facts, [183] though there may be a penalty in terms of costs if the evidence could have been introduced below. [184] In actual

tinction between new *demandes* and new *moyens* was quite important, since new matters could be used on appeal only if they could be interpreted to be new *moyens* rather than new *demandes*. In 1942, the rule against new claims was liberalized by providing that a claim with a new *cause* could be brought on appeal, provided it had the same purpose as the claim below. Hence, the distinction between claims (*demandes*) and *moyens* has lost much of its interest. *Cf.* CUCHE & VINCENT 466; MOREL 490; 1 DALLOZ, *op. cit. supra* note 176, at Nos. 19, 58, 59.

[179] See 8.12 *supra.*

[180] *E.g.*, CUCHE & VINCENT 467; GARSONNET & CÉZAR-BRU 336.

[181] See generally 6 GARSONNET & CÉZAR-BRU 330.

[182] 1 DALLOZ, *op. cit. supra* note 176, at No. 90. See also Dame Renoir v. Renoir, Cass. Civ., Feb. 19, 1952, [1952] J.C.P. 2. 7009 (intervening foreign judgment). New facts are traditionally considered as new *moyens*, not as new claims.

[183] 1 DALLOZ, *op. cit. supra* note 176, at No. 85; 6 GARSONNET & CÉZAR-BRU 339; Montagne v. Montagne, Cass. Civ., Feb. 14, 1951, [1951] D.J. 254 (*enquête* in divorce case involving testimony of witness which was not used by the court below); Bord v. Dame Raverot, épouse Bord, Cass. Civ., May 27, 1952, [1952] D.J. 506 (testimony as to new facts in a divorce case).

[184] See 8.20.f *infra.*

practice, the introduction of new documentary evidence before the *cour d'appel* is quite commonplace. Formal proof proceedings on appeal, such as *enquêtes* and *expertises*, although possible, are less frequent. Additional *expertises* seem to be more numerous than *enquêtes*. [185] On appeal, three experts are ordinarily appointed for an *expertise*. Since an *expertise* is frequently quite time-consuming, especially if three experts are involved, this practice is not conducive to the speedy determination of appeals. Nevertheless, there is little sentiment favoring a prohibition against the use of new evidence, probably because the evidence already in the record is often insufficient to allow a satisfactory determination of the issues. [186]

The raising of new issues of law creates difficult problems. New legal arguments may be advanced on appeal if the nature of the action is not changed basically, not if the new argument involves a substantial change in the theory of liability relied on below. This seems to be in substance the meaning of article 464 of the *Code de Procédure Civile* according to which a claim is new if it involves a new purpose, but not if it involves a new *cause*. For example, the plaintiff in a personal injury action, who has relied on negligence before the court below, may rely on absolute liability on appeal. [187] In an action involving land, a party may originally claim ownership on the basis of a record title and on appeal assert ownership on the basis of adverse possession. [188] On the other hand, it is not permissible to assert an easement over lands before the court of first instance and to modify this on appeal by claiming ownership. [189] A plaintiff suing a corporation for his wrongful dismissal

[185] In 1962, Me. J. Lot, chief clerk of the *Cour d'Appel* in Paris estimated that there was perhaps one new *enquête* for every 100–150 cases on appeal. A very cursory examination of some sample pages of the judgment-book of the court indicates that this figure is probably rather conservative; in evaluating it, it should also be kept in mind that French lawyers generally attempt to handle cases on the basis of documentary evidence if at all possible, so that the number of cases in which witnesses are heard is relatively small even in courts of first instance.

[186] By training and tradition, French lawyers limit their rôle in the gathering of facts; in addition, the rule of legal ethics preventing the interviewing of witnesses and the paucity of discovery devices often prevent full development of the facts before the case is brought before the courts of first instance. Leads may then develop that can be used only on appeal, so that the use of new evidence on appeal becomes almost a necessity. The institution has a certain potential for abuse, however. One experienced lawyer in Paris has stated that in cases in which divorce is sought because one of the spouses has found a new romantic interest, the plaintiff's lawyer occasionally lets the case drag on intentionally; by the time the case is on appeal, the two lovers have become impatient and have begun to live together, so that proof of adultery, *e.g.*, through use of a *constat d'huissier*, is easy.

[187] In other words, plaintiff may rely on CODE CIVIL art. 1382 (fault) in the court below, and on article 1384 (presumption of liability) on appeal. MOREL 492.

[188] MOREL 490.

[189] 1 DALLOZ, *op. cit. supra* note 176, at No. 33.

as chief executive officer may not argue on appeal that in dismissing him the corporation breached an entirely different agreement for the performance of certain technical services not comprised within his duties as chief executive officer.[190] A plaintiff in a tort action may not base his claim on *respondeat superior* before the lower court and on direct negligence of the principal on appeal.[191]

Cases involving actions to obtain annulment or rescission of contracts are most confused. Some allow the plaintiff to rely on a different legal theory[192] on appeal, while others do not.[193] A claim for money damages may be reduced. However, the plaintiff may not assert a lesser, but different, right, such as an easement instead of title.[194] The amount of damages demanded may not be increased on appeal, unless the increase is based on new facts.[195]

## 8.18. Exceptions to the Rule Restricting New Claims

**a. Statutory exceptions.** There are a number of express exceptions to the rule restricting the presentation of new claims on appeal. Most importantly, new defenses may always be raised on appeal, including

[190] Soc. anon. Manufacture moderne de lits v. Henno, Cass. Com., July 12, 1955, [1956] D.J. 40. The court emphasized the different rules of law applicable to a contract for the performance of technical services and to a contract between a corporation and its chief executive officer (*directeur général*).

[191] 6 GARSONNET & CÉZAR-BRU 334. This rule may not be followed today, since the amendment of article 464 of the CODE DE PROCÉDURE CIVILE in 1942 permits assertion on appeal of claims that have a *cause* different from the claims presented in the court below. See note 178 *supra*.

[192] *E.g.*, Dlle Thevan v. Berthet, Cour Lyon, Feb. 23, 1953, [1953] J.C.P. 7846 (note Rabut) (discussing what amounts to a new *cause* for a claim). The case involved an action to declare the sale of a farm void on the ground of *vileté de prix*, *i.e.*, substantial absence of consideration. On appeal, the plaintiff successfully demanded rescission on account of *lésion*, a legal concept which permits rescission of a contract for the sale of land if the price is 7/12th less than the true value. On the differences between the two, see 2 COLIN & CAPITANT 581–90; CODE CIVIL arts. 1118, 1685.

[193] *E.g.*, Dame Jary v. Masia, Cass. Civ., Jan. 3, 1951, [1952] S. 1. 58. In this case, the vendor sued in first instance for rescission of a sale of land on the ground of duress, but on appeal demanded rescission on account of *lésion*. This was held improper, since these bases for avoiding a contract are too different: A contract concluded under duress is completely void, while the purchaser, if the seller relies on *lésion* to avoid a contract, may always retain the property by offering to pay the difference between the price actually paid and a fair price as determined by experts. *Cf.* Simmard v. Administration de l'Enrégistrement, Cass. Com., June 29, 1948, [1948] S. 1. 141; Barruyer v. Morin, Cour Grenoble, Nov. 23, 1949, [1950] D.J. 423 (in both cases it was held improper, in an action for rescission, to rely on *lésion* in the first instance and on absence of consideration (*vileté de prix*) on appeal).

[194] 6 GARSONNET & CÉZAR-BRU 337; 1 DALLOZ, *op. cit. supra* note 176, at No. 43.

[195] Cie générale d'assurances v. Philippet, Cass. Civ., April 24, 1950, [1950] D.J. 450 (demand for increase of damages on appeal to compensate for decline in purchase power of money held improper); Dlle Monchausse, Cass. Com., Nov. 18, 1953, [1953] J.C.P. 4. 181. There are however, important exceptions to the rule that damages may not be increased on appeal. See 8.18.a *infra*.

defenses alleging payment, lack of title in plaintiff, invalidity of the contract which is the basis of the plaintiff's action, and the like.[196] However, this rule is inapplicable to defenses that are waived unless raised at the earliest possible moment during a suit, such as lack of competence.[197]

A counterclaim may be interposed for the first time on appeal, though apparently only by way of recoupment, not to obtain an affirmative decision.[198]

The rule allowing new defenses on appeal receives a particularly liberal interpretation in partition actions; all parties to such actions are allowed to formulate new claims relating to the property to be partitioned, since each claim is considered as a defense against the claims of all other co-tenants.[199]

Since the *cour d'appel* bases its decision on the facts as they exist at the time the case is submitted to it, damages not yet accrued at the time of the decision of the court of first instance may be demanded, including interest or rent which has become due since that date.[200] An accident victim, who suffered an aggravation of his condition after the court of first instance rendered its judgment, may likewise increase the amount of damages demanded.[201] The plaintiff may also request an increase in the damages awarded to him if there is an official devaluation of the currency.[202]

**b. Implied exceptions.** The rule restricting new claims on appeal is inapplicable to matters that cannot be raised before the court of first instance. Thus, it may always be contended on appeal that the judgment rendered by the court below is void because of some procedural

[196] Code de Procédure Civile art. 464; 1 Dalloz, *op. cit. supra* note 176, at 13; Dame Jeanton v. Consorts Parpillon, Cass. Com., July 17, 1950, [1951] S. 1. 50 (in action to fix boundary line, defense of prescription may be asserted for first time on appeal). The rule allowing new defenses on appeal is important if there is a default, since a defaulting defendant cannot obtain a reopening in cases which are appealable. See 7.04.a *supra*.

[197] See 7.08 *supra*. Of course, there is no waiver, if the defendant has defaulted below. In such a case, lack of competence may be raised for the first time on appeal.

[198] Whether an affirmative judgment may be rendered on a counterclaim interposed for the first time on appeal is controverted. *Cf.* Cuche & Vincent 467; 6 Garsonnet & Cézar-Bru 342; Morel 491.

[199] *E.g.*, Vuye v. Epoux Petremant, Cour Paris, Dec. 22, 1956, [1957] D.J. 137 (allegation that one of co-tenants made improvement which had to be taken into consideration); Hébraud, *Chronique*, 55 Rev. trim. dr. civ. 382 (1957).

[200] Code de Procédure Civile art. 464; Cuche & Vincent 468; Morel 491.

[201] *E.g.*, 1 Dalloz, *op. cit. supra* note 176, at No. 109.

[202] Soc. Hôtelière & Langlois v. Veuve Levavasseur, Cour Caen, April 16, 1947, [1949] D.J. 5 (when French franc was officially devaluated after final *conclusions* in wrongful death action filed, increase in amount of damages requested on appeal permitted). *But see* note 195 *supra*.

irregularity. In addition, changed circumstances justify requests for modification of provisional relief, such as provisional alimony, during appellate proceedings. [203] To some extent, it is also possible to request relief on appeal which is incidental to the main relief. Thus, parties to a divorce action, who have neglected to ask the court below to render a decision concerning the custody of their children, may do so on appeal. [204]

## 8.19. Scope of Appeal

**a. In case of final decisions not on the merits.** Appeals from decisions that, although not dealing with the merits, finally determine a case – for instance, dismissals on the ground of lack of competence, lack of standing to sue, statute of limitations, res judicata, and the like – create no problem if the *cour d'appel* decides to affirm. However, if the *cour d'appel* decides to reverse and to reject these defenses, the principle of the *double degré de juridiction* would require remand to afford the court of first instance an opportunity to pass on the merits and to render a decision that, in turn, would be appealable. [205] Nevertheless, moved on a practical plane by a desire to avoid delay caused by a remand [206] and on a theoretical plane by the concept of the *effet dévolutif,* the *cours d'appel* generally refuse to remand. When a court of first instance dismisses a claim because it is barred by the statute of limitations, [207] or by *res judicata,* [208] or because the plaintiff lacks standing to sue [209] and the *cour d'appel* decides that this holding is erroneous, it will usually proceed with the case and decide it on the merits, even though the court of first instance has not done so. Prior to 1958, an analogous procedure was followed in case of a dismissal for lack of competence. The creation of a special procedure for the transfer of cases

[203] *E.g.*, 6 Garsonnet & Cézar-Bru 344.

[204] 6 Garsonnet & Cézar-Bru 347.

[205] See note 2 *supra*. The prohibition against new claims on appeal (see 8.17 *supra*) and the rule which ordinarily restricts an appeal to matters comprised in the judgment appealed from (*cf.* 8.16 *supra*) would also seem to require remand.

[206] *Cf.* Motulski, *supra* note 174.

[207] Grégoire et autres v. Mantout frères, Cass. Req., April 8, 1895, [1895] S. 1. 334 (statute of limitations); Cochet v. Barnes, Cass. Soc., Jan. 21, 1950, [1950] D.J. 280 (special deadline applicable to rent control litigation).

[208] Mercier v. Catelain, Cass. Req., Oct. 25, 1905, [1906] S. 1. 460.

[209] Burette et autres v. Fieffé de Lièvreville, Cass. Req., June 26, 1860, [1860] D. 1. 440 (alleged lack of *qualité*). It has been argued that the rule stated in the text is applicable only if the dismissal is based on a defense related to the merits, a so-called *fin de non-recevoir liée au fond*, but not to purely procedural defenses. See 1 Solus & Perrot 297. The cases seem to take a broader view.

from incompetent to competent courts in 1958 eliminated most problems in this area. [210]

**b. In case of interlocutory decisions.** The principle of the *effet dévolutif*, which prevents an appellate court from remanding a case appealed to it, is fully applicable only to final decisions. In appeals from interlocutory orders, such as decisions ordering an *expertise* or a *comparution personnelle*, the appellate court ordinarily limits itself to examination of the interlocutory decision appealed from and remands the case for completion of the proceedings. There is one exception to this rule: If the *cour d'appel* reverses the interlocutory decision and the case is ready for decision, the court may, in its discretion, retain the case and decide it on the merits. This procedure is known as *évocation*. [211] The reason for its existence is said to be the fear that a court whose decision has been reversed may not be fair when a case is sent back to it. [212]

*Evocation* may not be used if the interlocutory decision has been affirmed, in which case there must always be a remand. [213] Furthermore, the parties have no right to *évocation*. The court may determine in its discretion whether to keep the case for adjudication on the merits; it may also retain part and remand the remainder. [214]

Presumably, the courts, when deciding whether or not to retain a case on the basis of *évocation*, use pragmatic criteria. A desire to expedite final resolution may lead the court to retain the case on the basis of *évocation*. However, when the reversal is due to a procedural mistake, the court may remand to impress the parties with the importance of observing all procedural rules. [215] Estimates as to the number of cases in which the courts exercise their right of *évocation* vary. [216]

[210] On the special procedure for transfer of cases from incompetent to competent courts, see 7.09.b *supra*.

[211] Code de Procédure Civile art. 473. *Evocation* came into French law from Canon law; before the French Revolution, it was a method used by the *Parlements* to increase their power at the expense of the feudal courts. See Perrot, *supra* note 174; 6 Garsonnet & Cézar-Bru 189. *Evocation* means in practice that, if a case pending before a court of first instance has progressed to a point at which a proof proceeding is ordered and this order is reversed on an interlocutory appeal, the *cour d'appel* may substitute itself for the court of first instance as to all further proceedings.

[212] *E.g.*, Cuche & Vincent 469.

[213] Soc. René Philippe v. Dame Leon, Trib. Seine, May 2, 1953, [1953] D.J. 380 (also stating in dictum that the parties may be able to waive the rule that there must be a reversal); 6 Garsonnet & Cézar-Bru 195.

[214] *Id.* at 190; 1 Dalloz, Répertoire de Procédure Civile et Commerciale, *Evocation*, at Nos. 3, 5, 33 (1955).

[215] *E.g.*, Veuve de Brinon v. Epoux Lachassagne, Trib. Montluçon, Nov. 9, 1951, [1952] D.J. 564.

[216] Perrot, *supra* note 174, states that *évocation* is used rather seldom. Cuche & Vincent, at 468–71, seem to be of a contrary opinion.

Formerly, the right of *évocation* could be exercised only if the case was ready for immediate decision. No separate proof proceeding was possible before the *cour d'appel.* [217] Under the present, more liberal, interpretation of the rule that the case must be ready for decision, it suffices if the parties have defined the issues by filing *conclusions* as to the merits in the court below; [218] the proof need no longer be complete. Thus, a *cour d'appel* in a custody case may reverse an interlocutory decision, order an *enquête sociale,* and decide the issue of custody on the basis of that proof measure. [219] The same is true of other methods of proof.

*Evocation* is possible only if the *cour d'appel* handling the case is, itself, territorially competent. [220]

Since 1942, the last sentence of article 473 of the *Code de Procédure Civile,* which deals with *évocation,* contains a final clause which allows a *cour d'appel* to retain a case on the basis of *évocation* even if it reverses a decision that is final. The meaning of this somewhat obscure clause has given rise to a great deal of dispute.

As noted, in case of final decisions, the *cour d'appel* must always deal with the merits and may never remand. [221] Consequently, in the view of certain authors, a special authorization to retain the case and deal with the merits is superfluous; they argue that the last clause of article 473 does not really refer to final decisions on the merits, but merely to decisions that finally determine various incidental matters that may arise during litigation. Others view the clause as limiting in a somewhat roundabout way the excessive scope given to the principle of the *effet*

[217] CODE DE PROCÉDURE CIVILE art. 473, as originally enacted, provided that the reversal of the lower court's interlocutory judgment and the final judgment on the merits had to be embodied in one decision. This precluded use of all proof procedures requiring a separate interlocutory judgment. The requirement that there be only one decision was dropped when article 473 was amended in 1942. *Cf.* Hébraud, note 135 *supra.*

[218] CUCHE & VINCENT 470; Veuve Vray v. Caisse régionale de la sécurité sociale de Lyon, Cass. Soc., Jan. 12, 1950, [1950] D.J. 229 (*évocation* may be used as long as parties have filed *conclusions* on merits in the court below). *Evocation* may not be used if in the court below the parties have filed only *conclusions* as to some preliminary issue, such as competence. Epoux Wendling v. Dame Thierry et Chausse, Cass. Civ., June 19, 1959, [1959] D.J. 473 (*conclusions* relating only to defense that same action pending in another court not sufficient basis for *évocation*).

[219] C. ès qualités v. Dame B., Cass. Civ., Feb. 21, 1961, [1961] D.J. 229. (with note Holleaux reviewing the historical development). *But see* CUCHE & VINCENT 470, arguing that the old law has not changed in spite of the 1942 amendment of article 473. However, Cuche & Vincent wrote before the case cited was decided.

[220] *E.g.,* Soc. Chocolat Vinay v. Omnès, Cour Paris, July 4, 1958, [1959] D. SOMM. 5. The rule is less important now, since there is a special procedure for the transfer of cases, which may apparently not be coupled with an *évocation.*

[221] See 8.16 *supra.*

*dévolutif* by making the rules governing in the case of interlocutory appeals applicable to appeals from final judgments. [222]

No real problem in the application of this provision arises if the decision of the *cour d'appel* is based on the merits, in which case remand would be pointless. However, difficulties are present if a lower court decision on the merits is reversed on procedural grounds only – for instance, because the *ajournement* was improperly served. Many courts state that in such an event failure to remand for new proceedings at which all rules must be observed would make rules of form meaningless. [223] Consequently, they hold that a *cour d'appel* may deal with the merits in such a case only if the conditions for *évocation* are present and that, since use of *évocation* is always discretionary, it is never compelled to do so. [224] Additional support for this position is derived from the principle *tantum devolutum quantum appellatum*, according to which the *acte d'appel* served by appellant defines the scope of the appeal. Under this principle, it would be improper to deal with the merits if the appellant requests merely reversal on procedural grounds.

Other courts, including the *Cour de Cassation*, disagree. According to their view, the *cours d'appel* must always render a decision on the merits if one has been rendered below, [225] provided one of the parties to the appeal requests such a decision in its *conclusions*. [226] Thus, it seems to be the majority rule that a *cour d'appel* reversing a lower court decision on the ground that the original *ajournement* by which the

[222] See CUCHE & VINCENT 472; 1 DALLOZ, *op. cit. supra* note 214, at No. 13.

[223] Motulski, *Les Rapports entre l'effet dévolutif de l'appel et l'évocation dans la jurisprudence récente de la Cour Suprême*, [1953] J.C.P. 1. 1095.

[224] In support of this contention, it has been argued that, if a decision is reversed for violation of a procedural rule, the proceedings below are void, so that there is nothing that can be brought before the *cour d'appel* by virtue of the *effet dévolutif* of an appeal. For a collection of authorities, see 1 DALLOZ, *op. cit. supra* note 214, at No. 13; Motulski, *supra* notes 174 and 223; Perrot, *supra* note 174.

[225] See the cases collected by the authors cited *supra* note 224. The *Cour de Cassation* strongly favors the idea that a *cour d'appel* should deal with the merits of every case brought before it. For a recent case, see The London Waterproof Co. v. Soc. des Etab. J. Jourdain, Cass. Civ., Dec. 12, 1957, [1958] J.C.P. 2. 10545 (note Motulski). This decision seems to permit a *cour d'appel* to deal with the merits on appeal from an interlocutory decision even though there has been no *évocation*. This would be contrary to all established rules. However, the case is by no means clear and has given rise to a great deal of discussion. See the appended note by Motulski and Raynaud, *Chronique*, 56 REV. TRIM. DR. CIV. 302 (1958).

[226] It is generally assumed that a *cour d'appel* may deal with the merits only if the party wanting to litigate the merits has put his opponent on notice by filing *conclusions* as to the merits. Motulski, *supra* note 174. This raises a problem as to the power of the appellant to limit the scope of the appeal. According to the principle *tantum devolutum quantum appellatum*, the appeal should deal only with matters raised in the notice of appeal; however, in the instant case, the respondent is apparently able to broaden the scope of the appeal to include all the issues litigated below, though the appellant requests reversal only on procedural grounds.

action was started was not properly served, or that some other procedural rule was not observed, or that the judgment below was not properly prepared, must give the parties an opportunity to repeat the defective proceedings before itself, rather than compel them to relitigate the case before a court of first instance. This solution may be due to a desire to save time. In view of the split in the cases, legislative clarification of the meaning of article 473 of the *Code de Procédure Civile* would be helpful. [227]

### 8.20. Procedure on Appeal

Procedure on appeal is substantially similar to procedure before the courts of first instance. The discussion that follows is generally limited to distinguishing characteristics of proceedings on appeal. [228]

**a. Representation.** In actions appealed to a *cour d'appel* from a *tribunal de grande instance, tribunal d'instance,* or commercial court, the parties are not represented by the *avoué* (or *agréé*) who represented them below, but by an *avoué* practising before the *cour d'appel* to which the appeal is taken. [229] In the *acte d'appel,* the appellant must elect domicile at the office of that *avoué,* at which all papers dealing with the appeal may be served on him. [230] The respondent must likewise elect domicile at the office of the *avoué* chosen by him. The number of *avoués* admitted to practice before the various *cours d'appel* in France is extremely small, especially in comparison with the large number of cases coming before these courts. [231] Except in the rather rare instances in which parties wish to argue their own cases, only *avocats* may present argument before the *cours d'appel* in cases appealed from the *tribunaux*

[227] If the conditions for *évocation* are present and the court decides to deal with the merits, appellate judges, by stating in their opinion that they exercise their right of *évocation* to the extent necessary, often avoid the problem of whether *évocation* must be used or whether the merits are before them by virtue of the *effet dévolutif.* But this device is of no avail if the appellate court decides to remand for a decision on the merits. This may be done whenever *évocation* is possible, but is not allowed if the whole case is before the appellate court by virtue of the *effet dévolutif.*

[228] *Cf.* CODE DE PROCÉDURE CIVILE art. 470 which states that, except as otherwise provided, the rules governing procedure before the *tribunaux de grande instance* apply before the *cours d'appel.*

[229] *Cf.* DÉCRET No. 58–1284 of Dec. 22, 1958, J.O. Dec. 23, 1958, p. 11579, [1959] D.L. 41, art. 37. On the functions of the *avoués*, see 2.06 *supra.* On the *agréés*, see 2.07 *supra.*

[230] CODE DE PROCÉDURE CIVILE art. 457. In spite of the election of domicile, a few documents, such as final judgments, must be served on the party personally, not on his *avoué.*

[231] There are only 51 *avoués* admitted to practice before the *cour d'appel* in Paris, even though this court handled over 12,000 civil cases during the 1960–61 judicial year. While not all of these cases required the services of an *avoué*, the majority did.

*de grande instance, tribunaux d'instance,* and commercial courts. [232] Since *avocats* are not restricted in their practice to one court the parties customarily retain the *avocat* who argued below. No *avoués* are needed for cases which have come to a *cour d'appel* from a labor court (*conseil de prud'hommes*), [233] social security court, [234] or rural lease court. [235] In such cases, a party may act as his own *avoué* and *avocat*, or, if he wishes, may request an *avocat* to attend to procedural matters. Certain officials of trade or labor organizations, co-employees, and employees of some government departments are also authorized to represent litigants in these cases. [236]

**b. Proceedings before the first hearing.** After he has been served with the *acte d'appel,* the respondent must appear. Both the time to appear and the manner of appearing are the same as before the *tribunal de grande instance.* [237] To put the case on the calendar, a *placet* similar to the one used before the *tribunal de grande instance* must be filed with the court. [238] The respondent can put pressure on the appellant if the latter does not proceed with reasonable promptness, [239] but in the case of appeals from final judgments there is no deadline for getting the case on the calendar if neither party wishes to take action. [240] In the case of appeals from interlocutory decisions, however, the appellant must put the case on the calendar within one month from the time the *acte d' appel* has been served; otherwise, his appeal becomes ineffective. [241]

[232] See DÉCRET No. 58–1284, *supra* note 229, art. 37. On the rôle of the *avocat*, see 2.03 *supra.*

[233] DÉCRET No. 58–1292 of Dec. 22, 1958, J.O. Dec. 23, 1958, p. 11621, [1959] D.L. 28, art. 90. The same rule seems applicable to matters appealed from *tribunaux d'instance* acting in the place of labor courts.

[234] DÉCRET No. 58–1291, *supra* note 33, art. 26.

[235] Décret No. 58–1293 of December 22, 1958, J.O. Dec. 23, 1958, p. 11627, [1959] B.L.D. 87, art. 24.

[236] See also 2.01 *supra.*

[237] Time to appear is ordinarily one week, subject to increases if the respondent lives outside metropolitan France. See 7.03 *supra.* The appearance is simply a notice from the respondent's *avoué* to the appellant's *avoué* that he has been retained by respondent and will represent him in the matter. See 7.03 *supra.* It should be remembered that on appeal both parties are represented by new *avoués*. For a form used for an appearance, see Appendix, Form No. 2.

[238] See 7.05 *supra.* The *placet* contains information about the parties and their counsel as well as a copy of the appellant's original *conclusions.*

[239] See 8.20.c *infra.*

[240] Except the general French rule that all proceedings are deemed abandoned if nothin is done for thirty years. Abandonment of the proceedings (*peremption*) is in effect substantially equivalent to affirmance of the judgment below. See CODE DE PROCÉDURE CIVILE art. 469.

[241] CODE DE PROCÉDURE CIVILE art. 452. This article contains the somewhat cryptic statement that in case of interlocutory appeals the appellant must, within one month from

After the filing of the *placet*, the case is put on the general calendar of the *cour d'appel*, but is not yet assigned to one of the panels. The parties then exchange their *conclusions* which are in essence summary statements of the parties' factual and legal contentions with some emphasis on the errors of fact or law allegedly made below. Since there are no specific rules governing the content of the *conclusions*, they vary a great deal. The liberal rules concerning the submission of amended *conclusions* are identical to those prevailing in the *tribunaux de grande instance*. For the first exchange of *conclusions*, the use of printed forms which state merely in very broad general terms that the opponent is wrong in law and fact, both as to substance and procedure, and that the judgment below must be affirmed or reversed, as the case may be, is not uncommon. [242] Later *conclusions* may be considerably more elaborate. Copies of all exchanged *conclusions* are filed with the court.

After the exchange of the first *conclusions*, the case is considered at issue (*en état*), [243] is assigned to one of the *chambres* of the *cour d'appel*, and is put on the calendar of that *chambre*. The clerk of the court must now obtain the file of the case from the court of first instance. [244] One of the judges of the court is assigned to the case as a reporting judge, with functions analogous to those of the *juge chargé de suivre la procédure* before the *tribunal de grande instance*. [245]

The case stays on the calendar of the *chambre* until its turn for a hearing approaches. In Paris, where the *cour d'appel* has a very heavy case load, this may take 18 months or even more. The actual delay varies with the *chambre* concerned. [246] The parties can expedite matters by petitioning the presiding judge of the *chambre* to have the case set down for a hearing. This is taken as a sign of the parties' interest in a prompt disposition which merits consideration. In the *cours d'appel* located in rural areas, waiting time may be only a few weeks. There are provisions for immediate hearings in certain matters requiring speed.[247]

the date of the appeal, effectively bring the case before the appellate court by a "simple act." There is general agreement that this means that the case must be put on the calendar by means of a *placet*. See 1 DALLOZ, *op. cit. supra* note 5, at No. 670. See also Hébraud, *supra* note 135, at 4. This rule is not applicable to decisions that are in part interlocutory and in part final. See 1 DALLOZ, *op. cit. supra* note 5, at 669 (giving some examples).

[242] See Appendix, Form No. 19.

[243] On the meaning of this term, see 7.06 *supra*.

[244] CODE DE PROCÉDURE CIVILE art. 79(12).

[245] See, *e.g.*, CUCHE & VINCENT 473.

[246] Information on the calendar practice of the Paris *Cour d'Appel* was kindly furnished by Me. Jean Lot, its chief clerk (*greffier titulaire de charge*).

[247] In such matters, a petition must be addressed to the presiding judge of the court, who will set the case down for a hearing; even the ordinary eight day period for an appearance

If the parties are not represented by *avoués*, the court fixes the date of the hearing and the clerk's office informs the parties of that date by mail. If the parties are represented by *avoués*, the clerk's office merely informs the *avoués* of the date at which the case will be set down for a hearing. The *avoués* must be present in court on that day. The cases are then called one by one, and the presiding judge fixes the date of the hearing for each. As far as possible, a date agreeable to both sides is selected. Since the case will be argued by the parties' *avocats* rather than by their *avoués*, the *avoués* must, of course, know on what dates their *avocats* will be able to appear in court. [248]

c. **Failure to proceed expeditiously and default.** If the appellant does not put the case on the calendar within eight days after respondent's appearance and does not serve his *conclusions* on the respondent within the same time, the respondent may serve a so-called *avenir* on the appellant which invites the appellant to come (*à venir*) before the court to argue the case or, at least, to serve his *conclusions*. In practice, the purpose of this document, though it states that a default may be taken against the appellant if he fails to appear, is merely to induce the appellant to file his *conclusions*. If the appellant disregards respondent's request, the respondent may summon the appellant again by a second *avenir* served not less than two weeks and a day after the first. If the appellant still neglects to file his *conclusions*, the respondent's *avoué* may request the court at its next sitting to declare the appellant in default and to render a judgment in favor of the respondent. Such a judgment is treated as a regular judgment rendered after litigation of the merits: It cannot be reopened by way of *opposition*. [249]

If the appellant does file his *conclusions* after having been served with the second *avenir*, the case may proceed in the regular manner; however, in four situations in which the hearing is likely to be brief, an immediate hearing may be had: (1) if the appeal is obviously unfounded; (2) if a proof measure, such as an *enquête* or *expertise* is likely to be

may be shortened. See DÉCRET of March 30, 1808, art. 18, reprinted in DALLOZ, CODE DE PROCÉDURE CIVILE 181 (61st ed. 1965). This so-called *assignation à bref délai* procedure is similar to an analogous procedure before the courts of first instance. See 7.03 *supra*.

[248] It is also the duty of *avoués* to inform their *avocats* of the date of the hearing.

[249] CODE DE PROCÉDURE CIVILE art. 262; 1 DALLOZ, *op. cit. supra* note 5, at No. 677; CUCHE & VINCENT 474. Service of the second *avenir* not earlier than 15 days after the first one is essential if the respondent wishes to obtain a default judgment. Lecourt v. Dlle Gaillard, Cass. Civ., June 16, 1947, [1948] S. 1. 93 (note Marin). For *avenirs* used to obtain a default judgment, see Appendix, Form No. 7 *infra*. A default judgment is requested in *conclusions* filed with the court.

necessary; (3) if the case seems urgent; and (4) if the case must be handled summarily. [250]

The rules applicable when the respondent fails to proceed are less clear. If the respondent fails to appear at all, he is presumably treated as a defendant who has failed to appear in an action brought before the *tribunal de grande instance*. If the *acte d'appel* has been served on the respondent in person, [251] a default judgment obtained against him is not subject to *opposition*. If the respondent has appeared, but thereafter fails to file his *conclusions*, the appellant may obtain a default judgment against him by following a procedure similar to that used against an appellant who fails to proceed. [252]

In the event neither party takes any action, the proceedings are considered abandoned after thirty years. In practice, this amounts to an affirmance of the judgment below. [253]

**d. Hearing.** On the day set for the hearing, the calendar for the cases to be heard that day is first called. The presiding judge asks both parties if they are ready. If they are not – for instance, because one of the *avocats* is otherwise engaged –, the case is put over until some other day agreeable to the court and the parties' *avoués*. [254] In the case of *cours d'appel* with a very crowded calendar, such as in Paris, this may mean a delay of several months. Requests for adjournments are apparently fairly frequent and disrupt calendars, especially in courts with heavy caseloads. Since such courts do not wish to lose time as a result of adjournments and it is assumed that a certain percentage of the scheduled cases will be adjourned, frequently more cases are scheduled for one day than can conveniently be handled. If the anticipated number of adjournments do not occur, it may be impossible to terminate the last case, which then has to be put over until some other day. Legislative attempts to solve the problem by reducing the number of requests for adjournments have not proved successful. [255] *Cours d'appel* outside

[250] Code de Procédure Civile art. 462. Compelling the appellant to an immediate hearing is apparently considered as a punishment for his tardiness.

[251] See, *e.g.*, Cuche & Vincent 475. On the procedure applicable when defendant fails to appear, see Code de Procédure Civile arts. 149–153, 7.04 *supra*.

[252] Code de Procédure Civile art. 463.

[253] Code de Procédure Civile art. 469.

[254] When the case is called, if one of the *avocats* cannot be present, his *avoué* must, of course, be in court to inform the court that the case cannot be argued that day. In Paris, it is not general practice for the *avoué* to come to an argument if his *avocat* is in court; in the smaller cities, both *avoués* and *avocats* are likely to come to every hearing.

[255] On the measures taken to reduce requests for adjournments, see 7.12 *supra*. One of the arguments used by *avoués* against *avocats* in the course of their somewhat muted rivalry is

the main metropolitan areas, which do not suffer from calendar congestion, schedule only as many cases for a morning or afternoon session as can conveniently be heard even if no case is adjourned. They do not experience difficulties in keeping their calendars in order and up to date.

After the calendar has been called, [256] the cases are argued one by one. Before the argument of each case, the reporting judge makes his report, which consists essentially of a reading of the judgment below and of a summary of the contentions of the parties. In most cases, this is done in a routine manner. [257] The argument is conducted as the argument before the *tribunal de grande instance.* The length of the hearing varies greatly, from about an hour to a whole afternoon or more. It depends not only on the difficulty of the case, but also on the location of the court. Courts with heavy caseloads, such as the Paris *Cour d' Appel*, are more inclined to insist on brevity. As a rule, questions of fact are stressed less, and questions of law more, than in first instance.

The special procedure for raising the defense of lack of competence before courts of first instance is not used before the *cours d'appel.* [258]

**e. Judgment *(arrêt).*** In rare and very simple cases, judgment is sometimes rendered immediately after the hearing; more frequently, the decisions of the *cours d'appel*, called *arrêts* to distinguish them from decisions of courts of first instance, which are called *jugements*, are handed down one to four weeks after the hearing. [259] Decisions are ordinarily read in open court.

If the appeal is not timely or defective for some other reason, it is dismissed without discussion of the merits. Otherwise, the various points raised by the parties must ordinarily be discussed in the de-

that *avocats*, since they may practice throughout France, are too often away on the day they are supposed to argue. This is not true of *avoués*, who may practice in only one place, and usually come to court every day.

[256] Once a week, each *chambre* devotes some time to setting down cases for a future hearing. See 7.12 *supra*. This is done after the cases to be heard that day have been called and before actual argument starts.

[257] See 1 DALLOZ, *op. cit. supra* note 5, at No. 674.

[258] CODE DE PROCÉDURE CIVILE art. 470. On this special procedure, see 7.09.b *supra*. Ordinarily, this issue will not be raised on the hearing of an appeal on the merits, since, if raised in time, it will already have been determined, and, if not raised in time, it is waived. Cases in which the defendant defaulted in first instance and cases in which an appeal was taken to a wrong *cour d'appel* – a somewhat unlikely occurrence – seem to constitute the only exceptions.

[259] In case of interlocutory appeals, the decision must be rendered within one month from the time the case has been brought before the court. CODE DE PROCÉDURE CIVILE art. 453. There is no express time limit as to other cases, but delays of more than one month are unusual.

cision.[260] Since a *cour d'appel* may order a new *enquête, expertise*, or other proof measure, the judgment may be interlocutory. If a new proof measure has been ordered, there must, of course, be a new hearing after its completion to permit the parties to discuss its results.[261]

The formal rules governing *arrêts* of the *cours d'appel* are substantially similar to those governing judgments of the *tribunaux de grande instance.* There are no concurring or dissenting opinions.[262] All decisions must be reached by a majority. In the unlikely event that there is an even division of votes – for instance, because each one of the three judges has come to a different result –, two additional judges must be added to the panel and the case must be argued again before them.[263] In spite of the rule that all French judgments must indicate the reasons for the decision reached,[264] the *cour d'appel*, if it affirms, may simply adopt the opinion of the court below.[265] Though opinions are similar in style to those of the *tribunaux de grande instance*, they tend to be somewhat briefer.

**f. Costs and appeal fine.** The decision of the *cour d'appel* must include a provision as to costs. Ordinarily, costs are imposed on the losing party.[266] However, a party that caused unnecessary costs on appeal – for instance, by demanding an *enquête* which could have been conducted while the case was pending in first instance – may be penalized by saddling him with them.[267]

If the court believes that the appellant's purpose in appealing was merely dilatory or abusive, it must impose upon him a fine of 100 francs to 10,000 francs (about $ 20 to $ 2,000). This fine is payable to the

[260] The general French rule that all judgments must embody the reasons for the decision reached also applies to *arrêts* of the *cours d'appel*. CODE DE PROCÉDURE CIVILE art. 141. Law of April 20, 1810, art 7. See also 7.13.c *supra*; 6 GARSONNET & CÉZAR-BRU 380. Failure to discuss a point (*moyen*) raised by one of the parties is ground for reversal by the *Cour de Cassation*. However, there is no duty to deal with each argument (*argument*) raised in support of a point (*moyen*). See 9.09 *infra*.

[261] See 6 GARSONNET & CÉZAR-BRU 368–69.

[262] See 7.13.c *supra*.

[263] CODE DE PROCÉDURE CIVILE art. 467. Article 468 provides that, if there are more than two different opinions, each with a different number of votes, the judges constituting the smallest minority must join the judges representing the largest number of votes. Under the present system, since the *cours d'appel* sit ordinarily in panels of three, and only rarely in panels of five (*audience solennelle*), this is not a very likely occurrence.

[264] See note 260 *supra*.

[265] 6 GARSONNET & CÉZAR-BRU 387–88. Sometimes, the courts write a detailed opinion, but terminate it with the statement that they also adopt the reasons of the court below that are not contrary to their views.

[266] CODE DE PROCÉDURE CIVILE art. 130. The court may impose part of the costs on a different party, but must indicate its reasons for doing so.

[267] 6 GARSONNET & CÉZAR-BRU 383.

government, not to the respondent. [268] Since an appeal interposed for an improper purpose is also considered a wrongful act, the court may grant the respondent damages in addition to costs. Such damages will ordinarily include expenses of litigation not taxable as costs.

Whether an appeal is dilatory or abusive is a question of fact which the *cour d'appel* determines in a non-reviewable fashion; however, no damages may ever be imposed upon a party that has prevailed on the appeal. [269]

**g. Execution of judgment on appeal.** Supervision over the execution of affirmed judgments belongs to the court of first instance, while supervision over the execution of judgments reversed in their entirety belongs to the *cour d'appel.* [270] The rule is apparently due to fear that a court whose judgment has been reversed may be biased in subsequent proceedings involving the same action. By its own terms, it is not applicable if a statutory provision assigns the execution of a particular judgment to a specific court. [271]

In France, everything that has to be done to make a court decision effective is said to relate to its execution. [272] Thus, execution is not restricted to matters that may arise upon execution of a money judgment by levy and sale, but includes registration of a divorce judgment in the marriage and birth records of the parties and numerous other matters. This broad interpretation of the term execution makes it sometimes doubtful whether a matter can be characterized as being part of execution and creates problems concerning the respective competence of the courts of first instance and of the appellate courts. Thus, at present, a request for an increase of support payments on account of changed circumstances is considered a new action, not a matter relating

[268] CODE DE PROCÉDURE CIVILE art. 471; CUCHE & VINCENT 475. At one time, the appellant, when taking an appeal, had to deposit security with the court to guarantee payment of the fine. 6 GARSONNET & CÉZAR-BRU 26. This rule was found objectionable and discontinued. See 1 DALLOZ, *op. cit. supra* note 5, at 700–08.

[269] *Id.* at 309–11.

[270] CODE DE PROCÉDURE CIVILE art. 472. If the affirmed judgment has been rendered by a court that may not deal with the execution of its own judgments – for instance, a commercial court –, its execution is within the province of the court that must handle such matters, *i.e.*, the *tribunal de grande instance.* 6 GARSONNET & CÉZAR-BRU 398; *cf.* CODE DE PROCÉDURE CIVILE arts. 442, 553.

[271] *E.g.*, Dame Pasqualiné-Saliceti v. Saliceti, Cass. Civ., May 15, 1945, [1945] D.J. 331 (*cour d'appel* may not appoint notary to undertake liquidation of marital community, since CODE CIVIL arts. 822 and 1476 assign liquidation of marital community, and all questions of partition of decedent's estates to the *tribunal de grande instance* at the last domicile of the decedent).

[272] See, *e.g.*, the note by Meurisse appended to Homel v. Amoux et Caisse de Sécurité Sociale, Cour Nancy, July 21, 1953, [1954] S. 2. 9.

to execution of the original judgment. Consequently, a claim for increased support must be brought before the competent court of first instance, even if the original support judgment was rendered by a *cour d'appel.* [273] On the other hand, the conduct of an *enquête* or *expertise* is considered as execution of the judgment authorizing it. If an interlocutory judgment of a court of first instance ordering an *expertise* is affirmed on appeal, the conduct of the *expertise* must therefore remain under the supervision of the lower court; conversely, if an interlocutory lower court judgment denying an *expertise* has been reversed, and an *expertise* ordered by the *cour d' appel,* the *cour d'appel* must have supervision over the *expertise,* though all proceedings subsequent to it are conducted by the court of first instance. [274]

In case of a partial reversal, the *cour d'appel* may, in its discretion, retain supervision over the execution of its judgment. It may also give the task of supervision to the court that rendered the original judgment, if that court is composed of different judges, or to a different court of first instance. [275] An example of a partial reversal is an affirmance on the question of liability, but a modification on the question of damages. [276]

## 8.21. Appeals from Decisions of Specialized Courts

**a. Appeals from *tribunaux d'instance.*** Ordinary rules are modified but little in case of appeals from decisions of the *tribunal d'instance.*

[273] *E.g.*, Zaoui v. Dlle Pat, Cass. Civ., July 21, 1954, [1955] D.J. 185 (with note Hébraud citing earlier cases contra holding that, since the claim for increased support was merely a matter relating to execution of the original decision, it had to be brought before the *cour d'appel* that rendered the decision).

[274] Clearly, a *cour d'appel* may retain supervision over the conduct of an *expertise* ordered by it after reversal of an interlocutory decision of a lower court denying it. See The London Waterproof Co. v. Jourdain, *supra* note 225 (even modification of scope of *expertise* is sufficient reversal to authorize the *cour d'appel* to retain supervision). However, some authors argue that in case of reversal of an interlocutory decision denying a proof measure, the *cour d'appel* should retain a discretionary power to give the court below supervision over the conduct of the proof measure ordered by the *cour d'appel,* since, unless there is to be an *évocation,* all following proceedings will be conducted by the court of first instance. 1 DALLOZ, RÉPERTOIRE DE PROCÉDURE CIVILE ET COMMERCIALE, *Exécution des Jugements et Actes,* at Nos. 186–88 (1955). This problem lost some of its importance as a result of the 1958 reforms, which prohibits interlocutory appeals from decisions ordering or denying *enquêtes.* Earlier, such appeals had been fairly frequent.

[275] CODE DE PROCÉDURE CIVILE art. 472.

[276] See, *e.g.*, La Compagnie Martiniquaise de Distribution d'Energie Electrique v. Epoux Privat, Cass. Civ., May 29, 1959, [1959] J.C.P. 2. 11179. See also Homel v. Anoux et Caisse de Sécurité Sociale, *supra* note 272 (reversal on question of division of damages but affirmance as to conduct of an expertise to evaluate total damages amount to partial reversal within rule allowing remand within the court's discretion). Other cases are cited at 1 DALLOZ, *op. cit. supra* note 274, at 169–76. Meurisse, *supra* note 272, argues that in case of partial reversal in which the affirmed and reversed portions of the judgment are independent of each other, the

Time to appeal is shorter. [277] The appealability of interlocutory decisions may be more restricted than in case of decisions of the *tribunaux de grande instance.* [278] Before the *cour d'appel,* the summary rather than the regular procedure must be used. [279]

**b. Appeals from commercial courts.** The summary procedure must be used in case of appeals from the commercial courts. In other respects, the ordinary rules governing appeals apply to appeals from commercial courts. [280] Consequently, *cours d'appel* may not refer commercial cases to *arbitres rapporteurs* to hear and report, [281] as is the common practice of some commercial courts. Of course, substantive commercial law must be applied by the appellate courts in commercial cases, including the more liberal commercial rules as to proof of contracts and other transactions. [282]

**c. Appeals from labor courts.** Parties appealing from a decision of a labor court need no *avoué.* [283] The case must be put on the calendar within one month after the date of the appeal. [284] Before the *cour d' appel,* the summary procedure, not the procedure proper to the labor courts, is used. [285] Except as specifically noted, other aspects of appeals from the labor courts are governed by ordinary rules. There is some controversy as to the procedure to be applied in case of default. [286]

**d. Appeals from rural lease courts.** As noted, no *avoué* is needed on appeal from a decision of a rural lease court. [287] The summary pro-

question of remand pursuant to article 472 should be considered independently for each portion of the judgment.

[277] See 8.06 *supra.*

[278] See 8.05.b *supra.*

[279] CODE DE PROCÉDURE CIVILE art. 404. At present, there is but little difference between the "regular" and the "summary" procedure. See 11.01 *supra.*

[280] CODE DE COMMERCE arts. 647, 648. On representation of parties, see 8.20.a *supra.*

[281] *E.g.*, Grandes Brasseries de Champigneulles v. Piacentini, Cass. Com., Dec. 26, 1951, [1952] D.J. 143; 6 GARSONNET & CÉZAR-BRU 376.

[282] See 7.37–7.38, 7.49 *supra.*

[283] DÉCRET No. 58–1292 of Dec. 23, 1958, J.O. Dec. 23, 1958, p. 11621, [1959] D.L. 28, art. 90.

[284] DÉCRET No. 58–1292, *supra* note 283, art. 89. Article 89 also requires the filing of the statement provided by CODE DE PROCÉDURE CIVILE art. 457.

[285] DÉCRET No. 58–1292, *supra* note 283, art. 90; DALLOZ, RÉPERTOIRE DE PROCÉDURE CIVILE ET COMMERCIALE, *Prud' Hommes*, at No. 177 (Supp. 1962).

[286] The question is whether the general rules governing defaults (CODE DE PROCÉDURE CIVILE arts. 149, 462) or the special rules governing default before the labor courts apply. For a collection of cases, see DALLOZ. *op. cit. supra* note 285; CUCHE & VINCENT 27 (Supp. 1961); Raynaud, *Chronique*, 59 REV. TRIM. DR. CIV. 182 (1960). On the appealability of interlocutory decisions of labor courts, see 8.05.b *supra.*

[287] DÉCRET No. 58–1293, J.O. Dec. 23, 1958, p. 11627, [1959] D.J. 61, art. 24.

cedure must be used. [288] It is apparently not necessary to file in the clerk's office the statement that is required in most other appeals. Otherwise, the general rules apply. [289]

**e. Appeals from decisions by judges sitting *en référé* and from decisions in non-rural landlord-tenant cases.** Appeals from decisions of judges sitting *en référé* and appeals in non-rural landlord-tenant matters are heard under the summary procedure. Time to appeal is usually short. [290] In most respects, ordinary rules apply. [291]

**f. Appeals in social security matters.** Appeals from the ordinary first instance commissions go to the *cour d'appel* of the region where the commission sits; appeals from the regional technical commissions go to the *Commission Nationale Technique.* [292] In neither case do the parties need the services of an *avoué*; the procedure is gratuitous. [293] The procedure on appeal from the first instance commission is basically similar to the procedure before the commission. [294] However, the remedy of *opposition,* not available before the first instance commission, is available to a defaulting defendant before the *cour d'appel* if both letters that must be sent to him by the clerk of the court to summon him to the hearing have been returned by the post office marked "not delivered." [295]

The procedure before the *Commission Nationale Technique* is entirely

[288] DÉCRET No. 58–1293, *supra* note 287, art. 24.

[289] DALLOZ, RÉPERTOIRE DE PROCÉDURE CIVILE ET COMMERCIALE, *Tribunaux Paritaires de Baux Ruraux*, at No. 107 (Supp. 1962).

[290] The time to appeal from *référé* decisions is two weeks. CODE DE PROCÉDURE CIVILE art. 809. As to litigation concerning leases of apartments used for residential or professional purposes and subject to rent control, see Law No. 48–1360 of Sept. 1, 1948, J.O. Sept. 2, 1948, p. 8659, [1948] D.L. 300, arts. 47–48 as amended by DÉCRET No. 58–1284 of Dec. 22, 1958, J.O. Dec. 23, 1958, p. 11579, [1959] D.L. 41, art. 38. These articles make CODE DE PROCÉDURE CIVILE art. 809 applicable to appeals in these rent control matters.

[291] There is, however, some dispute as to the applicability of the rule requiring service of two notices before obtaining a default judgment. See 8.20.c *supra*. See also 2 DALLOZ, RÉPERTOIRE DE PROCÉDURE CIVILE ET COMMERCIALE, *Référé Civil*, at No. 377 (1956 and Supp. 1962) (citing conflicting cases concerning the necessity for this procedure). Appeals from *référé* decisions are usually heard by a specialized panel of the *cour d'appel.*

[292] See 3.31 *supra.*

[293] DÉCRET No. 58–1291, *supra* note 33, art. 24 (appeal from first instance commission), art. 47 (appeal from regional technical commission). See also 7.19 *supra.*

[294] The *greffier* (clerk) calls parties and witnesses to the hearing by mail. Co-workers or co-employers and members of certain trade or labor organizations may act on behalf of the parties. Certain social security officials, though not parties, may make written or oral comments. The final decision is mailed to the parties by the clerk of the court. DÉCRET No. 58–1291, *supra* note 33, art. 25.

[295] DÉCRET No. 58–1291, *supra* note 33, art. 27. Time to ask for a reopening (*opposition*) is one month.

written. The file of the regional technical commission is transmitted to the National Commission and the parties are asked to submit a memorandum within twenty days. [296] The Commission decides on the basis of the documents in the file, but may order a new examination of a party by an expert. In such a case, the parties are entitled to see a copy of the expert's report. [297] There is no oral argument, however. In all cases, the entire file is reviewed by a physician belonging to the medical panel attached to the Commission before a final decision is rendered. [298]

## 8.22. The Reforms of 1965

As noted, [299] two decrees enacted late in 1965, after this book had gone to press, brought substantial changes to French civil procedure. *Décret* No. 65–1006, which is applicable throughout France, modifies many time limitations and the rules relating to the service of procedural documents. [300] To the extent they concern appeals, the changes effectuated by that *Décret* have been incorporated into this chapter. *Décret* No. 65–872 modifies a number of rules relating to procedure. Since, for the moment, it is applicable only before the *cours d'appel* in Aix, Caen, Lyon, Montpellier and Poitiers, while all other *cours d'appel* continue to be governed by the older rules, [301] the changes made by that *Décret* are set out here separately.

Generally speaking, the new rules that apply in the *tribunaux de grande instance* also apply in the *cours d'appel.* [302] A few rules operate only in the *cours d'appel*, however. Henceforth, the statement that the appellant must file in the clerk's office within one month after having taken an appeal serves more than mere statistical purposes. It is now to be accompanied by a *placet* and serves to put the case on the calendar. [303] The file to be kept by the clerk of the court must be more

[296] DÉCRET No. 58–1291, *supra* note 33, art. 45. *Appel* always stays execution. *Id.* art. 37.

[297] DÉCRET No. 58–1291, *supra* note 33, art. 47 (included are reports of medical examinations of a party by a physician, laboratory examinations of specimens, and the like).

[298] DÉCRET No. 58–1291, *supra* note 33, art. 46.

[299] See 7.58 *supra*.

[300] DÉCRET No. 65–1006, *supra* note 59.

[301] DÉCRET No. 65–872 of Oct. 13, 1965, J.O. Oct. 14, 1965, p. 9076, as corrected by J.O. Oct. 19, 1965, p. 9235, [1965] B.L.D. 600, art. 21, provides that the new *Décret* is, for the time being, to be applicable only before the courts listed in a regulation (*arrêté*) of the Minister of Justice. For the practical reasons for this provision, see the report of the Minister of Justice prefacing the *Décret*. The pertinet regulation is the ARRÊTÉ of Oct. 13, 1965, J.O. Oct. 14, 1965, p. 9076, [1965] B.L.D. 606.

[302] CODE DE PROCÉDURE CIVILE art. 470, as modified by DÉCRET No. 65–872, *supra* note 301, art.17.

[303] CODE DE PROCÉDURE CIVILE art. 457 as amended by DÉCRET No. 65–872, *supra* note 301, art. 13.

complete than before. [304] If either appellant or respondent fails to file his *conclusions* within the time fixed by the *conseiller des mises en état* established by this decree, his opponent may request the *conseiller des mises en état* to issue an order putting the case at issue. If both sides fail to file *conclusions* within the time limited, or if one side fails to do so and the other side does not request an order putting the case at issue, the case may be struck from the calender on the court's own motion. [305]

[304] CODE DE PROCÉDURE CIVILE art. 457–1 as inserted by DÉCRET No. 65–872, *supra* note 301, art. 14.

[305] CODE DE PROCÉDURE CIVILE arts. 462, 462–1, 463, as modified or added by DÉCRET No. 65–872, *supra* note 301, arts. 16, 17. Before the *cours d'appel* the judge performing the functions of the *juge des mises en état* is called *conseiller des mises en état* since all *cour d'appel* judges bear the title *conseiller*.

CHAPTER 9

# PROCEEDINGS BEFORE THE *COUR DE CASSATION*

This chapter describes the territorial competence of the *Cour de Cassation* (9.01–9.02), decisions subject to review (9.03–9.05), waiver of the right to review (9.06), grounds for review (9.07–9.12), the prohibition against raising new matter (9.13), private parties before the *Cour de Cassation* (9.14), the rôle of the *ministère public* (9.15), the method and time for filing a *pourvoi* (9.16–9.17), the effects of *pourvoi* on execution (9.18), procedures before the *Cour de Cassation* (9.19–9.22), preparation of the decision (9.23), effects of the decision (9.24), procedure on remand (9.25), proceedings on a second *pourvoi* (9.26), cases in which there is no remand (9.27), and the rôle of the *Cour de Cassation* in the development of the law (9.28).

## 9.01. Introduction

Standing at the apex of the structure of the ordinary courts, the *Cour de Cassation* has as its principal function review of lower court judgments on questions of law. The proceeding for seeking review of a lower court judgment by the *Cour de Cassation* is called *pourvoi.*

## 9.02. Territorial Competence of the *Cour de Cassation*

The *Cour de Cassation* is empowered to hear *pourvois* originating in any part of France (including Alsace-Lorraine, where procedure is still partially based on German Law) and the remaining French overseas possessions. Since August 28, 1962, the *Cour de Cassation* may not deal with *pourvois* originating in Algeria, unless they were pending at that date and concern the French state, or its agencies or subdivisions, or questions of French nationality. [1] Originally, the *Cour de Cassation* was to hear *pourvois* from most of the new countries in Africa south of the Sahara that had been granted independence by France, but, except for

[1] Judicial Protocol between France and Algeria of August 28, 1962, published by DÉCRET No. 62–1020 of August 29, 1962, J.O. August 30, 1962, p. 8506, [1962] D.L. 293, 89 CLUNET 1152 (1962), art. 18. Pursuant to the terms of the protocol, all cases from Algeria pending in the *Cour de Cassation* on August 28, 1962, were transferred to the Algerian authorities. DALLOZ, RÉPERTOIRE DE PROCÉDURE CIVILE ET COMMERCIALE, *Pays d'Outre Mer-Algérie*, No. 240 (Supp. 1963).

Gabon and the Tschad, these nations no longer permit review of their decisions by French tribunals. [2] It seems safe to assume that the remaining powers of the *Cour de Cassation* over decisions rendered in countries no longer under French control will disappear in the near future.

### 9.03. Decisions Subject to Review by the *Cour de Cassation*

As a general rule, all judicial decisions that are not subject to other methods of review, [3] if they are "judgments" as that term is understood in French law, [4] may be brought before the *Cour de Cassation.* Decisions relating to internal court administration are not ordinarily reviewable by the *Cour de Cassation*; [5] likewise, a mere reprimand given by the presiding judge of a commercial court to the court's chief clerk, since such action does not amount to rendering a judgment, is not subject to a *pourvoi.* [6] The availability of *pourvoi* against decisions rendered in non-adversary proceedings (so-called *juridiction gracieuse* [7]) is doubtful. [8]

In a few cases, a specific statutory provision restricts the right to file a *pourvoi.* Thus, certain decisions dealing with the administration of a

[2] The exchange of letters between the French Prime Minister and the Presidents of the various African states which terminated *pourvois* to the *Cour de Cassation* from the Ivory Coast and Mauretania is reprinted in 89 CLUNET 820–24 (1962); *cf.* DALLOZ, RÉPERTOIRE DE PROCÉDURE CIVILE ET COMMERCIALE, *Pays d'Outre Mer-Etats d'Afrique et Madagascar,* Nos. 52–54 (Supp. 1963). *Pourvois* from Africa were originally intended to go to a special temporary panel of the *Cour de Cassation,* called *chambre de la Communauté.* Under an agreement between France and Gabon published by DÉCRET No. 61–596 of May 17, 1961, J.O. June 14, 1961, p. 5355, [1961] D.L. 201, cases arising in Gabon go to the panel of the *Cour de Cassation* normally competent, not to the *chambre de la Communauté.*

[3] On the requirement that only decisions that are not subject to appel may be reviewed by the *Cour de Cassation,* see 9.04 *infra.*

[4] Article 15 of Law No. 47–1366 of July 23, 1947, J.O. July 24, 1947, p. 7142, [1947] D.L. 275, speaks of *pourvois* against *jugements* (judgments of lower courts) and *arrêts* (judgments of *cours d'appel*). On the many amendments to, and for commentary on, this law, see 3.32 n. 279 *supra.*

[5] 6 GARSONNET & CÉZAR-BRU 640; 1 DALLOZ, RÉPERTOIRE DE PROCÉDURE CIVILE ET COMMERCIALE, *Cassation,* at Nos. 164–65.

[6] *Id.* at No. 175.

[7] On the meaning of the term *juridiction gracieuse,* see 11.03.a *infra.*

[8] According to 6 GARSONNET & CÉZAR-BRU 641, a *pourvoi* is available in these matters only for violation of procedural rules. *Cf.* CUCHE & VINCENT 504. On the other hand, it is stated in 1 DALLOZ, RÉPERTOIRE DE PROCÉDURE CIVILE ET COMMERCIALE, *Chambre du Conseil,* at No. 58 (1955), that a *pourvoi* is available against decisions in non-adversary proceedings, since the 1944 legislation revising the procedure in the *Chambre de Conseil* (see 11.03.c *infra*) which specifically makes *appel* available must, by implication, be considered also to allow *pourvoi.* The problem was important mainly in adoption proceedings, where the right to file a *pourvoi* is now governed by specific statutory provision. See text at note 11 *infra.*

bankrupt's estate are not reviewable by the *Cour de Cassation.* [9] The same is true of some decisions concerning execution against real property. [10] In adoption cases, a *pourvoi* is allowed only against decisions that deny adoption, and even these decisions may be attacked only on procedural grounds. [11] Decisions in eminent domain cases condemning property may not be attacked on the ground of an error of substantive law, though they may be attacked before the *Cour de Cassation* on grounds of lack competence, procedural error, or *excès de pouvoir*; however, decisions concerning the amount of compensation are subject to the general rules. [12] There are also some restrictions in labor and rural lease cases. [13]

All methods of review, including *pourvois* to the *Cour de Cassation,* are excluded against decisions temporarily suspending an *officier ministériel* pending the outcome of a disciplinary or criminal proceeding against him. Final decisions imposing disciplinary penalties are subject to the ordinary methods of review. [14] A direct *pourvoi* against decisions of arbitral tribunals is impossible, though court decisions dealing with arbitral awards are reviewable by the *Cour de Cassation.* [15] Restrictions on the right to file a *pourvoi* are interpreted narrowly. They are found only on the basis of a clear statutory text. [16]

[9] CODE DE COMMERCE art. 457. No *pourvoi* – and, likewise, no *appel* – is possible against decisions appointing a trustee in bankruptcy, appointing a *juge-commissaire,* authorizing the sale of goods forming the assets of the bankrupt's estate, authorizing the continued operation of the bankrupt's business, and a few other decisions.

[10] CODE DE PROCÉDURE CIVILE art. 703 (decision fixing date for auction sale).

[11] CODE CIVIL art. 356. The rule is made applicable to the related procedure known as *adoption légitimative* by CODE CIVIL art. 369. Concerning the distinction between these two forms of adoption, see 4.33.b *supra.*

[12] ORDONNANCE No. 58–997 of October 23, 1958, J.O. October 24, 1958, p. 9694, [1958] D.L. 355, arts. 30, 38; Boré, *Le Pourvoi en cassation pour violation de la loi en matière d'expropriation dans le régime transitoire,* [1962] D. CHR. 155. On the meaning of the term *excès de pouvoir,* see 9.11 *infra.*

[13] No *pourvoi* appears possible against decisions of the labor courts for the Mediterranean fisheries (*prud' hommes pêcheurs de la Méditerrannée*), since these courts keep no written record of their proceedings which can be reviewed. See 1 DALLOZ, *op. cit. supra* note 5, at No. 154. In social security matters, the ordinary rules now seem to apply. DÉCRET No. 58–1291 of Dec. 22, 1958, J.O. Dec. 23, 1958, p. 11613, [1959] D.L. 49, art. 53. Decisions in rural lease matters do not seem subject to attack for procedural error generally, but only for lack of competence, through otherwise the general rules apply. DÉCRET No. 58–1293 of Dec. 22, 1958, J.O. Dec. 23, 1958, p. 11627, [1959] B.L.D. 87, art. 25.

[14] ORDONNANCE of Nov. 2, 1945, J.O. Nov. 3, 1945, p. 7367, [1945] D.L. 310, arts. 36 (temporary suspension), 37 (final determinations). For more details concerning disciplinary proceedings against *officiers ministériels,* see, *e.g.,* 2.06.e *supra.*

[15] See 11.11.c *supra.*

[16] See, *e.g.,* 1 DALLOZ, *op. cit. supra* note 5, at No. 146.

### 9.04. Non-Reviewability by other Means as a Condition for *Pourvoi*

As a general rule, a court decision is subject to a review by the *Cour de Cassation* only if no other method of review is available. [17] In particular, only a decision *en dernier ressort* (in last resort) – that is, a decision not subject to *appel* – may be brought before the *Cour de Cassation*. [18]

Decisions rendered by the *cours d'appel* (and also by the National Technical Social Security Commission), since they are not subject to a further appeal, [19] are subject to review by the *Cour de Cassation*. However, *pourvoi* against decisions of the various courts of first instance, such as the *tribunaux d'instance, tribunaux de grande instance,* labor courts, and social security courts, lies only if they may not be reviewed by *appel*. [20]

As far as the right to file a direct *pourvoi* from a court of first instance to the *Cour de Cassation* is concerned, it is immaterial whether a party which has the right to an *appel* exercizes it. No *pourvoi* is possible from a judgment of a court of first instance, even after the time for *appel* has elapsed, if *appel* was once available. [21] The rules stated are subject to only one significant exception: *Pourvois* based on *excès de pouvoir* lie against all judicial decisions, whether or not they are subject to any other form of review. [22]

Default judgments, as well as judgments rendered in contested actions, are subject to *pourvois* if all other conditions are met. No *pourvoi* may be filed against default judgments subject to *opposition*. However, the party against whom the default judgment has been entered may let the time limitation for *opposition* elapse and then file a *pourvoi*. [23] It is also possible to attack a default judgment by *opposition* and

[17] *E.g.*, 6 GARSONNET & CÉZAR-BRU 632.

[18] See Law No. 47–1366, *supra* note 4, art. 15 (*pourvoi* may be filed against decisions *en dernier ressort*); MOREL 507.

[19] Since the judicial reform of December 22, 1958, the *cours d'appel* and the National Technical Social Security Commission are substantially the only courts that hear *appels*, the right of the *tribunaux de grande instance* to hear *appels* having been abolished. *But see* 3.30 *supra*. An *appel* from an arbitral award goes to the *tribunal de grande instance* if the amount involved is less than 3000 francs (about $ 600); however, the right to file an *appel* against a decision of an arbitrator is generally waived; in the unlikely case that it is not, a *pourvoi* against a decision of a *tribunal de grande instance* on *appel* from an arbitral award is, of course, possible.

[20] On decisions of courts of first instance that are not subject to *appel*, see 8.04 *supra*. If the losing party to a decision rendered in first instance is in doubt whether he may file an *appel*, it is wise to file both a *pourvoi* and an *appel*, since a mistake in remedy is usually irremediable because of the running of the time limitations.

[21] *E.g.*, 6 GARSONNET & CÉZAR-BRU 636.

[22] On *excès de pouvoir*, see 9.11 *infra*.

[23] See, *e.g.*, Beaume v. Chauvet, Cass. Com., Nov. 8, 1950, [1951] D.J. 239; 6 GARSONNET

to file a *pourvoi* against the decision rendered after reopening if it is unfavorable.

Generally speaking, the rule that a *pourvoi* to the *Cour de Cassation* is available only against decisions that may not be reviewed in any other manner is applicable if the losing party may obtain a rehearing through *requête civile*: If that remedy is available, *pourvoi* is not. However, since the French Code of Civil Procedure authorizes *requête civile* in a few instances in which *pourvoi* is possible, there is a limited area of possible overlap. [24]

### 9.05. Review of Non-Final Decisions

Review by the *Cour de Cassation* is not limited to final judgments on the merits (*jugements au fonds*). In the discussion of other judgments subject to attack by *pourvoi*, a distinction must be drawn between judgments rendered by the full court and orders issued by a single judge granting or denying some form of provisional relief either *ex parte* (*sur requête*) or after an adversary hearing (*en référé*).

In case of decisions rendered by the full court, the old division of non-final decisions into *jugements préparatoires* and *jugements interlocutoires*, abandoned as far as the right to appel is concerned, [25] continues to be important: A *jugement interlocutoire* is subject to immediate review, [26] while a *jugement préparatoire* is reviewable only together with the final judgment on the merits. [27]

& CÉZAR-BRU 691; CUCHE & VINCENT 504. On the availability of *opposition*, see 7.04.a *supra*. Time for filing a *pourvoi* is ordinarily two months (see 9.17 *infra*), while the time limit for *opposition* is only one month. CODE DE PROCÉDURE CIVILE art. 158.

[24] See CODE DE PROCÉDURE CIVILE art. 480. The following grounds for *requête civile* may also lead to *pourvoi*: procedural error, judgment going beyond pleadings of parties, judgment failing to render a decision on one of the claims presented in the pleadings, and failure to forward file to *ministère public* when this is required. See also 10.11 *infra*.

[25] See 8.05.b *supra*.

[26] The judgment must be *en dernier ressort* (not appealable), and other methods of review must ordinarily be excluded. In practice, *jugements interlocutoires* may be brought before the *Cour de Cassation* in two cases: (1) if an interlocutory judgment was rendered by a court of first instance and an immediate appeal was taken to a *cour d'appel*, the decision on appeal is reviewable by *pourvoi*; (2) if a *jugement interlocutoire* has been rendered directly by a *cour d'appel* in a case pending before it, it may also be attacked by *pourvoi*.

[27] Law of the 2 brumaire year IV, art. 14, reprinted in DALLOZ, PETIT CODE DE PROCÉDURE CIVILE 220 (58th ed. 1962). *Cf.* note appended to Sté Purfina Française v. Cros, Cass. Soc., May 21, 1959, [1959] J.C.P. 2. 11275, stating that the *Cour de Cassation* does not consider article 14 abrogated by the 1942 legislation, which abolished the distinction between *jugements interlocutoires* and *jugements préparatoires* as far as *appels* were concerned. Since the distinction between these two types of judgments is hazy, it is usually advisable to bring an immediate *pourvoi* if there is any doubt that the decision may be *interlocutoire*: Since the time to file a *pourvoi* against a decision that is *interlocutoire* begins to run as soon as that decision has been served on the other side, the time for filing a *pourvoi* will ordinarily have expired long before a final decision on the merits has been obtained. See also note 29 *infra*.

The distinction between *jugements interlocutoires* and *jugements préparatoires*, is, unfortunately, unclear. Generally, a decision is considered *interlocutoire* if, to any extent, it prejudges the merits; other decisions are considered *préparatoires*. [28] Thus, since the appointment of an expert usually implies that the facts to be shown by means of an *expertise* are decisive, a decision appointing an expert is considered *interlocutoire*. [29] However, even decisions appointing experts may be *préparatoires*. [30] Since it has a purely procedural character, a decision granting a party an adjournment is considered *préparatoire*. [31] A decision referring a case to an *arbitre rapporteur* (referee) has likewise been considered *préparatoire*. [32] *Cour d'appel* decisions involving the new special procedure to determine objections to the competency of the court are always immediately reviewable. [33]

The right to obtain review of *référé* decisions has been in doubt for quite some time. Some old *Cour de Cassation* decisions seemed to deny its existence, but later decisions have permitted *pourvoi*. [34] The writers are divided. [35]

The rules concerning review of *ex parte* orders of a provisional nature (*ordonnances sur requête*) are likewise unclear. Absent a specific statutory provision to the contrary, [36] they are subject to review by the *Cour*

[28] *Cf.* 8.05.b *supra*: 6 GARSONNET & CÉZAR-BRU 691.

[29] *E.g.*, Tetard v. Godfroy, Cass. Req., July 9, 1945, [1946] D.J. 53 (since a decision appointing an expert is *interlocutoire*, the time for obtaining review does not commence upon rendition of the subsequent judgment on the merits).

[30] See the cases cited at 1 DALLOZ, *op. cit. supra* note 5, at No. 190. Decisions having to do with proof orders are not always *interlocutoires*. For another example of a decision relating to proof which is *préparatoire*, see Sté Purfina Française v. Cros, *supra* note 27 (desicion concerning alleged failure by one party to make documents available to other side (*non-communication de pièces*)). Traditionally, decisions ordering *enquêtes* have been considered as *interlocutoires*. However, since such decisions may now be brought before the *cours d'appel* only at the time of an appel on the merits (CODE DE PROCÉDURE CIVILE art. 258) and a decision *en dernier ressort* concerning an *enquête* will not be rendered too often apart from a decision on the merits, the question of whether they may be attacked by separate *pourvoi* is not very likely to arise.

[31] *E.g.*, Soc. coop. producteurs de blanquette de Limoux v. Dir. rég. séc. soc. de Montpellier, Cass. Civ., Feb. 27, 1958, [1958] D.J. 111 (adjournment to give one side more time).

[32] Banque Populaire, Industrielle et Commerciale de la Région Est de Paris v. Vves Paul et Pierre Chauvenet, Cass. Req., Feb. 19, 1946, [1946] S. 1. 54.

[33] CODE DE PROCÉDURE CIVILE art. 169.

[34] The not very numerous and generally fairly old cases are collected in 1 DALLOZ, *op. cit. supra* note 5, at Nos. 171–72.

[35] According to CUCHE & VINCENT 365, *pourvoi* is unqualifiedly possible. According to 6 GARSONNET & CÉZAR-BRU 445, a *référé* decision may be attacked before the *Cour de Cassation* only on account of lack of competence and *excès de pouvoir*.

[36] All methods of review are specifically excluded in the following cases: CODE DE PROCÉdure Civile art. 700 (*ex parte* order relating to publication of auction sale of real property); CODE DE PROCÉDURE CIVILE art. 776 (*ex parte* order relating to replacement of *avoué* in proceeding relating to priority among judgments); CODE DE PROCÉDURE CIVILE art. 969

*de Cassation* if they immediately affect the rights of the parties. Included in this group are certain *ordonnances* in succession matters and *ordonnances* concerning attachment (*saisie conservatoire*). But *ordonnances* which have no real effect on the rights of a party, such as orders appointing a particular *huissier* to serve a specific document (in an instance in which only a court-appointed *huissier* may make service) or replacing a delegated judge appointed to act in some proof proceeding, do not seem to be reviewable by means of *pourvoi*. [37]

### 9.06. Waiver of the Right to Review

The right to obtain a review by the *Cour de Cassation* may be lost by waiver. Express acquiescence in the decision below clearly constitutes waiver, but, though the courts are not inclined to imply acquiescence except in a very clear case, implied acquiescence will also suffice. [38] Service of a copy of the decision on one's opponent ordinarily signifies acquiescence. The same is not true, however, of execution of the judgment. Since a *pourvoi* does not effect a stay, a party who executed a judgment, as that term is understood in French law – in other words, a party who does something required by the decision –, does not waive his right to review if he expressly reserves it. [39] The same seems to be true of payment of costs. [40] However, participation in an *expertise* ordered by a court or other compliance with a court order without objections waives the right to review. [41] Since no immediate *pourvoi* may be taken from a *jugement préparatoire*, execution of such a judgment is never considered as acquiescence. [42]

### 9.07. Grounds for Review by the *Cour de Cassation*

The various statutes that regulate procedure before the *Cour de Cassation* list four grounds (often referred to as *moyens de cassation*) for review: (1) violation of rules of (substantive) law; [43] (2) violation of procedural rules prescribed "on pain of nullity"; [44] (3) inconsistency

(*ex parte* order relating to replacement of delegated notary or judge in partition). When all methods of review are excluded, a *pourvoi* is, of course, also unavailable.

[37] 1 DALLOZ, *op. cit. supra* note 5, at No. 167.

[38] See the note appended to Cie d'assurances la Concorde v. Soc. de Battelage de Manakara, Cass. Com., May 6, 1959, [1959] D. SOMM. 92 (stating that acquiescence is not to be presumed, but must be proved).

[39] 2 DALLOZ, *op. cit. supra* note 5, at Nos. 241–45.

[40] Cie d'assurances la Concorde v. Soc. de Battelage de Manakara, *supra* note 38.

[41] 2 DALLOZ, *op. cit. supra* note 5, at No. 247.

[42] Law of 2 brumaire year IV, *supra* note 27, art. 14.

[43] See 9.08 *infra*.

[44] See 9.09 *infra*.

between decisions between the same parties; [45] and (4) *excès de pouvoir.* [46] In addition to these four statutory bases (*moyens*) of review, there is a fifth, grounded only in case law, namely "lack of a legal basis" (*manque de base légale*). [47] The characteristic common to these grounds is that they all concern questions of law, either substantive or adjective: The *Cour de Cassation* does not review questions of fact. [48]

The rule that the *Cour de Cassation* may review only questions of law is probably followed more consistently in France than are analogous rules elsewhere. Its application has raised difficult problems. These complexities have been compounded by shifts in policy of the *Cour de Cassation.* Some eighty years ago, it began to widen its definition of law in order to exercise more effective control over the lower courts. [49] However, after World War II, in a desire to stem the flood of cases brought to it in the postwar period, the *Cour de Cassation,* with one notable exception, [50] returned to a more restrictive definition.

The powers of the *Cour de Cassation* to reverse findings of fact are quite limited. In making findings of fact, the lower courts are limited only by the rules regulating the admissibility of evidence. Even in determining admissibility of evidence a wide latitude is left to the lower courts, since the *Cour de Cassation* usually does not review a holding that, as required by law, a fact found is pertinent and material or that it is proven by consistent inferences. [51] The freedom of the lower courts to evaluate the evidence is limited only in one respect: When they base their findings on a written document in the record, such as the report of an expert, they may not distort it – that is, they may not give it a meaning that the *Cour de Cassation* finds to be patently wrong. In deciding whether a court has distorted the meaning of a document in the record, [52] the *Cour de Cassation* seems to proceed more or less on an *ad hoc* basis.

In contract cases, the rule that an otherwise unreviewable finding of fact becomes reviewable if it involves distortion of a document a-

[45] See 9.10 *infra.*
[46] See 9.11 *infra.*
[47] See 9.12 *infra.*
[48] MOREL 508; 6 GARSONNET & CÉZAR-BRU 645.
[49] For a more detailed discussion, see 1 DALLOZ, *op. cit. supra* note 5, at Nos. 1508–12.
[50] For this exception, see note 62 *infra.*
[51] See 7.26.c, 7.32 *supra.*
[52] *E.g.,* Lehay v. Auvinet, Cass. Civ., Dec. 6, 1955, [1956] D.J. 174 (although report of expert specifically stated that physician did not use ordinary precaution, court held him not liable, noting that the report did not eliminate the possibility that the patient would have suffered complication anyway); 1 DALLOZ, *op. cit. supra* note 5, at Nos. 2085–91. On experts' reports generally, see 7.54 *supra.*

chieves particular significance. Whether two parties have actually entered into an agreement is obviously a non-reviewable question of fact. [53] Further, the *Cour de Cassation* has held that questions of interpretation of a contract relate to the factual search for the intention of the parties and can therefore not be raised before the *Cour de Cassation*. [54] However, since 1873, the *Cour de Cassation* has qualified this rule by holding that it may reverse a decision that distorts the "clear and precise" meaning of a contract submitted by the parties. Again, no very clear criteria have been developed as to when a contract is "clear and precise" and as to when an erroneous interpretation amounts to distortion. [55] Thus, in a case in which an employment contract between a pilot stationed in the Far East and an airline stated expressly that all actions concerning the contract were to be brought in Paris, the *Cour de Cassation* reversed as constituting distortion a lower court holding – apparently based on the desire to relieve the pilot of this onerous clause – that the clause had become inapplicable because the firm had changed its address in Paris. [56] The *Cour de Cassation* also has shown a tendency to review the interpretation of contracts with widely used standard clauses – presumably, because the uniform interpretation of such clauses is highly desirable for commercial purposes. [57] In addition, it

[53] *E.g.*, Epoux Rosso v. Ahmed ben Assen Abdeloued, Cass. Soc., Feb. 13, 1958, [1958] D.J. 338 (whether employment contract was made is for lower court); *cf.* Soc. Emel v. Chevallier, Cass. Soc., Jan. 19, 1961, [1961] D.J. 238 (lower court determines whether order is final). Whether a contract results from the sending of the acceptance or from its receipt is also a question of fact which the lower courts determine in unreviewable fashion. 2 COLIN & CAPITANT 38.

[54] Immediately after the enactment of the CODE CIVIL, since CODE CIVIL art. 1134 states that agreements lawfully made have the effect of a law as between the parties, the *Cour de Cassation* held questions of contractual interpretation to be reviewable questions of law. However, by 1808, the *Cour de Cassation* had modified its position, holding that the interpretation of a contract presented a non-reviewable question of fact. 2 COLIN & CAPITANT at 82–83; *cf.* Cons. Gonnet v. Cons. de Ligne, Cass. Req., Nov. 7, 1928, [1928] S. 1. 61 (scope of power of attorney for lower courts).

[55] *Cf.* 2 COLIN & CAPITANT 82–83.

[56] Comp. aéronautique française d'Extrême Orient v. Lemaitre, Cass. Civ., Nov. 7, 1928, [1929] S. 1. 60. For an example of a more ambiguous clause found to be distorted, see also Vve Simonin v. Comp. d'assur. sur la vie Le Monde, Cass. Civ., March 16, 1925, [1925] S. 1. 166 (when life insurance policy provided that war risk was not covered unless special premium paid and lower courts held that this clause required insured to make special contract with insurance company if he wanted to be covered, *Cour de Cassation* reversed on ground of distortion and held that policy was clearly to continue in case of war, though insurance company became entitled to higher premium); 6 GARSONNET & CÉZAR-BRU 66.

[57] *E.g.*, Galatis v. Worms et Cie., Cass. Req., Oct. 26, 1942, [1944] S. 1. 21 (note Houin) (York-Antwerp rules embodied in bill of lading); Comp. d'assur. La Protectrice v. Senac, Cass. Civ., March 18, 1942, [1943] S. 1. 13 (note Houin) (standard clause in automobile policy). In the 1930's, when many countries enacted legislation banning contracts with gold or foreign currency clauses, the *Cour de Cassation* reviewed the interpretation of such clauses. The *procureur général* had urged the court to do so in order to provide uniform solutions for the questions raised by such clauses. 1 DALLOZ, *op. cit. supra* note 5 at Nos. 1531–32.

seems to exercise a right of review when tax consequences depend on interpretation of a contract [58] and, to some extent, in cases relating to the interpretation of wills. [59]

Recently, questions of distortion have become significant in another area. Traditionally, foreign law has been considered as a question of fact not subject to review by the *Cour de Cassation.* [60] An exception has been made only in a case involving legislation of the Allied Control Council for Germany, [61] perhaps because the enactments of that body on which France was represented, could not be considered as truly foreign law. A short time ago, however, the *Cour de Cassation* reviewed the interpretation of a foreign statute whose meaning it held to have been distorted. Although the basic law concerning the government of the Belgian Congo stated quite explicitly that Belgium and the Belgian Congo were to remain two distinct juridical entities with separate liabilities, the *cour d'appel* had held that Belgium and the Belgian Congo formed one entity. [62] The statute was brief and in French, so that no problem of translation existed. It remains to be seen whether the *Cour de Cassation* will be willing to exercise its powers of review in cases involving more complex foreign law problems. [63]

The reviewing power of the *Cour de Cassation* is more extensive as to questions of legal characterization of facts. Whether, in a tort case, the defendant has committed the acts alleged in the complaint [64] and what

[58] *Id.* at Nos. 2235–37.

[59] They, too, may be interpreted by the lower court free of any control by the *Cour de Cassation*, which, however, may intervene if a "clear and precise" clause is "distorted" by the courts. 3 COLIN & CAPITANT 905–06.

[60] *E.g.*, BATIFFOL 393–400.

[61] Epoux Guinguène v. Dlle Falk, Cass. Ass. Plén., Dec. 20, 1950, [1951] J.C.P. 2. 6058; 78 CLUNET 177 (1951); Plevin v. Le Ker, Cass. Soc., May 4, 1950, 78 CLUNET 177 (1951).

[62] Montefiore et Association Nationale des porteurs de valeurs mobilières v. Colonie du Congo Belge et Etat Belge, Cass. Civ., Nov. 21, 1961, 89 CLUNET 686 (1962) (with extensive note by Goldman discussing whole problem). In two earlier cases in which the *Cour de Cassation* had refused to interfere with findings of foreign law, it nevertheless had hinted that it might do so in a case of distortion. Consorts Fat Liou Sang. v. dame Tchong Si, Cass. Civ., June 13, 1960, [1960] D.J. 597 (note Malaurie), 88 CLUNET 440 (1961); Dame Ferrer y Vidal Alloy v. Moens, Cass. Civ., Nov. 4, 1958, 86 CLUNET 788 [1959] (note A.P.).

[63] As the note by Goldman, *supra* note 62, points out, the Montefiore case leaves it uncertain whether the *Cour de Cassation* will extend its review from an obvious misinterpretation of an unambiguous statute in the French language to misinterpretation of statutes not in French or to misinterpretations of rules based on case law or custom. A later case indicates that the *Cour de Cassation* will not interfere with lower court findings as to case law. Hocke v. Schubel, Cass. Com., March 4, 1963, 91 CLUNET 806 (1964).

[64] *E.g.*, Etabl. Clarac Frères v. Gachon, Cass. Soc., July 22, 1957, [1957] D.J. 674 (alleged unfair competition). The term tort is used in the text because it gives a good indication of the scope of the rule. However, the rule applies not only to instances that are considered as cases of tort (*délit* or *quasi-délit*), but also to some cases, such as cases of malpractice, in which liability is considered to rest on a contractual basis.

damages were suffered by the plaintiff [65] are questions of fact the lower courts decide free of effective supervision by the *Cour de Cassation.* However, although the decision of the court below may carry some weight, a determination that the facts found amount to fault on the part of the defendant is reviewable. [66] Questions of causation are likewise subject to review. [67]

The rule that the *Cour de Cassation* may review the legal qualification given to facts has some exceptions, especially in the field of domestic relations. The Civil Code permits divorce or separation on account of *excès, sévices et injures* – a term fairly similar to mental or physical cruelty –, but only if the acts of the guilty spouse amount to a serious and repeated violation of the duties arising from the marriage and render married life intolerable. [68] The *Cour de Cassation* does not interfere with determinations by lower courts as to whether the legal requirement of serious and repeated violations of marital duties, intended as a check on the very liberal attitude towards divorce of some French courts, has been met; as a result, this requirement has been largely ineffective. [69] Lower courts also are able to determine in unreviewable fashion whether an admission of paternity is unequivocal, [70] or whether a person is insane, or acting under undue influence. [71] Findings as to domicile likewise have a non-reviewable character. [72] However, a determination that a person is or is not a *commerçant* (merchant) is reviewable. [73]

[65] *E.g.*, 2 Colin & Capitant 214; 1 Dalloz, *op. cit. supra* note 5, at No. 1936. In some instances, the Civil Code prescribes a measure of damages. See, *e.g.*, Code Civil arts. 301 (alimony), 1953 (liability of innkeeper), 1153 (interest).

[66] 2 Colin & Capitant 219; Blondot v. Guyard, Cass. Civ., Nov. 17, 1936, [1937] S. 1. 53 (whether staying close to trailer after helping driver fix it is fault); Veuve Candelot v. Soc. Truchetet, Cass. Civ., Feb. 13, 1957, [1957] D. Somm. 62 (duty to warn that oil has been spilled on highway); Francheteau v. Vve Cornu, Cass. Civ., Jan. 18, 1957, [1957] D. Somm. 39 (throwing away old detonating cap in a dump); Nourrigat v. Pech, Cass. Civ., Feb. 28, 1910, [1911] S. 1. 329 (failure to protect gears); M. v. Demoiselle G., Cass. Civ., July 9, 1935, [1935] D.H. 444, [1936] S. 1. 29 (whether living with woman was seduction giving rise to damages on termination of relationship). *But see* X. v. Digonnet, Cass. Civ., Dec. 6, 1949, [1950] D.J. 141 (in action against notary for professional negligence finding of *cour d'appel* as to what experienced notary should have known would not be disturbed).

[67] The term causation is ambiguous – it refers both to causation as a matter of fact and to causation in the sense of proximate cause. See, *e.g.*, 2 Colin & Capitant 216–17. The precise scope of the reviewing power of the *Cour de Cassation* in matters of causation is not entirely clear. Nourrigat v. Pech, *supra* note 66, and the appended note.

[68] Code Civil art. 232.

[69] 2 Colin & Capitant 465–66, 468. The same rule applies to a finding of reconciliation, which constitutes a defense to a divorce action. 6 Garsonnet & Cézar-Bru 659.

[70] 1 Dalloz, *op. cit. supra* note 5, at Nos. 1604–05.

[71] *Id.* at No. 1658; 6 Garsonnet & Cézar-Bru 660.

[72] 2 Colin & Capitant 292; 6 Garsonnet & Cézar-Bru 659; 1 Dalloz, *op. cit. supra* note 5, at No. 1580. The same rule applies to residence.

[73] 1 Dalloz, *op. cit. supra* note 5, at No. 1914. The same rule applies in other commercial

It should also be noted that the social and criminal panels are more inclined to review qualifications given to facts by the courts below than the other three panels.

Application of the law to the facts as found and characterized below is always reviewable by the *Cour de Cassation*; [74] indeed, review of law application is its main field of endeavor.

### 9.08. Violation of Law as a Basis for Review

The statute that instituted the *Cour de Cassation* in 1790 granted the court the power to annul court decisions on the ground of express violation of law (*loi*). [75] Since the term *loi* refers to statutes rather than to law in general, this provision seemed to restrict the court to reversal of decisions contrary to a statutory text. However, the rule soon received a double extension. First, the *Cour de Cassation* began to reverse not only decisions directly contrary to a statute, [76] but also decisions that gave an erroneous interpretation to a statutory text or applied it in an incorrect fashion. Second, violation of rules of a not strictly statutory character also was recognized as a ground for review. [77] The term law (*loi*) was extended to include, in addition to all enactments that had a statutory character under the constitution in force at the time, [78] all decrees and regulations issued by the executive branch of the government by virtue of a general or special delegation of powers, such as *décrets*, *décrets-loi*, and *règlements d'administration publique*. Also included in this category were regulations issued by administrative officials, local as well as national, by virtue of their inherent powers. However, violation of a directive contained in a ministerial circular or

matters. Thus, in a bankruptcy case, the lower courts determine whether the facts alleged to constitute cessation of payments exist, but the *Cour de Cassation* determines whether these facts amount to cessation of payments. *Id.* at No. 1918.

[74] While the *Cour de Cassation* does not ordinarily review a finding that the acts of the defendant amount to serious, repeated, violations of marital duties that make the marital life intolerable, the court does check whether a divorce judgment recites one of the bases for divorce mentioned in the Code as the ground on which the divorce judgment is based. Likewise, the *Cour de Cassation* will not ordinarily review a finding concerning the intent of a testator, but does review whether the will violates the prohibition against certain substitutions (analogous to bequests of future interests). For this reason, it has been said that the *Cour de Cassation* does not review facts, but only judgments.

[75] Law of Nov. 27, 1790, reprinted in DALLOZ, PETIT CODE DE PROCÉDURE CIVILE 436 (58th ed. 1962), art. 3.

[76] Such decisions are rare. An example might be a decision granting a divorce on account of incompatibility or some other ground not recognized by the Civil Code.

[77] 6 GARSONNET & CÉZAR-BRU 646; MOREL 509.

[78] 6 GARSONNET & CÉZAR-BRU 648; CUCHE & VINCENT 509; MOREL 509. On the rules considered to be of statutory character, see 1.30–1.31 *supra*.

other publication destined mainly for internal administrative use is not a ground for review by the *Cour de Cassation.* [79]

It is unclear to what extent violation of customs, especially commercial customs, is a reviewable matter. Apparently, a violation of customs specifically referred to in a statute is reviewable, [80] but a violation of other customs is not.[81] The *Cour de Cassation* also reviews decisions that violate traditional rules of French law, such as *nul ne plaide par procureur,* or the *exceptio non adimpleti contractus,* or the rule prohibiting disclosure of confidential letters. Ordinarily, the *Cour de Cassation* will attempt to relate these rules to a statutory text, but occasionally it treats violation of these rules as an independent basis for reversal. [82]

Since case law is not an official source of law, [83] violation of case law is not formally a ground for review. However, in practice, if a decision is contrary to well-established case law, although the original formal statement of the bases (*moyens*) for the *pourvoi* will mention only the statute and not the cases, the brief (*mémoire*) submitted to the court as well as oral argument will make ample reference to case law. [84]

The rules stated also apply in litigation with international aspects. Treaties and executive agreements are recognized as formal sources of

[79] Cuche & Vincent 509; 6 Garsonnet & Cézar-Bru 652–53; Morel 509. For a very detailed listing of various types of regulations and other administrative enactments, see also 1 Dalloz, *op. cit. supra* note 5, at Nos. 1297–1325. Regulations enacted by local officials by virtue of their inherent powers include *arrêtés* of mayors and prefects. See generally 1.15, 1.17 *supra.*

[80] Cuche & Vincent 509; 1 Dalloz, *op. cit. supra* note 5, at Nos. 1329–30. Examples of customs specifically mentioned in statutes are Code Civil arts. 645 (local customs relating to water rights), 663 (local customs relating to party walls and division fences), 671 (local customs concerning distance trees must be from lot boundary), 674 (local custom concerning distance septic tanks and other annoying objects must be from lot boundary), 1159, 1160, and 1135 (conditions implied in contracts by custom).

[81] 1 Dalloz, *op. cit. supra* note 5, at Nos. 1346–49.

[82] See generally Morel 509; 1 Dalloz, *op. cit. supra* note 5, at 1346–49. On the rule *nul ne plaide par procureur,* see 6.04.d *supra.* On the *exceptio non adimpleti contractus* (litterally, defense of the non-fulfilled contract), which permits a party sued on a contract to use a breach by the other party as a defense, see 2 Colin & Capitant 104–06. On the privilege numerous confidential letters, see 7.48 *supra.* These general principles find their expression in covering cases. However, cases are thought of as being based on general principles rather than the reverse.

[83] See 1.32 *supra*; *cf.* 1 Dalloz, *op. cit. supra* note 5, at Nos. 1339–44.

[84] For example, Code Civil art. 1384 provides quite generally that a person is liable for objects under his control. On the basis of this rather vague provision, the *Cour de Cassation* has developed the whole French scheme of liability for automobile accidents, which imposes a presumption of liability on the owner except as against gratuitous passengers. If a lower court should hold a non-negligent owner liable to a gratuitous passenger, the formal statement of the *moyens* for the *pourvoi* will simply allege violation of Code Civil art. 1384, but the briefs (and sometimes oral argument) will discuss the applicable cases. The decision of the *Cour de Cassation* mentions only the statute or general rule on which the *pourvoi* was based, never a case. See 9.23 *infra.*

law analogous to statutes, and their violation is therefore ground for review by the *Cour de Cassation.* [85] The same is true of well-established rules of international law not based on any statute, such as those relating to sovereign immunity. [86]

In matters of personal status, the native inhabitants of French overseas possessions are usually governed by their own law. This customary law, if applicable to French nationals, is considered as French rather than foreign law, and its application is subject to review by the *Cour de Cassation.* [87] Finally, violation of French conflict rules is also ground for review by the *Cour de Cassation.*

Although violation of law (*loi*) is a ground for review, a mere erroneous statement about the applicable law in the opinion (*motifs*) is no basis for reversal if the case has been decided correctly. Such an error will usually be disregarded. [88]

### 9.09. Violation of Rules of Procedure *(Vice de Forme)*

Article 3 of the Law of 1790, [89] which gave the *Cour de Cassation* power to reverse decisions for express violation of statutes, also authorized the court to reverse decisions for violation of procedural rules "prescribed on pain of nullity." Subsequent laws of the revolutionary period reiterated this provision. [90] Under this provision, review lies if the enactment prescribing the rule of procedure allegedly violated states that its disregard is sanctioned with nullity. [91] In a few instances, however, the courts have held procedural rules so "essential" or "substantial" that, even in the absence of an express provision to that effect,

[85] MOREL 509; 6 GARSONNET & CÉZAR-BRU 649–50. In cases involving French foreign relations, the courts may not interpret treaties, but must obtain an authentic interpretation from the executive branch of the government. See 4.37.a *supra.*

[86] They are treated as other general principles of French law which are not based on any specific statute. See note 82 *supra.* On sovereign immunity, see 4.35 *supra.*

[87] 6 GARSONNET & CÉZAR-BRU 651. Since the loss of most former French colonies and the loss of Algeria, this rule has decreased in importance.

[88] MOREL 509–10; 6 GARSONNET & CÉZAR-BRU 655. At times, however, a mere defect in the opinion (*motifs*) may be the basis for reversal. See 9.11 *infra.*

[89] See 3.32 n. 273 *supra.*

[90] Notably, the Law of the 4 germinal year 2, art. 2, and the Constitutions of 5 fructidor year 3, art. 255, and 22 frimaire year 8, art. 66, reprinted in DALLOZ, PETIT CODE DE PROCÉDURE CIVILE at 203–04 (58th ed. 1962). These statutes permitted review by the *Cour de Cassation* for violation of the (relatively few) procedural rules established during the revolutionary period even if they were not prescribed "on pain of nullity."

[91] See, *e.g.*, 1 DALLOZ, *op. cit. supra* note 5. at No. 1422. There are numerous examples of such rules. See, *e.g.*, CODE DE PROCÉDURE CIVILE arts. 66 (*huissier* may not act on behalf of relatives), 70 (various formalities relating to service of process), 174 (judgments must be served on adverse parties before execution), 278 (formalities relating to *enquête*, but by implication only), 357 (stay of proceedings in case of claim that *avoué* acted without authorization (*désaveu*)), 559 (various formalities relating to garnishment proceedings), 715 (various formalities relating to execution on real property).

their non-observance results in nullity and opens the way for review by the *Cour de Cassation.* [92] Ordinarily, procedural error is a ground for reversal only if the error has caused prejudice. However, some formalities are considered so "essential" or "substantial" that reversal will follow their disregard even in the absence of a showing of prejudice. [93]

In case of a procedural error, immediate objection is ordinarily necessary to preserve the possibility of review. [94] Furthermore, because of the rule prohibiting the raising of new issues in the *Cour de Cassation,* procedural errors made in first instance must be raised again on *appel*: Otherwise, no review by the *Cour de Cassation* is possible. [95] *Pourvoi* based on a procedural error represents one of the relatively rare instances in which the *Cour de Cassation* examines the file of the case rather than merely the judgment. [96]

Article 480 of the French *Code de Procédure Civile* establishes a special procedure, known as *requête civile,* for reopening a case on a number of specified grounds, including violation of procedural rules. For example, *requête civile* is available if the judgment grants a recovery greater than that demanded or if the judgment does not deal with one

[92] See, *e.g.*, 1 SOLUS & PERROT 368 (formalities of service of process in proceeding pending before *tribunal d'instance,* although nullity not prescribed by CODE DE PROCÉDURE CIVILE art. 1, considered substantial); CUCHE & VINCENT 530 (*huissier* must sign all papers served by him, though no express statute so requires); *cf.* de Biré v. Soc. des argiles, faïences et réfractaires de Sognolles-en-Montois, Cass. Civ., April 21, 1958, [1958] D.J. 325 (illegal delegation of judicial functions by appointment of expert in case in which not nesessary). Violation of the basic principles of judicial organization ordinarily leads to nullity. CODE DE PROCÉDURE CIVILE art. 1030 prohibits declaring a procedure void except in cases expressly provided for by statute, but this article has been held inapplicable to the instances mentioned. On nullities generally, see 7.09.c *supra.*

[93] CODE DE PROCÉDURE CIVILE arts. 173 (generally), 715 (execution against real property). The Code articles themselves contain no exception for substantial formalities, but that exception has been read into them by the *Cour de Cassation.*

Among the rules generally considered as prescribing substantial formalities are those requiring (1) a statement of the date, address, and domicile of the recipient in an *exploit,* (2) an indication of the court in which an action is brought, and (3) the mailing of a registered letter to the defendant notifying him of the beginning of an action if the formal *exploit* has been left at the mayor's office. Among those prescribing formalities not considered substantial are the rules requiring (1) the typed name and address of the *huissier* in body of *exploit* if his rubber stamp is on the outside, (2) the first name and occupation of the plaintiff in the *exploit,* and (3) that service be made within specified hours. For a detailed list, see 1 SOLUS & PERROT 370–81, criticising the distinction made by the courts and arguing that a violation of a procedural rule should never result in nullity of a proceeding when no prejudice has been caused.

[94] CODE DE PROCÉDURE CIVILE arts. 173, 192.

[95] See 9.13 *infra.* See also Gervais v. Dame Gervais, Cass. Civ., June 15, 1955, [1956] D. SOMM. 73.

[96] 1 DALLOZ, *op. cit. supra* note 5, at No. 2092. CODE DE PROCÉDURE CIVILE art. 142, as amended in 1958, provides that failure to recite the accomplishment of a formality does not affect the validity of a judgment, if its accomplishment appears from other documents in the file. Before 1958, a formality not recited in the *qualités* of a judgment was conclusively considered not to have been accomplished.

of the claims contained in the *conclusions* of the parties. [97] Difficulties arise because the coverage of article 480 overlaps that of the statutes permitting *pourvoi* for violation of procedural rules and review by means of *pourvoi* is generally excluded whenever some other method of review is available. [98] The prevailing view seems to be that in case of procedural error on the part of the parties, such as improper service, *requête civile* must be used, while *pourvoi* is the correct remedy if the irregularity is committed by the judges. However, this distinction is not universally accepted. [99]

In four situations, a statute specifically provides that *pourvoi* to the *Cour de Cassation* rather than *requête civile* must be used: (1) when a judgment was rendered by less than the required number of judges; (2) when a judge who rendered a judgment did not participate in all the hearings of the case; (3) when the judgment was not rendered in public; and (4) when the judgment was not supported by *motifs* (opinion). [100] In practice, absence of *motifs* is a rather frequent basis for attack, since it can be used not only if no opinion has been written at all, but also if the opinion is seriously defective in contents – for instance, because it refers merely to a decided case to justify the decision [101] or because it fails to deal with a part of the *conclusions*. [102]

Lack of competence also is a basis for *pourvoi*, but since the reforms of 1958 it must ordinarily be raised by means of a special procedure at

[97] On *requête civile*, see 10.09–10.15 *infra*.

[98] The various methods for obtaining reopening, such as *opposition* and *requête civile*, are considered methods of review within the meaning of this rule. See 9.04 *supra*.

[99] For a discussion of the various views, see MOREL 510; CUCHE & VINCENT 510. For a more detailed discussion of the relationship between *requête civile* and *pourvoi*, see 10.11.b *infra*.

[100] Law of April 20, 1810, art. 75, reprinted in DALLOZ, PETIT CODE DE PROCÉDURE CIVILE 78, 221 (58th ed. 1962). On the *motifs* (opinion) that must accompany every judgment, see 7.13.c *supra*. On the bases for review by the *Cour de Cassation*, see also 1 DALLOZ, *op. cit. supra* note 5, at Nos. 1420–24; 6 GARSONNET & CÉZAR-BRU 684–85; CUCHE & VINCENT 510.

[101] *E.g.*, Soc. parisienne pour l'industrie électrique v. Laroche, Cass. Com., Oct. 31, 1961, [1962] D. SOMM. 76.

[102] *E.g.*, Renvoise v. Etat français, Cass. Com., March 23, 1949, [1949] D.J. 280. This is one of the instances in which the *Cour de Cassation* examines the file: It cannot determine whether all claims have been dealt with in the judgment, unless the *conclusions* as well as the judgment are examined. It should be noted in this connection that a court commits reviewable error if it distorts the *conclusions* – for instance, by treating a contract claim as a tort claim. See 1 DALLOZ, *op. cit. supra* note 5, at Nos. 2092–2117. The courts must deal with all separate claims presented in the *conclusions*, but need not deal with mere arguments. *Id.* at No. 2123–24. The distinction is not always easy to apply. See, *e.g.*, Joubert v. Veuve Jean, Cass. Civ., Nov. 21, 1956, [1957] D.J. 209 (if in automobile accident plaintiff relied on CODE CIVIL art. 1382 (fault), court needs not deal with related provisions of article 1384). There may be an absence of *motifs* in a few situations in addition to those discussed – for example, if the *motifs* and the decretal paragraph of the judgment are mutually exclusive. See 1 DALLOZ, *op. cit. supra* note 5, at Nos. 2173–90.

the beginning of the litigation. The parties may usually not raise it in a *pourvoi* directed against the final judgment on the merits. [103]

## 9.10. Inconsistent Judgments

The *Cour de Cassation* may review a judgment on the ground of "inconsistency of judgments" (*contrariété de jugements*) if it contradicts an earlier judgment rendered by a different court in a proceeding between the same parties on the same cause of action. [104] Both judgments must have been rendered by judicial rather than administrative courts, and both judgments must have been *en dernier ressort* – that is, may not be subject to *appel*. [105] Though inconsistency of judgments is the only basis for review by the *Cour de Cassation* mentioned in the French *Code de Procédure Civile* itself, [106] since two proceedings pending between the same parties in different courts are usually joined at an earlier stage, it is of limited practical importance. The *pourvoi* to the *Cour de Cassation* is always directed against the second of the two inconsistent judgments. Apparently, a *pourvoi* for inconsistency of judgments may be filed even if the issue of inconsistency was not raised in the court below. [107]

## 9.11. *Excès de Pouvoir*

The fourth ground for review is *excès de pouvoir*, which may be approximately defined as any action by which a court exceeds its lawful

[103] CODE DE PROCÉDURE CIVILE arts. 168–71; *cf.* 7.09.b *supra*. The special procedure is not applicable if an administrative court is competent, nor in proceedings *en référé* or in a preliminary hearing in divorce actions. CODE DE PROCÉDURE CIVILE arts. 171, 806; CODE CIVIL art. 238. A decision of a *cour d'appel* rendered in a special proceeding to determine competence may, of course, be reviewed by the *Cour de Cassation*, but the review must take place immediately, not after the final decision on the merits. Even in instances in which the parties are foreclosed from raising a question of competence before the *Cour de Cassation*, the court may raise it on its own motion, if public policy (*ordre public*) is particularly involved. See 7.09.b *supra*; CODE DE PROCÉDURE CIVILE art. 171.

[104] CODE DE PROCÉDURE CIVILE art. 504. If two inconsistent judgments between the same parties and involving the same cause of action are rendered by the same court, the proper remedy is *requête civile*. CODE DE PROCÉDURE CIVILE art. 480.

[105] 6 GARSONNET & CÉZAR-BRU 687. If a judgment of a judicial court contradicts an earlier administrative judgment, there is likely to be *excès de pouvoir*. See 9.11 *infra*. The requirement that the judgment brought before the *Cour de Cassation* must be *en dernier ressort* is merely an application of the general principle that the *Cour de Cassation* may review only decisions not otherwise reviewable; the rule that the first judgment must also be non-reviewable does not seem to make much sense in practice.

[106] See CODE DE PROCÉDURE CIVILE art. 504. Other bases for review are stated in various statutes of the revolutionary period. See notes 73, 88, and 98 *supra*.

[107] If the existence of a judgment between the same parties on the same cause of action is raised below, it may not be necessary to rely on "inconsistent judgments," since the *Cour de Cassation* may review for violation of the rule of res judicata embodied in article 1355 of the CODE CIVIL. MOREL 512.

powers. Until 1915, since decisions of the *juges de paix* were subject to review by the *Cour de Cassation* only on account of *excès de pouvoir*, it was sometimes quite important to distinguish between mere errors of law, or lack of competence, and a true case of *excès de pouvoir*. As the *Cour de Cassation* did not want to be too restricted in its review of *juge de paix* decisions, it gave the concept of *excès de pouvoir* a rather broad interpretation. [108] Since 1915, *juge de paix* (now *tribunal d'instance*) decisions are also reviewable on account of error of law, [109] and the distinction has lost much of its importance. [110] However, since the Minister of Justice may order the *ministère public* to bring any case before the *Cour de Cassation* for review if there is an *excès de pouvoir*, even if the *ministère public* has not been a party to the action before the court below, and even if the parties themselves may not file a *pourvoi*, the distinction continues to be of some significance. [111]

No statute provides a definition of *excès de pouvoir*, nor is it possible to derive one from the decisions of the *Cour de Cassation*, which has always taken a rather flexible attitude towards this concept. Some French authors state that there is *excès de pouvoir* if a court impinges upon the prerogatives of the legislative or executive branch of government. Thus, there is not much doubt that a court promulgating a rule of practice (except in the very narrow sphere in which French courts have a rule-making power) would be guilty of *excès de pouvoir*. [112] There is also an *excès de pouvoir* if a court interprets a treaty which may be interpreted only by the executive branch of the government, [113] or if it criticizes the *ministère public* [114] or addresses orders to administrative officials. [115]

However, the *Cour de Cassation* has gone further and found *excès de pouvoir* in a number of instances in which a court, although not interfering with administrative or legislative functions, acted improperly.

108 MOREL 511; 1 DALLOZ, *op. cit. supra* note 5, at 2542–48, 2555.

109 Law of December 22, 1915, J.O. Dec. 24, 1915, [1916] S. 4. 79 (with report on legislative history). Since the enactment of this law, the *Cour de Cassation* has restricted its interpretation of *excès de pouvoir*.

110 As a practical matter, parties filing a *pourvoi* frequently state that it is based on error of law, procedural error, and excess of power just to be on the safe side.

111 Law No. 47–1366, *supra* note 4, art. 52. See also 9.15 *infra*.

112 MOREL 511; 6 GARSONNET & CÉZAR-BRU 681. On the very limited powers of the courts to enact rules, see 1.35 *supra*.

113 *E.g.*, Procureur général v. Fournier, Cass. Civ., June 4, 1955, [1956] REV. CR. D.I.P. 66 (effect of war on 1923 treaty with Italy). On situations in which the courts may not interpret treaties, but must obtain a ruling from the executive, see 4.37.a *supra*.

114 6 GARSONNET & CÉZAR-BRU 682. The same is true of criticisms directed against circulars of the Minister of Justice.

115 *E.g.*, Epoux Lavin, Cass. Civ., March 4, 1958, [1958] D.J. 333 (order to modify birth certificate in manner not authorized by law).

Thus, *excès de pouvoir* has been found when a court failed to recognize the immunity enjoyed by a foreign state [116] or an international organization, [117] or criticized a foreign court, [118] or added unwarranted insulting statements concerning a third party to an opinion, or stated that it followed the case law of the *Cour de Cassation* only with disinclination. [119]

Mere error of law, on the other hand, is not *excès de pouvoir.* [120] Nor is lack of competence, though the distinction between *excès de pouvoir* and lack of competence is hazy. Apparently, there is lack of competence if a court renders a decision that should have been rendered by a different court, while there is *excès de pouvoir* if it acts without authority in some other fashion. When a decision of a lower court is reviewed by the *Cour de Cassation* on account of an error of law, an erroneous statement of law in the opinion is disregarded if the case has been decided correctly. Review on account of *excès de pouvoir* is possible, however, even if there is merely an improper statement in the opinion. [121] *Excès de pouvoir* is thus in effect one of the devices adopted during the revolutionary period to keep the courts in their place and prevent recurrence of the troubles created by the *Parlements*.

## 9.12. *Manque de Base Légale*

*Manque de base légale* (litterally, absence of a legal basis) as a basis for review is entirely the creation of the *Cour de Cassation*. A decision suffers from a lack of legal basis whenever the findings of fact contained in it are so defective or unclear that the *Cour de Cassation* cannot determine whether the law has been applied correctly to the facts found. [122] To a very limited extent, the requirement of a legal basis compensates for the absence of a detailed review of the record. Thus, in a tort case, a finding of fault is reviewable by the *Cour de Cassation*.

116 For a listing of cases, see 4.35 *supra*.

117 Procureur général près la Cour de Cassation v. Syndicat des copropriétaires la Société immobilière Alfred Dehodencq, Cass. Civ., July 6, 1954, [1955] D.J. 633 (note l'Huillier) (building owned by OEEC).

118 Procureur général près la Cour de Cassation, affaire Myzliwiecz, Cass. Req., March 18, 1935, [1935] D.H. 267 (derogatory remarks about Polish courts to justify refusal to grant request for taking testimony in Poland by letters rogatory held *excès de pouvoir*).

119 Morel 512; 6 Garsonnet &Cézar-Bru 682. A decision by a commercial court to meet in the home of its presiding judge rather than in the court house or a decision by a court not to meet until certain grievances are redressed may also be *excès de pouvoir*. At times, even serious violations of procedural rules have been called *excès de pouvoir*.

120 1 Dalloz, *op. cit. supra* note 5, at No. 2587. The distinction between *excès de pouvoir* and error of law is important only in the special type of *pourvoi* formulated by the *ministère public* at the request of the Minister of Justice. See text at note 111 *supra*.

121 1 Dalloz, *op. cit. supra* note 5, Nos. 2593–99.

122 See generally Morel 512; 1 Dalloz, *op. cit. supra* note 5, at No. 1454.

The requirement of a legal basis makes it impossible for a lower court to hamper this review by failing to state the ultimate facts on which its finding of fault is based. [123] The *Cour de Cassation* will reverse for lack of legal basis whenever an opinion is based on hypothetical statements, on statements expressing doubt, or on several facts stated in the alternative. [124] Likewise, a decision lacks a legal basis, if it imposes liability on a principal for an act of his agent without indicating whether the agent acted within the scope of his employment, or if it fails to state whether a certain agreement was in writing if a writing is required by law, or if it fails to recite sufficient facts to support all legal elements of the claim or defense involved. [125]

Since a defect in the opinion of the court is the basis for review in both cases, lack of a legal basis is often confused with an absence of *motifs*. There is, however, a distinction: When there is an absence of *motifs*, the opinion fails to deal with at least a portion of the case; when there is a lack of legal basis, the opinion deals with all the facts of the case, but is not sufficiently explicit. [126]

### 9.13. The Prohibition against Raising New Issues before the *Cour de Cassation*

The *Cour de Cassation* will not adjudicate new issues. This restriction is more severe than the analogous one prevailing in proceedings before the *cours d'appel*. During an appeal to a *cour d'appel*, an entirely new claim (*demande*) may not be raised but new facts may be pre-

[123] In a tort case there is a lack of legal basis if the opinion fails to recite with sufficient preciseness facts that show fault, causation, and damages. See M. v. Demoiselle G., supra note 66 (fault); Soc. Emel v. Chevallier, Cass. Soc., Jan. 19, 1961, [1961] D.J. 238 (fault); Epoux Rosso v. Ahmed ben Assen Abdeloued, *supra* note 53 (damages); MOREL 512.

[124] Soc. auxiliaire d'Entreprises électriques et de travaux publics v. Soullier, Cass. Soc., Oct. 25, 1957, [1958] D.J. 249 (court stated that it was possible that employer dismissed employee on account of union activities); Hugonnet v. Guignard, Cass. Civ., Jan. 9, 1957, [1957] D.J. 196 (automobile accident which court found could have been due to poor tires, or excessive speed, or error of driver instead of finding a specific negligent act).

[125] *E.g.*, MOREL 512; *cf.* Epoux Alexandre v. Roques, Cass. Civ., Jan. 6, 1930, [1931] S. 1. 289 (note Simmonet) (will contest decision lacks legal basis as it recites that legatee beat testator, but does not indicate whether beating was intended to obtain testator's signature on will).

[126] On absence of *motifs*, see 9.09 *supra*. A party filing a *pourvoi* is likely to assert an absence of *motifs* as well as lack of a legal basis. However, in case of absence of *motifs*, the *Cour de Cassation* reverses, merely citing article 7 of the Law of April 20, 1810, as the basis for its action; in case of lack of a legal basis, it discusses the applicable substantive law and notes in which respect the opinion reviewed is defective. See 1 DALLOZ, *op. cit. supra* note 5, at No. 1454. On the somewhat hazy distinction between absence of a legal basis and absence of *motifs*, see Cons. Wahab v. Soc. des Etablissements Maurel et Prom, Cass. Civ., May 19, 1958, [1958] D.J. 496 (failure by court to deal with issue raised in pleadings, although generally considered absence of *motifs*, reversed for lack of legal basis).

sented. [127] Before the *Cour de Cassation,* however, not only new claims but all new *moyens* are prohibited. [128] The term *moyen* refers to issues raised before the lower courts, not to the five bases for review, which are sometimes called *moyens de cassation.* The prohibition against new *moyens* means in practice that a *moyen* may be used only if raised before the court of first instance and the *cour d'appel,* or at least before the *cour d'appel.* A *moyen* used before a court of first instance, but abandoned on *appel,* may not be used before the *Cour de Cassation.* [129]

Unfortunately, the concept of *moyen,* in the sense used here, has no very clear contours. French authors state that a *moyen* is a proposition of law or fact wich may support a claim or defense and distinguish it from a mere argument (*argument*), but this distinction is very hard to apply in practice. [130] A few examples may serve to delineate more clearly the scope of the prohibition against raising new *moyens.*

It is undisputed that neither new documents nor new facts in general may be presented to the *Cour de Cassation.* This is a corollary of the rule that the *Cour de Cassation* must take the facts as found by the judgment under review. [131] However, the prohibition against new *moyens* also restricts the raising of new legal arguments. Thus, a party who has relied on French law before the courts below may not ask the *Cour de Cassation* to rule that foreign law is applicable. [132] Similarly, it is not permissible to raise the defenses of payment, compensation, or illegality of a contract for the first time before that court. [133] In the procedural field, a party who has not raised issues relating to the statute of limitations, *res judicata,* lack of capacity of a party, inadmissibility of evidence, improper service of the original process or of the notice of appeal below is precluded from raising them before the *Cour de Cassation.* [134]

[127] See 8.17 *supra.*

[128] Cuche & Vincent 511; Morel 513; 6 Garsonnet & Cézar-Bru 667.

[129] 6 Garsonnet & Cézar-Bru 667; 1 Dalloz, *op. cit. supra* note 5, at Nos. 875–76. Sometimes, the *Cour de Cassation* avoids the prohibition against new issues by holding that an allegedly new issue was implied in an issue presented below. 6 Garsonnet & Cézar-Bru 669.

[130] See 1 Dalloz, *op. cit. supra* note 5, at No. 849. Since French courts sit without a jury and courts of first and second instance both deal with the facts as well as the law, there is no great need to draw a distinction between factual and legal issues until a case goes to the *Cour de Cassation.*

[131] See 9.07 *supra*; *cf.* 1 Dalloz, *op. cit. supra* note 5, at No. 865.

[132] *E.g.,* Cie internationale des wagons-lits et des grands express européens v. Dame Duchinon, Cass. Civ., Jan. 5, 1961, [1961] D.J. 340.

[133] *E.g.,* Morel 515; 6 Garsonnet & Cézar-Bru 671. The same is true of the defense of provocation in a divorce case. Dame Vidal de Lirac v. Vidal de Lirac, Cass. Civ., Oct. 12, 1955, [1956] D. Somm. 30.

[134] *E.g.,* Librairie Hachette v. Epoux Chauvin, Cass. Soc., February 17, 1950, [1950] D.J. 278 (modification of *conclusions* not timely); Fonds de garantie automobile, Cass. Crim., Dec.

The prohibition against raising new matter is subject to a few exceptions. Since the prohibition is applicable only to issues that could have been raised below, one may always complain before the *Cour de Cassation* about defects inherent in the judgment under review, such as absence of a judge at the time the judgment was rendered, absence of *motifs*, or lack of a legal basis. [135] For the same reason, a party may raise issues before the *Cour de Cassation* that are related to issues raised by the court below on its own motion. [136]

Issues based on strong public policy (*ordre public*) may also be raised for the first time before the *Cour de Cassation*, even by the court on its own motion. [137] But since the *Cour de Cassation* does not engage in an independent examination of the facts, this may be done only if the facts on which the public policy argument is based are recited in the judgment under review. [138] The *Cour de Cassation* seems to apply the public policy exception mostly when rules are involved relating to court organization, the separation of powers doctrine, the non-retroactivity of laws, the basic rights of the parties to a fair hearing (*droits de la défense*), nationality, personal status, illegal preferences in bankruptcy, contracts for an immoral object, and contracts with gold clauses. [139]

New matters may also be raised for the first time if they involve new arguments rather than new *moyens*. Because there is no clear distinction between arguments and *moyens*, the rule is hard to apply. Indeed, legal arguments are sometimes called *moyens de pur droit* (purely legal *moyens*). Mere legal arguments may usually be considered by the lower courts on their own motion. In a sense, they are thus always before the court. This is said to be the reason why they are not considered really

7, 1961, [1962] D. Somm. 21 (improper appeal); Grieux v. Cie algérienne de crédit et de banque, Cass. Com., Feb. 1, 1961, [1961] D. Somm. 76 (use of ordinary instead of summary procedure); 6 Garsonnet & Cézar-Bru 670–71; 1 Dalloz, *op. cit. supra* note 5, at Nos. 1014–48.

135 Cuche & Vincent 214; 1 Dalloz, *op. cit. supra* note 5, at No. 1015. French courts have no inherent power to modify their own decisions; on the contrary, they are said to be "disseized" of a case as soon as a judgment has been rendered. *Cf.* 7.13.e *supra*.

136 1 Dalloz, *op. cit. supra* note 5, at No. 1258.

137 Cuche & Vincent 512; Morel 513; 6 Garsonnet & Cézar-Bru 673.

138 *E.g.*, Dame Cuffaut-Célérier v. Cuffaut, Cass. Civ., Oct. 21, 1954, [1955] D. Somm. 2 (public policy argument may be made initially before *Cour de Cassation* only if court below had opportunity to deal with underlying facts).

139 *E.g.*, 6 Garsonnet & Cézar-Bru 672; Morel 513; 1 Dalloz, *op. cit. supra* note 5, at Nos. 1126–75 (citing many cases). See also Caisse rég. assur. vieillesse de Lyon v. Serve, Cass. Civ., Nov. 24, 1955, [1956] D.J. 522 (non-retroactivity of laws). *But see* Grieux v. Cie algérienne de crédit et de banque, *supra* note 134 (no violation of public policy to use regular instead of summary procedure). *Cf.* also Bisbal v. Dame Bisbal, Cass. Civ., May 12, 1959, [1960] D.J. 611 (note Malaurie) (conflict of laws rules do not involve public policy, at least if reference is to foreign law).

new.[140] In practice, the rule seems to mean that issues that are never raised by the court on its own motion, such as statute of limitations, may not be raised for the first time before the *Cour de Cassation.*[141] On the other hand, it is apparently possible to invoke a legal rule closely related to the one invoked below. A plaintiff, who argues before a court of first instance for the admissibility of oral evidence on the basis of one of the exceptions to article 1341 of the Code Civil, may rely on another exception to that article before the *Cour de Cassation.*[142] In an action by a wife to declare void a transfer of property made by the husband to his concubine, the *Cour de Cassation* even allowed the concubine to argue that the transfer, while possibly void as against the wife, was not void as against the children, although she had denied below that the transfer was void at all.[143] Likewise, a defendant successfully argued before the *Cour de Cassation* that the plaintiff had no standing to sue because he lacked any genuine interest in the outcome, although this argument had not been made below.[144] Legal rules concerning the liability of heirs for debts of the decedent and the transferability of assets of a bankrupt were similarly invoked before the *Cour de Cassation* though they had not been relied on below.[145] According to one author, the *Cour de Cassation* refuses to listen to new issues that require either consideration of new facts or consideration of established facts in a new relationship. It is not certain whether all cases can be explained under this criterion.[146]

## 9.14. Private Parties before the *Cour de Cassation*

The party filing a *pourvoi* to the *Cour de Cassation* is generally referred to as the *demandeur en cassation,* while the party against whom the *pourvoi* is directed is called the *défendeur en cassation.* The use of

[140] Cuche & Vincent 512 nn. 1-2; Morel 513; 6 Garsonnet & Cézar-Bru 676; *cf.* Le Clech, *Moyens et arguments devant la Cour de Cassation,* [1951] J.C.P. 1. 939.

[141] See text at note 133 *supra.*

[142] 6 Garsonnet & Cézar-Bru 676.

[143] Dlle Porzio v. Consorts Rossi, Cass. Civ., Dec. 4, 1929, [1931] S. 1. 361.

[144] Epoux Alexandre v. Roques, *supra* note 125.

[145] Consorts Godin v. Consorts Pasquier, Cass. Civ., Dec. 18, 1939, [1940] S. 1. 10 (non-liability of heirs of husband for certain debts of matrimonial community); Guillou v. Lelong, Cass. Civ., Feb. 21, 1944, [1944] D. Anal. J. 58 (same rule); Mauger ès qual. v. Cons. Mazère, Cass. Com., Apr. 20, 1948, [1948] D.J. 375 (effect of bankruptcy on assignment of account).

[146] 1 Dalloz, *op. cit. supra* note 5, at Nos. 1263–65. Some of the difficulties may be due to uncertainty as to the policy basis for the rule prohibiting new issues before the *Cour de Cassation.* Neither the cases nor the authors seem to make it very clear whether it is merely an application of the more general rule that the *Cour de Cassation* does not deal with the facts – in which case it would be important only as to new factual issues –, or whether it is based on a desire to avoid dilatory tactics by compelling the parties to present all issues at an early stage of the litigation, which would justify its application to legal as well as factual issues.

these terms depends exclusively on the rôle of the parties before the *Cour de Cassation*: It is quite immaterial who was plaintiff or defendant before the court of first instance. [147]

Only persons who have been parties (or represented) [148] before the lower courts may be parties before the *Cour de Cassation*. In case of *pourvois* against decisions of a *cour d'appel*, it is necessary only to have been a party before that court; even a person who became a party after the proceedings in the court of first instance were started – for instance, by *tierce opposition* – may formulate a *pourvoi*. In other respects, the rule that only parties below may be parties to a *pourvoi* is treated as the analogous rule applicable to appeals. Who has been a party below must be determined from the recitals in the judgment submitted for review. [149]

Parties to a *pourvoi* also must have capacity and have an interest – that is, they must be aggrieved by the decision below. Again, the requirements of capacity and of interest are analogous to those imposed in case of appeals. However, since the *Cour de Cassation* does not consider new facts, an interest existing at the time the decision under review was rendered is sufficient. Events occurring thereafter are not material. The rule limiting *pourvois* to aggrieved parties means that the *Cour de Cassation* will not deal with purely theoretical errors of law. Thus, a party may not formulate a *pourvoi* on the ground that a judgment is defective for lack of an opinion, if he has obtained all the relief demanded in his pleadings; nor can a party formulate a *pourvoi* against a decision in a cross-appeal on the ground that the cross-appeal was defective if his opponent in the cross-appeal did not prevail. [150]

## 9.15. The *Ministère Public* as a Party Before the *Cour de Cassation*

The rôle of the *ministère public* before the *Cour de Cassation* is, to some extent, similar to its rôle before the lower courts. Whenever the *ministère public* has been a true party before the lower courts, it may file a *pourvoi* and has the position of a true party before the *Cour de Cassation*. In cases in which the *ministère public* has acted only as *par-*

[147] The plaintiff on appeal is called *appelant* (appellant); his opponent is called *intimé* (respondent). The use of these terms is restricted to proceedings before the *cours d'appel*; they are not used before the *Cour de Cassation*.

[148] As to representation, see 8.09 *supra*. The same rules are applicable to appeals and to *pourvois*.

[149] 6 GARSONNET & CÉZAR-BRU 621–22; CUCHE & VINCENT 505.

[150] CUCHE & VINCENT 505; 1 DALLOZ, *op. cit. supra* note 5 at Nos. 358–78; 6 GARSONNET & CÉZAR-BRU 624–26; *cf.* P. v. Wahl, Cass. Civ., Nov. 28, 1957, [1958] D.J. 411 (costs as alleged basis for "interest").

*tie jointe*, it may not file a *pourvoi*. However, the *ministère public* acts as *partie jointe* in every case before the *Cour de Cassation* in which it is not a true party, regardless of whether it was *partie jointe* below. While the *ministère public* acting as *partie jointe* before the lower courts often performs its functions in a somewhat cursory fashion, the report submitted by the *ministère public* in cases pending before the *Cour de Cassation* is ordinarily quite full and detailed. [151]

In a number of cases, the *ministère public* may act as a true party before the *Cour de Cassation* and file a *pourvoi* though it was not a true party below. Generally, it may do so in cases involving strong public policy (*ordre public*). Apparently, the criteria used to determine when public policy is sufficiently involved to permit the *ministère public* to file a *pourvoi* are identical to those used to determine whether it may file an appeal if it has not been a party in the first instance. [152] However, before the *Cour de Cassation*, the *ministère public* has additional powers. When the parties have let the time within which to file a *pourvoi* elapse, the *procureur général* at the *Cour de Cassation* may file a *pourvoi* "in the interest of the law." There is no time limitation on the right to file such a *pourvoi*. Only the *ministère public* participates in the proceedings if a *pourvoi* "in the interest of the law" has been filed: The parties do not participate, since they no longer have any right to formulate a *pourvoi*. At the same time, the parties are not affected by the decision rendered by the *Cour de Cassation*; the lower court decision remains binding between them. The purpose of *pourvoi* "in the interest of the law," as its name implies, is to avoid the perpetuation of erroneous precedents. [153] The decision whether or not to file a *pourvoi* "in the interest of the law" rests in the complete discretion of the *procureur général*, who seems to exercise it rather sparingly.

The *ministère public* may also file a *pourvoi* in a case of *excès de pou-*

[151] 1 DALLOZ, *op. cit. supra* note 5, at Nos. 347–48. On the rôle of the *ministère public* as *partie principale* and as *partie jointe*, see 3.08–3.10 *supra*.

[152] CUCHE & VINCENT 505; 1 DALLOZ, *op. cit. supra* note 5, at No. 347. On the rôle of the *ministère public* in cases involving public policy generally, see 3.10 *supra*. On its rôle before the *cours d'appel*, see 8.09 *supra*.

[153] Law No. 47–1366, *supra* note 4, art. 51; MOREL 515. Apparently, if the parties have waived the right to file a *pourvoi* by acquiescence, the *procureur général* may file a *pourvoi* "in the interest of the law" without awaiting expiration of the period within which a *pourvoi* may be filed. See 1 DALLOZ, *op. cit. supra* note 5, at Nos. 2504–29. The rule that in case of a *pourvoi* "in the interest of the law" the lower court decision remains binding on the parties even if reversed causes some difficulties in declaratory actions concerning nationality. See Proc. gén. près la Cour de Cassation (intérêt de la loi), aff. Laidner, July 6, 1948, [1948] D.J. 25 (note P.L.P.). Certain officials of the Ministries of Labor and Agriculture (regional social security directors) have a right to file *pourvois* in social security cases which is similar to the right of the *procureur général* in "interest of the law" cases. DÉCRET No. 58–1291 of Dec. 22, 1958, J.O. Dec. 23, 1958, p. 11613, [1959] D.L. 49, art. 54.

*voir.* [154] The decision to file a *pourvoi* in such a case must be made by the Minister of Justice; the *procureur général* may proceed only on the basis of a written order from the Minister. [155] Many of the ordinary rules governing *pourvois* are not applicable to a *pourvoi* for *excès de pouvoir* on order of the Minister of Justice. Such a *pourvoi* may be directed merely against a statement in the opinion: It is not necessary that the decision itself be erroneous. It may also be brought against court orders dealing with internal court administration. The *procureur général* need not, as in the case of a *pourvoi* "in the interest of the law," wait until the parties have let the time to file a *pourvoi* expire. [156] Again, unlike the case of *pourvoi* "in the interest of the law," if a *pourvoi* for *excès de pouvoir* is filed, the parties must be summoned before the *Cour de Cassation* and may participate in the proceedings. They need not be represented by an *avocat aux conseils.* The decision of the *Cour de Cassation* is binding on everybody. If the *pourvoi* is successful, the decision under review is declared void; the case is not, as in other situations, remanded to a different court for further proceedings. [157] The *pourvoi* for *excès de pouvoir* has a certain importance in the international field; it is used from time to time by the French government to raise the issue of sovereign immunity on behalf of foreign states. [158]

### 9.16. Method of Filing a *Pourvoi*

The method for initiating the proceedings before the *Cour de Cassation* is somewhat different in cases in which the parties need the services of an *avocat aux conseils* from what it is in cases in which such services are not needed. [159]

When the parties must be represented by an *avocat aux conseils,* a *pourvoi* is initiated by filing a petition in the office of the clerk of the *Cour de Cassation.* The petition bears the archaic name of *requête en forme de vu d'arrêt.* [160] It is a rather stereotyped document, which contains the name, occupation, and address of the party submitting it (the *demandeur en cassation*), the same data for his opponent (the *dé-*

[154] See 9.11 *supra.*

[155] Law No. 47–1366, *supra* note 4, art. 52.

[156] MOREL 515; 1 DALLOZ, *op. cit. supra* note 5, at Nos. 2533, 2591.

[157] Law No. 47–1366, *supra* note 4, arts. 52–53.

[158] See, *e.g.*, 4.35 n. 117 *supra.*

[159] On condemnation, rent control, and labor cases in which the services of an *avocat aux conseils* are not needed, see 1 DALLOZ, *op. cit. supra* note 5, at No. 651 and SUPP. 1964.

[160] Law No. 47–1366, *supra* note 4, art. 15. The name *requête en forme de vu d'arrêt* goes back to the 1738 ORDONNANCE on the procedure before the royal council. According to Morel, the name signifies that the petition is to contain all information needed to draft the decision of the court. MOREL 516.

*fendeur en cassation*), a description of the judgment to be reviewed, and a request that the judgment be reversed in whole or in part. There is no requirement that the legal grounds on which the request for reversal is based be indicated in this petition. They may be included in the brief that is submitted at a later phase of the proceedings. [161] As a practical matter, however, a summary statement of the grounds for review (*moyens de cassation*) is always included. Since *avocats aux conseils* do not want to limit their future freedom of action at this early stage, they often include not only a reference to the specific statute allegedly violated but add a clause to the effect that they attack the decision in all respects in which it aggrieves the petitioner and make an additional reference to *défaut de motifs*. [162] The petition must be signed by the *avocat aux conseils* who is submitting it. A copy of the judgment sought to be reviewed and of any other document necessary for a decision of the *pourvoi* must be attached to it. [163] The party petitioning for review does not have to serve a copy of the petition on his opponent. The duty to notify the other side rests with the clerk of the *Cour de Cassation*. [164]

When the services of an *avocat aux conseils* are not needed, a *pourvoi* is initiated by a declaration made in the clerk's office of the court that rendered the decision to be reviewed. [165] This procedure was apparently chosen because in instances in which no *avocats aux conseils* are required the amount in controversy is often small and the parties are frequently of limited means, so that a requirement of filing in Paris might impose a hardship. The clerk of the court with whom the petition has been filed must notify all adverse parties within two weeks and send the whole file of the case to the *Cour de Cassation* within three months. [166] The declaration must contain substantially the same infor-

[161] Law No. 47–1366, *supra* note 4, art. 21; 6 GARSONNET & CÉZAR-BRU 704–05. For a form, see Appendix, Form No. 21.

[162] 1 DALLOZ, *op. cit. supra* note 5, at No. 570.

[163] Law No. 47–1366, *supra* note 4, art. 15. Since the *Cour de Cassation* decides the case on the basis of the facts as found, the judgment below is usually the only document necessary. However, at times, additional documents may be required – for example, if a claim is made that the meaning of a document has been distorted. See 9.07 *supra*; *cf.* Martelly v. Dame Pellegrino et Ferrand, Cass. Civ., Nov. 9, 1955, [1956] D.J. 55; Reix v. Soc. R. Launont & Cie., Cass. Com., Feb. 8, 1950, [1950] D.J. 278 (if *cour d'appel* decides case by adopting opinion of court of first instance, latter must also be submitted).

[164] The clerk must notify the other side within two weeks by registered mail, return receipt requested. Law No. 47–1366, *supra* note 4, art. 18.

[165] The law contemplated that the party wishing to obtain review by the *Cour de Cassation* in a case in which the services of an *avocat aux conseils* are not needed would make an oral declaration at the clerk's office that would be reduced to writing by the clerk and signed by him and by the party. Law No. 47–1366, *supra* note 4, art. 36. As a practical matter, at least when the parties have been represented below by an *avoué*, a form prepared by the *avoué* is sometimes submitted to the clerk's office for signing and filing.

[166] Law No. 47–1366, *supra* note 4, arts. 36, 37.

mation as the petition used if the parties are represented by an *avocat aux conseils*, but, since a formal brief is not always filed, the specification of the alleged errors of the court below (*moyens de cassation*) assumes greater importance. [167] Whether a bare statement of one of the five grounds for review, such as error of law or absence of a legal basis, is sufficient, or whether there must be precise reference to the statute that has been violated, is controverted. [168] The petition must be reduced to writing by the clerk and signed by the party submitting it, or by an agent who has a special written power of attorney for the purpose as well as the clerk. [169]

## 9.17. Time for Filing a *Pourvoi*

In all ordinary proceedings before the *Cour de Cassation*, the time for filing a *pourvoi* is two months and one day from the date the judgment under review was served on the adverse party. [170] Service of the judgment on the adverse party's *avoué* is ordinarily not sufficient to make the time period run. [171] In case of default judgments, the time

[167] According to Law No. 47–1366, *supra* note 4, art. 37, either the declaration or the brief must contain a summary indication of the bases for the *pourvoi*.

[168] MOREL 519; 1 DALLOZ. *op. cit. supra* note 5, at Nos. 692–96.

[169] Law No. 47–1366, *supra* note 4, art. 36. This rule applies even if the declaration is made by an *avoué*, though an *avoué* does not need a written power of attorney in other circumstances. The power of attorney must have been given after the judgment to be reviewed was rendered and before the declaration concerning the *pourvoi* is made; it is subject to the usual requirements concerning stamp and *enregistrement* taxes. See Ropers, *La Procédure sans Avocat devant la Cour de Cassation*, [1951] J.C.P. 1. 956; Epoux Botté v. Commune de Servon, Cass. Com., May 4, 1962, [1962] D.J. 399 (power of attorney must be signed after lower court decision rendered); Trésaugue v. Rouet, Cass. Soc., Nov. 25, 1948, [1949] D.J. 28 (power of attorney not considered dated unless *enregistrement* tax paid). In case of corporate entities, the persons ordinarily acting as their representatives, such as the president, do not seem to need a special power of attorney. Soula v. Caisse rég. Séc. Soc. Limoges, Cass. Soc., Jan. 5, 1956, [1956] J.C.P. 2. 9241 (social insurance organization); Sté d'exploitation Forestière et Agricole de Cormontreuil v. Main, Cass. Soc., Jan. 12, 1956, [1956] J.C.P. 2. 9241 (note G.B.) (liquidator of business corporation (S.A.R.L.)). See also Appendix, Form No. 20.

[170] According to Law No. 47–1366, *supra* note 4, art. 17, the time period is two months, but article 56 of the same law adds that this period is *franc*, so that one day must be added. On a similar rule in the case of appeals, see 8.06 n. 63 *supra*. The time limitation mentioned applies also in proceedings in which the services of an *avocat aux conseils* are not needed. Law No. 47–1366, *supra* note 4, art. 36. In election cases involving the chambers of commerce and commercial courts, the time limitation is only ten days. DÉCRET No. 61–923 of Aug. 3, 1961, J.O. Aug. 18, 1961, p. 7750, [1961] D.L. 277, amended by DÉCRET No. 62–407 of April 11, 1962, J.O. April 12, 1962, p. 3790, [1962] D.L. 149, arts. 11, 36.

[171] *E.g.*, 6 GARSONNET & CÉZAR-BRU 694. Service on the *avoué* alone is sufficient in so-called *ordre* proceedings to determine priorities in the satisfaction of judgments. CODE DE PROCÉDURE CIVILE art. 764. In case of actions involving minors or incompetents, the judgment must be served on the appropriate guardian or other representative to start the time period running. 1 DALLOZ, *op. cit. supra* note 5, at No. 514.

period begins to run only from the date *opposition* is no longer possible. [172]

The day the judgment is served and the day the *pourvoi* is initiated at the appropriate clerk's office are not counted in computing the period. Thus, a *pourvoi* against a judgment served on March 4 is timely if filed on May 6 of the same year. If the last day available to file a *pourvoi* falls on a Saturday, Sunday, or holiday, the usual extensions apply. [173]

No extensions of the two months period are available to infants or incompetents. [174] However, the period is tolled for parties applying for legal aid (*assistance judiciaire*), until a decision on their application has been rendered by the legal aid office of the court. [175] Additional time is also granted to parties who do not have their domicile or residence in the territory in which the *pourvoi* must be instituted. Thus, an extension of time is available to parties residing outside of continental France, if they must institute the *pourvoi* at the *Cour de Cassation* in Paris or at a court clerk's office in France. If the *pourvoi* must be instituted at a court clerk's office in one of the French overseas possessions, an extension of time is available to parties not residing in the particular possession concerned. [176] In both cases, the time available to institute the *pourvoi* is extended by one month if the parties reside in a territory bordering upon the territory where it must be instituted; otherwise, five additional months are granted. [177]

[172] Law No. 47–1366, *supra* note 4, arts. 17 (regular proceedings), 36 (proceedings without *avocat aux conseils*).

[173] Law No. 47–1366, *supra* note 4, art. 56; MOREL 516; 1 DALLOZ, *op. cit. supra* note 5, at No. 495. Unlike a party who serves a judgment on an appeal, a person serving a judgment does not start the two month period running against himself; unless his opponent served him with the judgment, the party serving the judgment has thirty years to file a "cross" *pourvoi*, in accordance with the rule that nobody precludes himself (*nul ne se forclôt soi-même*). CUCHE & VINCENT 507. n. 2. The losing party does not have to wait until the judgment has been served upon it before filing a *pourvoi*. It is disputed whether a party who has filed a *pourvoi* and lost, but whose time to file a *pourvoi* has not yet run because no judgment has been served upon him, may file a second *pourvoi* on a different ground. See Ralier v. Etat français, Cass. Soc., March 13, 1958, [1958] D. SOMM. 116 (yes); Pasquet v. Tornier, Cass. Soc., Dec. 14, 1945, [1946] D. SOMM. 11 (no).

[174] *E.g.*, 6 GARSONNET & CÉZAR-BRU 697–98.

[175] Law No. 47–1366, *supra* note 4, art. 56. On the legal aid office of the *Cour de Cassation*, see 12.12 *infra*.

[176] If the services of an *avocat aux conseils* are needed, the *pourvoi* is instituted by filing a petition at the clerk's office of the *Cour de Cassation*; otherwise, the *pourvoi* is instituted by a declaration made at the clerk's office of the court which rendered the decision sought to be reviewed. See 9.16 *supra*.

[177] Law No. 46–1366, *supra* note 4, art. 54. This article also provides that Corsica, Algeria, Tunisia, and Morocco are to be considered as bordering upon France. The statute implies that Corsica is not part of continental France; yet, for the purposes of most other time limitations, Corsica is treated as part of France. 1 SOLUS & PERROT 408. The one-month extension seems to be available to residents of Belgium, Luxemburg, Germany, Switzerland, and Italy, while

In accordance with the general rule, the time for filing a *pourvoi* for parties having their domicile outside of France and being therefore served by delivery of a copy of the judgment to the *ministère public* begins to run on the date the judgment was delivered to the *ministère public*, not on the date actual notice of the judgment was received. [178] In a genuine case of impossibility to file a *pourvoi* in time on account of *force majeure*, the time limitations are not binding, but the *Cour de Cassation* takes a very strict view as to what constitutes impossibility. [179]

In actions with several parties, a separate *pourvoi* must ordinarily be filed by each party. However, a timely *pourvoi* by one party enables other parties to proceed before the *Cour de Cassation*, though they have not filed a *pourvoi*, if the parties are united by an "indivisible" or "solidary" obligation. [180]

## 9.18. Effect of *Pourvoi* on Execution of Judgment

Generally, the filing of a *pourvoi* neither affects the effectiveness of the judgment below nor stays its execution. [181] However, the party who executes a judgment that is or may be attacked by means of a *pourvoi* to the *Cour de Cassation* acts at his peril. If the judgment is reversed, full restitution must be made, and liability for damages attaches. [182] The rule is not entirely satisfactory, since it leaves the party filing the *pourvoi* unprotected if his opponent, after levying execution, becomes insolvent or absconds. In such a situation, an eventual success before the *Cour de Cassation* is a hollow victory. A system under which the party filing the *pourvoi* could prevent the execution

Great Britain is apparently not considered as bordering upon France, so that its residents may take advantage of the five-month extension, which, of course, is also applicable to residents of the United States. See 1 DALLOZ, *op. cit. supra* note 5, at No. 493.

[178] See 15.02 *infra*. However, if the party against whom the judgment has been rendered has a *de facto* domicile in France, he should be served there. 1 DALLOZ, *op. cit. supra* note 5, at No. 509.

[179] 1 DALLOZ, *op. cit. supra* note 5, at Nos. 532-33. *But see* 15.02.a *infra*.

[180] *Id.* at Nos. 528–30.

[181] Law of Nov. 27, 1790, *supra* note 75, art. 16. Before the Revolution, the King could grant a stay to parties who had appealed to his council. ORDONNANCE of June 28, 1738, 1.23.b *supra*, tit. IV, art. 29. See generally CUCHE & VINCENT 511; MOREL 516; 6 GARSONNET & CÉZAR-BRU 718.

[182] *E.g.*, 6 GARSONNET & CÉZAR-BRU 718. On the liability for damages, see Epoux Raynaud v. Soc. de Laiterie industrielle de Charne, Cass. Civ., July 9, 1958, [1958] D. SOMM. 152 (landlord who removed tenant from store as authorized by lower court was ordered to pay tenant as damages profits he would have made in the store after reversal of decision by *Cour de Cassation*).

of the judgment against him by posting security would be desirable, but is not available. [183]

In a limited number of instances in which the likelihood of irreparable harm is great, a *pourvoi* to the *Cour de Cassation* has the effect of a stay. This is especially true in divorce and separation cases. Judgments in these cases do not become effective as long as the time for filing a *pourvoi* is still running, and, once a *pourvoi* has been filed, their effectiveness is further delayed until the *Cour de Cassation* has rendered its decision. [184] This rule applies to both final decisions and most interlocutory orders, [185] except provisional orders concerning support or the custody of children *pendente lite*. These orders may be executed even if attacked before the *Cour de Cassation*. [186]

Decisions in *inscription de faux* proceedings which order the destruction or alteration of a document are likewise ineffective until the time for filing a *pourvoi* has elapsed or, if a *pourvoi* has been filed, until it has been decided. [187] A similar rule prevails in a few other instances of minor importance. [188] To safeguard the interests of the French treasury, a law also provides that no judgment rendered against the French Republic may be paid if it has been attacked by a *pourvoi*. This law is

[183] See generally 6 GARSONNET & CÉZAR-BRU 718–19; 1 DALLOZ, *op. cit. supra* note 5, at No. 724. There is a requirement for the posting of security in case of judgments against the French Republic. See text at note 189 *infra*.

[184] CODE CIVIL art. 248 (dealing with divorce procedure but also applicable to separation cases). Although this article merely states that the filing of a *pourvoi* suspends the effectiveness of the judgment under review, it is interpreted to imply that the judgment also remains ineffective while the time period available for filing a *pourvoi* is still running. Orlu v. Dame Orlu, Cour Poitiers, Nov. 25, 1935, [1936] D.H. 77; 1 DALLOZ, *op. cit. supra* note 5, at No. 732. The reason is the obvious undesirability of giving temporary effectiveness to a divorce judgment subject to possible reversal: Any marriage contracted in the interim might create serious complications.

[185] Included would be decisions dealing with the competence of the court and orders relating to proof proceedings. 1 DALLOZ, *op. cit. supra* note 5, at No. 730. *But see* Dame C. v. son mari, Cass. Civ., Feb. 22, 1961, [1961] D.J. 337 (note Holleaux) (when in a divorce case the court rendered a decision concerning certain affirmative defenses by wife, and in a second decision on a later date ordered an *enquête*, a *pourvoi* directed against the first decision did not stay the *enquête*).

[186] *E.g.*, Juchs v. Dame Juchs, Cour Colmar, Dec. 3, 1948, [1949] D.J. 152. Furthermore, the staying effect of a *pourvoi* in divorce cases does not mean that the *cour d'appel* retains power to modify provisional alimony or custody orders. Requests for such modifications must be directed to the court of first instance which made the original order. Reichart, Cour Colmar, Feb. 1, 1961, [1961] D.J. 65.

[187] CODE DE PROCÉDURE CIVILE art. 241. This article provides merely that the effect of a decision remains suspended during the period available to file a *pourvoi*; however, this rule is interpreted to mean that, once a *pourvoi* has been filed, the effectiveness of the decison continues to remain suspended until the *Cour de Cassation* has rendered judgment. 6 GARSONNET & CÉZAR-BRU 720.

[188] *E.g.*, the law protecting regional names, especially of wines (*appellations d'origine*). Law of May 6, 1919, J.O. May 8, 1919, p. 4726, [1922] D. 4. 6, amended by Law of July 22, 1927, J.O. July 2, 1927, [1928] D. 4. 41, art. 6. See also 1 DALLOZ, *op. cit. supra* note 5, at No. 740.

applicable to governmental enterprises, such as the Post Office, but not to municipalities. [189]

### 9.19. Procedure in Cases in which the Assistance of *Avocats* is Required

The procedure before the *Cour de Cassation* consists mainly of an exchange of writings. Oral argument plays a minor rôle. [190] Within six months of the date on which the party initiating the *pourvoi* has filed his petition with the clerk of the *Cour de Cassation*, he must submit to the court one copy of a document called *mémoire ampliatif* (literally, amplifying memorandum). [191] As its name implies, this document discusses in detail the bases for the *pourvoi* (*moyens de cassation*) mentioned in summary fashion in the original petition. It consists of a short summary of the facts, followed by a discussion of the applicable law and a prayer for relief. The discussion of the law is always related to one of the grounds for review. [192] The *mémoire* (brief) must be signed by the *avocat aux conseils* who prepared it. It is generally written in a concise style; usually, it is about ten double-spaced typewritten pages long. Briefs of more than fifteen pages are rare. Cases, especially *Cour de Cassation* cases, are cited in considerable numbers, but their facts are not given detailed attention. There is no requirement that the briefs be printed, and in fact this is never done. There is likewise no need to furnish a long record. It is usually sufficient to supply a copy of the judgment. Thus, a *pourvoi* to the *Cour de Cassation* is not very costly, at least as far as clerical expenses are concerned.

Not later than two months after the expiration of the period for filing the brief with the court, one copy must be served on each adverse party. [193] Failure timely to file the brief with the court or serve a copy

[189] Law of July 16, 1793, reprinted in DALLOZ, PETIT CODE DE PROCÉDURE CIVILE 219 (58th ed. 1962); 6 GARSONNET & CÉZAR-BRU 721. This law applies even to sums due by the French Republic in its capacity of employer under the general labor legislation. Etat Français v. Dame Agote, Cour Fort Laramy, Oct. 20, 1961, [1962] D.J. 407 (note Donnier).

[190] MOREL 516. See also text at note 203 *infra*.

[191] Law No. 47–1366, *supra* note 4, art. 19. This time limitation, as well as all other time limitations before the *Cour de Cassation*, is *franc* – that is, one day must be added to the six-month period. The other rules relating to extensions on account of Sundays and holidays, are also applicable. Law No. 47–1366, *supra* note 9, art. 56. See also 7.03 nn. 37–38 *supra*. Once the *mémoire* has been filed, the lower courts may no longer modify their decision, even to correct an obvious error. Mirault v. Sté de Grands Bazars de la Méditerranée, Cass. Civ., May 26, 1956, [1956] J.C.P. 2. 9447 (note G.B.) (erroneous statement about composition of court).

[192] On the five bases for review, see 9.07–9.12 *supra*.

[193] Law No. 47–1366, *supra* note 4, art. 19. Service is made in the regular fashion, through an *huissier*. In social security cases, one copy of the brief must be sent by mail to the Ministry of Labor or Agriculture (in the case of agricultural employees). DÉCRET No. 58–1291, *supra* note 153, art. 60.

on each adverse party leads to automatic dismissal of the case.[194]

The party against whom the *pourvoi* is directed has four months from the date of receipt of his opponent's brief to prepare an answering brief. After it has been served and, in any event, after the four-month period has elapsed, the case is assigned to the proper panel. Failure to file an answering brief does not lead to automatic loss of the case.[195] When the case is received by a panel, it is put on the panel calendar. When it is reached, the presiding judge of the panel assigns it to one of the judges, who studies the case and prepares a report and is therefore called the reporting judge. The report is based on the briefs of the parties, the judgment under review, and any other documents submitted by the parties, as well as the judge's own research. As it precedes the hearing, the report is never based on oral argument. The report must be ready within the time period fixed by the *bureau* of the *Cour de Cassation*. At present, this period is four months. When the report is ready, the reporting judge files it with, and returns the briefs and other documents to, the clerk of the court. Both parties may submit additional briefs until the report has been filed.[196]

After the various papers relating to the case have been received in the clerk's office, they are transmitted to the *procureur général* of the *Cour de Cassation*, who must submit his recommendations in every case brought before the *Cour de Cassation*. The *procureur général* assigns the case to one of his *avocats généraux*, who is required by law to prepare his recommendations in the briefest possible time; a decision of the *bureau* of the *Cour de Cassation* allows him two months for this purpose. After the *avocat général* has prepared his recommendations, he returns all papers to the clerk's office and has the case put on the calendar for the hearing. If he fails to submit his recommendations within the two-month period, the case may be put on the calendar at the request of the presiding judge.[197] The clerk of the court notifies the parties of the

[194] The case must be dismissed on the court's own motion on the basis of a certificate made by the clerk noting the failure to file the brief in time. Law No. 47–1366, *supra* note 4, art. 20.

[195] Law 47–1366, *supra* note 4, art. 22. The result of delay is thus more drastic for the party filing the *pourvoi* then for his opponent. If he does not submit his brief within six months, the party filing the *pourvoi* loses his case. His opponent risks merely that the case will be assigned to a reporting judge without his brief. This is not too serious, because supplemental briefs may be filed until the reporting judge has filed his report. *Cf.* Morel 519.

[196] Law No. 47–1366, *supra* note 4, arts. 23–24; 1 Dalloz, *op. cit. supra* note 5, at No. 589, 741. The reporting judge may take additional time for his report if he obtains the approval of the presiding judge. In preparing his report, the reporting judge may use the services of the research and documentation unit of the court.

[197] Law No. 47–1366, *supra* note 4, arts. 25–26. 1 Dalloz, *op. cit. supra* note 5, at Nos. 589, 745. Less time would be consumed if the reporting judge and the *avocat général* could work on the case at the same time, but this is impossible since only one copy of the briefs and other papers is available.

hearing date by mail. If the date is inconvenient for the parties, the parties may ask for a different date, but there may be only one such adjournment. [198]

A fair amount of time elapses before the hearing takes place, even if delays caused by calendar congestion in the *Cour de Cassation* are disregarded. Assuming that the parties make full use of the time periods available to them, the hearing can take place no earlier than twenty months from the date the judgment under review was served. [199] If one of the parties lives outside of France, this time period may be much longer, since the same one month and five months extensions available for filing *pourvois* also apply to the submission of briefs. [200]

At the hearing, the reporting judge first reads his report. [201] The report usually involves a fairly detailed analysis of the facts and law of the case, including a reference to other decisions in point. When printed it often takes several pages in the reports.

After the reading of the report, the *avocats aux conseils* for the various parties may present their oral arguments. [202] However, they usually prefer to rely merely on their written briefs. Oral argument is presented only in cases pending before the full court (*chambres réunies*) or the general civil bench (*assemblée plenière civile*) and in cases involving a particularly difficult problem. In presenting oral argument, the *avocats aux conseils* generally follow the format of their brief. First, they state briefly the facts of the case and then discuss the applicable law. Their general approach is rather different from the somewhat rambling and fact-centered approach used by *avocats* in the courts of first and second instance. Questions to counsel from the bench are unusual.

After termination of the oral argument, the *avocat général* assigned to the case orally presents his recommendations (*conclusions*), which are also more detailed than the often quite stereotyped *conclusions* of the *ministère public* before the courts of first or second instance. His presen-

[198] ORDONNANCE of Jan. 15, 1826, art. 35, reprinted in DALLOZ, PETIT CODE DE PROCÉDURE CIVILE (60th ed. 1964); 1 DALLOZ, *op. cit. supra* note 5, at Nos. 745–53. The presiding judge may grant a preference; otherwise, cases are heard in the order in which they appear on the calendar. ORDONNANCE of Jan. 15, 1826, *supra* art. 33.

[199] 1 DALLOZ, *op. cit. supra* note 5, at No. 589 (2 months to file the *pourvoi*, 6 months for filing the main brief, 2 more months to serve it on the other side, 4 months for the answering brief, 4 months for the report of the reporting judge, 2 months for the recommendations of the *avocat général*).

[200] Law No. 47–1366, *supra* note 4, arts. 54–55. See 9.17 *supra*.

[201] ORDONNANCE of Jan. 15, 1826, *supra* note 198, art. 36. The reporting judge sits next to the presiding judge, whatever his place may otherwise be.

[202] ORDONNANCE of Jan. 15, 1826, *supra* note 198, art. 37. The same article authorizes the parties to present brief remarks if the court consents. It is rarely invoked for this purpose.

tation terminates the proceeding. No further argument is allowed after the remarks of the *ministère public*, except when the *ministère public* is a true party and proceeds as any other party. [203]

A number of procedures in use before the lower courts do not exist, or are less important, before the *Cour de Cassation*. Thus, a defaulting party may not obtain reopening by *opposition* or otherwise. [204] Intervention is possible, but it is of no great significance. A party wishing to intervene before the *Cour de Cassation* and having the requisite interest may do so at any time before the hearing. Permission to intervene must be sought by petition addressed to the court. The granting of the petition is discretionary. The intervening party may not present independent arguments, but must restrict himself to supporting the arguments of one of the other parties. He may submit a brief, but the other parties need not serve him with copies of their briefs. [205]

With the consent of his opponent, the party having filed the *pourvoi* may abandon the proceedings. If the proceedings are abandoned without such consent, the court must render a decision certifying the abandonment. Such a decision subjects the party having filed the *pourvoi* to the same disadvantages as a decision against him on the merits.[206]

## 9.20. Procedure without *Avocats aux Conseils*

The procedure in cases in which the assistance of an *avocat aux conseils* is not required is designed to provide the parties with a simple and inexpensive method of obtaining review by the *Cour de Cassation*, which does not necessitate either their presence, or the appointment of a representative, in Paris. Furthermore, filing of papers in a court clerk's office replaces formal service by an *huissier*. The procedure must be used in all cases in which no *avocat aux conseils* is needed, even if one has in fact been retained. [207]

Not later than three months after the declaration instituting the

[203] ORDONNANCE of Jan. 15, 1826, *supra* note 198, art. 38; Law of 2 brumaire year IV, *supra* note 27, art. 21; MOREL 519; CUCHE & VINCENT 515.

[204] Law No. 47–1366, *supra* note 4, art. 31; *cf.* CUCHE & VINCENT 515; 6 GARSONNET & CÉZAR-BRU 740.

[205] 1 DALLOZ, *op. cit. supra* note 5, at Nos. 760–79; 6 GARSONNET & CÉZAR-BRU 753–54. On the requirement of interest in an intervening party, see Mazeaud, *Chronique*, 56 REV. TRIM. DR. CIV. 258 (1958) (discussing case in which organization of *avoués* was denied right to intervene in *pourvoi* involving *avoués*' fees on ground of lack of interest, no *avoués* being parties to litigation).

[206] In other words, he becomes liable for costs, the fine imposed on unsuccessful parties, and the indemnity. Law No. 47–1366, *supra* note 4, art. 57.

[207] On the cases in which no *avocat aux conseils* is needed, see note 159 *supra*.

*pourvoi*, [208] the clerk of the court in which it has been made must send the whole file of the case to the clerk of the *Cour de Cassation*. This file consists of the declaration itself, the decision to be reviewed, the decision of the court of first instance, and the *conclusions* of the parties before the courts of first instance and of appeal. [209]

If the decision to be reviewed refers to some other document on which it is based, this must also be furnished. These items may not be taken by the clerk from the court's own file of the case, but must be supplied by the party wanting to bring the case before the *Cour de Cassation*. [210] The number of documents required to be submitted to the *Cour de Cassation* is thus larger in instances in which an *avocat aux conseils* is not required, presumably because parties not assisted by counsel may be unable to select the documents necessary for decision. [211] Failure of the clerk to submit the file within the three-month period does not affect the rights of the parties. [212] The party initiating the *pourvoi* may submit a brief. The original and one copy for each defendant must be filed either in the court clerk's office in which the *pourvoi* was initiated or in the office of the clerk of the *Cour de Cassation*. Failure to file a brief does not lead to dismissal; it is assumed that, if no brief is filed, the reporting judge will compensate for its absence by a more detailed study of the case. If the briefs have been filed at the place in which the *pourvoi* has been initiated, they must be transmitted by the clerk of that court to the clerk of the *Cour de Cassation*. The latter forwards the copies destined for adverse parties by registered mail, return receipt requested, together with a notice that an answering brief may be submitted within two months. The answering brief may also be filed either at the place where the *pourvoi* was initiated or at the *Cour de Cassation* in Paris. If not filed at the *Cour de Cassation*, it is sent there by the clerk of the court with whom it was filed; as in the case of the main brief, the clerk of the *Cour de Cassation* mails out the copies destined for adverse parties. [213]

[208] When the services of an *avocat aux conseils* are not required, the *pourvoi* is initiated by the filing of a declaration at the clerk's office of the court which rendered the decision to be reviewed. See note 159 *supra*.

[209] Law No. 47–1366, *supra* note 4, art. 37.

[210] 1 DALLOZ, *op. cit. supra* note 5, at No. 681.

[211] In cases in which *avocats aux conseils* must be used, the law specifically requires only that the decision to be reviewed be filed, but in practice it is necessary to submit all documents needed for proper understanding of the *pourvoi*; these documents are selected by counsel.

[212] *E.g.*, Michel v. Veuve Saint Paul, Cass. Soc., June 2, 1950, [1950] D.J. 681.

[213] Law No. 47–1366, *supra* note 4, arts. 37–38; CUCHE & VINCENT 516–17. The briefs and other documents filed in the court clerk's office where the *pourvoi* has been initiated must be sent to the *Cour de Cassation* at the same time the file is sent. If the file has already been

After the answering brief has been submitted, or, if no briefs have been submitted, within four months from the date the file of the case arrived at the *Cour de Cassation*, the case is assigned to a panel for a hearing. [214] This is done on the court's own motion. However, briefs may still be submitted until the reporting judge has filed his report. [215]

After the case has been assigned to a panel, the procedure is the same as in ordinary cases. A reporting judge is appointed. Upon completion of his report, the file is submitted to the *ministère public* for its recommendations. The hearing begins with the report of the reporting judge. If *avocats aux conseils* have been retained by the parties, they present their arguments after the report of the reporting judge. The parties also have the right to present argument, but they may not use any other persons to present argument for them. As a general rule, however, there is no oral argument. The hearing concludes with the recommendations of the *avocat général* representing the *ministère public*. [216]

## 9.21. The Urgent Procedure

In a few instances, an urgent procedure instead of the regular procedure must be used. Under the urgent procedure, the time periods available for taking various procedural steps, mainly for the filing and service of briefs, are halved. However, the time for filing a *pourvoi* remains two months, and the additional one month and five months periods available to non-resident parties are likewise unaffected. [217] Except for the shortening of the time limitations, the urgent procedure is identical to the regular procedure. [218]

The urgent procedure must be used in all divorce, separation, and support cases, in all *référé* matters, in all cases in which the *référé* procedure is used though they are not *référé* matters (this includes many

sent to the *Cour de Cassation*, they must be forewarded to the court at once. A special division of the clerk's office at the *Cour de Cassation*, called *greffe social*, handles all cases in which the services of an *avocat aux conseils* are not needed. The clerk in whose office the *pourvoi* is initiated collects a fee as lump sum compensation for all mailing costs. Law No. 47–1366, *supra* note 4, art. 38.

[214] Law No. 47–1366, *supra* note 4, art. 38.

[215] 1 Dalloz, *op. cit. supra* note 5, at Nos. 700–14; Ropers, *supra* note 169.

[216] See Law No. 47–1366, *supra* note 4, art. 39 and 9.19 *supra*. The one and five month extensions for non-residents are available in the procedure without *avocats* as well as in the procedure with *avocats*. They are not as important, since frequently no papers will be filed except for the declaration initiating the *pourvoi* and the supporting documents.

[217] Law No. 47–1366, *supra* note 4, art. 34. Also reduced by half is the time period available to the reporting judge to prepare his report. See Cuche & Vincent 515; Morel 519. In contests involving the voting lists for elections concerning the chambers of commerce and commercial courts, the time to file a *pourvoi* is only ten days. Décret No. 61–923, *supra* note 170, art. 11.

[218] Law No. 47–1366, *supra* note 4, art. 35.

rent control controversies), and in *pourvois* directed against decisions of a *tribunal d'instance* not subject to appeal. It is also applicable in a few matters of an administrative character. [219] Additional statutes provide for use of the urgent procedure in cases involving leases for commercial purposes [220] and contests concerning the voting lists for elections to the chambers of commerce and commercial courts. [221]

## 9.22. Special Procedures

In addition to its primary function of reviewing lower court decisions on questions of law, the *Cour de Cassation* performs some other duties related mainly to its rôle as the hierarchical superior of all judicial courts in France. Special procedures have been created for its carrying out most of these functions.

The conclusive effect given public documents can be attacked only in an *inscription de faux* procedure, [222] which, to a limited extent, is available before the *Cour de Cassation* and may be used against the decision under review and the return (*exploit*) of the *huissier* who has served it. [223] For example, a decision not rendered by the required number of judges, although reciting erroneously that the required number of judges was present, cannot be attacked successfully before the *Cour de Cassation* until the recitals in the decision are shown to be incorrect by an *inscription de faux*. [224] No *inscription de faux* is possible before the *Cour de Cassation* against documents which were used in the courts below, since this would amount to the raising of new matters. [225]

The *inscription de faux* procedure is begun by a petition addressed to the presiding judge (*premier président*) of the *Cour de Cassation*. It must be signed by an *avocat aux conseils* if the case is one in which the services of such a person are required. [226] The presiding judge must obtain the recommendation of the *ministère public* and, within one

[219] Law No. 47–1366, *supra* note 4, art. 33. Rent control matters referred to here include controversies concerning apartments used for residential or professional use. Law. No 48–1360 of Sept. 1, 1948, J.O. Sept. 2, 1948, p. 8659, [1948] D.L. 300, art. 48. Included in the cases of an administrative character are decisions relating to certain educational matters and war orphans.

[220] DÉCRET No. 53–960 of Sept. 30, 1953, J.O. Oct. 1, 1953, p. 8618, [1953] D.L. 393, art. 30.

[221] DÉCRET No. 61–923, *supra* note 170, art. 11.

[222] See 7.44 *supra*.

[223] 1 DALLOZ, *op. cit. supra* note 5, at Nos. 794–98.

[224] Once the conclusive effect of the recitals in the judgment below has been overcome, it is subject to attack before the *Cour de Cassation* on the ground of violation of a procedural rule (*vice de forme*). See text at note 100 *supra*.

[225] 1 DALLOZ, *op. cit. supra* note 5, at No. 796. On the prohibition against raising new matters, see 9.13 *supra*.

[226] Law No. 47–1366, *supra* note 4, art. 46.

month, must hand down an order in which he either rejects it or gives permission to proceed. [227] If permission to proceed is given, a copy of the order must be served on adverse parties. At the same time, a demand for a statement whether the document in question will be used is also served. [228] If a positive answer is given within two weeks, the presiding judge sends the matter to a court selected by him for adjudication of the factual issues. Before that court, the general *inscription de faux* procedure is followed. [229]

The *Cour de Cassation* also hears *prise à partie* procedures to impose civil liability upon judges, if they are directed against an entire *cour d'appel* or *cour d'assises*, or against a panel of a *cour d'appel*. Presumably, it may also hear such proceedings directed against an individual member of the *Cour de Cassation*. [230] The procedure, which is always handled by one of the civil panels, is the same as in *prise à partie* procedures before a *cour d'appel*. [231]

If a case is pending in one court and a separate case involving the same cause of action (*litispendence*) or a related cause of action (*connexité*) is pending between the same parties in a different court, the two actions may be joined by a procedure known as *règlement de juges*. [232] If at least one of the actions is pending in a *cour d'appel*, this is done by the *Cour de Cassation*. The party seeking joinder of the two actions must first ask one of the lower courts to transfer the action to the other court. If that request is denied, the party notes an objection (*contredit*) to the decision in the court clerk's office. The presiding judge of the lower court thereupon sends the file of the case to the presiding judge of the *Cour de Cassation*. The *Cour de Cassation* proceeds as a *cour d'appel* in a similar instance. If the *Cour de Cassation* agrees that the two actions should be joined, its clerk sends the file of the case, together with a certified copy of the *Cour de Cassation*'s decision, to the clerk of the court which is to handle the matter. There, the case continues on its regular course. [233]

[227] Law No. 47–1366, *supra* note 4, art. 47. If the petition is rejected, the party submitting it must pay the same fine as a party who files an unsuccessful *pourvoi*. See 9.24 *infra*.

[228] Law No. 47–1366, *supra* note 4, art. 48.

[229] Law No. 47–1366, *supra* note 4, arts. 49–50. On the *inscription de faux* procedure in general, see 7.44 *supra*.

[230] Code de Procédure Civile art. 505. See also 3.17 *supra*.

[231] Law No. 47–1366, *supra* note 4, art. 45. See 3.17 *supra*. *Prise à partie* proceedings go to the first civil panel of the court.

[232] On the *règlement de juges* in general, see 7.09.b at note 122 *supra*.

[233] Code de Procédure Civile arts. 169, 172. The date for the hearing is set by the presiding judge of the *Cour de Cassation*. It may take place at once, without regard for the court calendar. The services of an *avocat aux conseils* are not needed. See 7.09.b *supra*.

During the French revolution, the *Cour de Cassation* received original competence in two additional situations: (1) the transfer of cases on account of a "legitimate suspicion" concerning the impartiality of a court, and (2) the transfer for reasons of public safety. [234] A case may be removed from a court on account of "legitimate suspicion" if there is reason to believe that the court may be prejudiced, even though one of the specific causes for the removal of a case, such as close relationship between a judge and a party, is not present. Removal on account of "legitimate suspicion" is permitted only in rather rare cases. [235] While the revolutionary law instituting this procedure gave original competence to the *Cour de Cassation* in all such cases and this law was never abrogated, the *Cour de Cassation* now hears such cases only if the proceedings are directed against a *cour d'appel*. The *cours d' appel* hear these cases if courts of first instance are involved. [236] No statute indicates what procedure must be used for the removal of civil cases on account of "legitimate suspicion." [237] Before 1958, the procedure then in force for *règlement de juges* was used; the matter was initiated by a petition to the *Cour de Cassation* and heard by the *chambre des requêtes* while it existed, thereafter by one of the civil panels. [238] However, the original *règlement de juges* procedure was abolished as part of the 1958 judicial reforms and replaced by an entirely different scheme which does not seem adaptable to the removal of cases for "legitimate suspicion." [239] Apparently, there have been no cases since 1958 so that it is difficult to say what procedure must now be applied. [240]

A case may be transferred from one court to another court for reasons of "public safety" if there is a danger that riots, mob violence, or like causes may make a fair hearing impossible. Such a transfer seems to occur fairly often in criminal cases, but is very rare in civil

[234] The transfer of cases on account of legitimate suspicion was authorized by the Constitution of the 22 frimaire, year VIII, art. 65; the transfer for reasons of public safety by Law of the 27 ventôse year VIII, art. 79. Both are reprinted in DALLOZ, PETIT CODE DE PROCÉDURE CIVILE 156 (58th ed. 1962).

[235] SOLUS & PERROT 684–85; 2 DALLOZ, RÉPERTOIRE DE PROCÉDURE CIVILE ET COMMERCIALE, *Renvoi*, at No. 32 (1956). On the transfer of cases for reasons specifically mentioned in the code, see CODE DE PROCÉDURE CIVILE arts. 368–77 (various relationships between parties and judges).

[236] SOLUS & PERROT 685–86; 2 DALLOZ, *op. cit. supra* note 235, at No. 314.

[237] There is such a statute for criminal cases. CODE DE PROCÉDURE PÉNALE art. 662.

[238] 2 DALLOZ, *op. cit. supra* note 235, at No. 50.

[239] DÉCRET No. 58–1281 of Dec. 22, 1958, J.O. Dec. 23, 1958, p. 11608, [1959] D.L. 45, art. 13. The revised *règlement de juges* procedure is now part of CODE DE PROCÉDURE CIVILE art. 172.

[240] For a discussion, see SOLUS & PERROT 685–86.

matters. [241] Apparently, it can take place only at the request of the *procureur général* at the *Cour de Cassation* and must always be handled by the *Cour de Cassation*. However, some authors state that such proceedings must be handled by the *cours d'appel* if the case to be transferred is pending before a court of first instance and by the *Cour de Cassation* if it is pending before a *cour d'appel*. [242] Presumably, the procedure is the same as in case of transfer for "legitimate suspicion."

### 9.23. Preparation of the Decision

Immediately upon conclusion of the hearing, the judges who participated in it discuss the case and vote on it. Formerly, this conference quite frequently took place in the courtroom itself, the judges standing in a circle (*rondeau*) around the presiding judge. At present, this method, ill-adapted to a conference of more than moderate length, is used less often. Ordinarily, the judges retire into their conference room (*chambre du conseil*) for their deliberations. Under long-established tradition, the representative of the *ministère public* is present at the conference, but does not vote. [243] The judges speak in well-established order: first the reporting judge, then the other judges in order of seniority, and, finally, the presiding judge. [244] The opinion is written by the reporting judge who gives it to the clerk of the court. [245] Decisions are always read aloud in the course of a public hearing.

The *Cour de Cassation* either rejects the *pourvoi*, which amounts to affirmance of the decision below, or breaks (*casse*) the decision under review and renders a decision of reversal (called *cassation*). The reversal may also be partial.

The decisions are short and follow a set pattern. First comes the heading, which indicates the names of the parties, the capacity in which they have been acting, and, by court and date, the decision under review. Then follows the opinion (*motifs*) which includes the decretal clause (*dispositif*). The names of the presiding judge, of the reporting judge, of the other judges, of the members of the *ministère public* and of

[241] On the procedure in criminal cases, see CODE DE PROCÉDURE PÉNALE art. 665; *cf.* 2 DALLOZ, *op. cit. supra* note 235, at No. 54.

[242] For a review of authorities, see SOLUS & PERROT 687; 2 DALLOZ, *op. cit. supra* note 235, at No. 55.

[243] *Id.* at No. 755.

[244] ORDONNANCE of Jan. 15, 1826, *supra* note 198, art. 40. This article also provides that nobody may speak unless he has received the presiding judge's permission and that nobody who speaks may be interrupted, except by the presiding judge for the purpose of admonishing him to return to the matter in hand if he departs from it.

[245] ORDONNANCE of Jan. 15, 1826, *supra* note 198, art. 41.

counsel who participated in the case are also given. [246] The opinion forms one sentence, which always begins with the words *La Cour* (The Court), followed by a number of clauses indicating the reasons for the decision, and terminates with the *dispositif* (decretal clause) which contains the main verb for the whole sentence.

There are a few differences between opinions affirming a judgment and opinions reversing it. An opinion for reversal always contains the word *vu* (having seen) followed by a reference to the statute or statutes involved in the case immediately after the words *La Cour*. Then follows the rest of the opinion, consisting of recitals of the facts of the case, the grounds given by the court below for its decision, the bases on which this decision is attacked, and the reasons for the *Cour de Cassation*'s position. Each of these recitals forms a dependent clause introduced by the word *attendu* (whereas), except the recital immediately following that of the reasons given by the court below for its decision. The latter begins with the words *mais attendu* (but whereas).

Judgments for affirmance follow the same general pattern, except that the *vu* clause with the reference to the statutes involved is omitted and that the words *mais attendu* (but whereas) follow the recital of the grounds for the *pourvoi*. These words thus indicate that the court disagrees with the statement preceding them. [247]

In practice, opinions show even more similarity than indicated, because passages from one opinion are often repeated verbatim (but without citation) in another. This practice seems to be due largely to the heavy case load of the *Cour de Cassation* and the duty to write an opinion in every case.

The brief, standardized, structure of a *Cour de Cassation* decision, which never contains a reference to precedent, gives the reader the impression that the decision of the court is the inescapable logical consequence of the statutory provisions involved. It dates back to the early years of the *Cour de Cassation*, when all legal problems were thought of as being resolvable by a comparatively simple process of logical deductions from statutory texts. However, it also offers a practical advantage. Since *Cour de Cassation* decisions are brief (and sometimes enigmatic), they do not, in advance of actual litigation, commit the court to a broadly stated legal principle, which the court may wish to modify later.

[246] Law No. 47–1366, *supra* note 4, art. 61; MOREL 520. See also 7.13.c *supra*.

[247] 1 DALLOZ, *op. cit. supra* note 5, at Nos. 2242–44; SZLADITS, A GUIDE TO FOREIGN LEGAL MATERIALS, FRENCH, GERMAN, SWISS 72, 73 (1959) (good general discussion of style of French opinions). See Appendix, Form No. 23.

## 9.24. Effects of the Decision

If the *Cour de Cassation* rejects the *pourvoi*, the decision below becomes final and unimpeachable. [248] There is no way in which a further review or rehearing may be obtained, even in case of default. [249]. Each rejection of a *pourvoi* must order the losing party to pay costs, including costs in the court below. The fees of the *avocats aux conseils* are not included in these costs, however. [250] In addition, a party who has brought an unsuccessful *pourvoi* is subject to a fine of 400 francs (about $ 80) for the benefit of the French treasury, but the court may reduce the fine to a fraction of this amount. It may also dispense entirely with payment of the fine, but must give reasons for its decision. Whenever the party having brought the *pourvoi* must pay the fine, an indemnity must also be paid to adverse parties. This indemnity is an addition to costs. It is always three fourths of the fine. Thus, if the maximum fine of 400 francs is imposed, the indemnity is 300 francs. Fine and indemnity are intended to discourage rash *pourvois*. [251]

A decision of reversal must be transcribed in the margin of the official record of the reversed decision. [252] The losing party is liable for costs, but need not pay a fine or special indemnity. The liability for costs does not depend on the outcome of the case upon remand. [253] In effect, a reversal (*cassation*) destroys the decision under review. It also destroys all other decisions that are based upon it. Thus, if an interlocutory decision granting an *expertise* is reversed, the later final decision based on the *expertise* also becomes void. [254] As a further conse-

[248] *E.g.*, 1 Dalloz, *op. cit. supra* note 5, at No. 2257–66. The effect of an affirmance is not weakened by a statement in the opinion that the court has disregarded an erroneous, but unnecessary, portion of the opinion below. Qualifying statements of this kind are rather frequent in *Cour de Cassation* opinions.

[249] Law No. 47–1366, *supra* note 4, art. 31; Morel 520; 1 Dalloz, *op. cit. supra* note 5, at No. 2251; *cf.* Hyacinthe v. Comptoir national d' escompte de Paris, Cass. Soc., April 27, 1944, [1944] D. Anal. J. 94 (no new *pourvoi* possible, if one rejected for formal reasons).

[250] Law No. 47–1366, *supra* note 4, art. 28; Morel 520.

[251] Law No. 47–1366, *supra* note 4, arts. 29 (regular procedure), 36 (procedure without *avocats*). The amount of the fine was regulated by Law No. 56–780, 3.32 n. 279 *supra*, art. 54. The fine is only 100 francs (about $ 20) in labor and social security matters. Even if the court decision fails to mention them, the fine and indemnity are due. Until 1956, every party filing a *pourvoi* had to deposit cash at the time of filing as security for the payment of the fine. The deposit was refunded if no fine was imposed. The deposit was abolished by Law No. 56–780, 3.32 n. 279 *supra*, art. 52.

[252] For this purpose, a copy is forwarded *ex officio* to the court that rendered the decision below. Law of 27 ventôse, year VIII, *supra* note 234, art. 85.

[253] See note 250 *supra*.

[254] Netter v. Epoux Vincent, Cass. Civ., May 30, 1956, [1956] D. Somm. 121; *cf.* Descous v. Vve Tardieu, Cass. Civ., Feb. 28, 1938, [1938] D.H. 209 (*cour d'appel* decided to liquidate company and appointed liquidator; a *pourvoi* was taken from this decision; while this *pourvoi* was pending, the *cour d'appel* received the report of the liquidator which it approved; in the meantime, the first decision was reversed by the *Cour de Cassation* which held that, as a conse-

quence, everything collected by a party in executing the reversed judgment must be returned – in the case of money, with interest. Damages may also be payable. Again, this duty of restitution is not dependent upon the outcome of the case upon a subsequent remand. [255] If there is a reversal, the case must be remanded to a court equal in rank to that which rendered the reversed decision. In the usual case in which a *cour d'appel* decision is involved, the remand is to another *cour d' appel*. The remand should be to the closest available court, but the *Cour de Cassation* is not bound by any strict rules. The decision must indicate the court to which the case is remanded. If a judgment is reversed for lack of competence, the remand is to the competent court, at least if the competent court is a judicial court located in France. [256]

### 9.25. Procedure on Remand

Before any steps may be taken on remand, the prevailing party must serve a copy of the *Cour de Cassation* decision on all adverse parties. [257] The procedure on remand is begun by a regular *ajournement* summoning adverse parties to appear before the court. The court on remand has the same powers as the court that rendered the original decision. However, the entire proceedings need not be repeated. If the reversal is for procedural error, the procedure is repeated from the stage at which the error occured. If the reversal is due to a mistake of the court in applying the law to the facts, although there will be a hearing on the law, the court may simply render a new decision on the basis of the existing record. [258] However, the parties may treat the proceedings as a new appeal, submit new pleadings (*conclusions*) and present new facts, even facts that occured after the decision of the *Cour de Cassation*. If desira-

quence, the second decision also became void). In case of partial reversal, only the portion of the decision directly affected becomes void, unless all portions of the decision are so closely related that they must stand or fall together, in which case the whole decisions falls. Veuve Delque v. Martel, Cass. Civ., March 5, 1957, [1957] D.J. 264; *cf.* Dugardin v. de Warenghien de Flory, Cass. Civ., Feb. 27, 1957, [1957] D.J. 231.

[255] MOREL 521; 1 DALLOZ, *op. cit. supra* note 5, at No. 2326; *cf.* 9.18 *supra*, especially note 182.

[256] Law of 27 ventôse, year VIII, *supra* note 234; 6 GARSONNET & CÉZAR-BRU 765; MOREL 521. There may be an occasional remand to a court of a different rank; for instance, if a case was erroneously brought before a *cour d'appel*, it might be remanded to the proper court. Cases coming from the *Cour d'Appel* in Colmar, which uses the special procedure for Alsace-Lorraine rather than the ordinary French procedure, are always remanded to that court, but to different judges. 1 DALLOZ, *op. cit. supra* note 5, at No. 2404. On problems raised as to remand by the abolition of many courts as part of the 1958 reforms, see Hébraud, *Chronique*, 57 REV. TRIM. DR. CIV. 577 (1959).

[257] This in accordance with the general rule that no decision may be executed, *i.e.*, put into effect, unless it has been served on the other party.

[258] Law of Nov. 27, 1790, *supra* note 75, art. 20; Law of 2 brumaire, year IV, *supra* note 27, art. 24; 6 Garsonnet & Cézar-Bru 768.

ble, there may be a new *expertise* or *enquête*. Even new defenses, such as the statute of limitations, may be raised. The parties are, however, precluded from relying on procedural defects already waived. [259] The *cour d'appel* which hears a case on remand from the *Cour de Cassation* always sits in solemn session; it is composed of at least two of its regular panels, and the judges wear their formal red gowns. [260]

The *cour d'appel* is not bound to follow the legal rule expounded by the *Cour de Cassation*, but will ordinarily do so. The court may impose costs on the losing party, but only the costs of the proceedings before it.

### 9.26. Proceedings on a Second *Pourvoi*

The party losing on remand may file a new *pourvoi* to the *Cour de Cassation*. If the second *pourvoi* is between the same parties acting in the same capacity, and is based on the same grounds (*moyens*) as the first *pourvoi*, such a *pourvoi* is referred to the full bench (*chambres réunies*) of the *Cour de Cassation*. [261] The case is referred to the *chambres réunies* only if the two divergent decisions – that of the court below and that of the *Cour de Cassation* – are based on the same facts. If new facts were brought before the court on remand, the two decisions are distinguishable rather than irreconcilable, and the case remains with the panel to which it was originally assigned. Transfer from a panel to the *chambres réunies* takes place on the initiative of the panel rather than that of the parties. The *chambres réunies* are always the ultimate judge as to whether a case is properly before them. If it is not, they may remand it to the proper panel. The procedure before the *chambres réunies* is similar to that before the regular panels. [262]

### 9.27. Cases in which there is no Remand

In a few instances, the *Cour de Cassation* may reverse without remanding the case to a lower court for further proceedings. This is always so in case of *pourvois* "in the interest of the law." There is likewise no remand following *pourvois* by the *procureur général* for *excès*

[259] Nicolau v. Dame Coste, née Aragno, Cass. Civ., May 29, 1953, [1953] D.J. 515 (offer made after reversal) 6 GARSONNET & CÉZAR-BRU 679; 1 DALLOZ, *op. cit. supra* note 5, at Nos. 2328–2442.

[260] Perhaps to underline the importance of its decision. A refusal to follow the holding of the *Cour de Cassation* results in a second *pourvoi* and a meeting of the full bench (*chambres réunies*) of the *Cour de Cassation*. See 3.32.d *supra*.

[261] Law No. 47–1366, *supra* note 4, art. 58. See also 3.32.d *supra*.

[262] The reporting judge is always selected from a panel other than that which rendered the original decision. Law No. 47–1366, *supra* note 4, arts. 58–60; 1 DALLOZ, *op. cit. supra* note 5, at Nos. 2490–93.

*de pouvoir*. The court simply annuls the offending decision. [263] Remand is also unnecessary in a few other cases in which nothing remains to be accomplished after reversal by the *Cour de Cassation*. Thus, under French law, a criminal judgment is conclusive also on the issue of civil liability in tort. If a plaintiff sues a defendant in damages on the basis of such a criminal conviction but the conviction is reversed while the civil proceedings are pending, the *Cour de Cassation* will reverse the civil judgment if a *pourvoi* is taken by the defendant. In such a case there is no remand, since the reversal of the criminal conviction has destroyed the entire basis for the plaintiff's suit, and further proceedings are useless. [264] Likewise, remand is not necessary if the *Cour de Cassation* reverses a *cour d'appel* decision because the appeal was not timely. Since this makes the decision of the court of first instance fully effective, there is no point in further proceedings. Sometimes, remand may also be unnecessary in *ex parte* proceedings. Oddly enough, a remand is necessary if a decision is attacked on account of "inconsistency of judgments." In such an event, it is sufficient to reverse the second decision to avoid any inconsistency; however, the case is always remanded. [265]

### 9.28. The Rôle of the *Cour de Cassation* in the Development of the Law

By adapting through interpretation often rather general statutory provisions to the needs of the times, the *Cour de Cassation* has contributed greatly to the development of French law, even in the absence of a formal doctrine of *stare decisis*. It is in large measure the merit of the *Cour de Cassation* that so many portions of the codes enacted at the beginning of the 19th century can still function today. [266]

[263] See 9.11 *supra*.

[264] Mutuelle générale française-Accidents v. Andrevon, Cass. Civ., [1958] D.J. 96 (automobile accident case). On the conclusiveness of criminal convictions in civil cases, see 3.23 *supra*.

[265] *Cf*. CUCHE & VINCENT 518; 1 DALLOZ, *op. cit. supra* note 5, at No. 2458.

[266] On the rôle of case law in France, see 1.32 *supra*.

## CHAPTER 10

# EXTRAORDINARY METHODS OF REVIEW

After having indicated the distinction between ordinary and extraordinary methods of review (10.01), this chapter describes *tierce opposition* (10.02–10.08) and *requête civile* (10.09–10.15), two extraordinary methods of review.

## 1. INTRODUCTION

### 10.01. The Distinction between Ordinary and Extraordinary Methods of Review

In France, judgments can be attacked only by means of the procedural devices specifically made available by statute. French courts do not claim to possess inherent power to revise their judgments, nor are judgments that have become final, because all *voies de recours* provided by statute have either been used or otherwise become unavailable, subject to collateral attack. [1]

Every procedural device for attacking a judgment, whether it seeks reconsideration of the judgment by the court that rendered it or review by a tribunal of higher rank, is a *voie de recours.* [2] French authors, following in this respect the terminology of the *Code de Procédure Civile,* usually divide *voies de recours* into two classes: (1) ordinary methods of review (*voies de recours ordinaires*), and (2) extraordinary methods of review (*voies de recours extraordinaires*). Ordinary methods of review include only *appel* and *opposition.* All other methods of review, in-

[1] This rule is frequently stated by use of the phrase *voies de nullité n'ont lieu contre jugements en France.* The rule is subject to a few, limited, exceptions. Collateral attack is possible against judgments that are non-existent, rather than merely void – for instance, decisions rendered by individuals not invested with judicial power. In practice, however, courts have been quite reluctant to consider a decision non-existent rather than void. A court may also be asked to correct an obvious minor error, such as a typographical mistake, or an error in a computation. Similarly, a court may be asked to clarify a decision that is so ambiguous that it cannot be executed. However, outside these cases courts do not have the power to grant a rehearing or modify their decisions, except pursuant to specific statutory authority. See 6 GARSONNET & CÉZAR-BRU 5–7; MOREL 471–72; *cf.* 4.02.b *supra* and 13.01 *infra.*

[2] 6 GARSONNET & CÉZAR-BRU 3. Devices to obtain reconsideration of a judgment by the court that rendered it are sometimes called *voies de rétractation,* while the term *voies de réformation* designates procedures for review of judgments by higher courts.

cluding not only *pourvois* to the *Cour de Cassation*, but also the methods of review called *requête civile* and *tierce opposition* which are discussed in this chapter, are extraordinary methods of review. [3]

Extraordinary methods of review (*voies de recours extraordinaires*) are said to have common features that distinguish them from ordinary methods of review: First, they are available only in cases specifically provided for; second, resort to them generally does not stay execution of the judgment attacked. [4] However, since there are now numerous exceptions to these rules, these distinguishing features are not particularly helpful.

The drafters of the *Code de Procédure Civile* expected that extraordinary methods of review [5] would be used quite sparingly. This expectation turned out to be ill-founded insofar as *pourvois* to the *Cour de Cassation* are concerned. However, the two procedural devices discussed in this chapter, *tierce opposition* and *requête civile*, are employed rather infrequently and at least in that sense retain their extraordinary character.

## 2. *TIERCE OPPOSITION*

### 10.02. Introduction

*Tierce opposition* (literally, third opposition) is a procedural device by which persons who were not parties to the action may attack a judgment that causes them prejudice. [6] Because judgments generally have no *res judicata* effect against persons who were not parties to the action, the need for this device has been drawn into doubt. However, *tierce opposition* may be useful, especially in view of the strict rules proscribing collateral attack upon a judgment. Thus, for example, *tierce opposition* enables a creditor to avoid a collusively obtained judgment that reduces the assets of his debtor. The somewhat uncertain contours of *tierce opposition* seem to be due mainly to historical factors. [7]

[3] *E.g.*, MOREL 473; CUCHE & VINCENT 443.

[4] 6 GARSONNET & CÉZAR-BRU 3–4; MOREL 473.

[5] French authors, following the terminology of the *Code de Procédure Civile*, include among *voies de recours extraordinaires* not only *pourvoi* to the *Cour de Cassation*, *requête civile*, and *tierce opposition*, but – mainly for historical reasons – also the special procedure to impose civil liability upon judges called *prise à partie*. *E.g.*, CUCHE & VINCENT 443. On *prise à partie*, see 3.17 *supra*.

[6] CODE DE PROCÉDURE CIVILE art. 474; CUCHE & VINCENT 483; 6 GARSONNET & CÉZAR-BRU 440.

[7] For a description of the historical development of this device, see 6 GARSONNET & CÉZAR-BRU 876–79; 2 DALLOZ, RÉPERTOIRE DE PROCÉDURE CIVILE ET COMMERCIALE, *Tierce Opposition*, at No. 1 (1956).

*Tierce opposition* is usually an independent proceeding called *tierce opposition principale.* Sometimes, however, a prior judgment may be attacked in a subsequent action by a person who was not a party to the prior action. Such an attack is called *tierce opposition incidente.* [8] It seems to be of infrequent occurence.

## 10.03. The Requirement of Prejudice

In addition to possessing the usual qualifications demanded of all litigants, such as capacity to sue and an interest in the outcome of the proceedings, [9] a person who wishes to resort to *tierce opposition* must show that the judgment he attacks has caused him prejudice. [10] In defining prejudice, the courts have been rather liberal. The criteria applied in determining the propriety of intervention in a pending lawsuit are generally also applied to determine the availability of *tierce opposition.* [11]

Clearly, a person is prejudiced by a judgment obtained through collusion between his debtor and some other person if it reduces the debtor's assets. [12] However, the prejudice need not be present and actual; future or possible prejudice may be sufficient. [13] Thus, if A sues B to recover a chattel that was actually bailed to A by C, C may attack the judgment ordering B to deliver the chattel to A by *tierce opposition.* While C, since he was not a party to the action, is not bound by the judgment declaring A to be the owner of the chattel and could, therefore, bring an action to get the chattel back from A, he does not have to assume the risk of A's losing the chattel pending the outcome of that action. [14] Similarly, since there is a danger that the husband may impair the family assets through future irresponsible dealings, a wife may object to a decision, made in a proceeding to which she was not a party, which removes an incapacity earlier imposed upon her husband on account of his insanity. [15] Indeed, even "moral" harm as distinguished

[8] CODE DE PROCÉDURE CIVILE art. 475.

[9] See 6.01–6.04 *supra.*

[10] CODE DE PROCÉDURE CIVILE art. 474; Soc. financière d'Expansion industrielle v. Soc. des Acacias, Cour Paris, June 24, 1929, [1931] D. 2. 15; Amidieu du Clos v. Navarre, Cass. Civ., Oct. 17, 1933, [1933] D.H. 553 (no *tierce opposition* possible when issue has become moot); 6 GARSONNET & CÉZAR-BRU 913–14. Whether there is prejudice is determined as of the time the court decides the *tierce opposition* proceeding, not as of the date on which the judgment under attack was rendered. Nicolau v. Dame Coste, Cass. Civ., May 29, 1953, [1953] D.J. 515.

[11] CUCHE & VINCENT 487; 2 DALLOZ, *op. cit. supra* note 7, at 66.

[12] *E.g.,* CUCHE & VINCENT 483.

[13] *E.g.,* Nicolau v. Dame Coste, *supra* note 10; MOREL 526.

[14] *Id.* at 524.

[15] 2 DALLOZ, *op. cit. supra* note 7, at No. 72.

from financial prejudice may form the basis for attack by *tierce opposition.* [16] However, this form of attack is not available against a decision that is objectionable merely because it constitutes an unwelcome judicial precedent. [17] Nor may such an attack be based on derogatory statements in the court's opinion: The harm must be caused by the decretal part of the decision. [18] Whether a judgment causes prejudice is ordinarily a question of fact the *Cour de Cassation* does not review. [19]

Of course, in order to be successful in a *tierce opposition,* a mere showing of prejudice does not suffice; the judgment must also be shown to be wrong. [20]

## 10.04. Persons Who May Resort to *Tierce Opposition*

*Tierce opposition* may not be used by a person who was a party to the action. Even a person who defaulted may not resort to *tierce opposition* as long as he was properly summoned. [21] On the other hand, a person who was a party to an action in one capacity may institute *tierce opposition* when acting in a different capacity. [22] Additional restrictions exist when no fraud is alleged.

**a. When no fraud is alleged.** When no fraud or collusion is alleged, not only parties, but also persons who were "represented" in the action, are precluded from attacking the resulting judgment by *tierce opposition.* [23] The term "representation," as used in this connection, is not well defined.

Clearly, a person in whose behalf litigation was conducted by a true agent, such as an attorney in fact, may not attack the resulting judgment by *tierce opposition.* [24] The same is true of the principal of an

[16] 6 GARSONNET & CÉZAR-BRU 914; MOREL 526. Organizations of notaries, *avoués,* and similar professional bodies sometimes use *tierce opposition* to attack a decision considered harmful to their membership as a whole. On the availability of this device in such cases, see 2 DALLOZ, *op. cit. supra* note 7, at Nos. 82–85.

[17] *E.g.,* Marchand v. Olano, Cour Rennes, Jan. 10, 1952, [1952] D. SOMM. 72; Raynaud, *Chronique,* 56 REV. TRIM. DR. CIV. 135–37 (1958).

[18] 2 DALLOZ, *op. cit. supra* note 7, at No. 92. However, *prise à partie* may be available against a judge who inserts unnecessary insulting statements in an opinion.

[19] 2 DALLOZ, *op. cit. supra* note 7, at No. 71.

[20] *E.g.,* MOREL 528.

[21] CODE DE PROCÉDURE CIVILE art. 474; 6 GARSONNET & CÉZAR-BRU 892.

[22] *Id.* at 893.

[23] CODE DE PROCÉDURE CIVILE art. 474.

[24] CUCHE & VINCENT 488; 2 DALLOZ, *op. cit. supra* note 7, at Nos. 152–66. Since under rules as to procedural capacity, actions are not brought by minors or incompetents directly, but by their parent or guardian acting as their representative, the rule is of some practical importance. However, minors, incompetents, and also public bodies, to which somewhat similar rules apply, may use *requête civile* in case of improper representation by the person charged with their representation. See 10.11.c *infra.*

undisclosed agent. A husband married under one of the various matrimonial *régimes* that leave him the power to administer the property of his wife is likewise considered the representative of the wife, with the result that the wife may not use *tierce opposition* against a judgment rendered in litigation conducted by her husband though affecting her interests. [25]

There is also representation in all cases of universal succession. Thus, heirs may not, by *tierce opposition*, attack a judgment rendered against the decedent. In the case of transfers of individual items of property, however, there is representation only as to judgments rendered before the transfer took place. Thus, the transferee of a plot of land may not attack a judgment concerning that plot rendered against his transferor before the transfer took place; however, he may use *tierce opposition* to attack a judgment rendered after the transfer. [26]

In the case of several obligations, one of the contracting parties does not represent the other contracting parties, and *tierce opposition* is available even to parties to an indivisible obligation who did not participate in the litigation concerning the obligation. [27] Generally speaking, a surety cannot attack a judgment rendered against his principal by way of *tierce opposition*. [28] Similarly, *tierce opposition* does not seem available to an accident insurance company to attack a judgment against the insured – at least, if the insurer was in control of the litigation. [29] Creditors, whether secured or unsecured, are always likewise represented by their debtor. [30]

**b. When fraud is alleged.** In case of fraud, *tierce opposition* is available even to persons represented by the parties to the action, although the parties themselves remain excluded. Apparently, fraud means collusion between the parties to the litigation. [31] In fact, *tierce opposition* seems

[25] Morel 523–24; 2 Dalloz, *op. cit. supra* note 7, at No. 171.

[26] Cuche & Vincent 488; Morel 526; 2 Dalloz, *op. cit. supra* note 7, at Nos. 208–14.

[27] *Id.* at Nos. 192–94.

[28] Cons. G. v. Crédit de l'Ouest, Trib. Com. Angers, Dec. 4, 1957, [1958] D.J. 378 (with extensive note Vincent). *But see* Caisse des dépôts et consignations v. Vve Conord, Cass. Civ., June 9, 1928, [1928] S. 1. 269 (semi-autonomous social security fund, which, to some extent is surety for employers' obligations under social security laws, may use *tierce opposition* to attack judgment concerning employer).

[29] Cie d'assurances Les Travailleurs français v. Cuzot, Trib. Charolles, March 7, 1952, [1953] D.J. 14 (note Besson). On the subsequent fate of the case, see 2 Dalloz, *op. cit. supra* note 7, at No. 139.

[30] *Cf.* Breton v. Consorts Debonnesset, Cass. Req., Jan. 11, 1938, [1938] D.H. 211; 6 Garsonnet & Cézar-Bru 906–08.

[31] Morel 526. For an older opinion to the effect that collusion is not necessary if there has been fraud in procuring the judgment, see 6 Garsonnet & Cézar-Bru 920–21.

useful mainly to creditors whose debtors' assets have been reduced by collusively obtained judgments. [32] It is likewise available to creditors whose security is reduced by a *séparation de biens* (judicial termination of the community property regime) obtained by the wife. [33]

## 10.05. Judgments Subject to Attack by *Tierce Opposition*

Almost all court decisions that are judgments are subject to attack by *tierce opposition*. However, this means of attack is not available against decisions that are judgments only in form – for instance, judgments that merely make a settlement agreement a matter of record. [34] *Tierce opposition* may be used against decisions of all courts of first instance as well as against decisions of the *cours d'appel*. Decisions of the *Cour de Cassation* are, however, immune from this form of attack. [35]

As a rule, the nature of the action does not affect the availability of *tierce opposition*. It may be used against judgments rendered in contested proceedings conducted in open court as well as against decisions rendered in non-litigious matters in the *chambre de conseil*. [36] It is also available against decisions in *exequatur* proceedings. [37]

According to some authors and courts, judgments that have an *in rem* effect and more particularly judgments relating to personal status, since they are effective against everybody, may not be attacked by *tierce opposition*. Others have argued that the very *in rem* effect of such judgments makes it desirable to give third parties an opportunity to attack them. [38]

The problem was particularly bothersome in connection with judgments of adoption. Natural parents of adopted children who were not parties to the adoption proceedings attempted fairly frequently to upset

[32] Cuche & Vincent 483.

[33] Code Civil art. 1447. Generally speaking, creditors may seize community property assets, even if brought into the community by the wife, in order to satisfy debts incurred by the husband. A court decision separating the property of the spouses (*séparation de biens*), since it reduces the assets they may reach, is therefore likely to harm creditors. *Cf.* Amos & Walton, Introduction to French Law 260 (2d ed. 1963).

[34] *E.g.*, B. v. T., Cass. Soc., Feb. 1, 1957, [1957] D. Somm. 120.

[35] 6 Garsonnet & Cézar-Bru 853; 2 Dalloz, *op. cit. supra* note 7, at Nos. 37–38.

[36] Cuche & Vincent 489; Morel 527; Epoux Genilloud v. Epoux Novak, Trib. Toulon, Dec. 18, 1957, [1958] D. Somm. 100. The availability of *tierce opposition* in non-litigious matters (*juridiction gracieuse*) is, however, controverted.

[37] 2 Dalloz, *op. cit. supra* note 7, at No. 6. On *exequatur* proceedings for the enforcement of foreign judgments, see also 14.01–14.04, 14.07 *infra*.

[38] To the effect that *tierce opposition* is not available as to judgments creating a new status, see, *e.g.*, Brancherie v. Dame Aubry, Cass. Req., May 17, 1943, [1943] S. 1. 107 (separation); Cons. Castan v. Epoux Loustdunau, Cour Paris, Nov. 19, 1953, [1954] D.J. 132 (note Savatier) (legitimation); 6 Garsonnet & Cézar-Bru 843. For the contrary opinion, see especially the note Savatier *supra*.

the adoption by resorting to *tierce opposition*, and the decisions on the availability of this form of attack were divided. [39] The controversy has been settled by a recent amendment to the *Code Civil* which permits the use of *tierce opposition* in adoption cases, but only within a relatively short period of time following the adoption. [40] Specific statutory provisions resolve similar problems in other cases. [41]

Even apart from such statutes, the most recent decision of the *Cour de Cassation* seems to permit recourse to *tierce opposition* by all persons who could have become parties in the original action. [42] This rule excludes *tierce opposition* against judgments in divorce and separation cases since in these actions only the spouses may be parties. [43] In other actions concerning personal status, the number of possible parties is greater, though it remains restricted. [44]

*Tierce opposition* is not available in proceedings to deprive a parent of his parental powers because such proceedings, though in the form of a civil action, have essentially a penal character. [45] *Tierce opposition* is further unavailable in all cases in which all methods of review are barred. [46]

*Tierce opposition* is available against final judgments as well as non-

[39] *Compare* Dame Therel v. Epoux Garet, Cass. Civ., May 13, 1958, [1958] D.J. 446 (not available) *with* Epoux Genilloud v. Epoux Novak, *supra* note 36 (available) (dictum); Raynaud, *supra* note 17, at 456.

[40] Code Civil art. 356 (as amended in 1963). *Tierce opposition* must be instituted within one year from the date on which the adoption was recorded in the adopted child's birth record. By virtue of Code Civil art. 369, this rule is also applicable to the special form of adoption known as *légitimation adoptive*.

[41] *E.g.*, Code Civil art. 54 (decisions of *tribunal de grande instance* affecting birth, death, and marriage records subject to attack by any interested party); Code de Procédure Civile art. 888 (judicial approval of decisions of family council subject to attack by any dissenting member of council). Special rules apply in bankruptcy cases. See 2 Dalloz, *op. cit. supra* note 7, at Nos. 39–40.

[42] 2 Dalloz, *op. cit. supra* note 7, at No. 53 (Supp. 1963); Durassow v. Durazzo-Durassow, Cass. Civ., March 28, 1962, [1962] D.J. 489.

[43] Cuche & Vincent 489; *cf.* Code Civil arts. 234, 306. This rule means in fact that the creditors of the husband cannot prevent the wife from obtaining a collusive divorce or separation designed to prevent creditors from seizing her assets for debts of her husband. *Tierce opposition* is, however, available to creditors if the wife brings a *séparation de biens* action which merely terminates the community of property between the spouses, but does not affect their marital status. See note 33 *supra*.

[44] *Tierce opposition* seems excluded in actions *en désaveu* through which a father may rebut the presumption that the child of his wife is his also, as he is the only person who may bring such an action (with a very limited exception for his heirs). Code Civil arts. 312, 317; *cf.* Cuche & Vincent 489. On other actions relating to personal status, see, *e.g.*, Code Civil arts. 329 (action to claim status of legitimate child, available to child and to its heirs, but to latter only under certain conditions); 1 Colin & Capitant 251–52 (listing persons who may be parties to various actions relating to personal status).

[45] 2 Dalloz, *op. cit. supra* note 7, at No. 60.

[46] These cases include various proceedings after judgment dealing with execution against property, and some bankruptcy matters. See 9.03 *supra*.

final judgments that are *interlocutoires*; it does not lie against judgments that are merely *provisoires* in nature. [47] Whether *tierce opposition* can be used to attack provisional orders made by a judge in the so-called *référé* procedure is debated. [48] It is generally assumed that *tierce opposition* is not available against provisional orders issued *ex parte* by a judge (*ordonnances sur requête*), although there are some cases to the contrary. [49] Usually, the proper remedy against an *ex parte* order is recourse to the judge sitting *en référé*. [50]

## 10.06. Time within which *Tierce Opposition* Must Be Instituted

The *Code de Procédure Civile* contains no provision of general applicability limiting the time within which *tierce opposition* must be instituted. Hence, the general statute of limitations usually applies, and *tierce opposition* may be brought at any time within thirty years from the date on which the judgment under attack was rendered. [51] Some authors even contend that *tierce opposition incidente* is not subject to any time limitation. [52]

In some instances, the general statute of limitations does not apply. A person who holds real property by virtue of a judgment acquires a perfect title through adverse possession in 10 or 20 years. [53] This title cannot be attacked by overthrowing the judgment through *tierce opposition*, once the ten or twenty year limitation period has run out. [54] *Tierce opposition* against an adoption must be brought within one year from the date on which the adoption was recorded in the margin of the

[47] *E.g.*, 6 GARSONNET & CÉZAR-BRU 852. On the distinction between judgments that are *interlocutoires* and judgments that are *provisoires*, see 8.05, 9.05 *supra*.

[48] Maurice v. Groupment auxiliaire des industries textiles, Cour Nancy, Feb. 1, 1946, [1946] D.J. 146 (yes); Soc. financière d'Expansion industrielle v. Soc. des Acacias, *supra* note 10 (no, but on special facts); Dame Hengy v. Poitevin, Trib. Clermont-Ferrand, May 21, 1951, [1951] D.J. 666 (generally no, but yes in instant case when decision actually on merits) (with extensive note collecting the cases).

[49] 2 DALLOZ, *op. cit. supra* note 7, at No. 14 (generally no). *But see* Perry v. Orban, Trib. Clermont-Ferrand, Jan. 23, 1954, [1954] D. SOMM. 39 (*tierce opposition* possible against *ex parte* order appointing *huissier* to determine whether divorced wife lives in concubinage).

[50] See 5.05 *supra*.

[51] 6 GARSONNET & CÉZAR-BRU 856; 2 DALLOZ, *op. cit. supra* note 7, at No. 298. The general thirty-year limitation period is provided for in CODE CIVIL art. 2262. The rule that the time to bring *tierce opposition* begins to run as soon as the judgment has been rendered is somewhat unusual; usually, the time to attack judgments begins to run only upon service of the judgment.

[52] 6 GARSONNET & CÉZAR-BRU 863; 2 DALLOZ, *op. cit. supra* note 7, at No. 298.

[53] On the circumstances under which ownership is acquired by adverse possession lasting ten or twenty years if the person in possession holds under a "just title," see CODE CIVIL art. 2265; AMOS & WALTON, *op. cit. supra* note 33, at 101–02. Persons in possession of chattels neither lost nor stolen are usually protected without having to wait for the running of any limitation period. CODE CIVIL art. 2279.

[54] *E.g.*, 6 GARSONNET & CÉZAR-BRU 857. On movables, see note 53 *supra*.

adopted child's official birth record. [55] Creditors of a husband who want to use *tierce opposition* to object to a *séparation de biens* judgment must likewise act within one year. [56] The time for instituting *tierce opposition* is particularly short against certain decisions in bankruptcy matters: When publication of the judgment is required, *tierce opposition* must be instituted within eight days only from the day on which the judgment under attack was published. [57]

*Tierce opposition* may always be brought as soon as the judgment under attack has been rendered. There is no waiting period. [58]

### 10.07. Manner of Initiating *Tierce Opposition*

*Tierce opposition principale* begins with the service of a regular *ajournement* (summons). If the judgment attacked has not yet been executed, the *ajournement* is served on both parties to the action; if the judgment has already been executed and there has been no collusion between winner and loser, although it may be advantageous to serve both parties, [59] it is sufficient if only the winning party be served.

*Tierce opposition principale* is always brought before the court that rendered the judgment attacked. [60] If an appeal was taken before *tierce opposition* was brought, the person bringing *tierce opposition* has substantially the position of a party intervening before the appellate court. [61]

A person who wishes to attack a judgment to which he has not been a party, but which is used against him in pending litigation, may bring *tierce opposition incidente*. If the court in which the litigation is pending is of lower rank than the court that rendered the judgment to be attacked, *tierce opposition incidente* is instituted by serving an *ajournement* in the court in which the original judgment was rendered. [62] If the rank of the court in which the action is pending is equal to or higher than that of the court that rendered the original judgment, *tierce opposition* is brought by means of ordinary pleadings (*conclusions*) in the

[55] Code Civil art. 356 (as amended in 1963). The rule is also applicable to *légitimation adoptive*. See note 40 *supra*.

[56] Code de Procédure Civile arts. 872–873. On *séparation de biens*, see also note 33 *supra*.

[57] Code de Commerce art. 454.

[58] 6 Garsonnet & Cézar-Bru 855.

[59] 6 Garsonnet & Cézar-Bru 868; 2 Dalloz, *op. cit. supra* note 7, at 294. It may be useful to serve both parties to the original action whenever the effects of the judgment as to these parties cannot be severed from its effects as to the person bringing *tierce opposition*.

[60] Code de Procédure Civile art. 475.

[61] 2 Dalloz, *op. cit. supra* note 7, at No. 309.

[62] Code de Procédure Civile art. 476.

court in which the action is pending. [63] If the latter court does not have subject matter competence – for instance, because the judgment under attack was rendered by a civil court, but the pending litigation involves commercial matters –, *tierce opposition* must be brought before the court that rendered the original judgment, and a formal *ajournement* is necessary. [64] When *tierce opposition incidente* is brought, the pending action may be stayed until the outcome of the proceedings. [65]

Courts ordinarily have discretionary power to stay the execution of a judgment attacked by way of *tierce opposition*; they exercise this power especially if irreparable harm may be caused by the execution. However, no stay of execution may be granted of a judgment ordering the defendant to be evicted from real property. [66]

### 10.08. Procedure and Judgment

Once *tierce opposition* has been initiated, it proceeds as any action involving the same subject matter. When the original judgment suffers from an error of fact or law, it will be annulled and a new judgment substituted in its stead; otherwise, the *tierce opposition* will be dismissed. Ordinarily, the annulled judgment remains effective as to the original parties, however. For instance, if creditors of the husband bring a *tierce opposition* against a judgment of *séparation de biens* and win, they may proceed as if the spouses were still married under the community property regime and seize the entire former community property to satisfy the debts of the husband, but, as between the spouses, the *séparation de biens* judgment remains in effect. [67] If the original judgment and the judgment rendered in the *tierce opposition* are "indivisible" – for instance, because they involve joint obligations or other matters in which both judgments cannot co-exist –, the original judgment must be annulled as to all parties. [68]

To discourage rash *tierce opposition*, a fine varying from 25 francs (about $ 5) to 100 francs (about $ 20) is imposed on the person who unsuccessfully initiated such a proceeding. Within the limits indicated,

[63] Code de Procédure Civile art. 475. Although this article states that in such a case *tierce opposition* is begun by a *requête* (petition), ordinary pleadings (*conclusions*) apparently will do. *E.g.*, 6 Garsonnet & Cézar-Bru 868.

[64] *E.g.*, Morel 527.

[65] Code de Procédure Civile art. 477.

[66] Code de Procédure Civile art. 478; *cf.* 2 Dalloz, *op. cit. supra* note 7, at Nos. 345–47.

[67] Morel 528; 2 Dalloz, *op. cit. supra* note 7, at Nos. 349–50. On *séparation de biens*, see note 33 *supra*.

[68] *Id.* at Nos. 354–56; Cuche & Vincent 493. In such cases, it is advisable to serve all parties to the original judgment. See note 59 *supra*.

the amount of the fine is in the discretion of the court. [69] The court may also impose upon the person who brought an unsuccessful *tierce opposition* [70] the duty to pay compensation to his opponent for damages suffered – for example, for damages sustained as a result of delay in the execution of his judgment. Apparently, very slight fault on the part of the person who brought the *tierce opposition* suffices for the imposition of the duty to pay damages. [71] In addition, the losing party, whether or not he brought *tierce opposition*, is liable for costs.

The general rules on review of judgments apply to review of judgments rendered in *tierce opposition* proceedings. [72]

### 3. *REQUÊTE CIVILE*

#### 10.09. Introduction

Formerly, a *requête civile* (polite petition) had to be initiated by petition. Since it was submitted to the same judges who had rendered the original judgment, the attorney preparing the petition had to be polite and cautious when indicating the errors made by the court to avoid antagonizing its members. Hence, the unusual name of this extraordinary means of attack on a judgment.

In pre-revolutionary law, *requête civile* was used rather frequently; there was no clear-cut distinction between errors that could be corrected only by *pourvoi* to the royal council and errors that a court could be asked to correct itself upon *requête civile*. [73]

In modern law, the scope of *requête civile* is circumscribed. As a rule, *requête civile* can be based only on statutorily specified procedural errors or on misconduct of a party. [74] Furthermore, complicated procedure makes the use of the device burdensome. [75]

Unfortunately, the *Code de Procédure Civile* has done little to clarify

[69] CODE DE PROCÉDURE CIVILE art. 479. The fine is payable to the government, not to adverse parties.

[70] CODE DE PROCÉDURE CIVILE art. 479.

[71] Préfet des Ardennes v. Lavocat, Cass. Soc., Dec. 3, 1953, [1954] D. SOMM. 32 (no malice necessary for damages); 2 DALLOZ, *op. cit. supra* note 7, at Nos. 366–67 (proof of harm sufficient and fault not necessary). Even in an ordinary action, damages may be imposed upon an unsuccessful plaintiff, but only if malice is shown. *Cf.* CUCHE & VINCENT 484.

[72] *Id.* at 494. For purposes of the availability of the various methods of review, the judgment in the *tierce opposition* is treated as the judgment it replaces.

[73] For a discussion of the history of *requête civile* and of the significance of this history for modern law, see Boyer, *Réflexions sur la requête civile*, 54 REV. TRIM. DR. CIV. 55 (1956); MOREL 500–01; 2 DALLOZ, RÉPERTOIRE DE PROCÉDURE CIVILE ET COMMERCIALE, *Requête Civile*, at Nos. 5–8 (1956).

[74] See 10.11 *infra*.

[75] See 10.13–10.14 *infra*.

the distinction between *pourvoi* and *requête civile*. According to some authors, the characteristic feature of *requête civile* is that it serves to remedy unintentional mistakes made by judges. However, this criterion does not always furnish a safe basis for distinction. [76]

## 10.10. Judgments that May Be Reviewed by *Requête Civile*

Only judgments *en dernier ressort* – that is, judgments not subject to appeal (*appel*) – may be reviewed on *requête civile*. [77] If a judgment was at any time reviewable by appeal, *requête civile* is excluded even after the time for an appeal has expired. [78] It is, however, usually of no significance which court rendered the judgment. Decisions of *tribunaux d'instance, tribunaux de grande instance,* commercial courts, and *cours d'appel,* if they are not appealable, are all subject to attack by *requête civile*. [79] Only decisions by the *Cour de Cassation* are excluded. [80]

*Requête civile* is also unavailable against awards of arbitrators if the parties, in their submission, waived all resort to the courts for review of the award. [81] Whether decisions of a judge sitting *en référé* may be reviewed by *requête civile* is controverted. According to the prevailing opinion, they may not. [82]

Default judgments, as well as judgments in contested cases, are subject to *requête civile*. The availability of *opposition* does not render

[76] *E.g.*, 6 GARSONNET & CÉZAR-BRU 782; MOREL 500. The increasing scope of *pourvoi* to the *Cour de Cassation* has restricted *requête civile*. On proposals for reform of *requête civile* that would clarify the relationship of that remedy to *pourvoi* and reduce the number of formalities, see 2 DALLOZ, *op. cit. supra* note 73, at No. 9.

[77] CODE DE PROCÉDURE CIVILE art. 480.

[78] Cie d'assurances La Participation v. Soc. des ateliers de construction d'Epluches, Cass. Civ., Nov. 27, 1952, [1953] D.J. 91 (judgment which was appealable not subject to *requête civile* even if parties lost right to appeal by failing to file timely notice of appeal or by some other contingency); Goffi v. Dame veuve Goffi, Cass. Civ., March 24, 1930, [1930] D.H. 285. The rules determining when a judgment is non-appealable for purposes of *pourvoi* to the *Cour de Cassation* also determine when a judgment is non-appealable for purposes of *requête civile*. 6 GARSONNET & CÉZAR-BRU 777. On these rules, see 9.04 *supra*.

[79] As a practical matter, *requête civile* will most often be used against decisions of *cours d' appel*, as these are never subject to *appel*. Judgments of the *tribunaux de grande instance* are almost always subject to appeal, and judgments of other lower courts are subject to appeal in most instances when the amount in controversy or the nature of the litigation is of any significance. See 8.04 *supra*.

[80] 2 DALLOZ, *op. cit. supra* note 73, at No. 204; MOREL 479.

[81] However, mere waiver of the right to appeal from an arbitral award does not waive the right to attack it by *requête civile*; there must be waiver of all remedies. 2 DALLOZ, *op. cit. supra* note 73, at No. 188. On the availability of *requête civile* in arbitration cases, see 11.11.c *infra*.

[82] *E.g.*, Epoux Demaniez v. Lemaître, Cour Paris, Nov. 12, 1951, [1951] D.J. 720 (no need for *requête civile* in case of *référé* decisions since they do not prejudge the merits and always involve urgent matters that cannot stand the slow pace of *requête civile*); Barrès-Laffite v. Ass. locataires de la résidence de Neuilly, Cour Paris, June 6, 1957, [1957] D. SOMM. 128; MOREL 479.

*requête civile* unavailable; however, *requête civile* cannot be used until the time for *opposition* has expired. [83]

## 10.11. Grounds for *Requête Civile*

*Requête civile* is available in only three cases: (1) when a party has been guilty of fraudulent or otherwise improper conduct, (2) when a procedural error has been committed, and (3) when a person belonging to specified privileged groups, which include infants, incompetents, and public bodies, has not been properly represented. [84]

**a. Improper conduct by a party.** Three types of misconduct of one's opponent may form the basis for attack by *requête civile,* if the misconduct was not discovered until after the judgment was rendered.

First, *requête civile* is always available in case of *dol* (fraud). [85] Fraud includes subornation of perjury, bribing an opponent's attorney, and intercepting an opponent's correspondence. [86] It is not quite clear to what extent mere silence may amount to fraud. [87] Whether there is fraud is usually a question of fact. *Requête civile* is not available unless the fraud had a substantial effect on the outcome of the case [88] and constituted intentional misconduct. [89]

Second, *requête civile* is also available if a party to the litigation held back a decisive document which was recovered by the other side after rendition of the judgment. [90] The party bringing *requête civile* must have been either unaware of the existence of the document before the judgment was rendered or prevented from obtaining it as a result of the absence of disclosure devices. [91] Thus, a party who does not make a decisive document available to his opponent runs the risk that the judgment to be obtained by it will later be attacked by *requête civile.*

[83] Code de Procédure Civile art. 480; Cuche & Vincent 496. Of course, default judgments must also be in last resort.

[84] Morel 502–04; Cuche & Vincent 497.

[85] Code de Procédure Civile art. 489(1).

[86] 2 Dalloz, *op. cit. supra* note 73, at Nos. 16–17; 6 Garsonnet & Cézar-Bru 783–84 (both sources listing several additional examples).

[87] *E.g.*, F. v. Dame G., Cour Pau, Oct. 27, 1953, [1954] D. Somm. 24 (even silence may be fraud); Dame Riff v. Lang, Cour Nancy, Feb. 11, 1952, [1952] D. Somm. 64 (*requête civile* available in divorce action in which plaintiff husband had covered up his own adultery). *But see* Coasne v. Klein, Cour Paris, June 5, 1946, [1946] D.J. 331 (note Lebon) (in action for wrongful death of wife, *requête civile* may not be based on failure of plaintiff husband to disclose his remarriage, since he may not have known whether this had any legal significance).

[88] 6 Garsonnet & Cézar-Bru 786–87.

[89] Coasne v. Klein, *supra* note 87.

[90] Code de Procédure Civile art. 480(10).

[91] 6 Garsonnet & Cézar-Bru 789–91. Concerning the rule *nemo tenetur edere contra seipsum* (nobody is compelled to produce (documents) against himself), see 5.02 n. 6 *supra.*

However, the risk is fairly small. *Requête civile* is available only if the document in question actually comes into the possession of the opponent after judgment. Since production of the document can generally not be compelled and *requête civile* is impossible unless the document is in the physical possession of the party instituting *requête civile*, [92] it does not help a party at all merely to learn that his opponent has withheld a decisive document.

Third, *requête civile* may be based on forgery. The forged document must have had a substantial influence on the outcome of the action, [93] but the forgery need not have been committed by one of the parties. However, the forgery must be established by an admission or by a civil or criminal judgment. [94] A mere allegation that a forged document was used is not sufficient. [95] The admission or the judgment establishing the forgery must have occurred after rendition of the judgment to be attacked.

**b. Procedural error.** The *Code de Procédure Civile* permits recourse to *requête civile* whenever a rule of form "prescribed on pain of nullity" has been violated and the parties have not waived their right to object. [96] The criteria used to determine what procedural rules are prescribed on pain of nullity are similar to those employed in determining when *pourvoi* to the *Cour de Cassation* for procedural error is possible. [97]

Unfortunately, since it is not always clear which remedy must be used, the availability of both *pourvoi* and *requête civile* as a remedy for procedural error has led to confusion. *Pourvoi* is the only proper method of review whenever it is specifically prescribed by statute. [98] In addition, *pourvoi* is the proper remedy whenever the judgment attacked suffers from an error of substantive law as well as a purely procedural error. [99] The *Cour de Cassation* has tended to increase the scope of *pour-*

[92] 2 DALLOZ, *op. cit. supra* note 73, at Nos. 41–49. *Requête civile* is available only if the document in question was retained by a party or the agent of a party until after judgment; the discovery of a document in the hands of a third person is no basis for *requête civile*.

[93] Veuve Guérin v. Epoux Bourdeleau, Cass. Civ., Jan. 16, 1958, [1958] D. SOMM. 56.

[94] CODE DE PROCÉDURE CIVILE art. 480(9); 6 GARSONNET & CÉZAR-BRU 787–89. For this purpose, the criminal conviction of the forger between the date the judgment under attack was rendered and the date on which *requête civile* was instituted will suffice.

[95] 2 DALLOZ, *op. cit. supra* note 73, at No. 57.

[96] CODE DE PROCÉDURE CIVILE art. 480(2).

[97] See 9.09 *supra*.

[98] See 9.09 *supra*. *Pourvoi* to the *Cour de Cassation* is the only remedy if the judgment was not rendered by the required number of judges, if one judge did not participate in all hearings of the case, if the judgment was not rendered in public, or if the judgment contains no opinion (*motifs*).

[99] *E.g.*, CUCHE & VINCENT 403.

*voi* further by sometimes construing a procedural into a substantive error. [100] However, when there is neither a specific statutory basis for using *pourvoi* nor an error of substantive law, the choice between *pourvoi* and *requête civile* is more difficult. It has been said that *requête civile* must be used if the error was committed by the parties and *pourvoi* if the error was committed by the court, or that *requête civile* is to be used in case of involuntary errors of the court and *pourvoi* in the case of voluntary errors. However, neither of these criteria can account for all the cases. [101]

*Requête civile* is also available when the judgment attacked grants what was not demanded in the pleadings [102] or goes beyond what was demanded in the pleadings. [103] In both instances, the judgment is characterized as being *ultra petita*. The determinative pleadings are the last pleadings that put the case *en état* (at issue).

A judgment is *ultra petita* if it awards damages to a workman under workmen's compensation legislation though the plaintiff demanded compensation under laws relating to occupational diseases, [104] or if it awards interest while none had been demanded, or if it awards damages higher than those demanded. [105] Further, although a court may raise on its own motion issues that involve strong public policy (*ordre public*), [106] *ordre public* may not be used by the court as a pretext to completely modify the plaintiff's claim; [107] if it does, it acts *ultra petita*. A court may grant something impliedly comprised within the plaintiff's pleadings; for instance, it may refuse to adjudge the plaintiff owner of a certain lot, but award him an easement of right of way, or in an annulment action it may state that a void marriage is at least "putatively" valid, even

[100] *E.g.*, Delacour v. Ecole normale sociale, Cass. Com., Dec. 7, 1954, [1955] D.J. 110 (extensive note Crémieu) (Code Civil art. 1134 stating that contracts are binding on parties if lawfully made used to construe error of law); Boyer, *supra* note 73, at 64–67.

[101] Voluntary error as used in this connection refers to an erroneous ruling made by a judge in the belief that the ruling was correct; involuntary error to a matter not brought to the attention of the court. *Cf.* 2 Dalloz, *op. cit. supra* note 73, at Nos. 82–86; Morel 503. As a practical matter, procedural error will not be available very often as a basis for *requête civile* since in a contested case the error is waived if not raised as soon as possible, and, if raised at once, the error is likely to be considered a conscious one (since the judges' attention was specifically drawn to it), thus making *pourvoi* rather than *requête civile* the proper means of attack.

[102] Code de Procédure Civile 430(3).

[103] Code de Procédure Civile art. 480(4).

[104] Caisse primaire de sécurité sociale de Paris v. Jamin, Cass. Soc., July 16, 1953, [1953] D.J. 633.

[105] 2 Dalloz, *op. cit. supra* note 73, at Nos. 109–14.

[106] *Cf.* Code de Procédure Civile art. 171 (court may raise the defense of lack of subject matter competence on its own motion when criminal or administrative court would be competent, in questions involving personal status, and in some other matters).

[107] Delort v. Rougier, Cass. Soc., March 18, 1955, [1956] D. Somm. 73.

though the parties' pleadings did not refer to this point.[108] It is generally assumed that in cases of *ultra petita*, unless the judgment under attack is also based on a substantive error, *requête civile* rather than *pourvoi* is the correct remedy.[109]

*Requête civile* is further available when the court has failed to deal with one of the claims (or defenses) presented by the parties.[110] This occurs, for example, when the court neither grants nor denies costs, though they have been demanded, or completely ignores a request for alimony *pendente lite* in a matrimonial action.[111] However, it is sufficient if the court grants or denies a claim (or defense) by implication.[112]

In those cases in which the files must be "communicated" to the *ministère public*, *requête civile* is also available if there was a failure to comply with that requirement.[113] It may be instituted by any losing party whenever the "communication" is required in the public interest; if it is required only in the interest of a private party, only the party for whose benefit the requirement exists may institute the proceeding.[114]

*Requête civile* is further the appropriate remedy when a court has rendered two contradictory judgments in the same matter between the same parties and both judgments are in last resort.[115] However, a *pourvoi* to the *Cour de Cassation* must be used if the two judgments have been rendered by two different courts.[116] The contradiction must be in the decretal part of the judgments, not merely in the opinions.[117]

[108] 2 DALLOZ, *op. cit. supra* note 73, at No. 104; Hanifa bent Benyoucef v. Amar ben Mussa, Trib. Blida, Dec. 31, 1931, [1932] D. 2. 113 (by holding marriage to be at least a putative marriage, the court was able to avoid making the children of the void marriage illegitimate).

[109] *Cf.* Delacour v. Ecole normale sociale, *supra* note 100. *Pourvoi* is also the proper remedy if the opinion is defective (*défaut de motifs*).

[110] CODE DE PROCÉDURE CIVILE art. 480(5).

[111] 2 DALLOZ, *op. cit. supra* note 73, at Nos. 134–35.

[112] *E.g.*, 6 GARSONNET & CÉZAR-BRU 769–97. The court must deal separately only with claims and defenses as such; it has no obligation to dispose of all arguments raised in support of a claim or defense. Furthermore, *requête civile* is the proper remedy only if there is no reference to a claim or defense in the decretal part of the decision; absence of discussion in the opinion (*défaut de motifs*) is a basis for *pourvoi* to the *Cour de Cassation*. See 9.09 *supra*.

[113] CODE DE PROCÉDURE CIVILE art. 480(8).

[114] 2 DALLOZ, *op. cit. supra* note 73, at Nos. 175–79. If, instead of merely neglecting to communicate the file to the *ministère public*, a party litigated as to whether communication was necessary, there would have been an error of law, and *pourvoi* to the *Cour de Cassation* would have been the proper remedy. *Id.* at 180. On *communication* to the *ministère public*, see 3.09 *supra*.

[115] CODE DE PROCÉDURE CIVILE art. 480(6).

[116] CODE DE PROCÉDURE CIVILE art. 504.

[117] *E.g.*, Veuve Duhaux v. Soc. nautique de Bayonne, Cour Pau, Jan. 2, 1952, [1952] D.J. 119.

Under the same circumstances, *requête civile* is also possible when a judgment contains several parts that contradict each other. [118]

**c. Inadequate representation of minors, incompetents, and public bodies.** Minors, persons judicially declared incompetents (*interdits*), and the French state and its subdivisions may bring *requête civile* if they were improperly represented in the action in which the judgment attacked was rendered. [119] There is improper representation whenever the rules governing proceedings by minors, incompetents, and persons similarly situated have not been followed. The courts have sometimes gone further and permitted *requête civile* when the person acting on behalf of an infant, incompetent, or the government was properly appointed but failed to raise a decisive issue of fact or law, or, by failing to act in time, permitted a default judgment to be entered. [120]

### 10.12. Time within which *Requête Civile* Must Be Instituted

In case of adult parties, *requête civile* must ordinarily be instituted within two months from the day on which the judgment to be reviewed was served. [121] In case of minors, this period begins to run only after re-service of the judgment after they have attained their majority. [122] An analogous rule applies to incompetents. [123] Persons residing outside of France are granted the usual extensions. [124] The rules determing when the time to appeal starts to run also determine when the running of the time for *requête civile* commences. [125] If a party dies while the two-month period is running, the period is tolled until the judgment is served again on his heirs. [126]

These time periods may be extended considerably when *requête civile*

[118] CODE DE PROCÉDURE CIVILE art. 480(7).

[119] CODE DE PROCÉDURE CIVILE art. 481.

[120] 6 GARSONNET & CÉZAR-BRU 792–94. On the family council, see AMOS & WALTON, INTRODUCTION TO FRENCH LAW 82–83 (2d ed. 1963).

[121] CODE DE PROCÉDURE CIVILE art. 483. The two-month period runs only against the party on whom the judgment was served, not against the party who served the judgment; in case of *requête civile*, the old rule that one cannot preclude oneself (*nul ne se forclôt soi-même*) still persists.

[122] CODE DE PROCÉDURE CIVILE art. 484.

[123] 2 DALLOZ, *op. cit. supra* note 73, at No. 227.

[124] Persons residing outside France but elsewhere in Europe have one additional month; persons residing in other parts of the world have two additional months. CODE DE PROCÉDURE CIVILE arts. 483, 1033–3.

[125] CODE DE PROCÉDURE CIVILE art. 483. See 8.07 *supra*.

[126] CODE DE PROCÉDURE CIVILE arts. 487, 447. Actually, time does not begin to run again until two weeks after service on the heirs. In all events, however, the heirs have at least "three months and forty days" from the date of death. For the analogous rule applicable to the appeal period, see 8.08 *supra*.

is based on the improper conduct of a party. In case of fraud or of forgery or decisive withheld documents discovered after rendition of the judgment, time for *requête civile* does not usually begin to run until discovery of the fraud or forgery or the recovery of the document.[127] If the fraud or forgery results in a criminal conviction, time begins to run only on the date of the conviction. [128] There must, in any event, be written proof of the date on which the fraud was discovered or the document recovered, but the courts are quite liberal in determining what constitutes written proof. [129] If *requête civile* is based on inconsistent judgments in the same court, the time for initiating it begins to run upon service of the second judgment. [130]

### 10.13. Manner in which *Requête Civile* is Instituted

A party wishing to institute a *requête civile* proceeding must meet the usual requirements concerning procedural capacity and interest, and must have been a party to, or at least have been "represented," in the proceeding to be reviewed. In all these respects, the rules governing *pourvois* to the *Cour de Cassation* apply. [131]

The *requête civile* procedure is cumbersome. First, a written opinion must be obtained, signed by three *avocats* who have practiced for at least ten years in the district (*ressort*) of the *cour d'appel* in which the proceeding is initiated. In the opinion, the *avocats* must indicate the grounds on which the *requête civile* is based and state why they believe it will be successful. Only the grounds mentioned in the opinion may later be relied upon. [132] The sum of 3 francs (about $ 0.60) must be deposited in court as security for the fine which is imposed if the proceeding is unsuccessful, and the sum of 1.50 francs (about $ 0.30) must be deposited as security for any judgment for damages. [133] These requirements were designed to discourage rash *requête civile* proceedings, but the sums are now so small that they lack significant deterrent effect.

Ordinarily, *requête civile* is commenced by service of an *ajourne-*

[127] Code de Procédure Civile art. 488; Vernet v. Telesphore, Cass. Civ., May 23, 1957, [1957] D.J. 481.

[128] *E.g.*, Gervais v. Société Les Enterprises Langlois-Murray, Cass. Com., June 11, 1951, [1951] D.J. 546 (with note indicating that there is some authority *contra*).

[129] Code de Procédure Civile art. 488; Morel 505; 2 Dalloz, *op. cit. supra* note 73, at Nos. 230–37 (all kinds of writings usable as proof of date, even if gross hearsay).

[130] Code de Procédure Civile art. 489.

[131] 6 Garsonnet & Cézar-Bru 777; *cf.* 9.14 *supra*.

[132] Code de Procédure Civile arts. 495, 499.

[133] Code de Procédure Civile art. 494. On the ultimate disposition of these deposits, see 10.14 *infra*.

*ment* [134] and copies of the opinion by the three *avocats* and the receipt for the deposits. [135] Traditionally, French attorneys obtain an *ex parte* order from the presiding judge of the court authorizing commencement of the *requête civile* before the *ajournement* is served. However, there is no statutory requirement for such an order. [136]

If the *requête civile* is brought within six months from the time the judgment under attack was rendered, it is not served on the party himself, as in a regular civil case, but on his *avoué*. After that date, there must be service on adverse parties, either personally or at their domicile. [137]

*Requête civile* is always instituted in the same court that rendered the judgment; it may be heard by the same or different judges. [138] However, in arbitration cases, if the right to *requête civile* is not waived, the proceeding is initiated in the court that would be competent to hear an appeal from the arbitrators' decision. [139]

*Requête civile* does not automatically stay execution of the judgment attacked, nor do the courts have the power to grant a stay. A person against whom a judgment of eviction has been rendered must even show that he has quit the premises before he may initiate a *requête civile*. [140]

### 10.14. The Two Phases of the Procedure: *Rescindant* and *Rescisoire*

After service of the *ajournement*, the *requête civile* generally proceeds

[134] Code de Procédure Civile art. 483. In the somewhat unusual case of a party who is faced with litigation in which an earlier judgment is used against him and who wishes to overcome the effect of that judgment by *requête civile*, ordinary *conclusions* (pleadings) are sufficient if the judgment to be attacked was rendered by the court in which the present proceedings are pending. Such a *requête civile* is called *requête civile incidente*. Code de Procédure Civile art. 493.

[135] Code de Procédure Civile art. 495.

[136] Morel 506; 2 Dalloz, *op. cit. supra* note 73, at No. 254. Such a petition was, however, required in the pre-revolutionary law.

[137] Code de Procédure Civile art. 492. If the *avoué* is served within the six-month period, he automatically continues to represent his client without any need for a new authorization or appearance. Code de Procédure Civile art. 496.

[138] Code de Procédure Civile art. 490. Even *requête civile incidente* is not instituted in the court in which the new proceeding is pending, but in the court that rendered the orginal judgment. Code de Procédure Civile art. 491. The court in which the current action is pending may stay its proceedings. See note 134 *supra*.

[139] Code de Procédure Civile art. 1026. The right to *requête civile* is often waived in arbitration cases.

[140] Code de Procédure Civile art. 497. However, if a judgment is attacked by *requête civile*, a person levying execution pursuant to the judgment acts at his peril; if the judgment is later declared void, he must return everything recovered by him. The rule that *requête civile* does not stay execution has a few exceptions: A stay occurs, if the judgment contains contradictions, if there are two contradictory judgments in the same court, or if the action is one for divorce or separation. 6 Garsonnet & Cézar-Bru 829.

as does an ordinary civil action in the court in which it is pending.[141] There are only two differences: (1) the procedure is divided into two phases, called *rescindant* and *rescisoire,* and (2) the files of the case must always be communicated to the *ministère public.*[142]

During the *rescindant* phase, the court decides whether the judgment under attack is void for the reason alleged and, in the affirmative case, renders judgment accordingly. The deposits for the fine and damages are ordered returned, and the restitution is ordered of anything recovered by the prevailing party under the judgment declared void.[143] The case then enters into the second or *rescisoire* phase, in which it is adjudicated *de novo.*[144]

If the court decides at the end of the *rescindant* phase that the judgment under attack is not subject to any infirmity, it renders a judgment against the person who instituted the *requête civile.* The deposit for the fine to the state and the deposit for damages are declared forfeited,[145] and the losing party is ordered to pay costs. If it finds that the *requête civile* was brought in bad faith and caused prejudice, the court may order payment of damages exceeding the minimal amount covered by the deposit.[146]

The two-phase procedure is not used when *requête civile* is based on the inconsistency of two judgments rendered by the same court, in which case the second judgment is simply annulled at the end of the *rescindant* procedure and the first judgment remains in full force and effect.[147] In other situations, this division must, however, be observed unless both parties, by covering both points in their pleadings, agree to simultaneous determination of both the validity of the judgment under attack and the merits.[148]

[141] The regular, not the summary, procedure must always be used during the *rescindant* phase. 2 DALLOZ, *op. cit. supra* note 73, at No. 283.

[142] *E.g.,* CUCHE & VINCENT 501 (two phases); CODE DE PROCÉDURE CIVILE art. 498 (*communication* to *ministère public*).

[143] CODE DE PROCÉDURE CIVILE art. 501. The duty to make restitution arises immediately upon the judgment determining the *rescindant* phase. The final outcome on the merits in the *rescisoire* phase is quite immaterial.

[144] During the second (*rescisoire*) phase, the same procedure is used in the original action; *communication* to the *ministère public* is necessary only if it was required in the original action. Before the *rescisoire* phase may be started, the judgment determining the *rescindant* phase must first be served on the losing side. 2 DALLOZ, *op. cit. supra* note 73, at Nos. 308–13. The loser on the *rescisoire* phase must pay costs, but these do not include the costs of the *rescindant* procedure.

[145] CODE DE PROCÉDURE CIVILE art. 500.

[146] CODE DE PROCÉDURE CIVILE art. 494; 2 DALLOZ, *op. cit. supra* note 73, at No. 297. For example, there may be lack of good faith if the party instituting *requête civile,* though knowing that his opponent obtained only what was lawfully his, accuses him of bad faith.

[147] CODE DE PROCÉDURE CIVILE art. 501.

[148] *E.g.,* MOREL 506. Combining the two phases of the procedure without the express or implied consent of both parties normally constitutes reversible error.

Division of the procedure into two phases may also be unnecessary if the issue determining the outcome of the *rescindant* phase of necessity determines the case on the merits. [149] Because it is often difficult to distinguish between the validity of a judgment as such and its correctness on the merits, some authors have suggested that the *rescindant* and *rescisoire* phase be combined in all cases.

## 10.15. Review of Judgments Rendered in *Requête Civile*

*Requête civile* may not be instituted a second time against the same judgment, even if it is based on different grounds, nor may *requête civile* be instituted against a judgment rendered in a *requête civile* proceeding. [150] A judgment rendered on *requête civile,* while not subject to appeal, [151] is reviewable by the *Cour de Cassation.* If rendered by default, it may be attacked by *opposition*; it is also subject to attack by *tierce opposition.* [152]

[149] For instance, if in an action on a note plaintiff prevails and defendant later attacks the judgment by *requête civile,* alleging the note to be a forgery, a decision in the *rescindant* phase declaring the note to be forged and annulling the judgment practically makes readjudication of the merits unnecessary since the only basis for plaintiff's cause of action, the note, has already been declared to be a nullity. *Cf.* F. v. Dame G., Cour Pau, Oct. 27, 1953, [1954] D. Somm. 24.

[150] Code de Procédure Civile art. 503. An *avoué* who disregards this rule – sometimes stated as *requête civile sur requête civile ne vaut* – may be liable for damages. The party against whom a *requête civile* was directed may, however, bring a new one if the issues are not foreclosed. 6 Garsonnet & Cézar-Bru 826–27.

[151] This is so, because *requête civile* is possible only against judgments not subject to appeal and the judgment on *requête civile* replaces the judgment attacked. Cie d'assurances La Participation v. Soc. des ateliers de construction d' Epluches, *supra* note 78.

[152] See generally 6 Garsonnet & Cézar-Bru 838–39; 2 Dalloz, *op. cit. supra* note 73, at Nos. 330–35; Morel 506.

CHAPTER 11

# SPECIAL PROCEEDINGS

This chapter describes summary proceedings (11.01), special procedures for the collection of small claims (11.02), proceedings in the *chambre du conseil* (11.03), procedure in divorce and separation cases (11.04), and arbitration (11.05–11.11).

## 11.01. Summary Proceedings before the *Tribunal de Grande Instance*

Summary proceedings for the determination of minor or uncomplicated claims have been in use in France since an early date and were continued by the *Code de Procédure Civile*. Originally, these proceedings were faster and less expensive than the regular proceedings before the *tribunal civil,* forerunner of the *tribunal de grande instance.* However, in the course of time, many of the existing differences between the two procedures were abolished. Because the differences between summary and regular proceedings had become attenuated, the 1955 draft of a revised Code of Civil Procedure omitted summary proceedings completely. [1] The 1958 reform legislation did not abolish summary proceedings, but, by unifying the *enquête* procedure, it eliminated their last major distinguishing feature. [2] Since the remaining differences between summary and regular procedure are of minor importance and since there now exists an even more expeditious procedure for the collection of small claims, summary proceedings are discussed only briefly.

**a. Availability.** Article 404 of the *Code de Procédure Civile* specifies five situations in which summary proceedings must be used.

[1] On the history of the summary procedure, see 2 Dalloz, Répertoire de Procédure Civile et Commerciale, *Procédure Sommaire,* Nos. 2–4 (1956). At the time of the enactment of the *Code de Procédure Civile,* summary procedures were distinguished from regular proceedings in that: (1) the written appointment procedure (which eventually fell into disuse and was abolished) could not be used; (2) witnesses were heard before the full court, not before a delegated judge; and (3) costs were less.

[2] See Décret No. 58–1289 of Dec. 22, 1958, J.O. Dec. 23, 1958, p. 11608, [1959] D.L. 45 (with Minister's Report at [1959] D.L. 335).

First, appeals from the *tribunaux d'instance* (formerly *juges de paix*) must be conducted in the manner prescribed for summary proceedings. These appeals, until 1958 brought before the regular courts of first instance, are presently instituted before the *cours d'appel*. Presumably, notwithstanding this change, the *cours d'appel* must use the summary procedure when hearing these appeals. [3]

Second, "pure personal claims based on an uncontested title" must be asserted in summary proceedings. The phrase quoted includes mainly contract claims based on a written instrument. There is some dispute as to the precise meaning of the term "uncontested title." According to one view, it requires that the authenticity of the written instrument not be contested, but does not prevent the presence of other issues. However, the majority view is that the summary procedure becomes unavailable whenever there is a dispute involving the basic elements of the transaction, such as capacity of the parties to contract or absence of fraud or duress. [4]

Third, "personal" claims involving less than 10 francs, whether or not based on a written instrument, must be pursued in summary proceedings. This rule is obsolete since small claims presently fall within the competence of the *tribunal d'instance*. [5]

Fourth, all provisional matters and matters requiring speed are handled in summary proceedings. The courts have wide discretion in deciding what matters require speed. [6] Included are applications for

[3] CUCHE & VINCENT 359; 2 DALLOZ, *op. cit. supra* note 1, SUPP. 1962, at No. 8. Appeals from the rural lease courts and labor courts must likewise be heard in a summary fashion by the *cour d'appel*; in these cases, no *avoué* need be appointed. See 2 DALLOZ, *op. cit. supra* note 1, SUPP. 1962, at No. 25–2 (in this paragraph, the numbers in the text correspond to the subdivisions of art. 404).

[4] MOREL 372; CUCHE & VINCENT 359. According to the majority view, summary proceedings may be used in disputes as to minor matters, such as the rate of interest or the due date, but not otherwise.

[5] Subdivision 3 of article 404 was usually interpreted broadly to apply to all in personam claims brought before the *tribunal civil* in which no appeal to the *cour d'appel* was possible because of the smallness of the amount involved; this amounted in practice to an upwards adjustment of the sum of 10 francs (1000 old francs) whenever the limits for appeal were raised. See MOREL 372. Since the 1958 reform in judicial organization, substantially all in personam claims that the *tribunal de grande instance* may hear are subject to appeal to the *cour d'appel*; claims for less than 3000 francs ordinarily fall within the competence of the *tribunal d'instance* and appeals to the *cour d'appel* are open for claims over 1500 francs. Subdivision 3 is thus obsolete even if, as suggested by CUCHE & VINCENT at 359, it is assumed that the 10 francs limit has by implication been changed to 1500 francs, see DALLOZ, RÉPERTOIRE DE PROCÉDURE CIVILE ET COMMERCIALE, *Compétence des Tribunaux de Grande Instance* No. 7 (Supp. 1962). The summary procedure is not applicable in proceedings before the *tribunal d'instance*, which are handled even more expeditiously.

[6] See MOREL 372; CUCHE & VINCENT 359. French law makes no formal distinction between actions and motions. The summary procedures may sometimes be used to handle an interlocutory application in an ordinary action.

alimony *pendente lite,* [7] suits involving attempts by parents to block the marriage of children, [8] and proceedings to obtain the cancellation of attachments. A court order shortening the defendant's time to appear does not automatically amount to a determination that the summary procedure must be used because speed is required. [9]

Fifth, summary proceedings must be used to adjudicate all actions for rent due, unless they fall within the competence of the rural lease court or *tribunal d'instance.*

Some statutes other than article 404 of the *Code de Procédure Civile* provide that specified matters must be handled "summarily" or by "summary procedure." It is not always clear whether these provisions require the use of the summary procedure or amount merely to an exhortation to the courts to proceed with dispatch. [10] However, the summary procedure does seem applicable in actions for a partition, [11] in actions by third parties to dissolve attachments on goods allegedly belonging to them, [12] and in some other cases relating to provisional remedies and execution. [13]

*Tierce opposition,* which enables a person who has not been made a party to an action to demand its reopening if he is affected by the judgment, is never treated as a summary proceeding, even if the original proceeding was summary. [14]

**b. Differences between regular and summary procedure.** The rules concerning the appointment of an *avoué,* the service of the summons, time to appear, costs, and most other matters are the same in summary and regular proceedings. [15] Summary procedure differs from regular

[7] But support proceedings are not to be handled under the summary procedure if a difficult factual question – for instance, a question of filiation – is involved. Texier v. Duvert, Cass. Req., July 26, 1865, [1865] D. 1. 495.

[8] On the procedure (*opposition*) by which parents and sometimes other relatives can temporarily block the marriage of their children and the action to obtain cancellation of this *opposition,* see CODE CIVIL arts. 172–79. Such actions must be determined within ten days. CODE CIVIL art. 177.

[9] 2 DALLOZ, *op. cit. supra* note 1, at Nos. 17–19; *cf.* Richard v. Pelletier, Cass. Req., Nov. 8, 1859, [1859] D. 1. 507 (summary procedure may be used in proceeding to validate garnishment (*action en validité de saisie-arrêt*), since claim of creditor is based on written contract).

[10] CUCHE & VINCENT 360.

[11] CODE CIVIL art. 823 (this applies to partition of a succession by co-heirs).

[12] CODE DE PROCÉDURE CIVILE art. 608.

[13] For a more complete list, see 2 DALLOZ, *op. cit. supra* note 1, at Nos. 21–25. The procedure used for the recovery of the *enregistrement* tax (this is handled by the regular, not the administrative courts) is also somewhat similar to the summary procedure. No appeal is allowed, but *pourvoi* is possible. DALLOZ, RÉPERTOIRE DE PROCEDURE CIVILE ET COMMERCIALE, *Enregistrement et timbre,* at Nos. 110–29 (Supp. 1965).

[14] Leroy v. Le Cornu, Cass. Civ., January 8, 1907, [1907] D. 1. 128.

[15] 2 DALLOZ, *op. cit. supra* note 1, at No. 27.

procedure only in the following particulars: (1) *conclusions* may be filed at any time, and the rule prohibiting new *conclusions* in the ten-day period immediately preceding the hearing (*audience*) is inapplicable; [16] (2) although it is done only in rare cases in which speed is very important, summary proceedings may be heard even during the courts' vacation period; [17] (3) summary proceedings do not have to await their turn on the calendar, but may be handled immediately; [18] (4) costs in summary proceedings are taxed in the final judgment, not in a special proceeding. [19]

An action brought in a summary proceeding when it should have been brought as a regular action, or *vice versa*, is irregular. However, the error cannot be invoked for the first time before the *Cour de Cassation*, nor may the courts rely on it on their own motion. [20]

## 11.02. Special Procedures for the Collection of Small Claims

**a. Collection of small commercial debts and debts based on negotiable instruments.** A special procedure for the collection of small commercial debts was introduced in 1937. It was modeled on a procedure in use in Alsace-Lorraine, where the German *Zivilprozessordnung* had been retained. The 1937 legislation, amended several times in subsequent years, [21] was revised in 1957. [22]

The procedure provided by this legislation is mainly a collection device which offers no particular advantage if the defendant interposes a defense. It may be used for the collection of commercial debts based

[16] *Id.* at No. 29; Morel 373. As to the rule that no more *conclusions* may be filed in the last ten days before the hearing, see Code de Procédure Civile art. 82.

[17] Décret No. 59–1078 of September 11, 1959, J.O. September 16, 1959, p. 9043, [1959] D.L. 595 art. 2; Morel 374; Cuche & Vincent 361. During the vacation period, which lasts from July 15 to September 15, some of the judges of each court are designated by the presiding judge to handle criminal cases and civil cases requiring speed.

[18] Morel 374; 2 Dalloz, *op. cit. supra* note 1, at 29. But even cases which are not summary in nature may now be given what amounts to a preference. Code de Procédure Civile art. 80.

[19] Code de Procédure Civile art. 543.

[20] Morel 374; 2 Dalloz, *op. cit. supra* note 1, Supp. 1962, at No. 5.

[20] Morel 374; 2 Dalloz, *op. cit. supra* note 1, Supp. 1962, at No. 5. But if the point is raised timely, the *Cour de Cassation* will reverse a decision erroneously rendered under the regular rather than the summary procedure. *E.g.*, Fabre v. Rabana, Cass. Civ., June 28, 1932, [1932] D.H. 461.

[21] For a listing of the various laws involved, see 2 Dalloz, Répertoire de Procédure Civile et Commerciale, *Procédure commerciale*, No. 52 (1956). For a description of the corresponding German procedure, see Kaplan, Von Mehren and Schaefer, *Phases of German Civil Procedure*, 71 Harv. L. Rev. 1192, 1265 (1958).

[22] Law No. 57–756 of July 4, 1957, J.O. July 7, 1957, p. 6690, [1957] D.L. 210. The law settled various problems which had arisen under prior legislation. See Delau–Deshayes, *Commentaire de la loi du 4 avril 1957 relativement au recouvrement de certaines créances*, [1957] D.L. 315. The procedures provided by this law for the collection of both civil and commercial debts are optional; a regular action may always be brought instead.

on contract that do not exceed the sum of 2500 francs (approximately $ 500), but is available without limitation as to amount if the debt is based on a promissory note or accepted draft. [23] The debtor must have his domicile or at least a residence in France, and service on him there must be possible. [24] The proceedings must always be brought in the commercial court at the debtor's domicile. An election of domicile clause in a contract has no effect. [25] The proceedings are initiated by a petition (*requête*) addressed to the president of the commercial court indicating the name and address of the debtor and the basis of the claim. Any available relevant documents must be attached. [26] If the president of the court finds the amount demanded to be due, he authorizes the clerk of the court to send an "order to pay" to the debtor; if he rejects the petition, the creditor's only remedy is a regular action against the debtor. The rejection of the petition is not reviewable. [27]

The "order to pay" is sent to the debtor by registered mail, return receipt requested, unless the amount involved is more than 1000 francs, in which case it must be served by an *huissier*. It amounts to a command by the court to pay the debt within two weeks or to file objections within the same period of time if there are defenses to the claim. If no objections are filed during the two-week period, the creditor may ask the president of the court to finally approve the petition. After this has been done, the clerk of the court puts the "executory formula" (authorization to levy execution) on it, thus converting it into a judgment for the sum demanded on which execution may be levied. [28] The creditor can obtain neither a review of this judgment by appeal nor a reopening by *opposition*. [29]

[23] Law of July 4, 1957, *supra* note 22, art. 1. The procedure is available only for money claims. As to the distinction between commercial and other matters and the competence of the commercial courts in general, see 4.39 *supra*. Since article 1 mentions only promissory notes and accepted drafts, claims based on checks cannot be enforced by this procedure.

[24] Law of July 4, 1957, *supra* note 22, art. 4.

[25] If there are several debtor-defendants, the proceeding must be brought at the domicile of one of them. Law of July 4, 1957, *supra* note 22, art. 9.

[26] This petition may either be mailed by registered mail, return receipt requested, to the president of the commercial court or it may be filed by the party or an agent with the clerk (*greffier*) of the commercial court. Law of July 4, 1957, *supra* note 22, art. 2.

[27] The authorization to send out the order to pay is simply noted at the bottom of the petition, which remains on file in the clerk's office during the proceedings. Law of July 4, 1957, *supra* note 22, art. 3.

[28] Law of July 4, 1957, *supra* note 22, art. 5. If the defendant files no objections, final approval of the petition by the president of the commercial court is ordinarily granted as a matter of course. The request for final approval is made by letter.

[29] However, the court may grant a delay. Law of July 4, 1957, *supra* note 22, art. 7. Final approval of the petition must be demanded within six months of the date it has been filed. Law of July 4, 1957, art. 8.

If the debtor wishes to assert defenses, he must file an objection (*contredit*) to the order to pay within two weeks. This is done by a simple letter to the clerk of the court. [30] After receipt of the letter, the clerk summons all parties to a hearing before the commercial court. [31] The court first appoints one of its members to attempt a settlement. If none can be obtained, the case is heard on the merits, in the regular fashion. [32] The debtor may appeal from such a judgment against him; however, if he has failed to appear at the hearing, [33] he may not demand a reopening of the case by *opposition*.

**b. The collection of small civil debts.** The 1957 law which revised the procedure for the collection of small commercial debts also created a very similar procedure for the collection of small civil debts. It may be used for the collection of all civil debts based on contract in which the claim is for a sum of money only, provided the amount is within the competence of the *tribunal d'instance*. [34] Election of domicile clauses in contracts are again inoperative. [35] The debtor must have his domicile, or at least a residence, in France, and service on him there must be possible. [36]

The procedure is substantially similar to that in use before the commercial court. The creditor addresses a petition to the judge of the *tribunal d'instance*. [37] If it is approved, the clerk issues an order to pay to the debtor. If the debtor fails to pay or to raise objection within two weeks, execution may be levied against his property, and neither appeal nor *opposition* are open. If the debtor files objections, the judge of

[30] The letter must be handed, not mailed, to the clerk; the debtor must also deposit court costs, which he recovers if he wins his case. See Law of July 4, 1957, *supra* note 22, art. 6. Reasons for objections to the order to pay may be stated in an informal manner. 2 DALLOZ, *op. cit. supra* note 21, at No. 61.

[31] The parties (including any co-debtors who have not filed objections) are summoned by registered mail, return receipt requested. On the hearing date, the court may not proceed unless it has the return receipts before it. At least eight days' notice must be given of the hearing, more in some cases. Law of July 4, 1957, *supra* note 22, art. 6.

[32] If the debtor files no objections, there is a saving of time and effort, but that advantage over the regular procedure is lost if the debtor files objections.

[33] Law of July 4, 1957, *supra* note 22, art. 6. Of course, appeal to the *cour d'appel* is possible only if the sum involved is more than 1500 francs ($ 300), since no appeal can be filed in in personam actions for a smaller sum. *Cf.* CUCHE & VINCENT, SUPP. 1961, at 20.

[34] Law of July 4, 1957, *supra* note 22, art. 11. This means that the sum demanded must be less than 3000 francs ($ 600), since that is the monetary limit of the competence of the *tribunal d'instance*. See 4.38 *supra*.

[35] Law of July 4, 1957, *supra* note 22, art. 19.

[36] Law of July 4, 1957, *supra* note 22, art. 14.

[37] The petition must be submitted in person or by an agent; it may not be mailed. Law of July 4, 1957, *supra* note 22, art. 12. The petition is similar to that which is submitted to the commercial court for the collection of commercial debts. A denial of the petition is again unreviewable; the creditor must bring an ordinary action.

the *tribunal d'instance* first attempts a settlement and then hears the case on the merits. An appeal from his decision is apparently possible but *opposition* is not. [38] The procedure for the collection of small civil debts, just as the procedure for the collection of small commercial debts, is thus useful mainly when the debtor is unlikely to interpose a defense.

## 11.03. Proceedings in the *Chambre du Conseil*

The term *chambre du conseil* in its literal sense denotes the room to which the judges of a court retire for their deliberations and from which the public is excluded. Even before the Revolution, the courts developed the custom of hearing certain matters, especially *ex parte* applications, in the *chambre du conseil.* Consequently, the term *chambre du conseil* received a secondary meaning – that of a separate part of the court specializing in such matters.

The *Code de Procédure Civile* of 1806 contained no rules governing proceedings in the *chambre du conseil.* Since its general provisions were not always adapted to the special proceedings heard there, a number of uncertainties arose, which became more vexing in the course of time as the number of matters handled in the *chambre du conseil* gradually increased. [39]

Existing uncertainties were partially removed by a Law of July 15, 1944, the first general legislation dealing with procedure in the *chambre du conseil.* [40] The law provided, in accordance with existing tradition, that the *chambre du conseil* was to handle: (1) all matters not involving adversary proceedings falling under the heading of *juridiction gracieuse,* which is also called *juridiction volontaire* and involves mainly applications to obtain court approval for transactions concerning infants, incompetents, decedent's estates, and the like; and (2) all adversary

[38] Law of July 4, 1957, *supra* note 22, arts. 15–19. Since the *tribunal d'instance* is a one-judge court, the attempt at settlement is made by the judge hearing the case, not by a delegated judge as in commercial cases. If an amount of more than 1500 francs, approximately $ 300, (rather than 1000 francs, as in commercial cases) is involved, the order to pay must be served by an *huissier* instead of by registered mail. For a general description of this procedure, see Dalloz, Répertoire de Procédure Civile et Commerciale, *Procédure devant le Tribunal d'Instance,* Nos. 37–2 – 37–10. (Supp. 1962).

[39] See generally 1 Dalloz, *Répertoire de Procédure Civile et Commerciale, Chambre du Conseil,* Nos. 1–5 (1956); Hébraud, *Commentaire, Loi du 15 Juillet 1944,* [1946] D.L. 333. The appealability of non-adversary decisions rendered in the *chambre du conseil* was one of the main points in doubt.

[40] Law of July 15, 1944, on the *Chambre du Conseil,* J.O. July 27, 1944, p. 1902, [1944] D. Anal. L. 82, validated by Ordonnance of October 9, 1945, J.O. October 10, 1945, p. 6375, [1945] D.L. 258. The law is brief and provides only a very general outline for the procedure to be followed.

proceedings as to which a statute expressly provides that they must be conducted in the *chambre du conseil* rather than in open court. [41]

Most proceedings heard in the *chambre du conseil* are within the competence of the *tribunal de grande instance* [42] and, on appeal, of the *cour d'appel*. Consequently, the term *chambre du conseil* in the sense of a specialized part of the court is used principally in connection with these two courts. The judges of every panel or *chambre* of a multi-panel court may hear cases in the *chambre du conseil*, [43] but in the larger courts some specialization is usual; thus, in Paris, *chambre du conseil* matters are ordinarily handled by the judges of the first panel of the *tribunal de grande instance*. [44]

**a. Competence in matters of *juridiction gracieuse*.** The *chambre du conseil* hears all non-adversary proceedings involving the exercise of so-called *juridiction gracieuse* or *volontaire*. Numerous authors have attempted to define this term. [45] The Law of July 15, 1944, also provides a definition. [46] However, none of these definitions is completely

[41] Law of July 15, 1944, *supra* note 40, art. 2.

[42] Most of these concern matters of personal status, such as proceedings relating to infants, incompetents, and similar matters. See 4.37 *supra*.

[43] Law of July 15, 1944, *supra* note 40, art. 1. The law does not state specifically that a member of the *ministère public* must be present when the court is sitting in the *chambre du conseil*, but this seems required since the *ministère public* must be heard in substantially all cases involving the *chambre du conseil*. See 1 DALLOZ, *op. cit. supra* note 39, at No. 9.

[44] Article 1 of the Law of July 15, 1944, which provides that all panels may hear cases in the *chambre du conseil* has been enacted to induce the courts to break with this tradition and assign *chambre du conseil* cases to all their panels (*chambres*). It does not seem to have had much effect, at least not in Paris. It is a subject of theoretical discussion whether a court sitting in the *chambre du conseil* has a separate identity or is merely the ordinary court sitting in a different room. 1 DALLOZ, *op. cit. supra* note 39.

[45] For a description of the various views, see 1 SOLUS & PERROT 448–55. Neither the term *juridiction volontaire* nor the term *juridiction gracieuse* is particularly fortunate. The term *juridiction volontaire* seems to imply that resort to the courts is voluntary when, in fact, it is just as necessary as in the case of ordinary litigation. The term *juridiction gracieuse* implies a discretionary power on the part of the courts to act or not; it is used because the *juridiction gracieuse* of the courts is outside their normal function, the decision of actual cases and controversies. However, courts exercising *juridiction gracieuse* are just as much compelled to render a decision in a matter properly before them as in ordinary litigated cases. On the French term *juridiction*, see 4.01 *supra*. Before 1944, the courts, in cases of doubt, in order to make appeals available, were inclined to classify proceedings as ordinary litigation rather than as proceedings of *juridiction gracieuse*, in which the appealability of decisions rendered was contested. 1 SOLUS & PERROT 447; Hébraud, *supra* note 39, at 336. Since 1944, all such decisions are appealable.

[46] The term *juridiction gracieuse*, as used in the Law of July 15, 1944, *supra* note 40, art. 2, embraces: (1) all matters in which there is no adversary and in which there can be no objection by third parties, and (2) all matters in which the parties are not in disagreement but are required by law to obtain a court decision. Even this definition is not complete. Some matters included within *juridiction gracieuse* affect the interests of third parties who are authorized to intervene. On the other hand, certain matters, such as collusive divorces, when the parties are in *de facto* agreement, have always been considered as true adversary proceedings. See Hébraud, *supra* note 39, at 335, 336. In order to avoid potential future liability, parties some-

satisfactory. The scope of *juridiction gracieuse* can probably best be gathered from a listing of the more important matters it covers. [47]

Resort to the *juridiction gracieuse* of the courts is often necessary in matters involving infants. Thus, the guardian of a minor may not incur a debt on behalf of the minor or mortgage or sell his real property, unless the family council has authorized him to do so and this decision has been approved by the court. [48] The same rule is applicable in the case of compromises of causes of action belonging to minors. [49] The court must likewise approve all adoptions. [50] Emancipations of minors must take place before the court, but there is no power of disapproval.[51] Sometimes, proceedings for the appointment of a committee for an incompetent are also considered part of the *juridiction gracieuse* of the courts; [52] the committee is subject to court supervision to the same extent as the guardian of an incompetent. [53]

*Ex parte* applications may be necessary under the rules relating to matrimonial property. Frequently, one spouse may dispose of property only with the consent of the other. If it is physically impossible to obtain consent, an application may be made to the court to authorize the contemplated transaction. [54] Court approval is always required for the sale of so-called dotal property, even if both spouses agree. [55] In the

times seek court approval for a transaction though such approval is not required by law. In such cases, approval is usually not granted. See, *e.g.*, Dame Lemarié, Trib. Rouen, Sept. 12, 1944, [1945] D.J. 196.

[47] In the cases listed in the text, court approval is usually required to safeguard the interests of infants, incompetents, or others not or not well able to protect themselves. However, sometimes, such as in emancipations, the court intervenes merely to give a matter greater solemnity and to provide a permanent record. On occasion, *juridiction gracieuse* involves a limited power to dispense from the operation of certain rules of law when their observance is difficult or impossible.

[48] Code Civil arts. 457–58.

[49] Code Civil art. 467. Since 1965, court approval is unnecessary.

[50] Code Civil arts. 353, 355. The same applies to the so-called *légitimation adoptive*. Code Civil art. 369. Although adoption is not necessarily restricted to minors, *légitimation adoptive* is.

[51] Code Civil art. 477. A declaration of emancipation of a minor is made before the *tribunal d'instance* rather than the *tribunal de grande instance*, which is ordinarily competent in matters of *juridiction gracieuse*.

[52] Since the incompetent is really the defendant, this is more doubtful, especially if the incompetent is able to take part in the proceedings. See Code Civil arts. 489–501.

[53] Code Civil art. 509. He must obtain the approval of the court sitting *en chambre du conseil* for the transactions described in the text at notes 48 and 49 *supra*. Dowries and marriage contracts of children of incompetents are also subject to court approval. Code Civil art. 511.

[54] Code Civil art. 217; *cf.* Code Civil art. 219 (court may authorize one spouse to represent other in matters affecting matrimonial property).

[55] Code Civil art. 1558; Code Civil art. 1559 (exchange of dotal property); Code Civil art. 1557 (use of dotal property if manner provided in marriage contract becomes impossible). Dotal property is property settled upon the husband, usually by the father of the bride, for the life of the marriage. The husband has the use and income of the property. Some of these rules have been changed by the 1965 reforms.

field of public records, which is minutely regulated, [56] an *ex parte* application is necessary to obtain a correction of erroneous birth, death, and marriage records. [57] If a person has died under circumstances making the issuance of a death certificate impossible, a declaration of death, which takes the place of such a certificate, may be obtained from the courts. [58]

In the area of succession, the *Code Civil* provides that every holographic will must be presented to the presiding judge of the local *tribunal de grande instance*, opened by him, and given to a *notaire* of his choice. [59] In some cases, court approval is also required before a person may take possession of an inheritance. [60] In certain instances, even if all parties agree, [61] court approval must be obtained for the partition of estate property among co-heirs.

Although some authors state that *ex parte* applications made in connection with pending or prospective litigation, such as requests for an attachment or other provisional remedy, also fall within the *juridiction gracieuse* of the courts, this view has not remained uncontested. [62] Furthermore, applications for such incidental relief are ordinarily governed by detailed special provisions in the *Code de Procédure Civile*, not by the Law of July 15, 1944, on the *chambre du conseil*. [63]

**b. Procedure in matters of *juridiction gracieuse*.** Proceedings in matters of *juridiction gracieuse* are ordinarily [64] begun by a petition (*requête*) submitted to the court by the *avoué* of the petitioner. [65] The law does not specify to which court the petition must be submitted;

[56] See 7.35 *supra*.

[57] CODE CIVIL art. 99; CODE DE PROCÉDURE CIVILE arts. 855–56. Very minor corrections, such as in spelling, may now be made by the registrar upon the authority of the *procureur de la République*.

[58] CODE CIVIL arts. 88–92.

[59] CODE CIVIL art. 1008.

[60] CODE CIVIL art. 1008.

[61] CODE CIVIL arts. 819, 822 (some of the co-heirs minors or incompetents). Upon the death of an intestate, under French law, the distributees (*héritiers*) of an intestate become automatically joint tenants of the estate. However, a subsequent partition is possible.

[62] See 1 SOLUS & PERROT 450–51. Those who do not wish to classify *ex parte* applications for incidental relief within *juridiction gracieuse* speak of *contentieux connexe* (related litigation).

[63] See especially 5.04–5.06 *supra*.

[64] The procedure described is the general procedure to be followed in non-adversary proceedings before the *chambre du conseil*. Individual statutes may provide for variations not described in the text.

[65] Law of July 15, 1944, *supra* note 40, art. 3. If the *ministère public* acts as petitioner, no *avoué* is needed. In some other cases, the services of an *avoué* may also be dispensed with. Coheirs who seek court approval for a partition and are not in disagreement may present a collective petition. CODE CIVIL art. 822; *cf.* note 61 *supra*. Collective petitions are also possible in some other instances. See, *e.g.*, CODE CIVIL art. 89 (collective petition for declaration of death of persons killed in common disaster).

usually, it will be the court at the petitioner's domicile. Some authors state that proceedings concerning a third party, such as proceedings to have somebody declared "absent," should be brought at the domicile of that person. [66]

Upon receipt of the petition, the presiding judge of the court must fix a date for the hearing of the case and appoint one of the judges of the court as reporting judge. [67] The petitioner's *avoué* must transmit his file to the *ministère public*. [68] The *ministère public* frequently takes an active, rather than a merely formal, part in the proceedings, especially when the rights of infants or incompetents are involved. In some cases, such as adoptions of infants under seven, or the correction of birth, death, or marriage registers, the *ministère public* may also act as petitioner. [69] In adoption cases, the parties often ask the *ministère public* to act in order to save expenses.

On the day of the hearing, from which the public is excluded, either the petitioner's *avoué*, or his *avocat*, or the petitioner himself, presents argument in favor of the petition. A member of the *ministère public* is also heard. [70] Although the Law of July 15, 1944, is silent about proof before the *chambre du conseil*, general principles apply. If the matter cannot be determined on the basis of the documentary evidence presented by the parties, an interlocutory decision may issue ordering an *enquête* for the hearing of witnesses, an *expertise*, or a similar proof pro-

[66] This is based on the idea that such a person is at least a potential defendant, and under CODE DE PROCÉDURE CIVILE art. 59 actions must ordinarily be brought at the domicile of the defendant. See 1 DALLOZ, *op. cit. supra* note 39, at No. 29, Hébraud, *supra* note 39, at 337. Sometimes, special legislation prescribes where the proceedings must be brought. See 4.33 *supra*.

[67] Law of July 15, 1944, *supra* note 40, art. 3; 1 DALLOZ, *op. cit. supra* note 39, at No. 34. On proceedings before the *chambre du conseil* generally, see also CUCHE & VINCENT 362–63.

[68] Article 3 of the Law of July 15, 1944, *supra* note 40, prescribes that, upon receipt of the petition, the presiding judge must order the *avoué* of the petitioner to transmit his file to the *ministère public*. According to some authors, this means that the *ministère public* must intervene in all proceedings before the *chambre du conseil*; others opine that this clause does not enlarge the instances in which the *ministère public* must intervene as a "joined "party under CODE DE PROCÉDURE CIVILE art. 83. See also 3.09 *supra*; 1 DALLOZ, *op. cit. supra* note 39, at No. 33. In practice, this makes little difference because nearly all matters coming before the *chambre du conseil* are covered by article 83 of the *Code de Procédure Civile*.

[69] See CODE CIVIL art. 353 (adoption of minor), art. 99 (registers of birth, death and marriage). For other instances, see 3.10 *supra*.

[70] Law of July 15, 1944, *supra* note 40, art. 3. Before the argument begins, although no such report is specifically required by law, the reporting judge makes his report, *i.e.*, summarizes the case. Hébraud, *supra* note 39, at 338. The law speaks only of remarks by the *avoué* at the hearing, but it is generally assumed that the petitioner or his *avocat* is also authorized to present argument. 1 DALLOZ, *op. cit. supra* note 39, at No. 34. If the interests of infants, incompetents, or other persons less able to defend themselves are not involved, nor a matter involving strong public policy or a novel point of law, the *ministère public* often limits his argument to a statement that he relies on the wisdom of the court.

ceeding. [71] In the case of certain proceedings involving the custody of infants, the court is not bound by the rule that it must not seek out information on its own, but may order an investigation of all conditions affecting the child by social workers, psychologists, and similar persons. [72]

Third parties may intervene in non-adversary proceedings before the *chambre du conseil.* This poses no problem if they support the position of the petitioner. If they oppose it, the law prescribes that they must be heard "in an adversary manner." [73] There is some dispute whether such an intervention transforms the non-adversary proceedings into a regular action which must be heard in open court. The better opinion seems to be that the proceedings must remain in the *chambre du conseil.* [74]

Unless a special statute prescribes that it be given in open court, the decision of the court must be rendered in the *chambre du conseil.* [75] Decisions in non-adversary proceedings do not have a true *res judicata* effect, as that term is understood in French law. A petitioner whose request for relief has been denied, may renew it, at least upon a showing of changed circumstances. [76] In addition, the rule *voies de nullité n'ont lieu contre jugements,* which prohibits collateral attack against judgments rendered in adversary proceedings, does not apply. [77]

**c. Review of decisions.** Decisions of the *chambre du conseil* in non-adversary matters may be appealed within one month from the service of the decision on the defendant or, if there is no defendant, on the *ministère public.* The appeal is always to the *chambre du conseil* of the appropriate *cour d'appel.* [78] An appeal may be filed by a petitioner whose petition has been denied or granted only in modified form. A

[71] See 7.51–7.56 *supra.*

[72] See, *e.g.*, Code Civil art. 372.

[73] Law of July 15, 1944, *supra* note 40, art. 3. The French term is *contradictoirement.*

[74] Morel 375; Hébraud, *supra* note 39, at 339; Ministère Public v. Me. X, Cour Lyon, January 8, 1951, [1951] D.J. 342 (proceedings remain in *chambre du conseil* in spite of intervention of other persons).

[75] Law of July 15, 1944, *supra* note 40, art. 3.

[76] Some authors speak of an attenuated *res judicata* effect. See 1 Solus & Perrot 457–58; *cf.* Ministère Public v. Me X., *supra* note 74 (petition may be renewed, but only on showing of changed factual circumstances, not upon allegation that court made error of law).

[77] 1 Solus & Perrot 460–61; Dlle Riembaud et Dame Barat v. Blet, Trib. Seine, March 28, 1945, [1946] D.J. 201 (action may be brought to declare adoption void) (this proceeding was brought before the revision of adoption legislation in 1958).

[78] Law of July 15, 1944, *supra* note 40, art. 6. In the ordinary case in which there is no defendant, in order to start the running of the appeal period, a copy of the judgment must be served on the *ministère public.* If the *ministère public* acts as petitioner and there is no defendant, time to appeal runs from the date of judgment. Ministère Public v. Me. X., *supra* note 74.

third party which has intervened in the proceedings may appeal if it has been aggrieved by the decision. In cases in which it is not a petitioner, the *ministère public* may appeal only if it is authorized to do so by a special statute or if public policy (*ordre public*) is particularily involved. [79] Whether a person who has not been a party to the proceedings in first instance but is affected by the decision may appeal is a controverted question. [80]

Legal scholars are generally agreed that, since *opposition* is reserved for defaulting defendants and, strictly speaking, there can be no defendant in a non-adversary proceeding, a person not a party who is affected by a non-adversary decision rendered in the *chambre du conseil* may not use the remedy of *opposition* to obtain a reopening. [81] However, according to these authors, the remedy of *tierce opposition,* by which third parties may obtain reopening of court decisions affecting them, is available. In non-adversary proceedings, the courts do not always distinguish between these two remedies. [82] Since the 1958 reform, the remedy of *opposition* is no longer open in cases in which appeal is possible. [83] It is not quite clear whether this means that persons affected by decisions in non-adversary proceedings in which they have not participated must appeal to preserve their rights or whether they can demand a reopening of the proceedings.

**d. Competence in adversary proceedings.** Since the principle that litigation should be conducted in open court is strong, fewer adversary than non-adversary matters are brought before the *chambre du conseil.* The desire to avoid scandal and protect the reputation of the parties seems to have been the main factor in determining what litigated matters must be handled by the *chambre du conseil.* For this reason, divorce and separation [84] and proceedings to deprive parents of their

[79] See 1 DALLOZ, *op. cit. supra* note 39, at No. 51.

[80] Although most courts hold that a person not a party to the proceedings in first instance may not appeal, some have authorized an appeal. See Hébraud & Raynaud, *Chronique,* 51 REV. TRIM. DR. CIV. 165–66 (1953).

[81] *E.g.,* Hébraud, *supra* note 39, at 346.

[82] 1 SOLUS & PERROT 465–66; 1 DALLOZ, *op. cit. supra* note 39, at No. 59; Veuve Jean Sauphar v. Veuve Lucien Sauphar; Trib. Seine, April 16, 1947, [1947] D.J. 324 (mother sought to have set aside by way of *tierce opposition* the declaration of death obtained by grandmother of person who had been deported to concentration camp; held, although *tierce opposition* may be used by a person not a party and mother has sufficient moral interest to have standing, petition denied in view of very strong evidence that person had been killed); *cf.* Cons. Castan v. Loustaunau, Cour Pau, November 19, 1953, [1954] D.J. 132 (court did not allow *tierce opposition* against decision legitimizing child, but on special grounds).

[83] See 7.04.a *supra.*

[84] CODE CIVIL arts. 239 (divorce), 310 (conversion of separation into divorce), 307 (separation – by reference to rules governing divorce).

parental authority [85] have been included. In matters involving matrimonial property, the *chambre du conseil* hears proceedings involving the abusive refusal of one spouse to consent to transactions which the other spouse wishes to undertake. [86] The *chambre du conseil* is also competent in matters involving the various law professionals. It hears actions by *avocats* for the recovery of fees [87] and disciplinary proceedings against all *officiers ministériels.* [88] Disciplinary proceedings against *avocats* are handled by the disciplinary councils of their professional organizations in first instance, but these decisions may be appealed to the *chambre du conseil* of the regional *cour d'appel.* [89] The appointment of receivers and similar persons charged with the temporary administration of property must likewise be made in the *chambre du conseil.* [90] To promote an informal atmosphere more favorable to settlement, the law prescribes that even in a proceeding conducted in open court the personal appearance of parties before the court (*comparution personnelle*) and attempts at settlement on the part of the court must be conducted in the *chambre du conseil.* [91]

In order to limit the number of non-public proceedings, the rules prescribing when an action must be handled in the *chambre du conseil* are interpreted narrowly. [92] Hearing a proceeding in the *chambre du conseil* when this is not authorized constitutes reversible error. Since the rule that court proceedings must be public involves strong public policy, the error is not waived by a failure to make a timely objection

[85] Law of July 24, 1889, [1890] D. 4. 15, as amended by Law of November 15, 1921, J.O. November 1, 1921, [1921] D. 4. 313, arts. 3–4. Parents may be deprived of their parental authority for a variety of crimes and for actions endangering the health, morals, or safety of their children.

[86] CODE DE PROCÉDURE CIVILE art. 862; CODE CIVIL art. 217. This procedure is analogous to the procedure mentioned *supra* note 54, except that it is adversary in nature since it involves a present and non-consenting rather than an absent spouse.

[87] Law No. 57–1429 of December 31, 1957, J.O. January 5, 1958, p. 194, [1958] D.L. 29, art. 4. For more details, see 2.03.e *supra.*

[88] Except to the extent that disciplinary proceedings are handled by the appropriate professional organization. See 2.06.e *supra* (*avoués*), 2.08.c (*huissiers*), 2.10.d (*notaires*).

[89] See 2.03.f *supra.*

[90] Law of July 14, 1944, *supra* note 40, art. 2.

[91] CODE DE PROCÉDURE CIVILE art. 80 (*conciliation*); CODE DE PROCÉDURE CIVILE art. 327 (*comparution personelle*); see 5.03, 7.53 *supra.* See also CODE DE PROCÉDURE CIVILE art. 963 (judicial sale of property of minors).

[92] See, *e.g.*, Weiller v. Dame Diplarkos, Cour Paris, December 15, 1948, [1949] D.J. 461 (action to declare Nevada divorce void must be brought in open court, not *chambre du conseil*); Dame Beaup v. Beaup, Cass. Civ., December 16, 1959, [1960] D. SOMM. 41 (challenge to competence of court in divorce action heard in open court); Vve Taillandier v. Vve Taillandier et autres, Trib. Riom, November 7, 1947, [1948] D.J. 50 (proceeding to oust guardian (*tuteur*) not to be brought in *chambre du conseil*; article 2 of Law of July 15, 1944, dealing with administrators of property of absent persons, incompetents, and the like must be interpreted strictly and is not applicable to guardian).

and may be raised for the first time before the *Cour de Cassation.* [93] When a court commits the converse mistake and hears in open court a case which belongs before the *chambre du conseil,* it also commits error, but, except in divorce cases, that error is waived by a failure to make a timely objection. [94] Joinder of an action which must be heard in the *chambre du conseil* with another action which must be heard in open court is probably improper. [95]

**e. Adversary procedure before the *chambre du conseil.*** The articles of the Law of July 15, 1944, dealing with adversary proceedings before the *chambre du conseil* contain only minor departures from the rules governing ordinary cases. However, additional variations occur in divorce and separation cases and some other situations. [96]

The ordinary rules of competence determine before which court an adversary proceeding in the *chambre du conseil* must be brought. [97] The proceedings are initiated by an *ex parte* petition in which the plaintiff requests the presiding judge of the court to fix a date for a hearing. The plaintiff must summon the defendant to this hearing. [98] From then on, the regular rules are largely applicable. [99] In the absence of an explicit contrary provision, judgments must be rendered in open court. [100] Judgments are always appealable. The appeal goes to the *chambre du conseil* of the regional *cour d'appel.* [101] In view of the availability of appeal, defaulting defendants may no longer obtain a reopening of the case by *opposition.* [102]

[93] 1 DALLOZ, *op. cit. supra* note 39, at No. 25.

[94] Hébraud, *supra* note 39, at 334; 1 DALLOZ, *op. cit. supra* note 39, at 26–27; Falgoux v. Dame Falgoux, Cass. Civ., Nov. 6, 1945, [1946] D.J. 4; Dame Chary v. Chary, Cass. Civ., January 29, 1946, [1946] D.J. 169 (error committed by hearing divorce case in part in open court not waived though both parties consented at the time).

[95] 1 DALLOZ, *op. cit. supra* note 39, at No. 23.

[96] On divorce proceedings, which vary significantly from other proceedings in the *chambre du conseil,* see 11.04 *infra.*

[97] See 1 DALLOZ, *op. cit. supra* note 39, No. 26. For a description of these rules, see CODE DE PROCÉDURE CIVILE art. 59 and 4.33 *supra.*

[98] Law of July 15, 1944, *supra* note 40, art. 4. Parties are summoned in the regular manner by an *huissier.*

[99] See generally MOREL 374.

[100] Law of July 15, 1944, *supra* note 40, art. 4.

[101] Law of July 15, 1944, *supra* note 40, art. 6. Time to appeal is one month from the date of service of the judgment on the defendant. *Cf.* Auribault v. Jaudon, Cour Paris, January 20, 1951, [1951] D.J. 122 (appeal from *chambre du conseil* always goes to *chambre du conseil* of *cour d'appel*).

[102] Article 5 of the Law of July 15, 1944, *supra* note 40, which authorized the remedy of *opposition* in cases before the *chambre du conseil* if the defendant was in default, was specifically abrogated by article 13 of DÉCRET No. 58–1289, J.O. December 23, 1958, p. 11608, [1959] D.L. 45.

## 11.04. Procedure in Divorce and Separation Cases

In France, divorce and separation are available for the same reasons: [103] adultery, [104] conviction for serious crimes, [105] and physical or mental cruelty. [106]

The procedure in divorce and separation cases is also largely the same, [107] but differs significantly from the regular procedure and from the procedure in the *chambre du conseil*. It has designedly been made cumbersome in order to afford numerous opportunities for reconciliation. Due in part to historical accident and in part to the close relationship between substance and procedure, the rules regulating procedure in divorce and separation cases are contained in the Civil Code rather than in the Code of Civil Procedure. [108]

**a. Capacity and standing to sue.** Minors may bring and defend divorce or separation actions without the assistance of a curator; however, a person legally declared a spendthrift needs such assistance. The committee of an incompetent may defend divorce and separation actions, but is not authorized to bring a divorce action on behalf of an incompetent unable to make known his own wishes. The committee may sue for separation. A person committed to an institution for the insane without having been declared incompetent may be sued for divorce or separation, but a guardian or *mandataire ad litem* must be appointed

[103] CODE CIVIL art. 306 provides that the grounds for separation are the same as those for divorce.

[104] CODE CIVIL art. 229 (adultery of wife), art. 230 (adultery of husband).

[105] CODE CIVIL art. 231. The spouse must have been sentenced to a penalty classified as *peine afflictive et infamante* which includes the death penalty and imprisonment for a period of five years or more. CODE PÉNAL arts. 7, 18, 19. A *peine afflictive et infamante* is imposed only for a serious felony. CODE PÉNAL art. 1.

[106] CODE CIVIL art. 232. The French term is *excès, sévices, et injures*. Under this article, a divorce may be granted only if there has been a serious or repeated violation of the obligations resulting from the marriage which makes continued maried life intolerable. However, the courts often pay mere lipservice to this restriction. Since the *Cour de Cassation* does not ordinarily review the record but merely the recitals in the judgment, a judgment is safe from reversal if it merely recites, without more, that the facts shown indicate that continued married life is impossible. 1 COLIN & CAPITANT 465–68. On the limited review of questions of fact by the *Cour de Cassation*, see also 9.07 *supra*.

[107] Articles 307 and 308 of the Civil Code make most of the provisions dealing with divorce procedure applicable to separation.

[108] The drafters of the Civil Code did not want to wait for the completion of the Code of Civil Procedure, which was not yet ready. On the history of divorce in France, see Rheinstein, *The Code and the Family*, in THE CODE NAPOLÉON AND THE COMMON-LAW WORLD 139, 141–46 (Schwartz ed. 1956); 1 COLIN & CAPITANT 451–57; 1 DALLOZ, RÉPERTOIRE DE PROCÉDURE CIVILE ET COMMERCIALE, *Divorce*, at Nos. 1–22 (1955). On the close connection between substance and procedure in divorce, see also 1 COLIN & CAPITANT 472.

for him. Presumably, the guardian may sue for separation, though not for divorce. [109]

Both divorce and separation actions are considered as strictly personal. They abate if either party dies before the judgment has become final. Heirs of a party have no standing to continue these actions. Neither action may be brought by the unpaid creditors of a spouse. [110]

**b. Competence.** The *tribunal de grande instance* has exclusive competence to hear divorce and separation actions. [111] In accordance with the general rule, they must be brought at the domicile of the defendant. [112] However, by operation of the law, the domicile of the wife is that of her husband, and she must be sued there. [113] The rule that divorce and separation actions must ordinarily be brought at the husband's domicile creates hardship if the husband has abandoned the household. In such instances the courts sometimes tend to find that the husband has not changed his domicile. [114]

**c. Joinder of actions and counterclaims.** Although a divorce and a separation may not be sought simultaneously, [115] a divorce action may

[109] 1 COLIN & CAPITANT 473–74; 1 DALLOZ, *op. cit. supra* note 108, Nos. 49–59. Article 307 of the *Code Civil* expressly authorizes the committee (*tuteur*) of an incompetent to bring a separation action on behalf of the incompetent. It is generally assumed that this implies that the *tuteur* is not authorized to bring a divorce action. See 1 COLIN & CAPITANT 506.

[110] 1 DALLOZ, *op. cit. supra* note 108, at 38–39. On the standing to sue of heirs and creditors generally, see 6.04 *supra.*

[111] See 4.37 *supra.*

[112] CODE DE PROCÉDURE CIVILE art. 59; 4.12 *supra.* The domicile is determined as of the time the initial petition is filed. 1 DALLOZ, *op. cit. supra* note 108, at No. 164; Dame B. v. B., Cour Bordeaux, June 7, 1946, [1947] D.J. 11. *But see* 1 COLIN & CAPITANT 473 (domicile determined as of time defendant is cited to conciliation hearing).

[113] CODE CIVIL art. 108. As a practical result, divorce and separation actions must ordinarily be brought at the husband's domicile. However, the wife's domicile is no longer that of the husband if the spouses are judicially separated, or if the wife has been authorized by the presiding judge of the court at the outset of a separation or divorce action to obtain a separate residence. On the other hand, a wife who has been authorized to live apart from her husband pursuant to CODE CIVIL art. 215 in order to protect her health or safety does not acquire a separate domicile. Savoye v. Dame Savoye, Cass. Com. Feb. 19, 1952, [1952] D.J. 289. See also 7.02.b n. 21 *supra.* If the domicile of the defendant is unknown or if he has no domicile or residence in France, the action may be brought at the plaintiff's domicile. See 4.08 *supra.*

[114] See, *e.g.*, Dame B. v. B., *supra* note 112 (husband who had left matrimonial domicile at Bordeaux to go live with his mistress in Paris and obtained job in Paris but continued to pay taxes and rent and to vote in Bordeaux still had domicile for purposes of a divorce action in Bordeaux). Occasionally, the courts speak of a matrimonial domicile, at which the action must be brought, but this does not seem to be a proper expression. See Villeret v. Villeret, Cass. Civ., March 11, 1959, [1959] D.SOMM. 69.

[115] See Dame Seuriot v. Seuriot, Cass. Civ., March 14, 1944, [1944] D. ANAL. J. 73 (plaintiff suing for divorce and a separation at the same time can be compelled to elect). If a divorce and a separation action have been brought at different times, plaintiff may be granted a divorce if he has abandoned the separation action at the time the divorce action goes to judgment. Lelouche v. Dame Lelouche, Cass. Civ., May 28, 1952, [1952] D.J. 776.

always be converted into a separation action. The converse is not true.[116] A defendant in a divorce action may file a counterclaim for divorce or a separate divorce action.[117] Counterclaims in divorce actions are very frequent, because they present a number of tactical advantages.[118] It is possible to interpose a counterclaim for separation in a divorce or in a separation action.[119] However, a person sued for separation may not counterclaim for divorce, but has to bring an independent action.

**d. Proceedings before the presiding judge of the court.** Divorce and separation actions are initiated by a petition addressed to the presiding judge of the court, requesting permission to summon the defendant to a conciliation hearing and the setting of a day for this hearing.[120] At the same time, the petitioner may request the court's permission to live separately from his spouse.[121] The petition is prepared by an *avoué* and submitted *ex parte*. In separation cases, the *avoué* who has drawn the petition submits it to the judge. In divorce actions, the plaintiff must submit the petition in person in order to give the judge a chance to talk to him and persuade him to discontinue the proceedings. If, as usual, the judge is unsuccessful, he must grant permission to cite the defendant to the conciliation hearing[122] and may grant the plaintiff permission to live apart from the defendant.[123]

[116] 1 DALLOZ, *op. cit. supra* note 108, at Nos. 96–100.

[117] *Id.* at No. 119.

[118] Divorce is considered a penalty for the misconduct of a spouse. See Rheinstein, *supra* note 108. As a result, the unsuccessful defendant may have to pay damages in addition to alimony (CODE CIVIL arts. 301 (divorce), 311 (separation)) and loses all benefits bestowed upon him by his spouse by ante-nuptial agreement or gift during marriage (CODE CIVIL art. 299). Besides, a counterclaim opens even wider possibilities for alleging misconduct of the plaintiff during a divorce action. Counterclaims are interposed by the filing of ordinary *conclusions*: There is no need for an additional petition, conciliation hearing, or summons. CODE CIVIL art. 239.

[119] 1 COLIN & CAPITANT 509.

[120] CODE CIVIL art. 234 (divorce); CODE DE PROCÉDURE CIVILE art. 875 (separation).

[121] See CODE CIVIL art. 236. French law does not recognize separation by agreement.

[122] CODE CIVIL art. 235 (judge must talk to plaintiff in divorce action). The rule creates a problem if the plaintiff is unable to come to court on account of illness or lives too far away from the defendant's domicile. In case of illness, article 234 of the *Code Civil* authorizes the judge to go to the plaintiff's home with his clerk to receive the petition. It is not entirely clear whether the *avoué* of the plaintiff may ask the court at the defendant's domicile to request another judge by letters rogatory to receive the petition. In very busy courts, divorce matters are usually not handled by the presiding judge of the court, who has numerous administrative duties, but by a judge delegated for that purpose. See generally 1 COLIN & CAPITANT 474; 1 DALLOZ, *op. cit. supra* note 108, at Nos. 189–206.

[123] CODE CIVIL art. 236 (divorce procedure made applicable to separation by article 307 of the *Code Civil*). At this stage, no statutory provision authorizes the judge to order the defendant to turn the plaintiff's personal effects over to the plaintiff, but it is sometimes argued that he may do so. See 1 DALLOZ, *op. cit. supra* note 108, at No. 892.

The plaintiff then summons the defendant to the conciliation hearing before the presiding judge. This must be done by an *huissier* specially designated by the presiding judge for the purpose. [124] The scope of the conciliation hearing has grown over the years. It is now used for three purposes: (1) to attack the competence of the court; (2) to attempt reconciliation of the spouses; and (3) to request various kinds of provisional relief. [125]

Upon penalty of waiver, objections to the competence of the court must be raised at the beginning of the conciliation hearing. [126] They may be raised by the *avocats* or *avoués* of the parties. [127] The special procedure provided by the 1958 reforms to raise questions of competence is not applicable in divorce and separation actions. [128] The presiding judge's decision is appealable to the *cour d'appel*.

After the challenge to the competence of the court has been determined – immediately if there has been no such challenge –, the court must attempt to reconcile the parties by hearing them both out of the presence of their *avocats* and *avoués*. If one spouse lives too far from the place where the court sits, a judge of another court may be requested by letters rogatory to interview that spouse and attempt a reconciliation. [129] Reconciliations are rare. [130]

After the reconciliation attempt, the parties may request the judge to grant various kinds of provisional relief. The parties' *avocats* or *avoués* may again be present and act on behalf of their clients. This stage of the proceedings usually serves to determine the custody of the children during the pendency of the action and visitation rights. In

[124] CODE CIVIL art. 237. Service must be made at least three days before the conciliation hearing. If the defendant lives abroad, the usual additional time periods apply. CODE DE PROCÉDURE CIVILE art. 1033–2.

[125] See the note Raynaud appended to Dame Ortiz–Patino v. Ortiz-Patino, Cour Paris, February 27, 1956, [1956] D.J. 487.

[126] CODE CIVIL art. 238; Dame Ortiz-Patino v. Patino, *supra* note 125; 1 DALLOZ, *op. cit. supra* note 108, at Nos. 168–69. This is in accord with the general rule that questions of competence must be raised early in the suit. See CODE DE PROCÉDURE CIVILE art. 168.

[127] CODE CIVIL art. 238. The parties need apparently not be present at this stage. *Cf.* 1 DALLOZ, *op. cit. supra* note 108, at No. 171. See also the note appended to Dame Bié v. Bié, Cass. Civ., Dec. 12, 1956, [1957] D.J. 389 (discussion of representation of parties at conciliation).

[128] CODE DE PROCÉDURE CIVILE art. 170.

[129] CODE CIVIL art. 238; CODE DE PROCÉDURE CIVILE art. 878. If a party lives abroad, letters rogatory may be sent to a French consul or to a foreign court. Article 238 of the *Code Civil* refers to divorce actions, but is made applicable to separation actions by article 307 of the *Code Civil*. Article 878 of the *Code de Procédure Civile*, which applies only to separation, is virtually identical to article 238 of the *Code Civil*, except that it does not mention challenges to the competence of the court. As far as separation is concerned, the conciliation hearing is thus governed by two duplicative, but slightly inconsistent, articles.

[130] 1 COLIN & CAPITANT 476. The defendant often defaults at the conciliation hearing. This does not prevent a continuation of the proceedings.

addition, either party may obtain provisional alimony. The wife may be granted a *provision ad litem*, a sum designed to help her meet court costs. Either spouse may now also be ordered to turn over personal effects, such as clothing and other everyday items, to the other. [131] Under the various French systems of matrimonial property, the husband may have the right to possession and management of property belonging to his wife. To prevent misappropriation, the judge may take various steps: Property may be put under seal pending preparation of an inventory; securities sometimes have to be put into a safe deposit box in a bank; and the judge may even appoint a receiver to supervise the activities of the husband. However, before a final judgment of divorce or separation has been obtained, the husband may not be deprived completely of all rights over matrimonial property. [132] If there are children of the marriage, the judge conducting the reconciliation hearing also appoints a social worker or similarly qualified person to investigate their situation and submit a report when the final decision as to their custody must be made. This investigation is usually referred to as *enquête sociale*.

If the judge's attempt to reconcile the parties has been unsuccessful, he may authorize the plaintiff to begin the regular divorce or separation action immediately or he may impose a waiting period of not more than six months. [133] The latter is done infrequently. [134]

**e. Proceedings.** Within twenty days after having received permission to begin the action, the plaintiff must summon the defendant by a regular *assignation*. If the summons is not served within the twenty day period, the provisional alimony and all other provisional measures

[131] Code Civil art. 238; Code de Procédure Civile art. 878 (separation). If speed is essential, provisional relief, such as provisions concerning the custody of the children, may be requested *en référé* from the presiding judge of the court. Dame Mantz-Boyer v. Boyer, Cass. Civ., Nov. 2, 1955, [1956] D.J. 153 (note Hébraud) (*référé* judge may grant grandmother visitation rights). If required by the welfare of the children, even relatives of the spouses or the *ministère public* may request the court to rule on their custody. See 1 Dalloz, *op. cit. supra* note 108, at Nos. 1032–34. Provisional alimony and *provision ad litem* are, at least to some extent, chargeable against sums payable by the husband to the wife following divorce or separation on account of the settlement of their mutual interests in the matrimonial property.

[132] These measures may be obtained on an *ex parte* application; they are not necessarily limited to the husband. Code Civil art. 242; *cf.* article 293 of the *Code Civil* (transactions by husband in fraud of wife's rights void if entered into after plaintiff authorized to summon defendant to conciliation hearing). See generally 1 Dalloz, *op. cit. supra* note 108, at Nos. 1105–24, and Rousseau v. Dame Rousseau, Cass. Civ., July 30, 1951, [1952] D.J. 57 (management of business being part of community property given to wife during pendency of action, but under control of court-appointed supervisor).

[133] Code Civil art. 238.

[134] 1 Dalloz, *op. cit. supra* note 108, at No. 266.

ordered at the conciliation hearing automatically terminate. [135] After service of the summons, a divorce or separation action is conducted substantially as any other action. However, the *audience* must take place in the *chambre du conseil.* [136] At any time during the pendency of the action, the court may modify the provisional measures taken by the presiding judge during the conciliation hearing or grant new ones. [137]

In divorce and separation cases, the general rules of evidence are somewhat modified. Admissions may be used only if they are corroborated and there is obviously no collusion. [138] The party-oath is not available. [139] Either spouse may use letters addressed to the other, unless they have been secured by improper means. [140] Relatives of parties, except descendants, may be heard as witnesses. [141] During the *enquête,* the defendant is not limited to disproving the facts of which he is accused, but may show misconduct on the part of the plaintiff in order to explain his own actions. [142] Inferences (*présomptions de fait*) may be used quite freely, but a husband may not compel his wife to take a blood grouping test to show her adultery. [143] A party wishing to rely on adultery as a ground for divorce often attempts to secure proof by obtaining an *ex parte* court order authorizing an *huissier* to go to the place were the adultery is allegedly to be committed, observe the adulterous activities, and prepare a report. An *huissier* armed with such

[135] CODE CIVIL art. 238. However, failure to summon the defendant within twenty days does not void the proceedings. The summons (*assignation*) is in the ordinary form.

[136] CODE CIVIL art. 239 (relating to divorce but made applicable in separation by virtue of article 879 of the *Code de Procédure Civile*). Matters relating to the divorce, such as alimony, or custody of children, must always be heard in the *chambre du conseil,* but a challenge to the competence of the court need not be decided there. Dame Beaup v. Beaup, Cass. Civ., Dec. 16, 1959, [1960] D. SOMM. 41. Actions to have a foreign divorce declared void are not heard in the *chambre du conseil.* See 14.05.b *supra.*

[137] Measures concerning the custody of children may be ordered not only at the request of the parties, but also at the request of members of the family and of the *ministère public.* CODE CIVIL art. 240. The *juge chargé de suivre la procédure* is not authorized to grant or modify alimony *pendente lite* or other provisional relief. 1 DALLOZ, *op. cit. supra* note 108, at No. 1036.

[138] See 7.52 *supra*; 1 COLIN & CAPITANT 483.

[139] See 7.56 *supra*; 1 DALLOZ, *op. cit. supra* note 108, at 498, 499.

[140] Improper means include the breaking open of locked containers and fraud. See 7.48 *supra*; 1 DALLOZ, *op. cit. supra* note 108, at Nos. 514–62; 1 COLIN & CAPITANT 483; P. v. Dame P., Cour Chambéry, Jan. 16, 1961, [1961] D.J. 343 (in divorce action by husband, letters written by wife to third party, which, apparently after quarrel with wife, third party had sent to husband's father, excluded).

[141] CODE CIVIL art. 245; 7.51.b *supra.*

[142] See Dame Dulac v. Dulac, Cass. Civ., April 5, 1954, [1955] D.J. 125. This will usually have to be done by way of an *enquête respective.*

[143] P..., Trib. Privas, Dec. 5, 1956, [1958] D.J. 492 (note Savatier) (since a blood grouping test might prove the child a bastard, it was not allowed). Savatier states in his note that not only letters but also other means of proof, such as pictures or recordings, must be excluded if obtained by fraud.

an order must be admitted to the building designated in it, except during the night. The written report of the *huissier*, called *constat* or *constat d'adultère*, may be used in the divorce or separation action, though it has only the effect of an inference, not that of actual testimony. [144] French judges are sometimes fairly lenient as to the quantum of proof necessary in divorce cases. [145]

The judgment in divorce and separation cases is rendered in open court, not in the *chambre du conseil*. In divorce cases – but apparently not in separation cases –, the court may impose an additional waiting period of not more than one year before rendering its judgment. [146] The final judgment granting a divorce may award the innocent party permanent alimony. In separation actions, alimony may be awarded even to the guilty spouse. Alimony is not necessarily restricted to the wife and is always modifiable. In addition to alimony, the court may award the successful plaintiff compensation for the misconduct of the defendant. [147] Appropriate provisions for the custody of the children and visitation rights must also be made. [148]

**f. Proceedings subsequent to judgment.** Both divorce and separation judgments are appealable from the *tribunal de grande instance* to the

[144] See 5.02 *supra*. The use of a *constat* as a kind of discovery device to establish adultery seems to be particularly frequent. In cases in which adultery amounts to a crime (if committed by the husband, only the maintenance of a concubine in the matrimonial domicile is punishable adultery: Code Pénal art. 339), the other spouse occasionally makes a complaint to the police and uses the police report of the investigation as proof of adultery. See generally Vouin, *Constats d'adultère*, [1949] D. Chr. 77.

[145] That is especially true if the allegations are "*excès, sévices et injures*," corresponding roughly to mental or physical cruelty. Because of the limited amount of proof which is ordinarily necessary, this has become the most popular ground for divorce. See the statistics in 1 Colin & Capitant 461; *cf.* note 106 *supra*.

[146] But, if the divorce is based on article 231 of the *Code Civil* (conviction for felony), this waiting period may not be imposed. Code Civil art. 246; 1 Dalloz, *op. cit. supra* note 108, at Nos. 643–50. Some decisions have wrongly allowed imposition of the additional waiting period before judgment even in separation actions: Article 246 of the *Code Civil* is not one of the articles dealing with divorce procedure that have been made applicable to separation by articles 307 and 308 of the *Code Civil*. See 2 Dalloz, Répertoire de Procédure Civile et Commerciale, *Séparation de corps*, No. 47 (1956).

[147] Code Civil art. 301 (divorce), art. 311 (separation). Alimony in divorce may not exceed one third of a spouse's income. In case of need, since the obligation of mutual support and assistance contained in article 212 of the *Code Civil* is not completely destroyed by the separation, a separation judgment may award alimony even to the guilty spouse. Alimony following divorce, however, is regarded as in the nature of damages for misconduct. 1 Colin & Capitant 499, 510–11.

[148] Unless the *enquête sociale* ordered by the presiding judge indicates that another solution will be better for the children, custody must be given the successful plaintiff. Code Civil art. 302. Both parents must continue to contribute to the support of their children after divorce and may supervise their upbringing and education, regardless of who has been awarded custody. Code Civil art. 303.

*cour d'appel.* [149] Appeals are heard in the *chambre du conseil.* The divorce judgment is not final – that is, not fully effective – until either the time to appeal has expired or an appeal has been taken and decided. Parties cannot impart immediate effectiveness to a divorce judgment by waiving the right to appeal. [150] However, the right to appeal may be waived in separation actions. If a divorce or separation case has been taken to the *cour d'appel,* its finality is further suspended until time to file a *pourvoi* to the *Cour de Cassation* has run out or the *pourvoi* has been decided. [151]

A judgment of divorce or separation must be posted at the *tribunal de grande instance* and the commercial court; it must also be published in a local paper. Within fifteen days after a divorce or separation judgment has become final, the *avoué* of the plaintiff must serve copies of the judgment on the registrars of births, deaths, and marriages, the so-called *officiers de l'état civil,* at the places of birth of both parties and at the place of their marriage. The divorce or separation judgment must be mentioned in the margin of the birth and marriage records. Third parties are not bound by the divorce or separation until these marginal notations have been made. If there is no marriage record in France because the parties have been married abroad, the judgment is inscribed in the marriage registers of the first *arrondissement* in Paris. [152]

**g. Conversion of separation into divorce.** After a separation has been in effect for three years, either party may file a suit to convert the separation into a divorce. [153] The procedure is similar to that in *chambre du conseil* matters generally. The action must be brought before the *tribunal de grande instance* of the defendant's domicile. Since the parties

[149] CODE CIVIL art. 248. Not only final judgments, but also interlocutory decisions (with the exception of the original *ex parte* decision authorizing the plaintiff to cite the defendant to the conciliation hearing), are appealable. The ordinary rules as to time to appeal apply (1 month, subject to extension on account of distance). See 1 DALLOZ, *op. cit. supra* note 108, at Nos. 825–27, 831. CODE CIVIL art. 248 authorizes counterclaims even on appeal.

[150] CODE CIVIL art. 250.

[151] CODE CIVIL art. 248.

[152] CODE CIVIL art. 252. Under the French system of matrimonial property, the husband often has the right to manage property belonging to the wife, or community property belonging to both of them, and to some extent the wife also has the right to represent the husband, but these rights terminate with the divorce or separation. Thus, it is important for a third party to know whether the husband (or sometimes the wife) has authority to act. Merchants who obtain a divorce or separation must also serve a copy on the clerk of the commercial court where they are registered in the commercial register, so that the judgment may be noted in that register. DÉCRET No. 58–1355 of Dec. 27, 1958, J.O. Dec. 29, 1958, p 11971, [1959] D.L. 137.

[153] CODE CIVIL art. 310 (1). The three-year period runs from the date the separation judgment has become final, *i.e.*, is no longer subject to any review. 1 COLIN & CAPITANT 513.

may have moved since the rendering of the separation judgment, this is not necessarily the same court that has granted the separation.[154] The plaintiff, after having obtained an order from the presiding judge of the court fixing a date for the hearing, summons the defendant, giving him at least eight days' notice. The hearing takes place in the *chambre du conseil.* Conversion of a separation into a divorce is a matter of right. The court has no power to deny it unless the judgment of separation itself has become ineffective as a result of reconciliation. Unless there is an issue as to reconciliation, the hearing will therefore be largely a formality.[155] The court hearing the action for the conversion of a separation into a divorce may grant alimony or damages. If the court granting the separation has already awarded alimony, requests for modification of the alimony must be addressed to that court, however. The same seems to be true of decisions relating to the custody of children.[156]

The judgment converting a separation into a divorce is rendered in open court.[157] An appeal lies to the *chambre du conseil* of the *cour d' appel.*[158] The parties may give the judgment immediate effectiveness by waiving the right to appeal. A judgment converting a separation into a divorce is treated as a regular divorce judgment as far as its recording in the birth and marriage registers is concerned.

**h. Conflict of laws rules.** Under French conflict of laws rules, provided both spouses are of the same nationality, the national law of the spouses determines on what grounds a divorce or separation may be granted.[159] However, French courts will refuse to grant a divorce on a ground considered against local public policy.[160] If the spouses are of

[154] 2 DALLOZ, RÉPERTOIRE DE PROCÉDURE CIVILE ET COMMERCIALE, *Séparation de corps,* at No. 82. The domicile of the defendant in the action to convert the separation into a divorce governs, whether or not he has been the defendant in the separation action.

[155] 2 DALLOZ, *op. cit. supra* note 154, at Nos. 59–65; 1 COLIN & CAPITANT 514.

[156] 2 DALLOZ, *op. cit. supra* note 154, at Nos. 85–91. Article 310 of the *Code Civil* provides that alimony granted the successful spouse by the separation judgment remains in effect. Since the obligation of mutual aid and support inherent in the marriage relationship terminates with the divorce, alimony granted the guilty spouse in a separation case comes to an end if the separation is converted into a divorce. See 1 COLIN & CAPITANT 516.

[157] CODE CIVIL art 310.

[158] CODE CIVIL art 249.

[159] BATIFFOL 513; DELAUME, AMERICAN FRENCH PRIVATE INTERNATIONAL LAW 100 (2nd ed. 1961).

[160] The scope of this exception is not clear. There is general agreement that French courts will not grant a divorce based on consent or unilateral repudiation, even if available under the national law of the spouses. Some authors go further and contend that a divorce may not be granted in France for a reason based on foreign law unless the same reason is available under French law. Some court decisions, which in granting a divorce based on foreign law state that the foreign law is similar to the French, support this view. BATIFFOL 516–17; D. v. D., Trib.

different nationality, their domiciliary law will be applied. [161] The law of the forum seems applicable in the rare instances in which spouses of different nationality have no common domicile. [162]

French law is applied to questions of procedure, including proof, unless there is a close relationship between substantive and procedural matters. [163]

The nationality of the spouses also governs the conversion of a separation into a divorce. French courts will convert into a divorce a separation awarded abroad, even if this cannot be done in the country where the separation has been awarded, provided the applicable national law authorizes such a conversion. [164] However, there must have been a true separation judgment, not a mere separation by common agreement. [165] A spouse having acquired French nationality subsequent to a

Seine, April 27, 1933, 61 CLUNET 900 (1934). *But see* Fatma Kaci v. Hamache, Trib. Seine, March 26, 1956, [1956] J.C.P. 2. 9318, 84 CLUNET 762 (1957) (Algerian governed by Muslim law who moved to France with wife was allowed to divorce her by unilateral repudiation; case stresses that application of Muslim law to Arabs in Algeria is result of French, not foreign, statute). However, a divorce will not be granted if the national law does not allow it. BATIFFOL 518.

[161] Rivière v. Roumiantzeff, Cass. Civ., April 17, 1953, [1953] J.C.P. 2. 7863, 80 CLUNET 860 (1953) (Ecuadorian law applied in case of French and Russian nationals domiciled in Ecuador); Dame Lewandowski v. Lewandowski, Cass. Civ., [1955] D.J. 540, 83 CLUNET 146 (French law applied in case of husband of Polish nationality and French wife domiciled in France). Spouses of different nationalities may obtain a divorce in France if domiciled there, even if the national law of one of the spouses does not allow a divorce. Dame Del Torchio v. Del Torchio, Cass. Civ., Nov. 17, 1958, [1959] D.J. 80, 86 CLUNET 466 (1959) (French law applied to divorce of French domiciliaries, though one spouse Italian national and Italian law prohibits divorce). In Amat, épouse Corcos v. Corcos, Cass. Civ., Feb. 22, 1961, 88 CLUNET 734 (1961) the *Cour de Cassation* implied that a divorce could be granted under the French law of the domicile even if the different national laws of the spouses would prohibit it. The question of what law must be used to determine the domicile is not clear: Presumably, it is the French law of the forum. See, *e.g.*, D. v. D., *supra* note 160. Indeed, in the Tarwid decision, *infra* note 162, the *Cour de Cassation* suggested that for the purposes of the instant rule domicile might be a question of pure fact not affected by rules related to domicile as a matter of law. However, there is some authority that foreign law should be used if the domicile is abroad. DELAUME, *op. cit. supra* note 159, at 76.

[162] Tarwid v. Dame Wirtensohn, Cass. Civ., May 15, 1961, [1961] D.J. 436 (note Holleaux), 88 CLUNET 736 (1961). *But see* BATIFFOL 514–15.

[163] On proof, especially admissions, see 11.04.e *supra*. *But see* Lang v. Dame Lang, Cour Colmar, Dec. 13, 1927, 56 CLUNET 154 (1928) (in Alsace, where German Code of Civil Procedure applicable, in view of close relationship with substance, French law governs competency of witnesses in divorce action). On the difficulties arising when the applicable foreign law provides for a special procedure (such as the intervention of religious authorities) which arguably is a matter of substance but is not practicable in France, see BATIFFOL 520–23.

[164] Epoux Pastre, Cass. Req., Nov. 13, 1928, 56 CLUNET 426 (1929) (separation judgment rendered in England between French nationals); BATIFFOL 527–28. The foreign separation judgment need not be subjected to the *exequatur* procedure in France, but, as in an *exequatur* procedure, the French court will check whether the foreign court had jurisdiction according to French notions of international jurisdiction, and whether the law applied by the foreign court was that which would have been applied under French conflict of laws rules. Fossati v. Dame Nardi, Trib. Alpes Maritimes, Oct. 25 1927, 55 CLUNET 645 (1928).

[165] 2 DALLOZ, *op. cit. supra* note 154, at No. 112.

separation may obtain a conversion of the separation into a divorce, regardless of his prior nationality. [166]

The effect of foreign divorces in France is discussed in a subsequent chapter. [167]

## 11.05. Arbitration – Introduction

Arbitration was used even before the French Revolution. For example, disputes between members of a partnership had to be settled by arbitration. The early leaders of the revolution favored and extended arbitration, which they considered as the most reasonable method of resolving controversies. This revolutionary experiment did not prove satisfactory so that the scope of arbitration was again restricted by the Code of Civil Procedure of 1806. However, compulsory arbitration for disputes involving members of a company was continued.

The Code of Civil Procedure regulated only the submission to arbitration of existing controversies. Since it did not deal with clauses providing for the arbitration of future controversies, doubts arose as to the validity of these clauses. Around 1845, the *Cour de Cassation,* in a series of decisions, held such arbitration clauses invalid, thus reducing the importance of arbitration. A few years later, compulsory arbitration of disputes among members of a company was abolished. Since the *Cour de Cassation* upheld arbitration clauses inserted in international contracts if valid under the law governing the contract, [168] arbitration remained important mainly in international commercial transactions.

After extensive debate, a law declaring arbitration clauses lawful in commercial matters was enacted in 1925. [169] Shortly before the Second World War, when all collective labor disputes were subjected to compulsory arbitration, arbitration received a further extension. Compulsory arbitration was replaced after the Second World War [170] by

[166] *E.g.*, Fossati v. Dame Nardi, *supra* note 164; BATIFFOL 527; 2 DALLOZ, *op. cit. supra* note 154, at Nos. 113–14.

[167] See 14.05 *infra.*

[168] On the history of arbitration in France, see 1 ROBERT, ARBITRAGE CIVIL ET COMMERCIAL 7–9 (3d ed. 1961) [hereinafter ROBERT]; CUCHE & VINCENT 614, 618. For English discussions of the French law of arbitration, see Robert, *France*, in UNION INTERNATIONALE DES AVOCATS, INTERNATIONAL COMMERCIAL ARBITRATION 240 (n.d.); INTERNATIONAL CHAMBER OF COMMERCE, COMMERCIAL ARBITATION AND THE LAW THROUGHOUT THE WORLD, Sec. F (1949); Cartier, *Arbitration in France*, 3 ARB. J. (N.S.) 25 (1948); Domke, *Arbitral Clauses and Awards, Recent Developments in French Law*, 17 TULANE L. REV. 447 (1943).

[169] Law of December 31, 1925, J.O. Jan. 4, 1926, [1926] S. LOIS ANNOT. 57–58 (with extensive discussion of legislative history). The bill legalizing arbitration clauses was first introduced in 1907; it encountered quite strong opposition.

[170] See 4.40 *supra*, especially n. 403; Heneman, *The French Superior Court of Arbitration*, 9 BROOKLYN L. REV. 33 (1939) (discussing system of compulsory arbitration); Colton, *The*

special machinery for the voluntary arbitration of collective labor disputes,[171] which, however, does not seem to be much used.[172] Since arbitration clauses in individual employment contracts are illegal,[173] labor arbitration plays a minor rôle.[174] Commercial arbitration predominates. A number of trade associations encourage voluntary resort to arbitration by providing arbitral tribunals.[175] Compulsory arbitration is required only in disputes between journalists and newspapers and in certain matters arising out of post-World War II nationalizations.[176]

## 11.06. Submission of Existing Controversies *(Compromis)*

Although French law distinguishes between the *compromis,* the submission to arbitration of an existing controversy, and the *clause compromissoire,* the arbitration clause relating to future disputes,[177] the legal restrictions on the submission of existing controversies also apply to arbitration clauses.

**a. Matters that may be submitted to arbitration.** Many, but not all, disputes may be submitted to arbitration.[178] Neither divorce and

*Rejection of Compulsory Arbitration in France, the New Law on the Settlement of Labor Disputes,* 6 ARB. J. (N.S.) 42 (1951) (discussing developments following second World War).

[171] Law of Feb. 11, 1950, J.O. Feb. 12, 1950, p. 1673, [1950] D.L. 52, as amended by Law No. 57–833 of July 26, 1957, J.O. July 28, 1957, p. 7459, [1957] D.L. 226; Colton, *supra* note 170.

[172] 3 DURAND, TRAITÉ DU DROIT DU TRAVAIL 999 (1956), calls arbitration of collective labor disputes in France an almost complete failure. Mediation is used more extensively, however. Rules governing arbitration of collective labor disputes in France differ from rules applicable to other forms of arbitration. Awards need no *exequatur* by the president of the court to be enforcible and they can be reviewed only by a special court called *Cour Supérieur d'Arbitrage. Id.* at 1005. Because of its limited importance, the special procedure for the arbitration of collective labor disputes is not discussed here.

[173] *E.g.,* Baud v. Soc. anon. d'étude et expansion de la parfumerie de luxe, Cass. Civ., June 20, 1957, [1958] BULL. CIV. II. 500, [1958] D. SOMM. 16.

[174] In addition to the factors mentioned, the existence of the *conseils de prud'hommes* (labor courts), created for the purpose of handling individual labor disputes, reduces the significance of labor arbitration. See 4.40 *supra.* Since the judges of these courts are ordinarily laymen representing employers and employees (see 3.27 *supra*), the atmosphere of these courts approximates that of arbitration. Furthermore, it is doubtful whether even existing controversies subject to the competence of the labor courts may be submitted to arbitration.

[175] These include the International Chamber of Commerce in Paris, commodity exchanges in Paris and Strasbourg, and the trade associations of the coffee and spice, leather, cotton, and cocoa business. There is also a maritime arbitral tribunal. For exact names and addresses, see UNION INTERNATIONALE DES AVOCATS, *op. cit. supra* note 168, at 241; 1 ROBERT 15–16.

[176] On other areas in which arbitration is of some significance, see 11.07 *infra.*

[177] See generally UNION INTERNATIONALE DES AVOCATS, *op. cit. supra* note 168, at 12 (giving a comparative view; the French text of this bi-lingual work is much clearer on this point than the English text).

[178] CODE DE PROCÉDURE CIVILE art. 1003 provides that all persons may submit to arbitration disputes concerning rights of which they may dispose freely.

separation matters, nor questions of personal status, such as legitimacy, are arbitrable. Submission of disputes concerning gifts and bequests granting the beneficiary an annuity or the right to live in a certain building is also prohibited. [179] In addition, there are prohibitions of more general scope. Arbitration is not possible as to matters which are *hors commerce* – that is, not subject to purchase and sale. [180] All matters in which the *ministère public* must act in its *amicus curiae* capacity are likewise not arbitrable. [181] Covered by this prohibition are controversies concerning the French Republic, its public domain, and municipalities, gifts and bequests for the benefit of the poor, questions relating to the so-called dotal property of married women, [182] and questions concerning the validity of patents. [183]

In matters involving strong public policy or *ordre public*, arbitration is likewise excluded. [184] This prohibition is important in areas affected by legislation imposing maximum prices or other restrictions upon free bargaining. [185] The extent to which it excludes arbitration is subject to some controversy. Thus, the laws regulating the renting of residential

[179] CODE DE PROCÉDURE CIVILE art. 1004. The provision concerning gifts or bequests relating to annuities and the right to occupy space in a building was apparently inserted in the Code because such bequests are sometimes used as a means to provide for aged relatives who might need the protection of the judiciary. The provision of article 1004 relating to such gifts and bequests is considered to apply to all matters of support. 1 ROBERT 39. Questions of personal status include not only divorce and separation, which are mentioned specifically in the Code, but also disputes concerning the validity of marriage, filiation, and related problems. 1 DALLOZ, RÉPERTOIRE DE PROCEDURE CIVILE ET COMMERCIALE, *Arbitrage*, at No. 78 (1955).

[180] Submission of a controversy is considered a contract, and, under article 1128 of the *Code Civil*, matters *hors commerce* may ordinarily not be the object of a contract. See 1 ROBERT 39. Not only rights relating to marriage and other family relations are considered *hors commerce*, but also governmental property (*domaine public*) and things the manufacture or sale of which is prohibited for reasons of public health or national security, such as certain weapons. However, these legal restrictions do not necessarily amount to a complete prohibition: Arbitration is illegal only to the extent that it interferes with the purpose of the legal restriction. Thus, since it would be a way to elude the control of the Ministry of Justice, arbitration of disputes relating to the purchase price of *offices ministériels* is probably not permitted. See 2.04 *supra*. But other disputes relating to the sale of such offices are presumably arbitrable. See 1 ROBERT 41. As a practical matter, the rule that matters *hors commerce* are not subject to arbitration seems to impose few restrictions that are not already imposed by some other more specific rule.

[181] CODE DE PROCÉDURE CIVILE art. 1004. As to the matters that are "communicable" to the *ministère public*, see also 3.09 *supra*.

[182] See CODE CIVIL art. 83, listing most matters that are "communicable."

[183] Law of July 5, 1844, concerning patents, 1844 DUVERGIER, RECUEIL DES LOIS 553, art. 36 (prescribing that all actions to declare a patent void, or to cancel it, must be "communicated" to the *ministère public*). As to the possible inclusion of cases relating to trade marks, see 1 ROBERT 42.

[184] Matters involving strong public policy (*ordre public*) are "communicable" to the *ministère public* under the terms of article 83 of the *Code Civil*.

[185] Such legislation always involves *ordre public* (public policy). *Cf.* 1 ROBERT 35–38 (discussion of the impact of public policy on arbitrability).

and farm property do not bar arbitration, [186] but stricter rules may be applicable when maximum prices for food products are involved. [187]

Arbitration is forbidden in controversies involving sales or pledges of a *fonds de commerce* – a going business – or the dissolution of a company lacking legal existence. [188] Both rules seem due to a fear of collusive acts detrimental to creditors.

**b. Persons lacking capacity to submit disputes to arbitration.** Only a person having legal capacity to dispose of a right may submit a dispute involving it to arbitration. [189] Consequently, neither infants nor incompetents may submit a dispute to arbitration. [190] The same prohibition applies to the guardians and committees of such persons. [191] However, it is not applicable to so-called emancipated minors, who have been authorized to operate an independent business. It is also inapplicable to persons with minor mental disabilities, the so-called *prodigues*. [192] Since married women now have full legal capacity, they may submit disputes to arbitration. However, the prevalence of marital property systems under which the husband manages some part of his wife's property is a practical limitation upon this right. Only the husband may submit to arbitration disputes that involve property under his management. If the dispute involves transactions going beyond

[186] Vouillaume v. Veuve Vix, Cass. Civ., Dec. 30, 1954, [1955] D.J. 321 (dispute involving apartment subject to rent control may be submitted to arbitration); Lechet (*sic*), Cour Angers, March 27, 1953, [1954] D.J. 407 (note Savatier) (arbitration of case involving legislation relating to farm tenancies) (*semble*). Some authors state that a dispute is not arbitrable if a particular type of court is exclusively competent to adjudicate it. This formula seems to have little practical utility. It has been used (without much success) as an argument for excluding arbitration in rural lease cases. It is also used as an argument against the arbitrability of disputes falling within the competence of the labor courts. 1 ROBERT 44–47.

[187] Tissot v. Neff, Cass. Com., Nov. 29, 1950, [1951] D.J. 170 (in dispute involving sale of barley, price of which was regulated, the court below, before ruling on validity of arbitral award, should have determined whether award was based on price exceeding legal limitations); Soc. anonyme agricole v. Torris, Cour Paris, Feb. 9, 1954, [1954] D.J. 192 (arbitration not possible in dispute involving sale of barley, since its price subject to government regulation).

[188] 1 ROBERT 42. For a general discussion of matters which are not arbitrable, see also MOREL 544–45; CUCHE & VINCENT 615–16.

[189] See note 178 *supra*; *cf.* generally CUCHE & VINCENT 616.

[190] MOREL 545. One reason for this rule is that cases involving infants and incompetents are "communicable" to the *ministère public* under article 83 of the *Code de Procédure Civile* and that matters which are "communicable" are not arbitrable. The term incompetents refers to *interdits*, persons legally declared incompetent and for whom a committee has been appointed.

[191] 1 ROBERT 20–21. The *tuteur* (guardian or committee) ordinarily appears as the formal party in a law suit involving the infant or incompetent; the name of the infant or incompetent is not mentioned in the reported title of the action. See 6.03.c, 6.04.c *supra*.

[192] 1 DALLOZ, *op. cit. supra* note 179, at Nos. 31–34.

day-to-day management of the property, the consent of the wife is required. [193]

Neither the French Republic, nor its territorial subdivisions or public authorities, may submit disputes to arbitration, unless specifically authorized by law. [194] By way of exception, arbitration is permissible if the dispute involves payment for public works or supplies furnished public agencies. [195]

A trustee in bankruptcy may submit estate claims to arbitration, provided he has obtained the consent of the *juge commissaire* who supervises the bankruptcy proceedings. [196] The same rule is applicable in case of a *règlement judiciaire*, which resembles American arrangement proceedings. [197]

Agents need a special power to submit a controversy to arbitration. A general power of attorney is insufficient, [198] even for *avocats* or *avoués*. [199] Originally, a special power was also required for officers of corporations. At present, if the by-laws authorize them to do so, corporate officers may submit to arbitration disputes involving day-to-day business. [200]

[193] MOREL 545; 1 ROBERT 22. Cases involving dotal property are "communicable" to the *ministère public* under article 83 of the *Code de Procédure Civile*: This is an additional reason for the rule.

[194] *E.g.*, Société nationale de vente des surplus, Conseil d'Etat, Dec. 13, 1957, [1958] D.J. 517 (extensive discussion of the topic in the reprinted conclusions of the *commissaire du gouvernement* Gazier and the note by l'Huillier). The case held an agency of the French government created for the purpose of selling American surplus property incapable of submitting a dispute to arbitration though it had the form of an ordinary commercial firm and was authorized by executive regulation to arbitrate. These restrictions may not be applicable in disputes arising out of international contracts. See Sté Myrtoon Steam Ship v. Agent Judiciaire du Trésor, Cour Paris, April 10, 1957, [1957] J.C.P. 2, 10078 (note Motulsky). *But see* Agent Judiciaire du Trésor public v. Galakis, Trib. Gde Inst. Seine, June 25, 1959, 87 CLUNET 488 (1960). Under French conflict of laws rules, capacity is ordinarily governed by nationality; whether this rule would be applied if capacity to submit a dispute to arbitration were involved is not clear.

[195] Law of April 17, 1906, J.O. April 17, 1906, (1906–1910) S. LOIS ANNOT. 283, art. 69. The law is interpreted strictly. By its terms, it applies only to the French Republic and its *départements* and municipalities. It does not benefit other public agencies.

[196] CODE DE COMMERCE art. 499. If the claim is indeterminate or exceeds 1500 francs (approximately $ 300), the commercial court must also approve (*homologuer*) the submission. The bankrupt and the other party are entitled to be heard. Once a person has been declared bankrupt, since all his rights are transferred to the trustee, he loses the right to submit any disputes to arbitration.

[197] CODE DE COMMERCE art. 507. In these proceedings, there is no trustee; the debtor himself continues in possession and administers his property as would a trustee, but an administrator is appointed who must approve his actions.

[198] See CODE CIVIL art. 1889, providing that an agent may not act beyond the powers granted to him, and that the power to settle a dispute does not include the power to submit it to arbitration.

[199] 1 DALLOZ, *op. cit. supra* note 179, at Nos. 43–45. An *avocat* or *avoué* ordinarily needs no written power of attorney.

[200] 1 ROBERT 27–29.

**c. Form and contents of submission.** Every submission must indicate the names of the arbitrators selected by the parties and the issues to be arbitrated. [201] It may be in the form either of an agreement signed by the parties or of a notarial act. A statement made by the parties before the arbitrators that they want to submit a specified controversy to arbitration is also a sufficient submission, if it is taken down in writing by the arbitrators and signed by them and the parties. [202]

These rules have been interpreted in a fairly liberal manner. It suffices if one party addresses a letter stating his claim and demanding arbitration to the other party and the other party signs that letter at the bottom. [203] Even an oral submission may be effective if it can be proved by an admission in court or a party-oath; however, testimonial proof may not be used. [204] Since the submission is treated as a contract, it may be modified by agreement of the parties: Its scope may be enlarged or restricted. Defects in the submission may be cured at a later date by the preparation of a new document. [205] In addition to the clauses required by law, a submission may contain rules for the conduct of the arbitration proceedings.

**d. Time at which submission must be made.** A submission presupposes an actual controversy. A clause in a contract of sale providing for the determination of the sale price by a third person is not considered the submission of a controversy to arbitration. [206] But once a controversy exists, there is no limitation on the time at which it may be submitted to arbitration. This may be done before suit is brought, while the case is pending before a court of first instance, or even when the case has reached a *cour d'appel.* [207]

## 11.07. Arbitration Clauses

**a. Validity.** Clauses providing for the arbitration of future controversies arising out of a contract, called *clauses compromissoires*, are valid only in a limited number of instances. Since the Law of December

[201] CODE DE PROCÉDURE CIVILE art. 1006. If that rule is not observed, the submission is void.

[202] CODE DE PROCÉDURE CIVILE art. 1005. A written statement that on a specified date named parties appeared before the named arbitrators and declared that they wanted to submit the specified controversy to their arbitration and that the arbitrators accepted their assignment would be sufficient.

[203] Dame Moizant v. Dame Roussel-Eloy, Cour Poitiers, Dec. 20, 1950, [1951] D.J. 103.

[204] MOREL 545; CUCHE & VINCENT 616.

[205] MOREL 546; 1 ROBERT 55–56.

[206] 1 ROBERT 13–15.

[207] CUCHE & VINCENT 617.

31, 1925, they are effective in contracts between merchants, as that term is defined in French law, provided they concern the merchants' business. They may also be inserted in contracts concerning transactions that are commercial in nature, whether or not the contracting parties are merchants. Finally, the Law of December 1925 authorizes the use of an arbitration clause in the by-laws of a commercial *société* or company for disputes between its members or shareholders. [208] Arbitration clauses are thus available in most of the cases falling within the competence of the commercial courts. For this reason, arbitration clauses are sometimes said to be available in commercial matters generally. However, commercial courts are competent in a number of instances in which arbitration clauses are not authorized. [209] These include the so-called mixed matters, actions which are commercial as to one party, but not as to the other. [210] Arbitration clauses are also valid in certain contracts relating to shipping, such as marine insurance policies [211] and bills of lading. [212]

Outside the field of business transactions, arbitration clauses are valid in collective labor agreements. [213] They may also be included in so-called *règlements de co-propriété*, agreements between the co-owners

[208] CODE DE COMMERCE art. 631, last paragraph, as added by the Law of December 31, 1925, *supra* note 169. This paragraph, which authorizes arbitration clauses, contains no list of matters in which such clauses are permissible. It states merely that arbitration clauses are permissible in the matters covered by the preceding paragraphs of the article, which define the competence of the commercial court. Arbitration clauses relating to controversies between members or shareholders of a company may cover disputes relating to the mutual obligations of members or shareholders, management responsibility, or dissolution, but not disputes arising out of an alleged lack of legal existence (*nullité*) of the company. 1 ROBERT 102–04; 1 DALLOZ, RÉPERTOIRE DE PROCÉDURE CIVILE ET COMMERCIALE, *Clause Compromissoire*, Nos. 13–14 (1955). An arbitration clause may validly be inserted only in the *statuts* of a commercial company. Its insertion in the *statuts* of a company which is not commercial has no effect. *E.g.*, Sté Coopérative Agricole Vinification de Lespignon v. Fabre, Cour Montpellier, Sept. 29, 1959, [1960] J.C.P. 2. 11401 (note G.M.) (agricultural co-operative being non-commercial, arbitration clause is void, but clause providing that no action may be brought until attempt at settlement made by committee of co-operative had proved unsuccessful is valid). Nevertheless, the use of arbitration clauses by agricultural co-operatives is frequent. 1 ROBERT 138. On the distinction between civil and commercial companies, see 4.39.b *supra*.

[209] See 4.39 *supra*.

[210] *E.g.*, Baud v. Soc. anon. d'étude et expansion de la parfumerie de luxe, Cass. Civ., June 20, 1957, (1957) BULL. CIV. 2. 500, [1958] D. SOMM. 16 (employment contract for fixed period of time); Sté Utilco v. Sté des Ets. Law, Cour Paris, Dec. 17, 1957, [1958] J.C.P. 2. 10778 (note Motulsky) (licensing of patent by inventor to business firm). Some older cases hold that in mixed contracts only the non-merchant may rely on the lack of validity of the arbitration clause, but the more recent cases decide that an arbitration clause in a mixed contract is absolutely void and that both parties may assert its nullity. See the note by Motulsky, *supra*, and generally 1 ROBERT 108; CUCHE & VINCENT 619.

[211] CODE DE COMMERCE art. 332.

[212] See Law of April 2, 1936, on the carriage of goods by sea, J.O. April 11, 1936, [1937] D. 4. 1, art. 10.

[213] Law of February 11, 1950, *supra* note 171, art. 9, renumbered art. 21 by Law No. 57–833, *supra* note 171. See also note 172 *supra*.

of co-operatively owned apartment houses. [214] There seems to be little agitation favoring extension of arbitration clauses to other non-commercial matters. [215]

Valid arbitration clauses are subject to the restrictions applicable to submissions, both as to subject matter and capacity of persons. Thus, no minor or incompetent may enter into an arbitration clause, nor is such a clause lawful in a contract entered into with the French Republic or one of its territorial subdivisions or public authorities.[216] The invalidity of an arbitration clause is waived if both parties proceed to arbitration without objection. [217] Adult heirs of a decedent who has signed an arbitration clause are bound by it. [218]

**b. Validity under conflict of laws rules.** French courts take a liberal attitude towards arbitration clauses inserted in contracts with international ramifications and give them effect if they are valid under the law governing the contract. [219] In determining which law governs, French courts rely largely on the intention of the parties, at least if the intended law has a relationship with the contract. The courts sometimes hold that a stipulation for arbitration in a particular country indicates that the parties want the law of that country applied to their contract. [220] An otherwise invalid arbitration clause inserted in a purely internal French contract may not be validated by a provision that the contract shall be subject to a specified foreign law. However, even a contract signed in France between French firms may validly include a stipulation to such effect if the contract relates to an inter-

[214] Ownership of co-operative apartment houses, which have become very numerous in recent years, is frequently arranged so that each owner-tenant owns the apartment he occupies, and is a co-tenant, in a stated ratio, of all common ways and other not individually owned parts of the house. The *règlement de co-propriété* deals with the rights and duties of the owner-tenants, and with those of the *syndic*, who is their agent for the management of the building. Law of June 28, 1938, J.O. June 30, 1938, [1939] D. 4. 73, art. 8 (note Chevallier). The arbitration clause is, of course, not binding on third parties suing the owners of the building.

[215] According to some authors, it is dangerous to let non-businessmen who may not be able to appreciate fully what they are doing sign an arbitration clause. See 1 ROBERT 100 n. 1. Opposition to extension of arbitration is sometimes quite strenuous. See the note G.M. appended to Sté Coopérative Agricole Vinification de Lespignon v. Fabre, *supra* note 208.

[216] See 11.06.b *supra*.

[217] 1 ROBERT 108.

[218] *Id.* at 113. The reason for the rule is that minors are not allowed to submit a controversy to arbitration.

[219] Except in case of possible violation of public policy (*ordre public*), this will be true even if the clause is not valid under French internal law. 1 ROBERT 139–40; 1 DALLOZ, *op. cit. supra* note 179, at Nos. 175–78.

[220] BATIFFOL 648.

national transaction. [221] To contracts containing a valid choice of foreign law clause even the rules prohibiting arbitration of controversies involving the French Republic seem inapplicable. [222]

The recent Convention of Establishment between France and the United States provides that arbitration clauses involving American and French nationals or firms do not become unenforcible merely because the place selected for arbitration is outside the territory of one of the contracting parties or because the arbitrators are not nationals of the country where the clause is sought to be enforced. [223] The treaty codifies general French practice: In France, foreign nationals may be arbitrators, and arbitration of controversies with international elements may take place in a foreign country even if that country is not the domicile of either party. [224]

c. **Form of arbitration clauses.** There are no separate rules concerning the form of arbitration clauses. Arbitration clauses that are part of a contract [225] are governed by the formal rules applying to the contract. [226] Since there are no formal requirements for ordinary commercial contracts, [227] arbitration clauses inserted in such contracts may be proved in any manner. [228] Even the designation of an arbitrator

[221] Mardelé v. W. & H. Mueller et Cie, Cass. Civ. Feb. 19, 1930, [1930] D.H. 228 (contract clause for arbitration in London held valid, though it would have been invalid under internal French law at time of transaction). *But see* Sté Mueller et Cie v. Roux, Cour Limoges, Oct. 12, 1928, [1931] D. 2. 49 (note Baudouin) (facts similar to those of preceding case).

[222] Sté Myrtoon Steam Ship v. Agent Judiciaire du Trésor, *supra* note 194 (French government must abide by arbitration clause contained in charter party for Greek ship chartered by France in London). Capitaine du S.S. San Carlo v. Office national interprofessional des céréales, Cour Aix, May 5, 1959, [1960] REV. ARBIT. 28, 87 CLUNET 1076 (1960), *aff'd* Cass. Civ., April 14, 1964, [1964] D.J. 637 (same facts). *But see* Agent Judiciaire du Trésor v. Galakis, Trib. Gde. Inst. Seine, June 25, 1959, 87 CLUNET 488 (1960).

[223] Convention of Establishment with France, November 25, 1959, (1960) 2 U.S.T. & O.I.A. 2398, T.I.A.S. No. 4625, art. III (2).

[224] DELAUME, AMERICAN FRENCH PRIVATE INTERNATIONAL LAW 175 (2d ed. 1961) (questioning practical usefulness of treaty provision). On the capacity of foreigners to be arbitrators, see 11.08 *infra*.

[225] Parties to a contract may agree on an arbitration clause subsequent to the conclusion of the main contract, but the agreement is subject to the rules governing the main contract.

[226] The formal rules governing submissions of existing controversies are not applicable to arbitration clauses. 1 DALLOZ, *op. cit. supra* note 208, at 32; MOREL 548, CUCHE & VINCENT 620; Palombe et Thomas v. Société des Etablissements Delamare et Montier, Dec. 12, 1938, [1939] D.H. 163.

[227] On the formal requirements for a few commercial contracts, see 7.38, 7.42 *supra*.

[228] 1 ROBERT 134. Since most arbitration clauses are inserted in commercial contracts, this is in fact a very liberal rule. An arbitration clause may be embodied in correspondence, or, if the offer contains an arbitration clause, may even be found in the acceptance of goods and part payment, Wallenborn v. Bouis, Cass. Civ., Jan. 9, 1933, [1933] D.H. 164. If there is a "battle of forms," it will ordinarily be a question of fact whether there has been a meeting of the minds on the arbitration clause. 1 ROBERT 135.

is not an absolute necessity. [229] A reference to the rules of an arbitration center incorporates them into the contract. [230] Nevertheless, careful drafting of arbitration clauses is advisable since they are sometimes interpreted in a restrictive manner.

**d. Effects of arbitration clauses; appointment of arbitrator by court.** The courts are incompetent to adjudicate controversies covered by a valid arbitration clause. [231] However, in disputes subject to arbitration, provisional relief may be granted by a judge sitting *en référé*. [232] An arbitration clause may be waived by the joint action of both parties;[233] it is waived if the defendant fails to demand dismissal at the beginning of an ordinary action. [234]

An arbitration clause obligates the parties to sign a submission indicating the names of the arbitrators and the matters in dispute. [235] At one time, it was held that a party failing to sign such a submission could be penalized only by imposition of a duty to pay damages. At present, the courts appoint an arbitrator on behalf of a party in default or use other methods specifically to enforce the agreement to arbitrate. [236] The appointment of an arbitrator by the court does not,

[229] Palombe et Thomas v. Société des Etablissements Delamère et Moutier, *supra* note 226. The parties may, and often do, designate an arbitration center as arbitrator or as the agency that is to nominate arbitrators. Cuche & Vincent 620.

[230] 1 Robert 127. See also Buck v. Constantine, Cour Paris, Jan. 22, 1957, [1957] D.J. 566.

[231] Morel 549; *cf.* 4.29 *supra.*

[232] Cie d'assurances La Vigilance v. Dumas, Cass. Civ., Dec. 4, 1953, [1954] D.J. 108 (appointment of receiver). An application for interlocutory relief may be addressed to arbitrators, but since this method is not very satisfactory, resort to the *référé* procedure is more advisable. See the note by Garaud appended to Vigneron, Cass. Com., Jan. 11, 1960, [1960] J.C.P. 2. 11764.

[233] Gins v. Chemin, Cass. Civ., Oct. 29, 1934, [1934] D.H. 602 (arbitration clause waived when plaintiff started court action and defendant did not appoint his arbitrator). *But see* Cie d'assurances L'Alsacienne-Vie v. Laniot, Cass. Civ., Jan. 22, 1946, [1946] D.J. 239 (after plaintiff had demanded arbitration and appointed his arbitrator, but defendant had failed to appoint his arbitrator, plaintiff made no further effort to compel arbitration but started to sue on the merits; defendant's objection that the courts are incompetent when there is an arbitration clause sustained).

[234] Code de Procédure Civile art. 168 provides that lack of competence must be raised by the parties at the beginning of the suit before any other issue (excepting security for costs). Arbitration clauses do not seem to justify dismissal of an action on the court's own motion under article 171 of the *Code de Procédure Civile.* See 7.09.b *supra.* The procedure for transfer of a case from an incompetent to a competent court seems inapplicable in the case of arbitration; there must be a dismissal. Cuche & Vincent, Supp. 1961, at 17.

[235] *E.g.*, 1 Dalloz, *op. cit. supra* note 208, at No. 44.

[236] Appointment of an arbitrator by the court is the usual method, but a recalcitrant party may also be compelled to appoint an arbitrator by imposition of a penalty called *astreinte.* An arbitration clause may provide for the appointment of arbitrators by a specified third party if one side fails to appoint his arbitrator. An application for the appointment of an arbitrator must be addressed to the court that would have heard the controversy in the absence of an arbitration clause – usually, to the commercial court. It may be made either to

theoretically, obviate the preparation of a written submission indicating the matter in dispute. However, the courts generally hold that the matter in controversy is sufficiently indicated by the arbitration clause and correspondence between the parties relating to the dispute. [237]

## 11.08. The Arbitrators

The Code of Civil Procedure contains few rules relating to arbitrators; most are judge-made. The parties may designate one, two, or more arbitrators, [238] who need not be French nationals. However, infants or incompetents are excluded. When organizations enjoying corporate personality are named as arbitrators, a person designated by the governing body of the organization acts on its behalf. Individual judges may be appointed arbitrators, but an entire court apparently may not. [239] The same circumstances that disqualify a judge [240] also disqualify an arbitrator. [241] However, the disqualification of arbitrators appointed by the parties in the submission may be demanded only on the basis of events occurring after its execution. A party may not nominate itself, but technical advisers or legal counsel for a party may probably be nominated as arbitrators. [242]

the full court or to a judge sitting *en référé*. 1 ROBERT 120–23; CUCHE & VINCENT 620. On the *astreinte*, see also 13.06 *infra*.

[237] 1 ROBERT 124–26; 1 DALLOZ, *op. cit. supra* note 208, at 44. The arbitration clause, together with a copy of a letter from the party demanding arbitration to the other, indicating on what issues arbitration is demanded, may be a sufficient substitute for a submission if the court appoints the arbitrator. At the time of the signing of a contract containing an arbitration clause, parties sometimes attempt to prevent future refusals to arbitrate by exchanging signed submissions containing blank spaces for the names of the arbitrators and the description of the issues in controversy, to be filled in by the party desiring arbitration when a controversy arises. This procedure is probably invalid. See, *e.g.*, L. v. S., Cour Paris, Dec. 11, 1959; L. v. V., Cour Paris Jan. 12, 1960, [1960] J.C.P. 2. 11513 (note R. B.).

[238] MOREL 550.

[239] *Id.* at 549; 1 ROBERT 76–81. According to CUCHE & VINCENT, a minor may be appointed as arbitrator. See CUCHE & VINCENT 621. The rule making the nationality of arbitrators immaterial has been incorporated in art. III (2) of the Convention of Establishment with France, *supra* note 223.

[240] CODE DE PROCÉDURE CIVILE art. 378 disqualifies a judge: (1) if he or his wife is a relative of one of the parties; (2) if he or his children are involved in a controversy similar to that before the court; (3) if they are creditors or debtors of a party; (4) if he or his relatives and one of the parties were involved in litigation; (5) if he has acted as counsel, judge, or arbitrator in the matter, or been a witness in the case, or received presents from one of the parties, or been his guest.

[241] CODE DE PROCÉDURE CIVILE art. 1014; MOREL 550; 1 ROBERT 159–60. If an arbitrator requested to disqualify himself does not do so, a proceeding may be initiated before the *tribunal de grande instance* to disqualify him. *Id.* at 161. Unless the submission has provided for the replacement of arbitrators, the disqualification of an arbitrator terminates the arbitration. See CODE DE PROCÉDURE CIVILE art. 1012. Demands for the disqualification of an arbitrator seem to be made very rarely.

[242] It would probably be considered a violation of public policy if a party attempted to act as his own arbitrator. See generally MOREL 550; 1 ROBERT 77–79.

Arbitrators need not accept their assignment. They may resign for good cause after acceptance, provided the actual arbitration has not yet begun. [243] The unanimous consent of all parties is required for the revocation of an arbitrator, once he has been appointed. [244] Unauthorized withdrawal of an arbitrator may make him liable in damages to the parties. [245]

Arbitrators are entitled to a fee. Usually, an agreement concerning the fee is reached before the beginning of the arbitration proceedings. If this has not been done, the arbitrators may apply to the court for taxation of their fees after rendering their award. Arbitrators may not tax their own fees in the award unless the submission authorizes them to do so. [246]

### 11.09. Procedure before Arbitrators

The Code of Civil Procedure provides that, unless – as is usually done – the parties have stipulated otherwise, arbitrators must apply existing rules of substantive and adjective law. [247] The parties may agree that the arbitrators shall not be bound by ordinary rules of procedure, or that they need not follow rules of substantive law, or both. Arbitrators not bound to follow rules of substantive law are generally referred to as *amiables compositeurs.* [248] Specific authorization to act as *amiable compositeur* implies the power to disregard ordinary rules of procedure. However, arbitrators may never disregard substantive or procedural rules involving public policy. Thus, both sides must always receive an adequate opportunity to be heard, and written documents must be submitted to the other side before they are introduced. [249] Even when there is no waiver of procedural rules, the procedure before arbitrators differs somewhat from the regular procedure before the *tribunal de grande instance.* The proceedings are not initiated by an *a-*

[243] CODE DE PROCÉDURE CIVILE art. 1014. Acceptance may be formal or informal – *e.g.*, by beginning the arbitration. 1 ROBERT 87–88.

[244] CODE DE PROCÉDURE CIVILE art. 1008.

[245] Arbitrators may become liable to the parties not only for impermissible withdrawal from the arbitration, but also for other misconduct. Arbitrators must be sued in a regular damage action; the *prise à partie* procedure used to impose liability upon judges is not applicable to arbitrators. 1 ROBERT 88.

[246] *Id.* at 245; 1 DALLOZ, *op. cit. supra* note 179, at 495.

[247] CODE DE PROCÉDURE CIVILE arts. 1009, 1019.

[248] CODE DE PROCÉDURE CIVILE art. 1019. Translated literally, the term *amiable compositeur* means friendly conciliator; however, the *amiable compositeur* is a true arbitrator, not a mere conciliator. Arbitrators appointed pursuant to an arbitration clause contained in an ocean bill of lading may not be given the power of *amiables compositeurs* entitled to disregard rules of law. Law of April 2, 1936, *supra* note 212, art. 10.

[249] 1 ROBERT 149–51; MOREL 551; CUCHE & VINCENT 622–23.

*journement,* and the parties do not have to be represented by an *avoué,* though they may use legal counsel if they wish. However, compliance with the rules requiring interlocutory decisions for the various proof proceedings and the regulations concerning time limitations and contents of legal papers is necessary. [250] If there is more than one arbitrator, all arbitrators must act together, unless the submission expressly authorizes delegation of functions. [251] French arbitrators customarily prepare minutes after each hearing in which they describe the events that have taken place. Stenographic transcripts are not usual.

**a. Scope of the arbitrators' powers.** The powers of arbitrators are limited by the submission. An award dealing with matters not covered by the submission is void. However, the arbitrators are authorized to interpret the clauses of the submission that define their powers. [252] A third person not a party to the submission may not be impleaded, nor may such a person intervene in a pending arbitration unless all parties consent. A counterclaim based on matters not covered by the submission may not be interposed. [253]

If the validity of an authentic document is questioned, arbitrators must stay their proceedings until an *inscription de faux* procedure has been brought and decided. They may not decide a question of personal status, such as the validity of a marriage, if it is raised incidentally in the course of an arbitration: A stay is required until the decision of a competent court has been obtained. The same is true if a criminal prosecution is initiated involving the same facts as the arbitration. [254]

Difficult problems arise if the submission or arbitration clause is alleged to be invalid because of fraud, duress, or mistake or because of violation of a rule of law. According to some decisions, arbitrators may deal with such issues even though they raise questions as to the very existence of their powers, but other decisions deny them this right. [255]

[250] MOREL 552; 1 ROBERT 171.

[251] CODE DE PROCÉDURE CIVILE art. 1011.

[252] *E.g.*, MOREL 551.

[253] 1 ROBERT 161–68.

[254] CODE DE PROCÉDURE CIVILE art. 1016 (*inscription de faux* in criminal matters); 1 ROBERT 167. On the *inscription de faux* procedure, see 7.44 *supra.* Arbitrators may conduct a *vérification d'écritures* procedure. On the rule preventing arbitrators from acting once criminal proceedings have been started, see also 3.23 *supra.* This rule is interpreted restrictively; an arbitrator may – if feasible – sever that part of the proceeding having criminal implications and render an award as to the remainder. Société de constructions aéronautiques du Midi v. Dewoitine, Cour Paris, July 8, 1942, [1944] D. CHR. J. 23.

[255] The *Cour d'Appel* in Paris has consistently followed that rule. Other *cours d'appel* have held to the contrary. Decisions by the *Cour de Cassation* are split. However, some of the more recent cases deny the arbitrators the right to decide whether the agreement which is

Generally, it is possible to bring a declaratory judgment action before the start of arbitration proceedings to have the arbitration clause or submission declared void. [256] If court proceedings have been started, an arbitration has to be stayed until the validity of the submission or arbitration clause has been determined. [257] A determination of the validity of a submission or arbitration clause by arbitrators is always reviewable by the courts, even when the right to appeal has been waived. [258]

**b. Proof before arbitrators.** Even when the parties have waived adherence to ordinary rules of procedure, the development of evidence before French arbitrators often seems to take place in the gradual fashion characteristic of an ordinary civil action. Usually, the presentation of written evidence presents no problems. [259] If witnesses are to be heard and the parties have not released the arbitrators from following the Code, or if a witness is likely to be recalcitrant, the arbitrators must render an interlocutory decision and proceed according to the rules established for *enquêtes* in the *Code de Procédure Civile.* Testimonial compulsion is available only if the arbitrators have ordered an *enquête* by an interlocutory decision that has been sanctioned by the court in an exequatur proceeding. Unless the submission provides otherwise, whether or not there is a formal *enquête*, witnesses are always heard by all arbitrators at the same time. The parties and their counsel should be present when the witnesses are heard. [260]

Formal *expertises* are used less frequently in arbitrations than in regular law suits, since the arbitrators themselves are often specialists,

the very basis of their powers is valid and require a stay until that question has been decided by the court. The cases on both sides of the question are collected in 1 ROBERT 154 n. 3; 1 DALLOZ, *op. cit. supra* note 179, at 178. The procedure for the appointment of an arbitrator does not seem to be used to decide this issue.

[256] See Buck v. Constantine, *supra* note 230 (court recognized possibility of bringing independent action before start of arbitration, but held this was not possible since the rules of the International Chamber of Commerce, incorporated in the arbitration clause, provided that the arbitrators were also to decide questions relating to the validity of the underlying agreement).

[257] Vigneron (sic), *supra* note 230 (with note Garaud reviewing the cases on the question). The case is in accord with other *Cour de Cassation* decisions holding that arbitrators should not decide the validity of an agreement forming the basis of their powers.

[258] MOREL 553.

[259] On the law applicable to written evidence, see 7.34–7.50 *supra.* Even if formal rules of law have been waived, documentary evidence must be submitted to the other side before it is used, in accordance with the rules governing the *communication des pièces*, mentioned 7.34 *supra.*

[260] 1 ROBERT 172–73. On the *exequatur* procedure for the enforcement of arbitral decisions, see 11.10.b *infra.* Concerning the penalties which may be imposed upon recalcitrant witnesses, see 7.51.c *supra.*

especially in commercial disputes. The parties may provide in their submission that the arbitrators shall seek the advice of a designated expert. A formal order authorizing an *expertise* is necessary if the arbitrators are bound to follow the regular procedure.

Arbitrators are authorized to view the premises, and parties may be interrogated through a formal *comparution personnelle*. Frequently, the latter is unnecessary, however, since the parties are generally present during arbitration hearings and the arbitrators can ask informal questions whenever appropriate. The availability of the party-oath in arbitration is doubtful. [261]

**c. Premature termination.** A number of events can bring an arbitration to an end before an award has been rendered. These include the death of a party if there are minors among his heirs [262] and the refusal of an arbitrator to accept his assigment or his death or withdrawal. However, the submission may provide a method for the replacement of arbitrators who are unwilling or unable to serve. [263] Unless the parties have provided a different time limit, an arbitration terminates three months after the date of the submission. [264] This rule is useful because an arbitration, like an ordinary action, may take the form of an extended series of hearings. The time allowed for the arbitration may be extended by express or implied agreement of the parties. [265] The death of a party or any other event leading to a stay of the arbitration extends the period available for its completion by the period of the stay. [266] The parties may not present new evidence or new memoranda

[261] 1 ROBERT 175–76. Some quite old cases authorize the use of the party-oath. 1 DALLOZ *op. cit. supra* note 179, at No. 170.

[262] CODE DE PROCÉDURE CIVILE art. 1013. The rule is based on the idea that the heirs of a party, not an executor or administrator, are substituted for a decedent (see 6.04.a *supra*) and that minors may not submit cases to arbitration (see 11.06.b *supra*).

[263] CODE DE PROCÉDURE CIVILE art. 1012. The parties may make various arrangements for the replacement of an arbitrator, *e.g.*, that they will select a replacement or that the remaining arbitrators shall do so; they may also provide that the remaining arbitrator or arbitrators shall decide the controversy.

[264] CODE DE PROCÉDURE CIVILE art. 1007.

[265] See CODE DE PROCÉDURE CIVILE art. 1012; 1 ROBERT 64–65; CUCHE & VINCENT 617–18. There may be an implied extension – for example, if both parties proceed with the arbitration after the expiration of the three-month period. Absent active participation in the arbitration, failure by one side to protest if the other proceeds with arbitration after the expiration of the period does not constitute implied consent to an extension. Etabl. Dupuis et Fils v. Soc. A.D.E.M.E.V., Cour Paris, Feb. 9, 1961, [1961] D.J. 283.

[266] Death of a party extends the period by the time given to the heirs to decide on acceptance of the inheritance. CODE DE PROCÉDURE CIVILE art. 1013. On extension in case of stay by *inscription de faux* or criminal proceedings, see CODE DE PROCÉDURE CIVILE art. 1015.

during the last two weeks of the arbitral period.[267] An award is void if it has been rendered after the arbitration has terminated.

**d. Law governing arbitral procedure.** The rule that all questions of procedure are governed by the law of the forum is not always applied in the case of arbitrations conducted in France involving international transactions. In such a case, the arbitrators may apparently follow the procedural law selected by the parties.

### 11.10. The Award

A majority of the arbitrators must concur in the award, which must be in writing and be signed by all the arbitrators. If some refuse to sign after a decision has been reached, the other arbitrators must make a notation to that effect on the award; otherwise, the award is invalid.[268] Dissenting opinions are not possible.[269] If compliance with rules of procedure has not been waived, the award must contain all recitals required by the Code of Civil Procedure for judgments.[270] Even in case of waiver, the arbitrators must write an opinion indicating the contentions of the parties and the reasons for their decision. The arbitrators may award costs; they must make a decision concerning the allocation of costs if the submission requires them to do so.[271] An award is considered an authentic act. Recitals by the arbitrators concerning matters they have personally observed or done may not be controverted except in an *inscription de faux* procedure.[272] With the signing of the award, the arbitrators' powers are at an end; they may not reopen the case or amend their own decision.[273]

[267] Code de Procédure Civile art. 1016.

[268] Code de Procédure Civile art. 1016; Morel 553. The signatures of the arbitrators need not be notarized.

[268] However, the arbitrators may insert a clause in the award stating that it represents the decision of a majority. 1 Robert 200.

[270] See Code de Procédure Civile art. 141, requiring that a judgment contains the names of the judges, the names, occupations and residences of the parties, the nature of the claim, a summary of the arguments of the parties, the reasons for the decision, and the actual decision. French law does not distinguish between the opinion, the decision, and the judgment. See 7.13.c *supra*.

[271] 1 Robert 151, 201. Some cases hold that arbitrators need not write an opinion if they have the power of *amiable compositeurs*.

[272] Morel 555. But this seems true only if the arbitrators do not exceed their powers. On authentic acts, see 7.43 *supra*.

[273] 1 Robert 203. However, a correction of a mistake seems possible. Furthermore, arbitrators may be able to amend an award if all the parties consent. See 1 Dalloz, *op. cit. supra* note 179, at Nos. 350–53.

**a. Effect of even division among arbitrators.** In France, parties often select two arbitrators rather than one or three. If the two arbitrators cannot reach a common decision, the arbitration comes to an end [274] and the proceedings have, in fact, been useless. However, parties may agree in the submission that, in case of even division among the arbitrators, a third person, called *tiers arbitre,* [275] shall be selected to break the tie. The submission may provide for the appointment of the *tiers arbitre* by an outside person or agency, by the court, by the two arbitrators, or by the parties. [276] If the *tiers arbitre* is to be appointed by the two arbitrators and these cannot agree, he may be appointed by the court. [277]

The *tiers arbitre* is not a third independent arbitrator. He must follow the opinion of one of the arbitrators. To enable him to do so, the arbitrators must prepare statements setting out their views. The *tiers arbitre* must examine these statements and confer with the two arbitrators. He does not hear new evidence. Unless the parties stipulate otherwise, his decision must be rendered within one month. [278]

**b. Enforcement *(exequatur)* and *res judicata* effect of awards.** If the losing party does not comply with the award voluntarily, the prevailing party must obtain a so-called *exequatur* in order to be able to levy execution. [279] The *exequatur* order also gives the award *res judicata* effect. Furthermore, only awards sanctioned by *exequatur* may be reviewed by the courts through appeal or *opposition.* [280]

[274] Code de Procédure Civile art. 1012.

[275] *Tiers arbitre* means literally third arbitrator; the ancient term *tiers* instead of the modern term *troisième* is retained to distinguish the *tiers arbitre,* whose only function is to break a tie and who does not participate in the arbitration proper, from a true third (*troisième*) arbitrator. *Cf.* Cuche & Vincent 625; Morel 553.

[276] Morel 553; 1 Robert 185.

[277] Code de Procédure Civile art. 1017. This is done upon *ex parte* application of either party addressed to the presiding judge of the *tribunal de grande instance* at the place where the award was to be rendered. Appointment by the presiding judge of the commercial court, though irregular, is a waivable defect. Dame Moizant v. Dame Roussel-Eloy, Cour Poitiers, Dec. 20, 1950, [1951] D.J. 103.

[278] Code de Procédure Civile art. 1018. Arbitrators may either prepare a joint statement setting out their differences or two separate statements. The Code apparently contemplates a formal conference between the *tiers arbitre* and the two arbitrators. However, these rules are interpreted liberally; it is sufficient if the *tiers arbitre* learns the views of the two arbitrators in some fashion – for example, by conferring with them separately. Dame Moizant v. Dame Roussel-Eloy, *supra* note 277. In case of a tie between two arbitrators, the parties may also appoint a new arbitrator and authorize him to make his own independent evaluation of the issues, but he would not be a *tiers arbitre.*

[279] Translated literally, *exequatur* means "let it be executed." *Cf.* Morel 555.

[280] *E.g.,* Meunié v. Centre national de commerce extérieur, Cass. Com., Dec. 22, 1959, [1960] D.J. 685 (only *exequatur* gives *res judicata* effect; no appeal possible until after *exequatur*); Soc. auxiliaire française des pétroles v. Cie. française de raffinage, Cour Paris, March

To receive the *exequatur*, the award must be filed in the office of the clerk of the *tribunal de grande instance* competent for the area in which the award has been rendered. This should be done by the arbitrators within three days of the rendering of the award, but later filing is not fatal. With the award, it is ordinarily necessary to file the submission, formal statements of the parties, and all interlocutory decisions.

The party desiring the *exequatur* addresses an *ex parte* petition to the presiding judge of the court. [281] The judge grants the *exequatur*, unless the award shows on its face that it contravenes public policy or is otherwise void. Accordingly, the *exequatur* proceeding is not an effective method for review of arbitral decisions. Denial of *exequatur* is appealable. [282]

If voluntary compliance is not expected, an *exequatur* proceeding is necessary even for interlocutory decisions. An arbitration award which has received the *exequatur* is treated substantially as a judgment. A copy of the award and *exequatur* must be served on adverse parties to start running the time periods within which a review of the award may be obtained. [283]

### 11.11. Review of Arbitral Decisions

The rules governing the review of arbitral decisions are complex. This is due to some extent to terminology, [284] but also to the availability of the remedy of appeal, which involves the possibility of adjudication *de novo* by an appellate court, a procedure inconsistent with the idea of arbitration. In addition, a special remedy for the review of arbitral decisions, called *opposition en nullité*, is only partially co-ordi-

17, 1960, [1960] D.J. 699 (same holding). Some authors oppose the view that an award does not have *res judicata* effect until after the *exequatur*. 1 ROBERT 205–06; CUCHE & VINCENT 625.

[281] CODE DE PROCÉDURE CIVILE art. 1020. The same article provides that the award must be filed in the office of the clerk of the *cour d'appel* if the case was submitted to arbitration while pending on appeal. Some court clerks require the filing of all papers mentioned in the text; others require only the filing of the award. It is not entirely clear whether the filing of all papers is required by law. See 1 ROBERT 208. On the *exequatur* procedure generally, see *id.* at 212–17.

[282] The *exequatur* order is simply put at the foot of the original award. The matter need not be referred to the *ministère public*. A dispute concerning the execution of the award must be brought before the court that ordered the *exequatur*. CODE DE PROCÉDURE CIVILE art. 1021.

[283] MOREL 556; CODE DE PROCEDURE CIVILE art. 102; *cf.* 11.11 *infra*. An *enregistrement* tax is payable on arbitral awards having received the *exequatur*, though the *exequatur* itself is tax free. A stamp tax is also due. These taxes are identical to the taxes on judgments. This may discourage arbitration. *Cf.* 12.06 *infra*.

[284] See 11.11.a *infra*.

nated with the appeal procedure. Suggestions for simplification have been made, but so far have not been put into effect. [285]

**a. *Opposition en nullité.*** Ordinarily, *opposition* is a remedy by which a party in default may obtain reopening of his case. It is not available in arbitration, since parties to an arbitration are never considered in default. [286] However, the special remedy of *opposition en nullité,* also called *opposition à l'ordonnance d'exequatur,* exists to obtain the annulment of an arbitral award suffering from a procedural defect. This remedy has nothing to do with default.

The remedy is available: (1) if an award has been rendered in the absence of a valid submission; (2) if procedural rules regulating the conduct of the arbitrators specified in the submission have been violated; [287] (3) if an award has been rendered after premature termination of the arbitration; [288] (4) if some arbitrators have not signed the award; [289] (5) if the *tiers arbitre* has not conferred with the two arbitrators; [290] or (6) if the award goes beyond the terms of the submission. [291]

*Opposition en nullité* is conducted as an ordinary action. It is brought before the court that has rendered the order of *exequatur* [292] and is begun by a regular *ajournement.* No special limitation period, only the general thirty-year statute of limitations, applies. However, a party waives the right to *opposition en nullité* by formal acquiescence in the award, by executing the award voluntarily, or by failing to object to its execution by legal process. [293] An *opposition en nullité* stays exe-

[285] It has been suggested that the *opposition en nullité* should be abolished, leaving only appeal available. 1 ROBERT 228. The use of the *exequatur* procedure as a method of review does not seem to have been contemplated, perhaps because it is not well adapted to adjudication of the issues *de novo,* a procedure firmly anchored in French law, which can be avoided in arbitration only if waived by the parties. On review of arbitral decisions in collective labor disputes, see 11.05 n. 172 *supra.*

[286] CODE DE PROCÉDURE CIVILE art. 1016.

[287] CODE DE PROCÉDURE CIVILE art. 1028 (1). This subdivision includes awards not based on rules of law when the parties have not waived the rule that arbitrators must base their decision on existing rules of law. 1 ROBERT 231.

[288] CODE DE PROCÉDURE CIVILE art. 1028 (2). On events prematurely terminating arbitration, see 11.09.c *supra.*

[289] CODE DE PROCÉDURE CIVILE art. 1028 (3) (except where a minority of the arbitrators refuses to sign after a decision has been reached and their refusal has been noted in the award in accordance with article 1016 of the *Code de Procédure Civile*); *cf.* 11.10 *supra.*

[290] CODE DE PROCÉDURE CIVILE art. 1028 (4); *cf.* 11.10.a *supra.*

[291] CODE DE PROCÉDURE CIVILE art. 1028 (5).

[292] CODE DE PROCÉDURE CIVILE art. 1028.

[293] 1 ROBERT 236; CUCHE & VINCENT 627. Whether an award may be declared void in an ordinary declaratory judgment action, is controverted. On the manner in which objection to an execution must be made, see 13.13.c *infra.*

cution of the award, unless the prevailing party has been granted provisional execution by the arbitrators. The rules applicable to provisional execution of judgments apply to provisional execution of arbitral awards. [294]

The *opposition en nullité*, if successful, leads to a judgment declaring the award void.

**b. Appeal from arbitral awards.** Unless waived, an appeal lies from arbitral awards, regardless of the amount involved. An appeal from an award, as an appeal from a judgment, involves a re-examination of the facts as well as of the law and the possibility of introducing new evidence. The time to appeal is one month. [295] The appeal must be taken to a *cour d'appel* unless the case would have been within the competence of the *tribunal d'instance* if brought before a court rather than arbitrated. In that event, the appeal goes to the *tribunal de grande instance.* [296] No appeal to a court is possible if the case was submitted to arbitration while pending on appeal or if an appeal was taken to an appellate arbitral tribunal. The ordinary rules of procedure governing appeals apply. [297] As in the case of judgments, the appeal stays execution of the award, unless provisional execution has been granted. [298]

The right to appeal may be waived by an express stipulation in the submission or arbitration clause. Waiver is also implied in a clause giving the arbitrators the right to act as *amiables compositeurs* or to disregard rules of law.

Waiver of the right to appeal is ineffective if rules involving strong public policy or *ordre public* have been violated during the arbitration – for instance, if a party has not received an adequate opportunity to be heard or if documentary evidence or memoranda handed to the arbitrators by one party have not first been submitted to the other. [299]

[294] See 8.15 *supra.* Provisional execution may be granted only if mentioned in the submission as a possible issue.

[295] On appeals generally, see ch. 8 *supra.*

[296] CODE DE PROCÉDURE CIVILE art. 1023. Before the 1958 reforms, the *tribunal civil,* predecessor of the *tribunal de grande instance,* heard all appeals from the *juges de paix* (predecessors of the *tribunal d'instance*) and certain lower courts, but since 1958 all these appeals go to the *cours d'appel.* It is not clear whether the drafters of the 1958 amendments forgot to change the article dealing with appeals from arbitral awards or whether they intentionally preserved the power of the *tribunal de grande instance* in this matter, now the only case in which it may act in an appellate capacity. *Cf.* 3.30 *supra.*

[297] *Cf.* CODE DE PROCÉDURE CIVILE art. 1025, providing that, as on appeal from a judgment, an unsuccessful appellant may be subjected to a fine.

[298] CODE DE PROCÉDURE CIVILE art. 1024. On provisional execution, see 8.15 *supra.*

[299] Appeal is the remedy to be used if minimum procedural safeguards, referred to in France as rights of the defense or *droits de la défense,* have been violated. Though analogous to American ideas of due process, this principle has no constitutional sanction. *Cf.* Alloncle v.

In such a case, the appeal leads to annulment of the award, not to a hearing *de novo*.

Since many of the grounds for *opposition en nullité* also involve public policy, there is a certain duplication of remedies.[300] If available, *opposition en nullité* must be used,[301] but selection of the proper procedure is not always easy. Lack of competence on the part of the arbitrators must be raised by appeal,[302] but *opposition en nullité* is the appropriate remedy if the award was rendered after expiration of the time available for the arbitration.[303] Appeal and *opposition en nullité* are not mutually exclusive; in a proper case, both may be invoked at the same time.

**c. Other methods of review.** No *pourvoi* directly from an arbitral award, even if sanctioned by an *exequatur* order, may be taken to the *Cour de Cassation*. However, judgments dealing with arbitral matters may be taken to the *Cour de Cassation* if they cannot be reviewed by ordinary appeal.[304] The regular rules governing all *pourvois* apply.

According to the *Code de Procédure Civile*, the remedy of *requête civile* is available to review arbitral decisions. Though ordinarily brought before the court that has rendered the decision, a different rule prevails in arbitration, since arbitrators lose all their powers once they have made their award: *Requête civile* is brought before the court that must hear an appeal from the arbitral award.[305] *Requête civile*, not much used even in the case of judgments, seems of even less importance in the case of arbitral decisions.[306]

Soc. anon. Bolinders, Cour Paris, Feb. 27, 1958, [1958] D.J. 489; Société auxiliare des pétroles v. Cie française du raffinage, *supra* note 280. See also Bottos v. Prévost, Cour Paris, Feb. 7, 1957, [1957] D.J. 251 (in spite of waiver of right to appeal, appeal remains possible if the arbitrators have not written an opinion indicating the reasons for their decision); Société de constructions aéronautiques du Midi v. Dewoitine, Cour Paris, July 8, 1942, [1944] D. Chr. J. 23 (right to appeal probably not affected by waiver if arbitrators proceeded in matter in which criminal prosecution pending).

300 An appeal, when possible in spite of a waiver of the right to appeal, leads to the same result as an *opposition en nullité*, *i.e.*, the annulment of the award, not a new decision on the merits.

301 See 1 Robert 227.

302 Casanova v. Serratrice, Cass. Com., Nov. 10, 1947, [1948] D.J. 16. Lack of competence of arbitrators is usually due to a submission which is void. Appeal also is the proper remedy if less than all the arbitrators have acted during some phase of the arbitration, though the submission does not allow a delegation of powers. 1 Robert 228. But *opposition en nullité* must be used if not all the arbitrators have signed the award. Code de Procédure Civile art. 1028 (1).

303 See 11.09.c *supra*.

304 Code de Procédure Civile art. 1028.

305 Code de Procédure Civile art. 1026.

306 *Requète civile* may not be used for violation of rules of procedure, if the parties have agreed that the arbitrators shall not be bound by those rules; nor is it available if the arbi-

Although the question is disputed, it seems that third parties who are affected by an award may be able to obtain a reopening by addressing a *tierce opposition* to the court that has power to grant an *exequatur* order. [307]

trators have dealt with matters not mentioned in the submission, when *opposition en nullité* is the proper remedy. CODE DE PROCÉDURE CIVILE art. 1027. This leaves mainly fraud on the part of the arbitrators as a basis for the remedy. *Cf.* CUCHE & VINCENT 630; 1 ROBERT 147-48; 223–26.

[307] The provision of article 1022 of the *Code de Procédure Civile* that arbitral awards are not binding on third parties has been invoked as an argument for exclusion of *tierce opposition*. In spite of article 1022, however, third parties, such as creditors, affected by a collusively obtained award, may probably bring *tierce opposition*. It is brought before the court that would have heard the dispute in the absence of arbitration. See CUCHE & VINCENT 630; 1 ROBERT 241–42.

CHAPTER 12

# LITIGATION EXPENSES AND LEGAL AID

This chapter describes amounts of litigation expenses (12.01–12.07), their allocation (12.08–12.10), and legal aid (12.11–12.17).

## 1. AMOUNTS OF LITIGATION EXPENSES

### 12.01. Introduction

Litigation costs are usually low in cases in which the litigants are likely to be of modest means. For example, in the social security courts, in which no fees or taxes of any kind are collected and assistance of professional counsel is not required, litigation is practically free of costs. [1] Expenses of litigation are also quite moderate before the labor courts (*conseils de prud'hommes*), [2] the farm tenancy courts (*tribunaux paritaires de baux ruraux*), and the *tribunal d'instance*. [3]

Costs are more substantial before the commercial courts and the *tribunaux de grande instance*. However, before all courts, the availability of legal aid enables even poor persons freely to engage in litigation.

Litigation expenses encompass: (1) expenses incurred in the preparation of a case; (2) fees payable to the parties' counsel and their process servers; (3) fees payable to court clerks; (4) witness' and expert's fees and travel expenses; and (5) taxes. Most of these expenses are regulated by complex official schedules.

[1] DÉCRET No. 58–1291 of Dec. 22, 1958, J.O. Dec. 23, 1958, p. 11613, [1959] D.L. 49, art. 57; CUCHE & VINCENT 599 n. 1. On the inexpensive nature of litigation in France generally, see the note Gavalda appended to Lewis v. Epoux Cunningham, Cour Paris, Feb. 9, 1962, 52 REV. CR. D.I.P. 81 (1963), in which costs of litigation in England and France are compared. Professor Gavalda indicates that total costs in a French lawsuit – the losing party's own as well as those it must pay to the prevailing party – will ordinarily not exceed 10 percent of the amount in litigation.

[2] In proceedings before these courts, professional counsel is not required (see 2.01–2.02 *supra*), and no stamp or *enregistrement* taxes are collected. However, service of original process by an *huissier* is sometimes required.

[3] Taxes and clerk's fees are substantially less than the corresponding fees charged in the *tribunal de grande instance*. Professional counsel is not required. See 2.01 and 7.16 *supra*.

## 12.02. Expenses Incurred in the Preparation of a Case

Expenses incurred in the preparation of a case are usually small, mainly because French counsel do not engage in wide-ranging factual investigations. [4] The cost of a *constat d'huissier* is modest, [5] and other preparation is quite often limited to obtaining copies of police reports and similar documents. Only if an *expertise* is conducted as a kind of discovery device are costs likely to be of any significance: The fees of an expert may reach about 500 francs (about $ 100), or even more. [6]

## 12.03. Fees Payable to Parties' Counsel and Their Process Servers

**a. Fees of *avocats* and *avoués*.** Fees charged by *avocats* vary widely and are not subject to official regulation. *Avoués*, however, must abide by an official – fairly modest – fee schedule. [7]

*Avoués* practicing before a *tribunal de grande instance* are entitled to a flat fee of 25 francs (about $ 5) for each case. [8] If the subject matter of the dispute can be evaluated in money, they receive, in addition, a proportional fee based on the amount in controversy or, sometimes, on the amount of damages awarded. [9] The fee is 3 percent of all amounts up to 7000 francs (about $ 1,400), but this percentage decreases for amounts in excess of that sum. It is only one fourth of one percent for amounts in excess of 60,000 francs (about $ 12,000). [10] In divorce actions and other proceedings in which the matter in controversy cannot, or cannot easily, be evaluated in money, the proportional fee is replaced by a fee which varies between one and twenty times the fixed fee. The variable fee must be fixed by the presiding judge at the time of rendition of the judgment. [11] If the case cannot be terminated with

[4] On preparation before suit, see 5.01–5.02 *supra*.

[5] The *huissier* is entitled to a fee of 22.50 francs (about $ 4.50) for each three hour period devoted to the *constat*. In addition, the regular stamp and *enregistrement* taxes must be paid. See 12.06 *infra*.

[6] See 12.05.a *infra*.

[7] See 2.06.d *supra*.

[8] Only half the fee is payable if the case is not contested or the amount in controversy is below 3000 francs (about $ 600). *Avoués* before a *cour d'appel* are entitled to a fee of 37.50 francs (about $ 7.50). DÉCRET No. 60–323 of April 2, 1960, J.O. April 7, 1960, p. 3194, [1960] D.L. 133, arts. 2, 70.

[9] In tort cases, the proportional fee is based on the amount in controversy if it is 3000 francs (about $ 600) or less; if it exceeds this amount, the fee is based on the damages actually awarded. DÉCRET No. 60–323, *supra* note 8, art. 11. There are fairly elaborate rules for evaluating different types of claims and converting periodic payments into present value. DÉCRET No. 60–323, *supra* note 8, arts. 9–10, 12.

[10] DÉCRET No. 60–323, *supra* note 8, art. 4. The proportional fee before the *cour d'appel* is one third higher. DÉCRET No. 60–323, *supra* note 8, art. 71.

[11] DÉCRET No. 60–323, *supra* note 8, arts. 13–14. The *avoués* request the presiding judge to determine the variable fee at the end of the case. For this purpose, they indicate, on a form

one *audience*, additional fees, usually amounting to one-half or one-fourth the fixed fee, become payable for each *incident*. [12] *Avoués* are entitled to reimbursement for certain expenses actually incurred. [13] Additionally, they receive a kind of lump sum compensation for mailing expenses and stationery, which varies from 11 to 80 francs (about $ 2,20 to $ 16). [14] Disregarding compensation for expenses, the fees payable to *avoués* may not, ordinarily, exceed 10 percent of the amount involved in litigation. [15]

**b. Fees of *huissiers*.** The *huissier audiencier* calling the calendar is entitled to a moderate fee. [16]

For preparing an original and duplicate original *ajournement*, notice of appeal, or other paper requiring formal service (such as a judgment), *huissiers* are entitled to a fee of 8.40 francs (about $ 1.70). This fee is slightly higher for proceedings pending before a *cour d'appel*, the *Conseil d'Etat*, or the *Cour de Cassation*. [17] For each copy served by an *huissier*, one-fourth of the fee mentioned is due. [18] For formal service of papers, *huissiers* are entitled in addition to 12.55 francs (about $ 2.50) as compensation for mailing expenses and stationery [19] and to a flat fee as lump sum compensation for travel expenses. [20] They further receive reimbursement for stamp and *enregistrement* taxes paid by them.

established by the professional organization of the *avoués*, to what fee they believe themselves entitled.

[12] DÉCRET No. 60–323, *supra* note 8, arts. 20, 23–24. In case of impleader, the *avoué* for the impleading party receives, in addition to the fee to which he is entitled on account of the main action, one half the fixed and proportional fee. DÉCRET No. 60–323, *supra* note 8, art. 21.

[13] DÉCRET No. 60–323, *supra* note 8, arts. 65–67.

[14] DÉCRET No. 60–323, *supra* note 8, art. 68. The actual amount of this fee depends on the amount of the regular fee to which the *avoué* is entitled.

[15] DÉCRET No. 60–323, *supra* note 8, art. 81.

[16] DÉCRET No. 58–1040 of Oct. 30, 1958, J.O. Nov. 5, 1958, p. 10020, [1958] D.L. 374, as amended by DÉCRET No. 61–1295 of Dec. 4, 1961, J.O. Dec. 5, 1961, p. 11159, [1961] D.L. 357, art. 7. The fee is 0.95 francs (about $ 0.20) for each case before the *tribunal d'instance*, 1.85 francs (about $ 0.35) for each case before the commercial court and the *tribunal de grande instance*, 2.65 francs (about $ 0.55) for each case before a *cour d'appel* and 3.60 francs (about $ 0.75) for each case in the *Cour de Cassation*.

[17] DÉCRET No. 58–1040, *supra* note 16, art. 2. The fee is 10.30 francs (about $ 2.10) before the *cours d'appel*, *Conseil d'Etat*, or *Cour de Cassation*.

[18] DÉCRET No. 58–1040, *supra* note 16, art. 1.

[19] DÉCRET No. 58–1040, *supra* note 16, art. 4. However, the *huissier* is entitled to reimbursement for expenses of registered mail if the use of registered mail is required by law.

[20] Irrespective of the distance actually traveled, each *huissier* serving a paper must receive from his client twenty-nine times the cost of a first class train ticket for one kilometer. The sum is paid into a fund which reimburses *huissiers* for their actual expenses. DÉCRET No. 58–1040, *supra* note 16, arts. 15–21. At present, the sum payable under this head amounts to 3.48 francs (about $ 0.70).

Separate provisions govern the fees of *huissiers* who levy execution. The fees for the (informal) service of pleadings (*conclusions*) and other *actes d'avoué à avoué* are modest. [21]

## 12.04. Fees of Court Clerks

Court clerks are ordinarily entitled to three different kinds of fees: First, for putting the case on the calendar following the filing of the *placet*, the *greffier* of a *tribunal de grande instance* receives a fee of 7.20 francs (about $ 1.50); [22] second, for transcribing and keeping the *minute* of a judgment, whether definitive or not, he receives a fee of 7 francs (about $ 1.40); [23] third, for issuing the *grosse* of any judgment, he is entitled to a fee of 2 francs (about $ 0.40) per typed page and, for issuing any other copy, 1 franc (about $ 0.20) per typed page. [24] The parties must also reimburse the clerk for the cost of the tax stamps he must affix to the *grosse* and to other copies delivered by him, and the clerk is further entitled to a flat fee of 4 francs (about $ 0.80) as compensation for the stamps he must affix to the original *minute* of the judgment which he keeps on file. [25]

## 12.05. Fees of Experts and Witnesses

**a. Fees of experts.** There is no set schedule of fees for experts, though the courts examine their fees rather closely. While experts' fees are not very high, they are considered a real burden by many French litigants and are probably the only element of total litigation expenses which has engendered substantial adverse comment. Experts' fees vary so much, depending on the expert and the type of investigation involved, that it is difficult to give any figures. A fee of 500 francs (about $100) is not unusual for a medical expert. Expert accountants seem to charge somewhat higher, and most other experts somewhat lower, fees than physicans. [26]

[21] The fee for serving an *acte d'avoué à avoué* is ordinarily the same as the fee, mentioned *supra* note 16, for calling a case. DÉCRET No. 58–1040, *supra* note 16, art. 7.

[22] DÉCRET No. 58–465 of May 3, 1958, J.O. May 6, 1958, p. 4431, [1958] D.L. 205, as amended by DÉCRET No. 59–598 of May 5, 1959, J.O. May 6, 1959, p. 4825, [1959] D.L. 486, art. 6, and annexed schedule. The corresponding fees are: 3 francs (about $ 0.60) before the *tribunal d'instance*, 4 francs (about $ 0.80) before the *tribunal de commerce* and 10 francs (about $ 2.00) before a *cour d'appel*.

[23] DÉCRET No. 58–465, *supra* note 22, as amended, art. 7, and annexed schedule. The corresponding fees are 5 francs (about $ 1.00) for the commercial courts and *tribunaux d'instance* and 7.20 francs (about $ 1.45) for the *cours d'appel*.

[24] DÉCRET No. 58–465, *supra* note 22, as amended, art. 3, and annexed schedule. The fee for a regular copy (*expédition*) is the same in all courts; the fee for the *grosse* is 1 franc per page (about $ 0.20) in the commercial courts and *tribunaux d'instance*.

[25] DÉCRET No. 58–465, *supra* note 22, art. 12.

[26] See 7.54 *supra*.

**b. Witnesses.** Witnesses are entitled to a witness fee of 5.50 francs (about $ 1.10) in Paris and 4 francs (about $ 0.80) elsewhere as well as to the price of a second class train ticket if travel of more than 4 km (about 3 miles) is required. If travel exceeds 20 km (about 16 miles) or if more than one day of absence from home is involved, a small additional fee may be due. [27] Parties required to be present in court for a *comparution personnelle* are entitled to the same fees witnesses receive. [28]

## 12.06. Taxes

Two taxes, intended to help defray the costs of operating the court system, are collected from litigants in French courts. They are the stamp tax and the *enregistrement* tax. These taxes are not payable in various social matters, and indigents may obtain partial relief under the system of *assistance judiciaire* (legal aid). [29] However, in an ordinary case before the *tribunal de grande instance,* they add significantly to the cost of litigation.

**a. Stamp taxes.** The stamp tax is a tax on legal documents. The present rate is 2.50 francs (about $ 0.50) per letter-size page. It may be paid by affixing the proper amount of stamps unto the instrument before use, by using pre-stamped paper sold by the government, or by the use of a stamp-tax meter machine. [30]

Stamps must be used for *ajournements* and other documents (*exploits*) subject to formal service by *huissiers* in divorce or other actions involving personal status and in actions involving a subject matter having a monetary value. An exemption is granted in personal actions concerning movable property if the amount in controversy is less than 1500 francs (about $ 300). [31]

[27] Witnesses in civil cases are generally entitled to the fees and expenses provided for witnesses in criminal cases. See DÉCRET No. 49–1251, of August 27, 1949, J.O. Sept. 20, 1949, p. 9391, [1949] D.L. 401. The fee schedule for witnesses in criminal cases is contained in CODE DE PROCÉDURE PÉNALE arts. R. 129–38.

[28] When no *comparution personnelle* has been ordered, parties who must travel to the place where the court is sitting are entitled to travel expenses, but only for one such trip in first instance and one on appeal. See DÉCRET No. 49–1251, *supra* note 27.

[29] See 12.11–12.17 *infra.*

[30] 1 DALLOZ, ENCYCLOPÉDIE DE PROCÉDURE CIVILE ET COMMERCIALE, *Enregistrement et Timbre,* at No. 49 (1955). The tax-stamp meter machine is an adaptation of the postage meter machine.

[31] Law No. 63–254 of March 15, 1963, J.O. March 17, 1963, p. 2579, [1963] D.L. 97, arts. 6–7, 39, 56. The stamp tax is due for each page of the original *ajournement,* and for each page of every copy, but not for the duplicate original which the *huissier* returns to his client. The amount payable for stamp taxes can become substantial if the initial *ajournement* is long or if there are many parties to be served. See 7.02 *supra.* A stamp tax is not due in connection with proceedings before the labor or social security courts (see CODE GÉNÉRAL DES IMPÔTS art. 1098), nor in connection with certain election matters.

No stamp tax is due for pleadings (*conclusions*) and notices informally exchanged between *avoués* (*actes d'avoué à avoué*). [32] However, tax stamps must be affixed both to the original (*minute*) of a judgment and to all formal copies, as well as to records of proof proceedings and similar documents prepared by court clerks. [33]

**b. *Enregistrement* taxes.** An *enregistrement* tax of 5 francs (about $ 1) is due on *ajournements* and other papers subject to formal service by an *huissier*. [34] In addition, judgments and orders of most courts are subject to an *enregistrement* tax, which amounts to 10 francs (about $ 2) for interlocutory and *référé* decisions and 50 francs (about $ 10) for final decisions [35] rendered by a *tribunal de grande instance*. Since there may be several decisions in the course of a law suit, the total *enregistrement* tax may amount to a substantial sum. No *enregistrement* tax is due in cases before the social security or labor courts, nor in certain election matters. [36]

The *enregistrement* tax must be paid within one month after rendition of the judgment; plaintiff and defendant are jointly and severally liable for its payment; as a practical matter, the prevailing party pays the tax and subsequently attempts to collect it from the losing party. [37] At the time the *enregistrement* tax on a judgment is paid, unpaid *enre-*

[32] Law No. 63–254, *supra* note 31, art. 36.

[33] But not to the informal copy of the judgment which the clerk may deliver to the *avoués* merely for informational purposes, and which cannot be used to levy execution. See 1 DALLOZ, *op. cit. supra* note 30, at No. 48–2 (Supp. 1964).

[34] Law No. 63–254, *supra* note 31, arts. 3–4. The *enregistrement* tax is payable only for instruments subject to the stamp tax. See note 31 *supra*. On *enregistrement* in general, see 7.40 *supra*.

[35] The complete schedule is as follows: Non-final or *référé* decisions of the *tribunal d'instance* and the *tribunal paritaire de baux ruraux* (farm tenancy court): 5 francs (about $ 1); final decisions of the *tribunal d'instance* and *tribunal paritaire de baux ruraux*, and non-final and *référé* decisions of the *tribunal de grande instance* and commercial court: 10 francs (about $ 2); final decisions of the *tribunal de grande instance* and the commercial court, and non-final decisions of the *cours d'appel*: 50 francs (about $ 10); final decisions of the *cours d'appel* and non-final decisions of the *Cour de Cassation*: 100 francs (about $ 20); final decisions of the *Cour de Cassation*: 200 francs (about $ 40). For decisions of the *cours d'appel* and *Cour de Cassation*, the tax is reduced to one half in the case of appeals or *pourvois* against decisions of the *tribunal d'instance* or *tribunal paritaire de baux ruraux*. In some cases, higher taxes may be due. Law No. 63–254, *supra* note 31, art. 4. On the distinction between non-final and final judgments (which need not necessarily be final in the common law sense), see 7.13.d *supra*.

[36] The tax is payable only in the instances listed in note 35 *supra*. *Cf.* CODE GÉNÉRAL DES IMPÔTS art. 1098.

[37] About two weeks after rendition of the judgment, the clerk of the court sends the *avoué* for the prevailing part a notice indicating the tax due. To facilitate payment of the tax, in Paris there are *enregistrement* tax offices in the court house. See generally 1 DALLOZ, *op. cit. supra* note 30, at No. 28; 1 RAVIART, TRAITÉ FORMULAIRE DE PROCÉDURE GÉNÉRALE 228–29 (1956).

*gistrement* taxes on any contracts or other documents used during the litigation must also be paid. [38]

c. ***Droits de plaidoirie.*** The *enregistrement* tax office also collects a so-called *droit de plaidoirie* of 15 francs (about $ 3) payable in every case in which an *avocat* appears. This fee remains the same, regardless of the number of non-final judgments rendered during the case. However, a separate fee of 7.50 francs (about $ 1.50) is payable for each *référé* application. The *droits de plaidoirie* are paid into a retirement fund for *avocats.* [39]

### 12.07. Total Cost of a Lawsuit

The total litigation expenses in a French lawsuit vary greatly, depending upon the complexity of the matter. By way of example, there are set forth below the total costs in a contract action. It is assumed that the amount in controversy is 20,000 francs (about $ 4,000), that both the *ajournement* and the judgment are three pages long, and that the case can be decided on the basis of documentary evidence only, so that one formal *audience* will suffice. Under these circumstances, the total expenses would be about as follows:

| | |
|---|---|
| *avoué*'s fee | 515.00 francs (about $ 103.00) |
| *huissier*'s fees for service of *ajournement* and of judgment | 33.10 francs (about $ 6.65) |
| clerk's fees | 23.20 francs (about $ 4.65) |
| fees of *huissier audiencier* for calling calendar and serving various *actes d'avoué à avoué* (estimated) | 9.25 francs (about $ 1.85) |
| stamp and *enregistrement* taxes on *ajournement* and judgment | 101.50 francs (about $ 20.25) |
| *droit de plaidoirie* | 15.00 francs (about $ 3.00) |
| Total | 697.05 francs (about $ 139.40) |

[38] *Id.* at 230. The files handed to the court by the *avocats* (see 7.12.b *supra*) must remain in the court clerk's office two weeks after rendition of the judgment for inspection by the *enregistrement* officials. Although the *enregistrement* tax on the judgment becomes part of costs and must ultimately be paid by the losing party, the primary liability for the *enregistrement* tax on a document used as evidence rests on the party who originally prepared it.

[39] Décret No. 65–379 of May 19, 1965, reprinted in Code de Procédure Civile 671 (62d ed. Dalloz 1966). The *référé* rate also applies in cases before the *tribunal d'instance*.

To the total, the *avocat*'s fee and preliminary expenses must be added. Additional expenses arise if execution must be levied to enforce the judgment or if proof proceedings are necessary. Total expenses will be somewhat more than doubled if an appeal is taken to a *cour d'appel* since the fees before that court are higher than those before the *tribunal de grande instance*. However, there are no separate expenses for preparing a record, whether printed or not, and no expenses for preparing printed briefs.

## 2. ALLOCATION OF LITIGATION EXPENSES

### 12.08. Who is Liable for Costs

Until 1958, the losing party had to bear his own as well as his opponent's costs and fees. The *Code de Procédure Civile* permitted only limited exceptions. These rules were liberalized in 1958. At present, the court has a discretionary power in the allocation of costs. [40] However, normally costs continue to be imposed upon the losing party. If the court orders any other party to bear the costs, it must give its reasons. [41]

If both parties prevail in part and lose in part, the courts have, and had, a large degree of discretionary power in the allocation of costs. [42] In practice, the expenses of both sides are pooled and the court divides them among the parties on an equitable basis. [43] The courts also have a discretionary power not to grant costs in actions between spouses or other close relatives. [44] As a matter of case law, the *ministère public* and other public agencies acting in a governmental capacity are never liable for costs. [45] Furthermore, the prevailing party is not entitled to receive reimbursement for expenses that are due to its own fault. [46]

Costs may be imposed only upon a true party. Guardians and similar

[40] Code de Procédure Civile art. 130. The theoretical basis for the right to recover costs is a matter of controversy. For various theories, see Morel 530–31; Cornu & Foyer 387.

[41] Code de Procédure Civile art. 130, as amended by Décret No. 58-1289 of Dec. 22, 1958, J.O. Dec. 23, 1958, p. 11608, [1959] D.L. 49.

[42] Code de Procédure Civile art. 131.

[43] 2 Dalloz, Répertoire de Procédure Civile et Commerciale, *Frais et Dépens*, at No. 391 (1956).

[44] Code de Procédure Civile art. 131. The rule includes, in addition to spouses, ascendants, descendants, brothers and sisters, and in-laws in the same degrees.

[45] 2 Dalloz, *op. cit. supra* note 43, at Nos. 334–40; Cuche & Vincent 604.

[46] The same is true if the action was brought "in the exclusive interest of the prevailing party," in other words without a real need. Morel 533; 2 Dalloz, *op. cit. supra* note 43, at Nos. 360–67.

representatives are never personally liable for costs, [47] except in cases of neglect of duty or other wrongdoing. [48]

## 12.09. Expenses That May be Taxed as Costs

As a rule, to the extent they are prescribed by law, the fees of *avoués* and *huissiers*, as well as of court clerks, may be taxed as costs. The same is true of stamp and *enregistrement* taxes paid on *ajournements*, judgments, and similar documents. However, past due *enregistrement* taxes on documents used as evidence may generally not be recovered from the losing party even if they were paid during the litigation.

No party receives reimbursement for the fees he paid his own *avocat*. The same is true of fees paid to an *avoué* for legal consultations or other services not regulated by the official fee schedule. Expenses incurred in the preparation of the case – for instance, for a *constat* – may be recovered from the losing party if they are directly related to the suit. [49] The cost of unnecessary or void procedural documents are borne by the *avoué* or *huissier* who caused the unnecessary expense. [50]

The prevailing party may be able to recover expenses not ordinarily included in taxable costs by claiming that his opponent's conduct in resisting a clearly well-founded claim or in bringing an obviously unfounded action is so outrageous that it amounts to a tort for which damages should be paid in the form of compensation for litigation expenses not ordinarily included in taxable costs. If the court agrees, it may grant such damages, indicating in its opinion the facts on which it bases its decision. [51]

Costs may be awarded to a party only if they have been requested in its *conclusions*. [52] As a practical matter, the request for costs is embodied in a boilerplate clause. Damages not ordinarily taxable as costs must likewise be requested by *conclusions*. In its judgment, the court merely orders that the losing party bears the costs; it does not ordinarily specify the amount of costs to be recovered. On the basis of the order, the *avoué* prepares a detailed schedule of costs and fees which is served on the losing side at the same time as the judgment. If there is a

[47] 2 DALLOZ, *op. cit. supra* note 43, at No. 341.

[48] CODE DE PROCÉDURE CIVILE art. 132.

[49] Witnesses' fees, experts' fees, travel expenses for witnesses or for the court (in the case of a *descente sur les lieux*) are included in taxable costs. See, *e.g.*, MOREL 531; 2 DALLOZ, *op. cit. supra* note 43, at 405–09.

[50] CODE DE PROCÉDURE CIVILE art. 132.

[51] 2 DALLOZ, *op. cit. supra* note 43, at Nos. 410–11, 424. Damages granted under this head include the *enregistrement* taxes and penalties which should have been paid by the party producing the documents.

[52] *But see* CORNU & FOYER 387.

controversy, an application for taxation of the costs may be made to one of the judges who heard the case. [53] Costs are ordinarily paid at the end of the entire case. However, costs in certain proceedings, for instance proceedings concerning the competence of the court, are taxed separately on the basis of the outcome of that proceeding. [54]

## 12.10. *Distraction* of Costs in Favor of the Prevailing Party's *Avoué*

Clients are primarily responsible for payment of the fees and expenses of their *avoués*. However, if the *avoué* of the prevailing party has paid substantial expenses out of his own funds, he may ask the court to order the losing party to pay the costs not to his client but directly to him. This is known as the *distraction* of costs and fees. [55] It may be requested at any time before judgment, but in practice the demand for *distraction* is incorporated in a boilerplate clause in the original *conclusions* or, in the case of the plaintiff's *avoué*, in the *ajournement*. Although the *avoué* requesting *distraction* must make an affirmation that he has paid most of the litigation expenses out of his own pocket, the courts are usually satisfied with a statement in the *conclusions* that he is ready to make such an affirmation. [56] *Distraction* may be requested only in proceedings in which the use of an *avoué* is mandatory. The availability of *distraction* in *référé* proceedings is controverted. [57]

If *distraction* is granted, costs are taxed in the name of the prevailing party's *avoué*, who may recover them by levying execution against the losing party. The granting of *distraction* does not deprive the *avoué* of his primary claim against his own client. [58]

*Distraction* is not available to law professionals other than *avoués*.

[53] CUCHE & VINCENT 604–05; MOREL 535. In Paris, the professional organization (*chambre*) of *avoués* exercises semi-official control over costs and fees claimed by their members. In summary matters and before the various courts in which no *avoués* are acting, the costs are computed by the clerk of the court and mentioned in the judgment itself. CODE DE PROCÉDURE CIVILE art. 534. See generally 2 DALLOZ, RÉPERTOIRE DE PROCÉDURE CIVILE ET COMMERCIALE, *Taxe* (1956).

[54] MOREL 533; CODE DE PROCÉDURE CIVILE art. 169. If there is an appeal, the outcome of the appeal ordinarily determines who pays the costs. On the allocation of costs in the case of a *pourvoi* to the *Cour de Cassation*, see 9.24–9.25 *supra*.

[55] CODE DE PROCÉDURE CIVILE art. 133. The *distraction* must be granted in the same judgment which grants costs. There is some controversy whether distraction is basically a lien or a direct action. See CORNU & FOYER 388; MOREL 537.

[56] 2 DALLOZ, *op. cit. supra* note 43, at No. 433; CUCHE & VINCENT 606.

[57] 2 DALLOZ, *op. cit. supra* note 43, at Nos. 436–37, and SUPP. 1964; MOREL 538.

[58] CODE DE PROCÉDURE CIVILE art. 133.

## 3. LEGAL AID
## *(ASSISTANCE JUDICIAIRE)*

### 12.11. Introduction

Legal aid (*assistance judiciaire*), which is based on close co-operation between the legal professions and government authorities, [59] is used very widely. [60] The general availability of *assistance judiciaire* is one of the reasons why in France there has been no need for a contingent fee system. Since the present system imposes a very substantial burden on the legal professions, reforms have been suggested, but so far without success. [61]

### 12.12. Organization of Legal Aid Offices

For proceedings before courts of first instance, the question of wether legal aid (*assistance judiciaire*) should be granted is decided by legal aid offices (*bureaux d'assistance judiciaire*) established at the seat of each *tribunal de grande instance*. Ordinarily, each *bureau* consists of a representative of the local *enregistrement* tax office, a representative of the *préfet*, a member selected by the local *ordre* of *avocats*, a member selected by the local *chambre* of *avoués*, and a member selected by the *tribunal de grande instance* from among various law professionals or retired *magistrats*. If necessary, the Ministry of Justice may create several sections for *bureaux* handling numerous cases, each section having the membership of a regular *bureau*.

At the seat of each *cour d'appel*, there is a *bureau* handling requests for legal aid in matters before the *cour d'appel* and appeals from the

[59] See generally Schweinburg, *Legal Assistance Abroad*, 17 U. CHI. L. REV. 270 (1949); Jacoby, *Legal Aid to the Poor*, 53 HARV. L. REV. 940 (1940); Hassard-Short, *Legal Aid for the Poor*, 23 J. COMP. LEGIS. (3d ser.) 27, 37 (1941).

[60] Thus, in 1959, 25,323 new cases were put on the calendar of the *tribunal de grande instance* in Paris. In 16,210 of these, an application for legal aid was made; it was granted in 8,819 instances and rejected in 1,584 instances. The remaining applications were withdrawn, or the case settled, or the matter transferred elsewhere. 1 SOLUS & PERROT 961. For additional statistics, see 1 DALLOZ, RÉPERTOIRE DE PROCÉDURE CIVILE ET COMMERCIALE, *Assistance Judiciaire*, at No. 4 (1955).

[61] *Id.* at No. 5; 1 SOLUS & PERROT 961. In an average year, each *avoué* before a court of first instance in Paris is likely to handle about 85 legal aid cases. Reform plans have included a proposal to make persons able to pay a limited sum liable for reduced fees, and a proposal to have municipalities pay part of the costs of legal aid out of their welfare budgets. 1 SOLUS & PERROT 976–77.

The first detailed legislation concerning legal aid in France is the Law of Jan. 22, 1851, Bull. Off. 346, No. 2680, [1851] D. 4. 25. It was substantially modified by Law of July 10, 1901, J.O. July 12, 1901, [1902] D. 4. 9, by Law of Dec. 4, 1907, J.O. Dec. 5, 1907, [1908] D. 4. 1, and, more recently, by DÉCRET No. 58–1289, *supra* note 41. *Cf.* 1 Solus & Perrot 960–61.

local legal aid offices. Its membership, though somewhat more numerous, is analogous to that of the local *bureaux*.

There is also a *bureau* for litigation before the *Cour de Cassation* and one for litigation pending before the *Conseil d'Etat* or the *Tribunal des Conflits*. [62]

In addition, a kind of appellate legal aid office (*bureau supérieur d'assistance judiciaire*) has been created at the Ministry of Justice. It is composed of representatives of various government departments, the *Cour de Cassation*, the *Conseil d'Etat*, and the organization of *avocats aux conseils*. It hears appeals from decisions of the legal aid offices at the seat of the *cours d'appel* and from decisions of the legal aid offices of the *Cour de Cassation* and *Conseil d'Etat*. [63]

## 12.13. Persons Entitled to Legal Aid

Legal aid is broadly available. Natural persons, as well as certain charitable foundations, public bodies, and associations, may obtain legal aid if their resources are insufficient for the contemplated litigation. [64] There is no arbitrary income limit; the granting of legal aid depends on the anticipated expenses of the suit as well as on the resources of the applicant. [65]

Legal aid *bureaux* are rather liberal in deciding requests for legal aid. However, they have a tendency to consider the merits of the case as well as the resources of the applicant: Legal aid is not ordinarily granted if the applicant wishes to institute litigation without a reasonable chance of success. [66] In a few cases, legal aid is awarded automatically, regardless of the means of the applicant. [67]

The Convention of Establishment of 1959 makes United States nationals eligible for legal aid in France. [68] Whether, absent a treaty, legal aid is available to persons who are not French nationals is disputed. [69]

Legal aid is available to litigants in all civil cases, regardless of the

[62] Law of Jan. 22, 1851, as amended, *supra* note 61, arts. 3, 5, 6.

[63] Law of Jan. 22, 1851, as amended, *supra* note 61, art. 12.

[64] Law of Jan. 22, 1851, as amended, *supra* note 61, art. 1.

[65] 1 Solus & Perrot 963.

[66] *E.g.*, Morel 540; Cuche & Vincent 611. Thus, *assistance judiciaire* is unlikely to be granted to permit commencement of an action obviously barred by the statute of limitations.

[67] For instance, to World War II political or military prisoners. For a listing, see 1 Solus & Perrot 964.

[68] Convention of Establishment with France, Nov. 25, 1959, (1960) 2 U.S.T. & O.I.A. 2398, T.I.A.S. No. 4625, art. III, para. 1.

[69] The prevailing opinion is that legal aid is available to persons who are not French nationals. 1 Dalloz, *op. cit. supra* note 60, at Nos. 193–97. For a list of treaties dealing with legal aid, see *id.* at Nos. 199–201 and Supp. 1964; *cf.* Batiffol 816.

court in which the action is pending, as well as to civil parties in criminal cases. It is not restricted to contested matters and may also be granted in matters falling within *juridiction gracieuse.* [70]

## 12.14. Procedure for Obtaining Legal Aid

A person desiring legal aid must address an oral or written request to the *procureur de la République* competent for the district in which he is domiciled or to the mayor of his home community. No particular formalities are required, [71] but the request must be accompanied by a certified copy of the applicant's tax return and by a declaration in which the applicant affirms that, on account of the insufficiency of his resources, he is unable to protect his interests in court. The declaration must enumerate all sources of income of the applicant. [72] It is also customary to attach to the application some documents affirming the merits of the applicant's proposed action.

The application and supporting documents are forewarded to the *bureau* of the *tribunal de grande instance* competent for the area in which the applicant lives. This *bureau* hears the applicant and investigates his financial resources. It also invites the applicant's opponent to make comments and may attempt to settle the case. If the action is pending or is to be brought before the local *tribunal de grande instance* or before a lower court in its district, the *bureau* decides whether or not to grant *assistance judiciaire*; if the action is pending in another area, the file that has been collected is transmitted to the appropriate *bureau.* [73] A *bureau* rejecting an application must indicate the reasons for its action. [74]

[70] Article 1 of the Law of Jan. 22, 1851, as amended, *supra* note 61, provides that *assistance judiciaire* is available for litigation, including ex parte and *référé* matters, before the *tribunaux de grande instance, tribunaux d'instance,* commercial courts, administrative courts, *cours d'appel, Cour de Cassation, Conseil d'Etat,* and *Tribunal des Conflits* and for civil parties in criminal cases. Legal aid is authorized for proceedings before the labor courts by article 78 of DÉCRET No. 58–1292 of Dec. 22, 1958, J.O. Dec. 23, 1958, p. 11621, [1959] B.L.D. 77.

[71] Law of Jan. 22, 1851, as amended, *supra* note 61, art. 8. If the request is addressed to the mayor, he transmits it to the *procureur,* who, in turn, sends it to the legal aid bureau.

[72] Law of Jan. 22, 1851, as amended, *supra* note 61, art. 10. The truth of the declaration must be affirmed before the mayor of the applicant's home community, though the mayor has no right to investigate its truthfulness. He may, however, point out to the applicant that the making of false statements constitutes a criminal offense. 1 SOLUS & PERROT 965. If the applicant presents the so-called *carte sociale d'économiquement faible* (a kind of identification paper for low-income persons), he is automatically entitled to legal aid. CODE DE LA FAMILLE art. 162.

[73] Law of Jan. 22, 1851, as amended, *supra* note 61, arts. 8, 11. If the applicant does not live in the *arrondissement* in which the *bureau* meets, he may be heard by a judge of the local *tribunal d'instance.*

[74] Law of Jan. 22, 1851, as amended, *supra* note 61, art. 12. If the *bureau* lacks a quorum, it may nevertheless grant legal aid on a temporary basis if the matter is urgent. In urgent

An applicant may never appeal a denial of *assistance judiciaire*, but the *ministère public* may appeal decisions rendered by a local *bureau* to the *bureau* at the seat of the *cour d'appel* and may appeal decisions of the *cours d'appel, Cour de Cassation,* and *Conseil d'Etat bureaux* to the appeal *bureau* in the Ministry of Justice. Decisions of the legal aid *bureaux* are not subject to judicial review. [75]

If an appeal or *pourvoi* is taken against a person who was granted legal aid before the lower court, legal aid continues automatically for the purpose of the appeal or *pourvoi*. If the person having been granted legal aid wishes to take an appeal or *pourvoi*, he must make a new application for legal aid. The decision whether to grant or withhold legal aid must be made by the *bureau* at the appropriate appellate court. [76]

## 12.15. Effects of Grant of Legal Aid

A person to whom legal aid has been granted is entitled to the free services of an *avocat, avoué,* and *huissier*. The *bureau* granting legal aid must forward a copy of its decision to the court in which the action is pending or to be brought. The presiding judge of the court then invites the presiding officers of the local organizations of *avocats, avoués,* and *huissiers* to designate an *avocat, avoué,* and *huissier* who will act for the person having been granted legal aid. [77] At one time, it seems to have been customary to designate *avocats stagiaires* in legal aid matters. Under present practice, experienced *avocats* are usually designated in difficult cases. The members of the various legal professions take their duties under the legal aid scheme seriously. [78]

cases, even one single member of the *bureau* may grant temporary legal aid. Law of Jan. 22, 1851, as amended, *supra* note 61, art. 6.

[75] Law of Jan. 22, 1851, as amended, *supra* note 61, art. 12. In practice, the *ministère public* will generally appeal if requested to do so by a party whose application has been denied. 1 Raviart, Traité Formulaire de Procédure Générale 160 (8th ed. 1956).

[76] Law of Jan. 22, 1851, as amended, *supra* note 61, art. 9. If the applicant did not have legal aid in first instance, he may request it for the appeal or *pourvoi*, but in that case there is a preliminary investigation by his local aid *bureau* which transmits the file to the *bureau* at the appropriate appellate court for decision. An application for legal aid addressed to the *Cour de Cassation* legal aid *bureau* tolls the time period available for taking a *pourvoi*. Law No. 47–1366 of July 23, 1947, J.O. July 24, 1947, p. 7142, [1947] D.L. 275, art. 56.

[77] If the action is pending before the *Cour de Cassation*, an *avocat aux conseils* and an *huissier* are designated; if the action is pending before one of the courts before which the services of *avocats* and *avoués* are not required, only an *huissier* is appointed. Law of Jan. 22, 1851, as amended, *supra* note 61, art. 13. In an appropriate case, a notary may also be appointed. It will be remembered that article 15 of the law requires all cases in which legal aid has been granted to be communicated to the *ministère public*. See 3.09 *supra*.

[78] On the detailed procedures used in the designation of *avocats, avoués,* and *huissiers*, see 1 Raviart, *op. cit. supra* note 75, at 160. The designated *avocat* may not refuse or terminate his co-operation without the approval of the presiding officer (*bâtonnier*) of his bar association. 1 Dalloz, *op. cit. supra* note 60, at No. 109 (Supp. 1964).

Persons having been granted legal aid need not pay court clerk's fees. In addition, the government advances witness' fees, expert's fees and travel expenses. A beneficiary of legal aid does not have to pay stamp or *enregistrement* taxes on *ajournements*, judgments, and other procedural documents. The same is true even of documents which the beneficiary wishes to use as evidence and for which stamp and *enregistrement* taxes should have been paid earlier. All documents must, however, be taken to the tax office where the sums are noted that would be due in the absence of legal aid. [79]

## 12.16. Allocation of Costs in Legal Aid Cases

**a. If the beneficiary wins.** If the person who has been granted legal aid prevails and judgment for costs goes against his opponent, the opponent must be pay all normal costs that would have been payable had there been no grant of *assistance judiciaire*. These costs are collected by the government and distributed to the various persons entitled thereto. Ordinarily, the *avoué* representing a legal aid client will, therefore, get paid if his client wins. Since the *avocat*'s compensation is not part of taxable costs, even a successful *avocat* does not get paid by his client's opponent. However, he may demand a fee from his client if the recovery he has obtained is so substantial that legal aid would not have been granted had the client had these funds at the beginning of the litigation. [80]

**b. If the beneficiary loses.** If the person having been granted legal aid does not prevail, the fees of the *avocat, avoué, huissier* and court clerk will generally remain unpaid. [81] The same is true of the stamp and *enregistrement* taxes which should have been paid on the procedural documents served during the litigation. However, after the end of the suit, the government may collect stamp and *enregistrement* taxes for documents used as evidence. The government may likewise try to recover witness' fees, travel expenses, and the like which it has advanced. [82] In the nature of things, an attempt to recover these funds is frequently unsuccessful.

[79] Law of Jan. 22, 1851, *supra* note 61, art. 14. Most documents prepared in France are subject to a stamp and an *enregistrement* tax. If the tax has not been paid, the documents may not be produced in court. Since at the time documents are prepared payment of the tax is often neglected, the tax must be paid when litigation arises. See generally 7.40 *supra*.

[80] Law of Jan. 22, 1851, as amended, *supra* note 61, arts. 17–18.

[81] Such persons may demand payment if legal aid is withdrawn, see 12.17 *infra*.

[82] Law of Jan. 22, 1851, *supra* note 61, arts. 14, 19. If the opponent of the party who has received legal aid prevails and obtains a judgment for costs, he may try to recover costs from

## 12.17. Withdrawal of Legal Aid

In two cases, the *bureau* which has granted legal aid may withdraw it: first, if the applicant has made false statements in order to obtain legal aid, and second, if his financial position has substantially improved after the grant of legal aid. The *bureau* may act on its own motion or at the request of the *ministère public* or an adverse party. The person concerned must always be heard. Legal aid may be withdrawn at any time, even after the end of the proceedings for which it has been granted. If legal aid is withdrawn, the applicant must pay the various fees and taxes he would have had to pay in the absence of legal aid. [83]

the beneficiary of legal aid, but the latter is likely to be judgment - proof. CUCHE & VINCENT 612.

[83] Law of Jan. 22, 1851, as amended, *supra* note 61, arts. 21–24.

CHAPTER 13

# RES JUDICATA AND ENFORCEMENT OF JUDGMENTS

This chapter discusses the French doctrine of *res judicata*, including the scope of the basic rule (13.01–13.02), and the manner of invoking its applicability (13.03). It continues with a discussion of procedures for enforcement of judgments, embracing the remedy of specific performance (13.04–13.05) and the *astreinte* device (13.06), as well as procedures for enforcement against property (13.07–13.16). The description of enforcement against property deals with the various types of enforcement proceedings (13.08), the binding nature of rules on enforcement (13.09), judicial competence in enforcement proceedings (13.10), the time at which enforcement may commence (13.11), property subject to and exempt from enforcement (13.12), enforcement against movables (13.13), enforcement against intangibles (13.14), enforcement against immovable property (13.15), and distribution of the proceeds of enforcement proceedings (13.16).

## 1. *RES JUDICATA*

### 13.01. Introduction

In the *Code Civil*, the *res judicata* effect of a judgment is defined in the section on presumptions. [1] The rule of *res judicata* is grounded in the policy that there must be an end to litigation (*lites finiri oportet*). [2] The *res judicata* effect of a judgment may be invoked offensively as well as defensively; [3] defensive reliance on the rule takes the form of a defense called *exception de la chose jugée*.

The rule of *res judicata* also has a procedural aspect: Every judg-

[1] CODE CIVIL art. 1351 contains the basic rule. It is part of Section III (which deals with presumptions) of Chapter VI (which deals with proof) of Title III (which deals with contracts) of Book 3 (which deals with means of acquiring ownership).

[2] See 2 COLIN & CAPITANT 525; CUCHE & VINCENT 61; MOREL 450; 1 PLANIOL & RIPERT, TREATISE ON THE CIVIL LAW 34–35 (Part 2) (Louisiana State Law Institute Translation 1959).

[3] Although French authors state that a French judgment does not ordinarily create new rights but merely defines the existing legal relationship (*e.g.*, CUCHE & VINCENT 69), a French judgment has in fact a bar and a merger effect. For a more detailed discussion of the problem, see Millar, *The Premises of the Judgment as Res Judicata in Continental and Anglo American Law*, 39 MICH. L. REV. 1, 5 (1940); *cf.* CUCHE & VINCENT 62; CORNU & FOYER 460; note 2 *supra*; Lemaître v. Veuve Ledent, Cass. Civ., June 16, 1937, [1937] D.H. 517. If there are two inconsistent judgments, the *res judicata* effect attaches to the second judgment. Lanfranchi v. Grimaldi, Cass. Civ., Feb. 10, 1953, [1953] J.C.P. 2. 7636 (note Perrot).

ment benefits from a presumption of regularity and validity. [4] This presumption gains in importance as the various means of review are exhausted or become time-barred. In the case of a judgment still subject to *appel* or *opposition*, it can be overcome fairly easily. Once only the so-called extraordinary methods of review are available, its rebuttal becomes much more difficult. When all means of review are barred, since *voies de nullité n'ont lieu en France contre jugements* (collateral attack is not possible against judgments in France [5]), a judgment is completely immune against attack, even if it was rendered by an incompetent court or is subject to a serious procedural defect.

A judgment becomes *res judicata* as soon as it has been rendered. It is immaterial that execution may not yet be levied upon it, or that it is still open to attack by *opposition* or appeal. However, attack by an appeal or *opposition* suspends its *res judicata* effect. The mere taking of a *pourvoi* to the *Cour de Cassation* or recourse to any of the other so-called extraordinary methods of review does not, although reversal does, deprive a judgment of its *res judicata* effect. [6]

Judgments by courts of first instance that are still subject to appeal or *opposition* are said to have the *autorité de la chose jugée* (authority of *res judicata*). Once appeal or *opposition* has been used or becomes barred by lapse of time, a judgment is said to have *force de la chose jugée*. When all methods of review have been exhausted or become time-barred, a judgment is said to be irrevocable. [7]

## 13.02. The Scope of the Rule of *Res Judicata*

**a. The judgment must be definitive and adjudicate a „contentious'' matter.** Only judgments rendered in „contentious'' matters (*affaires contentieuses*) have the *autorité de la chose jugée*. *Res judicata* effect does not attach to decisions rendered in *ex parte* matters (that is, those involving the exercise of *juridiction gracieuse*), such as decisions authorizing guardians to take certain steps concerning the property of their wards. It also does not attach to a decision that notes merely that a

[4] 2 Planiol & Ripert, *op. cit. supra* note 2, at 34–35.

[5] Bouchet v. Lamberty, Cass. Civ., Feb. 25, 1964, [1964] D.J. 312 (decision by court incompetent *ratione materiae res judicata*). See 4.02. b *supra*.

[6] *E.g.*, Morel 450.

[7] 2 Colin & Capitant 527; Cuche & Vincent 63; Morel 451–52. Since an appeal leads to readjudication of the case on the merits, the presumption of regularity and validity is of relatively minor importance in the case of judgments subject to this method of review. The scope of *pourvoi* to the *Cour de Cassation* and of *tierce opposition* and *requête civile* is, however, much more limited. See 8.01, 9.01, 10.01 *supra*.

party reserves the right to take other legal steps later and therefore does not resolve a controversy. [8]

In order to have *res judicata* effect, a judgment must be final (*définitif*) in the sense that it settles a point in controversy, although it need not be a judgment on the merits rendered at the end of the litigation: A judgment resolving a question of competence is entitled to *res judicata* effect even though the litigation on the merits continues. However, judgments granting merely provisional relief, such as alimony *pendente lite*, do not have such an effect, since they are subject to modification upon a showing of changed circumstances; the same is generally true of judgments rendered by a judge sitting *en référé* and of judgments relating to proof that are merely *préparatoires*. [9]

**b. *Res judicata* effect attaches only to the decretal part of a judgment.** The *res judicata* effect of a French judgment attaches only to its decretal part (*dispositif*), not to the opinion (*motifs*). However, the opinion, if it is "closely related" to the decretal portion of the judgment, may be consulted to determine the scope of *res judicata*. [10]

**c. Only the parties to the original action are bound by *res judicata*.** As a general rule, only the original parties are later bound by the *res judicata* effect of the judgment. Furthermore, a party who does not sue in the same capacity is not bound. [11]

These rules are subject to a few exceptions. A person who has been "represented" in the litigation is bound by the resulting judgment. Universal successors of a party, such as heirs or universal legatees, are always "represented" by their ancestor. Transferees of an item of property are bound by a judgment concerning the item if the judgment was rendered before the transfer, but not if it was rendered thereafter.

[8] MOREL 450; Suzineau v. Lambert, Cass. Civ., Jan. 2, 1959, [1959] D.J. 35 (statement in judgment that party has reserved its rights not binding). The same rule is generally applied to decisions merely incorporating an agreement of the parties.

[9] 2 COLIN & CAPITANT 526–27; MOREL 451. On the meaning of *définitif*, see also 7.13.d *supra*.

[10] A passage in the opinion is closely related to the decretal part of the judgment if it explains its scope. See, *e.g.*, Commission administrative des Hospices de Vichy v. Administration de l'enregistrement, Cass. Com., March 21, 1950, [1950] D.J. 381 (in litigation concerning parties' rights concerning royalties on certain mineral water springs, opinion of earlier judgment between the same parties may be consulted in order to determine which springs were included in that judgment); Richou, *Autorité de la chose jugée attachée aux motifs des décisions judiciaires à l'égard des parties*, [1962] J.C.P. I. 1962. See generally Millar, *supra* note 3, at 10–12, 15–18.

[11] CODE CIVIL art. 1351. See generally Boyer, *Les effets des jugements à l'égard des tiers*, 49 REV. TRIM. DR. CIV. 163 (1951).

Jointly and severally liable debtors "represent" each other and, subject to some exceptions, a debtor represents his unsecured creditors. [12]

By special statute, the effects of a judgment concerning one of a group of bondholders may be extended to other bondholders, [13] and a judgment concerning the proper designation of origin of wine (*appellation contrôlée*) rendered as to one grower in an area is binding on all growers in the same area. [14]

Judgments creating a new personal status, such as divorce, separation, and bankruptcy judgments, [15] and judgments in matters of nationality [16] are binding on third parties as well as on the parties to the original proceeding.

**d. The subsequent action must have the same „object''.** The *Code Civil* states that *res judicata* applies only to the "object" of the original judgment. [17] According to the textwriters, this means that the second action is barred only if it seeks adjudication of the same right to the same physical object. A person who has lost in an action in which he claimed title to a building may later claim a life estate (*usufruit*). Similarly, a person who has lost a "possessory" action concerning a plot of land may later claim title.

Difficulties arise when claims are closely related. A person who has claimed a debt and lost on the ground that nothing was due him may not later sue for the interest. On the other hand, a person who sued to obtain interest on a debt and lost may later claim the capital if the existence of the debt was not an issue in the earlier action. Ordinarily, an action for rent does not bar another action for rent accrued after the beginning of the first action. [18]

[12] 2 Colin & Capitant 531–32; Morel 450. There is likewise representation whenever litigation is conducted on behalf of a person by an agent, guardian, or the like. Creditors are bound by a judgment rendered against their debtor only to a limited extent. In the case of fraud on their rights, they may attack it.

[13] Décret-Loi of Aug. 8, 1935, J.O. Aug. 9, 1935, [1935] D. 4. 221.

[14] Law of July 22, 1927, J.O. July 27, 1927, [1928] S. Lois Annot. 1319.

[15] *E.g.*, Brancherie v. dame Aubry, Cass. Req., May 17, 1943, [1943] S. 1. 107 (separation); Lafond v. Ministère Public, Trib. Nantes, July 31, 1947, [1948] D.J. 382 (judgment depriving father of parental rights) (note Chéron). The appended note indicates that it is doubtful to what extent the rule applies to judgments that do not create a new state of facts (such as divorce judgments), but merely establish an existing fact (such as paternity judgments). See generally Cornu & Foyer 460; Cuche & Vincent 70. A judgment of bankruptcy (*faillite*), since it deprives the bankrupt of the right to dispose of his property, is considered to establish a new status. Judgments concerning property rights only are not usually binding on third parties.

[16] Ordonnance of Oct. 19, 1945 (Code of French Nationality), J.O. Oct. 20, 1945, p. 6700, [1945] D.L. 10, art. 136.

[17] Code Civil art. 1351.

[18] 2 Colin & Capitant 528–29; 2 Planiol & Ripert, *op. cit. supra* note 2, at 36. For ex-

**e. The subsequent action must have the same *cause* as the prior action.** The *Code Civil* limits the effect of *res judicata* to subsequent actions having the same *cause.* [19] Although its precise meaning is uncertain, the term *cause* seems to refer to the ultimate facts on which the actions are based. Thus, a party who has unsuccessfully attacked a will for defect of form may renew his attack on the ground of lack of testamentary capacity. [20] Likewise, the various bases for paternity actions mentioned in article 340 of the *Code Civil* are independent *causes.* [21] A tort action based on the liability for fault rule of article 1382 of the *Code Civil* does not exclude another action based on the absolute liability rule of article 1384. [22] However, attacks on a contract based on the existence of various formal defects must be made in one action.[23]

## 13.03. Manner of Invoking *Res Judicata*

The *res judicata* effect of a judgment must be invoked by a party. Since it is not considered a matter strongly affected by public policy (*ordre public*), it may not be raised on the court's own motion. While *res judicata* is often called in French the *exception de la chose jugée,* it is not an *exception* in the technical sense of the word, nor, according to some authors, a *fin de non-recevoir.* Thus, the defense of *res judicata* is not covered by article 168 of the *Code de Procédure Civile* which requires all *exceptions* and *fins de non-recevoir* to be raised at the outset of the litigation. [24] Apparently the *res judicata* effect of a prior judgment may be invoked at any time before final judgment, though not for the first time before the *Cour de Cassation.* [25]

amples, see Hébraud, *Chronique*, 63 REV. TRIM. DR. CIV. 164 (1964) (discussing case involving a two-car collision in which a judgment rendered in favor of the owner of one car for damages to his vehicle did not bar a later action by the owner of the second car, although the parties in both actions were the same); Huynh Thi Ngheh v. Trien Mang, Cass. Civ., May 14, 1935, [1935] D.H. 427 (property claimed originally on ground that plaintiff was heir of decedent may be claimed later on ground that property actually belonged to plaintiff's mother).

[19] CODE CIVIL art. 1351.

[20] COLIN & CAPITANT 527–29; CUCHE & VINCENT 64; 2 PLANIOL & RIPERT, *op. cit. supra* note 2, at 38–39.

[21] *E.g.*, Vincent v. Gazanion, Cour Rennes, Jan. 16, 1950, [1950] D.J. 22, *aff'd* Cass. Civ., March 10, 1953, [1953] J.C.P. 7601 (fraudulent seduction and later participation in cost of upbringing of child). Paternity actions are permissible in France only in certain specific situations, such as seduction or father's participation in costs of upbringing child.

[22] Bordenave v. Lachia, Cass. Civ., Nov. 14, 1934, [1935] D.H. 52.

[23] 2 PLANIOL & RIPERT, *op. cit. supra* note 2, at 40.

[24] *Cf.* CORNU & FOYER 460; CUCHE & VINCENT 66–67. On the various types of defenses and the time when they must be raised, see 7.08–7.09 *infra*. Generally, only matters affected by public policy (*ordre public*) may be raised by the courts on their own motion.

[25] *E.g.*, Etablissements Arnaud v. Soc. française des corps gras, Cass. Com., Feb. 16, 1953, [1953] D.J. 303.

## 2. SPECIFIC PERFORMANCE

### 13.04. Cases in Which Specific Performance is Possible

As a general rule, the plaintiff is entitled to specific performance of the defendant's obligation rather than to mere money damages. [26] However, this rule has a number of exceptions, based in part on reasons of public policy and in part on the absence of effective means of compelling specific performance.

**a. Obligations to transfer title to property.** Usually, a distinction is made between obligations "to give" (*de donner*) and obligations "to do" (*de faire*). [27] Obligations "to give," which are obligations to transfer title to property, [28] ordinarily raise no problems of enforcement. In the case of land or of ascertained goods, unless the parties have agreed otherwise, the mere conclusion of a contract of sale transfers title, [29] so that court intervention is usually unnecessary. If the defendant, who is no longer the owner after the conclusion of the contract, refuses to give up possession of the land or goods at the time stipulated in the agreement, he may be expelled from the land or the goods may be seized by an *huissier*. [30] If the contract provides that the passing of title depends on the signing of an additional document and the defendant unjustifiedly refuses to sign such a document, the court may render a judgment that will have the effect of passing title. [31] In the case of unascertained fungible goods, the plaintiff may purchase their equivalent on the open market and charge the defendant for the difference in price. [32]

**b. Obligations to perform or not to perform a specific act.** The drafters of the *Code Civil*, fearing that specific performance of an obligation "to

[26] *E.g.*, 1 Dalloz, Répertoire de Procédure Civile et Commerciale, *Exécution des jugements et actes*, at No. 2 (1956). For discussions in English, see Newman, Equity and the Law 71–74 (1961); Schlesinger, Comparative Law 119–21 (2d ed. 1959); Von Mehren, The Civil Law System 772–93 (1957); Dawson, *Specific Performance in France and Germany*, 57 Mich. L. Rev. 495 (1959); Jackson, *Specific Performance of Contracts in Louisiana*, 24 Tul. L. Rev. 401 (1950); Szladits, *The Concept of Specific Performance in Civil Law*, 4 Am. J. Comp. L. 208, 214–20 (1955).

[27] This distinction, said to have been devised by Pothier, is often hazy. Jackson, *supra* note 26, at 412.

[28] *E.g.*, 2 Colin & Capitant 115; 2 Planiol & Ripert, *op. cit. supra* note 2, at 104.

[29] Code Civil art. 1138.

[30] 2 Planiol & Ripert, *op. cit. supra* note 2, at 104; Cuche & Vincent, Voies d'Exécution et Procédures de Distribution 7 (8th ed. 1961) [to avoid confusion with the text on civil procedure by the same authors, this work is hereinafter cited as Cuche, Exécution].

[31] 2 Colin & Capitant 116.

[32] *E.g.*, Amos & Walton, Introduction to French Law 180 (2d ed. 1963).

do" – that is, an obligation to perform or to refrain from performing a specific act or acts – might result in a restraint upon personal liberty, [33] provided in article 1142 of the *Code Civil* that damages would be the only remedy against non-performance of such an obligation. [34] However, the Code itself contains a number of exceptions [35] to this broad principle.

If the defendant fails to meet the obligation of performing a certain work, the court may authorize the plaintiff to have the work performed at the defendant's expense. [36] In an emergency, the plaintiff may even act without court authorization if he can show that the work was performed as cheaply as possible. [37] It is largely discretionary with the courts whether to authorize this type of substituted performance. Money damages only will be awarded if the defendant's obligation has a strictly personal character. [38]

If the defendant has erected a construction he was under obligation not to build – for instance, a wall interfering with an easement of light–, the court may authorize the plaintiff to remove the structure at the defendant's expense. [39] Again, it is largely discretionary with the court whether to do this or award damages only. [40]

Even beyond this, the courts have ordered specific performance in a variety of situations: to protect a trade name; to prevent interference with a right of way; to prevent interference with plaintiff's radio reception; and in similar circumstances. [41]

Specific performance is excluded only if the obligation of defendant is personal in nature, such as to paint a picture, [42] or if specific performance is impossible or may lead to unseemly results. As a rule, the

[33] Newman, *op. cit. supra* note 26, at 71.

[34] The rule is sometimes stated in Latin as *nemo praecise cogi potest ad factum* (nobody can be specifically compelled to do something). See generally 2 Colin & Capitant 111; 2 Planiol & Ripert, *op. cit. supra* note 2, at 105–06.

[35] See, *e.g.*, Cuche, Exécution 8, stating that the rule as formulated in Code Civil art. 1142 is much too absolute.

[36] Code Civil art. 1144. An example would be an agreement by the landlord to repair the demised premises. See, *e.g.*, Consorts Saas-Leprince v. Epoux Le Trividic, Cass. Soc., June 5, 1953, [1953] D.J. 601.

[37] *E.g.*, Houbron v. Vendis, Cass. Soc., Dec. 7, 1951, [1952] D.J. 144.

[38] There are no precise rules as to when money damages must be awarded. Unduly high cost of performance may sometimes lead the courts to award money damages only. *E.g.*, Von Mehren, *op. cit. supra* note 26, at 773.

[39] Code Civil art. 1143.

[40] *E.g.*, 2 Colin & Capitant 116; 2 Planiol & Ripert 105.

[41] For a list of examples, see Dawson, *supra* note 26, at 519 n. 63. For other examples, see Von Mehren, *op. cit. supra* note 26, at 786–87.

[42] *Cf.* Eden v. Whistler, Cass. Civ., March 14, 1900, [1900] S. 1. 489.

courts enjoy a wide discretion and seem to be affected to some extent by the equities of the situation.[43]

## 13.05. Procedural Difficulties in the Enforcement of Judgments of Specific Performance

**a. Absence of contempt power.** Though modern French jurists no longer seem to share the *Code Civil*'s reluctance to permit specific enforcement of obligations "to do," a number of procedural rules make it difficult to enforce orders for specific performance. The main obstacle is the absence of a true contempt power.[44] A judge in a civil case may not order the imprisonment of a party for violation of his orders, except to a very limited extent when necessary to preserve order in the courtroom itself.[45] In addition, in civil cases, imprisonment for debt (body execution) has been illegal since 1867.[46]

**b. The final judgment terminates the court's power over a case.** The power of a court to act in a case terminates once the court has rendered its final judgment. Unless there has been a formal reopening through *opposition* or *tierce opposition*, the court may not thereafter take any action in respect of the case, except in order to clarify its judgment.[47] Proceedings concerning the enforcement of a judgment by execution are considered new proceedings. Except in some cases, in which the *tribunal d'instance* is competent, they must be brought in the *tribunal de grande instance* even if the decision to be enforced has been rendered by another court, such as a commercial or labor court. Further proceedings to enforce a judgment are ordinarily brought in the place in which the property to be levied on is located, though the judgment was rendered by a court located elsewhere.[48] These rules have hampered development of effective specific performance procedures.[49]

[43] 2 Colin & Capitant 117; Cuche, Exécution 8. To some extent, the customs of the times are taken into consideration. See 1 Dalloz, *op. cit. supra* note 26, at No. 3. A person who, though his tortious conduct, has caused injury to property is ordinarily liable only for damages and cannot be compelled to restore the property. *Cf.* Soc. immobilière du Béarn v. Ville de Pau, Cass. Civ., March 15, 1948, [1948] D.J. 346. But this rule has not been followed unanimously. See the examples given by Dawson, *supra* note 26, at 520 n. 63.

[44] On the traditional reluctance to give French judges strong powers, see Pekelis, *Legal Techniques and Political Ideologies: A Comparative Study*, 41 Mich. L. Rev. 665, 669–72 (1943); Newman, *op. cit. supra* note 26, at 71.

[45] See Code de Procédure Civile arts. 89–91; *cf.* 7.12.c *supra*.

[46] Imprisonment as a remedy in civil cases was made illegal in 1867. See 2 Planiol & Ripert, *op. cit. supra* note 2, at 106–07; 2 Dalloz, *op. cit. supra* note 26, at No. 4.

[47] See 7.13.e *supra*.

[48] See 4.37–4.38 and 4.26 *supra*.

[49] *E.g.*, Brodeur, *The Injunction in French Jurisprudence*, 14 Tul. L. Rev. 211–12 (1940).

**c. Enforcement of judgments by *huissiers* and the police.** Comparatively few difficulties are encountered if a judgment can be executed by an *huissier*. This will ordinarily be the case when the defendant must deliver a specified chattel or give up possession of land. A chattel that should have been delivered may be seized by the *huissier*; likewise, the *huissier* may dispossess the seller of land who refuses to move out after title has passed or the tenant who overstays. [50] Execution by an *huissier* (sometimes called execution *manu militari*) has even been held appropriate in certain domestic relations cases. [51] However, this type of execution will not be used when it is likely to cause scandal. Thus, the courts will not order an actor bodily removed from the stage by bailiffs or the police, though his performance may violate an agreement that gives another theater exclusive rights to his services. [52]

If in executing a judgment the *huissier* encounters resistance, he may request the aid of the police. The "executory formula" at the end of a judgment specifically requires all officers and commanders of the police and armed forces to lend their assistance when requested. [53] However, on occasion the executive branch of the government has directed police officials not to assist in the execution of certain judgments. This has happened with some frequency in the period following World War II. Because of the severe housing shortage, assistance in the enforcement of judgments ordering tenants to vacate an apartment was frequently denied. Under case law developed by the *Conseil d'Etat*, the French Republic is ordinarily liable in damages if its authorities refuse to render assistance in the enforcement of a valid judgment. [54] However, this is of limited benefit to a plaintiff whose judgment remains unexecuted, especially since the prosecution of a damage claim before the administrative tribunals is time-consuming. [55]

Self-help is not permitted in France as a means for enforcing a judgment. [56]

[50] *Cf.* NEWMAN, *op. cit. supra* note 26, at 72.

[51] At times, husbands have even obtained court orders requiring wives who had wrongfully left the matrimonial domicile to be forcibly returned with the help of bailiffs and the police. It is questionable whether this would be done today. See 2 DALLOZ, *op. cit. supra* note 26, at No. 2.

[52] Likewise, the police will not be ordered forcibly to prevent an illegal stockholders' meeting. See generally AMOS & WALTON, INTRODUCTION TO FRENCH LAW 182 (1963); 2 COLIN & CAPITANT 117; Dawson, *supra* note 26, at 517.

[53] DÉCRET No. 47–1047 of June 12, 1947, J.O. June 13, 1947, p. 5487, [1947] S. 5. 942, as amended by DÉCRET No. 58–1289 of Dec. 22, 1968, J.O. Dec. 23, 1958, p. 1160, [1959] D.L. 45.

[54] *E.g.*, Soc. anon. des anciens Etablissements E. Borderel, Cons. d'Etat, Nov. 30, 1956, [1957] D.SOMM. 73; *cf.* Consorts Perrin, Cons. d'Etat, Feb. 10, 1950, [1950] D.J. 457.

[55] *Cf.* VON MEHREN, *op. cit. supra* note 26, at 775–76.

[56] Thus, a landlord may not enforce a judgment of eviction against his tenant by removing

### 13.06. *Astreinte*

**a. Development of the *astreinte*.** A person who fails specifically to perform an obligation may be held liable in damages. On the basis of this rule, the French courts have gradually developed a device designed to induce compliance with court orders requiring specific performance by adding to such orders a clause ordering payment of a specified amount of damages for each specified period of time – usually, a day – the judgment debtor delays their execution. This device came to be known as *astreinte*.

Although it is recognized that the *astreinte* is designed to compel compliance with a court order, since it is difficult to find a statutory basis for this practice outside the court's right to award damages, many cases stress the damages aspect of this remedy. This has hampered its development as an effective enforcement device. [57]

There are two kinds of *astreinte*: the definitive *astreinte* and the provisional *astreinte*.

**b. The definitive *astreinte*.** A definitive *astreinte* is the sum that the defendant is ordered to pay for each day or other time unit of delay in the execution of the judgment. Since the courts must fix the *astreinte* on the basis of the actual damage likely to be suffered by the plaintiff as a result of the defendant's non-performance, the effectiveness of the definitive *astreinte* as a means of coercion is limited. [58] However, as a rule, the *Cour de Cassation* does not review the amount of damages granted by lower courts. This means in practice that courts imposing an *astreinte* frequently will resolve all doubts concerning the amount of actual harm to the plaintiff in the plaintiff's favor. [59]

**c. The provisional *astreinte*.** The provisional *astreinte* is used more frequently than the definitive *astreinte*. The choice between the two is discretionary with the court. [60] A provisional *astreinte*, like a definitive *astreinte*, is the sum the judgment debtor must pay for each specified

the roof of the building in order to induce the tenant to leave. See the case cited in 1 DALLOZ, *op. cit. supra* note 26, at No. 10.

[57] See generally 2 COLIN & CAPITANT 132–37; NEWMAN, *op. cit. supra* note 26, at 73; Brodeur, *supra* note 49, at 214–15; Dawson, *supra* note 26, at 512–16.

[58] *E.g.*, Pinchon v. Dassier, Cass. Soc., Nov. 30, 1950, [1951] J.C.P. 2. 6089; 2 COLIN & CAPITANT 134. This rule is due to the damage origin of the *astreinte*.

[59] See the note by Holleaux appended to Soc. X. v. P., Cass. Civ., Oct. 20, 1959, [1959] D.J. 537, at 538.

[60] *E.g.*, Marinetti v. Marinetti, Cour Paris, Feb. 16, 1961, [1961] J.C.P. 2. 12146 (note Mazeaud).

unit of time he delays the judgment's execution. However, in the case of a provisional *astreinte*, the amount mentioned by the court is only provisional: The sum the defendant must actually pay is definitely settled ("liquidated") only when the defendant has performed or when performance has become impossible. At the time of "liquidation," the sum due may be increased or – as happens more frequently – decreased by the court. [61]

When imposing a provisional *astreinte*, the courts traditionally do not limit it to the anticipated actual damages caused by the delay. They usually specify a high enough amount to induce the defendant to obey the court's mandate. Hence, the provisional *astreinte* is sometimes called *astreinte comminatoire* (threatening *astreinte*).

In the past, a number of *Cour de Cassation* cases had required that the courts, in finally "liquidating" the *astreinte*, base their award on the actual damages suffered by plaintiff. As a result, persons without competent legal advice were often induced into quick compliance with a court order by a high provisional *astreinte*, while those better counselled refused to be intimidated, since they knew that, no matter how high the provisional *astreinte*, they would not have to pay a sum in excess of the plaintiff's actual damages. [62] In 1959, however, the *Cour de Cassation* decided that in "liquidating" an *astreinte* the courts were not limited by the amount of actual damages suffered by plaintiff and that, since the *astreinte* was basically a means of compulsion, the defendant's financial means and the reasons for his resistance to the court's mandate could properly be taken into consideration. [63] This decision has made the *astreinte* considerably more effective.

**d. Courts that may order an *astreinte*.** The *astreinte* is not considered one of the procedures for executing a judgment. Hence, the rule that these procedures are within the exclusive competence of the *tribunal de grande instance* (or sometimes, the *tribunal d'instance*) does not apply. An *astreinte* may be ordered by any court, including the specialized courts. It may be ordered for the first time by a *cour d' appel* [64] as well as by a judge sitting *en référé*. [65] Since the provisional *astreinte* is not

[61] 2 COLIN & CAPITANT 134; Fréjaville, *L'Astreinte*, [1949] D.CHR. 1; Holleaux, *supra* note 59. For example, performance will be considered as impossible when a specific object, which the defendant was to deliver, has been destroyed or sold to a bona fide purchaser.

[62] See generally Dawson, *supra* note 26, at 512–16.

[63] Soc. X. v. P., *supra* note 59.

[64] 1 DALLOZ, RÉPERTOIRE DE PROCÉDURE CIVILE ET COMMERCIALE, *Astreinte*, at Nos. 1–4 (1955).

[65] *E.g.*, Ville de Marseille v. d'Authier de Sisgau, Cass. Com., April 17, 1956, [1956] J.C.P. 2. 9330 (note Vellieux).

"final" until "liquidated," the rule that a court may not deal with a case after it has rendered a final judgment is inapplicable. [66]

**e. Cases in which an *astreinte* may be imposed.** An *astreinte* may be imposed in all cases in which specific performance may be ordered. For example, it may be imposed to prevent waste [67] or to compel the repair of a roof, [68] the removal of an encroaching structure, [69] or the return of a child. [70]

*Astreinte* does not have to be the only available remedy. It is sometimes used in cases involving encroaching structures or repairs in which the court may authorize the plaintiff to perform the work at the expense of the defendant. [71] The *astreinte* has been used frequently to enforce judgments of eviction. The choice of the appropriate remedy lies within the discretion of the court.

French authors usually state that *astreinte* is not available to enforce a judgment for a sum of money and that execution against the property of the defendant is an adequate, and generally preferable, remedy. [72] Recently, however, the *Cour de Cassation* has upheld the imposition of an *astreinte* to enforce a judgment for a sum of money. The defendant was a French municipality, against which the ordinary methods of execution by levy and sale could not be used. It is not clear to what extent this was a material factor. [73]

In an appropriate case, an *astreinte* designed to induce specific performance of an obligation may be coupled with an award of damages for the delay in performance up to the time of judgment. [74]

**f. Collection of amounts due pursant to provisional *astreinte*.** According to traditional doctrine, the plaintiff may not collect any sums under a provisional *astreinte* until the *astreinte* has been "liquidated." An *astreinte* may not be "liquidated" until the defendant has performed

[66] For an early case, see Vimont v. Cally, Cass. Req., Nov. 22, 1841, [1842] S. 1. 170.

[67] Déjardin v. Charpentier, Cour Douai, Aug. 28, 1844, [1845] S. 2. 293.

[68] *Cf.* Gode v. Castagnié, Cour Bordeau, Nov. 29, 1950, [1951] D. Somm. 27.

[69] Soc. X. v. P., *supra* note 59.

[70] *E.g.*, the famous Beauffremont case, discussed by Dawson, *supra* note 26, at 514.

[71] *E.g.*, Soc. X. v. P., *supra* note 59 (removal of structure). The *astreinte* has been used to compel the return of specific chattels, which could have been seized by an *huissier*. Marinetti v. Marinetti, *supra* note 60. See generally Brodeur, *supra* note 49, at 221; Jackson, *supra* note 26, at 416–18.

[72] *E.g.*, 2 Colin & Capitant 132.

[73] Ville de Marseille v. d'Authier de Sisgau, *supra* note 65. On the extent to which an *astreinte* may be possible against public bodies in France, see the appended note by Vellieux and Fréjaville, *supra* note 61; *cf.* Von Mehren, *op. cit. supra* note 26, at 256–57.

[74] Reinier v. Soc. Bronzavia, Cass. Civ., July 12, 1960, [1960] D. Somm. 95.

or performance has become impossible. This rule, by allowing the defendant a large measure of control in determining when payment must be made, reduces the effectiveness of the *astreinte.* For this reason, courts occasionally "liquidate" the *astreinte* at periodic intervals, thus subjecting the defendant to periodic payments and periodic court appearances until he performs. There is no unanimity as to the legality of this practice. [75] As a means of enforcing judgments of eviction, it is specifically prohibited by a law enacted in 1949. [76]

Some but not all courts also permit plaintiffs to collect amounts that have accrued under a provisional *astreinte* by levying execution on the defendant's property, although the *astreinte* has not yet been liquidated. This increases the pressure upon the defendant, although the plaintiff must return any sums exceeding the amount awarded him when the *astreinte* is finally "liquidated." [77]

The courts do not "liquidate" a provisional *astreinte* automatically, but only upon demand by the plaintiff. The *Cour de Cassation* treats a demand for "liquidation" of an *astreinte* as a new action which must be initiated before a court of first instance, even if the *astreinte* was pronounced by a *cour d'appel.* [78] This rule, which seems based on the notion that the *astreinte* is basically an award of damages, is not in accord with the modern view of the *astreinte* as a means of coercion. [79]

**g. Effectiveness of the *astreinte*.** American writers, in discussing the *astreinte,* tend to question its effectiveness. [80] Since the 1959 decision of the *Cour de Cassation,* French law professionals no longer share this scepticism. Nevertheless, French scholars, though conceding the practical utility of the device, express reservations, because there is no general legislative authority warranting its use, because the case law relating

[75] CUCHE EXÉCUTION 12; 1 DALLOZ, *op. cit. supra* note 64, at 12–13.

[76] Law No. 49–972 of July 21, 1949, J.O. July 22, 1949, p. 7183, [1949] D.L. 328. This law provides that only provisional (not definitive) *astreintes* may be used in such cases, that only actual damages may be awarded when the *astreinte* is liquidated, and that the difficulties of the tenant must be taken into consideration in determining the amount of the "liquidated" damages.

[77] *E.g.,* Soulard v. Le Corre, Trib. Gd. Inst. Nantes, Feb. 8, 1962, [1963] D. SOMM. 24; Savatier, *L'exécution des condamnations au payment d'une astreinte,* [1951] D. CHR. 37. It is suggested in CUCHE, EXÉCUTION at 12 that the plaintiff be allowed to use provisional remedies such as attachment, against the defendant, but not execution.

[78] Soc. Production d'Energie Electrique de la Sioule v. Consorts Pradon, Cass. Civ., Nov. 7, 1958, [1959] D. SOMM. 24. It may be noted in this connection that the amount of the *astreinte* as finally "liquidated" has no effect on appealability; the sum originally demanded controls. Guinier v. Vauzelle, Cour Paris, March 2, 1963, [1963] D.J. 722.

[79] Raynaud, *Chronique,* 60 REV. TRIM. DR. CIV. 147, 148–49 (1962).

[80] *E.g.,* Dawson, *supra* note 26, at 524–25; SCHLESINGER, *op. cit. supra* note 26, at 121; VON MEHREN, *op. cit. supra* note 26, at 782.

to the *astreinte* is inconsistent, and because the *astreinte* is, in fact, a civil penalty, an institution that is unknown to the French law of damages. Hence, legislative regulation of this device is sometimes suggested. [81] In a very limited class of cases, the *astreinte* has received legislative sanction. [82]

### 3. ENFORCEMENT AGAINST PROPERTY

### 13.07. General Rules concerning Enforcement against Property

Execution may be levied on the basis of any *titre exécutoire* – that is, either a judgment or a notarial document. Just as court clerks may put the "executory formula" directing *huissiers* to levy execution on copies of judgments filed in their office, so notaries may put the "executory formula" on documents prepared by them. [83] Execution may be levied only on account of a claim that is certain – that is, not seriously contested –, due, and liquidated – that is, for a fixed amount. [84] These conditions are ordinarily fulfilled in the case of a judgment. However,

[81] Colin & Capitant, though conceding the usefulness of the *astreinte*, state flatly that it is illegal. 2 COLIN & CAPITANT 134–35. The *astreinte* has been defended by others. See, *e.g.*, Esmein, *L'origine et la logique de la jurisprudence en matière d'astreintes*, 2 REV. TRIM. DR. CIV. 1 (1903). Esmein and others argue that French judges have retained a general power of command analogous to the imperium of Roman judges. *Cf.* Fréjavile, *supra* note 61. Some authors base the *astreinte* on CODE DE PROCÉDURE CIVILE art. 1036, which authorizes the courts to "... issue injunctions, suppress writings ...," but the context suggests that this article refers only to the power of the courts to keep the proceedings orderly. For an example, see Debouvry v. Richard, Cour Amiens, March 24, 1964, [1964] D.J. 403 (court order striking out defamatory part of pleading); *cf.* CUCHE, EXÉCUTION 10; LABORDE-LACOSTE, PRÉCIS ELÉMENTAIRE DES VOIES D'EXÉCUTION 24–26 (2d ed. 1939). Mazeaud approves the *astreinte*, but would like the award to go to the state, as in the case of a fine. See Mazeaud, *supra* note 60. Evidently, the law relating to the *astreinte* is still in a state of flux.

[82] ORDONNANCE No. 59–62 of Jan. 3, 1959, J.O. Jan. 8, 1959, p. 547, [1959] D.L. 211, art. 2 (*astreinte* to compel removal of structures interfering with easements established in connection with airports and with aids for aerial navigation); DÉCRET No. 59–139 of Jan. 7, 1959, J.O. Jan. 9, 1959, p. 664, [1959] D.L. 267, art. 3 (*astreinte* to compel employers to pay over to social security organizations contributions deducted by them from employees' pay); *cf. supra* note 76.

[83] The terms "enforcement" and "execution" are here used interchangeably. Specifically, the term "execution", when used, does not indicate a writ issued by the court in enforcement proceedings. *But see* N.Y.C.P.L.R. § 5230 (1965). On *titres exécutoires*, see CUCHE, EXÉCUTION 25–26; CRÉMIEU, TRAITÉ ELÉMENTAIRE DE PROCÉDURE CIVILE ET VOIES D'EXÉCUTION 170 (1956). If the *juge chargé de suivre la procédure* or the court succeeds in settling the case, the settlement agreement (*procès-verbal de conciliation*) may be the basis for execution. CODE DE PROCÉDURE CIVILE art. 82. Arbitral awards (except in the case of labor arbitration) must be approved by the court in an *ex parte* proceeding before they can be the basis for execution. CODE DE PROCÉDURE CIVILE art. 1020; *cf.* CUCHE, EXÉCUTION 29. French judgments or notarial acts may be executed anywhere in France. If they are in proper form – that is, certified by the clerk or notary –, no further authentication is required. CODE DE PROCÉDURE CIVILE art. 547. On the enforcement of foreign judgments, see ch. 14 *infra*. Certain administrative decisions may also be the basis for execution.

[84] CODE DE PROCÉDURE CIVILE art. 550; CUCHE, EXÉCUTION 23–24; CRÉMIEU, *op. cit. supra* note 83, at 169.

if the debtor is in default, execution may also be levied on the basis of a notarial document containing a loan agreement providing for repayment of a definite sum on a specified day. No court proceedings reducing the debt to a judgment are required, [85] though this course of action remains possible and may be desirable because a judgment creates a lien on the debtor's real property. [86]

## 13.08. Types of Proceedings for Enforcement against Property

Seizures for the purpose of bringing property under judicial control are known as *saisies*. This term embraces both seizures that are merely provisional remedies, such as attachments, and seizures leading to sale of the property.

*Saisie-exécution* for enforcement against chattels, *saisie immobilière* for enforcement against land, *saisie-brandon* for enforcement against growing crops, and several related procedures serve only as means of enforcement. *Saisie-arrêt* (garnishment) may be used as a provisional remedy as well as a means of enforcement. *Saisie conservatoire* (attachment) and some of its variations are predominantly provisional remedies. [87]

French rules concerning enforcement against property are highly complex and slightly antiquated. [88] Only the more important rules are discussed here. [89]

## 13.09. Imperative Nature of Rules Governing Enforcement

Rules concerning enforcement against property involve a strong public policy, must be observed strictly, and generally cannot be varied by agreement of the parties. In particular, a clause authorizing a

[85] For a form of such an agreement, see LABORDE–LACOSTE, *op. cit. supra* note 81, at 84–85. The right of notaries to prepare documents which can be used as a basis for execution has a historical basis: At one time notaries were court clerks. That right is now based on the Law of the 25 ventôse year XI, art. 19, reprinted in DALLOZ, CODE CIVIL at 485–90 (63d ed. 1964). Execution based on notarial instruments has not given rise to the objections occasioned by cognovit notes in the United States, probably because the traditional professional standards of the notaries prevent fraud and oppression. *Cf.* LABORDE-LACOSTE, *op. cit. supra* note 81, at 10 n. 2.

[86] CUCHE, EXÉCUTION 24; CODE CIVIL art. 2123 (lien on land of judgment debtor results from French judgment, and foreign judgment must be rendered effective in France by French decision or arbitral award reduced to judgment). To be effective against third parties, the judgment lien (*hypothèque judiciaire*) must be recorded.

[87] 1 DALLOZ, *op. cit. supra* note 26, at No. 7; CRÉMIEU, *op. cit. supra* note 83, at 165.

[88] For example, the "ceremony of the three candles" is used to determine who is the highest bidder when land is sold on execution. CODE DE PROCÉDURE CIVILE arts. 705–706. Further, a forced sale of land must be announced "at the sound of the trumpet, the beating of drums, or the ringing of bells." CODE DE PROCÉDURE CIVILE art. 700; see 13.15.d *infra*.

[89] For a discussion of provisional remedies, see 5.04–5.06 *supra*. Some of the time limitations mentioned in this chapter were modified recently. See 7.59 *supra*.

mortgage creditor to sell the mortgaged premises without judicial proceedings (*clause de voie parée*) is illegal, [90] as is an agreement authorizing a pledgee upon default of the debtor to retain as owner the goods pledged to him (*pacte commissoire* or *contrat pignoratif*). [91] However, the *Cour de Cassation* interprets these restrictions narrowly and has upheld *clauses de voie parée* and *pactes commissoires* that were not part of the original loan agreement. [92]

## 13.10. Judicial Competence in Matters of Enforcement

As a rule, only the *tribunal de grande instance* may deal with questions of enforcement. [93] However, the *tribunal d'instance* is exclusively competent in matters of wage garnishments [94] and disputes relating to enforcement of judgments that are within its subject-matter competence. [95] The specialized courts, such as the commercial courts, on the other hand may never adjudicate questions concerning enforcement of their judgments. [96]

Because the term "execution of judgments" varies in meaning, the scope of these rules is uncertain. Sometimes, the term refers to execution by levy and sale. At other times, it refers to other acts performed in obedience to a judgment; thus, the actual accounting is said to be the "execution" of a judgment ordering an accounting. Interlocutory proof judgments are executed by conducting the proof proceeding. The statutorily required recording of the summary of a divorce judgment in the margin of the parties' birth and marriage records is sometimes also considered an aspect of the execution of the divorce judgment. Generally speaking, the rule that only the *tribunal de grande instance* may deal with the execution of judgments applies only to exe-

[90] CODE DE PROCÉDURE CIVILE art. 742; *cf.* CODE CIVIL art. 2088.

[91] CODE CIVIL art. 2078, providing that the pledgee may be authorized by the court to sell the pledged article at auction, or to have it evaluated by an expert and keep it. In either case, he must return the difference between the debt and the value as found by the expert or the price realized on auction to the debtor. Apparently, the pledge agreement may authorize the pledgee to use either of these two procedures without court proceedings. CUCHE, EXÉCUTION 50.

[92] *E.g.*, CUCHE, EXÉCUTION 49–50.

[93] *E.g.*, 1 DALLOZ, *op. cit. supra* note 26, at 140.

[94] CODE DU TRAVAIL, bk. I, art. 64.

[95] DÉCRET No. 58–1284 of Dec. 22, 1958, J.O. Dec. 23, 1958, p. 11579, [1959] D.L. 41, art. 3. However, the *tribunal d'instance* does not deal with execution against immovables.

[96] On the commercial courts, see specifically CODE DE PROCÉDURE CIVILE arts. 442, 553. However, the *juge d'instance* as presiding officer of a *tribunal paritaire de baux ruraux* (farm tenancy court) may deal provisionally with matters concerning the execution of the judgments of his court pursuant to his *référé* powers. DÉCRET No. 58–1293 of Dec. 22, 1958, J.O. Dec. 23, 1958, p. 11627, [1959] B.L.D. 87, art. 20.

cution against property, not to execution in the other broader senses here indicated. [97]

The special problems that arise in connection with execution of judgments rendered by *cours d'appel* are discussed elsewhere. [98]

Special rules of territorial competence apply in disputes governing execution of judgments. In particular, all proceedings concerning execution against land must be conducted at the court of its location. [99]

## 13.11. When Judgments May Be Enforced

Unless the court grants a grace period, [100] judgments may ordinarily be executed immediately upon service of the judgment. [101] In case of default judgments, however, unless provisional execution is available, execution is not permissible as long as appeal or *opposition* is possible. [102] The extent to which the availability or use of the various methods of review may result in a stay of execution has been discussed elsewhere. [103]

Execution against a third party, such as a garnishee, is possible only after the judgment is no longer subject to attack by appeal or *opposition*. [104]

No levy is permitted before six o'clock in the morning, or after nine o'clock at night, nor on Sundays or legal holidays, except by

[97] 1 DALLOZ, *op. cit. supra* note 26, at 140–55.

[98] The pertinent rule is contained in CODE DE PROCÉDURE CIVILE art. 472. On its interpretation, see 8.20.g *supra*.

[99] CODE DE PROCÉDURE CIVILE arts. 677–78. Other rules of territorial competence are discussed in connection with the several procedures for the execution of judgments.

[100] The court has a discretionary power to grant a stay of execution of up to one year, if this seems appropriate in view of the economic condition of the debtor. Such a stay may also be granted by a single judge sitting *en référé*. CODE CIVIL art. 1244. If the stay is granted by the court, it must be part of the original judgment. CODE DE PROCÉDURE CIVILE arts. 122–23. No stay may be granted if the debtor is a bankrupt or a fugitive from justice (*en contumace*), or if levies have already been made at the request of other creditors, or if he has impaired the security of his debtor. Grace periods may not be granted in cases involving negotiable instruments. CODE DE COMMERCE art. 182

[101] *E.g.*, 1 DALLOZ, *op. cit. supra* note 26, at Nos. 74–75. However, a tender of the amount due, if made in the manner prescribed by the Civil Code, prevents execution. CODE CIVIL arts. 1257–59. On the manner the judgment must be served, see 7.13 *supra*.

[102] CODE DE PROCÉDURE CIVILE art. 155. Immediate execution is possible if authorized by the court.

[103] On appeal, see 8.14 *supra*. On *pourvoi* to the *Cour de Cassation*, see 9.18 *supra*. On *tierce opposition*, see 10.02–10.08 *supra*. On *requête civile*, see 10.09–10.15 *supra*. On *opposition*, see 7.04.a *supra*.

[104] CODE DE PROCÉDURE CIVILE art. 548. The term execution is used in the text in a broad sense. Article 548 includes among third parties depositaries of funds, officials of the public land records office (if they have to cancel a mortgage or take some other steps pursuant to the judgment), and officials charged with the keeping of the birth, death, and marriage registers if they must record the judgment in their official records. See 1 DALLOZ, *op. cit. supra* note 26, at 113–17.

special permission.[105] The limitation period on judgments is thirty years.[106]

## 13.12. Property Subject to, and Exempt from, Enforcement

**a. Land and movable property.** Article 2092 of the *Code Civil* provides that a person having contracted an obligation is bound with all his movable and immovable property. This means in substance that a creditor may, at his option, levy on his debtor's immovable, movable, or intangible property. Except in the case of minors and incompetents,[107] movable property need not be exhausted before immovable property is levied upon.[108] But immovables which are the joint property of several heirs may not be levied upon by a creditor of one of them until partition has taken place.[109] Further, a creditor whose claim is secured by a mortgage must proceed against the mortgaged property before he proceeds against other immovables of his debtor.[110] The mortgagee does not have a special procedure at his disposal. He must proceed by *saisie immobilière* as any other creditor,[111] though he is entitled to a preference in the distribution of the sale price, based on the rank of his mortgage, and may levy upon the mortgaged property even if it has come into the hands of a third party.[112]

**b. Property exempt from execution.** Property that may not be alienated is exempt from execution. Such property includes property in the public domain,[113] immovables that are "dotal" property,[114] rights attached to a particular person (such as *usage* and *habitation*),[115] and the usufruct parents have in the property of their children.[116] For all

[105] CODE DE PROCÉDURE CIVILE art. 1037.

[106] 1 DALLOZ, *op. cit. supra* note 26, at No. 79. This is based on the general thirty-year limitation period provided by CODE CIVIL art. 2262.

[107] CODE CIVIL art. 2207 permits the sale of a minor's or incompetent's immovables only if his movables are insufficient.

[108] *E.g.*, CRÉMIEU, *op. cit. supra* note 83, at 167; 2 PLANIOL & RIPERT, *op. cit. supra* note 2, at 109, 120.

[109] CODE CIVIL art. 2205. The creditors may request a partition.

[110] CODE CIVIL art. 2209.

[111] This was not always so. See 2 PLANIOL & RIPERT, *op. cit. supra* note 2, at 118.

[112] CRÉMIEU, *op. cit. supra* note 83, at 168.

[113] 2 DALLOZ, RÉPERTOIRE DE PROCÉDURE CIVILE ET COMMERCIALE, *Insaisissabilité*, at No. 15 (1956); *cf.* CODE CIVIL arts. 537–38.

[114] CODE CIVIL art. 1554. However, the ante-nuptial agreement by which the *dot* has been set up may permit alienation. CODE CIVIL art. 1556. There are a few other exceptions. The 1965 reforms have abolished the dotal system as to marriages concluded after their effective date.

[115] *Usage* and *habitation* involve the personal non-transferable right to live in a particular building, or to receive the crops, fruits, and other proceeds of land for personal use. CODE CIVIL arts. 630–34.

[116] Parents have a right to the income derived from the property of their minor children,

practical purposes, property subject to a "fideicommissary substitution" (a kind of future interest) falls in the same class.[117] To the extent that property may be exempted by gift or bequest, the same rule applies.[118] A Law of 1909, modelled after American legislation, permits the creation of homestead farms not subject to execution, but few such homesteads have been created.[119]

Other property is exempt from execution as a matter of governmental convenience. Since the French Revolution, statutes have provided that government obligations shall be exempted from levy. According to the *Cour de Cassation*'s interpretation, attachment of funds in the hands of the government is not possible, but bonds may be seized. The practical result of this interpretation is that bearer bonds are subject to levy and sale, but that registered bonds, which cannot be sold without the co-operation of the government, are not. Amounts due public contractors are exempt from execution, except for the claims of laborers and suppliers of materials. Another exemption benefits the fees of jurors and witnesses.[120] Property of foreign states or diplomatic representatives is also exempt from execution.[121]

To preserve the free flow of commerce, negotiable instruments, with minor exceptions, are not subject to levy,[122] nor are ships ready to sail.[123]

Various items of property have been exempted from levy and sale as a matter of social policy. Bedding and clothing necessary for the debtor and his family may not be sold, nor may food required by him and his family for one month; also exempt are the necessary tools of

subject to the obligation to use the income primarily for the upbringing of the child. CODE CIVIL arts. 384–85. Hence, their right as such may not be sold, but any income not needed for the support of the child is subject to seizure. 2 DALLOZ, *op. cit. supra* note 113, at No. 6.

[117] *Id.* at No. 12; *cf.* CODE CIVIL arts. 1048–49.

[118] Under CODE DE PROCÉDURE CIVILE art. 581, a donor or testator may declare that his gift or bequest shall not be levied upon by the creditor of the beneficiary, but only to the extent the beneficiary is not entitled to the property in any event as a forced heir. With court approval, creditors whose claim arose after the date of the gift or after the death of the testator may seize such property. CODE DE PROCÉDURE CIVILE art. 582.

[119] Law of July 12, 1909, J.O. July 13, 1909, [1910] D. 4. 1; CUCHE, EXÉCUTION 37. On the general topic discussed in this paragraph, see also 2 PLANIOL & RIPERT, *op. cit. supra* note 2, at 111.

[120] CUCHE, EXÉCUTION 38–40; 2 DALLOZ, *op. cit. supra* note 113, at 24–29. On bonds of the *Crédit Foncier*, see *id.* at No. 25; on accounts in the French National Bank (*Banque de France*), see *id.* at No. 26.

[121] See 4.35 *supra.*

[122] CODE DE COMMERCE arts. 140 (bills of exchange), 185 (promissory notes). Decree-Law of Oct. 30, 1935, J.O. Oct. 31, 1935, [1935] D. 4. 467, art. 32 (checks). There are certain exceptions, such as in case of bankruptcy.

[123] CODE DE COMMERCE art. 215. There is an exception for debts incurred in connection with the impending voyage.

craftsmen, books, and instruments of professional people up to 1500 francs (about $ 300) in value and one cow or two goats or three sheep. [124] These items are subject to sale on behalf of creditors having furnished necessaries, but families receiving certain government welfare benefits enjoy complete immunity. [125] Wages and salaries, including those paid by the government, are exempted on a sliding scale. Amounts up to 3,000 francs (about $ 500) per annum are subject to execution only to the extent of five per cent; the percentage increases for sums above this amount and all amounts exceeding 15,000 francs (about $ 3,000) may be levied upon. [126] Certain government payments, including those to *légion d'honneur* members and to holders of military decorations, are totally exempt. [127]

Proceeds resulting from the exploitation of a copyright are subject to execution, except to the extent they are needed by the author, his spouse, and descendants for their support. [128] Unpublished manuscripts, works of art, as well as family correspondence, souvenirs and the like are not subject to execution. The same is true of the *droit moral* of an author. Patents, however, may be sold by creditors. [129] Support payments are exempt from execution, except at the request of creditors who furnished necessaries. [130]

### 13.13. Enforcement Against Movables *(Saisie-Exécution)*

**a. Property subject to *saisie-exécution*.** *Saisie-exécution* may be used to levy execution on corporeal movable property in the possession of the debtor. It may also be used to levy execution on instruments incorporating a debt, such as bearer bounds, but not for execution a-

[124] Code de Procédure Civile art. 592.

[125] Code de Procédure Civile art. 593. Necessary bedding and clothing is always exempt. Social security pensions paid on account of industrial accidents are exempt from execution, except on account of support or alimony claims. Moreau v. Dame Azar, Cass. Soc., March 5, 1964, [1964] D.J. 285.

[126] Code du Travail, bk. 1, art. 60a; Décret No. 64–1098 of Oct. 28, 1964, J.O. Nov. 1, 1964, p. 9799, [1964] D.L. 343. The complete scale is as follows: up to 3000 francs (about $ 500), 5 per cent; from 3000 francs to 6000 francs (about $ 1200), 10 percent; from 6000 francs to 9000 francs (about $ 1800), 20 percent; from 9000 to 12,000 francs (about $ 2,400), 25 percent; from 12,000 francs to 15,000 francs (about $ 3000), one third. On execution on salaries paid by the government, see also Code de Procédure Civile art. 561.

[127] Cuche, Exécution 43–44.

[128] Law No. 57–298 of March 11, 1957, J.O. March 14, 1957, p. 2723, [1957] D.L. 102, art. 69; Law No. 57–803 of July 19, 1957, J.O. July 20, 1957, p. 7172, [1957] D.L. 219. For details, see 2 Dalloz, *op. cit. supra* note 113, at No. 17 (Supp. 1964).

[129] Cuche, Exécution 44–46

[130] Code de Procédure Civile arts. 581–82. Awards of damages for injury to property are subject to execution as are personal injury awards for loss of wages, but awards for pain and suffering are not. However, the law on this point is unsettled. Mauro v. Cie d'assur. Le Soleil, Cour Aix-en-Province, Dec. 19, 1963, [1964] D.J. 295.

gainst other intangibles.[131] *Saisie-exécution* is neither available for execution against fixtures, which are considered part of the land, nor for execution against growing crops.[132] *Saisie-exécution* may be conducted entirely without court intervention if no complications arise.

**b. The order to pay *(commandement).*** Before an execution is possible, an *huissier* must serve an order to pay (*commandement*) on the debtor. The order is similar to the *exploit* by which an action is instituted. If the document on which execution is based has not already been served, it must be served at the same time.[133] In the *commandement* the creditor must "elect a domicile" in the locality in which execution is to take place – in other words, he must agree that all papers concerning the execution may validly be served upon him upon a designated agent in that locality.[134] If the debtor is willing to pay when served with the order, the *huissier* may accept payment.[135]

**c. The levy *(procès-verbal de saisie).*** The actual levy may not take place until at least one day has passed after the service of the order to pay. It is conducted by an *huissier*. If the *huissier* is not granted access to the building where he wishes to levy, he may obtain the assistance of the authorities.[136] First, the *huissier* asks the debtor again to pay (*itératif commandement*). If no payment is forthcoming, he seizes property that is subject to levy and appoints a custodian who is to safeguard it. The *huissier* himself may not be the custodian, but one of his clerks may be; the debtor may be appointed custodian if the creditor consents. If the debtor suggests a solvent custodian, he must be appointed.[137]

[131] 2 DALLOZ, RÉPERTOIRE DE PROCÉDURE CIVILE ET COMMERCIALE, *Saisie-Exécution* 32–34, 55. Property in the possession of a bailee and intangibles can be reached only through *saisie-arrêt*.

[132] *Saisie-brandon* must be used to levy on growing crops. See 13.13.g *infra*. *Saisie immobilière* must be used to levy on fixtures. See 13.15 *infra*.

[133] CODE DE PROCÉDURE CIVILE art. 583. The order to pay informs the creditor that execution will take place unless he pays.

[134] CODE DE PROCÉDURE CIVILE art. 584.

[135] The *huissier* needs no special power of attorney, but he must have the *grosse* of the judgment or of the notarial instrument, which bears the "executory formula" in his possession.

[136] CODE DE PROCÉDURE CIVILE arts. 583, 585, and 587. The party on whose behalf the *huissier* acts may not be present, but the *huissier* may ask two witnesses (*recors*) to accompany him.

[137] CODE DE PROCÉDURE CIVILE arts. 596–98. Unless all parties agree, cash is not given to the custodian, but must be deposited with the *Caisse des Dépôts et Consignations*. CODE DE PROCÉDURE CIVILE art. 590. If farm animals and utensils are to be levied upon, a receiver may be appointed to take care of them. CODE DE PROCÉDURE CIVILE art. 594.

After appointment of the custodian, the *huissier* prepares a report (*procès-verbal de saisie*) in which he describes his activities and lists the property he has seized. He must also indicate the day on which the sale is to take place. The report must be signed by the *huissier* and the custodian. [138] If the proceedings take place at the home of the debtor and he is present, a copy must be given to him; if he is absent, a copy must be left with a servant or relative. If the proceedings do not take place at the debtor's home, a copy of the *procès-verbal* must be served on him in the regular manner. [139] If the *huissier* does not find goods sufficient to warrant the expenses of an execution sale, he must note this in his report and discontinue the proceedings. [140]

The preparation of the *procès-verbal* by the *huissier* constitutes the actual levy. Thereafter, the goods listed in the *procès-verbal* are considered to be in the custody of the court, even if the debtor keeps them as custodian. The custodian, even if he is the debtor, is criminally liable if he disposes of the goods and is accountable for any income they produce. [141]

If the *huissier* proceeds pursuant to a default judgment, the debtor may orally inform the *huissier* that he demands a reopening (*opposition*), if that remedy is available. The *huissier* must then stay further proceedings and note the debtor's statement in his report. [142] The debtor may also request the *huissier* to discontinue proceedings for other reasons – for instance, because the *huissier* attempts to levy on goods the debtor believes are exempt from execution or because of a formal defect in the proceeding. Though they have nothing to do with the reopening of a default judgment, such objections are also referred to as *opposition*. In the case of objections of this nature, the *huissier*, if he believes that the debtor's objections are well founded, will ordinarily stay the proceedings. The *huissier*'s principal, by summoning the debtor before a judge sitting *en référé*, may obtain a quick decision on whether the execution should be continued. If the *huissier* believes the debtor's objections are illfounded, he may continue the proceedings. It is then up to the debtor to seek a stay by bringing the matter before a judge sitting *en référé*. [143]

[138] CODE DE PROCÉDURE CIVILE arts. 586, 588, 589, and 599.

[139] CODE DE PROCÉDURE CIVILE arts. 601–02.

[140] This is known as *procès-verbal de carence*, *i.e.*, report of absence of goods. CUCHE, EXÉCUTION 61.

[141] CODE DE PROCÉDURE CIVILE arts. 603–04; CODE PÉNAL art. 400; CUCHE, EXÉCUTION 61–63.

[142] CODE DE PROCÉDURE CIVILE art. 162; *cf.* 7.04.a *supra*.

[143] CODE DE PROCÉDURE CIVILE art. 607. After completion of the *procès-verbal de saisie*,

**d. The sale.** At least eight days must elapse between the preparation of the *procès-verbal de saisie* and the actual sale of the property. [144] The sale must be announced by at least four posters and ordinarily also by an advertisement in a newspaper. Ordinarily, the sale must be conducted either in a public market, or in a room for auction sales, or at the place where the goods have been levied upon. [145] When there are *commisseurs-priseurs,* [146] they conduct the sale. The goods must be sold at auction. Successful bidders must pay cash; if they cannot pay, the goods are auctioned again. [147] After the sale, the *commisseur-priseur* conducting the sale prepares a report (*procès-verbal*), which, in effect, serves as document of title for the purchasers. [148]

**e. Remedies of third parties claiming rights in the property seized.** A third party claiming ownership or an other *in rem* right in property levied upon may demand that his property be excluded from the sale. If the third party should be present while the *huissier* is preparing his *procès-verbal,* the claim may be made at that time; it should be noted by the *huissier* in his report and submitted to a judge sitting *en référé.* Upon completion of the *huissier*'s report, the third party may claim the objects by serving a formal *ajournement* on the debtor and creditor as well as on the custodian of the goods. The writ must indicate the bases for the third party's claim. The dispute is adjudicated by the court at the place where the levy has taken place. The sale of the property is stayed pending litigation of the dispute. [149] After the sale, the third party must proceed against the purchaser by an ordinary action (*action en revendication*). [150] The high degree of protection granted persons who have acquired movable property in good faith makes this a precarious undertaking. [151]

**f. Rights of other creditors.** If an *huissier* wishing to levy on a debtor's goods finds that a levy has already been made, he may not make an

the debtor must bring a formal action if he wishes to raise objections. 2 Dalloz, *op. cit. supra* note 131, at Nos. 236–43; Cuche, Exécution 67.

[144] Code de Procédure Civile art. 613.

[145] Code de Procédure Civile arts. 617–18.

[146] However, securities will be sold through a broker. On *commissaires-priseurs,* see 2.11.a *supra.*

[147] Code de Procédure Civile art. 624.

[148] *Cf.* Code de Procédure Civile arts. 623, 625.

[149] Code de Procédure Civile art. 608; 2 Dalloz, *op. cit. supra* note 131, at Nos. 269–83.

[150] *Id.* at No. 284.

[151] See Code Civil art. 2279, under which a bona fide acquirer of movable property ordinarily gets a good title unless the property has been lost or stolen.

additional levy on the same goods. However, he may request the custodian to indicate, and he may levy on, goods that have not been seized. The creditor on whose behalf the original levy was made must then be requested to proceed to the sale of the goods comprised by both levies. [152] In effect, there is a joinder of the two proceedings. The proceeds of the sale are later distributed *prorata*.

In addition, by a so-called *opposition sur le prix de la vente,* any creditor of a person whose goods are being attached may reserve his right to participate in the proceeds of an eventual sale. [153] He does not need an "executory title." To make *opposition sur le prix de la vente,* a creditor must serve a notice of his *opposition* on the creditor on whose behalf the levy is taking place and on the person conducting the sale. In the instrument, he must agree to service of all papers upon him through an agent in the locality where the sale is taking place. [154] Until the time of the distribution of the funds realized on the sale, a creditor who has made *opposition sur le prix de la vente* may ordinarily not interfere with the proceedings. However, such a creditor, as well as a creditor who has made an additional levy, may sell the seized goods if the creditor who started the original proceedings delays the sale for too long. [155]

**g. *Saisie-brandon.*** The procedure for execution on growing crops is substantially similar to the procedure used in the case of movables. However, the levy (*procès-verbal de saisie*) may not take place earlier than six weeks before the maturity of the crops. [156] The *garde champêtre,* a kind of municipal watchman charged with preventing damage to fields, must ordinarily be appointed custodian. [157]

### 13.14. Enforcement Against Intangibles *(Saisie-Arrêt)*

**a. General scope of *saisie-arrêt.*** By *saisie-arrêt,* a creditor may reach claims of his debtor against third parties. *Saisie-arrêt* may be based on any money claim, whether or not due or liquidated. By *saisie-arrêt,* the creditor may also reach chattels of his debtor that are not in the latter's possession. [158]

[152] Code de Procédure Civile art. 611.
[153] *Cf.* 13.16.b *infra.*
[154] Code de Procédure Civile art. 609.
[155] Code de Procédure Civile arts. 610, 612. The goods should be sold within eight days.
[156] Code de Procédure Civile art. 626.
[157] Code de Procédure Civile art. 628.
[158] Code de Procédure Civile art. 557 speaks of sums or goods belonging to the debtor which are in the hands of a third party. *Saisie-arrêt* is frequently used to reach goods in the

*Saisie-arrêt* is a provisional remedy as well as a means of execution. [159]

**b. Persons in whose hands property or funds may be attached.** *Saisie-arrêt* may be used to reach property or funds in the hands of any "third party." The precise meaning of the term "third party" is subject to dispute. A person who is merely a cashier for the debtor is not, but an agent may be, a third party. [160] If the creditor is indebted to the debtor and he cannot set off one claim against the other, the creditor may attach by *saisie-arrêt* a debt owed by him to the debtor (*saisie-arrêt sur soi-même*). [161]

**c. The preliminary phase of *saisie-arrêt*.** *Saisie-arrêt* consists of two phases. First, the funds are frozen in the hands of the third party; then, a court order is obtained directing the third party to make payment to the creditor. To freeze the funds, the creditor [162] serves a notice on the third party. The notice indicates the judgment or other basis for the creditor's claim and the amount involved. It must also contain an election of domicile at the place where the third party resides. The third party must indicate to the *huissier* serving the notice what assets of the debtor he holds and whether there has been any previous attachment. [163] Third parties living outside France must be served personally, or service must be made at their domicile. So-called *signification à parquet* is not available. [164] After the service of the notice, the

hands of carriers. In some cases it is doubtful whether property is in the hands of a third party or of the debtor. According to the majority view, a bank is merely the lessor of a safe deposit box; property in the box is therefore in the depositor's possession and cannot be reached through *saisie-arrêt*. See Cuche, Exécution 128–30 (1956). An ordinary account in a bank is subject to *saisie-arrêt* but certain accounts involving mutual transactions are not. *Id.* at 148.

[159] On *saisie-arrêt* as a provisional remedy, see 5.06.a *supra*.

[160] Cuche, Exécution 125–26 (suggesting that a third party is involved whenever the owner of the funds must resort to judicial proceedings to recover them, a criterion not accepted by the courts).

[161] It is the purpose of this procedure to obtain a set-off where it would otherwise be unavailable. Cuche, Exécution 130–32.

[162] The party seeking to obtain a *saisie-arrêt* is designated here as the creditor. *Saisie-arrêt* as a method of execution, like all other methods of execution, may be used to enforce the provisions of a notarial instrument as well as a judgment. As a provisional remedy, it may be used to secure payment of any obligation, whether or not based on a written instrument. See 5.06.a *supra*. The combination of a provisional remedy with execution has resulted in a rather complex procedure.

[163] Code de Procédure Civile art. 559.

[164] Code de Procédure Civile art. 560.

third party may no longer surrender the funds to the person to whom they are owed. [165]

**d. The final phase of the *saisie-arrêt (action en validité).*** Within eight days of service of the notice on the third party, the creditor must inform the debtor of the proceedings. Within the same time limit, the creditor must begin an action against the debtor before the *tribunal de grande instance* at the debtor's domicile to obtain a judicial declaration that the attachment is valid and that the third party must pay over the funds he holds to the creditor (*action en validité*) [166] With the permission of a judge sitting *en référé*, the debtor may avoid the effects of a *saisie-arrêt* by depositing the amount claimed by the creditor with the *Caisse des dépôts et consignations.* [167] He is likely to do this if the amount claimed by the creditor is much smaller than the sum owed by the third party.

Notice of the *action en validité* must be given to the third party within eight days; [168] at the same time, he must be requested to make a formal declaration in court indicating in detail the amounts he owes the debtor, any payments on account, and all previous attachments. [169] If the declaration of the third party is not contested, the *action en validité* takes its course. [170]

First, the claim of the creditor against the debtor is examined by the court, although this is a mere formality if the *saisie-arrêt* is based on a judgment. In addition, the court examines the validity of the previous proceedings. If there are no irregularities, the court renders a judgment

[165] 2 DALLOZ, RÉPERTOIRE DE PROCÉDURE CIVILE ET COMMERCIALE, *Saisie-Arrêt,* at No. 122 (1956).

[166] If the notice is not given and the *action en validité* not started within eight days, the *saisie-arrêt* becomes void; the third party may pay over the funds. In the unusual case in which the debtor does not live in the *département* in which the court hearing the *action en validité* is sitting, the additional time periods granted by CODE DE PROCÉDURE CIVILE art. 1033-2 apply. CODE DE PROCÉDURE CIVILE arts. 563–67.

[167] CODE DE PROCÉDURE CIVILE art. 567. This is known as *cantonnement.*

[168] CODE DE PROCÉDURE CIVILE art. 564. The additional time periods of CODE DE PROCÉDURE CIVILE art. 1033-2 are available.

[169] CODE DE PROCÉDURE CIVILE art. 573. The request for the formal declaration is made at this stage of the proceedings if the *saisie-arrêt* is used as a means of enforcing a judgment or notarial instrument; otherwise, it must be made after the *action en validité.* CODE DE PROCÉDURE CIVILE art. 568. The declaration must be made at the clerk's office of the place where the action is pending if the third party is present there; otherwise, the third party may make the declaration before a judge of the *tribunal d'instance* at his domicile. CODE DE PROCÉDURE CIVILE arts. 570–71. The third party must annex all pertinent documents to his declaration. CODE DE PROCÉDURE CIVILE art. 574. If the third party fails to make the declaration, he may be held liable for the entire amount claimed by the creditor. CODE DE PROCÉDURE CIVILE art. 577.

[170] CODE DE PROCÉDURE CIVILE art. 576.

declaring the *saisie-arrêt* valid and ordering the third party to pay the funds it holds over to the judgment creditor. [171] By a separate action or by a counterclaim in the *action en validité*, the debtor may request cancellation of the *saisie-arrêt*. [172] If a dispute about the amounts due the debtor by the third party results from the latter's declaration, the third party may request that it be resolved by the court at the third party's domicile. [173]

If additional *saisies-arrêt* involving the same funds occur before judgment in the *action en validité*, the funds must be distributed *prorata* among the various parties. [174]

**e. Enforcement against stocks and bonds.** The *Code de Procédure Civile* contains no special rules concerning execution against stocks and bonds. Since bearer instruments are considered to embody the underlying right, they are treated as chattels and can be reached by *saisie-exécution* if they are in the possession of the debtor. If they are held by a broker on his behalf, they may be reached by *saisie-arrêt*. Frequently, however, persons in France deposit bearer instruments [175] with an organization called SICOVAM, which operates as a warehouse or clearinghouse for bearer securities. Transactions in securities between persons who are depositors in the SICOVAM do not involve physical transfer of documents, merely appropriate entries in their accounts. A person wishing the return of his securities is entitled only to securities of the same kind, not to the identical securities he deposited. The receipts evidencing the deposit of securities with SICOVAM are not negotiable. All deposits in SICOVAM are made through a broker, bank, or similar intermediary. [176] By law, securities deposited with SICOVAM cannot be reached through *saisie-arrêt*, [177] though it seems possible to direct a *saisie-arrêt* against the broker or bank which is acting

[171] CODE DE PROCÉDURE CIVILE art. 579; 2 DALLOZ, *op. cit. supra* note 165, at Nos. 188–201.

[172] Such a demand may also be addressed to a judge sitting *en référé*. 2 DALLOZ, *op. cit. supra* note 165, at Nos. 224–29.

[173] CODE DE PROCÉDURE CIVILE art. 570.

[174] CODE DE PROCÉDURE CIVILE art. 575. On the distribution of the proceeds of execution, see 13.16.b *infra*.

[175] In France, as in Europe generally, bearer stock is used much more frequently than in the United States. On the distinction between bearer and registered (nominal) stock in French law, see CHURCH, BUSINESS ASSOCIATIONS UNDER FRENCH LAW 286–91 (1960).

[176] The description of the SICOVAM given here is highly simplified. For a more detailed discussion, see CHURCH, *op. cit. supra* note 175, at 291–94.

[177] DÉCRET No. 49–1105 of August 4, 1949, J.O. Aug. 6, 1949, p. 7726, [1949] D.L. 369, art. 8.

as intermediary before the deposit with SICOVAM is effectuated. [178]

In France, order instruments are not used as investment securities. [179] Registered instruments (*titres nominatifs*) do not embody the underlying right. Hence, registered bonds may be reached through *saisie-arrêt* against the issuer. Some courts permit *saisie-arrêt* directed against the issuing corporation as a means of levying execution against registered shares of stock. The prevailing opinion, however, is that, since the issuing corporation is not a creditor of its stockholders, *saisie-arrêt* is not available. Sometimes, *saisie-exécution* against the instrument itself is used, though registered stock does not embody the stockholder's right in the corporation. However, seizure of the instrument prevents the stockholder from selling his shares unless he obtains a duplicate and, in addition, even registered shares give the bearer a right to the dividends. [180]

**f. Wage garnishments.** To reduce expenses and formalities required of employers who might otherwise be tempted to dismiss employees whose wages are being garnished, the procedure for wage garnishments has been made simpler than the regular *saisie-arrêt*. The proceedings are brought before the *tribunal d'instance* at the employee's residence. Before any further action is taken, an attempt at settlement must be made by the court. [181] If the settlement attempt is unsuccessful, the judge of the *tribunal d'instance* authorizes the garnishment by an order that is mailed to the employer by the clerk of the court. This prevents further payment of wages to the extent they are not exempt from execution. [182] Other creditors may join the proceedings later and share in the funds. [183]

The employer must notify the court of the amount of the employee's wages and of the existence of any prior garnishment orders. On three days' notice, the clerk must call all parties to a hearing before the judge of the *tribunal d'instance*. At the hearing, the judge decides on the validity of the *saisie-arrêt* and on other issues that may have arisen. If the *saisie-arrêt* is valid, the judge renders a decision requiring the

[178] CUCHE, EXÉCUTION 215.

[179] CHURCH, *op. cit. supra* note 175, at 262.

[180] CUCHE, EXÉCUTION 215–17. The bearer of a registered share cannot be required to prove his identity when demanding payment of dividends. Dividends are not mailed to "stockholders of record," but are paid at the offices of the company or of its agents, upon presentation of the stock certificate, which is then stamped. CHURCH, *op. cit. supra* note 175, at 301.

[181] CODE DU TRAVAIL, bk. I, art. 64.

[182] CODE DU TRAVAIL, bk. I, arts. 64a–64b.

[183] CODE DU TRAVAIL, bk. I, art. 65.

employer to make the appropriate wage deductions. To facilitate the employer's bookkeeping problems, he may pay the amounts collected by him to the clerk of the court at quarterly intervals. They are paid to the creditors by the clerk. [184]

## 13.15. Enforcement Against Immovable Property *(Saisie Immobilière)*

**a. Reach.** *Saisie immobilière* may be used against any kind of property that can be mortgaged, including land, mining rights, water rights, fixtures, and rights in land, such as *usufruit.* [185] When *saisie immobilière* is used to enforce a mortgage, it may be directed against the mortgaged premises even if they are no longer in the hands of the original mortgagor, though a third party may require that recourse be had first to mortgaged property still belonging to the mortgagor. [186]

The debtor may obtain a stay of execution against immovable property by showing that one year's rental income from the property will be sufficient for payment of the debt. [187] A third party who is the defendant in a proceeding for execution against immovables merely as owner of premises mortgaged by a prior owner may avoid the proceedings by abandoning the premises to the plaintiff, by paying off the debt and becoming subrogated to the plaintiff's claim, or by following a procedure known as *purge.* [188]

The procedure for execution against immovables is complex. Court intervention [189] is required in every case. All proceedings must be conducted through an *avoué.*

**b. The order to pay *(commandement).*** To start the execution procedure, the creditor must serve an order to pay (*commandement*) on the debtor. The order must contain a description of the property to be levied on. It is generally similar to the order to pay used in case of execution against movables. [190] A copy of the order must be recorded in

[184] Code du Travail, bk. I, arts. 66–70.

[185] Code Civil art. 2204; Cuche, Exécution 227–29.

[186] Code Civil art. 2209.

[187] Code Civil art. 2212.

[188] Cuche, Exécution 234. On the *purge* procedure which, for all practical purposes, involves paying off the secured creditors, see Code Civil arts. 2181–92.

[189] The competent court is the *tribunal de grande instance* at the situs of the property. If property extends over more than one district, the court at the place where the main building is located is competent. Code Civil art. 2211; Code de Procédure Civile art. 675.

[190] Code Civil art. 2217; Code de Procédure Civile art. 673. The *commandement* must contain the usual election of domicile clause.

the public land records office within ninety days of its service. The recording of the order to pay has the same effect as the *procès-verbal de saisie* in a case of execution against movables. It puts the property in the constructive custody of the court. Thereafter, the owner may not make any disposition of the property; even subsequent leases are not binding on the creditors. [191] Additional orders to pay served by other creditors are not independently recorded, but merely mentioned in the margin of the record of the original order. [192]

**c. The *cahier des charges*.** Within forty days of the recording of the *commandement*, the *avoué* for the levying party must prepare a document, called *cahiers des charges*, that lists the conditions of the sale, including the time and place of sale, the minimum bid, and gives a description of the property. This document must also recite the basis for the execution, whether a judgment or notarial instrument, and all proceedings up to its date. It is filed in the court clerk's office. [193] Within eight days thereafter, the owner of the property and all lienholders as they appear in public land records must be served with a notice inviting them to examine the *cahiers des charges* and to annex to it any objections they may have. [194] If any party files objections – for example, because it considers the minimum bid too low –, a hearing is held and the court renders a judgment in which it may order modification of the *cahiers des charges*. Objections based on irregularities in the proceedings must be raised at the same time. [195]

**d. The sale.** After all disputes concerning the *cahier des charges* have been resolved, a notice of sale must be published in one of the papers of the district in which the land is located. The sale must also be announced by posters. The presiding judge of the *tribunal de grande instance* may order additional announcements to be made; he may also permit the use of fewer announcements. The announcements must be made between the fifteenth and the thirtieth day before the sale. [196]

[191] Code de Procédure Civile arts. 674, 686 (generally), 684 (leases). The owner is liable for damages, and may even be criminally liable if he commits any waste. Code de Procédure Civile art. 683. Ordinarily, the owner remains in possession of the premises until the sale, but a judge sitting *en référé* may order him expelled. Code de Procédure Civile art. 681. Any income produced by the property is considered as real property and must be preserved for the levying creditors. Code de Procédure Civile arts. 682, 684.

[192] Code de Procédure Civile art. 680.

[193] Code de Procédure Civile art. 688.

[194] Code de Procédure Civile art. 689.

[195] Code de Procédure Civile arts. 690, 727.

[196] Code de Procédure Civile arts. 696–700.

The sale must be conducted in court, before a full three-judge panel. If irregularities have occured in the procedure, they must be raised before bidding starts. [197] Prospective purchasers must bid through an *avoué*; an *avoué* may not bid for a party who is notoriously insolvent.[198] If no bid is forthcoming, the property is struck down to the levying party for the minimum bid mentioned in the *cahier des charges*. If bids are made, the property is struck down to the highest bidder. [199] *Avoués* making bids need not disclose the identity of their principal, but the successful *avoué* must do so within three days. [200] The successful bidder must pay not only the price, but also the costs of the proceedings which must be announced before bidding starts. [201] Any person authorized to bid may demand a second auction sale by offering to take the property for a price exceeding the price realized at the first auction by at least ten per cent if the bidding at the second auction produces no higher price. [202]

After the conclusion of the bidding, the court renders a judgment that becomes the successful bidder's title. [203] It bears the "executory formula," so that the bidder, if necessary, will be able to expel the former owner with the aid of an *huissier*. [204] The judgment also enables the persons at whose request the sale has taken place to levy execution against the bidder if he fails to pay the purchase price. If the purchase price is not paid, the sale may be repeated and the property struck down to a different bidder. [205] The judgment transferring the title must be recorded in the public land records office. [206]

[197] CODE DE PROCÉDURE CIVILE art. 728. For good cause, the sale may be adjourned. CODE DE PROCÉDURE CIVILE arts. 702–04.

[198] CODE DE PROCÉDURE CIVILE arts. 704, 711. There are also rules as to conflicts of interest.

[199] The highest bidder is determined with the help of candles burning approximately one minute. These are lighted one after the other while the bidding continues. After the bidding has stopped, two more candles are lighted in succession. If no more bids are made until these have gone out, the court strikes the property down to the last bidder.

[200] CODE DE PROCÉDURE CIVILE art. 707.

[201] CODE DE PROCÉDURE CIVILE arts. 701, 714.

[202] CODE DE PROCÉDURE CIVILE arts. 709–10.

[203] CODE DE PROCÉDURE CIVILE arts. 712, 716. Actually, the complete title consists of a copy of the judgment and of the *cahier des charges*.

[204] 2 DALLOZ, RÉPERTOIRE DE PROCÉDURE CIVILE ET COMMERCIALE, *Saisie Immobilière*, at No. 254 (1956); CUCHE, EXÉCUTION 284.

[205] This is known as *folle enchère* (foolish auction), because the original high bidder was foolish to bid if he did not have the funds to pay. CODE DE PROCÉDURE CIVILE arts. 733–40.

[206] The judgment itself passes title as between the parties, but recording is required to make it effective against third parties; in addition, the property may be auctioned off again if the successful bidder fails to record within two months. CODE DE PROCÉDURE CIVILE art. 716.

**e. Nature of purchaser's title.** Generally, the title acquired by the purchaser is no better than that of the former owner: The purchaser's title is subject to the infirmities of the prior owner's title, and all easements or similar restrictions remain in effect. However, the recording of the judgment transferring the title to the high bidder cancels all mortgages; the mortgagees retain only a preference upon distribution of the purchase price. [207] The previous owner is liable to the purchaser in warranty if the purchaser is evicted by a third party. If the eviction takes place after the purchaser has paid the purchase price to the creditors, he may recover it in an action for unjust enrichment. [208]

**f. Conversion of execution sale into voluntary sale.** At any time after the recording of the order to pay (*commandement*), the owner of the property levied upon may ask that the forced sale in court be converted into a voluntary sale. If all parties agree, they submit a collective petition to the presiding judge of the *tribunal de grande instance* who makes an order approving the conversion, establishing the modalities of the sale, and appointing a single judge of the court, or more frequently a *notaire*, to conduct the sale. [209] The property must still be sold at auction, but, since *notaires* are usually experts in matters of land transactions, is likely to bring a higher price than if it were sold by the court. [210] If there is no agreement between the parties, the owner must summon them before the court and demand the conversion. In the absence of an agreement, the court may apparently not appoint a notary to conduct the sale, but must designate a judge. However, even a "voluntary" sale before one judge involves fewer formalities than a sale by the full court. [211]

## 13.16. Distribution of the Proceeds of Execution: *Ordre* and *Contribution*

There are two procedures for the orderly distribution of funds realized on an execution sale: *ordre* and *contribution*. [212] *Ordre* is used for distribution of the proceeds of a sale of land if there are lien creditors.

[207] Code de Procédure Civile art. 717.
[208] Cuche, Exécution 289. A third party may assert his title against the purchaser at the auction sale at any time within the applicable limitation period. However, there is a special procedure (*action en distraction*) by which a party claiming to have a superior right to the premises being levied upon may claim them. Code de Procédure Civile arts. 725–26.
[209] Code de Procédure Civile arts. 744–45.
[210] Cuche, Exécution 336.
[211] Code de Procédure Civile arts. 745a–48e; Cuche, Exécution 336–38.
[212] Bankruptcy is restricted to *commerçants*. On who are merchants, see 4.39.b *supra*.
[213] See generally Cuche, Exécution 341–43.

*Contribution* is used to distribute the proceeds of a sale of movables or the proceeds of a sale of land if there are no lien creditors. [213]

**a. *Ordre*.** As its name indicates, *ordre* is used to distribute the proceeds of a sale to secured creditors in the order in which their security ranks. In each *tribunal de grande instance*, one or more judges are specially designated by the presiding judge of the regional *cour d'appel* to handle *ordre* proceedings. [214]

Eight days after the party to whom the property has been struck down has recorded the judgment that gives him title to the property, the creditor who initiated the *saisie immobilière* must file a list of all creditors with recorded liens in the court clerk's office and request that *ordre* proceedings be initiated. The designated judge summons all creditors with recorded liens as well as the former owner and the successful bidder before him and attempts to get an agreement of all parties concerning the distribution of the funds. If an agreement is reached, he makes an order accordingly and delivers a form to the various creditors, which they must give to the successful bidder, or, if the bidder has deposited the funds in the *Caisse des dépôts et consignations*, to the latter institution, to receive their share of the price. [215]

If there is no agreement and fewer than four creditors are involved, a simplified *ordre* procedure is used. All parties are summoned before the full (three-judge) court for a hearing at which the secured creditors state their claims and produce supporting documents. The court then renders a decision indicating how the available funds must be distributed. [216]

If there are four or more creditors, in the absence of an amicable settlement, the regular *ordre* procedure is used. The secured creditors are summoned to file statements of their claims and supporting documents within forty days. [217] If they do not comply with the summons, their claims are barred. When the forty-day period is over, the designated judge prepares a tentative report in which he lists the creditors in the order in which their claims must be satisfied. The creditors must examine the report and file objections within thirty days. If timely

[214] CODE DE PROCÉDURE CIVILE art. 749.

[215] CODE DE PROCÉDURE CIVILE arts. 750–51. On the procedure the high bidder must follow when depositing the funds instead of holding them until the end of the *ordre* procedure, see CODE DE PROCÉDURE CIVILE arts. 777–78.

[216] CODE DE PROCÉDURE CIVILE art. 773.

[217] This mailing is based on the list of creditors with recorded liens filed earlier in the court clerk's office. CODE DE PROCÉDURE CIVILE arts. 752–53.

objections are not filed, the tentative report becomes the final report which becomes the basis for distribution of the funds. [218]

If objections to the tentative report are raised – for instance, on the ground that one of the creditors listed ahead of the objecting creditor did not have a valid lien or had only a lien subordinate to that of the objector –, the matter is transferred to the full court for a hearing on the issue. [219] The parties submit *conclusions*; any documents they wish to use must be filed in the court clerk's office at least three days before the hearing. At the argument, the *ministère public* is entitled to be heard. The judgment is subject to appeal, but time to appeal is very short. [220]

After time to appeal has run out or after the decision of the appellate court has been rendered, the designated judge prepares his final report which, if there have been objections, is based on the judgment rendered by the full court. [221] In a limited number of cases, the final report by the designated judge may be brought before the full court for review – for instance, if the final report is not in accord with a judgment rendered upon contest of the tentative report, or the final report is not in accordance with the tentative report although there was no contest, or the final report contains a mistake by the designated judge. Review by the full court must be demanded within eight days of the service of the final report. The procedure before the full court is identical to that used in case of a contest on the preliminary report. [222]

After this method of review has been used or after it has become time-barred, a summary of the final report must be filed in the public land records office. [223] At the same time, the clerk delivers to those creditors whose secured claim entitles them to share in the proceeds a

[218] CODE DE PROCÉDURE CIVILE arts. 754–56, 759. The costs of litigation have first priority, then come various general liens, then the mortgages according to their rank. CRÉMIEU, *op. cit. supra* note 83, at 233.

[219] CODE DE PROCÉDURE CIVILE art. 758.

[220] CODE DE PROCÉDURE CIVILE arts. 760–66. Time to appeal is only ten days if the appellant lives in the place where the court is located; otherwise, one day is added for each 50 kilometers (about 31 miles) of distance. The summary procedure is used in the *cour d'appel* as well as in the court of first instance. *But see* 7.59 *supra*.

[221] CODE DE PROCÉDURE CIVILE art. 765. On costs, see CODE DE PROCÉDURE CIVILE art. 766. The claims of the creditors are satisfied in the order mentioned in note 218 *supra*. If any funds remain after all secured creditors have been satisfied, they may be distributed *pro rata* to unsecured creditors in a *contribution* proceeding.

[222] This method of review is also known as *opposition*, though it has nothing to do with the reopening of default judgments. CODE DE PROCÉDURE CIVILE art. 767. On the situations in which review is possible, see CUCHE, EXÉCUTION 405.

[223] CODE DE PROCÉDURE CIVILE art. 769.

form upon presentation of which they must be paid by the purchaser of the land. [224]

**b. *Contribution.*** *Contribution,* or more properly *distribution par contribution,* is used for the distribution of funds realized upon an execution sale of movable property if the funds are insufficient to satisfy all creditors or upon sale of immovable property on which no creditors have liens. [225] Since, traditionally, liens on movable property have played only a minor rôle in French law, the available funds are usually distributed so that each creditor bears a *pro rata* share of the loss; hence, the name of the procedure. [226] It is generally similar to the *ordre* procedure. *Contribution* procedures are conducted by the *tribunal de grande instance* that dealt with the execution. However, the *tribunal d' instance* is competent for amounts of less than 1500 francs (about $ 300) and for the distribution of all funds realized from wage garnishments, regardless of the amount involved. [227]

If the procedure is brought before a *tribunal de grande instance,* it is largely in the hands of the same judge who also conducts *ordre* procedures. First, there is an attempt at amicable settlement. [228] If no settlement can be reached within one month, the *commisseur priseur* or other individual who conducted the execution sale must deposit the proceeds of the sale, minus his fees, with the appropriate agency. [229] All the creditors who participated in the *saisie* and all those who reserved their right to participate in the distribution of funds by *opposition sur le prix de la vente* are then summoned to file their claims against the debtor and supporting documents in court. If they have a lien or preference, they must so indicate. A landlord having a landlord's lien is not required to participate in the *contribution* procedure; he may obtain an immediate determination of the amount to which he is entitled by a judge sitting *en référé.* [230] On the basis of the claims and

[224] CODE DE PROCÉDURE CIVILE art. 770. If the purchaser has paid the funds into the *Caisse des Dépôts et Consignations,* the form is presented to that organization.

[225] Actually, only the claims of creditors who levied execution or reserved their right to participate in the distribution of funds by *opposition sur le prix de la vente* are taken into consideration. See generally CUCHE, EXÉCUTION 421–22; 1 DALLOZ, RÉPERTOIRE DE PROCÉDURE CIVILE ET COMMERCIALE, *Distribution par Contribution,* Nos. 1–16 (1955).

[226] The procedure is called distribution by contribution because, in the distribution of the available funds, everybody (with the exception of preferred creditors) contributes his *pro rata* sacrifice towards the total loss.

[227] CUCHE, EXÉCUTION 422; *cf.* 13.10 *supra.*

[228] CODE DE PROCÉDURE CIVILE art. 656.

[229] CODE DE PROCÉDURE CIVILE art. 657. Funds are usually deposited with the *Caisse des Dépôts et Consignations.*

[230] CODE DE PROCÉDURE CIVILE arts. 659–61.

documents submitted by the parties, the judge prepares a preliminary report listing the amounts to which the various preferred and ordinary creditors are entitled. If no objections are raised, the preliminary report becomes the final report on which the distribution of funds is based. [231] If objections are raised, the matter is transferred to the full three-judge court for a hearing on the objections. As far as the matters in contest are concerned, the final report which is then prepared is based on the judgment of the court. [232]

In the case of funds realized from wage garnishments, the distribution of available funds is determined by the judge of the *tribunal d' instance* after a summary hearing. [233]

[231] CODE DE PROCÉDURE CIVILE arts. 663–65.

[232] CODE DE PROCÉDURE CIVILE arts. 666–72. The procedure for the hearing and the rules as to appeal are similar to those applicable in *ordre* procedures.

[233] CODE DU TRAVAIL bk. I, art. 70; *cf.* 13.14.f *supra.* The procedure in other cases within the competence of the *tribunal d'instance* is similar.

CHAPTER 14

# RECOGNITION AND ENFORCEMENT OF FOREIGN JUDGMENTS

This chapter discusses the requirements for recognition and enforcement in France of foreign judgments and arbitral awards. Discussion of the procedure for obtaining an *exequatur* (14.01–14.04) precedes treatment of foreign judgments relating to personal status that do not need an *exequatur* to be recognized (14.04). The chapter concludes with a description of the circumstances in which, and the procedure by which, foreign arbitral awards are recognized and enforced (14.06) and with a brief summary on international agreements dealing with the recognition and enforcement of foreign judgments and arbitral awards to which France is a party (14.07).

## 14.01. Introduction

Absent an international agreement to the contrary, a foreign judgment, in order to have *res judicata* effect or to be enforceable in France, needs a so-called *exequatur* from a French court. [1] The procedure for obtaining an *exequatur* is similar to that followed in a regular civil action. [2] For all practical purposes, an *exequatur* transforms a foreign into a domestic judgment. [3]

These rules are subject to one exception: Foreign judgments relating to personal status have *res judicata* effect in France without *exequatur*. However, they need an *exequatur* if they are to be enforced against persons and property in France. [4]

Foreign judgments without an *exequatur* are not wholly without effect in France. The liberal French rules of evidence make it possible

[1] On the enforcement of foreign judgments, see CODE DE PROCÉDURE CIVILE art. 546 and CODE CIVIL art. 2123. On their *res judicata* effect, see BATIFFOL 828. The beneficiary of a foreign judgment that has not received an *exequatur* may sue in France on his original caus of action. Soc. Wilhelm Gammersbach v. Gordon et Simon, Cass. Civ., Oct. 8, 1940, 67 CLUNET 108 (1945). For a brief historical survey and a summary of the reasons for the *exequatur* procedure, see BATIFFOL 826; *cf.* generally DELAUME, AMERICAN-FRENCH PRIVATE INTERNATIONAL LAW 160 (2d ed. 1961); Philononenko, *Contribution à la théorie générale d'exécution des jugements en droit français et belge*, 64 CLUNET 429 (1937).

[2] See 14.04 *infra*.

[3] In spite of the different terminology, there is, therefore, little difference between an *exequatur* proceeding and an American action on a foreign judgment. BATIFFOL 827.

[4] See 14.05 *infra*.

to use almost any writing as proof of the facts therein recited. [5] Hence, a foreign judgment that has not received the *exequatur* may be used as evidence in a French proceeding involving the same subject matter. However, since it does not have *res judicata* effect, it is not binding and conclusive evidence. [6] Furthermore, a foreign judgment without *exequatur* may be considered sufficient evidence of a claim to entitle its holder to obtain an appropriate provisional remedy, such as attachment (*saisie-arrêt*), in France. An *exequatur* must, however, be obtained before actual execution takes place. [7] In addition, a foreign judgment is sometimes considered as a fact that may have legal consequences in France quite apart from any *exequatur*. A party evicted from property in the United States as a result of the judgment of an American court may sue the person liable to him on a warranty of title in France without prior *exequatur* if the French courts are otherwise competent. [8]

The rules applicable to the recognition and enforcement of foreign judgments are largely judge-made. Statutes deal with this topic only to a limited extent. [9]

## 14.02. Judgments That Need, and Judgments That May Be Given, an *Exequatur*

Unless a treaty provides otherwise, as a rule, all judgments of foreign courts, in order to be effective in France, need an *exequatur*. [10] Whether a court is considered foreign depends on the sovereignty in whose name it renders its justice, not on the place in which it sits. [11] Courts of international organizations are treated as foreign courts, but special rules apply to the Court of Justice of the European Communities. [12]

A purely criminal judgment of a foreign court may not receive an

[5] See 7.31 *supra*.

[6] *E.g.*, Rougeron v. Veuve Rougeron, Cass. Civ., June 19, 1963, 91 CLUNET 555 (1964); Bachmann v. Dame Vigier, Cour Paris, April 10, 1959, 48 REV. CR. D.I.P. 364 (1959), 87 CLUNET 488 (1960); Reverchon v. époux Guelton, Trib. Gde Inst. Seine, May 29, 1963, 91 CLUNET 315 (1964).

[7] Dame Buchel v. Veuve Garabedian, Trib. Seine, Feb. 1, 1956, 84 CLUNET 150 (1957).

[8] See generally BATIFFOL 865; 2 DALLOZ, RÉPERTOIRE DE PROCÉDURE CIVILE ET COMMERCIALE, *Jugement Etranger*, at Nos. 21–34 (1956).

[9] CODE DE PROCÉDURE CIVILE art. 546 provides that foreign judgments may be enforced in France only if the requirements of CODE CIVIL arts. 2123 and 2128 are met. CODE CIVIL art. 2123 states that a foreign judgment gives rise to a lien in France only if it has received an *exequatur*. Article 2128 provides merely that agreements concluded in foreign countries do not give rise to a mortgage in France unless there is a treaty or law to the contrary. All other rules relating to the recognition and enforcement of judgments are entirely judge-made.

[10] For exceptions, see text at notes 4–8 *supra*.

[11] Hence, a judgment of an American military court sitting in France is considered a foreign judgment and the judgments of French consular courts were treated as French judgments. BATIFFOL 831.

[12] See 14.07.b *infra*.

*exequatur.* [13] However, in many foreign countries, the victim of a wrongful act may join a criminal proceeding against the perpetrator of the act and receive an award of damages in that proceeding. This award is not considered a criminal judgment and may be enforced in France. [14] The same is probably true of purely private penalties in civil actions. [15] Administrative decisions may, generally, not be given an *exequatur.* [16]

### 14.03. Conditions for Grant of *Exequatur*

In a recent case, the *Cour de Cassation* has listed five requirements to be met before a foreign judgment may be given an *exequatur*: (1) it must have been rendered by a court having jurisdiction; (2) the procedure followed must have been regular; (3) the foreign court must have applied the law applicable under French conflict of laws rules; (4) there may be no fraud on the law; and (5) it must be possible to execute the judgment in the country in which it was rendered. [17]

**a. Jurisdiction.** The judgment of a foreign court will be given an *exequatur* only if that court had (international) jurisdiction under pertinent French rules. This means primarily that a foreign judgment will not receive an *exequatur* if the French courts had general competence to adjudicate the dispute. Hence, since under articles 14 and 15 of the *Code Civil* French courts are almost always competent in cases in which at least one party is a French national, foreign judgments involving French nationals will ordinarily not be enforced in France. Similarly, if the parties had agreed to give exclusive competence to a French court, a foreign judgment rendered in disregard of that agreement will not be granted an *exequatur.* [18]

While it is reasonably settled that a foreign judgment will not be

[13] Batiffol 832; Reverchon v. époux Guelton, *supra* note 6.

[14] *E.g.*, Lintermans v. dame Clercq, Cour Paris, May 2, 1958, 86 Clunet 156 (1958). The court decisions are not unanimous, however. Sometimes, a decision of a foreign criminal court creating a civil disability is enforced in France. See Receveur-Percepteur du 10e arrondissement de Paris v. Lajarrige, Cour Rennes, July 20, 1953, 83 Clunet 690 (1956) (recognizing judgment of Belgian military tribunal appointing receiver for defendant's property as punishment for pro-German activities during war).

[15] Batiffol 834.

[16] Israilovici Triad v. Procureur de la République, Trib. Gde Inst. Seine, Nov. 27, 1963, 91 Clunet 313 (1964) (administrative decision of Roumanian authorities changing plaintiff's name cannot receive *exequatur* in France).

[17] Munzer v. dame Jacoby-Munzer, Cass. Civ., Jan. 7, 1964, 91 Clunet 302 (1964) (note Goldman), [1964] J.C.P. 2. 13590 (note Ancel).

[18] Batiffol 842–44; 2 Dalloz, *op. cit. supra* note 8, at Nos. 36–39. On the scope of articles 14 and 15 of the Code Civil, see 4.03–4.07 *supra*. On waiver of reliance on these articles, see 4.09 and 4.27–4.30 *supra*. On the impact of treaties on the competence of French courts, see 4.34 *supra*.

enforced if a French court would have been competent to adjudicate the dispute, it is still debated to what extent France should impose on foreign countries its own jurisdictional standards in cases in which no French court is competent. According to many authors, when French courts are clearly not competent, the competence of a foreign court should be determined under its own law and the findings of the foreign court as to its competence respected, especially when they have become *res judicata* in the foreign country. [19] There is, however, no universal agreement on this point. Migratory divorces of American nationals seem sometimes to have been denied effect [20] because the action was not brought before the court of the domicile of the defendant, the competent court under French law. [21]

**b. A proper procedure.** A judgment of a foreign court will be recognized only if the foreign court used a proper procedure. This means primarily that the foreign judgment must comply with minimum standards of fairness as prescribed by French *ordre public* (public policy): The defendant must have been served in a manner calculated to give him actual notice and he must receive adequate time to appear and prepare his defense. [22] Since French courts must write opinions for all of their decisions, foreign judgments not accompanied by an opinion have, in the past, sometimes been refused recognition on the ground that this absence rendered them contrary to French public policy, but at present this rule seems no longer prevalent. However, the papers submitted during the *exequatur* proceeding must enable the French

[19] BATIFFOL 845; 2 DALLOZ, *op. cit. supra* note 8, at No. 37; Goldman, *supra* note 17, at 305; Lundwall v. dame Villada y Sanchez, Cour Paris, Feb. 4, 1958, 47 REV. CR. D.I.P. 389 (1958) (note H.B.), 85 CLUNET 1016 (1958) (note Ponsard); *cf.* Oppenheimer v. Haymann, Trib. Seine, Nov. 4, 1954, 82 CLUNET 650 (1955) (note A.P.).

[20] See 14.05.d *infra*.

[21] *Cf.* 4.01.e and 4.03 *supra*. Related to this problem is the question of whether a foreign court having jurisdiction under French standards of (international) jurisdiction must also be competent under its own law. It is generally agreed that it must. Obviously, a judgment void in its country of origin should not be enforced in France. According to many authors, when examination into the question of competence is foreclosed in the foreign country by *res judicata*, estoppel, or similar doctrines, a French court may not review the competence of the foreign court under the foreign court's own law. However, there is some opinion *contra*. BATIFFOL 846; *cf.* époux Fatton, Trib. Besancon, July 23, 1937, 65 CLUNET 490 (1938).

[22] *E.g.*, BATIFFOL 850; 2 DALLOZ, *op. cit. supra* note 8, at No. 42. French courts will not enforce a foreign judgment in an action in which the defendant was served only by publication, if the plaintiff knew the defendant's address and could have used a method of service better calculated to give the defendant actual notice. Cie Naviera Baracaldesa v. Lloyd de France, Trib. Seine, Jan. 18, 1929, 56 CLUNET 1056 (1929). If the defendant actually receives timely notice of proceedings against him, it is not too important what method of service is used, provided it complies with the laws applicable where the action is pending. *E.g.*, S.A. Wouters et Cie v. Robert-Bérin, Trib. Gde Inst. Seine, Dec. 12, 1961, 89 CLUNET 1032 (1962). For a more detailed discussion of service, see 15.07 *infra*.

court to make sure that the foreign judgment meets all requirements. [23]

It has been argued that, even if the procedure followed meets the French minimum standards, a French court may refuse to enforce a foreign judgment when it can be shown that the foreign court made a mistake in applying its own laws of procedure. According to a more recent view, however, such mistakes must be disregarded when the foreign judgment is effective in the country in which it was rendered because the procedural defect has been cured by waiver, estoppel, *res judicata* or the application of similar principles. [24]

In some matters involving a close relationship between substance and procedure, such as divorce, if under French conflict of laws rules the foreign forum may not apply its own substantive laws, even strict compliance with the foreign procedural rules is not always sufficient to-ensure recognition of the judgment in France. [25]

**c. Application of the proper law under French choice of law rules.** French court decisions, especially those dealing with peronal status matters, give effect to a foreign judgment only if the foreign court applied the law applicable under French choice of law rules. [26] This requirement, which has been criticized, seems particularly unjustified when French choice of law rules do not demand application of French law. [27] In such circumstances, the interest of the French courts in the application of the correct choice of law rule is minimal.

[23] BATIFFOL 851; 2 DALLOZ, *op. cit. supra* note 8 at No. 45. A judgment accompanied by an opinion containing statements insulting to France would probably be refused enforcement. Cases denying *exequatur* because of the absence of an opinion are listed in the note by Sialelli to Blunt v. Mirles, Trib. Corbeil, March 5, 1952, 80 CLUNET 128 (1953). For the more recent rule, see Société Roechlingsch Eisen und Stahlwerke v. Verreries de Trois-Fontaines, Cass. Civ., July 11, 1961, [1961] D.J. 577 (note Holleaux), 89 CLUNET 184 (1962); Gamsaragan v. Sté Duthion & Cie., Cour Paris, May 5, 1961, 49 REV. CR. D.I.P. 388 (1960), 88 CLUNET 1120 (1961). See also 14.04.b *infra*.

[24] *E.g.*, 2 DALLOZ, *op. cit. supra* note 8, at No. 41 (and Supp. 1964); Goldman, *supra* note 17, at 307. For a case following the more recent view, see Lestrade de Kyron v. Roussel, Cour Paris, Feb. 2, 1961, 50 REV. CR. D.I.P. 566 (1961) (note Franceskakis).

[25] Since French courts require the foreign court to apply the substantive law applicable under French choice of law rules, if under French conflict of laws rules French substantive law would be applicable, a French court will not recognize a foreign divorce based on the admission of one spouse, because reliance on an admission, though a procedural question, has a bearing on the substantive French rule prohibiting divorce by agreement. Figué v. dame Figué, Cass. Civ., June 17, 1958, [1958] J.C.P. II. 10761 (note Louis-Lucas), 86 CLUNET 1114 (1959) (note Goldman). See also 14.03.c *infra*.

[26] BATIFFOL 851; 2 DALLOZ, *op. cit. supra* note 8, at Nos. 46–47; Rivière v. Roumiantzeff, Cass. Civ., April 17, 1953, [1953] J.C.P. 2. 7863, 80 CLUNET 860 (1953). In matters of personal status, French conflict of laws rules frequently require the application of the law of the parties' nationality. See 11.03.c *supra*.

[27] Goldman, *supra* note 8, at 307; Nadelmann, *French Courts Recognize Foreign Money-Judgments: One Down and More to Go*, 13 AM. J. COMP. L. 72 (1964); 2 DALLOZ, *op. cit. supra* note 8, at No. 49.

In one respect, the rule here stated receives a liberal application. If the law actually applied by the foreign court and the law applicable under French choice of law rules lead to the same result, the foreign judgment is effective in France. [28] Thus, because adultery – the only basis for divorce in New York – is also a ground for divorce under French law, a judgment of a New York court granting a divorce to a French couple under New York law will be recognized in France, though French choice of law rules require that French law be applied in all divorce actions in which both parties are French nationals. [29]

**d. No violation of French public policy *(ordre public)* or "fraud on the law".** A foreign judgment is not recognized if it violates French public policy (*ordre public*). The scope of this rule is hard to define. However, foreign judgments are treated more liberally than foreign laws. [30] Thus, although divorce by consent is not permissible in France and French courts will not grant such a divorce even though it may be legal under the law applicable under French choice of law rules, a foreign divorce judgment based on the consent of the parties may be recognized in France. [31] On the other hand, a provision in a New York divorce decree, which prohibited remarriage of the defendant within three years of the judgment, has been considered as violative of French public policy. [32]

The meaning of the term *ordre public* may vary with the times. For example, in the past, foreign paternity judgments that had not been rendered in compliance with the strict conditions of the *Code Civil* were sometimes refused enforcement on the ground that their recognition would violate public policy, but the more recent trend is to the contrary. [33]

A judgment ordering payment of a civil penalty is apparently effective in France. [34] Foreign judgments that contradict an existing French judgment between the same parties (or even another foreign

[28] BATIFFOL 853; 2 DALLOZ, *op. cit. supra* note 8, at No. 48.

[29] Dame Cureau v. Cureau, Trib. Seine, May 14, 1956, 84 CLUNET 146 (1957); *cf.* Oppenheimer v. Haymann, *supra* note 19.

[30] BATIFFOL 854; 2 DALLOZ, *op. cit. supra* note 8, at Nos. 50–51.

[31] Rivière v. Roumiantzeff, *supra* note 26; Cau v. Sieur Grossel, Trib. Seine, Oct. 20, 1956, 86 CLUNET 454 (1959); Mason v. dame Henrioux, Trib. Gde Inst. Seine, Oct .17, 1961, 89 CLUNET 708 (1962). Even a divorce by unilateral repudiation, valid under the applicable (Iranian) law, was recognized in France when it was in effect the result of an agreement of the parties. Martino v. Salahuddin, Trib. Gde Inst. Seine, April 17, 1962, 90 CLUNET 150 (1963).

[32] Dame Cureau v. Cureau, *supra* note 29.

[33] *Compare, e.g.*, Hengsberger v. Escoffier, Trib. Draguignan, Feb. 18, 1938, 65 CLUNET 785 (1938), *with* Bach v. Blankenhorn, Cass. Civ., April 11, 1945, 67 CLUNET 596 (1945).

[34] S.A. Wouters et Cie v. Robert-Bérin, *supra* note 22.

judgment having received a French *exequatur*) are always considered in violation of *ordre public.* [35]

A foreign judgment will not be enforced in France if it involves "fraud on French law." There is "fraud on the law," when parties change their nationality, domicile, or residence merely for the purpose of obtaining the application of a law different from that which would normally be applied in impending litigation. [36] The concept of "fraud on the law," however, does not have a very precise meaning. It is sometimes said that a fraud on any law other than French law does not impair the effectiveness of a foreign judgment. [37] However, some American migratory divorces seem to have been refused recognition because they amounted to fraud on the law of the parties' domicile. [38]

**e. Enforceability in country of origin.** To receive an *exequatur,* a foreign judgment need not be final. Foreign alimony or custody decrees will be enforced in France though they are subject to prospective modification in the country of origin. [39] However, the judgment must be *exécutoire* – in other words, capable of immediate enforcement in the place of its origin. Unless there is a stay of execution, neither the possibility nor the actual solicitation of review by appeal or otherwise prevents the grant of an *exequatur*. However, as a practical matter, French courts do stay *exequatur* proceedings in case of appeal in the country of origin until the appeal has been decided. [40]

## 14.04. *Exequatur* Proceedings

**a. Competent court.** An *exequatur* proceeding is always broughtbefore the *tribunal de grande instance,* regardless of the subject matter adjudicated by the foreign judgment. The proceedings are conducted before

[35] *E.g.*, Patino v. dame Patino, Cass. Civ., May 15, 1963, 90 CLUNET 1016 (1963). On a patent case, see Forest v. Punski, Cass. Civ., April 5, 1960, 50 REV. CR. D.I.P. 389 (note Weser).

[36] 2 DALLOZ, *op. cit. supra* note 8, at No. 52.

[37] *E.g.*, Oppenheimer v. Haymann, *supra* note 19 (though residents of Argentina went to Uruguay to obtain divorce unavailable in Argentina, divorce judgment is valid, since under French conflict of laws rules French law should have been applied and under French internal law parties could have obtained a divorce).

[38] See 14.05.d *infra.*

[39] Hence, it is unnecessary to let alimony arrears accumulate and then sue in the foreign country to obtain a judgment for the arrears before bringing proceedings in France. Epoux Parmentier, Trib. Lille, Feb. 14, 1951, 78 CLUNET 910 (1951); BATIFFOL 849. In fact, French law has a policy against accumulation of alimony arrears, though this does not affect the validity of foreign judgments for such arrears. Munzer v. dame Jacoby-Munzer, *supra* note 17.

[40] Abramovith v. De Wind, Trib. Seine, Nov. 21, 1956, 47 REV. CR. D.I.P. 119 (1958); 1 DALLOZ, *op. cit. supra* note 8, at Nos. 92–93 (and Supp. 1964).

a regular panel in open court, not in the *chambre du conseil.* [41] The court at the defendant's domicile or residence is territorially competent, but that competence is not exclusive. If the judgment debtor has no domicile or residence in France, the action may be brought where his property can be levied upon or at some other place in France that has a reasonable contact with the case. [42]

**b. Documents to be submitted.** The documents submitted in an *exequatur* proceeding must enable the court to ascertain whether the judgment meets the conditions for enforcement. [43] In case of an American decision, it is therefore not sufficient to submit merely the formal judgment. The opinion as well as the findings of fact and conclusions of law should also be provided. If these do not provide the requisite information, copies of the summons, the proof of service, the pleadings, and of other procedural papers should be submitted. If a typed or printed record exists, submission of the whole record will sometimes be the best approach. All papers should be properly certified by the clerk of the court. The clerk's signature must be authenticated by the territorially competent French consul. The French consul's signature must, in turn, be authenticated by the French Ministry of Foreign Affairs. A chain certification of the clerk's signature by higher American officials is apparently not necessary. French courts seem to be lenient as to the requirement of authentication. Documents that are not in the French language must be accompanied by a translation prepared by a French sworn (court) interpreter. [44]

**c. Procedure.** A proceeding to obtain an *exequatur* is conducted as a regular civil action. Absent a treaty provision to the contrary, it must be initiated by an ordinary *ajournement* served on the judgment debtor. It has been argued, however, that an *exequatur* proceeding may be joined with another action between the same parties by the filing of supplemental pleadings (*conclusions*). The pleadings should recite the decretal part of the foreign judgment. No communication to the *ministère public* is necessary. The case is always argued in open court, even

[41] BATIFFOL 837; 2 DALLOZ, *op. cit. supra* note 8, at No. 80.

[42] Forest v. Punski, *supra* note 35; 4.32.a *supra.*

[43] *E.g.*, Société Boden & Haac v. Union commerciale africaine, Trib. Seine, March 15, 1956, 84 CLUNET 144 (1957); Gamsaragan v. Sté Duthion, *supra* note 23.

[44] In addition, when appropriate, a certificate of no appeal should be supplied. See generally JURISCLASSEUR DE DROIT INTERNATIONAL, FASC. 584, at Nos. 36–38 (1963); 2 DALLOZ, *op. cit. supra* note 8, at Nos. 89–91. On authentication of American documents for use in France, see 15.05 *infra.*

when recognition of a divorce judgment is sought. [45] Ordinary rules apply as to appeal and other methods of review. [46]

**d. The power of revision.** During the *exequatur* proceedings, the court must examine whether the requirements for enforcement are met. However, in the past, French courts, assuming and exercising a *pouvoir de révision* (power of revision), also examined the merits of the foreign judgment and refused to grant an *exequatur* if, in their view, the case was decided incorrectly, either on the law or on the facts. The party seeking the exercise of this power had the burden of showing that the judgment was wrong on the merits. [47] The power of revision did not permit modification of the judgment submitted to the French court, but only denial of an *exequatur*. However, the *exequatur* could be granted for a reduced amount and a separable provision of a judgment could be refused enforcement, though *exequatur* was granted as to the rest. [48]

The assumption and exercise of a power of revision has been criticized by many authors. It was abandoned by the *Cour de Cassation* in cases dealing with personal status more than a hundred years ago, [49] but has been re-affirmed repeatedly as to money judgments. In the last ten years, the Paris *Cour d'Appel* has refused to follow the case law of the *Cour de Cassation* in this respect, [50] and, of late, the *Cour de Cassation* itself seems to have abandoned the idea that a French court may examine the merits of a foreign judgment that meets the rather far-reaching requirements for recognition. [51] It is not too clear to what extent this new ruling affects the power of the French courts to grant an *exequatur* for a reduced amount or to excise the part of a judgment considered in violation of public policy. [52] The traditional right of

[45] BATIFFOL 836–40; 2 DALLOZ, *op. cit. supra* note 8, at Nos. 78–88.

[46] *Id.* at No. 119.

[47] See generally BATIFFOL 856–60.

[48] BATIFFOL 861; 2 DALLOZ, *op. cit. supra* note 8, at Nos. 95–103.

[49] Bulkley v. Bulkley, Cass. Civ., Feb. 2, 1860, [1860] D. 1. 57.

[50] Charr v. Hazim Ulusahim, Cour Paris, Oct. 21, 1955, [1956] D.J. 61, 83 CLUNET 164 (1956). For a comment, see Nadelmann, *Recognition of Foreign Judgments in France*, 5 AM. J. COMP. L. 248 (1956). See also Lestrade de Kyron v. Roussel, *supra* note 24.

[51] First, in a dictum in Michel de Hohenzollern v. Mircea Lambrino, Cass. Civ., Jan. 8, 1963, 90 CLUNET 1032 (1963); then, in a case concerning a New York judgment for alimony arrears, which the court apparently did not consider to involve a matter of personal status, Munzer v. dame Jacoby-Munzer, *supra* note 17. For a more detailed survey of this development, see the note Goldman appended to the Munzer case and Nadelmann, note 27 *supra*. At least one French author has had reservations about the wisdom of abandoning *révision au fond*. Raynaud, *Le contrôle des jugements étrangers, La règle du roi Carol*, [1963] D. CHR. 129.

[52] Presumably, since the Munzer case expressly preserves the right of the French courts to deal with public policy, the new rule affects the courts' right to reduce damages, but not the

French courts to modify custody and related decisions if new facts are shown [53] probably remains unaltered.

e. **Effect of *exequatur*.** A foreign judgment becomes *res judicata* and enforceable the moment it receives an *exequatur*. The scope of its *res judicata* effect as well as the methods of enforcement are determined by French law. [54] An *exequatur* gives a foreign alimony or support judgment effectiveness also as to future payments. [55]

### 14.05. Judgments Relating to Personal Status

Foreign judgments relating to personal status do not need an *exequatur* to be recognized in France. However, French courts will give such judgments effect only if they satisfy the requirements for the grant of an *exequatur*. [56]

a. **Meaning of "judgments relating to personal status."** All judgments in matrimonial actions, including judgments of divorce, separation, and annulment, are "judgments relating to personal status" within the meaning of the rule stated. The phrase also includes most other decisions relating to domestic relations, such as judgments of adoption, filiation judgments, and judgments relating to family names or titles of nobility. Judgments affecting personal capacity, such as those appointing a guardian or committee are also included, though a foreigner can not rely on a foreign declaration of incompetency to avoid a contract made in France if the French party was excusably ignorant of the declaration. [57] Foreign probate proceedings, or proceedings for the appointment of a receiver or liquidator, and, to some extent, a trustee in bankruptcy, fall into the same category. [58]

right to excise part of a judgment which is considered in violation of public policy. For an application of this rule, see dame Cureau v. Cureau, *supra* note 29 (New York divorce given effect in France, but not provision in decree prohibiting remarriage for three years).

[53] *E.g.*, Grunberg v. dame Charrier, Trib. Gde Inst. Seine, April 2, 1963, 91 CLUNET 116 (1964).

[54] BATIFFOL 828–30.

[55] See also note 39 *supra*.

[56] BATIFFOL 867–88; 2 DALLOZ, *op. cit. supra* note 8, at No. 56; Rivière v. Roumiantzeff, *supra* note 26; Ermolieff v. Popoff, Cass. Civ., June 16, 1958, [1958] J.C.P. 2. 10716, 86 CLUNET 156 (1959).

[57] BATIFFOL 267–71; 2 DALLOZ, *op. cit. supra* note 8, at Nos. 57–59. See also note 56 *supra*.

[58] *E.g.*, Bensa v. Coleman, Cour Paris, July 4, 1958, 86 CLUNET 1122 (1959) (English probate judgment); Société Blumenthal Ries v. Sarson, Cour Paris, May 29, 1963, 91 CLUNET 119 (1964) (English decision appointing receiver for corporation); Leffert Holz v. Union des Juifs pour la résistance et l'entr'aide, Trib. Seine, March 7, 1957, 85 CLUNET 134 (1958) (decision appointing New York Superindendent of Insurance liquidator of fraternal benefit association).

Some authors go further and give recognition without *exequatur* to all judgments having an *in rem* effect – that is, an effect against the whole world –, but their view does not seem to have received widespread acceptance. [59]

**b. Effect of judgments relating to personal status.** Foreign judgments relating to personal status have complete *res judicata* effect in France. Thus, a party to a foreign divorce judgment may not bring a new divorce or separation action in France. [60] In theory, at least, a foreign divorce also enables both spouses to remarry in France. In practice, however, *officiers de l'état civil* who perform the (compulsory) civil marriage ceremony sometimes refuse to act unless the foreign divorce has first been registered in the French vital statistics records in the same manner as a French divorce judgment and refuse to register the judgment unless it has received an *exequatur*. [61] A foreign divorce or separation judgment has the same effects as a French judgment on the rights of spouses married under the French community property system. [62]

Since judgments appointing guardians, committees of incompetents, administrators, executors, receivers, or liquidators are treated as judgments relating to personal status, such officials may act in France immediately after their appointment by a foreign court; there is no need for ancillary proceedings in France. [63] Foreign trustees in bankruptcy may sue in France in connection with the foreign assets of the bankrupt; however, a declaration of bankruptcy by a foreign court does not affect assets in France. [64]

When reliance is placed on a foreign status judgment – for instance when it is invoked as *res judicata* –, the court must examine whether the

[59] BATIFFOL 869.

[60] *E.g.*, Ermolieff v. Popoff, *supra* note 56.

[61] See, *e.g.*, the note by Ponsard appended to dame Ollard v. Ministre des Affaires étrangères, Trib. Seine, Jan. 3, 1958, 86 CLUNET 776 (1959), and the note by Loussouarn appended to dame Strazzera v. Galea, Trib. Gde Inst. Seine, Nov. 8, 1961, 52 REV. CR. D.I.P. 601 (1963). Refusal of French *officiers de l'état civil* to register a foreign divorce judgment until it has received the *exequatur* seems based on an administrative directive (INSTRUCTION GÉNÉRALE CONCERNANT L'ETAT CIVIL art. 514), but there is no legal justification for the refusal to perform a marriage ceremony, since CODE CIVIL art. 296 now permits remarriage immediately after a divorce. On French vital statistics registers in general, see 7.35 *supra*. On the requirement of registration of all French divorce and separation judgments in the public registers, see 11.04.f *supra*. It is possible, without resorting to *exequatur*, to compel an *officier de l'état civil* to register a foreign divorce by a proceeding directed against him.

[62] In other words, the foreign divorce judgment starts the running of the time period for "accepting the community." BATIFFOL 879.

[63] See cases cited note 58 *supra*; *cf.* 6.04.d *supra*.

[64] BATIFFOL 872–73; 2 DALLOZ, *op. cit. supra* note 8, at No. 70.

judgment would be entitled to an *exequatur*. [65] Persons who fear that a foreign status judgment they consider invalid may be used against them, but do not wish to wait until their opponent acts, sometimes bring a proceeding to have the foreign judgment declared void. This proceeding, which is essentially a declaratory judgment action, is ordinarily referred to as an *action en inopposabilité*. [66]

**c. When *exequatur* is necessary.** An *exequatur* is required for a foreign status judgment if it is to be the basis of an "execution against property or a coercion of persons." For example, an *exequatur* must be obtained before one of the methods of forced execution may be used.

The expression "execution against property or coercion against persons" is given a broad meaning. There is coercion of persons whenever a person in France is required to do a specific act on the basis of a foreign judgment – for instance, to publish a retraction of a defamatory statement, to refrain from using a name, or to deliver custody of children. Although there seems to be an "execution against property" whenever a foreign judgment leads to modification of the parties' property rights in France, the precise scope of this expression is not clear. [67]

Even when there is no legal necessity for obtaining an *exequatur*, it is sometimes useful to do so – for instance, to avoid any later dispute as to the validity of the foreign judgment. The judgment in the *exequatur* action will be *res judicata* as to the issue of validity. An *exequatur* will also be helpful in registering the judgment in the French vital statistics records. [68] In addition, French banks and other financial institutions occasionally refuse to recognize a foreign status judgment unless it has received an *exequatur*. [69] But since an *exequatur* is not essential, *exequatur* proceedings initiated in such cases have at times

[65] BATIFFOL 877; 2 DALLOZ, *op. cit. supra* note 8, at No. 72; dame Renoir v. Renoir, Cass. Civ., Feb. 19, 1952, [1952] J.C.P. 2. 7009; Rivière v. Roumiantzeff, *supra* note 26; De Katchaloff v. Chanial, Cour Paris, April 16, 1953, 82 CLUNET 128 (1955).

[66] *E.g.*, Weiller v. dame Diplarkos, Cour Paris, Dec. 15, 1948, [1949] D.J. 461, *aff'd sub nom.* Epoux Russel v. Weiller, Cass. Civ., Jan. 22, 1951, 40 REV. CR. D.I.P. 167 (1951); dame Perugia v. Perugia, Trib. Gde Inst. Seine, Dec. 16, 1963, 91 CLUNET 326 (1964). See also the note by Bellet appended to dame S. v. G., Cour Paris, Nov. 7, 1957, 48 REV. CR. D.I.P. 319 (1959).

[67] BATIFFOL 875–76; 2 DALLOZ, *op. cit. supra* note 8, at Nos. 65–68. The refusal of French registrars (*officiers de l'état civil*) to register a foreign divorce is sometimes justified on the ground that registration involves coercion of persons. *Id.* at No. 69.

[68] *E.g.*, Dormoy v. dame Feer, Trib. Gde Inst. Seine, May 21, 1963, 91 CLUNET 118 (1964). The question has been raised whether a declaratory judgment action could be used instead, but, since the same facts would have to be shown in both actions, it is largely academic.

[69] Bellet, *supra* note 66.

been dismissed on the ground that the party seeking the *exequatur* lacked the requisite "interest." [70]

**d. Effect of American divorce judgments in France.** American divorce judgments rendered by a court sitting at the real domicile of at least one of the spouses are recognized in France if the general requirements for the recognition of foreign judgments are met.[71] Migratory divorces, obtained in Nevada, Mexico, or other divorce havens, are frequently denied effect, however. When the parties are French nationals, this refusal is likely to be based on the ground that the Nevada or Mexican court did not apply French law, as required by French choice of law rules. [72] In instances not involving French nationals, the decision is sometimes based on the ground that the domiciliary law of the parties, applicable under French choice of law rules, was not applied. [73] Other decisions have been based on the ground that under applicable American jurisdictional concepts a divorce may be rendered only by a court at the actual domicile of one of the parties. This reasoning has been followed even in cases in which both spouses had appeared in the divorce action and the divorce would have been recognized by the state of their actual domicile. [74] These decisions have been criticized for showing greater respect for American jurisdictional standards than is shown by American courts. [75] The awareness of members of the French judiciary of the liberal attitude of certain states and of Mexico towards

[70] 2 DALLOZ, *op. cit. supra* note 8, at Nos. 120–25; dame S. v. G., *supra* note 66 (wife seeking *exequatur* of Nevada divorce merely to ensure that its validity will not be questioned later lacks interest); dame Strazzera v. Galea, *supra* note 61 (spouse seeking *exequatur* of foreign divorce judgment in order to obtain its registration in French vital statistics records has a sufficient interest, though registration not absolutely necessary to enable her to remarry in France).

[71] *E.g.*, dame Cureau v. Cureau, *supra* note 29; dame Scharf v. Algazy, Trib. Gde Inst. Seine, May 17, 1961, 89 CLUNET 440 (1962) (New York judgment granting provisional alimony held effective in France, even though court applied New York law and alimony subject to modification, since New York law the same as French law and judgment is effective in New York).

[72] *E.g.*, époux Russel v. Weiller, *supra* note 66. See also 14.03.c. *supra.*

[73] *E.g.*, Gunzburg v. dame Schrey, Trib. Gde Inst. Seine, May 14, 1962, 90 CLUNET 110 (1963) (note Bredin), *aff'd* Cour Paris, June 18, 1964, 91 CLUNET 810 (1964). Under French choice of law rules, the law of the domicile of the parties must be applied if they are of different nationality; otherwise, the law of their common nationality (citizenship) must be applied. In the case of United States citizens residing in the United States, this would, of course, also be the law of their domicile. *Cf.* 11.04.h *supra.*

[74] Guinle v. Sherwood, Trib. Seine, Nov. 28, 1956, 84 CLUNET 148 (1957) (*exequatur* refused but case continued to permit proof of bona fide domicile in Nevada); Gunzburg v. dame Schrey, *supra* note 73. Sometimes, the decision is based on lack of proper service on the defendant. Bradford, Trib. Seine, June 29, 1938, 66 CLUNET 61 (1939).

[75] Bredin, *supra* note 73.

divorce seems to be the main reason for the difficulties encountered by American migratory divorces in France. [76]

### 14.06. Recognition and Enforcement of Arbitral Awards

There is more similarity between the treatment of domestic and that of foreign arbitral awards than between the treatment of foreign judgments and that of foreign arbitral awards. Enforcement of both foreign and French awards is sought in a proceeding before a single judge, initiated by an *ex parte* application (*requête*). French courts do not assert a *pouvoir de révision* as to foreign arbitral awards; these awards have *res judicata* effect. [77] But special rules exist as to the conditions for the enforcement of foreign awards and the methods for their review.

**a. Definition of foreign awards.** There is dispute as to what awards are to be considered foreign. Sometimes, the place at which the arbitral tribunal was sitting is said to be the determining factor. According to the prevailing opinion, however, an award is foreign if it is not rendered pursuant to French law. [78] Significantly, under French conflict of laws rules, parties are usually able to choose the law they wish to apply to an arbitration if the transaction has international elements. [79]

**b. Conditions for enforcement.** To be enforceable, a foreign award must be based on a valid submission or arbitration clause. Ordinarily, the validity of the submission or arbitration clause depends on the law chosen by the parties. [80] A recent decision holds that the validity of an arbitration clause is not necessarily dependent on the validity of the underlying contract. [81]

[76] *E.g.*, Prince A. v. C., Trib. Seine, Jan. 11, 1956, 45 Rev. cr. D.I.P. 128 (1956) (note Bellet) (emphasizing the doubtful reputation of the Nevada courts). Refusal to recognize a divorce has also been based on the idea that a migratory divorce amounts to a "fraud on the law" of the true domicile. Gunzburg v. dame Schrey, *supra* note 73. It should be noted that in Paris all cases involving foreign judgments go to the same (fifth) panel of the *Tribunal de Grande Instance*. Its members therefore have considerable experience in dealing with American judgments.

[77] See Batiffol 834; 2 Dalloz, *op. cit. supra* note 8, at 144. On arbitration in France in general, see 11.05 – 11.11 *supra*. On enforcement of French awards, see 11.10.b *supra*.

[78] Batiffol 835; 2 Dalloz, *op. cit. supra* note 8, at Nos. 147–50.

[79] See 11.07.b and 4.29 *supra*.

[80] See 11.07.b *supra*; Batiffol 847; 2 Dalloz, *op. cit. supra* note 8, at No. 153; Compagnie marchande de Tunisie v. Société Costa de Marfil, Cour Paris, March 27, 1962, 51 Rev. cr. D.I.P. 528 (1962) (note Mezger), 90 Clunet 468 (1963).

[81] Société des Etablissements Raymond Gosset v. Société Carapelli, Cass. Civ., May 7, 1963, [1963] D.J. 545 (note Robert), 91 Clunet 82 (1964). Older cases seemed to hold that the validity of an arbitration clause always depends on the validity of the agreement in which it is embodied.

The French rule that arbitration clauses are valid only in commercial contracts is inapplicable if the contract is subject to foreign law, but a foreign award will not be enforced in cases in which France has a strong public policy against arbitration. [82]

Whenever, by the terms of the arbitral agreement, the arbitrators are not bound to decide according to strict rules of law, a foreign arbitral award will be enforced in France though the arbitrators did not observe French choice of law rules. [83] Parties must be duly summoned and receive an adequate opportunity to present their case, but a foreign arbitral award will not be rejected on procedural grounds if the procedure followed is in accordance with the law chosen by the parties. [84] According to the current view, the absence of an opinion does not invalidate the award. [85]

**c. Procedure for enforcement.** Enforcement of a foreign arbitral award is sought in a proceeding initiated by an *ex parte* petition (*requête*) to the presiding judge of the *tribunal de grande instance* of the place where the award is to be enforced. The procedure is the same as in the case of a French award. [86] It may be followed whether or not the foreign award has been reduced to judgment in the foreign country. If the award has been reduced to judgment in the foreign country, it also seems possible to seek a regular *exequatur* for the judgment embodying the award. [87]

[82] 2 DALLOZ, *op. cit. supra* note 8, at Nos. 154–55. There exists a strong public policy against arbitration in divorce or separation cases and in cases involving French economic legislation (exchange control, price control, and the like) and, according to some authorities, in cases that must be "communicated" to the *ministère public. E.g.*, Société Jean Tardits v. Korn Og Foderstof Kompagniet, Cour Orléans, May 15, 1961, 89 CLUNET 140 (1962) (note Goldman); Société Varimex v. Société Pathé-Marconi, Cour Paris, Jan. 9, 1962, [1962] J.C.P. 2. 12478, 90 CLUNET 158 (1963) (note J.B.S.).

[83] *E.g.*, 2 DALLOZ, *op. cit. supra* note 8, at No. 157. On the requirement that foreign courts may apply the law applicable under French conflict of laws rules, see 14.03.c *supra*.

[84] *E.g.*, Gerstlé v. Société Merry Hull & Co., Cour Paris, May 30, 1963, 91 CLUNET 85 (1964) (appointment of defendant's arbitrator by American Arbitration Association proper, as defendant failed to act.)

[85] Compagnie marchande de Tunisie v. Société Costa de Marfil, *supra* note 80; Société Elmassian v. Société Veuve Henri Broutchoux, Cour Nancy, Jan. 29, 1958, 47 REV. CR. D.I.P. 148 (1958), 86 CLUNET 128 (1959); Loussouarn, *De l'Exéquatur des sentences étrangères non motivées*, [1957] D. CHR. 191.

[86] For details of this procedure, see 11.10.b *supra*. The enforcement of a French or foreign arbitral award through an *ex parte* proceeding is sometimes referred to as *exequatur*. It should not, however, be confused with the *exequatur* procedure for foreign judgments which, in essence, is a regular civil action. See generally Robert, *France*, in UNION INTERNATIONALE DES AVOCATS, INTERNATIONAL COMMERCIAL ARBITRATION 240, 264 (1956).

[87] *E.g.*, Société Elmassian v. Société Veuve Henri Broutchoux, *supra* note 85 (*exequatur* of English judgment enforcing English award); Weisbaum and Sons v. Archaimbault, Cour Paris, Oct. 20, 1959, 48 REV. CR. D.I.P. 716 (1959) (note E.B.), 87 CLUNET 456 (1960) (note Bredin); Sartre v. The Respectful Cy., Trib. Gde Inst. Seine (Vice-Président), Feb. 20, 1961,

French rules governing review of domestic arbitral decisions are complex and not well co-ordinated. As a rule, unless the right to appeal has been waived, an appeal (*appel*) may be taken from an arbitral award. The appeal leads to a rehearing of the entire case. An award defective for the limited reasons specified in article 1028 of the *Code de Procédure Civile* may also be reviewed by a plenary action. [88]

Application of these rules to foreign awards causes difficulties. There is general agreement that a regular appeal from a foreign award may not be taken to a French court. [89] On the other hand, the procedure for the enforcement of foreign awards, since it is conducted *ex parte*, does not guarantee that the award meets the requirements for its recognition in France. For that reason, in an action brought under article 1028, some courts will ascertain whether all requirements for the validity of the award are met, although article 1028, by its own terms, limits review to certain specified matters. [90] In some instances, parties faced with a foreign arbitral award recognized in France after an *ex parte* proceeding have taken recourse to the remedy of *tierce opposition* or have tried to prevent enforcement of the award by *référé* proceedings. [91] Clarification of the proper rules by legislation is desirable.

## 14.07. International Agreements Concerning the Recognition and Enforcement of Judgments and Arbitral Awards

France is a party to a number of bilateral and multilateral agreements dealing with the recognition of foreign judgments and arbitral awards. While some of these agreements were concluded mainly to eliminate the *pouvoir de révision* of the French courts and have therefore decreased in significance, they frequently contain other useful provisions. Generally, they give foreign judgments *res judicata* effect without *exequatur*, making resort to the *exequatur* procedure necessary

51 REV. CR. D.I.P. 522 (1962), 88 CLUNET 1128 (1961) (enforcement of award by *ex parte* proceeding, though award reduced to judgment in New York). *Ex parte* enforcement of an award is obviously faster and less expensive than enforcement of a foreign judgment by a regular *exequatur* action.

[88] For a more detailed discussion of these and several less important remedies, see 11.11 *supra*.

[89] 2 DALLOZ, *op. cit. supra* note 8, at No. 166; Société Jean Tardits v. Korn Og Foderstof Kompagiet, *supra* note 82.

[90] *E.g.*, Gerstlé v. Société Merry Hull & Co., *supra* note 84.

[91] For a general discussion, see Bredin, *La paralysie des sentences arbitrales étrangères par l'abus des voies de recours*, 89 CLUNET 638 (1962). See also Sté Myrtoon Steamship v. Agent judiciaire du Trésor, Cour Paris, April 10, 1957, 85 CLUNET 1002 (1958) (remedy under article 1028 limited to cases mentioned); Société des Etablissements Raymond Gosset v. Société Carapelli, *supra* note 81 (same holding but permitting person objecting to enforcement of foreign arbitral award to obtain review of *ex parte* decision recognizing award in France by *tierce opposition*). On the remedy of *tierce opposition* in general, see 10.02–10.08 *supra*.

only when enforcement of the foreign judgment is sought. They may also define standards of jurisdiction, eliminate the requirement that French choice of law rules be observed, or prescribe what documents are necessary for the enforcement of a judgment. [92]

**a. Bilateral agreements.** The Franco-British agreement concerning the recognition of judgments [93] is of particular interest because it attempts to cover the problems which arise when judgments rendered in a civil law country are to be enforced in a common law country and *vice versa*. It applies only to judgments of higher courts and excludes from its coverage matters relating to personal status – such as marriage, divorce, and matrimonial property –, succession, liquidation of companies, and bankruptcy. [94]

Judgments covered by the convention have *res judicata* effect without *exequatur* if they fulfill the following conditions. First, they must be rendered by a court having jurisdiction according to the law of the state in which recognition or enforcement is sought. However, the convention provides that the court at the defendant's residence or place of business or, in an action concerning land or in an *in rem* action concerning personal property, the court of the situs always has jurisdiction, and that lack of jurisdiction or competence under the law of the country of the judgment's origin may be raised only if the issue is not *res judicata* in that country. Second, the defendant must have been given due notice of the proceedings against him, and the proceedings must be free of fraud. Third, recognition must be denied if it would violate the forum's public policy or the judgment is contrary to another judgment in the same matter rendered in the state in which recognition is sought. Violation of choice of law rules is no ground for denial of recognition. [95]

[92] For a general discussion, see BATIFFOL 880; 2 DALLOZ, *op. cit. supra* note 8, at Nos. 132–42; Ropers, *La reconnaissance et l'exécution réciproque des décisions de justice à l'intérieur du marché commun*, [1962] J.C.P. 1. 1679 (listing many treaties).

[93] Convention between France and the United Kingdom, Jan. 18, 1934, J.O. May 30, 1936, 171 L.N.T.S. 183, 62 CLUNET 1115 (1935). See generally BATIFFOL 889–90; Audinet, *L'exécution des jugements étrangers en Angleterre*, 62 CLUNET 805 (1935).

[94] Convention between France and the United Kingdom, *supra* note 93, art. 2. Higher courts include the High Court in England, the *tribunaux civils* (now *tribunaux de grande instance*) in France, and courts of corresponding and higher rank. With the exceptions noted, the agreement applies to all civil and commercial matters and, in criminal cases, to judgments granting civil damages. When the convention does not apply, the general rules control.

[95] Convention between France and the United Kingdom, *supra* note 93, arts. 3–4. A default judgment is to be recognized only if the defendant has received actual notice of the proceedings against him. In order to determine whether British courts have international jurisdiction under French law, French courts sometimes apply French rules of territorial competence by analogy. *E.g.*, Consorts Erlebach v. Société Veuve Chachaty, Trib. Gde Inst. Seine, Feb. 12, 1962, 90 CLUNET 154 (1963).

To be enforceable in the other country, judgments must be subjected to the regular procedure for the enforcement of judgments. The foreign judgment must have *res judicata* effect and must be subject to execution in the country of origin.[96] A certified copy of the judgment must be submitted, but consular authentication is not necessary.[97] The court must restrict its examination to the points mentioned; it has no power to review the merits of the judgment. Because of the much greater litigation expenses in Great Britain, the agreement provides that judgments for costs and disbursements may be reduced to ten per cent of the principal amount recovered.[98] The Franco-British agreement seems to be working quite well.

France has also concluded bilateral agreements for the recognition of judgments with other European countries, namely Belgium, Italy, Monaco, and Switzerland.[99] All except the agreement with Switzerland give judgments within their coverage *res judicata* effect without *exequatur* if certain conditions are fulfilled.[100] Furthermore, if these conditions are met, an *exequatur*, if requested, must be granted.[101] The conditions include the usual requirements of jurisdiction in the court of rendition, due notice to the defendant, and absence of violation of public policy.[102] The agreement with Monaco provides that jurisdiction is to be determined according to the law of the country in which enforcement is sought;[103] the other agreements specify the jurisdictional rules that must be complied with. In substance, these rules eliminate

[96] Convention between France and the United Kingdom, *supra* note 93, art. 5.

[97] Convention between France and the United Kingdom, *supra* note 93, art. 8; Etablissements George J. Smith, Cour Paris, July 7, 1959, 87 CLUNET 1072 (1960).

[98] Convention between France and the United Kingdom, *supra* note 93, art. 5; Lewis v. époux Cunningham, Cour Paris, Feb. 9, 1962, 52 REV. CR. D.I.P. 81 (1963) (note Gavalda), 90 CLUNET 148 (1963); London Film v. Poznanski, Trib. Seine, Feb. 10, 1938, 65 CLUNET 303 (1938) (in calculating costs for which *exequatur* may be granted, fees of barrister and various preliminary and investigative expenses of parties must be eliminated).

[99] Convention between France and Belgium on Competence and Execution of Judgments, July 8, 1899, J.O. Aug. 1, 1900, 29 MARTENS N.R.G. (2d ser.) 419, JURISCLASSEUR DE DROIT INTERNATIONAL fasc. 591 (1960); Convention between France and Italy on the Execution of Judgments, June 3, 1930, J.O. Nov. 26, 1933, [1934] D. 4. 38; Convention between France and Monaco, Oct. 5, 1957, J.O. Jan. 14, 1960, p. 421, [1960] D.L. 57; Convention between France and Switzerland on Competence and the Execution of Judgments, June 15, 1869, J.O. Jan. 19, 1870, p. 119, BULL. DES LOIS No. 17, 264, [1869] S. 5. 735.

[100] Convention between France and Belgium, *supra* note 99, art. 11; Convention between France and Italy, *supra* note 99, art. 1; Convention between France and Monaco, *supra* note 99, art. 16.

[101] The Agreement between France and Switzerland, *supra* note 99, imposes the standard conditions for enforcement without referring to *res judicata*.

[102] *E.g.*, Convention between France and Belgium, *supra* note 99, art. 11; Convention between France and Italy, *supra* note 99, art. 1; Convention between France and Switzerland *supra* note 99, art. 17.

[103] Convention between France and Monaco, *supra* note 99, art. 16.

the effect of articles 14 and 15 of the *Code Civil.* [104] The agreements also require due service upon the defendant, absence of violation of public policy, and non-contrariety of the foreign judgment with a judgment in the country in which recognition is sought. [105] Their coverage is not limited to money judgments. The agreements with Belgium, Italy, and Switzerland specifically cover arbitral awards. [106] Some of these agreements provide for an accelerated *exequatur* procedure. [107]

The agreements on international co-operation in litigation concluded between France and her former colonies and overseas possessions frequently include provisions for the mutual recognition and enforcement of judgments. They usually provide that decisions rendered in one of the contracting countries shall automatically be given *res judicata* effect and an *exequatur* in the other contracting country if the standard conditions as to jurisdiction, non-violation of public policy, and due notice are met. [108] Under some agreements, the presiding judge of the

[104] Convention between France and Belgium, *supra* note 99, arts. 1–10; Convention between France and Italy, *supra* note 99, arts. 10–25; Convention between France and Switzerland, *supra* note 99, arts. 1–14. There is one distinction between the French-Italian treaty and the French treaties with Belgium and Switzerland. The latter lay down rules of general competence that must be observed by courts in both the country of origin and the country in which recognition is sought, so that their disregard also constitutes reversible error in the country in which the judgment was rendered. The treaty with Italy, on the other hand, merely provides rules of (international) jurisdiction that determine whether a judgment rendered in one of the contracting states must be recognized in the other contracting state, and that do not affect the validity of the judgment in the country of origin. For a critique, see Weser, *Faut-il réviser la Convention franco-italienne du 3 juin 1930 sur l'exécution des jugements*, 43 REV. CR. D.I.P. 451, 693 (1954), 44 REV. CR. D.I.P. 63 (1955). On the effect of these agreements on the competence of courts, see 4.34 *supra*. See generally BATIFFOL 881–88. In one unusual case, the rule of the French-Italian treaty was used to determine internal French competence, however. Soc. Ludiprim di Costanzo v. Cooperative Ortofrutte coltori Ravennati, Cour Paris, Feb. 4, 1964, [1964] D.J. 497.

[105] See note 102 *supra*.

[106] Agreement between France and Belgium, *supra* note 99, art. 15; Agreement between France and Italy, *supra* note 99, art. 5; Agreement between France and Switzerland, *supra* note 99, art. 15.

[107] The Agreement between France and Belgium, *supra* note 99, art. 12, provides for the use of the summary procedure. Under the Agreement between France and Switzerland, *supra* note 99, art. 16, the *exequatur* procedure is initiated by a petition addressed to the *chambre du conseil* of the court where enforcement is to take place. However, a copy of the petition must be served on the defendant.

[108] *E.g.*, Judicial Convention between France and Cameroon, Nov. 13, 1960, J.O. Aug. 9, 1961, p. 7429, 88 CLUNET 1216 (1961), arts. 35–40; Convention on Co-Operation in Judicial Matters between France and the Republic of the Ivory Coast, April 24, 1961, J.O. Feb. 6, 1962, p. 804, 89 CLUNET 802 (1962); Convention on Co-operation in Judicial Matters between France and the Islamic Republic of Mauretania, June 19, 1961, J.O. Feb. 6, 1962, p. 1324, 89 CLUNET 824 (1962) (agreement identical in its terms to the agreement between France and the Ivory Coast); Convention on Judicial Co-Operation, Exequatur, and Extradition between France and Morocco, Oct. 5, 1957, J.O. Jan. 14, 1960, p. 421, [1960] D.L. 57, 87 CLUNET 614 (1960); Protocol concerning a simplified Exequatur Procedure in Civil and Commercial Matters between France and Viet-Nam, J.O. Sept. 15, 1954, J.O. May 3, 1959, p. 4758, 87

court of the country in which enforcement is sought may grant an *exequatur* in the expeditious *référé* proceedings. Review of the merits is excluded. Occasionally, even administrative decisions are covered. [109]

The United States has no agreement with France concerning the enforcement of judgments. However, the Convention of Establishment of 1959 provides that arbitration clauses contained in contracts entered into by individuals or corporations who are nationals of the contracting parties shall not be considered void because arbitration is to take place outside the territory of the contracting parties and the nationality of one or more of the arbitrators is not that of a contracting party. An arbitral award rendered pursuant to such a clause may not be considered void and unenforceable merely for the reasons that the award was rendered outside the territory of the contracting parties and the nationality of one or more of the arbitrators is not that of a contracting party. [110] The agreement does not seem to go beyond what would otherwise be the law.

**b. Multilateral agreements.** France is a party to a number of multilateral agreements which concern the enforcement of foreign judgments or arbitral awards, though the main purpose of most of these agreements is directed towards other ends. The Hague Convention of 1954 provides that judgments for costs and disbursements rendered in one of the contracting states against a plaintiff dispensed from posting security for costs under the terms of the convention shall be enforced in the other contracting states on a mere diplomatic request, without hearing the parties, and without expenses, though states may agree that the request for enforcement be made directly by a party. [111] The Hague

CLUNET 260 (1960). Judicial Convention between France and Togo, July 10, 1963, J.O. June 10, 1964, p. 4990, [1964] D.L. 198. Jurisdiction is usually to be determined according to the law of the state in which enforcement is sought. Hence, absent a waiver, articles 14 and 15 of the *Code Civil* remain in effect and prevent recognition in France of judgments rendered abroad against a French national. Sometimes, these agreements provide that compliance with the choice of law rules of the state in which recognition is sought is not required, provided these choice of law rules do not require application of the law of the state in which recognition is sought. Protocol between France and Viet-Nam, *supra*, art. 2. See also Agreement between France and Algeria, June 27, 1964, J.O. August 17, 1965, 92 CLUNET 985 (1965).

[109] Conventions between France and the Ivory Coast and France and Mauretania, *supra* note 108, art. 38 (*référé* procedure), art. 45 (*exequatur* of administrative decisions to be granted by administrative tribunals). Some agreements also provide for recognition of arbitral awards. Agreement between France and Morocco, *supra* note 108, art. 22; Protocol between France and Viet-Nam, *supra* note 108, art. 8.

[110] Convention of Establishment with France, Nov. 25, 1959, T.I.A.S. No. 4625, [1960] 2 U.S.T. & O.I.A. 2398, 401 U.N.T.S. 75, art. III (2).

[111] Convention relating to Civil Procedure signed at the Hague, March 1, 1954, J.O. Sept. 30, 1959, p. 9429, 87 CLUNET 590 (1960), 286 U.N.T.S. 243 (1958), [1959] D.L. 608, arts. 18–19.

Convention does not deal with the enforcement of judgments generally.

The so-called "CIV" agreement for the transportation of passengers and baggage by railroad and the "CIM" agreement for the transportation of goods by railroad provide that judgments rendered in one of the contracting states in matters governed by these conventions shall be recognized and enforced in the other contracting states. [112] The Convention on the Enforcement of Support Obligations Abroad sets up a scheme for the enforcement of support obligations which is rather similar to the Uniform Support of Dependents Act in the United States. [113]

The treaties establishing the European Communities (Economic Community, Coal and Steel Community, and Euratom) provide that decisions of the Court of Justice of the European Communities shall be enforceable in the member states upon mere administrative certification. The powers of the certifying officials are limited to examination of the authencity of the judgment submitted to them. [114] The treaty establishing the European Economic Community also provides that the members states shall enter into negotiations looking towards agreements facilitating the mutual enforcement of judgments. [115] Preliminary discussions have taken place, and a draft treaty is in the process of preparation. [116]

France is a party to the 1958 New York Convention on the Recognition and Enforcement of Foreign Arbitral Awards, [117] and to its

The parties to the Convention are listed in 2 DALLOZ, RÉPERTOIRE DE PROCÉDURE CIVILE ET COMMERCIALE, *Commission Rogatoire*, at No. 65 (Supp. 1964). The Convention on Judicial Co-Operation with the Federal Republic of Germany, May 6, 1961, J.O. Oct. 4, 1961, p. 9237, [1961] D.L. 317, arts. 8–10, implementing the Hague Convention, provides that the parties themselves may address requests for the execution of judgments for costs to the courts.

[112] Conventions for the Transportation of Passengers and Baggage by Railroad, and for the Transportation of Goods by Railroad, Oct. 25, 1952, J.O. June 28, 1955, p. 6394, 241 U.N.T.S. 336, art. 55.

[113] Convention concerning the enforcement of Support Obligations Abroad, June 20, 1956, J.O. Oct. 12, 1960, p. 9311, 88 CLUNET 588 (1961), [1960] D.L. 354, 268 U.N.T.S. 3 (1956).

[114] Treaty establishing the European Coal and Steel Community, April 18, 1951, J.O. Sept. 5, 1952, p. 8778, 79 CLUNET 952 (1952), [1952] D.L. 312, 261 U.N.T.S. 140, arts. 44, 92; Convention establishing the European Economic Community, March 25, 1957, J.O. Feb. 2, 1958, p. 1188, 85 CLUNET 480, 816 (1958), [1958] D.L. 73, 298 U.N.T.S. 11, arts. 187, 192; Convention establishing the European Atomic Energy Community (Euratom), March 25, 1957, 86 CLUNET 534, 882 (1959), [1958] D.L. 87, 298 U.N.T.S. 167, arts. 159, 164. This was implemented by DÉCRET No. 54–387 of April 25, 1954, J.O. April 6, 1954, p. 3262, [1954] D.L. 154, amended by DÉCRET No. 57–321 of March 13, 1957, J.O. March 19, 1957, p. 2885, [1957] D.L. 111.

[115] Treaty establishing the European Economic Community, *supra* note 144, art. 220.

[116] Ropers, *supra* note 92. See also Weser, *Litigation on the Common Market Level*, 13 AM. J. COMP. L. 44, 45 (1964).

[117] Convention for the Recognition and enforcement of Foreign Arbitral Awards, June 10, 1958, J.O. Sept. 6, 1959, p. 8726, 87 CLUNET 600 (1960), [1959] D.L. 581, 300 U.N.T.S. 3.

predecessors, the Geneva Agreements of 1923 and 1927. [118] The United States is not a party to either. The New York Convention permits signatories to restrict its operation to other signing states and to matters considered commercial by their own law. [119] France has adopted both restrictions. Under the Convention, each state must recognize arbitration clauses and submissions that are in writing. Courts in member states must dismiss actions brought before them in violation of a valid submission or arbitration clause [120] and shall enforce foreign awards through locally available procedures. [121] The validity of an arbitration clause must be determined under the law chosen by the parties. If no law has been chosen by the parties, the law of the place at which the award was made controls. An award may not be enforced if a party was not duly notified of the proceedings against it, if the award deals with matters not submitted to the arbitrators, or if the arbitral tribunal was constituted in a manner not in accordance with the arbitral agreement or the applicable law. [122] By and large, the agreement does not seem to go far beyond what is current practice in the relations between the United States and France.

France has also signed the European Convention on International Commercial Arbitration, April 21, 1961, E/ECE/423, but does not yet seem to have ratified it. *Cf.* Robert. *La convention européene sur l'arbitrage commercial international signée a Genève le 21 avril 1961*, [1961] D. CHR. 173.

[118] See Bredin, *La Convention de New York du 10 juin 1958 pour la reconnaissance et l'exécution des sentences arbitrales étrangères*, 87 CLUNET 1002 (1960); *Cf.* Sultan, *The United Nations Arbitration Convention and United States Policy*, 53 AM. J. INT. L. 807 (1959).

[119] Convention for the Recognition and Enforcement of Foreign Arbitral Awards, *supra* note 110, art. 1(3).

[120] Convention for the Recognition and Enforcement of Foreign Arbitral Awards, *supra* note 117, art. 2. An exchange of letters or telegrams constitutes a sufficient writing.

[121] Convention on the Recognition and Enforcement of Foreign Arbitral Awards, *supra* note 117, art. 3.

[122] Convention for the Recognition and Enforcement of Foreign Arbitra Awards, *supra* note 117, art. 5. Subdivision 2 of this article provides that an award need not be enforced if it is contrary to the public policy or does concern a matter that is not arbitrable under the law of the country in which enforcement is sought.

CHAPTER 15

# INTERNATIONAL CO-OPERATION IN LITIGATION *

After a brief introduction (15.01), this chapter surveys procedures of international co-operation in litigation, including those relating to service of French documents abroad (15.02) and of foreign documents in France (15.07), the taking of testimony abroad (15.03) and in France (15.08), obtaining tangible evidence abroad (15.04) and in France (15.09), proof of French official records abroad (15.05) and of foreign official records in France (15.10), and proof of foreign law in France (15.06) and of French law abroad (15.11).

## 1. INTRODUCTION

### 15.01. Sources of Rules

In France, only a few isolated statutes and decrees deal with international co-operation in litigation. The Code of Civil Procedure contains provisions concerning service of process in foreign countries [1] and requires foreign plaintiffs to post security. [2] A decree regulating the duties of consuls deals briefly with service of documents and execution of letters rogatory. [3] Instructions concerning administrative practice are contained in a few circulars of the Ministry of Justice. These circulars, which are fragmentary, [4] although binding on the *ministère public*, do not bind the courts.

* The author wishes to express his indebtedness to the Honorable LOUIS LEGORJU, *Vice-Président au Tribunal de Grand Instance* in Paris, and to Professor CHRISTIAN GAVALDA of the University of Dijon, who provided valuable comments and suggestions.

1 CODE DE PROCÉDURE CIVILE arts. 69(10), 1033–3 (service abroad); CODE DE PROCÉDURE CIVILE art. 1033–2 (time to appear, appeal, or file *opposition* in case of non-resident). See also CODE DE PROCÉDURE CIVILE arts. 158–3 (*opposition* by non-resident), 445–2 (appeal by non-resident).

2 CODE DE PROCÉDURE CIVILE arts. 166–67; CODE CIVIL art. 16. See 6.03.b *supra*.

3 DÉCRET No. 46–2390 of Oct. 23, 1946, J.O. Oct. 29, 1946, p. 9201, [1946] D.L. 437. Of minor significance is DÉCRET No. 62–1461 of Nov. 27, 1962, J.O. Dec. 6, 1962, p. 11938, [1963] D.L. 1 concerning the notarial functions of consuls.

4 One of the more recent ones is the Circular of the Minister of Justice of May 20, 1925, 1925 BULLETIN DU MINISTÈRE DE LA JUSTICE 30, 54 CLUNET 241 (1927). While it deals mainly with co-operation with Austria, it also contains provisions relating to co-operation in general and summarizes some earlier circulars. For a list of circulars, see Japiot, *Commission Rogatoire (Matière Civile)*, in 4 DE LAPRADELLE & NIBOYET, RÉPERTOIRE DE DROIT INTERNATIONAL 73, 77 (1929).

France is a party to the Hague Conventions of 1905 and 1954. [5] It is also an adherent to a number of multi-lateral agreements concerning support, birth, death, and marriage records, and related topics, which deal incidentally with matters of international co-operation in litigation. [6] In addition, France has concluded a large number of bilateral agreements [7] relating to such matters as service of process, execution of letters rogatory, security for costs, and legal aid for indigent parties. With some countries, France has concluded additional agreements concerning exchange of information relating to marriage, birth, and death records, authentication of official documents, and related topics. [8] The most comprehensive agreements exist between France and many of her former colonies. Ordinarily, these cover not only the topics mentioned

[5] Convention relating to Civil Procedure signed at The Hague, March 1, 1954, J.O. Sept. 30, 1959, p. 9429, 87 CLUNET 590 (1960), [1959] D.L. 608, 286 U.N.T.S. 243 (1958). As to the states that adhere to it, the Agreement replaced The Hague Agreement of July 17, 1905, 2 Martens (3d ser.) 243, J.O. May 2, 1909. The parties to the 1954 Agreement are listed in 1 DALLOZ, RÉPERTOIRE DE PROCÉDURE CIVILE ET COMMERCIALE, *Commission Rogatoire*, at No. 65 (Supp. 1963).

[6] Convention concerning extracts (multilingual summaries) of birth, death, and marriage records, signed at Paris, Sept. 27, 1956, J.O. Jan. 9, 1958, p. 291, [1958] D.L. 31, 299 U.N.T.S. 211 (1958); Convention concerning the authentication of birth, death, and marriage certificates and their free delivery, signed at Paris, Sept. 26, 1956, J.O. August 2, 1959, p. 8614, [1959] D.L. 577; Convention relating to the exchange of information concerning birth, death, and marriage records signed at Istanbul, Sept. 4, 1958, J.O. Nov. 19, 1959, p. 11064, [1959] D.L. 644; Convention concerning the recognition of natural children signed at Rome, Sept. 14, 1961, J.O. July 24, 1962, p. 7286, 89 CLUNET 1148 (1962), [1962] D.L. 242; Convention concerning enforcement of support obligations, signed at New York, June 20, 1956, J.O. Oct. 12, 1960, p. 9311, 88 CLUNET 588 (1961), [1960] D.L. 354, 268 U.N.T.S. 3 (1956).

[7] These treaties are listed at 1 DALLOZ, *op. cit. supra* note 5, at No. 65 (1955 and Supp. 1964) and 1 SOLUS & PERROT 350 (1961). Among the more recent agreements with European powers, the following may be mentioned: Convention between France and Belgium, March 1, 1956, J.O. June 29, 1959, p. 6183, [1959] D.L. 524, 87 CLUNET 296 (1960), amended by Exchange of Letters, J.O. Oct. 21, 1960, p. 9559; Convention between France and Italy, Jan. 2, 1955, J.O. May 17, 1959, p. 5078, [1959] J.C.P. 3. 24603, 87 CLUNET 288 (1960); Convention between France and Sweden, March 7, 1956, J.O. July 24, 1959, p. 7350, 87 CLUNET 621 (1960); Convention between France and Germany (Federal Republic), May 6, 1961, J.O. Oct. 10, 1961, p. 9237, [1961] D.L. 317. The agreements with Germany and Sweden merely implement The Hague Convention, *supra* note 5.

Of particular interest are the treaties with Great Britain. See Agreement between France and Great Britain concerning co-operation in litigation, Feb. 2, 1922, J.O. June 20, 1922, p. 6446, 49 CLUNET 485 (1922), [1923] S. 5. 959. With minor modifications, the convention is also applicable between France and Northern Ireland, the Irish Republic, Australia, Canada, and Scotland. JURISCLASSEUR DE DROIT INTERNATIONAL, fasc. 589–B, No. 6 (1961). See also Agreement between France and Great Britain concerning the admission of documents without authentication, April 3, 1937, J.O. May 30, 1937, 65 CLUNET 137 (1938); Convention between France and Great Britain concerning security for costs, April 15, 1936, J.O. February 2, 1949, p. 1184, 73–76 CLUNET 408 (1949), [1949] D.L. 118.

[8] See, *e.g.*, the Agreement between France and Switzerland of August 26, 1926, concerning the exchange of information concerning birth, death, and marriage certificates and the admission of such certificates into evidence without authentication, J.O. Oct. 26, 1926, 54 CLUNET (1927). On agreements concerning the enforcement of judgments, see 14.07 *supra*.

thus far, but also include provisions for co-operation in the criminal, and sometimes the administrative, field. [9]

Conventions between the United States and France have only a limited impact on international co-operation in litigation. There is an agreement concerning the extradition of criminals, [10] and tax treaties contain some provisions concerning exchange of information between tax authorities. [11] The only treaty provision of significance in the civil field is Article VI of the Consular Convention of 1853, which authorizes United States consuls in France and French consuls in the United States to take "*declarations*" of their nationals. [12] The recent Convention of Establishment is limited to some provisions concerning legal aid and the enforcement of arbitral awards. It also guarantees to nationals, including corporations, of both contracting parties, easy access to the courts. [13]

## 2. CO-OPERATION SOUGHT BY FRANCE

### 15.02. Service of French Documents in a Foreign Country

**a. In the absence of a treaty.** Service of an *ajournement* (summons) on a defendant with a known residence outside France is regulated by

[9] Provisions relating to co-operation in litigation are often included in the agreements providing for the transfer of the French judicial services to the new countries and the use of French judges pending the creation of an adequate domestic judiciary. The similarity between the judicial systems in France and her former colonies or possessions make co-operation easier. See, *e.g.*, Judicial protocol between France and Algeria of August 28, 1962, J.O. Aug. 30, 1962, p. 8506, [1962] D.L. 293, 89 CLUNET 1152 (1962); Judicial convention between France and Cameroon, signed Nov. 13, 1960, J.O. Aug. 9, 1961, p. 7429, 7443, 88 CLUNET 1216 (1961); Agreement concerning co-operation in judicial matters between France and the Ivory Coast, signed April 24, 1961, J.O. Feb. 6, 1962, p. 804, 89 CLUNET 802 (1962); Agreement on judicial co-operation between France and Laos, Oct, 22, 1953, J.O. May 3, 1959, p. 4758, 87 CLUNET 254 (1960); Agreement on judicial co-operation between France and the Malagasy Republic of June 27, 1960, J.O. July 20, 1960, p. 6607, 87 CLUNET 1118 (1960), [1960] D.L. 301; Agreement on judicial co-operation with Mauretania (completely identical to agreement with Ivory Coast, see 89 CLUNET 824 (1962)); Judicial Convention between France and Togo, July 10, 1963, J.O. June 10, 1964, p. 4990, [1964] D.L. 198; Protocols on judicial co-operation and exequatur between France and Viet-Nam, Sept. 15, 1954, J.O. May 3, 1959, p. 4758, 87 CLUNET 260, 264 (1960).

[10] Extradition Convention with France, January 6, 1909, 37 STAT. 1526 (1913), T.S. No. 561.

[11] Tax Treaty with France, October 18, 1946, 64 STAT. (3) B3 (1950), T.I.A.S. No. 1982, tit. 3, arts. 8–15, modified by Protocol of May 17, 1948, 64 STAT. (3) B28 (1950), T.I.A.S. No. 3844. On United States-French tax conventions generally, see DELAUME, AMERICAN-FRENCH PRIVATE INTERNATIONAL LAW 50–54 (2d ed. 1961).

[12] Consular Convention with France, February 23, 1853, 10 STAT. 992 (1853), 1 MALLOY 528.

[13] Convention of Establishment with France of Nov. 25, 1959, [1960] 2 U.S.T. & O.I.A. 2398, T.I.A.S. No. 4625. The convention does not deal with service of process and letters rogatory or depositions; the annexed protocol specifically states that it does not affect security for costs (art. 3).

article 69, subdivision 10, of the Code of Civil Procedure. By analogy, the provisions of this article have been extended to all documents, such as judgments and notices of appeal, of which formal service is required. [14] Article 69(10) applies to all persons – natural as well as corporate – residing outside France, whatever their nationality. However, the method of service for which it provides may not be used to serve a foreign national who has a domicile or residence in France and therefore can be served there in the regular fashion. A contractual consent to service in France, through what is known in France as an election of domicile clause, has the same effect as an actual domicile in France: It excludes application of article 69(10). This article is also inapplicable to companies on which service in France can be made at a branch establishment. Furthermore, use of the procedure provided by article 69(10) is not essential. If the party to be served happens to be in France, service may, and if possible should, be made by an *huissier* in the regular manner. [15]

Service under article 69(10) is made by an *huissier*. He must be paid his statutory fee and the cost of the stamps that must be affixed to the document to be served. [16] The *huissier* proceeds to the office of the *ministère public* attached to the court in which the action is to be brought or, in the case of a judgment or other paper served in a pending action, to the office of the *ministère public* attached to the court in which the action is pending. If the action is pending or is to be brought in a commercial or other court to which no *ministère public* is attached, the *huissier* proceeds to the office of the *ministère public* attached to the court of general competence (*tribunal de grande instance*) in whose district the court is situated. The *huissier* delivers a copy of the paper to the official in charge (*procureur de la République*, *procureur général*) or to one of his assistants and asks him to sign the original. He completes the return by inserting the details of service both on a duplicate original and the original and then files the original in his office and

[14] Vickers v. Boutigny, Cass. Civ., June 30, 1955, [1956] D.J. 465 (notice of appeal); 1 SOLUS & PERROT 348; BATIFFOL 823; note by Goldman appended to Mathys v. Renaudin, Cour Amiens, March 27, 1962, 89 CLUNET 986 (1962). Service on the *ministère public* is unavailable in one instance: In the case of attachment or garnishment of property in the hands of a third party, it is not permissible to serve the notice of attachment or garnishment on a third party residing outside of continental France through the *ministère public*. CODE DE PROCÉDURE CIVILE art. 560. On international co-operation in connection with service of process, see generally Rigaux, *La signification des actes judiciaires à l'étranger*, 52 REV. CR. D.I.P. 448 (1963).

[15] 1 DALLOZ, RÉPERTOIRE DE PROCÉDURE CIVILE ET COMMERCIALE, *Exploit*, at Nos. 290–95 (1955).

[16] On service of process in France, and applicable taxes and fees, see 7.02, 12.03, and 12.06 *supra*. For recent changes, see 7.58 *supra*.

gives the party who requested the service the duplicate original. The copy served is, of course, left in the office of the *ministère public.* Ordinarily, no translation need accompany the papers served. [17] On the day he served the *procureur,* the *huissier* must send a copy of the document to the defendant by registered mail, return receipt requested. [18] Since the offices of the *ministère public* at the various courts are known as *parquets* in France, such service is customarily referred to as *signification à parquet.*

If the addressee of a document served on the *ministère public* resides in a country with which France has no agreement relating to international co-operation in litigation, the document is forwarded to the Ministry of Justice. The Ministry of Justice transmits it to the Ministry of Foreign Affairs, which checks whether it is in due form and attaches a form (*bordereau*) which must later be signed by the recipient or on which the French embassy or consulate must note the reasons for non-delivery. [19] The Ministry then sends the document and form to the French embassy or consulate abroad for transmittal to the addressee. [20] However, transmittal of the document to the addressee is not considered formal service. The applicable decree states specifically that it is for informational purposes only (*à titre de simple renseignement*). [21] Time to appear begins to run upon delivery of the document to the *ministère public,* but, since the effective date of *Décret* No. 65–1006, this rule prevails only if the return receipt for the copy of the document mailed by the *huissier* to the defendant shows that the latter received actual notice. Absent the return receipt, time to appear begins to run only when the defendant receives actual notice. But if no proof is available within three months that the defendant received the document, the court may, nevertheless, grant a default judgment if it finds that all useful steps to inform the defendant were taken. In an appropriate case, it may order other measures for this purpose or take other steps to protect the parties' rights. [22] Thus, the former harsh

[17] A few countries require that a translation accompany the French original if service is to be made in a formal manner by their authorities. JURISCLASSEUR DE DROIT INTERNATIONAL, fasc. 583, No. 59 (1960). Under the French-British Convention of 1922, *supra* note 7, art. 3, the original paper to be served, two copies, a translation into English, and a copy of the translation must be submitted if service is to be made in Britain through the intermediary of the High Court. The Hague Agreement of 1954, *supra* note 5, art. 3, requires a translation only if service is to be made in some special form.

[18] CODE DE PROCÉDURE CIVILE art. 1033–3, as added by DÉCRET No. 65–1006, of Nov. 26, 1965, J.O. Dec. 2, 1965, p. 10664, [1965] B.L.D. 678.

[19] JURISCLASSEUR DE DROIT INTERNATIONAL, fasc. 583, No. 49 (1960).

[20] CODE DE PROCÉDURE CIVILE art. 69 (10).

[21] DÉCRET No. 46–2390, *supra* note 3, art. 2.

[22] CODE DE PROCÉDURE CIVILE art. 1033–3.

and criticized [23] rule that only service on the *ministère public* is legally relevant [24] has been softened considerably.

In the absence of treaty, there are no special rules as to the manner in which the consulate or embassy must transmit the papers it receives. In those countries in which local authorities are willing to deliver documents through the police or other public officials, the papers are transmitted to the appropriate local authorities with a request that they effectuate delivery.

In countries that do not object to a foreign diplomatic or consular official's effectuating delivery, addressees who live within a reasonable distance of a French embassy or consulate are advised by mail that a legal document is waiting for them and are asked to pick it up. When they do, they must sign the form attached to the paper by the French Foreign Ministry. This rather convenient form of service is unavailable in a few countries, which view service of legal papers as involving an exercise of sovereignty forbidden to foreign authorities. Some countries, however, permit French consuls to serve papers on French nationals.

If the addressee lives at a distance from the consulate or embassy, the consulate will sometimes mail the document and request that the form attached by the Ministry of Foreign Affairs be signed and returned. The French Consulate General in New York sometimes seems to use the services of American process servers. After service has been effected, the signed form from the Ministry of Foreign Affairs is returned to Paris. If service could not be effected, the papers to be served and the form are returned with an explanation on the form. In the past, the Ministry of Foreign Affairs in Paris does not always seem to have informed the parties who requested service when the delivery was effectuated. [25]

[23] BATIFFOL 824; 1 SOLUS & PERROT 354; *cf.* Mathys v. Renaudin, Cour Amiens, March 27, 1962, 89 CLUNET 986 (1962) (note Goldman), 52 REV. CR. D.I.P. 91 (1963) (note Gavalda).

[24] Dame Viret v. Viret, Cass. Civ., Feb. 23, 1962, 89 CLUNET 986 (1962) (service of a judgment on *ministère public* starts running of appeal period, notwithstanding rule contained in agreement with Morocco, where defendant resided, that local authorities making service must return proof of service). See also Krishana & Cie. v. Sté David & Cie, Cass. Civ., Nov. 30, 1938, 1939 REV. CR. D.I.P. 312 (1939) (similar holding involving service in England); dame Sfintescu v. Sfintescu, Cass. Civ., Feb. 7, 1964, [1964] D.J. 247, 91 CLUNET 596 (1964).

[25] JURISCLASSEUR DE DROIT INTERNATIONAL, fasc. 583, No. 54 (1960). At present, the receipt must be returned to the *huissier*. For an example of a paper delivered by an American process server at the request of the French consulate in New York, see Dame d'Esterno v. d'Esterno, Cass. Civ., Feb. 17, 1961, [1961] BULL. CIV. No. 136, p. 100, 88 CLUNET 1106 (1961) (note J.B.S.). A Circular of the Ministry of Justice, referring specifically to Austria, but apparently stating a general rule, instructs French consuls who serve papers themselves, rather than through the use of local authorities not to use any "compulsion." Circular of the Ministry of Justice of May 20, 1925, *supra* note 4.

**b. Under treaties.** Service in the manner prescribed by article 69(10) is slow because the papers go through many official hands before they are delivered to the addressee. It is not unusual for three months to elapse between the time a paper is served on the *ministère public* by an *huissier* and the time it is actually received by the addressee. [26] For this reason, some international agreements provide for more efficient methods of delivery. Under agreements with many of the former French colonies, [27] the document may be forwarded directly by the French *ministère public* to its counterpart in the foreign country. The local *ministère public* then has the document delivered to the addressee through a police officer. [28] The Agreement with Germany provides that papers to be served there must be forwarded by the French *ministère public* to the presiding judge of the German court (*Amtsgericht* or *Landgericht*) in whose district the recipient lives. The German court effectuates delivery through one of its own officials. [29] When delivery is to be made in Great Britain, papers served on the *ministère public* are transmitted through channels to the French Embassy in London, which forwards them to the Senior Master of the High Court who has the documents delivered by a British process server. [30] Some agreements permit the mailing of documents directly from one country to the addressee in the other country, [31] and some specifically authorize

[26] According to knowledgeable French lawyers, this is approximately the time it takes for a paper to reach the United States. The JURISCLASSEUR DE DROIT INTERNATIONAL, fasc. 583, at No. 66 (1960), states that the following periods elapse between the time a document is sent out by the French Foreign Ministry and the time the Ministry receives proof of service (a period which is not identical to the one mentioned in the text):

| | |
|---|---|
| United States | 3–6 months |
| Argentina | 2–4 months |
| Venezuela | 4 months or more |
| Japan | 2–4 months |
| Spain | 3–6 months |

[27] French authors seem somewhat in doubt whether CODE DE PROCÉDURE CIVILE art. 69 (10) is applicable to the former French colonies which became part of the French Community or rather article 69(9) which governs service in colonies and is somewhat less complex. It would seem, however, that the former colonies, even if they still co-operate with France, must be considered as sovereign states so that article 69(10) is applicable. See 1 SOLUS & PERROT 349 n. 5; JURISCLASSEUR DE DROIT INTERNATIONAL, fasc. 583, No. 52 (1960). In practice, the problem is largely academic because the treaties between France and these countries regulate service of process in fair detail.

[28] *E.g.*, Agreements with the Ivory Coast and Mauretania, *supra* note 9, art. 1; Judicial Protocol with Algeria, *supra* note 9, art. 21. Most of these agreements also permit various other forms of service.

[29] Agreement with the Federal Republic of Germany, *supra* note 7, art. 1.

[30] Convention with Great Britain, *supra* note 7, art. 3; *cf.* Harwood, *Service and Evidence Abroad under English Civil Procedure, Part I, the Rules of the Supreme Court*, 29 GEO. WASH. L. REV. 497, 501–02 (1961).

[31] *E.g.*, The Hague Convention, *supra* note 5, art. 6 (with the proviso that the country to which the paper is sent may object).

service by consuls, [32] or by agents or representatives of parties. [33] Formal letters rogatory are never used for the service of French papers abroad. [34] Absent a specific provision, the existence of a treaty does not modify the rule determining when service is complete. [35]

c. **Default judgments.** If a non-resident defendant served under article 69(10) receives notice of the action brought against him after his time to appear has elapsed but before a default judgment is entered, he may, nevertheless, appear and litigate the case on the merits. However, presumably, he can raise an objection based on lack of proper service only if the service on the *ministère public* was defective, not if the copy was not mailed, and only if he suffered actual prejudice. [36] Such an objection must be raised at once, before any discussion of the merits. [37] Improper service has no effect on the competence of a French court. [38]

If a default judgment has been entered, [39] the defendant may ordinarily obtain a hearing on the merits by appealing from the default judgment or obtaining a reopening of the case through a procedure known as *opposition*. [40] If one of these means of attack is not used, however, the default judgment becomes unimpeachable. [41]

To start the time period for appeal or *opposition* running, the default judgment must be served upon the defendant in the same manner as an *ajournement*. Time for appeal or *opposition* begins to run

[32] *E.g.*, The Hague Convention, *supra* note 5, art. 6. Treaties specifically authorize French consuls to serve papers in Austria, Australia, Canada, Czechoslovakia, Great Britain, Ireland and the Netherlands, but in some of these countries only on French nationals. JURISCLASSEUR DE DROIT INTERNATIONAL, fasc. 589 B, No. 12 (1961).

[33] Most of the agreements with former French colonies, *supra* note 9, so provide, but limit this practical form of service to nationals of the country from which the service issues.

[34] Under French law, letters rogatory are proper only in matters relating to proof. See note 140 *infra*.

[35] Dame Viret v. Viret, *supra* note 24; Krishana & Cie. v. Sté David & Cie., *supra* note 24. But under the Agreement on Judicial Co-operation between France and Sweden, *supra* note 7, art. 2, service is complete when the paper is actually received by its addressee in Sweden, or two weeks after it has been given to the Swedish authorities by the French Consulate, whichever is earlier. An analogous provision is contained in the treaty on Judicial Co-operation between France and Monaco, Sept. 21, 1949, J.O. April 2, 1953, p. 3121, 81 CLUNET 852 (1954), [1953] DL. 113, art. 8.

[36] Under CODE DE PROCÉDURE CIVILE art. 70, the requirements of article 69 (requiring service of the document on the *procureur*), but not those of article 1033–3 (requiring mailing to the addressee) are prescribed "on pain of nullity."

[37] CODE DE PROCÉDURE CIVILE art. 173; *cf.* 7.08, *supra*; Patino v. sa femme, Cour Paris, July 1, 1959, 49 REV. CR. D.I.P. 192 (1960), 87 CLUNET 424 (1960).

[38] See 4.02.a and 7.09.c *supra*.

[39] *Cf.* 1 SOLUS & PERROT 354 n. 2 and note 26 *supra*.

[40] See 7.04.a *supra*.

[41] See 13.01 *supra*.

upon service upon the *ministère public*, but only if it is a shown by the return receipt that the defendant actually received the copy of the judgment mailed by the *huissier*. Absent the return receipt, the time for appeal or *opposition* begins to run with the recipt of the judgment by the defendant. If there is no proof of such receipt within three months of the service on the *ministère public*, the plaintiff may petition the presiding judge of the court for permission to levy execution. If the presiding judge believes that all useful steps to inform defendant of the judgment against him have not been taken, he must order additional steps for that purpose. If he believes that all useful steps have been taken, he must make an order granting permission to execute and noting the date on which the time for *opposition* expired. In cases in which execution was levied before the time for appeal or *opposition* expired because "provisional execution" was available by court order or as a matter of law, the first act of execution starts the running of the applicable time periods. [42]

**d. Service on defendants without a known address anywhere.** In case of defendants whose whereabouts are unknown entirely, the *huissier* must proceed under article 69(8), not article 69(10), of the *Code de Procédure Civile*. Service is effected by delivering a copy of the instrument to the *ministère public* of the court in which the action is pending. The *ministère public* must investigate the whereabouts of the defendant and, if feasible, attempt to deliver the document to him through the police. [43] This method of service should be used only if the person on whose behalf service is made has given the *huissier* all information in his possession concerning the whereabouts of the defendant and if the *huissier* himself made whatever investigations to locate the defendant required by "prudence, vigilance, and good faith". [44]

If a judgment must be served in such a manner, time to appeal or make *opposition* runs from the time the defendant received actual notice of the judgment if the *procureur* was, in fact, successful in finding him. If he is unsuccessful, the plaintiff may petition the presiding judge of the court for permission to levy execution. He must grant it upon receiving a report from the *procureur* concerning his lack

[42] CODE DE PROCÉDURE CIVILE arts. 158–3, 158–4, 1033–3, as added by DÉCRET No. 65–1006, *supra* note 18.

[43] CODE DE PROCÉDURE CIVILE art. 69(8).

[44] Raynaud, CHRONIQUE, 61 REV. TRIM. DR. CIV. 391, 392 (1962); 1 SOLUS & PERROT 356–58; 1 DALLOZ, RÉPERTOIRE DE PROCÉDURE CIVILE ET COMMERCIALE, *Exploit.* at Nos. 174–77 (1956).

of success in locating the defendant. In his order, the judge notes when the time for appeal or *opposition* ran out. If there was execution of the judgment because "provisional execution" was available, time for appeal or *opposition* starts to run with the first act of execution. [45]

## 15.03. Taking Testimony in a Foreign Country for Use in France

The Code of Civil Procedure provides very broadly that whenever a court which ordered an *enquête*, an *expertise*, or other proof-taking proceeding is unable to execute it because of distance, it may appoint another court or judge to proceed in its place. [46] In addition, most of the code titles dealing with the various proof proceedings, such as *enquête* and *expertise*, contain provisions authorizing courts, which, on account of distance, cannot conduct proof proceedings themselves, to request other courts to do so. [47] A request to that effect is called a *commission rogatoire* (letters rogatory). [48] The pertinent code articles do not make specific mention of letters rogatory destined for foreign countries and are brief as to the procedure to be followed. As a consequence, the rules relating to letters rogatory destined for foreign countries are in considerable measure formed by judicial practice. Although the specific references to *commissions rogatoires* in the French codes relate to the procedure in the court of first instance (*tribunal de grande instance*) and the commercial court, [49] letters rogatory may undoubtedly issue in civil cases pending in other courts. [50]

Letters rogatory destined for foreign countries may be addressed to a foreign court, or, unless that country objects to the execution of letters rogatory by French consuls, to a French consulate in the country in which the evidence is to be obtained. Theoretically, letters rogatory

[45] Code de Procédure Civile art. 158–2.

[46] Code de Procédure Civile art. 1035. Such a delegation is mandatory whenever the proof proceeding involved has to take place outside the district in which the court is competent, since French judges may not act outside their territorial verge. Morel 380.

[47] Code de Procédure Civile art. 121 (decisory oath), art. 256 (*enquête*), art. 333 (examination of a party, *i.e.*, *comparution personnelle*); Code de Commerce art. 16 (*représentation* of books of account).

[48] The only articles in which the words *commission rogatoire* are used are Code de Procédure Civile art. 333 and Code de Commerce art. 16. The provisions cited in the preceding footnote state merely that one court may delegate (*commettre*) another court in its place. However, the term *commission rogatoire* is freely used by authors in all circumstances covered by these provisions. *E.g.*, 1 Dalloz, *op. cit. supra* note 5, at Nos. 1–4. The term *commission rogatoire* is used only in connection with proof proceedings, never in connection with service of process.

[49] See note 47 *supra*.

[50] For the courts directly governed by the Code of Civil Procedure, namely the *tribunal d'instance*, the *tribunal de grande instance*, the *cour d'appel*, and the commercial court, Code de Procédure Civile art. 1035 seems to provide sufficient authority permitting the use of letters rogatory.

may be used for the conduct of any of the several proof proceedings known to French law. [51] In practice, they are granted with some frequency only for the purpose of examining a witness (*enquête*) or obtaining the report of an impartial expert (*expertise*).

As a rule, parties to a French lawsuit may not conduct a formal proof proceeding outside of France without a court-ordered *commission rogatoire*. [52] However, nothing prevents the parties from obtaining informal *ex parte* statements from willing witnesses or experts in foreign countries. Since a hearsay rule is unknown in French law, such statements are admissible in French lawsuits, except in certain instances. [53]

**a. Examination of witnesses.** The Code of Civil Procedure prescribes no special procedure for obtaining letters rogatory requesting the examination of a witness. The general procedure for obtaining an order authorizing an *enquête* is used. Regular pleadings (*conclusions*) are submitted requesting that the witness or witnesses indicated be heard on specified issues. If the witness is outside France, the *conclusions* will also request that the court issue letters rogatory directed to a foreign court or to a French consulate. The court will grant the request if the conditions for hearing a witness in a French civil proceeding are met – that is, if oral testimony is admissible in the case, if the evidence sought is necessary as well as pertinent and material, and if the witness is competent. The order will describe in fair detail the issues on which the witness is to be heard. [54]

If the letters rogatory are to be executed by a foreign court, the party who has obtained the order must prepare a translation [55] and submit both the order and the translation to the *ministère public* attached to the court that issued the order. [56] The *ministère public* checks the order and, if a translation is required, whether it is attached. It also inquires whether the parties wish to be informed of the date of

[51] French authors generally state that letters rogatory are available in connection with all proof proceedings (*mesures d'instruction*). See, *e.g.*, Japiot, *supra* note 4, at 75. For a detailed discussion of letters rogatory in general, see Gavalda, *Les Commissions Rogatoires Internationales en Matière Civile et Commerciale*, 53 REV. CR. D.I.P. 15 (1964).

[52] The various types of proof proceedings known to French law are viewed as judicial acts (*actes juridictionnels*) which may take place only pursuant to court order before a judge or at least a public official. *Cf.* Goldman, *De l'obtention des Preuves à l'Etranger*, INTERN. BAR ASS'N, 5TH CONF. REP. 68, 74 (1954).

[53] See 7.31 *supra.*

[54] See 7.51 *supra.*

[55] JURISCLASSEUR DE DROIT INTERNATIONAL, fasc. 583, at No. 14 (1960). A translation is, of course, unnecessary, if the letters are sent to a French speaking country or if a treaty provides otherwise.

[56] Submission of letters rogatory by foreign counsel directly to the foreign court is unusual.

the execution of the letters rogatory, so that they or their representatives may be present. If the letters rogatory are to be executed by a foreign court likely to make a charge to the French Government, the parties are asked whether they are willing to bear this expense. After these steps have been taken, the *ministère public* prepares a letter of transmittal to be attached to the court order. [57]

In the absence of a treaty providing otherwise, both order and letter of transmittal are forwarded by the *ministère public* to the Ministry of Justice which transmits them to the Ministry of Foreign Affairs. There, both papers are checked again in the office dealing with matters of international co-operation in litigation. Letters directed to a foreign court are sent to the French diplomatic representative in the foreign country, which submits them to the foreign office of the particular country with the request that they be executed and returned. The French authorities have, of course, no control over the manner of execution of such letters. Because in the past the United States Department of State has been unwilling to transmit letters rogatory submitted by foreign countries – a practice liberalized but recently –, letters rogatory directed to a court in the United States are sent to the local French consulate, which presents them to the appropriate United States District Court through its American counsel. They are executed by a commissioner appointed by the court. Since a fee must be paid to the commissioner, letters rogatory addressed to an American court are transmitted only if the parties have undertaken to bear the cost involved. Executed letters rogatory are returned to the French Foreign Ministry for transmittal to the proper authorities. If execution was impossible, the French embassy returns the papers to the Foreign Ministry with an explanation of the reasons that prevented execution.

Letters rogatory directed to a French consular officer are similarly forwarded to their destination by the French Foreign Ministry. Of course, French consular officers have no coercive powers and therefore the use of consuls for the execution of letters rogatory is ordinarily practicable only in the case of co-operative witnesses. [58] Circulars of

[57] JURISCLASSEUR DE DROIT INTERNATIONAL, fasc. 583, at No. 11; *cf. id.*, fasc. 589 B, at No. 30 (1961).

[58] French consuls do not summon witnesses by a subpoena or other document threatening reprisals in case of non-appearance, but merely invite witnesses to appear. JURISCLASSEUR DE DROIT INTERNATIONAL, fasc. 583, at No. 31 (1960). Two old lower court cases have refused the issuance of letters rogatory to French consuls on the ground that the examination of witnesses involved a "judicial act" which could not be performed by an executive official such as a consul. No recent case seems to have questioned the right of consuls to examine witnesses. *Cf.* Gavalda, *supra* note 51, at 24–25.

the French Ministry of Justice suggest recourse to consuls only if the letters can be executed "easily." [59] In addition, consuls must "invite" witnesses to testify, they may not "summon" them. [60] Some countries do not permit French consuls to execute letters rogatory at all, and in others they may examine only French nationals. [61] In the United States, French consuls are completely free to examine any person, regardless of his nationality. [62]

When examining witnesses, a French consul follows French law, proceeding as a French judge conducting an *enquête*; he examines the witness on the issues listed in the court order under oath and prepares a summary of the testimony. A certified copy of the summary and the court order appointing the consul to take the testimony are returned to the Ministry of Foreign Affairs in Paris, which transmits them to the court that issued the letters rogatory. [63] French parties favor recourse to French consuls for the execution of letters rogatory, because French procedure is used in conducting the examination and the expenses involved are reasonable. [64] The latter consideration is significant, because many cases in which letters rogatory are sent to the United States involve domestic relations problems or other litigation in which the amount in controversy is small. Furthermore, the French Consulate General in New York, at any rate, infrequently encounters unco-operative witnesses. [65]

**b. Examination of experts.** It has always been assumed that the appointment of an impartial expert [66] in a foreign country can be obtained through the use of letters rogatory addressed to a French consul or a foreign court. [67] In the 1930's, when many workers from Poland and

[59] See, *e.g.*, the Circular of May 20, 1925, concerning co-operation with Austria, *supra* note 4, and the Circular of the Ministry of Justice of Feb. 10, 1910, cited in 1 DALLOZ, *op. cit. supra* note 5, at No. 64.

[60] See note 58 *supra*.

[61] See JURISCLASSEUR DE DROIT INTERNATIONAL, fasc. 589 B, at No. 31 (1961).

[62] SMIT & MILLER, INTERNATIONAL CO-OPERATION IN CIVIL LITIGATION, A REPORT ON PRACTICES AND PROCEDURES PREVAILING IN THE UNITED STATES 10 (1962). The Consular Convention with France, *supra* note 12, art. VI, sanctions the taking of depositions of nationals by consuls.

[63] JURISCLASSEUR DE DROIT INTERNATIONAL, fasc. 583, at Nos. 32–33 (1960).

[64] *Id.* at Nos. 30–31 (discussing relative advantages of use of French consuls and foreign courts for execution of letters rogatory).

[65] Information kindly supplied by the French Consulate General in New York by letter of October 29, 1963, The letter indicates that an average of about 30 letters rogatory are executed annually by the French Consulate General in New York. However, it seems that in 1954 the consulate received about 150 letters, over half of them in criminal cases. LeLièvre, in LETTERS ROGATORY 13 (Grossman ed. 1956).

[66] For a general discussion of the *expertise* procedure, see 7.54 *supra*.

[67] *E.g.*, JURISCLASSEUR DE DROIT INTERNATIONAL, fasc. 583, No. 17 (1960).

Czechoslovakia came to France on a temporary basis, medical experts were sometimes appointed in such a manner in actions for benefits under the French employer's liability law which were often filed by these workers after their return home. [68] It is not entirely clear to what extent the appointment of an expert in a foreign country is still possible. Since its revision in 1944, the Code of Civil Procedure has provided that, absent a treaty to the contrary, an expert must be a French national. [69] This rule would make it impossible to appoint an expert in a foreign country unless a qualified French national happened to be available there. It has been suggested that the rule requiring experts to be French nationals may be inapplicable if an expert is to be appointed in a foreign country. [70] Cases in point are lacking so far, but several treaties seem to recognize the possibility of the appointment of experts through letters rogatory. [71] If the appointment of a foreign national as an expert is permissible, nothing prevents the issuance of letters rogatory to a French consul in a foreign country for such a purpose. As far as French law is concerned, the procedure for the conduct of an *expertise* abroad through letters rogatory is substantially similar to the procedure for the examination of a witness. [72] While the taking of testimony through letters rogatory is usually not very costly, a number of conventions entered into between France and other civil law countries provide that the country requesting the appointment of an expert must pay his fees.

**c. Examination of parties.** Under French procedure, parties may be examined in a *comparution personnelle*, but are not put under oath. [73]

[68] Sometimes, French courts have refused to permit the appointment of a foreign physician as an expert on the ground that the proceedings could have been instituted while the worker was still in France. Doubts as to the impartiality of foreign experts may have been at the root of these holdings. See, *e.g.*, Andel v. Houillères de Ronchamp, Cour Besançon, Oct. 6, 1934, 63 CLUNET 137 (1936); Malek v. Mines d'Anzin, Cour Douai, July 12, 1933, 61 CLUNET 855 (1934). *But see* Compagnie des Mines de Courrières v. Smarzynski, Cass. Req., Dec. 13, 1933, 61 CLUNET 858 (1934).

[69] CODE DE PROCÉDURE CIVILE art. 306, as amended by Law of July 15, 1944, J.O. July 27, 1944, p. 1903, [1944] D. ANAL. L. 82. The reason for the requirement may be that under French procedure experts are officers of the court.

[70] 1 DALLOZ, RÉPERTOIRE DE PROCÉDURE CIVILE ET COMMERCIALE, *Expertise*, at No. 356 (1956).

[71] *E.g.*, The Hague Convention, *supra* note 5, art. 16 (state requesting appointment of expert may be required to pay his fees); Convention with Germany, *supra* note 7, art. 6 (same); Convention with Cameroon, *supra* note 9, art. 12 (same).

[72] While a witness is sworn orally, an expert merely signs a written form containing an oath. CODE DE PROCÉDURE CIVILE art. 309. When an expert is appointed by a consul, the consul must return this form, together with the expert's report and the papers forwarded him by the French ministry of Foreign Affairs, after the *expertise* is concluded. JURISCLASSEUR DE DROIT INTERNATIONAL, fasc. 583, at No. 34 (1960).

[73] CODE DE PROCÉDURE CIVILE arts. 324–36; *cf.* 7.53 *supra.*

The *comparution personnelle* is designed chiefly to enable the court to obtain a first-hand impression of the parties and to hear their stories from their own mouths. For this reason, a *comparution personnelle* must ordinarily take place before the court in which the action is pending and the use of the letters rogatory to effectuate a *comparution personnelle*, even inside France, is permitted only in "exceptional circumstances." [74] There is a dearth of authority on what facts constitute "exceptional circumstances." There would seem to be no reason, however, why a French consul in the United States could not be asked by letters rogatory to examine a party to a French law suit. The expenses involved in a transatlantic journey would probably be considered sufficient to constitute "exceptional circumstances." [75] While there is no way of penalizing a witness who fails to testify before a French consul, there is some inducement for a party invited to appear for a *comparution personnelle* to comply with the invitation. When a party fails to appear or to answer questions, the court may draw unfavorable inferences from its refusal to answer or appear and may even authorize the opponent to furnish oral evidence in a situation in which normally a writing is required. [76]

It may, however, be doubted whether an American court could conveniently execute letters rogatory addressed to it in connection with a *comparution personnelle*. In a *comparution personnelle*, there are no specific interrogatories; rather, the judge is supposed to engage in independent probing of his own. [77] Even American courts authorized to use foreign procedure when rendering assistance to a foreign court [78] may have difficulties in performing this unaccustomed task.

**d. Treaties concerning letters rogatory.** While compliance with letters rogatory by a foreign court is ordinarily considered a matter of courtesy rather than of obligation, France is a party to a number of agreements

[74] CODE DE PROCÉDURE CIVILE art. 333 (letters rogatory to court of domicile or residence of a party possible in exceptional circumstances).

[75] CODE DE PROCÉDURE CIVILE art. 333 implies that the exceptional circumstances exist if the trip to the court is too expensive or burdensome.

[76] CODE DE PROCÉDURE CIVILE art. 336 (dealing not with letters rogatory, but with *comparution personnelle* generally).

[77] See generally 7.53 *supra*.

[78] This authorization is specifically granted in the UNIFORM INTERSTATE AND INTERNATIONAL PROCEDURE ACT § 3.02(a), 9B U.L.A. 72 (Supp. 1963). An analogous amendment to 28 U.S.C. § 1782 (1958) was enacted on October 3, 1964. Public Law 88–619, 78 STAT. 995 (1964). The Hague Convention, *supra* note 5, in its only direct reference to the examination of parties, states that a state executing letters rogatory shall not be bound to use coercion when a party, as opposed to a witness, is to be examined.

that make the execution of letters rogatory mandatory. [79] They also simplify the procedures applicable in the absence of a convention. Typically, they provide that in the transmittal of letters rogatory diplomatic channels may be by-passed. Often, letters may be transmitted directly to the foreign court by the *ministère public*, [80] although sometimes the intervention of a French consul is required. As a rule, these treaties authorize the execution of letters rogatory by consuls if no compulsion is used, but some limit this authorization to cases in which only French nationals are to be heard. [81] Ordinarily, the agreements also contain special provisions as to costs, [82] methods of compulsion to be used against recalcitrant witnesses, [83] and translations required to be submitted with the original papers. [84] Sometimes, they state that, upon request, a court executing letters rogatory shall use special procedures that do not violate its own law. [85]

The treaty between France and Great Britain provides that French

[79] For a list of the more important agreements, see notes 5–9 *supra*; JURISCLASSEUR DE DROIT INTERNATIONAL, fasc. 589 B, No. 41 (1961). Although these agreements generally make it an obligation to comply with letters rogatory, they all contain exceptions for situations in which their execution would violate the security, public policy, or sovereignty of the state whose co-operation is sought. See, *e.g.*, The Hague Convention *supra* note 5, art. 11; Convention with Great Britain, *supra* note 7, art. 6.

[80] *E.g.*, Agreement with Germany, *supra* note 7, art. 4; Agreement with Cameroon, *supra* note 9, art. 6; Judicial Protocol with Algeria, *supra* note 9, art. 26. The Hague Convention, *supra* note 5, art. 9, does not authorize the transmittal of letters rogatory directly from court to court. It authorizes transmittal through consuls instead of diplomatic channels, but permits a state to demand transmittal through diplomatic channels. A recent Circular of the French Ministry of Justice seems to require that all letters rogatory, even those destined for a country in which transmittal directly to the court is authorized, be channelled through the Ministry. JURISCLASSEUR DE DROIT INTERNATIONAL, fasc. 589 B, at No. 33 (1961).

[81] By treaty, French consuls may take depositions both of their own nationals and of nationals of their host country in Austria, Czechoslovakia, Great-Britain, Holland, Morocco, and Spain. JURISCLASSEUR DE DROIT INTERNATIONAL, fasc. 589 B, No. 31 (1961). The other bilateral treaties authorize consuls to hear only their own nationals. *E.g.*, Convention with Germany, *supra* note 7, art. 7. Sometimes, treaties require that consuls executing letters rogatory state expressly, when asking witnesses to appear, that no compulsion is used. See, *e.g.*, Agreement with Germany, *supra* note 7, art. 7. The Hague Convention, *supra* note 5, art. 15, states that consuls may execute letters rogatory if a bilateral agreement so provides, or if the state on whose territory the consul is acting does not object.

[82] The Hague Convention, *supra* note 5, provides in article 16 that the state that executes letters rogatory shall not demand any fees, except for reimbursement of witnesses and experts' fees and possible extra expenses caused by the execution of letters rogatory in a special manner requested by the foreign country. Similar provisions are found in many other treaties. Sometimes the country executing letters rogatory agrees to bear even witnesses fees. See Agreement with Germany, *supra* note 7, art. 6 (only reimbursement for experts' fees). The multilateral agreement on support proceedings, *supra* note 6, art. 7, excludes the payment of all costs.

[83] Thus, The Hague Convention, *supra* note 5, art. 11, requires the country executing letters rogatory to use the same methods of compulsion it uses in purely domestic proceedings.

[84] The Hague Convention, *supra* note 5, art. 10, requires all papers to be accompanied by a translation attested either by a consular officer of the state requesting assistance or by a sworn interpreter of the state in which assistance is requested.

[85] *E.g.*, The Hague Convention, *supra* note 5, art. 14.

letters rogatory adressed to a British court shall be transmitted to the Senior Master of the High Court by the French Consul General in London. Requests for the examination of witnesses may be received and executed by consuls without regard to the nationality of the witnesses. The treaty specifically authorizes the consul to administer an oath and to demand the production of documents. Parties are authorized to be present when witnesses are examined. [86] Interestingly, the agreement also provides that a court of the state whose co-operation is sought may appoint a person proposed by the requesting state, including a consul, to take depositions and may compel the attendance of witnesses and the production of documents before the person so appointed, but only if the law of the state whose co-operation is sought authorizes this. [87] As a result, French consuls executing letters rogatory in Great Britain who are faced with recalcitrant witnesses sometimes ask a British court to appoint them as commissioners to take the deposition because they can then obtain application of British compulsory measures to the witness. However, this results in a fair amount of expense, and French consuls do not seek to be appointed as commissioners except on specific authorization by the parties, who must undertake to bear all expenses. Since France does not consider the appointment of British consuls as commissioners to be authorized by French law, it does not grant reciprocal facilities to British litigants. [88] Although there is no treaty on co-operation in litigation between France and the United States, United States District Courts, and many state courts, will, upon request, appoint French consuls or persons suggested by them as commissioners to take testimony. [89]

**e. Proceedings after return of letters rogatory.** After the letters rogatory have been executed and the minutes of the testimony returned to the French court [90] and filed in the clerk's office, the court proceeds in the same manner as following any other *enquête*. There is a hearing (*audience*) at which counsel for the parties argue about the impact of the testimony. They may also ask the court to exclude letters rogatory if

[86] Convention with Great Britain, *supra* note 7, arts. 6–7. The agreement, like The Hague Convention, states that a court executing letters rogatory shall, upon request, use a special form.

[87] Convention with Great Britain, *supra* note 7, art. 8.

[88] JURISCLASSEUR DE DROIT INTERNATIONAL, fasc. 589 B, No. 34 (1962).

[89] See SMIT & MILLER, *op. cit. supra* note 62, at 9–10.

[90] Executed letters rogatory are ordinarily retransmitted from the French consulate or embassy to the Ministry of Foreign Affairs, hence to the Ministry of Justice, which sends them to the appropriate *ministère public*, but foreign courts which received letters directly from a local *ministère public* will also return them that way.

for some reason they are invalid. [91] The mere use of foreign procedure by the court executing letters rogatory, such as the use of a form of oath unknown to French law, does not vitiate the testimony. [92] The letters may, however, be held void if the foreign court violated French public policy (*ordre public*) in their execution – for instance, by permitting the disclosure of information considered privileged under French law. [93]

In most countries, the execution of French letters rogatory does not require major expenditures on the part of the litigants. Under the Hague Convention, a country executing letters rogatory may make a charge only for actual expenditures incurred, such as witnesses' fees. Some countries do not even demand reimbursement for such fees, and under some treaties letters rogatory are executed free of charge. [94]

### 15.04. Obtaining Tangible Evidence in a Foreign Country for Use in France

Although the matter is not entirely free from doubt, witnesses – not parties – may be asked to produce documents in court when testifying. [95] Similarly, a request for production of documents by witnesses may be embodied in letters rogatory. A number of treaties at least impliedly sanction such a procedure. [96]

Under French procedure, third parties who are not witnesses can be compelled to produce documents only in a limited number of instances: (1) if the document relates to property jointly owned by its holder and the person desiring its production; (2) if the holder of the document has an obligation of warranty towards the person wishing to obtain production of the document; and (3) if the holder of the document has been guilty of some fraud. [97]

Public officials, including notaries, are under a duty to deliver copies of documents in their custody to all persons legally entitled to receive

[91] Code de Procédure Civile arts. 274–78; *cf.* 7.51.e *supra.*

[92] *Cf.* 1 Dalloz, *op. cit. supra* note 5, at No. 62.

[93] *E.g.*, Dame Ancel v. Ancel, Cass. Req., Nov. 22, 1916, [1918] S. I. 121 (statement by physician involving privileged communication). A French court might also refuse to recognize letters rogatory as valid if the foreign court had refused one of the parties the right to participate in the procedure, or had acted unfairly. Batiffol 808–09.

[94] See note 82 *supra*; Jurisclasseur de Droit International, fasc. 589 B, No. 41 (1961).

[95] 2 Dalloz, Répertoire de Procédure Civile et Commerciale, *Preuve*, at No. 181. *But see* 12 Aubry & Rau, Droit Civil 71 (6th ed. Esmein 1958).

[96] Convention with Germany, *supra* note 7, art. 7 (consuls may examine their own nationals as witnesses and demand the production of documents); Convention with Great Britain, *supra* note 7, art. 7 (similar).

[97] 12 Aubry & Rau, *op. cit. supra* note 95; 2 Dalloz, *op. cit. supra* note 95, at No. 182. *But see id.* at No. 183 (listing a few isolated cases in which courts have held liable for damages persons who refused without good reason to produce a document needed in litigation by somebody else).

them. [98] In an appropriate case, a court order may be obtained for this purpose. The pertinent procedures apply only to French public officials and French notaries. They cannot be used to compel production of documents that are not in France. [99]

The *Code de Commerce* specifically authorizes commercial courts of the place in which an action is pending to request other commercial courts to examine books of account of *commerçants* pursuant to a *représentation* procedure, if the books are kept at a distance from the place in which the court is sitting. [100] Although this provision seems to contemplate only the appointment of another French court for the purpose, in an appropriate case letters rogatory may perhaps be directed to a French consul or a foreign court. [101] Apparently, however, no attempt has so far been made to obtain in this manner the production of commercial books located in the United States. [102]

## 15.05. Obtaining Proof of Foreign Official Documents for Use in France

As a general rule, foreign documents are given the same probative effect in France they have at their place of origin (*locus regit actum*). [103] The rule is not necessarily applicable to the question of the admissibility of a document, however. [104] As to French nationals who were born

[98] CODE DE PROCÉDURE CIVILE art. 853. As a rule, copies of notarial acts may be delivered only to parties, their heirs, and assigns. On who is entitled to copies of other documents, see 15.10 *infra*.

[99] CODE DE PROCÉDURE CIVILE arts. 839–40 (compelling notary to deliver copy of notarial document to party thereto), arts. 846–52 (procedure for court authorization to obtain copy of notarial document when application not made by party), art. 853 (liability of court clerks and public officers refusing to deliver copies of public document); DÉCRET No. 62–921 of Aug. 3, 1962, J.O. Aug. 9, 1962, p. 7918, [1962] D.L. 272, art. 9 (permission to obtain complete copy of birth, death, or marriage record). A French litigant anticipating a need for a document in the custody of an American public officer may use appropriate American procedures to secure a copy.

[100] CODE DE COMMERCE art. 16. On the *représentation* (production) of books of account, see 7.49 *supra*.

[101] Since the Commercial Code refers to other commercial courts and since the pertinent article 16 is part of title II of the French Commercial Code, which deals generally with the manner in which French merchants must keep their books, there may be a question whether this article permits a demand for the production of commercial books kept outside France through letters rogatory. However, French authors generally assume that such letters may be used in connection with all proof proceedings. See, *e.g.*, JURISCLASSEUR DE DROIT INTERNATIONAL, fasc. 583, at Nos. 7, 17 (1960).

[102] On possible assistance by courts in the United States, see SMIT & MILLER, *op. cit. supra* note 62, at 22–25.

[103] See 7.57 *supra*.

[104] As a rule, the law of the place where the document has been prepared will also determine its admissibility. See, *e.g.*, Consorts Justomond v. époux Delbreil, Cour d'Appel Bordeaux, Dec. 21, 1886, [1887] D. 2. 163 (official birth or marriage certificates, which are admissible evidence only in purely domestic French situation, not required in proceeding involving person who had lived in Louisiana; evidence usable in Louisiana to prove birth or marriage may be used). *Accord*, Dussauce v. Dussauce, Cour Paris, Jan. 20, 1873, [1873] D. 2. 59. At

outside of France or who married or died there, problems concerning the effect of foreign birth, death, or marriage certificates are often avoided because French consulates keep marriage, birth, and death records for French nationals in their districts, and copies of such records are equivalent to copies prepared by French registrars (*officiers de l' état civil*).[105] Occasionally, the probative effect of a foreign official document is regulated by treaty.[106]

Absent a treaty to the contrary, a foreign official document which is to be used in France must be properly authenticated (*légalisé*), translated, and provided with the appropriate tax stamps. The precise statutory basis for the requirement of authentication of foreign official documents is somewhat obscure.[107] A *Décret* authorizes French consuls to certify the signatures of all public officers in their consular district, whether the public officer is the officer who has prepared or authenticated the document or whether he is merely an authenticating officer himself.[108] As a practical matter, French consuls do not seem to require chain certifications. The French Consulate General in New York, for instance, will certify directly the signatures of all American public officers, such as registrars of vital statistics and notaries public, who are located in its consular district (New York, Connecticut, and Northern New Jersey). It will also certify the signature of all French nationals whose signature it has in its signature card file.[109] In authenticating a foreign public document, the French consul certifies that the document was prepared by the competent authority and indicates the official position of the public officer whose signature he certifies.[110]

times, however, the law applicable to the substance of the transaction (if different), or the law of the forum may have a bearing on the admissibility of evidence in France. See, *e.g.*, BATIFFOL 460, 533, 809–14; *cf.* Société les Films Roger Richebé v. Société Roy Export Co., Cass. Civ., May 28, 1963, 90 CLUNET 1004 (1963) (assignment of copyright in American film valid if American form of copyright assignment used, though assignment made in Paris).

105 See CODE CIVIL art. 47, most recently amended by DÉCRET No. 62–921, *supra* note 99.

106 See, *e.g.*, The Rome Agreement on the recognition of illegitimate children, *supra* note 6, which provides that a recognition made by the father in one of the contracting countries shall have the same effect in another contracting country as a recognition made there.

107 DÉCRET No. 46–2390, *supra* note 3, authorizes, but does not require, French consuls to authenticate documents. An older decree dealing with this topic was abrogated by the 1946 *Décret*. See note Sialelli to Dornen v. Batzenschlager, Trib. Blida, March 13, 1957, 85 CLUNET 128 (1958).

108 DÉCRET No. 46–2390, *supra* note 3, art. 3.

109 Information kindly supplied by the French Consulate General in New York by letter dated October 29, 1963.

110 JURISCLASSEUR DE DROIT INTERNATIONAL, fasc. 544, at No. 98 (1960) (discussing vital statistics records, but apparently applicable generally); DÉCRET No. 46–2390, *supra* note 3, art. 3 (requirement that position of official be stated). French law does not prescribe the form an authentication (*légalisation*) must take.

111 DÉCRET No. 46–2390, *supra* note 3, art. 4.

The signature of a French consul must, in turn, be certified by the French Foreign Ministry in Paris before the document may be used in France.[111] As to some states, authentication of a document by a French consul resident in the country of origin of the document may be replaced by authentication by a consul of that country resident in France. Again, certification of the consul's signature by the French Foreign Ministry is required.[112]

The attitude of the French courts towards authentication seems to be rather flexible. Often, they admit an unauthenticated foreign document, especially if there is no real issue as to its genuineness or if it is not feasible to produce an authenticated copy.[113] Authentication is required for foreign documents that have to be submitted to a French registrar of vital statistics (*officier de l'état civil*). If it is impossible to supply properly authenticated documents to the registrar, the local *procureur de la République* may, however, grant a dispensation from the requirement of authentication by consul and Foreign Ministry.[114]

Documents in foreign languages must be translated. French consulates are usually ready to translate documents submitted to them for authentication. Alternatively, the party submitting the document may have it translated and request the consulate to authenticate the translation. A document not already translated when it arrives in France must be translated there by an official French "sworn" interpreter or by a consul of the country in which the document originated.[115]

Foreign documents submitted to a French court or administrative official are subject to French stamp taxes. The expense involved is relatively minor, however.[116]

France is a party to the European conventions on birth, death, and

[112] Supplement to the *Instruction Générale* of the Minister of Justice concerning vital statistics records, issued April 12, 1962, J.O. May 13, 1962, p. 4741, reprinted in JURISCLASSEUR DE DROIT INTERNATIONAL, fasc. 544, at p. 1 (Supp. 2–1963), Nos. 525–26. This seems to be a general rule, although the circular speaks only of vital statistics records.

[113] *E.g.*, de Bioncourt, Cass. Req., June 28, 1937, 64 CLUNET 807 (1937) (adoption judgment issued in Russia before Revolution accepted without authentication when authentication seemed difficult or impossible and there was some proof of genuineness of document). See also cases mentioned in the note Sialelli to Dornen v. Batzenschlager, *supra* note 107, and 1 DALLOZ, RÉPERTOIRE DE PROCÉDURE CIVILE, *Actes de l'Etat Civil*, at No. 90 (1955).

[114] 1962 Supplement to INSTRUCTION GÉNÉRALE, *supra* note 112, at No. 528.

[115] JURISCLASSEUR DE DROIT INTERNATIONAL, fasc. 544, at No. 107 (1960). On the authority of French consulates to prepare and attest translations, see DÉCRET No. 46–2390, *supra* note 3, art. 6. At least as to vital statistics records, translation of documents by the French consulate seems to be the normal procedure.

[116] JURISCLASSEUR DE DROIT INTERNATIONAL, fasc. 544, at No. 110; Guilhot, *Le régime fiscal des actes de l'état civil dressés à l'étranger ou concernant des étrangers*, 64 CLUNET 244 (1937). The stamp tax is based on the number of pages in the document and the size of the paper. Documents containing a business transaction may, in addition, become subject to the much more burdensome *enregistrement* tax.

marriage certificates. One of these conventions provides for special multilingual forms to be used by registrars of vital statistics to supply summary information on birth, death, or marriage for use in the contracting states. The required information, apart from names, is provided by means of special symbols. The document must be signed by the issuing officer and bear his official seal. Neither translation nor authentication is required. The other convention provides for the mutual recognition of copies of birth, death, and marriage records without authentication, provided the documents are signed and bear the seal of the issuing officer. [117] In addition, France is a party to a number of bilateral agreements exempting birth, death, and marriage certificates, and sometimes other documents as well, from any requirement of authentication if signed by the appropriate officer and sealed with the seal of his office. [118] Often, these agreements also provide for administrative co-operation in keeping vital statistics records current. [119]

[117] Agreements of Sept. 26 and Sept. 27, 1956, *supra* note 6. As a result, birth, death, and marriage records from Belgium, (West) Germany, Holland, Luxemburg, Switzerland, and Turkey may be used in France without authentication. See 1962 Supplement to INSTRUCTION GÉNÉRALE, *supra* note 112, at No. 511. Authentication is also unnecessary for all copies of declarations of paternity issued pursuant to the multilateral convention concerning the recognition of illegitimate children. See note 6 *supra*.

[118] For a list of countries concerned, see 1962 Supplement to the INSTRUCTION GÉNÉRALE, *supra* note 112, at No. 527. The Agreement with Great Britain, *supra* note 7, provides for the mutual recognition, without authentication, of vital statistics records, patent office records, and other public documents and judgments if they are signed by the appropriate public official and bear the seal of the office or court concerned. Other bilateral treaties usually exempt only vital statistics records from the requirement of authentication. See, *e.g.*, Convention with Switzerland of August 26, 1926, J.O. Oct. 26, 1926, 54 CLUNET 249 (1927). Similar provisions can be found in many of the agreements between France and her former colonies mentioned *supra* note 9. See, *e.g.*, Agreement between France and Cameroon, art. 23, and the Agreement with the Ivory Coast, art. 21. The Agreement between France and Czechoslovakia, J.O. Feb. 12, 1928, 58 CLUNET 550 (1931), art. 15, provides for a simplified form of authentication: Documents need not be authenticated by a consul; authentication by a court or a member of the central administration of the country of origin is sufficient.

[119] Such agreements usually provide that each contracting state will periodically transmit to the other contracting state information concerning births, deaths, and marriages of nationals of that state. They may also provide that registrars of vital statistics shall promptly inform the appropriate consul of the other contracting state of the death of any person having the consul's nationality. There may be further clauses concerning the free delivery of birth, death, and marriage certificates to governmental organizations of the other state and concerning national treatment of indigent nationals of the other state as far as remission of fees payable on account of birth, death, and marriage certificates is concerned. *Cf.* Agreements, *supra* note 118. A provision concerning the free delivery of birth, death, and marriage certificates is also contained in The Hague Convention, *supra* note 5, art. 25. For French administrative rules on these matters, see INSTRUCTION GÉNÉRALE of the Ministry of Justice concerning vital statistics records of Sept. 21, 1955, J.O. Sept. 22, 1955, p. 9322, at No. 384, and 1962 Supplement, *supra* note 112, at No. 510.

## 15.06. Proof of Foreign Law in France

A party wishing to rely on foreign law must refer to it in his *conclusions* (pleadings) and prove it. [120] Absent any reference to foreign law in the *conclusions* and absent any proof on the subject, French courts have no duty to apply foreign law, [121] but will ordinarily apply French law, even if under pertinent French conflict of laws rules the use of foreign law would be required. [122] However, although French courts are under no duty to take judicial notice of foreign law, they occasionally do so. [123]

Since cases brought before intermediate appellate tribunals (*cours d' appel*) are heard *de novo*, parties may ordinarily rely and submit evidence on foreign law before such tribunals even though they have not done so before the courts of first instance.

French law is extremely flexible as to the methods that may be used to prove foreign law. The standard method of proof is a *certificat de coutume*, which is, in effect, a memorandum on the applicable foreign law prepared on behalf of a party by a person familiar with such law. There is no requirement that the certificate be issued by an official body or agency. A *certificat de coutume* seems to be admitted on the same basis as other certificates of experts. [124] Statutes and other documenta-

[120] *E.g.*, BATIFFOL 385–86.

[121] For some recent cases, see Dame Bertoncini v. Bertoncini, Cass. Civ., July 11, 1961, 51 REV. CR. D.I.P. 124 (1962), 90 CLUNET 132 (1963); Allemes v. Demoiselle Auzou, Cour Paris, April 6, 1962, [1962] D.J. 617, 90 CLUNET 134 (1963), 52 REV. CR. D.I.P. 364 (1963) (note Batiffol).

On the basis of dictum appearing in Comp. algérienne de crédit et de banque v. Chemouny, *infra* note 123, Batiffol has suggested in a brief note that a court may have a duty to take judicial notice of foreign law if a question of public policy is involved. There is also dictum in the Allemes case, *supra*, implying that a court must take judicial notice of foreign law in case of fraud. *But see* Bisbal v. Dame Bisbal, *infra* note 122.

[122] *E.g.*, Belaieff v. Gillet, Cass. Civ., Jan. 7, 1929, 56 CLUNET 1248 (1929); Bisbal v. Dame Bisbal, Cass. Civ., May 12, 1959, 49 REV. CR. D.I.P. 62 (1960) (critical note Batiffol); Allemes v. Demoiselle Auzou, *supra* note 121; *cf.* BATIFFOL 391–92. In Bisbal, two Spanish nationals were able to obtain a divorce in France by not pleading Spanish law, although under French conflict of laws rules nationality governs the availability of divorce and Spanish law prohibits divorce.

[123] For recent cases in which judicial notice was taken, see Comp. algérienne de crédit et de banque v. Chemouny, Cass. Civ., March 2, 1960, 49 REV. CR. D.I.P. 97 (1960) (note H.B.), 88 CLUNET 408 (1961); Hasenpout v. Veuve Outkewicz, Cour Paris, March 18, 1954, 45 REV. CR. D.I.P. 116 (1955) (note Batiffol). See also cases cited in BATIFFOL 391; Chevallier, *Remarques sur l'utilisation par le juge de ses informations personnelles*, 61 REV. TRIM. DR. CIV. 5, at 9–10 (1962). For a general discussion, see Giuliano, *Le traitement du droit étranger dans le procès civil dans les systèmes juridiques continentaux*, 14 REVUE INTERNATIONALE DE DROIT COMPARÉ 5 (1962).

[124] See, *e.g.*, Cie Naviera Baracaldesa v. Lloyd de France, Trib. Seine, Jan. 18, 1929, 56 CLUNET 1056 (1929); *cf.* 7.31 and 7.54.a *supra*. The practice has been criticized because of the difficulty of impeaching the qualifications of the person who prepared the *certificat de coutume*. *Cf.* BATIFFOL 385 n. 8. Ordinarily, each party will submit a *certificat de coutume*, leaving it to the court to resolve any conflict.

ry evidence of the foreign law are also used, [125] especially when such evidence is immediately in point. Treatises by recognized authors may likewise be employed. [126] In a recent case, which involved complex problems of American law, the court even resorted to an *expertise,* appointing three impartial experts to examine all the documents submitted in the case and determine their validity and effect in the light of the applicable American law. [127] Oral testimony, on the other hand, is not used as a means of proof of foreign law.

Findings of courts of first instance as to the content of the applicable law are subject to review by an intermediate appellate tribunal (*cour d' appel*). [128] The *cours d'appel* and courts of first instance possess a considerable measure of freedom in determining the weight to be given to proof adduced by the parties.

The *Cour de Cassation,* treating questions of foreign law as questions of fact – which it may not examine – usually does not review findings of foreign law. [129] There are only very limited exceptions to this rule. The *Cour de Cassation* has reviewed the interpretation given by the lower courts to a decision of the Allied Control Council for Germany, perhaps on the ground that a decision of that inter-allied body was, in a sense, French law. [130] In a recent case, the *Cour de Cassation* also reversed a *cour d'appel* decision which disregarded the French text of a Belgian statute submitted by one of the parties. The *Cour de Cassation* held that the lower court had committed reversible error by "distorting" the Belgian statute. [131] Whether this decision means that the *Cour de Cas-*

[125] See, *e.g.*, Montefiore v. Colonie du Congo Belge, Cass. Civ., Nov. 21, 1961, 89 CLUNET 687 (1962) (Belgian statute); DELAUME, AMERICAN-FRENCH PRIVATE INTERNATIONAL LAW 171 (2d ed. 1961).

[126] Epoux Landauer v. Corniglion-Molinier, Cass. Civ., April 26, 1950, 77 CLUNET 1192 (1950) (French text on American law as proof of matrimonial property law of Indiana).

[127] Soc. Algérienne des pétroles Mory v. Soc. Emerson Steamship Corp., Cour Rennes, February 6, 1962, 90 CLUNET 408 (1963). The case involved the priorities of numerous creditors – French, American, and others – in a fund resulting from the sale, under order of a French court, of an American tanker subject to an American ship mortgage and various other liens. The three impartial experts were given the order to collect all pertinent documents, receive the declarations of the parties, investigate the applicable American law, determine the validity and effect of the documents (mainly the mortgage) in the light of that law, prepare a report on their findings, and file it. The case well illustrates the scope of a French *expertise.*

[128] BATIFFOL 393–97.

[129] *Ibid*; Dame Barbara v. Messina, Cass. Civ., Dec. 7, 1949, 77 CLUNET 176 (1950); De Marchi della Costa v. De Bagneux, Cass. Civ., March 7, 1938, 65 CLUNET 784 (1938); Guez v. Ben Attar, Cass. Req., November 7, 1933, 62 CLUNET 88 (1935); *cf.* 9.07 *supra.*

[130] Epoux Guinguèns v. Dlle Falk, Cass. Ass. Plén., Dec. 20, 1950, [1951] J.C.P. 2. 6058, 78 CLUNET 176 (1951).

[131] Montefiore v. Colonie du Congo Belge, *supra* note 125.

*sation* will be ready to review lower court findings as to foreign law even in a less clear situation is uncertain. [132]

Treaties on international co-operation in litigation to which France is a party occasionally contain provisions tending to simplify proof of foreign law, but these provisions do not seem to be very significant. [133]

### 3. CO-OPERATION RENDERED BY FRANCE

### 15.07. Service of Foreign Documents in France

No statute forbids the service in France of summonses, notices, and similar papers issued in connection with civil proceedings pending in foreign countries, effectuated by foreign officials, court appointees, or private persons. Furthermore, as a rule, the French government does not object to such service on any other ground. However, French courts will refuse to enforce foreign judgments unless the method of service and foreign procedure generally meet minimum standards of fairness.[134]

French authorities ordinarily stand ready to assist in the service of foreign documents in France. A request for service – together with the document to be served – may be sent to the diplomatic representative in Paris of the country in which the action is pending. He transmits both the request and the document to be served to the French Foreign Ministry, which attaches a covering form (*bordereau*) and sends both items to the *ministère public* for the district in which the person to be served resides. If no particular instructions have been given, the *ministère public* requests a local policeman or *gendarme* to effectuate service simply by delivering the document to the addressee. The policeman must ask the addressee to sign the *bordereau* and, if a duplicate of the paper to be served is to be returned, also the duplicate. The *bordereau* and any duplicate are then returned to the *ministère public*, which sends

[132] See note Goldman, *supra* note 125. For another evaluation, see Franceskakis, *La loi étrangère à la Cour de Cassation*, [1963] D. CHR. 7. A later decision is somewhat inconclusive. Chemouny v. dame Krieff, Cass. Civ., Feb. 19, 1963, 90 CLUNET 1016 (1963) (note Malaurie) (lower court may freely interpret foreign law, the *Cour de Cassation* noting that foreign law had not been "distorted").

[133] See, *e.g.*, the Agreement with Czechoslovakia, *supra* note 118, art. 16, stating that the Ministries of Justice of the two countries shall, if requested by diplomatic channels, certify whether a statute mentioned in the request is still in force.

[134] See generally BATIFFOL 850; *cf.* Cie Naviera Baracaldesa v. Lloyd de France, Trib. Seine, Jan 18, 1929, 56 CLUNET 1056 (1929) (default judgment obtained in Spain after service by publication not recognized in France, since service by publication not adequate method of notifying a defendant whose actual address is known). See also Denton v. Hall, Cour Toulouse, Jan. 29, 1872, [1872] D. 2. 236; Shepard's Bush Exhibition v. Very, Cour Paris, March 1, 1917, 44 CLUNET 1405 (1917) (English judgment based on service by private individual in France enforced).

them back to the Foreign Ministry. If the policeman cannot effectuate service, he must state the reasons on the *bordereau*. [135] French authorities will attempt to comply with requests that service be effectuated in a special manner, if that manner is not prohibited by French law.

Service of foreign documents is also regulated in a number of international conventions, the pertinent provisions of which have been discussed in connection with the service of French documents abroad. [136] The French Government seems quite willing to effectuate service in the manners prescribed by these conventions, even if the country requesting service has no treaty with France. [137]

Service through the *ministère public* and the local police is quite expeditious. No costs are involved; the services of the policeman or *gendarme* are free. [138] Nor are there any particular formal requirements An informal request by the appropriate diplomatic or consular authority is sufficient; [139] formal letters rogatory are unnecessary and, indeed, improper. [140] Absent a treaty provision to the contrary, a translation of the document to be served is not required, although it may be desirable for other reasons. [141] It is not clear whether service of documents through the *ministère public* and the police can be obtained at the request of a private litigant. Probably, a French public servant, such as an official of the *ministère public*, will insist that he be approached by a foreign official.

If a more solemn method of service than simple delivery by a police officer is required, the foreign diplomatic or consular representative may request that formal service of the document be effectuated through an *huissier*. In such a case, the local *ministère public* will instruct an *huissier* to make service. [142] This type of service is not gratuitous, however. The *huissier*'s fee – which is fairly moderate – must be paid by the

[135] JURISCLASSEUR DE DROIT INTERNATIONAL, fasc. 583, at Nos. 37–39 (1960).

[136] On service under international agreements, see JURISCLASSEUR DE DROIT INTERNATIONAL, fasc. 589 B, at No. 23 (1961); *cf.* 15.02.b *supra*. These agreements usually try to save time by permitting the transmittal of documents directly from the foreign court to the appropriate French *ministère public*. See, *e.g.*, Convention with the German Federal Republic, *supra* note 7, art. 1.

[137] *Acte judiciaire et extra-judiciaire*, in 1 DE LAPRADELLE & NIBOYET, RÉPERTOIRE DE DROIT INTERNATIONAL Nos. 67–68 (1929).

[138] JURISCLASSEUR DE DROIT INTERNATIONAL, fasc. 583, at Nos. 39 (cost), 41 (speed) (1960).

[139] The Hague Convention, *supra* note 5, art. 1, requires that requests for service indicate the names of the parties, the capacity in which they act, the authority which has issued the paper to be served, the nature of the paper, and the address of the recipient.

[140] Letters rogatory may be used only in connection with proof proceedings. See 1 DALLOZ, RÉPERTOIRE DE PROCÉDURE CIVILE ET COMMERCIALE, *Commission Rogatoire*, Nos. 6–10 (1955).

[141] JURISCLASSEUR DE DROIT INTERNATIONAL, fasc. 583, at No. 41 (1960).

[142] JURISCLASSEUR DE DROIT INTERNATIONAL, fasc. 589 B, at No. 25 (1961).

authority requesting service. In addition, stamp and registration taxes may be due on documents served by the *huissier*. Payment of these expenses must be guaranteed when service is requested. Ordinarily, it will also be necessary to supply a French translation of the document to be served, attested either by a French "sworn" interpreter or by a diplomatic or consular representative of the country from which the document emanates. [143] In making service, the *huissier*, as a quasi-public French officer, will follow French law; he will serve a copy, file the original in his office, and return the duplicate original. [144] Hence, absent a different treaty rule, it is advisable to supply at least three copies of the paper to be served and of the translation. When service is effectuated through an *huissier*, the *huissier*'s certificate constitutes the official proof of service which is returned to the requesting authority.[145] Service through an *huissier* is the standard method of service under the Anglo-French treaty, unless resort is had to service by a consular officer. [146]

Private litigants may also approach a French *huissier* directly and ask him to serve a document. [147] Some international agreements expressly sanction this practice. [148]

The Hague Convention permits the mailing of documents from the state in which the action is pending directly to the person to be served in another contracting state, "provided the state of destination does not object." [149] In a number of cases, French courts have stated that France does not object to this type of service and have enforced foreign judgments rendered after the defendant in France had been served by

[143] See, *e.g.*, Circular of the Ministry of Justice of May 20, 1925, *supra* note 4. The circular deals specifically with relations between France and Austria, but seems to state a rule of general applicability. Presumably, a translation attested by a French consulate in the country of origin of the paper would also be satisfactory. The rules indicated are sometimes modified by treaty. Thus, in the case of documents coming from Germany, the French authorities will prepare a translation, but the costs of translation must be reimbursed. Convention with Germany, *supra* note 7, art. 3.

On the *huissier's* fee, see 12.03.b *supra*. On the taxes that must be paid, see 7.02.a *supra*. Since the stamp tax varies with the size of paper, it is advisable to use standard letter size paper rather than American legal size paper.

[144] See 7.02.b *supra*.

[145] JURISCLASSEUR DE DROIT INTERNATIONAL, fasc. 583, at No. 39 (1960).

[146] Convention with Great Britain, *supra* note 7, arts. 3–4.

[147] See LEREBOURS-PIGEONNIÈRE, DROIT INTERNATIONAL PRIVÉ 459 (7th ed. 1959).

[148] See, *e.g.*, Protocol with Algeria, *supra* note 9, art. 25; Convention with Cameroon, *supra* note 9, art. 5; Convention with the Ivory Coast, *supra* note 9, art. 28.

[149] The Hague Convention, *supra* note 5, art. 6. On other agreements providing expressly for service by mail, see JURISCLASSEUR DE DROIT INTERNATIONAL, fasc. 589 B, at No. 27 (1961).

mail. [150] It may be assumed that there will, likewise, be no objection if a summons in a civil action is mailed into France from a country which is not a signatory of the Hague Convention.

A number of treaties specifically authorize consuls to serve process in civil actions on their own nationals. Agreements with Austria, Czechoslovakia, Great Britain, and The Netherlands authorize consuls to serve any person in France, including French nationals. [151]

### 15.08. Taking Testimony in France for Use in a Foreign Country

**a. Without intervention of French authorities.** No statute regulates the taking of testimony in France in connection with a civil case pending in a foreign country.

Testimony for use in foreign civil proceedings may be taken either before a private person or before a foreign consul or court appointee. As a rule, the French Government has not objected to any of these manners of taking testimony. [152] Although the Consular Convention of 1853 between France and the United States authorizes consuls merely to take the "declarations" of their own nationals, [153] American consuls have freely examined nationals of countries other than the United States. [154] When persons holding an official or quasi-official position are to be examined, the permission of the French Government must, however, be obtained. [155]

[150] Société S.E.O. v. Pons, Trib. Gde Inst. Seine, Dec. 8, 1959, 87 CLUNET 1068 (1960); *cf.* S.A. Wouters et Cie v. Robert-Bérin, Trib. Gde Inst. Seine, Dec. 12, 1961, 89 CLUNET 1032 (1962).

[151] JURISCLASSEUR DE DROIT INTERNATIONAL, fasc. 589 B, at No. 26 (1961). See also Agreements referred to in note 32 *supra.*

[152] There is authority to the effect that the taking of testimony by private persons for use in litigation pending outside France may be a violation of French sovereignty. Japiot, *Commission Rogatoire*, in 4 DE LAPRADELLE & NIBOYET, RÉPERTOIRE DE DROIT INTERNATIONAL 73 (1929); Gavalda, *Les commissions rogatoires internationales en matière civile et commerciale*, 53 REV. CR. D.I.P. 15, 33 (1964). However, there appears to be no recorded instance in which the French government has objected to the taking of depositions before a private individual.

The French government does not object to the taking of depositions by foreign consuls, at least when, as in the case of the United States, French consuls are given similar rights. Gavalda, *supra* at 32 n. 2; JURISCLASSEUR DE DROIT INTERNATIONAL, fasc. 589 B, at No. 44 (1961). At one time, though, the French Ministry of Justice seems to have taken the position that consuls may not take depositions in France, absent a treaty. Japiot, *supra* at 79.

In the ten-month period from January through October 1963, the American Embassy in Paris took 29 depositions of French as well as American nationals. The French government has voiced no objections. Information supplied by the American Embassy in Paris by letter dated October 31, 1963.

[153] See Convention, *supra* note 12, art. VI.

[154] See note 152 *supra.*

[155] *Cf.* People v. Lothringer, N.Y.L.J. Aug. 20, 1963, p. 8 (Sup. Ct. Queens Co.) (French authorities refused to permit officials involved in extradition proceeding to give testimony before the United States consul pursuant to order of New York court).

A foreign consular officer may not use compulsion in taking testimony in France. Furthermore, perjury before a foreign consular official is probably not a crime under French law. [156]

**b. Execution of letters rogatory.** Testimonial evidence for use in civil proceedings abroad may also be requested by letters rogatory. France is a party to a number of international agreements under which the execution of letters rogatory is mandatory. [157] However, even in the absence of a treaty, French courts and public authorities ordinarily comply with requests for the taking of testimony issued out of foreign countries. They will refuse to execute such letters only: (1) if the foreign court lacks adjudicatory power; [158] (2) if the action violates French public policy; [159] or (3) if the security and sovereignty of France may be endangered by the execution of the letters. [160] The significance of the last two exceptions is probably quite limited. However, the requirement that the foreign courts have adjudicatory power in accordance with pertinent French concepts – if followed consistently – may limit the availability of letters rogatory, since, under French law, a foreign court rarely has such power in an action in which one of the parties is a French national. [161]

Letters rogatory must be addressed to the *tribunal de grande instance* for the district in which the witness to be heard lives. Unless a treaty provides for a more expeditious method of transmittal, they must be submitted to the French Foreign Ministry by the diplomatic representative of the country requesting assistance. American litigants wishing to obtain evidence in France must submit the letters to the

[156] See *Les auteurs d'une déposition mensongère faite en France sous la forme d'un affidavit devant le consul des Etats Unis ou devant un notaire français peuvent-ils être poursuivis en France par la juridiction répressive?*, 57 Clunet 254 (1930); *cf.* Jones, *Letters Rogatory in Federal Practice*, in Letters Rogatory 73, 76 (Grossman ed. 1956).

[157] See, *e.g.*, treaties mentioned in note 7 *supra*.

[158] Gavilloux v. Dlle H., Trib. Gde Inst. Seine, March 29, 1960, [1961] J.C.P. II. 12161 (no execution of letters rogatory issued by Swiss court not competent under French-Swiss agreement on judicial competence).

[159] The scope of this restriction is not clear. In B. v. Z., Trib. Boulogne, Aug. 14, 1908, 37 Clunet 818 (1910), a French court refused to execute letters rogatory in a paternity case on the ground that paternity actions violated French public policy. Less than a year later, another court came to the opposite conclusion. Ramsdorf, Trib. St. Malo, July 15, 1909, 38 Clunet 190 (1911). Since French internal restrictions on paternity actions were eased in 1912 and again in 1955, it is quite unlikely that a French court would now refuse to execute letters rogatory in filiation proceedings. *Cf.* Batiffol 809 (public policy exception to have very limited application in connection with execution of letters rogatory).

[160] Jurisclasseur de Droit International, fasc. 589 B, at no. 47 (1961).

[161] See 4.03–4.07 *supra*.

United States Department of State together with a deposit to cover the fee charged for the transmittal of the documents. [162]

The French Foreign Ministry refers all incoming letters rogatory to the Ministry of Justice, which forwards them to the *ministère public* attached to the *tribunal de grande instance* to which they are addressed. The *ministère public* checks whether that court is territorially competent; if it is not, the *ministère public* forwards the letters to the proper court and so informs the requesting authority. It also checks whether the letters are accompanied by a translation and, in the event the execution of the letters is not free of charge, whether there is an undertaking to reimburse the French Republic for costs incurred. Furthermore, the *ministère public* makes sure that execution of the letters will not infringe on French sovereignty, security, or public policy. [163]

Although the overwhelming majority of letters rogatory is executed without question, their transmittal by the *ministère public* does not mean that the court is bound to execute them. The court may still determine that their execution would violate French public policy or be otherwise illegal. [164]

A French court which has received letters rogatory may be requested not to execute them either in a formal declaratory judgment proceeding or in a petition to the presiding judge of the court sitting *en référé*. [165] Letters rogatory may be, but rarely are, submitted through French *avoués* instead of through diplomatic channels. [166]

Incoming letters rogatory are always transmitted to the *président* of the court. He assigns one of the judges of his court to execute them. In Paris, the execution of letters rogatory is usually assigned to the same judge, who is an expert in these matters. The judge, by order, sets a day for the execution of the letters. He usually tries to comply with

[162] On applicable American procedures, see SMIT & MILLER, *op. cit. supra* note 62, at 52–54.

[163] 1 DALLOZ, RÉPERTOIRE DE PROCÉDURE CIVILE ET COMMERCIALE, *Commission Rogatoire*, No. 61 (1955); JURISCLASSEUR DE DROIT INTERNATIONAL, fasc. 589 B, at No. 46 (1961). Some control is also exercised by the Ministry of Foreign Affairs and the Ministry of Justice. The translation should ordinarily be provided by the foreign court, but if letters rogatory are submitted to the French Ministry of Foreign Affairs without a translation, the latter will sometimes supply one.

[164] *E.g.*, Bemberg v. Représentant du Fisc de Buenos Aires, Trib. Seine, Feb. 24, 1949, 39 REV. CR. D.I.P. 627 (1950) (note Loussouarn), [1949] S. 2. 101 (note Niboyet) (court refused to examine books of French company as requested by Argentine fiscal authorities because use of letters rogatory for tax purposes would violate French public policy).

[165] For an example of a *référé* proceeding, see Bemberg v. Représentant du Fisc de Buenos Aires, *supra* note 164. For an example of a plenary action, see Gavilloux v. dlle H., *supra* note 158. Some treaties provide that difficulties arising in execution of letters rogatory shall be settled diplomatically.

[166] GOYET, LE MINISTERE PUBLIC 254 (3d ed. 1955). For a rare case in which an *avoué* submitted a letter rogatory, see Ramsdorf, *supra* note 159.

any reasonable request for a date convenient to the witness. If the parties are to be represented by counsel, an attempt will be made to select a date convenient to counsel as well. The American Embassy in Paris is willing to assist American counsel in making necessary arrangements.[167] After the day for the execution of letters has been determined, the judge returns the file to the *ministère public*. The *ministère public* then sends notices to the witnesses asking them to appear at the appointed time. These notices are delivered to their addressees by the police. After the notices have been sent out, the file is returned to the court. Failure to appear does not carry a penalty, although most witnesses appear or at least inform the court why they cannot come. If necessary, the hearing is rescheduled by the judge. If a witness fails to appear without giving any reason for his absence, the letters are returned to the requesting authority. If the requesting authority again asks that the witness be heard and demands that the measures of compulsion provided by French law be applied, the witness is treated as a recalcitrant witness in a French civil proceeding: He may be fined or even be physically brought to court by the police.[168] It is not entirely clear whether this somewhat lengthy procedure is necessary. French courts are probably willing to employ means of coercion immediately, if the original letters rogatory specify clearly that coercion should at once be applied against recalcitrant witnesses. If such a request is made, it is prudent to include an undertaking to reimburse the French Government for any expenses caused by the imposition of coercive measures.

An examination of witnesses pursuant to letters rogatory is always conducted by the appointed judge, assisted by a *greffier* (clerk). Counsel for the parties may be present, but in fact rarely are. The judge first asks the witness for his name and other personal data, verifies these by requesting identification papers, and dictates the witness' name and personal data to the clerk. The clerk takes these down at once by typewriter. French courts attempt to apply the rules regarding privileged communications and incapacities to testify that are in force where the action is pending. Most civil-law countries therefore include an excerpt from their statutes governing privileged communications with letters rogatory sent to France. The judge reads these statutes to the witness and asks if they apply to him. If the witness replies in the affirmative,

[167] See letter of October 31, 1963, *supra* note 152.

[168] *Cf.* JURISCLASSEUR DE DROIT INTERNATIONAL, fasc. 589 B, at No. 48 (1961). On measures of coercion against recalcitrant witnesses in civil cases, see CODE DE PROCÉDURE CIVILE art. 269.

he is excused. On the other hand, it seems certain that the French court will not permit a physician or other person who has received a confidential communication in a professional capacity to reveal it even if the information is not privileged where the action is pending. The disclosure of such communications is prohibited by the French Penal Code. [169] It is also unclear whether French courts will examine parties under oath as witnesses. [170]

Following these preliminaries, the witness is sworn. He promises to "speak the truth," and is liable to rather severe punishment if he lies.[171] After the witness has been sworn, the judge begins his interrogation. Courts from other civil-law countries generally limit themselves to a general indication of the topic to be inquired into, so that the judge asking the questions usually does a considerable amount of independent probing. The judge dictates each answer to the clerk, who takes it down on his typewriter. The answer is not summarized, but reproduced rather fully; nevertheless, the judge has a tendency to polish the answer to make it clearer and more literate.

If requested to do so, French courts may apply special procedures as long as these are not illegal in France. [172] Thus, if an appropriate request to that effect is contained in letters rogatory, they will examine witnesses pursuant to detailed interrogatories and cross-interrogatories and dictate to the clerk the precise answers given. Since the answers of witnesses are dictated not to a stenographer but directly to a clerk equipped with a typewriter, the interrogatories should be framed so that they can be answered in rather brief sentences.

It is far less certain whether French judges would permit counsel for the parties to examine and cross-examine witnesses orally. This procedure is definitely not permitted in French civil cases, in which the witness must always be interrogated by the court. If an attorney wishes to put a question to the witness, he must submit the question to the judge and request the judge to ask it. [173]

After the interrogation is over, the answers are read to the witness,

[169] CODE PÉNAL art. 378; *cf.* 7.51.b *supra*.

[170] This procedure is unknown under French law. Since parties may be examined (but not put onder oath) in the *comparution personnelle* procedure and may be asked to take the so-called decisory oath, the examination of parties as witnesses would probably not be considered a violation of public policy. French courts will also ask a party to take the decisory oath if requested to do so by letters rogatory. For an example, see Ramsdorf, *supra* note 159.

[171] On the form of the oath in civil cases, see CODE DE PROCÉDURE CIVILE art. 283. On the penalty for perjury in civil and administrative cases, see 7.51.c n. 556 *supra*.

[172] JURISCLASSEUR DE DROIT INTERNATIONAL, fasc. 583, at No. 21 (1960).

[173] CODE DE PROCÉDURE CIVILE art. 265; *cf.* 7.51.c *supra*. With special permission, a foreign attorney may appear in a French court if he is assisted by a French *avocat*.

and he is asked if he wishes to make any changes. If he does, the changes are made in the appropriate places and are initialled by the witness, the judge, and the clerk. The entire deposition, prepared in duplicate, is then signed by all the participants. If the witness demands his witness fee, the court must see to it that it is paid by the *receveur* (the appropriate official of the French treasury). Under some treaties, the sum paid may be recovered from the foreign country involved. [174]

Completed depositions are returned to the *ministère public* from where they are transmitted to the diplomatic representative of the requesting country by way of the French Ministries of Justice and of Foreign Affairs. If a treaty provides for a more direct method of return, it is, of course, used. [175]

France does not charge any fees for the execution of letters rogatory unless the requesting country asks that the depositions be taken in some special manner. In that event, the costs must be borne by the requesting country. [176] A request to follow submitted interrogatories strictly and to dictate answers verbatim would probably not give rise to special costs. Sometimes, the question of costs is regulated by treaty. [177]

## 15.09. Obtaining Tangible Evidence in France for Use in a Foreign Country

Voluntary production of tangible evidence in France in connection with civil proceedings pending in a foreign country is lawful as long as French penal laws, such as those prohibiting the disclosure of confidential information acquired in a professional capacity [178] or the disclosure of national defense secrets, [179] are not violated. To the extent warranted by the applicable foreign procedural rules [180] persons asked to appear before a foreign consul in France to give testimony by way of a deposition may also be requested to produce documents in their possession. [181]

[174] JURISCLASSEUR DE DROIT INTERNATIONAL, fasc. 589 B, at No. 50 (1961); *cf.* CODE DE PROCÉDURE CIVILE art. 279. The witness fee is 5,50 francs (about $ 1.10). Travel expenses may also have to be paid. CODE DE PROCÉDURE PÉNALE arts. R. 129–38.

[175] JURISCLASSEUR DE DROIT INTERNATIONAL, fasc. 589 B, at No. 48 (1961).

[176] See, *e.g.*, The Hague Convention, *supra* note 5, art. 16.

[177] See text at note 94 *supra*.

[178] CODE PÉNAL art. 378.

[179] CODE PÉNAL arts. 75–78 (forbidding disclosure of secrets relating to national defense).

[180] See Smit, *International Aspects of Federal Civil Procedure*, 61 COLUM. L. REV. 1031, 1053–54 (1961).

[181] The Agreement with Great Britain, *supra* note 7, art. 7, expressly sanctions this practice.

When tangible evidence is not produced voluntarily, recourse to letters rogatory may become necessary. Unfortunately, French methods for compelling the production of documentary and other tangible evidence are rather restricted.

Since witnesses in domestic French cases may be asked to produce tangible evidence in their hands when testifying, it is presumably possible to obtain the production of documents when the examination of witnesses takes place pursuant to letters rogatory. Likewise, the production of commercial books of account is probably obtainable in France, since French judges are likely to analogize such a request to a demand for the *représentation* of books of account which is possible under French law. It is not clear whether French courts will compel the production of other tangible evidence in the hands of parties or third persons not witnesses, except in the limited cases in which this is permissible under internal French rules.

### 15.10. Obtaining Proof of French Official Records

The most important public records kept in France are the birth, marriage, and death records, collectively known as *actes de l'état civil.* [182]

There is no separate public register indicating under what matrimonial property regime (community property, separate property, and their variations) spouses are married. However, the marriage record indicates whether they have concluded an ante-nuptial agreement, and if so, before what notary, and at what time. [183] Further inquiries can then be made at the appropriate notary's office.

Land records are kept by an official called (somewhat inappropriately) *conservateur des hypothèques*. These records resemble American land records more than a German *Grundbuch*: [184] Entry in the land records serves mainly as a notice to third parties rather than as a means of transfer of title. Full copies of the actual documents are kept only in the case of transfers of title; documents creating liens or mortgages are

[182] See 7.35 *supra*. For a brief description of *actes de l'état civil* in English, see also AMOS & WALTON, INTRODUCTION TO FRENCH LAW 37 (2d ed. 1963).

[183] CODE CIVIL art. 76. Standard community property rules apply to couples who have not entered into an ante-nuptial agreement (*contrat de marriage*). Until recently, modification of the contract after marriage was not possible. See CODE CIVIL arts. 1387–98.

[184] *Conservateur des hypothèques* means, literally, preserver of mortgages. Originally, only mortgages were recorded in France. For a brief description of the French system, see AMOS & WALTON, *op. cit. supra* note 182, at 106–09, and 1 COLIN & CAPITANT 7–14. The German system, somewhat modified, is in force in the Alsace-Lorraine region of France.

recorded in summary form.[185] To facilitate access to the records, owner and property (lot) indexes are kept on card files.[186] Only notarial documents may be recorded in France. Notarial documents prepared by foreign notaries must be authenticated by a French consul and deposited with a French notary before they can be used.[187]

Another important repository of public records is the commercial court at which the *registre du commerce* (commercial register) is kept. This register lists all individuals in the district who qualify as *commerçants* (merchants) under French law, and also all companies of the district, and all branches of companies located elsewhere. Foreign corporations having a branch in France must be registered.[188] Fairly detailed indications must be given in connection with the registration of each commercial enterprise.[189] Corporations must also file their articles of incorporation (*actes de société*) in the clerk's office of the appropriate *tribunal de commerce*.[190]

An office called *Institut National de la Propriété Industrielle* (National Institute of Industrial Property) now maintains central records duplicating those kept in commercial courts and makes it possible to obtain information on business enterprise throughout France.[191] Official

[185] The inscription (recording of a summary) of liens and mortgages is governed principally by CODE CIVIL arts. 2146–54. The general rules concerning the French land records system and the transcription (recording, or rather filing and indexing) of the entire documents transferring ownership or similar interests are contained in DÉCRET No. 55–22 of Jan. 4, 1955, J.O. Jan. 7, 1955, p. 346, [1955] D.L. 44, since amended in details.

[186] DÉCRET No. 55–22, *supra* note 185, art. 1.

[187] DÉCRET No. 55–22, *supra* note 185, art. 4, as amended by DÉCRET No. 59–89 of Jan. 7, 1959, J.O. Jan. 8, 1959, p. 579, [1959] D.L. 239. On mortgages, see CODE CIVIL arts. 2127–28. When documents prepared by foreign notaries are involved, the paper actually recorded is a copy of the foreign original prepared by the notary with whom the original has been deposited. It should be remembered that in foreign countries French consular officers may exercise notarial functions. See DÉCRET No. 62–1461, *supra* note 3.

[188] DÉCRET No. 58–1355 of Dec. 27, 1958, J.O. Dec. 29, 1958, p. 11971, [1959] D.L. 137, arts. 1–3. Physical persons must register in the clerk's office of the court competent for the district in which they have their main establishment; companies (*sociétés*) where their *siège social, i.e.*, their administrative center, is located. Supplemental registration is required in each district in which branch establishments are located. DÉCRET No. 58–1355, *supra*, art. 5; *cf.* 3.26, 4.39.b *supra*.

[189] These include information on the identity, nationality, capacity of the registrant, and the matrimonial property regime under which he is married, the name under which the enterprise is operated, its location and "... all other elements of the legal position of the registrant, and of his commercial activities which third parties need to know in order to deal with him in all security or the publication of which is in the general interest." DÉCRET No. 58–1355, *supra* note 188, art. 6. More detailed specifications are contained in regulations supplementing the *Décret*. The commercial register indicates (among other things) who has a general power to bind the firm involved.

[190] Law of July 24, 1867, on *sociétés par actions*, (1867) BULL. DES LOIS No. 45328, [1867] D. 4. 98, arts. 55–64; Law of March 7, 1925, as amended, on *sociétés à responsabilité limitée*, J.O. March 8, 1925, (1921–1925) S. LOIS ANNOT. 1801, art. 12. The requirement of filing of *actes de société* applies only to *sociétés anonymes* and *sociétés à responsabilité limitée*.

[191] DÉCRET No. 58–1355, *supra* note 188, art. 2.

registers of patents and trademarks are also kept by the *Institut National de la Propriété Industrielle*, which, in addition, maintains files of designs and models. It publishes an official bulletin for its announcements (*Bulletin officiel de la propriété industrielle*). [192]

Usually, any person willing to pay the appropriate fee may obtain a copy of a public record kept in France. However, some important special rules exist. In order to avoid embarrassment to illegitimate children, complete copies of birth and marriage records are available only to the parties therein mentioned, their descendants, ascendants, spouses, guardians, or committees (*tuteurs*). Other persons need a court order if they wish to obtain a complete copy. [193] However, anybody can obtain an *extrait* (summary) of any birth or marriage record. In the case of a birth record, the summary indicates the name of the child, the date and place of its birth, and, if possible, the date of the child's marriage; the summary of the marriage record indicates the name of the spouses, their birth places and dates, their occupations, the date and place of the marriage, and the existence of an ante-nuptial agreement. [194] Somewhat more detailed summaries may be issued without order to heirs of parties and public officials or agencies. [195] Copies of death records may be issued to anybody without court order. [196]

Anybody may obtain copies or summaries of matters recorded in the commercial registers and of articles of incorporation, with unimportant exceptions. In an appropriate case, a certificate that no entry could be found will also be issued. [197]

Court clerks must deliver copies of judgments to any person. [198] Copies of other documents filed in a civil action may be obtained only by the parties, except on court order. Copies of other papers filed in

[192] Law No. 51–444 of April 19, 1951, J.O. April 20, 1951, p. 3964, [1951] D.L. 104, as supplemented by DÉCRET No. 51–1469 of Dec. 22, 1951, J.O. Dec. 27, 1951, p. 12934, [1952] D.L. 29. French legislation on designs is reprinted in *France*, in 1 DESIGN LAWS AND TREATIES OF THE WORLD (1960).

[193] DÉCRET No. 62–921, *supra* note 99, art. 9. Application to obtain a complete copy must be made to the judge of the local *tribunal d'instance*; if he refuses, it may be referred to the presiding judge of the competent *tribunal de grande instance* using the *référé* procedure.

[194] DÉCRET No. 62–921, *supra* note 99, art. 10.

[195] DÉCRET No. 62–921, *supra* note 99, art. 1.

[196] DÉCRET No. 62–921, *supra* note 99, art. 9.

[197] DÉCRET No. 54–37 of Jan. 6, 1954, J.O. Jan. 14, 1954, p. 565, [1954] D.L. 78, art. 23. These may be obtained either from the clerk of the competent commercial court (for enterprises in his district) or from the *Institut national de la propriété industrielle* for enterprises anywhere in France. However, generally speaking, no information on enterprises registered before 1953 can be obtained from the latter office.

[198] CODE DE PROCÉDURE CIVILE art. 1040.

criminal cases may be obtained only with the consent of the public prosecutor (*procureur de la République* or *procureur général*). [199]

Notaries must deliver copies of papers in their custody to the parties and their successors or assigns; they may deliver copies to other persons only pursuant to court order. [200]

Public records or copies of such records are ordinarily signed by the official who keeps them or one of his deputies, and bear the seal of his office. The judges of the *tribunaux d'instance* and the presiding judges of the *tribunaux de grande instance* are authorized to authenticate the signatures of notaries and of officials keeping birth, death, and marriage records (*officiers de l'état civil*) in their districts. [201] Since officials of the *ministère public* attached to the various *tribunaux de grande instance* in France supervise court clerks, *notaires* (notaries), and *officiers de l'état civil* in their districts, questions that foreign officials might have concerning the genuineness of the signature on a document presented to them for authentication, or concerning the actual office held by the signatory, are best directed to the appropriate *ministère public.* [202]

### 15.11. Proof of French Law

At present, all French statutory and quasi-statutory materials (*lois* and *décrets*) must be published in the French official gazette, the *Journal Officiel.* This publication indicates on its face that it is an official publication of the French Republic. [203]

It will generally be very difficult to obtain official editions of older statutes, however. The last official edition of the Civil Code, for instance, dates from 1816. [204] All decisions of the *Cour de Cassation* in civil cases are presently published officially in its *Bulletin,* but only a fraction of the criminal decisions are published, and before 1947 even decisions in civil cases were published only on a limited basis. [205] Decisions of the lower courts are not usually published officially, and de-

[199] CODE DE PROCÉDURE PÉNALE arts. R. 155–56. In criminal cases, even the parties need the approval of the *procureur* to obtain copies of documents other than judgments and the initial complaint.

[200] See notes 98–99 *supra.*

[201] Law of May 2, 1861, [1861] D. 4. 54.

[202] *Cf.* GOYET, LE MINISTÈRE PUBLIC 49 (3d ed. 1955).

[203] The *Journal Officiel* has been published since 1871. Until 1931, statutes were also officially reprinted in the *Bulletin des Lois.* For a listing of the various official publications which contained French statutes from 1799 to date, see SZLADITS, A GUIDE TO FOREIGN LEGAL MATERIALS 56 n. 37 (1959).

[204] See CODE CIVIL ii (63d ed. Dalloz 1964).

[205] See 3.32.i *supra.*

cisions of the *Conseil d'Etat* (highest tribunal in administrative matters) are published only in a semi-official edition.[206]

In actual practice, official publications are used infrequently by French practitioners and judges. The latter prefer instead to rely on the reporting services of private law publishers.[207]

No agency in France is authorized to furnish official certificates concerning French law, except in a very limited sense: French consuls may, on request, furnish a citation to a French statutory text directly relating to the inquiry, but without making any personal comment.[208]

[206] On French law reports, see SZLADITZ, *op. cit. supra* note 203, at 61–77, and 1.38 *supra*.
[207] See 1.38 *supra*.
[208] DÉCRET No. 46–2390, *supra* note 3, art. 7.

# APPENDIXES

APPENDIX

# SAMPLE PROCEDURAL DOCUMENTS *

This appendix contains a number of procedural documents, most of which relate to two actual cases: (1) an action between the owners of two adjoining apartment houses, involving as additional parties some of the owners of individual apartments purchased under a condominium-type arrangement, and (2) a divorce action. The English translations of the documents endeavor to preserve as much as possible their French style.

The names of the parties and their attorneys, as well as the dates, have been changed. In actual practice, ordinary letter-size paper without a backing is usually used for these documents.

* The compilation of this appendix has been made possible by the co-operation of *Maître* RENÉ DESPRÉS, *avoué* at the *Cour d'Appel* in Paris, *Maître* JEAN LOT, *greffier titulaire de charge* of the *Cour d'Appel* in Paris, *Maître* JEAN PONELLE, *avoué* at the *Tribunal de Grande Instance* in Paris, and *Maître* JULIETTE VEILLER-DURAY, *avocat* at the *Cour d'Appel* in Paris. Their kind assistance is gratefully acknowledged.

## Form No. 1

## *ASSIGNATION* OR *AJOURNEMENT*[1]

In the margin:
(1) Tax stamp
(2) Rubber stamp of *huissier* and of *avoué*
(3) Computation of fee for stamps

Madame Rivière
v.
Boulevard Roses Building Co.

In the year one thousand nine-hundred fifty-eight, on the thirtieth of June, at the request of Mrs. Suzanne Rivière, domiciled at Rennes, for whom a domicile is elected at Paris, 7 rue des Camélias, at the office of *Maître* Pierre Blanc, *avoué* at the court of first instance in Paris, who appears for her and will represent her in connection with this writ and its consequences,

I, the undersigned André Bontemps, *Huissier* at the court of first instance in Paris, and residing in that city at No. 5, rue de Genève, have summoned: the Boulevard Roses Building Co., whose seat is at 1 Boulevard Roses, in the person of its legal representative living at the said seat, where I have gone and, in the absence of any official of the said company, spoken to the janitor, who admitted to be such,

to appear in eight "free" days, as prescribed by law, through an *avoué* duly appointed, at a hearing before the President and judges of the court of first instance at Paris, in the regular courtroom for the said hearings, in the Palace of Justice in Paris, at the hour of noon (and otherwise a default shall be taken at once), in order to:

Whereas Mrs. Rivière is the owner of a building located at Paris, 3 Boulevard Roses, which she inherited from Mr. Rivière, her predecessor in title, who had acquired the property by a notarial instrument drawn by Mr. Merlin, notary, the second of June 1895, and had built the building which stands there now,

Whereas in the course of the year 1951 the Boulevard Roses Building Co. began construction work at 1 Boulevard Roses,

Whereas, *first of all*, that it appeared that the location of the said building involved an error and encroached upon the frontage of 3 Boulevard Roses,

Whereas the two adjoining landowners agreed, through the intermediary of their architects, to instruct Mr. Compas and Mr. Tangent, surveyors, to establish the exact boundary line,

Whereas they rendered their formal report the fourth of April 1954 and over the objections raised by the Boulevard Roses Building Co., confirmed their report, to wit, that the latter company has encroached, with its building, by 20 and 20/100 square meters on the property of 3 Boulevard Roses, *i.e.*, 1 meter on a depth of 19 meter and 50/100 towards No. 1 and 20 meter 90/100 towards No. 3,

That the 17 meter frontage has been reduced to 16 meters,

Whereas, until to-day, in spite of numerous friendly requests, the plaintiff has not been able to obtain compensation for its loss, which, in view of the value of the land, cannot be less than twenty thousand francs,

Whereas, *in the second place*, the Boulevard Roses Building Co. has increased the height of the party wall by one story, which has serious consequences,

Whereas excavations have been made underneath a wall belonging to the plaintiff in order to establish foundations which are deeper, and it is absolutely necessary for the plaintiff to receive complete assurances, all the while reserving her rights,

Whereas, on the other hand, the chimneys of No. 3 now have a poor draft, so

[1] On the contents and function of this document, see 7.02 *supra*.

that the plaintiff will undoubtedly be compelled to build them up to the level of the new building,

Whereas the plaintiff is well justified to demand, on account of the said increase in height, 5000 francs of damages on a provisional basis, and the appointment of an expert to determine the amount of damage done, the nature and quality of the objectionable construction work, and the prejudicial consequences it has,

FOR THESE REASONS:

May the court declare that Mrs. Rivière's action is well-founded and properly brought,

Grant an award of damages against the Boulevard Roses Building Co. in favor of Mrs. Rivière for twenty thousand francs for the harm caused by the encroachment of 20 and 20/100 square meters upon land belonging to Mrs. Rivière at 3 Boulevard Roses,

Grant an award of provisional damages in favor of Mrs. Rivière of five thousand francs for the damage caused by the increase in height of the partition wall,

Grant the appointment of such expert as the Presiding Judge may be pleased to appoint, who in case of unavailability or refusal to serve shall be replaced upon a simple *ex parte* petition, and whose duty it shall be to examine the incriminated construction, elevation in height of the wall, and excavation underneath the party wall, to say whether they are executed in conformity with an approved practice, establish the prejudice they have caused to the building at 3 Boulevard Roses, hear the parties in their allegations and explanations, reconcile them if possible, and if not, file a report at the court clerk's office, so that the parties may claim, and the court decide what shall be right.

Award all costs against the Boulevard Roses Building Co.

And we reserve all our rights most expressly.

And may they not ignore it.

And talking to the person mentioned above, I have left him a copy of the above in a closed envelope bearing on one side only the name and address of the defendant and on the other only the seal of my office, and I have signed, in accordance with law, the indications given above relating to service

(signed) André Bontemps

Cost 480 francs

Used for the copy, two sheets of stamp size paper

(signed) André Bontemps

### Form No. 2

## NOTICE OF APPEARANCE [1]

*Maître* . . . , [2] *avoué* at the court of first instance in Paris, announces to *Maître* . . . , [3] *avoué* at the same court and representing . . . , [4]
That he has received the power and obligation to represent and appears for . . . , [5]
In connection with the writ served upon him on the . . . 19. . by . . . , [6] *huissier*,
Without, however, in any way approving the claim contained in the said writ, but on the contrary, reserving most expressly all procedural and substantive defenses, affirmative and otherwise, on the facts as well as on the law.

And may he not ignore it.
Of which we give you notice.

*Maître* . . . [7]

On the other side, the return of service will be endorsed as follows by means of a rubber stamp: [8]

I, the undersigned *huissier-audiencier*, have served this document upon, and left a copy with, *Maître* . . . , [9] at his domicile by speaking to his clerk.

. . . [10]

[1] Through this form, which is generally printed or mimeographed, defendant's *avoué* notifies plaintiff's *avoué* that he appears for defendant.

[2] Name of defendant's *avoué*.

[3] Name of plaintiff's *avoué*.

[4] Plaintiff's name, address, and occupation.

[5] Defendant's name, address, and occupation.

[6] Name of *huissier* who served the *ajournement* on plaintiff.

[7] Name and address of *avoué* appearing for defendant.

[8] Notices of appearance and most other documents exchanged in the course of litigation with the exeption of *ajournements*, judgments, and notices of appeal) are served by *avoués* upon each other through a *huissier-audiencier*. In practice, the *huissier-audiencier* merely deposits such documents (collectively known as *actes du palais*) in the mailbox which each *avoué* has in the court house.

[9] Name of plaintiff's *avoué*.

[10] Signature of *huissier*, and date.

### Form No. 3

***PLACET*** [1]

| | | |
|---|---|---|
| Case distributed<br>to the ... panel<br>on ... 19..<br>No. | Filed in the clerks' office:<br>... | Variable fee<br>evaluated at ...<br>times the fixed fee<br>or ... francs.<br>The Treasurer of<br>the Association of<br>*Avoués*. |

## Request for a Hearing

For ... [2]

Nature of the claim
or matter: ...

Date of the writ: ...

Name of *huissier*: ...

Object of claim: ...

Amount in controversy,
calculated or
evaluated: ...

or

[In this space, the *avoué* of the party asking that the case be put on the calendar recopies his original *conclusions*]

Hearing fee: ...

Hearing date: ...

Reporting Judge: ...

Date of Judgment: ... 19..

General Calendar No.: ...

*Maître* ... [3]

[1] This so-called *placet* must be filed in the court clerk's office, in order to place the case on the calendar. A standard printed form is used. On the *placet*, see also 7.05 *supra*.

[2] Here, the name of plaintiff or other party requesting that the case be put on the calendar is inserted.

[3] Name of plaintiff's *avoué*.

### Form No. 4

## NOTICE OF LISTING ON THE CALENDAR[1]

Clerk's Office of the Court of First Instance of the Seine

| | |
|---|---|
| For ... [2] | *Maître* ... [3] |
| Against ... [4] | *Maître* ... [5] |

The following fees have been collected by the clerk's office for placing the above matter on the calendar:

| | |
|---|---|
| Putting case on calendar | francs 7.20 |
| Lump sum compensation for mailing cost | francs 4.30 |
| Fee of the *Huissiers-Audienciers* for calling case | francs 1.85 |
| Fee of the *Chambre* of the *avoués* | francs 12.00 |
| Total | francs 25.35 |

Case put on the calendar under No. ...

Paris, the ... [6]

Case assigned to panel No. ...

[1] This form is given by the clerk of the court to the *avoué* of the party who has requested that the case be put on the calendar. It indicates the number of the case on the general calendar and the panel to which the case has been assigned; it is also a receipt for the fees collected at the time the *placet* is filed. On this notice, see also 7.05 *supra.*

[2] Plaintiff's name.

[3] Name of plaintiff's *avoué.*

[4] Defendant's name

[5] Name of defendant's *avoué.*

[6] Date.

### Form No. 5

## NOTICE OF LISTING ON CALENDAR AND REQUEST TO APPEAR[1]

## Court of First Instance of the Seine

... Panel

*Maître* [2] ..., *avoué*, is hereby notified that the case ... [3] against ...[4] has been put on the calendar the ... [5] under No. ... and that the case will be called before the *juge chargé de suivre la procédure* the ... [6] at ... [7] o'clock.

Please be present at that hearing and take note that his notice will not be repeated.

[1] This form is sent by the clerk of the court to the *avoué* of the party having put the case on the calendar (usually plaintiff). It indicates the number of the case on the panel calendar and the date of the hearing before the *juge chargé de suivre la procédure*. On this form, see also 7.06 *supra*.

[2] Name of *avoué* to whom the notice is addressed.

[3] Plaintiff's name.

[4] Defendant's name.

[5] Date on which the case was put on the calendar.

[6] Date of hearing.

[7] Time of hearing

## Form No. 6

### *AVENIR* [1]

At the request of ..., [2] who has *Maître* ... [3] as his *avoué*,

*Maître* ..., [4] *avoué* for ..., [5] is summoned to appear the ... [6] at a hearing before the Presiding Judge and the Judges constituting panel No. ... of the court of first instance of the Seine, sitting in the Palace of Justice in Paris, at the regular hours for hearings, in order to argue the case between the parties, which was assigned to the panel mentioned and bears No. ... on the general calendar of the court.

Notice is hereby given that, if you are not present and do not file your pleadings, all steps will be taken that the law allows.

And we reserve all our rights.
And may you not ignore it.

*Maître* ... [7]

[1] By its terms, this form invites the defendant to appear before the full court. In fact, it is used to summon the defendant's *avoué* to appear at a hearing before the *juge chargé de suivre la procédure*. On the *avenir*, see also 7.06 *supra*.

[2] Name of plaintiff.

[3] Name of plaintiff's *avoué*.

[4] Name of defendant's *avoué*.

[5] Name of defendant.

[6] Date of hearing.

[7] Name and address of plaintiff's *avoué*.

**Form No. 7**

## *AVENIR*[1]

Article 154 *bis* of the Code of Civil Procedure

[The balance of this form is similar to the preceding form, except that the last paragraph reads:]

You are hereby given notice that, if you are not present and do not file your pleadings within fifteen days, judgment will be taken against you which will have all the effects of a contested judgment in accordance with Article 154 *bis* of the Code of Civil Procedure.

[1] This form must be served if the first *avenir* has produced no effect. See also 7.06 *supra*.

## Form No. 8

## *CONCLUSIONS* [1]

To the Presiding Judge and Judges composing the second panel of the court of first instance of the Seine

| | | |
|---|---|---|
| FOR: | The *Boulevard Roses Building Co.* | |
| | Defendant and plaintiff on impleader | ... *Noir* [2] |
| AGAINST: | Mrs. *Dupont* | |
| | Mrs. *Durant* | |
| | Mr. *Petit*, administrator | ... *Blanc* [2] |
| | Plaintiffs | |
| | Mr. and Mrs. *Poivre*, third-party defendants | ... *Rouge* [2] |

MAY IT PLEASE THE COURT:

Whereas, by virtue of the rules of adverse possession, it does not appear that the plaintiffs have a valid claim;

FOR THESE REASONS:

May the court hold for the Boulevard Roses Building Co., in accordance with the pleadings filed earlier by it;

Declare the plaintiffs' claim extinguished by adverse possession;

Hold them liable for all costs, granting *Maître Noir* a lien thereon in accordance with law.

And we reserve all our rights.
And justice will be done.

[1] The frequently uninformative character of French pleadings (*conclusions*), especially answers, is shown by this document asserting a defense of adverse possession. See also 7.08 *supra*.

[2] The names that follow the dots are those of the parties' *avoués*.

**Form No. 9**

## SUMMONS IN IMPLEADER [1]

In the year Nineteen Hundred and Fifty-Nine, and the twentieth of April,

At the request of the Boulevard Roses Building Co., whose seat is at 1 Boulevard Roses, and which is acting through its administrator residing at the said seat, and for which a domicile is chosen in Paris, 6 rue du Pont, at the office of *Maître* Noir, *avoué* at the court of first instance of the Seine, who appears for it and shall represent it for the present summons and further proceedings,

I, Fernand Pain, *Huissier* at the court of first instance of the Seine, residing at 522 Avenue des Fleurs, have left herewith, and served upon:

Mrs. Jeanne Bougie, the spouse of Mr. Edward POIVRE, the spouses having adopted by contract the *régime* of separation of property, who resides in Paris, at 9 Rue des Résedas, where I went and – having found neither the party, nor a relative or servant of the party, nor a neighbor willing to accept service and sign the original – spoke to the janitor,

and upon Mr. Edward POIVRE, in his own name, as well as in his capacity of husband to the extent necessary for the validity of the proceedings concerning Mrs. POIVRE, and who resides at Paris, 9 Rue des Résedas, where I went and spoke to the janitor,

a copy of a writ, served by Bontemps, *huissier* in Paris on June 30, 1958, at the request of Mrs. Rivière, [2] and a copy of a pleading dated November 1, 1958,

reserving all rights, so that they may not ignore it,

and at the request of the party aforesaid, who has elected a domicile as aforesaid, and appointed its *avoué* as aforesaid, I, the abovementioned *huissier*, who have signed this instrument, have summoned the abovementioned Mrs. Bougie, wife of Mr. POIVRE, and Mr. POIVRE to appear in eight "free" days as provided by law, through a duly appointed *avoué* at a hearing before the Presiding Judge and the Judges of the court of first instance of the Seine, sitting in the Palace of Justice in Paris, at the hour of noon (and default may be taken at once) for the purpose of:

Whereas Mrs. Bougie has, by an instrument prepared by *Maître* Plume, notary at Neuilly on February 28, 1954, sold to the Boulevard Roses Building Co. 880/1000 of a plot of 508 square meters abutting in front upon the Boulevard Roses for a length of 23 meters and 32 centimeters, at the rear upon a property located at 92 Avenue Paul, on one side upon a property located at 3 Boulevard Roses and on the other side upon the Avenue Pierre,

Whereas the rights of the Boulevard Roses Building Co. are threatened by Mrs. Rivière, as it appears from a writ served on behalf of the said Madame Rivière on June 30, 1958 by Bontemps, *huissier*,

Whereas the Boulevard Roses Building Co. may implead Mrs. Bougie, and such an impleader is justified on the merits because of her rights and her obligation of warranty

FOR THESE REASONS,

May the court declare the claim of the Boulevard Roses Building Co. procedurally proper and justified on the merits,

[1] This form is used to implead a party. It has no special title in France. The formalities for its service are the same as those for service of an original *ajournement*. See also 7.14.b *supra*.

[2] The writ referred to here is the original *ajournement* in the action, a copy of which is always served along with the summons in the impleader action.

adjudge that Mrs. Bougie, wife of Mr. Poivre, is liable in warranty to the Boulevard Roses Building Co.,

adjudge that the said lady will have to be liable for any judgment rendered against the Boulevard Roses Building Co., in the unlikely case of such an event,

and hold Mrs. Bougie, wife of Mr. Poivre, and Mr. Poivre liable for all costs.

And we reserve all our rights. And may they not ignore it. And I have left a copy (of this instrument) in a sealed envelope bearing on one side merely the name and address of the party, and on the other, across the flap of the envelope, the stamp of my office, all this done through my sworn clerk, whose return has been countersigned by me on the original in accordance with law.

Cost: Twenty-one francs and twenty-five hundredths.

(signed): Fernand Pain

## Form No. 10

## NOTICE OF PROCEEDINGS TAKEN[1]

Boulevard Roses Building Co.
v.
DUPONT & DURANT

At the request of the *Boulevard Roses Building Co.* having *Maître* Noir as its *avoué*,

a copy of:

(1) a summons claiming warranty against Mr. and Mrs. POIVRE on behalf of the Boulevard Roses Building Co. in connection with a claim made by Mrs. Rivière,

(2) a notice of appearance by *Maître* Rouge, *avoué* for Mr. and Mrs. POIVRE,

are hereby served upon *Maître* BLANC, *avoué* for Mrs. DUPONT and Mrs. DURANT.

And we reserve all our rights.
And may they not ignore it.
(signed) Noir

[1] To complete the impleader, a copy of the writ served on the third-party defendant, and a copy of the notice of appearance of the third-party defendant's *avoué* are served upon the other parties to the action with this covering form. See also 7.14.b *supra*.

### Form No. 11

### *CONCLUSIONS* [1]

To the Presiding Judge and Judges of the second panel of the court of first instance of the Seine.

| | | |
|---|---|---|
| For: | Boulevard Roses Building Co. | |
| | DEFENDANT | ... NOIR [2] |
| Against: | 1) Mrs. DUPONT | |
| | 2) Mrs. DURANT | |
| | 3) Mr. PETIT | |
| | 4) Mrs. RIVIÈRE | |
| | PLAINTIFFS | ... BLANC [2] |
| | 5) Mr. and Mrs. POIVRE | |
| | DEFENDANTS | ... ROUGE [2] |

May it Please the Court:

Whereas by a writ served by Bontemps, *huissier* in Paris, dated August 30, 1958, Mrs. DUPONT, Mrs. DURANT, and Mr. PETIT have started an action for the same purpose as the action initiated by Mrs. RIVIÈRE by a writ served by Bontemps, *huissier*, on June 30, 1958, and which bears number 35873 on the calendar, an action into which the defendant has impleaded Mr. and Mrs. POIVRE, its assignors, because of their obligation of warranty,

Whereas the new action bears the number 38874 on the special calendar of the second panel,

Whereas the actions having calendar numbers 35873 and 38874 should be joined so that one single judgment may be rendered in both cases,

Whereas the claims, allegations, and pleadings of Mrs. DUPONT, Mrs. DURANT and Mr. PETIT should be dismissed for reasons of substance as well as procedure,

Whereas, in fact, Mrs. RIVIÈRE has never abandoned her action which should be dismissed for the reasons stated in our pleading dated November 3, 1958,

Whereas the claims of Mrs. DUPONT, Mrs. DURANT, and Mr. PETIT, who stand in the shoes of Mrs. RIVIÈRE cannot be on any better footing than the claim of Mrs. RIVIÈRE, their assignor,

FOR THESE REASONS:

May the court hold for defendant in accordance with its earlier pleading,

*On the demand for joinder*:

May the court order the two actions joined so that one and the same judgment may be rendered in the entire case,

*On the claims of* DUPONT, DURANT, *and* PETIT:

May the court dismiss the claims, allegations, and pleadings of DUPONT, DURANT, and PETIT,

Hold against them,

And hold them liable for all costs, granting a lien thereon to *Maître* NOIR in accordance with law,

And we reserve all our rights,
And justice will be done.
(signed) NOIR

[1] This is another example of a defensive pleading; in this case, joinder of two related actions and dismissal on the merits is requested. See also 7.08 *supra*.

[2] The names following the dots are those of the parties' *avoués*.

**Form No. 12**

## *CONCLUSIONS* [1]

To the Presiding Judge and Judges composing the second panel of the court of first instance of the Seine.

| | | | |
|---|---|---|---|
| For: | | Mr. and Mrs. POIVRE, Third-party defendants | Claude ROUGE |
| Against: | (1) | The Boulevard Roses Building Co. Third-party plaintiff, Defendant in the main action | *Maître* NOIR |
| | (2) | ... [2] | |

MAY IT PLEASE THE COURT:

Wheras Mrs. Rivière, owner of a building located at 3 Boulevard Roses, has, by writ dated June 30, 1958, sued the Boulevard Roses Building Co.

(1) for the sum of 20,000 francs, the value of the strip of land belonging to her and on which the Boulevard Roses Building Co. is said to have constructed its own building,

(2) for the sum of 5,000 francs as damages for building upon the wall separating the two properties,

Whereas by writ dated April 20, 1959, the Boulevard Roses Building Co. has impleaded the third-party defendants,

Whereas ..., [3]

1. ON THE EXTENT OF THE WARRANTY OWED BY MR. AND MRS. POIVRE TO THE BOULEVARD ROSES BUILDING CO.

Whereas the agreement of exchange between Mr. and Mrs. Poivre and the Boulevard Roses Building Co., dated February 28, 1954, provides as follows:

"Conditions: The present exchange is made under the conditions usual in such circumstances, and in particular under the following conditions, which the contracting parties agree to observe:

"To accept the exchanged properties in their present condition ... without regard to any error ... or insufficiency in the description of the property ... or in the area, no deficiency, even exceeding one twentieth, giving right to any recourse ...,"

Whereas it follows that Mr. and Mrs. POIVRE are not liable in warranty to the Boulevard Roses Building Co. because the property conveyed encroached upon the property of 3 Boulevard Roses.

2. ON THE EXTENT OF THE LIABILITY OF MR. AND MRS. POIVRE.

Whereas Mr. and Mrs. POIVRE cannot be held liable for damages caused by the increase in height given to the wall separating the two properties, this being solely the work of the Boulevard Roses Building Co. which started this construction after the agreement of exchange.

[1] This is an example of more detailed *conclusions*, and of *conclusions* in which an authorization for a hearing of witnesses (*enquête*) is requested. See also 7.08 and 7.51.a *supra*.

[2] Here follow the names of the other parties to the action and their *avoués*.

[3] The following recital again lists the various parties to the action and the capacities in which they are acting.

3. ON THE ACQUISITION BY ADVERSE POSSESSION OF THE LITIGATED STRIP OF LAND BY MR. AND MRS. POIVRE.

Whereas in her writ dated June 30, 1958, Mrs. POIVRE herself recognizes that it is only in 1951, at the time the Boulevard Roses Building Co. started its construction work and the surveyors made their survey, that she learned about the encroachment of 1 meter by the lot at 1 Boulevard Roses upon the lot at 3 Boulevard Roses,

Whereas the findings of the expert have confirmed that this situation is more than thirty years old and hence Mr. and Mrs. POIVRE have acquired that strip of land by adverse possession,

Whereas, in fact, the building at 3 Boulevard Roses was built more than thirty years ago and was constructed 1 meter from the lot line of 1 Boulevard Roses,

Whereas on the other hand, the buildings on the Boulevard Roses are all built with a front yard 5 meters deep and the City of Paris had required all owners to build fences or walls to enclose front yards and the rest of the property,

Whereas the expert has stated in his report:

"The fences enclosing the front yards were built in accordance with the specifications, without regard to whether the length of the frontage, under the contract of sale, actually was 17 meter and 22.57 meter. The fence on the side of the properties enclosing the front yard dates from the same period, 1877.

"This is shown by its nature, its looks, and its old appearance.

"Since fences were put along the frontage of No. 1 and No. 3, and on a small part of the side of the property, as indicated above, the strip of land of 1 meter width was thus closed off against the street, and, as it were, landlocked,"

Whereas it is thus established that the owners of 1 Boulevard Roses have effectively confirmed their possession of the 1 meter strip of land by enclosing it within fences in front and on the sides as early as *1877*,

Whereas this situation is also established by the erection of partition walls separating Nos. 1 and 3, since the surveyors of the parties, Mr. COMPAS and Mr. TANGENT, have specified:

"We assume that by a mistake of the builders, the building at No. 3 was built at the site of the partition wall, thus abandoning a strip of 1 meter, which was later incorporated into the building at No. 1,"

Whereas the existence of such a partition wall is also confirmed by the sales agreement dated February 14, 1876, which provided:

"The area sold herewith includes half the width of the walls separating the property sold from the adjoining lots,"

Whereas the existence of partition walls on the line which at present separates the two lots is also confirmed by various witnesses,

Whereas it is therefore established that the owners of 1 Boulevard Roses have, for more than thirty years, been in peaceful and effective possession of the strip of land in litigation which became "enclosed" in their property, while nothing could reveal to them the existence of this encroachment, which, besides, is also incorporated in the tax maps,

Whereas it is only by a manifestly erroneous interpretation of the law that the honorable expert believes that he can suggest that only a mere "license" was involved,

Whereas it is, on the contrary, certain that the two adjoining landowners ignored the encroachment until 1951, when a comparison of the property titles and the actual measurements revealed to them the difference of 1 meter in the frontage of the two lots,

Whereas the peaceful and effective possession of the land in litigation for more than thirty years has given title by adverse possession to the owners of 1 Boulevard Roses,

ALTERNATIVELY

Whereas Mr. and Mrs. POIVRE offer to prove the following facts through a regular *enquête*:

(1) The lot at 1 Boulevard Roses was enclosed in its present area since 1876, and at any rate for more than thirty years before 1951, by partition fences and walls,

(2) The owners of 1 Boulevard Roses had the effective and peaceful enjoyment of the strip of land in litigation since these fences were put up,

FOR THESE REASONS:

May the Court:

(1) Say and adjudge that the exchange agreement concluded between the third-party defendants and the Boulevard Roses Building Co. on February 28, 1954, excluded any obligation of warranty for error in the area sold,

Say and adjudge as a result that the third-party defendants owe no warranty to the Boulevard Building Co., because the property conveyed by them to the Boulevard Roses Building Co. encroached upon the No. 3 Boulevard Roses;

(2) Say and adjudge that the third-party defendants are in no way liable on account of the construction put upon the party wall between No. 1 and No. 3 Boulevard Roses,

(3) Say and adjudge that the owners of 1 Boulevard Roses have had, for more than thirty years, peaceful and effective possession of the strip of land in litigation, that strip of land having been enclosed by walls and fences since 1876,

Say and adjudge that the owners of 1 Boulevard Roses have therefore acquired that strip of land by adverse possession under the terms of Article 2262 of the Civil Code.

ALTERNATIVELY

May the court authorize the third-party defendants to prove the following facts by a regular *enquête*:

(1) The lot at 1 Boulevard Roses was enclosed in its present area since 1876, and at any rate for more than thirty years before 1951, by partition fences and walls.

(2) The owners of 1 Boulevard Roses had effective and peaceful enjoyment of the strip of land in litigation since these fences were put up.

As a consequence, may the court adjudge Mrs. RIVIÈRE's main action unfounded on the merits and

Say and adjudge that the impleader against Mr. and Mrs. POIVRE should be dismissed,

Dismiss as a consequence all the claims, defenses, and pleadings of the Boulevard Roses Building Co., Mrs. RIVIÈRE, and all other parties,

And hold them jointly and severally liable for all costs, granting a lien thereon to *Maître* Claude ROUGE, *avoué*, in accordance with law.

And we reserve all our rights.
And justice will be done.

**Form No. 13**

## ANSWER IN IMPLEADER[1]

To the Presiding Judge and Judges composing the second panel of the court of first instance of the Seine

Rivière v. Boulevard Roses Bldg. Co.

| | | |
|---|---|---|
| For: | 1) Mrs. Rivière[7] | |
| | 2) . . . [2] | |
| | plaintiffs | *Maître* Blanc [3] |
| Against: | The Boulevard Roses Building Co. | |
| | defendant | *Maître* Noir [3] |
| | Mr. and Mrs. Poivre | |
| | Third-party defendants | *Maître* Rouge [3] |

MAY IT PLEASE THE COURT:

Whereas by pleadings dated March 30, 1960, the spouses Poivre, impleaded by the Boulevard Roses Building Co., have claimed that they have become owners, by the effect of adverse possession under Article 2262 of the Civil Code, of the encroaching strip of land, but have not even contested the existence of the encroachment,

Whereas such a claim cannot be accepted and the Boulevard Roses Building Co. has caused the plaintiffs damage under this part of their claim, as well as under other parts of the claim,

FOR THESE REASONS:

May the court declare the third-party defendants entire claims, defenses, and pleadings procedurally improper and unfounded on the merits,

Hold them liable for the costs of that part of the action, granting *Maître* Blanc a lien thereon in accordance with law.

And we reserve all our rights.
And justice will be done.

[1] This pleading (*conclusions*) in reply to the third-party defendant's *conclusions* is a good example of the informal character of French pleadings. See also 7.08 *supra*.

[2] Here, the names of the other parties are listed.

[3] These are the names of the parties' *avoués*.

## Form No. 14

## *CONCLUSIONS* TO DISMISS [1]

To the Presiding Judge and Judges of the twentieth panel of the court of first instance of the Seine.

For: Mr. Jean Lenormand, born in Paris, 1st *arrondissement*, the 1st of January, 1900, living at 1 Rue de la Concorde, in Paris, plaintiff in the main action,
defendant on the counterclaim Jean Plume [2]

Against: Mrs. Lenormand
defendant in the main action,
plaintiff on the counterclaim Pierre Tome [2]

MAY IT PLEASE THE COURT:

Whereas, by a writ served by *Maître* Grand, *huissier* in Paris, dated June 29, 1961, the plaintiff has brought a divorce action against his wife,

Whereas by a pleading dated November 16, 1961, Mr. Lenormand has introduced a counterclaim against her husband for the same purpose,

Whereas, to support her claim, Mrs. Lenormand alleges a certain number of facts and offers to prove them,

Whereas these facts are neither relevant nor admissible, and their proof should not be ordered,

Whereas the counterclaim is procedurally defective and unfounded on the merits, and should not prevail,

FOR THESE REASONS:

May the court say that the facts alleged by Mrs. Lenormand in support of her counterclaim are neither pertinent nor admissible, that their proof should not be ordered, and consequently,

Dismiss the counterclaim of Mrs. Lenormand,

And, accepting plaintiff's claim, render judgment for plaintiff in accordance with the terms of his original writ,

And hold Mrs. Lenormand liable for all costs, granting *Maître* Plume a lien thereon in accordance with law.

And we reserve all our rights.
And justice will be done.

[1] These *conclusions* represent a reply to a counterclaim in a divorce action. See also 7.08 *supra*.

[2] Names of the parties' *avoués*.

### Form No. 15

## REQUEST FOR PRODUCTION OF DOCUMENT [1]

At the request of ... [2]
Having *Maître* ... [3] as its avoué,
*Maître* ..., [4] *avoué* of ..., [5] is hereby requested to produce within twenty-four hours at most, either informally on receipt of the *avoué* of the requesting party or by means of the court clerk's office, all the documents which he wishes to use in the action pending between the parties, and especially

... [6]

Giving him notice that, in case of failure to act in accordance with this request within the time limit indicated, all steps provided by law will be taken.

And may he not ignore it.

[1] This form is used to demand production of the original of a document relied upon by the other side. See also 7.34 *supra*.
[2] Name of party requesting production.
[3] Name of *avoué* of party requesting production.
[4] Name of *avoué* of party holding document.
[5] Name of party holding document.
[6] Description of document to be produced.

### Form No. 16

## NOTICE OF CALENDER CALL [1]

Court of First Instance of the Seine
Panel No. Division No.

*Maître* ..., [2] *avoué*

is notified that the case between ... [3]
and ... [4]
has been put on the calendar ...
has been struck from the calendar on ...
will come on for a hearing on ...
will be called on ... to fix a date for argument
will come on the ... for argument.

Paris, the ... [5]

[1] This form is used by the clerk's office to notify *avoués* of the date on which a particular case will be called to set it down for a definite hearing date and also for various other notifications – for instance, to inform them that their case was struck from the calendar because neither side appeared when it was called. See also 7.12.a *supra*.

[2] Name of *avoué* to whom notice is addressed.

[3] Name of plaintiff.

[4] Name of defendant.

[5] Date.

## Form No. 17

## NOTICE OF APPEAL [1]

In the year nineteen hundred and sixty ... and the ... [2]

At the request of ... [3]

For whom a domicile is elected at the office of *Maître* ..., [4] who appears for the above-named appellant on the appeal and this summons, and and will represent him in connection whit its consequences,

I, the undersigned ... [5]

have served upon, and stated and declared to, ... [6]

That the appellant formally appeals by these presents from a judgment rendered on ... [7] on account of the procedural defects by which it may be affected and also on account of the wrong which it causes to the appellant.

And at the request of the same person mentioned above, who elects domicile as above, I, the above mentioned *huissier*, have summoned the above-mentioned respondent to appear by *avoué* in ... [8] days, as provided by law, before the Presiding Judge and Judges of the first panel of the Court of Appeal in Paris, which sits in that city in the Palace of Justice, in the ordinary hearing room for such hearings, at the hour of noon, [9] so that,

For the reasons given before the court of first instance, those to be submitted to the court, and any others to be supplied:

The court may receive the appeal of the appellant, and in doing so quash the judgment appealed from, correct it, and relieve the appellant from all portions and headings aggrieving the appellant,

On the merits, the court may hold in accordance with the appellant's pleadings in the court of first instance and in accordance with all the pleadings he reserves the right to present to this Court,

And in case of a decision rendered by default, may the court order immediate execution in spite of a possible demand for a reopening, the matter being urgent,

And declare that, in case of default of the respondent, Articles 150, 151, and 153 of the Code of Civil Procedure will be applied,

And hold the respondent liable for all costs in first instance and on appeal,

And we expressly reserve all our rights.

And so that they may not ignore it, I have left a copy of this instrument as mentioned above.

... [10]

COST: ... [11]

[1] This form serves as a notice of appeal. It is served in a formal manner, similar to that used to serve an *ajournement*. Ordinarily, printed forms are used. See also 8.13.a *supra*.

[2] Date.

[3] Name of appellant.

[4] Name of appellant's *avoué* on the appeal.

[5] Name and address of *huissier* serving the notice of appeal.

[6] Name and address of respondent, and, as in the case of an *ajournement*, description of method by which he has been served.

[7] Description of judgment appealed from by date and court.

[8] Number of days before respondent must appear are here specified.

[9] In fact, within the time indicated, the respondent merely must appoint an *avoué*; no hearing before the court takes place as yet.

[10] Signature of *huissier*.

[11] List of *huissier's* fees and expenses.

**Form No. 18**

## REGISTRATION OF APPEAL[1]

Office of *Maître* ... [2]
Request for Registering of Appeal
Case: ... [3]

*Maître* ..., [4] *avoué* at the Court of Appeal, residing in Paris, at ... [5]
Requests registration at the clerk's office of an appeal taken at the request of:
... [6]
served upon:
... [7]
from a judgment rendered by the ... [8] on ... [9]

Dated ... 19..

[1] This form must be filed in the clerk's office of the *cour d'appel* after the notice of appeal (Form No. 17) has been served upon the respondent. See 8.13.a *supra.*
[2] Name of appellant's *avoué* on appeal.
[3] Names of the parties.
[4] Name of appellant's *avoué* on appeal.
[5] Office address of appellant's *avoué* on appeal.
[6] Name and address of appellant.
[7] Name and address of respondent.
[8] Name of court that rendered the judgment appealed from.
[9] Date of judgment appealed from.

### Form No. 19

## ANSWER ON APPEAL [1]

Court of Appeal Paris
... Panel
General Calendar No. ...
Panel Calander No. ...
Served on ...
Object of the litigation: ... [2]

***CONCLUSIONS***

For: ... [3]
Respondent
... [4]
Against: ... [5]
Appellant
... [6]

MAY IT PLEASE THE COURT:

In dealing with this appeal from a judgment rendered ... [7]

May the court declare the appeal void and of no effect, and alternatively also procedurally defective,

And even more in the alternative, hold for respondents in accordance with their pleadings before the court of first instance as to lack of competence, formal defects or other procedural defects of the claim of the opponent, and, even more in the alternative, on any other grounds, especially as they may relate to the original writ, the pleadings in first instance being reasserted here only to the extent they are important on this appeal,

And may the court, in addition, adopt the opinion of the court of first instance to the extent it is not contrary to the above,

And invalidate the appeal: Order that the judgment appealed from shall be fully effective and executed to the extent it is not contrary to what has been said above,

And may the court hold the appellants liable for the costs of provisional execution and the costs of this appeal, granting a lien thereon to *Maître* ..., [8] as provided by law.

And we reserve all our rights, especially to further indicate and make more precise our allegations as to defects of form and procedural defects concerning the appeal, and all other grounds we have previously invoked, and also to take a cross-appeal from the judgment mentioned, or to bring an additional claim or a counterclaim or any other claim and to change our pleadings at any stage of the proceedings.

And the Court will do justice.

[1] This is an example of respondent's first answering *conclusions*. Generally, a printed form is used. See also 8.20.b *supra*.

[2] Brief description of nature of action.

[3] Name of respondent.

[4] Name of respondent's *avoué* on appeal.

[5] Name of appellant.

[6] Name of appellant's *avoué* on appeal.

Description of judgment appealed from by date and court that rendered it.

[8] Name of respondent's *avoué*.

## Form No. 20

## *POURVOI*[1]

In the year ..., and the ... there appeared at the clerk's office of the Court of Appeal in Paris, before us, the undersigned chief clerk

(date) ... [2]

Law residing at ... [3]

of ...[4] Acting in his own personal name, [5]

Who declared to us that he was taking a *pourvoi* to the *Cour de Cassation* against a decision rendered after appearance by both sides on ... [6] in a case pending between the party mentioned above and ... [7]

...[8] Respondent on the *pourvoi*,

...[9] Which decision was served upon the appellant on ... [10]

And we have read to the appellant Article thirty-seven of the Law of July 23, 1947,

And the appellant gave his summary reasons for taking the *pourvoi* as follows:

... [11]

(And the appellant declared that he reserved the right to supply the bases for his *pourvoi* in a memorandum to be furnished by him within the time provided by law,)[12]

And we have invited the appellant to supply the documents listed in the above-mentioned Article 37 as soon as possible and have informed him that the file will be transmitted to the *Cour de Cassation* no later than three months from the date of the present declaration.

Of which we have prepared these minutes which the appellant has signed with us, the chief clerk, after they had been read to him.

(Signature of appellant and chief clerk)

[1] When the services of an *avocat aux conseils* are not required, a *pourvoi* to the *Cour de Cassation* is taken by making an oral declaration in the clerk's office of the *cour d'appel* that rendered the judgment to be reviewed. The declaration is recorded by the clerk on this form. See also 9.16 *supra*.

[2] Name of appellant or, if he does not appear personally, of person appearing for him.

[3] Address of person making declaration.

[4] Date of law on which *pourvoi* is based.

[5] If the appellant has not appeared in person, this sentence is crossed out and replaced by the sentence "acting for (name of appellant) pursuant to a power of attorney given on ..."

[6] Date of decision against which *pourvoi* is taken.

[7] Name and address of respondent on *pourvoi*.

[8] Name of appellant on *pourvoi*.

[9] Name of respondent on *pourvoi*.

[10] Date on which decision against which *pourvoi* is taken was served on appellant.

[11] Here, the grounds for the *pourvoi* are set forth in summary fashion and the following paragraph is crossed out, *or* the paragraph reading "And the appellant gave his summary reasons for taking the *pourvoi* as follows" is crossed out.

[12] This paragraph may be used in lieu of the preceding one. See note 11 *supra*.

## Form No. 21

## *POURVOI*[1]

In the year one thousand nine hundred and sixty five and the ... [2]

*Pourvoi* for Mr. ... [3]

Against Mr. ... [4]

Mr. .. [5] requests the reversal of a *Cour d'Appel* decision rendered against him, in a case pending between himself and Mr. ... [6] by the *Cour d'Appel* in ... [7] on the ... 19... [8] That decision has erroneously applied Article ... [9] of the law of ... [10] and violated Article ... [11] of the law of .... [12]

These violations and false applications of law consisted in ... [13]

For these reasons the undersigned requests that it may please the Court to reverse and quash the above-mentioned decision of the *Cour d'Appel* of ...; [14] put the parties into the position in which they were before the rendition of the said decision; order, if necessary, the restitution of sums that may have been paid by virtue of the said decision; remand the parties to such other *Cour d'Appel* as the Court may desire, all this with costs; and we reserve the right to modify, amplify, or restrict these our requests.

Documents Attached: ... [15]

(Signature of *avocat aux conseils*)

[1] This form is used to initiate a *pourvoi* to the *Cour de Cassation* in cases in which the services of an *avocat aux conseils* are needed. It is submitted to the *Cour de Cassation* by the appellant's *avocat aux conseils*. See also 9.16 *supra*.

[2] Day of the month.

[3] Name of appellant on *pourvoi*.

[4] Name of respondent on *pourvoi*.

[5] Name, occupation, and address of appellant on *pourvoi*.

[6] Name, occupation, and address of respondent on *pourvoi*.

[7] Name of court that rendered the decision against which *pourvoi* is taken.

[9] Date of decision against which *pourvoi* is taken.

[9] Numbers of articles of the statute erroneously applied. If no allegation of erroneous application of a statute is made, this sentence is crossed out.

[10] Date of statute allegedly applied erroneously.

[11] Numbers of articles of statute allegedly violated. If no allegation of a violation or erroneous application of a statute is made, this sentence is crossed out.

[12] Date of statute allegedly violated.

[13] Here, the errors of the court below, on which the *pourvoi* is based, are briefly listed. They are later amplified in the *mémoire ampliatif*.

[14] Name of court that rendered the decision against which *pourvoi* is taken.

**Form No. 22**

## JUDGMENT BY COURT OF FIRST INSTANCE[1]

(Tax stamps)[2] From the minutes of the clerk's office of the court of first instance of the Seine. French Republic. In the name of the French people.

| | | |
|---|---|---|
| 20th Panel | 12345/61 | J. PLUME, *avoué* for Mr. LENORMAND, Jean |
| 2d Division | Summons: June 29, 1961 Divorce | residing at 6, Rue des Colombes, PARIS |
| Jan. 3, 1963 | No. 4 | P. TOME, *avoué* for Mrs. LENORMAND, *née* Claudette Allègre, author, residing at 6 Blvd. des Cigales, PARIS |

THE TRIBUNAL,

having held a hearing in its conference room on December 23, 1963, and having heard Mr. SAGE, Judge, in his report, and the arguments and requests of LOQUACE, *avocat*, assisted by PLUME, *avoué* for Mr. LENORMAND, and TOME, *avoué* for Mrs. LENORMAND, *née* Allègre, and having heard the State's attorney, and having held its conference on the case in accordance with law, and using the ordinary (non-summary) procedure, and acting as a court of first instance, and having remanded the case to the public hearing of to-day for the reading of the present judgment, [3] .................................... Whereas Mr. Jean LENORMAND has entered into a marriage with Claudette ALLEGRE before the registrar of the first arrondissement of the City of Paris on June 20, 1949, and Whereas by the terms of a marriage contract drawn by ENCRIER, notary in Paris on June 1, 1949, the parties have adopted the system of separate property, Whereas there is no issue of their marriage, Whereas by a writ served by GRAND, *huissier*, dated June 29, 1961, Mr. LENORMAND has brought a divorce action against his wife, Whereas by a pleading dated November 16, 1961 Mrs. LENORMAND has denied the facts alleged by her husband and has brought a counterclaim for divorce, Whereas by a pleading dated January 10, 1962, the husband has denied the facts alleged by his wife, .................................... *On the husband's main claim*, Whereas Mr. LENORMAND alleges, in support of his claim for divorce, the cruel attitude of his wife and in particular that "since 1954, his wife, using her occupation of author as a pretext, has abandoned the matrimonial domicile, and has not reappeared there for long periods of time, that since August 1959 she has completely abandoned the family domicile," And whereas in answer to his request, made in October 1959 through PAPIER, *huissier* in Paris, to return home, she stated that "she considered his request, made by *huissier*, that she should love her husband and live with him as ridiculous, that these things and he himself had long been dead for her, and that he could have avoided that step and its expenses," Whereas Mr. LENORMAND produces letters from his wife which leave no doubts as to her feelings for him, (as she writes) "I would like you to know once and for all that I will under no circumstances live with you again, everything is dead between us, we can do

[1] This form represents the formal copy or *grosse* of a judgment of a court of first instance. The law requires that, to prevent unauthorized insertions, it be written without blank spaces; hence, it is usually written without paragraphing, and if paragraphs are used, unused portions of lines are filled in by dashes. See also 7.13 *supra.*

[2] In this space, the tax stamps are affixed.

[3] Here, ordinarily a recital follows that the court was composed of the same judges at the time of the reading of the judgment and at the time of the hearing. For reasons unknown, it was omitted in this case.

nothing about it, this is beyond hope, our past experience is conclusive on this point and it is better that we each try to live our separate lives," ..........

*On the counterclaim of the wife*, Whereas, in support of her counterclaim the wife alleges the following facts: that for several years Mr. LENORMAND has treated her with a coldness and indifference making their actual separation inevitable, Whereas Mr. LENORMAND has made it plain to the wife that their break appeared as a great relief to him, and has informed his wife about his feelings in a brutal manner and without restraint, writing to her in a letter: "you are almost the lowest type of a woman. Though your departure was a great relief for me and was the beginning of a peace I thought lost forever, I want to clarify our situation," Whereas the letters written by Mr. LENORMAND leave no doubts as to the feelings of the latter and as to his clearly manifested will to cease all relations with his wife, Whereas in a letter written to Mrs. LENORMAND on January 3, 1960, he says: "the peace to which your absence has accustomed me and which I mentioned in my first letter has increased and becomes a peace of happiness. To have lost you makes me free and gives me the hope that I may associate my life with a human being that, in any event, will be better than you," Whereas the facts established by both spouses amount to the cruel acts constituting a serious and repeated violation of the obligations resulting from the marriage bond and making the continuation of married life intolerable, which authorize the granting of a divorce to the spouses LENORMAND at the request and in favor of each of them, ..........

FOR THESE REASONS, and considering the court order of March 3, 1961, noting that the spouses could not be reconciled and authorizing them to live apart, (the tribunal) declares the spouses LENORMAND-ALLEGRE divorced at the request and in favor of each of them, and holds both sides to be at fault with all legal consequences of such fact, orders the decretal paragraph of this judgment to be recorded in the margin of the marriage record of the spouses LENORMAND in the mayor's office of the first *arrondissement* of Paris and in the margin of all other records where this is required by law, appoints the President of the Chamber of Notaries in Paris, with power of subdelegation, to proceed to the liquidation of the matrimonial property of the parties and Mr. SAGE, judge, to report to the court on the said liquidation if court approval should be sought, orders that in case of unavailability of the said judge and notary, they will be replaced by order of the Presiding Judge on simple *ex parte* petition, holds that the combined expenses of both parties must be borne in equal shares by each of them, granting to the parties' *avoués* a lien thereon,

decided and adjudged in the Twentieth Panel of the Court of First Instance of the Seine, on January 3, 1963, by Mr. LEPONT, Vice-President, and Mr. SAGE and Mr. BIEN, Judges, in the presence of Mr. ASTUT, Assistant State Attorney, and with the assistance of Mr. LACOTE, Clerk of the Court.

(Signed) LEPONT, LACOTE

In consequence, the French Republic orders all *huissiers* who may receive a request to that effect to execute this judgment, all procurators general and state's attorneys at the courts of first instance to see to it that it is executed, all commanders and officers of the police and armed forces to lend their assistance when they receive a lawful request for that purpose.

In witness thereof the present judgment has been signed by

(Signature of clerk)

**Form No. 23**

## JUDGEMENT BY *COUR DE CASSATION* [1]

## The Court

Having heard the report of Judge Ancel, the arguments of *Maître* Le Prado, attorney for Munzer, and of *Maître* de Ségogne, attorney for Mrs. Munzer, as well as the report of advocate-general Ithier, and having held its conference on the case immediately thereafter in accordance with law,

On appellant's third objection:

Whereas this objection, which constitutes new matter, has been raised only on July 18, 1963, though the *pourvoi* was filed on July 25, 1962, and consequently, by virtue of Articles 19 and 21 of the Law of July 23, 1947, may not be considered;

Declares that appellant's third objection may not be considered;

On appellant's first objection:

Whereas it appears from the judgment under review that on June 29, 1926, a judgment was rendered in the State of New York granting a separation to the spouses Munzer-Jacoby and awarding the wife weekly alimony of $ 35.–, that under another judgment rendered by the same court on April 10, 1958, Mr. Munzer was to pay the sum of $ 76.987, representing alimony arrears from November 10, 1939, to January 19, 1958, to Mrs. Munzer-Jacoby, and that Mrs. Munzer requested *exequatur* of these two judgments, as Mr. Munzer had established his residence in Nice;

Whereas the judgment under review is attacked for the reason that it granted this request (for *exequatur*), although, so it is argued in the *pourvoi*, it is a rule of public policy that arrears of alimony may not be claimed and in addition French law protects alimony debtors against stale claims and suits that are difficult to decide or that have become inconvenient as a result of the lapse of time by the statute of limitations contained in Article 2277 of the Civil Code;

But whereas the judgment under review states with good reason that the instant case "involves merely the enforcement of rights regularly acquired abroad" and the requirements of public policy, which applies only in its attenuated form, are therefore less great; and the principle that alimony arrears may not be claimed may be considered as not affected by public policy considered from that point of view and, besides, is a simple presumption which disappears upon proof to the contrary, while the rule of Article 2277, though it is a means of discharging a debtor without payment, does not apply automatically, may be waived, and may not be applied by the judge on his own motion; whereas the decision under review correctly concludes, on the basis of this analysis, that the foreign judgment, enforcement of which was sought in France by Mrs. Munzer-Jacoby is not contrary to public policy in its international sense; so that the arguments of appellant's first objection are not well founded;

On appellant's second objection:

Whereas the *pourvoi* attacks the judgment under review because the *Cour d' Appel* decided that it had no power to review the American decision brought to it for *exequatur* on the merits, because a separation judgment with all its effects is not subject to such a power of revision on the merits, though the *pourvoi* argues that, even if there is no power of revision on the merits in matters affecting

[1] This form contains a translation of the judgment of the *Cour de Cassation* in Munzer v. dame Jacoby Munzer, Cass. Civ., Jan. 7, 1964, 91 CLUNET 302 (1964); *cf.* 9.23 *supra*.

personal status, that exception, which must necessarily receive a narrow interpretation, is inapplicable to that part of the decision which determines the alimony payable by Mr. Munzer;

But whereas the decision under review states correctly that, to grant the *exequatur*, the French judge must make certain that five conditions are fulfilled, namely that the foreign court which rendered the judgment had jurisdiction, that the procedure followed before that court was regular, that the law which was proper under French conflict of laws rules was applied, and that the decision is in accord with public policy and does not amount to a fraud on the law, and whereas this examination, which sufficiently guarantees the protection of the French legal order and of French interests, which is the purpose of the whole institution of the *exequatur*, represents the scope and the limit of the powers of the judge asked to grant enforcement in France of a foreign decision and that judge is not to review the decision on the merits;

Whereas in the instant case the *Cour d'Appel* decides that the judgments submitted to its examination comply with the conditions for the grant of an *exequatur*, so that, in granting enforcement of both judgments in France, the decision under review, far from having violated the statutes mentioned in the *pourvoi*, has on the contrary applied them correctly and has a legal basis;

For these reasons,

Rejects the appeal . . .

# INDEX

F

G

I

T

GPSR Compliance

*The European Union's (EU) General Product Safety Regulation (GPSR) is a set of rules that requires consumer products to be safe and our obligations to ensure this.*

*If you have any concerns about our products, you can contact us on ProductSafety@springernature.com*

In case Publisher is established outside the EU, the EU authorized representative is:

Springer Nature Customer Service Center GmbH
Europaplatz 3
69115 Heidelberg, Germany

**Batch number: 10830941**

Printed by Printforce, the Netherlands